OXFORD

The Oxford Dictionary of
Foreign Words and Phrases

Jennifer Speake is a freelance writer and editor of reference books, including *The Concise Oxford Dictionary of Proverbs* (with John Simpson, 3rd edn. 1998) and the *The Oxford Dictionary of Idioms* (1999).

The Oxford Dictionary of

Foreign Words and Phrases

Edited by JENNIFER SPEAKE

OXFORD
UNIVERSITY PRESS

Great Clarendon Street, Oxford OX2 6DP

Oxford University Press is a department of the University of Oxford.
It furthers the University's objective of excellence in research, scholarship,
and education by publishing worldwide in

Oxford New York

Athens Auckland Bangkok Bogotá Buenos Aires Calcutta
Cape Town Chennai Dar es Salaam Delhi Florence Hong Kong Istanbul
Karachi Kuala Lumpur Madrid Melbourne Mexico City Mumbai
Nairobi Paris São Paulo Singapore Taipei Tokyo Toronto Warsaw

Oxford is a registered trade mark of Oxford University Press
in the UK and in certain other countries

Published in the United States
by Oxford University Press Inc., New York

First published 1997
First published in paperback 1998
Reissued in new covers 2000

British Library Cataloguing in Publication Data
Data available

Library of Congress Cataloging in Publication Data
Data available

ISBN 0-19-280112-0

10 9 8 7 6 5

Printed in Great Britain by
Clays Ltd, St Ives plc

Contents

Preface

The Oxford Dictionary of Foreign Words and Phrases records the influx of words from a variety of other languages into both American and British English, concentrating especially on those introduced during the course of the twentieth century. Older dictionaries in this field tend to have a preponderance of French and Latin expressions; many of these are indeed still current and are represented in the present work by 1990s citations, but the English language is now open to new words on a worldwide basis. Many recent introductions reflect an unprecedented cultural eclecticism, particularly in what might be called 'lifestyle' words—those dealing with areas such as fashion, cuisine, ethnic music, and recreation.

There is nothing new about sources for foreign words being indicative of historical or cultural events. The influx of French military terms in the early eighteenth century, for instance, can be linked to the Continental campaigns of the Duke of Marlborough. More recently, the British Raj in India spawned a large number of Anglo-Indian terms for the various functionaries and institutions necessary to keep the wheels of empire turning. However, neither of these two categories is heavily represented in late twentieth-century speech, *nouvelle cuisine* being more fashionable than fortification and *karma* having a higher profile than imperial administration.

The criteria for currency that have been applied in the selection of entries mean that there is a bias in favour of words first introduced during this century. An exception to this is the large category of words, particularly from the classical languages, that are recent introductions or revivals with exclusively scientific senses; these are excluded on the grounds that they do not fulfil the other criterion of currency, namely that the word may be encountered in non-specialist literature. However, many other words have both technical and more general senses, and in such cases the technical senses are generally included or mentioned in the entry, as the evolution of the various senses once they have entered the language is often interesting in itself. For instance, *flèche*, which occurs in Middle English with its basic French meaning of 'arrow', soon became obsolete after its first introduction (most probably because it duplicated an already established word); reintroduced from Modern French with a variety of special applications, it has fared better. Terms that have been introduced purely as terms of art in particular sports or other fields of activity and have remained so (or have not had time to move beyond their restricted area) have been excluded; admitting terms for bullfighting passes or judo throws would have considerably increased the proportion of, respectively, Spanish and Japanese entries.

Introduced expressions have met with varying fortunes in English, but certain patterns can be seen. On the whole, phrases tend to be more resistant to naturalization than single words. At one end of the scale of naturalization, many words, especially those from Old French and Latin, have become totally assimilated in spelling, pronunciation, and plural form, and are thus no longer thought of as foreign in any sense other than the purely etymological. Others (such as *restaurant*) are nearing the end of this process of assimilation, with only some slight variation in standard pronunciation as a gesture towards an alien origin. Others, particularly Latin and French phrases, have remained obstinately 'foreign' over several centuries.

Italicization is a helpful but not infallible clue to the extent of assimilation, the rule of thumb being that the more 'foreign' a word is felt to be the more likely it is to be distinguished in this way. However, italics are generally retained in practice even for well-established words where there might be any possibility of confusion with an English word, as between *pace* (Latin ablative singular of *pax* used as a preposition) and 'pace' English noun and verb. Practice regarding italics however varies between British and American English and between publisher and publisher. For this reason, and to avoid the appearance of prescription, no attempt has been made to distinguish between italic and non-italic in the headwords in this dictionary.

Retention of accents is another indicator of awareness of the foreign origin of a word, since the native English writer has a strong tendency to drop them. In this respect the spelling *detour*, to take a common example, is well down the route to total assimilation, but the pronunciation still has a faint echo of the original *détour*.

How far spelling can move away from the original before a word can be said to be wholly Anglicized is not only a matter of the dropping or retention of accents. Various words from the Romance languages have doubled or single consonants in the original and the opposite in the usual English spelling: examples are *concessionnaire* in French, but 'concessionaire' in English, *improvvisatore* in Italian, but 'improvisatore' in English; on the other hand it is 'commando' in English but *comando* in Portuguese. Some variation in unstressed vowels also appears (*imprimitura* in Italian, but predominantly 'imprimatura' in English). However, in none of these cases does the fluctuation in spelling seriously affect the perception of the word as 'foreign'.

More latitude has been allowed in the case of words transcribed from non-Roman alphabets, and significant variants have been noted. For instance, Greek *kappa*, formerly often transcribed as *c*, is now more frequently rendered *k*, particularly in specialist contexts. Variation between *s* and *sh* and between *c* and *ch* occurs in transliterations from various languages of the Indian subcontinent. Attempts by users to make transliterations conform to English spelling norms have not disqualified words, since they generally do not disguise the alien origin of the word itself.

To keep the dictionary within reasonable bounds, several whole categories of words have been excluded, unless there is some strong reason to make an exception for a particular member of the class. If a word has a transferred meaning in English or is sufficiently at home to be used figuratively, it is generally included; thus, made-up words, even those with impeccable classical Greek or Latin elements such as *homophobia*, *megalomania*, are usually not admitted, but *utopia* is included. A very few other words such as *braggadocio* that are not genuine foreign words at all have been allowed in on the basis of their being so easily mistaken for a genuine borrowing. Also in are Latin phrases such as *infra dig.* that are seldom or never given their full form in English usage. Currencies, obsolete coins, weights and measures, and scientific units are excluded, but exceptions are made for *shekel* and *sou* on account of their metaphorical uses. Plant and animal names do not have entries unless they are also the names of a commodity that is widely traded or used; thus *jojoba* and *vicuña* are both in.

Evidence for use in the latter part of the twentieth century almost always guarantees inclusion, although some items which duplicate good English expressions and which are therefore unlikely to move beyond an entirely literary ambience have been omitted (e.g. *dialogue des sourds* smacks of affectation as an alternative to 'dialogue of the deaf'). Sometimes a foreign expression fulfils a valid function as a euphemism: *faux marbre* sounds considerably more up-market than *fake* (or *false*) *marble*. Words that are current but used only in the context of the country of origin have been looked at individually on the basis of likelihood of applications outside the particular national context; for example, *ragazza* as a word for 'girl' is most unlikely to be encountered anywhere except in a text specifically about or set in Italy, while *wagon-lit* on the other hand is much less country-specific. Greetings and polite forms of address have generally been excluded on similar grounds, *gnädige Frau* and such expressions belonging more properly in a foreign-language phrase book.

The tables given in the Appendix break down the headwords in the *Dictionary* by country of origin and century of introduction. They are intended as a snapshot of the foreign expressions for which there is evidence in twentieth-century texts and are in no sense a statistical exercise. Dates are given in abbreviated form, following the scheme used for the *New Shorter Oxford English Dictionary* (see below).

OE	Old English	pre-1149
ME	Middle English	1150–1349
LME	late Middle English	1350–1469
L15	late fifteenth century	1470–1499
E16	early sixteenth century	1500–1529
M16	mid sixteenth century	1530–1569
L16	late sixteenth century	1570–1599
E17	early seventeenth century	1600–1629
M17	mid seventeenth century	1630–1669
L17	late seventeenth century	1670–1699
E18	early eighteenth century	1700–1729
M18	mid eighteenth century	1730–1769
L18	late eighteenth century	1770–1799
E19	early nineteenth century	1800–1829
M19	mid nineteenth century	1830–1869
L19	late nineteenth century	1870–1899
E20	early twentieth century	1900–1929
M20	mid twentieth century	1930–1969
L20	late twentieth century	1970–

Pronunciation Guide

Guidance on pronunciation follows the International Phonetic Alphabet system (IPA), and is based on the pronunciation associated especially with southern England (sometimes referred to as 'Received Pronunciation'). Many foreign words and phrases, however, have widely varying pronunciations, ranging from the wholly naturalized to a conscious attempt to reproduce what the speaker believes to be the 'foreign' pronunciation, and it is neither feasible nor particularly helpful to include every possibility.

Stress

ˈ indicates primary stress on the following syllable
ˌ indicates secondary stress on the following syllable

Consonants and Semivowels

b, d, f, h, k, l, m, n, p, r, s, t, v, w, and *z* all have their usual English values. Other sounds are represented by the following symbols:

ɡ get	x lo*ch*	ð *th*is	j *y*es
tʃ *ch*ip	ŋ ri*ng*	ʃ *sh*e	dʒ *j*ar
θ *th*in	ʒ deci*s*ion	ç (German) e*ch*t	
ɲ (French) seig*n*eur		ɥ (French) n*u*it	

(r) indicates an *r* that is sometimes sounded when a vowel follows, as in *cha-chaing*.

Vowels

The following symbols represent vowel sounds that appear in English and foreign languages:

short vowels	*long vowels* (ː *indicates length*)	*diphthongs*
a c*a*t	ɑː *ar*m	ʌɪ m*y*
ɛ b*e*d	ɛː h*air*	aʊ h*ow*
ə *a*go	əː h*er*	eɪ d*ay*
ɪ s*i*t	iː s*ee*	əʊ n*o*
i cos*y*	ɔː s*aw*	ɪə n*ear*
ɒ h*o*t	uː t*oo*	ɔɪ b*oy*
ʌ r*u*n		ʊə p*oor*
ʊ p*u*t		ʌɪə f*ire*
		aʊə s*our*

(ə) signifies the indeterminate sound as in the final syllables of *garden*, *carnal*, and *rhythm*.

The following symbols are used for vowel sounds that do not occur in English:

short vowels		*long vowels* (**:** *indicates length*)	
ɑ	(French) p*a*ssé		
e	(French) démod*é* (Italian) dolc*e*	eː	(German) W*e*hrmacht (Italian) comm*e*dia
o	(French) *au*berge (German) Bildungsr*o*man (Italian) am*o*rett*o*	oː	(German) verb*o*ten (Italian) cass*o*ne
ɔ	(French) b*o*rné (German) D*o*ppelgänger (Italian) d*o*nna		
œ	(French) b*oeu*f	œː	(French) accouch*eur*
ø	(French) bl*eu*	øː	(French) berc*eu*se (German) Gasth*ö*fe
u	(French) bij*ou* (Italian) fig*u*rante		
y	(French) cr*u*	yː	(German) gem*ü*tlich

The following symbols are used for other sounds that do not occur in English:

nasalized vowels (˜ *indicates nasality*)		*diphthongs*	
ɒ̃	(French) cord*on* bleu	aɪ	(German) Gl*ei*chschaltung
ɑ̃	(French) *en*		
ɛ̃	(French) dist*in*gué	ɔy	(German) Hakenkr*eu*z
ɔ̃	(French) c*on*gé		

aa /ˈɑːɑː/ *noun* M19 **Hawaiian** (ʻ*a*-ʻ*a*). *Geology* Rough, clinkery, scoriaceous lava. Cf. PAHOEHOE.

aba /ˈabə/ *noun* (also **abba**) E19 **Arabic** (ʻ*abā*ʼ). A sleeveless outer garment of various forms, worn by Arabs. Cf. ABAYA.

abacus /ˈabəkəs/ *noun* plural **abaci** /ˈabəsʌɪ/, **abacuses** M16 **Latin** (from Greek *abakos*, *abax* slab, originally drawing-board covered with dust, from Semitic: cf. Hebrew *ʼābāq* dust). **1** M16 *Architecture* The upper member of a capital, supporting the architrave. **2** L17 A calculating frame, *especially* one with balls sliding on wires. **3** L18 *Classical Antiquities* A sideboard.

■ The word was first introduced (LME) in its antique sense of 'a board strewn with sand, for drawing figures, etc.' but this sense is not found after the medieval period.

à bas /a bɑ/ *interjection* M19 **French**. Down with . . . !

■ Always followed by the name of a person or thing.

abatis /ˈabətɪs/ *noun* (also **abattis** /əˈbatɪs/) plural **abat(t)is**, **abatises** M18 **French** (from Old French *abatre*, ultimately from Latin *batt(u)ere* to beat). *Military* A defence formed by placing felled trees lengthwise one over the other with their branches towards the enemy line. Also, a barricade of barbed wire.

abattoir /ˈabətwɑː/ *noun* E19 **French** (from *abattre* to fell). A slaughterhouse.

abaya /əˈbeɪjə/ *noun* M19 **Arabic**. An ABA.

Abba /ˈabə/ *noun* LME **ecclesiastical Latin** (from New Testament Greek, from Aramaic *ʼabbā* father). *Christian Church* **1** LME *Abba, father*: an invocation to God as Father (Mark 14:36 etc.). **2** M17 A title given to bishops and patriarchs in the Syrian Orthodox and Coptic Churches.

abba see ABA.

abbé /ˈabeɪ/, *foreign* /abe/ (*plural same*) *noun* M16 **French** (from ecclesiastical Latin *abbat-* abbot). In France: an abbot, a secular priest, or *loosely* anyone, with or without official duties, who is entitled to wear ecclesiastical dress.

ab extra /ab ˈɛkstrə/ *adverb phrase* M17 **Late Latin**. From outside.

ab initio /ab ɪˈnɪʃɪəʊ/ *adverb phrase* E17 **Latin**. From the beginning.

1996 *Spectator* An unthinking agnosticism is taken for granted everywhere, so atheists are seldom called on to put their case *ab initio*.

ab intra /ab ˈɪntrə/ *adverb phrase* L17 **Modern Latin**. From inside.

Abitur /abiˈtuːr/ *noun* (also **abitur**) M20 **German** (abbreviation of *Abiturientenexamen* leavers' examination). In Germany: a set of examinations taken in the final year of secondary school (success in which formerly ensured a university place).

Abiturient /ˌabituriˈɛnt/ *noun* (also **abiturient**) plural **Abiturienten** M19 **German** (from Modern Latin *abiturire* to wish to leave). A candidate for the ABITUR.

ablaut /ˈablaʊt/ *noun* M19 **German** (from *ab* off + *Laut* sound). *Philology* Vowel change in related words, *especially* that in Indo-European, which survives in English in, e.g., *sing, sang, sung, song*.

abonné /abɔne/ *noun* plural pronounced same L19 **French** (past participle of *abonner* to subscribe). A subscriber; a season-ticket holder.

abonnement /abɔnmɑ̃/ *noun* plural pronounced same L19 **French** (from *abonner* to subscribe). A subscription, as for a newspaper etc.; a season ticket.

ab origine /ab əˈrɪdʒɪni/ *adverb phrase* M16 **Latin** (from *ab* from + *origine* ablative of *origo* beginning, source). From the beginning; from the creation of the world.

abortus /əˈbɔːtəs/ *noun* plural **aborti** /əˈbɔːtʌɪ/, **abortuses** M19 **Latin** (= miscarriage). *Medicine* **1** M19 Abortion. **2** E20 An aborted foetus.

ab ovo /ab ˈəʊvəʊ/ *adverb phrase* L16 **Latin** (= from the egg). From the (very) beginning.

abrazo /aˈbraθo/, /aˈbraso/, /əˈbrɑːzəʊ/ *noun* plural **abrazos** /aˈbraθos/,

/a'brasos/, /ə'brɑ:zəʊz/ E20 **Spanish**. An embrace, a hug, especially as a salutation.

abri /ə'bri:/ *noun* E19 **French**. A shelter; *specifically* in *Archaeology*, an overhanging rock affording shelter.

abscissa /ab'sɪsə/ *noun* plural **abscissae** /ab'sɪsi:/, **abscissas** L17 **Modern Latin** (*abscissa* use as noun (sc. *linea* line) of feminine past participle of *abscindere* to cut asunder). **1** L17 *Mathematics* Originally, the portion of a line between a fixed point on it and the point of intersection with an ordinate. Now, the distance of a point from the *y*-axis measured parallel to the *x*-axis. **2** L19 *Botany absciss layer*, a distinctive layer of cells at which separation occurs on leaf-fall.

abseil /'abzʌɪl/, /'abseɪl/ *noun & intransitive verb* M20 **German** (*abseilen*, from *ab* down + *Seil* rope). **1** M20 *Mountaineering* (Make) a descent of a steep rock-face by means of a doubled rope fixed at a higher point. **2** L20 (Make) a similar descent from a helicopter.

absinth /'absɪnθ/ *noun* (also (in sense 2 usually) **absinthe**) LME **French** (*absinthe* from Latin *absinthium* from Greek *apsinthion* wormwood). **1** LME Wormwood, the plant *Artemisia absinthium* or its essence; *figuratively* bitterness, sorrow. **2** M19 A green liqueur made (at least originally) from wine and wormwood. **b** L19 A green colour resembling that of the liqueur.

absit omen /'absɪt ˌəʊmən/ *interjection* L16 **Latin** (= may this (ill) omen be absent). May this evil foreboding not become fact.

absurdum /əb'sə:dəm/ *noun* plural **absurda** /əb'sə:də/ M19 **Latin** (neuter singular of *absurdus* absurd, used as noun). An absurd or illogical conclusion or condition. See also REDUCTIO AD ABSURDUM.

ab urbe condita /ab ˌə:beɪ kɒn'dɪtə/ *adverbial phrase* E17 **Latin** (= since the foundation of the city). (In the Roman annual dating system) since the founding of Rome.

■ The traditional date of the founding of Rome was 753 BC, which was the point of departure for the computation of dates. A variant form of the phrase is *anno urbis conditae* in the year of the founding of the city. Both version are abbreviated AUC.

AC abbreviation of APPELLATION CONTRÔLÉE.

academia /akə'di:mɪə/ *noun* M20 **Latin** (from Greek *akadem(e)ia*, adjective from *Akademos*). The world of higher learning; the university environment or community.

■ Akademos was the man or demigod who gave his name to the garden just outside ancient Athens where Plato conducted his philosophical school.

acanthus /ə'kanθəs/ *noun* M16 **Latin** (from Greek *akanthos*, from *akantha* thorn, perhaps from *akē* sharp point). **1** M16 Any of several erect herbaceous plants belonging to the genus *Acanthus* (family Acanthaceae), having decorative spiny leaves; especially *Acanthus spinosus*, native to the Mediterranean region. **2** M18 *Architecture* A conventionalized form of the leaf of *Acanthus spinosus*, used to decorate Corinthian and Composite capitals; hence, a similar decorative motif used on furniture and fabrics.

a cappella /a kə'pɛlə/, /ɑ:/ *adjective & adverb phrase* L19 **Italian** (= in chapel style). Of choral music or choirs: unaccompanied. Cf. ALLA CAPELLA.

■ Used both as a premodifier and postpositively (see quotations).

1995 *Times* No doubt the uninviting weather had something to do with it [the smallness of the audience], although admittedly it is difficult to imagine a programme of 20th-century German and Dutch *a cappella* music ever causing a traffic jam in Smith Square.
1996 *Times* He [sc. Bruce Springsteen] remained at the Ivy the other night until all other diners had left, then regaled staff with a short concert *a cappella*.

accelerando /əkˌsɛlə'randəʊ/, /əˌtʃɛlə'randəʊ/ *adverb, adjective, & noun* E19 **Italian**. *Music* E19 **A** *adverb & adjective* (A direction:) with gradual increase of speed. **B** *noun* L19 plural **accelerandos, accelerandi**. A gradual increase of speed; a passage (to be) played with a gradual increase of speed; also *figurative*.

B 1996 *Bookseller* There are fewer and fewer prerequisites to studying the humanities, but . . . the entrance exams in mathematics and physics for the first-year student, were what, less than 15 years ago, would have been post-doctoral research. That is your accelerando.

acciaccatura /əˌtʃakə'tʊərə/, *foreign* /atˌtʃakka'tu:ra/ *noun* plural **acciaccaturas, acciaccature** /atˌtʃakka'tu:re/ E19 **Italian** (from *acciaccare* to crush). *Music* A grace-note performed quickly before an essential note of a melody.

accidie /'aksɪdi/ *noun* ME **Anglo-Norman** (= Old French *accide* from medieval Latin *accidia*, alteration of late Latin ACEDIA). Sloth, torpor, apathy. Now also, despair.

■ Became obsolete (E16), but subsequently revived (L19).

accouchement /əˈkuːʃmɒ̃/, *foreign* /akuʃmɑ̃/ *noun* L18 **French** (from *accoucher* to give birth). Childbirth.

accoucheur /akuːˈʃəː/, *foreign* /akuʃœr/ (*plural same*) *noun* M18 **French** (from *accoucher* to give birth). A man (formerly also a woman) who acts as midwife.

accra /ˈakrə/, /əˈkrɑː/ *noun* (also **akkra**, **akara** /əˈkarə/, and other variants) L19 **Yoruba** (*àkàrà* bean cake). A West African and West Indian fritter made with black-eyed peas or a similar pulse.

acedia /əˈsiːdɪə/ *noun* E17 **Late Latin** (*acedia* from Greek *akēdia*, from *a-* not + *kēdos* care, concern). ACCIDIE.

Aceldama /əˈkɛldəmə/, /əˈsɛldəmə/ *noun* M17 **Greek** (*Akeldama* from Aramaic *ḥăqel dĕmā* field of blood). A scene of bloodshed; a place of slaughter.

achar /əˈtʃɑː/ *noun* L16 **Hindustani** (ultimately from Persian *āchār*). Pickles, as prepared in the Indian subcontinent.

acharnement /aʃarnəmɑ̃/, /əˈʃɑːnmɒ̃/ *noun* M18 **French** (from *acharner* to give a taste of flesh (to dogs etc.)). Bloodthirsty fury; ferocity, gusto.

acharya /ɑːˈtʃɑːrjə/ *noun* E19 **Sanskrit** (*ācārya* master, teacher). In the Indian subcontinent: (a title given to) a spiritual teacher or leader; *transferred* a mentor.

à cheval /a ʃəval/, /ɑː ʃəˈval/ *adverb phrase* M19 **French** (= on horseback). With one foot on each side; with a stake risked equally on two chances.

achkan /ˈatʃk(ə)n/ *noun* E20 **Hindustani** (*ackan*). A knee-length coat, buttoned in front, worn by men in the Indian subcontinent.

acme /ˈakmi/ *noun* L16 **Greek** (*akmē* highest point). The highest point; the point or period of perfection.

■ Long after its introduction into English it was consciously used as a Greek word and written in Greek letters. It was formerly also used in the specific senses of 'the period of full growth; the flower or full bloom of life' (L16–M19) and 'the crisis of an illness' (M17–M19).

à contrecœur /a kɔ̃trəkœr/ *adverb phrase* E19 **French** (literally, 'against the heart'). Against one's will, reluctantly.

1996 *Spectator* A pragmatist, he accepted, *contre coeur*, the liberalisation of the economy as the only alternative to bankruptcy . . .

acropolis /əˈkrɒpəlɪs/ *noun* E17 **Greek** (*akropolis*, from as *akros* tip, peak + *polis* city). The citadel or elevated fortified part of a Greek city, especially of Athens.

acroterion /akrəˈtɪərɪən/ *noun* plural **acroteria** /akrəˈtɪərɪə/ (also **acroter** /ˈakrətə/, plural **acroters**; **acroterium** /akrəˈtɪərɪəm/, **acroteria** /akrəˈtɪərɪə/; **akroterion** /akrəˈtɪərɪən/, **akroteria** /akrəˈtɪərɪə/) M17 **Greek** (*akrōtērion* extremity. Variants from French *acrotère* and (its source) Latin *acroterium* from Greek). *Architecture* **1** *collectively singular* and (usually) in *plural* Ornaments in ranges on roofs of classical buildings. **2** E18 A pedestal for a statue or the like on the centre or side of a pediment.

acte gratuit /akt gratɥi/ *noun phrase* plural **actes gratuits** (pronounced same) M20 **French**. A gratuitous, random, or inconsequent action.

■ The concept of the *acte gratuit* was given currency by the works of the French novelist and essayist André Gide (1869–1951) and explored in such works as *Les Caves du Vatican* (1914).

1933 'Rebecca West' *St Augustine* It was simply a demonstration against order . . . ; in fact, it was an *acte gratuit* of the sort that fills M. André Gide with such ecstasy.

actio in distans /ˌaktɪəʊ ɪn ˈdɪstanz/ M19 **Latin** (= action on something apart). The exertion of force by one body upon another separated from it by space; *figurative* the exertion of influence from afar.

actualité /aktɥalite/ *noun* L20 **French** (= current events). Objective, existing facts.

■ As an alternative to 'truth' in the euphemism 'economical with the *actualité*' (i.e. lying).

acumen /ˈakjʊmən/, /əˈkjuːmən/ *noun* L16 **Latin** (= point, acuteness, from *acuere* to sharpen, from *acus* needle). **1** L16 Sharpness of wit; penetration of perception; keenness of discrimination. **2** L18 *Botany* A tapering point.

■ Of the two pronunciations, /əˈkjuːmən/ is the older and more etymological.

AD abbreviation of ANNO DOMINI.

adage /ˈadɪdʒ/ *noun 1* M16 **French** (from Latin *adagium*, from *ad* to + an early form of *aio* I say). A saying expressing common experience, a folk maxim.

adage /adɑʒ/ *noun 2* plural pronounced same **M20 French** (from Italian, as next). ADAGIO noun 2.

1996 *Spectator* . . . the standard sequence of the various parts of the pas de deux, namely *adage*, variations and coda . . .

adagio /ə'dɑ:(d)ʒɪəʊ/ *adverb, adjective, & noun* **L17 Italian** (from *ad agio* at ease). *Music* **A** *adverb & adjective* L17 In slow time, leisurely. **B** *noun* plural **adagios**. **1** M18 A musical piece or movement in slow time. **2** M18 A dance or ballet movement in slow time.

adat /'adat/ *noun* **L18 Malay** (from Arabic *'āda*). Custom, or customary law, in the Islamic regions of South-East Asia, especially in contrast to Islamic religious law.

■ Also in the phrase *adat law*.

ADC abbreviation of AIDE-DE-CAMP.

ad captandum vulgus /ad kapˌtandəm 'vʌlgəs/ *adverb & adjective phrase* **M18 Latin** (= for alluring the crowd). (Designed) to appeal to the emotions (of the rabble).

■ Also used in the abbreviated form *ad captandum*.

addendum /ə'dɛndəm/ *noun* plural **addenda** /ə'dɛndə/ **L17 Latin** (neuter gerundive of *addere* to add). A thing to be added, especially because of omission; an appendix, an addition; *singular* and (especially) in *plural* (occasionally treated as *singular*), additional matter at the end of a book.

addio /ad'di:o/ *interjection* **L18 Italian** (from *a* to + *Dio* god: cf. ADIEU, ADIOS). Goodbye.

■ Formerly in general use in the subscription of letters etc.

ad eundem /ad ɪ'ʌndəm/ *adverb phrase* **E18 Latin** (= to the same (degree)). (Admitted) to the same degree or rank at another university or institution.

à deux /a dø/ *adverb & adjective phrase* **L19 French**. Of, for, or between, two. Cf. FOLIE À DEUX, MÉNAGE.

ad hoc /ad 'hɒk/ *adverb & adjective phrase* **M17 Latin** (literally, 'to this'). For this particular purpose; special(ly).

1996 *Spectator* [In] 1899, government ministries were relatively small affairs, but the ad hoc jumble of Georgian buildings that housed them in Whitehall was deemed neither to be efficient, nor to reflect the dignity of the largest empire the world had ever seen.

ad hominem /ad 'hɒmɪnɛm/ *adverb & adjective phrase* **L16 Latin** (= to the person). Of an argument etc.: directed to the individual, personal; appealing to an opponent's known personal views rather than reason.

■ Such an argument, which plays upon an opponent's own premisses, seeking to draw from them a conclusion that is rejected by that same opponent, is a legitimate debating tactic, unlike the kind of ARGUMENTUM AD HOMINEM which is really no more than a personal attack.

ad idem /ad 'ɪdɛm/ *adverb phrase* **L16 Latin** (= to the same thing). On the same point, in agreement.

adieu /ə'dju:/ *interjection & noun* **LME French** (Anglo-Norman *adeu*, Old French *adieu*, from *à* to + *Dieu* god: cf. ADDIO, ADIOS). **A** *interjection* LME Goodbye. *Archaic*. **B** *noun* LME plural **adieus**, **adieux** /ə'dju:z/. A leave-taking; a parting word; a farewell.

ad infinitum /ad ˌɪnfɪ'nʌɪtəm/ *adverb & adjective phrase* **E17 Latin** (literally, 'to infinity'). Without limit, for ever.

ad interim /ad 'ɪntərɪm/ *adverb & adjective phrase* **L18 Latin** (*ad* to + *interim* adverb 'meanwhile' used as noun). For the meantime.

adios /adɪ'əʊs/, /adɪ'ɒs/ *interjection* **M19 Spanish** (*adiós*, from *a* to + *Dios* god: cf. ADIEU, ADDIO). Goodbye.

1996 *Times* . . . Señor Nuñez has decided that since he had neither cups nor courtesy from the coach, it is time to say *adios* to Mr Cruyff.

ad lib /ad 'lɪb/ *adverb, adjective, verb & noun* (also **ad-lib**, when used as attributive adjective or verb) **E19 Latin** (abbreviation of next). **A** *adverb* E19 AD LIBITUM. **B** *adjective* E20 Extemporized; spontaneous. **C** *transitive & intransitive verb* E20 To speak extempore, to improvise. **D** *noun* M20 Something extemporized; an ad-lib remark.

ad libitum /ad 'lɪbɪtəm/ *adverb & adjective phrase* **E17 Latin**. According to pleasure; to any desired extent.

■ Often used in the abbreviated form AD LIB.

adjective phrase **1995** *New Scientist* The joke—though it wasn't a funny joke—in our lab is that the most deadly thing we've tested has been a perfectly healthy diet given in ad libitum amounts. We literally kill them [sc. the rats] with kindness.

ad litem /ad 'lʌɪtɛm/ *adverb & adjective phrase* **M18 Latin** (= for the lawsuit). *Law* Of a guardian, etc.: appointed to act, in a lawsuit, on behalf of a child or other incapable person.

ad nauseam /ad 'nɔ:zɪam/, /ad 'nɔ:sɪam/ *adverb phrase* M17 **Latin** (literally, 'to sickness'). To a disgusting or tiresome extent.

■ The phrase was earlier (E17) introduced in the form *ad nauseam usque* (right up to sickness), and also occurs as *usque ad nauseam*, but these have been superseded by the shorter form.

1996 *Times* As we argued ad nauseam at the time, the Government should have consulted the people when the Maastricht treaty was drummed through Parliament . . .

adobe /ə'dəʊb(ɪ)/ *noun* M18 **Spanish** (from *adobar* to plaster, from Arabic *aṭ-ṭūb*, from *al* the + *ṭūb* bricks). **1** M18 An unburnt brick dried in the sun. **b** E19 A house built of such bricks. *United States*. **2** L18 Clay or earth prepared for making into such bricks or suitable for this purpose.

ad personam /ad pə:'səʊnam/ *adverb & adjective phrase* M20 **Latin** (literally, 'to the person'). Personal(ly); on an individual basis.

ad referendum /ad rɛfə'rɛndəm/ *adverb phrase* L18 **Modern Latin** (literally, 'for reference'). Subject to the assent of a higher authority.

ad rem /ad 'rɛm/ *adverb & adjective phrase* L16 **Latin** (literally, 'to the matter'). To the point; to the purpose.

adsuki variant of ADZUKI.

adsum /'adsʌm/ *interjection* L16 **Latin** (1st singular present indicative of *adesse* to be present). I am present.

■ As an answer to a roll-call etc.

ad usum Delphini /ad, ju:səm dɛl'fmɪ/ *adjective phrase* L18 **Latin** (= for the use of the Dauphin). Originally, designating or pertaining to an edition of the classics prepared for the use of the son of Louis XIV of France; hence, expurgated.

ad valorem /ad və'lɔ:rɛm/ *adverb & adjective phrase* L17 **Latin** (= according to the value). Of taxes: in proportion to the estimated value of goods.

adversaria /advə'sɛ:rɪə/ *noun plural* E18 **Latin** (use as noun of neuter plural (sc. *scripta* writings) of *adversarius* facing one). Miscellaneous remarks and observations; *collectively singular* a commonplace-book.

ad vivum /ad 'vi:vəm/ *adverb & adjective phrase* M17 **Latin** (= according to the living (model)). (Painted) from life.

1996 *Country Life* . . . this *ad vivum* rendering captures perhaps better than any other, the physical presence and psychology of the future King.

advocatus diaboli /advə,kɑ:təs di:'abəli:/, /advə,keɪtəs dʌɪ'abəlʌɪ/ *noun phrase* E19 **Modern Latin** (literally, 'devil's advocate'). *Roman Catholic Church* The official whose function is to put the case against a person's beatification or canonization; *transferred* a person who provokes argument or debate by supporting the opposing side or by pointing out the weaknesses in his or her own case.

■ The phrase, particularly in its transferred sense, is now much more familiar in its English form: 'devil's advocate'.

1933 *Music and Letters* It is a pleasant thing to play *advocatus diaboli* with the knowledge that one is going to allow oneself to cross over to the angels' bench later.

adytum /'adɪtəm/ *noun* plural **adyta** /'adɪtə/ E17 **Latin** (from Greek *aduton* use as noun of neuter singular of *adutos* impenetrable). The innermost part of a temple; a private chamber, a sanctum.

adzuki /əd'zu:ki/ *noun* (also **adsuki**, **azuki**) E18 **Japanese** (*azuki*). A bushy leguminous plant, *Vigna angularis*, cultivated in China and Japan; the edible bean of this plant.

■ Also in the phrase *adzuki bean*.

aegis /'i:dʒɪs/ *noun* (also **egis** (chiefly United States)) E17 **Latin** (from Greek *aigis* shield of Zeus). **1** E17 A shield, defensive armour, *especially* that of Jupiter or Minerva. **2** L18 *figurative* Protection; an impregnable defence.

■ Most frequently in the phrase *under the aegis of* 'under the protection of' (see quotation).

1996 *Country Life* Here under the aegis of Jan Brueghel, Roelandt Savery and Bosschaert we can see the format evolving.

aegrotat /ʌɪ'grə(ʊ)tat/, /'i:grə(ʊ)tat/, /i:'grə(ʊ)tat/ *noun* L18 **Latin** (*aegrotat* 3rd singular present indicative of *aegrotare* to be ill, from *aeger* sick, ill). In universities, a certificate that a student is too ill to attend an examination etc.; an examination pass or (*North America*) a credit awarded to a student having such a certificate.

aetatis /ʌɪ'tɑ:tɪs/, /i:'teɪtɪs/ *adjective* (usually abbreviated as **aet.**) /ʌɪt/, /i:t/ or **aetat** /'ʌɪtat/, /'i:tat/ E19 **Latin**. Of or at the age of.

■ The formula *aetatis*, *aetatis suae*, or one of the abbreviations, plus a figure, is found much earlier, in England and elsewhere, inscribed on portraits to give the age of the sitter. The full formula *anno aetatis suae* is also occasionally found.

affaire /afɛr/ *noun* plural pronounced same E19 **French**. A temporary sexual relationship outside marriage; a love affair. Also *generally* a sensational event, case, or scandal.

■ Originally more usual in its full form *affaire de* (or *du*) *cœur* /də/, /dy/, /kœr/ (literally, 'affair of the heart'). In its more general sense, used with the definite article (either French or English), followed by the name of the person(s) involved (see quotation 1995).

1958 A. Wilson *Middle Age of Mrs. Eliot* It would be so awful to have one of those office affaires that they have in the women's mags. **1995** *Times* Robbed of its most lurid aspect—money—*l'affaire* O.J. [sc. Simpson] may now serve a more contemplative purpose.

affairé /afere/ *adjective* E20 **French**. Busy; involved.

affaire de (or **du**) **cœur** see AFFAIRE.

affiche /afiʃ/ (*plural same*); /ə'fi:ʃ/ *noun* E19 **French**. A notice affixed to a wall etc.; a poster.

affidavit /afɪ'deɪvɪt/ *noun* M16 **Medieval Latin** (= he/she has affirmed, 3rd person singular perfect indicative of *affidare* to declare on oath). *Law* A written statement, confirmed by oath, to be used as evidence.

■ In legal phraseology a deponent *swears* an affidavit, the judge *takes* it; in popular use, however, the deponent *takes* or *makes* it.

1996 *Oldie* For my part, once I am sure that everyone knows who I am talking about, I shall sign an affidavit that all the characters are fictitious, and publish the book anonymously.

afflatus /ə'fleɪtəs/ *noun* M17 **Latin** (from *afflat-* past participial stem of *afflare*, from *ad* on + *flare* to blow). The communication of supernatural knowledge; divine impulse; (especially poetic) inspiration.

aficionado /afɪsjə'nɑ:dəʊ/, *foreign* /a,fiθjo 'nado/, *noun* plural **aficionados** /a,fɪsjə 'nɑ:dəʊz/, *foreign* /a,fiθjo'nados/ M19 **Spanish** (= amateur, use as noun of past participle of *aficioner* to become fond of, from *afición* from Latin *affectio* favourable disposition). **1** M19 A devotee of bullfighting. **2** L19 An ardent follower of any activity or interest.

1 1996 *Spectator* For those of us who are *aficionados*, it is satisfying to report that the bullfight is flourishing today as never before. **2 1996** *Times* Dennis Potter *aficionados* may care to take notice of Keeley Hawes . . . who will be making something of a splash as the female star of *Karaoke*.

à fond /a fɔ̃/ *adverb phrase* E19 **French** (literally, 'to bottom'). Thoroughly, fully.

a fortiori /eɪ fɔ:tɪ'ɔ:rʌɪ/, /fɔ:tɪ'ɔ:ri:/ *adverb phrase* E17 **Latin**. With yet stronger reason; more conclusively; even more so.

1961 *New Scientist* Anyone who . . . loses his sight after leaving school—or *a fortiori* in mid-career—cannot easily escape feelings of deep dismay.

afreet /'afri:t/ *noun* (also **afrit**, **efreet** /'ɛfri:t/) L18 **Arabic** (*'ifrīt*, colloquial *'afrīt*). A powerful jinnee in Arabian stories and Muslim mythology.

aga /'ɑ:gə/ *noun* (also **agha**) M16 **Turkish** (*ağa* master, lord from Mongolian *aqa*). An Ottoman title, now abolished, for (originally) a military commander and (later) officials of various ranks. Now, a title of respect for landowners among Turkish village people.

agal /a'gɑ:l/ *noun* M19 **Arabic** (representing Bedouin pronunciation of Arabic *'iḳāl* bond, rope for hobbling a camel). A fillet worn around the head by Bedouin Arabs to keep the KEFFIYEH in position.

agape /'agəpi/ *noun* plural **agapae** /'agəpi:/, **agapes** E17 **Greek** (*agapē* brotherly love). **1** E17 A love-feast held by early Christians in connection with the Eucharist; *transferred* a parochial feast at a festival time. **2** M19 Christian love, charity.

agapemone /agə'pi:məni/, /agə'pɛməni/ *noun* M19 **Greek** (irregular formation from *agapē* love + *monē* abode). An abode of love; an establishment where free love is practised.

■ Originally with capital initial, the name of a community founded in Somerset, England, *c.*1850 by H. J. Prince.

agar-agar /,eɪgɑ:r'eɪgɑ:/ *noun* (in sense 2 usually simply **agar**) E19 **Malay**. **1** E19 Any of certain South-East Asian seaweeds from which a gelatinous substance is extracted. **2** M19 The substance itself, used especially to make soups and to form biological culture media.

agenda /ə'dʒɛndə/ *noun plural*, also used as *singular* (less commonly in singular **agendum** /ə'dʒɛndəm/) E17 **Latin** (plural of *agendum*, use as noun of gerundive of *agere* to do). **1** E17 *plural* Things to be done; matters of practice. **2** M18 *collective singular* A memorandum book. *archaic*.

3 L19 As *plural*, items of business to be considered at a meeting or to be otherwise attended to. As *singular*, a list of such items.

agent provocateur /aʒɑ̃ prɔvɔkatœr/ *noun phrase* plural **agents provocateurs** (pronounced same) L19 **French** (= provocative agent). An agent employed to tempt suspected persons into committing an incriminating act.

1996 *Times* Either try persuading people that cycling is a realistic mode of transport in London. Or—forgive me for sounding like an *agent provocateur*—start shooting motorists.

aggiornamento /adˌdʒorna'mento/, /əˌdʒɔːnə'mɛntəʊ/ *noun* M20 **Italian**. Bringing up to date, especially of Roman Catholic Church policy by and after the Second Vatican Council (1962–5).

agio /'adʒɪəʊ/ *noun* plural **agios** L17 **Italian** (*ag(g)io*). **1** L17 The percentage charged for changing paper money into cash, or an inferior for a more valuable currency; the excess value of one currency over another. **2** E19 *loosely*. Money-changing.

agiotage /'adʒɪətɪdʒ/ *noun* L18 **French** (from *agioter* to speculate, from Italian *ag(g)io* from as preceding). Money-changing business; speculation in stocks; stock-jobbing.

agitato /adʒɪ'tɑːtəʊ/ *adverb, adjective, & noun* E19 **Italian**. *Music* **A** *adverb & adjective* E19 (A direction:) in an agitated manner. **B** *noun* E19 plural **agitati** /ɑdʒɪ'tɑːti/, **agitatos**. A passage (to be) played or sung in an agitated manner. *rare*.

agitprop /'adʒɪtprɒp/, /'agɪtprɒp/ *noun* (also **Agitprop**) E20 **Russian** (from *agit(atsiya)* agitation + *prop(aganda)* propaganda). *History* Soviet Communist propaganda; the system or activity of disseminating this.

agloo, **aglu** see IGLOO.

agnolotti /ˌanjə'lɒti/ *noun plural* L20 **Italian**. Pasta made into cases with meat or other stuffing. Cf. RAVIOLI.

agnomen /ag'nəʊmɛn/ *noun* M17 **Latin** (*agnomen*, from *ad* to + *(g)nomen* name). A name given or acquired during the course of one's life, a nickname; *Roman History* a fourth name occasionally given as an honour.

Agnus Dei /ˌagnʊs 'deɪiː/, *in sense 1 also* /ˌanjʊs/; /ˌagnəs 'diːʌɪ/ *noun phrase* LME **Latin** (= Lamb of God). *Christian Church* **1** LME Part of the Mass beginning with the words *Agnus Dei*; a musical setting of this. **2** LME A figure of a lamb bearing a cross or flag, as an emblem of Christ. **b** L16 A cake of wax stamped with such a figure and blessed by the Pope.

■ In sense 2 the Agnus Dei is the emblem of St John the Baptist in art, who is very often depicted with it and holding a scroll with the words *ECCE AGNUS DEI* 'Behold the Lamb of God'.

a gogo /ə 'gəʊgəʊ/ *adverb & postpositive adjective phrase* M20 **French** (*à gogo*). In abundance, galore. *colloquial*.

agon /'agəʊn/ *noun* plural **agones** /ə'gəʊniːz/ E17 **Greek** (*agōn* contest). *Greek History* **1** E17 A public celebration comprising athletic games; a contest for the prize at such games or *transferred* elsewhere. **2** L19 A verbal contest between two characters in a play.

agonistes /agə'nɪstiːz/ *postpositive adjective* L17 **Greek** (= contestant). Who is an agonist.

■ First used in the title of John Milton's *Samson Agonistes* (1671) and imitated by later authors.

agora /'agɒrə/ *noun* plural **agorae** /'agɒriː/, **agorai** /'agɒrʌɪ/, **agoras** L16 **Greek**. *Greek History* An assembly; a place of assembly, *especially* a market-place.

1996 *Times* If there was ever an opportunity to create a new European *agora*, the Net's unsupervised electronic anarchy is surely the place.

agoraphobia /ˌag(ə)rə'fəʊbɪə/ *noun* L19 **pseudo-Greek** (from AGORA + -PHOBIA). Irrational terror of open spaces.

■ Coined by the German psychologist Carl Westphal in 1871.

agraphon /'agrəfən/ *noun* plural **agrapha** /'agrəfə/ L19 **Greek** (neuter of *agraphos* unwritten). A saying attributed to Jesus but not in the canonical Gospels. Usually in *plural*.

agrément /agremɑ̃/ *noun* plural **agréments**, **agrémens** (pronounced same) E18 **French**. **1** E18 In *plural* Agreeable qualities, circumstances, etc. **2** L18 *Music* In *plural* Grace-notes; embellishments. **3** E20 Official approval given to a diplomatic representative of another country.

1 1996 *Spectator* The continentals like to have their *agréments*, the comfortable pleasures of civilisation without its pomp.

aguardiente /ˌagwardi'ente/, /əˌgwɑːdɪ'ɛnti/ *noun* E19 **Spanish** (from *agua* water + *ardiente* fiery). Coarse Spanish brandy; in

Spanish-speaking areas of America, a similar distilled liquor, *especially* one made from sugar cane.

AH see under HEGIRA.

ahimsa /əˈhɪmsɑː/ *noun* L19 **Sanskrit** (from *a* non- + *hiṃsā* violence). The doctrine in Hindu, Buddhist, and Jain philosophy that there should be no violence or killing of any living creature, however humble.

à huis clos /a yi klɔ/ *adverb phrase* E17 **French**. In secret, IN CAMERA.

aide-de-camp /eɪddəˈkɒ̃/, *foreign* /ɛddəkɑ̃/ *noun* (also **aid-de-camp**, **aide de camp**) plural **aides-de-camp**, **aids-de-camp** (*chiefly United States*), /eɪdzdəˈkɒ̃/, *foreign* /ɛddəkɑ̃/ L17 **French** (= camp adjutant). *Military* An officer acting as a confidential assistant to a senior officer, or assisting on a ceremonial occasion; *transferred* anyone acting in a similar capacity to a more senior person.

■ Often abbreviated in military use to ADC.

1996 *Times* The culprits were John Redwood, MP for Wokingham, and his ebullient *aide de camp*, Hywel Williams.

aide-mémoire /ˌeɪdmɛmˈwɑː/; *foreign* /ɛdmemwɑr/ *(plural same) noun* M19 **French**. (A book or document serving as) an aid to the memory; (in diplomats' use) a memorandum.

1995 *Spectator* Then I had a bright idea and dug out of a trunk all my account books going back to the 1950s. They are a wonderful *aide-mémoire*.

aigre-doux /ɛgrədu/, /ɛgrəˈduː/ *adjective* (also **aigre-douce** /ɛgrədus/, /ɛgrəˈduːs/) LME **French**. Compounded of sweet and sour; bitter-sweet.

aigrette /ˈeɪgrɛt/, /eɪˈgrɛt/ *noun* M18 **French**. An egret's plume; a tuft of feathers or hair; a spray of gems etc. worn on the head.

aiguille /ˈeɪgwiːl/ *noun* M18 **French** (= needle). A sharply pointed peak of rock, especially in the Alps.

aikido /ʌɪˈkiːdəʊ/ *noun* M20 **Japanese** (*aikidō*, from *ai* together, unify + *ki* spirit + *dō* way). A Japanese form of self-defence and martial art, developed from ju-jitsu and involving holds and throws.

aileron /ˈeɪlərɒn/ *noun* E20 **French** (diminutive of *aile* wing). A movable aerofoil used to control the balance of an aircraft in flight, usually a hinged flap in the trailing edge of a wing.

aioli /ʌɪˈjəʊli/, *foreign* /ajɔli/ *noun* E20 **French** (from Provençal *ai* garlic + *oli* oil). Mayonnaise seasoned with garlic.

akara, **akkra** variants of ACCRA.

akroterion variant of ACROTERION.

akvavit variant of AQUAVIT.

à la /ɑː lɑː/, *foreign* /a la/ *preposition phrase* L16 **French** (abbreviation of À LA MODE). In the manner, method, or style of.

■ Followed by a French noun in standard phrases (see following entries), but also often with an English noun (see quotation).

1995 *Spectator* And how long can the Labour leader go on talking about newness *à la* Newt before someone notices that, unlike with Mr Gingrich, there is no real radicalism behind the rhetoric?

à la bonne femme see BONNE FEMME.

à la broche /ɑː lɑː ˈbrɒʃ/, *foreign* /a la brɔʃ/ *adverb & adjective phrase* E20 **French**. (Cooked) on a spit; spit-roasted. Cf. À LA BROCHETTE.

à la brochette /ɑː lɑː brɒˈʃɛt/, *foreign* /a la brɔʃɛt/ *adverb & adjective phrase* M19 **French**. (Cooked) on a skewer. Cf. À LA BROCHE.

à la carte /ɑː lɑː ˈkɑːt/, *foreign* /a la kart/ *adverb & adjective phrase* E19 **French**. By the bill of fare; ordered as a separately priced item or as separately priced items from a menu, not as part of a table d'hôte meal.

à la daube /ɑː lɑː dəʊb/, *foreign* /a la dob/ *adverb & adjective phrase* E18 **French**. (Of poultry, meat, or game) stewed, braised.

à la Florentine /ɑː lɑː ˈflɒr(ə)ntiːn/, *foreign* /a la flɔrɑ̃tin/ *adverb & adjective phrase* E20 **French** (= in the Florentine manner). (Of eggs, fish, etc.) served on a bed of spinach or with a spinach sauce.

■ Now generally just 'Florentine'.

à la fourchette /ɑː lɑː fʊəˈʃɛt/, *foreign* /a la furʃɛt/ *adverb & adjective phrase* E19 **French**. (Of a meal) requiring the use (only) of a fork.

à la lanterne /ɑː lɑː lɑ̃tɛrn(ə)/ *interjection* L18 **French** (= to the lantern). Away with (them)!

■ The phrase is a quotation from the refrain of the French Revolutionary song 'Ça ira'. It records the Revolutionary mobs' practice of hanging their victims from the street lamps.

1995 *Country Life* Did they hear the trundle of the tumbrels on Blenheim's drive and distant cries of 'A la lanterne' from the streets of Woodstock?

alameda /alə'meɪdə/ *noun* L18 **Spanish**. In Spain and Spanish-speaking areas: a public walk, shaded with trees; an ALLÉE.

à la mode /ɑ: lɑ: 'məʊd/, *foreign* /a la mɔd/ *adverb & adjective phrase* L16 **French** (= in the fashion). **1** L16 In or according to the fashion; fashionable. **2** *Cookery* **a** M17 Of beef: braised or made into a rich stew, usually with wine. **b** E20 Of food: served with ice cream. Chiefly *United States*.

■ Also in use (M–L17) as a noun (phrase), usually as one word, meaning 'a fashion, a temporary mood' or (M17) 'a thin glossy usually black silk'.

1 1996 *Spectator* He ends with a chapter describing what the book might have been, if it had been longer . . . All very much *à la mode*, but why not save the space and cut the price to the public?

à la page /a la paʒ/, /ɑ: lɑ: 'pɑ:ʒ/ *adverb & adjective phrase* M20 **French** (literally, 'at the page'). Up to date, up to the minute.

à la russe /ɑ: lɑ: 'ru:s/, *foreign* /a la rys/ *adverb & adjective phrase* (also **à la Russe**) E19 **French**. In the Russian manner.

■ In the mid nineteenth century *à la russe* often alluded to the then new-fangled custom in smart society of serving meals on a table dressed with flowers and dessert, with the individual courses brought in from another room or served from side-tables.

alba /'albə/ *noun* E19 **Provençal** (ultimately from Latin *albus* white). A medieval Provençal song at dawn. Cf. AUBADE.

albarello /albə'rɛləʊ/ *noun* plural **albarelli** /albə'rɛli/ L19 **Italian** (*alberello* pot, phial). A majolica jar used especially as a container for drugs.

1995 *Country Life* The form of the *albarello* came from Persia in the 15th century, and was popular with northern European potteries as well as the makers of maiolica.

albedo /al'bi:dəʊ/ *noun* plural **albedos** M19 **ecclesiastical Latin** (= whiteness, from Latin *albus* white). The proportion of incident radiation reflected by a surface, especially of a planet or moon.

albergo /al'bɛrgo/, /al'bə:gəʊ/ *noun* plural **alberghi** /al'bɛrgi/, /al'bə:gi:/ E17 **Italian**. An Italian inn. Cf. AUBERGE.

albino /al'bi:nəʊ/ *noun & adjective* E18 **Spanish and Portuguese** (from *albo* white). **A** *noun* plural **albinos** **1** E18 A human being having a congenital deficiency of pigmentation in the skin and hair, which are white, and the eyes, which are usually pink. **2** E19 An abnormally white animal or plant. **B** *adjective* E19 Congenitally lacking in pigmentation; abnormally white.

■ Originally applied by the Portuguese to albinos among African Blacks.

album /'albəm/ *noun* E17 **Latin** (= blank tablet, use as noun of neuter of *albus* white). **I** A blank book for the insertion of collected items. **1** E17 A blank book in which people other than the owner insert autographs, memorial verses, etc. **2** M19 A blank book for the insertion of stamps, photographs, etc. **II 3** E20 A holder for a set of discs or tape recordings; an integral set of discs or tapes; a disc or tape comprising several pieces of music etc.

■ First taken into English from the German use of the Latin phrase *album amicorum* album of friends, i.e. an autograph book.

albumen /'albjʊmɪn/ *noun* (also **albumin** in sense 3) L16 **Latin** (from *albus* white). **1** L16 The white of an egg. **2** L17 *Botany* The nutritive material surrounding the embryo in some plant seeds; the endosperm. **3** E19 Soluble protein, such as that in egg-white.

alcade variant of ALCALDE.

alcaide /al'kʌɪdi/, *foreign* /al'kaide/ *noun* (also **alcaid, alcayde**) E16 **Spanish** (from Arabic *al-ḳā'id* the leader, the commander). The governor of a Spanish, Portuguese, Moorish, etc., fortress; a jailer.

alcalde /al'kaldi/, *foreign* /al'kalde/ *noun* (also **alcade** /al'kɑ:d/, *foreign* /al'kad/) M16 **Spanish** (*alcalde* (French *alcade*) from Arabic *al-ḳāḍī* the judge). A mayor, magistrate, or similar administrative officer in Spain, Portugal, and parts of South America and the south-western United States.

alcayde variant of ALCAIDE.

alcazar /alkə'zɑ:/, *foreign* /al'kaθar/, /al'kasar/ *noun* plural **alcazars** /alkə'zɑ:z/, **alcazares** /al'kaθares/, /al'kasares/ E17 **Spanish** (*alcázar* from Arabic *al-ḳaṣr* the castle). A Spanish palace or fortress.

alcheringa /altʃə'rɪŋgə/ *noun* L19 **Aranda** (= in the dream-time). A golden age in the mythology of some Australian Aborigine groups.

aldea /al'deɪə/, *foreign* /al'dea/ *noun* E17 **Portuguese** (*aldeia*, Spanish *aldea* from Arabic *al-ḍay'a*, from *al* the + *ḍay'a* agricultural village, farm). A small village or a farm in Portugal, Spain, or one of their former territories.

al dente /al 'dɛnti/, *foreign* /al 'dɛnte/ *adverb & adjective phrase* M20 **Italian** (literally, 'to the tooth'). Of pasta, vegetables, etc.: (cooked) so as to be still slightly firm when bitten.

> **1995** *Spectator* [The] pasta, although it had swollen wonderfully with the pale coral juices of the seafood, was just a bit too *al dente*.

aleatico /alɪ'atɪkəʊ/ *noun* (also **Aleatico**) E19 **Italian**. A sweet Italian red wine.

aleph /'ɑːlɛf/ *noun* ME **Hebrew** (*'ālep*, literally, 'ox'; cf. ALPHA). **1** ME The first letter of the Hebrew, Phoenician, and other Semitic alphabets. **2** E20 *Mathematics* A transfinite cardinal numeral.

alfa /'alfə/ *noun* (also **halfa** /'halfə/) M19 **Arabic** (*ḥalfā'*, colloquial *ḥalfa*). Esparto grass.

alfalfa /ˌal'falfə/ *noun* M19 **Spanish** (from Arabic *al-fasfaṣa* a green fodder). A leguminous plant, *Medicago sativa*, cultivated for green fodder; lucerne.

alfilaria /ˌalfɪlə'riːə/ *noun* M19 **Mexican Spanish** (from Spanish *alfiler* pin, with reference to the long-beaked carpels). In the United States: the common stork's-bill, *Erodium cicutarium*, grown as fodder; pin clover.

alforja /al'fɔːhə/, *foreign* /al'fɔrxa/ *noun* Also formerly written **alforge** E17 **Spanish** (*alforja*, Portuguese *alforge* from Arabic *al-ḵurj* the saddle-bag). In Spain, Portugal, Latin America, and other areas of Spanish influence (as the south-western United States): a wallet, a saddle-bag.

alfresco /al'frɛskəʊ/ *adverb & adjective* (also **al fresco**) M18 **Italian** (*al fresco*). **A** *adverb* **1** M18 In the open air. **2** M18 *Art* In fresco. **B** *adjective* E19 Open-air.

> **B 1996** *Times: Weekend* This situation, naturally, has many possibilities, especially when complicated by extra-mural, even *al fresco*, couplings, one of which leads to a sacking.

alga /'algə/ *noun* plural **algae** /'alʤiː/, /'algiː/ M16 **Latin** (= seaweed). Originally, seaweed; now, any of a large group of non-vascular mainly aquatic cryptogams capable of photosynthesis, including seaweeds and many unicellular and filamentous organisms. Also *collectively*, the mass formed by such organisms.

alguacil /algwə'sɪl/, *foreign* /algwa'θil/, /algwa'sil/ *noun* plural **alguacils** /algwə'sɪlz/, *foreign* **alguaciles** /algwa'θiles/, /algwa'siles/ (also **alguazil** /algwə'zɪl/ plural **alguazils** /algwa'zɪlz/, **alguaziles** /algwə'ziːləz/) E16 **Spanish** ((earlier *alguazil*) from Arabic *al-wazīr*, from *al* the + *wazīr* vizier). **1** E16 In Spain: an officer of justice, a warrant-officer, a sergeant. In Latin America or other areas of Spanish influence: a sheriff, a constable. **2** *Bullfighting* E20 A mounted official at a bullfight.

alhaji /al'haʤi/ *noun* (also as a title **Alhaji**) M20 **Hausa** (from Arabic *al* the + *ḥajj* pilgrimage). In West Africa: a Muslim who has been to Mecca as a pilgrim.

alias /'eɪlɪəs/ *adverb & noun* LME **Latin** (= at another time, otherwise). **A** *adverb* LME Otherwise called or named; called at other times. **B** *noun* E17 A name by which a person is or has been called on other occasions; an assumed name.

> **B 1996** *Times: Magazine* So, for whom is Grace an alias?

alibi /'alɪbʌɪ/ *adverb, noun, & verb* L17 **Latin** (= elsewhere). **A** *noun* L18 A plea by the person accused of an act that he or she was elsewhere when it took place; evidence to support such a plea; *colloquially* an excuse of any kind. **B** *transitive & intransitive verb* E20 Provide an alibi, offer an excuse, (for).

■ *Alibi* was originally used in English as an adverb, following the Latin, but during the late eighteenth century this usage became obsolete and was superseded by the modern nominal usage.

aliquot /'alɪkwɒt/ *adjective & noun* L16 **French** (*aliquote* from Latin *aliquot* some, several, from *alius* one of two + *quot* how many). Originally *Mathematics*. **A** *adjective* L16 That is contained in the whole an integral number of times. Chiefly in *aliquot part*. **B** *noun* E17 An aliquot part, integral factor; *loosely* any fraction of a whole, a sample.

alla breve /alə 'breɪvi/ *adverb, adjective, & noun phrase* M18 **Italian** (= according to the breve). *Music* With increased speed, at two minim beats in a bar instead of four crotchets; such a tempo or time signature.

alla cappella /alə kə'pɛlə/ *adverb & adjective phrase* M18 **Italian**. Of choral music or choirs: unaccompanied.

■ Introduced earlier than A CAPPELLA.

alla marcia /ˌalə 'mɑːtʃə/ *adverb, adjective, & noun phrase* L19 **Italian**. *Music* (A piece, movement, etc.) in the style of a march.

allargando /alɑː'gandəʊ/ *adverb, adjective, & noun* L19 **Italian** (= broadening). *Music* **A** *adverb & adjective* L19 (A direction:) getting slower and slower and often also fuller in tone. **B** *noun* M20 plural **allargandi** /alɑː'gandi/, **allargandos**. A passage (to be) so played.

allée /ale/ *noun* plural pronounced same M18 **French**. A walk or passage in a garden, park, etc., usually flanked and shaded by trees or shrubs; an alley.

1996 *Country Life: Garden Year* The grotto is approached through an ominously dark *allée* of tall yews extending south of the house.

allegretto /alɪ'grɛtəʊ/ *adverb, adjective, & noun* M18 **Italian** (diminutive of ALLEGRO). *Music* **A** *adverb & adjective* M18 (A direction:) in fairly quick time, but not as quick(ly) as allegro. **B** *noun* L19 plural **allegrettos**, **allegretti** /alɪ'grɛti/. A movement or piece in fairly quick time. Also, a short movement or piece in quick time.

allegro /ə'leɪgrəʊ/, /ə'lɛgrəʊ/ *adverb, adjective, & noun* L17 **Italian** (= lively, gay). *Music* **A** *adverb & adjective* L17 (A direction:) in quick time; *transferred* (of forms of words and phrases) used in speech and shortened (e.g. *we'll* for *we will*). **B** *noun* M18 plural **allegros**, **allegri** /ə'leɪgri/. A movement or piece in quick time.

allemande /'almɑːnd/, /almɑ̃d/ (*plural same*) *noun* L17 **French** (= German (feminine)). **1** L17 A piece of music for a German dance or in its rhythm, *especially* one which forms a movement of a suite. **2** E18 Any of various German dances. **b** E19 A figure in square dancing in which adjacent dancers link arms or join hands and make a full or partial turn. Also used as a call to dancers to execute this figure turning in the specified direction. **3** *Cookery* E19 A rich velouté sauce thickened with egg yolks.

■ The earliest sense (M17) in which *Allemande* was used in English was 'a German woman', but this is not attested outside this period.

allumette /aluː'mɛt/, *foreign* /alymɛt/ (*plural same*) *noun* E17 **French** (from *allumer* to set light to). A match for lighting or setting things alight.

■ Rare before the nineteenth century.

alluvium /ə'l(j)uːvɪəm/ *noun* plural (now *rare*) **alluvia** /ə'l(j)uːvɪə/, **alluviums** M17 **Latin**, (neuter of *alluvius* washed against, from *ad* to + *luere* to wash). A deposit of clay, silt, sand, etc., left by flowing water, as in a river valley or delta.

Alma Mater /ˌalmə 'mɑːtə/, /'meɪtə/ *noun phrase* (also **alma mater**) plural **Alma Maters**, (*rare*) **Almae Matres** /ˌalmʌɪ 'mɑːtrɛz/, /ˌalmiː 'meɪtriːz/ M17 **Latin** (= bounteous mother, a title given to various Roman goddesses, especially Ceres and Cybele). **1** M17 Someone or something providing nourishment and care. **2** L17 *especially* A university or school as regarded by its past and present members.

2 1996 *Spectator* After representing the Emperor and Empress . . . at King George VI's coronation, and visiting his *alma mater* at Oxford, he [sc. the Crown Prince] returned to Japan . . .

aloe vera /ˌaləʊ 'vɛːrə/ *noun phrase* L20 **Latin** (= true aloe). A plant resembling a cactus from which an extract used in skin care and other health products is obtained.

1989 A. Tan *Joy Luck Club* A cutting of aloe vera that Lena gave me did not belong anywhere because we had no other succulents.

aloha /ə'ləʊhə/ *interjection & noun* E19 **Hawaiian**. Used in Hawaii especially at greeting or parting: love, affection; an utterance of this.

à l'outrance variant of À OUTRANCE.

alpaca /al'pakə/ *noun* L18 **Spanish** (from Aymara *allpaca*). A domesticated Peruvian animal, *Lama pacos*, resembling the llama, with long fine woolly hair and usually brown and white colouring; the wool of the alpaca; fabric or a garment made from this.

alpargata /alpɑː'gɑːtə/ *noun* E19 **Spanish**. An ESPADRILLE.

alpenhorn /'alpənhɔːn/ *noun* L19 **German** (= Alp-horn). A long wooden horn used by Alpine herdsmen.

alpenstock /'alpənstɒk/ *noun* E19 **German** (= Alp-stick). A long iron-tipped staff used in mountain-climbing.

alpha /'alfə/ *noun* ME **Latin** (from Greek). **1** ME The first letter (*A, a*) of the Greek alphabet; the beginning of anything. **2** E17 Denoting the first in a numerical or other sequence. **3** *attributive Science* M18 First, most important; as in *Astronomy* (preceding the genitive of the Latin name of the constellation) designating the chief star in a constellation; thus *Alpha Centauri* is the brightest star in the constellation Centaurus. **4** E20 (A person gaining) a first-class mark in an examination etc.

■ In sense 1 *alpha* often appears in the phrase *the alpha and (the) omega*, which originally referred to God (see Revelation 1:8), but now is also used in the transferred sense of 'the beginning and the end' (see quotation 1996). In scientific terminology *alpha* has specialist applications in Chemistry, Medicine, and Computing, as well as Astronomy.

1 1996 *Times* The 100 metres is the alpha and omega of sport.

3 1995 *New Scientist* If the female deigns to mate, the honour goes to the senior partner, or alpha male. The junior, or beta male reaps his reward years later: when the alpha dies, the beta inherits his mentor's alpha status, and recruits his own apprentice.

al segno /al 'sɛnjəʊ/ *adverb phrase* L18 **Italian** (= to the sign). *Music* (A direction:) go back (= DAL SEGNO) or continue to the point indicated by the sign.

alter ego /ˌaltər 'ɛgəʊ/, /ˌɒltər/, /'iːgəʊ/ *noun phrase* plural **alter egos** M16 **Latin** (= other self). A person's second self; an intimate friend; a representative of another person.

1996 *Times* If . . . Anne is ever-faithful Auden to Kallman's rake, then the poet could not have asked for a more sympathetic alter ego.
1996 *Oldie* 'Simply put, one of the greatest writers ever.' This is Scott Turow's considered judgment on Ruth Rendall and her alter ego Barbara Vine.

althorn /'althɔːn/ *noun* M19 **German** (*alt* alto + *horn* horn). *Music* A wind instrument of the saxhorn family.

altiplano /altɪ'plɑːnəʊ/, *foreign* /alti'plano/ *noun* E20 **Spanish**. The high tableland of central South America.

alto /'altəʊ/ *noun & adjective* L16 **Italian** (= high (sc. song) from Latin *altus* high). *Music* **A** *noun* plural **altos** **1a** L16 The highest adult male voice, with range above the tenor, the counter-tenor voice; a part written for such a voice. **b** E19 A female voice of similar range, a contralto voice; a part written for such a voice. **2** L18 A person who has a counter-tenor or contralto voice. **3** L19 An alto wind instrument (see **B**). **B** *adjective* E18 Designating, pertaining to, or intended for a counter-tenor or contralto voice. Also, designating that member of a group of similar instruments with a range or relative pitch comparable to an alto voice (among wind instruments usually the second or third highest member of the family).

alto-relievo /ˌaltəʊrɪ'liːvəʊ/ *noun* (also **alto-rilievo** /ˌaltəʊrɪ'ljeɪvəʊ/) plural **alto-relievos** M17 **Italian** (*alto-rilievo*). (A sculpture, moulding, carving, etc., in) high relief.

alumna /ə'lʌmnə/ *noun* plural **alumnae** /ə'lʌmniː/ L19 **Latin** (feminine of next). A female graduate or former student of a school, college, university, or other educational institution.

alumnus /ə'lʌmnəs/ *noun* plural **alumni** /ə'lʌmnʌɪ/, /ə'lʌmniː/ M17 **Latin** (= nursling, pupil, from *alere* to nourish). Formerly, a pupil. Now *specifically*, a (male) graduate or former student of a school, college, university, or other educational institution.

a.m. abbreviation of ANTE MERIDIEM.

ama /'amə/ *noun* plural same M20 **Japanese**. A Japanese woman who dives for shellfish and edible seaweed.

amah /'ɑːmə/ *noun* M19 **Portuguese** (*ama* nurse). In parts of the Indian subcontinent and the Far East: a wet-nurse, a children's nurse, a house-servant.

amanuensis /əˌmanjʊ'ɛnsɪs/ *noun* plural **amanuenses** /əˌmanjʊ'ɛnsiːz/ E17 **Latin** (from *a manu* in *servus a manu* slave at hand + *-ensis* belonging to). A person who writes from dictation or copies manuscript; a literary assistant.

■ The Latin phrase *servus a manu* was used by Suetonius (Life of Julius Caesar: 74) and by the Latin legal writers to denote a slave who acted as a secretary.

amateur /'amətə/, /'amətjʊə/ *noun & adjective* L18 **French** (from Italian *amatore* from Latin *amator* lover). **A** *noun* **1** L18 A person who is fond *of* something; a person who has a taste for something. **2** L18 A person who practises something, especially an art or game, only as a pastime; an unpaid player, performer, etc. (opposed *professional*); also (*depreciative*), a dabbler. **B** E19 *attributive* or as *adjective* Done by amateurs, not professional; also (*depreciative*), unskilful.

ambiance /ɑ̃bjɑ̃s/ *noun* M20 **French** (from *ambiant* from Latin *ambire* to go round). Environment, ambience; also *specifically*, the combination of the accessory elements of a painting to support the main effect of a piece.

■ The Anglicized *ambience* tends to be used in general contexts, with *ambiance* suggesting a more contrived or specially created atmosphere, as in the *ambiance* of a club or restaurant (see quotation).

1996 *Times* Now there are theme restaurants: hang the food, feel the ambiance is the premise on which they operate.

ambiente /ambi'ente/, /ambɪ'ɛnti/ *noun* E20 **Italian and Spanish**. Surroundings, ambience.

ambo /'ambəʊ/ *noun* plural **ambos** also written in Latin form **ambones** /am'bəʊni:z/ M17 **Medieval Latin** (from Greek *ambōn* rim, edge of a cup). The pulpit or reading-desk in early Christian churches; an oblong enclosure with steps at both ends.

ambrosia /am'brəʊzjə/ *noun* M16 **Latin** (from Greek = immortality, elixir of life, from *ambrotos* immortal; in Dioscurides and Pliny applied to one or more herbs). **I 1** M16 *Classical Mythology* The food, drink, or unguent of the gods. **2** E17 (Honey and) pollen used as food by bees, bee-bread. **3** M17 Something divinely sweet to taste or smell. **4** L17 Water, oil, and fruits mixed as a libation; also, a perfumed or flavoured drink. **5** L19 A fungal product which forms the food of the pin-hole borer. **II 6** M16 Wood-sage and certain other plants. Now only as Modern Latin name of a genus of plants of the Compositae family.

ameba variant of AMOEBA.

âme damnée /ɑm dɑne/ *noun phrase* plural **âmes damnées** (pronounced same) E19 **French** (= damned soul). A devoted adherent; a stooge.

ameer mainly US variant of AMIR.

amende honorable /amɑ̃d ɔnɔrabl/ *noun phrase* plural **amendes honorables** (pronounced same) E17 **French** (= honourable reparation). Public or open apology and reparation; an instance of this.

a mensa et thoro /eɪ ˌmɛnsɑ: ɛt 'tɔ:rəʊ/ *adverb & adjective phrase* E17 **Latin** (= from table and bed). *Law*. Formerly (before 1857) of a divorce: decreed by an ecclesiastical court on grounds sanctioned by law (having the effect of a modern judicial separation).

à merveille /a mɛrvɛj/ *adverb phrase* M18 **French** (= to a marvel). Admirably, wonderfully.

âmes damnées plural of ÂME DAMNÉE.

amicus curiae /aˌmʌɪkəs 'kjʊərɪi:/ *noun phrase* plural **amici curiae** /aˌmi:si: 'kjʊərɪi:/ E17 **Modern Latin** (= friend of the court). *Law* A disinterested adviser who assists the court by drawing attention to points that might otherwise fail to be mentioned.

1996 *Times* At the High Court's Chancery Division, the Government will argue that the traitor [sc. George Blake] has no right to royalties . . . Lord Lester of Herne Hill has been appointed *amicus curiae* to ensure Blake gets a fair hearing.

amigo /ə'mi:gəʊ/ *noun* plural **amigos** M19 **Spanish**. A friend, a comrade.

■ Frequently used as a colloquial form of address, mainly in the United States.

1996 *Times* Herro thought the 'amigos' who had been with the brothers since time began . . . would never walk away from their fat-cat accoutrements, pensions, chauffeured cars, and so on. But they did.

amir /ə'mi:ə/ *noun* (also **ameer**) L16 **Persian and Urdu** (from Arabic *'amīr* commander, governor, prince, from *amara* to command; cf. EMIR). A title of various Muslim rulers.

amnesia /am'ni:zjə/ *noun* L18 **Greek** (*amnēsia* forgetfulness). Loss of memory.

amoeba /ə'mi:bə/ *noun* (also **ameba**) plural **amoebas**, **amoebae** /ə'mi:bi:/ M19 **Modern Latin** (from Greek *amoibē* change, alternation). A single-celled aquatic protozoan, characterized by a constantly changing shape.

amok /ə'mɒk/ *adjective, noun, & adverb* (also **amuck** /ə'mʌk/, (earliest) **am(o)uco**) E16 **Portuguese** (*am(o)uco* from Malay *amuk* fighting furiously, in a homicidal frenzy). **A** *adjective* E16 In a homicidal frenzy. *rare*. Only in E16. **B** *noun* **1** M17 A Malay in a homicidal frenzy. **2** M19 A homicidal frenzy; an act of running amok. **C** *adverb* L17 *run amok*, run about in a frenzied thirst for blood; go on a destructive rampage; rush wildly and heedlessly.

amole /ə'məʊli/ *noun* M19 **Mexican Spanish**. The root of any of several plants of Mexico and the southern United States, used as a detergent; any of these plants.

amontillado /əˌmɒntɪ'lɑ:dəʊ/, /əˌmɒntɪl'jɑ:dəʊ/ *noun* (also **Amontillado**) plural **amontillados** E19 **Spanish** (from *Montilla* a town in southern Spain). Formerly, a wine of the sherry type produced in Montilla. Now, a medium sherry of a matured type. Also, a drink or glass of either of these wines.

amoretto /amə'rɛtəʊ/, *foreign* /amo'retto/ *noun* plural **amoretti** /amo'rɛtti/, **amoretto(e)s** /amə'rɛtəʊz/ L16 **Italian** (diminutive of *amore* love). **1** L16–E18 A sweetheart; a love poem. **2** E17 A cupid.

amorino /amə'ri:nəʊ/, *foreign* /amo'ri:no/ *noun* plural **amorini** /amə'ri:ni/, **amorinos** M19 **Italian** (diminutive of *amore* love). A cupid.

1996 *Times* Last month the auction house predicted a sale of £1 million plus for the *amorino*, discovered in a garden in Wales.

amoroso /amə'rəʊsəʊ/ *noun, adverb, & adjective* E17 **Spanish and Italian** (from medieval Latin *amorosus* amorous). **A** *noun* plural **amorosi** /amə'rəʊsi/, **amorosos** **1** E17–E19 A lover; a gallant. **2** L19 A type of sweetened oloroso sherry. **B** *adverb & adjective* L18 *Music* (A direction:) tender(ly).

amour /ə'mʊə/, *foreign* /amur/ *noun* ME **Old and Modern French** (from Latin *amor*). **1** ME Love; affection. Now *rare* except in AMOUR COURTOIS, AMOUR PROPRE. **2** LME–E18 In *plural*. Sexual or romantic love. **3** L16 A love affair, especially a secret one.

3 1996 *Times* The final swapping of amours [in *Twelfth Night*] does not seem a tricky matter.

amour courtois /amur kurtwa/ *noun phrase* L19 **French** (= courtly love). A highly conventionalized medieval code of love and etiquette first developed by the troubadours among the chivalric aristocracy of southern France.

amourette /amʊə'rɛt/, *foreign* /amurɛt/ (*plural same*) *noun* E19 **French**. **1** E19 A brief or unimportant love affair. **2** M19 A cupid, an amoretto.

amour propre /ˌamʊə 'prɒpr(ə)/, *foreign* /amur prɔpr/ *noun phrase* (also **amour-propre**) L18 **French**. Self-esteem; vanity.

1996 *Times* [N]ot only is hurling yourself about the court and going for every shot healthier both for body and for *amour-propre*, it is the best excuse there is for losing to those younger than you.
1996 *Spectator* Although it would be a blow to the *amour propre* of Mr Preston and friends to sell the Sunday paper after only three years, they may have to do so.

amphisbaena /ˌamfɪs'bi:nə/ *noun* LME **Latin** (from Greek *amphisbaina*, from *amphis* both ways + *bainein* to go, walk). **1** LME A fabled serpent with a head at each end and able to move in either direction. **2** M19 A wormlike burrowing lizard of the genus *Amphisbaena*.

■ Pliny describes the mythical serpent in the eighth book of his *Natural History*, and Lucan (*Pharsalia* ix.719) lists it amongst the poisonous monsters of Libya that sprang from the dripping blood of the gorgon Medusa's severed head.

amphora /'amf(ə)rə/ *noun* plural **amphorae** /'amf(ə)ri:/, **amphoras** ME **Latin** (from Greek *amphoreus*, or French *amphore*). **1** ME A Greek or Roman two-handled vessel. **2** LME A Greek or Roman liquid measure of varying capacity.

ampoule /'ampu:l/ *noun* M17 **Modern French**. **1** M17 An AMPULLA 2. *rare*. **2** E20 A small sealed glass vessel for holding sterilized materials for injection, poisons, air-sensitive chemicals, etc.

ampulla /am'pʊlə/ *noun* plural **ampullae** /am'pʊli:/ LME **Latin** (diminutive of *ampora* variant of AMPHORA). **1** LME *Roman Antiquities* A small two-handled globular flask or bottle. **2** L16 A vessel for holding consecrated oil or for other sacred uses. **3** M19 *Anatomy* A vessel or cavity shaped like the ancient ampulla.

amuck variant of AMOK.

amuse-gueule /amyzgœl/ *noun* L20 **French** (literally, 'amusement for the mouth'). A snack, an appetizer.

1996 *Spectator* Before our starters came an amuse-gueule.

anabasis /a'nabəsɪs/ *noun literary* plural **anabases** /a'nabəsi:z/ E18 **Greek** (= going up, from *ana-* up + *basis* going. A military advance, an up-country march.

■ The original *anabasis* was that of ten thousand Greek auxiliaries under the Persian Cyrus the Younger into Asia in 401 BC. The Athenian writer Xenophon narrated the story of the ill-fated expedition, which turned into a *katabasis* or retreat in which he played a conspicuous role, in his *Anabasis*.

anacoluthon /ˌanəkə'lu:θɒn/, /ˌanəkə'lu:θ(ə)n/ *noun* plural **anacolutha** /ˌanəkə'lu:θə/ E18 **Late Latin** (from Greek *anakolouthon* neuter singular of adjective = lacking sequence, from as *an-* not + *akolouthos* following). A sentence or construction lacking grammatical sequence.

anacrusis /anə'kru:sɪs/ *noun* plural **anacruses** /anə'kru:si:z/ M19 **Modern Latin** (from Greek *anakrousis* prelude, from *anakrouein*, from as *ana-* not + *krouein* to strike). **1** M19 *Prosody* An unstressed syllable at the beginning of a verse. **2** E20 *Music* An unstressed note or unstressed notes before the first strong beat of a phrase.

anaesthesia /anɪs'θiːzjə/ *noun* (also **anesthesia**) E18 **Modern Latin** (from Greek *anaisthēsia*, from as *an-* not + *aisthēsis* sensation). Absence of sensation; *especially* artificially induced inability to feel pain.

anagnorisis /anəg'nɒrɪsɪs/ *noun* plural **anagnorises** /anəg'nɒrɪsiːz/ L18 **Greek** (*anagnōrisis*). Recognition; the dénouement in a drama.

analemma /anə'lɛmə/ *noun* plural **analemmae**, /anə'lɛmiː/, **analemmas** M17 **Latin** ((Vitruvius) = sundial, from Greek *analēmma* support, (base of a) sundial). **1** M17 (An astronomical instrument incorporating) an orthographic projection of the sphere on the plane of the meridian. **2** M19 A figure representing the sun's daily declination and the difference between the right ascension of the mean sun and that of the true sun, drawn especially on terrestrial globes.

analgesia /an(ə)l'dʒiːzjə/ *noun* E18 **Greek** (*analgēsia* painlessness, ultimately from *an-* not + *algeein* to feel pain). *Medicine* Absence or reduction of ability to feel pain; relief of pain, especially by drugs.

anamnesis /anəm'niːsɪs/ *noun* plural **anamneses** /anəm'niːsiːz/ L16 **Greek** (*anamnēsis* remembrance). **1** L16 The recalling of things past; reminiscence. **2** L19 *Christian Church* That part of the Eucharistic canon in which the sacrifice of Christ is recalled. **3** L19 A patient's account of his or her medical history.

anamorphosis /anə'mɔːfəsɪs/ *noun* plural **anamorphoses** /anə'mɔːfəsiːz/ E18 **Greek** (*anamorphōsis* transformation). **1** E18 A distorted projection or drawing of anything, which appears normal when viewed from a particular point or by means of a suitable mirror. **2** M19 *Botany* and *Zoology* Progression to a higher type. Now *specifically* development of the adult form through a series of small changes.

anaphora /ə'naf(ə)rə/ *noun* L16 **Latin and Greek** (branch I, Latin from Greek = repetition, from as *ana-* back, again + *pherein* carry; branch II Late Greek). **I 1** L16 *Rhetoric* The repetition of the same word or phrase in several successive clauses. **2** M20 *Linguistics* The use of an expression which refers to or stands for an earlier word or group of words. **II 3** M18 *Christian Church* The part of the Eucharist at which the oblation is made.

anastrophe /ə'nastrəfi/ *noun* M16 **Greek** (*anastrophē* turning back, from as *ana-* back + *strephein* to turn). *Rhetoric* Inversion or unusual order of words or clauses.

anathema /ə'naθəmə/ *noun* plural **anathemas**, in sense 3 also **anathemata** /anə'θiːmətə/ E16 **ecclesiastical Latin** ((as senses 1 and 2) from Greek originally 'a thing devoted' (sense 3), later 'an accursed thing', originally variant of *anathēma* votive offering, from *anatithenai* to set up). **1** E16 Something or someone accursed or assigned to damnation; something or someone detested. **2** L16 The formal act or formula of consigning to damnation; the curse of God; the curse of the Church, excommunicating a person or denouncing a doctrine etc.; a denunciation of alleged impiety, heresy, etc.; an imprecation. **3** L16 Something devoted or consecrated to divine use. Now *rare*.

anchoveta /antʃə'vɛtə/ *noun* M20 **Spanish** (diminutive of *anchova*). A Pacific anchovy, *Cetengraulis mysticetus*, used as bait or to make fish-meal.

ancien régime /ɑ̃sjɛ̃ reʒim/ *noun phrase* L18 **French** (= former regime). The system of government in France before the Revolution of 1789. Also *transferred*, the old system or style of things.

> **1995** *Spectator* Sponsored by the Home Office under the auspices of the Centre of Criminological Research at the University of Oxford, it [sc. the researchers' visitation] set the fear of God into Grendon's *ancien régime*.

ancona /an'koːna/, /an'kəʊnə/ *noun* plural **ancone** /an'koːne/, /an'kəʊni/ L19 **Italian** (from medieval Latin, of uncertain origin: perhaps alteration of Greek *eikona* accusative of *eikōn* icon). An altarpiece, *especially* one consisting of a group of paintings connected by architectural structure.

andante /an'danti/ *adverb, adjective, & noun* E18 **Italian** (present participle of *andare* to go). *Music* **A** *adverb & adjective* E18 (A direction:) (originally) distinct(ly); (now) moderately slow(ly). **B** *noun* L18 A moderately slow movement or piece.

andantino /ˌandan'tiːnəʊ/ *adverb, adjective, & noun* E19 **Italian** (diminutive of preceding). *Music* **A** *adverb & adjective* E19 (A direction:) (originally) rather slower than andante; (now usually) with less of andante, i.e. rather quicker than andante.

B *noun* M19 plural **andantinos**. A movement or piece rather quicker (originally slower) than an andante.

andouille /ɑ̃duj/ *noun* plural pronounced same E17 **Old and Modern French** (of unknown origin). A kind of pork sausage, usually served as an hors d'oeuvre.

andouillette /ɑ̃dujɛt/ *noun* plural pronounced same (also **andouillet**) E17 **French** (diminutive of preceding). A sausage made from a paste of minced veal, bacon, and other ingredients.

angekok /ˈaŋgɪkɒk/ *noun* M18 **Eskimo** ((Greenlandic) *angakkoq*). An Eskimo sorcerer or medicine man.

angelus /ˈandʒ(ə)ləs/ *noun* M17 **Latin** (from the opening words *Angelus domini* the angel of the Lord). **1** M17 A devotional exercise commemorating the Incarnation, said by Roman Catholics at morning, noon, and sunset. **2** M19 The bell rung at the times for the angelus. More fully *angelus bell*.

angina pectoris /anˌdʒʌɪnə ˈpɛktərɪs/ *noun* M18 **Latin** (*angina* quinsy (from Greek *agkhonē* strangling, assimilated to Latin *angere* to squeeze) + *pectoris* of the chest). *Medicine* Severe pain in the chest, and often also the arms and neck, due to inadequate blood supply to the heart muscles.

■ *Angina* alone was earlier (M16) used of any condition marked by a suffocating, oppressive pain or discomfort, especially quinsy. It is now rare in this sense and is current only as a shortened form of *angina pectoris*.

anglice /ˈaŋglɪsi/ *adverb* (also **Anglice**) E17 **Medieval Latin** (from Latin *Anglus* English). In (plain) English.

angst /aŋst/ *noun* E20 **German**. Anxiety, neurotic fear; guilt, remorse.

1995 *Times* 'Oh, I'm seriously rich,' hoots Rhys Jones, not altogether seriously. 'I am covered in angst because I am so rich.'

an-hua /anˈhwɑː/ *noun & adjective* E20 **Chinese** (*ànhuā*, from *àn* obscure + *huā* flower). (Of) a type of decoration of Chinese porcelain or fabrics that is visible only by transmitted light.

anima /ˈanɪmə/ *noun* E20 **Latin** (= (i) air, breath, life; (ii) mind, soul). *Psychoanalysis* The inner self (opposed to PERSONA). Also, the source of the feminine component of a personality. Cf. ANIMUS.

anima mundi /ˌanɪmə ˈmʌndʌɪ/, /ˈmʊndiː/ *noun phrase* L16 **Medieval Latin** (= soul of the world; apparently formed to render Greek *psukhē tou kosmou*). A power supposed to organize the whole universe and to coordinate its parts.

■ The concept is first found in the writings of the French philosopher and theologian Peter Abelard (1079–1142), who was accused in 1140 by his detractors of identifying it with the Holy Spirit. The phrase was introduced into English philosophical discourse in the seventeenth century by the alchemist Thomas Vaughan in *Anima Magica Abscondita* (1650), who defined it as 'the universal spirit of Nature', and given wider currency by the Cambridge Platonist Ralph Cudworth (1617–88) in *The True Intellectual System of the Universe* (1678) and by the writings of John Locke.

animus /ˈanɪməs/ *noun* E19 **Latin** (= spirit, mind). **1** E19 Actuating feeling, animating spirit, usually hostile; animosity shown in speech or action. **2** E20 *Psychoanalysis* The source of the masculine component of a personality. Cf. ANIMA.

1 1995 *Spectator* The greatest animus felt by British, Australian and New Zealand troops alike was against the politicians.

anis /ani(s)/ *noun* L19 **French**. A liqueur or aperitif flavoured with aniseed; occasionally, aniseed.

ankh /aŋk/ *noun* L19 **Egyptian** (= life, soul). An object resembling a cross, but with a loop in place of the upper limb, used in ancient Egyptian art as a symbol of life.

■ Also called CRUX ANSATA.

ankus /ˈaŋkəs/ *noun* L19 **Hindustani** (*ā̃kus*, *aṅkas* from Sanskrit *aṅkuśa*). In the Indian subcontinent: an elephant-goad.

anlaut /ˈanlaʊt/ *noun* L19 **German** (from *an* on + *Laut* sound). *Philology* The initial sound of a word.

anno aetatis suae see under AETATIS.

Anno Domini /ˌanəʊ ˈdɒmɪnʌɪ/, /ˈdɒmɪni/ *adverb & noun phrase* M16 **Latin** (= in the year of the Lord). **A** *adverb* M16 Of the Christian era. Usually written AD. **B** *noun* **1** L17 A particular year. **2** L19 Advanced or advancing age. *colloquial*.

B.2 1906 E. V. Lucas *Fireside and Sunshine* When the time came for A. to take the bat he was unable to do so. *Anno Domini* asserted itself.

annulus /ˈanjʊləs/ *noun* plural **annuli** /ˈanjʊlʌɪ/, /ˈanjʊliː/ M16 **Latin** (late form of *anulus* diminutive of *anus* ring). Chiefly

Mathematics and *Botany* A ring, a circle that is not filled in; *specifically* a partial veil forming a collar round the stalk in some agarics.

annus horribilis /ˌanəs hɒˈrɪbɪlɪs/ *noun phrase* L20 **Modern Latin** (= horrible year; formed after ANNUS MIRABILIS). A dreadful or miserable year.

■ The phrase leapt into circulation after H.M. the Queen used it with reference to 1992, a year of much-publicized matrimonial troubles within the British royal family and a serious fire at Windsor Castle.

1995 *Times* Against this background, the EU has let itself in for an *annus horribilis* in 1998.

annus mirabilis /ˌanəs mɪˈrɑːbɪlɪs/ *noun phrase* M17 **Modern Latin** (= wonderful year). A remarkable or auspicious year.

■ The origin of the phrase is the title of Dryden's poem *Annus Mirabilis: The Year of Wonders* (1667), which chronicled events in 1666, including British naval battles against the Dutch and the Great Fire of London. Dryden's use of *mirabilis* as 'remarkable in both good and bad senses' has tended to be superseded by the more positive sense of 'marvellous' (see quotation), a tendency reinforced by the currency of ANNUS HORRIBILIS in the 1990s.

1995 *Spectator* All peoples have their *annus mirabilis*, the crucial period of their history which defines them . . . : great political or constitutional acts, like 1776 to the Americans or 1789 to the French, or great military events like 1812 in Russia . . . or 1813 in Prussia.

anomie /ˈanəmi/ *noun* (also **anomy**) M20 **French** (from Greek *anomia*, from *anomos* lawless). Lack of the usual social standards in a group or person.

■ The term was resurrected in its current sense by the French sociologist Emile Durkheim in *Suicide* (1897). It occurs in English in technical sociological contexts, but also more generally (see quotation).

1995 *Spectator* Today, . . . travelling to work by car is guaranteed to whip up anger, alienation and *anomie*.

anonym /ˈanənɪm/ *noun* (also **anonyme**) E19 **French** (*anonyme* from Greek *anōnumos* anonymous). **1** E19 An anonymous person or publication. **2** M19 A pseudonym.

anorak /ˈanərak/ *noun* E20 **Eskimo** (Greenlandic *annoraaq*). **1** A hooded jacket made of skin or cloth and worn by Eskimos and so by others in polar regions; a similar weatherproof garment worn elsewhere. **2** A person who wears an anorak; an obsessive hobbyist. *derogatory*.

2 1995 *Times* Should they pick up a point or three at Barnsley on Saturday, it will be a sad day for expectant anoraks everywhere.

anorexia /anəˈrɛksɪə/ *noun* M17 **Late Latin** (from Greek *an-* no + *orexis* appetite). *Medicine* Absence of appetite.

■ First introduced in 1598 in the French form *anorexie*, which, like the Anglicized form *anorexy*, is now obsolete. *Anorexia* now very often refers to the specific complaint of ANOREXIA NERVOSA.

anorexia nervosa /anəˌrɛksɪə nəːˈvəʊsə/ *noun phrase* L19 **Late Latin** (= nervous anorexia) Chronic anorexia induced by emotional disturbance.

Anschauung /ˈanʃaʊʊŋ/ *noun* plural **Anschauungen** /ˈanʃaʊʊŋən/ M19 **German** (= looking at). **1** M19 *Philosophy* (especially *Kantian*) A sense-perception, an intuition, an immediate apprehension by sense. **2** E20 An outlook, an attitude, a point of view. Cf. WELTANSCHAUUNG.

Anschluss /ˈanʃlʊs/ *noun* E20 **German** (from *anschliessen* to join, annex). Union, annexation; *specifically* the annexation of Austria by Germany in 1938.

1958 *Economist* Ability to opt to join the Commonwealth might give certain states a valuable policy counter, when other forms of Anschluss seem to be in the offing.

an sich /an zɪç/ *adjective & adverb phrase* M19 **German**. In itself; in the abstract; not in relation to anything else. See also DING AN SICH.

anta /ˈantə/ *noun* plural **antae** /ˈantiː/, **antas** L16 **Latin**. *Architecture* A square pilaster at either side of a door or at the corner of a building. Cf. ANTES, IN ANTIS.

ante /ˈanti/ *noun* E19 **Latin** (= before). **1** E19 In poker and similar games: a stake put up by a player before drawing cards. **2** L19 *transferred* An advance payment; a sum of money for a payment.

■ Chiefly North American. Often in the phrase *upping* (or *to up*) *the ante*, that is, 'raising the stakes'.

2 1996 *Times* That would have balanced the market and raised the negotiating ante.

ante-bellum /antɪˈbɛləm/ *adjective* (also **antebellum**) M19 **Latin** (*ante bellum* before the war). Occurring or existing before a particular war, especially (*United States*) the American Civil War. Opposed to POST-BELLUM.

1996 *Times* Kenneth Greenberg's aim is to enlarge our understanding of a dead world . . . The world? The antebellum slave South.

antefix /ˈantɪfɪks/ *noun* (also in Latin form **antefixum** /ˈantɪfɪksəm/, plural **antefixa** /ˈantɪfɪksə/) M19 **Latin** (*antefixum*, from as *ante-* before + use as noun of *fixus* fixed). *Classical Architecture* An ornament on an eave or cornice to conceal the ends of tiles; also, as ornamental head etc. making a spout from a gutter. Usually in *plural*.

ante meridiem /ˌantɪ məˈrɪdɪəm/ *adjective & adverb phrase* M16 **Latin**. Before midday; between midnight and the following noon.

■ Abbreviated to *a.m.*

ante-mortem /antɪˈmɔːtəm/ *adjective* L19 **Latin** (*ante mortem* before death). Made before death. Cf. POST-MORTEM.

antenna /anˈtɛnə/ *noun* plural **antennae** /anˈtɛniː/ (especially sense 4) **antennas** M17 **Latin** (alteration of *antemna* sailyard, used in plural as translation of Aristotle's *keraioi* 'horns' of insects). **1** M17 *Zoology* Either of a pair of sensory appendages on the heads of insects, crustaceans, and some other arthropods; a feeler. **2** M19 *figurative* In *plural*. Receptive senses, means of exploration. **3** M19 *Botany* Either of a pair of projections on the male flowers of certain orchids. **4** E20 A metal wire, rod, or other structure used to transmit or receive radio or other electromagnetic waves; an aerial. Chiefly *United States* and *in technical use*.

2 1996 *Spectator* He had developed sensitive antennae over the years as to when a man was on the way out and who was to succeed him . . .

4 1995 *New Scientist* Instead [of fuel tanks], slung beneath its [sc. the airship's] belly is a giant, square receiving antenna designed to convert microwaves into electric power.

antependium /antɪˈpɛndɪəm/ *noun* L16 **Medieval Latin** (from as *ante-* before + Latin *pendere* to hang). A veil or hanging for the front of an altar.

antepenultima /ˌantɪpɪˈnʌltɪmə/ *noun* plural **antepenultimae** /ˌantɪpɪˈnʌltɪmiː/, **antepenultimas** L16 **Late Latin** ((*syllaba*) *antepaenultima*, from as *ante-* before + *penultima* feminine of *paenultimus* last but one). *Prosody* The last syllable but two of a word or verse.

ante rem /ˈantɪ rɛm/ *adjective & adverb phrase* L19 **Medieval Latin** (= before the thing). *Philosophy* Prior to the existence of something else; *specifically* (of a universal) prior to the particular; of or pertaining to the theory that the universal is logically prior to the particular. Cf. IN RE 2, POST REM.

■ The phrase occurs in the writings of the thirteenth-century scholastic philosopher Albertus Magnus.

antes /ˈantɪz/ *noun plural* L16 **French** (representing Latin *antae* plural of ANTA). *Architecture* Square pilasters.

anthemion /anˈθiːmɪən/ *noun* plural **anthemia** /anˈθiːmɪə/ M19 **Greek** (= flower). A figure or ornament resembling a stylized honeysuckle.

anthrax /ˈanθraks/ *noun* L19 **Latin** (= carbuncle, from Greek *anthrax*, *anthrak-* coal, carbuncle). *Medicine* Infection with the bacterium *Bacillus anthracis*, which in animals usually takes the form of a fatal acute septicaemia, and in humans usually affects the skin, causing development of a pustule, or the lungs, causing a form of pneumonia.

■ Originally (LME) with its Latin sense, but this is now rare or obsolete.

anthropophagi /anθrəˈpɒfəgʌɪ/, /anθrəˈpɒfədʒʌɪ/ *noun plural* M16 **Latin** (*anthropophagus* from Greek *anthrōpophagos* man-eating). Cannibals.

■ The singular *anthropophagus* is rare.

anti /ˈanti/ *noun & adjective* L18 **Greek** (*anti* = opposite, against). **A** *noun* L18 Someone who is opposed to someone or something; *especially United States* an anti-Federalist. **B** *adjective* M19 Against or antagonistic to someone or something.

■ The use of *anti-* as a prefix in words adopted (ultimately) from Greek, and in English words modelled on these, long predates the use of *anti* as an independent word, and as a prefix *anti-* has been freely used with nouns and adjectives in the twentieth century with the sense 'opposite, against, preventing'.

A 1996 *Spectator* In those days, the antis were marginal figures, more numerous than the League of Empire loyalists but with hardly greater purchase on the future.

antipasto /antɪˈpastəʊ/ *noun* plural **antipasti**, /antɪˈpasti/, **antipastos** E17 **Italian**. An appetizer, an hors d'oeuvre.

■ Rare before the mid twentieth century. Also used figuratively (see quotation).

1996 *Times* An artistic *antipasto* can stimulate the appetite for more substantial fare.

antipodes /anˈtɪpədiːz/ *noun plural* (sense 3 also treated as *singular*) (also **Antipodes**) LME **French** (or late Latin from Greek plural of *antipous* having the feet opposite, from as *anti-* opposite + *pous*, *pod-* foot).

1 LME–M19 Those who live on the opposite side of the earth to each other or to oneself. **2** M16 Places on the surface of the earth directly or diametrically opposite to each other; a place diametrically opposite to another, *especially* Australasia as the region on the opposite side of the earth to Europe. **3** E17 Exact opposites. Also as *singular*. (Followed by *of*, *to*.)

■ Formerly pronounced as a trisyllable /ˈantɪpəʊdz/; present pronunciation follows Greek and Latin.

antistrophe /anˈtɪstrəfi/ *noun* M16 **Late Latin** (from Greek *antistrophē*, from *antistrephein* to turn against). **1** M16 *Rhetoric* The repetition of words in inverse order. **2** E17 The returning movement, from left to right, in Greek choruses and dances, answering to the strophe; the lines of choral song recited during this movement; *transferred* any choral response. **3** E17 An inverse correspondence.

antithesis /anˈtɪθəsɪs/ *noun* plural **antitheses** /anˈtɪθəsiːz/ LME **Late Latin** (from Greek, from *antitithenai*, from as *anti*- against + *tithenai* to set, place: cf. THESIS). **1** *Grammar* **a** The substitution of one case for another. Only in LME. **b** L16–M17 The substitution of one sound for another. **2** E16 *Rhetoric* (An) opposition or contrast of ideas, expressed by parallelism of words which are the opposites of, or strongly contrasted with, each other. Also, repetition of the same word at the end of successive clauses. **3** M16 The second of two opposed clauses or sentences; a counter-thesis. **4** E17 Direct or striking opposition of character or function (*of*, *between* two things). **5** M17 The direct opposite, a complete contrast, (*of*, *to*). **6** L19 In Hegelian philosophy: the negation of the THESIS as the second stage in the process of dialectical reasoning. Cf. SYNTHESIS 2.

antonomasia /ˌantənəˈmeɪzɪə/ *noun* M16 **Latin** (from Greek, from *antonomazein* to name instead, from as *anti*- instead + *onoma* name). The substitution of an epithet etc. or the name of an office or dignity, for a proper name (e.g. *the Iron Lady* for Margaret Thatcher). Also, conversely, use of a proper name to express a general idea (e.g. *Jezebel* for 'a wicked woman').

AOC see under APPELLATION CONTRÔLÉE.

à outrance /a utrɑ̃s/ *adverb phrase* Also **à l'outrance** /a lutrɑ̃s/, **à toute outrance** /a tut utrɑ̃s/ E17 **French** (= to beyond bounds). To the death; to the bitter end.

1996 *Spectator* . . . he [sc. President Clinton] may find it difficult to shift the blame onto the opposition as he did so brilliantly when Newt Gingrich unwisely engaged him in war *à outrance* over the budget.

Apache *in senses A.1, B.1* /əˈpatʃi/; *in senses A.2, B.2* /əˈpaʃ/, *foreign* /apaʃ/ (*plural of noun same*) *noun & adjective* (senses A.2, B.2 also written **apache**) M18 **Mexican Spanish** (probably from Zuñi *Ápachu*, literally, 'enemy'; senses A.2, B.2 through French). **A** *noun* plural **Apaches**, same. **1** M18 A member of an Athapaskan Indian people of New Mexico and Arizona; the language of this people. **2** E20 A violent street ruffian, originally in Paris. **B** *attributive* or as *adjective* **1** M19 Of or pertaining to the Apache or their language. **2** E20 Designating a vigorous dance for two associated with street ruffians or apaches.

aparejo /apəˈreɪhəʊ/ *noun* plural **aparejos** M19 **Spanish** (= preparation, harness, tackle). A pack-saddle.

■ Only in United States.

apartheid /əˈpɑːtheɪt/ *noun* M20 **Afrikaans** (literally, 'separateness', from Dutch *apart* apart + *-heid* -hood). The former South African (policy of) racial segregation of the White inhabitants from the remainder. Also *transferred* and *figurative*, any other form of segregation.

1996 *Times* Men became more involved in parenting and women entered the workplace. But the end of sexual apartheid brought its own problems.

aperçu /apɛrsy/ (*plural same*), /apɛːˈsjuː/ *noun* E19 **French**. A summary, a conspectus; an insight, a revealing glimpse.

1995 *Spectator* Nowhere, though, have I seen mentioned one of Amis's best *aperçus* . . . that the surest harbinger of boredom and *longueurs* is the question, perfunctory and ominous—'Red or white, sir?'

aperitif /əˈpɛrɪtiːf/, /əpɛrɪˈtiːf/ *noun* (also **apéritif** /aperitif/ (*plural same*)) L19 **French** (*apéritif* (noun and adjective) from medieval Latin *aperitivus* (adjective) variant of late Latin *apertivus*, from *apertus* open). An alcoholic drink taken as an appetizer. Also *figurative*.

apex /ˈeɪpɛks/ *noun* plural **apexes**, **apices** /ˈeɪpɪsiːz/ E17 **Latin**. **1** The tip, top, peak, or pointed end of anything; the vertex of a triangle, cone, etc.; *Botany* the growing point of a shoot etc. **2** L18 *Astronomy* The point on the celestial sphere towards which the sun is moving. Also *solar apex*.

apfelstrudel /ˈapf(ə)lˌʃtruːd(ə)l/ *noun* M20 German (from *Apfel* apple + STRUDEL). A flaky pastry with a spicy apple filling.

■ Also very frequently in partially Anglicized form *apple strudel*.

aphasia /əˈfeɪzɪə/ *noun* M19 **Greek** (from *aphatos* speechless, from *a-* without + *phanai* to speak). Loss or impairment of the faculty of speech or of understanding of language (or both), due to cerebral disease or damage.

aplomb /əˈplɒm/ *noun* L18 **French** (from *à plomb* according to the plummet). **1** L18 Perpendicularity; steadiness. Now *rare* or *obsolete*. **2** E19 Self-possession, coolness; assurance.

2 1996 *Spectator* Some ministers stamp their personality on their department with such aplomb that, ever after, they become archetypes.

apocatastasis variant of APOKATASTASIS.

Apocrypha /əˈpɒkrɪfə/ *noun* (usually treated as *singular*; rarely as *plural*, with *singular* **Apocryphon** /əˈpɒkrɪfɒn/) (also **apocrypha**) LME **ecclesiastical Latin** (neuter plural (sc. *scripta* writings) of *apocryphus* from Greek *apokruphos* hidden, from *apokruptein* to hide). A writing or statement of doubtful authorship or authenticity; *specifically* **a** those Old Testament books included in the Septuagint and Vulgate which are not included in the Hebrew Scriptures, and which were excluded from the Protestant canon at the Reformation; **b** *New Testament Apocrypha*, various early Christian writings parallel to but excluded from the New Testament canon.

apodyterium /ˌapədɪˈtɪərɪəm/ *noun* plural **apodyteria** /ˌapədɪˈtɪərɪə/ E17 **Latin** (from Greek *apodutērion*, from *apoduein* to strip). *Classical History* A room adjacent to a bath or palaestra where clothes were deposited.

à point /a pwɛ̃/ *adverb phrase* E20 **French** (= to the point). Especially *Cookery*. At or to exactly the right point; just enough, without overcooking or undercooking.

apokatastasis /ˌapə(ʊ)kəˈtastəsɪs/ *noun* (also **apocatastasis**) L17 **Greek** (= re-establishment). Restoration, renewal; *specifically* in *Theology* the ultimate salvation of all moral beings.

apo koinou /ˌapəʊ ˈkɔɪnuː/, /ˈkɔɪnaʊ/ *adjective & adverb phrase* L19 **Greek** (literally, 'in common'). *Grammar* Designating a construction comprising two clauses having an unrepeated word or phrase in common; so as to form such a construction.

apologia /apəˈləʊdʒɪə/ *noun* L18 **Latin**. A written defence of one's own (or someone else's) opinions or conduct.

■ The currency of *apologia* is largely due to the impact of John Henry Newman's *Apologia pro Vita Sua* (1864), charting his intellectual and spiritual progress from Anglicanism to Roman Catholicism. The complete phrase is sometimes used of an autobiography, especially one by a controversial figure.

1996 *Times* . . . we are told that there is respect for human rights in China. To prove it (and this gets very macabre), the Chinese Government has published a weird kind of *apologia*.

aporia /əˈpɔːrɪə/, /əˈpɒrɪə/ *noun* M16 **Late Latin** (from Greek, from *aporos* impassable). **1** M16 *Rhetoric* The expression of doubt. **2** L19 A doubtful matter, a perplexing difficulty.

a posteriori /eɪ/, /ɑː/, /pɒˌstɛrɪˈɔːrʌɪ/, /pɒˌstɪərɪɔːrʌɪ/ *adverb & adjective phrase* E17 **Latin** (= from what comes after). **1** E17 Of reasoning: (by) proceeding from effects to causes; inductive(ly), empirical(ly). Opposed (to) A PRIORI. **2** M18 From behind; on the buttocks. *facetious*.

1 1991 W. Charlton *The Analytic Ambition* This general belief is dispositional. It could be applied in action or prediction but here it is applied in *a posteriori* inference.

apotheosis /ˌəpɒθɪˈəʊsɪs/ *noun* plural **apotheoses** /ˌəpɒθɪˈəʊsiːz/ L16 **ecclesiastical Latin** (from Greek *apotheōsis*, from *apotheoun* to deify, from *apo-* + *theos* god). **1** L16 (Elevation to) divine status. **2** E17 Glorification or exaltation of a person, principle, or practice; canonization; idealization. **3** M17 Ascension to glory, resurrection, triumph; highest development, culmination.

apparat /apəˈrɑːt/ *noun* M20 **Russian** (through German from Latin *apparatus* from *apparare* to make ready). The Communist Party machine in the former USSR and other countries.

apparatchik /apəˈratʃɪk/ *noun* plural **apparatchiki** /apəˈratʃɪki/, **apparatchiks** M20 **Russian** (from preceding). **1** M20 A member of the APPARAT; a Communist agent. **2** L20 *transferred* An implementer of party or official policy; an executive officer.

2 1996 *Spectator* What usually happens now is that the prime minister assembles a committee of favoured ministers, placemen and apparatchiks to decide the date.

apparatus criticus /apəˌreɪtəs 'krɪtɪkəs/ *noun phrase* plural **apparatus critici** /apə ˌreɪtəs 'krɪtɪsʌɪ/ M19 **Modern Latin.** A collection of material, as variant readings and other palaeographical and critical matter, for the textual study of a document.

1996 *Spectator* On what grounds is this a *Selected* and not a *Collected*? How much surviving comic verse [of A. E. Housman's] do we in fact have? We are not going to find out from the present *apparatus criticus*, so to dignify it.

appellation contrôlée /apɛlasjɔ̃ kɔ̃trole/ *noun phrase* M20 **French** (= controlled appellation). (A guarantee of) the description of a bottle of French wine (or other item of food) in conformity with statutory regulations as to its origin.

■ Abbreviated to AC. Also *appellation d'origine contrôlée* /apɛlasjɔ̃ dɔriʒin kɔ̃trole/, abbreviated to AOC.

1996 *Times* Without any form of *appellation contrôlée*, the quality of what we are served in the name quickly deteriorates.

appliqué /ə'pli:keɪ/ *noun & verb* M18 **French** (use as noun of past participle of *appliquer* from Latin *applicare* to apply (to)). Chiefly *Needlework*. **A** *noun* M18 (A piece of) ornamental work cut out from one material and affixed to the surface of another; the technique of ornamenting in this way. **B** *transitive verb* L19 Decorate in this way. Chiefly as *appliquéd* participial adjective.

appoggiatura /əˌpɒdʒə'tʊərə/ *noun* plural **appogiature**/əˌpɒdʒə'tʊəreɪ/ M18 **Italian** (from *appoggiare* to lean upon, rest). *Music* A grace-note just above or below a primary note, which it precedes and delays; the use of such notes.

après /'apreɪ/, *foreign* /aprɛ/ *preposition* M20 **French.** After.

■ Combined with English words in (jocular) imitation of APRÈS-SKI, as *après-bath*, *après-sex*, etc.

après coup /'apreɪ ku:/ *adverb phrase* M19 **French** (literally, 'after stroke'). After the event; as an afterthought.

après nous le déluge /apre nu lə delyʒ/ *adverb phrase* M19 **French** (literally, 'after us the flood'). (Used to express the feeling that) the present state of affairs or order of things will not long survive us.

■ Attributed in the *Mémoires* of Mme de Hausset (1824) to Mme de Pompadour (1721–64), mistress of King Louis XV of France, who had premonitions of catastrophe after the French defeat by the Prussians at Rossbach in 1757. It is very often quoted by English speakers in the version *après moi le déluge*.

1995 *Times* Evidently, the only way we can truly face our own demise is by hoping that, so to speak, *après moi, le déluge*. If we have to go, then we want everyone to go with us.

après-ski /ˌapreɪ'ski:/ *noun & adjective* M20 **French.** (Worn, done, etc., at) the time when skiing is over for the day at a resort.

a priori /eɪ prʌɪ'ɔ:rʌɪ/, /ɑ: prɪ'ɔ:ri/ *adverb & adjective phrase* L16 **Latin** (*a priori* from what is before). **1** L16 Of reasoning: (by) proceeding from causes to effects; deductive(ly). Opposed to A POSTERIORI. **2** E19 *loosely* Presumptive(ly); without previous investigation; as far as one knows. **3** M19 *Philosophy* Of knowledge or concepts: not derived from sensory experience; innate(ly).

2 1995 *Spectator* What would be limited is the phenomenon by which European law could be said to apply *a priori*, regardless of national legislatures.

3 1996 *Times* His *a priori* melancholic disposition becomes whipped into a religious fever.

apropos /aprə'pəʊ/, /'aprəpəʊ/ *adverb, adjective, & preposition* (also **à propos** /a prɔpo/) M17 **French** (*à propos*, from à to + *propos* purpose). **A** *adverb* **1** M17 To the point; fitly, opportunely. **2** M18 In respect or as a relevant association *of* (now less commonly, *to*). **b** M18 *absolutely* Incidentally, by the way. **B** *adjective* M17 Pertinent, appropriate, opportune. (Followed by *of*, *to*.) **C** *preposition* M20 Concerning, with regard to. *colloquial*.

C 1996 *Times A propos* the medicinal habits of Florence Nightingale . . . , there is convincing evidence in biographical literature that she took laudanum . . .

à propos de bottes /aprə'pəʊ də bɔt/ *adverb phrase* M18 **French** (= with regard to boots, i.e. to something quite irrelevant). Without rhyme or reason, motiveless.

apsara /'ʌpsərɑ:/ *noun* (also **upsara**) M19 **Hindi** (*apsarā* from Sanskrit *apsarās*). *Hindu Mythology* Any of a class of celestial nymphs, frequently regarded as the wives of the gandharvas or heavenly musicians.

aqua fortis /ˌakwə ˈfɔːtɪs/ *noun phrase* (also **aquafortis**) L15 **Latin** (= strong water). Nitric acid; originally, any powerful solvent. Now *archaic*.

aqua regia /ˌakwə ˈriːdʒə/ *noun phrase* (also formerly **aqua regis**) E17 **Latin** (= royal water). *Chemistry* A concentrated mixture of nitric and hydrochloric acids, able to dissolve gold, platinum, etc.

aquarelle /akwəˈrɛl/ *noun* M19 **French** (from Italian *acquarella* watercolour, from *acqua* from Latin *aqua* water). A style of painting in thin, usually transparent, watercolours; a painting in this style.

aquarium /əˈkwɛːrɪəm/ *noun* plural **aquaria** /əˈkwɛːrɪə/, **aquariums** M19 **Modern Latin** (use as noun of neuter singular of *aquarius* pertaining to water, after VIVARIUM). An artificial pond or tank (usually with transparent sides) for keeping live aquatic plants and animals; a place containing such tanks.

aquavit /akwəˈviːt/ *noun* (also **akvavit** /akvəˈviːt/) L19 **Norwegian, Swedish, Danish** (*akvavit* AQUA VITAE). An alcoholic spirit distilled from potatoes or other starch-containing plants.

aqua vitae /ˌakwə ˈvʌɪtiː/, /ˈviːtʌɪ/, /ˈviːtiː/ *noun phrase* (also **aqua-vitae**) LME **Latin** (= water of life: cf. French *eau de vie*). Alcoholic spirits, especially of the first distillation.

arabesque /arəˈbɛsk/ *noun & adjective* M17 **French** (from Italian *arabesco*, from *arabo* Arabic). **A** *noun* **1** M17 Decorative work of a kind which originated in Arabic or Moorish art, consisting of flowing lines of branches, leaves, scrollwork, etc., fancifully intertwined; an ornamental design of this kind. **2** M19 *Ballet* A posture in which the body is bent forwards and supported on one leg with the other leg extended horizontally backwards, with the arms extended one forwards and one backwards. **3** M19 *Music* A passage or composition with fanciful ornamentation of the melody. **B** *adjective* L18 Of ornamental design: decorated with arabesques (sense 1).

arak /ˈarək/ *noun* (also **arrack**) E17 **Arabic** (*ʻaraḳ* sweat, especially in *ʻaraḳ at-tamr* fermented and distilled juice of dates). In Eastern countries: an alcoholic spirit of local manufacture, especially distilled from the sap of the coco palm or from rice.

arbiter elegantiae /ˌɑːbɪtə ɛlɪˈgantɪʌɪ/ E19 **Latin** (= judge of elegance). An authority on matters of taste or etiquette.

■ First introduced in the form *arbiter elegantiarum* 'judge in matters of taste', which was current in English in the nineteenth century, but the singular form of the genitive, *elegantiae*, is now usual. It has classical sanction in being applied by Tacitus (*Annales* xvi.18) to Titus Petronius, *elegantiae arbiter* at the court of Nero.

arboretum /ɑːbəˈriːtəm/ *noun* plural **arboreta** /ɑːbəˈriːtə/, (chiefly *North American*) **arboretums** E19 **Latin** (= place with trees, from *arbor* tree). A place devoted to the cultivation and exhibition of rare trees; a botanical tree-garden.

arbor vitae /ˌɑːbə ˈvʌɪtiː/, /ˈviːtʌɪ/ *noun phrase* (also (especially in sense 1) **arborvitae** plural same) E17 **Latin** (= tree of life). E17 Any of a number of North American or Far Eastern evergreen conifers, belonging chiefly to the genus *Thuja*.

Arcades ambo /ˌɑːkədiːz ˈambəʊ/ *noun phrase* E19 **Latin** (= both Arcadians, i.e. both pastoral poet-musicians). Two people of the same (often literary or aesthetic) tastes, profession, or character.

■ The phrase is a quotation from Virgil (*Eclogues* vii. 4) and, following Byron (see quotation), is frequently used derogatorily with overtones of 'idle layabouts' or worse.

1821 *Don Juan* With Raucocanti lucklessly was chain'd The tenor . . . 'Arcades ambo,' *id est*—blackguards both.

arcanum /ɑːˈkeɪnəm/ *noun* plural **arcana** /ɑːˈkeɪnə/ L16 **Latin** (use as noun of neuter singular of *arcanus* concealed). Usually in *plural*. **1** L16 A hidden thing; a mystery, a profound secret. **2** E17 *specifically* Any of the supposed secrets of nature sought by alchemists; a marvellous remedy, an elixir. *archaic*.

1 1996 *Spectator* One has always heard it bruited that such [obscene] compositions survive, shrouded away on the duskier, dustier shelves of the British and Cambridge Libraries . . . surely the age has now come when the arcana may finally be opened?

archi plural of ARCO.

archon /ˈɑːkən/ *noun* plural **archons**, **archontes** /ɑːˈkɒntiːz/ L16 **Greek** (*arkhōn*, *arkhont-* ruler, use as noun of present participle of *arkhein* to rule). **1** L16 The chief magistrate, or, after the time of Solon, each of the nine chief magistrates, of ancient Athens. **2** M18 A ruler, a president. **3** M18 A power subordinate to God, held by some of the Gnostics to have created the world.

arco /'arko/, /'ɑ:kəʊ/ *noun, adverb & adjective* M18 **Italian**. *Music* **A** *noun* M18 plural **archi** /'arki/, **arcos** /'ɑ:kəʊz/. A bow for a stringed instrument. **B** *adverb & adjective* E19 (A direction:) resuming use of the bow after a pizzicato passage.

à rebours /a rəbur/ *adverb phrase* E20 **Old French** (*à* from + *rebors* (modern *rebours*) rough, perverse, the wrong side, etc., from popular Latin *rebursum*, Latin *reburrum* rough-haired, bristly). In the wrong way, against the grain; through perversity.

■ *Rebours* was formerly naturalized in the Scottish phrase *at rebours*. The adoption of the phrase in its modern form may be on account of its having been the title of an influential book (1884) by the French novelist Joris-Karl Huysmans.

areg plural of ERG.

arête /ə'rɛt/, /ə'reɪt/ *noun* E19 **French** (from Latin *arista* ear of corn, fish-bone or -spine). A sharp mountain ridge with steep sides.

argot /'ɑ:gəʊ/ *noun* M19 **French** (of unknown origin). The jargon, slang, or peculiar phraseology of a social class or group; originally, rogues' and thieves' cant.

1996 *Times* European football has always had its own argot too . . .

argumentum ad hominem /ɑ:gjʊ ˌmɛntəm ad 'hɒmɪnɛm/ *noun phrase* M17 **Latin**. An argument, usually vilificatory, attacking the personal circumstances or character of an opponent rather than employing sound reasoning to make the point. Cf. AD HOMINEM.

■ In attributive use often shortened to *ad hominem*; see quotation.

1995 *Times* Ad hominem attacks smack of an insolence intolerable to most leaders . . .

argumentum e silentio /ɑ:gjʊˌmɛntəm eɪ sɪ'lɛntɪəʊ/, /sɪ'lɛnʃɪəʊ/ *noun phrase* (also **argumentum ex silentio** /ɑ:gjʊˌmɛntəm ɛks sɪ'lɛntɪəʊ/, /sɪ'lɛnʃɪəʊ/) M20 **Latin** (= argument from silence). A conclusion based on silence, i.e. on lack of contrary evidence.

■ The more (classically) correct *argumentum ex silentio* is also found.

1962 *Listener* Doesn't Dr Needham . . . give the Chinese the benefit of a doubt, sometimes, with an *argumentum e silentio*?

Arhat /'ɑ:hat/ *noun* (also **Arahat** /'arəhat/, **arahat**) L19 **Sanskrit** (*arhat*, Pali *arahat* meritorious). *Buddhism* and *Jainism* A saint of one of the highest ranks.

aria /'ɑ:rɪə/ *noun* E18 **Italian** (from Latin *aera* accusative of *aer* from Greek *aēr* air). *Music* A long song for one voice usually with accompaniment; *especially* such a song in an opera, oratorio, etc.

arietta /arɪ'ɛtə/ *noun* E18 **Italian** (diminutive of ARIA). *Music* A short tune or song.

arioso /arɪ'əʊsəʊ/ *adjective, adverb, & noun* E18 **Italian** (from ARIA). *Music* **A** *adjective* E18 Melodious, songlike, cantabile; having something of the quality of an aria. Also as *adverb* as a direction. **B** *noun* L19 plural **ariosos**. A piece of vocal or instrumental music of this kind.

armada /ɑ:'mɑ:də/ *noun* (also **armado** and in sense 1b **Armada**) M16 **Spanish** (from Proto-Romance *armata* army). **1** M16 A fleet of warships. **b** L16 *specifically* The Spanish Armada, the fleet sent by Philip II of Spain to attack England in 1588. **2** L16–M17 A single warship. **3** E18 *transferred* and *figurative* A large army or airborne force; a large fleet of vessels of any kind.

■ Formerly pronounced /a:'meɪdə/.

armamentarium /ˌɑ:məmɛn'tɛ:rɪəm/ *noun* plural **armamentaria** /ˌɑ:məmɛn 'tɛ:rɪə/ L19 **Latin** (= arsenal, armoury). The medicines, equipment, and techniques available to a medical practitioner.

arme blanche /arm blɑ̃ʃ/ *noun phrase* plural **armes blanches** (pronounced same) L19 **French** (literally, 'white arm'). A cavalry sword or lance; the cavalry.

armiger /'ɑ:mɪdʒə/ *noun* M16 **Latin** (= bearing arms, from *arma* arms). An esquire: originally, a person who attended a knight to bear his shield; now, a person entitled to heraldic arms.

armilla /ɑ:'mɪlə/ *noun* plural **armillae** /ɑ:'mɪli:/, **armillas** M17 **Latin** (diminutive of *armus* shoulder). **1** M17 An ancient astronomical instrument consisting of a graduated ring or hoop fixed in the plane of the equator (*equinoctial armilla*), sometimes crossed by another in the plane of the meridian (*solstitial armilla*). **2** L17 A coronation stole; an armil. **3** E18 Chiefly *Archaeology*. A bracelet, an armlet.

armoire /ɑ:'mwɑ:/ *noun* L16 **French**. A cupboard, a wardrobe; *especially* one that is ornate or antique.

arpeggio /ɑːˈpɛdʒɪəʊ/ *noun* plural **arpeggios** E18 **Italian** (from *arpeggiare* to play on the harp, from *arpa* harp). *Music* The sounding of the notes of a chord in (usually rapid upward) succession, not simultaneously; a chord so sounded.

1996 *Country Life* . . . the playfulness of Opus 110 dissolved into a moment of perfect stillness before the joyous arpeggios came bubbling back.

arrack variant of ARAK.

arrêt /arɛ/ (*plural same*), /əˈrɛt/ *noun* M17 **French**. An authoritative sentence or decision, *specifically* of the monarch (*historical*) or parliament of France.

arrière-pensée /arjɛrpɑ̃se/ *noun* plural pronounced same E19 **French** (literally, 'behind-thought'). A concealed thought or intention; an ulterior motive; a mental reservation.

arrivisme /arrivism/ *noun* (also in Anglicized form **arrivism**) M20 **French** (from Old French *ariver* to arrive, ultimately from Latin *ad* to + *ripa* shore). The behaviour or character of an ARRIVISTE.

arriviste /arivist/ *noun* plural pronounced same (also in Anglicized form **arrivist**) E20 **French** (from as preceding). An ambitious or self-seeking person.

1995 *Spectator* The shameless effrontery with which these two power-greedy *arrivistes* bought and sold office for votes quite takes one's breath away.

arrondissement /arɔ̃dismɑ̃/ *noun* plural pronounced same E19 **French** (from *arrondiss-* lengthened stem of *arrondir* make round). In France: an administrative subdivision of a city or department.

arroyo /əˈrɔɪəʊ/ *noun* plural **arroyos** M19 **Spanish**. A steep gully, a watercourse. *North American*.

arsis /ˈɑːsɪs/ *noun* plural **arses** /ˈɑːsiːz/ LME **Late Latin** (from Greek = lifting, raising, from *airein* to raise). The syllable or part of a metrical foot that is stressed (originally, *Classical Prosody*, by raised pitch or volume); the unstressed beat in barred music. Opposed to THESIS I sense 1.

art brut /ar bryt/ *noun phrase* M20 **French** (literally, 'raw art'). Primitive or pseudo-primitive art.

■ *L'Art brut* was the title of an exhibition of paintings in Paris in 1949, which included works by children and psychiatric patients.

1996 *Economist Art brut*—raw art—is the term that the French artist and collector Jean Dubuffet coined to describe works by intuitive artists outside the common run.

artel /ɑːˈtɛl/ *noun* L19 **Russian** (*artel'*). A Russian or Soviet collective enterprise of craftsmen or skilled workers.

artiste /ɑːˈtiːst/ *noun* E19 **French**. A performing artist; a professional singer, dancer, actor, etc.

art nouveau /ɑː nuːˈvəʊ/, *foreign* /ar nuvo/ *noun phrase* E20 **French** (literally, 'new art'). A decorative style in French and English art of the late nineteenth century characterized by ornamented and flowing lines. Cf. JUGENDSTIL.

1996 *Spectator* Bakst's original setting for the 1906 exhibition in Paris . . . gives a lift to some overripe Russian art nouveau sculpture.

aryballos /arɪˈbaləs/ *noun* M19 **Greek** (*aruballos* bag, purse, oil-flask). *Greek Antiquities* A globular flask with a narrow neck used to hold oil or unguent.

ascesis /əˈsiːsɪs/ *noun* (also **askesis** /əˈskiːsɪs/) L19 **Greek** (*askēsis* exercise, training, from *askein* to exercise). The practice of self-discipline.

ashram /ˈaʃrəm/ *noun* E20 **Sanskrit** (*āśrama* hermitage). **1** E20 In the Indian subcontinent: a hermitage, a place of religious retreat. **2** M20 *transferred* Any group with shared spiritual or social aims living together.

askari /əˈskɑːri/ *noun* plural **askaris**, same L19 **Arabic** (*'askarī* soldier). An East African soldier or police officer.

askesis variant of ASCESIS.

asphyxia /əsˈfɪksɪə/ *noun* M19 **Modern Latin** (from Greek *asphuxia*, from *a-* without + *sphuxis* pulsation). *Medicine* The condition of defective aeration of the blood caused by failure of the oxygen supply; suffocation.

■ Earlier (E18) in the sense of 'stoppage of the pulse', but there is no apparent evidence of this outside dictionaries.

assai /aˈsʌɪ/ *adverb* E18 **Italian**. *Music* (In directions:) very.

assegai /ˈasəgʌɪ/ *noun* (also **assagai**) E17 **French** (*azagaie* (now *zagaie*, *sagaie*)) or Portuguese (*azagaia*, Spanish *azagaya* from colloquial Arabic *az-zaġāya from al* the + Berber *zaġāya* spear). An iron-bladed spear with a hardwood shaft used for stabbing or as a missile by South African indigenous peoples.

assemblé /asɑ̃ble/ *noun* plural pronounced same L18 **French** (past participle of *assembler* to bring together). *Ballet* A leap in which the feet are brought together before landing.

assemblée /asɑ̃ble/ *noun* plural pronounced same E18 **French**. An assembly; *especially* a gathering of polite society for recreational purposes.

assiette /asjɛt/ (*plural same*), /asɪˈɛt/ *noun* M18 **French** (= plate, course of a meal; seat, site; bed, foundation). A prepared dish of food.

■ Usually with qualifying word or phrase, as in *assiette anglaise* 'a platter of assorted cold meats'.

ataman /ˈatəman/ *noun* M19 **Russian**. A Cossack leader. Cf. HETMAN.

ataraxia /atəˈraksɪə/ *noun* M19 **Greek** (= impassiveness, from *a-* not + *tarassein* to disturb). Imperturbability; ataraxy.

atelier /əˈtɛlɪeɪ/ *noun* L17 **French**. A workshop or studio, especially of an artist or couturier.

1995 *Times* Gone are the days when . . . the *ateliers* of craftspeople were busy, not just with clothes and hats for a wedding, but with custom-made jewels.

a tempo /ɑː ˈtɛmpəʊ/ *adverb phrase* M18 **Italian** (= in time). *Music* (A direction:) in the tempo indicated previously, before the direction to deviate from it.

à terre /a tɛr/ *adverb & adjective phrase* E20 **French**. Chiefly *Ballet*. On the ground.

atlantes /atˈlantiːz/ *noun plural* E17 **Greek** (*Atlas, Atlant-*, the Titan supposed to hold up the pillars of the universe, and a mountain range in western North Africa also regarded mythically as supporting the heavens). *Architecture* Male figures used as pillars to support an entablature.

■ The singular form of the word, meaning 'a person who supports a great burden' was introduced via Latin (L16) and soon afterwards (M17) became the name for 'a collection of maps or charts bound in a volume'. In this sense, and in other senses derived from it, *atlas* has long been entirely naturalized. The connection between the world-supporting Titan and the book of maps was first made in the mid sixteenth century, when Antonio Lafreri, a French publisher working in Rome, put together collections of maps to his customers' specifications and bound them with a standard titlepage depicting Atlas carrying the world on his shoulders. The use of 'Atlas' as a title for a book of maps originated with the Flemish geographers Gerhard and Rumold Mercator, whose complete 107-map *Atlas* was published in 1595. The Mercator *Atlas* in various versions and editions so dominated European cartography in the first half of the seventeenth century (it appeared in English in 1636) that the name became used generically for all such books.

atman /ˈɑːtmən/ *noun* L18 **Sanskrit** (*ātman*). *Hindu Philosophy* The self as the subject of individual consciousness, the soul; the supreme personal principle of life in the universe.

atole /əˈtəʊli/ *noun* M17 **American Spanish** (from Nahuatl *atolli*). Gruel or porridge made of maize or other meal.

■ Chiefly United States.

à tort et à travers /a tɔr e a travɛr/ *adverb phrase* M18 **French** (= wrongly and across). At random, haphazardly.

à toute outrance variant of À OUTRANCE.

atrium /ˈeɪtrɪəm/ *noun* plural **atria** /ˈeɪtrɪə/, **atriums** L16 **Latin**. **1** L16 *Architecture* A central court, originally that of an ancient-Roman house; a covered court or portico; (a building with) a large light-well; a central hall or glassed-in court in a building. **2** L19 *Anatomy* and *Zoology* Any of various chambers into which one or more passages open; *specifically* (**a**) either of the two upper chambers of the heart into which the veins conduct blood; (**b**) the tympanic chamber of the ear.

1 1995 *Times* Office accommodation for tenants has a separate entrance with escalators leading up to a glass and cream-coloured marble atrium.

à trois /a trwa/ *adjective & adverb phrase* L19 **French**. Shared by, or in a group of, three people. Cf. MÉNAGE À TROIS.

1996 *Spectator* In 1956 Gottfried, Budge and I went to dine *à trois* wearing black tie.

attaché /əˈtaʃeɪ/ *noun* E19 **French** (past participle of *attacher* to attach). A junior official attached to the staff of an ambassador etc.; a representative of his or her government in a foreign country.

■ Frequently in the combination *attaché case* a small rectangular case, usually with a handle, for carrying documents.

attar /ˈatə/ *noun* (also (earlier) **otto** /ˈɒtəʊ/) M17 **Persian** (*ʿiṭr*, Arabic *ʿiṭr*, colloquial Arabic *ʿaṭar* perfume, essence). A fragrant volatile essence, *especially* (more fully *attar of roses*) that obtained from rose-petals.

attentat *in sense 1 foreign* /atɑ̃ta/; (*plural same*); *in sense 2* /əˈtɛntət/ *noun* (also (now only in sense 2) **attentate** /ə'tɛnteɪt/) E17 **Old and Modern French** (or medieval Latin *attentatum*, from *attentatum* past participial stem of *attentare* variant of Latin *attemptare* to attempt). **1** E17 An attack; an attempted assassination. **2** E18 *Law* Something wrongfully done by a judge in a proceeding, pending an appeal.

attentisme /atɑ̃tism/ *noun* M20 **French** (from *attente* wait, waiting). The policy of waiting to see what happens.

attrait /atrɛ/ *noun* E20 **French** (from *attraire* to attract). *Theology* Vocation; inclination.

aubade /əʊ'bɑːd/, *foreign* /obad/ (*plural same*) *noun* L17 **French** (from Spanish *albada*, from *alba* (= French *aube*) dawn). A piece of music or a poem written to be heard at or appropriate to dawn.

auberge /əʊ'bɛːʒ/; *foreign* /obɛrʒ/ (*plural same*) *noun* L16 **French** (from Provençal *alberga* lodging). An inn, *especially* one in France.

aubergine /'əʊbəʒiːn/ *noun & adjective* L18 **French** (from Catalan *alberginia*, from Arabic *al-bāḏinjān*, from *al-* the + Persian *bādingān, bādinjān* from Sanskrit *vātiṃgaṇa*). **A** *noun* **1** L18 The fruit of the eggplant, *Solanum melongena*, eaten as a vegetable; the plant itself. Cf. BRINJAL. **2** L19 A dark purple colour typical of the skin of the fruit. **B** *adjective* L19 Of the colour aubergine, dark purple.

aubusson /obysɔ̃/ *noun* (also more correctly **Aubusson**) plural pronounced same E20 **French** (Aubusson = a town in central France). Tapestry or (especially) a tapestry carpet woven at Aubusson.

AUC abbreviation of AB URBE CONDITA.

au contraire /o kɔ̃trɛr/, /əʊ kɒn'trɛː/ *adverb phrase* M18 **French**. On the contrary.

1995 D. Lodge *Therapy* Don't get the idea that I'm an enthusiast for British Rail's Inter-City service to London. *Au contraire*, as Amy would say.

au courant /o kurɑ̃/ *adverb & adjective phrase* M18 **French**. In an informed position; aware of current developments.

■ Usually followed by *with*, *of*, but can also be used absolutely.

1996 *Times* . . . to find out what the in-your-face young are wearing, or were ten minutes ago when in-your-face was still an *au courant* fashion statement . . .

auditorium /ɔːdɪ'tɔːrɪəm/ *noun* plural **auditoriums, auditoria** /ɔːdɪ'tɔːrɪə/ E17 **Latin**. **1** E17 *general* A place for hearing. *rare*. **2** M19 *specifically* The part of a theatre, lecture-hall, or other public building occupied by the audience; (*North America*) such a building as a whole.

au fait /əʊ feɪ/, *foreign* /o fɛ/ *adverb & predicative adjective phrase* M18 **French** (literally, 'to the fact', 'to the point'). Thoroughly conversant (*with*), well instructed (*in*), expert or skilful (*at*).

1996 *Times: Weekend* The Tuscans are not entirely au fait with the idea of walking for pleasure.

Aufklärung /'aʊfklɛːrʊŋ/ *noun* E19 **German** (literally, 'clearing up'). The intellectual and philosophical movement in eighteenth-century Europe that promoted reason and individualism against traditional religion and ancient authority; the Enlightenment.

au fond /o fɔ̃/ *adverb phrase* L18 **French**. At bottom, basically.

1996 *Spectator* . . . Mrs Lancaster was *au fond* nostalgic, a sentiment she vehemently denies possessing . . .

au grand sérieux /o grɑ̃ serjø/ *adverb phrase* M19 **French**. In all seriousness. Cf. AU SÉRIEUX.

au gratin /o grɑtɛ̃/ *adverb & predicative adjective phrase* E19 **French** (from *au* with the + GRATIN). *Cookery* Sprinkled with breadcrumbs and/or grated cheese and browned.

auguste /'ɔːguːst/; *foreign* /ogyst/ (*plural same*) *noun* E20 **French** (from German *August*, male forename, (*slang*) clown, fool). A circus clown wearing ill-fitting or dishevelled clothes.

au mieux /o mjø/ *adverb phrase* M19 **French** (= at the best). On the best of, or on very intimate, terms *with* (someone).

aumônière /omonjɛr/ *noun* plural pronounced same E19 **French** (feminine of *aumônier* almoner). A purse carried at the waist.

au naturel /o natyrɛl/ *adverb phrase* E19 **French**. In the natural state; cooked plainly; uncooked.

1996 *New Scientist* Now the company is paying people to look for weedy pastures around the state [sc. Nebraska] and pick the [milkweed] pods *au naturel*.

au pair /əʊ pɛː/ *adjective & noun phrase* L19 **French** (= on equal terms). **A** *adjective phrase* L19 Of arrangements between two parties: paid for (entirely or largely) by mutual services. Of a person: party to such an arrangement; *specifically* (of a (usually foreign) girl) undertaking domestic duties in return for room and board. **B** *noun* M20 An au pair girl.

au pied de la lettre /o pje də la lɛtr/ *adverb phrase* L18 **French** (= to the foot of the letter). Down to the last detail; literally.

aura /ˈɔːrə/ *noun* plural **auras**, (*rare*) **aurae** /ˈɔːriː/ LME **Latin** (from Greek = breath, breeze). **1** LME A gentle breeze, a zephyr. *archaic* and *poetic*. **2** M18 A subtle emanation or exhalation; a surrounding glow; *figurative* an atmosphere diffused by or attending a person, place, etc.; a distinctive impression of character or aspect. **3** L18 A premonitory sensation experienced before an epileptic fit.

> **2 1996** *Oldie* Esther, who is also a medium, says she can tell whether an animal is sick by its aura.

aureola /ɔːˈriːələ/ *noun* plural **aureolae**, /ɔːˈriːəli/, **aureolas** L15 **Latin** (feminine (sc. *corona* crown) of *aureolus* adjective, diminutive of *aureus* golden, from *aurum* gold). A celestial crown; a halo; an aureole.

au reste /o rɛst/ *adverb phrase* E17 **French**. As for the rest.

au revoir /o rəvwɑr/, /əʊ rəˈvwɑː/ *interjection & noun phrase* L17 **French** (literally, 'to the seeing again'). (Goodbye) until we meet again; a farewell for the present.

aurora /ɔːˈrɔːrə/ *noun* (also **Aurora**) plural **aurorae** /ɔːˈrɔːriː/, **auroras** LME **Latin** (*Aurora* the Roman goddess of the dawn). **1** LME The rising light of the morning; the dawn. **b** *figurative* M19 The beginning, the early period. **2** M17 A rich orange colour, as of the sky at sunrise. **3** E18 A luminous phenomenon, often taking the form of variable streamers or resembling drapery, seen in the upper atmosphere of high northern (*borealis*) and southern (*australis*) latitudes.

aurora australis /ɔːˌrɔːrə ɔːˈstreɪlɪs/ M18 **Latin** (= southern dawn). The aurora of the southern polar regions, the southern lights.

■ Coined after AURORA BOREALIS.

aurora borealis /ɔːˌrɔːrə bɔːrɪˈeɪlɪs/ E18 **Latin** (= northern dawn). The aurora of the northern polar regions, the northern lights.

■ The phrase was coined to describe the phenomenon in 1621 by the French physicist and philosopher Pierre Gassendi (1592–1655).

au sérieux /o serjø/ *adverb phrase* M19 **French**. Seriously. Cf. AU GRAND SÉRIEUX.

Auslese /ˈaʊsleːzə/ *noun* (also **auslese**) plural **Auslesen** /ˈaʊsleːzən/, **Ausleses** M19 **German** (from *aus* out + *lese* picking, vintage). A white wine made (especially in Germany) from selected bunches of grapes picked later than the general harvest.

auteur /otœr/ *noun* plural pronounced same M20 **French** (= author). *Cinema* A director who so greatly influences the films directed as to be able to rank as their author.

> **1995** *Spectator* But then why would anyone go hire a writer when everyone keeps telling him that he's an *auteur*?

auto /ˈauto/ *noun* plural **autos** /ˈautos/ M16 **Spanish and Portuguese** (from Latin *actus* act). **1** M16 An AUTO-DA-FÉ. **2** L18 A play (by a Spanish or Portuguese author).

autobahn /ˈɔːtəbɑːn/, *foreign* /ˈaʊtobaːn/ *noun* plural **autobahns**, **autobahnen** /ˈaʊtobaːnən/ M20 **German** (from *Auto* automobile + *Bahn* road). In Germany, Switzerland, or Austria: a motorway.

> **1996** *Independent* Germany gave us prototypical motorways in Hitler's *Autobahn*.

auto-da-fé /ˌautodaˈfe/, /ˌɔːtəʊdɑːˈfeɪ/, /ˌaʊtəʊdaˈfeɪ/ *noun* plural **autos-da-fé** /ˌautosdaˈfe/, /ˌɔːtəʊzdɑːˈfeɪ/, /ˌaʊtəʊzdɑːˈfeɪ/, **auto-da-fés** E18 **Portuguese** (= act of the faith (Spanish *auto de fe*)). (The execution of) a judicial sentence of the Inquisition; *especially* the public burning of a heretic; *transferred* a public burning.

> **1997** G. Kepel *Allah in West* . . . television viewers saw the scenes [of the burning of Rushdie's *Satanic Verses*] differently: they recalled engravings of Inquisition bonfires or black-and-white images of Nazis burning books . . . whilst commentators in the Western press used these images to wax indignant about the *auto-da-fé* . . .

autogiro /ɔːtəʊˈdʒʌɪrəʊ/ *noun* (also **autogyro**) plural **autogiros** E20 **Spanish** (from as *auto-* self + *giro* gyration). A type of aircraft having a propeller and freely rotating horizontal vanes.

automat /ˈɔːtəmat/ *noun* L17 **German** (from French *automate* from Latin AUTOMATON). **1** L17 An *automaton* **2** E20 A cafeteria in which food is obtained from a slot-machine; a slot-machine.

■ Sense 2 is chiefly a United States usage.

automaton /ɔːˈtɒmət(ə)n/ *noun* plural **automatons**, **automata** /ɔːˈtɒmətə/ E17 **Latin** ((also *automatum*) from Greek, use as noun of neuter of *automatos* acting of itself). **1** E17 Something having the power of spontaneous motion; *especially* a living being viewed as a machine. **2** M17 A piece of mechanism with concealed motive power, *especially* one simulating a living being; a robot. **3** L17 A living being whose actions are purely involuntary or mechanical; a person behaving without active intelligence or mechanically in a set pattern or routine. **4** M20 *Computing* A machine whose responses to all possible inputs are specified in advance.

autopista /ɔːtəˈpiːstə/, *foreign* /autoˈpista/ *noun* M20 **Spanish** (from *auto* automobile + *pista* track, PISTE). In Spain and Spanish-speaking countries: a motorway.

autoroute /ˈɔːtəruːt/, *foreign* /otorut/ (*plural same*) *noun* M20 **French** (from *auto* automobile + *route* road). In France: a motorway.

autostrada /ɔːtəˈstrɑːdə/, *foreign* /auto ˈstrɑːda/ *noun* plural **autostradas, autostrade** /autoˈstrɑːde/ E20 **Italian** (from *auto* automobile + *strada* road from Latin STRATUM). In Italy: a motorway.

avalanche /ˈavəlɑːnʃ/ *noun & verb* L18 **French** (from Romansh, alteration of Alpine French dialect *lavanche* (of unknown origin), by blending with *avaler* descend: cf. Provençal *lavanca*, Italian *valanga*). **A** *noun* **1** L18 A large mass of snow, rocks, and ice, moving swiftly down a mountainside. **2** *transferred* and *figurative* M19 A sudden onrush or descent; a rapidly descending mass. **b** *Physics* M20 A process of cumulative ionization in which each electron and ion generates further charged particles. Also more fully *Townsend avalanche*. Frequently *attributive*. **B** *intransitive verb* L19 Descend in or like an avalanche.

avant-garde /ˌavɒ̃ˈgɑːd/ *noun & adjective* LME **French** (from *avant* forward, before + *garde* guard). **A** *noun* **1** LME The vanguard of an army. Now *archaic* or *historical*. **2** E20 The pioneering or innovative writers, artists, etc., in a particular period. **B** *adjective* E20 Of or pertaining to the artistic avant-garde; progressive, ultra-modern.

A.2 1996 *Times* The punk singer, who wowed the avant-garde of Madrid in the frenzied years after Franco's death, has mellowed into a chubby 45-year-old in jeans and a stripey jumper.

B 1996 *Country Life* [Stockhausen's] *Gruppen* has always been considered an avant-garde landmark.

avant la lettre /avɒ̃ la lɛtr/ *adverb phrase* M20 **French** (literally, 'before the letter'). Before the word, definition, etc., was invented.

1995 *Spectator* He was a Eurosceptic *avant la lettre*.

avatar /ˈavətɑː/ *noun* L18 **Sanskrit** (*avatāra* descent, from *ava* off, away, down + *tar-* to pass over). **1** L18 *Hindu Mythology* The descent of a god to earth in incarnate form. **2** E19 An incarnation or embodiment (of another person, an idea, etc.). **3** E19 A manifestation to the world as a ruling power or as an object of worship; *generally* a manifestation, a phase.

2 1995 *Times* Most are interpreted as avatars of anti-imperialism, which requires some dedicated pummelling into shape.

3 1995 *New Scientist* For example, members of the online communities . . . can create avatars for themselves, complete with the body and head of their choice—which is more flexibility than you get offline in real life.

ave /ˈɑːvi/, /ˈɑːveɪ/ *noun & interjection* (also *Ave* in sense A.1) ME **Latin** (as imperative singular of *avere* to be or fare well, used as an expression of greeting or farewell). **A** *noun* **1** ME An AVE MARIA. **b** ME A bead on a rosary (as used for counting the number of aves recited). **2** E17 A shout of welcome or farewell. **B** *interjection* LME Hail! Farewell!

■ The earliest use of the noun was short for AVE MARIA.

ave atque vale /ˌɑːveɪ atkwi ˈvɑːleɪ/ *interjection* M19 **Latin** (= hail and farewell). Hello and goodbye, hail and farewell.

■ The concluding words of Catullus' graveside address to his dead brother (*Carmina* ci.10), the exclamation is now sometimes used jocularly as a greeting to someone whom one has seen or will see for only a short time.

Ave Maria /ˌɑːvi məˈriːə/, /ˌɑːveɪ məˈriːə/ *interjection & noun phrase* (also **Ave Mary** /ˈmɛːri/) ME **Latin** (= hail, Mary!). **1** ME The angel's greeting to the Virgin Mary combined with that of Elizabeth (cf. Luke 1:28, 42), used as a devotional recitation; the prayer to the Virgin as Mother of God beginning with these words; a recitation of this devotional phrase or prayer (often shortened to AVE). **2** L16 (The time of) the ave-bell.

avoirdupois /avədəˈpɔɪz/, /ˌavwɑːdjʊ ˈpwɑː/ *noun* ME **Old French** (*aveir de peis* goods of weight, from *ave(i)r* (modern *avoir*) use as noun of *avoir* to have (from Latin *habere*) + *de* of + *peis*, *pois* (modern *poids*) weight. **1** ME–L17 Merchandise sold by weight. **2** L15 A system of weights based on a pound (the *avoirdupois pound*) of 16 ounces or 7,000 grains. More fully *avoirdupois weight*. **3** L16 Weight, heaviness; *colloquially* excess bodily weight.

■ The substitution of *du* for the earlier *de* was established in the seventeenth century.

3 1995 *Times* It may be wish-fulfilment or simply *avoirdupois*, but Paula Yates's famously tiny waist seems to have expanded.

avoué /avwe/ *noun* plural pronounced same E19 **French**. **1** E19 A person who holds the advowson of an ecclesiastical house or benefice; an advowee. **2** E19 A French solicitor.

awabi /ə'wɑːbi/ *noun* E18 **Japanese**. The Japanese abalone, *Haliotis gigantea*.

axiomata media /aksɪˌɒmətə 'miːdɪə/ *noun phrase plural* M19 **Modern Latin** (= middle principles). *Philosophy* Principles above simple empirical laws but below the highest generalizations or fundamental laws.

■ The phrase is Francis Bacon's in his *Novum Organum* (I.xix), published in Latin in 1620. It was introduced into English philosophical discourse by J. S. Mill in the mid nineteenth century.

ayah /'ʌɪə/ *noun* L18 **Portuguese** (*aia* feminine of *aio* tutor). A nurse or maidservant, especially of Europeans in India, South-east Asia, etc.

1996 *Times: Weekend* Olive, like many children born in colonies and brought up by an *ayah*, has divided loyalties.

ayahuasca /ˌaja'waska/ *noun* L20 **South American Spanish** (From Quechua *ayawáskha* from *aya* corpse + *waskha* rope). A hallucinogenic drug made from the bark of a tropical vine found in the Amazon basin; the vine itself. Also called *yagé*.

1991 M. Talbot *Holographic Universe* He had to take a shamanic sacred drink made from a hallucinogenic plant known as *ayahuasca*, the 'soul vine'.

ayatollah /ʌɪə'tɒlə/ *noun* (also (as a title) **Ayatollah**) M20 **Persian** (from Arabic *'āyatu-llāh* miraculous sign of God). A Shiite religious leader in Iran; *figurative* a dogmatic leader, an influential or powerful person.

ayurveda /ɑːjə'veɪdə/ *noun* (also **Ayurveda**) E20 **Sanskrit** (*āyur-veda* science of life, medicine). An ancient Indian health system.

1995 *Guardian: Weekend* Ayurveda recommends that red meat in particular is to be avoided as it is extremely hard to digest.

azan /ə'zɑːn/ *noun* M19 **Arabic** (*'aḏān* announcement). The Muslim call to ritual prayer, often made by a muezzin or broadcast through loudspeakers from the minaret of a mosque.

azotea /aθo'tea/, /azo'tea/ *noun* E19 **Spanish**. In Spain and Spanish-speaking countries: the flat roof of a house used as a terrace.

azuki variant of ADZUKI.

azulejo /aθu'lexo/, /asu'lexo/, /azjʊ'leɪhəʊ/ *noun* plural **azulejos** /aθu'lexos/, /asu 'lexos/, /azjʊ'leɪhəʊz/ M19 **Spanish** (from *azul* blue). A kind of coloured glazed tile used in Spanish buildings.

baas /bɑ:s/ *noun* L18 **Dutch**. In South Africa: a (usually White) employer, master, overseer, etc.

■ The word was first used in English in 1625 (*Purchas his Pilgrimes* I. ii. 117) for a sea-captain: 'Our Baase (for so a Dutch capitaine is called)'. It travelled to South Africa with the Dutch settlers of that country and became, in both Afrikaans and South African English, the normal form of address used by Black or Coloured South Africans for those in authority (hence BAASSKAP).

baasskap /'bɑ:skap/ *noun* M20 **Afrikaans** (from Dutch *baasschap*, from BAAS + *-schap* -ship). Domination, especially of non-Whites by Whites.

baba /'bɑ:bɑ:/ *noun* E19 **French** (from Polish, literally, 'married (peasant) woman'). A rich sponge cake; *specifically* one served in a rum syrup. More fully *rum baba* or *baba au rhum*.

babiche /bə'bi:ʃ/ *noun* E19 **Canadian French** (from Micmac *a:papi:č*). In North America: thongs or thread made of rawhide, sinew, etc.

babu /'bɑ:bu:/ *noun* (also **baboo** or (as title) **Babu**) L18 **Hindustani** (*bābū*). **1** L18-E19 Originally, a Hindu title of respect. Later, a Hindu gentleman. **2** M19 *History* An Indian clerk or official who could write English; *derogatory* an Indian, especially in Bengal, who had had a superficial English education; *attributive* the ornate and often unidiomatic English written by such a person.

2 *attributive* **1936** C. S. Lewis *Allegory of Love* The fantastical 'babu' ornaments of the style [of the *De Nuptiis*] were admired.

babushka /bə'bʊʃkə/ *noun* M20 **Russian** (= grandmother). **1** M20 In Russia: a grandmother, an old woman. **2** M20 A headscarf folded diagonally and tied under the chin. Chiefly *North American*.

bac abbreviation of BACCALAUREATE or BACCARAT.

bacalao /baka'lao/ *noun* (also **bacalhau** /baka'ʎau/) M16 **Spanish** (*bacal(l)ao*, Portuguese *bacalhau*). Codfish, especially dried or salted.

baccalaureate /bakə'lɔ:rɪət/ *noun* M17 **French** (*baccalauréat* or medieval Latin *baccalaureatus*, from *baccalaureus*, originally with reference to *bacca lauri* laurel berry). **1** M17 The university degree of bachelor. **2** L20 (A qualification awarded for satisfactory performance in) a set of examinations intended to qualify successful candidates for higher education in any of several countries; hence also known as the *International Baccalaureate*.

■ *Bac* or *bachot*, the colloquial French abbreviations of *baccalauréat*, are also found.

baccarat /'bakərɑ:/ *noun* (also **baccara**) M19 **French** (*baccara*, of unknown origin). A gambling card-game, played between a banker and one punter, or several punters in turn, in which the best one- or two-card hand is that yielding the highest remainder when its total face value is divided by 10.

bach /bɑ:x/ *noun* L19 **Welsh** ((dialect) literally, 'little'). Dear, beloved; little one; friend.

■ Chiefly vocative and often placed appositionally after personal names.

bachot abbreviation of BACCALAUREATE.

bacillus /bə'sɪləs/ *noun* plural **bacilli** /bə'sɪlʌɪ/, /bə'sɪli:/ L19 **Late Latin** (= little rod, diminutive of *baculus* rod, stick). Any rod-shaped bacterium; *loosely* any pathogenic bacterium.

backfisch /'bakfɪʃ/ *noun* plural **backfische** /'bakfɪʃə/ L19 **German** (literally, 'fish for frying'). A girl in late adolescence, a teenage girl.

1966 *Observer* Marlene Dietrich . . . conjures up the little Berlin *backfisch* . . . who auditioned for 'The Blue Angel'.

backsheesh variant of BAKSHEESH.

bacterium /bak'tɪərɪəm/ *noun* plural **bacteria** /bak'tɪərɪə/ M19 **Modern Latin** (from Greek *baktērion* diminutive of *baktēria* staff, cane). Any of the very widely distributed group *Bacteria* of microscopic prokaryotic mainly single-celled organisms, many of which are symbiotic or pathogenic in animals and plants.

badigeon /bə'dɪʤ(ə)n/ *noun* M18 **French** (of unknown origin). A composition used to fill up gaps in stone or wood.

■ Now United States.

badinage /ˌbadɪˈnɑːʒ/ *noun & verb* M17 **French** (from *badiner* to joke, from *badin* fool from Provençal, from *badar* to gape, from Proto-Romance). **A** *noun* M17 Humorous banter or ridicule. **B** *verb* E19 Banter playfully.

1996 *Spectator* The jokes and the badinage now were for real; and so were the author's anxieties.

badmash /ˈbʌdmɑːʃ/ *noun* M19 **Urdu** (from Persian, from *bad* evil + Arabic *maʻāš* means of livelihood). In the Indian subcontinent: a rascal, a hooligan.

bagarre /bagar/ *noun* plural pronounced same L19 **French**. A tumult; a scuffle, a brawl.

bagasse /bəˈgas/ *noun* E19 **French** (from Spanish *bagazo*). The residue left after the extraction of juice from sugar cane or sugar beet.

bagatelle /bagəˈtɛl/ *noun* M17 **French** (from Italian *bagatella* perhaps diminutive of Latin *baca* berry, or from Italian *baga* baggage). **1** M17 A trifle, a thing of no value or importance; a negligible amount. **2** M18 A piece of verse or music in a light style. **3** E19 A game in which small balls are struck (usually by a mechanical striker operated by the player) towards numbered holes on a board with a semicircular end.

1 1996 *Spectator* What if I had confused a treaty? Phooey, a mere bagatelle.

bagel /ˈbeɪg(ə)l/ *noun* (also **beigel** /ˈbʌɪg(ə)l/) E20 **Yiddish** (*beygel*). A usually hard ring-shaped roll of bread.

bagnio /ˈbɑːnjəʊ/ *noun* plural **bagnios** L16 **Italian** (*bagno* from Latin *balneum* bath). **1** L16 An oriental prison; a slave-house. Now only *historical*. **2** E17–E19 A bath, a bathing-house. **3** E17 A brothel.

baguette /baˈgɛt/ *noun* E18 **French** (from Italian *bacchetto* diminutive of *bacchio* from Latin *baculum* staff). **1** E18 *Architecture* A small moulding of semicircular section, like an astragal. **2** E20 A gem, usually a diamond, cut in a long rectangular shape. **3** M20 A long narrow French loaf.

bahada variant of BAJADA.

bahut /bay/ *noun* plural pronounced same M19 **French**. An ornamental chest or cabinet.

baignoire /bɛɲwar/ *noun* plural pronounced same M19 **French** (= bath-tub). A box at a theatre on the same level as the stalls.

bain-marie /ˌbanməˈriː/, *foreign* /bɛ̃mari/ *noun* plural **bains-marie** (pronounced same) E18 **French** (translation of medieval Latin *balneum Mariae* translation of medieval Greek *kaminos Marias* furnace of Maria, a supposed Jewish alchemist). A vessel of hot water in which cooking-pans and their contents are slowly heated; a double saucepan. Also, a dish prepared in this.

bajada /bəˈhɑːdə/ *noun* (also **bahada**) M19 **Spanish** (= descent, slope). A broad slope of alluvial material at the foot of an escarpment.

■ Originally south-western United States but subsequently more general (see quotation).

1960 B. W. Sparks *Geomorphology* The whole slope from the range to the infilled playa lake is usually termed a piedmont. The upper part is often, but not always, a rock-cut surface, normally termed a pediment, while the lower part is an aggradation feature formed of detritus from the ranges and termed a bahada.

baklava /ˈbɑːkləvə/ *noun* M17 **Turkish**. An originally eastern Mediterranean dessert made of thin pieces of flaky pastry, honey or syrup, and nuts.

baksheesh /bakˈʃiːʃ/ *noun* (also **backsheesh**) M18 **Persian** (ultimately from *bakšīš* from *bakšīdan* to give). In Eastern countries: a gratuity, a tip.

balafon /ˈbalafɒn/ *noun* L20 **African**. A West African musical instrument similar to a xylophone.

1991 P. Matthiessen *African Silences* The group included . . . three players of the balafon, a kind of xylophone with hardwood strips.

balalaika /baləˈlʌɪkə/ *noun* L18 **Russian** (of Tartar origin). A musical instrument of the guitar kind, with a triangular body and from two to four strings, popular in Slavonic countries.

balancé /balɑ̃se/ *noun* plural pronounced same L18 **French** (= balanced (sc. *pas* step)). *Dancing* A swaying step from one foot to the other.

bal costumé /bal kɔstyme/ *noun phrase* plural **bals costumés** (pronounced same) E19 **French**. A fancy-dress ball.

baldachin /ˈbaldəkɪn/, /ˈbɔːldəkɪn/ *noun* (also **baldaquin**) M17 **Italian** (*baldacchino*, ultimately from *Baldacco* Italian form of *Baghdad*). A canopy supported on columns or fixed to a roof or wall, and placed over an altar, throne, or doorway.

■ When first introduced into English (L16), *baldacchino* denoted rich brocade of a type that had originally been made in Baghdad. It was later (M17) transferred to describe a canopy made out of this material, and in current usage the canopy can be of any material.

ballabile /ba'lɑ:bile/ *noun* plural **ballabili** /ba'lɑ:bili/ M19 **Italian** (from *ballare* to dance). A dance by the *corps de ballet* or by the chorus in an opera; a piece of music for this; any piece of instrumental music suggestive of a dance.

ballade /ba'lɑ:d/ *noun* LME **French** (from Provençal *balada* dance, song, or poem to dance to, from *balar* to dance). **A** *noun* **1** LME A poem (originally for singing with accompaniment) of one or more triplets of stanzas having 7, 8, or 10 lines, each usually ending with the same refrain line, and an envoy; more *generally*, a poem divided into stanzas of equal length, usually of 7 or 8 lines. Also *collectively*, poetry of this form. **2** M19 *Music* An extended, usually dramatic, piece usually for the piano.

ballerina /balə'ri:nə/ *noun* plural **ballerinas** L18 **Italian** (feminine of *ballerino* dancing-master, from *ballare* to dance). *Ballet* A female dancer, *especially* one who undertakes a leading role in classical ballet.

ballet /'baleɪ/, /'bali/ *noun* M17 **French** (from Italian *balletto* diminutive of *ballo* ball). (A theatrical performance of) dancing and mime to music; a company performing this.

ballet blanc /'baleɪ blɑ̃/ *noun phrase* M20 **French** (= white ballet). A ballet in which the female dancers wear long white tutus.

1996 *Spectator La Sylphide* is conventionally regarded as the work that introduced Romantic elements on stage such as the long white tutus—hence the term *ballet blanc* or 'white ballet' used to describe that particular genre . . .

ballista /bə'lɪstə/ *noun* plural **ballistae** /bə'lɪsti:/, **ballistas** E16 **Latin** (ultimately from Greek *ballein* to throw). A large military engine used in antiquity for hurling stones and other missiles.

ballon /balɔ̃/ *noun* plural pronounced same M19 **French**. **1** M19 Elasticity and buoyancy in dancing; smooth passage from step to step. **2** M20 A spherical glass for brandy, a brandy balloon.

1 1995 *Times* Tetsuya Kumakawa as the Blue Boy turns and jumps with the flashy *ballon* and clarity that has made him such a hit . . .

ballon d'essai /balɔ̃ desɛ/ *noun phrase* plural **ballons d'essai** (pronounced same) L19 **French** (= trial balloon). An experiment to see how a new policy or project will be received; a tentative proposal.

1942 *Mind* A good deal of Hume's theory of belief is rather a *ballon d'essai* than meant altogether seriously.

ballonné /balɔne/ *noun* plural pronounced same L18 **French** (past participle of *ballonner* to swell or puff out, distend). A bouncing step in dancing.

bal masqué /bal maske/ *noun phrase* plural **bals masqués** (pronounced same) M18 **French**. A masked ball.

bal musette /bal myzɛt/ *noun phrase* plural **bals musettes** (pronounced same) E20 **French**. In France: a popular dancehall (with an accordion band).

balsa /'bɒlsə/ *noun* E17 **Spanish** (= raft). **1** E17 A raft or fishing boat, used chiefly on the Pacific coasts of South America. **2** M19 A tropical American tree, *Ochroma pyramidale* (more fully *balsa tree*); its strong, very light wood, used for rafts, floats, etc. (more fully *balsa-wood*).

balti /'bɔ:lti/, /'balti/ *noun* L20 **Urdu** (*bāltī bucket*). A type of Indian cuisine apparently originating in Northern Pakistan and served in metal pans.

1994 *Guardian* Among the 8,000 restaurants now doing business, previous vogues have been superseded by balti (bucket) cuisine. 'Balti is the current fashion and it hasn't peaked yet,' he said.

bambino /bam'bi:no/, /bam'bi:nəʊ/ *noun* plural **bambini** /bam'bi:ni/, **bambinos** E18 **Italian** (diminutive of *bambo* silly). In Italy: a young child or baby; *specifically* an image of the infant Jesus in swaddling-clothes.

banco /'baŋkəʊ/ *interjection* L18 **French** (from Italian). In baccarat etc.: expressing a player's willingness to meet single-handed the banker's whole stake. Cf. VA BANQUE.

bandar-log /'bʌndələʊg/ L19 **Hindustani** (*bā̃dar*, from Sanskrit *vānara* rhesus monkey + *log* people, from Sanskrit *loka*). The monkeys collectively; *figurative* a group of irresponsible chatterers.

bandeau /ˈbandəʊ/, *foreign* /bɑ̃do/ *noun* plural **bandeaux** /ˈbandəʊz/, *foreign* /bɑ̃do/ E18 **French** (from Old French *bandel* diminutive of *bande*). A band or strip of material, *especially* one used for binding a woman's hair.

banderilla /bandeˈriʎa/, /bandəˈrɪljə/ *noun* plural **banderillas** /bandeˈriʎas/, /bandəˈrɪljəz/ L18 **Spanish** (diminutive of *bandera* banner). *Bullfighting* A decorated dart thrust into a bull's neck or shoulders during a bullfight.

banderillero /banderiˈʎero/, /bandərɪˈljɛːrəʊ/ *noun* plural **banderilleros** /banderiˈʎeros/, /bandərɪˈljɛːrəʊz/ L18 **Spanish** (from BANDERILLA). *Bullfighting* A bullfighter who uses banderillas. Also called PEON.

banderole /ˈbandərəʊl/ *noun* (also **banderol**; /ˈbandərəʊl/, /ˈbandər(ə)l/; (especially in sense 2, earlier form) **bannerol** /ˈbanərəʊl/, /ˈbanər(ə)l/) M16 **French** (*ban(n)erole*, later *banderole*, from Italian *banderuola* diminutive of *bandiera* banner). **1** M16 A long narrow flag with a cleft end, flown from the masthead of a ship. **2** M16 A rectangular banner borne at the funerals of public figures and placed over the tomb. **3** L16 An ornamental streamer of the kind attached to a knight's lance. **4** E17 A ribbon-like scroll bearing a device or inscription.

bandobast variant of BUNDOBUST.

bandolero /bandəˈlɛːrəʊ/ *noun* plural **bandoleros** M17 **Spanish**. A Spanish bandit.

bania /ˈbʌnɪə/ *noun* L18 **Hindustani** (*baniyā* from Sanskrit *vāṇija*). A Hindu trader or merchant.

banian variant of BANYAN.

bannerol variant of BANDEROLE.

banquette /baŋˈkɛt/ *noun* E17 **French** (from Italian *banchetta* diminutive of *banca* bench, shelf). **1** E17 A raised step or way running along the inside of a rampart, at the bottom of a trench, etc., on which soldiers stand to fire at the enemy. **2** M19 A long upholstered seat along a wall.

banyan /ˈbanɪən/, /ˈbanjən/ *noun* (also **banian**) L16 **Portuguese** (from Gujarati *vāṇiyo* man of the trading caste, from Sanskrit *vāṇija* merchant). **I 1** L16 A BANIA. **2** M17 An Indian broker or steward attached to a firm or individual. **3** E18 In full *banyan shirt* etc. A loose flannel shirt or jacket. **II 4** M17 In full *banyan tree*. An Indian fig tree, *Ficus benghalensis*, the branches of which root themselves over a wide area.

■ *Banyan* has tended this century to supersede the generally preferred earlier spelling *banian*. In sense 4 the word was originally applied by Europeans to a particular tree of the species growing in a port on the Persian Gulf, under which Hindu merchants had set up a shrine; in 1634 Sir Thomas Herbert wrote of 'A tree . . . named by us the Bannyan Tree, from their adorning and adoring it with ribbons and streamers of varicoloured Taffata' (*Travels* II (1638)). The tree is not known by this name in any Indian language.

banzai /banˈzʌɪ/ *interjection & adjective* L19 **Japanese** (= ten thousand years (of life to you)). **A** L19 *interjection* A form of acclamation used by the Japanese especially to their Emperor, a cheer used in battle etc. **B** E20 *attributive* or as *adjective* (As if) shouting 'banzai'; uproarious; (of an attack by Japanese) reckless. *slang*.

banzuke /banˈzuːki/ *noun* L20 **Japanese**. The ranking list of sumo wrestlers.

baragouin /baragwɛ̃/, /barəˈgwɪn/ *noun* E17 **French**. Gibberish; unintelligible jargon.

baraza /bəˈrɑːzə/ *noun* L19 **Kiswahili**. In East Africa: a place of public audience or reception; a meeting, a reception.

barbette /bɑːˈbɛt/ *noun* L18 **French** (from *barbe* beard + diminutive *-ette*). A platform in a fort or ship from which guns fire over a parapet etc. and not through an embrasure.

barbotine /ˈbɑːbətɪn/, /ˈbɑːbətiːn/ *noun* M19 **French**. (Pottery ornamented with) a slip of kaolin clay.

barcarole /ˈbɑːkərəʊl/, /bɑːkəˈrəʊl/ *noun* (also **barcarolle** /ˈbɑːkərɒl/) L18 **French** (*barcarolle* from Venetian Italian *barcarola* related to *barcarolo* gondolier, from *barca* boat). A song sung by Venetian gondoliers; a piece of music in imitation of such songs or suggestive of the rocking motion of a boat.

barchan /ˈbɑːk(ə)n/ *noun* (also **barchane**, **barkhan**, **barkan**) L19 **Turkic** (*barkhan*). A shifting crescent-shaped sand-dune, concave on the leeward side.

barège /barɛʒ/ *noun & adjective* E19 **French** (from *Barèges* a village in south-west France). **A** *noun* E19 plural pronounced same. (A garment made of) a gauzelike fabric of silk and wool. **B** *adjective* M19 Made of barège.

barkan, **barkhan** variants of BARCHAN.

bar mitzvah /bɑː 'mɪtsvə/ *noun phrase* (also **Bar mitzvah**) M19 **Hebrew** (*bar miṣwāh* son of commandment). (A religious initiation ceremony for) a Jewish boy aged thirteen, regarded as liable to observe the religious precepts and eligible to take part in public worship. Cf. BAT MITZVAH.

barouche /bə'ruːʃ/ *noun* E19 **German** (dialect *Barutsche* from Italian *baroccio* (Spanish *barrocho*) two-wheeled, ultimately from Latin *birotus*, from *bi-* two + *rota* wheel). A four-wheeled horse-drawn carriage with a collapsible half-hood, a seat in front for the driver, and seats facing each other for passengers. Chiefly *historical*.

barre /bɑː/ *noun* E20 **French**. **1** E20 *Music* (A finger used as) a CAPOTASTO. **2** M20 A waist-level horizontal bar to help dancers keep their balance during some exercises.

barré /bare/ *adjective & noun* plural of noun pronounced same L19 **French** (past participle of *barrer* to bar). *Music* (A chord) played with strings stopped by a CAPOTASTO or finger.

barrera /ba'rrera/ *noun* E20 **Spanish** (= barrier). *Bullfighting* (The row of seats nearest to) the barrier encircling a bullring.

barrette /ba'rɛt/ *noun* E20 **French** (diminutive of BARRE). A bar-shaped clip or ornament for a woman's or girl's hair.

> **1996** *Times* Jil Sander and Prada favoured twisted buns sometimes held in place with a slim barrette.

barrio /'barɪəʊ/ *noun* plural **barrios** M19 **Spanish** (perhaps from Arabic). A ward or quarter of a town or city in Spain and Spanish-speaking countries; a Spanish-speaking quarter of a United States town or city.

bas bleu /bɑ blø/ *noun phrase* plural **bas bleus** (pronounced same) L18 **French** (translation from English). A bluestocking; a serious-minded and learned woman.

bascule /'baskjuːl/ *noun* L17 **French** ((earlier *bacule*) = see-saw, from stem of *battre* to beat + *cul* buttocks). A lever apparatus of which one end is raised when the other is lowered.

basha, **bashaw** variants of PASHA.

basho /'baʃəʊ/ *noun* plural same, **bashos** L20 **Japanese**. A sumo wrestling tournament.

basilica /bə'sɪlɪkə/, /bə'zɪlɪkə/ *noun* M16 **Latin** (branch I, literally, 'royal palace' from Greek *basilikē* use as noun of feminine of *basilikos* royal, from *basileus* king; branch II from Greek *basilika* neuter plural of *basilikos*). **I** *singular* (pl. **basilicas**, (*rare*) **basilicae** /bə'sɪlɪkiː/) **1** M16 *History* A large oblong hall or building, with double colonnades and a semicircular apse, used for courts of law and public assemblies. **2** M16 A building of this form used as a Christian church. Also, used as the title of certain churches granted privileges by the Pope. **II** *plural* **3** M17 *History* (**Basilica**) *The* 9th-century Byzantine legal code initiated by the emperor Basil I.

basmati /bas'mɑːti/, /bɑːz'mɑːti/ *noun* M19 **Hindustani** (*bāsmatī* literally, 'fragrant'). A kind of rice with very long thin grains and a delicate fragrance. More fully *basmati rice*.

basse-taille /bɑstaj/ *noun* L19 **French** (from *basse* feminine of *bas* low + *taille* cut). A technique of applying translucent enamels to metal reliefs so that the shade of the enamel is darkest where the relief is most deeply cut.

bassetto /bə'sɛtəʊ/ *noun* plural **bassettos** E18 **Italian** (diminutive of BASSO). A violoncello.

bassinet /basɪ'nɛt/ *noun* (also **bassinette**) M19 **French** (diminutive of *bassin* basin). A wicker cradle or pram with a curved hood.

■ A buttercup is called a bassinet in Normandy, and *bacinetz* occurs in a 1509 French list of vernacular flower names. In English too, *bassinet* was for a long time (L16–E18) used solely in a botanical context, with Lyte's 1578 herbal referring to the marsh marigold as the 'Brave Bassinet'; later herbalists recorded it as a dialect name for a geranium or various species of ranunculus.

basso /'basəʊ/ *noun & adjective* plural **bassos**, **bassi** /'basi/ E18 **Italian** (= low, from Latin *bassus*). *Music* Bass.

basso buffo /ˌbasəʊ 'bʊfəʊ/ plural **bassi buffi** /ˌbasi 'bʊfi/, **bassos buffos** E20 **Italian** (BASSO + *buffo* buffoon). *Music* A bass singer who takes comic parts in opera.

basso cantante /ˌbasəʊ kan'tanteɪ/ plural **bassi cantanti** /ˌbasi kan'tanti/ L19

Italian (BASSO + *cantante*, literally, 'singing'). *Music* (A singer with) a voice in the upper register of the bass range.

basso continuo /ˌbasəʊ kən'tɪnjʊəʊ/ plural **basso continuos** E18 Italian (BASSO + CONTINUO). *Music* A figured bass, a thorough bass.

basso ostinato /ˌbasəʊ ɒstɪ'nɑːtəʊ/ plural **basso ostinatos** L19 Italian (BASSO + OSTINATO). *Music* A short passage usually in the bass, constantly repeated with varying melody and harmony, a ground bass.

basso profundo /ˌbasəʊ prə'fʌndəʊ/ (occasionally **profondo** /prə'fɒndəʊ/) plural **bassi profundi** /ˌbasi prə'fʌndi/, **bassos profundos** M19 Italian (BASSO + *profundo*, literally, 'deep'). *Music* (A singer with) a very deep and rich voice.

basso-relievo /ˌbasəʊrɪ'liːvəʊ/ *noun* (also **basso-rilievo** /ˌbasəʊrɪ'ljeɪvəʊ/) plural **basso-relievos** M17 Italian (*basso-rilievo*). (A sculpture, carving, etc. in) low relief; bas-relief.

basta /'basta/ *interjection* L16 Italian. Enough! No matter!

bastide /ba'stiːd/ *noun* E16 Old French (Provençal *bastida* (medieval Latin *bastida*) use as noun of feminine past participle of *bastir* to build). **1** E16 *History* A fortified village or town. **2** E18 A country house in southern France.

2 1996 *Times Magazine* . . . centuries-old village houses, abandoned *mas* or farmhouses, grand *bastides*, dressed up for today's tastes but retaining their nobility.

basuco /bə'zuːkəʊ/, /bə'suːkəʊ/ *noun* (also **basuko**, **bazuco**, **bazuko**) L20 Colombian Spanish (perhaps connected with Spanish *basura* waste; or with Spanish *bazucar* to shake violently). A cheap form of impure cocaine made from adulterated coca paste and highly addictive when smoked as a drug.

■ The explosive effect of *basuco* has led to an alternative suggestion for the etymology, linking it with the English word *bazooka*, adopted in Spanish and applied figuratively to the drug and then borrowed back into English in a slightly altered form. Other names for the drug, which first appeared in the English-speaking world in the mid 1980s, are *little devil* and *Suzuki*.

1985 C. Nicholl *The Fruit Palace* There's a big internal market; a lot of coke and basuko used by the street boys.

batardeau /batardo/ *noun* plural **batardeaux** /batardo/ M18 French (earlier *bastardeau* diminutive of Old French *bastard* of unknown origin). A coffer-dam. Also, a wall built across the moat or ditch surrounding a fortification.

batata /bə'tɑːtə/ *noun* M16 Spanish (from Taino). Sweet potato.

bateau /'batəʊ/, *foreign* /bato/ *noun* plural **bateaux** /'batəʊz/, *foreign* /bato/ E18 French (= boat). A light riverboat, especially of a flat-bottomed kind used in Canada. Cf. BATEAU-MOUCHE.

■ *Bateau* is also used attributively as an alternative to 'boat' in *bateau neck*, *bateau-necked*, etc., used of a garment with shallow curved neckline running from shoulder to shoulder.

bateau-mouche /batomuʃ/ plural **bateaux-mouches** (pronounced same) E20 French. A riverboat which takes sightseers on the Seine in Paris.

bathos /'beɪθɒs/ *noun* E18 Greek (= depth). **1** E18 *Rhetoric* Ludicrous descent from the elevated to the commonplace; anticlimax. **2** E19 A comedown; a performance absurdly unequal to the occasion.

■ First introduced (M17) with its original Greek meaning of 'depth, lowest phase, bottom', *bathos* is now rare or obsolete in this sense, which has been superseded by the two senses above. Alexander Pope was primarily responsible for sense 1 in *Peri Bathous: or the Art of Sinking in Poetry* (1727), a parody of the work by the ancient Greek rhetorician Longinus *On the Sublime*.

2 1996 *Country Life* The series attempted to marry the bathos of the quiz show to the nitpicking of scholarship.

batik /'batɪk/, /bə'tiːk/ *noun & adjective* L19 Javanese (literally, 'painted'). **A** L19 *noun* A method (originally used in Java) of making coloured designs on textiles by waxing the parts not to be dyed; (a garment made of) a fabric dyed by this method. **B** E20 *attributive* or as *adjective* Executed or ornamented by this method.

batiste /bə'tiːst/ *noun & adjective* E19 French ((earlier *batiche*) perhaps from base of *battre* to beat). (Of) a fine light cotton or linen fabric like cambric.

bat mitzvah /bɑːt 'mɪtsvə/ *noun phrase* (also **Bat mitzvah**) M20 Hebrew (*baṯ miṣwāh* daughter of commandment, after BAR MITZVAH). (A religious initiation ceremony for) a Jewish girl aged twelve years and one day, regarded as the age of religious maturity.

baton /ˈbat(ə)n/, *in senses 4 and 6 also foreign* /bɑtɔ̃/ *noun* E16 **French** (*bâton* (earlier *baston*) = Provençal, Spanish *baston* Italian *bastone* from Proto-Romance, from late Latin *bastum* stick). **1** E16 A stick or staff used as a weapon. **b** L19 A police officer's cudgel, *especially* a relatively long one. **2** L16 A staff carried as symbol of office, *especially* that of a field marshal. **3** *Heraldry* M18 A narrow truncated bend. **4** *Music* L18 A conductor's wand; a drum-major's stick. **5** M19 A long loaf or stick of bread. **6** E20 A short stick carried in a relay race and passed from one participant to the next.

■ Although *baton* or *batton* was used by Scots writers in the sixteenth century, the commoner spelling in England until the nineteenth century was *batoon*. *Baton* in the general sense 1 is now much less common than in its various specialized senses.

battement /batmɑ̃/ *plural same*, /ˈbatmɒ̃/ *noun* M19 **French** (= beating). *Dancing* Any of a number of beating leg movements. Cf. GRAND BATTEMENT, PETIT BATTEMENT.

batterie /batri/ *noun* plural pronounced same E18 **French**. **1** *Dancing* E18 A movement in which the feet or calves are beaten together during a leap. **2** L18 Abbreviation of BATTERIE DE CUISINE. **3** *Music* M20 Percussion instruments in an orchestra or band.

■ French *batterie* in its commoner senses (electrical or military) has been fully assimilated in English as *battery*, but it is retained in more specialist meanings, such as 'drum-kit' (see sense 3).

batterie de cuisine /batri də kɥizin/ *noun phrase* L18 **French** (= articles for cookery). Apparatus or utensils for preparing or serving a meal.

battue /bəˈt(j)uː/; *foreign* /baty/ (*plural same*) *noun* E19 **French** (use as noun of feminine past participle of *battre* to beat). **1** E19 A driving of game towards the guns by beaters; a shooting-party on this plan. **2** *transferred* **a** M19 A thorough search. **b** M19 A wholesale slaughter.

batture /bəˈtjʊə/ *noun* E19 **French**. **1** E19 A stretch of river shore, usually formed by deposition, between the natural embankment and the low-water mark. **2** E19 A sand bar in a river.

■ Both senses North American; sense 2 Canadian.

battuta /bəˈtuːtə/ *noun* E18 **Italian** (from *battere* to beat). *Music* The beating of time; a strong beat; the regular beat.

Bauhaus /ˈbaʊhaʊs/ *noun* E20 **German** (*Bau* building + *Haus* house). (The principles of) a German school of architecture and design founded in 1919 by Walter Gropius and closed in 1933.

bavaroise /bavəˈwaːz/, *foreign* /bavarwaz/ *noun* (also **bavarois** /bavəˈwɑː/, *foreign* /bavarwa/) M19 **French** (use as noun of feminine adjective *bavaroise* Bavarian). A dessert containing gelatin and whipped cream, served cold.

bayadère /beɪjəˈdɛː/, /beɪjəˈdɪə/ *noun* L16 **French** (from Portuguese *bailadeira*, from *bailar* to dance, related to medieval Latin *ballare* to dance). **1** L16 A Hindu dancing-girl (especially at a southern Indian temple). **2** M19 A striped textile fabric.

bayou /ˈbʌɪuː/ *noun* M18 **American French** (from Choctaw *bayuk*). In the southern United States: a marshy offshoot of a river, lake, etc.

bazaar /bəˈzɑː/ *noun* L16 **Italian** (*bazarro* from Turkish from Persian *bāzār* market). **1** L16 An oriental market. **2** E19 A large shop, or arcade of shops, selling fancy goods, bric-à-brac, etc. **3** E19 A sale of miscellaneous new or second-hand goods in aid of charity.

bazuco, **bazuko** variants of BASUCO.

béarnaise /beɪəˈneɪz/, *foreign* /bearnɛz/ *adjective* (also **Béarnaise**) L19 **French** (feminine of *béarnais* of Béarn, a region of south-west France). A rich white sauce flavoured with tarragon. In full, *béarnaise sauce* (also *sauce béarnaise*).

beau /bəʊ/ *noun* plural **beaux** /bəʊz/, **beaus** L17 **French** (use as noun of adjective, ultimately from Latin *bellus* fine, beautiful). **1** L17 A fashionable man, a ladies' man; a fop, a dandy. **2** E18 A lady's male companion, a suitor; a boyfriend, a lover. Now chiefly *North America*.

beau geste /bəʊ ʒɛst/ *noun phrase* plural **beaux gestes** (pronounced same) E20 **French** (= splendid gesture). A display of magnanimity; a generous act.

beau ideal /bəʊ ʌɪˈdɪəl/ *noun phrase* E19 **French** (*beau idéal* = ideal beauty). One's highest or ideal type of excellence or beauty; the perfect model.

■ Now often misunderstood to mean 'beautiful ideal'.

Beaujolais nouveau /ˌbəʊʒəleɪ nuːˈvəʊ/, *foreign* /boʒɔlɛ nuvo/ L20 **French** (= new Beaujolais). A light, usually red, burgundy wine of the latest vintage from the Beaujolais district of France.

beau monde /bəʊ ˈmɒnd/, *foreign* /bo mɔ̃d/ *noun phrase* L17 **French** (= fine world). (The world of) fashionable society.

1995 *Times* Teresa Lady Rothschild was never deeply interested in the glittering *beau monde* which circled around the international banking dynasty into which she married.

beau rôle /bo rol/ *noun phrase* plural **beaux rôles** (pronounced same) L19 **French** (= fine role). A fine acting part; the leading part.

beau sabreur /bo sɑbrœr/ *noun phrase* plural **beaux sabreurs** (pronounced same) M19 **French** (= fine (or handsome) swordsman). A gallant warrior, a handsome or dashing adventurer.

■ Originally a sobriquet of Joachim Murat (1767–1815), French cavalry officer and brother-in-law of Napoleon.

beauté du diable /bote dy djɑbl/ *noun phrase* M19 **French** (= devil's beauty). Superficial attractiveness.

1997 *Country Life* Lartigue . . . would find the Riviera repellent now: there is not even a *beauté du diable* in the imperfections that are left.

beaux arts /boz ɑr/ *noun & adjective phrase* (also **beaux-arts**) E19 **French** (*beaux-arts*). **A** *noun phrase plural* E19 Fine arts. **B** *adjective phrase* E20 Of or pertaining to the classical decorative style maintained by the *École des Beaux-Arts* especially in the nineteenth century.

beaux esprits plural of BEL ESPRIT.

beaux gestes plural of BEAU GESTE.

beaux yeux /boz jø/ *noun phrase* E19 **French**. Beautiful eyes; admiring glances; favourable regard.

bebung /ˈbeːbʊŋ/ *noun* L19 **German** (= trembling). *Music* A pulsating or trembling effect given to a sustained note.

beccafico /bɛkəˈfiːkəʊ/ *noun* plural **beccaficos** E17 **Italian** (from *beccare* to peck + *fico* fig). Any of a number of small birds (warblers, etc.) esteemed as a delicacy in the Mediterranean region.

béchamel /ˈbeɪʃəmɛl/, *foreign* /beʃamɛl/ *noun* M18 **French**. *Cookery* A fine savoury white sauce, frequently made with added cream or milk. More fully *béchamel sauce*.

■ Called after the Marquis de *Béchamel*, steward of Louis XIV.

bêche-de-mer /bɛʃdəˈmɛː/ *noun* plural same, **bêches-de-mer** /bɛʃdəˈmɛː/ L18 **pseudo-French** (from Portuguese *bicho do mar*, literally, 'worm of the sea'). **1** L18 A sea cucumber eaten as a Chinese delicacy. **2** L19 An English-based pidgin used formerly as a trade language and contact vernacular in the southwest Pacific. Also *bêche-de-mer English* or *beach-la-mar*.

Bedouin /ˈbɛdʊɪn/ *noun & adjective* (also **Beduin**, **beduin**) LME **Old French** (*beduin* (modern *bédouin*) ultimately (through medieval Latin *beduini* plural) from Arabic *badawī*, plural *badawīn* (from *badw* desert) nomadic desert tribes). **A** *noun* **1** LME An Arab of the desert. **2** M19 A person living a nomadic life. **B** *adjective* M19 Of the desert or Bedouins; nomadic, wandering.

Bedu /ˈbɛduː/ *noun & adjective* plural of noun same E20 **Arabic** (*badw*). (Of) a Bedouin; *collective* (of) Bedouins.

beebee variant of BIBI.

Beerenauslese /ˈbeːrənˌaʊsleːzə/ *noun* (also **beerenauslese**) plural **Beerenauslesen**, /ˈbeːrənˌaʊsleːzən/, **Beerenausleses** E20 **German** (from *Beeren* berries, grapes + AUSLESE). A white wine made (especially in Germany) from selected individual grapes picked later than the general harvest.

béguin /begɛ̃/ *noun* plural pronounced same E20 **French**. An infatuation, a fancy.

■ *Avoir le béguin de* (or *pour*) is 'to have a crush on' in colloquial French.

beguine /beɪˈgiːn/ *noun 1* (also **béguine**) LME **Old and Modern French** (*béguine* (Middle Dutch, Middle High German *begīne*), medieval Latin *Beguina*, perhaps ultimately from Middle Dutch verb meaning 'to mutter (prayers)'). A member of a lay sisterhood in the Low Countries, formed in the twelfth century and not bound by vows.

beguine /bɪˈgiːn/ *noun 2* E20 **American French** (from French BÉGUIN). (The distinctive rhythm of) a dance of West Indian origin.

begum /ˈbeɪgəm/ *noun* (also (as title) **Begum**) M17 **Urdu** (*begam* from Early Turkic *begim*, from *beg* bey + 1st person singular possessive suffix *-im*). In the Indian subcontinent: a Muslim noblewoman or lady of high rank. Also (**Begum**), a title given to a married Muslim woman (= Mrs).

beignet /ˈbɛnjeɪ/, /bɛnˈjɛ/, *foreign* /bɛɲɛ/ (*plural same*) *noun* M19 **French.** A fritter; *specifically* (*United States*) a square of fried dough sprinkled with icing sugar and eaten hot. Usually in *plural*.

1995 *Observer* The French beignets, golden balls of molten cheese, must rank high in the world of the fritter fancier . . .

bel canto /bɛl ˈkantəʊ/ *noun phrase* L19 **Italian** (= fine song). (A style of) singing characterized by full rich broad tone, legato phrasing, and accomplished technique.

1996 *Spectator* Not only is his voice beautiful, but he always sings beautifully—'bel canto', in other words . . .

bel esprit /bɛl ɛspri/ *noun phrase* plural **beaux esprits** /boz ɛspri/ M17 **French** (= fine mind). A brilliant or witty person.

belle /bɛl/ *noun* E17 **French** (feminine of *bel*, BEAU, from Latin *bella* feminine of *bellus* beautiful). A beautiful woman, *especially* the outstanding beauty of a place, time, etc.

belle époque /bɛl eɪˈpɒk/ *noun phrase* (also **belle epoque**, **Belle Epoque**) plural **belles époques** /bɛlz eɪˈpɒk/ M20 **French** (= fine period). A period of settled comfort and prosperity.

■ Originally and specifically used of the period in France from the late nineteenth century to the war of 1914–18; see quotation at DOUCEUR DE VIVRE.

belle laide /bɛl lɛd/ *noun phrase* (also **belle-laide**) plural **belles laides** (pronounced same) E20 **French** (from feminine adjectives *belle* beautiful + *laide* ugly). An attractive though ugly woman. Cf. JOLIE LAIDE.

transferred **1956** L. E. Jones *Edwardian Youth* Like that of an ugly woman with many lovers, Balliol's uncomeliness only serves to underline the greatness and ardour of her soul . . . and her lovers at Eton . . . were long past the stage of minding . . . the physical failings of that fascinating *belle-laide*.

belles-lettres /bɛllɛtr/ *noun plural* (occasionally treated as *singular*) M17 **French** (literally, 'fine letters'). Studies or writings of a purely literary character, *especially* essays, criticism, etc. Originally more widely, literature generally, the humanities.

belote /bəˈlɒt/ *noun* (also **belotte**) M20 **French.** A card-game like pinochle, played with a 32-card pack, popular in France; the combination of king and queen of trumps in this game.

■ Perhaps from F. Belot, a Frenchman said to have developed the game.

bema /ˈbiːmə/ *noun* plural **bemas**, **bemata** /biːmətə/ L17 **Greek** (*bēma* a step, a raised place to speak from). **1** L17 *Christian Church* The altar part or sanctuary in ancient and Orthodox churches; the chancel. **2** E19 *Greek Antiquities* The platform from which Athenian orators spoke.

benedicite /bɛnɪˈdʌɪsɪti/ *interjection & noun* ME **Latin** (2nd person plural imperative of *benedicere* to wish well to, bless, from *bene* well + *dicere* to say). **A** *interjection* **1** ME Expressing a wish: God bless you! **2** ME Expression of astonishment: Good gracious! **B** *noun* **1** ME An invocation of a blessing; *especially* a grace at table. **2** M17 *Christian Church the Benedicite*, the canticle beginning *Benedicite, omnia opera* 'O all ye works [of the Lord], bless ye [the Lord]', known also as 'The Song of the Three Children', which is an alternative to the *Te Deum* at matins in the *Book of Common Prayer*.

bene esse /ˈbɛnɪ ɛsi/ *noun phrase* E17 **Modern Latin.** Well-being, welfare, especially opposed to ESSE.

benthos /ˈbɛnθɒs/ *noun* L19 **Greek** (= depth of the sea). The flora and fauna of the bottom of the sea (or of a lake).

ben trovato /ben troˈvɑːto/ *adjective phrase* L19 **Italian** (literally, 'well found'). Of a story etc.: happily invented; appropriate though untrue.

■ *Se non è vero, è molto ben trovato* 'if it is not true, it is a happy invention' was apparently a well-known saying in sixteenth-century Italy, being found for example in the writings of Giordano Bruno. Smollett used the phrase in 1771 in the form *ben trovata*.

1952 R. M. Hare *Language of Morals* We might say that to tell a story about someone, which every one knows is *ben trovato*, is not *lying*.

1996 *Spectator* Beaverbrook, who was a fund of good stories (*ben trovato* anyhow), was the source for the famous story of an old friend visiting Bottomley in prison finding him mending mailbags, as was usual then.

berceau /bɛrso/ *noun* plural **berceaux** (pronounced same) L17 **French** (literally, 'cradle'). An arbour; a shaded or leafy walk.

berceuse /bɛrsøz/, /bɛːˈsəːz/ *noun* plural pronounced same L19 **French** (from *bercer* to rock + feminine agent-suffix *-euse*). *Music* A lullaby; an instrumental piece with a gently rocking rhythm.

beret /ˈbɛreɪ/, /ˈbɛri/ *noun* E19 **French** (*béret* from south-west French dialect and Old Provençal *berret*). A round felt or cloth cap that lies flat on the head, covering it closely (as traditionally worn by Basque peasantry); such a cap forming part of military uniform.

beretta variant of BIRETTA.

berg /bəːɡ/, *foreign* /berx/ *noun* E19 **Afrikaans** (from Dutch (= Old English *beorg* barrow, hill)). A mountain; a mountain range.

bergère /bɛrʒɛr/ *noun* plural pronounced same M18 **French** (= shepherdess). A long-seated upholstered armchair fashionable in the eighteenth century. Also, a chair with canework seat, back, and sides.

1995 *Country Life* There are at least two types of *bergère*. One is a rectangular seat with high arms sweeping up to the back, which may be caned or covered in leather . . . .The second type is the 'curricle', which is a rounded, and usually slightly smaller, version of the same thing.

bergerette /bəːʒəˈrɛt/ *noun* LME **French** (from *berger* shepherd). A pastoral or rustic song about shepherds, for dancing to.

bergschrund /ˈbəːɡʃrʊnd/ *noun* M19 **German** (from *Berg* mountain + *schrund* cleft). A crevasse or gap at the junction of a glacier or snowfield with a steep upper slope.

bersaglieri /ˌbersaʎˈʎeːri/, /ˌbɛːsɑːlɪˈɛːriː/ *noun plural* M19 **Italian** (from *bersaglio* target). Highly trained Italian infantry, originally riflemen or sharpshooters.

bertillonage /bɛrtijɔnaʒ/ *noun* L19 **French** (*bertillonnage*). The system of identification of criminals by anthropometric measurements, etc.

■ The system is named after its inventor, the French criminologist Alphonse Bertillon (1853–1914), who introduced it in 1882. It was soon supplemented, and in the early years of the twentieth century superseded, by fingerprinting.

beta /ˈbiːtə/ *noun* ME **Latin** (from Greek). **1** ME The second letter (B, β) of the Greek alphabet. **2** L17 Denoting the second in a numerical sequence. **3** *attributive Science* L19 (Frequently written β); as in *Astronomy* (preceding the genitive of the Latin name of the constellation) designating the second brightest star in a constellation. **4** E20 A second-class mark in an examination etc.

■ Like *alpha*, *beta* has a number of specialist applications in scientific terminology and often appears in the same context to designate the entity secondary to the *alpha* one; see quotation at ALPHA.

betel /ˈbiːt(ə)l/ *noun* M16 **Portuguese** (from Malayalam *veṟṟila*). The leaf of a climbing evergreen shrub, *Piper betle*, which is chewed in the East with acreca-nut parings and a little lime. Also (more fully *betel pepper*), the plant itself.

bête noire /beɪt ˈnwɑː/, *foreign* /bɛt nwar/ *noun phrase* plural **bêtes noires** (pronounced same) M19 **French** (literally, 'black beast'). The bane of someone's life; an insufferable person or thing; an object of strong or obsessive aversion.

1995 *Spectator* [F. R. Leavis's] *bête noire*, David Cecil at Oxford, taught literature as something to be enjoyed without benefit of Leavisite scrutiny.

bethel /ˈbɛθ(ə)l/ *noun* E17 **Hebrew** (*bēṯ ēl* from *bēṯ* house of + *'ēl* god). **1** E17 A place where God is worshipped. **2** E19 *transferred* A Nonconformist chapel; a seamen's church.

bêtise /bɛtiz/, /beɪˈtiːz/ *noun* (also **betise**) plural pronounced same E19 **French** (= stupidity, from *bête* foolish, from Old French *beste* beast). An ill-judged or ill-timed remark or action; a piece of folly.

1996 *Spectator* They . . . at once went to Zimbabwe where their *betises* included, in an attempt to portray the sundowner life, a room full of ancient people served by a black man in a fancy uniform, in the kind of grand house that scarcely existed then. Wrong on every count.

beur /bœr/ *noun* L20 **French**. In France: a child of immigrant parents, born in France.

beurre manié /bœr manje/, /bəː manˈjeɪ/ *noun phrase* M20 **French** (= handled butter). *Cookery* A mixture of flour and butter used for thickening sauces or soups.

beurre noir /bœr nwar/, /bəː ˈnwɑː/ *noun phrase* M19 **French** (= butter). *Cookery* A sauce made by heating butter until it is brown, usually mixing it with vinegar.

bévue /bevy/ *noun* plural pronounced same. L17 **French**. A blunder.

bey /beɪ/ *noun* (also (as title) **Bey**) L16 **Turkish** (modern form of *beg* governor). The governor of a district or province in the Ottoman Empire. Also (**Bey** following name) formerly used in Turkey and Egypt as a courtesy title.

bezesteen /'bɛzɪsti:n/ *noun* M17 **Turkish** ((perhaps through French or Italian, from Turkish) *bezesten* (now *bedesten*) covered market for fine cloth and valuables, from Persian *bazistān*, from *baz* (Turkish *bez*) from Arabic *bazz* cloth + suffix of place *-istān*). An exchange, bazaar, or market-place in the Middle East.

bhajan /'bʌdʒ(ə)n/ *noun* E20 **Sanskrit** (*bhajana*). *Hinduism* A devotional song.

bhaji /'bɑ:dʒi/ *noun* L20 **Hindi** (*bhāji* fried vegetables from Sanskrit *bhrajj* to fry) . In Indian cooking, a fritter, generally made with onions, but also with other vegetables.

bhakta /'bʌktə/ *noun* E19 **Sanskrit**. *Hinduism* A religious devotee.

bhakti /'bʌkti/ *noun* M19 **Sanskrit**. *Hinduism* Religious devotion or piety as a means of salvation.

bhang /bɑ:ŋ/ *noun* (also **bang**) L16 **Persian and Urdu** (*bang* (through Portuguese *bangue*), later assimilated to Hindustani *bhāṅ* from Sanskrit *bhaṅg*). A preparation of the cannabis or Indian hemp plant (*Cannabis sativa*) used as an intoxicating or hallucinogenic drug or for medicinal purposes.

bhangra /'bɑ:ŋgrə/ *noun* M20 **Panjabi** (*bhāngrā*). **1** M20 A type of Punjabi folk-dance for men associated with the harvest. **2** L20 A style of popular (especially dance) music combining Punjabi folk music with rock and roll or disco music.

■ In Britain *bhangra* (also known as *bhangra beat*), originated in the Asian communities in the 1980s, but by the end of the decade had won a wider following.

2 1987 *Independent* An up and coming group . . . set the seemingly incompatible rhythmic stridency of funk and Bhangra dance to a compulsive harmony.

bhikkhu /'bɪku:/ *noun* (also **bhikku**) M19 **Pali** (*bhikkhu* from as BHIKSHU). A Buddhist mendicant or religious devotee.

bhikshu /'bɪkʃu:/ *noun* plural **bhikshus**, same E19 **Sanskrit** (*bhikṣu* beggar, from *bhikṣ* beg). A brahminical or Buddhist mendicant or religious devotee. Cf. BHIKKHU.

bianco sopra bianco /ˌbjaŋko ˌsopra 'bjaŋko/ *noun phrase* L19 **Italian** (literally, 'white upon white'). A form of white decoration upon white porcelain.

■ Earlier in English (M19) in the elliptical form *sopra bianco*.

bibelot /'bɪbələʊ/, *foreign* /biblo/ (*plural same*) *noun* L19 **French** (from reduplication of *bel* beautiful). A small curio or artistic trinket.

1996 *Times* Nor can he tell us who is the famous actress and beauty who slid bibelots into her handbag at Sir Harold Acton's villa outside Florence . . .

biberon /bibrɔ̃/ *noun* plural pronounced same M19 **French**. A drinking-vessel with elongated spout, formerly used by travellers, invalids, and children.

bibi /'bi:bi:/ *noun* (also **beebee**) E19 **Urdu** (*bībī* from Persian). In the Indian subcontinent: a mistress of a household; a non-European female consort.

bibliotheca /ˌbɪblɪə'θi:kə/ *noun* E18 **Latin** (from Greek *bibliothēkē* library, from *biblion* book + *thēkē* repository). A collection of books or treatises; a library; a bibliographer's catalogue.

■ Following St Jerome, *bibliotheca* was used in both medieval Latin and Old English to mean 'the Bible'. In Anglo-Latin it occurs interchangeably with *biblia* in an eleventh-century catalogue of the library of Lindisfarne, but by time of the compilation of the thirteenth-century Durham catalogue only *biblia* appears. By the end of that century the Middle English *bibul* and its many variants, from which Modern English *bible* derives, had replaced *bibliotheca* in the vernacular. The modern reintroduction into English of *bibliotheca* in a bibliographical sense is thus entirely separate from the earlier biblical sense and relies on learned Latin usage. *Bibliotheca annua* (1700–4), an annual catalogue of English and Latin books published in England, was an early example. Since the nineteenth century *bibliotheca* has been used in titles of series (e.g. *Bryophytorum bibliotheca*; *Bibliotheca Americana Vetustissima*) or individual bibliographies (e.g. *Bibliotheca arcana* (1885), a catalogue of banned erotica; *Bibliotheca chemica* (1906), a catalogue of alchemical works).

bibliothèque /bibljɔtɛk/ *noun* plural pronounced same M16 **French** (from as BIBLIOTHECA). A library.

■ Formerly naturalized, but now treated as French.

bidet /ˈbiːdeɪ/ *noun* M17 **French** (from earlier sense 'pony', from *bider* to trot, of unknown origin). **1** M17 A small horse. *archaic.* **2** L18 A shallow oval basin on a low stand used for washing especially the genital and anal regions.

■ The evolution of sense 2 from sense 1 is explained in Grose's definition of *bidet* in his *Dictionary of the Vulgar Tongue* (1785): 'commonly pronounced biddy, a kind of tub, contrived for ladies to wash themselves; for which purpose they bestride it like a little French poney, ... called in France bidets.

bidon /bidɔ̃/ *noun* plural pronounced same M19 **French**. A container for liquids; a petrol tin, oil can, etc.

1964 E. Ambler *Kind of Anger* Get the car filled up. Adèle left me two *bidons* for emergencies.

bidonville /ˈbiːd(ə)nvɪl/; *foreign* /bidɔ̃vil/ (*plural same*) *noun* M20 **French** (from BIDON + *ville* town). A shanty-town built of oil drums etc., *especially* a slum on the outskirts of a French or North African city.

bien entendu /bjɛ̃n ɑ̃tɑ̃dy/ *adverb phrase* M19 **French** (from *bien* well + *entendu* past participle of *entendre* to hear, understand). Of course; that goes without saying.

bien-être /bjɛ̃nɛtr/ *noun* M19 **French** (from *bien* well + *être* to be). A state of well-being.

biennale /biːɛˈnɑːli/ *noun* M20 **Italian** (from Latin *biennis* of two years). A large art exhibition or music festival, especially one held every two years.

■ Originally a specific festival, the Biennale, held biennially in Venice, Italy.

biennium /bʌɪˈɛnɪəm/ *noun* plural **bienniums**, **biennia** /bʌɪˈɛnɪə/ E20 **Latin** (from as *bi-* two + *annus* year). A period of two years.

bien pensant /bjɛ̃ pɑ̃sɑ̃/ *adjective & noun phrase* Also **bien-pensant** (plural pronounced same) E20 **French** (*bien* well, *pensant* present participle of *penser* to think). (A person who is) right-thinking.

■ Often with a derogatory implication of timorous or mindless compliance with current intellectual or moral fashion (see quotations).

noun phrase **1995** *Times* In this form of journo-speak, a Tory 'right winger' is someone who believes in: hanging, low taxes, large armies, standards in schools, ... and a rag-bag of other items which offend the *bien pensants*.

adjective phrase **1996** *Spectator* I ask him if Ms Roddick's liberal embrace of every *bien-pensant* cause does not lead to jumping on every passing bandwagon.

bienséance /bjɛ̃seɑ̃s/ *noun* L17 **French** (from *bien* well + *séant*, from *seoir* to befit). Decorum.

bierhaus /ˈbiːrhaʊs/ *noun* plural **bierhäuser** /ˈbiːrhɔyzər/ M20 **German** (from *Bier* beer + *Haus* house). In a German-speaking country: a public house or alehouse.

Bierstube /ˈbiːrʃtuːbə/, *noun* plural **Bierstuben** /ˈbiːrʃtuːbən/, **Bierstubes** E20 **German** (from *Bier* beer + *Stube* room). A German tavern, taproom, or bar. Cf. WEINSTUBE.

bigarade /bɪgəˈrɑːd/ *foreign* /bigarad/ (*plural same*) *noun* E18 **French** (from Provençal *bigarrado*). The Spanish bitter orange.

bigarreau /ˈbɪgərəʊ/ *noun* plural **bigarreaus**, **bigareaux** (pronounced same) E17 **French** (from *bigarré* variegated). A variety of sweet cherry, usually heart-shaped and with firm flesh. In full *bigarreau cherry*.

bijou /ˈbiːʒuː/, *foreign* /biʒu/ *noun & adjective* M17 **French** (from Breton *bizoù* finger-ring, from *biz* finger). **A** *noun* M17 plural **bijoux** /ˈbiːʒuː(z)/, *foreign* /biʒu/. A jewel, a trinket. **B** *adjective* M19 Small and elegant.

B 1996 *Bookseller* Shops dealing exclusively in English language books in the south of France tend to be bijou in size.

bijouterie /biʒutri/ *noun* E19 **French**. Jewellery, trinkets, etc.

Bildungsroman /ˈbɪldʊŋzroˌmɑːn/ *noun* plural **Bildungsromane** /ˈbɪldʊŋzroˌmɑːnə/ E20 **German** (from *Bildung* education + *Roman* novel). A novel dealing with one person's formative years or spiritual education.

1995 *Times* His long, indulgent autobiography, *What's It All About?*, is a kind of *bildungsroman* about how Maurice Joseph Micklewhite, Jr. became Michael Caine.

billabong /ˈbɪləbɒŋ/ *noun* M19 **Aboriginal** (*Billibang* Bell River, from *billa* water + *bang* channel dry except after rain). In Australia: a branch of a river, forming a blind channel, backwater, or stagnant pool.

billet-doux /bɪlɪˈduː/ *noun* plural **billets-doux** /bɪlɪˈduːz/ L17 **French** (literally, 'sweet note'). A love-letter.

■ Now chiefly jocular.

biltong /ˈbɪltɒŋ/ *noun* E19 **Afrikaans** (from Dutch *bil* buttock + *tong* tongue). In South Africa: lean meat cut into strips and dried.

bimbo /ˈbɪmbəʊ/ *noun* plural **bimbos, bimboes** E20 **Italian** (= small child, baby). **1** E20 A chap, *especially* a young and foolish one. **2** E20 A young woman, *especially* one that is sexually attractive but empty-headed.

■ Now used in a slang and almost always derogatory sense, *bimbo* was originally a direct borrowing from Italian. P. G. Wodehouse used it in sense 1 (see quotation 1947), but it was already current in the 1920s with the sense of a pretty but brainless tart. *Bimbo* was revived in the 1980s media to designate a young woman who has an affair with a rich or famous man and then sells the 'revelations' to the popular press. The word has also spawned a number of derivatives: *bimbette* (a teenage bimbo), *bimboy* (a male bimbo), *bimboland*, etc.

1 1947 P. G. Wodehouse *Full Moon* . . . bimbos who went about the place making passes at innocent girls after discarding their wives.

2 1988 *Independent* In the strict sense the bimbo exists on the fringes of pornography, and some cynics might say she has the mental capacity of a minor kitchen appliance.

binghi /ˈbɪŋʌɪ/ *noun* M19 **Aboriginal**. An Aborigine.

■ Originally a neutral word (R. Dawson in *Present State of Australia* (1831) mentions having been greeted by Aborigines as 'bingeye, or brother'), *binghi* has become an Australian slang term and usually derogatory.

bint /bɪnt/ *noun* M19 **Arabic** (= daughter, girl). A girl, a woman; (formerly) a girl friend.

■ Mainly servicemen's slang, used by personnel stationed in Egypt and elsewhere in the Middle East during the two world wars; usually derogatory.

1958 K. Amis *I Like It Here* As the R.A.F. friend would have put it, you could never tell with these foreign bints.

biretta /bɪˈrɛtə/ *noun* (also **beretta, birretta**) L16 **Italian** (*berretta* or Spanish *birreta*, feminine diminutives corresponding to Old Provençal *berret* beret, based on late Latin *birrus, birettum* hooded cape or cloak, perhaps of Celtic origin). A square cap worn by Roman Catholic ecclesiastics (black by priests, purple by bishops, red by cardinals) or by other clergymen.

biriani variant of BIRYANI.

birretta variant of BIRETTA.

biryani /bɪrˈjɑːni/, /bɪrɪˈɑːni/ *noun* (also **biriani** and other variants) M20 **Urdu** (from Persian *biryānī*, from *biriyān* fried, grilled). A dish of the Indian subcontinent consisting of spiced meat or vegetables and cooked rice.

bis /bis/ *adverb* E17 **French and Italian** (from Latin *bis* twice). Encore; again; twice; *specifically* as a direction in a musical score indicating that a passage is to be repeated.

bismillah /bɪsˈmɪlə/ *interjection & noun* L18 **Arabic** (*bi-smi-llāh(i)*, the first word of the Koran). (The exclamation) in the name of God: used by Muslims at the beginning of any undertaking.

bisque /bɪsk/ *noun 1* M17 **French** (of unknown origin). In various games, especially tennis, croquet, and golf, (the allowing of) a point or stroke to be scored or taken when desired as a handicapping advantage.

bisque /bɪsk/ *noun 2* M17 **French** (from Old French *bescuit, besquit*, ultimately from Latin *bis* twice + *coctus* past participle of *coquere* to cook). A variety of unglazed white porcelain used for statuettes etc. Also porcelain that has undergone firing but no other treatment; biscuit.

bisque /bɪsk/, /biːsk/ *noun 3* (also **bisk** /bɪsk/) M17 **French** (= crayfish soup). A rich soup usually made from shellfish but also from birds etc.

bistre /ˈbɪstə/ *noun* (also **bister**) E18 **French** (of unknown origin). (The colour of) a brown pigment prepared from soot.

bistro /ˈbiːstrəʊ/, /ˈbɪstrəʊ/ *noun* (also **bistrot**) plural **bistros** E20 **French**. A small wine-bar or restaurant.

bivouac /ˈbɪvʊak/, /ˈbɪvwak/ *noun & verb* E18 **French** (probably from Swiss German *Bîwacht*, literally, 'extra watch'). **A** *noun* E18 Originally, a night-watch by a whole army. Later, a temporary encampment, usually for the night, without tents; the place of such an encampment. **B** *intransitive & intransitive verb* E19 in *pass*. Inflected **bivouack**. Remain in the open air (especially during the night) without tents etc.

■ The Swiss word is said to have been used in Aargau and Zürich to denote a patrol of citizens to assist the ordinary town watch.

bizarre /bɪˈzɑː/ *adjective & noun* M17 **French** (from Italian *bizzarro* angry, of unknown origin. Cf. Spanish and Portuguese *bizarro* handsome, brave). **A** *adjective* **1** M17 Eccentric, fantastic, grotesque. **2** M18 Designating variegated forms of garden flowers, as carnations, tulips, etc. **B** *noun* **1** L18 A bizarre carnation, tulip, etc. **2** M19 *absolutely The* bizarre quality of things; bizarre things.

blague /blag/ *noun* M19 **French**. Humbug, claptrap.

blagueur /blagœr/ *noun* plural pronounced same L19 **French** (from BLAGUE). A pretentious talker; a joker, a teller of tall stories.

blanc /blɑ̃/ *noun* plural pronounced same M18 **French** (= white). **1** M18 White paint, especially for the face. Now *archaic* or *historical*. **2** M19 A type of light-coloured stock or gravy.

blancbec /blɑ̃bɛk/ *noun* plural pronounced same M19 **French** (literally, 'white beak'). A raw youngster, a greenhorn.

blanc de blanc /blɑ̃ də blɑ̃/ *noun phrase* M20 **French**. A (usually sparkling) white wine made from white grapes only.

blanc de chine /blɑ̃ də ʃin/ *noun phrase* L19 **French**. A white glazed Chinese porcelain, especially of the Ming period. Also called Dehua after its place of origin.

blanc de perle /blɑ̃ də pɛrl/ *adjective phrase* L19 **French**. Pearl-white.

blanc fixe /blɑ̃ fiks/ *noun phrase* M19 **French**. Barium sulphate, especially as used in paints.

blancmange /bləˈmɒnʒ/, /bləˈmɑːnʒ/ *noun* (also (earlier) **blancmanger**) LME **Old French** (*blanc mangier* (modern *blanc-manger*), from *blanc* white + *mang(i)er* food, use as noun of *mang(i)er* to eat.). **1** LME–L15 A dish of white meat or fish in a cream sauce. **2** M16 An opaque jelly made with isinglass or gelatin and milk or (now usually) cornflour and milk, often flavoured and sweetened.

■ The terminal 'r' was dropped in the eighteenth century.

blanquette /blɑ̃kɛt/ *noun* plural pronounced same M18 **French** (from Old French *blanchet* from *blanc, blanche* white). A dish of light meat, especially veal, cooked in a white sauce.

blasé /ˈblɑːzeɪ/ *adjective* E19 **French**. Cloyed with or tired of pleasure; bored or unimpressed by things from having seen or experienced them too often.

1996 *Oldie* We have also survived scares about yoghurt . . . , microwave cookers, television sets, computers, salami (contains nitrate), etc, and have now got blasé about it all.

bled /blɛd/ *noun* M20 **French** (from colloquial (Algerian) Arabic, corresponding to classical Arabic *balad* vast stretch of country, *bilād* land, country). In north-west Africa: uncultivated land behind a fertile populated area.

bleu-du-roi /blødyrwa/ *noun & adjective* (also **bleu-de-roi** /blødərwa/) M19 **French** (= king's blue). (Of) the ultramarine blue of Sèvres porcelain.

blin /blɪn/ *noun* plural **blini**, **bliny** /ˈblɪni/, **blinis** /ˈblɪnɪz/ L19 **Russian**. A kind of pancake, frequently stuffed. Cf. BLINTZE.

blintze /blɪn(t)s/ *noun* E20 **Yiddish** (*blintse* from Russian *blinets* diminutive of *blin*). A BLIN.

blitzkrieg /ˈblɪtskriːg/ *noun* (also **Blitzkrieg**) M20 **German** (from *Blitz* lightning + *Krieg* war). A violent campaign intended to bring about speedy victory.

■ Used specifically of the German military campaigns in World War Two, *Blitzkrieg* is usually found in the abbreviated form *Blitz* with reference to the Luftwaffe's bombardment of British cities. Both *blitzkrieg* and *blitz* are in general metaphorical use (see quotation).

1996 *New Scientist* The Japanese blitzkrieg on Western markets was in full swing in the early 1980s.

bloc /blɒk/ *noun* E20 **French** (= block, from Middle Dutch *blok*, Middle and Modern Low German *block*, of unknown origin). A combination of nation-states, parties, groups, or people, formed to promote a particular interest.

blond /blɒnd/ *adjective & noun* (also **blonde**) L15 **Old and Modern French** (from medieval Latin *blundus, blondus* yellow, perhaps of Germanic origin). **A** *adjective* L15 (Especially of the hair) of a light golden-brown colour, flaxen, fair; (of the complexion) light-coloured with fair hair. **B** *noun* M18 A person (especially a woman) with blond hair and complexion.

■ The feminine form of the adjective *blonde* was introduced from French in the seventeenth century, but the masculine/feminine distinction is often not observed in English usage, with *blonde* being used of both men and women.

blouson /'blu:zɒn/, *foreign* /bluzɔ̃/ (*plural same*) *noun* E20 **French**. A short jacket fitting loosely on the body like a blouse.

blutwurst /'blʌtwə:st/ *foreign* /'blʊtvʊrst/ *noun* M19 **German** (from *Blut* blood + *Wurst* sausage). (A) black pudding.

bocage /bə'kɑ:ʒ/, *foreign* /bɔkɑʒ/ (*plural same*) *noun* L16 **French**. **1** L16 Wooded country interspersed with pasture (in France); a thicket, a wood. **2** *Ceramics* E20 (A, the) representation of silvan scenery (especially a leafy tree stump or flowery arbour) as a decorative element but also as a support for a figure during firing. Frequently *attributive*.

boccaro /'bɒkərəʊ/ *noun* (also **bucaro**, **buccaro** /'bʌkərəʊ/) plural **boccaros** L19 **Spanish** (*búcaro* from Portuguese *púcaro* clay cup, ultimately from Latin *poculum* cup). A scented red unglazed earthenware of a type originally made in Mexico and imitated in Spain and Portugal.

bodega /bə'di:gə/, *foreign* /bo'dega/ *noun* M19 **Spanish** (from Latin *apotheca* from Greek *apothēkē* storehouse; *cf.* BOUTIQUE). (Originally in Spain) a shop selling wine.

bodegón /bode'gon/ *noun* plural **bodegones** /bode'gones/ M19 **Spanish** (from BODEGA, as originally representing a bodega scene). A Spanish picture representing still life or a genre subject.

Boer /bɔ:/, /'bəʊə/, /bʊə/ *noun & adjective* (also **boer**) M19 **Dutch** (*boer* farmer). **A** *noun* M19 A South African of Dutch descent, an Afrikaner; *History* an early Dutch inhabitant of the Cape. **B** *attributive* or as *adjective* Of, made by, or typical of Boers.

boerewors /'bɔ:rəvɔ:s/ *noun* M20 **Afrikaans** (from *boer* farmer + wors *sausage*). (A) coarse sausage made with beef and pork.

> **1950** L. G. Green *Land of Afternoon*
> Boerewors is another farm product which some still make in the old way; a sausage in which the meat has been pounded with a wooden stamper rather than minced.

bœuf /bœf/ *noun* E20 **French** (= beef). *Cookery* Used in the names of various beef dishes.

bœuf bourguignon /bœf burgiɲɔ̃/ *noun phrase* E20 **French** (= beef of Burgundy). *Cookery* A casserole of beef cooked slowly in red wine.

bois brûlé /bwa bryle/ *noun phrase* plural **bois brûlés** (pronounced same) E19 **French** (= burnt wood). In North America: a half-breed, especially one of French and American Indian descent.

boiserie /bwɑzri/ *noun* M19 **French**. Wainscoting, wooden panelling.

boîte /bwat/ *noun* plural (pronounced same) E20 **French** (= box). A small (French) restaurant or nightclub.

bolas /'bəʊləs/ *noun singular* (with plural **bolases**) or *plural* (also *singular* **bola** /'bəʊlə/) E19 **Spanish and Portuguese** (plural of *bola* ball). A missile (chiefly South American) consisting of balls connected by a strong cord, which is thrown to entangle the legs of a quarry.

bolero /bə'lɛ:rəʊ/, *in sense 2 also* /'bɒlərəʊ/ *noun* plural **boleros** L18 **Spanish**. **1** L18 A lively Spanish dance; a piece of music for this dance. **2** L19 A short jacket just reaching the waist, worn by men in Spain; a woman's short open jacket, with or without sleeves.

boletus /bə'li:təs/ *noun* (also Anglicized as **bolet** /bə'lɛt/, **bolete** /bə'li:t/) E16 **Latin** (*boletus* from Greek *bōlitēs*, perhaps from *bōlos* lump). A mushroom or toadstool of the large genus *Boletus*, having the undersurface of the cap full of pores.

Bolshevik /'bɒlʃɪvɪk/ *noun & adjective* (also **bolshevik**) E20 **Russian** (*bol'shevik* = member of the majority, from *bol'she* greater, from *bol'shoĭ* big). **A** *noun* **1** E20 *History* A member of the majority faction of the Russian Social-Democratic Party, which in 1903 favoured extreme measures; an advocate of proletarian dictatorship in Russia by soviets; a Russian Communist. **2** E20 *general* A socialist revolutionary. **B** *adjective* E20 Of or pertaining to Bolsheviks or Bolshevism.

bolson /'bəʊls(ə)n/ *noun* M19 **Spanish** (*bolsón* augmentative of *bolsa* purse). A basin-shaped depression surrounded by mountains, especially in the southern United States and Mexico.

■ Originally United States; cf. Bolsón de Mapimí, the name of a high desert in Mexico.

bolus /'bəʊləs/ *noun* M16 **Late Latin** (from Greek *bōlos* clod, lump of earth). **1** M16 A large pill of medicine. Often *contemptuous* or *archaic* except in *Veterinary Medicine*. **2** L18 A small rounded mass of anything, especially of masticated food at the moment of swallowing. **3** M20 *Medicine* A single dose of a pharmaceutical preparation given intravenously.

boma /'bəʊmə/ *noun* L19 **Kiswahili**. In East Africa: a defensible enclosure, especially for animals; hence, a police or military post; a magistrate's office.

bombachas /bɒm'batʃəz/ *noun plural* M20 **South American Spanish** (from *bombacho* loose-fitting, wide). Baggy trousers worn in some South American countries.

bombe /bɒmb/, *foreign* /bɔ̃b/ (*plural same*) *noun* L19 **French** (= bomb). A conical or cup-shaped confection, frequently frozen.

bombé /bɔ̃be/ *adjective* E20 **French** (past participle of *bomber* to swell out). Especially of furniture: rounded, convex.

bombilla /bɒm'bɪljə/ *noun* M19 **American Spanish** (diminutive of Spanish *bomba* strainer). A tube with a strainer at the end, from which maté is drunk in South America.

bombora /bɒm'bɔːrə/ *noun* M20 **Aboriginal**. In Australia and New Zealand: a dangerous stretch of water where waves break over a submerged reef.

bon /bɔ̃/ *adjective* L16 **French** (= good (masculine; cf. BONNE)). Good.

■ In various phrases used in English (see entries below).

bona fide /ˌbəʊnə 'fʌɪdi/ *adverb & adjective phrase* M16 **Latin** (= with good faith (ablative of next)). (Acting or done) in good faith; sincere(ly), genuine(ly).

1996 *Times* We hear echoes of it in Top 40 songs, but we seldom, if ever, see a bona fide gospel singer in the chart shows.

bona fides /ˌbəʊnə 'fʌɪdiːz/ *noun phrase* L18 **Latin** (= good faith). **1** L18 Good faith, freedom from intent to deceive. **2** M20 (erroneously treated as plural) Guarantees of good faith, credentials.

bonanza /bə'nanzə/ *noun & adjective* E19 **Spanish** (= fair weather, prosperity, from Latin *bonus* good). **A** *noun* E19 A run of good luck, an unexpected success; prosperity; a source of great wealth or good fortune. **B** *adjective* L19 Greatly prospering or productive.

■ Originally used among miners in the United States for 'a rich find' or 'lucky strike'.

1996 *Country Life* Daffodil growers . . . , who missed their usual £10 million bonanza on Mothering Sunday because cold weather delayed flowering, are setting their sights on Easter.

bon appétit /bɔn apeti/, /bɒn apə'tiː/ *interjection* M19 **French**. Good appetite!

■ Used as a salutation to people about to eat.

bon-bon /'bɒnbɒn/ *noun* L18 **French** (literally, 'good-good'). A piece of confectionery, a sweet.

bonbonnière /bɔ̃bɔnjɛr/ *noun* plural pronounced same E19 **French**. A fancy box for holding sweets.

1996 *Country Life* As an amusement, I would far rather have had a bonbonnière by an unidentified 18th-century German factory. It was of a crouching and concentrating cat . . .

bond /bɔnt/ *noun* (also **Bond**) L19 **Afrikaans** (from Dutch (= German *Bund*), from *binden* bind). In South Africa: an Afrikaner league or association, especially the extreme nationalist *Broederbond*.

bondieuserie /bɔ̃djøzri/ *noun* plural pronounced same M20 **French** (from *bon* good + *Dieu* God). A church ornament or devotional object, *especially* one of little artistic merit; such objects collectively.

■ The French journalist and novelist Jules Vallès (1832–85) is credited with the invention of the term.

bon enfant /bɔn ɑ̃fɑ̃/ *noun phrase* M19 **French** (literally, 'good child'). An agreeable companion.

bongo /'bɒŋgəʊ/ *noun* plural **bongo(e)s** E20 **American Spanish** (*bongó*). Either of a pair of small drums, usually held between the knees and played with the fingers. Also *bongo-drum(s)*.

bon gré mal gré /bɔ̃ gre mal gre/ *adverb phrase* E19 **French** (literally, 'good will, bad will'). (Whether) willingly or unwillingly.

bonheur du jour /bɔnœr dy ʒur/ *noun phrase* plural **bonheurs du jour** (pronounced same) L19 **French** (literally, 'happiness of the day'). A small writing-table, usually fitted to hold toilet accessories, popular in eighteenth-century France.

bonhomie /'bɒnəmiː/ *noun* (also formerly written **bonhommie**) L18 **French** (from *bonhomme* good man, from medieval Latin *bonus homo* + suffix *-ie*). Good-natured friendliness, geniality.

1992 A. Lambert *A Rather English Marriage* Reginald was bluff and cheery, spreading enough *bonhomie* to fuel a party.

bonito /bə'niːtəʊ/ *noun* plural **bonitos** (also **boneta** /bə'niːtə/) L16 **Spanish**. Any of various striped tuna, especially *Sarda sarda* of the Atlantic and Mediterranean.

bonjour /'bɔ̃ʒur/ *interjection* L16 **French**. Good day! Hallo!

■ Used as a general greeting.

bon mot /bɔ̃ mo/ *noun phrase* plural **bons mots** (pronounced same) M18 **French** (literally, 'good word'). A witty remark, a clever saying.

1995 *Spectator* When King Louis-Philippe was told that Talleyrand had died he was heard to mutter: 'Died, has he? I wonder what he meant by that.' It seems a shame to deprive Louis-Philippe of some of his few recorded *bons mots* and ascribe it to Talleyrand, who has plenty to his credit.

bonne /bɔn/ *adjective & noun* E16 **French** (feminine of BON). **A** *adjective* E16 Good. **B** *noun* L18 A (French) nursemaid or personal servant.

■ Use as an adjective has long been restricted to certain phrases adopted from French (see below) and the nominal use too is now rare.

bonne bouche /bɔn buʃ/ *noun phrase* (also **bonne-bouche**) plural **bonnes bouches** (pronounced same) M18 **French** (literally, 'good mouth'). A dainty morsel, a titbit, especially one at the end of a meal; also *figurative*.

■ In French the sense is 'a pleasing taste in the mouth', which has been understood in English as the delicacy that gives this.

1996 *Times* Let us begin with a *bonne-bouche* before we tuck in.

bonne femme /bɔn fam/ *adjective phrase* E19 **French** (literally, 'in the manner of a good housewife'). *Cookery* (Of a dish of food) prepared in a particular way.

■ Also in the fuller form *à la bonne femme*, both used postpositively, as in 'sole *bonne femme*'.

bonne fortune /bɔn fɔrtyn/ *noun phrase* plural **bonnes fortunes** (pronounced same) E19 **French** (literally, 'good fortune'). A lady's favours, seen as a cause for self-congratulation on the part of their receipient.

bonsai /'bɒnsʌɪ/ *noun* plural same E20 **Japanese** (from *bon* tray + *sai* planting). The (Japanese) practice of cultivating artificially dwarfed potted plants or small trees; a plant or tree cultivated by this method.

bon ton /bɔn tɔ̃/ *noun phrase* M18 **French** (literally, 'good tone') . The fashionable world.

bon vivant /bɔ̃ vivɑ̃/ *noun phrase* plural **bons vivants** (pronounced same) L17 **French** (literally, '(a person) who lives well'). A gourmand, an epicure.

■ In contemporary usage *bon vivant* and BON VIVEUR appear interchangeably in a general sense of someone with a self-indulgent lifestyle (see quotation).

1996 *Times* Nor does it mean that the *bon vivant* has renounced his ways. 'Don't worry, . . . [the] fun and sex are not over yet.'

bon viveur /bɔ̃ vivœr/ *noun phrase* plural **bons viveurs** (pronounced same) M19 **pseudo-French** (formed after BON VIVANT). A person who indulges a taste for the good things of life.

1995 *Spectator* Roy Hattersley, politician, man of letters, *bon viveur*, is one of public life's polymaths.

bon voyage /bɒn vwa'jɑːʒ/ *interjection* L17 **French** (literally, 'good journey'). Pleasant journey!

■ Used as a farewell to a person about to travel.

bonze /bɒnz/ *noun* L16 **French** (*bonze* or Portuguese *bonzo* probably from Japanese *bonzō*, *bonsō* priest). A Japanese or Chinese Buddhist religious teacher.

boomerang /'buːməraŋ/ *noun & verb* L18 **Aboriginal** (perhaps modified: cf. Kamilaroi *būmarin*). **A** *noun* **1** L18 A thin curved hardwood missile (of a kind) used by Australian Aborigines as a hunting weapon, *especially* one that can be thrown so as to return to the thrower. **2** M19 *figurative* A scheme etc. that recoils on its originator. **B** *intransitive verb* L19 Act as a boomerang; *figurative* recoil on the originator.

boondock /'buːndɒk/ *noun* M20 **Tagalog** (*bundok* mountain). Rough or isolated country; remote parts.

■ North American slang, originally used by service personnel. It appears infrequently in the singular, more usually in the plural, and often in the phrase *(out) in the boondocks*.

bordello /bɔː'dɛləʊ/ *noun* plural **bordellos** L16 **Italian** (from medieval Latin *bordellum*). A brothel.

1996 *Times* The management skills involved in running a chain of hotels, discotheques, pubs or theme restaurants are no different from those needed for bordellos.

bordereau /bɔːdə'rəʊ/, *foreign* /bɔrdəro/ *noun* plural **bordereaux** /bɔːdə'rəʊz/, *foreign* /bɔrdəro/ L19 **French** (diminutive of *bord* board). A memorandum of contents, a schedule, a docket.

borné /bɔrne/ *adjective* L18 **French** (past participle of *borner* to limit). Limited in scope, intellect, outlook, etc.

bortsch /bɔːtʃ/ *noun* (also **borsch** /bɔːʃ/, **borstch** /bɔːstʃ/) E19 **Russian** (*borshch*). A Russian or Polish soup of various ingredients including beetroot and cabbage.

bosquet /ˈbɒskɪt/ *noun* (also **bosket**) M18 **French** (from Italian *boschetto* diminutive of *bosco* wood; cf. BOUQUET). A plantation of small trees in a garden, park, etc.; a thicket.

bossage /ˈbɒsɪdʒ/ *noun* E18 **French** (from *bosse* boss). *Architecture* Projecting stonework, bosses; *especially* a type of rustic work.

bossa nova /ˌbɒsə ˈnəʊvə/ *noun phrase* M20 **Portuguese** (*bossa* tendency, *nova* feminine singular of *novo* new). A style of Brazilian music related to the samba; a dance to this music.

1995 *Spectator* A 'bossa' is a hump on an ox's back, and thus idiomatically 'bossa nova' means something like 'new commotion' or 'new wrinkle'.

botargo /bəˈtɑːgəʊ/ *noun* plural **botargo(e)s** L16 **Italian** (from (medieval) Greek *arghotarakho*, perhaps through Pontic dialect *ovotarakho*). A relish made of the roe of the mullet or tuna.

boucan /ˈbuːk(ə)n/ *noun* (also **buccan** /ˈbʌk(ə)n/) E17 **French** (from Tupi *mukem*, *mocaém*). **1** E17 In South America: a wooden frame for cooking, smoking, or drying meat over an open fire. **2** M19 Meat cooked or cured on such a frame. **3** M19 An open floor on which coffee beans etc. may be spread out to dry.

bouchée /buʃe/ *noun* plural pronounced same M19 **French** (= mouthful, from *bouche* mouth). A small baked confection.

■ Usually in plural.

bouclé /ˈbuːkleɪ/ *adjective & noun* L19 **French** (= buckled, curled). (Fabric) woven with a knotted and curled appearance; (yarn) of looped or curled ply.

boudin /ˈbuːdɪn/, *foreign* /budɛ̃/ (*plural same*) *noun* E20 **French**. *Geology* Any of a number of roughly parallel elongated sections resulting from the fracturing of a rock stratum during folding.

■ Although recorded earlier (M19) with its current French meaning of 'a black pudding', *boudin* has never been entirely naturalized in this sense.

boudoir /ˈbuːdwɑː/ *noun* L18 **French** (literally, 'place to sulk in', from *bouder* to pout, sulk). A (woman's) small private room.

bouffant /ˈbuːfɑ̃/ *noun & adjective* E19 **French** (present participle of *bouffer* to swell). **A** *noun* E19 A puffed-out part of a dress etc.; a puffed-out hairstyle. **B** *adjective* L19 Of a dress, hairstyle, etc.: puffed out.

A 1996 *Times* Hoddle has come a long way since the days when he sported first a Keeganesque bouffant and then hair straggling sweatily down his neck.

bougie /ˈbuːʒi/ *noun* M18 **French** (from *Bougie* (Arabic *Bijāya*) a town in Algeria which carried on a trade in wax). **1** M18 A wax candle. **2** M18 *Medicine* A rod or tube for exploring or dilating the passages of the body.

bouillabaisse /buːjəˈbeɪs/, *foreign* /bujabɛs/ *noun* M19 **French** (from Modern Provençal *bouiabaisso*). A Provençal dish of fish stewed in water or white wine. Also *figurative*.

1996 *Times* Emerging from this *bouillabaisse* of complaints, however, is one certainty.

bouilli /ˈbuːji/, *foreign* /buji/ *noun* E17 **French** (use as noun of past participle of *bouillir* to boil). Boiled or stewed meat, especially beef.

■ Since the mid eighteenth century often Anglicized as *bully*, especially when referring to beef in the form used for army rations.

bouillon /ˈbuːjɒ̃/, *foreign* /bujɔ̃/ *noun* M17 **French** (from *bouillir* to boil). Broth, thin soup. See also COURT BOUILLON.

boule /ˈbuːli/ *noun 1* M19 **Greek** (*boulē* senate). A legislative body of ancient or modern Greece.

boule /buːl/, *foreign* /bul/ *noun 2* plural **boules** *in sense 2* /buːl/, *in sense 3* /buːlz/, *foreign* /bul/ E20 **French** (= bowl). **1** E20 A form of roulette. **2** E20 (*singular* and in *plural*) A French form of bowls played on rough ground, usually with metal bowls. **3** M20 A small pear-shaped mass of synthetic sapphire, ruby, etc., made by fusing suitably tinted alumina.

boul(l)e variant of BUHL.

boulevard /ˈbuːləvɑːd/, *foreign* /bulvar/ (*plural same*) *noun* M18 **French** ((originally) = rampart, (later) a promenade on the site of this). A broad street (especially in France) with rows of trees planted along it; *United States* a broad main urban road.

boulevardier /bulvardje/ *noun* plural pronounced same L19 **French** (from *boulevard* + *-ier*). A person who frequents (French) boulevards.

bouleversé /bulvɛrse/ *adjective* M19 **French** (past participle of *bouleverser* to turn as a ball, from as BOULE (*noun 2*) + *verser* to turn). Amazed, upset, completely taken aback.

1995 *Times* The rest of the world was *bouleversé* by this week's letter from Pope John Paul lauding feminism and apologising to women for centuries of hardship and exclusion.

bouleversement /bulvɛrsəmɑ̃/ *noun* plural pronounced same L18 **French** (from as preceding). An inversion, *especially* a violent one; an upset, an upheaval.

bouquet /bʊ'keɪ/, /bəʊ'keɪ/, /'bʊkeɪ/ *noun* E18 **French** ((earlier = clump of trees), from dialectal variant of Old French *bos*, *bois* wood). **1** E18 A bunch of flowers, *especially* a large attractive one for use at a ceremony. **b** E20 *figurative* A compliment. **2** M19 The perfume of wine etc. **3** M19 A BOUQUET GARNI. **4** L19 A number of rockets etc. fired together.

bouquet garni /bʊkeɪ 'gɑːni/ *noun phrase* M19 **French** (literally, 'garnished bouquet'). *Cookery* A bunch of assorted herbs for flavouring.

bouquetier /bʊkə'tɪə/, *foreign* /buktje/ *noun* L18 **French**. A small holder for a posy of flowers, especially one to be carried in the hand.

bourdon /'bʊəd(ə)n/ *noun* (also **burdoun**) ME **Old and Modern French** (= drone, from Proto-Romance, of imitative origin). **1** ME The bass or undersong of a melody. **2** M19 A low-pitched stop in an organ or harmonium; the drone pipe of a bagpipe. **3** E20 The lowest-pitched in a peal of bells.

■ *Bourdon* in sense 1 soon merged with the same sense of *burden* and is now rare or obsolete with its original meaning; sense 2 is a reintroduction.

bourg /bʊəg/ *noun* LME **Old and Modern French** (from medieval Latin *burgus* borough). A town or village under the shadow of a castle (*historical*); an ancient town in continental Europe.

bourgade /burgad/ *noun* plural pronounced same E17 **French** (from as preceding + *-ade*). A large village or straggling unwalled town in Europe.

bourgeois /'bʊəʒwɑː/, *foreign* /burʒwa/ *adjective & noun* M16 **French**. **A** *adjective* **1** M16 Of, pertaining to, characteristic of, or resembling, the bourgeois (see sense B below); middle-class; conventionally respectable and unimaginative, humdrum; selfishly materialistic; capitalistic, reactionary. **2** E20 Of French wine: next in quality to wines classified as the best. **B** *noun* plural same. **1** L17 Originally, a (French) citizen or freeman of a city or burgh, as distinct from a peasant or a gentleman. Now, any member of the middle class. **2** L19 In Communist or socialist writing: a capitalist, an exploiter of the proletariat. *derogatory.* **3** M20 A socially or aesthetically conventional person, a philistine. *derogatory.*

bourgeoise /'bʊəʒwɑːz/, *foreign* /burʒwaz/ *noun & adjective* plural of noun pronounced same L18 **French** (feminine of preceding). **A** *noun* L18 A female bourgeois. **B** *adjective* M20 Of a female: bourgeois.

bourgeoisie /ˌbʊəʒwɑː'ziː/, *foreign* /burʒwazi/ *noun* E18 **French** (from BOURGEOIS). The bourgeois collectively; the middle class.

bourrée /'bʊəreɪ/, *foreign* /bure/ (*plural same*) *noun* L17 **French**. A lively dance of French origin, resembling the gavotte; a piece of music for this dance or in its rhythm, *especially* one which forms a movement of a suite.

■ In a *bourrée step* the dancer moves sideways, with one foot crossing behind or in front of the other.

bourse /bʊəs/ *noun* L16 **French**. A money market; *especially* (the Bourse) the Paris stock exchange; *transferred* an exchange.

1996 *Times* For diplomats used to trading sovereignty for influence in the Brussels *bourse*, the thought that sovereignty might be retrieved, and independence asserted, is deeply uncongenial.

boustrophedon /baʊstrə'fiːd(ə)n/, /buːstrə'fiːd(ə)n/ *adverb & adjective* E17 **Greek** (= as the ox turns in ploughing, from *bous* ox + *strophos* twist + adverbial suffix *-don*). (Written) from right to left and from left to right in alternate lines.

boutade /buː'tɑːd/ *noun* E17 **French** (from *bouter* to thrust). A sudden outburst or outbreak.

boutique /buːˈtiːk/ *noun* M18 **French** (from Old Provençal *botica* (Italian *bottega*) from Latin *apotheca* from Greek *apothēkē* storehouse: cf. BODEGA). A small shop. Now usually a shop, or a department in a large store, selling (especially fashionable) clothes or accessories.

bouton /ˈbuːtɒn/ *noun* M19 **French** (= button). **1** M19 A round pearl with a flat back. In full *bouton pearl*. **2** M20 *Anatomy* An enlarged part of a nerve fibre or cell, especially an axon, where it forms a synapse.

boutonnière /ˌbuːtɒnˈjɛː/, *foreign* /butɔnjɛr/ (*plural same*) *noun* L19 **French**. A flower or posy worn in a lapel buttonhole.

1996 *Times: Weekend* Reno is noted for being a wedding factory town, where one enterprising local chapel offers an all-inclusive nuptial special for $129 . . . in addition to a free *boutonnière* for the groom . . .

bouts rimés /buː riːˈmeɪ/ *noun phrase plural* E18 **French** (= rhymed endings). Rhyming words upon which verses are (to be) composed.

bouzouki /bʊˈzuːki/ *noun* M20 **Modern Greek** (*mpouzouki*: cf. Turkish *bozuk* spoilt, i.e. roughly made (instruments)). In Greece: a form of long-necked lute much used in traditional folk music.

boyar /bəʊˈjɑː/ *noun* L16 **Russian** (*boyarin* grandee). *History* A member of an order of Russian aristocracy (abolished by Peter the Great), next in rank to a prince.

braai /ˈbrɑːɪ/ *noun & verb* M20 **Afrikaans** (abbreviation of next). **A** *noun* M20 In South Africa: a barbecue, a BRAAIVLEIS. **B** *transitive & intransitive verb* M20 Grill (meat) over an open fire.

braaivleis /ˈbrɑːɪfleɪs/ *noun* M20 **Afrikaans** (= grilled meat, from *braai* to grill + *vleis* meat). In South Africa: meat grilled over an open fire; a picnic, barbecue, etc., at which meat is cooked in this way.

braggadocio /bragəˈdəʊtʃɪəʊ/ *noun* plural **braggadocios** L16 **pseudo-Italian** (fictional name formed from *brag* or *braggart* + Italian augmentative suffix *-occio*). **1** L16 A loud-mouthed braggart, an idle boaster. **2** M18 Empty boasting, bluster.

■ *Braggadocchio* is the name of a cowardly braggart in Spenser's *Faerie Queene*, the first part of which was published in 1590: 'Proud *Braggadocchio*, that in vaunting vaine / His glory did repose, and credit did maintaine' (III.viii.11).

1996 *Spectator* He drank unwisely and not too well, went in for a deal of Celtic fist-flaying and had a bully's *braggadocio* . . .

brahmacharya /brɑːməˈtʃɑːrɪə/ *noun* E20 **Sanskrit** (*brahmacarya*, from *bráhman* prayer, worship + *carya* conduct). Purity of life, especially regarding sexual matters.

■ Frequently used with reference to the life and teachings of M. K. Gandhi, through whose writings the word entered English.

brahman /ˈbrɑːmən/ *noun* (also **brahma** /ˈbrɑːmə/, **brahm**, **Brahman**) L18 **Sanskrit** (*bráhman* sacred utterance). In Hindu philosophy: the ultimate reality underlying all phenomena.

brandade /brɑ̃dad/ *noun* E19 **French** (from Modern Provençal *brandado*, literally, 'thing which has been moved or shaken'). A Provençal dish made from salt cod.

brasserie /ˈbrasəri/ *noun* M19 **French** ((originally = brewery), from *brasser* to brew). A (French) saloon selling beer and usually food; *generally* an informal restaurant.

brassière /ˈbrasɪə/, /ˈbrazɪə/ *noun* (also **brassiere**) E20 **French** (= child's reins, camisole, etc.). A woman's shaped undergarment worn to support the breasts.

■ The abbreviation *bra* is almost universal in informal contexts.

bratwurst /ˈbratwəːst/, /ˈbratvəːst/ E20 **German** (from *Brat* a spit (*braten* roast etc.) + *Wurst* sausage). (A) mild-flavoured German pork sausage.

brava /ˈbrɑːvə/ *noun & interjection* E19 **Italian** (feminine of *bravo*). (A cry addressed to a woman or girl meaning) excellent, well done!

bravo /ˈbrɑːvəʊ/ *noun 1* plural **bravo(e)s** L16 **Italian**. A hired ruffian; a desperado.

bravo /brɑːˈvəʊ/, /ˈbrɑːvəʊ/ *interjection & noun 2* M18 **French** (from as preceding: cf. BRAVA). **A** *interjection* M18 Excellent, well done! **B** *noun* plural **bravos**. M19 A cry of 'bravo!', a cheer.

B 1996 *Country Life* There was silence at the close, broken finally by bravos.

bravura /brəˈv(j)ʊərə/ *noun & adjective* M18 **Italian** (from *bravo* brave). **1** *Music* M18 (A passage or style, especially of singing) requiring exceptional powers of execution. **2** E19 (A performance that is) brilliant or ambitious; (a display that is) daring, dash(ing).

2 1996 *Spectator* But behind all the bravura lies a new novelist of prodigious talent; one whose voice, only audible when his own comedy has subsided, is a moving, melancholic one.

breccia /ˈbrɛtʃə/, /ˈbrɛtʃɪə/ *noun* L18 **Italian** (= gravel, rubble, cognate with French *brèche*, German *brechen* from Germanic base of break). *Geology* Rock consisting of angular fragments cemented together e.g. by lime.

brei /brʌɪ/ *noun* M20 **German** (= pulp, mush, jelly). *Biology* A homogenized pulp of organic tissue prepared for experimental work.

breitschwanz /ˈbrʌɪtʃvɑːnts/ *noun* E20 **German** (= broad tail). The lustrous pelt of a young karakul lamb.

breloque /brəˈləʊk/ *noun* M19 **French**. A small ornament fastened to a watch-chain; a trinket.

bretelle /brəˈtɛl/ *noun* M19 **French** (= strap, sling, (in plural) trouser-braces). Each of a pair of ornamental straps extending over the shoulders from the belt on the front of a dress to the belt on the back. Usually in *plural*.

bric-à-brac /ˈbrɪkəbrak/ *noun* (also **bric-a-brac**, **bricabrac**) M19 **French** (from *à bric et à brac* at random). Miscellaneous old ornaments, trinkets, small pieces of furniture, etc; antiquarian knick-knacks.

1996 *Spectator* For many years the great auction houses of London sold only fine art in all its forms. If you wanted to dispose of the bric-à-brac of life you had to look for others to sell it for you.

bricolage /brɪkəˈlɑːʒ/, *foreign* /brɪkɔlɑʒ/ (*plural same*) *noun* M20 **French** (from *bricoler* to do odd jobs, repair, from as next). Construction or creation from whatever is immediately available for use; something constructed or created in this way, an assemblage of haphazard or incongruous elements.

bricole /ˈbrɪk(ə)l/, /brɪˈkəʊl/ *noun* E16 **Old and Modern French** (from Provençal *bricola* or Italian *briccola*, of unknown origin). **1** E16 An engine or catapult for discharging stones or bolts. *obsolete* except *historical*. **2** L16 A rebound of the ball from a side-wall or cushion in real tennis, billiards, etc.

bricoleur /brɪkəˈləː/; *foreign* /brikɔlœr/ (*plural same*) *noun* M20 **French** (= handyman, from *bricoler* to do odd jobs). A person who engages in BRICOLAGE; a constructor or creator of bricolages.

brillante /brɪˈlanteɪ/ *adverb & adjective* M18 **Italian**. *Music* (A direction:) in a showy or sparkling style.

brinjal /ˈbrɪndʒɑːl/ *noun* E17 **Anglo-Indian** (ultimately from Portuguese *berinjela*, from as AUBERGINE). Especially in the Indian subcontinent: an aubergine.

brio /ˈbriːəʊ/ *noun* M18 **Italian**. Vivacity, liveliness, verve.

1996 *Country Life* At a time when the RSC has been looking a bit wobbly, it restores some much-needed brio and confidence to Stratford Shakespeare.

brioche /briːˈɒʃ/, /ˈbriːɒʃ/ *noun* E19 **French**. A small usually round sweet cake made with light yeast dough.

briquette /brɪˈkɛt/ *noun & verb* (also **briquet**) L19 **French** (diminutive of *brique* brick). **A** *noun* L19 A small block or slab, especially of compressed coal-dust or other inflammable material for use as fuel. **B** *transitive verb* L19 Form into briquettes.

brisé /brize/ *noun* plural pronounced same L18 **French** (past participle of *briser* to break). *Ballet* A movement in which the feet or legs are lightly beaten together in the air.

brise-soleil /brizsɔlɛj/, /ˌbriːzsɒˈleɪ/ *noun* plural pronounced same M20 **French** (literally, 'sun-breaker'). A device (such as a perforated screen, louvre, etc.) for shutting out direct or excessive sunlight.

brocard /ˈbrəʊkəd/, *foreign* /brɔkar/ (*plural same*) *noun* M16 **French** (or medieval Latin *brocardus*, appellative use of the Latinized form of the proper name *Burchart*). **1** M16 A cutting speech, a gibe. *rare*. **2** E17 An elementary legal principle or maxim.

■ Burchart was an eleventh-century bishop of Worms and the compiler of volumes of ecclesiastical rules and regulations.

broché /ˈbrəʊʃeɪ/, *foreign* /brɔʃe/ *adjective & noun* L19 **French** (past participle of *brocher* to stitch). (A material, especially silk) woven with a pattern on the surface.

brochette /brɒˈʃɛt/ *noun* L15 **French** (diminutive of *broche* spit). **1** L15 A small skewer or spit; *specifically* a skewer on which chunks of meat are cooked (cf. À LA BROCHETTE). **2** M19 A pin or bar used to fasten medals, orders, etc., to clothing; a set of decorations worn in this way.

brochure /ˈbrəʊʃə/, /brɒˈʃʊə/ *noun* M18 **French** (literally, 'stitching, stitched work', from *brocher* to stitch + *-ure*). A booklet or pamphlet, especially giving information about the amenities of a place etc.

■ The literal French meaning refers to the fact that, before the days of staplers, such a pamphlet would have been made by stitching a few sheets of paper together.

broderie anglaise /ˌbrəʊd(ə)rɪ ɒŋˈgleɪz/ *noun phrase* M19 **French** (= English embroidery). Open embroidery on linen, cambric, etc.; fabric so embroidered.

brogan /ˈbrəʊg(ə)n/ *noun* M19 **Irish** (*brógán*, Gaelic *brógan* diminutive of *bróg* brogue). A coarse stout leather shoe reaching to the ankle.

bronco /ˈbrɒŋkəʊ/ *noun & adjective* (also **broncho**) M19 **Spanish** (= rough, rude). **A** *noun* M19 plural **broncos**. A wild or half-tamed horse, especially of the western United States. **B** *adjective* M19. Wild, uncontrollable, rough. *United States, colloquial.*

brouhaha /ˈbruːhɑːhɑː/ *noun* L19 **French**. A commotion, a sensation; uproar, hubbub.

brouillon /brujɔ̃/ *noun* plural pronounced same L17 **French**. A rough draft.

bruit /bruːt/, *in sense 4 foreign* /brɥi/ (*plural same*) *noun* LME **Old and Modern French** (use as noun of past participle of *bruire* to roar, from Proto-Romance alteration of Latin *rugire* to roar, by association with Proto-Romance source of 'bray'). **1** LME Noise, clamour. **2** LME Rumour, report. **3** L15–E17 Fame, reputation. **4** M19 *Medicine* Any sound (especially an abnormal one) heard in auscultation.

brunet /bruːˈnɛt/, /brʊˈnɛt/ *noun & adjective* (also (feminine) **brunette**) M16 **French** (*brunet* masculine, *brunette* feminine, diminutive of *brun* brown). (A White person) with a dark complexion or (now usually) brown hair. Of the complexion: dark.

■ The form *brunette*, especially a woman or girl, is far more frequent than the masculine form.

brusque /brʊsk/, /bruːsk/ *adjective* (also **brusk**) M17 **French** (= lively, fierce, harsh, from Italian *brusco* sour, tart, use as adjective of noun = Spanish, Portuguese *brusco* butcher's broom (a spiny bush) from Proto-Romance). Rough or rude in manner or speech; blunt, off-hand, abrupt.

■ Earliest (only in E17) in the sense of 'tart'.

brut /bruːt/, *foreign* /bryt/ *adjective* L19 **French**. Of wine: unsweetened, very dry.

brutum fulmen /ˌbruːtəm ˈfʌlmən/ *noun phrase* plural **bruta fulmina** /ˌbruːtə ˈfʌlmɪnə/ E17 **Latin** (literally, 'unfeeling thunderbolt'). A mere noise; an ineffective act, an empty threat.

■ The phrase *bruta fulmina et vana* 'insensate and ineffectual thunderbolts' occurs in Pliny's *Natural History* II.xliii.

bubo /ˈbjuːbəʊ/ *noun* plural **buboes** LME **Latin** (from Greek *boubōn* groin, swelling in the groin). A swollen inflamed lymph node especially in the groin or armpit.

bucaro, **buccaro** variants of BOCCARO.

buccan variant of BOUCAN.

buccra variant of BUCKRA.

bucellas /bjuːˈsɛləs/ *noun* E19 **Portuguese** (name of a village near Lisbon). A Portuguese white wine; a drink of this.

buckaroo see VAQUERO.

buckling /ˈbʌklɪŋ/ *noun* E20 **German** (*Bückling* bloater). A smoked herring.

buckra /ˈbʌkrə/ *noun* (also **buccra** and other variants) M18 **Ibibio and Efik** ((*m*)*bakara* European, master). (A Blacks' name for) a White man, a master.

■ Used in the West Indies and southern United States and frequently derogatory.

buffet /ˈbʊfeɪ/, *in sense 1 also* /ˈbʌfɪt/ *noun* E18 **French** (from Old French *buf(f)et*, of unknown origin). **1** E18 A sideboard or recessed cupboard for china, plate, etc. **2** L18 (A place offering) a service of food from a sideboard or counter where guests or customers can help themselves.

buffo /ˈbʊfəʊ/ *noun & adjective* M18 **Italian** (= puff of wind, buffoon, from *buffare* to puff, from Proto-Romance verb of imitative origin). **A** *noun* M18 plural **buffos**. A comic actor, a singer in OPERA BUFFA. **B** *adjective* L18 Comic, burlesque.

bugaku /ˈbʊgakuː/ *noun* L19 **Japanese** (from *bu* dancing + *gaku* music). A Japanese classical dance in which pure dance form and symmetry are emphasized, and masks are used.

buhl /buːl/ *noun & adjective* (also **boul(l)e**, **Buhl**) E19 **German** (*buhl*, French *boule*, from André Charles *Boulle* (1642–1732), French cabinet-maker). (Of) brass, tortoise-shell, etc., worked into ornamental patterns for inlaying; (work) inlaid thus.

bulgur /ˈbʌlgə/ *noun* (also **bulghur**) M20 **Turkish** (= Persian *bulġūr* bruised grain). Cracked wheat, BURGHUL.

bund /bʊnd/, *foreign* /bʊnt/ *noun* (also **Bund**) plural **bunds**, **bunde** /ˈbʊndə/ M19 **German**. A German league, confederacy, or association. Cf. BOND.

bundobust /ˈbʌndəbʌst/ *noun* (also **bandobast**) L18 **Urdu** (from Persian *band-o-bast* tying and binding). In the Indian subcontinent: arrangements, organization.

Bunraku /ˈbʊnrakuː/, *foreign* /ˈbunraku/ *noun & adjective* E20 **Japanese**. (Of, pertaining to, or characteristic of) Japanese puppet drama, *specifically* as practised by the Bunraku-za company.

bunyip /ˈbʌnjɪp/ *noun* M19 **Aboriginal**. In Australia: a fabulous monster of swamps and lagoons.

bureau /ˈbjʊərəʊ/ *noun* plural **bureaux** /ˈbjʊərəʊz/, **bureaus** L17 **French** (Old French *burel*, originally = woollen stuff, baize (used for covering writing-desks), probably from *bure*, variant of *buire* dark brown, from Proto-Romance alteration of Latin *burrus* fiery red, from Greek *purros* red). **1** L17 A writing-desk with drawers for papers etc. **b** E19 A chest of drawers. *North America*. **2** L17 An office, especially for the transaction of public business; a department of public administration. **b** E20 An office or business with a specified function; an agency for the coordination of related activities, the distribution of information, etc.

burette /bjʊˈrɛt/ *noun* (also **buret**) M19 **French**. A graduated glass tube with tap, used for measuring small quantities of liquid in chemical analysis.

burghul /bəːˈguːl/ *noun* (also **burgul**) E20 **Arabic** (*burġul* from Persian *burġūl* variant of *bulġūr*). Wholewheat partially boiled and then dried; a dish made from this.

burin /ˈbjʊərɪn/ *noun* M17 **French** (related to Italian *burino* (*bulino*), perhaps connected with Old High German *bora* boring-tool). A tool for engraving on copper or wood.

burka /ˈbʊəkə/ *noun* M19 **Urdu** (Persian *burḳaʻ* from Arabic *burḳuʻ*). A Muslim woman's long enveloping garment worn in public. Also, a yashmak.

burlesque /bəːˈlɛsk/ *adjective, noun, and verb* M17 **French** (from Italian *burlesco*, from *burla* ridicule, joke, fun, of unknown origin). **A** *adjective* **1** M17–M19 Jocular, odd, grotesque. **2** M17 Derisively or amusingly imitative; mock-heroic or mock-pathetic; bombastic. (Now chiefly of literary composition or dramatic representation.) **B** *noun* **1** M17 Derisively or amusingly imitative literary or dramatic composition, bombast; mock-seriousness; an instance or example of this; (a) parody; (a) caricature. **2a** M19 *History* The concluding portion of a blackface minstrel entertainment, containing dialogue and sketches. *United States*. **b** L19 A variety show, frequently featuring striptease. Originally and chiefly *United States*. **C** *transitive verb* L17 Imitate to deride or amuse; parody; caricature.

burnous /bəːˈnuːs/ *noun* (also **burnoose** and other variants) L16 **French** (from Arabic *burnus*, *burnūs*). An Arab or Moorish hooded cloak; a fashion garment resembling this.

burra /ˈbʌrə/ *adjective* E19 **Hindustani** (*baṛā*, *barā* great, greatest). In the Indian subcontinent: high-ranking, great.

■ Occurs only in phrases such as *burra sahib* and *burra memsahib*, used to refer to important people.

burrito /bʊˈriːtəʊ/ *noun* plural **burritos** M20 **American Spanish** (diminutive of BURRO). A tortilla rolled round a filling of spiced beef and other ingredients.

burro /ˈbʊrəʊ/ *noun* plural **burros** E19 **Spanish**. A small donkey used as a pack-animal. Chiefly *North American*.

bushido /ˈbuːʃɪdəʊ/, /bʊˈʃiːdəʊ/ *noun* L19 **Japanese** (= military knight's way). The code of honour and morals evolved by the samurai.

bustier /ˈbʌstɪeɪ/, /ˈbʊstɪeɪ/, *foreign* /bystje/ (*plural same*) *noun* L20 **French** (from *buste* bust). A close-fitting usually strapless bodice or top worn by women.

■ The revival of the *bustier* as a fashion item in the 1980s was closely associated with the rock star Madonna, who frequently wore one for her public appearances.

1987 *London Evening News* . . . bustiers in scarlet and black sat atop wafts of brightly coloured chiffon skirts for evening.

butoh /'buto/ *noun* L20 **Japanese** ('dark art'). A Japanese dance style influenced by Western dance.

1996 *Spectator* Dramatic tension and the exploration of man's dark inner depths should also be the ingredients of *butoh*, the Japanese theatre art halfway between dance and drama.

butte /bju:t/ *noun* M19 **French.** *Physical Geography* In North America: an isolated hill with steep sides and a flat top, similar to but narrower than a MESA.

bwana /'bwɑ:nə/ *noun* L19 **Kiswahili.** In East Africa: master, sir.

■ Frequently used, particularly in colonial times, as a term of respectful address by a Black person to a White man.

c., ca. abbreviations of CIRCA.

caba /kə'bɑː/ *noun* (also **cabas** /kə'bɑːs/) M19 **French** (*cabas* basket, pannier). A small satchel or handbag. Chiefly *United States*.

cabaia variant of KEBAYA.

cabala variant of CABBALA.

caballada /kabə'ljɑːdə/ *noun* **M19 Spanish** (from *caballo* horse). A drove of horses or mules.

■ United States; earlier in the form CAVAYARD.

caballero /kabə'ljɛːrəʊ/ *noun* plural **caballeros** M19 **Spanish** (= French *chevalier*, Italian *cavaliere*). A Spanish gentleman.

cabana /kə'bɑːnə/ *noun* (also **cabaña** /kə 'bɑːnjə/) L19 **Spanish** (*cabaña* from late Latin *capanna*, *cavana* cabin). A cabin; *specifically* a shelter at a beach or swimming pool. Chiefly *United States*.

1957 F. Richards *Practise to Deceive* He asked why Lane had gone into the bath-house cabaña.

cabane /kə'bɑːn/ *noun* **M19 French**. **1** M19 A hut, a cabin. *French Canadian*. **2** E20 A pyramidal structure supporting the wings of an aircraft.

cabaret /'kabəreɪ/; *in sense 1 also foreign* /kabarɛ/ (*plural same*) *noun* **M17 Old and Modern French** (originally Walloon and Picard, from Middle Dutch variant of *camaret*, *cambret* from Old Picard *camberet* little room). **1** M17 A public house in France etc. **2** E20 An entertainment provided in a restaurant etc. while customers are at table; a restaurant, nightclub, etc., providing such entertainment.

cabas variant of CABA.

cabbala /kə'bɑːlə/, /'kabələ/ *noun* (also **cabala**, **kabbala**, and (in sense 1) with initial capital) E16 **Medieval Latin** (*cab(b)ala* from rabbinical Hebrew *qabbālāh* tradition, from *qibbēl* to receive, accept). **1** E16 The esoteric and mystical Jewish tradition, first transmitted orally, of which the Zohar (thirteenth century) is the basic text. **2** *generally* **a** M–L17 (An) oral tradition. **b** M17 (An) esoteric doctrine; (a) mystic interpretation; occult lore.

cabildo /ka'bildo/, /kə'bɪldəʊ/ *noun* plural **cabildos** /ka'bildos/, /kə'bɪldəʊz/ E19 **Spanish** (from late Latin *capitulum* chapter-house). In Spain and Spanish-speaking countries: a town hall or town council.

cabob variant of KEBAB.

cabochon /'kabəʃɒn/ *adjective & noun* **M16 Old and Modern French** (diminutive of *caboche*, Picard variant of Old French *caboce* head, of unknown origin). (A gem) polished but not faceted.

■ Also in the phrase EN CABOÇHON.

cabotage /'kabətɑːʒ/, /'kabətɪdʒ/ *noun* M19 **French** (from *caboter* to coast along (a shore), perhaps ultimately from Spanish *cabo* cape, promontory). **1** M19 Coastal trade. **2** M20 The reservation to a country of (especially air) traffic operation within its territory.

cabotin /kabɔtɛ̃/ *noun* (feminine **cabotine** /kabɔtin/) plural pronounced same E20 **French** (= strolling player, perhaps from as preceding from resemblance to vessels travelling from port to port). A third-rate or low-class actor.

cabriole /'kabrɪəʊl/, *foreign* /kabrijɔl/ (*plural same*) *noun* L18 **French** (from *cabrioler*, earlier *caprioler*, from Italian *capriolare* to leap; cf. CAPRIOLE). **1** L18 A springing dance step in which one leg is extended and the other brought up to it. **2** L18 *History* More fully *cabriole chair*. A kind of small armchair. **3** L18 A CABRIOLET sense 1. Chiefly *historical*. **4** L19 A kind of curved leg characteristic of Chippendale and Queen Anne furniture.

cabriolet /'kabrɪəleɪ/ *noun* **M18 French** (from as preceding). **1** M18 A light two-wheeled hooded one-horse chaise. Chiefly *historical*. **2** L18 A bonnet or hat shaped like a cabriolet. **3** E20 A motor car with a folding top.

cache /kaʃ/ *noun & verb* L18 **French** (from *cacher* to hide). **A** *noun* **1** L18 A hiding place for goods, provisions, ammunition, treasure, etc. **2** M19 A hidden store of provisions etc. **3** M20 An auxiliary computer memory from which high-speed retrieval is possible. Also *cache memory*. **B** *transitive verb* E19 Place or store in a cache.

B 1986 *Personal Computer World* Window images are normally cached in a form to allow fast screen redraw.

cache-peigne /kaʃpɛɲ/ *noun* plural pronounced same L19 **French** (from *cacher* to hide + *peigne* comb). A bow or other trimming for a hat, usually worn at the back.

cache-pot /kaʃpo/ (*plural same*), /'kaʃpɒt/ *noun* L19 **French** (from *cacher* to hide + *pot* pot). An ornamental holder for a flower-pot.

cache-sexe /kaʃsɛks/ (*plural same*), /'kaʃsɛks/ *noun* E20 **French** (from *cacher* to hide + *sexe* sex). A covering for the genitals.

cachet /'kaʃeɪ/ *noun* E17 **French** (from *cacher* (in sense 'press', represented now in *écacher* to crush) from Proto-Romance alteration of Latin *coactare* to constrain). **1** E17 A seal for letters, documents, etc. Now *rare* or *obsolete*. **2** M19 A characteristic or distinguishing mark; a characteristic feature or quality conferring prestige or distinction; high status. **3** L19 A small digestible case enclosing a dose of medicine.

2 1995 *Times* Suddenly perfume is losing its luxury cachet and becoming an everyday purchase—and buyers are no longer showing brand loyalty.

cachou /'kaʃu:/, /kə'ʃu:/ *noun* L16 **French** (from Portuguese *cachu* from Malay *kacu*). **1** L16 Catechu, any of various astringent tannin-rich vegetable extracts used especially in tanning. **2** E18 A lozenge taken to sweeten the breath.

cacique /kə'si:k/ *noun* M16 **Spanish or French** (from Taino). **1** M16 A West Indian or South American Indian native chief. **2** L19 In Spain or Latin America: a political boss.

cacodemon /kakə'di:mən/ *noun* (also **cacodaemon**) L16 **Greek** (*kakodaimōn* from as *kako-* evil + *daimōn* genius). **1** L16 An evil spirit. **2** E18 A malignant or deprecated person.

cacoethes /kakəʊ'i:θi:z/ *noun* M16 **Latin** (from Greek *kakoēthes* use as noun of adjective *kakoēthes* ill-disposed, from as *kako-* evil + ETHOS). An evil habit; a passion or 'itch' for doing something inadvisable.

■ Although also formerly used of a malignant tendency in a medical sense, *cacoethes* mainly occurs in English with reference to the Latin poet Juvenal (*Satire* vii): *tenet insanabile multos / scribendi cacoethes* 'the incurable itch to write grips many'.

cadastre /kə'dastə/ *noun* L18 **French** (from Modern Provençal *cadastro* from Italian *catast(r)o* earlier *catastico* from late Greek *katastikhon* list, register, from *kata stikhon* line by line). A register of property showing the extent, value, and ownership, of land for taxation.

cadeau /kado/ *noun* plural **cadeaux** plural pronounced same L18 **French**. A gift.

cadenza /kə'dɛnzə/ *noun* M18 **Italian**. *Music* A (sometimes improvised) flourish or passage for a solo instrument or voice, usually near the close or between the divisions of a movement; *specifically* such a passage in a concerto in which the main themes of the movement (usually the first or last) are developed.

cadet /kə'dɛt/ *noun* E17 **French** (earlier *capdet* from Gascon dialect (= Provençal *capdel*) from Proto-Romance diminutive of Latin *caput* head). **1** E17 A younger son or brother; also occasionally (a member of) a younger branch of a family. **b** M17 *The* youngest son or brother. **2** M17 *History* A gentleman who entered the army without a commission, to learn the profession. **3** L18 A student in a naval, military, or air force college. **4** M19 A young man learning sheep-farming. *New Zealand*. **5** L19 A member of a corps receiving elementary military or police training.

cadi /'kɑ:di/, /'keɪdi/ *noun* (also **kadi**, **qadi**) L16 **Arabic** ((*al-*)*ḳāḍī*). A civil judge in a Muslim country.

cadre /'kɑ:də/, /'kɑ:dr(ə)/, /'kadri/ *noun* M19 **French** (from Italian *quadro* from Latin *quadrus* square). **1** M19 A frame, a framework; a plan. *rare*. **2** M19 *Military* **a** A permanent establishment of trained personnel forming a nucleus for expansion at need. **b** M19 (A list of) the complement of the officers of a regiment etc. **3** M20 (A member of) a group of workers acting to promote the aims and interests of the Communist Party. **b** M20 In the People's Republic of China: an office-holder in a Party, governmental, or military organization.

caduceus /kə'dju:sɪəs/ *noun* plural **caducei** /kə'dju:sɪʌɪ/ L16 **Latin** (*caduceus*, *caduceum* from Doric Greek *karuk(e)ion* = Attic *kērukeion* neuter adjective used as noun, from *kērux* herald). *Classical History* A Greek or Roman herald's wand; *specifically* the wand carried by the messenger-god Hermes or Mercury, usually represented with two serpents twined round it.

caesura /sɪ'zjʊərə/ *noun* M16 **Latin** (*caesura*, from *caes-* past participial stem of *caedere* to cut). **1** M16 *Prosody* A break or pause between words within a metrical foot in classical prosody or near the middle of a line in English etc. prosody. **2** L16 *generally* A break, a stop, an interruption.

cafard /ka'fɑ:/, *foreign* /kafar/ *noun* M16 **French** (= cockroach, hypocrite, probably from late Latin *caphardum*). **1** M16–M17 A hypocrite. **2** E20 Melancholia.

café /'kafeɪ/, /'kafi/; *also jocular or slang* /kaf/, /keɪf/ *noun* (also **cafe** and (reflecting slang pronunciation) **caf(f)**) E19 **French** (= coffee (house)). A coffee-house; a teashop; an informal restaurant; a bar (*United States*).

■ Both the 'coffee' and the 'coffee-house' senses of the French occur in various phrases used in English (see entries below).

café au lait /kafe o lɛ/ *noun & adjective phrase* M18 **French** (= coffee with milk). **A** *noun phrase* M18 Coffee with milk, white coffee. **B** *adjective phrase* E20 Of the light brown colour of this.

café chantant /kafe ʃɑ̃tɑ̃/ *noun phrase* plural **cafés chantants** (pronounced same) M19 **French** (literally, 'singing café'). A café with live musical entertainment.

café complet /kafe kɔ̃plɛ/ *noun phrase* plural **cafés complets** (pronounced same) M20 **French** (literally, 'complete coffee'). A light breakfast including coffee and usually croissants. Cf. THÉ COMPLET.

café noir /kafe nwar/ *noun phrase* M19 **French** (= black coffee). Coffee without milk, black coffee.

cafeteria /kafɪ'tɪərɪə/ *noun* M19 **American Spanish** (*cafetería*, from *café* coffee). A coffee-house; a restaurant; now *especially* a self-service restaurant as part of the facilities in a workplace, institution or public building.

■ Originally United States, but apparently spread to Europe in the 1920s, when the *Glasgow Herald* (30 July 1925) observed that 'Cafeterias, although a commonplace in America, are just beginning to have a hold in Paris.'

cafetière /kaftjɛr/ *noun* plural pronounced same M19 **French** (from *café* coffee). A coffee-pot; a coffee-making machine; a coffee-percolator.

1996 *Times Magazine* Every household member believes that he or she is the only person who ever . . . deals with coffee-grounds in the cafetière . . . .

cafila /'kɑ:fɪlə/ *noun* L16 **Arabic** (*ḳāfila*). A company of travellers in the Middle East, a caravan.

■ *Coffle*, an eighteenth-century derivation from *ḳāfila*, refers specifically to a line of slaves or animals fastened together.

caftan /'kaftan/, /kaf'tɑ:n/ *noun* (also **kaftan**) L16 **Turkish** (*kaftan* from Persian *ḳaftān*, partly through French *cafetan*). **1** L16 An Eastern man's long tunic with a waist girdle. **2** M20 A long loose dress; a loose-fitting shirt.

2 1996 *Times* Quant simply was not a kaftan sort of person, nor was she a glitzy shoulder-padded woman either.

cagnotte /kaɲɔt/ *noun* L19 **French**. Money reserved from the stakes for the bank at certain gambling games.

cagoule /kə'gu:l/ *noun* (also **kagoule**) M20 **French** (literally, 'cowl'). A hooded thin waterproof garment pulled on over the head.

caique /kʌɪ'i:k/, /keɪ'i:k/ *noun* E17 **French** (*caïque* from Italian *caicco* from Turkish *kayik*). **1** E17 A light rowing boat or skiff used on the Bosporus. **2** M17 An eastern Mediterranean sailing vessel.

caisson /'keɪs(ə)n/, /kə'su:n/ *noun* L17 **French** (= large chest, from Italian *cassone* with assimilation to *caisse* case). **1** L17 A large watertight chamber open at the bottom, from which the water is kept out by air pressure, used in laying foundations under water. **b** M19 A floating vessel used as a dock gate. **2** E18 An ammunition chest; an ammunition wagon.

calabrese /'kaləbri:s/, *noun* M20 **Italian** (= Calabrian). A variety of usually green sprouting broccoli.

calamari /kalə'mɑ:ri/ *noun plural* L20 **Italian** (plural of *calamaro* squid). Squid, especially as used in cooking.

calando /kə'landəʊ/, *foreign* /ka'lando/ *adverb* E19 **Italian** (= slackening). *Music* Gradually decreasing in speed and volume.

caldarium /kal'dɛ:rɪum/ *noun* plural **caldaria** /kal'dɛ:rɪə/ M18 **Latin**. *History* A (Roman) hot bath or bathroom.

caldera /kal'dɛ:rə/, /kal'dɪərə/ *noun* L17 **Spanish** (from late Latin *caldaria* pot for boiling). A volcanic crater of great size;

specifically one whose breadth greatly exceeds that of the vent(s) within it.

calembour /kalɑ̃bur/ *noun* (also **calembourg** /kalɑ̃bur/ plural pronounced same E19 **French**. A pun.

calinda /kəˈlɪndə/ *noun* M18 **American Spanish**. A Black American dance found in Latin America and the southern United States.

calliope /kəˈlʌɪəpi/ *noun* M19 **Greek** (*Kalliopē* (literally, 'beautiful-voiced') the Muse of epic poetry). A set of steam-whistles producing musical notes, played by a keyboard like that of an organ. Also *steam calliope*. *North American*.

callus /ˈkaləs/ *noun & verb* M16 **Latin** (more commonly *callum*). **A** *noun* **1** M16 A thickened and hardened part of the skin or soft tissue, a callosity. **2** L17 *Medicine* The bony healing tissue which forms around the ends of broken bone. **3** L19 *Botany* A hard formation of tissue; new tissue formed over a wound. **B** *verb intransitive* Form a callus (*over*).

calotte /kəˈlɒt/ *noun* M17 **French** (perhaps related to *cale* caul). **1** M17 A skullcap, especially as worn by Roman Catholic priests. **2** L19 A snowcap, an ice-cap.

caloyer /ˈkalɔɪə/, *foreign* /kaloje/ (*plural same noun* L16 **French** (from Italian *caloiero* from ecclesiastical Greek *kalogēros*, from *kalos* beautiful + *gērōs* old age). A Greek Orthodox monk.

calque /kalk/ *noun & verb* M20 **French** (= copy, tracing, from *calquer* to trace, from Italian *calcare* from Latin *calcare* to tread). **A** *noun* M20 A loan-translation (*of*, *on*). **B** *transitive verb* M20 Form as a calque. Usually in *passive* (followed by *on*).

■ A modern example of a calque is 'that goes without saying', which is calqued on French *cela va sans dire*.

1957 G. V. Smithers *Kyng Alisaunder Fecche mood* . . . is evidently a calque on OF. *porter ire*, as in *Chanson de Roland*.

calumet /ˈkaljʊmɛt/ *noun* L17 **French** (dialectal variant of *chalumeau* from late Latin *calamellus* diminutive of *calamus* reed). An American Indian tobacco-pipe with a clay bowl and reed stem, smoked especially as a sign of peace; *transferred* and *figurative* a symbol of peace.

calvados /ˈkalvədɒs/ *noun* E20 **French** (*Calvados*, a department in Normandy, France). Apple brandy, traditionally made in the Calvados region; a drink of this.

calyx /ˈkalɪks/, /ˈkelɪks/ *noun* plural **calyces** /ˈkalɪsiːz/, **calyxes** L17 **Latin** (*calyx*, *-yc-* from Greek *kalux* shell, husk, pod, from base of *kaluptein* to hide). *Botany* A whorl of leaves (sepals), forming the outer case of a bud or the envelope of a flower.

calzone /kalˈtsəʊni/ *noun* L20 **Italian** (literally, 'trousers'). In Italian cookery, pizza dough with a stuffing of savoury ingredients.

camaieu /kamajø/ *noun* plural pronounced same L16 **French**. **1** L16–L18 A cameo. **2** E18 A method of monochrome painting.

camaraderie /kaməˈrɑːd(ə)ri/, /kaməˈrɑːd(ə)riː/ *noun* M19 **French** (from *camarade* comrade). The mutual trust and sociability of comrades.

1995 *Spectator* Banter goes on across tables. The camaraderie is palpable and so is the air. Everybody smokes.

camarilla /kaməˈrɪlə/, /kaməˈrɪljə/ *noun* M19 **Spanish** (diminutive of *camara* chamber). A cabal, a clique.

camaron /kaməˈrəʊn/, /ˈkamər(ə)n/ *noun* L19 **Spanish** (*camarón* shrimp). A freshwater shrimp or prawn resembling a crayfish.

cambré /kɑ̃bre/ *adjective* E20 **French** (past participle of *cambrer* to camber, from Old French *cambre* from dialect variant of *chambre* arched, from Latin *camur* curved inwards). Curved, arched; *Ballet* (of the body) bent from the waist sideways or backwards.

cameo /ˈkamɪəʊ/ *noun* plural **cameos** LME **Old French** (*came(h)u*, *camahieu* (modern CAMAIEU): cf. medieval Latin *camahutus* etc. Later influenced by Italian *cam(m)eo*, corresponding to medieval Latin *cammaeus*). **1** LME A small piece of relief-carving in onyx, agate, etc., usually with colour-layers, the lower of which serves as ground; a relief design of similar form. **2** M19 A short literary sketch or acted scene; (more fully *cameo part*) a small character part in a play, film, etc.

2 1950 E. Crispin *Frequent Hearses* A cameo part . . . the film equivalent of a bit part on the stage.

camera lucida /ˌkam(ə)rə ˈluːsɪdə/ *noun phrase* plural **camera lucidas** M18 **Latin** (= bright chamber). An instrument by which the rays of light from an object are reflected by a prism and produce an image on paper placed beneath the instrument, traceable with a pencil.

camera obscura /ˌkam(ə)rə ɒbsˈkjʊərə/ *noun phrase* plural **camera obscuras** E18 **Latin** (= dark chamber). A darkened box or enclosure with an aperture for projecting an image of external objects on a screen placed at the focus of the lens; a building containing such a box or enclosure.

camisole /ˈkamɪsəʊl/ *noun* E19 **French** (from Italian *camiciola* or Spanish *camisola*, diminutive of (respectively) *camicia*, *camisa* from late Latin *camisia*). **1** E19 *History* A type of sleeved short jacket worn by men. **2** M19 *History* A short loose jacket worn by women when dressed in négligé. **3** M19 A woman's underbodice, usually straight with shoulder-straps and embroidered or otherwise ornamentally trimmed.

Camorra /kəˈmɔːrə/, /kəˈmɒrə/ *noun* (also **camorra**) M19 **Italian** (perhaps from Spanish *camorra* dispute, quarrel). A secret society akin to the Mafia operating in the Neapolitan district; *generally* any organized body engaged in extortion or other dishonest activities.

camouflage /ˈkaməflɑːʒ/ *noun and verb* E20 **French** (from *camoufler* (thieves' slang) to cover up, from Italian *camuffare* disguise, deceive, perhaps associated with French *camouflet* whiff of smoke in the face). **A** *noun* E20 The disguising or concealment of guns, ships, aircraft, etc., by obscuring with splashes of various colours, foliage, netting, smokescreens, etc.; the disguise so used; *generally* any means of disguise or evasion. **B** *verb transitive* E20 Conceal by camouflage.

campagna /kamˈpɑːnjə/, *foreign* /kam ˈpaɲɲa/ *noun* (also **campa(g)nia**) L16 **Italian** (from late Latin *campania*). Open country.

■ Now rare except with reference to the Campagna di Roma. In the mid seventeenth century the word was also briefly used with the sense of 'military campaign'.

1996 *Country Life* Its long, curving terrace looks over the once heavily wooded Warwickshire plain . . . , as if it were an English version of the Roman *campagna*.

campana /kamˈpɑːnə/ *noun* E17 **Late Latin** (*campana* bell). **1** E17 A bell; a bell-shaped flower. Now *rare* or *obsolete*. **2** E19 A bell-shaped vase.

campanile /kampəˈniːli/ *noun* M17 **Italian** (from *campana* bell + *-ile*). A (usually lofty and detached) bell-tower, especially in Italy.

campesino /kampeˈsino/, /kampəˈsiːnəʊ/ *noun* plural **campesinos** /kampeˈsinos/, /kampəˈsiːnəʊz/ M20 **Spanish**. In Spain and Spanish-speaking countries: a peasant farmer.

campo /ˈkampəʊ/ *noun* plural **campos** M19 **American Spanish or Portuguese** (= field, open country, from Latin *campus*). In South America (especially Brazil): a grass plain with occasional stunted trees; a savannah.

■ Frequently in plural.

campus /ˈkampəs/ *noun* L18 **Latin**. The grounds and buildings of a college, university, etc., especially where forming a distinct area; a separate part of a university; university or college life.

■ Originally used of the grounds of Princeton University, New Jersey, then of similar open spaces in other United States universities, and now worldwide.

canaille /kanaj/ *noun* L16 **French** (from Italian *canaglia*, literally, 'pack of dogs', from *cane* dog). *The* rabble, *the* populace.

canapé /ˈkanəpeɪ/, /ˈkanəpi/ *noun* L19 **French**. **1** L19 A piece of bread, toast, etc., with a small savoury on top. **2** L19 A sofa, a settee.

■ In sense 2 the history of the Romance word *canapé* is closely linked to that of English *canopy*, both of them deriving from medieval Latin *canopeum* baldachin, a variant of classical Latin *conopeum* bed with net curtains, from Greek *kōnōpeion* Egyptian bed with mosquito curtains, from *kōnōps* mosquito. In English the sense of *canopy* has adhered to the 'curtain' sense of the Latin, while *canapé* in the Romance languages (Spanish and Portuguese as well as French) has retained the primary sense of 'couch, sofa'. By the late eighteenth century sense 1, now by far the more familiar in English, had evolved in French.

canard /kəˈnɑːd/, /kanɑd/ *noun* M19 **French** (literally, 'duck'). **1** M19 A false report, a hoax. **2** E20 An extra surface attached to an aircraft, hydrofoil, etc., for stability or control. Also, an aircraft fitted with this.

1 1995 *New Scientist* This is a common misunderstanding and is a canard on a par with the belief that long ago insurance companies which provided fire engines would not put out fires unless the building displayed their company's mark.

canasta /kə'nastə/ *noun* M20 **Spanish** (= basket, ultimately from Latin *canistrum* bread (or flower) basket). A two-pack card-game of the rummy family and of Uruguayan origin, usually played by four in two partnerships; a meld of seven or more cards in this game.

cancan /'kankan/ *noun* M19 **French** (reduplication of *canard* duck). A lively dance of French origin, originally a form of quadrille, now performed by a woman and involving high kicks, usually while holding up the front of the skirts.

cancellandum /kansə'landəm/ *noun* plural **cancellanda** /kansə'landə/ E20 **Latin** (neuter gerundive of *cancellare* to cancel). *Printing* A leaf for which another is substituted. In full *cancellandum leaf*. Cf. next.

cancellans /'kanselanz/ *noun & adjective* E20 **Latin** (present participle of *cancellare* to cancel). *Printing* **A** *noun* E20 A leaf which replaces another. Cf. preceding. **B** *adjective* M20 Designating a leaf, sheet, fold, etc., which replaces another, or a slip which cancels text.

cancrizans /'kaŋkrɪzanz/ *adjective, adverb, & noun* L18 **Medieval Latin** (present participle of *cancrizare* to walk backwards, from Latin *cancer* crab). *Music* (Designating, pertaining to, in the manner of) a canon in which the theme or subject is repeated backwards in the second part.

candelabrum /kandɪ'lɑːbrəm/, /kandɪ'leɪbrəm/ *noun* plural **candelabra** /kandɪ'lɑːbrə/, **candelabrums** (also **candelabra**, plural same, **candelabras**) E19 **Latin** (from *candela* candle). A large usually branched ornamental candlestick or lamp-holder carrying several lights.

candida /'kandɪdə/ *noun* (also *Candida*) M20 **Modern Latin** (feminine of Latin *candidus* white). **1** M20 A yeastlike fungus of the genus *Candida*, especially *C. albicans*. **2** L20 *Medicine* and *Veterinary Medicine* Infection with candida, especially one causing vaginal or oral thrush; candidiasis.

1990 *News of the World* Certain food's OK for the Candida, but bad for the liver.

canephora /kə'nɛf(ə)rə/, /kə'niːf(ə)rə/ *noun* plural **canephorae** /kə'nɛf(ə)riː/ E17 **Latin** (*canephora* feminine, from Greek *kanēphoros*, from *kaneon* basket + *-phoros* carrying). In ancient Greece, each of the maidens who carried on their heads baskets bearing sacred things used at certain feasts; in *Architecture*, a caryatid representing or resembling such a maiden.

cannelloni /kanə'ləʊni/ *noun plural* M20 **Italian** (augmentative plural of *cannello* stalk). Rolls of pasta filled with meat or cheese and seasonings; an Italian dish consisting largely of this and usually a sauce.

cannelure /'kan(ə)ljʊə/ *noun* M18 **French** (from *canneler* to groove, flute, from *canne* reed). A groove or fluting, especially around a bullet etc.

cañon variant of CANYON.

cantabile /kan'tɑːbɪli/ *adverb, adjective, & noun* E18 **Italian** (= that can be sung). *Music* **A** *adverb & adjective* E18 In a smooth flowing style, as if singing. **B** *noun* M18 Cantabile style; a piece or movement in this style.

cantaloup /'kantəluːp/ *noun* (also **cantaloupe**) L18 **French**. A small round ribbed variety of melon, with orange flesh. Also called *rock melon*.

■ The French name is taken from *Cantaluppi*, the name of the place near Rome, where, on its introduction from Armenia, the melon was first grown in Europe.

cantata /kan'tɑːtə/ *noun* E18 **Italian** ((sc. *aria* air), feminine past participle of *cantare* to sing). *Music* An extended composition for one or more voices with instrumental accompaniment; original, a narrative recitative or sequence of recitatives and ariettas, for solo voice; later, a choral work resembling a short oratorio.

cantatrice /'kantətriːs/ *noun* E19 **French and Italian** (from Latin *cantatrix*). A female professional singer.

cante hondo /ˌkante 'xondo/, /ˌkanteɪ 'hɒndəʊ/ *noun phrase* (also **cante jondo**) M20 **Spanish** (= deep song). Flamenco singing, songs, of a predominantly mournful or tragic character.

canti fermi plural of CANTO FERMO.

cantilena /kantɪ'leɪnə/, /kantɪ'liːnə/ *noun* M18 **Italian** (or Latin *cantilena*). *Music* A simple or sustained vocal melody, or an instrumental passage performed in a smooth lyrical style. Also, the (highest) melodic part in a composition.

cantina /kan'tiːnə/ *noun* L19 **Spanish and Italian**. In Spain, Spanish-speaking countries, and the south-western United States: a bar-room, a saloon; in Italy: a wine-shop.

canto /'kantəʊ/ *noun* plural **cantos** L16 **Italian** (literally, 'song', from Latin CANTUS). **1** L16 Each of the divisions of a long poem. **2** E17–E18 A song, a ballad. **3** E18 *Music* The upper part or melody in a composition.

canto fermo /ˌkantəʊ ˈfəːməʊ/ *noun phrase* plural **canti fermi** /ˌkanti ˈfəːmi/ L16 **Italian** (translating medieval Latin CANTUS FIRMUS). *Music* Originally, an unadorned melody, plainsong; later *specifically* a melody used as a basis for counterpoint. Now also, an existing melody, taken as a basis for a new polyphonic composition.

canton /ˈkantən/, *in sense 1 also* /kanˈtɒn/ *noun* E16 **Old and Modern French** (from Provençal from oblique case of Proto-Romance variant of Latin *cant(h)us*). A subdivision of a country; a small district; *specifically* one of the several States which form the Swiss confederation.

cantor /ˈkantɔː/, /ˈkantə/ *noun* M16 **Latin** (= singer, from *canere* to chant). **1** M16 A precentor in a church. **2** L19 An official who sings liturgical music and leads prayer in a synagogue, a HAZZAN.

cantoris /kanˈtɔːrɪs/ *adjective* M17 **Latin** (genitive of CANTOR). Of or pertaining to the north side of the choir of a church where the precentor usually sits; *Music* to be sung by the cantorial side in antiphonal singing (cf. DECANI).

cantus /ˈkantəs/ *noun* plural **cantus** /ˈkantuːs/, /ˈkantəs/ L16 **Latin** (= song). *Early Music* A song, a melody, especially in church music. Also, the highest voice in a polyphonic song.

cantus firmus /ˌkantəs ˈfəːməs/ *noun phrase* plural **cantus firmi** /ˈfəːmʌɪ/ M19 **Medieval Latin** (= firm song). *Music* CANTO FERMO.

canyon /ˈkanjən/ *noun* (also **cañon**) M19 **Spanish** (*cañón* tube, pipe, gun barrel, etc. augmentative of *caña* from Latin *canna* reed). A deep gorge (especially in the United States or Mexico), frequently with a stream at its bottom.

canzona /kanˈtsəʊnə/ *noun* L19 **Italian** (from next). (A musical setting of the words of) a canzone; an instrumental piece resembling a madrigal in character.

canzone /kanˈtsəʊni/ *noun* plural **canzoni** /kanˈtsəʊni/ L16 **Italian** (= song (corresponding to Old and Modern French *chanson*) from Latin *cantio(n-)* singing, from *cant-* past participle of *canere* to sing). An Italian or Provençal song or ballad; a style of lyric resembling a madrigal.

caoine /ˈkiːnə/ *noun* E18 **Irish** (from *caoinim* I wail). An Irish funeral song accompanied by wailing in lamentation of the dead.

caoutchouc /ˈkaʊtʃʊk/ *noun & adjective* L18 **French** (from obsolete Spanish *cauchuc* from Quechua *kauchuk*). (Of) unvulcanized natural rubber.

capable de tout /kapabl də tu/ *adjective phrase* L19 **French**. Capable of anything; without scruple or restraint.

cap-à-pie /kapəˈpiː/ *adverb* E16 **Old French** (*cap a pie* (Modern French *de pied en cap*)). From head to foot, fully (armed, ready, etc.). Now *archaic*.

capataz /kapaˈtaθ/, /kapaˈtas/ *noun* plural **capataces** /kapaˈtaθes/, /kapaˈtases/ E19 **Spanish** (irregular from Latin *caput* head). In Spain or Spanish-speaking America: an overseer, a superintendent, a boss.

capeador /ˌkapɪəˈdɔː/ *noun* E20 **Spanish** (from *capear* to trick a bull with a cape, from *capa* cloak). *Bullfighting* A person who aids a bullfighter by distracting the bull with his cloak.

capitonné /kapɪtɔne/ *adjective* L19 **French** (past participle of *capitonner* to upholster, quilt). Designating or characterized by a style of upholstery or embroidery in which the material is drawn in at intervals to present a quilted appearance.

capo /ˈkapəʊ/ *noun* plural **capos** M20 **Italian** (from Latin *caput* head). The head of a crime syndicate or one of its branches. Chiefly *United States*.

capo abbreviated form of CAPOTASTO.

capot /kəˈpɒt/ *noun & verb* M17 **French** (perhaps from *capoter* dialectal variant of *chapoter* to castrate). *Piquet* **A** *noun* M17 The winning of all the tricks by one player; a score awarded for this. **B** *transitive verb* M17 Win all the tricks from.

■ Formerly stressed on the first syllable. *Capot* is the source of the German *kaputt*, from which the dated English slang KAPUT is taken.

capot /ˈkapəʊ/, /kəˈpɒt/; *foreign* /kapo/ (*plural same*) *noun* L17 **French** (masculine form of CAPOTE). A long hooded cloak worn by soldiers, travellers, etc.

capotasto /kapəʊˈtastəʊ/ *noun* plural **capotastos** (also **capo tasto**) L19 **Italian** (literally, 'head stop': cf. TASTO). *Music* A movable bar attached to the finger-board of a stringed instrument to make possible the simultaneous adjustment of the pitch of all the strings.

■ Generally known as a *capo*.

capote /kə'pəʊt/ *noun* E19 **French** (diminutive of *cape* cape, cloak). **1 a** E19 A long hooded cloak worn by soldiers, travellers, etc. **b** M19 A long mantle worn by women. **2** E19 A bonnet with a soft crown and stiff projecting brim.

capouch variant of CAPUCHE.

cappuccino /kapʊ'tʃi:nəʊ/ *noun* plural **cappuccinos** M20 **Italian**. (A cup of) coffee with milk, especially made with espresso coffee and topped with white foam.

capriccio /kə'prɪtʃɪəʊ/ *noun* plural **capriccios** E17 **Italian**. **1** E17–E19 A CAPRICE, a whim. **2** M17–M19 A sudden movement; a trick, a prank, a caper. **3** L17 A thing or work of lively fancy in art etc.; *especially* a lively usually short musical composition, more or less free in form.

capriccioso /kəprɪtʃɪ'əʊsəʊ/ *adverb* M18 **Italian**. *Music* (A direction:) in a free and impulsive style.

caprice /kə'pri:s/ *noun* M17 **French** (from Italian *capriccio*, literally, 'head with the hair standing on end', (hence) horror; later (by association with *capra* goat) sudden start, from *capo* head + *riccio* hedgehog, ultimately from Latin *(h)ericius* urchin). **1** M17 An unaccountable change of mind or conduct; a whim; a freakish fancy. **b** M17 Inclination or disposition to such changes etc.; capriciousness. **2** E18 A CAPRICCIO.

capriole /'kaprɪəʊl/ *noun & verb* L16 **French** ((now *cabriole*), from Italian *capriola*, from *capriolare* to leap, from *capriolo* roebuck, from Latin *capreolus* diminutive of *caper* goat). **A** *noun* **1** L16 A leap or caper, especially as made in dancing (cf. CABRIOLE 1). **2** *Equestrianism* L16 A trained horse's horizontal leap with the hind legs kicking vigorously. **B** *intransitive verb* L16 Perform a capriole; skip, leap, caper.

capuche /kə'pu:ʃ/ *noun* (also **capouch**) L16 **French** ((now *capuce*) from Italian *cappuccio*). The hood of a cloak, *especially* that of a Capuchin.

caput mortuum /ˌkapət 'mɔ:tu:əm/ *noun phrase* M17 **Latin** (= dead head). **1** A death's head, a skull. Only in M17. **2** M17 *Alchemy* The residue remaining after distillation or sublimation. **3** E18 Worthless residue.

carabinero /ˌkarabi'nero/, /ˌkarəbɪ'nɛ:rəʊ/ *noun* plural **carabineros** /ˌkarabi'neros/, /ˌkarabɪ'nɛ:rəʊz/ M19 **Spanish** (literally, 'carabineer'). A (Spanish) customs or revenue officer; a (Spanish) frontier guard.

carabiniere /ˌkarabi'njere/, /ˌkarəbɪ'njɛ:ri/ *noun* plural **carabinieri** /ˌkarabɪ'njeri/ M19 **Italian** (literally, 'carabineer'). An Italian soldier in a corps serving as a police force.

1995 *Times* Away from skiing, Tomba is facing possible expulsion from the Italian *carabinieri* after a photographer, who had sold nude photographs of him to a magazine, alleged that the Italian had thrown a heavy glass trophy at him after a World Cup race on Sunday.

caracole /'karəkəʊl/ *noun* (also **caracol** /'karəkɒl/) E17 **French** (*caracol(e)* snail's shell, spiral). *Equestrianism* E17 A half-turn or wheel to the right or left by a horse or rider. Formerly also, a series of such turns alternately to right and left.

■ The word was also formerly used in English for short periods in senses deriving directly from its basic French meanings: 'a spiral shell' (only E17) and in architectural contexts 'a helical staircase' (E18).

caracul variant of KARAKUL.

carafe /kə'raf/, /kə'rɑ:f/ *noun* L18 **French** (from Italian *caraffa*, of unknown origin). A glass bottle for water or wine at a table, in a bedroom, etc.

caramba /kə'rambə/, *foreign* /ka'ramba/ *interjection* M19 **Spanish**. Expressive of surprise or dismay.

carambole /'kar(ə)mbəʊl/ *noun & intransitive verb* L18 **Spanish** (*carambola* (whence French *carambole* red ball in billiards), apparently from *bola* ball). (Make) a cannon in billiards.

cara sposa /ˌkɑ:ra 'spo:za/ *noun phrase* plural **care spose** /ˌkɑ:re 'spo:ze/ L18 **Italian**. (One's) dear wife; a devoted wife. Cf. CARO SPOSO.

caravanserai /karə'vansərʌɪ/, /karə'vansəri/ *noun* (also **caravansary**, **caravansery**, and other variants) L16 **Persian** (*kārwānsarāy*, from *kārvān* (desert) caravan + SERAI). An Eastern inn with a large inner court where caravans rest.

carcinoma /kɑ:sɪ'nəʊmə/ *noun* plural **carcinomas**, **carcinomata** /kɑ:sɪ-

'nəʊmətə/ E18 **Latin** (from Greek *karkinōma* from *karkinos crab* + suffix *-oma*). *Medicine* A cancer; now *specifically* a malignant tumour of epithelial origin.

care spose plural of CARA SPOSA.

caret /'karət/ *noun* L17 **Latin** (3rd person singular present indicative of *carere* to be without, lack). A mark (strictly ^) placed below a line of writing or printing, in a margin, etc., to show the place of an omission.

carezza variant of KAREZZA.

cargador /kɑːgə'dɔː/ *noun* plural **cargadores** /kɑːgə'dɔːrɪz/ E19 **Spanish** (from *cargo* cargo). In Spanish-speaking parts of America: a porter.

caries /'kɛːriːz/ *noun* plural same L16 **Latin**. Decay of a tooth or bone.

carillon /'karɪljən/, /'karɪlɒn/, /kə'rɪljən/ *noun* L18 **French** (alteration of Old French *car(e)ignon*, *quarregnon*, from Proto-Romance = peal of four bells). **1** L18 A set of bells sounded either from a keyboard or mechanically. **2** L18 A tune played on such bells. **3** E19 A musical instrument or part of an organ designed to imitate a peal of bells.

carioca /karɪ'əʊkə/ *noun* M19 **Portuguese**. **1** M19 A native of Rio de Janeiro, Brazil. **2** M20 A Brazilian dance resembling a samba; a piece of music for this dance.

cariole variant of CARRIOLE.

cari sposi plural of CARO SPOSO.

carissima /ka'rissima/ *adjective* M19 **Italian** (superlative of *cara* dear). A term of endearment to a woman: dearest, darling.

carmagnole /karmaɲɔl/ *noun* plural pronounced same L18 **French**. **1** L18 A popular song and round dance of the French Revolutionary period. **2** L18 A French revolutionary soldier; *transferred* an author of mischief.

■ In French, originally a style of jacket popular during the French Revolution, the name probably ultimately deriving from Carmagnola, a town in Piedmont.

carnet /'kɑːneɪ/, *foreign* /karnɛ/ (*plural same*) *noun* E19 **French**. **1** E19 A notebook *rare*. **2** E20 A permit; *specifically* **(a)** one allowing a motorist to drive across a frontier; **(b)** one allowing use of some campsites.

caro sposo /'kɑːro 'spoːzo/ *noun phrase* plural **cari sposi** /ˌkɑːri 'spoːzi/ L18 **Italian**. (One's) dear husband; a devoted husband. Cf. CARA SPOSA.

carousel /karə'sɛl/, /karə'zɛl/ *noun* (also **carrousel**) M17 **French** (*carrousel* from Italian *carosello*, *garosello*). **1** M17 *History* A kind of tournament in which variously dressed companies of knights engaged in plays, chariot races, exercises, etc. **2** L17 A merry-go-round; a roundabout. Chiefly *North American*. **3** M20 A rotating delivery or conveyor system, *especially* one in an airport for the delivery of passengers' luggage.

carriole /'karɪəʊl/ *noun* (also **cariole**) M18 **French** (from Italian *carriuola*, diminutive of *carro* car). **1** M18 A small open carriage for one; a covered light cart. Chiefly *historical*. **2** E19 A kind of sledge used in Canada.

carrousel variant of CAROUSEL.

carte /kɑːt/ *noun* LME **French** (from Latin *c(h)arta* papyrus leaf, paper). **1** LME–M18 A charter, a document; an exposition; a chart, a diagram. **2** L15 A playing-card; in *plural*, a game of cards. *Scottish*. **3** E19 A bill of fare. Cf. À LA CARTE. **4** M19 A CARTE-DE-VISITE.

carte blanche /kɑːt 'blɑːnʃ/, *foreign* /kart blɑ̃ʃ/ *noun phrase* plural **cartes blanches** /kɑːts 'blɑːnʃ/, *foreign* /kart blɑ̃ʃ/ L17 **French** (= blank paper). **1** L17 A blank sheet of paper to be filled in as a person wishes; *figurative* full discretionary power granted. **2** E19 *Cards* In piquet and bezique, a hand containing no court-cards as dealt, and attracting a compensatory score.

■ The figurative use of sense 1 is now the one usually encountered (see quotation 1996).

1996 *Times* That is greatly to the credit of the company, which gave *carte blanche* to . . . an experienced American business academic who spent 60 days coming up with a more down-to-earth 'audit' than sceptics might have expected.

carte-de-visite /ˌkɑːtdəvɪ'ziːt/ *noun* plural **cartes-de-visite** (pronounced same) M19 **French** (= visiting-card). A small photographic portrait mounted on a card. Now *archaic* or *historical*.

carte d'identité /kart didɑ̃tite/ *noun phrase* plural **cartes d'identité** (pronounced same) E20 **French**. An identity card.

carte du pays /kart dy pei/ *noun phrase* plural **cartes du pays** (pronounced same) M18 **French** (literally, 'map of the country'). (A statement of) the state of affairs.

cartel *branch I* /ˈkɑːt(ə)l/, *branch II* /kɑːˈtɛl/ *noun* (branch I also **chartel**) M16 **French** (branch I from Italian *cartello* placard, challenge, diminutive of *carta* from Latin *c(h)arta*; branch II from German *Kartell* from French). **I 1** M16 A written challenge. In full *cartel of defiance*. Now *archaic* or *historical*. **2** L17 *History* A written agreement relating to the exchange or ransom of prisoners; an exchange or ransom of prisoners; (in full *cartel ship*) a ship commissioned for the exchange of prisoners. **3** L17 *generally* A paper or card bearing writing or printing. **II 4** L19 A combination between political parties to promote a mutual interest. **5** E20 A manufacturers' agreement or association formed to control marketing arrangements, regulate prices, etc.

cartes blanches, **cartes-de-visite**, etc. plural of CARTE BLANCHE, CARTE-DE-VISITE, etc.

cartonnage /ˈkɑːt(ə)nɪdʒ/ *noun* (also **cartonage**) M19 **French** (from *carton* cardboard (from Italian *cartone* augmentative of *carta*, from Latin *c(h)arta* paper) + *-age*). *Egyptology* A mummy-case made of tightly fitting layers of linen or papyrus glued together.

carton-pierre /kartɔ̃pjɛr/ *noun* M19 **French** (literally, 'cardboard (of) stone'). Papier mâché made to resemble stone or bronze.

cartouche /kɑːˈtuːʃ/ *noun* E17 **French** (from Italian *cartoccio* from *carta* paper). **I 1a** E17 A case for containing propellent explosive, a cartridge. *obsolete* except *historical*. **b** E17–M18 A case of wood, pasteboard, etc., for cannon-balls. **II 2a** E17 *Architecture* A scroll-shaped ornament; a tablet representing a scroll with rolled-up ends or edges, with or without an inscription. **b** L18 A painting or drawing of a scroll with rolled-up ends, with or without a text; an ornate frame in the shape of such a scroll. **3** M19 *Egyptology* An elongated oval with a straight bar at the end containing the hieroglyphic names and titles of rulers.

casbah variant of KASBAH.

cascara sagrada /kaˈskɑːrə səˌgrɑːdə/ *noun phrase* L19 **Spanish** (*cáscara sagrada*, literally, 'sacred bark'). The bark of a Californian buckthorn, *Rhamnus purshiana*; an extract of this, used as a purgative.

■ Often shortened to *cascara*.

casha variant of KASHA.

casino /kəˈsiːnəʊ/ *noun* plural **casinos** M18 **Italian** (diminutive of *casa* house, from Latin *casa* cottage). **1** M18 Originally, a public room used for social meetings; *especially* a public music or dancing saloon. Now, a building for gambling, often with other amenities. **2** M18 A summer-house (*specifically* in Italy).

■ See also CASSINO, originally a variant of *casino*.

2 1996 *Spectator* [Sir William Hamilton] took a *casino* on the beach at Posillipo for sea-bathing . . .

casque /kɑːsk/ *noun* L17 **French** (from Spanish *casco*). **1** L17 A piece of armour to cover the head; a helmet. Now *historical* or *poetical*. **2** L18 *Zoology* A helmet-like structure, as in the cassowaries and hornbills.

cassareep /ˈkasəriːp/ *noun* M19 **Caribbean**. A thick brown syrup prepared by boiling down the juice of the cassava with sugar, spices, etc.

cassata /kəˈsɑːtə/ *noun* E20 **Italian**. A Neapolitan ice-cream containing fruit and nuts.

casse /kas/ *noun* L19 **French** (from *casser* to break). Souring of certain wines, accompanied by the loss of colour and the throwing of a sediment.

casserole /ˈkasərəʊl/ *noun & verb* E18 **French** (extension of *cassole* diminutive of *casse* from Provençal *casa*, from late Latin *cattia* ladle, pan, from Greek *kuathion*, *kuatheion* diminutive of *kuathos* cup). **A** *noun* A covered heatproof vessel in which food is cooked and served (now also *casserole dish*, *pan*, etc.); (a dish of) food cooked in this. **B** *transitive verb* M20 Cook in a casserole.

cassette /kəˈsɛt/ *noun* L18 **French** (diminutive of *casse*, *caisse* case). **1** L18 A casket. Now *rare*. **2** L19 A container for transporting photographic plates; a frame or holder for an X-ray plate or film. **3** M20 A container for a spool of magnetic tape, photographic film, etc., fashioned so as to be immediately usable on insertion into equipment designed for it; (now usually) such a container together with its tape, film, etc.; a video or audio magnetic recording on such a tape etc. **4** L20 *Genetics* A block of genetic material which can be inserted or moved as a unit, *especially* one which is expressed only at one location.

cassino /kəˈsiːnəʊ/ *noun* L18 **Italian** (variant of CASINO). A two-handed card-game in which players match or combine cards exposed on the table with cards from their hands. Also, either of two high-scoring cards in this game, (*a*) *big cassino*, (now *rare*) *great cassino*, the ten of diamonds, (*b*) *little cassino*, the two of spades.

cassis /kaˈsiːs/, /ˈkasɪs/ *noun* L19 **French** (= blackcurrant, apparently from Latin *cassia*). A (frequently alcoholic) syrup made from blackcurrants and used to flavour drinks etc.

cassolette /kasəˈlɛt/ *noun* (also **cassolet**) M17 **French** (from Provençal *casoleta* diminutive of *casola*, from *casa*; cf. CASSEROLE). **1** M17 A vessel in which perfumes are burned. **2** E19 A box with a perforated cover for diffusing the odour of perfume in it. **3** E19 A small casserole dish; (a dish of) food cooked in this.

cassone /kaˈsəʊni/, *foreign* /kasˈsoːne/ *noun* plural **cassones** /kaˈsəʊniz/, **cassoni** /kasˈsoːni/ L19 **Italian** (augmentative of *cassa* chest). A large Italian coffer, especially to hold a bride's trousseau.

cassoulet /ˈkasʊleɪ/ *noun* M20 **French** (diminutive of dialect *cassolo* stew-pan, tureen). A ragout of meat and beans.

castrato /kaˈstrɑːtəʊ/ *noun* plural **castrati** /kaˈstrɑːti/ M18 **Italian** (use as noun of past participle of *castrare* to castrate). *History* An adult male singer castrated in boyhood so as to retain a soprano or alto voice.

castrum /ˈkastrəm/ *noun* plural **castra** /ˈkastrə/ M19 **Latin**. A Roman encampment or fortress.

casus belli /ˌkɑːsʊs ˈbɛliː/, /ˌkeɪsəs ˈbɛlʌɪ/ *noun phrase* M19 **Latin** (from *casus* case + *belli* genitive of *bellum* war). An act or situation justifying or precipitating war.

1996 *Spectator* There must be clear provocation, a satisfactory *casus belli*.

casus foederis /ˌkɑːsʊs ˈfɔɪdərɪs/, /ˌkeɪsəs ˈfiːdərɪs/ *noun phrase* L18 **Latin** (from *casus* case + *foederis* genitive of *foedus* treaty). An event which, under the terms of a treaty of alliance, entitles one of the allies to help from the other(s).

catafalque /ˈkatəfalk/ *noun* (also (now *rare*) **catafalco** /katəˈfalkəʊ/, plural **catafalco(e)s**) M17 **French** (from Italian *catafalco*, of unknown origin). **1** M17 A decorated structure fashioned so as to carry the coffin or effigy of a distinguished person during a funeral service or for a lying in state. **2** M19 A structure on which a coffin is drawn in procession.

catalogue raisonné /katalɔg rezɔne/ *noun phrase* plural **catalogues raisonnés** (pronounced same) L18 **French** (= reasoned catalogue). A descriptive catalogue with explanations or comments; *figurative* an exhaustive account.

1996 *Country Life* Paul McCarron has produced a *catalogue raisonné* of the prints of Martin Lewis . . . *figurative*

1995 *Spectator* That is the import of *The Sleaze File* by Judith Cook, a new *catalogue raisonné* of British scandal and microscandal over the last two or three years.

catalysis /kəˈtalɪsɪs/ *noun* plural **catalyses** /kəˈtalɪsiːz/ M17 **Modern Latin** (from Greek *katalusis*, from *kataluein* to dissolve). **1** M–L17 Dissolution, destruction. **2** M19 *Chemistry* The action or effect of a substance in increasing the rate of a reaction without itself being consumed; an instance of this.

catamaran /ˌkatəməˈran/, /ˈkatəməran/ *noun* E17 **Tamil** (*kaṭṭumaram*, literally, 'tied wood'). **1** E17 A raft or float of logs tied side by side with the longest in the middle; a raft of two boats fastened side by side; a sailing boat with two hulls side by side. **2** E19 *History* A naval weapon consisting of a floating chest packed with gunpowder. **3** M19 A quarrelsome woman. *colloquial*.

catastasis /kəˈtastəsɪs/ *noun* plural **catastases** /kəˈtastəsiːz/ M16 **Greek** (*katastasis* settling, appointment, from as *cata-* + *stasis*). The third part of the ancient drama, in which the action is heightened for the catastrophe.

catechesis /katɪˈkiːsɪs/ *noun* plural **catecheses** /katɪˈkiːsiːz/ M18 **ecclesiastical Latin** (from Greek *katēkhēsis* instruction by word of mouth, from *katēkhein*). **1** M18 Oral instruction given to catechumens; catechizing. **2** M18 A book for the instruction of catechumens.

catechumen /katɪˈkjuːmɛn/ *noun* LME **Old and Modern French** (*catéchumène* or ecclesiastical Latin *catechumenus* from Greek *katēkhoumenos* being instructed, present participle passive of *katēkhein*). A Christian convert under instruction before baptism. Also, a young Christian preparing for confirmation.

catharsis /kə'θɑːsɪs/ *noun* (in sense 2 also **katharsis**) plural **catharses** /kə'θɑːsiːz/ E19 **Modern Latin** (from Greek *katharsis*, from *kathairein* to cleanse, from *katharos* pure). **1** E19 *Medicine* Purgation. **2** M19 (A) purification of the emotions by vicarious experience, especially through drama, or, in psychotherapy, by abreaction.

■ In sense 2 from Aristotle's *Poetics*.

cathedra /kə'θiːdrə/ *noun* LME **Latin** (from Greek *kathedra* chair). A seat; *specifically* the chair of a bishop in his church; the episcopal see.

■ Most commonly in the phrase EX CATHEDRA.

catheter /'kaθɪtə/ *noun* (also **katheter**) E17 **Late Latin** (*catheter* from Greek *kathetēr*, from *kathienai* to send or let down). *Medicine* A tube which can be passed into the bladder or other body cavity or canal to allow the draining of fluid.

cathexis /kə'θɛksɪs/ *noun* E20 **Greek** (*kathexis* holding, retention). *Psychoanalysis* The concentration or accumulation of libidinal energy on a particular object.

■ A rendering of Freud's German term *(Libido)besetzung*.

caudillo /kaʊ'diːljəʊ/ *noun* plural **caudillos** M19 **Spanish** (from late Latin *capitellum* diminutive of *caput* head). In Spain and Spanish-speaking countries: a head of State, a military or political leader.

cause célèbre /koz selɛbr/ *noun phrase* plural **causes célèbres** (pronounced same) M18 **French**. A notorious legal case; *generally* a controversy or scandal that attracts much attention.

1996 *Times* The rape of Artemisia Gentileschi is a cause célèbre in art history.

causerie /kozri/ *noun* plural pronounced same E19 **French** (from *causer* to talk). Informal (especially literary) talk; a chatty article in a magazine or journal.

causes célèbres plural of CAUSE CÉLÈBRE.

causeuse /kozøz/ *noun* plural pronounced same M19 **French** (from *causer* to talk). A small sofa for two people.

cavaliere servente /kava'ljeːre ser 'vɛnte/ *noun phrase* M18 **Italian** (literally, 'gentleman-in-waiting'). The lover or solicitous admirer of a (married) woman.

cavallard variant of CAVAYARD.

cavatina /kavə'tiːnə/ *noun* E19 **Italian**. *Music* A short simple song; a songlike piece of instrumental music, usually slow and emotional.

cavayard /'kavɪjɑːd/ *noun* (also **cavallard** /'kav(ə)ljɑːd/, **cavy-yard**, and other variants) E19 **Spanish** (alteration of CABALLADA). A drove of horses or mules. *United States*.

cave /'keɪvi/ *noun & interjection* LME **Latin** (imperative singular of *cavere* to beware). **A** *noun* **1** LME–L15 A warning; an injunction. **2** E20 *keep cave*, act as a lookout. *school slang*. **B** M19 *interjection* As a warning cry: look out! *school slang*.

cavea /'keɪvɪə/ *noun* plural **caveae** /'keɪvɪiː/ E17 **Latin** (= a hollow). *Roman Antiquities* The (concave) auditorium of a theatre; a theatre.

caveat /'kavɪat/, /'keɪvɪat/ *noun* M16 **Latin** (3rd person singular present subjunctive of *cavere* to beware). **1** M16 A warning, a proviso; *specifically* in *Law* a process or notice suspending or delaying proceedings. **2** L16–L17 A precaution.

■ Also formerly as a transitive verb (M17) in legal terminology or an intransitive verb (M17) in fencers' jargon meaning 'disengage'. Current verbal use is confined to the phrase CAVEAT EMPTOR.

1 1996 *Times* I started to offer Wiesenthal Lord Shawcross's objections, but he stopped me with a caveat about using the euphemism 'war criminals'.

caveat emptor /ˌkavɪat 'ɛmptɔː/ *interjection* E16 **Latin**. (A maxim:) let the buyer beware!

■ A robust antique principle that the purchaser, rather than the seller, is responsible for making sure that the quality of the goods purchased is satisfactory. Frequently invoked in the context of horse-dealing—the earliest recorded use in English is in J. Fitzherbert's *A newe tracte . . . for all husbande men* (1523)—it fails to find much favour under modern consumer protection legislation.

1950 T. H. Marshall *Citizenship and Social Class* The principle of *caveat emptor* is at least plausible when you are buying a horse.

cavy-yard variant of CAVAYARD.

cedilla /sɪ'dɪlə/ *noun* (formerly (L16–M19) also **cerilla** L16 **Spanish** ((now *zedilla*), diminutive of *zeda* letter Z). The diacritic mark ¸ written under *c* to show that it is sibilant /s/ or /ts/, as before *a, o, u* in French and Portuguese and (formerly)

Spanish; a similar mark under *c* and *s* indicating a manner of articulation in various other contexts, as distinguishing the voiceless from the voiced consonants in Turkish.

ceilidh /ˈkeɪli/ *noun* L19 **Irish** (*céilidhe* (now *céilí*), Gaelic *cēilidh*, from Old Irish *céilide* visit, act of visiting, from *céile* companion). An informal gathering for (especially Scottish or Irish) folk music, dancing, song, etc.

ceinture /sɛ̃tyr/ *noun* plural pronounced same LME **French** (from Latin *cinctura*, from *cinctus* past participle of *cingere* to gird). A girdle, a cincture.

■ Fell into disuse after the Middle English period, but was reintroduced in the early nineteenth century as part of the enthusiasm for all things Gothic and medieval.

celadon /ˈsɛlədɒn/ *noun & adjective* M18 **French** (*céladon*). **A** *noun* **1** M18 A pale greyish shade of green. **2** M19 A glaze of this colour used on (especially Chinese) pottery or porcelain; ceramic ware thus glazed. **B** L19 *attributive* or as *adjective* Of this colour; covered with this glaze.

■ From the name of the shepherd-hero of D'Urfé's immensely popular pastoral romance *L'Astrée* (1607–27).

celebret /ˈsɛlɪbrɛt/ *noun* M19 **Latin** (= let him celebrate, 3rd person singular present subjunctive of *celebrare* to celebrate). *Roman Catholic Church* A document granting permission by a bishop to a priest to celebrate mass in a particular parish.

celesta /sɪˈlɛstə/ *noun* L19 **pseudo-Latin** (apparently based on French CÉLESTE). *Music* A small keyboard instrument in which hammers strike on steel plates, producing an ethereal bell-like sound.

celeste /sɪˈlɛst/ *noun* L19 **French** (*céleste* from Latin *caelestis* from *caelum* heaven). **1** L19 A stop on the organ and harmonium with a soft tremulous tone (French *voix céleste*). Also, a form of soft pedal on a piano. **2** M20 A CELESTA.

cella /ˈkɛlə/ *noun* plural **cellae** /ˈkɛliː/ L17 **Latin.** *Architecture* The internal section of a Greek or Roman temple housing the hidden cult image; a similar part of other ancient temples.

cembalo /ˈtʃɛmbələʊ/ *noun* plural **cembalos** M19 **Italian** (abbreviation of CLAVICEMBALO). A harpsichord.

cenacle /ˈsɛnək(ə)l/ *noun* LME **Old and Modern French** (*cénacle* from Latin *cenaculum*, from *cena* dinner). **1** LME A dining-room; *specifically* the room in which the Last Supper was held. **2** L19 A place where a discussion group, literary clique, etc., meets; the group itself.

cenobium variant of COENOBIUM.

cenote /seˈnote/ *noun* M19 **Yucatan Spanish** (from Maya *tzonot*). A natural underground reservoir of water, such as occurs in the limestone of Yucatan, Mexico.

census /ˈsɛnsəs/ *noun* E17 **Latin** (from *censere* to assess). **1** E17–M19 A tax, a tribute; *especially* a poll tax. **2** M17 *History* The registration of citizens and their property in ancient Rome, usually for taxation purposes. **3** M18 An official enumeration of the population of a country etc., or of a class of things, usually with statistics relating to them.

cento /ˈsɛntəʊ/ *noun* plural **centos** E17 **Latin** (literally, 'patchwork garment'). **1** E–M17 A piece of patchwork; a patchwork garment. **2** E17 A hotchpotch, a medley; *specifically* a composition made up of quotations from other authors.

centrifuge /ˈsɛntrɪfjuːdʒ/ *adjective, noun, & verb* E18 **French** (from Modern Latin *centrifugus* centrifugal). **A** *adjective* E18–E19 Moving or tending to move away from the centre, centrifugal. **B** *noun* L19 A centrifugal machine; *especially* a device for effecting separation, usually of one liquid from another or of a solid from a liquid, by rapid rotation. **C** E20 *transitive verb* Subject to centrifugal motion; separate by means of a centrifuge.

centum see PER CENTUM.

cep /sɛp/ *noun* (also **cèpe** /sɛp/ (*plural same*)) M19 **French** (*cèpe* from Gascon *cep* tree-trunk, mushroom, from Latin *cippus* stake). An edible boletus.

cerebellum /sɛrɪˈbɛləm/ *noun* M16 **Latin** (diminutive of CEREBRUM). *Anatomy* The larger part of the hindbrain, responsible for the control of muscle tone and balance.

1996 *Oldie* We are all so dull, without discernment . . . But flabby cerebellums, arise! Address yourselves to a new noise.

cerebrum /ˈsɛrɪbrəm/ *noun* E17 **Latin** (= brain). *Anatomy* The larger, anterior part of the brain, responsible for voluntary activity and mental processes.

cerilla obsolete variant of CEDILLA.

cerise /sɛˈriːz/, /sɛˈriːs/ *adjective & noun* M19 **French** (= cherry). (Of) a light clear red.

ceroon variant of SERON.

cervelat /ˈsəːvəlɑː/ *noun* E17 **French** ((now *cervelas*) from Italian *cervellata* Milanese sausage). A kind of smoked pork sausage.

cervix /ˈsəːvɪks/ *noun* plural **cervices** /ˈsəːvɪsiːz/ M18 **Latin**. *Anatomy* The neck; a part of an organ resembling or forming a neck; *specifically* the narrow passage forming the lower end of the womb adjacent to the vagina.

c'est la guerre /ˌseɪ la ˈgɛː/ *interjection* E20 **French** (= that's war). (An expression of resignation:) that's the kind of thing that happens!

c'est la vie /ˌseɪ la ˈviː/ *interjection* E20 **French**. (An expression of resignation:) that's life!

1995 *Country Life* Thanks to my inattention, and a low-flying helicopter . . . , I was bucked off this morning. *C'est la vie.*

cestui /ˈsɛti/ *noun* M16 **Anglo-Norman and Old French** (from Proto-Romance, from Latin *ecce* lo! + *iste* that (one), with element *-ui* as in *cui* dative of *quis* who). *Law* The person (who), he (who).

■ Only in the following legal phrases: *cestui que trust, cestui que use* the person for whose benefit something is given in trust to another; *cestui que vie* a person for whose lifetime an estate or interest in property is held by another.

cestus /ˈsɛstəs/ *noun 1* plural **cesti** /ˈsɛstʌɪ/ M16 **Latin** (from Greek *kestos* use as noun of participial adjective = stitched). A (bridal) belt or girdle for the waist, *especially* that of Aphrodite or Venus.

cestus /ˈsɛstəs/ *noun 2* plural same L17 **Latin** (*caestus*, from *caedere* to strike). *History* A covering for the hand made of thongs of bull-hide loaded with metallic strips, used by boxers in ancient Rome.

ceteris paribus /ˌkeɪtərɪs ˈparɪbəs/, /ˌsɛtərɪs ˈparɪbəs/, /ˌsiːtərɪs ˈparɪbəs/ *adverb phrase* E17 **Modern Latin**. Other things being equal or unchanged.

1995 *Spectator* The new Rowntree Trust report merely gives the latest gloss on the problem. Thousands of years from now, Rowntree-type people will be producing, *ceteris paribus*, similar gloomy reports.

ceviche variant of SEVICHE.

cha-cha /ˈtʃɑːtʃɑː/ *noun & verb* (also **cha-cha-cha** /tʃɑːtʃɑːˈtʃɑː/ M20 **American Spanish**. **A** *noun* M20 A type of ballroom dance to a Latin American rhythm; a piece of music for this dance. **B** *transitive verb* M20 Perform this dance.

1996 *Times* Ballroom dancing is divided into Latin (cha-cha, jive, rumba, samba, paso doblé) and Modern . . .

chacham variant of HAHAM.

chaconne /ʃəˈkɒn/ *noun* L17 **French** (from Spanish *chacona*). A moderately slow musical composition on a ground bass, usually in triple time; a dance to this music.

1996 *Country Life* . . . a theme by Bach is worked into a *chaconne* which is one of the wonders of 19th-century music.

chacun à son goût /ʃakœ̃ a sɔ̃ gu/ *interjection* L19 **French**. Everyone to his or her taste.

■ Also occasionally in the form usual in French: *à chacun son goût*.

1996 *Country Life* People must think I'm totally halfwitted. There are some who would give their eye-teeth to fish this beautiful stretch of river. But *chacun à son goût*.

chadar /ˈtʃɑːdə/ *noun* (also **chaddar**, **chador**, **chuddar** /ˈtʃʌdə/, and other variants) E17 **Urdu** (*chādar, chaddar* from Persian *čādar* sheet, veil). A large piece of material worn as a long shawl or cloak especially by Muslim women in the Indian subcontinent and Iran.

chaebol /keɪˈbɒl/ *noun* L20 **Korean**. In South Korea: a large business conglomerate comparable to the Japanese ZAIBATSU.

chagrin /ˈʃagrɪn/ *noun & verb* M17 **French** (literally, 'rough skin', of unknown origin). **A** *noun* **1** M17–M19 Anxiety; melancholy. **2** E18 Vexation arising from disappointment or failure; acute annoyance. **B** also /ʃəˈgriːn/ *transitive verb* M17 Affect with chagrin. Usually in *passive*.

■ The spelling *shagreen* of the noun is an obsolete (L17–M19) variant that is now used solely in senses that retain the literal French meaning, being applied to a kind of untanned leather with a rough granular surface (often dyed green) or to the rough scaly skin of sharks or rays especially as used for polishing.

chaîné /ʃɛne/ *noun* M20 **French** (= linked). *Ballet* A quick step or turn from one foot to the other, or a series of these, performed in a line.

chaise /ʃeɪz/ *noun* plural pronounced same M17 **French** (variant of *chaire* chair). **1** M17 A pleasure or travelling carriage, especially a light open one for one or two people. Chiefly *historical*. **2** M20 A CHAISE LONGUE.

chaise longue /ʃeɪz ˈlɒŋg/, *foreign* /ʃɛz lɔ̃g/ *noun phrase* plural **chaise longues** /ʃeɪz ˈlɒŋgz/, **chaises longues** /ʃeɪz ˈlɒŋg(z)/, *foreign* /ʃɛz lɔ̃g/ E19 **French** (= long chair). A kind of sofa with a backrest at only one end.

chaise percée /ʃɛz pɛrse/ *noun phrase* plural **chaises percées** (pronounced same) M20 **French** (= pierced chair). A chair incorporating a chamber-pot.

chaitya /ˈʧʌɪtjə/ *noun* L19 **Sanskrit** (*caitya* (resembling) a funeral pile, mound, etc., from *citā* funeral mound). A Buddhist place or object of reverence.

chakra /ˈʧʌkrə/ *noun* L18 **Sanskrit** (*cakra*; cf. Greek *kuklos* cycle). **1** L18 A thin knife-edged disc of steel formerly used as a weapon by Sikhs. **2** L19 A discus or mystic circle depicted in the hands of Hindu deities. **3** L19 *Yoga* Each of the centres of spiritual power in the human body. **4** M20 The circular emblem on the flag of the Indian Union.

chal /ʧal/ *noun* M19 **Romany** (= person, fellow). A male Gypsy. Also *Romany chal*.

chalet /ˈʃaleɪ/ *noun* L18 **Swiss French** (diminutive of Old French *chasel* farmstead from Proto-Romance derivative of Latin *casa* hut, cottage). A Swiss mountain cowherd's hut; a Swiss peasant's wooden cottage; a house with a widely overhanging roof; a small villa; a small house in a holiday camp etc.

chalifa variant of KHALIFA.

challah /ˈhɑːlə/, *foreign* /ˈxɑːlɑː/ *noun* L20 **Hebrew**. Jewish ceremonial bread for the Sabbath.

chalumeau /ʃalymo/ *noun* plural **chalumeaux** /ʃalymo/ E18 **French** (from late Latin *calamellus* diminutive of *calamus* reed). A musical pipe of reed or straw; an instrument having a reed mouthpiece, *especially* the forerunner of the clarinet. Also (in full *chalumeau register*), the lowest register of the clarinet.

chalutzim variant of HALUTZIM.

cham /kam/ *noun* LME **French** (*cham*, *chan* from Turkic *ḳān* KHAN). A khan. Now only *transferred* and *figurative*, an autocrat, a dominant critic, etc.

■ The transferred use alludes to an expression of the Scottish author Tobias Smollett, who, in a letter to John Wilkes in 1759, referred to Samuel Johnson as the 'great Cham of literature'.

chambranle /ʃɑ̃brɑ̃l/ *noun* plural pronounced same E18 **French**. *Architecture* An ornamental bordering around a door, window, or fireplace.

chambré /ʃɒmbreɪ/, *foreign* /ʃɑ̃bre/ *adjective* M20 **French** (past participle of *chambrer* to bring to room temperature, from Old French *chambre* from Latin *camera* room). Of wine: at room temperature. Usually *predicative*.

1952 B. Pym *Excellent Women* My only fear is that it will scarcely be chambré by the time I shall want to drink it.

chametz variant of HAMETZ.

chamois /ˈʃamwɑː/; *in senses A2 and B2, usually* /ʃami/ *noun & adjective* (senses A2 and B2 also **shammy** /ˈʃami/) plural of noun same /ˈʃamwɑːz/, /ˈʃamɪz/ M16 **Old and Modern French** (probably ultimately from Swiss Proto-Romance; cf. Gallo-Latin *camox*). **A** *noun* M16 **1** A goatlike antelope, *Rupicapra rupicapra*, found in the mountains of Europe and Asia Minor. **2** L16 Soft pliable leather from the chamois or (now more usually) from sheep, goats, deer, etc.; a piece of this for polishing etc. More fully *chamois leather*. **B** *attributive* or as *adjective*. **1** E17 Made of chamois leather. **2** M17 Of the colour of chamois leather; yellowish brown.

champignon /ʧamˈpɪnjən/, /ˈʃampɪnjɒ̃/; *foreign* /ʃɑ̃piɲɔ̃/ (*plural same*) *noun* L16 **French** ((earlier *champaignon*), diminutive of *champagne*). A mushroom; a toadstool. Now *specifically* (*a*) the edible field mushroom *Agaricus campestris*; (*b*) an agaric, *Marismius oreades*, which often forms fairy-rings.

champlevé /ˈʃampləveɪ/, *foreign* /ʃɑ̃ləve/ *adjective & noun* M19 **French** (from *champ* field + *levé* raised). (Designating) enamelwork in which the colours in the pattern are set into hollows made in the surface of the metal base. Cf. CLOISONNÉ.

1996 *Country Life* An example . . . is a Limoges engraved copper, gilt and *champlevé* enamel statue of the Virgin and Child.

chancre /ˈʃaŋkə/ *noun* L16 **French** (from Latin *cancer* crab). *Medicine* A painless ulcer, *especially* one occurring on the genitals and resulting from syphilis.

chandelier /ʃandəˈlɪə/ *noun* M17 **French** (from *chandelle* candle, from Latin *candela*). **1** M17 *Military* A wooden frame filled with fascines to form a traverse in sapping. **2** M18 A branched hanging support for several lights, originally candles.

changement /ʃɑ̃ʒmɑ̃/ *noun* plural pronounced same M19 **French** (from *changer* to change). *Ballet* A jump during which the dancer changes the position of the feet. In full *changement de pieds* /ʃɑ̃ʒmɑ̃də pje/ (literally, 'changing of feet').

chanson /ʃɑ̃sɔ̃/ *noun* plural pronounced same L15 **Old and Modern French** (from Latin *cantio* song). A French song.

chanson de geste /ʃɑ̃sɔ̃ də ʒɛst/ *noun phrase* plural **chansons de geste** (pronounced same) M19 **French** (= song of heroic deeds). Any of a group of medieval French epic poems dealing with chivalric and heroic subjects.

■ The earliest was the *Chanson de Roland*, written about 1100.

chansonette /ʃɑ̃sɔnɛt/ *noun* plural pronounced same E19 **French**. A short song.

chansonnier /[ʃɑ̃sɔnje/ *noun* plural pronounced same L19 **French**. In France: a writer or performer of songs, especially of satirical songs in a cabaret; a collection of (French) songs.

chantage /ʃɑ̃taʒ/, /ˈʧɑːntɪʤ/ *noun* L19 **French**. Extortion of money by blackmail.

chanterelle /ˈʧɑːntərɛl/, /ʧɑːntəˈrɛl/ *noun 1* E17 **French** (from *chanter* from Latin *cantare* frequentative of *canere* to sing). **1** A decoy-bird. Only in E17. **2** L18 The highest-pitched string of a plucked or bowed musical instrument.

chanterelle /ʧɑːntəˈrɛl/ *noun 2* (also **chantarelle**) L18 **French** (from Modern Latin *cantharellus* diminutive of *cantharus* from Greek *kantharos* drinking-vessel). A yellow funnel-shaped edible fungus, *Cantharellus cibarius*.

chanteuse /ʃɑ̃tøz/ *noun* plural pronounced same M19 **French**. A female singer of popular songs, originally in France.

1996 *Times Magazine* Stylistically, the work is a throwback to the golden age of confessional chanteuse à la Joni Mitchell . . .

chaparejos /ʃapəˈreɪhəʊs/, /ʧapəˈreɪhəʊs/ *noun plural* (also **chaparreras** /ʃapəˈrɛːrəs/, /ʧapəˈrɛːrəs/) M19 **Mexican Spanish** (*chaparreras*, from *chaparra*, *chaparro* dwarf evergreen oak). Tough leather over-trousers worn by cowboys for protection against spiny vegetation.

■ *Chaparejos* is a later form than *chaparreras* and is probably influenced by Spanish *aparejo* 'equipment'. In the United States the abbreviation *chaps* has been commonly used from the late nineteenth century onwards.

chaparral /ʃapəˈral/, /ʧapəˈral/ *noun* M19 **Spanish** (from as above). In United States: a thicket of dwarf evergreen oaks; dense tangled brushwood.

chaparreras variant of CHAPAREJOS.

chapatti /ʧəˈpɑːti/, /ʧəˈpati/ *noun* (also **chapati**, **chupatti**, and other variants) E19 **Hindustani** (*capātī*, from *capānā* to flatten, roll out, ultimately from Dravidian). In Indian cookery: a small flat thin cake of coarse unleavened bread.

chapeau-bras /ʃapobra/ *noun* plural **chapeaux-bras** (pronounced same) M18 **French** (from *chapeau* (Old French *c(h)apel*, from Latin *cappellum* diminutive of *cappa* cap) hat + *bras* arm). A three-cornered flat silk hat able to be carried under the arm.

chapelle ardente /ʃapɛl ardɑ̃t/ *noun phrase* plural **chapelles ardentes** (pronounced same) E19 **French** (= burning chapel). A chamber prepared for the lying-in-state of a distinguished person, and lit up with candles, torches, etc.

chaperon /ˈʃapərəʊn/ *noun & verb* (also **chaperone**) LME **Old and Modern French** (from *chape* cape, hood, ultimately from Latin *caput* head). **A** *noun* **1** LME A hood, a capital. *obsolete* except *historical*. **2** L17–L18 A small escutcheon placed especially on the forehead of a horse drawing a hearse. **3** E18 A person who ensures propriety, *especially* a married or older woman accompanying a young unmarried woman on social occasions. **B** L18 *transitive verb* Act as a chaperon to.

chappal /ˈʧap(ə)l/ *noun* (also **chappli** /ˈʧapli/) L19 **Hindustani** (*cappal*, *caplī*). In the Indian subcontinent: a sandal, especially of leather.

chaprassi /ʧəˈprasi/ *noun* plural **chaprassi(e)s** (also **chuprassy**) E19 **Urdu** (*chaprāsī*, from *chaprās* official badge, from Persian *čaprāst*). In the Indian subcontinent: an attendant, a messenger, a household official.

charabanc /'ʃarəbaŋ/ *noun* (also **char-à-banc**) E19 **French** (*char-à-bancs* literally, 'carriage with seats'). A long and light vehicle with transverse seats looking forward; a motor coach. Now *archaic* or *jocular*.

charade /ʃə'rɑːd/ *noun* L18 **French** (from Modern Provençal *charrado* conversation, from *charra* chatter, perhaps of imitative origin). **1** L18 A written or (now usually) acted clue from which a syllable of a word or a complete word is to be guessed. **b** M19 (in *plural* usually treated as *singular*) A game of guessing words from such clues. **2** L19 *figurative* An absurd pretence.

charcuterie /ʃarkytri/ (*plural same*), /ʃɑː'kuːt(ə)riː/ *noun* M19 **French** (from *char* (modern *chair*) *cuite* cooked flesh). Cold cooked meats; a shop selling these; a (French) pork-butcher's shop.

1996 *Times* He is capable of appreciating the elaborate display of a *charcuterie* . . .

chargé /'ʃɑːʒeɪ/; *foreign* /ʃarʒe/ (*plural same*) *noun* M19 **French**. Abbreviation of CHARGÉ D'AFFAIRES.

chargé d'affaires /ˌʃɑːʒeɪ da'fɛː/, *foreign* /ʃarʒe dafɛr/ *noun phrase* plural **chargés d'affaires** (pronounced same) (also **chargé des affaires**) M18 **French** (= (a person) in charge of affairs). **1** M18 A minister who transacts diplomatic business during the temporary absence of an ambassador; a State's representative at a minor foreign court or government. **2** L18 *generally* A person temporarily in charge.

charisma /kə'rɪzmə/ *noun* plural **charismata** /kə'rɪzmətə/ M17 **ecclesiastical Latin** (from Greek *kharisma*, *-mat-*, from *kharis* favour, grace). **1** M17 *Christian Theology* A divinely conferred power or talent. **2** M20 A capacity to inspire devotion and enthusiasm; aura.

2 1996 *Times* In the entertainment world, the Sagittarian's charisma is matched by a determination to be different, to stamp originality on the most mundane or unlikely material.

charivari /ʃɑːrɪ'vɑːri/ *noun* M17 **French** (of unknown origin). A cacophonous mock serenade in derision of an unpopular person, marriage, etc.; a discordant medley of sounds, a hubbub.

■ The variant *shivaree* (M19) is mainly found in the United States.

charlotte /'ʃɑːlət/ *noun* L18 **French** (possibly the feminine name). A pudding made of stewed fruit with a casing or covering of bread, biscuits, sponge cake, or breadcrumbs.

■ Usually with defining word, as in *apple charlotte*, *rhubarb charlotte*, etc. Cf. CHARLOTTE RUSSE.

charlotte russe /'ʃɑːlət ˌruːs/ *noun phrase* plural **charlottes russes**, **charlotte russes** M19 **French** (= Russian CHARLOTTE). A pudding with flavoured custard or cream inside a moulded sponge cake or biscuit casing.

charmeuse /ʃɑː'məːz/, *foreign* /ʃarmøz/ *noun* E20 **French** (feminine of *charmeur* charmer, from Old French *charme* charm, from Latin *carmen* song, incantation). A soft smooth silky dress-fabric.

charoset(h) variants of HAROSETH.

charpoy /'ʧɑːpɔɪ/ *noun* M17 **Urdu** (*chārpāī* from Persian). In the Indian subcontinent: a light bedstead.

charqui /'ʧɑːki/ *noun* E17 **American Spanish** (*charqui*, *charque* from Quechua *cc'arki*). Meat, especially beef, cut into thin slices and dried in the wind and sun.

■ English travellers to the New World in the seventeenth century apparently adopted the word from the Spanish, corrupting it in the process; from these corruptions the word *jerky* emerged (M19) to become the term widely used in North America. The South African equivalent is BILTONG; cf. PEMMICAN.

charro /'ʧɑːrəʊ/ *noun* plural **charros** E20 **Mexican Spanish** (from Spanish = rustic). A Mexican cowboy, *especially* one elaborately dressed.

chartreuse /ʃɑː'trəːz/, *foreign* /ʃartrøz/ (*plural same*) *noun* E19 **French** (feminine of *Chartreux*). **1** E19 *Cookery* A dish turned out from a mould, of meat, vegetables, or (now more usually) of fruit enclosed in jelly etc. **2** M19 A green or yellow liqueur of brandy and aromatic herbs etc., originally made by the monks of La Grande Chartreuse, near Grenoble, France. **3** L19 An apple-green colour.

chasid variant of HASID.

chasse /ʃas/, /ʃɑːs/ *noun 1* LME **French** (*châsse* reliquary). A case for the relics of a saint.

chasse /ʃas/, /ʃɑːs/ *noun 2* plural **chasses** /ʃas/, /ˈʃɑːsɪz/ M18 **French** (abbreviation of *chasse-café*, literally, 'chase-coffee'). A liqueur taken after coffee, tobacco, etc.; a chaser.

■ The full form *chasse-café* (E19) is now rare.

chassé /ʃase/ (*plural same*), /ˈʃaseɪ/ *noun* E19 **French** (literally, 'chasing, chase'). A sliding step in which one foot displaces the other in dancing.

■ A mainly North American alteration is *sashay* (noun and verb), '(to perform) a *chassé* in square dancing'; as a verb *sashay* also has a general colloquial sense of 'to walk with an ostentatiously gliding or swinging step' (see quotation at DERRIÈRE).

1995 *Times* A group of couples appear, confident in their skaters' *chassé* steps, with only one of the men later falling over.

chassé croisé /ʃase krwaze/ *noun phrase* L19 **French** (literally, 'crossed chassé'). A dance movement comprising a double chassé causing partners to change position; *figurative* an elaborate reversal of position, especially a mix-up in which people trying to meet constantly miss one another.

chasseur /ʃaˈsəː/; *foreign* /ʃasœr/ (*plural same*) *noun* M18 **French** (from *chasser* to hunt). **1** M18 *History* A soldier (especially French) equipped and trained for rapid movement. **2** M18 An attendant dressed in military style. Now *rare* or *obsolete*. **b** L19 A hotel messenger, especially in France. **3** L18 A huntsman.

■ The French equivalent of the German JÄGER.

chassid variant of HASID.

chassis /ˈʃasi/, /ˈʃasiː/ *noun* plural same /ˈʃasɪz/, /ˈʃasiːz/ M17 **French** (*châssis* from Proto-Romance, from Latin *capsa* case). **1** M17–E18 A window frame, a sash. **2** M19 The sliding base-frame of a mounted gun. **3** E20 The base-frame of a motor vehicle etc. **4** M20 A frame carrying radio etc. equipment. **5** M20 The human or animal frame, the body. *slang*.

château /ˈʃatəʊ/, *foreign* /ʃato/ *noun* plural **châteaux** /ˈʃatəʊz/, *foreign* /ʃato/ M18 **French**. A large country house in France (formerly also elsewhere); *especially* one giving its name to wine made in its neighbourhood.

■ Sometimes also used jocularly with the owner's name of an ostentatious or pretentious house anywhere, e.g. Château Jones.

1996 *Times Magazine* Buying en primeur . . . is often the only chance that claret lovers will get to buy their favourite châteaux.

Chateaubriand /ʃatobrijɑ̃/ *noun* plural pronounced same L19 **French**. A thick fillet beefsteak, grilled and garnished with herbs etc.

■ Called after François René, Vicomte de *Chateaubriand* (1768–1848), French writer and statesman. Also *Chateaubriand steak* or *steak à la Chateaubriand*.

chatelaine /ˈʃatəleɪn/ *noun* M19 **French** (*châtelaine* feminine of *châtelain*). **1** M19 A female castellan (*historical*); the mistress of a castle or (country) house. **2** M19 *History* A set of short chains attached to a woman's belt for carrying keys, a watch, a pencil, etc.

1 1995 *Times* If the chatelaine had spent all day lying down zonked out with Valium, these were suppers that required a minimum of preparation.

chaton /ʃatɔ̃/ *noun* plural pronounced same L16 **French** (from German *Kasten* case (Old and Middle High German *kasto*)). The part of a finger-ring in which a stone is set or on which a device is engraved.

chatoyant /ʃəˈtɔɪənt/, *foreign* /ʃatwajɑ̃/ *noun & adjective* L18 **French** (present participle of *chatoyer*) to shimmer. (Of) iridescent undulating lustre.

■ Now *rare*.

chaud-froid /ʃəʊˈfrwɑː/, *foreign* /ʃofrwa/ (*plural same*) *noun* L19 **French** (literally, 'hot-cold'). A dish of cold cooked meat or fish in a jelly or sauce.

chaukidar variant of CHOKIDAR.

chaussée /ʃose/ *noun* plural pronounced same E19 **French**. In France, Belgium, etc.: a causeway; a high road.

chaussure /ʃosyr/ *noun* LME **French** (Anglo-Norman *chaucer* = Old French *chaucier* (modern *chaussure*), Provençal *causier* shoe; cf. medieval Latin *calceatura*). Footwear.

■ Formerly naturalized with the spelling *chawcer* and variants, but reintroduced as a borrowing from Modern French in the nineteenth century.

chayote /ˈtʃeɪəʊti/, *noun* L19 **Spanish** (from Nahnatl *chayotli*). A tropical American vine, *Sechium edule*, cultivated elsewhere for its fruit; the succulent fruit of this vine. Also called *chocho*.

chaz(z)an variants of HAZZAN.

chechia /ˈʃeɪʃɪə/ *noun* M19 **French** (*chéchia* from Maghribi pronunciation of Arabic *šāšiyya*, from Arabic *Šāš* Tashkent in Uzbekistan). A red felt cap worn in North-west Africa.

cheder variant of HEDER.

cheechako /tʃiːˈtʃɑːkəʊ/ *noun* L19 **Chinook Jargon** (= newcomer). A recently arrived immigrant to the mining districts of North America; a greenhorn.

■ North American colloquial.

chee-chee variant of CHI-CHI.

chef /ʃɛf/ *noun* E19 **French** (= head). A person (usually a man) who is (usually the chief) cook in a hotel, restaurant, etc.

■ Also in combinations such as *sous-chef* 'under-chef', COMMIS *chef*, etc.

chef d'école /ʃɛf dekɔl/ *noun phrase* plural **chefs d'école** (pronounced same) M19 **French** (= head of school). The initiator or leader of a school or style of music, painting, literature, etc.

1995 *Spectator* He found himself an unwilling and unsuitable *chef d'école*—unsuitable because his search for a modern language in painting became increasingly idiosyncratic.

chef d'équipe /ʃɛf dekip/ *noun phrase* plural **chefs d'équipe** (pronounced same) L20 **French** (= head of team; cf. ÉQUIPE). The manager of a sports team responsible for practical arrangements especially when travelling.

1996 *Times* Long after she [sc. Pat Smythe] had been forced to give up showjumping she remained involved in the sport as an international selector, and sometimes, chef d'equipe of British teams abroad.

chef-d'œuvre /ʃɛdœvr/ *noun* plural **chefs-d'œuvre** (pronounced same) E17 **French** (= chief (piece) of work). The greatest work of an artist etc.; a masterpiece.

chef d'orchestre /ʃɛf dɔrkɛstr/ *noun phrase* plural **chefs d'orchestre** (pronounced same) M19 **French** (= head of orchestra). The leader or conductor of an orchestra.

chela /ˈtʃeɪlə/ *noun* M19 **Hindustani** (*celā*). A disciple, a pupil, *specifically* in Hinduism.

chemin de fer /ʃ(ə)mɛ̃ də fɛr/, /ʃəˈmɑ̃ də fɛː/ *noun* L19 **French** (= railway, literally, 'road of iron'). A form of baccarat.

chemise /ʃəˈmiːz/ *noun* ME **Old and Modern French** (from late Latin *camisia* shirt, nightgown). **1** ME A garment for the upper body; *especially* a woman's loose-fitting undergarment or dress hanging straight from the shoulders. **2** E18 *History* A wall with which a bastion etc. is lined as a fortification. **3** L19 *History* A loose covering for a book.

chemisette /ˌʃɛmɪˈzɛt/ *noun* E19 **French** (diminutive of CHEMISE). **1** E19 A bodice, resembling the upper part of a chemise. **2** E19 A piece of muslin, lace, etc., used to fill in the open front of a woman's dress.

chenille /ʃəˈniːl/ *noun* M18 **French** (literally, 'hairy caterpillar', from Latin *canicula* diminutive of *canis* dog). Velvety cord with pile all round, used in trimming and bordering dresses and furniture.

cheongsam /tʃɪɒŋˈsam/, /tʃɒŋˈsam/ *noun* M20 **Chinese** (Cantonese (= Mandarin *chángshān*)). A Chinese woman's garment with a high neck and slit skirt.

cherchez la femme /ʃɛrʃe la fam/ *interjection* L19 **French** (= look for the woman). The principle that there is certain to be a woman behind an untoward event.

■ A catchphrase of Alexandre Dumas *père* in *Les Mohicans de Paris* (1864).

1996 *Times* [Lady Hollis] was credited with influencing Alan Howarth's decision to cross the floor—a canard put out by credulous Tories playing *cherchez la femme*.

chère amie /ʃɛr ami/ *noun phrase* plural **chères amies** /ʃɛrz ami/ L18 **French** (literally, 'dear (woman) friend'). A female lover; a mistress.

cherem /ˈxerem/, /ˈherem/ *noun* (also **herem**) E19 **Hebrew** (*ḥērem* from *ḥāram* devote, put under a curse). Excommunication from the Synagogue and the Jewish community.

cherimoya /tʃɛrɪˈmɔɪə/ *noun* (also **chirimoya** /tʃɪrˈmɔɪə/) M18 **Spanish** (from Quechua, from *chiri* cold, refreshing + *muya* circle). (The pulpy edible fruit of) a small tree, *Annona cherimola*, native to the Andes of Peru and Ecuador.

cher maître /ʃɛr mɛtr/ *noun phrase* plural **chers maîtres** (pronounced same) E20 **French** (literally, 'dear master'). (A flattering form of address to) a famous writer.

■ Often used ironically (see quotation).

1995 *Country Life* For me at least, *cher maître*, you do not always succeed.

chernozem /ˈtʃəːnəzɛm/ *noun* (also **chernosem**) M19 **Russian** (from *chërnyĭ* black + Slavonic base *zem-* (cf. Russian *zemlya*) earth). A dark, humus-rich, fertile soil characteristic of temperate or cool grassland.

■ Originally used of the soil of the Russian steppes, now generally for soils of this type.

chétif /ʃetif/ *adjective* E20 **French**. Puny, sickly, thin; miserable, wretched.

chetnik /ˈtʃɛtnɪk/ *noun* E20 **Serbo-Croat** (*četnik*, from *četa* band, troop). A guerrilla fighter in the Balkans; (*historical*) one of a royalist force led by General Draža Mihajlović in occupied Yugoslavia, 1941–5.

chevachee variant of CHEVAUCHÉE.

cheval /ʃəval/, /ʃəˈval/ *noun* plural **chevaux** /ʃəvo/, /ʃəˈvəʊ/ L15 **French** (= horse, frame). Horse; frame.

■ Never independently naturalized in English, *cheval* occurs in the combination *cheval-glass* (a tall glass set on a pivot in an upright frame) and in various phrases; see À CHEVAL, CHEVAL DE BATAILLE, CHEVAUX DE FRISE.

cheval de bataille /ʃəval də batɑj/ *noun phrase* plural **chevaux de bataille** /ʃəvo də batɑj/ E19 **French** (literally, 'battle-horse'). An obsession, a pet subject; something made boring by repetition or overuse.

■ Native English equivalents are 'hobby-horse' or 'warhorse', depending on context; see quotation for 'warhorse' sense.

1942 E. Blom *Music in England* The chief *chevaux de bataille* for new sopranos [are] the heroines in 'La Sonnambula' and 'Lucia di Lammermoor'.

chevalet /ʃəvale/ *noun* plural pronounced same E19 **French** (diminutive of CHEVAL). **1** A trestle for a bridge. Only in E19. **2** L19 The bridge of a bowed musical instrument.

chevalier /ʃɛvəˈlɪə/, *foreign* /ʃəvalje/ (*plural same*) *noun* LME **Anglo-Norman** (*chevaler*, Old and Modern French *chevalier*, from medieval Latin *caballarius*, from Latin *caballus* horse). **1** LME *History* A horseman, *especially* a mounted knight. **2** M17 A chivalrous man, a gallant. **3** E18 A member of certain orders of knighthood, or of the French Legion of Honour, etc.

■ Sometimes in the phrase *chevalier sans peur et sans reproche* literally, 'a knight without fear or stain', a perfect gentleman; see also SANS PEUR.

chevauchée /ʃəvoʃe/ *noun* Also formerly written **chevachee** LME **French** (from Old French *chevauchiee* expedition on horseback, past participial formation on *chevauchier* (modern *chevaucher*) from Late Latin *caballicare* to ride, from *caballus* horse). *History* A mounted raid.

1995 *Spectator* These *chevauchées* involved the English soldiery running amok, marauding, looting, raping and laying waste the countryside.

chevaux de frise /ʃəvo də friz/ *noun phrase* L17 **French** (literally, 'horses of Friesland'). Iron spikes closely set in timber, originally to repel cavalry; a similar device, often with the spikes rotating around a rod, now set along the tops of walls, fences, etc. to deter intruders.

■ The name is an ironical reference to the fact that the Frieslanders possessed no cavalry and relied upon such devices to beat off the cavalry of others. Although the phrase is plural in form it is often treated as singular.

chevelure /ʃəvlyr/ *noun* plural pronounced same LME **Old French** (*chevelëure* (modern *chevelure*), from Latin *capillatura*, from *capillatus* haired, from *capillus* hair). **1** LME The hair of the head, a head of hair; (formerly) a wig. **2** L17 A halo around a star etc.; a comet's coma.

chevet /ʃəˈveɪ/, *foreign* /ʃəvɛ/ (*plural same*) *noun* E19 **French** (= pillow). The apsidal termination of the east end of a church.

cheville /ʃəvij/ *noun* plural pronounced same L19 **French** (= peg, pin, plug). **1** L19 A meaningless or redundant word or phrase inserted to round off a sentence or complete a verse. **2** L19 A peg in a stringed musical instrument.

chevra variant of HEBRA.

chèvre /ʃɛvr/ *noun* M20 **French** (= goat, especially she-goat). French goat's-milk cheese.

chevron /ˈʃɛvrən/ *noun* LME **Old and Modern French** (from Proto-Romance, from Latin *caper* goat; cf. Latin *capreoli* pair of rafters). **1** *Heraldry* LME A charge consisting of a bent bar of an inverted V shape. **b** E17 This shape used in decorative art etc. **2** L16 A beam or rafters, *especially* in *plural*, the rafters of a roof that meet at an angle at the ridge. **3** E19 A badge in a V shape (whether inverted or not) on a uniform to denote rank and length of service; a V-shaped stripe.

chez /ʃe/, *before a vowel* /ʃez/ *preposition* M18 **French** (from Old French *chiese* from

Latin *casa* cottage). At the house or home of.

> **1996** *Spectator* The predominant political leaning *chez* Hart suggested that a special musical selection was called for—perhaps a K-Tel collection of Top Tunes for Troubled Tories.

chiaroscuro /kɪˌɑːrəˈskʊərəʊ/ *noun & adjective* M17 **Italian** (from *chiaro* clear, bright + *oscuro* dark, obscure). **A** *noun* plural **chiaroscuros**. **1** M17 A style of painting in which only light and shade are represented; black and white. **2** L17 The treatment or disposition of the light and shade, or brighter and darker masses, in a picture; an effect or contrast of light and shade in a picture or in nature. **3** E19 *figurative* The use of contrast in literature etc. **B** M19 *attributively* or as *adjective* In chiaroscuro.

chiasmus /kʌɪˈazməs/, /kɪˈazməs/ *noun* plural **chiasmi** /kʌɪˈazmʌɪ/ M17 **Modern Latin** (from Greek *khiasmos* from *khiazein* mark with a chi, from *khi* chi. **1** M17 *generally* A diagonal or crosswise arrangement. *rare*. **2** L19 *Rhetoric* The inversion in a second phrase or clause of the order of words in the first.

chibouk /tʃɪˈbuːk/ *noun* (also **chibouque**) E19 **French** ((*chibouque* from) Turkish *çubuk*, (earlier) *çıbık* tube, pipe). A long Turkish tobacco-pipe.

chic /ʃiːk/ *noun & adjective* M19 **French** (probably from German *Schick* skill). **A** *noun* M19 Stylishness; elegance in dress; skill, effectiveness. **B** *adjective* M19 Stylish, elegant.

chicane /ʃɪˈkeɪn/ *noun* L17 **French** (from as next). **1** L17 Trickery or subterfuge in legal matters, chicanery. **2** L17–M18 An instance of chicanery; a subterfuge, a quibble. **3** L19 *Cards* A hand without trumps or without cards of one suit as dealt. **4** M20 An artificial barrier or obstacle, especially a sharp double bend, on a motor-racing track.

chicane /ʃɪˈkeɪn/ *verb* L17 **French** (*chicaner* to pursue at law, quibble, of unknown origin). **1** L17 *intransitive verb* Employ chicanery; quibble, cavil. **2** L18 *transitive verb* Quibble over; argue *away* by chicanery. *rare*. **3** M19 *transitive verb* Deceive by chicanery, cheat, (*into, out of*, etc.).

chicano /tʃɪˈkɑːnəʊ/, /ʃɪˈkɑːnəʊ/, /tʃɪˈkeɪnəʊ/, /ʃɪˈkeməʊ/ *noun & adjective* (also **Chicano**) M20 **Spanish** (alteration of *mejicano* Mexican, from *Méjico* Mexico). **A** *noun* M20 plural **chicanos** (feminine **chicana** /tʃɪˈkɑːnə/) A North American of Mexican origin. **B** *adjective* M20 Of or pertaining to chicanos; Mexican American.

chicha /ˈtʃɪtʃə/ *noun* E17 **American Spanish** (from Cuna). In South and Central America: a fermented liquor made from maize.

chicharron /tʃiːtʃəˈrəʊn/, *foreign* /tʃitʃaˈrron/ *noun* plural **chicharrones** /tʃiːtʃəˈrəʊnɪz/, *foreign* /tʃitʃaˈrrones/ M19 **American Spanish** (*chicharrón*). A piece of crackling, served as a delicacy in Mexico, parts of the southern United States, etc.

chichi /ˈʃiːʃiː/ *noun & adjective* E20 **French**. **A** *noun* E20 Showiness, fussiness; affectation; a frilly or showy thing. **B** *adjective* M20 Showy, frilly, fussy; affected.

chi-chi /ˈtʃiːtʃiː/ *adjective* (also **chee-chee**) L18 **Anglo-Indian** (perhaps from Hindustani *chī-chī* fie!). (Especially of a girl or woman) half-caste, Eurasian; (of speech) characteristic of the English formerly spoken by some Eurasians in India.

■ Usually derogatory in application, *chi-chi* mimicks an affected expression supposed by the Europeans to be used by Eurasians.

chicken variant of CHIKAN.

chicle /ˈtʃɪk(ə)l/, /ˈtʃɪkli/ *noun* L19 **American Spanish** (from Nahuatl *tzictli*). The coagulated latex of the sapodilla, *Manilkara zapota*, and several related trees, which forms the basis of chewing-gum.

chiffon /ˈʃɪfɒn/ *noun & adjective* M18 **French** (from *chiffe* rag). **A** *noun* **1** M18 In *plural* Trimmings or other adornments of women's dress. *archaic* **2** L19 A light diaphanous plain-woven fabric of silk, nylon, etc. **B** E20 *attributively* or as *adjective* Made of chiffon; light in weight.

chiffonier /ʃɪfəˈnɪə/ *noun* (also **chiffon(n)ière**) M18 **French** (*chiffonnier*, *chiffonière*, transferred use of CHIFFONNIER). A movable low cupboard with a sideboard top.

chiffonnade /ʃɪfəˈnɑːd/, *foreign* /ʃifɔnad/ (*plural same*) *noun* L19 **French**. A selection of shredded or finely cut vegetables, used especially as a garnish for soup.

chiffonnier /ʃifɔnje/ *noun* plural pronounced same M19 **French**. A collector of scraps, a rag-picker.

chignon /ˈʃiːnjɒ̃/ *noun* L18 **French** (originally = nape of the neck, from Proto-Romance variant of Latin *catena* chain). A coil or mass of hair worn by women at the back of the head.

chikan /'ʧɪk(ə)n/ *noun* (also **chicken**) L19 **Urdu** (*chikan* from Persian *čikin*). A type of hand-embroidery of the Indian subcontinent.

chilli /'ʧɪli/ *noun* (also **chile**, **chili**) plural **chil(l)ies**, **chiles** E17 **Spanish** (*chile* from Nahuatl *chilli*). The (dried) red pod of the pepper *Capsicum annuum* var. *longum*, used in sauces, relishes, etc., and made into a hot cayenne; cayenne made from these dried pods. Also *chilli pepper*.

chilli con carne /ˌʧɪli kɒn 'kɑ:ni/ *noun phrase* (also **chile con carne**, **chili con carne**) M19 **Spanish** (= chilli with meat). A Mexican dish of minced beef, beans, and chilli.

chilli relleno /ˌʧɪli rɛ'ljeɪnəʊ/ *noun phrase* **Spanish** (= stuffed chilli). A stuffed green pepper.

■ Sometimes abbreviated to *relleno* plural *rellenos* (E20).

chimera /kʌɪ'mɪərə/, /kɪ'mɪərə/ *noun* (also **chimaera**) LME **Latin** (*chimaera* from Greek *khimaira* she-goat, monster, from *khimaros* he-goat). **1** LME *Greek Mythology* A fire-breathing monster, with a lion's head, a goat's body, and a serpent's tail. **2** LME A grotesque monster represented in painting etc. **3a** E16 A bogey, a horrible phantasm. **b** L16 A wild or fanciful conception. **c** M19 A thing of hybrid character. **4** E19 (Usually **chimaera**.) Any cartilaginous fish of the family Chimaeridae. **5** E20 *Biology* An organism whose cells are not all derived from the same zygote.

chin variant of TCHIN.

chinchilla /ʧɪn'ʧɪlə/ *noun* E17 **Spanish** (probably from Aymara or Quechua). **I 1** E17 A South American rodent of the genus *Chinchilla*, with very soft grey fur. **2** L19 A cat of a silver-grey breed. **3** E20 A rabbit of a variety bred for its grey fur. **II 4** E19 The fur of the South American chinchilla or of the chinchilla rabbit.

chiné /ʃi:'neɪ/ *noun & adjective* M19 **French** (past participle of *chiner*, from *Chine* China). (A fabric) given a mottled pattern of (supposedly) Chinese style by colouring the warp or weft threads, or both, before weaving.

chino /'ʧi:nəʊ/ *noun & adjective* M20 **American Spanish** (= toasted). **A** M20 *noun* plural **chinos** A cotton twill cloth, usually khaki-coloured; in *plural*, trousers made of this. **B** M20 *adjective* Of this cloth.

■ Originally United States.

chinoiserie /ʃɪn'wɑ:zəri/, *foreign* /ʃinwazri/ (*plural same*) *noun* L19 **French** (from *chinois* Chinese + *-erie*). A Chinese or imitation Chinese artistic object, piece of furniture, etc.; the imitation of Chinese motifs in furniture etc.

1996 *Country Life* ... although chinoiserie is often thought of as a minor and frivolous flourish to the European decorative arts, it affected almost every palace and great house from the Danish Rosenborg Slot in the 17th century to the Brighton Pavilion ...

chipolata /ʧɪpə'lɑ:tə/ *noun* L19 **French** (from Italian *cipollata* dish of onions, from *cipolla* onion). In full *chipolata sausage*. A small (often spicy) sausage.

chipotle /tʃɪ'pɒtleɪ/ *noun* L20 **Mexican Spanish**. A kind of dried and smoked chilli used in Mexican cooking.

chi-rho /kʌɪ'rəʊ/ *noun* M19 **Greek** (twenty-second letter of the alphabet *chi* + seventeenth letter *rho*). A monogram representing the first two letters of Greek *Khristos* Christ.

■ The *chi-rho* was adopted in AD 312 by the Byzantine emperor Constantine the Great as a device for his military banners, following on a vision in which he was told 'By this sign you shall conquer'. During the following centuries the *chi-rho* became ubiquitous in Christian art.

chirimoya variant of cherimoya.

chitarrone /kɪtə'rəʊni/ *noun* plural **chitarroni** /kɪtə'rəʊni/ M18 **Italian** (augmentative of *chitarra* guitar). A double-necked lute of great length, a theorbo.

chiton /'kʌɪtɒn/, /'kʌɪt(ə)n/ *noun* E19 **Greek** (*khitōn*; in sense 1 through Modern Latin *Chiton* genus name). **1** E19 A mollusc of the class Polyplacophora, characterized by a broad oval foot and a symmetrical dorsal shell composed of a series of eight overlapping plates. **2** M19 A long woollen tunic worn in ancient Greece.

chocolatier /ʧɒkə'latɪə/, *foreign* /ʃɔkɔlatje/ (*plural same*) *noun* L19 **French** (from *chocolat* (or Spanish *chocolate* from Nahuatl *chocolatl* item of food made from caocao seeds)). A maker or seller of chocolate.

chokidar /'tʃaʊkɪdɑ:/ *noun* (also **chaukidar** /'tʃaʊkɪdɑ:/) E17 **Urdu** (*chaukīdār*, from Hindustani *cauki* toll, police station + Urdu and Persian *-dār* keeper). In the Indian subcontinent; a watchman.

chola see CHOLO.

cholent /ˈtʃɒl(ə)nt/, /ˈʃɒl(ə)nt/ *noun* M20 **Yiddish** (*tscholnt*; cf. SCHALET). A Jewish Sabbath dish of slowly baked meat and vegetables, prepared on a Friday and cooked overnight.

choli /ˈtʃəʊli/ *noun* E20 **Hindustani** (*colī*). An Indian woman's short-sleeved bodice of a type worn under a SARI.

cholo /ˈtʃəʊləʊ/ *noun* (also **Cholo**; feminine **chola** /ˈtʃəʊlə/) plural **cholos** M19 **American Spanish** (from *Chololl‌án*, now *Cholula*, a district of Mexico). An Indian of Latin America; a mestizo; *United States* (frequently *derogatory*) a lower-class Mexican.

chometz variant of HAMETZ.

chopsuey /tʃɒpˈsuːɪ/ *noun* L19 **Chinese** ((Cantonese) *tsaâp suì* mixed bits). A Chinese dish of pieces of meat or chicken fried with rice, onions, etc., often made with leftover food.

choragus /kɒˈreɪgəs/ *noun* (also **choregus**) plural **choragi** /kɒˈreɪgʌɪ/, /kɒˈreɪgiː/ E17 **Latin** (from Greek *khoragos*, *khorēgos*, from *khoros* chorus + *agein* to lead). Chiefly *Greek History* The leader of a chorus, or of any group; *specifically* at Athens, a person who defrayed the cost of bringing out a chorus.

chorea /kɒˈrɪə/ *noun* L17 **Latin** (from Greek *khoreia* dance). *Medicine* Jerky involuntary movements; a disease with symptoms of this kind.

chorizo /tʃəˈriːzəʊ/ *noun* plural **chorizos** M19 **Spanish**. A Spanish sausage of which the chief ingredient is pork.

chose jugée /ʃoz ʒyʒe/ *noun phrase* plural **choses jugées** (pronounced same) L19 **French**. A settled or decided matter; something it is idle to discuss.

chota /ˈtʃəʊtə/ *adjective* E19 **Anglo-Indian** (Hindustani *choṭā*). Small, little; younger, junior.

■ Occurs often in such phrases as *chota hazri* (a light early breakfast) and *chota peg* (a small drink of whisky).

chott variant of SHOTT.

chou /ʃuː/, *foreign* /ʃu/ *noun* (also **choux** (pronounced same)) plural **choux** E18 **French** (= cabbage, from Latin *caulis*). **1** E18 A small ball of pastry filled with cream etc. **2** L19 A rosette or ornamental knot of ribbon, chiffon, etc., on a woman's hat or dress.

choucroute /ʃukrut/ *noun* M19 **French** (from German dialect *Surkrut* SAUERKRAUT, assimilated to French CHOU). A kind of pickled cabbage.

chouette /ʃuːˈɛt/ *noun* L19 **French** (literally, 'barn owl'). A player in a two-handed game (e.g. backgammon, piquet) who plays against a number of others successively or in combination, especially as a means of enabling three players to compete with one another.

chou moellier /ˌʃuː ˈmɒlɪə/ *noun phrase* E20 **French** (= marrow-filled cabbage). A kind of kale grown as fodder, marrow-stem. *Australia and New Zealand*.

choux see CHOU.

chow mein /tʃaʊ ˈmeɪn/ *noun phrase* L19 **Chinese** (*chǎo miàn fried noodles*). A Chinese dish of fried noodles usually in a sauce with shredded meat and vegetables.

chroma /ˈkrəʊmə/ *noun* L19 **Greek** (*khrōma* colour). Purity or intensity as a colour quality, especially in colour television etc.

chronique scandaleuse /krɔnik skɑ̃daløz/ *noun phrase* plural **chroniques scandaleuses** (pronounced same) M19 **French**. A compilation or body of gossip, scandal, etc.

chuddar variant of CHADAR.

chulo /ˈtʃulo/, /ˈtʃuːləʊ/ *noun* plural **chulos** /ˈtʃulos/, /ˈtʃuːləʊz/ L18 **Spanish**. *Bullfighting* A bullfighter's assistant.

chuño /ˈtʃuɲo/, /ˈtʃuːnjəʊ/ *noun* E17 **American Spanish** (from Quechua *ch'uñu*). (Flour prepared from) dried potatoes, as eaten by Andean Indians.

chupatti variant of CHAPATTI.

chuppah /ˈxʊpə/ *noun* (also **chuppaha**) L19 **Hebrew** (*ḥuppāh* cover, canopy). A canopy beneath which Jewish marriage ceremonies are performed.

chuprassy variant of CHAPRASSI.

churinga variant of TJURUNGA.

churrasco /tʃʊˈrasko/, /tʃʊˈraskəʊ/ *noun* L20 **South American Spanish** (probably from dialect *churrascar* to burn; cf. Spanish *soccarar* to scorch). A grilled dish, usually of meat.

chutzpah /ˈxʊtspə/, /ˈhʊtspə/ *noun* L19 **Yiddish** (from Aramaic *ḥuṣpā*). Shameless audacity, gall. *slang*.

1995 *Times* Celtic oratory—brooding, bombastic, and with a touch of Hergé's Captain Haddock . . . —meets a metropolitan Londoner's smoothness, zest and chutzpah.

chypre /ʃipr/ *noun* L19 **French** (= Cyprus, where perhaps originally made). A heavy perfume made from sandalwood.

ciabatta /tʃəˈbɑːtə/, *foreign* /tʃaˈbatta/ *noun* plural **ciabattas**, **ciabatte** /tʃaˈbaːtte/ L20 **Italian** ((dialect) literally, 'slipper' (from the shape of the loaf)). A type of moist aerated Italian bread made with olive oil; a loaf of this.

ciao /tʃaʊ/ *interjection* E20 **Italian** (dialectal alteration of *schiavo* (I am your) slave, from medieval Latin *sclavus* slave). Hello; goodbye.

■ A colloquial expression widespread in continental Europe, now also used as a casual greeting between Anglophones.

cibol variant of CIBOULE.

ciborium /sɪˈbɔːrɪəm/ *noun* plural **ciboria** /sɪˈbɔːrɪə/ M16 **Medieval Latin** (from Greek *kibōrion* cup-shaped seed-vessel of the Egyptian water lily, a drinking-cup made from this; sense 1 probably influenced by Latin *cibus* food). **1** M16 *Christian Church* A receptacle for the reservation of the Eucharist, shaped like a shrine, or a cup with an arched cover. **2** M18 *Architecture* A canopy; a canopied shrine.

ciboule /ˈsɪb(ə)l/ *noun* (also **cibol**) M17 **French**. The Welsh onion, *Allium fistulosum*, which resembles a spring onion.

cicada /sɪˈkɑːdə/ *noun* LME **Latin** (*cicada*, *cicala*). Any of the family Cicadidae of large-winged homopteran insects, the males of which make shrill chirping sounds.

■ The Old Provençal name *cigala* (cf. French *cigale*) was the usual form in English during the seventeenth and eighteenth centuries.

cicatrice /ˈsɪkətrɪs/ *noun* (also (especially *Medicine and Botany*) **cicatrix** /ˈsɪkətrɪks/) plural **cicatrices** /ˈsɪkətrɪsɪz/, *especially Medicine and Botany* /sɪkəˈtrʌɪsiːz/ LME **Old and Modern French** (or Latin *cicatrix*, *cicatric-*). **1** LME The scar of a healed wound, burn, etc.; a scar on the bark of a tree. **b** E19 *Botany* A scar. **2** L16 A mark or impression resembling a scar.

cicerone /tʃɪtʃəˈrəʊni/, /sɪsəˈrəʊni/ *noun & verb* plural **ciceroni** /tʃɪtʃəˈrəʊni/, /sɪsəˈrəʊni/ **cicerones** E18 **Italian** (from Latin name *Cicero*, *-onis*). **A** *noun* E18 A guide who understands and explains antiquities etc.; any learned guide. **B** *transitive verb* L18 Act as a cicerone to.

■ Marcus Tullius Cicero (106–43 BC) was renowned for his learning, and it is surmised that English Grand Tourists dubbed the local Italian antiquaries who showed them round the sites *cicerones*, that is 'Ciceros'. The actual historical origin of the word is uncertain, as the earliest English use of *cicerone* (Addison was apparently the first, in 1726) antedates its appearance in Italian dictionaries.

1996 *Country Life* He made a good profit on the . . . 'Portland' vase bought from the Roman cicerone James Byres for £1,000 . . .

cicisbeo /tʃɪtʃɪzˈbeɪəʊ/ *noun* plural **cicisbei** /tʃɪtʃɪzˈbeiː/, **cicisbeos** E18 **Italian** (of unknown origin). A married (originally Italian) woman's male companion or lover.

ci-devant /sidvɑ̃/ *adjective & adverb* E18 **French**. Former(ly).

■ Used with the person's earlier name or status.

cigala see under CICADA.

cilantro /θiˈlantro/, /siˈlantro/ *noun* L20 **Spanish**. Coriander. *North American*.

cilium /ˈsɪlɪəm/ *noun* plural **cilia** /ˈsɪlɪə/ E18 **Latin**. **1** E18 An eyelash; (the edge of) an eyelid. **2** L18 A delicate hair like an eyelash, e.g. on the margin of a leaf, or the wing of an insect. **3** M19 A hairlike appendage, usually motile, which is found in numbers on the surfaces of some cells, and in many organisms is used in locomotion.

cimbalom /ˈsɪmb(ə)l(ə)m/ *noun* (also **zimbalom** /ˈzɪmb(ə)l(ə)m/) L19 **Hungarian** (from Italian CYMBALO). A dulcimer.

cinéaste /ˈsɪneɪast/, *foreign* /sineast/ (*plural same*) *noun* (also **cineast(e)** /ˈsɪnɪast/) E20 **French** (from *ciné* cine + *-aste* as in *enthousiaste* enthusiast). An enthusiast for or devotee of the cinema.

1995 *Spectator* It is outwardly the unfilmable script, far more imaginary than real, of a would-be English cinéaste, one Richard Arthur Thornby (RAT), currently lecturing in Texas on the cinema.

cinematheque /sɪnɪməˈtɛk/ *noun* (also **cinémathèque** /sinematɛk/ (*plural same*)) M20 **French** (*cinémathèque*, from *cinéma* cinema, after *bibliothèque* library). A library of cinema films; a (national) repository of old films. Also, a small cinema showing artistic films.

cinéma-vérité /sinemɑverite/, /ˌsɪnɪmə ˈvɛrɪteɪ/ *noun* M20 **French**. (The making of) films which avoid artificiality and have the appearance of real life.

ciné-vérité /sineverite/, /sɪnɪˈvɛrɪteɪ/ *noun* M20 **French**. CINÉMA-VÉRITÉ.

cinq-à-sept /sɛ̃k a sɛt/ *noun* (also **cinq à sept**) L20 **French** (literally, 'five to seven'). A visit to a mistress or a brothel, traditionally made between five and seven p.m.

> **1996** *Spectator* The English like to stand around a pool table and guffaw rather loudly. Continental men prefer *le cinq à sept*.

cinquecento /ˌtʃɪŋkwɪˈtʃɛntəʊ/ *noun* M18 **Italian** (= five hundred). The sixteenth century in Italy; the Italian style of art of this period, with reversion to classical forms.

cipolin /ˈsɪpəlɪn/ *noun* (also **cipollino** /ˌtʃɪpəˈliːnəʊ/, plural **cipolinos**) L18 **French** ((*cipolin* from) Italian *cipollino*, from *cipolla* onion (Latin *cepa*); so called from the resemblance of its foliated structure to the coats of an onion). An Italian marble interfoliated with veins of talc, mica, quartz, etc., showing alternations of (especially white and green) colourings.

cippus /ˈsɪpəs/ *noun* plural **cippi** /ˈsɪpʌɪ/ E18 **Latin** (= post, stake). *Architecture* A low column, usually bearing an inscription, used by the ancients as a landmark, funerary monument, etc.

■ Earlier (E17) in the sense of 'the stocks', but this sense does not seem to have survived into the eighteenth century.

circa /ˈsəːkə/ *preposition* M19 **Latin**. About, approximately in or at (with dates etc.).

■ Frequently in abbreviated form before a date: *c.* or *ca.*

circiter /ˈsəːsɪtə/ *preposition* L19 **Latin**. About, CIRCA.

■ Used with dates.

circulus vitiosus /ˌsəːkjʊləs vɪʃɪˈəʊsəs/, /vɪtɪˈəʊsəs/ *noun phrase* plural **circuli vitiosi** /ˌsəːkjʊlʌɪ vɪʃɪˈəʊsʌɪ/, /vɪtɪˈəʊsʌɪ/ E20 **Latin**. A vicious circle.

ciré /ˈsiːreɪ/ *adjective & noun* E20 **French** (= waxed). (Fabric) with a smooth polished surface, obtained especially by heating and waxing.

cire perdue /sir pɛrdy/ *noun phrase* L19 **French** (= lost wax). A method of casting bronze by pouring molten metal over a wax-surfaced core within a mould, to form a model in the space created by the melting and running out of wax.

cirque /səːk/ *noun* E17 **French** (from Latin *circus* circle, circus, corresponding to Greek *kirkos* ring, circle). **1** E17 Circus. **2** L17 A circle, a ring, a circlet. *literary*. **3** M19 *Physical Geography* A large bowl-shaped hollow of glacial origin at the head of a valley or on a mountainside.

cirrus /ˈsɪrəs/ *noun* (also **cirrhus**) plural **cirri** /ˈsɪrʌɪ/ E18 **Latin** (= curl, fringe). **1** E18 A curl or tuft of hair. *rare*. **2** E18 *Botany* A tendril. **3** M18 *Zoology* A slender, filamentary appendage, e.g. the limb of a cirripede, a barbel of certain fishes. **4** E19 *Meteorology* A cloud-type occurring at high altitude and having the appearance of wispy filamentous tufts.

cithara /ˈsɪθ(ə)rə/, /ˈkɪθ(ə)rə/ *noun* (also **kithara** /ˈkɪθ(ə)rə/) L18 **Latin** (from Greek *kithara*). An ancient Greek and Roman stringed musical instrument akin to the lyre, having two arms rising vertically from the soundbox.

civet /sivɛ/ *noun* plural pronounced same E18 **French** (earlier *civé*, from *cive* chive). A highly seasoned stew of hare, venison, or other game.

clachan /ˈklax(ə)n/ *noun* LME **Gaelic and Irish** (*clachán*). In Scotland and Northern Ireland: a small village, a hamlet.

clair-de-lune /klɛrdəlyn/, /klɛːdəˈluːn/ *noun* L19 **French** (literally, 'moonlight'). A soft white or pale blue-grey colour; a Chinese porcelain glaze of this colour.

clairschach /ˈklɑːʃəx/ *noun* (also **clarschach**) L15 **Irish** (*cláirseach*, Gaelic *clàrsach*). The traditional Celtic harp strung with wire.

clairvoyance /klɛːˈvɔɪəns/ *noun* M19 **French** (from as next). **1** M19 The supposed faculty of perceiving, as if by seeing, what is happening or exists out of sight. **2** M19 Keenness of mental perception: exceptional insight.

clairvoyant /klɛːˈvɔɪənt/ *adjective & noun* (occasionally feminine **clairvoyante**) L17 **French** (from *clair* clear + *voyant* present participial adjective of *voir* to see). **A** *adjective* **1** L17 Clear-sighted, perceptive. *rare*. **2** M19 Having or exercising the faculty of clairvoyance; pertaining to clairvoyance. **B** *noun* **1** L18 A clear-sighted person. *rare*. **2** M19 A person having the faculty of clairvoyance.

claque /klak/, /klɑ:k/; *foreign* /klak/ (*plural same*) *noun* M19 **French** (from *claquer* to clap). A hired body of applauders; *transferred* a body of devoted or sycophantic followers.

1995 *Times* [The organizers] of events decreed that before every open race there would be competitions for juveniles and juniors. This encourages the young to participate, feeds talent into the sport and provides an enthusiastic claque to cheer on the stars.

claqueur /klɑ:'kə:/, *foreign* /klakœr/ (*plural same*) *noun* M19 **French** (from *claquer* to clap). A member of a claque.

claro /'klɑ:rəʊ/ *noun* plural **claros** L19 **Spanish** (= light, clear). A light-coloured cigar.

clarschach variant of CLAIRSCHACH.

classico /'klasɪkəʊ/ *adjective* L20 **Italian**. Of an Italian wine: superior, in an established style of excellence.

■ Used after the name of a wine, as in *Bardolino classico*.

clave /kleɪv/, /klɑ:v/ *noun* E20 **American Spanish** (from Spanish *clave* keystone, from Latin *clavis* key). *Music* Either of a pair of hardwood sticks used to make a hollow sound.

■ Usually in plural.

clavecin /'klavɪsɪn/ *noun* E19 **French** (from medieval Latin *clavicymbalum* from *clavis* key + *cymbalum* cymbal). A harpsichord, especially in or from France.

clavicembalo /klavɪ'ʧɛmbələʊ/ *noun* plural **clavicembalos** M18 **Italian** (from as CLAVECIN). A harpsichord, especially in or from Italy.

clementine /'klɛm(ə)ntʌɪn/, /'klɛm(ə)nti:n/ *noun* E20 **French** (*clémentine*). A variety of tangerine grown especially in North Africa.

clepsydra /'klɛpsɪdrə/ *noun* plural **clepsydras**, **clepsydrae** /'klɛpsɪdri:/ LME **Latin** (from Greek *klepsudra*, from *kleps-* combining form of *kleptein* to steal + *hudōr* water). An instrument used in antiquity to measure time by the flow of water; a water-clock.

cliché /'kli:ʃeɪ/ *noun* M19 **French** (use as noun of past participle of *clicher* to stereotype, perhaps of imitative origin). **1** M19 *History* A metal stereotype or electrotype block. **2** L19 *figurative* A stereotyped expression, a hackneyed phrase or opinion; a stereotyped character, style, etc.

2 1996 *Spectator* [The] novel . . . simultaneously underlines and overturns whole layers of class clichés.

clientele /ˌkli:ɒn'tɛl/, *foreign* /kliɑ̃tɛl/ *noun* (also **clientèle**) M16 **Latin and French** (either, directly from Latin *clientela*, from *cliens*, *-ntis* (earlier *cluens*) client, use as noun of present participle of *cluere* to hear, obey; or, later, from French *clientèle* from Latin). **1** M16–L19 Clientship; patronage. **2** L16 A body of clients, a following; the customers (of a shop); the patrons (of a theatre etc.); persons seeking the professional advice of a lawyer, architect, etc.

clique /kli:k/ *noun* E18 **Old and Modern French** (from *cliquer* to make a noise, from Middle Dutch *klikken* to click). A small exclusive group; a coterie.

■ Possibly related to CLAQUE.

cloaca /kləʊ'eɪkə/ *noun* plural **cloacae** /kləʊ'eɪki:/, **cloacas** L16 **Latin** (*cloaca*, *cluaca* related to *cluere* to cleanse). **1** L16 An underground conduit for drainage, a sewer. Also, a water-closet. **2** M19 *Zoology* A common cavity for the release of digestive and urogenital products in birds, reptiles, amphibians, most fish, and monotremes.

clobiosh variant of KLABERJASS.

clochard /klɔʃar/ *noun* plural pronounced same M20 **French** (from *clocher* to limp). In France: a beggar, a vagrant.

1996 *Times* When, after the war, he went back to France, he lived for years—legend has it—more or less as a *clochard*, looked after, for a time, by the French Communist Party.

cloche /klɒʃ/, /kləʊʃ/ *noun* L19 **French** (= bell). **1** L19 A bell-glass; a small translucent (especially glass) cover for forcing or protecting outdoor plants. **2** E20 A woman's close-fitting bell-shaped hat. In full *cloche hat*.

cloisonné /klwazɔne/ *adjective & noun* M19 **French** (past participle of *cloisonner* to partition, from *cloison* division). More fully *cloisonné enamel*. (Designating) enamel-work or -ware in which the colours in the pattern are separated by thin strips of metal attached to the base. Cf. CHAMPLEVÉ.

cloqué /'kləʊkeɪ/ *noun* (also Anglicized as **cloky** /'kləʊki/) E20 **French** (literally, 'blistered'). A fabric with an irregularly raised or embossed surface.

clou /klu/ *noun* L19 **French** (literally, 'nail, stud'). The chief attraction, the point of greatest interest, the central idea.

1959 *Observer* The *clou* of the ballet is to be found in these four female solos.

cocasse /kɔkas/ *adjective* M19 **French**. Droll; ridiculous.

coccyx /'kɒksɪks/ *noun* plural **coccyxes, coccyges** /'kɒksɪdʒiːz/ L16 **Latin** (from Greek *kokkux* (originally) cuckoo (from its resemblance (in humans) to a cuckoo's beak)). *Anatomy* The small triangular bone forming the lower end of the spinal column in humans and some apes; the analogous part in birds or other vertebrates.

coco-de-mer /ˌkəʊkəʊdə'mɛː/ *noun* E19 **French** (= coco from the sea (as having been first known from the nuts found floating in the sea)). A tall palm tree *Lodoicea maldivica*, native to the Seychelles; its immense woody nut.

cocotte /kɒ'kɒt/ *noun* M19 **French** (sense 1 from a child's name for a hen; sense 2 from French *cocasse* from Latin *cucuma* cooking vessel). **1** M19 A fashionable prostitute. *archaic*. **2** E20 A small fireproof dish for cooking and serving an individual portion of food.

coda /'kəʊdə/ *noun* M18 **Italian** (from Latin *cauda* tail). **1** M18 *Music* An independent and often elaborate passage introduced after the end of the main part of a movement. **b** L19 *transferred* and *figurative* A concluding event, remark, literary passage, etc. **2** E20 *Ballet* The final section of a classical *pas de deux*; the concluding dance of a whole ballet.

codetta /kəʊ'dɛtə/ *noun* M19 **Italian** (diminutive of CODA). *Music* A short coda; a short passage connecting sections of a movement or fugue.

codex /'kəʊdɛks/ *noun* plural **codices** /'kəʊdɪsiːz/, /'kɒdɪsiːz/ L16 **Latin** (*codex*, *codic-* block of wood, block split into leaves or tablets, book). **1** L16–M18 A legal code; *generally* a set of rules on any subject. **2** L18 A manuscript volume, especially of ancient texts. **3** M19 A collection of pharmaceutical descriptions of drugs, preparations, etc.

coenobium /sɪ'nəʊbɪəm/ *noun* (also **cenobium** (mainly United States)) plural **coenobia** /sɪ'nəʊbɪə/ E19 **ecclesiastical Latin** (from Greek *koinobion* community life, convent, from *koinos* common + *bion* life). **1** E19 A monastic house, a coenoby. **2** L19 *Biology* A cluster of unicellular organisms, e.g. green algae, that behaves as a colony.

cogida /ko'xiða/, /kə'hiːdə/ *noun* E20 **Spanish** (literally, 'a gathering of the harvest', use as noun of feminine past participle of *coger* to seize, from Latin *colligare* to bind together). *Bullfighting* A tossing of a bullfighter by a bull.

cogito /'kɒdʒɪtəʊ/ *noun* M19 **Latin** (= I think, 1st person present of *cogitare* to cogitate). *Philosophy* The principle establishing the existence of the thinker from the fact of his or her thinking or awareness.

■ The principle derives from the formula *cogito, ergo sum* 'I think (*or* I am thinking), therefore I am' of the French philosopher René Descartes (1596–1650).

cognitum /'kɒgnɪtəm/ *noun* plural **cognita** /'kɒgnɪtə/ L19 **Latin** (neuter past participle of *cognoscere* to know). *Philosophy* An object of cognition.

cognomen /kɒg'nəʊmən/ *noun* plural **cognomens**, (earlier) **cognomina** E17 **Latin** (*cognomen* from as *co-* with + (g)*nomen* name). **1** E17 A surname; a nickname; *loosely* an appellation, a name. **2** L19 *Roman History* The third personal name of a Roman citizen (as Marcus Tullius *Cicero*); a fourth name or personal epithet (as Publius Cornelius Scipio *Africanus*).

cognoscente /koɲo'ʃɛnte/, /kɒnjə'ʃɛnti/ *noun* plural **cognoscenti** /koɲo'ʃɛnti/ M18 **Italian** ((now *conoscente*), literally, 'a person who knows', Latinized form of *conoscente* from Latin *cognoscent-* present participial stem of *cognoscere* to know). A connoisseur; a discerning expert.

1995 *Country Life* This steep, deep and funky resort [sc. Taos] is an extraordinary amalgam of Swiss, Pueblo Indian and Spanish cultures and attracts skiing *cognoscenti* from round the globe.

cohabitation /kəʊˌhabɪ'teɪʃ(ə)n/, *in sense 3 foreign* /kɔabitasjɔ̃/ *noun* LME **French**. **1** LME Living together; community of life. *archaic*. **2** M16 Living together as husband and wife, especially without legal marriage. **3** *Politics* L20 An alliance dictated by expediency between office-holders of differing political views (originally in France).

■ Fully naturalized in senses 1 and 2, the word in its general literal meaning, as used in Middle English, is now almost entirely superseded by the particular sense 2. As a recent introduction from the French political scene, sense 3 is often written in italics to differentiate it from sense 2 and is therefore accorded a version of the French pronunciation.

3 1995 *Times* That experience will be all the more important in dealings with the new Duma, where the election result will force *cohabitation à la russe*.

cohue /kɔy/ *noun* plural pronounced same M19 **French**. A mob, an unruly crowd.

coiffeur /kwɑːˈfəː/, /kwɒˈfəː/, *foreign* /kwafœr/ (*plural same*) *noun* M19 **French** (from *coiffer* to dress the hair). A hairdresser.

coiffure /kwɑːˈfjʊə/, /kwɒˈfjʊə/, *noun also foreign* /kwafyr/ (*plural same*) *noun & verb* M17 **French** (*coiffe* from Old French *coife* head-dress, from late Latin *cofia* helmet). **A** *noun* M17 The way the hair is arranged or (formerly) the head decorated or covered; a hairstyle, a head-dress. **B** *transitive verb* E20 Dress or arrange hair, coiff. Chiefly as *coiffured* participial adjective.

coitus /ˈkəʊɪtəs/ *noun* M19 **Latin**. Copulation.

cojones /koˈxones/, /kəˈhəʊneɪz/ *noun plural* M20 **Spanish** (plural of *cojón* testicle). Testicles; *figurative* courage, guts.

■ Colloquial, and in figurative use often euphemistic for 'balls' (see quotation 1996).

1932 E. Hemingway *Death in the Afternoon* It takes more cojones to be a sportsman where death is a closer party to the game.

1996 *Times Magazine* Corrigan is working his *cojones* off to give us kidneys, liver, sweetbreads, anything that has not been banned which might be banned.

col /kɒl/ *noun* M19 **French** (from Latin *collum* neck). **1** M19 A depression in the summit-line of a mountain chain; a saddle between two peaks. **2** L19 *Meteorology* An area of lower pressure between two anticyclones.

collage /kɒˈlɑːʒ/ *noun* E20 **French** (= gluing). An abstract form of art in which photographs, pieces of paper, string, matchsticks, etc., are placed in juxtaposition and glued to a surface; a work in this form; *figurative* a jumbled collection of impressions, events, styles, etc.

collectanea /kɒlɛkˈtɑːnɪə/, /kɒlɛkˈteɪnɪə/ *noun* M17 **Latin** (*collectanea* neuter plural (from *collect-*, past participial stem of *colligere* to assemble) as used as adjective in *Dicta collectanea* of Caesar, and as noun in *Collectanea* of Solinus). As *plural*, passages, remarks, etc., collected from various sources. As *singular*, a miscellany.

collegium /kəˈliːdʒɪəm/ *noun* plural **collegia** /kəˈliːdʒɪə/ L19 **Latin**. **1** L19 A society of amateurs for performing music, now *especially* one attached to a German or American university. In full *collegium musicum* /ˈmjuːzɪkəm/, plural *collegia musica* /ˈmjuːzɪkə/. **2** E20 *History* (representing Russian *kollegiya*) An advisory or administrative board in Russia.

colloquium /kəˈləʊkwɪəm/ *noun* plural **colloquia** /kəˈləʊkwɪə/, **colloquiums** L16 **Latin** (from as *co(l)-* with + *loqui* to speak). **1** L16–M18 A conversation, a dialogue. **2** M19 A conference; *specifically* an academic conference or seminar.

colluvium /kəˈl(j)uːvɪəm/ *noun* M20 **Latin**. *Physical Geography* Material which accumulates at the foot of a steep slope.

colon /kɒˈlən/ *noun* E17 **French** (from Latin *colonus*). **1** E17 A husbandman. *rare*. **2** M20 *History* A colonial settler or farmer, especially in a French colony.

colophon /ˈkɒləf(ə)n/ *noun* E17 **Late Latin** (from Greek *kolophōn* summit, finishing touch). **1** E17 A crowning or finishing touch. *rare*. **2** L18 A statement, sometimes with a device, at the end of a manuscript or printed book, giving information about its authorship, production, etc. **b** M20 A publisher's or printer's imprint; *loosely* a publisher's device, especially on a title-page.

coloratura /kɒlərəˈtjʊərə/, /kɒlərəˈtʊərə/ *noun* M18 **Italian** (from late Latin *coloratura*, from *colorat-* past participial stem of *colorare* to colour). **1** M18 Florid passages in vocal music, with runs, trills, etc.; the singing of these. **2** M20 A singer of coloratura, especially a soprano.

1 1996 *Spectator* Thus Zerbinetta's display piece in *Ariadne auf Naxos* is every bit as riveting as the frustrated composer's outcry earlier on . . . its coloratura expresses the feelings of a free spirit . . .

colossus /kəˈlɒsəs/ *noun* plural **colossi** /kəˈlɒsʌɪ/ **colossuses** LME **Latin** (from Greek *kolossos* applied by Herodotus to the statues of Egyptian temples). **1** LME A statue of considerably more than life size. **2** E17 A gigantic or overawing person or thing; an empire etc. personified as standing astride over dominions.

■ The Colossus of Rhodes, a gigantic statue of the Hellenistic period that is said to have-

straddled the harbour entrance on the island of Rhodes, was one of the Seven Wonders of the World.

2 1996 *New Scientist* Freud was a colossus, a massive intellect, the keenest clinical observer of mental disorders in the past 200 years.

colostrum /kəˈlɒstrəm/ *noun* (also (earlier) **colostra**) L16 **Latin**. The first milk of a mammal after giving birth.

colportage /ˈkɒlpɔːtɪdʒ/ *noun* M19 **French** (from *colporter* to hawk, peddle (see next)). The work of a colporteur; the peddling of books, newspapers, bibles, etc.

colporteur /ˈkɒlpɔːtə/, /kɒlpɔːˈtəː/ *noun* L18 **French** (from *colporter*, probably alteration of *comporter* from Latin *comportare* transport, from as *com-* with + *portare* to carry). A pedlar of books, newspapers, etc., *especially* one employed by a religious society to distribute bibles and other religious tracts.

columbarium /kɒl(ə)mˈbɛːrɪəm/ *noun* plural **columbaria** /kɒl(ə)mˈbɛːrɪə/, **columbariums** M18 **Latin** (*columbarium*, from *columba* dove + *-arium*). **1** M18 A vault or building with niches for the reception of cinerary urns; a niche in such a vault etc. **2** E19 A pigeon-hole; a columbary.

coma /ˈkəʊmə/ *noun 1* plural **comae** /ˈkəʊmiː/ E17 **Latin** (from Greek *komē* hair of the head). **1** E17 *Botany* The top of a plant; *especially* a terminal tuft of bracts or leaves; a leafy crown of branches; a tuft of silky hairs at the end of some seeds. **2** M18 *Astronomy* The diffuse hazy region surrounding the nucleus of a comet. **3** M19 An optical aberration causing the image of an off-axis point to be flared, like a comet with a diverging tail; the flared image itself.

coma /ˈkəʊmə/ *noun 2* M17 **Modern Latin** (from Greek *kōma*, *kōmat-*, related to *koitē* bed, *keisthai* to lie down). *Medicine* A prolonged state of unconsciousness from which the patient cannot be roused. Also *figurative*.

comble /kɔ̃bl/ *noun* plural pronounced same M19 **French** (from Latin *cumulus* heap). A culminating point, a crowning touch.

comédie humaine /kɔmedi ymɛn/ plural **comédie humaines** pronounced same L19 **French** (literally, 'human comedy'). The sum of human activities; a literary portrait of this.

■ The title given by Honoré de Balzac (1799–1850) to his series of novels on nineteenth-century French society.

comédie larmoyante /kɔmedi larmwajɑ̃t/ plural **comédie larmoyantes** pronounced same E19 **French** (literally, 'weeping comedy'). A sentimental, moralizing comedy.

■ Applied originally to the plays of P. C. Nivelle de La Chausée (1692–1754), which were very fashionable in eighteenth-century France.

comedienne /kəˌmiːdɪˈɛn/, /kəˌmɛdɪˈɛn/ *noun* (also **comédienne** /kəˌmeɪdɪˈɛn/) M19 **French** (feminine of *comédien* comedian). A female comedian.

comédie noire /kɔmedi nwar/ plural **comédie noires** pronounced same M20 **French** (literally, 'black comedy'). A macabre or farcical rendering of a violent or tragic theme.

■ Now more common in English translation, 'black comedy', but cf. NOIR.

comes /ˈkəʊmiːz/ *noun* plural **comites** /ˈkəʊmɪtiːz/ M18 **Latin** (= companion, from *com-* with + *ire* to go). *Music* An answering or imitating voice in a canon or fugue; the answer itself. Opposed to DUX sense 1.

commando /kəˈmɑːndəʊ/ *noun* plural **commandos** L18 **Portuguese** ((now *comando*), from *commandar* to command). **1** L18 A party, originally of Boers or burghers in South Africa, called out for military purposes, a militia; a unit of the Boer army made up of the militia of an electoral district; a raiding-party, a raid; participation in such a raid. **2** M20 (A member of) a unit of British amphibious shock troops; (a member of) a similar unit elsewhere.

comme ci, comme ça /kɔm si kɔm sa/ *adverb & adjective phrase* M20 **French** (literally, 'like this like that'). So-so, middling(ly).

commedia dell'arte /kɔmˌmeːdia dɛll ˈarte/, /kɒˌmɛdɪə dɛlˈɑːteɪ/ *noun phrase* L19 **Italian** (= comedy of art). The improvised popular comedy in Italian theatres between the sixteenth and eighteenth centuries with stock characters.

comme il faut /kɔm il fo/, /kɒm iːl fəʊ/ *adverb & predicative adjective phrase* M18 **French** (literally, 'as it is necessary'). Proper(ly), correct(ly), as it should be (especially of behaviour).

1984 A. Brookner *Hotel du Lac* It was implied that prolonged drinking, whether for purposes of business or as a personal indulgence, was not *comme il faut* . . .

commendatore /ˌkɒmɛndəˈtɔːri/ *noun* L19 **Italian.** A knight of an Italian order of chivalry.

commère /kɔmɛr/, /ˈkɒmɛː/ *noun* plural pronounced /kɔmɛr/, /ˈkɔmɛːz/ E20 **French.** A female COMPÈRE.

commis /ˈkɒmi/ *noun* plural same (pronounced same, /ˈkɒmiːz/) L16 **French** (use as noun of past participle of *commettre* to entrust). **1** L16–E19 A deputy, a clerk. **2** M20 A junior waiter or chef.

commissar /kɒmɪˈsɑː/ *noun* LME **French** (*commissaire* from medieval Latin *commissarius* commissary; in sense 2 from Russian *komissar* from French). **1** LME–M18 A deputy, a delegate, a commissary. Chiefly *Scottish.* **2** E20 *History* The head of a government department in the former USSR; also *transferred,* a powerful official.

2 1996 *Spectator* She assumed that because she was a commissar, she could exercise rights which she wished to deny to her constituents.

commissionaire /kəˌmɪʃəˈnɛː/ *noun* (also **commissionnaire** M17 **French** (*commissionnaire* from Latin *commissio(n-)* from *commiss-* past participial stem of *committere* to commit. **1** M17 A person entrusted with small commissions; a messenger. Now *rare.* **2** M19 A uniformed door-attendant at a theatre, hotel, office, etc.

■ The Corps of Commissionaires was founded in London in 1859 as an organization through which pensioned (originally wounded) soldiers could find light employment as messengers, porters, etc.

2 1996 *Times* The commissionaire, mistaking him for a bum, refused him access.

communard /ˈkɒmjʊnɑːd/ *noun* L19 **French.** A member of a commune; *especially* (**Communard**) an adherent of the Paris Commune (the socialist government March–May 1871); a communalist.

communautaire /ˌkɒmjʊnəʊˈtɛː/ *adjective* L20 **French.** Attentive to or serving the best interests of the wider community (often with reference to the European Community).

1995 *Spectator* [A united Ireland] simply isn't going to come about in any foreseeable future unless the Protestants are physically expelled from Ulster, and that would be a little tricky for the Irish to carry out in their new enlightened and *communautaire* pose.

communiqué /kəˈmjuːnɪkeɪ/ *noun* M19 **French** (use as noun of past participle of *communiquer* to communicate). An official communication; *especially* an official statement reporting on a meeting, conference, etc.

compactum /kəmˈpaktəm/ *noun* E20 **Latin** (use as noun of neuter of *compactus* past participle of *compingere* to put together). A structure or device intended to hold a number of articles; a container; *specifically* a wardrobe.

compadre /kɒmˈpɑːdri/ *noun* M19 **Spanish** (= godfather, (hence) benefactor, friend). Companion, friend.

■ Chiefly United States, often used as a form of address. The extension of meaning from 'godfather' to 'friend' is paralleled in the evolution of the native English word *gossip* from late Old English *godsibb* (from *god* God + *sib* kin) meaning a 'godparent' to mid-fourteenth-century *gossip* 'a familiar acquaintance'. (The usual modern sense of *gossip* follows from the restriction of the word to specifically *female friends,* and thence to mean the sort of talk enjoyed by women amongst themselves.)

compagnon de voyage /kɔ̃paɲɔ̃ də vwajaʒ/ *noun phrase* (also **compagnon du voyage** /kɔ̃paɲɔ̃ dy vwajaʒ/) plural **compagnons de voyage** (pronounced same) M18 **French.** A travelling companion, a fellow traveller.

compendium /kəmˈpɛndɪəm/ *noun* plural **compendiums, compendia** /kəmˈpɛndɪə/ L16 **Latin** (originally, 'profit, saving', from *compendere* to weigh together). **I 1** L16 A work presenting in brief the essential points of a subject; a digest, an epitome. **2** E17 *figurative* An embodiment in miniature. **3** M17–E19 Saving of labour, space, etc. **II 4** L19 An assortment, a varied collection. **5** L19 In full *compendium of games.* A box containing assorted table-games. **b** E20 A package of stationery for letter-writing.

compère /ˈkɒmpɛː/ *noun & verb* (also **compere**) M18 **French** (originally, 'godfather in relation to the actual parents', from medieval Latin *compater* from *com-* with + *pater* father). **A** *noun* **1** An elderly man who lavishes gifts on a younger woman. Only in M18. **2** E20 A person in a cabaret act, radio or television show, etc., who introduces the performers, comments on the turns, etc. **B** *transitive & intransitive verb* M20 Act as compère (to a show).

compluvium /kəm'plu:vɪəm/ *noun* plural **compluvia** /kəm'plu:vɪə/ M19 **Latin** (from *compluere* to flow together). *Roman Antiquities* A square opening in the roof of the atrium, through which fell the rainwater collected from the roof.

compos mentis /ˌkɒmpɒs 'mɛntɪs/ *adjective phrase* E17 **Latin**. In one's right mind, having control of one's mind, not mad. Cf. NON COMPOS MENTIS.

■ Usually used predicatively and sometimes shortened to *compos* (E19).

1996 *Spectator* . . . even drunks have their sober and *compos mentis* lulls . . .

compote /'kɒmpəʊt/, /'kɒmpɒt/ *noun* (also **compôte**) L17 **French** (Old French *composte* from Latin *compos(i)ta*, *compos(i)tum* use as noun of feminine and neuter past participle of *componere* to place together, compound). **1** L17 (A dish of) fruit preserved or cooked in a syrup; a fruit salad, stewed fruit, especially with or in a syrup. **2** M18 A dish of stewed pigeon. **3** L19 A COMPOTIER.

compotier /kɔ̃pɔtje/ *noun* plural pronounced same M18 **French** (from as preceding). A bowl-shaped dessert dish with a stem; a dish for stewed fruit etc.

compte rendu /kɔ̃t rɑ̃dy/ *noun phrase* plural **comptes rendus** (pronounced same) E19 **French** (= account rendered). A report, a review, a statement.

comptoir /kɔ̃twar/ *noun* plural pronounced same E18 **French**. A commercial agency or factory in a foreign country.

comte /kɔ̃t/ (*plural same*), /kɒnt/, /kɒmt/ *noun* E17 **French**. A French nobleman corresponding in rank to an English earl.

comtesse /kɔ̃tes/ (*plural same*), /kɔ̃'tɛs/, /'kɒmtes/ *noun* E20 **French** (from as preceding + feminine suffix *-esse*). A French noblewoman corresponding in rank to an English countess.

con abbreviation of CONTRA.

con amore /kɒn ə'mɔ:reɪ/, *foreign* /kɔn a 'mo:rɛ/ *adverb phrase* M18 **Italian** (= with love). With devotion or zeal; *Music* (a direction:) with tenderness.

con brio /kɒn 'bri:əʊ/, *foreign* /kɔn 'brio/ *adverb phrase* E19 **Italian**. *Music* (A direction:) with vigour. Also *figurative*.

1996 *Times* He also signed autographs by the dozen—it is, incidentally, a signature that is bold, sweeping and exuberant, written *con brio*.

conceptus /kən'sɛptəs/ *noun* M18 **Latin** (= conception, embryo, from *concept-* past participial stem of *concipere* to conceive). The product of conception in the womb, especially in the early stages of pregnancy.

concertante /kɒntʃə'tanti/ *adjective & noun* plural of noun **concertanti** /kɒntʃə 'tanti/ E18 **Italian** (participial adjective of *concertare* to bring into agreement or harmony). *Music* Formerly, (designating) those instrumental parts present throughout a piece of music. Now, (a piece of music) containing one or more solo parts (usually of less prominence or weight than in a concerto) playing with an orchestra; also, designating such a part.

concerti plural of CONCERTO.

concerti grossi plural of CONCERTO GROSSO.

concertino /kɒntʃə'ti:nəʊ/ *noun* plural **concertinos** L18 **Italian** (diminutive of CONCERTO). *Music* **1** L18 A small or short concert. *rare*. **2** E19 The solo instrument(s) in a concerto. **3** L19 A simple or short concerto.

concerto /kən'tʃə:təʊ/, /kən'tʃɛ:təʊ/ *noun* plural **concertos, concerti** /kən'tʃə:ti/ E18 **Italian** (from *concertare* to bring into agreement or harmony). *Music* Originally, a composition for various combinations of instruments. Now, a composition (in the classical form usually in three movements) for one, or sometimes more, solo instruments accompanied by orchestra.

concerto grosso /kənˌtʃə:təʊ 'grɒsəʊ/ *noun phrase* plural **concerti grossi** /kən ˌtʃə:ti: 'grɒsi:/ E18 **Italian** (= big concerto). *Music* A baroque concerto characterized by the use of a small group of solo instruments alternately with the full orchestra; a modern imitation of this.

concessionaire /kənˌsɛʃə'nɛ:/ *noun* (also **concessionnaire**) M19 **French** (*concessionnaire*, from Latin *concessio(n)-* (from *concess-* past participial stem of *concedere* to concede) + *-aire*). The holder of a concession or grant, especially of the use of land or trading rights.

concierge /'kɒnsɪɛ:ʒ/; *foreign* /kɔ̃sjɛrʒ/ (*plural same*) *noun* M16 **French** (from Old French *cumcerges* etc. = medieval Latin *consergius*, probably ultimately from Latin *conservus* fellow slave). **1** M16 The warden of a house, castle, or prison; (the title of) a high official in France and other European states, having custody of a royal palace etc. *obsolete* except *historical*. **2** L17 A doorkeeper, porter, etc., for a block of flats or other building, especially in France.

2 1996 *Times Magazine* Sympathetic Karen at concierge's desk calls doctor.

concordat /kən'kɔːdat/ *noun* E17 **French or Latin** (*concordatum* use as noun of neuter past participle of *concordare* to agree on). An agreement, a compact; *especially* one between the Vatican and a secular government relating to matters of mutual interest.

1996 *New Scientist* The lot of contract researchers was improved last week when universities and major research sponsors signed a concordat to give them some of the benefits enjoyed by permanent staff . . .

concours d'élégance /kɔ̃kur delegɑ̃s/ *noun phrase* plural same M20 **French** (= contest of elegance). A parade of motor vehicles in which prizes are awarded for the most elegant-looking.

■ Sometimes shortened to *concours*, especially when used attributively (see quotation).

1996 *Times* . . . Rolls-Royce would complete the work to *concours* condition and deliver the car 'in perfect working order, free of charge' in return for the right to use it for publicity.

conde /'kɔnde/ *noun* (also **Conde**) M17 **Spanish** (from Latin *comes, comitis* companion). A Spanish count.

condominium /kɒndə'mɪnɪəm/ *noun* E18 **Modern Latin** (from as *con-* with (others) + *dominium* rule). **1** E18 Joint control of a State's affairs vested in two or more other States. **2** M20 A set of flats, group of cottages, etc., rented or bought by a group of people; a unit of property so held. *North American.*

condor /'kɒndɔː/ *noun* E17 **Spanish** (*cóndor* from Quechua *kuntur*). Either of two very large vultures, *Vultur gryphus*, native to the Andes of South America (more fully *Andean condor*), and *Gymnogyps californianus*, of the mountains of California (more fully *Californian condor*).

condottiere /kɔndot'tjere/ *noun* plural **condottieri** /kɔndot'tjeri/ (also **condottiero**) L18 **Italian** (from *condotta* a contract, from feminine past participle of *condurre* to conduct, from as next). *History* A leader or member of a troop of mercenaries (originally and especially in Italy).

conférencier /kɔ̃ferɑ̃sje/ *noun* plural pronounced same L19 **French**. A lecturer, a public speaker; a (leading) member of a conference; a compère.

confetti /kən'fɛti/ *noun* E19 **Italian** (plural of *confetto* comfit, bonbon). Coloured paper shapes showered on the bride and bridegroom by the guests at a wedding. In Italy (the earlier sense), real or imitation bonbons thrown during carnival etc.

■ Originally plural but now usually treated as singular.

confiture /'kɒnfɪtjʊə/; (*foreign*) /kɔ̃fityr/ (*plural same*) *noun* M16 **French** (Old French *confit*). A preparation of fruit preserved in sugar; a confection.

■ The word was a rare import from Old French in the Middle English period with the meaning of 'a preparation of drugs'. In its present sense the forms *confiture* and *comfiture* were both used until the form in *-n-* was readopted (E19) from Modern French.

confrater /kən'freɪtə/ *noun* L16 **Medieval Latin**. A member of a brotherhood, especially of monks.

confrère /'kɒnfrɛː/ *noun* LME **French** (Old French from medieval Latin CONFRATER). **1** LME–L17 A fellow member of a fraternity. **2** M18 A fellow member of a profession, scientific body, etc.

2 1996 *Bookseller* His is a surprisingly Thatcherite credo, given how many of his confrères are running for cover in the face of the impending Tory bloodbath.

confrérie /kɔ̃freri/ *noun* plural pronounced same E19 **French** (from as preceding). A religious brotherhood; an association or group of people having similar interests, jobs, etc.

conga /'kɒŋgə/ *noun & verb* M20 **American Spanish** (from Spanish feminine of *congo* of or pertaining to the Congo). **A** *noun* **1** M20 A Latin American dance usually performed by people in single file who take three steps forward and then kick. **2** M20 In full *conga drum*. A tall, narrow, low-toned drum that is beaten with the hands. **B** *intransitive verb* L20 (past tense and participle **conga'd**, **congaed**). Perform the conga.

congé /kɔ̃ʒe/ (*plural same*), /'kɔ̃ʒeɪ/, /'kɒnʒeɪ/ *noun* (also (now *rare*) **congee** /'kɒndʒiː/) LME **Old French** (*congié* (modern *congé*) from Latin *commeatus* passage, leave to pass, furlough, from *commeare* to go and come). **1** LME Permission (for any act). **2** LME Ceremonious leave-taking. **3** L15–L18 Formal permission to depart. **4** L16 A bow. *archaic.* **5** M19 (from Modern

French) Unceremonious dismissal. Chiefly *jocular*.

1 1996 *Oldie* The primary articulation of the building gives congé to the decorative colour on the straight and curved planes, simple though they may be.

2 1996 *Spectator* What came to mind was not the anger of a statesman, but rather Tinkerbell in a huff. I made my *congés*.

con moto /kɒn 'məʊtəʊ/, *foreign* /kɔn 'moto/ *adverb phrase* E19 **Italian** (= with movement). *Music* (A direction:) with spirited movement.

connoisseur /kɒnə'sə:/ *noun* E18 **French** ((now *connaisseur*), from Old French *conoiss-* present participial stem of *conoistre* (modern *connaître*) to know). A person with a thorough knowledge and critical judgement of a subject, especially one of the fine arts; an expert in any matter of taste, e.g. wines, foods.

■ Often followed by *of, in*.

1996 *Country Life* Happily, this exhibition now re-unites more than 200 objects associated with Hamilton, attesting to the excellence of the connoisseur's taste . . .

conoscente /konoʃ'ʃɛnte/ *noun* plural **conoscenti** /konoʃ'ʃɛnti/ M18 **Italian**. COGNOSCENTE.

conquistador /kɒŋ'kwɪstədɔ:/ *noun* plural **conquistadors, conquistadores** /kɒŋˌkwɪstə'dɔ:rɪz/ M19 **Spanish**. A conqueror; *specifically* any of the Spanish conquerors of Mexico and Peru in the sixteenth century.

1995 *New Scientist* Pauling's style was that of a conquistador in the realm of science, much as Freud had claimed to be.

consensus /kən'sɛnsəs/ *noun* M17 **Latin** (= agreement, from *consens-* past participial stem of *consentire* to assent). Agreement or unity of or *of* opinion, testimony, etc.; the majority view, a collective opinion; (an agreement by different parties to) a shared body of views.

1996 *Country Life* Life is moving faster than the consensus of how to behave.

conservatoire /kən'sə:vətwɑ:/, *foreign* /kɔ̃sɛrvatwar/ (*plural same*) *noun* L18 **French** (from Italian CONSERVATORIO). An academy of music or other performing arts, especially in France or elsewhere in continental Europe.

■ Such an academy may also be called a CONSERVATORIO and CONSERVATORIUM in other parts of Europe (see below), while *conservatory* in this sense is chiefly North American.

conservatoria plural of CONSERVATORIUM.

conservatorio /kənˌsə:və'tɔ:rɪəʊ/ *noun* plural **conservatorios** L18 **Italian** (from late Latin *conservatorium* use as noun of neuter of adjective *conservatorius* from *conservat-* past participial stem of *conservare* to conserve). An (Italian or Spanish) academy of music or other performing arts. Cf. CONSERVATOIRE, CONSERVATORIUM.

conservatorium /kənˌsə:və'tɔ:rɪəm/ *noun* plural **conservatoriums, conservatoria** /kənˌsə:və'tɔ:rɪə/ M19 **German and Modern Latin** (from as CONSERVATORIO *noun*). An academy of music or other performing arts, especially in Germany, Austria, or Australia. Cf. CONSERVATOIRE, CONSERVATORIO.

consigne /kɔ̃siɲ/ *noun* plural pronounced same M19 **French** (from *consigner* to give instructions to a sentinel). **1** M19 An order given to a sentinel; a password. *rare*. **2** L19 A left-luggage office in France.

consolatio /kɒnsə'leɪʃɪəʊ/, /kɒnsə'lɑ:tɪəʊ/ *noun* plural **consolationes** /kɒnsəˌleɪʃɪ'əʊni:z/, /kɒnsəˌleɪtɪ'əʊni:z/ M20 **Latin**. A book, poem, etc. written to expound philosophical or religious themes as comfort for the misfortunes of life.

■ The much-translated *De Consolatione Philosophiae* of the Roman statesman Boethius (died AD 524) was the model for the *consolatio* genre in later European literature.

console /'kɒnsəʊl/ *noun* M17 **French** (perhaps from *consolider* to consolidate). **1** M17 *Architecture* An ornamental flat-sided bracket or corbel, usually incorporating a volute at each end. **2** E19 A table supported by consoles, and either fixed to a wall or free-standing. In full *console table*. **3** L19 A cabinet containing the keyboards, stops, and pedals of an organ. **4** E20 A cabinet for audio equipment, a television set, etc. **5** M20 A cabinet or panel where switches, meters, and controls are grouped together.

consommé /kən'sɒmeɪ/ *noun* E19 **French** (use as noun of past participle of *consommer* from Latin *consummare* to finish up). A clear soup, originally made by boiling meat slowly for a long time.

con sordino /kɒn sɔ:'di:nəʊ/ *adverb & adjective phrase* E19 **Italian**. *Music* (Played) with a mute or (*con sordini* /kɒn sɔ:'di:ni:/) mutes.

consortium /kən'sɔːtɪəm/ *noun* plural **consortia** /kən'sɔːtɪə/, **consortiums** E19 Latin (from *consors, consort-* having an equal share with). **1** E19 Partnership, association. *rare.* **2** M19 *Law.* The companionship, affection, and assistance which each spouse in a marriage is entitled to receive from the other. **3** L19 An association of organizations or States formed for commercial or financial purposes. **4** M20 A group; an assortment.

3 1996 *New Scientist* The main vehicle for this 'collaboration' between government and industry was the research and development consortium.

conspectus /kən'spɛktəs/ *noun* M19 Latin (from *conspectus* past participial stem of *conspicere* to view). **1** M19 A comprehensive mental survey. **2** M19 A summary, a synopsis.

consul /'kɒns(ə)l/ *noun* LME Latin (related to *consulere* to take counsel). **1** LME *History* **a** A magistrate in ancient Rome. **b** E19 Each of the three chief magistrates of the French Republic, from 1799 to 1804, the first of whom was head of State. **2** L15 *History* A medieval earl or count. **3** E16–M18 A member of a council. **4** E16–L18 A foreign official or magistrate; *specifically* a representative head of the merchants of a particular nation resident in a foreign town. **5** M16 An agent appointed by a State to reside in a foreign town to protect the interests of the State's subjects and assist its commerce.

contadina /konta'diːna/, /kɒntə'diːnə/ *noun* plural **contadine** /konta'diːne/, /kɒntə'diːni/, **contadinas** E19 Italian (feminine of next). An Italian peasant girl or peasant woman.

contadino /konta'diːno/, /kɒntə'diːnəʊ/ *noun* plural **contadini** /konta'diːni/, **contadinos** M17 Italian (from *contado* county, (peasant population of) agricultural area round a city). An Italian peasant or countryman.

conte /kɔ̃t/ *noun* plural pronounced same L19 French. A short story; as a form of literary composition, *specifically* a medieval narrative tale.

1996 *Bookseller* [Authors' agents] were always ready with scurrilous gossip or a mucky *conte*.

contessa /kɒn'tɛsə/ *noun* (also (especially in titles) **Contessa**) E19 Italian (from medieval Latin *comitissa*). An Italian countess.

conteur /kɔ̃tœr/ *noun* plural pronounced same M19 French (from CONTE). A composer of *contes*; a narrator.

continua plural of CONTINUUM.

continuo /kən'tɪnjʊəʊ/ *noun* plural **continuos** E18 Italian (= continuous). A figured bass, a thorough bass, (= BASSO CONTINUO; an accompaniment, usually for keyboard, improvised from this. Also, the instrument(s) playing this part.

continuum /kən'tɪnjʊəm/ *noun* plural **continua** /kən'tɪnjʊə/ M17 Latin (use as noun of neuter singular of Latin *continuus* continuous, unbroken). A continuous thing, quantity, or substance; a continuous series of elements passing into each other; *Mathematics* the set of real numbers.

contra /'kɒntrə/ *adverb, preposition, & noun* LME Latin (= against (adverb and preposition), ablative feminine of a comparative from *com, cum* with). **A** *adverb* LME On or to the contrary; contrariwise. Chiefly in *pro and con(tra)* 'for and against'. **B** *preposition* LME Against. **C** *noun* **1** LME The opposing or opposite (side); an opposing factor or argument. **2** (Also *Contra.*) L20 A counter-revolutionary in Nicaragua, *especially* one opposing the government.

■ Often in abbreviated form in the noun phrase *pros and cons* (the points for and against (something)). See also quotation under PRO.

contrabasso /kɒntrə'basəʊ/ *noun* plural **contrabassos, contrabassi** /kɒntrə'basi/ E19 Italian. **1** E19 A double-bass, a contrabass. **2** M19 (A part within) the octave below the normal (bass) range, a contrabass.

contrafactum /kɒntrə'faktəm/ *noun* plural **contrafacta** /kɒntrə'faktə/ M20 Modern Latin (use as noun of neuter past participle of medieval Latin *contrafacere* to counterfeit). *Early Music* A rearrangement of a vocal composition whereby the music is retained and the words altered.

contrafagotto /ˌkɒntrəfə'gɒtəʊ/ *noun* plural **contrafagotti** /ˌkɒntrəfə'gɒti/ L19 Italian (now *controfagotto*). Double bassoon.

contralto /kən'traltəʊ/ *noun & adjective* M18 Italian (from as *contra-* + ALTO). *Music* **A** *noun* (plural **contraltos**) M18 The lowest female voice or (formerly) highest adult male voice; a singer having such a voice;

a part written for such a voice. **B** *adjective* M18 Possessing, belonging to, or written for a contralto voice.

1996 *Times* Heroines were supposed to be fragile blondes with light voices. Rawlings had raven hair, striking but not pretty looks and a mellow contralto voice.

contra mundum /ˌkɒntrə ˈmʌndəm/ *adverb phrase* M18 **Latin**. Against the world; defying or opposing everyone.

1995 *Country Life* Perhaps journalists and country people should gang up together. Us *contra mundum*.

contrapposto /kontrapˈposto/ *noun* plural **contrapposti** /kontrapˈposti/ E20 **Italian** (past participle of *contrapporre* from Latin *contraponere* to contrapose). In the visual arts, an arrangement of a figure in which the action of the arms and shoulders contrasts as strongly as possible with that of the hips and legs; a twisting of a figure on its own axis.

contra proferentem /ˌkɒntrə prɒfəˈrɛntɛm/ *adverb phrase* E20 **Latin**. *Law* Against the party which proposes or adduces a contract or a condition in a contract.

contrayerva /ˌkɒntrəˈjəːvə/ *noun* M17 **Spanish** (literally, 'counter-herb', i.e. one used as an antidote, from *contra-* against + *yerva* (now *hierba*) herb). (The root of) any of several tropical American plants used medicinally (formerly against snakebites).

contre cœur variant of À CONTRECŒUR.

contrecoup /ˈkɔ̃ːtrəkuː/ *noun* M18 **French** (from *contre* against + *coup* blow). **1** M18 A repercussion, an adverse consequence. *rare*. **2** M19 *Medicine* An injury of a part (especially one side of the brain) resulting from a blow on the opposite side.

contredanse /ˈkɒntrədɑːns/, *foreign* /kɔ̃trədɑ̃s/ (*plural same*) *noun* (also **contradance**) E19 **French** (alteration of *country dance* by association with *contre* against, opposite). A country dance, *especially* a social dance of which quadrille is a variant; a piece of music for such a dance.

contre-jour /ˈkɒ̃ːtrəʒʊə/ *noun* E20 **French** (from *contre* against + *jour* daylight). *Photography* Back-lighting.

■ Usually attributive.

contretemps /ˈkɒ̃ːtrətɒ̃ː/, /ˈkɒntrətɒ̃ː/ *noun* plural pronounced same L17 **French** (originally 'motion out of time', from *contre* against + *temps* time). **1** L17 *Fencing* Originally, a thrust made at an inopportune moment or at the same time as one's opponent makes one. Now, a feint made with the intention of inducing a counter-thrust. **2** E18 An unexpected or untoward occurrence, especially of an embarrassing kind; a hitch, a mishap. **b** M20 A disagreement, an argument, a dispute. *colloquial*. **3** E18 *Dancing* A (ballet) step danced on the offbeat. Also, an academic ballet step involving a partial crossing of the feet and a small jump from a knees-bent position.

convenance /kɔ̃vnɑ̃s/ *noun* plural pronounced same L15 **French** (from *convenir* from Latin *convenire* to agree with). **1** L15–L17 Agreement, concurrence. *rare*. **2** M19 Conventional propriety or usage; in *plural*, the proprieties.

conversazione /ˌkɒnvəsatsɪˈəʊni/ *noun* plural **conversaziones**, **conversazioni** /ˌkɒnvəsatsɪˈəʊni/ M18 **Italian** (= conversation). **1** M18 In Italy: an evening gathering for conversation and recreation. **2** L18–L19 An at-home. **3** L18 A social gathering for discussion of the arts, literature, etc.; an educational soirée.

3 1995 *New Scientist* It [sc. the Royal Albert Hall] was to host science *conversaziones* and agricultural, industrial and scientific exhibitions.

conversus /kənˈvəːsəs/ *noun* plural **conversi** /kənˈvəːsʌɪ/ L18 **Latin**. *History* A lay member of a monastery or convent, *especially* one entering monastic life as a mature person.

cooee /ˈkuːɪ/, /ˈkuːiː/ *noun, interjection, & verb* (also **cooey**) L18 **Aboriginal**. **A** *noun & interjection* L18 (A call or cry) used as a signal to draw attention to the caller. **B** *intransitive verb* E19 Utter this call.

■ Chiefly Australia and New Zealand, imitative of a signal used by Aborigines and copied by settlers.

coon-can /ˈkuːnkan/ *noun* L19 **Spanish** (perhaps from *con quién?* with whom?). A card-game of Mexican origin, for two players and ancestral to (gin) rummy. Formerly also, a form of this played with two packs each with two jokers.

coontie /ˈkuːnti/ *noun* (also **coontah** /ˈkuːntə/) L18 **Seminole** (*kunti*). In the United States: any of several low-growing palmlike cycads of the genus *Zamia*, native to tropical and subtropical America; the arrowroot yielded by these plants.

copaiba /kəʊˈpʌɪbə/ *noun* (also **copaiva** /kəʊˈpʌɪvə/) E17 **Portuguese** (*copaîba* (whence Spanish *copaiba*) from Tupi *copaiba*, Guarani *cupaiba*). A balsam of aromatic odour and acrid taste obtained from South American leguminous trees of the genus *Copaifera* and used in medicine and the arts. Formerly also, a tree yielding this.

copal /'kəʊp(ə)l/ *noun* L16 **Spanish** (from Nahuatl *copalli* incense). A hard translucent odoriferous resin obtained from various tropical trees and used to make a fine transparent varnish. Also *gum copal*.

coperta /kə'pəːtə/ *noun* L19 **Italian** (= covering, from *coprire* from Latin *coperire*, *cooperire* to cover). A transparent lead glaze given as a final glaze to some majolica.

copita /kəʊ'piːtə/ *noun* M19 **Spanish** (diminutive of *copa* from popular Latin *cuppa* cup). A tulip-shaped sherry glass of a type traditionally used in Spain; a glass of sherry.

copra /'kɒprə/ *noun* L16 **Portuguese and Spanish** (from Malayalam *koppara*). Dried coconut kernels, from which oil is obtained.

copula /'kɒpjʊlə/ *noun* E17 **Latin** (= connection, linking of words, from as *co-* + *apere* to fasten). **1** E17 *Logic* and *Grammar* That part of a proposition which connects the subject and the predicate. **2** M17 A connection, a link.

coq au vin /kɒk əʊ vɛ̃/ *noun phrase* M20 **French** (literally, 'cock in wine'). Chicken cooked in wine.

coque /kɒk/ *noun 1* E19 **French** (= shell). A loop, a looped bow. Now *specifically* a small loop of ribbon in the trimming of a woman's hat.

coque /kəʊk/ *noun 2* (also **coq** /kɒk/) E20 **French** (*coq* cock). A cock's feather used in the trimming of a hat etc. In full *coque feather*.

coquet /kɒ'kɛt/ *noun & adjective* L17 **French** (diminutive of *coq* cock; as adjective = forward, wanton, gallant). **A** *noun* L17 A man given to flirting or coquetry. **B** *adjective* L17 Coquettish.

■ The noun was formerly (L17–E19) both masculine and feminine; later the feminine became COQUETTE.

coquet /kɒ'kɛt/ *verb* (also **coquette**) L17 **French** (*coqueter*, from as preceding). **1** *intransitive & transitive verb* L17 with *it*. Of a woman, or (formerly) a man: flirt (*with*). **2** *transitive verb* Flirt with. Only in 18. **3** *intransitive verb* L18 Dally, trifle, or toy (*with* a matter etc.)

coquette /kɒ'kɛt/ *noun & adjective* M17 **French** (feminine of COQUET (noun)). **A** *noun* **1** M17 A woman who trifles with men's affections; a woman given to flirting or coquetry. **2** M19 A crested hummingbird of the genus *Lophornis*. **B** *adjective* M18 COQUET (adjective).

A.1 1996 *Spectator* . . . she can mock, tease, play the coquette . . .

coquillage /kɔkijaʒ/ *noun* M19 **French** (literally, 'shell-fish'; see next). Decoration in the form of shells or shellfish, *especially* on furniture.

coquille /kɔkij/ *noun* L19 **French** (from medieval Latin from medieval Greek *kokhulia* plural of *kokhulion* for Greek *kogkhulion*, from *kogkhē* conch). (Scallop) shell.

1995 D. Lodge *Therapy* The scallop shell, or *coquille* . . . is the traditional symbol of the pilgrimage to Santiago.

coquina /kəʊ'kiːnə/ *noun* M19 **Spanish** (= shellfish, cockle, from Old Spanish *coca* from medieval Latin by-form of Latin *concha* shell). A soft white limestone composed of broken marine shells cemented together and used for building in the West Indies and Florida. Also *coquina rock*, *coquina stone*.

coquito /kəʊ'kiːtəʊ/ *noun* plural **coquitos** M19 **Spanish** (diminutive of *coco* coconut). The Chilean wine palm, *Jubaea chilensis*, which yields palm honey and fibre. Also *coquito palm*.

coradgee variant of KORADJI.

corah /'kɔːrə/ *noun & adjective* E19 **Hindi** (*korā* new, unbleached). **A** *noun* E19 An Indian-pattern silk handkerchief. **B** *adjective* L19 Of silk: undyed.

coram /'kɔːrəm/ *preposition* M16 **Latin**. Before, in the presence of.

■ Occurs in various archaic legal phrases used in English, such as CORAM JUDICE, *coram nobis* 'in our presence', *coram populo* 'in the presence of the people' (i.e. in public).

coram judice /ˌkɔːrəm 'juːdɪsi/ *adverb phrase* E17 **Latin** (= in the presence of a judge). In a properly constituted or an appropriate court of law.

cor anglais /kɔːr 'ɑːŋgleɪ/, /kɔːr 'ɒŋgleɪ/ *noun phrase* L19 **French** (literally, 'English horn'). A musical instrument like an oboe but lower in pitch; a player of this. Also, an organ reed-stop of similar quality.

corbeau /'kɔːbəʊ/ *noun & adjective* E19 **French** (= crow, raven). In the drapery trade, (of) a dark green colour verging on black.

corbeille /kɔː'beɪ/ *noun* E19 **French**. An elegant basket of flowers or fruit.

cordelle /kɔː'dɛl/ *noun & verb* E16 **French** (diminutive of *corde* rope, from Latin *chorda* from Greek *khordē* gut, string (of musical instrument)). **A** *noun* **1** E16–E17 A rope, especially on a ship. *Scottish*. **2** E19 A ship's towing-line. *North American* **B** *transitive & intransitive verb* E19 Give a tow (to) with a cordelle. *North American*.

cordillera /kɔːdɪ'ljɛːrə/ *noun* E18 **Spanish** (from *cordilla* diminutive of *cuerda* from Latin *chorda* cord). Each of a series of parallel mountain ridges or chains, especially in the Andes; an extensive belt of mountains, valleys, etc., especially as a major continental feature.

cordon bleu /ˌkɔːdɔ̃ 'bləː/ *noun & adjective phrase* M18 **French** (*cordon* ribbon + *bleu* blue). **A** *noun* plural **cordons bleus** (pronounced same). M18 (A person having) a supreme distinction; *specifically* a first-class cook. **B** *adjective* M20 Of cooking: first-class.

■ In French history, a blue ribbon signified the highest order of chivalry under the Bourbon kings.

cordon sanitaire /ˌkɔːdɔ̃ sanɪ'tɛː/ *noun phrase* plural **cordons sanitaires** (pronounced same) M19 **French** (*cordon* ribbon, band + *sanitaire* sanitary). A guarded line placed between an area affected by disease and adjacent unaffected areas in order to prevent the infection from spreading. Also *figurative*.

■ Earlier (E19) simply *cordon*.

1996 *Spectator* Working in oils is a messy, smelly business which demands a *cordon sanitaire* from the rest of the household.

cordovan /'kɔːdəv(ə)n/ *adjective & noun* L16 **Spanish** (*cordován* (now *cordobán*) noun, *cordovano* adjective, from *Córdova* (now *Cordoba*) from Latin *Corduba* Córdoba). **A** *adjective* L16 Of or pertaining to the city of and province of Córdoba in Spain; made of cordovan. **B** *noun* L16 **1** A kind of pliable fine-grained leather used especially for shoes, made originally at Córdoba from goatskin and now from horsehide. **2** M17–E19 A skin of this leather.

cornada /kor'nada/, /kɔː'nɑːdə/ *noun* plural **cornadas** /kor'nadas/, /kɔː'nɑːdəz/ M20 **Spanish** (from *cuerno* from Latin *cornu* horn). *Bullfighting* The goring of a bullfighter by a bull; a wound so caused.

corniche /'kɔːnɪʃ/, /kɔː'niːʃ/ *noun* M19 **French**. A road along the edge of a cliff; any coastal road with panoramic views. Also *corniche road*.

cornucopia /kɔːnjʊ'kəʊpɪə/ *noun* E16 **Late Latin** (*cornucopia* from Latin *cornu copiae* horn of plenty (a mythical horn able to provide whatever is desired)). **1** E16 A goat's horn depicted as a horn of plenty, overflowing with flowers, fruit, and corn; an ornamental vessel or other representation of this. **2** E17 *figurative* An overflowing stock; an abundant source.

corps /kɔː/, *foreign* /kɔr/ *noun* plural same /kɔz/, *foreign* /kɔr/ L16 **French** (from Latin CORPUS body). **1** L16 A tactical division of an army; an organized body of troops assigned to a special duty or a particular kind of work (medical, ordnance, intelligence, etc.). See also ESPRIT DE CORPS. **2** M18 A body of people engaged (collectively or as individuals) in a particular activity. **3** L19 A students' society in a German university.

■ The first appearance of *corps* in English was in the phrase CORPS DE GARDE. It was apparently first used as an independent word by Addison in 1711 in the *Spectator* in a letter peppered with up-to-the-minute military jargon, which was largely the product of the Duke of Marlborough's campaigns in Europe. It was probably at first pronounced as the English word *corpse*, and Johnson's *Dictionary* (1755) gives *corps* and *corpse* as alternative spellings. The desirability of distinguishing between the two sorts of 'body' has ensured that the French pronunciation and spelling have been retained for the 'group of people' sense.

corps à corps /kɔr a kɔr/ *adverb phrase* L19 **French** (= body to body). In close, especially bodily, contact; *Fencing* the position of two fencers so close that their bodies are in contact.

corps de ballet /kɔr də balɛ/, /ˌkɔːr də 'baleɪ/ *noun phrase* plural same E19 **French**. *Dance* The company of supporting dancers in a ballet.

transferred **1995** *Spectator* Those tough veterans had to sit down each year to be confronted by a *corps de ballet* of golden nymphs prancing down the table and saluting them with trumpets, laurel wreaths and skeins of silk.

corps de garde /kɔr də gard/, /kɔːr də 'gɑːd/ *noun phrase* plural same L16 **French**.

A small body of soldiers set as a guard; the post they occupy, a guard-house.

corps d'élite /kɔr delit/, /kɔː deɪ'liːt/ *noun phrase* plural same L19 **French**. A body of specially picked men; a select group.

corps de logis /kɔr də lɔʒi/ *noun phrase* plural same M17 **French** (literally, 'body of dwelling'). *Architecture* The main (part of a) building; the central block of a house.

corps diplomatique /kɔr diplɔmatik/, /ˌkɔː dɪpləmə'tiːk/ *noun phrase* plural **corps diplomatiques** (*pronounced same*) L18 **French**. The body of ambassadors and their staff attached to a particular seat of government; the diplomatic corps.

corpus /'kɔːpəs/ *noun* plural **corpora** /'kɔːp(ə)rə/, **corpuses** LME **Latin** (= body). **1** LME The body of a person or animal. Now *jocular*. **2** L17 *Anatomy* Any of various masses of tissue in the body that have a distinct structure or function. (Chiefly in technical terms such as *corpus callosum* etc.) **3** E18 A body or collection of writing, knowledge, etc.; the whole body *of* a particular category of literature etc. **b** M20 *specifically* A body of spoken or written material on which a linguistic analysis is based. **4** M19 Principal or capital, as opposed to interest or income. *archaic*. **5** M20 *Botany* The inner layers of cells in an apical meristem.

3 1996 *Oldie* Some exercise of this sort . . . needs to be applied to the corpus of architectural criticism.

corral /kə'rɑːl/ *noun & verb* L16 **Spanish and Old Portuguese** (*corral*, Portuguese *curral*: cf. KRAAL). **A** *noun* **1** L16 An enclosure for horses, cattle, etc. Chiefly *North American*. **2** M19 An enclosure in which to trap and capture wild animals. **3** M19 A defensive enclosure formed of wagons in an encampment. **B** *verb* inflected *-ll-*. **1** *transitive & intransitive verb* M19 Form (wagons) into a corral. **2** *transitive verb* M19 Shut up (as) in a corral, confine. **3** *transitive verb* M19 Obtain, get hold of. *North American colloquial*.

corrida /kɔː'riːdə/, *foreign* /ko'rrida/ *noun* L19 **Spanish** (literally, 'course (of bulls)'). A bullfight; bullfighting. In full *corrida de toros* /də 'tɔːrəʊz/, *foreign* /ðe 'toros/.

corrigendum /kɒrɪ'dʒɛndəm/ *noun* plural **corrigenda** /kɒrɪ'dʒɛndə/ E19 **Latin** (neuter gerundive of *corrigere* to correct). Something requiring correction, *specifically* in a book. In *plural especially* errors listed with the corrections alongside.

corroboree /kə'rɒbəri/ *noun* L18 **Aboriginal**. **A** *noun* **1** L18 A night-time dance of Australian Aborigines, which may be either festive or warlike; a song or chant for this. **2** L19 A noisy gathering; a disturbance.

corsetière /'kɔːsɪtjɛː/ *noun* M19 **French** (feminine of *corsetier*, from as Old French *cors* (modern *corps*) body + *-ière*). A woman who makes or fits corsets.

Corso /'kɔːsəʊ/ *noun* (also **corso**) plural **Corsos** L17 **Italian** (= course, main street from Latin *cursus* course). In Italy and some other Mediterranean countries: a procession of carriages; a social promenade; a street given over to this, or where races etc. were formerly held.

cortège /kɔː'teɪʒ/ *noun* M17 **French** (from Italian *corteggio*, from *corteggiare* to attend court, from *corte* court). A train of attendants; a procession of people, especially mourners.

cortex /'kɔːtɛks/ *noun* plural **cortices** /'kɔːtɪsiːz/ LME **Latin** (= bark). **1** LME An outer layer of a part in an animal or plant; *specifically* (*Anatomy*) the outer layer of the cerebrum, composed of folded grey matter and playing an important role in consciousness; *Botany* a layer of plant tissue between the epidermis and the central vascular tissue. **2** M17–M18 *figurative* An outer shell or husk. **3** L17 The bark of a tree, or the peel or rind of a plant, as used medicinally; *specifically* cinchona bark.

cortile /kor'tiːle/, /kɔː'tiːli/ *noun* E18 **Italian** (derivative of *corte* court). An enclosed usually roofless and arcaded area within or attached to an Italian building.

1984 A. G. Lehmann *European Heritage* . . . for all the classical exhibition in the *cortile*, when it comes to furnishing their private apartments, the Medici lean rather towards the tastes of a European market, not a classical revival at all.

corvée /'kɔːveɪ/ *noun* ME **Old and Modern French** (= Provençal *corroada* from Proto-Romance use as noun (sc. *opera* work) of Latin *corrogata* neuter plural past participle of *corrogare* to summon). A day's unpaid work required of a vassal by a feudal lord; forced labour exacted as a tax, *specifically* that on public roads in France before 1776; *figurative* an unpleasant duty, an onerous task.

corvette /kɔː'vɛt/ *noun* M17 **French** (ultimately diminutive of Middle and Modern Dutch *korf* basket, kind of ship). *History*

1 M17 Originally, a kind of small French vessel using both oars and sail. Later, a warship with a flush deck and one tier of guns. Now *historical*. **2** M20 An escort vessel smaller than a frigate used especially for protecting convoys against submarines in the war of 1939–45.

coryphaeus /kɒrɪˈfiːəs/ *noun* plural **coryphaei** /kɒrɪˈfiːʌɪ/ E17 **Latin** (from Greek *koruphaios* chief, chorus-leader, from *koruphē* head, top). **1** E17 The leader of a chorus. **2** E17 The leader of a party, sect, school of thought, etc.

coryphée /ˈkɒrɪfeɪ/ *noun* E19 **French** (from as preceding). A leading dancer of a CORPS DE BALLET.

coryza /kəˈrʌɪzə/ *noun* E16 **Latin** (from Greek *koruza* nasal mucus, catarrh). Acute catarrhal inflammation of the nose; *especially* the common cold.

Cosa Nostra /ˌkəʊzə ˈnɒstrə/ *noun phrase* M20 **Italian** (= our thing). The American branch of the Mafia.

cosmos /ˈkɒzmɒs/ *noun* ME **Greek** (*kosmos* order, ornament, world). **1** ME The universe as an ordered whole. **2** M19 Harmony, order. **3** L19 An ordered system of ideas etc.

costa /ˈkɒstə/ *noun* (also **Costa**) M20 **Spanish** (= coast). A coast, *especially* one developed as a holiday resort.

■ On the pattern of genuine place-names such as *Costa Brava* or *Costa del Sol*, jocular usage creates pseudo-Spanish names such as *Costa Geriatrica* (a sea-side resort or area mainly populated by elderly people) or *Costa del Crime* (an area favoured by criminals for enjoying their ill-gotten gains in luxury while remaining beyond the reach of extradition laws).

1995 *Times: Weekend* Goa is a long way yet from becoming another Spanish costa but the beach will become crowded and there will no longer be any sense of solitude.

costumier /kɒˈstjuːmɪə/ *noun* M19 **French** (from *costumer* to costume). A person who makes or deals in costumes; *especially* a person who sells or hires out theatrical costumes and properties.

coteau /kɒˈtəʊ/, *foreign* /kɔto/ *noun* plural **coteaus, coteaux** /kɒˈtəʊz/ M19 **French** (= slope, hillside from Old French *costel*, from *coste* (modern *côte* rib, from Latin *costa*). Any of various kinds of elevated geographical features, as a plateau, a divide between valleys, etc. *North American*.

coterie /ˈkəʊt(ə)ri/ *noun* E18 **French** ((in Old French = tenants holding land together), ultimately from Middle Low German *kote* cote, cottage). **1** E18 A small exclusive group with common interests; *especially* a select social group. **2** E19 A meeting of such a group.

cotillion /kəˈtɪljən/ *noun* (in sense 1 also **cotillon** /kəˈtɪljən/, *foreign* /kɔtijɔ̃/ (*plural same*)) E18 **French** (*cotillon* petticoat, dance, diminutive of *cotte* coat). **1** E18 Any of several dances with elaborate steps and figures. **2** L19 A formal ball, *especially* one at which débutantes are presented. *United States*.

cotta /ˈkɒtə/ *noun* M19 **Italian** (from Proto-Romance, from Frankish, of unknown origin). *Christian Church* A short surplice.

1996 *Oldie* I . . . feel deeply uncomfortable with its atmosphere of unguents, incense, bells, mortifications and prayers directed at a world infected with cassocks and cottas . . .

cottage orné see under ORNÉ.

couac /kʊˈak/ *noun* L19 **French** (imitative). *Music* A quacking sound made by bad blowing on the clarinet, oboe, or bassoon.

couchant /ˈkaʊtʃ(ə)nt/ *adjective* LME **Old and Modern French** (present participle of *coucher* to couch, lie down). **1** LME Especially of an animal: lying down. **2** E16 *Heraldry* Of an animal: lying on its belly with its head up, lodged. Usually *postpositive*, as in *lion couchant*.

couchee /ˈkuːʃeɪ/, *foreign* /kuʃe/ (*plural same*) *noun* L17 **French** (*couché* variant of *coucher* lying down, going to bed, use as noun of *coucher* to couch). An evening reception.

■ The opposite of a LEVEE noun 1.

couchette /kuːˈʃɛt/, *foreign* /kuʃɛt/ (*plural same*) *noun* E20 **French** (literally, 'little bed', diminutive of *couche*). A railway carriage in which the seats convert into sleeping-berths; such a berth.

coudé /kuːˈdeɪ/ *adjective & noun* L19 **French** (past participle of *couder* to bend at right angles, from *coude* elbow from Latin *cubitum* cubit). (Of, pertaining to, or designating) a telescope in which the rays are bent to focus at a fixed point off the axis.

coulée /kuːˈleɪ/, /ˈkuːli/ *noun* (also **coulee**, (sense 1) **coulie** /ˈkuːli/) E19 **French** (= (lava) flow, from Latin *colare* to filter, strain, (in Proto-Romance) flow, from *cōlum* strainer). **1** E19 (The bed of) an intermittent stream; a dry valley; a gulch or valley with steep sides. *North American dialect.* **2** M19 *Geology* A stream of molten or solidified lava.

couleur de rose /kulœr də roz/ *noun & adjective phrase* LME **French** (= rose colour). **A** *noun phrase* LME Rose-colour, pink; *figurative* optimism, cheerfulness. **B** *adjective phrase* L18 Rose-coloured, pink; *figurative* optimistic, cheerful.

coulis /ˈkuːli/ *noun* L20 **French** (see next). A thin, flowing sauce.

1996 *Spectator* . . . a cassata . . . was very good, though I was less keen on the strawberry coulis draped around it.

coulisse /kuːˈliːs/ *noun* E19 **French** (use as noun of feminine of *coulis* sliding (from *coulisser* to slide); cf. *portcullis* literally, 'sliding door'). **1** E19 *Theatre* Each of the side scenes of a stage; *singular* and (usually) in *plural*, the space between them, the wings. **2** M19 A groove in which a sluice-gate or other movable partition slides up and down. **3** L19 The body of outside dealers on the Paris Bourse; similar dealers in other stock exchanges; the place where they deal. **4** E20 A corridor; *figurative* a place of informal discussion or negotiation.

4 1968 D. Torr *Treason Line* The real business of the conference would begin . . . in the *coulisses*.

couloir /ˈkuːlwɑː/, *foreign* /kulwar/ (*plural same*) *noun* E19 **French** (= channel, from *couler* to pour, from Latin *colare* to filter). A steep gully on a mountainside.

coup /kuː/, *foreign* /ku/ (*plural same*) *noun* LME **Old and Modern French** (from medieval Latin *colpus* from Latin *colaphus* from Greek *kolaphos* blow with the fist; in branch II reintroduced from French in figurative sense and also in a number of phrases (see below)). **I 1** LME–M16 A blow given or received in combat. **II 2** L18 A stroke or move that one makes; *especially* a notable or strikingly successful move. **b** M19 A COUP D'ÉTAT. **c** M19 *History* Among North American Indians: the act of touching an enemy, as a deed of bravery; the act of first touching an item of the enemy's in order to claim it. **3** L18 *Billiards* The direct pocketing of the cue-ball, which is a foul stroke.

coup de fors /ku də fɔrs/ *noun phrase* plural **coups de fors** (*pronounced same*) M19 **French** (literally, 'stroke of force'). A sudden violent action.

coup de foudre /ku də fudr/ *noun phrase* plural **coups de foudre** (*pronounced same*) L18 **French** (literally, 'stroke of lightning'). A sudden unforeseen event; a revelation; love at first sight.

coup de grâce /ˌkuː də ˈgrɑːs/ *noun phrase* plural **coups de grâce** (*pronounced same*) L17 **French** (literally, 'stroke of grace'). A blow by which someone or something that has been mortally hurt is mercifully killed; *figurative* a decisive finishing stroke.

1996 *Times* It was de Villiers who administered the *coup de grâce*, dismissing Cork, Martin and Gough in successive overs . . .

coup de main /ku də mɛ̃/ *noun phrase* plural **coups de main** (*pronounced same*) M18 **French** (literally, 'stroke of hand'). Chiefly *Military* A sudden onslaught; a surprise attack.

coup d'état /kuː deɪˈtɑː/, *foreign* /ku deta/ *noun phrase* plural **coups d'état** /kuːz deɪ ˈtɑː/, *foreign* /ku deta/, **coup d'états** /kuː deɪˈtɑːz/ M17 **French** (literally, 'blow of State'). A violent or illegal change in government. Formerly also, any sudden and decisive stroke of State policy.

■ Now often abbreviated to *coup* in all but the most formal contexts.

1996 *Spectator* Andreotti was once asked whether there could be a coup d'état in Italy. 'No,' he replied. 'There is no état.'

coup de théâtre /ku də teɑtr/ *noun phrase* plural **coups de théâtre** (*pronounced same*) M18 **French** (literally, 'stroke of theatre'). **1** A theatrical hit. **2** A sudden dramatic turn of events or action, *originally* in a play, now also *figurative* (see quotations).

2 1995 *Spectator* . . . the finale of the scene—where the Prince's girlfriend is shot dead—looks rather forced, instead of being a *coup de théâtre*.

2 *figurative* **1995** *Times* Tony Blair's most unexpected *coup de théâtre* this week was his announcement of a deal with British Telecom . . .

coup d'œil /ku dœj/ *noun phrase* M18 **French** (literally, 'stroke of eye'). A comprehensive glance; a general view; *Military* the faculty or action of rapidly assessing a position and sizing up its advantages etc.

1996 *Country Life* Also, they [sc. the rooms] are seen at the correct angles in the first views, with the chimneypieces being part of the first *coup d'œils* in all of them.

coupe /kuːp/ *noun 1* L19 **French** (= goblet from medieval Latin *cuppa*). **1** L19 A shallow dish; a short-stemmed glass. **2** E20 A dessert of ice-cream, fruit, etc., served in a glass coupe.

coupe /kuːp/ *noun 2* E20 **French** (= felling, from *couper* to cut, slash). A periodic felling of trees; an area so cleared.

coupé /ˈkuːpeɪ/ *noun* (in sense 3b also **coupe** /kuːp/) E18 **French** (past participle of *couper* to cut; in branch II abbreviation of *carrosse coupé*, literally, 'cut carriage'). **I 1** E18 *Dancing* Formerly, *coupee*, a kind of bowing step. Now, a step in ballet in which one foot displaces another and weight is transferred to it. **2** L19 *Fencing* A movement of the sword similar to a disengage, but effected by drawing the sword along and over the point of the opponent's. **II 3a** M19 A four-wheeled carriage with a seat for two inside and an outside seat for the driver. Chiefly *historical*. **b** E20 An enclosed two-door motor car with two or four seats and (now) usually a sloping rear.

courante /kʊˈrɒ̃(n)t/, /kʊˈrɑːnt/ *noun* (also **courant** /kʊˈrant/) L16 **French** (use as noun of feminine present participle of *courir* to run). **1** L16 A court dance of the sixteenth and seventeenth centuries characterized by glides and light hops, a coranto. **2** L16 *Music* A piece of music for this dance; a piece of music in triple time, *especially* one which forms a movement of a suite.

courbette /kʊəˈbɛt/ *noun* M17 **French** (from Italian *corvetta*). *Equestrianism* A leap in *haute école* in which a trained horse rears up and jumps forward on the hind legs without the forelegs' touching the ground.

coureur /kurœr/ *noun* plural pronounced same E18 **French** (= (wood-)runner). *History* A woodsman, trader, etc., of French origin in Canada and the northern United States. In full *coureur de bois* /də bwa/.

courge /kʊəʒ/ *noun* M19 **French** (= gourd from Old French *cohourde* from Latin *cucurbita*). A basket for holding live bait, towed behind a fishing boat.

courgette /kʊəˈʒɛt/ *noun* M20 **French** (from as preceding). A small variety of vegetable marrow. Also called ZUCCHINI.

course libre /kurs libr/ *noun phrase* plural **courses libres** (pronounced same) M20 **French** (= free course). A bullfight, as in France, in which the bull is baited but not killed.

court bouillon /kur bujɔ̃/ *noun phrase* M17 **French** (from *court* short + BOUILLON). A stock made from wine, vegetables, etc., in which fish is boiled.

couscous /ˈkuːskuːs/ *noun* (also **kouskous**, **couscoussou** /ˈkuːskuːsuː/) E17 **French** (from Arabic *kuskus*, *kuskusū* millet grain, probably of Berber origin). A spicy North African dish of crushed wheat or coarse flour steamed over broth, frequently with meat or fruit added; the granules of flour from which this dish is made.

couture /kuːˈtjʊə/ *noun* E20 **French** (from Old French *cousture* sewing from late Latin *consutura*, from Latin *consutus* past participle of *consuere* to sew together). **1** Dressmaking; (the design and making of) fashionable garments, especially French ones. **2** Abbreviation of HAUTE COUTURE.

2 *attributive* **1995** *Times* How many women have the money to buy a couture dress?

couvade /kuːˈvɑːd/ *noun* M19 **French** (from *couver* to hatch from Latin *cubare* to lie). A custom in some cultures by which a man takes to his bed and goes through certain rituals when his wife bears a child.

■ Adopted in French in this sense (M19) owing to a misunderstanding of the expression *faire le couvade* 'to sit doing nothing' in earlier writers.

couverture /ˈkuːvətjʊə/ *noun* M20 **French** (= covering). (A layer of) chocolate for coating sweets and cakes.

couvre-pied /kuvrəpje/ (*plural same*) *noun* (also **couvre-pieds** /kuvrəpje/) E19 **French** (literally, 'cover foot', from *couvrir* to cover). A rug to cover the feet.

coyote /ˈkɔɪəʊt/, /kɔɪˈəʊti/ *noun & verb* plural same, **coyotes** M18 **Mexican Spanish** (from Nahuatl *coyotl*). **A** *noun* M18 A small nocturnal wolflike animal, *Canis latrans*, of western North America, noted for its mournful howling. Also called *prairie-wolf*. **B** *intransitive verb* M19 *Mining* Make a small lateral tunnel from a shaft etc. *United States slang*.

■ The sense of the verb refers to the small tunnels dug out by the coyote; in California the phrase *coyote diggings* described such lateral shafts.

cracovienne /krəkəʊvɪˈɛn/ *noun* M19 **French** (feminine adjective from *Cracovie* Kraków (Cracow), a city in southern Poland). A lively Polish dance; a ballet dance in a Polish style. Also called *krakowiak*.

cranium /ˈkreɪnɪəm/ *noun* plural **crania** /ˈkreɪnɪə/, **craniums** LME **Medieval Latin** (from Greek *kranion* skull). **1** LME The bones enclosing the brain; the bones of the whole head, the skull. **2** M17 The head. *jocular*.

2 1996 *Times Magazine* Never having had a book to promote before, *Like a Virgin* is chorusing through my cranium . . .

crannog /ˈkranəg/ *noun* E17 **Irish** (*crannóg*, Gaelic *crannag* timber structure, from *crann* tree, beam). In Scotland and Ireland: an ancient fortified settlement constructed in a lake or marsh on an artificial island made from timber.

craquelure /ˈkrakljʊə/, *foreign* /kraklyr/ *noun* E20 **French**. A network of small cracks in the pigment or varnish on the surface of a painting.

crèche /krɛʃ/, /kreɪʃ/ *noun* L18 **French** (from Old French *creche* wooden feeding rack for animals, from Proto-Romance from Germanic base related to *crib*). **1** L18 A model of the infant Jesus in the manger with attending figures, often displayed at Christmas. **2** M19 A day nursery for infants and young children.

■ *Crib* is now the more usual word for sense 1.

credenza /krɪˈdɛnzə/ *noun* L19 **Italian** (from medieval Latin *credentia* from Latin *credent-* present participial stem of *credere* to believe; see quotation 1996). A sideboard, a cupboard, a buffet.

1996 *Country Life* . . . although I knew what a credenza was—a sideboard or display cabinet with a blind door flanked by shelves or glazed cupboards—I was unsure of the derivation. A 'credence' in English furniture terminology began as a church table . . . but now means something more like a card-table. Although the Italian *credenza* shares the same origin, it developed into a sideboard, and the name was anglicized when such cabinets became popular in the 19th century.

credo /ˈkriːdəʊ/, /ˈkreɪːdəʊ/ *noun* plural **credos** ME **Latin** (*credo* I believe). **1** ME The Apostles' Creed, the Nicene Creed, (from their first word). Now *especially* a musical setting of the Nicene Creed. **2** L16 *generally* A creed, a set of opinions or principles.

2 1996 *Bookseller* To any critic they can always call on their shabby mass-market credo, 'If that's what people want, who am I to patronise them by offering what someone else might think is better?'

creese variant of KRIS.

crémaillère /kremajɛr/ *noun* plural pronounced same E19 **French** (formerly *cramaillère*, from *cramail* pot-hanger, chimney-hook). *Fortification* A zig-zag or indented inside line of a parapet.

crème /krɛm/ (*plural same*), /kreɪm/ *noun* (also **crême**) E19 **French** (= cream). **1** E19 Cream; a cream, a custard. Used especially in names of desserts and liqueurs (see following entries). **2** M19 The CRÈME DE LA CRÈME.

crème brûlée /krɛm bryle/, /kreɪm ˈbruːleɪ/ *noun phrase* L19 **French** (literally, 'burnt cream'). A cream or custard dessert topped with caramelized sugar.

crème caramel /krɛm karamɛl/, /kreɪm ˈkarəmɛl/ *noun phrase* E20 **French**. A custard dessert topped with caramel. Cf. CRÈME RENVERSÉE.

■ Earlier (M19) as *crème au caramel*.

crème Chantilly /krɛm ʃɑ̃tiji/, /kreɪm ʃanˈtɪli/ *noun phrase* (also *crème chantilly*) E20 **French**. Whipped cream flavoured with vanilla and sweetened.

■ Earlier (L19) as *crème à la Chantilly*. Chantilly is the name of a town in France, not far from Paris.

crème de cacao /krɛm də kakao/, /ˌkreɪm də ˈkəˈkaʊ/ *noun phrase* M20 **French**. A chocolate-flavoured liqueur.

crème de la crème /krɛm də la krɛm/, /kreɪm də lɑː kreɪm/ *noun phrase* M19 **French** (literally, 'cream of the cream'). The pick of society; the élite in any field.

1996 *Spectator* In 1988, they played Liverpool, then seen as the *crème de la crème* of Europe, in the FA Cup Final.

crème de menthe /krɛm də mɑ̃t/, /kreɪm də ˈmɑːnt/, /kreɪm də ˈmɒnθ/ *noun phrase* E20 **French**. A peppermint-flavoured liqueur.

crème de noyau /krɛm də nwajo/, /kreɪm də ˈnwʌɪəʊ/ *noun phrase* L19 **French**. An almond-flavoured liqueur.

crème fraîche) /krɛm frɛʃ/ *noun phrase* (also **creme fraiche**) L20 **French**. *Cookery* Soured cream.

1996 *Country Life* . . . one of my favourites is tartare of salmon with a *crème fraîche*, horseradish and dill sauce . . .

crème renversée /krɛm rɑ̃vɛrse/, /kreɪm ˈrɛnvəːseɪ/ *noun phrase* E20 **French** (literally, 'inverted cream'). A custard made in a mould and then turned out, often with a caramel topping (*crème caramel renversée*).

cremona variant of CROMORNE.

creole /ˈkriːəʊl/ *noun & adjective* (also (especially in strict use of sense A. 1 and corresponding uses of the adjective) **Creole**) E17 **French** (*créole*, earlier *criole* from Spanish *criollo* probably from Portuguese *crioulo* Black born in Brazil, home-born slave, from *criar* to nurse, breed, from Latin *creare* to create). **A** *noun* **1** E17 A descendant of European settlers or (occasionally) of Black slaves, in the West Indies or Central or South America; a descendant of French settlers in the southern United States, especially Louisiana. Also *loosely*, a person of mixed European and Black descent. **2** L19 A former pidgin language that has developed into the sole or native language of a community. **B** *adjective* **1** M18 That is a creole; of, pertaining to, or characteristic of a creole or creoles. **2** M18 Of a plant or animal: bred or grown in the West Indies but not of indigenous origin.

crêpe /kreɪp/ *noun & adjective* (also **crepe**) L18 **French** (earlier *crespe*, use as noun of Old French *crespe* curled, frizzed, from Latin *crispus* curled). **A** *noun* **1** L18 A fine cotton or gauzelike fabric with a crinkled surface. **2** E20 A type of raw rubber rolled into thin sheets with a wrinkled surface, used for shoe-soles etc. More fully *crêpe rubber*. **3** E20 A very thin pancake. **B** *attributive* or as *adjective* Made of crêpe; resembling crêpe.

■ The Anglicized spelling *crape* was current in the seventeenth century in sense A.1, but later came to be restricted to a specific kind of black silk cloth used especially for mourning dresses and funereal drapes.

crêpe de Chine /kreɪp də ʃiːn/ *noun phrase* L19 **French**. A fine crêpe of silk or similar fabric. Also called *China crêpe*.

crêpeline /ˈkreɪpəliːn/ *noun* (also **crêpoline**) L19 **French** (diminutive of CRÊPE). A thin light dress-material made of silk or silk and wool.

crêpe Suzette /kreɪp suːˈzɛt/ *noun phrase* plural **crêpes Suzette** (*pronounced same*) E20 **French**. A thin dessert pancake served hot in a sauce that usually contains spirit or liqueur.

crépinette /kreɪpɪˈnɛt/ *noun* L19 **French** (diminutive of *crêpine* caul). A kind of flat sausage consisting of minced meat and savoury stuffing wrapped in pieces of pork caul.

crêpoline variant of CRÊPELINE.

crépon /ˈkreɪpən/ *noun & adjective* L19 **French** (from as CRÊPE *noun & adjective*). (Made of) a fabric resembling crêpe, but heavier.

crepusculum /krɪˈpʌskjʊləm/, /krɛˈpʌskjʊləm/ *noun* (also Anglicized as **crepuscle** /ˈkrɛpʌs(ə)l/, **crepuscule** /ˈkrɛpəskjuːl/) LME **Latin** (related to *creper* dusky, dark). The period of half-dark at the beginning or end of the day; twilight, dusk.

crescendo /krɪˈʃɛndəʊ/ *adverb, adjective, noun, & verb* L18 **Italian** (present participle of *crescere* to increase from Latin *crescere* to grow). **A** *adverb & adjective Music* L18 (A direction:) with a gradual increase in loudness. **B** *noun* plural **crescendos**, **crescendi**. **1** *Music* L18 A gradual increase in loudness; a passage (to be) played or sung with such an increase. **2** L18 A progressive increase in force or effect. **3** E20 A climax. **C** *intransitive verb* Increase gradually in loudness or intensity.

> **A 1995** *Spectator* . . . the composer Percy Grainger used the word 'louden', where less Australian musicians are content with 'crescendo' . . .

cresson /krɛsɔ̃/ *noun* M17 **French** (= cress). **1** In *plural* Cress. *rare* (only M17). **2** L19 A shade of green resembling that of watercress.

cretin /ˈkrɛtɪn/ *noun* L18 **French** (*crétin* from Swiss French *creitin*, *crestin* from Latin *Christianus*). **1** L18 *Medicine* A person afflicted with cretinism. **2** L19 A fool; a person who behaves stupidly.

cretonne /krɛˈtɒn/, /ˈkrɛtɒn/ *noun* L19 **French** (of unknown origin). A strong unglazed fabric printed on one or both sides with a (usually large floral) pattern, used for chair covers, curtains, etc.

crevasse /krɪˈvas/ *noun* E19 **French** (Old French *crevace*). **1** E19 A (usually deep) fissure or chasm in the ice of a glacier; *transferred* a deep crack or chasm. **2** E19 A breach in the bank or levee of a river, canal, etc. *United States*.

criard /kriar/ *adjective* (also (French feminine) **criarde** /kriard/) M19 **French**. Shrill; garish.

criblé /krible/ *noun & adjective* L19 **French** (from Old French *crible* from popular

Latin variant of Latin *cribrum* sieve). (Designating) a type of engraving with small punctures or depressions on a wood or metal ground. Cf. MANIÈRE CRIBLÉE.

■ The technique of using metalworkers' punches to create stippled areas on a printing plate was one of the earliest used in Renaissance metal engraving. The effect was to have patterns of white dots (likened to the holes of a sieve) against the black ground of the print.

cri de cœur /kri də kœr/ *noun phrase* plural **cris de cœur** (pronounced same) E20 **French** (= cry of or from the heart). An appeal in distress.

1996 *Times* Newcastle's social sides are not going down without a final *cri de coeur* for the essential amateurism which they . . . believe can co-exist with professional rugby.

crime passionnel /krim pasjɔnɛl/ *noun phrase* plural **crimes passionnels** (pronounced same) E20 **French**. A crime, especially murder, due to sexual jealousy.

criollo /krɪˈɒləʊ/ *noun & adjective* (also **Criollo**) plural of noun **criollos** L19 **Spanish** (= native to the locality). **1** L19 (Designating or pertaining to) a native of Spanish South or Central America, especially one of pure Spanish descent. **2** E20 (Designating) a cacao tree of a variety producing thin-shelled beans of high quality. **3** M20 (Designating) any of various South or Central American breeds of domestic animal, *especially* a small horse bred from native South American and Arab stock, or cattle of Spanish ancestry.

crise /kriz/ *noun* plural pronounced same LME **French**. Crisis.

■ Formerly fully naturalized, it now occurs only in the following phrases or as an abbreviation of them.

crise de conscience /kriz də kɔ̃sjɑ̃s/ *noun phrase* M20 **French**. A crisis of conscience.

crise de nerfs /kriz də nɛr/ *noun phrase* (also **crise des nerfs**) E20 **French** (= crisis of nerves). An attack of nerves; a fit of hysterics.

1970 *New Yorker* She has been a splendid advertisement for the benefits of a happy marriage—conspicuously more relaxed, far less subject to those old *crises des nerfs*.

critique /krɪˈtiːk/ *noun* Originally **critic** M17 **French** (ultimately from Greek *kritikē* (sc. *tekhnē*) the critical art, criticism). **1** M17 Criticism; *especially* the art of criticism. **2** M17 A criticism; *especially* a critical analysis, article, or essay.

crochet /ˈkrəʊʃeɪ/, /ˈkrəʊʃi/ *noun & verb* M19 **French** (diminutive of *croc* with *-ch-* from *crochié, crochu* hooked). **A** *noun* M19 A kind of knitting done using a single hooked needle to form intertwined loops; knitted material made in this way. **B** *verb* **1** *transtitive verb* L19 Make in crochet. **2** *intransitive verb* L19 Do crochet work.

croisette /krwaˈzɛt/ *noun* L17 **French** (diminutive of *croix* cross). A small cross.

croissant /ˈkrwasɒ̃/ *noun* L16 **French**. L19 A flaky pastry roll in the shape of a crescent.

■ Earlier (L16–L17) found as an occasional variant of *crescent*, especially with reference to the crescent moon, *croissant* is now solely used for the pastry roll.

cromlech /ˈkrɒmlɛk/ *noun* L17 **Welsh** (from *crom* feminine of *crwm* bowed, arched + *llech* (flat) stone). A dolmen; any megalithic chamber-tomb.

cromorne /krəʊˈmɔːn/ *noun* (also **cremona**) E18 **French** (from German KRUMMHORN). An organ reed stop, usually of 8-ft pitch, suggestive of a krummhorn or (later) a clarinet in sound.

croque-monsieur /ˈkrɔk məˌsjəː/ *noun* M20 **French**. A toasted ham-and-cheese sandwich.

croquette /krɒˈkɛt/ *noun* E18 **French** (from *croquer* to crunch). A small ball or roll of vegetable, minced meat, or fish (to be) fried in breadcrumbs.

croquis /krɔki/, /krəʊˈkiː/ *noun* plural same /krɔki/, /krəʊˈkiːz/ E19 **French** (from *croquer* to sketch). A rough draft; a sketch.

crostini /krɒsˈtiːnɪ/ *noun plural* L20 **Italian**. Snacks consisting of bread, usually toasted or fried, with a savoury topping.

crotale /ˈkrəʊt(ə)l/ *noun* M20 **French** (from Latin CROTALUM). A small tuned cymbal; a kind of castanet or clapper; a crotalum.

crotalum /ˈkrɒt(ə)l(ə)m/, /ˈkrəʊt(ə)l(ə)m/ *noun* plural **crotala** /ˈkrɒt(ə)lə/, /ˈkrəʊt(ə)lə/ L18 **Latin** (from Greek *krotalon*). An ancient clapper or castanet the two halves of which were struck together with the finger and thumb.

croupade /kruˈpeɪd/ *noun* M17 **French** (from Italian *groppata* (with assimilation to French *croupe* croup). *Equestrianism* In *haute école* a single leap with the horse's hind legs brought up under the belly.

Also, a high kick with the hind legs while the forelegs remain on the ground.

croupier /'kru:pɪə/, /'kru:pɪeɪ/ *noun* E18 **French** ((originally a person who rides behind on a horse's croup), from *croupe* from Proto-Romance from Germanic base related to *crop*). **1** A person who stands behind a gambler to give support and advice. Only in E18. **2** M18 A person who rakes in and pays out the money or tokens at a gaming-table. **3** L18 An assistant chairman sitting at the lower end of the table at a public dinner.

croustade /krʊ'stɑ:d/ *noun* M19 **French** (from Old French *crouste* (modern CROÛTE) or Italian *crostata* tart (from *crosta* crust)). A crisp piece of bread or pastry hollowed to receive a savoury filling.

croûte /krut/ *noun* plural pronounced same E20 **French**. A crisp piece of toasted or fried bread; a croûton. See also EN CROÛTE.

croûton /'kru:tɒn/, /krutɔ̃/ (*plural same*) *noun* (also **crouton**) E19 **French** (from CROÛTE). A small piece of toasted or fried bread served with soup or as a garnish.

cru /kry/ (*plural same*), /kru:/ *noun & adjective* (also **crû**) E19 **French** (from *crû* past participle of *croître* grow). *Wine* (The grade or quality of wine produced in) a French vineyard or wine-producing region; (designating) French wine of a specified quality.

■ Often in phrases (see quotation); see also CRU CLASSÉ, GRAND CRU, PREMIER CRU.

1966 P. V. Price *France, Food & Wine Guide* Just below the classed growths come the *crus bourgeois* . . . then the *crus artisans*.

cru classé /kry klase/, /kru: 'klaseɪ/ *noun phrase* plural **crus classés** (pronounced same) M20 **French** (= classed growth). *Wine* A Bordeaux wine belonging to one of the highest official categories.

crudités /krydite/, /'kru:dɪteɪ/ *noun plural* M20 **French**. *Cookery* Assorted raw vegetables as an hors d'oeuvre.

crumhorn variant of KRUMMHORN.

crux /krʌks/ *noun* plural **cruxes** /'krʌksɪz/, **cruces** /'kru:si:z/ M17 **Latin** (= cross). **1** M17 (A representation of) a cross. Chiefly in CRUX ANSATA. **2** E18 A difficult matter, a puzzle; the decisive point at issue; the central point. **3** M19 (Usually **Crux**) (The name of) the constellation of the Southern Cross.

crux ansata /krʌks an'seɪtə/ *noun phrase* plural **cruces ansatae** /'kru:si:z an'seɪti:/ M19 **Latin** (= cross with a handle). An ANKH.

crwth /kru:θ/ *noun* M19 **Welsh** (cf. Gaelic *cruit* harp, violin, Irish *cruit* small harp, Old Irish *crot* harp, cithara). An old Celtic musical instrument with three, or later six, strings which was held against the chest and played by bowing and plucking.

■ Adopted earlier (ME) as *crowd*.

csardas /'tʃɑ:dɑ:ʃ/, /'zɑ:dəs/ *noun* (also **czardas**) plural same M19 **Hungarian** (*csárdás*, from *csárda* inn). A Hungarian dance usually having a slow start and a rapid wild finish, with many turns and leaps; a piece of music for this dance.

cuadrilla /kwad'riʎa/, /kwɒd'ri:ljə/ *noun* plural **cuadrillas** /kwad'riʎas/, /kwɒd 'ri:ljəz/ M19 **Spanish**. A company of people; *especially Bullfighting* A matador's team.

cuartel /kwar'tel/, /kwɔ:'tɛl/ *noun* M19 **Spanish** (from *cuarta* quarter, from *cuarto* fourth, from Latin *quartus*). In Spain and Spanish-speaking countries: a military barracks.

cuesta /'kwɛstə/ *noun* E19 **Spanish** (= slope, from Latin *costa*). Originally (*United States dialect*), a steep slope that terminates a gently sloping plain; a plain in this configuration. Now (*Geography*), a ridge with a gentle slope on one side and a steep one on the other, a scarp and dip.

cui bono /kwi: 'bɒnəʊ/, /ku:ɪ 'bɒnəʊ/, /ku:ɪ 'bəʊnəʊ/ *interjection* (*interrogative*), *adjective & noun phrase* E17 **Latin** (= to whom (is it) a benefit?). **A** *interjection* (*interrogative*) E17 What is the purpose (of)? Who stands to gain (and so might be responsible)? **B** *adjective phrase* M18 Of or pertaining to the question *cui bono?* **C** *noun phrase* M19 The question *cui bono?*

A 1996 *Spectator* Then, from the 1960s to the 1980s, yet more scholars . . . put the attribution back to Raphael and authenticated the Dürer inscription, to the general satisfaction. *Cui bono*? Well, it gave large numbers of dons and students . . . something to do.

cuir-ciselé /kwɪə'si:zleɪ/, *foreign* /kyirsizle/ *adjective* M20 **French** (= engraved leather). (Of a design on a leather binding) cut in relief with a pointed tool; having such a design.

cuisine /kwɪ'zi:n/ *noun* L18 **French** (= kitchen, from Latin *coquina*, *cocina*, from *coquere* to cook). A culinary establishment; cookery as an art, especially as characteristic of a particular country or establishment. Cf. HAUTE CUISINE, NOUVELLE CUISINE.

cuivré /'ki:vreɪ/, *foreign* /kyivre/ *adverb & noun* M20 **French** (past participle of *cuivrer* to play with a brassy tone, from *cuivre* copper, from late Latin *cuprum*). *Music* (With) a harsh strident tone (in a brass instrument).

cul-de-sac /'kʌldəsak/, /kʊldə'sak/ *noun* plural **culs-de-sac** (pronounced same), **cul-de-sacs** M18 **French** (= sack-bottom). **1** M18 *Anatomy* A vessel, tube, sac, etc., open only at one end; the closed end of such a vessel. **2** L18 A street, passage, etc., closed at one end; a blind alley; *Military* a position in which an army is hemmed in on all sides except behind.

> **2** *figurative* **1995** *New Scientist* Lock up the DNA libraries and information will simply not be available to other researchers. Life-saving research could then become stuck in a cul-de-sac.

culet /'kju:lɪt/ *noun* (also (earlier) **collet** /'kɒlɪt/) L17 **French** (diminutive of *cul* bottom). **1** L17 The horizontal base of a diamond, formed by the blunting of a point, when the stone is cut as a brilliant. **2** M19 A piece of armour for protecting the hinder part of the body below the waist.

culmen /'kʌlmɛn/ *noun* M17 **Latin** (contraction of *columen* top, summit, etc). **1** M17 The top, the summit; *figurative* the acme, the culminating point. **2** M19 The upper ridge of a bird's bill.

culotte /kju:'lɒt/, *foreign* /kylɔt/ *noun* plural pronounced same M19 **French** (= knee-breeches; cf. SANSCULOTTE). **1** M19 Knee-breeches. *rare*. **2** E20 *singular* and (usually) in *plural*. A woman's garment that hangs like a skirt but has separate legs, as in trousers; a divided skirt. **3** E20 A fringe of soft hair on the back of the fore-legs of some dogs.

culpa /'kʌlpə/ *noun* M19 **Latin**. *Law*. Neglect resulting in damage, negligence.

> ■ See also FELIX CULPA.

cultus /'kʌltəs/ *noun* M17 **Latin** (from past participial stem of *colere* to honour with worship). **1** Worship. *rare*. Only in M17. **2** M19 A system of religious worship or ritual; a cult.

cum /kʌm/ *preposition* LME **Latin** (= with). **1** LME Combined with. Used in names of combined parishes (e.g. Horton-cum-Studley). **2** With. Chiefly in Latin phrases and English ones imitating them (e.g. cum dividend). **3** And also. Denoting a combined role or nature (see quotation).

> **3** **1996** *New Scientist* . . . she [sc. Sylvia Earle] co-founded Deep Ocean Technology and Deep Ocean Engineering, . . . apparently running them as director-cum-secretary from her kitchen table.

cum laude /kʌm 'lɔ:di/, /kʌm 'laʊdeɪ/ *adverb & adjective phrase* L19 **Latin** (= with praise). (Of a degree, diploma, etc.) with honours, with distinction.

> ■ Chiefly North American; cf. MAGNA CUM LAUDE, SUMMA CUM LAUDE.

cumulus /'kju:mjʊləs/ *noun* plural **cumuli** /'kju:mjʊlʌɪ/, /'kju:mjʊli:/ M17 **Latin**. **1** M17 A heap, a pile; an accumulation; the conical top of a heap. **2** E19 *Meteorology* (A cloud-type consisting of) rounded masses of cloud heaped on each other and having a horizontal base at usually a low altitude. Also *cumulus cloud*.

cunnilingus /kʌnɪ'lɪŋgəs/ *noun* L19 **Latin** (= a person who licks the vulva, from *cunnus* female external genitals + *lingere* to lick). Stimulation of a woman's genitals with the tongue.

cupidon /'kju:pɪdɒn/, *foreign* /kypidɔ̃/ (*plural same*) *noun* (also **Cupidon**) E19 **French** (from Latin *Cupido* Cupid, the personification of desire, the god of love). A beautiful youth; a cupid, an Adonis.

> ■ *Cupid* or *cupid* has been the normal form since Late Middle English, and *cupidon* is chiefly poetical.

cupola /'kju:pələ/ *noun* M16 **Italian** (from late Latin *cupula* little cask, small burying-vault, diminutive of *cupa* cask). **1** M16 A rounded vault or dome forming the roof of (part of) a building; *specifically* a small rounded dome forming or adorning a roof; the ceiling of a dome. **b** M17 Something likened to such a dome. **2** E18 A tall usually cylindrical furnace, open at the top and tapped at the bottom, for melting metal that is to be cast. Also *cupola furnace*. **3** E19 *Anatomy* The small dome-shaped end of the cochlear duct. **4** M19 A revolving dome for protecting mounted guns on a warship etc. **5** E20 *Geology* A small dome-shaped projection on the top of a larger igneous intrusion.

curandero /kuran'dero/ *noun* plural **curanderos** /kuran'deros/ (feminine **curandera** /kuran'dera/) M20 **Spanish** (from *curar* to cure, from Latin *curare*). In Spain and Latin America: a healer who uses folk remedies.

curare /kjʊ'rɑːri/ *noun* L18 **Spanish and Portuguese** (from Carib word represented also by *wourali*). A resinous bitter substance obtained from the bark and stems of various tropical and subtropical South American plants of the genus *Strychnos*, which paralyses the motor nerves and was formerly used as an arrow poison by South American Indians and now in surgery etc. to relax the muscles.

curé /kyre/ *noun* plural pronounced same M17 **French** (from medieval Latin *curatus* a person who has a cure or charge (of a parish)). In France and French-speaking countries: a parish priest.

curettage /kjʊə'rɛtɪdʒ/, /kjʊərɪ'tɑːʒ/ *noun* L19 **French** (from as next). *Surgery* The scraping or cleaning of an internal surface of an organ or body cavity with a curette.

■ Often in the phrase *dilatation and curettage* (colloquially abbreviated *d&c*), a common operation on the womb which consists of this.

curette /kjʊə'rɛt/ *noun & verb* M18 **French** (from *curer* to take care of, clean, from Latin *curare* to heal). *Surgery* **A** *noun* M18 A small instrument resembling a scoop used to remove material by a scraping action, especially from the womb. **B** L19 *transitive & intransitive verb* Scrape or clean with a curette.

curia /'kjʊərɪə/ *noun* (also in sense 3 **Curia**) plural **curiae** /'kjʊərɪiː/, **curias** E17 **Latin.** **1** E17 *History* Each of the ten divisions into which each of the three tribes of ancient Rome was divided; the senate of an ancient Italian town, as distinguished from that of Rome. **2** E18 A court of justice, counsel, or administration, especially of the Roman Catholic Church or (*historical*) under the feudal system. **3** M19 *The Curia* Vatican tribunals, congregations, and other institutions through which the Pope directs the work of the Roman Catholic Church; *the* government departments of the Vatican.

curiosa /kjʊərɪ'əʊsə/ *noun plural* L19 **Latin** (*curiosa* neuter plural of *curiosus*). Curiosities, oddities; *specifically* erotic or pornographic books.

1996 *Independent on Sunday* It has beautiful women: . . . an absent-minded, gloriously disorganised, plump and pretty *assistante* sprung to life from the pages of some piece of Victorian *curiosa*.

curiosa felicitas /kjʊərɪˌəʊsə fə'lɪsɪtɑːs/ *noun phrase* M18 **Latin** (literally, 'careful felicity'). A studied appropriateness of expression.

■ The phrase is a quotation from Petronius (*Satyricon* cxviii).

currach /'kʌrə(x)/ *noun* (also **curragh**, **corrack**) LME **Irish** (Gaelic *curach* small boat, coracle). In Ireland and Scotland: a small boat made of slats or laths covered with watertight material (formerly hide, now usually tarred canvas).

curragh /'kʌrə(x)/ *noun* M17 **Irish** (*currach* marsh, Manx *curragh* moor, bog, fen). In Ireland and the Isle of Man: marshy waste ground.

currente calamo /kəˌrɛnteɪ 'kaləməʊ/ *adverb phrase* L18 **Modern Latin** (literally, 'with the pen running on'). Extempore; without deliberation or hesitation.

curriculum /kʌ'rɪkjʊləm/ *noun* plural **curricula** /kʌ'rɪkjʊlə/ E19 **Latin** (= running, course, race-chariot, from *currere* to run). A course of study at a school, university, etc.; the subjects making up such a course.

curriculum vitae /kʌˌrɪkjʊləm 'viːtʌɪ/, /'vʌɪtiː/ *noun phrase* plural **curricula vitae** /kʌ'rɪkjʊlə/ E20 **Latin** (from as preceding + Latin *vitae* of life). A brief account of one's life or career, especially as required in an application for employment.

■ In job advertisements and colloquial contexts usually abbreviated to *c.v.*

1996 *Times* None of the usual 'seeking other business opportunities', no attempt to deny a rift or gild the *curriculum vitae* for the benefit of future employers.

cursillo /kur'siʎo/; /kʊə'siːjəʊ/, /kur'siːljəʊ/ *noun* plural **cursillos** /kur'siʎos/, /kur'sijəʊz/, /kur'siːljəʊz/ M20 **Spanish** (literally, 'little course'). A short course of study etc., *specifically* of intensive religious studies and exercises, originally for Roman Catholics in Spain.

cursor /'kəːsə/ *noun* ME **Latin** (= runner, from *currere* to run). **1** ME–M17 A runner, a running messenger. **2** L16 A part of a mathematical or surveying instrument which can be slid back and forwards; *specifically* the transparent slide with a fine line with which the readings on a slide-rule are taken. **3** M20 A movable visual marker forming part of a VDU display, showing where the next character to be keyed will appear.

cursus /ˈkəːsəs/ *noun* plural same, **cursuses** M18 **Latin** (= course, from *currere* to run). **1** M18 *Archaeology* A neolithic structure consisting of a long straight avenue, usually closed at the ends, formed by two earthen banks with a ditch on the outer side of each. **2** M19 A stated order of daily prayer or worship. **3** E20 One of the cadences which mark the ends of sentences and phrases, especially in Greek and Latin prose. **4** E20 Abbreviation of CURSUS HONORUM.

cursus honorum /ˌkəːsəs ɒˈnɔːrəm/ *noun phrase* plural same E20 **Latin** (= course of honours). An established hierarchy of positions through which a person may be promoted.

1995 *Spectator* His [sc. Isaiah Berlin's] *cursus honorum* (Fellow of All Souls, headship of an Oxford College . . . President of the British Academy and O.M.), might seem to make him a paid-up member of the establishment.

cuspidor /ˈkʌspɪdɔː/ *noun* M18 **Portuguese** (= spitter, from *cuspir* to spit, from Latin *conspuere*). A spittoon. Chiefly *North American*.

custos /ˈkʌstɒs/ *noun* plural **custodes** /kʌˈstəʊdiːz/, (originally) **custoses** /kʌˈstəʊsiːz/ LME **Latin**. A keeper, a guardian, a custodian.

■ Now chiefly in titles from Modern Latin, as in *custos rotulorum* (literally, 'keeper of the rolls'), a title given to the chief Justice of the Peace in an English county, who has nominal responsibility for the records of the commission of the peace in that county.

cutcha variant of KUTCHA.

cuvée /kjuːˈveɪ/, *foreign* /kyve/ (*plural same*) *noun* M19 **French** (= vatful, from *cuve* from Latin *cupa* cask, vat). The contents of a vat of wine; a particular blend or batch of wine.

cuvette /kjuːˈvɛt/ *noun* L17 **French** (diminutive of *cuve* vat). **1** L17 *Fortification* A trench along the middle of a dry ditch. **2** E18 A shallow vessel for holding liquid; a transparent vessel with flat sides for holding a spectrophotometric sample etc. **3** M19 A large clay basin or crucible used in making plate glass. **4** E20 *Geology* A basin in which sedimentation is occurring or has occurred.

cwm /kʊm/ *noun* M19 **Welsh** (= coomb). A bowl-shaped valley or hollow in (Welsh) mountains; *Physical Geography* A CIRQUE.

cyanosis /sʌɪəˈnəʊsɪs/ *noun* plural **cyanoses** /sʌɪəˈnəʊsiːz/ M19 **Modern Latin** (from Greek *kuanōsis* blueness). *Medicine* A blue discoloration of the skin due to deficient oxygenation of the blood.

cyma /ˈsʌɪmə/ *noun* M16 **Modern Latin** (from Greek *kuma* billow, wave, wavy moulding, from *kuein* to become pregnant). **1** M16 *Architecture* An ogee moulding of a cornice. **2** E18 *Botany* A CYME.

cymatium /sɪˈmatɪəm/, /sɪˈmeɪʃəm/ *noun* plural **cymatia** /sɪˈmatɪə/, /sɪˈmeɪʃə/ M16 **Latin** (*cymatium* ogee, Ionic volute from Greek *kumation* diminutive of *kuma* CYMA). *Architecture* A CYMA.

cymbalo /ˈsɪmbələʊ/ *noun* plural **cymbalos** L19 **Italian** (*cembalo, cimbalo* from Latin *cymbalum* cymbal; cf. CIMBALOM). A dulcimer.

cyme /sʌɪm/ *noun* (in sense 1 also written **cime**) E18 **French** (*cyme, cime* summit, top, from popular form of Latin CYMA). **1** The unopened head of a plant. *rare*. Only in E18. **2** L18 *Botany* An inflorescence (frequently forming a more or less flat head) in which the primary axis bears a single flower which develops first, flowers of secondary and higher order axes developing successively later.

czar variant of TSAR.

czardas variant of CSARDAS.

czarevich, **czarevna**, etc. variants of TSAREVICH, TSAREVNA, etc.

da capo /dɑː 'kɑːpəʊ/ *adverb phrase* E18 **Italian** (= from the beginning). *Music* (A direction:) repeat from the beginning.

dacha /'datʃə/ *noun* (also **datcha**) M19 **Russian** (= grant of land). In Russia: a small country house or villa.

1996 *Oldie* The Russians, who did not enjoy their time in Yemen, built *dachas* and Black Sea style hotels.

dacoit /də'kɔɪt/ *noun* L18 **Hindustani** (*ḍakait*, from *ḍākā* gang-robbery). A member of an Indian or Myanmar (Burmese) band of armed robbers.

dado /'deɪdəʊ/ *noun* plural **dados** M17 **Italian** (= die, cube, from Latin *datum*). *Architecture* **1** M17 The plain portion of a pedestal between the base and the cornice. **2** L18 The lower part of an interior wall when faced or coloured differently from the upper part.

daemon /'diːmən/, /'dʌɪməʊn/ *noun* (also formerly **demon**) M16 **Latin** (medieval Latin *demon*, Latin *daemon* from Greek *daimōn* divinity, genius). **1** *Greek Mythology* M16 A being of a nature between that of the gods and men, a spirit; the soul of a deceased person regarded as a minor divinity. **2** E17 An attendant or indwelling spirit; a DAIMON.

■ *Demon*, meaning specifically 'an evil spirit' or 'devil', was naturalized in Middle English, and this spelling was also occasionally used in Early Modern English in the senses above. However, the usefulness of being able to differentiate between an evil spirit and other morally neutral entities taken over from pagan classical religion ensured that the spelling *daemon* has survived in the latter senses. A similar consideration lay behind the later (M19) introduction of DAIMON.

dagesh /'dɑːgɛʃ/ *noun* M16 **Hebrew** (*dāḡēš*). *Hebrew Grammar* A point or dot placed within a Hebrew letter, denoting either that it is doubled or that it is not aspirated.

dagga /'dagə/ *noun* L17 **Afrikaans** (from Nama *daχa*). In South Africa: Indian hemp used as a narcotic; any indigenous plant of the genus *Leonotis* which is similarly used.

dagoba /'dɑːgəʊbə/ *noun* E19 **Sinhalese** (*dāgaba* from Pali *dhātu-gabbha* receptacle for relics). A stupa or dome-shaped structure containing Buddhist relics.

daimon /'dʌɪməʊn/ *noun* M19 **Greek** (*daimōn*). An attendant or indwelling spirit, one's genius.

■ The direct transliteration of the Greek is intended to evoke the pagan classical concept of the personal spirit, unencumbered by the nuances of the earlier usages of *d(a)emon*; see also DAEMON.

daimyo /'dʌɪmɪəʊ/, /'dʌɪmjəʊ/ *noun* (also **daimio**) plural **daimyos** E18 **Japanese** (from *dai* great + *myō* name). *History* In feudal Japan: any of the chief land-owning nobles, vassals of the shogun.

dak /dɑːk/, /dɔːk/ *noun* (also **dawk**) E18 **Hindustani** (*ḍāk*). In the Indian subcontinent: originally, post or transport by relays; now, postal service, delivery of letters, mail.

dal variant of DHAL.

dalles /dalz/ *noun plural* L18 **French** (plural of *dalle* conduit, tube, etc.). In the western United States: rapids where a river is compressed into long narrow troughlike channels.

dal segno /dal 'semjəʊ/ *adverb phrase* L19 **Italian** (= from the sign). *Music* (A direction:) go back to the point indicated by the sign (not the beginning). Cf. AL SEGNO.

dame de compagnie /dam də kɔ̃paɲi/ *noun phrase* plural **dames de compagnie** (pronounced same) L18 **French** (literally, 'lady of company'). A paid female companion.

dame d'honneur /dam dɔnœr/ *noun phrase* plural **dames d'honneur** (pronounced same) E19 **French** (literally, 'lady of honour'). A maid of honour, a lady-in-waiting.

damna plural of DAMNUM.

damnatio memoriae /dam,nɑːtɪəʊ mə 'mɔːrɪiː/ *noun phrase* M20 **Latin** (= condemnation of the memory). The attempt to obliterate the memory of a dead person by erasing inscriptions mentioning him or her, destroying statues and memorials, etc.

1985 H. Schutz *Romans in Central Europe* Nero's name had been erased after his death when the Roman Senate condemned his memory, the *damnatio memoriae.*

damnosa hereditas /dam,nəʊsə hɪ 'rɛdɪtas/ *noun phrase* M19 **Latin** (= inheritance that causes loss). An inheritance, tradition, etc., bringing more burden than profit.

1955 *Times* The rule that an executor was not compelled to accept a *damnosa hereditas* did not provide a reliable guide.

damnum /'damnəm/ *noun* plural **damna** /'damnə/ E19 **Latin** (= hurt, harm, damage). *Law* A loss, a wrong.

dan /dan/ *noun* M20 **Japanese**. Each of the (numbered) grades in the advanced level of proficiency in judo, karate, etc. (also *dan grade*; a person who has reached (a specified grade of) this level. Cf. KYU.

danse du ventre /dɑ̃s dy vɑ̃tr/ *noun phrase* plural **danses du ventre** (pronounced same) L19 **French**. A belly-dance.

danse macabre /dɑ̃s makabr/*noun phrase* plural **danses macabres** (pronounced same) L19 **French**. The dance of death; a musical piece or passage representing or suggestive of this.

■ Earlier (LME) Anglicized as *dance (of) macabre* (cf. MACABRE). As an allegory, the Dance of Death (called TOTENTANZ in German-speaking areas) was very popular in the late Middle Ages. Medieval and Renaissance representations of it show Death in the form of a skeleton approaching young and old, rich and poor, powerful and obscure, and leading them all away in a dance to the grave; the most famous of these images is the series of 50 woodcuts by Hans Holbein the Younger designed in the early 1520s and published at Lyons in 1538.

figurative **1996** *Spectator* . . . less like all-out war, more like a stately minuet between the command structure of the British state and that of the IRA, a *danse macabre* whose ritual bows to certain unwritten understandings about the rules of engagement.

danseur /dɑ̃sœr/ *noun* plural pronounced same E19 **French** (from *danser* to dance). *Ballet* A male dancer.

danseur noble /dɑ̃sœr nɔbl/ *noun phrase* plural **danseurs nobles** (*pronounced same*) M20 **French** (from as *danseur* + *noble* noble). *Ballet* A male dancer as partner of a ballerina.

1996 *Spectator* Wildor is now a complete ballerina . . . . Similarly, Trevitt is a true *danseur noble* who coped brilliantly with the complexities of the part . . .

danseuse /dɑ̃søz/ *noun* plural pronounced same E19 **French**. A female dancer; a ballerina.

dariole /'darɪəʊl/ *noun* LME **Old and Modern French**. **1** LME An individual sweet or savoury dish of various kinds; now *specifically* one made in a dariole mould. **2** M19 A small metal mould shaped like a flower-pot and used for making such a dish. In full *dariole mould*.

darshan /'dɑːʃən/ *noun* E20 **Hindi** (pronunciation of Sanskrit *darśana* sight, seeing, from *dṛś-* to see). In the Indian subcontinent etc.: the opportunity or occasion of seeing a holy person or the image of a deity.

Dasein /'dɑːzeɪn/ *noun* M19 **German** (from *dasein* to exist, from *da* there + *sein* to be). *Philosophy* In Hegelian terms, existence, determinate being; in existentialism, human existence, the being of a person in the world.

dashiki /'dɑːʃɪki/ *noun* M20 **West African** (probably Yoruba from Hausa: cf. Krio *da(n)shiki*). A loose brightly coloured West African shirt, also worn by Blacks in America etc.

data /'deɪtə/ *noun* M17 **Latin** (plural of DATUM). *plural and collective singular* **1** M17 Things given or granted; things known or assumed as facts, and made the basis of reasoning or calculation. **2** L19 Facts, especially numerical facts, collected together for reference or information. **3** M20 The quantities, characters, or symbols on which operations are performed by computers and other automatic equipment, and which may be stored and transmitted in the form of electrical signals, records on magnetic, optical, or mechanical recording media, etc.

2 1996 *New Scientist* Much of the modern craze for collecting data is to avoid having to admit that we are just using our judgment.

datcha variant of DACHA.

datum /'deɪtəm/ *noun singular* plural **data** /'deɪtə/ M18 **Latin** (neuter past participle of *dare* to give). A thing given or granted; a thing known or assumed as a fact, and made the basis of reasoning or calculation; a fixed starting-point for a series of measurements etc.

■ Now much more frequent in the plural DATA.

daube /dəʊb/, *foreign* /dob/ (*plural same*) *noun* E18 **French**. A braised meat (usually beef) stew with wine, spices, etc.

dauphin /ˈdɔːfɪn/, /ˈdəʊfã/ *noun* (also **Dauphin**) LME **French** ((Old French *daulphin*), family name of the lords of Viennois or Dauphiné). **1** LME *History* (The title of) the eldest son of the King of France, from 1349 to 1830. **2** A dolphin. *rare*. Only in L16.

■ See also AD USUM DELPHINI.

dazibao /ˈdɑːdzəbaʊ/ *noun* plural same M20 **Chinese** (*dàzìbào*, from *dà* big + *zì* character + *bào* newspaper, poster). In the People's Republic of China: a wall-poster written in large characters expressing an (especially political) opinion.

débâcle /deɪˈbɑːk(ə)l/, /dɪˈbɑːk(ə)l/ *noun* (also **debacle**) E19 **French** (from *débâcler* to unbar, from *dé-* + *bâcler* to bar). **1** E19 A breaking-up of ice in a river; a sudden flood or rush of water carrying along debris. **2** M19 A sudden and ignominious collapse or defeat; a humiliating and embarrassing situation.

2 1996 *Times Magazine* Fred Vermorel emerges from this débâcle as a sad individual trading on the reflected glory of his association with people from a bygone time.

débat /deba/ *noun* plural pronounced same L19 **French** (= debate). A poetic discussion between persons, personifications, or abstractions, on a question of morality, politics, or love, common in medieval European literature.

debitage /dɛbɪˈtɑːʒ/ *noun* M20 **French** (*débitage* cutting of stone). *Archaeology* Waste material produced in the making of prehistoric stone implements.

débouché /debuʃe/ *noun* plural pronounced same M18 **French** (from *déboucher* from *dé-* de- + *bouche* mouth (after synonymous Italian *sboccare*)). An opening where troops etc. (may) emerge; *generally* an outlet.

debris /ˈdɛbriː/, /ˈdeɪbriː/ *noun* (also **débris**) E18 **French** (*débris*, from *débriser* to break down, break up, from *dé-* + *briser* to break). The remains of anything broken down or destroyed (originally *in figurative use*, of institutions, States, etc.); fragments, wreckage, ruins; accumulated waste matter; *Geology* fragmentary material accumulated from the breakdown of rocks etc.

début /ˈdeɪb(j)uː/, /ˈdɛb(j)uː/; /deɪˈbjuː/, /dɛˈbjuː/ *noun* (also **debut**) M18 **French** (from *débuter* to lead off). Entry into society; the first appearance in public of a performer etc.

débutant /ˈdɛbjʊtɒ̃/, /ˈdeɪbjʊtɒ̃/ *noun* (also **debutant**) E19 **French** (present participle of *débuter* to lead off). A male person making his début.

débutante /ˈdɛbjʊtɑːnt/, /ˈdeɪbjʊtɑːnt/ *noun* (also **debutante**) E19 **French** (feminine of *débutant*: see preceding). **1** E19 A female performer etc. making her début. **2** E19 A young woman making her social début; *loosely* a young woman in fashionable society.

decalage /ˈdiːkəlɑːʒ/ *noun* E20 **French** (*décalage* displacement, from *décaler* to displace). *Aeronautics* The difference in the angle of incidence between two aerofoils on an aeroplane.

decani /dɪˈkeɪnʌɪ/ *adjective* M18 **Latin** (genitive of *decanus* dean). Of or pertaining to the south side of the choir of a church where the dean usually sits; *Music* to be sung by the decanal side in antiphonal singing (cf. CANTORIS).

decemvir /dɪˈsɛmvə/ *noun* LME **Latin** (singular of *decemviri*, originally *decem viri* ten men). **1** LME In *plural* A council or ruling body of ten. Originally and *especially* (*Roman History*) either of two bodies of magistrates appointed in 451 and 450 BC respectively. **2** E18 A member of such a body.

decennium /dɪˈsɛnɪəm/ *noun* plural **decennia** /dɪˈsɛnɪə/, **decenniums** L17 **Latin** (from *decennis*, from *decem* ten + *annus* year). A period of ten years, a decade.

déclassé /deklase/ (*plural same*), /deɪˈklaseɪ/ *adjective & noun* (feminine **déclassée**) L19 **French** (past participle of *déclasser* to (re)move from a class). (A person who is) reduced or degraded in social class or status.

1995 *Spectator* Forte (having for so long been accused of being too *déclassé* to own the Savoy) could point out the incongruity of a company whose most famous hostelry is the Rover's Return in *Coronation Street* becoming the landlord of the Grosvenor House in Park Lane.

décolletage /dekɔltaʒ/, /deɪkɒlˈtɑːʒ/ *noun* L19 **French** (from *décolleter* to expose the neck). **1** L19 The low-cut neckline of a woman's garment. **2** L19 Exposure of the neck and shoulders by such a neckline.

2 1995 *Times Pride and Prejudice* convinced a nation of bra burners that a heaving décolletage was the only way to attract a Mr Darcy in time for Christmas.

décolleté /dekɔlte/, /deɪˈkɒl(ə)teɪ/ *adjective* (also **décolletée**) M19 **French** ((feminine *décolletée*), from *décolleter* to expose the neck, from *dé-* + *collet* collar of a dress etc). Of a (woman's) garment: having a low-cut neckline. Of a woman: wearing a low-necked garment. Also *figurative*, daring, slightly improper.

décor /ˈdeɪkɔː/ *noun* (also **decor**) L19 **French** (from *décorer* to decorate). **1** L19 The scenery and furnishings of a theatre stage; the set. **2** E20 (The overall effect of) the decoration and furnishings of a room, building, etc.

decorum /dɪˈkɔːrəm/ *noun* M16 **Latin** (use as noun of neuter singular of *decorus* seemly). **1** M16 Suitability of artistic or literary style to the subject; congruity, unity. **2** L16 Suitability to the dignity or circumstances of a person or occasion. *archaic*. **3** L16 Propriety of behaviour or demeanour; seemliness; etiquette.

3 1996 *Times* Correct posture, dress and decorum was all.

découpage /dekupaʒ/ *noun* plural pronounced same M20 **French** (from *découper* to cut up, cut out). **1** M20 The decoration of a surface with cut-out paper patterns or illustrations; an object so decorated. **2** M20 *Cinematography* The cutting or editing of a film.

1 1977 A. Jeffs *Creative Crafts* As découpage traveled through Europe in the 18th century, it was enthusiastically adopted by the women of the courts who amused themselves by imitating the then fashionable Chinese lacquerwork.

decrescendo /diːkrɪˈʃɛndəʊ/ *adverb, adjective, noun & intransitive verb* plural of noun **decrescendos** E19 **Italian** (present participle of *decrescere* to decrease). DIMINUENDO.

decretum /dɪˈkriːtəm/ *noun* plural **decreta** /dɪˈkriːtə/ E17 **Latin**. A decree.

de facto /deɪ ˈfaktəʊ/, /diː/ *adverb & adjective phrase* E17 **Latin** (= of fact). (Existing, held, etc.) in fact, in reality; in actual existence, force, or possession, whether by right or not.

■ Often used as the opposite to DE JURE.

1996 *Times* Old Compton Street on a Saturday night has become a *de facto* pedestrian precinct. It is thronged with people and almost impossible to drive down.

defluvium /dɪˈfluːvɪəm/ *noun* E19 **Latin** (*defluvium* loss by flowing or falling away). *Medicine* A complete shedding of hair, fingernails, etc., as a result of disease.

dégagé /degaʒe/, /deɪˈgɑːʒeɪ/ *adjective* (feminine **dégagée**) L17 **French** (past participial adjective of *dégager* to set free). Unconstrained, relaxed; detached, unconcerned.

degras /ˈdɛgrəs/ *noun* (also **dégras** /ˈdeɪgras/) L19 **French** (*dégras*, from *dégraisser* to remove grease from). **1** L19 A dark wax or grease obtained when fish-oils are rubbed into hides and recovered, used in the dressing of leather; a preparation containing this or synthesized in imitation of it; moellon. **2** L19 Wool-grease, wool-fat; a crude mixture of wax and fats obtained by scouring wool or treating it with organic solvents. *United States*.

dégringolade /degrɛ̃gɔlad/ *noun* plural pronounced same L19 **French** (from *dégringoler* to descend rapidly). A rapid descent or deterioration; decadence.

1996 *Spectator* After the happy Venetian years before the last war and the hardly less happy postwar ones . . . , there followed the ghastly and grotesque *dégringolade* of the final years.

de haut en bas /də o ɑ̃ bɑ/ *adverb and adjective phrase* L17 **French** (= from above to below). Condescending(ly) or patronizing(ly).

1995 *Spectator* Maynard Keynes . . . had a very *de haut en bas* view that he knew best what forms of culture should be supported (opera and ballet) . . .

dehors /dəɔr/, /dəˈhɔː/ *preposition* E18 **French** (in Old French used as a preposition (Modern French as adverb and noun)). *Law* Outside of; not within the scope of.

Dei gratia /deɪɪ ˈgrɑːtɪə/, /diːʌɪ ˈgreɪʃə/ *adverb phrase* E17 **Latin**. By the grace of God.

déjà entendu /deʒa ɑ̃tɑ̃dy/, /ˌdeɪʒɑː ɒ̃tɒ̃ ˈduː/ *noun phrase* (also **déjà-entendu**) M20 **French** (= already heard, after DÉJÀ VU). A feeling (correct or illusory) that one has already heard or understood the words, music, etc., currently under attention.

1995 *Spectator* From the moment Tony Blair uttered the fatal words, 'We will be opening discussions . . . about how we meet the goal of ensuring that every child has access to a laptop computer', the sense of *dejà-entendu* became almost too much to bear.

déjà lu /deʒa ly/, /ˌdeɪʒɑː 'luː/ *noun phrase* M20 **French** (= already read, after next). A feeling that one may have read the present passage, or one very like it, before.

déjà vu /deʒa vy/, /ˌdeɪʒɑː 'vuː/ *noun phrase* E20 **French** (= already seen). **1** E20 *Psychology* The illusory feeling of having already experienced the present moment or situation. **2** M20 The (correct) impression that something similar has been previously experienced; tedious familiarity.

2 1995 *Spectator* Huddled in the international departure lounge at Waterloo underneath a Eurostar board proudly exhibiting its cancelled trains, I felt a sudden nostalgic twinge of *déjà-vu* [sic].

déjeuner /deʒœne/ (*plural same*), /'deɪʒəneɪ/ *noun* L18 **French** (use as noun of infinitive = to break one's fast). **1** L18 A morning meal (early or late) in France or elsewhere; breakfast or (usually) lunch. **2** L18 A set of cups, saucers, plates, etc., for serving breakfast, breakfast service.

■ *Petit déjeuner* is commonly used for 'breakfast'.

de jure /diː 'dʒʊəri/, /deɪ 'jʊəreɪ/ *adverb & adjective phrase* M16 **Latin** (= of law). (Existing, held, etc.) rightfully, according to law.

■ Frequently used in contexts where it is the opposite to DE FACTO.

dekko /'dɛkəʊ/ *noun* plural **dekkos** L19 **Hindustani** (*dekho* polite imperative of *dekhnā* to look). A look.

■ Originally army slang. Although the word also existed (L19) as a transitive and intransitive verb, the verbal sense is usually expressed by *have* (or *take*) *a dekko*.

délassement /delɑsmɑ̃/ *noun* plural pronounced same E19 **French** (from *délasser* to relax, from *dé-* + *las* weary). Relaxation.

del credere /dɛl 'kreɪdəri/, /dɛl 'krɛdəri/ *adjective, adverb, & noun phrase* L18 **Italian** (= of belief, of trust). *Commerce* (Subject or relating to) a selling agent's guarantee, for which a commission is charged, that the buyer is solvent.

délicatesse /delikatɛs/ *noun* L17 **French** (from *délicat* delicate). Delicacy.

delicatessen /ˌdɛlɪkə'tɛs(ə)n/ *noun* L19 **German** (*Delikatessen* plural or Dutch *delicatessen* plural, from as preceding). **1** L19 Cooked meats, cheeses, and unusual or foreign prepared foods. **2** M20 A shop, or shop counter or department, selling delicatessen.

■ Originally in the United States. Sense 2 is often abbreviated colloquially to *deli*, which in Australia has undergone an extension of meaning to 'a small shop open long hours and selling perishable goods, newspapers, etc.'

delirium /dɪ'lɪrɪəm/ *noun* plural **deliriums**, **deliria** /dɪ'lɪrɪə/ M16 **Latin** (from *delirare* to deviate, be deranged, from *de-* + *lira* ridge between furrows). **1** M16 A disordered state of the mind resulting from disease, intoxication, etc., characterized by incoherent speech, hallucinations, restlessness, and often extreme excitement. **2** M17 Great excitement; ecstasy, rapturous frenzy.

delirium tremens /dɪˌlɪrɪəm 'triːmənz/, /dɪˌlɪrɪəm 'trɛmənz/ *noun phrase* E19 **Modern Latin** (= trembling delirium, from as DELIRIUM + *tremens* present participial adjective of *tremere to shake*). Delirium accompanied by tremors and terrifying illusions, usually as a symptom of withdrawal in cases of chronic alcoholism.

■ A term invented by a Dr T. Sutton in 1813 for a type of delirium that was worsened by bleeding but alleviated by opium; later medical writers established its modern sense.

delta /'dɛltə/ *noun* ME **Latin** (from Greek). **1** ME The fourth letter (Δ, δ) of the Greek alphabet. **2** M16 A tract of alluvial land, often more or less triangular in shape, enclosed or traversed by the diverging mouths of a river; originally (*the Delta*) *specifically* that of the River Nile. **3** M17 A triangle; a triangular area or formation. Usually *attributive*, as in *delta connection* (*Electricity*) and *delta wing* (*Aeronautics*). **4** L18 Denoting the fourth in a numerical sequence: *attributive Science* (frequently written δ) as *Astronomy* (preceding the genitive of the Latin name of the constellation): the fourth brightest star in a constellation; (**b**) *delta rays*, rays of low penetrative power consisting of slow electrons released from atoms by other particles; (**c**) *delta rhythm*, *delta waves*, slow electrical activity of the unconscious brain. **5** E20 A fourth-class or poor mark in an examination etc.

de luxe /dɪ 'lʌks/, /'lʊks/, /də/ *adjective phrase* E19 **French** (= of luxury). Luxurious, sumptuous; of a superior kind.

■ Used either postpositively (see quotation 1996) or as a premodifier (see quotation 1970). Cf. POULE DE LUXE.

1970 K. Chesney *Victorian Underworld* These places were often little businesses engaged in

a de luxe trade, glovers, bonnet makers, perfumers and so on.
1996 *Spectator* Margaret Cooper, at the age of about 500 and as pretty as springtime, is a catalyst *de luxe*.

démarche /demarʃ/ (*plural same*), /deɪ ˈmɑːʃ/ *noun* M17 **French** (from *démarcher* to take steps, from *dé-* + *marcher* to march). A step, a proceeding; *especially* a diplomatic action or initiative.

1996 *Spectator* John Lloyd . . . and Barry Cox . . . urged Mr Blair to stand against John Smith . . . . Mr Blair was right to disregard their advice . . . But the Cox/Lloyd *démarche* is interesting . . .

déménagement /demenaʒmɑ̃/ *noun* L19 **French**. The removal of household possessions from one place to another; moving house.

démenti /demɑ̃ti/ *noun* plural pronounced same L16 **French** (from *démentir* to contradict, from *dé-* from + *mentir* to lie). A contradiction, a denial; now *especially* an official denial of a published statement.

dementia /dɪˈmɛnʃə/ *noun* L18 **Latin** (from *demens* insane, from *de-* + *mens* mind). **1** L18 *Psychiatry* Chronic mental and emotional deterioration caused by organic brain disease. **2** L19 Madness, folly.

demi-caractère /ˌdɛmɪkarəkˈtɛː/, *foreign* /dəmikaraktɛr/ (*plural same*) *noun & adjective* L18 **French** (literally, 'half character'). *Ballet* **A** *noun* L18 A dance retaining the form of the character dance but executed with steps based on the classical technique. Also, a dancer of demi-caractères. **B** *adjective* E19 Of, pertaining to, or designating dancing of this kind.

demi-glace /ˈdɛmɪglas/ *noun* E20 **French** (literally, 'half-glaze'). *Cookery* A meat-stock from which the liquid has been partially evaporated. In full *demi-glace sauce*.

demilune /ˈdɛmɪluːn/ *noun & adjective* E18 **French** (literally, 'half-moon'). **A** *noun* **1** E18 *Fortification* An outwork resembling a bastion, with a crescent-shaped gorge. **2** M18 A half-moon, a crescent; a crescent-shaped body. **B** *adjective* L19 Crescent-shaped, semilunar.

demi-mondaine /dəmimɔ̃dɛn/ (*plural same*), /ˌdɛmɪmɒnˈdeɪn/ *noun* L19 **French** (from as next). A woman of the DEMI-MONDE.

1996 *Spectator* Most of my romantic entanglements have been less *demi-mondaine* than mundane.

demi-monde /dəmimɔ̃d/, /dɛmɪˈmɒnd/, /ˈdɛmɪmɒnd/ *noun* M19 **French** (literally, 'half world'). The class of women of doubtful reputation and social standing; the class of kept women or *loosely* of prostitutes; *transferred* any social group regarded as behaving with doubtful propriety or legality.

■ *Le Demi-monde* was the title of a novel (1855) by the younger Alexandre Dumas.

1988 K. Adler *Unknown Impressionists* La Grenouillère was well known as a favourite place for Parisian bourgeois men to meet women of the demi-monde . . . .

de minimis /deɪ ˈmɪnɪmiːs/ *adverb and adjective phrase* E17 **Latin** (= about the smallest things (*de* about + use as noun of ablative plural of *minimus* least, smallest)). About petty details.

■ An elliptical use of the Latin legal tag *de minimis non curat lex* 'the law does not concern itself with petty matters', which is used as an injunction not to become overconcerned about trivia.

1996 *Times* At that level we must be getting very close to a *de minimis* argument.

demi-pension /dəmipɑ̃sjɔ̃/ *noun* M20 **French**. Originally in France and French-speaking countries: (the price of) bed, breakfast, and one other meal at a hotel etc.; half-board.

attributive **1995** D. Lodge *Therapy* We were on *demi-pension* terms at the hotel.

demi-saison /dəmisɛzɔ̃/ *adjective* M18 **French** (literally, 'half season'). Of a style or fashion intermediate between that of the past and that of the coming season.

demi-sec /dɛmɪˈsɛk/, *foreign* /dəmisɛk/ *adjective* M20 **French** (literally, 'half-dry'). *Wine* Medium dry.

demitasse /ˈdɛmɪtas/, *foreign* /dəmitas/ (*plural same*) *noun* M19 **French** (literally, 'half-cup'). (The contents of) a small coffee-cup.

demi-vierge /dəmivjɛrʒ/ *noun* plural pronounced same E20 **French** (literally 'half-virgin'). A woman who behaves licentiously while remaining a virgin.

■ From the title of the novel *Les demi-vierges* (1874) by M. Prévost.

démodé /demɔde/, /deɪˈməʊdeɪ/ *adjective* L19 **French** (past participle of *démoder* to send, go out of fashion, from *dé-* from +

mode fashion). Out of fashion, unfashionable.

demoiselle /dɛmwɑːˈzɛl/ *noun* E16 **French.** **1** E16 A young lady, a girl. *archaic.* **2** L17 A Eurasian and North African crane, *Anthropoides virgo*, with elongated black breast-feathers and white neck-plumes. Now usually more fully *demoiselle crane.* **3** M19 A dragonfly or (*especially*) a damselfly. **4** L19 A damselfish.

de mortuis /deɪ ˈmɔːtuːiːs/ *noun phrase* **Latin** (= about the dead). (An injunction not to speak ill) of the dead.

■ An elliptical form of the Latin saying *de mortuis nil nisi bonum* '(say) nothing but good of the dead'. The saying is traditionally ascribed to Chilon of Sparta, one of the sages of ancient Greece.

1995 *Times* It is a real moment of casting-off for Jane who, ever a lady, is afflicted by *de mortuis*.

demos /ˈdiːmɒs/ *noun* plural **demi** /ˈdiːmʌɪ/ L18 **Greek** (*dēmos*). **1** L18 A district of ancient Attica, Greece; a deme. *rare.* **2** M19 (**Demos**) The common people of an ancient Greek State; (a personification of) the populace, especially in a democracy.

dengue /ˈdɛŋgi/ *noun* (also **denga** /ˈdɛŋgə/) E19 **West Indian Spanish** (from Kiswahili *denga, dinga* (in full *kidinga-popo*), identified with Spanish *dengue* fastidiousness, prudery, with reference to the stiffness of the neck and shoulders caused by the disease). A debilitating tropical viral disease. Also *dengue-fever.*

dénigrement /denigrəmɑ̃/ *noun* L19 **French.** Blackening of character, denigration.

de nos jours /də no ʒur/ *postpositive adjective phrase* E20 **French** (= of our days). Of the present time; contemporary.

1995 *Times* Much was made in the late Eighties about comics being the rock stars *de nos jours* and so forth.

denouement /deɪˈnuːmɒ̃/, /deɪˈnuːmɒŋ/ *noun* (also **dénouement**) M18 **French** (from *dénouer* (earlier *desnouement* to untie, from *des, dé-* + *nouer* to knot). The unravelling of the complications of a plot, or of a confused situation or mystery; the final resolution of a play, novel, or other narrative.

1996 *Times* The denouement [of *An Ideal Husband*] depends on the accidental discovery of a brooch the villainess has stolen, by the very man who years before bought it.

de nouveau /də nuvo/ *adverb phrase* L18 **French** (= from new). Afresh, starting again from the beginning. Cf. next.

de novo /deɪ ˈnəʊvəʊ/, /diː/ *adverb phrase* E17 **Latin** (= from new). Starting again from the beginning.

1995 *Country Life* A splendid example of a private Jacobean chapel built *de novo* for Anglican worship is that at Hatfield House, Hertfordshire, created for Robert Cecil, 1st Earl of Salisbury, in 1607–12.

deoch an doris /dɒx (ə)n ˈdɒrɪs/, /dɒk/ *noun phrase* (also **doch an doris**) M17 **Gaelic** (*deoch an doruis* (Irish *deoch an dorais*) a drink at the door). In Scotland and Ireland: a drink taken at parting, a stirrup-cup.

Deo gratias /deɪəʊ ˈgrɑːtɪəs/, /ˈgrɑːʃɪəs/ *interjection* L16 **Latin** (= (we give) thanks to God). Thanks be to God.

Deo volente /ˌdeɪəʊ vɒˈlɛnteɪ/ *adverb phrase* M18 **Latin.** God willing; if nothing prevents it.

■ Abbreviated to *d.v.*.

dépaysé /depeize/ *adjective* (feminine **dépaysée**) E20 **French** (= (removed) from one's own country). Removed from one's habitual surroundings.

depot /ˈdɛpəʊ/ *noun* (also (now *rare*) **depôt**) L18 **French** (*dépôt*, Old French *depost* from Latin *depositum* use as noun of neuter past participle of *deponere* to place, put away). **1 a** L18–M19 The action or an act of depositing. *rare.* **b** M19 A deposit, a collection, a store. Now *specifically* (*transferred* from sense 4 below) a localized accumulation of a substance in the body. **2** L18 A military establishment at which stores are deposited, recruits or other troops assembled, etc.; *especially* a regimental headquarters. **3** L18 A place where goods etc. are deposited or stored, often for later dispatch; a warehouse, an emporium. **b** M19 A place where vehicles, locomotives, etc., are housed and maintained and from which they are dispatched for service; *North American* a railway or bus station. **4** E20 A site in the body at which a particular substance naturally concentrates or is deposited.

de profundis /deɪ prəˈfʊndiːs/ *noun & adverb phrase* LME **Latin** (= from the depths)). **A** *noun* LME A psalm of penitence; *specifically* Psalm 130 (129 in the Vulgate); *generally* a cry of appeal from the depths (of sorrow, humiliation, etc.). **B** *adverb phrase* LME Out of the depths (of sorrow etc.).

■ The initial words of Psalm 130 (129 in the Vulgate): 'Out of the deep have I called unto thee O Lord' (Book of Common Prayer). *De Profundis* was the title of Oscar Wilde's posthumously published apologia written after being sentenced to a term of imprisonment in Reading Gaol, and modern use of the phrase often contains an unspoken allusion to Wilde's work (see quotation).

A 1996 *Times* Johnson has given us an excellent Profession of Faith: his *De Profundis* has yet to come.

déraciné /derasine/ (*plural same*), /deɪ'rasmeɪ/ *adjective & noun* (feminine **déracinée**) E20 **French** (= uprooted, past participial adjective of *déraciner*). **A** *adjective* E20 Uprooted from one's environment; displaced geographically or socially. **B** *noun* E20 A *déraciné* person.

derailleur /dɪ'reɪlə/, /dɪ'reɪljə/ *noun* M20 **French** (*dérailleur*, from *dérailler* to cause (a train) to run off the rails). A bicycle gear in which the ratio is changed by switching the line of the chain (while pedalling) so that it jumps to a different sprocket.

de rigueur /də rigœr/, /də rɪ'gəː/ *predicative adjective phrase* M19 **French** (literally, 'of strictness'). Required by custom or etiquette.

1995 *Spectator* It was *de rigueur* to dream on the eve of a battle, before giving birth to a hero, or before one's own assassination.

dernier /dɛrnje/, /'dəːnjeɪ/ *adjective* E17 **French** (from Old French *derrenier*, from *derrein* last). Last, ultimate, final.

■ Formerly fully naturalized, but now only in phrases (see below).

dernier cri /dɛrnje kri/, /ˌdəːnjeɪ 'kriː/ *noun phrase* (also **le dernier cri**) L19 **French** (literally, '(the) last cry'). The very latest fashion.

1996 *Times* I loathed every minute of the staging, while recognising that it is probably the *dernier cri* (this week) of the producer's art.

dernier mot /dɛrnje mo/, /ˌdəːnjeɪ 'məʊ/ *noun phrase* (also **le dernier mot**) M19 **French**. The last word.

dernier ressort /dɛrnje rəsɔr/, /dəːnjeɪ rə'sɔː/ *noun phrase* (also **le dernier resort**) M17 **French**. A last refuge; *originally* the ultimate court of appeal.

derrière /dɛrjɛr/, /dɛrɪ'ɛː/ (*plural same*) *noun* L18 **French** (= behind). The buttocks.

■ Usually only in jocular or colloquial use.

1995 *Times* At the autumn fashion collections, hourglass girls sashayed down the catwalk all décolletage and derrière with only a wasp waist to separate them.

dervish /'dəːvɪʃ/ *noun* L16 **Turkish** (*derviş* from Persian *darvīš* poor, a religious mendicant). A Muslim (*specifically* Sufi) religious man who has taken vows of poverty and austerity; *specifically* (more fully *dancing, whirling, howling*, etc., *dervish*) one whose order includes the practice of dancing etc. as a spiritual exercise.

desaparecido /ˌdesapare'sido/ *noun* plural **desaparecidos** /ˌdesapare'sidos/ L20 **Spanish** (= (one who has) disappeared). In Argentina: a person who disappeared during the period of military rule between 1976 and 1983, presumed killed by members of the armed services or the police; a child removed from his or her arrested parents and placed with another family without consent.

■ By extension, the word is now also applied to any persons who have vanished or been separated from their real families under totalitarian regimes in South America.

1987 *New Yorker* People whose children or husbands or wives were *desaparecidos* —disappeared ones—would go to Cardinal Arns, and the Cardinal would stop whatever he was doing and drive to the prisons, the police, the Second Army headquarters.

désaxé /dezakse/ *adjective & adverb* E20 **French**. Of a motor-car crankshaft: (set) out of line with the centre of the cylinder.

descamisado /ˌdeskami'sado/, /dɛsˌkamɪ'sɑːdəʊ/ *noun* plural **descamisados** /ˌdeskami'sados/, /dɛsˌkami'sɑːdəʊz/ M19 **Spanish** (= shirtless). *History* An extreme liberal in the Spanish Revolutionary War of 1820–3; *transferred* an impoverished revolutionary.

■ A similar sartorial deficiency gave rise to the earlier French Revolutionary equivalent, SANSCULOTTE.

1979 J. M. Taylor *Evita Perón* His speech declared Eva the martyr of the descamisados, an example given by God to the Argentinian people of self-sacrifice and faith.

déshabillé /dezabije/ (*plural same*) *noun* (also **deshabille, déshabille** /deɪzə'biːl/, /deɪza'biːjeɪ/, **dishabille** /dɪsə'biːl/) L17 **French** (*déshabillé* use as noun of past participle of *déshabiller* to undress). **1** L17 The state of being casually or only partially dressed. Chiefly in *in dishabille*, EN DÉSHABILLÉ. **2** L17 A garment or costume of a casual or informal style.

desideratum /dɪˌzɪdəˈrɑːtəm/, /dɪˌzɪdəˈreɪtəm/, /dɪˌsɪdəˈrɑːtəm/ *noun* plural **desiderata** /dɪˌzɪdəˈrɑːtə/, /dɪˌzɪdəˈreɪtə/, /dɪˌsɪdəˈrɑːtə/ M17 **Latin** (use as noun of neuter singular of past participle of *desiderare* to feel the lack of, desire). A thing for which desire is felt; a thing lacked and wanted, a requirement.

1995 *Spectator* Stalin's demands changed remarkably little between 1939 and 1945; all that altered was his ability to obtain his desiderata.

détente /deɪˈtɑ̃ː(n)t/, /deɪˈtɑ̃(n)t/, /deɪˈtɑːnt/, /deɪˈtɒnt/ *noun* E20 **French** (= loosening, relaxation). The easing of strained relations, especially between States.

détenu /deɪtəˈnuː/; *foreign* /detəny/ (*plural same*) *noun* (also **detenu**) E19 **French** (use as noun of past participle of *détenir* to detain). A detainee, now especially in the Indian subcontinent.

detour /ˈdiːtʊə/ *noun & verb* (also **détour** /ˈdeɪtʊə/) M18 **French** (*détour* change of direction, from *détourner* to turn away). **A** *noun* M18 A deviation from one's route, a roundabout way; a digression. **B** *verb* **1** *intransitive* M19 Make a detour. **2** *transitive* E20 Send by a detour. **3** *transitive* M20 Bypass, make a detour round.

détraqué /detrake/ *adjective & noun* (feminine **détraquée**) E20 **French** (past participial adjective of *détraquer* to put out of order, derange). **A** *adjective* E20 Deranged; crazy; psychopathic. **B** *noun* E20 plural pronounced same. A deranged person, a psychopath.

detritus /dɪˈtrʌɪtəs/ *noun* L18 **Latin** (*detritus* rubbing away, from *deterere* to wear away; in sense 2 after French *détritus*). **1** L18–E19 Wearing away by rubbing; disintegration. **2** E19 Matter produced by detrition; *especially* material eroded or washed away, as gravel, sand, silt, etc. **3** M19 Debris of any kind.

de trop /də tro/, /də ˈtrəʊ/ *adjective phrase* M18 **French** (literally, 'excessive'). Not wanted, unwelcome, in the way.

1996 *Oldie* But now blackboards and chalk are rapidly becoming *de trop*, replaced by whiteboards and markers.

detur /ˈdɪːtə/ *noun* L18 **Latin** (= let there be given). Any of several prizes of books given annually at Harvard University.

■ *Detur* is the first word of the inscription accompanying these books.

deus absconditus /ˌdeɪəs abˈskɒndɪtəs/, /ˌdiːəs/ *noun phrase* M20 **Latin** (= hidden god). *Theology* A divine being that is inaccessible to human perception.

■ Cf. Isaiah 45:15 'Verily thou art a God that hidest thyself, O God of Israel . . . '

deus ex machina /ˌdeɪəs ɛks ˈmakɪnə/, /ˌdiːəs ɛks ˈmakɪnə/ *noun phrase* L17 **Modern Latin** (translation of Greek *theos ek mēkhanēs*, literally, 'god from the machinery'). A power, event, or person arriving in the nick of time to solve a difficulty; a providential (often rather contrived) interposition, especially in a novel or play.

■ The 'machine' was originally the device by which deities were suspended above the stage in the theatre in classical antiquity. The phrase is generally used in its entirety but also occurs abbreviated to *ex machina*, with another agent of providence substituted for *deus* (see quotation 1996(2)).

attributive **1996** *Spectator* The *deus ex machina* resolution of the drama may provide one of the most feeble dénouements in all opera . . .

1996 *Times* In this ideal scenario, growth in Europe turns up and deficits come down without anyone on this side of the Atlantic having to do anything. EMU ex machina.

deva /ˈdeɪvə/ *noun* E19 **Sanskrit** (= a god, (originally) a shining one). Any of a class of deities in Vedic mythology; any of the lower-level gods in Hinduism and Buddhism.

devadasi /deɪvəˈdɑːsi/ *noun* E19 **Sanskrit** (*devadāsī*, literally, 'female servant of a god' (cf. preceding)). A hereditary female dancer in a Hindu temple.

développé /devlɔpe/ *noun* plural pronounced same E20 **French** (use as noun of past participle of *développer* to develop). A ballet movement in which one leg is raised and then fully extended.

dévot /devo/ (*plural same*), /deɪˈvəʊ/ *noun* (feminine **dévote** /devɔt/ (*plural same*), /deɪˈvɒt/) E18 **French** (use as noun or adjective). A devotee; a devout person.

dey /deɪ/ *noun* (also (especially in titles) **Dey**) M17 **French** (from Turkish *dayl* maternal uncle, used also as a courtesy title). *History* (The title of) any of the supreme rulers of Algiers, 1710–1830. Also, (the title of) the local ruler of Tunis or Tripoli under nominal Ottoman suzerainty.

dhal /dɑːl/ *noun* (also **dal**) L17 **Hindustani** (*dāl*). Split pulses (especially the seed of the pigeon-pea, *Cajanus cajan*), a common ingredient in Indian cookery.

dhamma /ˈdɑːmə/, /ˈdʌmə/ *noun* E20 **Pali** (from as *dharma*). Especially among Theravada Buddhists, DHARMA.

dhania /ˈdaniə/ *noun* E20 **Hindi** (*dhaniyā*). In Indian cookery: coriander.

dharma /ˈdɑːmə/, /ˈdəːmə/ *noun* L18 **Sanskrit** (= something established, decree, custom; cf. DHAMMA). In *Hinduism*: social or caste custom, right behaviour, law; justice, virtue; natural or essential state or function, nature. In *Buddhism*: universal truth or law, especially as proclaimed by Buddha.

dharmsala /ˈdɑːmsɑːlə/, /ˈdəːmʃɑːlɑː/ *noun* (also **dharmasala** /ˈdɑːməsɑːlə/, /ˈdəːməʃɑːlɑː/) E19 **Sanskrit** (representing Hindustani pronunciation of Sanskrit *dharmaśālā*, from *dharma* + *śālā* house). In the Indian subcontinent: a building devoted to religious or charitable purposes, *especially* a rest-house for travellers.

dhobi /ˈdəʊbi/ *noun* (also **dhoby**, **dhobie**) M19 **Hindustani** (*dhobī*, from *dhob* washing). In the Indian subcontinent: a washerman or washerwoman.

dhoti /ˈdəʊti/ *noun* (also formerly **dhootie** /ˈduːti/ and other variants) E17 **Hindustani** (*dhotī*). A cloth worn by male Hindus, the ends being passed through the legs and tucked in at the waist.

dhow /daʊ/ *noun* (also **dow**) L18 **Arabic** (*dāwa*, probably related to Marathi *ḍāw*). A lateen-rigged sailing vessel of the Arabian Sea, with one or two masts. Formerly also *loosely*, an Arab slaver or other vessel.

diable /djɑbl/ *interjection & noun* L16 **French** (from ecclesiastical Latin *diabolus* devil). **A** *interjection* L16 Expressing impatience, amazement, dismay, etc. **B** *noun* M19 (*le diable*) DIABOLO. Now *rare* or *obsolete*.

diable au corps /djɑbl o kɔr/ *noun phrase* L19 **French** (literally, 'devil in the body'). Restless energy; a spirit of devilry.

diablerie /dɪˈɑːbləri/ *noun* (also **diablery**) M18 **French** (from as DIABLE). **1** M18 Dealings with the Devil; sorcery, witchcraft. **b** M19 *figurative* Mischievous fun, devilment. **2** E19 The mythology or lore of devils; a description or representation of devils. **3** M19 The realm of devils.

1 1996 *Spectator* Fool! Ass! How had it happened? Was it some mysterious electric agency? Or was it *diablerie* playing tricks with my subconscious mind?

diabolo /dɪˈabələʊ/, /dʌɪˈabələʊ/ *noun* plural **diabolos** E20 **Italian** (from ecclesiastical Latin *diabolus* devil). A game in which a two-headed top is thrown up and caught on a string stretched between two sticks; the top used in this game.

diabolus in musica /dɪˈɑːbələs ɪn ˌmjuːzɪkə/ *noun phrase* M20 **Latin** (literally, 'the devil in music'). *Music* The interval of the diminished fifth.

■ So called because of its displeasing or unsettling effect.

attributive **1995** J. D. Barrow *Artful Universe* An acoustic form of this perceptual ambiguity exists with musical chord sequences displaying the *diabolus in musica* phenomenon.

diaeresis /dʌɪˈɪərɪsɪs/, /dʌɪˈɛrɪsɪs/ *noun* (also **dieresis**) plural **diaereses** /dʌɪˈɪərɪsiːz/ L16 **Latin** (from Greek *diairesis* noun of action from *diairein* to take apart, divide). **1** L16 The division of one syllable into two, especially by the resolution of a diphthong into two simple vowels. **2** E17 The sign ¨ placed over a vowel to indicate that it is pronounced separately, as in *Brontë*, *naïve*. **3** M19 *Prosody* A break in a line where the end of a foot coincides with the end of a word.

diamanté /dɪəˈmɒnteɪ/, *foreign* /djamɑ̃tɛ/ (*plural of noun same adjective & noun*) E20 **French** (past participle of *diamanter* to set with diamonds, from *diamant* diamond). (Material) given a sparkling effect by means of artificial gems, powdered crystal, etc.

Diaspora /dʌɪˈasp(ə)rə/ *noun* (also **diaspora**) L19 **Greek** (from *diaspeirein* to disperse, scatter). The dispersion of Jews among the Gentile nations; all those Jews who live outside the biblical land of Israel; (the situation of) any body of people living outside their traditional homeland.

dibbuk variant of DYBBUK.

dictum /ˈdɪktəm/ *noun* plural **dicta**, /ˈdɪktə/, **dictums** L16 **Latin**. **1** L16 A saying, an utterance; *especially* one that claims some authority, a pronouncement. **2** L18 *Law* An expression of opinion by a judge which is not essential to the decision and so has no binding authority as precedent. See also OBITER DICTUM. **3** E19 A common saying; a maxim.

1 1996 *Spectator* Conan Doyle's dictum—'When you have eliminated the impossible, whatever remains, *however improbable*, must be the truth'—simply doesn't apply.

didgeridoo /ˌdɪdʒ(ə)rɪˈduː/ *noun* (also **didjeridoo**, **didgeridu**) E20 **Aboriginal** (of imitative origin). A long tubular wooden musical instrument of the Australian Aborigines which is blown to produce a resonant sound.

dieresis variant of DIAERESIS.

dies irae /ˌdiːeɪz ˈɪərʌɪ/, /ˌdiːeɪz ˈɪəreɪ/ *noun phrase* E19 **Latin** (= day of wrath). A thirteenth-century Latin hymn that was formerly an obligatory part of the requiem mass in the Roman Catholic Church; a musical setting of this part of the mass; *hence* the Day of Judgement or *transferred* any day of reckoning.

■ The text of which *Dies irae* is the opening phrase is attributed to Thomas of Celano (*c.*1250).

dies non /ˈdʌɪiːz ˌnɒn/ *noun phrase* plural same E19 **Latin** (literally, 'a non day'). A day that does not count because there has been no (specific) activity or because it cannot be used for a particular purpose.

■ Used in its original legal sense, it is an abbreviated form of the following, but it is also applied in other contexts.

dies non juridicus /ˌdʌɪiːz nɒn dʒʊə ˈrɪdɪkəs/ *noun phrase* plural **dies non juridici** /ˌdʌɪiːz nɒn dʒʊəˈrɪdɪsʌɪ/ E17 **Latin** (literally, 'day not judicial'). *Law* A day on which no legal business is enacted.

differentia /dɪfəˈrɛnʃɪə/ *noun* plural **differentiae** /dɪfəˈrɛnʃɪiː/ L17 **Latin**. A distinguishing mark or characteristic, *especially* (*Logic*) that distinguishing a species from others of the same genus.

difficile /ˈdɪfɪsiːl/, *foreign* /difisil/ *adjective* LME **French** (from Latin *difficilis*, from *dif-* not + *facilis* easy). **1** LME–L17 Requiring physical or mental effort or skill. **2** L15–M17 Hard to understand; obscure. **3** M16 Of a person: not easy to get on with, stubborn, unaccommodating.

difficilior lectio /dɪfɪˌkɪlɪɔː ˈlɛktɪəʊ/ *noun phrase* plural **difficiliores lectiones** /dɪfɪkɪlɪˈɔːreɪz lɛktɪˌəʊneɪz/ E20 **Latin** (from the maxim *difficilior lectio potior* the harder reading is to be preferred). *Textual Criticism* The more difficult or unexpected of two variant readings and therefore the one that is less likely to be a copyist's error; (the principle of) giving preference to such a reading.

1996 *Spectator* A. E. H.[ousman], who would devote four pages of acerbic minutiae to the re-instatement of a *difficilior lectio* in Manilius, would have expired foaming on the spot.

digamma /dʌɪˈgamə/ *noun* L17 **Latin** (from Greek, from *di-* twice + *gamma* (from the shape of the letter, a GAMMA with a doubled cross-stroke)). The sixth letter of the original Greek alphabet, probably equivalent to W, later disused.

digestif /diʒɛstif/ (*plural same*), /dʌɪˈdʒɛstɪf/ *noun* E20 **French**. Something which promotes good digestion, especially a drink taken after a meal.

diktat /ˈdɪktat/ *noun* M20 **German** (from Latin *dictatum* use as noun of neuter past participle of *dictare* to dictate). **1** M20 A severe settlement, especially one imposed by a victorious nation on a defeated one. **2** M20 A dictate; a categorical assertion.

2 1996 *Times* The essence of civilised behaviour is anyway to override the diktats of nature.

dilemma /dɪˈlɛmə/, /dʌɪˈlɛmə/ *noun* E16 **Latin** (from Greek *dilēmma*, from as *di-* twice + *lēmma* assumption, premiss). **1** E16 In *Rhetoric*, a form of argument involving an opponent in choice between two (or more) alternatives, both equally unfavourable. In *Logic*, a syllogism with two conditional major premisses and a disjunctive minor premiss. **2** L16 A choice between two (or several) alternatives which are equally unfavourable; a position of doubt or perplexity.

dilettante /dɪlɪˈtanti/ *noun & adjective* plural **dilettanti**, /dɪlɪˈtanti/, **dilettantes** M18 **Italian** (use as noun of verbal adjective from *dilettare* from Latin *delectare* to delight). **A** *noun* M18 A lover of the fine arts; a person who cultivates the arts as an amateur; a person who takes an interest in a subject merely as a pastime and without serious study, a dabbler. **B** *adjective* M18 Of, pertaining to, or characteristic of a dilettante; amateur.

■ The English use of the word is linked to the eighteenth-century British fashion for wealthy young aristocrats to travel to Italy on the so-called Grand Tour to study the remains of classical antiquity there and to purchase sculptures, coins, and other objects for their personal collections. In 1733–4 'some gentlemen who had travelled in Italy, desirous of encouraging, at home, a taste for those objects which had contributed so much to their entertainment abroad' founded the Society of Dilettanti. Despite Horace Walpole's unkind observation that the nominal qualification for membership of the Dilettanti was 'having been in Italy, and the real one, being drunk', the society subsequently financed some major expeditions and publications and generally played a key role in developing British knowledge of the ancient world.

A 1996 *Spectator* . . . the show is an oasis of antique elegance and calm—where would-be dilettanti can take wistful refuge from the mêlée of not-so-grand tourists in the Museum's entrance hall, and wish themselves transported to 18th-century Naples.

dilruba /dɪl'ru:bə/ *noun* E20 **Hindustani** (*dilrubā* = robber of the heart). An Indian musical instrument with a long neck, three or four strings played with a bow, and several sympathetic strings.

diminuendo /dɪˌmɪnjʊ'ɛndəʊ/ *noun, verb, adverb, & adjective* L18 **Italian** (= diminishing, present participle of *diminuire* from Latin *deminuere* to lessen). *Music* **A** *noun* L18 plural **diminuendos, diminuendi** /dɪˌmɪnjʊ'ɛndi/. A gradual decrease in loudness; a passage (to be) played or sung with such a decrease. **B** *intransitive verb* L18 Become quieter; grow less. **C** *adverb & adjective* E19 (A direction:) with a gradual decrease in loudness.

dim sum /dɪm 'sʌm/ *noun phrase* (also **dim sim** /dɪm 'sɪm/ and other variants) plural **dim sum(s)** etc. M20 **Chinese** (Cantonese) (*tím sam*, from *tím* dot + *sam* heart). A Chinese snack consisting of different hot savoury pastries.

dinanderie /dinɑ̃dri/ *noun* M19 **French** (from *Dinant* (formerly *Dinand*), a town near Liège, Belgium + *-erie*). Domestic and other utensils of brass (frequently embossed) made in late medieval times in and around Dinant; ornamental brassware from other parts, including India and the eastern Mediterranean region.

dinero /dɪ'nɛ:rəʊ/ *noun* plural **dineros** L17 **Spanish** (= coin, money from Latin *denarius* a silver coin). **1** *History* L17 A monetary unit in Spain and Peru, now disused. **2** M19 Money. *United States slang.*

Ding an sich /dɪŋ an 'zɪç/ *noun phrase* M19 **German** (= thing in itself). *Philosophy* A thing as it really is, apart from human observation or experience of it. Cf. NOUMENON.

diorama /dʌɪə'rɑ:mə/ *noun* E19 **French** (from as Greek *dia* through + *orama* view (after *panorama*). **1** E19 A scenic painting, viewed through a peephole, in which changes in lighting, colour, etc., are used to suggest different times of day, changes in weather, etc.; a building in which such paintings are exhibited. **2** E20 A small-scale tableau in which three-dimensional figures are shown against a painted background; a museum display of an animal etc. in its natural setting; a scale model of an architectural project in its surroundings. **3** M20 *Cinematography* A small-scale set used in place of a full-scale one for special effects, animation, etc.

diploma /dɪ'pləʊmə/ *noun & verb* M17 **Latin** (from Greek = folded paper, from *diploun* to make double, fold, from *diploos* double). **A** *noun* plural **diplomas**, (*rare*) **diplomata** /dɪ'pləʊmətə/. **1** M17 A State paper, an official document; a charter; in *plural*, historical or literary muniments. **2** M17 A document conferring some honour, privilege, or licence; a certificate of a university, college, or (*North American*) school degree or qualification; such a degree or qualification. **B** *transitive verb* M19 Award a diploma to. Chiefly as *diplomaed, diploma'd* participial adjective.

Directoire /dɪ'rɛktwɑ:/, *foreign* /dirɛktwar/ (*plural of noun same*) *noun & adjective* L18 **French** (from Late Latin *directorium* use as noun of neuter singular of *directorius* from *director* person who directs). **A** *noun* L18 *History* The French Directory (1795–9). **B** *adjective* L19 Also **directoire**. Of, pertaining to, or resembling an extravagant style of fashion, decorative art, etc., prevalent at the time of the Directory and characterized especially by an imitation of Greek and Roman modes.

■ The adjective is often found in the phrase *directoire knickers* (women's knee-length knickers elasticated at the knee and waist).

dirigisme /diriʒism/ *noun* (also **dirigism** /'dɪrɪdʒɪz(ə)m/) M20 **French** (from *diriger* from Latin *dirigere* to direct). The policy of State direction and control in economic and social matters.

1996 *Times* French dirigisme preserved their oyster. English *laisser faire* turned the oyster from poor man's food into an impossible luxury.

dirigiste /diriʒist/ *adjective & noun* M20 **French** (as preceding). (A proponent) of DIRIGISME.

adjective **1995** *New Scientist* But it is surely off-beam to suggest an outright ban is somehow less dirigiste than piecemeal regulation.

noun **1995** *Times* The European Community, which had been designed to make Europe more competitive, was already moving towards a bureaucratic model based on those old European *dirigistes* Bismarck and Colbert.

dirndl /ˈdəːnd(ə)l/ *noun* M20 **German** (dialect, diminutive of *Dirne* girl). **1** M20 A dress in the style of Alpine peasant costume with a bodice and full skirt. **2** M20 A full skirt with a tight waistband. More fully *dirndl skirt*.

dis aliter visum /ˌdɪs alɪtə ˈviːsəm/ *interjection* M20 **Latin**. The gods decided otherwise.

■ Quoted from Virgil *Aeneid* ii.428.

1948 R. Coupland *Zulu Battle Piece* The Zulu war, [Frere] had written, must begin and end with 'a sharp and decisive success'. *Dis aliter visum.*

discobolus /dɪˈskɒbələs/ *noun* plural **discoboli** /dɪˈskɒbəlʌɪ/, /dɪˈskɒbəliː/ E18 **Latin** (from Greek *diskobolos*, from as *discus* + *-bolos* throwing, from *ballein* to throw). *Classical History* A discus-thrower; a statue representing one in action.

discothèque /ˈdɪskətɛk/ *noun* (also **discotheque**) M20 **French** (originally = record-library (after *bibliothèque*)). A place or event at which recorded pop music is played for dancing.

■ Now almost universally abbreviated to *disco*.

discus /ˈdɪskəs/ *noun* M17 **Latin** (from Greek *diskos*). **1** M17 A heavy thick-centred disc or plate thrown in ancient and modern athletic sports; the sporting event in which it is thrown. **2** L17–E18 Any disc or disc-shaped body.

diseuse /diːˈzəːz/, *foreign* /dizøz/ *noun* plural pronounced same L19 **French** (= talker, feminine of *diseur*, from *dire* to say). A female artiste who specializes in monologue.

dishabille variant of DÉSHABILLÉ.

disinvoltura /ˌdisinvɔlˈtuːra/ *noun* M19 **Italian** (from *disinvolto* unembarrassed, from *disinvolgere* to unwind). Self-assurance; lack of constraint.

disjecta membra /dɪsˌjɛktə ˈmɛmbrə/ *noun phrase plural* (also **disiecta membra**) E18 **Latin**. Scattered remains.

■ Alteration of Latin *disjecti membra poetae* 'limbs of a dismembered poet' (Horace *Satires* I.iv.62). The word order *membra disjecta* is apparently a later (M20) variant.

dissensus /dɪˈsɛnsəs/ *noun* M20 **Latin** (= disagreement; or from *dis-* + (*con*)*sensus*). Widespread dissent; the reverse of consensus.

distingué /dɪˈstaŋgeɪ/, *foreign* /distɛ̃ge/ *adjective* (feminine **distinguée**) E19 **French**. Having an air of distinction; having a distinguished appearance or manner.

distinguo /dɪˈstɪŋgwəʊ/ *noun* plural **distinguos** L19 **Latin** (= I distinguish). A distinction in thought or reasoning.

distrait /dɪˈstreɪ/, /ˈdɪstreɪ/, *foreign* /distrɛ/ *adjective* (feminine **distraite** /dɪˈstreɪt/, /ˈdɪstreɪt/, *foreign* /distrɛt/) LME **French** (from Old French *destrait* past participle of *destraire* from Latin *distrahere* to distract). **1** Only in LME. Distracted in mind. **2** LME–L16 Divided, separated. **3** M18 Absent-minded; not paying attention.

■ Sense 3 represents a re-borrowing from French after *distrait* had become obsolete in English in its two earlier senses.

3 1996 *Spectator* On my visit, . . . the place was crowded, though emptying, and the young, slightly inept staff *distrait.*

dithyramb /ˈdɪθɪram(b)/ *noun* (also in Latin form **dithyrambus** /ˌdɪθɪˈrambəs/, plural **dithyrambi** /ˌdɪθɪrambʌɪ/) E17 **Latin** (*dithyrambus* from Greek *dithurambos*). **1** E17 An ancient Greek choric hymn, vehement and wild in character; a Bacchanalian song. **2** M17 A passionate or inflated poem, speech, or writing.

ditto /ˈdɪtəʊ/ *adjective, adverb, & noun* plural of noun **dittos** E17 **Italian** (dialect (Tuscan) variant of *detto* said, from Latin *dictus* past participle of *dicere* to say). **1** In or of the month already named; the aforesaid month. Only in 17. **2** L17 In the same way, similar(ly); the same; (the) aforesaid; (the same as, another of) what was mentioned above or previously. *colloquial* except in lists etc. (where usually represented by dots or commas under the matter repeated). **b** *noun* L19 A symbol representing the word 'ditto'. Also *ditto mark*. **3** *noun* M18 Cloth of the same material. Chiefly in *suit of dittos*, a suit of clothes of the same material and colour throughout. *archaic*. **4** *noun* L18 Something identical or similar; an exact resemblance; a repetition. **5** E20 (also **Ditto**) (Proprietary name for) a duplicator, a small offset press for copying.

2 1996 *Times* Anyway, neither Carman, QC, nor Gray, ditto, is going to beg his bread in the gutter . . .

diva /ˈdiːvə/ *noun* L19 **Italian** (from Latin *diva* goddess). A distinguished female (especially operatic) singer; a prima donna.

1995 *Times* In person, she [sc. Dawn Upshaw] has few diva tendencies. The morning after her Berlin recital, she came to her interview minutes after stepping from the shower—hair still wet, face scrubbed.

divan /dɪ'vɑn/, /dʌɪ'van/, /'dʌɪvan/ *noun* L16 **French** (or Italian *divano*, from Turkish *dīvān* from Persian *dīvān* brochure, anthology, register, court, bench; cf. DOUANE). **1** L16 An oriental council of State; *specifically* (*historical*) the privy council of the Ottoman Empire. **b** E17 Any council. *archaic*. **2** L16 The hall where the Ottoman divan was held; an oriental court of justice or council-chamber. **3** L17 In oriental countries: a room entirely open at one side towards a court, garden, river, etc. **4** E18 (Now the usual sense.) A couch or bed without a head- or footboard. Originally, a low bench or a raised part of a floor forming a long seat against the wall of a room. **5** E19 (A smoking-room attached to) a cigar-shop. *archaic*. **6** E19 An anthology of poems in Persian or other oriental language; *specifically* a series of poems by one author, with rhymes usually running through the alphabet.

divertimento /dɪˌvəːtɪ'mɛntəʊ/, /dɪˌvɛːtɪ'mɛntəʊ/ *noun* plural **divertimenti** /dɪˌvəːtɪ'mɛnti/, **divertimentos** M18 **Italian** (= diversion). **1** M18 An amusement. Long *rare*. **2** E19 *Music* A composition primarily for entertainment, *especially* a suite for a small group of instruments or a single instrument; a light orchestral piece.

divertissement /ˌdiːvɛː'tiːsmɔ̃/, *foreign* /divertismɑ̃/ (*plural pronounced same*) *noun* E18 **French** (from *divertiss-* stem of *divertir* to divert). **1** A short ballet or other entertainment between acts or longer pieces. **b** L19 A DIVERTIMENTO sense 2. **2** E19 An entertainment.

1.a 1996 *Spectator* . . . the ballroom scene is constructed as a conventional 19th-century *divertissement*, where the well-regulated choral dancing frames virtuoso duets . . .

divisi /di'viːsi/ *adverb, adjective, & noun* M18 **Italian** (= divided, plural past participial adjective of *dividere* to divide). *Music* **A** *adverb & adjective* M18 (A direction:) with a section of players divided into two or more groups each playing a different part. **B** *noun* M20 (The use of) *divisi* playing or scoring.

divorcee /dɪvɔː'siː/ *noun* (also (earlier) **divorcé**, feminine **divorcée**, /dɪvɔː'seɪ/ (*plural same*)), /dɪvɔː'seɪ/) E19 **French** (partly from *divorcé(e)* use as noun of past participial adjective of *divorcer* to divorce, partly from *divorce* + *-ee* after the French). A divorced person.

dix-huitième /dizɥitjɛm/ *adjective & noun* E20 **French** (= eighteenth). (Of or pertaining to) the eighteenth century.

dixit /'dɪksɪt/ *noun* L16 **Latin** (= he has said). An utterance or statement (quoted as) already made.

djellaba(h) variant of JELLABA.

djibba(h) variant of *jibba*; see JUBBA.

djinn see JINNEE.

Dobos Torte /'dɒbɒʃ ˌtɔːtə/ *noun phrase* (also **Dobos Torta**, **dobos torte**) plural **Dobos Torten** /'tɔːt(ə)n/ E20 **German** (*Dobostorte*, from J. C. *Dobós* (1847–1924), Hungarian pastry-cook + *Torte* tart, pastry, cake; cf. Hungarian *dobostorta*). A rich cake made of alternate layers of sponge and chocolate or mocha cream, with a crisp caramel topping.

docent /'dəʊs(ə)nt/ *foreign* /do'tsɛnt/ *noun* L19 **German** (*Docent*, *Dozent*, from Latin *docent-* present participial stem of *docere* to teach). **1** L19 Originally, a *Privatdozent* (formerly in German universities, a teacher paid by the students taught). Now, in certain United States universities and colleges, a member of the teaching staff below professorial rank. **2** E20 A (usually voluntary) guide in a museum, art gallery, or zoo. Chiefly *United States*.

doch an doris variant of DEOCH AN DORIS.

doctorand /'dɒktərand/ *noun* (also in Latin form **doctorandus** /dɒktə'randəs/, plural **doctorandi** /dɒktə'randʌɪ/) E20 **German** (from medieval Latin *doctorandus*). A candidate for a doctor's degree.

doctrinaire /ˌdɒktrɪ'nɛː/ *noun & adjective* E19 **French** (from *doctrine* + *-aire*). **A** *noun* **1** E19 *History* In early nineteenth-century France, a member of a political movement which supported constitutional government and the reconciliation of the principles of authority and liberty. **2** M19 A person who tries to apply principle without allowance for circumstance; a pedantic theorist. **B** *adjective* M19 Pertaining to or of the character of a doctrinaire; determined to apply or promote a doctrine in all circumstances; theoretical and unpractical.

B 1996 *Country Life* [It] would be easy to imagine this tear-jerking technique being used for propaganda purposes. A clever, doctrinaire film-maker could have a wonderful time with fox cubs.

doek /dʊk/ *noun* L18 **Afrikaans** (= cloth). In South Africa: a cloth, *especially* a head-scarf.

dogana /dəʊ'gɑːnə/ *noun* M17 **Italian**. In Italy (and Spain): a custom-house; the customs.

dogaressa /dəʊgə'rɛsə/ *noun* E19 **Italian** (irregular feminine of DOGE). *History* The wife of a doge.

doge /dəʊ(d)ʒ/ *noun* M16 **French** ((monosyllabic) from Italian (disyllabic) from Venetian Italian *doze* ultimately from Latin *dux, duc-* leader). *History* The chief magistrate in the former republics of Venice and Genoa.

dogma /'dɒgmə/ *noun* plural **dogmas**, **dogmata** /'dɒgmətə/ M16 **Late Latin** (from Greek *dogma, dogmat-* opinion, decree, from *dokein* to seem good, think). **1** M16 An opinion, a belief; *specifically* a tenet or doctrine authoritatively laid down, especially by a Church or sect; an arrogant declaration of opinion. **2** L18 A whole body of doctrines or opinions, especially on religious matters, laid down authoritatively or assertively.

2 1996 *Times* Treasury dogma opposes all tax allowances.

dojo /'dəʊdʒəʊ/ *noun* plural **dojos** M20 **Japanese** (from *dō* way, pursuit + *-jō* a place). A room or hall in which judo or other martial arts are practised; an area of padded mats for the same purpose.

dolce far niente /ˌdoltʃe far ni'ɛnte/ *noun phrase* E19 **Italian** (= sweet doing nothing). Delightful idleness.

■ Also in the shortened form FAR NIENTE.

dolce vita /ˌdoltʃe 'viːta/, /ˌdəʊltʃeɪ 'viːtə/ *noun phrase* M20 **Italian** (= sweet life). A life of luxury, pleasure, and self-indulgence.

■ Frequently preceded by *the* or *la* /la/.

1996 *Country Life* . . . his talent and prospects were regularly undermined by his taste for *la dolce vita*.

doli capax /ˌdɒlɪ 'kapaks/ *adjective phrase* L17 **Latin** (from *doli* genitive singular of *dolus* guile, fraud + *capax* capable). *Law* Capable of having the wrongful intention to commit a crime.

doli incapax /ˌdɒlɪ ɪn'kapaks/ *adjective phrase* L17 **Latin** (from as DOLI CAPAX). *Law* Not *doli capax*, especially because under fourteen years old.

attributive **1996** *Times* . . . the House of Lords shied away from changing the *doli incapax* rule concerning the criminal liability of children.

dolman /'dɒlmən/ *noun* (in sense 1 also written (earlier) **doliman** L16 **French** (in sense 1 from French *doliman*; in sense 2 from French *dolman* from German from Hungarian *dolmány*; both ultimately from Turkish *dolama(n)*). **1** L16 A long Turkish robe open in front and with narrow sleeves. **2** L19 A hussar's jacket worn with the sleeves hanging loose. **3** L19 A woman's mantle with dolman sleeves. **4** M20 A loose sleeve made in one piece with the body of a coat etc. In full *dolman sleeve*.

dolmas /'dɒlməs/ *noun* plural **dolmades** /dɒl'mɑːdɛz/ (also **dolma**, plural **dolmas**) L17 **Modern Greek** (*ntolmas* from Turkish *dolma*, from *dolmak* to fill, be filled). In the cookery of Greece, Turkey, and other East European countries: a dish of seasoned chopped meat and rice enclosed in a vine leaf, cabbage, pepper, etc.

dolmen /'dɒlmɛn/ *noun* M19 **French** (perhaps from Cornish *tolmen* hole stone). A megalithic structure found especially in Britain and France, consisting of a large flat stone supported on stone slabs set vertically in the ground forming a burial chamber, probably originally covered by an earth mound.

dolmus /'dɒlmʊʃ/ *noun* M20 **Turkish** (*dolmuş* filled, (as noun) dolmus). In Turkey: a shared taxi.

dolus /'dɒləs/ *noun* E17 **Latin**. *Law* Deceit; intentional damage. Cf. DOLI CAPAX.

dom /dəʊm/ *noun* M19 **German** (from Latin *domus* house). In Germany, Austria, and other German-speaking areas: a cathedral church.

domaine /də'meɪn/ *noun* M20 **French**. A vineyard.

■ Often in the phrase *domaine-bottled*, indicating that the wine has been bottled at the estate where the grapes of which it is made were grown.

domine /'duːmɪni/, /'dʊəmɪni/ *noun* (also (especially as a title) **Domine**) M16 **Latin** (vocative of *dominus* lord, master; cf. DOMINEE, DOMINIE). **1** M16–L17 Lord, master; sir: used in respectful address to a clergyman or a member of one of the professions. **2** E17 DOMINIE sense 1. Now *rare* or *obsolete*. **3** M17 A member of the clergy, a pastor; *especially* a pastor of the Dutch Reformed Church. (Cf. DOMINEE, DOMINIE 2). *archaic*.

dominee /'duːmɪni/, /'dʊəmɪni/ *noun* (also (especially as a title) **Dominee**) M20 **Afrikaans and Dutch** (from Latin DOMINE). In South Africa: a pastor of the Dutch Reformed Church.

dominie *in sense 1* /ˈdɒmmi/; *in senses 2 and 3* /ˈdəʊmmi/, /ˈdɒmmi/ *noun* L17 **Latin** (alternative form of DOMINE). **1** L17 A schoolmaster. Now chiefly *Scottish*. **2** L17 A pastor of the Dutch Reformed Church; (*dialect*) any minister. *United States*. **3** E19 A variety of large apple. More fully *dominie apple*. *United States*.

dominium /dəˈmmɪəm/ *noun* M18 **Latin**. *Law* Lordship, ownership, dominion.

■ Chiefly in the phrases *dominium directum* 'direct ownership' and *dominium utile* 'ownership of use', differentiating the rights of the owner and those of the tenant who has the use only of something.

domino /ˈdɒmməʊ/ *noun & interjection* L17 **French** (= hood worn by priests in winter (also in Spanish, = a masquerade garment), probably ultimately from Latin *dominus* lord, master, but unexplained). **A** *noun* plural **domino(e)s**. **1** L17 A garment worn to cover the head and shoulders; *specifically* a loose cloak with a mask for the upper part of the face, worn to conceal the identity at masquerades etc. **2** M18 A person wearing a domino. **3** L18 Each of a set of small oblong pieces, usually 28 in number and marked with 0 to 6 pips in each half, used in various matching and trick-taking games; in *plural* (treated as *singular*) or *singular*, the game played with such pieces. **4** M19 (From the interjection.) The end, the finish. Chiefly in *be all domino*, be all up (*with*). *slang*. **5** M19 Paper printed with a design from a woodblock and coloured, used as wallpaper etc. In full *domino paper*. **B** *interjection* M19 Notifying that one has matched up all one's dominoes; *transferred* notifying or registering the end of something.

■ The phrases *domino effect* and *domino theory*, much used in the mid twentieth century, allude to what happens when a row of dominoes (sense 3) is stood on end and the first one pushed over, resulting in the speedy collapse of the remainder; in political terms this is what Western governments feared would happen, particularly in South-east Asia but also in Africa, if one country became Communist-controlled.

don /dɒn/ *noun* E16 **Spanish** ((in sense 1c Italian) from Latin *dominus* lord, master). **1** E16 (**Don**) Used as a title of respect preceding the forename of a Spanish man (originally one of high rank) or (formerly, *jocular*) preceding the name or designation of any man. **b** E17 A Spanish lord or gentleman. **c** M20 A high-ranking or powerful member of the Mafia. *North American slang*. **2** L16 A distinguished or skilled man; a man who is outstanding in some way. *archaic*. **3** M17 At British universities, especially Oxford and Cambridge: a head, fellow, or tutor of a college; a member of the teaching staff.

donatio mortis causa /dəˌneɪʃɪəʊ ˌmɔːtɪs ˈkɔːzə/ *noun phrase* plural **donationes mortis causa** /dəˌneɪʃɪˈəʊniːz/ M17 **Latin** (= gift by reason of death). *Law* A (revocable) gift of personal property made in expectation of the donor's imminent death and taking effect thereafter.

doner kebab /ˌdɒnə kɪˈbab/, /ˌdəʊnə/, /kəˈbab/, /kəˈbɑːb/ *noun phrase* M20 **Turkish** (*döner kebap*, from *döner* rotating + *kebap* KEBAB). A Turkish dish consisting of spiced lamb roasted on a vertical rotating spit and sliced thinly.

donga /ˈdɒŋgə/ *noun* L19 **Nguni**. **1** L19 A ravine or watercourse with steep sides. *South Africa*. **2** E20 A broad shallow depression in the ground. *Australia*. **3** E20 A makeshift shelter; a temporary dwelling. *Australia*.

donnée /dɔne/, /ˈdɒneɪ/ *noun* (also **donné**) L19 **French** (feminine past participial adjective of *donner* to give). **1** L19 A subject, theme, or motif of a literary work. **2** L19 A datum, a given fact; a basic assumption.

1 1995 *Spectator* In a preface, Vansittart reveals that he received the *donné* for his novel some 50 years before actually embarking on it.

dop /dɒp/ *noun* L19 **Afrikaans** (of uncertain origin). **1** L19 In South Africa: brandy, especially of a cheap or inferior kind. In full *dop brandy*. **2** M20 A tot of liquor, especially of wine as given to farm labourers in the Cape Province of South Africa.

doppelgänger /ˈdɔpəlˌgɛŋər/, /ˈdɒp(ə)lˌgɛŋə/, /ˈdɒp(ə)lˌgaŋə/ *noun* (also **doppelganger**) M19 **German** (literally, 'doublegoer'). A supposed spectral likeness or double of a living person.

1962 O. Sitwell *Tales My Father Taught Me* I was never able myself to discern the mysterious stranger, and my own feeling was that he must be . . . my father's Narcissus-like *doppelgänger*, a projection from and of his own personality . . .

doppione /dopˈpjoːne/, /dɒpɪˈəʊni/ *noun* plural **doppioni** /dopˈpjoːni/ M20 **Italian** (from *doppio* double). *Early Music* A double-bore woodwind instrument of the Italian Renaissance.

dormeuse /dɔrmøz/ (*plural same*), /dɔːˈməːz/ *noun* M18 **French** (feminine of *dormeur*, literally, 'sleeper', from *dormir* to sleep). **1** A cap or hood worn in bed. Only in M18. **2** E19 A travelling-carriage adapted for sleeping in; *obsolete* except *historical*. **3** M19 A kind of couch or settee.

dos-à-dos /dozado/, /dəʊzəˈdəʊ/ *adverb, noun, & adjective* (also **do-se-do** /dəʊzɪˈdəʊ/, /dəʊsɪˈdəʊ/, **do-si-do**) M19 **French** (from *dos* back). **A** *adverb* M19 Back to back. **B** *noun* plural same. M19 A seat, carriage, etc., so constructed that the occupants sit back to back. *archaic*. **C** *adjective* M20 Designating binding or books in which two volumes are bound together facing in opposite directions and sharing a central board.

dot /dɒt/ *noun* M19 **Old and Modern French** (from Latin *dos, dot-*). A dowry only the income from which is at the husband's disposal.

dotaku /ˈdəʊtakuː/ *noun plural* (also **dōtaku**) E20 **Japanese**. Prehistoric Japanese bronze objects, shaped like bells and usually decorated with geometric or figurative designs.

douane /duːˈɑːn/ *noun* M17 **French** (from Italian *do(g)ana* from Arabic *dīwān* office, from Old Persian *dīwān* DIVAN). A customhouse in France or other Mediterranean country.

douanier /duːˈɑːnɪeɪ/ *noun* M18 **French** (from as preceding). A customs officer, *especially* one at a douane.

doublé /duble/ *adjective* M19 **French** (past participle of *doubler* to line). Covered or lined *with*; (of a book) having a doublure; plated *with* precious metal.

double entendre /ˌduːb(ə)l ɒ̃ːˈtɒ̃ːdr(ə)/, *foreign* /dubl ɑ̃tɑ̃dr/ *noun phrase* plural **double entendres** (pronounced same) L17 **French** (now obsolete (modern *double entente*) = double understanding). A double meaning; an ambiguous expression; a phrase with two meanings, one usually indecent. Also, the use of such a meaning or phrase.

> **1996** *Spectator* It seemed as if only I was vulgar enough to be aware of the *double entendre*; one or two other ladies confessed that they were plonkers too.

double entente /dubl ɑ̃tɑ̃t/ *noun phrase* plural **doubles ententes** (pronounced same) L19 **French**. A DOUBLE ENTENDRE.

doublure /dəˈblʊə/, /duˈblʊə/, *foreign* /dublyr/ (*plural same*) *noun* L19 **French** (= lining, from *doubler* to line). An ornamental lining, usually of leather, on the inside of a book-cover.

douçaine /duːˈseɪn/ *noun* M20 **French** (from *douce* sweet). *Early Music* A soft-toned reed instrument.

douce /duːs/ *adjective* ME **Old French** (*dous* (modern *doux*), feminine *douce* from Latin *dulcis* sweet). **1** ME Pleasant, sweet. (Formerly a stock epithet of France.) Now *Scottish* and *northern* (*dialect*). **2** E18 Quiet, sober, sedate. *Scottish* and *northern* (*dialect*).

douceur /dusœr/, /duːˈsəː/ *noun* LME **French** (from Proto-Romance variant of Latin *dulcor* sweetness). **1** LME Originally, sweetness of manner, amiability, (of a person). Now, agreeableness, charm (chiefly in DOUCEUR DE VIVRE). **2** L17–E19 A complimentary speech or turn of phrase. **3** M18 A conciliatory present; a gratuity, a bribe. **4** L20 A tax benefit available to a person who sells a work of art by private treaty to a public collection rather than on the open market.

> **3 1996** *Times: Magazine* Journalists . . . take a stern, principled, even po-faced stance against bribery, corruption, inducements and *douceurs*.

douceur de vivre /dusœr də vivr/ *noun phrase* (also **douceur de (la) vie** /dusœr də (la) vi/) M20 **French** (literally, 'sweetness of living'). The pleasure or amenities of life.

> **1995** *Spectator L'Heure de Gloire* is also a panorama of the Belle Epoque and the years of *douceur de vivre* that were brought to an end by the first world war.

douche /duːʃ/ *noun & verb* M18 **French** (from Italian *doccia* conduit pipe, from *docciare* to pour by drops, from Proto-Romance from Latin *ductus* duct). **A** *noun* M18 (The application of) a jet of (especially cold) liquid or air to a part of the body, as a form of bathing or for medicinal purposes; *specifically* the flushing of the vagina, as a contraceptive measure. Also, a syringe or similar device for producing such a jet. **B** *verb* **1** *transitive verb* M19 Administer a douche to. **2** *intransitive verb* M19 Take a douche; *specifically* take a vaginal douche, especially as a contraceptive measure.

dow variant of DHOW.

doyen /ˈdɔɪən/, /ˈdwɑːjɑ̃/ *noun* L17 **French** (Old French *d(e)ien* from Late Latin *decanus* chief of a group of ten, from Latin *decem* ten, after *primanus* member of the first legion). The most senior or most prominent of a particular category or body of people.

■ Found as a rare borrowing from Old French in the Late Middle English period, with the sense of 'a leader or commander of ten', the word became obsolete after this period and was then reintroduced from Modern French in its modern sense. The English word *dean* (from Anglo-Norman *de(e)n*) is closely related.

1996 *Oldie* Any art critic who goes on the telly to talk about art runs the risk of being compared with the doyen of telly-savants, the late Lord Clark.

doyenne /'dɔɪɛn/, /dɔɪ'ɛn/, /dwɑː'jɛn/ *noun* M19 **French** (feminine of DOYEN). The most senior or prominent woman in a particular group or category of people, a female doyen.

1996 *Times* Elma Browne, the wartime doyenne of London nightclubs, was impressed and offered her a two-week engagement at the Pigalle Club . . .

dragée /'drɑːʒeɪ/, *foreign* /draʒe/ (*plural same*) *noun* L17 **French** (Old French *dragie*, from medieval Latin *drageia*, *dragetum*, perhaps from Latin *tragemata* sweetmeats, from Greek). A sweet consisting of a centre covered with some coating, *especially* a sugared almond etc. or a chocolate; a small silver-coated sugar ball for use in cake decoration; a sweet used as a vehicle for a medicine or drug.

drageoir /draʒwar/ *noun* plural pronounced same M19 **French** (from as preceding). A box for holding sweets.

dramatis personae /ˌdramətɪs pəː'səʊnʌɪ/, /ˌdramətɪs pəː'səʊniː/ *noun plural* (frequently treated as *singular*) M18 **Latin** (= persons of the drama). The (list of) characters in a play; *figurative* the participants in an event etc.

1996 *Spectator Rebecca* . . . is the only one of these films in which the terror seems to rise organically from character and psychology and situation—rather than just being imposed on the *dramatis personae* by the dictates of the formula.

figurative **1996** *Times* The *dramatis personae* are the usual cast of Catalan and Basque nationalists.

dramaturge /'dramatəːdʒ/ *noun* (also **dramaturg** /drama'təːg/) M19 **French** (*dramaturge*, German *Dramaturg*, from Greek *dramatourgos*, from *dramat-* drama + *-ergos* worker). A dramatist; *specifically* a reader and literary editor etc. to a permanent theatrical company.

Drang /draŋ/ *noun* M19 **German**. Strong tendency, pressure; urge, strong desire.

■ Chiefly in phrases DRANG NACH OSTEN, STURM UND DRANG.

Drang nach Osten /ˌdraŋ nax 'ɔstən/ *noun phrase* E20 **German** (literally, 'drive towards the east'). *History* The German imperialist policy of eastward expansion; *transferred* any political or economic drive eastwards.

dreidel /'dreɪd(ə)l/ *noun* (also **dreidl**) M20 **Yiddish** (*dreydl*, from Middle High German *dræ(je)n* (German *drehen*) to turn). A four-sided spinning-top with a Hebrew letter on each side; a game of put-and-take played with this, especially at Hanukkah. Chiefly *North American*.

dressage /'drɛsɑːʒ/, /'drɛsɑːdʒ/ *noun* M20 **French** (literally, 'training', from *dresser* to train, drill). The training of a horse in obedience and deportment; the execution by a horse of precise movements in response to its rider.

droit /drɔɪt/, *foreign* /drwa/ *noun* LME **Old and Modern French** (from Proto-Romance use as noun of variant of Latin *directum* neuter of *directus* past participle of *dirigere* to direct, guide). **1** LME A right; a legal claim; something to which one has a legal claim; a due. **2** L15–M16 Law, right, justice; a law.

droit de seigneur /ˌdrwɑː də sɛn'jəː/, *foreign* /drwɑ də sɛɲœr/ *noun phrase* (also **droit du seigneur**) E19 **French** (literally, 'lord's right'). An alleged custom whereby a medieval feudal lord might have sexual intercourse with a vassal's bride on the latter's wedding-night.

1996 *Times Droit de seigneur* may be harder to trace in fact than in *The Marriage of Figaro*, but it represents the popular myth of lordly immorality.

dromos /'drɒmɒs/ *noun* plural **dromoi** /'drɒmɔɪ/ M19 **Greek**. *Greek Antiquities* An avenue or entrance-passage to an ancient temple, tomb, etc., often between rows of columns or statues.

droshky /'drɒʃki/ *noun* (also **drosky** /'drɒʃki/) E19 **Russian** (*drozhki* plural, diminutive of *drogi* wagon, hearse, plural of *droga* centre pole of a carriage). A low open horse-drawn carriage used especially in Russia; any horse-drawn passenger vehicle.

druzhina /'drʊʒiːnə/ *noun* plural **druzhinas**, **druzhiny** /'drʊʒiːni/ L19 **Russian**

(from *drug* friend + group suffix *-ina*). *History* **1** L19 The retinue or bodyguards of a Russian prince. **2** M20 In the former USSR: a military or police unit; *specifically* a detachment of volunteers assuming police powers.

duce /'du:tʃeɪ/ *noun* (also **Duce**) E20 **Italian**. A leader.

■ *Il* (Italian = the) *Duce* was the title assumed by Benito Mussolini (1883–1945), creator and leader of the Fascist State in Italy; hence *duce* in English usage generally has derogatory overtones (see quotation).

1996 *Times* Monday night saw Sir James Goldsmith, *duce* of the mono-policy Referendum Party, taking his message to the young ladies of the Kit Kat Club . . .

duchesse /du:'ʃɛs/, /'dʌtʃɪs/, /'dʌtʃɛs/, *foreign* /dyʃɛs/ (*plural same*) *noun* (also **Duchesse**) L18 **French** (from medieval Latin *ducissa* feminine from Latin *dux* leader). **1** L18 A chaise longue consisting of two facing armchairs connected by a detachable footstool. **2** M19 A dressing-table with a pivoting mirror. More fully *duchesse dressing-chest*, (*dressing*)*-table*. **3** L19 More fully *duchesse satin*, *satin duchesse*. A soft heavy kind of satin.

■ Also in several English phrases: e.g. *duchesse lace* (a kind of fine Brussels lace worked in large sprays); *duchesse potatoes* (mashed potatoes mixed with egg, moulded into small cakes and baked or fried); *duchesse set* (lace mats for a dressing-table); *duchesse sleeve* (a two-thirds-length sleeve with an elaborate trim).

duende /du:'ɛndeɪ/, *foreign* /'dwende/ *noun* E20 **Spanish**. **1** E20 A ghost, an evil spirit. **2** M20 Inspiration, magic.

duenna /dju:'ɛnə/ *noun* M17 **Spanish** (*dueña*, *duenna* from Latin *domina* lady, mistress). **1** M17 An older woman acting as governess and companion to one or more girls, especially within a Spanish family. **2** E18 A chaperon.

duettino /dju:ɛ'ti:nəʊ/ *noun* plural **duettinos** M19 **Italian** (diminutive of next). A short duet.

duetto /dju:'ɛtəʊ/ *noun* plural **duettos** E18 **Italian** (from Latin *duo* = two). *Music* A duet.

dulciana /dʌlsɪ'ɑ:nə/ *noun* L18 **Medieval Latin** (from Latin *dulcis* sweet). *Music* A small-scaled, soft, open metal diapason usually of 8-ft length and pitch.

dulia /djʊ'lʌɪə/ *noun* LME **Medieval Latin** (from Greek *douleia* servitude, from *doulos* slave). *Roman Catholic Church* The veneration properly given to saints and angels.

■ Cf. HYPERDULIA and LATRIA. Similar distinctions in degrees of veneration obtain in the Orthodox Churches, *dulia* being the honour paid to icons as representative of the saints.

duma /'du:mə/, /'dju:mə/ *noun* L19 **Russian**. *History* A Russian elective municipal council; *specifically* the elective legislative council of state of 1905–17; the Russian parliament.

dum casta /dʌm 'kastə/ *noun & adjective phrase* L19 **Latin** (abbreviation of *dum sola et casta vixerit* as long as she shall live alone and chaste). *Law* (Designating) a clause conferring on a woman a benefit which is to cease should she (re)marry or cease to lead a chaste life.

dummkopf /'dʊmkɒpf/ *noun* (also **domcop**) E19 **German** (from *dumm* stupid + *Kopf* head; obsolete variant *domcop* from Dutch). A stupid person, a blockhead.

■ Slang, originating in the United States.

duo /'dju:əʊ/ *noun* plural **duos** L16 **Italian** ((whence also French) from Latin = two). **1** L16 *Music* A duet. **2** L19 Two people; a couple; *especially* a pair of entertainers.

duodecimo /ˌdju:əʊ'dɛsɪməʊ/ *noun & adjective* M17 **Latin** ((*in*) *duodecimo* in a twelfth (sc. of a sheet), from Latin *duodecimus* twelfth). **A** *noun* plural **duodecimos** M17 A size of book or paper in which each leaf is one-twelfth of a standard printing-sheet. (Abbreviation *12mo*.) **B** L18 *attributive* or as *adjective* Of this size, in duodecimo; *figurative* diminutive.

duodenum /dju:ə'di:nəm/ *noun* LME **Medieval Latin** (*duodenum* (so called from its length = twelve fingers' breadth), from Latin *duodeni* distributive of *duodecim* twelve). *Anatomy* The first portion of the small intestine immediately beyond the stomach.

duomo /'dwəʊməʊ/, *foreign* /'dwomo/ *noun* (also (earlier) **domo**) plural **duomos** /'dwəʊməʊz/, **duomi** /'dwomi/ M16 **Italian**. An Italian cathedral.

durbar /'də:bɑ:/ *noun* E17 **Urdu** (from Persian *darbār* court). **1** E17 A public levee held by an Indian ruler or by a British ruler in India. Also, the court of an Indian ruler. **2** E17 A hall or place of audience where durbars were held.

durchkomponiert /ˌdʊrçkɔmpo'ni:rt/ *adjective* L19 **German** (from *durch* through

+ *komponiert* composed). *Music* (Of composition) having a formal design which does not rely on repeated sections; *especially* (of song) having different music for each stanza; through-composed.

du reste /dy rɛst/ *adverb phrase* E19 French (literally, 'of the rest'). Besides, moreover.

durgah /'dəːgə/ *noun* L18 Persian (*dargāh* royal court). In the Indian subcontinent: the tomb and shrine of a Muslim holy man.

du tout /dy tu/ *adverb phrase* E19 French (abbreviation of PAS DU TOUT). Not at all; by no means.

duumvir /djuː'ʌmvə/ *noun* plural **duumvirs**, in Latin form **duumviri** /djuː'ʌmvɪrʌɪ/ E17 Latin (singular from *duum virum* genitive plural of *duo viri* two men). In *Roman History*, either of a pair of coequal magistrates or officials; *generally* either of two people with joint authority, a coalition of two people.

duvet /'djuːveɪ/, /'duːveɪ/ *noun* M18 French (= down) A thick soft quilt used instead of other bedclothes. Also called *continental quilt*, PLUMEAU.

dux /dʌks/ *noun* plural **duces** /'djuːsiːz/, **duxes** M18 Latin (= leader). **1** M18 *Music* The subject of a fugue or canon; the leading voice or instrument in a fugue or canon. Opposed to COMES. **2** L18 The top pupil in a class or school. Chiefly in *Scotland*, *New Zealand*, and *South Africa*.

duxelles /'dʌks(ə)lz/, *foreign* /dyksɛl/ *noun* L19 French (Marquis *d'Uxelles*, seventeenth-century French nobleman). *Cookery* A mixture of finely chopped shallots, parsley, onions, and mushrooms, *especially* used to flavour a sauce.

d.v. abbreviation of DEO VOLENTE.

dybbuk /'dɪbʊk/ *noun* (also **dibbuk**) plural **dybbukim** /'dɪbʊkɪm/, **dybbuks** E20 Yiddish (*dibek* from Hebrew *dibbūq*, from *dāḇaq* to cling, cleave). In Jewish folklore, a malevolent wandering spirit that enters and possesses the body of a living person until exorcized.

dyspepsia /dɪs'pɛpsɪə/ *noun* E18 Latin (from Greek *duspepsia*, from *duspeptos* difficult of digestion, from *dus-* + *peptos* cooked, digested). Indigestion; abdominal pain or discomfort associated with taking food.

dysphoria /dɪs'fɔːrɪə/ *noun* M19 Greek (*dusphoria* malaise, discomfort, from *dusphoros* hard to bear, from *dus-* + *pherein* to bear). A state of unease or discomfort; *especially* an unpleasant state of mind marked by malaise, depression, or anxiety. Opposed to EUPHORIA.

dyspnoea /dɪsp'niːə/ *noun* (also **dyspnea**) M17 Latin (from Greek *duspnoia*, from *dus-* + *pnoē* breathing). *Medicine* Difficulty in breathing or shortness of breath, as a symptom of disease.

dystopia see UTOPIA.

eau /əʊ/, *foreign* /o/ *noun* plural **eaux** pronounced same E19 French. Water.

■ Occurs in English only in various phrases, mainly the names of liquids used in medicine or perfumery (see following, also JET D'EAU, SALLE D'EAU).

eau-de-Cologne /ˌəʊdəkəˈləʊn/ *noun* (also **eau de Cologne**) E19 French. A lightly scented perfume made mainly from alcohol and essential oils, originally produced at Cologne, Germany.

eau de Javel /ˌəʊ də ʒaˈvɛl/ *noun phrase* (also **eau de Javelle**) E19 French. A solution of sodium or potassium hypochlorite, used as a bleach or disinfectant.

■ Also called *Javelle water*. Javel was a village just outside Paris, now a suburb, where this solution was first used.

eau-de-Nil /ˌəʊdəˈniːl/, *foreign* /odnil/ *noun phrase* L19 French (literally, 'water of (the) Nile'). A pale greenish colour (purportedly resembling the waters of the River Nile).

eau de toilette /ˌəʊ də twɑːˈlɛt/, *foreign* /o də twalɛt/ *noun phrase* E20 French (= toilet water). A dilute form of perfume.

eau-de-vie /əʊdəˈviː/, *foreign* /odvi/ *noun phrase* (also **eau de vie**) M18 French (literally, 'water of life'). Brandy.

eau sucrée /əʊ ˈsuːkreɪ/, *foreign* /o sykre/ *noun phrase* E19 French (literally, 'sugared water'). Water with sugar dissolved in it.

ébauche /eboʃ/ *noun* plural pronounced same E18 French. **1** E18 A sketch; a rough-hewn sculpture; a first draft. **2** E20 A partly finished watch movement.

ébéniste /ebenist/ *noun* plural pronounced same E20 French (from *ébène* ebony). An ebonist; *specifically* a French cabinet-maker who veneers furniture (originally with ebony).

éboulement /ebulmɑ̃/ *noun* plural pronounced same E19 French (from *ébouler* to crumble). A crumbling and falling of rock etc.; a landslide.

écarté /eɪˈkɑːteɪ/, *foreign* /ekarte/ *noun* E19 French (past participle of *écarter* to discard, from *é-* + *carte* card). **1** E19 A card-game for two people in which cards may be exchanged for others and those from the two to the six are excluded. **2** E20 *Ballet* A pose with one arm and one leg extended, the body being at an oblique angle to the audience.

ecce /ˈɛki/, /ˈɛtʃeɪ/, /ˈɛksi/ *interjection* LME Latin. Lo!; behold.

■ Especially in the following phrases.

Ecce Homo /ˌɛki ˈhəʊməʊ/ *interjection & noun phrase* E17 Latin. **A** *interjection* Behold the Man! **B** *noun phrase Art* A portrayal of Jesus wearing the crown of thorns.

■ The source is the Latin text of the account of the presentation of Jesus to the crowd after his trial by Pontius Pilate: 'Then came Jesus forth, wearing the crown of thorns, and the purple robe. And Pilate saith unto them, Behold the man!' (John 19:5).

ecce signum /ˌɛki ˈsɪɡnəm/ *interjection* L16 Latin. Behold the sign!

echelon /ˈɛʃəlɒn/, /ˈeɪʃəlɒn/ *noun* (also **echellon**) L18 French (*échelon*, from *échelle* ladder, from Latin *scala*). **1** L18 An arrangement of troops or equipment in parallel lines such that the end of each line is stepped somewhat sideways from that in front; *generally* a formation of people or things arranged, individually or in groups, in a similar stepwise fashion. Also *echelon arrangement*, *echelon formation*, etc. Cf. EN ÉCHELON. **2** E19 Each of the divisions of an echelon formation. **b** E19 Each of the subdivisions of the main supply service for troops in warfare. **3** M20 (A group of people occupying) a particular level in any organization.

echinus /ɪˈkʌɪnəs/ *noun* plural **echini** /ɪˈkʌɪnʌɪ/ LME Latin (sense 1 from Greek *ekhinos* hedgehog, sea urchin; the origin of sense 2 (also in Latin and Greek) is unknown). **1** LME A sea urchin. Now *specifically* a member of the genus *E. chinus*, which includes the common edible sea urchin *E. esculentus*. **2** M16 *Architecture* An ovolo moulding next below the abacus of a capital.

echt /ɛçt/ *adjective & adverb* E20 German. Authentic(ally), genuine(ly), typical(ly).

1995 *Spectator* 'He [sc. Newt Gingrich] doesn't say he's a conservative, he says he's allied to the conservatives' is how Paul Weyrich, head of the *echt*-conservative Free Congress Foundation, explains the relationship.

éclair /eɪˈklɛː/, /ɪˈklɛː/ *noun* M19 **French** (literally, 'lightning'). A small finger-shaped cake of choux pastry, filled with cream and iced, especially with chocolate icing.

éclaircissement /eklɛrsismɑ̃/ *noun* plural pronounced same M17 **French** (from *éclairciss-* lengthened stem of *éclaircir* to clear up, from as *ex-*, *clair* clear *-ment*). A clarification of what is obscure or misunderstood; an explanation.

éclat /ɛˈklɑː/, /ˈeɪklɑː/, *foreign* /ekla/ *noun* L17 **French** (from *éclater* to burst out). **1** L17 Radiance, dazzling effect (now only *figurative*); brilliant display. **2** L17–L19 Ostentation, publicity; public exposure, scandal; a sensation. **3** M18 Social distinction; celebrity, renown. **4** M18 Conspicuous success; universal acclamation. Chiefly as *with* (*great* etc.) *éclat*.

1 1996 *Times* Puccini's La Rondine, staged with old-fashioned theatrical *éclat* by John Copley . . . , was almost as enjoyable.

écorché /ˈɛkɔːʃeɪ/, *foreign* /ekɔrʃe/ (*plural same*) *noun* M19 **French** (past participle of *écorcher* to flay). *Art* An anatomical subject treated so as to display the musculature.

écossaise /ɛkɒˈseɪz/, *foreign* /ekɔsɛz/ *noun* plural pronounced same M19 **French** (feminine of *écossais* Scottish). (A dance to) a lively tune in duple time.

écrevisse /ekrəvis/ *noun* plural pronounced same M18 **French**. A crayfish.

ecru /ˈeɪkruː/, /ɛˈkruː/ *adjective & noun* M19 **French** (*écru* raw, unbleached). (Of) the colour of unbleached linen; light fawn.

ecuelle /ɛˈkwɛl/ *noun* (also **écuelle**) M19 **French** (*écuelle* ultimately from Latin *scutella* small dish). **1** M19 A two-handled soup bowl. **2** L19 The process or apparatus by which oils are extracted from the peel of citrus fruit.

editio princeps /ɪˌdɪʃɪəʊ ˈprɪnsɛps/ *noun phrase* plural **editiones principes** /ɪˌdɪʃɪ ˌəʊniːz ˈprɪnsɪpiːz/ E19 **Modern Latin** (from Latin *editio* publication + *princeps* first). The first printed edition of a book.

effendi /ɛˈfɛndi/ *noun* E17 **Turkish** (*efendi* from Modern Greek *aphentē* vocative of *aphentēs* from Greek *authentēs* lord, master). A man of education or social standing in an eastern Mediterranean or Arab country. Frequently (usually *historical*) as a title of respect or courtesy in Turkey or (former) Turkish territory.

effluvium /ɪˈfluːvɪəm/ *noun* plural **effluvia** /ɪˈfluːvɪə/, **effluviums** M17 **Latin** (from *effluere*, from *ef-* + *fluere* to flow). **1** M17–E18 A flowing out. **2** M17 Chiefly *History*. An outflow or stream of imperceptible particles, especially as supposedly transmitting electrical or magnetic influence etc. **3** M17 An (especially unpleasant) exhalation affecting the lungs or the sense of smell.

efreet variant of AFREET.

e.g. abbreviation of EXEMPLI GRATIA.

égalité /egalite/ *noun* L18 **French** (= equality, from *égal* from Latin *aequalis* equal). The condition of having equal rank, power, etc. with others.

■ Historically, as part of the rallying cry of the French Revolution: *Liberté, égalité, fraternité* 'Liberty, equality, brotherhood'.

églomisé /eglɔmize/ *adjective & noun* plural of noun pronounced same L19 **French** (from *Glomy*, eighteenth-century Parisian picture-framer). **A** *adjective* L19 Of glass: decorated on the back with engraved gold or silver leaf or paint. Frequently in VERRE ÉGLOMISÉ. **B** *noun* L19 (A panel of) verre églomisé.

ego /ˈiːgəʊ/, /ˈɛgəʊ/ *noun* plural **egos** E19 **Latin** (= I (pronoun)). **1** E19 *Metaphysics* Oneself, the conscious thinking subject. **2** L19 *Psychoanalysis* That part of the mind which has a sense of individuality and is most conscious of self. **3** L19 Self-esteem, self-importance.

3 1997 *Daily Telegraph* Mum can nurture her ego by fulfilling the career role set for her . . .

eheu fugaces /ˌeɪhjuː fuːgɑːsiːz/ *interjection* M19 **Latin** (= alas, the fleeting (years are hurrying by)). An expression of regret for the rapidity with which life passes.

■ The words are from the opening line of one of Horace's *Odes* (II.xiv).

eid /iːd/ *noun* (also **id**) L17 **Arabic** (*ʿīd* festival, from Aramaic). A Muslim feast-day; *specifically* that at the breaking of the fast at the end of Ramadan (cf. ID UL-FITR).

eidolon /ʌɪˈdəʊlɒn/ *noun* plural **eidola** /ʌɪˈdəʊlə/, **eidolons** M17 **Greek** (*eidōlon*). **1** An emanation considered by atomic philosophers to constitute the visible image of an object. *rare*. Only in M17.

2 E19 A spectre, a phantom. Also, an idealized image.

Einfühlung /ˈʌɪnfyːlʊŋ/, /ˈʌɪnfuːləŋ/ *noun* E20 **German** (from *ein-* into + *Fühlung* feeling, from *fühlen* to feel). Empathy.

eisteddfod /ʌɪˈstɛðvɒd/, /ʌɪˈstɛdvəd/ *noun* plural **eisteddfods**, **eisteddfodau** /ʌɪˈstɛðvɒdʌɪ/ E19 **Welsh** (= session). A congress of Welsh bards; a gathering for competitions in Welsh poetry, music, etc.

Eiswein /ˈʌɪsvʌɪn/ *noun* M20 **German** (from *Eis* ice + *Wein* wine). Wine made from ripe grapes picked while covered with frost.

ejecta /ɪˈdʒɛktə/ *noun plural* (treated as *plural* or *singular*) L19 **Latin** (neuter plural of past participle of *e(j)icere* to eject). **1** L19 Matter that is thrown out of a volcano or a star. **2** L19 Material discharged from the body, *especially* vomit.

■ An earlier (M19) synonym for sense 1 was *ejectamenta*.

ejido /eˈxido/, /eɪˈhiːdəʊ/ *noun* plural **ejidos** /eˈxidos/, /eɪˈhiːdəʊz/ L19 **Mexican Spanish** (from Spanish = common land (on the road leading out of a village), from Latin *exitus* going out). In Mexico: a cooperative farm; a piece of land farmed communally.

ek dum /eɪk ˈdʌm/ *adverb phrase* (also **ek dam**) L19 **Hindustani** (from *ek* one + Urdu *dam* breath). At once, immediately.

élan /eɪˈlɒ̃/, /eɪˈlan/, *foreign* /elɑ̃/ *noun* M19 **French**. Vivacity, vitality; energy arising from enthusiasm.

1996 *Country Life* Boucher's two canvases with their dramatic *élan* and beautifully painted landscape backgrounds are the best of the series.

élan vital /elɑ̃ vital/, /eɪˈlɒ̃ viːˈtɑːl/ *noun phrase* E20 **French**. An intuitively perceived life-force; any mysterious creative principle.

■ The French philosopher Henri Bergson (1859–1941) posited the *élan vital*, as opposed to inert matter, in *L'Evolution créatrice* (1907); as philosophical concept it has frequently been attacked for its lack of content (see quotation), but the phrase remains current in English in more general use.

1996 *Times L'évolution créatrice* has had much less impact than it deserves. Perhaps, nearly 100 years later, people will now realise that the *élan vital* exists on Mars.

élégante /elegɑ̃t/ *noun* plural pronounced same L18 **French** (feminine of *élégant* elegant). A fashionable woman.

elenchus /ɪˈlɛŋkəs/ *noun* plural **elenchi** /ɪˈlɛŋkʌɪ/ M17 **Latin** (from Greek *elegkhos* argument of refutation). *Logic* A syllogism in refutation of a syllogistic conclusion; a logical refutation.

elephanta /ɛlɪˈfantə/ *noun* (also **elephanter** /ɛlɪˈfantə/) E18 **Portuguese** (*elephante*, feminine *elephanta* from Proto-Romance variant of Latin *elephantus*, *elepha(n)s* from Greek *elephas*, elephant-ivory, elephant). A violent storm at the end (or the beginning) of a monsoon.

élite /eɪˈliːt/, /ɪˈliːt/ *noun & adjective* (also **elite**) L18 **French** (use as noun of feminine of obsolete past participle of *élire*, *eslire* from Proto-Romance variant of Latin *eligere* to elect). **A** *noun* **1** L18 The choice part, the best, (of society, a group of people, etc.); a select group or class. **2** E20 (Usually *elite*.) A size of type used on typewriters, having twelve characters to the inch. **B** *attributive adjective* M19 Of or belonging to an élite; exclusive.

A.1 1996 *Spectator* Gone are the good old days: now only Soho . . . is the resting place of the élite.

El Niño /ɛl ˈniːnjəʊ/ *noun phrase* (also **el Niño**, **El Nino**) L19 **Spanish** (*El Niño* (*de Navidad*) the (Christmas) child, with reference to beginning in late December). Formerly, an annual warm southward current off northern Peru. Now, an irregularly occurring southward current in the equatorial Pacific Ocean, associated with weather changes and ecological damage; these associated phenomena.

1992 *Economist* The effects of El Nino are not limited to the countries of the Pacific rim.

éloge /elɔʒ/ *noun* plural pronounced same M16 **French** (from Latin *elogium* short saying or epitaph, altered from Greek *elegeia* elegy; apparently confused with *eulogium* eulogy). **1** M16–E19 A commendation; an encomium. **2** E18 A discourse in honour of a deceased person; *especially* that pronounced on a member of the French Academy by his successor.

Elysium /ɪˈlɪzɪəm/ *noun* L16 **Latin** (from Greek *Elusion* (sc. *pedion* plain)). **1** L16 *Classical Mythology* The home of the blessed after death. **2** L16 A place or state of perfect happiness.

email ombrant /ɛˌmeɪl ˈɒmbrənt/, *foreign* /emajɔ̃brɑ̃/ *noun phrase* (also **émail ombrant**) plural **email ombrants**, **émaux**

ombrants /emoz ɔ̃brɑ̃/ L19 **French** (*émail ombrant*, from *émail* enamel + *ombrer* to shade). A form of decoration in which a coloured glaze is laid over intagliated earthenware or porcelain to give a monochrome picture.

emakimono /ɪˌmakɪˈməʊnəʊ/ *noun* plural same M20 **Japanese** (from *e* painting, picture + *makimono* scroll). A Japanese scroll containing pictures representing a narrative; a pictorial MAKIMONO.

émaux ombrants plural of EMAIL OMBRANT.

embarcadero /ɛmˌbɑːkəˈdɛːrəʊ/ *noun* plural **embarcaderos** M19 **Spanish** (from *embarcar* to embark). A wharf, a quay. *United States*.

embargo /ɛmˈbɑːgəʊ/, /ɪmˈbɑːgəʊ/ *noun & verb* (also formerly **imbargo**) E17 **Spanish** (from *embargar* to arrest, impede, from Proto-Romance, from Latin *in-* + *barra* bar). **A** *noun* plural **embargoes**. **1** E17 An order prohibiting ships from entering or leaving a country's ports, usually issued in anticipation of war. **2** M17 An official, usually temporary, prohibition of a particular commercial activity, or of trade in general, with another country. **3** L17 *generally* A prohibition, an impediment. **B** *transitive verb* **1** M17 Seize, confiscate; *specifically* seize, requisition, or impound (ships, goods, etc.) for the service of the State. **2** M18 Place (ships, trade, etc.) under an embargo.

embarras /ɑ̃bara/ *noun* plural pronounced same M17 **French**. Embarrassment.

■ Now in English only in phrases below.

embarras de choix /ɑ̃bara də ʃwa/ *noun phrase* L19 **French** (literally, 'embarrassment of choice'). More choices than one knows what to do with.

embarras de richesse /ɑ̃bara də riʃɛs/ *noun phrase* (also **embarrass de richesses**) M18 **French** (literally, 'an embarrassment of riches'). More resources, pleasures, etc., than one knows what to do with.

■ *L'embarras des richesses* (1726) was the title of a work by the Abbé d'Allainval, and the earliest recorded use in English (1751) is in one of Lord Chesterfield's letters. *Richesse* as an independent noun is found earlier (ME–L17) with the meanings 'wealth' or 'richness' and also (L15) 'a group of martens', but it has long been archaic as an independent noun.

1995 *Spectator* There is an *embarras de richesse* of rose gardens to visit in June.

embolus /ˈɛmbələs/ *noun* plural **emboli** /ˈɛmbəlʌɪ/, /ˈɛmbəliː/ M17 **Latin** (= piston of a pump, from Greek *embolos* peg, stopper). **1** M17–M18 *Mechanical* Something inserted or moving in another; *especially* the piston of a syringe. **2** M19 *Medicine* The blood clot or other object or substance which causes embolism.

embonpoint /ɑ̃bɔ̃pwɛ̃/ *noun & adjective* L17 **French** (phrase *en bon point* in good condition). **A** *noun* L17 Plumpness. **B** *adjective* E19 Plump.

■ In quotation as euphemism for 'cleavage'.

A 1995 *Times* It was Kissinger's bad luck, but our good fortune, that a photographer caught the moment as the learned doctor peered, astonished, at the Princess's embonpoint.

embouchure /ɑ̃buʃyr/, /ˈɒmbʊʃʊə/ *noun* M18 **French** (from *s'emboucher* reflexive, to discharge itself by a mouth, from *emboucher* put in or to the mouth, from as *em-* + *bouche* mouth). **1** M18 *Music* The manner in which a player's mouth and lips are placed when playing a woodwind or brass instrument. **b** M19 The mouthpiece of a musical instrument, especially of a flute. **2** L18 The mouth of a river; the opening of a valley on to a plain.

1.a 1996 *Times* But my composer friend was right about my trombone-playing. . . . The problem is my *embouchure*, you see: it's just not the same with a false tooth.

embourgeoisé /ɑ̃burʒwaze/ *adjective* M20 **French** (past participle of *embourgeoiser* to make or become BOURGEOIS). That has been bourgeoisified.

embourgeoisement /ɑ̃burʒwazmɑ̃/ *noun* M20 **French** (from *embourgeoiser* to make or become BOURGEOIS). Bourgeoisification.

1996 *Spectator* He [sc. Liam Gallagher] is undergoing the same *embourgeoisement* which affected the late John Lennon when he embraced domesticity and started baking his own bread.

embrasure /ɪmˈbreɪʒə/, /ɛmˈbreɪʒə/ *noun* E18 **French** (from obsolete *embraser* (modern *ébraser*) to widen (a door or window opening), of unknown origin). **1** *Military* E18 An opening in a parapet that widens towards the exterior, made to fire a gun through. **2** M18 A slanting or bevelling of the wall on either side of a door or window opening so as to form a recess; the area contained between such walls. **3** *Dentistry* M20 The angle between adjacent teeth where their two surfaces curve inwards towards the line of contact.

embusqué /ãbyske/ *noun* plural pronounced same E20 **French** (past participle of *embusquer* from Old French *embuschier* to ambush). A person who avoids military service by obtaining a post in a government office or the like.

emeritus /ɪ'mɛrɪtəs/ *adjective* M18 **Latin** (past participle of *emereri* to earn (one's discharge) by service, from *e-* + *mereri* to deserve). Honourably discharged from service; (of a former office-holder, especially a professor) retired but allowed to retain his or her title as an honour.

■ Often postpositive (see quotation).

1995 *Spectator* Sir Michael Richardson, Savoy director emeritus and pastmaster dealmaker, is just the man to go round with the hat.

émeute /emøt/ *noun* L18 **French** (from Old French *esmote*, from *esmeu* (modern *ému*) past participle of *esmovoir* (modern *émouvoir*), after *meute* crowd, uprising). A popular rising or disturbance.

emigré /'ɛmɪgreɪ/ *noun & adjective* (also **émigré**) L18 **French** (*émigré*, past participle of *émigrer* from Latin *emigrare* to emigrate). **A** *noun* L18 Originally, a French emigrant, *especially* one from the Revolution of 1789–99. Now, any emigrant, *especially* a political exile. **B** *adjective* E20 That is an emigré; composed of emigrés.

emincé /emɛ̃se/ *noun* E20 **French** (use as noun of past participle of *émincer* to slice thinly). A dish consisting of thinly sliced meat in sauce.

éminence grise /eminɑ̃s griz/ *noun phrase* plural **éminences grises** (pronounced same) M20 **French** (literally, 'grey eminence'. A person who exercises power or influence though holding no official position. Also, a confidential adviser.

■ Originally applied to the Capuchin Père Joseph, confidential agent of the French statesman Cardinal Richelieu (1585–1642).

1995 *New Scientist* A young researcher talking about her work today would be an invaluable resource for some future investigator about to interview the same person when an elderly *éminence grise* of science.

emir /ɛ'mɪə/ *noun* L16 **French** (*émir* from Arabic *'amīr*). **1** L16 A male descendant of Muhammad. Now *rare*. **2** M17 A title of certain Muslim rulers; an Arab prince, governor, or commander.

empanada /ɛmpə'nɑːdə/, *foreign* /empa 'nada/ *noun* M20 **Spanish** (use as noun of feminine past participle of *empanar* to bake or roll in pastry, from as *em-* + *pan* bread, from Latin *panis*). *Cookery* A turnover with a filling of meat, cheese, or vegetables.

empiecement /ɪm'piːsm(ə)nt/, /ɛm 'piːsm(ə)nt/ *noun* L19 **French** (*empiècement*, from as *em-* + *piece* piece). A piece of material inserted in a garment for decoration.

emplacement /ɪm'pleɪsm(ə)nt/, /ɛm 'pleɪsm(ə)nt/ *noun* E19 **French** (from as *em-* + *place* place). **1** E19 *Military* A defended or protected position where a gun or missile is placed ready for firing. **2** E19 Situation, position; *specifically* that of a building. **3** M19 The action of putting or settling into place.

employé /ɒm'plɔɪeɪ/, *foreign* /ɑ̃plwaje/ (*plural same*) *noun* (feminine **employée**) E19 **French** (past participial adjective of *employer* to employ). A person who works for an employer.

■ Now naturalized in the later (M19) form *employee*.

emporium /ɛm'pɔːrɪəm/, /ɪm'pɔːrɪəm/ *noun* plural **emporiums**, **emporia** /ɛm 'pɔːrɪə/ L16 **Latin** (from Greek *emporion*, from *emporos* merchant, from as *em-* + verbal stem *por-*, *per-* to journey). **1** L16 A centre of commerce; a market. **2** M19 A shop, *especially* one that sells unusual or fancy goods. Chiefly *jocular*.

empressé /ɑ̃prɛse/ *adjective* (feminine **empressée**) M19 **French** (past participial adjective of *empresser* to urge, (reflexive) be eager, (in Old French) to press, crowd in). Eager, zealous; showing EMPRESSEMENT.

empressement /ɑ̃prɛsmɑ̃/ *noun* E18 **French** (from *empresser* (see preceding)). Eagerness; effusive friendliness.

enamorata, **enamorato** variants of INAMORATA, INAMORATO.

en attendant /ɑ̃ atɑ̃dɑ̃/ *adverb phrase* M18 **French**. In the meantime, while waiting.

en avant /ɑ̃ avɑ̃/ *adverb & interjection phrase* E19 **French**. Forward, onwards.

en beau /ɑ̃ bo/ *adverb phrase* E19 **French**. In a favourable manner; in the best light. Cf. EN NOIR.

en bloc /ɑ̃ blɔk/, /ɒn blɒk/ *adverb & adjective phrase* M19 **French** (literally, 'as a block'). **A** *adverb phrase* M19 As a whole; collectively, all together. **B** *adjective phrase* E20 Performed or made *en bloc*.

A 1984 A. G. Lehmann *European Heritage* . . . the civil service moves, *en bloc*, and with no changes, from serving the Kaiser to serving the republic—equally without enthusiasm.

en brosse /ɑ̃ brɔs/ *adverb & adjective phrase* E20 **French** (literally, 'as a brush'). (Of hair) cut short and bristly.

1996 *Times: Weekend* Middle-aged men wore Newcastle United shirts, ear-rings, hair *en brosse* or back-to-front baseball caps.

en cabochon /ɑ̃ kabɔʃɔ̃/ *adverb phrase* E19 **French**. Of a gem: cut as a CABOCHON, with curved surfaces rather than facets.

enceinte /ɑ̃sɛ̃t/, /ɒ̃'sãt/ *noun* plural pronounced same E18 **French** (from Latin *incincta* feminine past participle of *incingere* to gird in). The main enclosure or enclosing wall of a fortified place.

enceinte /ɑ̃sɛ̃t/, /ɒ̃'sãt/ *adjective* (also (in legal use) **ensient**) E17 **French** (from medieval Latin *incincta* ungirded, from Latin *in-* + *cincta* feminine past participle of *cingere* to gird). Of a woman: pregnant.

■ Now archaic or euphemistic.

enchaînement /ɑ̃ʃɛnmɑ̃/ *noun* plural pronounced same M19 **French** (literally = a chaining up, a concatenation). *Ballet* A sequence of steps.

enchilada /ɛntʃɪ'lɑːdə/ *noun* M19 **American Spanish** (feminine of *enchilado* past participle of *enchilar* to season with chili). A usually meat-filled tortilla served with chilli sauce.

enchiridion /ˌɛnkʌɪ'rɪdɪən/ *noun* LME **Late Latin** (from Greek *egkheiridion*, from as *en-* + *kheir* hand + diminutive suffix *-idion*). A handbook, a manual.

encierro /en'sjerro/ *noun* plural **encierros** /en'sjerros/ M19 **Spanish** (literally, 'shutting in', from *en-* (from as *in-*) + *cierre* shutting). The driving of bulls through the streets of a Spanish town from a corral to the bullring.

en clair /ɑ̃ klɛr/ *adverb & adjective phrase* L19 **French**. (Transmitted, written, etc.) in ordinary language, not in code or cipher; also *figurative*.

figurative **1995** *Spectator* Franks worked *en clair*, Goodman in code.

enclave /'ɛnkleɪv/, *formerly also* /ɑ̃klav/ *noun* M19 **French** (from Old and Modern French *enclaver* to enclose, from popular Latin *in-* + *clavis* key). **1** M19 A region belonging to a country but surrounded by another country as viewed by the latter. **2** M20 A culturally or socially distinct minority group in society or place.

encoignure /ɑ̃kwaɲyr/ *noun* plural pronounced same M19 **French** (from as *en-* + *coin* corner). A piece of usually ornamental furniture made with an angle to fit into a corner.

encomium /ɛn'kəʊmɪəm/ *noun* plural **encomiums**, **encomia** L16 **Latin** (from Greek *egkōmion* eulogy, use as noun of neuter of adjective (sc. *epos* speech), from as *en-* + *komos* revel). A formal or high-flown expression of praise; a panegyric.

■ Earlier (M16) Anglicized as *encomy*.

1996 *Bookseller* I was miffed, incidentally, not to be among the luminaries asked to provide a 10th birthday encomium for Serpent's Tail.

encore /'ɒŋkɔː/ *interjection, noun & verb* E18 **French**. (= still, again). **A** *interjection* E18 Again! **B** *noun* M18 An audience's demand for an item to be performed again or for a further item after the programme finale in a concert, etc. Also an item (to be) performed thus. **C** *transitive verb* M18 Call for a repetition.

■ The origin is uncertain. The Italian equivalent *ancora* 'still' was also formerly used (E18) but neither it nor *encore* occurs in this context in the original languages.

encourager les autres see POUR ENCOURAGER LES AUTRES.

en croûte /ɑ̃ krut/ *adverb & adjective phrase* L20 **French**. (Cooked) in a pastry crust.

en daube /ɑ̃ dob/ *adverb & adjective phrase* L20 **French** (cf. DAUBE). Stewed, braised.

en déshabillé /ɒn deɪza'biːjeɪ/, *foreign* /ɑ̃ dezabije/ *adjective & adverb phrase* (also Anglicized as **en déshabille** /ɒn deɪzə'biːl/, **en dishabille** /ɒ̃ dɪsə'biːl/) L17 **French** (from preposition *en* + *déshabillé* dishabille). In a state of undress or of partial dress; casually dressed.

en échelon /ɑ̃n eʃlɔ̃/ *adjective & adverb phrase* (also **en echelon**) E19 **French**. (Arranged) in an ECHELON.

en évidence /ɑ̃n evidɑ̃s/ *adverb phrase* E19 **French**. In or at the forefront; conspicuously.

en face /ɑ̃ fas/ *adverb phrase* M18 **French**. **1** M18 With the face to the front, facing forwards. Cf. EN REGARD. **2** M20 *Bibliography* On the facing page.

en famille /ɑ̃ famij/, /ɒn fa'mi:/ *adverb phrase* E18 **French**. At home, with one's family; as one of the family, informally.

1996 *Times: Weekend* Though mostly in their fifties or sixties, there was a sprinkling of teenagers *en famille*.

enfant gâté /ɑ̃fɑ̃ gɑte/ *noun phrase* plural **enfants gâtés** (pronounced same) E19 **French** (= spoilt child). A person given undue flattery or indulgence.

enfantillage /ɑ̃fɑ̃tijaʒ/ *noun* E19 **Old and Modern French** (from Old French *enfantil* from Latin *infantilis* of an infant). A childish action or prank.

enfant terrible /ɑ̃fɑ̃ tɛribl/ *noun phrase* plural **enfants terribles** (pronounced same) M19 **French** (= terrible child). A person who causes embarrassment by ill-considered, or unorthodox behaviour or speech; an unconventional person.

1996 *Country Life* Seven years on, Mr Barr has lost none of his impishness; he remains one of the *enfants terribles*, the young Turks of the wine-writing world, still tweaking the nose of the Establishment . . .

en fête /ɑ̃ fɛt/ *predicative adjective phrase* M19 **French**. Prepared for or engaged in holiday-making or celebration.

enfilade /ɛnfɪ'leɪd/, /'ɒnfɪlɑ:d/ *noun & verb* E18 **French** (from *enfiler* to thread on a string, pierce or traverse from end to end, from as *en-* + *fil* thread). **A** *noun* **1** *Military* **a** The situation of a post such that it commands the whole length of a line. Only in E18. **b** L18 Gunfire directed along a line from end to end (also *enfilade fire*); an act of firing in this way. **2** E18 A suite of rooms with doorways in line with each other; a vista between rows of trees etc. **B** *transitive verb* E18 *Military* Subject to enfilade; cover the whole length of (a target) with a gun or guns.

A.2 1995 *Country Life* Hopetoun's Great Apartment is arranged in a standard enfilade running north from the entrance hall, and incorporating a spectacular five-bay drawing room . . .

engagé /ɑ̃gaʒɛ/, /ˌɒŋga'ʒeɪ/ *noun & adjective* E19 **French** (past participle of *engager* to engage). **A** *noun* E19 *History* A boatman hired by a fur-trader or explorer; an engagee. *North American*. **B** *adjective* M20 Of writers, artists, etc., or their works: showing social or political commitment.

1996 *Spectator* They know where they are with other directors: Truffaut? Wry. Godard? *Engagé*.

en garçon /ɑ̃ garsɔ̃/ *adverb phrase* E19 **French**. As or in the manner of a boy or a bachelor.

engobe /ɑ̃gɔb/ *noun* M19 **French**. A mixture of white clay and water applied as a coating to pottery to cover the natural colour or to provide a ground for decoration; a slip.

en grande tenue /ɑ̃ grɑ̃d təny/ *adverb phrase* M19 **French**. In full dress, *especially* full military dress.

en grand seigneur /ɑ̃ grɑ̃ sɛɲœr/ *adverb phrase* E19 **French**. In the manner of a nobleman.

engrenage /ɑ̃grənaʒ/ *noun* plural pronounced same E20 **French** (literally, 'gearing', from *engrener* to feed corn into (a threshing-machine), throw into gear). **1** E20 A set of circumstances that trap one; an organization or society regarded as full of snares. **2** M20 The process of preparing for effective joint action.

2 1963 *Economist* 'Good Europeans' . . . sought consolation in the . . . theory of *engrenage* (getting into gear).

en gros /ɑ̃ gro/ *adverb phrase* E18 **French**. In general, in broad terms.

en l'air /ɑ̃ lɛr/ *adverb phrase* E18 **French** (= in the air). **1** E18 *Ballet* While leaping vertically. **2** E19 *Military* While unsupported.

en masse /ɑ̃ mas/, /ɒn mas/ *adverb phrase* L18 **French**. In a mass; all together, as a group.

1996 *Spectator* Rereading the stories *en masse* brings out Rose Tremain's strengths as a short story writer . . .

en noir /ɑ̃ nwar/ *adverb phrase* M19 **French**. On the black side; in the worst light. Cf. EN BEAU.

ennui /ɒn'wi:/, *foreign* /ɑ̃nɥi/ *noun* M18 **French** (from Latin *in odio* in *mihi in odio est* it is hateful to me). Mental weariness and dissatisfaction arising from lack of occupation or interest; boredom.

1996 *Country Life* [February] epitomises that rural ennui which is distinguished by its lack of distinguishedness.

ennuyant /ɑ̃nɥijɑ̃/ *adjective* L18 **French** (present participle of *ennuyer*; see next). That gives rise to ennui; boring, tedious.

ennuyé /ɑ̃nɥije/ *adjective* (feminine **ennuyée**) M18 **French** (past participial adjective of *ennuyer* to bore, from ENNUI). Affected with ennui; bored.

enosis /ɪˈnəʊsɪs/, /ˈɛnəsɪs/ *noun* M20 **Modern Greek** (*henōsis*, from *hena* one). Political union, *especially* that proposed between Greece and Cyprus.

en pantoufles /ɑ̃ pɑ̃tufl/ *adverb phrase* E20 **French** (literally, 'in slippers'). Relaxed, off guard; in a free and easy manner or atmosphere.

en papillote see PAPILLOTE.

en passant /ɑ̃ pɑsɑ̃/, /ɒ̃ paˈsɒnt/ *adverb phrase* E17 **French**. In passing, by the way.

1996 *Bookseller* Michael Schwanhauser of Walthari in Freiburg commented almost *en passant* that his twice-weekly orders for British books arrived within four days.

en pension /ɑ̃ pɑ̃sjɔ̃/ *adverb and adjective phrase* E19 **French**. Living as a boarder, in lodgings.

■ Formerly (L16 onwards) Anglicized as *in* or *on pension*; cf. PENSION.

en permanence /ɑ̃ pɛrmanɑ̃s/ *adverb phrase* M19 **French**. Permanently.

en place /ɑ̃ plas/ *adverb phrase* E19 **French**. In place, in position.

en plein /ɑ̃ plɛ̃/ *adverb phrase* L19 **French** (= in full). *Gambling* Entirely on one number or side; with the whole of one's bet.

en plein air /ɑ̃ plɛn ɛr/ *adverb phrase* L19 **French**. In the open air.

■ Especially with reference to the working methods of the French Impressionist painters, as compared with their academic *confrères* who worked in studios and from posed models; cf. PLEIN AIR.

1988 K. Adler *Unknown Impressionists* Many of them wished to learn from Pissarro's example, . . . and they watched him at work, often *en plein air*, and discussed ideas about art.

en poste /ɑ̃ pɔst/ *adverb phrase* M20 **French**. In an official diplomatic position (at a specified place).

1996 *Spectator* Nathaniel Hawthorne, who actually did get a cushy job as consul, turned out nothing while he was *en poste*.

en primeur /ɑ̃ primœr/ *adverb & adjective phrase* L20 **French**. (Of vegetables) fresh, new; (of wine) young, especially before bottling. Cf. PRIMEUR.

1996 *Country Life* If you have not bought *en primeur* before, get as many merchants' lists as you can and compare the tasting notes.

en prince /ɑ̃ prɛ̃s/ *adverb phrase* L17 **French**. Like a prince; in a princely or luxurious manner.

en principe /ɑ̃ prɛ̃sip/ *adverb phrase* E20 **French**. In principle.

en prise /ɑ̃ priz/ *adverb phrase* E19 **French**. *Chess* In a position to be taken.

enragé /ɑ̃raʒɛ/, /ˌɒnraˈʒeɪ/ *adjective & noun* (also **enrage**) (feminine **enragée**) E18 **French** (past participle of *enrager* to enrage). **A** *adjective* E18 Furiously angry. **B** *noun* L18 An enraged person; a fanatic.

B 1995 *Spectator* Journalists (and intellectuals in general) have an important responsibility for the creation of a more civilised climate of opinion, so that semi-educated *enrages* do not take to the bomb or the gun each time they grow angry on the basis of undigested gobbets of information.

en rapport /ɑ̃ rapɔr/ *adjective phrase* E19 **French**. In (close and harmonious) relationship (*with*); in harmony (*with*). Cf. RAPPORT.

en regard /ɑ̃ rəgar/ *adverb phrase* E20 **French**. *Bibliography* On the facing page. Cf. EN FACE.

en règle /ɑ̃ rɛgl/ *adverb phrase* E19 **French**. In order, according to form.

en retraite /ɑ̃ rətrɛt/ *adverb phrase* M19 **French**. In retirement.

en revanche /ɑ̃ rəvɑ̃ʃ/ *adverb phrase* E19 **French**. In return, as compensation; in revenge.

1996 *Spectator* The best solution would be for you to wait until your friends visit you *en revanche* and then, as they leave, set a trap for them . . .

en route /ɑ̃ rut/, /ɒn ruːt/ *adverb phrase* L18 **French**. On the way.

1996 *Spectator* On one occasion, . . . the Prince marched through the meeting in a towel *en route* to the bathroom.

ens /ɛnz/ *noun* plural **entia** /ˈɛntɪə/, /ˈɛnʃɪə/ M16 **Late Latin** (*ens* use as noun of present participle formed from *esse* to be, on the supposed analogy of *absens* absent, to translate Greek *on* use as noun of present participle of *einai* to be). **1** M16 *Philosophy* etc. Something which has existence; a being, an entity, as opposed to an attribute or quality. **2** L16–M18 The essence; the essential part.

■ Used in various phrases relating especially to Christian medieval theology and scholastic philosophy; thus *ens necessarium* (a necessarily existent being, i.e. God), *ens rationis* (a being having no existence outside the mind), *ens reale* (a being that exists independently of any finite mind), etc.

ensemble /ɒn'sɒmb(ə)l/, *foreign* /ɑ̃sɑ̃bl/ (*plural same*) *noun* M18 **Old and Modern French** (from Proto-Romance from Latin *insimul*, from *in-* into, in + *simul* at the same time). **1** M18 (The parts of) a thing viewed as a whole. **2** E19 The unity of performaance achieved by a group of artistes. **b** E20 A group of stage artistes who perform together; *especially* the supporting actors or dancers as opposed to the principals. **c** E20 A scene on stage in which the whole cast appears. **d** M20 A group of singers or musicians, especially soloists, who perform together. **3** E20 A set of (usually women's) clothes that harmonize and are worn together. **4** E20 *Science* A notional collection of systems of identical constitution but not necessarily in the same state.

■ Originally (LME) introduced in the adverbial sense of 'together, at the same time', which it retains in French, but this has long been rare in English. Sense 1 is found slightly earlier in the phrase TOUT ENSEMBLE.

2.b 1996 *Country Life* Once a small ensemble of distinct individuals, this company now resembles a large precision instrument . . .

ensient variant of ENCEINTE.

ensilage /'ɛnsɪlɪʤ/, /ɛn'sʌɪlɪʤ/ *noun & verb* L19 **French** (from *ensiler* from Spanish *ensilar*, from *en-* + *silo* silo). **A** *noun* **1** L19 The process of making silage. **2** L19 Silage. **B** *transitive verb* L19 Treat (fodder) by ensilage; turn into silage.

en suite /ɒn 'swi:t/, *foreign* /ɑ̃ sɥit/ *adverb, adjective, & noun phrase* (also (especially as adjective & noun phrase) **ensuite** /ɒ̃swi:t/) L18 **French**. **A** *adverb phrase* **1** L18 In agreement or harmony (*with*). Now *rare* or *obsolete*. **2** E19 In a row, with one room leading into another; as part of the same set of rooms. (Followed by *with*.) **b** M20 As part of the same set of objects. (Followed by *with*.) **B** *adjective phrase* M20 Of a room: that is en suite; forming part of the same set, immediately adjoining. **C** *noun phrase* L20 An en suite room, *especially* an en suite bathroom.

B 1995 D. Lodge *Therapy* She'd already bagged the master bedroom with the *en suite* bathroom.

entasis /'ɛntəsɪs/ *noun* plural **entases** /'ɛntəsi:z/ M17 **Modern Latin** (from Greek, from *enteinein* to strain). *Architecture* A slight bowing of the shaft of a column (introduced to correct the visual illusion of concavity).

entente /ɒn'tɒnt/, *foreign* /ɑ̃tɑ̃t/ *noun* M19 **French**. A friendly understanding, especially between States; a group of States sharing such an understanding.

1995 *Times* France has its own, largely German, reasons for wanting a new entente with Britain; both countries know that a close bilateral relationship is essential.

entente cordiale /ɑ̃tɑ̃t kɔrdjal/, /ˌɒntɒnt kɔ:dɪ'ɑ:l/ *noun phrase* plural **ententes cordiales** (pronounced same) M19 **French**. An entente, *specifically* (*historical*) that arrived at by France and Britain in 1904.

1995 *Times* But the selection of a chap with such a friendly disposition towards Europe can only serve to strengthen the new *entente cordiale* between John Major and Jacques Chirac.

entia plural of ENS.

entourage /'ɒntʊrɑ:ʒ/, /ˌɒntʊ(ə)'rɑ:ʒ/ *noun* M19 **French** (from *entourer* to surround, from *entour* surroundings, use as noun of adverb = 'round about'). A group of people in attendance on or accompanying someone important. Also, surroundings, environment.

en tout cas /ɑ̃ tu kɑ/ *noun & adjective phrase* L19 **French** (= in any case or emergency). **A** *noun phrase* L19 A parasol which also serves as an umbrella. **B** *adjective & noun phrase* M20 (*En-Tout-Cas*) (Proprietary name designating) a hard tennis-court.

entr'acte /'ɒntrakt/, *foreign* /ɑ̃trakt/ (*plural same*) *noun* M19 **French** (now obsolete (modern *entracte*), from *entre* between + *acte* act). The interval between two acts of a play; a performance or entertainment which takes place during an interval.

entrain /ɑ̃trɛ̃/ *noun* M19 **French**. Enthusiasm, animation.

1954 E. Jenkins *Tortoise and Hare* She wanted to put her head out of the window, but that would have shown too much *entrain*.

en train /ɑ̃ trɛ̃/ *adverb phrase* L18 **French**. Afoot, under way; in or into the swing of something; occupied (*with*).

en travesti /ɑ̃ travɛsti/ *adverb phrase* M20 **pseudo-French**. *Theatre* In the dress of the opposite sex.

■ The phrase is not recorded in French, and represents the misunderstanding as a noun of French *travesti*, the past participle of *travestir* (from Italian *travestire*, from *trans* (a)cross + *vestire* to clothe).

1996 *Spectator* Carabosse, traditionally performed by a man *en travesti*, becomes an unbearable over-gesticulating drag queen.

entrechat /ãtrəʃa/ (*plural same*), /'ɒntrəʃɑː/ *noun* L18 **French** (from Italian (*capriola*) *intrecciata* complicated (caper)). *Ballet* A leap in which a dancer strikes the heels together or crosses the feet a number of times while in the air.

entrecôte /'ɒntrəkəʊt/, *foreign* /ãtrəkot/ (*plural same*) *noun* M19 **French** (literally = between rib). A boned steak cut off the sirloin. More fully *entrecôte steak*.

entredeux /ãtrədø/ *noun* plural pronounced same M19 **French** (literally = between two). An insertion of lace, linen, etc., in sewing.

entrée /'ɒntreɪ/, *foreign* /ãtre/ (*plural same*) *noun* E18 **French**. **1** E18 *Music* **a** A piece of instrumental music, usually resembling a march, forming the first part of a suite or divertissement, or introducing a character etc. on stage. **b** L18 A group of dances on one theme in seventeenth- and eighteenth-century French ballet; an act of a seventeenth- or eighteenth-century French opera-ballet. **2** M18 The action or manner of entering. **b** E19 The entrance of the performers in a play, circus, or other large show. **3** M18 The privilege or right of entrance; admission, especially to an exclusive social or professional circle. **4** M18 A dish served between the fish course and the main meat course; *North American* the main dish of a meal.

> **3 1996** *Times* His upper-class accent and eminently recognisable surname . . . had not only given him an entré to the profession, it had allowed him to land a good royal story . . .

entrée en matière /ãtre ã matjɛr/ *noun phrase* M20 **French** (literally, 'entry into the matter'). An opening remark or statement; the beginning of a literary work.

> **1930** E. F. Thomas *Nevertheless the Duke* 'I have known you before!' . . . As an entrée en matière it was, to say the least, time-worn.

entremet /ãtrəmɛ/ *noun* plural **entremets** pronounced same L15 **French** (*entremets*). **1** L15 In *plural*. Side dishes. **2** M18 *singular* and in *plural* (treated as *singular* or *plural*). A sweet dish; a dessert; *rare* a side dish.

entre nous /ãtrə nu/ *adverb phrase* L17 **French**. Between ourselves; in private.

entrepôt /'ɒntrəpəʊ/, *foreign* /ãtrəpo/ (*plural same*) *noun* E18 **French** ((earlier *entrepost*, *entrepos*), from *entreposer* to store, from *entre* among + *poser* to place). **1** E18 A storehouse for the temporary deposit of goods, provisions, etc.; *rare* temporary deposit. **2** M18 A commercial centre to which goods are brought for import and export, and for collection and distribution.

entrepreneur /ˌɒntrəprə'nəː/ *noun* E19 **French** (from *entreprendre* to undertake). **1 a** E19 A director of a musical institution. **b** M19 A person who organizes entertainments, especially musical performances. **2** M19 A person who undertakes or controls a business or enterprise and bears the risk of profit or loss; a contractor who acts as an intermediary.

entresol /'ɒntrəsɒl/, *foreign* /ãtrəsɔl/ (*plural same*) *noun* (also **entersole**, **intersole**) E18 **French** (from Spanish *entresuelo*, from *entre* between + *suelo* storey). A low storey between the ground floor and the first floor of a building; a mezzanine storey.

Entscheidungsproblem /ɛnt'ʃaɪdʊŋz 'proˌbleːm/, /ɛnt'ʃʌɪdʊŋgzˌprɒbləm/ *noun* M20 **German** (= decision problem). *Mathematics* and *Logic* The problem of finding a way to decide whether a formula or class of formulas is true or provable within a given system of axioms.

en ventre sa mère /ã vãtr sa mɛr/ *adverb phrase* (also **en ventre sa mere**) L18 **French** (= in its mother's womb). *Law* In the womb.

environs /ɪn'vʌɪrənz/, /ɛn'vʌɪrənz/, /'ɛnvɪrənz/ *noun plural* M17 **French** (plural of *environ* surrounding(s)). The district surrounding a place, especially an urban area. (Followed by *of*.)

envoi /'ɛnvɔɪ/ *noun* (also (earlier) **envoy**) LME **Old and Modern French** (from *envoyer* to send, from phrase *en voie* on the way). The concluding part of a literary work, *especially* a short stanza concluding a ballade; *archaic* an author's concluding words, dedication, etc.; *generally* a conclusion.

> **1996** *Country Life* She ended with a brief piece by Elgar . . . an apt *envoi* to an evening where landscape, architecture and music met in peculiarly English harmony.

eo ipso /ˌeɪəʊ 'ɪpsəʊ/ *adverb phrase* L17 **Latin** (ablative of *idipsum* the thing itself). By that very act (or quality); through that alone; thereby. Cf. IPSO FACTO.

eo nomine /ˌeɪəʊ 'nəʊmɪni/, /'nɒmɪneɪ/ *adverb phrase* E17 **Latin** (ablative of *id nomen* that name). Under that name; that is so called; explicitly.

épatant /epatã/ *adjective* E20 **French** (present participial adjective of *épater* to flabbergast). Shocking (to conventional persons); daring.

épater /epate/ *transitive verb* E20 **French** (= flabbergast). Startle, shock.

■ Only used in the infinitive, especially in phrase below or English phrases based upon it.

épater les bourgeois /epate lɛ burʒwɑ/ *adverb phrase* (also **épater le bourgeois**) E20 **French** (= to amaze the bourgeois). To shock the narrow-minded or conventional.

■ 'Je les ai épatés, les bourgeois' is attributed to Alexandre Private d'Anglemont (d. 1859).

1995 *Times* Because it takes more than a urinal to *épater les bourgeois* now, the real things that are being hauled into galleries grow ever more provocative: turds, frozen foetuses and used sanitary towels . . .

épaulement /epolmɑ̃/ *noun* plural pronounced same M19 **French** (see next). *Ballet* A stance in which one shoulder is turned forward and the other drawn back, with the head facing over the forward shoulder; correct positioning of the shoulders.

epaulette /ˈɛpəlɛt/, /ˈɛpɔːlɛt/, /ɛpəˈlɛt/ *noun* (also **epaulet**) L18 **French** (*épaulette* diminutive of *épaule* shoulder, from Latin *spatula*, (in Late Latin) shoulder-blade). **1** L18 An ornamental shoulder-piece worn on a military or other uniform, usually as a sign of rank. **b** E19 A military officer; a commission. **2** E19 A small shoulder-plate on a suit of armour. **3** M19 A loop or tab on the shoulder of a coat; a piece of trimming on the shoulder of a dress etc.

épée /ˈeɪpeɪ/, *foreign* /epe/ (*plural same*) *noun* L19 **French** (= sword, from Old French *espee*). A sharp-pointed duelling-sword used (blunted) for fencing; the art of fencing with this.

ephemera /ɪˈfɛm(ə)rə/, /ɪˈfiːm(ə)rə/, /ɛˈfɛm(ə)rə/ *noun* plural **ephemeras**, **ephemera** /ɪˈfɛm(ə)riː/, /ɪˈfiːm(ə)riː/, /ɛˈfɛm(ə)riː/ L17 **Medieval Latin** (from use as noun of feminine of late Latin *ephemerus* from Greek *ephēmeros* lasting only one day). **1** Originally, a winged insect that lives only one day; an EPHEMERON. Now, a winged insect of the genus *Ephemera*, a mayfly. **2** M18 A person or thing of short-lived usefulness or interest.

ephemeris /ɪˈfɛm(ə)rɪs/, /ɪˈiːm(ə)ris/ *noun* plural **ephemerides** /ɛfɪˈmɛrɪdiːz/ E16 **Latin** (from Greek, from *ephēmeros* lasting only a day. A table or book of tables giving information about celestial bodies on a daily or regular basis over a particular period; an astronomical almanac.

ephemeron /ɪˈfɛm(ə)rɒn/, /ɪˈfiːm(ə)rɒn/ *noun* plural **ephemerons**, **ephemera** /ɪˈfɛm(ə)rə/, /ɪˈfiːm(ə)rə/ L16 **Greek** (neuter of *ephēmeros* lasting only one day. **1** L16 A winged insect that lives only one day or spends only one day in its winged form; cf. EPHEMERA 1. **2** L18 A short-lived person, institution, or production. **3** M20 As *ephemera (plural)*. Printed or written items intended for short-term use, as tickets, posters, etc.

3 1995 *Spectator* The ephemera of rock and roll now plays an important part in the social history of the 20th-century's last half.

épicerie /episri/ *noun* plural pronounced same E20 **French**. In France: a grocer's shop.

epigramme /ˈɛpɪgram/ *noun* M18 **French** (*épigramme*, apparently a fanciful use of *épigramme* = epigram). *Cookery* A small piece of meat, usually lamb, served as an entrée.

epithalamium /ˌɛpɪθəˈleɪmɪəm/ *noun* (also (earlier) **epithalamion** /ˈɛpɪθəˈleɪmɪən/) plural **epithalamiums**, **epithalamions**, **epithalamia** /ˌɛpɪθəˈleɪmɪə/ L16 **Latin** (from Greek *epithalamion* use as noun of neuter of *epithalamios* nuptial, from as *epi-* + *thalamos* bridal chamber). A song or poem in celebration of a wedding.

epitome /ɪˈpɪtəmi/, /ɛˈpɪtəmi/ *noun* (also (*non-standard*) **epitomy**) E16 **Latin** (from Greek *epitomē*, from *epitemnein* to cut into, cut short, from as *epi-* + *temnein* to cut). **1** E16 A summary or abstract of a written work; a condensed account. **2** E16 A thing that represents another in miniature; a person who or thing which embodies a quality etc.; a typical example.

epode /ˈɛpəʊd/ *noun* E17 **French** (*épode* or Latin *epodos* from Greek *epōidos*, from as *epi-* + *ōidē* ode). **1** E17 A Greek lyric poem composed of couplets in which a long line is followed by a shorter; a serious poem. **2** L17 The part of a Greek lyric ode following the strophe and antistrophe.

éponge /epɔ̃ʒ/ *noun* E20 **French** (from Latin *spongia* sponge). Sponge cloth.

epos /ˈɛpɒs/ *noun* M19 **Latin** (from Greek = word, song, from *ep-* stem of *eipein* to say). **1** M19 Epic poetry; an epic poem; *especially* narrative poetry embodying a nation's conception of its past history. **2** M19

Something in real life regarded as a fit subject for an epic poem.

épris /epri/ *adjective* (feminine **éprise** /epriz/) L18 **French** (past participial adjective of ((*s'*)*éprendre* to become attached or enamoured, from as *es-* + Latin *prehendere* to seize). Enamoured (*of*); taken *with*.

1949 C. Hare *When Wind Blows* As if anybody else could not see that Mr. Ventry is *épris* of Nicola.

epsilon /ˈɛpsɪlɒn/, /ɛpˈsʌɪlɒn/ *noun* E18 **Greek** (*e psilon*, literally, 'bare e', short e written ε). **1** E18 The fifth letter (E, ε) of the Greek alphabet; *Astronomy* (preceding the genitive of the Latin name of the constellation) the fifth brightest star in a constellation. **2** E20 An examiner's fifth-class mark; a person of low intelligence.

epyllion /ɪˈpɪlɪən/, /ɛˈpɪlɪən/ *noun* plural **epyllia** /ɪˈpɪlɪə/, /ɛˈpɪlɪə/ L19 **Greek** (*epullion* diminutive of EPOS). A narrative poem resembling an epic in style or matter but of shorter extent.

équipe /ekip/ *noun* (also **equipe**) plural pronounced same M20 **French** (= group, team, from as *équiper* to equip (cf. Anglo-Norman *eskipeson*, medieval Latin *eschipare* to man (a vessel)), probably from Old Norse *skipa* to man (a vessel), fit up, from *skip* ship). A motor-racing stable; a team, especially of sports players.

equivoque /ˈiːkwɪvəʊk/, /ˈɛkwɪvəʊk/ *noun* (also **equivoke**) LME **Old and Modern French** (*équivoque* or late Latin *aequivocus*). **1** L16–M17 A thing which has the same name as something else. **2** E17 An expression capable of more than one meaning; a pun; wordplay, punning. **3** E19 The fact of having more than one meaning or interpretation; ambiguity.

■ Earlier (LME–M17) as an adjective meaning 'equivocal'.

erbswurst /ˈəːbzwəːst/ *noun* L19 **German** (from *Erbse* pea + *Wurst* sausage). *Cookery* Seasoned pease-meal compressed into a sausage shape and used for making soup.

erg /əːg/ *noun* plural **areg** /ˈarɛg/ L19 **French** (from Arabic *'irḳ*, *'erg*). An area of shifting desert sand-dunes, especially in the Sahara.

ergo /ˈəːgəʊ/ *adverb* LME **Latin**. Therefore.

■ Later (L16) there was also a nominal sense of *ergo*, meaning 'a use or occurrence of *ergo*, as in a logical conclusion', but this sense has long been rare.

1995 *Spectator* Thus, if the US Federal Government committed a crime (the Waco massacre), everyone who works for the Federal Government shares in its guilt; ergo it is permissible to bomb a Federal Government building because the people in it are by definition guilty.

ergot /ˈəːgɒt/ *noun* L17 **French** (= cock's spur, from Old French *ar(i)got*, *argoz* of unknown origin). **1** L17 A disease of rye and certain other grasses in which the seeds become replaced by hard black sclerotia of a fungus, giving the appearance of cock's spur: a sclerotium, or sclerotia, of this kind; a fungus causing such a disease. **2** M19 (A preparation or extract of) the dried sclerotia of this fungus used medicinally for the alkaloids they contain, especially to induce contraction of the uterus. **3** L19 A small horny protrusion on the back of the fetlock of most horses.

erh hu /əː ˈhuː/ *noun phrase* (also **erhu**) E20 **Chinese** (*èrhú*, from *èr* two + *hú* bowed instrument). A Chinese two-stringed musical instrument played with a bow.

Erlebnis /ɛrˈleːpnɪs/ *noun* plural **Erlebnisse** /ɛrˈleːpnɪsə/ E20 **German** (literally, 'experience', from *leben* to live). A conscious experience undergone, as opposed to the content or the memory of one.

Eros /ˈɪərɒs/, /ˈɛrəʊz/ *noun* plural **Erotes** /ɪˈrəʊtɛz/, **Eroses** /ˈɪərɒsɪz/, /ˈɛrəʊzɪz/ (also **eros**) L17 **Latin** (from Greek). **1** L17 Love; the god of love, Cupid; earthly or sexual love. **2** E20 In Freudian psychology: the urge for self-preservation and sexual pleasure.

errata /ɛˈrɑːtə/, /ɛˈreɪtə/ *noun* L16 **Latin** (plural of ERRATUM). **I 1** L16 *plural* of ERRATUM. **II** *singular* plural **errata's**, **erratae** /ɛˈrɑːtəz/. **2** M17 A list of errors in a text.

erratum /ɛˈrɑːtəm/, /ɛˈreɪtəm/ *noun* plural **errata** /ɛˈrɑːtə/ M16 **Latin** (= error, use as noun of neuter past participle of *errare* to err). An error in a printed or written text; *especially* one noted in a list appended to a book or published in a subsequent issue of a journal.

ersatz /ˈəːsats/, /ˈɛːsats/, *foreign* /ɛrˈzats/ *adjective & noun* L19 **German** (= compensation, replacement). **A** *adjective* L19 Made or used as a (usually inferior) substitute for something else. **B** *noun* L19 An ersatz thing.

A 1996 *Spectator* . . . to judge from recent Australian movies, the old pro-British cringe, which was at least rooted in historical and cultural reality, has been replaced by an *ersatz* Americanisation, rooted in nothing but commercial calculation.

eruv /ə'rʌv/ *noun* plural **eruvim** /ərʌ'vim/ L20 **Hebrew.** An area marked out by a community of observant Jews within which they are allowed to move on the Sabbath without contravening the restrictions on Sabbath activity.

1993 *Guardian* Most major American cities now have eruvim—the White House is even in Washington's.

escargot /ɛ'skɑːgəʊ/, /ɪ'skɑːgəʊ/ *noun* plural pronounced same L19 **French** (from Old French *escargol* from Provençal *escaragol*). A snail as an article of food.

escarole /'ɛskərəʊl/ *noun* E20 **French** (from Italian *scar(i)ola* from late Latin *(e)scariola*, from Latin *escarius* used as food, from *esca*). A variety of endive with broad undivided leaves, used in salads.

■ Mainly North American.

esclandre /ɛsklɑ̃dr/ *noun* plural pronounced same M19 **French** (from ecclesiastical Latin *scandalum* scandal). Unpleasant notoriety; a scandal, a scene.

escopette /ɛskə(ʊ)'pɛt/ *noun* E19 **Spanish** (*escopeta* (assimilated to French *escopette* from Italian) from Italian *schioppetto* diminutive of *schioppo* carbine, from medieval Latin *sclop(p)us* harquebus). A kind of carbine formerly used in Mexico and the southern United States. *United States History.*

escritoire /ˌɛskriː'twɑː/ *noun* L16 **Old French** (= study, writing-box (modern *écritoire* writing-desk) from medieval Latin SCRIPTORIUM). A writing-desk with drawers etc., a bureau.

esophagus variant of OESOPHAGUS.

esoterica /ɛsə'tɛrɪkə/, /iːsə'tɛrɪkə/ *noun plural* E20 **Greek** (*esōterika* neuter plural of *esōterikos* esoteric). Items or publications intended only for the initiated or appropriate only to an inner circle; esoteric details.

espacement /ɪ'speɪsm(ə)nt/, /ɛ'speɪsm(ə)nt/ *noun* M19 **French** (from *espacer* to space out). **1** M19 The action of spacing, or of placing at suitable intervals. **2** M20 The distance at which trees or crops are set apart when planted.

espada /e'spada/, /ɛ'spɑːdə/ *noun* plural **espadas** /e'spadas/, /e'spɑːdəz/ L19 **Spanish** (from Latin *spatha* sword). A matador.

■ Although introduced originally (E18) in its literal sense of 'a Spanish sword', the word did not achieve currency and was later reintroduced in its present sense.

espadrille /ɛspə'drɪl/, /'ɛspədrɪl/ *noun* L19 **French** (from Provençal *espardi(l)hos*, from *espart* esparto). A light canvas shoe with plaited fibre sole, originally worn in the Pyrenees; an ALPARGATA.

espagnole /ɛspaŋɔl/ *noun* M19 **French** (literally, 'Spanish' (feminine), from Old French *espaignol*, *espaigneul*). A simple brown sauce. In full *espagnole sauce*.

espagnolette /ɪˌspanjə'lɛt/, /ɛˌspanjə'lɛt/ *noun* E19 **French** (from *espagnol* Spanish; see preceding). A kind of bolt used for fastening French windows, in which a single handle operates fasteners at the top and bottom of the window.

espalier /ɪ'spaljə/, /ɛ'spaljə/ *noun* M17 **French** (from Italian *spalliera*, from *spalla* shoulder, from Latin *spatula*, (in late Latin) shoulder-blade). **1** M17 A fruit tree or ornamental shrub trained on a lattice or a framework of stakes. **2** A row of trees or shrubs trained in this way. Only in E18. **3** M18 A lattice or framework, or one of the stakes, on which a tree or shrub is trained.

esparto /ɛ'spɑːtəʊ/, /ɪ'spɑːtəʊ/ *noun* plural **espartos** M19 **Spanish** (from Latin *spartum* from Greek *sparton* rope). A tough grass, *Stipa tenacissima*, growing in Spain and North Africa and used in paper-making. Also *esparto grass*.

espièglerie /ɛspjɛgləri/ *noun* E19 **French** (from *(Ul)espiegle* frolicsome, from Dutch *Uilenspiegel* (= German *Eulenspiegel*), from *uil* owl + *spiegel* mirror, from Latin *speculum*). Mischievousness; roguishness.

■ Till Eulenspiegel was a mythical fourteenth-century German peasant whose exploits and practical jokes were recounted in a collection of satirical tales first published in the early sixteenth century. The English noun *owlglass* (M16) is also a translation of *Eulenspiegel*.

esplanade /ɛsplə'neɪd/, /ɛsplə'nɑːd/ *noun* L16 **French** (from Italian *spianata* from feminine of Latin *explanatus* flattened, levelled, past participle of *explanare*). **1** L16 *Fortification* **a** The glacis of a counterscarp. Formerly, an area of flat ground on the top of a rampart. **b** E18 A level open space separating a citadel from the town that it commands. **2** L17 Any level open space, but *especially* one where the public may walk; a road along the sea front of a resort.

espressivo /ˌɛsprɛˈsiːvəʊ/ *adverb & adjective* L19 **Italian** (from Latin *expressus* distinctly presented, past participle of *exprimere* to express). *Music* (Performed) with expression of feeling.

espresso /ɛˈsprɛsəʊ/ *noun* (also **expresso** /ɛkˈsprɛsəʊ/) plural **espressos** M20 **Italian** ((*caffè*) *espresso*, from *espresso* squeezed, pressed out, from Latin *expressus* (see preceding)). **1** M20 Coffee made by forcing steam through ground coffee beans. **2** M20 A coffee bar etc. where such coffee is sold. Also *espresso bar, espresso café*, etc.

esprit /ɛspri/, /ɛˈspriː/, /ˈɛspriː/ *noun* L16 **French** (from Latin *spiritus* spirit). Vivacity; wit.

1995 *Times* So you walk back to the Rigaud portrait [of Lord Nelson], the slight figure with colourless hair and arched brows and a face full of nervous *esprit* and determination.

esprit de corps /ɛˌspriː də ˈkɔː/, /ˌɛspriː/ *noun phrase* L18 **French**. Regard for the honour and interests of the group or organization to which one belongs; team spirit.

1995 *Spectator* An *esprit de corps* was emerging fast. As we sped into the Channel Tunnel, the businessman on the next table cracked open a bottle of champagne and handed round paper cups.

esprit de l'escalier /ɛspri də lɛskalje/ *noun phrase* (also **esprit d'escalier**) E20 **French** (literally, 'wit of the staircase'). A clever remark or rejoinder that only occurs to one after the opportunity for making it is past.

■ The phrase was coined by the French *philosophe* Denis Diderot (1713–84) in *Paradoxe sur le Comédien*. The staircase was the one descending from the salon, and *esprit d'escalier* was the witty saying that came to mind only as one was departing down it.

1995 *Times Magazine* With my usual dunderheaded *esprit d'escalier* I will realise later that the correct response is simply to walk on past . . .

esprit fort /ɛspri fɔr/ *noun phrase* plural **esprits forts** (pronounced same) M18 **French** (= strong spirit). A strong-minded person, *especially* one who claims independence from conventional thinking on religious or philosophical topics.

esquisse /ɛskis/ *noun* plural pronounced same M18 **French** (from Italian *schizzo*). A rough or preliminary sketch.

esraj /ɛˈsrɑːdʒ/ *noun* E20 **Bengali** (*esrāj*). A three- or four-stringed Indian musical instrument with added sympathetic strings.

esse /ˈɛsi/ *noun* M16 **Latin** (use as noun of *esse* to be). Essential nature, essence, especially as opposed to BENE ESSE.

estacade /ɛstakad/ *noun* plural pronounced same E17 **French** (from Spanish *estacada*, from *estaca*, from Proto-Romance, from Germanic base of *stake*). A dyke made of piles or stakes in water or marshy ground in order to impede an enemy.

estaminet /ɛstaminɛ/ *noun* plural **estaminets** pronounced same E19 **French** (from Walloon *staminé* byre, from *stamo* pole to which a cow is tethered in a stall, probably from German *Stamm* stem, trunk). Originally, a café where smoking was allowed. Now, a small unpretentious café selling wine, beer, etc.

estancia /ɛˈstansɪə/, *foreign* /eˈstanθia/, /eˈstansia/ *noun* M17 **Spanish** (literally, 'station' = Old French *estance* dwelling, from medieval Latin *stantia*, from Latin *stant-* present participial stem of *stare* to stand). A cattle-ranch in Latin America or the southern United States.

1996 *Oldie* In the pampas cattle and sheep farmers made their fortunes on huge estancias.

estocada /estoˈkada/, /ɛstəˈkɑːdə/ *noun* E20 **Spanish** (from *estoque* sword (from Old and Modern French *estoc*) short sword for thrusting + *-ada*). *Bullfighting* The sword-thrust that finally kills the bull.

estouffade /ɛstufad/ *noun* plural pronounced same L19 **French** (from Italian *stuf(f)ata* past participle of *stufare* to stew, from *stufa* stove, from popular Latin, ultimately from Greek *tuphos* smoke). (A dish of) meat cooked very slowly in its own vapour.

estrade /ɛˈstrɑːd/ *noun* L17 **French** (from Spanish *estrado*, from Latin STRATUM, literally, 'something spread or laid down', neuter past participle of *sternere* to throw down). Originally, a slightly raised platform or dais for persons of rank to sit or recline on. Later, any dais.

■ The Spanish equivalent *strado* was an earlier introduction into English (L16) than *estrade* and was used with the same two senses, but is now rare.

estrog variant of ETROG.

estrus variant of OESTRUS.

estufa /e'stufa/ *noun* M19 **Spanish** (corresponding to Old French *estuve* (modern *étuve*)). **1** M19 An underground chamber in which a fire is kept permanently alight, used as a place of assembly by the Pueblo Indians. **2** L19 A heated chamber in which Madeira is stored and matured.

et /ɛt/ *conjunction* ME **Latin**. And.

■ In Modern English only in medieval and Modern Latin phrases; see ET AL., ET CETERA, etc.

eta /'iːtə/ *noun* LME **Greek** (*ēta*). **1** LME The seventh letter (H, η) of the Greek alphabet. **2** Frequently written (η). **a** L18 *attributive Astronomy* (Preceding the genitive of the Latin name of the constellation) denoting the seventh brightest star in a constellation. **b** M20 *Physics* A meson with zero isospin and spin and a mass of 549 MeV. In full *eta meson*.

etagere /ɛtə'ʒɛː/ *noun* (also **étagère**) plural pronounced same M19 **French** (*étagère*, from *étage* shelf, stage). A piece of furniture with a number of open shelves on which to display ornaments etc.

et al. /ɛt al/ *adverb phrase 1* L19 **Latin** (*et* and + abbreviation of *alii, aliae, alia* masculine, feminine, and neuter plural of *alius* other). And others.

■ Often used in bibliographies in cases of works by several authors; the formula 'Smith et al.' avoids having to list all the authors' names in full.

1996 *Spectator* [There] is a long succession of recreated theatrical 'flats' . . . with original costumes and astonishingly flamboyant designs by Bakst, Benois, Goncharova *et al.*

et al. /ɛt al/ *adverb phrase 2* **Latin** (*et* and + abbreviation of ALIBI elsewhere). And elsewhere.

étalage /etalaʒ/ *noun* plural pronounced same E20 **French** (from *étaler* to display). A display, a show.

etamine /'ɛtəmiːn/ *noun* (also **étamine**) E18 **French** (*étamine*). A lightweight open-weave fabric of coarse yarn, now usually cotton or worsted.

étang /etɑ̃/ *noun* plural pronounced same M19 **French** (from Old French *estanc*, ultimately from base of *stanch*, origin unknown). A shallow pool or small lake, *especially* one resulting from the blocking of streams by sand-dunes along the French Mediterranean coast.

etatism /ɛ'tɑːtɪz(ə)m/ *noun* (also **étatisme** /etatism/) E20 **French** (*étatisme*, from *état* state). The extreme authority of the State over the individual citizen.

et cetera /ɛt'sɛt(ə)rə/, /ɪt'sɛt(ə)rə/ *adverb, noun, & verb* (also **etcetera**, **et caetera**) ME **Latin** (from *et* and + *cetera* the rest, neuter plural of *ceterus* remaining over). **A** *adverb* ME And the rest; and similar things; and so on; and the customary continuation. Also reduplicated. **B** *noun* **1** L16 (An instance of) the adverb *et cetera*. **2** L16 Something not mentioned explicitly for reasons of propriety. Formerly *specifically* (in *plural*) trousers. **3** M17 A number of unspecified things or persons. **4** (In *plural*.) (The usual) additions, extras, sundries. **C** *verb* M19 Replacing a suppressed verb.

■ Often abbreviated to *etc* or *&c.*

ethos /'iːθɒs/ *noun* M19 **Greek** (*ēthos* nature, disposition). The characteristic spirit of a culture, era, community, institution, etc., as manifested in its attitudes, aspirations, customs, etc.; the character of an individual as represented by his or her values and beliefs; the prevalent tone of a literary work in this respect.

1996 *Country Life: Garden Year* . . . we open six days a week from spring to autumn. This means that the public are very much a part of the ethos in which we live and work.

ethrog variant of ETROG.

etiquette /'ɛtɪkɛt/, /ɛtɪ'kɛt/ *noun* M18 **French** (*étiquette* label, etiquette). The conventional rules of personal behaviour in polite society; the prescribed ceremonial of a court; the formalities required in diplomatic intercourse; the order of procedure established by custom in the armed services, Parliament, etc.; the unwritten code restricting professional persons in what concerns the interests of their colleagues or the dignity of their profession.

■ Also formerly (M19) in the primary French sense of 'a label, ticket', but this is rare in English. The sense of 'a rule of etiquette', 'an observance prescribed by etiquette' was also briefly (L18–E19) current in English, generally in the plural. From the word's history in French it is not entirely clear how the transition between between the primary and secondary senses was effected, although the English colloquial expressions 'just the ticket' and 'not quite the ticket' (*ticket* here meaning 'the accepted (or needed) thing') suggest how it could have come about. Modern Romance languages have adapted the word from

French in the secondary sense: Italian *etichetta*, Spanish *etiqueta*.

étourderie /eturdəri/ *noun* M18 **French** (from next). Thoughtlessness, carelessness; a thoughtless act, a blunder.

1958 I. Murdoch *Bell* His love affairs appeared as the *étourderies* of a much younger man.

étourdi /eturdi/ *adjective & noun* (feminine **étourdie**) plural pronounced same L17 **French** (past participial adjective of *étourdir* to stun, make dizzy). (A person who is) thoughtless or irresponsible.

étrenne /etrɛn/ *noun* plural pronounced same E19 **French** (from Old French *estreine* ultimately from Latin *strena*). A New Year's gift; a Christmas-box.

etrier /ˈeɪtrɪə/, *foreign* /etrije/ (*plural same*) *noun* (also **étrier**) M20 **French** (*étrier* stirrup, etrier). *singular* and in *plural*. A short rope ladder with a few solid rungs, used by climbers.

etrog /ˈɛtrɒg/ *noun* (also **ethrog**, **estrog** /ˈɛstrɒg/) plural **etrogs**, **etrogim** /ˈɛtrɒgɪm/ L19 **Hebrew** (*ʾeṯrōg*). A citron fruit as used ritually in the Jewish Feast of Tabernacles.

et seq. /ɛt sɛk/ *noun phrase* plural **et seqq.** (pronounced same) L19 **Latin** (*et* and + present participle of *sequi* to follow; abbreviation of *et sequentes* (Latin masculine and feminine plural of *sequens*) and *et sequentia* (neuter plural of *sequens*)). And following.

Et tu, Brute /ɛt ˈtuː ˌbruːteɪ/ *interjection* L16 **Latin** (= and you, Brutus). (An expression of) reproach to a friend who has betrayed one's trust and gone over to the enemy.

■ The words spoken by Caesar in Shakespeare's *Julius Caesar* (III.i) when he sees his friend Brutus amongst his assassins. Another name is sometimes jocularly substituted for that of Brutus (see quotation 1995(2)).

1995 *Times* The cry *Et tu, Brute?* has been the death rattle of many a fallen king.

1995 *Times* The penalty shoot-out, the Boland decision, and all such pack-'em-in modifications to a sport . . . betray competition for fun. Each one is a betrayal: a knife in the heart of sport. *Et tu,* Illingworth?

étude /ˈeɪtjuːd/, /eɪˈtjuːd/, *foreign* /etyd/ (*plural same*) *noun* M19 **French** (= study). An instrumental piece, especially for the piano, which concentrates on a particular aspect of technique or allows a display of virtuosity.

etui /ɛˈtwiː/ *noun* (also **etwee**) E17 **French** (*étui*, Old French *estui* prison, from Old French *estuier* to shut up, keep, save). A small usually ornamental case for needles etc. Formerly also, a case for surgical instruments.

euchre /ˈjuːkə/ *noun & verb* E19 **German** (dialect *Jucker(spiel)*). **A** *noun* **1** E19 A card-game for two to four players in which the highest cards are the joker (if used), the jack of trumps, and the other jack of the same colour in a pack with the lower cards removed, the aim being to win at least three of the five tricks played. **2** M19 An instance of euchring or being euchred. **B** *transitive verb* **1** E19 Prevent (a bidder) from winning three or more tricks at euchre, thereby scoring points oneself. **2** M19 Cheat, trick, (*into*, *out of*); deceive, outwit. **3** M20 Exhaust; ruin, finish, do for, (a person). Usually in *passive*. *Australian*.

eudaimonia /ˌjuːdʌɪˈmɒnɪə/ *noun* E20 **Greek** (from as *eudemon* from as *eu-* good + *daimōn* genius). *Philosophy* Happiness or well-being consisting in the full realization of human potential, *especially* (in Aristotle's ethics) in rational activity exhibiting excellence.

eunomia /juːˈnəʊmɪə/ *noun* M19 **Greek** (from as *eu-* good + *-nomia* state of law). A political condition of good law well administered.

eupepsia /juːˈpɛpsɪə/ *noun* E18 **Greek** (*eupepsia* digestibility, from *eupeptos*, from *eu-* good + *peptein* to digest). Good digestion; absence of indigestion.

euphoria /juːˈfɔːrɪə/ *noun* /ˈjuːf(ə)ri/ L17 **Modern Latin** (from Greek, from *euphoros* borne well, healthy, from as *eu-* good + *pherein* to bear). Originally, a state of well-being, especially as produced in a sick person by a medicine. Now, a strong feeling of well-being, cheerfulness, and optimism, *especially* one based on overconfidence or overoptimism; a mood marked by this, as symptomatic of a mental illness or the influence of drugs.

1996 *Spectator* After a while one feels a terrific euphoria, and, looking for more, one switches to whiskey or vodka.

eureka /jʊ(ə)ˈriːkə/ *interjection & noun* (also **Eureka**) E17 **Greek** (*heurēka*, 1st person singular perfect of *heuriskein* to find). **A** *interjection* E17 Expressive of exultation at a sudden discovery. **B** *noun* **1** M17 A cry of *eureka!* **2** M19 A fortunate discovery. **3** E20 (**Eureka**) (Proprietary name for) an alloy of copper and nickel used for electrical filament and resistance wire.

■ The exclamation supposedly uttered by the Sicilian Greek philosopher Archimedes (*c.*287–*c.*212 BC) when he hit upon a method of determining the purity of gold, an inspiration which, according to tradition, occurred to him as he was taking a bath.

euthanasia /juːθəˈneɪzɪə/ *noun* E17 **Greek** (from as *eu-* good + *thanatos* death). **1** E17 A gentle and easy death. **2** M18 A means of bringing about such a death (chiefly *in figurative use, of* something). **3** M19 The action of bringing about such a death, especially of a person who requests it as a release from incurable disease.

événement /evenmɑ̃/ *noun* plural pronounced same M20 **French** (= event, happening). Politically motivated civil disorder involving mass demonstrations.

■ Usually plural. The word became current in English with reference to the French strikes and student riots of 1968 and received a further boost from the wave of strikes and demonstrations in France in 1995, though it is no longer necessarily confined to the French political scene (see quotation 1995(2)).

1995 *Times* The French media are full of comparisons with the *événements* of 1968, when students and workers suddenly took to the streets for no very obvious reason.
1995 *Spectator* The next few months will show whether the Ilidza *événements* join the heady days of Belgrade 1941 in the annals of Serb defiance.

évolué /evɔlɥe/ *noun & adjective* plural of noun pronounced same M20 **French** (past participle of *évoluer* to evolve). (Characteristic of or designating) an African who has had a European education or has adopted European ways or attitudes.

Ewigkeit /ˈeːvɪçkaɪt/, /ˈeɪvɪgkʌɪt/ *noun* (also **ewigkeit**) L19 **German**. Eternity; infinity.

ex /ɛks/ *noun & adjective* plural **exes**, **ex's** /ˈɛksɪz/ E19 **Latin** (from prefix *ex-* former(ly)). **A** *noun* E19 A person who formerly held a position etc. denoted by the context; *specifically*, a former husband or wife. **B** *adjective* E19 Former; outdated.

ex /ɛks/ *preposition* M19 **Latin** (= out of). **1** *Commerce* M19 Of stocks and shares: without, excluding. **2** Of goods: (sold) direct from (a ship, warehouse, etc.) **3** L19 Of an animal: out of (a specified dam).

exacta /ɪgˈzaktə/, /ɛgˈzaktə/ *noun* M20 **American Spanish** (*quiniela exacta* exact quinella). *Betting* In North America: a PERFECTA.

exalté /ɛgzalte/ *adjective & noun* (feminine **exaltée**) plural of noun pronounced same M19 **French** (past participial adjective of *exalter* to exalt, from as *ex-* up(wards) + *altus* high). (A person who is) elated or impassioned.

ex animo /ɛks ˈanɪməʊ/ *adverb phrase* E17 **Latin** (= from the soul, from as *ex* (preposition) + *animo* ablative of *animus* soul). Heartily, sincerely.

ex ante /ɛks ˈanti/ *adjective & adverb phrase* M20 **Modern Latin** (from as *ex* (preposition) + *ante* before). Chiefly *Economics* **A** *adjective phrase* M20 Based on prior assumptions or expectations; predicted, prospective. **B** *adverb phrase* M20 Before the event, in advance, beforehand.

■ The opposite of EX POST.

B 1992 *New York Review of Books Ex ante*, the thing looks dubious. *Ex post* it is, disconcertingly, a surprising success . . .

ex cathedra /ɛks kəˈθiːdrə/, /ɛks ˈkaθɪdrə/ *adverb & adjective* E17 **Latin** (= from the (teacher's) chair, from *ex* (preposition) + *cathedra* chair). **A** *adverb* E17 Authoritatively; as an official pronouncement; *especially* (*Roman Catholic Church*) with the full weight of the Pope's office as divinely appointed guardian of Christian faith and morals. **B** *adjective* E19 Authoritative, official; given *ex cathedra*; dogmatic.

B 1996 *New Scientist* Something of a pattern emerges about deception that will reassure the ex cathedra theoreticians.

excelsior /ɛkˈsɛlsɪɔː/ *interjection & noun* (also **Excelsior**) L18 **Latin** (comparative of *excelsus* from *ex-* + *celsus* lofty). **A** L18 *interjection* Go higher! **B** *noun* **1** M19 Curled shavings of soft wood for stuffing, packing, etc. Originally *United States*. **2** L19 A person who or thing which reaches or aspires to reach higher. **3** E20 A very small size (3 points) of type. Chiefly *United States*.

exceptis excipiendis /ɛkˌsɛptɪs ɛkˌsɪpɪˈɛndɪs/ *adverb phrase* L19 **Late Latin** (from ablative plural of Latin *exceptus* past participle, and of *excipiendus* gerundive, of *excipere* to except). With appropriate exceptions.

excreta /ɪkˈskriːtə/, /ɛkˈskriːtə/ *noun plural* M19 **Latin** (use as noun of neuter plural of *excretus* past participle of *excernere* to excrete). Waste matter discharged from the body; *especially* faeces, urine.

excursus /ɪk'skəːsəs/, /ɛk'skəːsəs/ *noun* plural **excursuses**, **excursus** /ɪk 'skəːsuːs/ E19 **Latin** (= excursion, from *excurs-* past participial stem of *excurrere* to run out). **1** E19 A fuller treatment in an appendix of some point in the main text of a book, especially an edition of the classics. **2** M19 A digression within a narrative in which some point is discussed at length.

exeat /'ɛksɪat/ *noun* E18 **Latin** (= let him or her go out, 3rd person singular present subjunctive of *exire* to go out). **1** E18 A permission for temporary absence from a college or other institution. **2** M18 A permission granted by a bishop to a priest to move to another diocese.

1 1984 A. Brookner *Hotel du Lac* The tall thin beauty with the dog was never visible in the daytime and it was impossible to imagine her doing anything except eating ice cream and smoking, like a child on an exeat from school.

exedra /'ɛksɪdrə/, /ɪk'siːdrə/, /ɛk'sɪdrə/ *noun* (also **exhedra** /'ɛkshɪdrə/, /ɪks 'hiːdrə/, /ɛks'hɪdrə/) plural **exedrae** /'ɛksɪdriː/ E18 **Latin** (from Greek, from as *ex-* + *hedra* seat). **1** E18 *Classical History* A hall or arcade with seats, attached to a palaestra or a private house and used for conversation. **b** M19 *generally* An apse, a recess, a large niche. **2** E18 A CATHEDRA.

exegesis /ɛksɪ'dʒiːsɪs/ *noun* plural **exegeses** /ɛksɪ'dʒiːsiːz/ E17 **Greek** (*exēgēsis*, from *exēgeisthai* to interpret). (An) exposition, especially of Scripture; an explanatory note or discourse.

1996 *Spectator* And his films resist the easy exegesis of critics . . .

exempla plural of EXEMPLUM.

exempli gratia /ɪg,zɛmpli 'greɪʃə/, /ɛg ,zɛmpli/ *adverb phrase* M17 **Latin** (from genitive of *exemplum* example + ablative of *gratia* grace). For example; for instance.

■ Abbreviated to *e.g. Exempli gratia* and its ubiquitous abbreviation have entirely superseded *exempli causa* (literally, 'by reason of example'), although the latter was the earlier (M16) in English.

exemplum /ɪg'zɛmpləm/, /ɛg'zɛmpləm/ *noun* plural **exempla** /ɪg'zɛmplə/ L19 **Latin**. An example; *especially* an illustrative or moralizing story.

exequatur /ɛksɪ'kweɪtə/ *noun* E17 **Latin** (= let him or her perform, 3rd person singular present subjunctive of *exequi* to carry out, execute). **1** E17 *Roman Catholic Church* A government's authorization for a bishop to exercise his office in its territory, or for any papal enactment to take effect there; a claim by a government that such authorization is required or can be withheld. **2** L18 An official recognition of a consul by a foreign government, authorizing him or her to exercise office.

exergue /ɪk'səːg/, /ɛk'səːg/, /'ɛksəːg/ *noun* L17 **French** (from medieval Latin *exergum*, from Greek *ex-* + *ergon* work). *Numismatics* A small space on a coin or medal, usually on the reverse below the principal device, for the date, the engraver's initials, etc.; the inscription placed there.

exeunt /'ɛksɪʌnt/ *verb & noun* L15 **Latin** (3rd person plural present indicative of *exire* to go out). **A** *intransitive verb* (*defective*) (A stage direction:) (actors, or the characters whose names follow) leave the stage. Cf. EXIT. **B** A collective exit; a departure by more than one person.

■ Also in the phrase *exeunt omnes* 'all leave the stage' at the end of a scene or play.

B 1996 *Times* Usually when the critics slink off to the pub during the last act, their excuse to the paying customers they are forcing to stand up for their exeunt is that they have to catch the early editions.

ex gratia /ɛks 'greɪʃə/ *adverb & adjective phrase* M18 **Latin** (from *ex* from + *gratia* grace). (Done, given, etc.) as a favour or without (especially legal) compulsion.

1996 *New Scientist* We can only ask that the government provide ex gratia payments to all affected.

exhedra variant of EXEDRA.

ex hypothesi /,ɛks hʌɪ'pɒθəsʌɪ/ *adverb phrase* E17 **Modern Latin** (from Latin *ex* by + ablative of late Latin HYPOTHESIS). According to the hypothesis (made); supposedly.

exigeant /egziʒɑ̃/ *adjective* (feminine **exigeante** /egziʒɑ̃t/) L18 **French** (present participial adjective of *exiger* from Latin *exigere* to exact). Exacting, demanding.

exit /'ɛksɪt/, /'ɛgzɪt/ *noun* L16 **Latin** (*exitus*; cf. EXIT (verb 1)). **1** L16 A departure of an actor etc. from the stage during a scene; *figurative* a person's death. **2** M17 *generally* A departure from any place or situation. Also, freedom or opportunity to depart. **3** L17 A means of egress, especially from a public building; an outlet, a way out. **b** M20 A place where traffic can leave a motorway etc.; a slip-road provided at such a place. **4** M20 *Cards* (especially *Bridge*) The action of deliberately losing the lead; a card enabling one to do this.

exit /'ɛksɪt/, /'ɛgzɪt/ *verb 1* (*intransitive*) *defective* M16 **Latin** (3rd person singular present indicative of *exire* to go out, from as *ex-* out + *ire* to go). (A stage direction:) (the last speaker, or the character whose name follows) leaves the stage. Cf. EXEUNT.

exit /'ɛksɪt/, /'ɛgzɪt/ *verb 2* E17 **Latin** (from EXIT (noun)). **1** *intransitive verb* E17 Make one's exit or departure, especially from a stage; leave any place; *figurative* die. **2** *intransitive verb* M20 *Cards* (especially *Bridge*). Lose the lead deliberately. **3** *transitive verb* L20 Leave, get out of.

ex-libris /ɛks'lɪbrɪs/, /ɛks'li:brɪs/, /ɛks 'lʌɪbrɪs/, /ɛks'li:bri:s/ *noun* plural same L19 **Latin** (literally, 'out of the books *or* library (of—)'). An inscription, label, etc., indicating the owner of a book; *especially* a bookplate.

ex machina see DEUS EX MACHINA.

ex nihilo /ɛks 'ni:hɪləʊ/, /'nʌɪhɪləʊ/ *adverb phrase* L16 **Latin**. Out of nothing.

1996 *New Scientist* Atheists are equally alarmed, because the notion of the Universe coming into being from nothing looks suspiciously like the creation, *ex nihilo*, of Christianity.

exodus /'ɛksədəs/ *noun* OE **ecclesiastical Latin** (*Exodus* from Greek *exodos*, from as *ex-* out + *hodos* way). **1** OE (*Exodus*) (The name of) the second book of the Bible, relating the release of the Israelites from their bondage in Egypt and their journey to Canaan. **2** E17 A departure, usually of many people; an emigration; *specifically* the departure of the Israelites from Egypt.

ex officio /ˌɛks ə'fɪʃɪəʊ/ *adverb, adjective, & noun* M16 **Latin** (from *officium* duty, office). **A** *adverb* & (usually with hyphen) *adjective* M16 (That is such) by virtue of one's office. **B** *noun* E19 A person serving ex officio.

exordium /ɪg'zɔ:dɪəm/, /ɛg'zɔ:dɪəm/ *noun* plural **exordiums**, **exordia** /ɪg'zɔ:dɪə/ L16 **Latin** (from *exordiri* to begin). The beginning of anything; *especially* the introductory part of a discourse or treatise.

exotica /ɪg'zɒtɪkə/, /ɛg'zɒtɪkə/ *noun plural* L19 **Latin** (neuter plural of *exoticus* exotic). Exotic things.

1995 *Country Life* This year's hot summer is not principally responsible for the increase in insect life . . . The exotica survived because of the mildness of the winter.

ex parte /ɛks 'pɑ:ti/ *adverb & adjective phrase* (as adjective frequently **ex-parte**) E17 **Latin** (= from a *or* the side). **A** *adverb phrase* **1** E17 Originally, on the part of. Now (*Law*), on behalf of. **2** L17 *Law* On behalf of or with reference to only one of the parties concerned (and without notice to the adverse party). **B** *adjective phrase* **1** L18 *Law* Of an application, injunction, deposition, etc.: made, issued, etc., by or for only one party in a case. **2** E19 Of a statement etc.: one-sided, partial.

ex pede Herculem /ɛks ˌpɛdi 'hə:kjʊlɛm/ *adverb phrase* M17 **Latin** (= Hercules from his foot). Inferring the whole of something from an insignificant part.

■ The ancient Greek mathematician Pythagoras is supposed to have calculated the height of the hero Hercules from the size of his foot.

experimentum crucis /ɪkˌspɛrɪmɛntəm 'kru:sɪs/, /ɛkˌspɛrɪmɛntəm 'kru:kɪs/, *noun phrase* M17 **Modern Latin** (= crucial experiment). A decisive test showing which of several hypotheses is correct.

explication de texte /ɛksplikasjɔ̃ də tɛkst/ *noun phrase* plural **explications de texte** (pronounced same) M20 **French**. A detailed textual examination of a literary work; the making of such examinations.

explicit /'ɛksplɪsɪt/ *noun* M17 **Late Latin** (either = here ends, 3rd person singular indicative of *explicare* to unfold (plural *expliciunt*); or abbreviation of *explicitus est liber* = the book is finished). The end; the conclusion.

■ Originally used by medieval scribes to denote the end of a Latin manuscript or work, *explicit* was sometimes also placed (ME–M19) at the end of an printed book, chapter, etc.

exposé /ɪk'spəʊzeɪ/, /ɛk'spəʊzeɪ/, *foreign* /ɛkspoze/ (*plural same*) *noun* (also **expose**) E19 **French** (past participle of *exposer* to set out, display). **1** E19 An orderly statement of facts. **2** E19 A showing up or revelation of something discreditable.

2 1996 *Spectator* . . . his relentless research has produced something much more than an exposé of a single rogue . . .

ex post /ɛks 'pəʊst/ *adjective & adverb phrase* M20 **Modern Latin** (from as preposition *ex* + Latin *post* after). Chiefly *Economics*. **A** *adjective phrase* M20 Based on past events or actual results; occurring afterwards; actual rather than predicted; retrospective. **B** *adverb phrase* M20 After the event; retrospectively.

■ The opposite of EX ANTE (see quotation at *ex ante*).

ex post facto /ˌɛks pəʊst ˈfaktəʊ/ *adverb & adjective phrase* M17 **Latin** (erroneous division of Latin *ex postfacto* in the light of subsequent events, from *ex* from, out of + ablative of *postfactum* that which is done subsequently). **A** *adverb phrase* M17 After the event, after the fact; retrospectively. **B** *adjective phrase* L18 Done after another thing; *especially* (of a law) applied retrospectively.

expresso variant of ESPRESSO.

ex professo /ɛks prəˈfɛsəʊ/ *adverb phrase* L16 **Latin** (from as preposition *ex* + ablative of *professus* use as noun of past participial stem of *profiteri* to declare). By profession; professedly.

ex proprio motu /ɛks ˌprəʊprɪəʊ ˈməʊtuː/, /ˌprɒprɪəʊ/ *adverb phrase* L17 **Late Latin** (= by own motion). MOTU PROPRIO; *specifically* in *Law*, by decision of a court without anyone's application.

ex relatione /ɛks rɪˌleɪʃɪˈəʊni/ *prepositional phrase* E17 **Latin**. *Law* By relation of; according to the report of, as reported by.

ex silentio /ɛks sɪˈlɛntɪəʊ/, /ɛks sɪˈlɛnʃɪəʊ/ *adverb phrase* E20 **Latin** (= from silence). By or from a lack of evidence to the contrary.

extempore /ɪkˈstɛmp(ə)ri/, /ɛk ˈstɛmp(ə)ri/ *adverb, noun, & adjective* M16 **Latin** (*ex tempore* on the spur of the moment, from as preposition *ex* + *tempore* ablative of *tempus* time). **A** *adverb* **1** M16 Without premeditation or preparation; impromptu. (Now chiefly of speaking or of performing music.) **2** L16–M17 At once, immediately. **B** *noun* L16–E19 An unprepared improvised speech, composition, or performance. **C** *adjective* **1** E17 Of a speech, musical performance, etc.: spoken or done without preparation, especially without written notes. Of a speaker or performer: performing without preparation. **2** M17 Occasional; sudden, unprepared for. (Now only of personal actions, with some notion of sense 1.) **3** L17 Makeshift, contrived for the occasion.

extra dictionem /ˌɛkstrə dɪktɪˈəʊnɛm/ *adverb phrase* E19 **Latin** (translation of Greek *exō tēs lexeōs* outside the wording). Of a logical fallacy: not arising from the wording used to express it.

■ A subdivision of logical fallacy noted by Aristotle in his *Sophistici Elenchi* (ch. 4); it is sometimes also called in Latin *in re* in the matter. Opposed to IN DICTIONE.

extrados /ɪksˈtreɪdɒs/, /ɛksˈtreɪdɒs/ *noun* L18 **French** (from Latin *extra* outside + French *dos* back). *Architecture* The upper or outer curve of an arch; *especially* the upper curve of the voussoirs which form the arch. Cf. INTRADOS.

extraordinaire /ɪkˌstrɔːdɪˈnɛː/, /ɛkˌstrɔːdɪ ˈnɛː/, *foreign* /ɛkstraɔrdinɛr/ *postpositive adjective* M20 **French**. Remarkable, outstanding; (of a person) unusually active or successful in a specified respect.

1996 *Times* This brings up the unfortunate truth that Roger Daltry, trout-farmer extraordinaire, is cooler than Cobain . . .

exuviae /ɪgˈzjuːvɪiː/, /ɛgˈzjuːvɪiː/ *noun plural* M17 **Latin** (= clothing stripped off, skins of animals, spoils, from *exuere* to divest oneself of). Cast skins, shells, or other shed outer parts of animals, whether recent or fossil; *specifically* (*Zoology*) sloughed skins; *figurative* remnants, remains.

ex vivo /ɛks viːvəʊ/ *adjective & adverb phrase* (also **ex-vivo**) L20 **Latin**. *Biology* (Performed, obtained, or occurring) outside a living organism.

■ Opposed to IN VIVO.

1995 *New Scientist* Most trials, including the ADA treatments, have relied on the 'ex vivo' approach. Scientists take cells from patients, insert the key gene and return the altered cells to the patient.

ex-voto /ɛksˈvəʊtəʊ/ *noun & adjective* plural of noun **ex-votos** L18 **Latin** (*ex voto* from *ex* out of, from + *voto* ablative singular of *votum* vow). (Designating) something offered in fulfilment of a vow previously taken.

ezan /ɛˈzʌn/ *noun* M18 **Persian and Turkish** (pronunciation of Arabic *'aḏān*). The Muslim call to prayer; the AZAN.

f abbreviation of FORTE (*musical direction*).

fabliau /ˈfablɪəʊ/, /fablijo/ *noun* plural **fabliaux** /ˈfablɪəʊz/, /fablijo/ E19 **French**. *Literature* A verse tale, often burlesque in character, from the early period of French poetry.

■ The word is also used to denote a similar verse tale of sex and trickery in medieval English, particularly the tales of the Miller, Reeve, Summoner, Merchant, and Shipman in Chaucer's *Canterbury Tales*.

façade d'honneur /fasad dɔnœr/ *noun phrase* plural **façades d'honneur** (pronounced same) M20 **French**. *Architecture* The principal front of a building, esp. of a large formal building.

facetiae /fəˈsiːʃɪiː/ *noun plural* E16 **Latin** (plural of *facetia* jest). **1** E16 Witticisms; humorous sayings. **2** M19 *Bookselling* Pornography.

Fach /fax/ *noun* (also **fach**) M19 **German** (= compartment, division, shelf). A line of business or work; a department of activity.

facia variant of FASCIA senses 4, 5.

faciendum /fakɪˈɛndəm/, /feɪʃɪˈɛndəm/ *noun* plural **facienda** /fakɪˈɛndə/, /feɪʃɪˈɛndə/ M19 **Latin** (= thing to be done, neuter gerundive of *facere* to make, do). *Philosophy* A thing that should be done.

facies /ˈfeɪʃɪiːz/ *noun* plural same E17 **Latin** (= face). **1** L19 *Medicine* The appearance of the face, esp. when characteristic of a particular illness. **2** E18 *Science* A general aspect, appearance, or character. **b** M19 *Geology* The character of a rock formation. **c** E20 *Ecology* The characteristic set of species in a habitat.

facile princeps /ˌfasɪlɪ ˈprɪnsɛps/ *adjective & noun phrase* M19 **Latin** (= easily first). (A person who is) easily first; the acknowledged chief or leader.

facilis descensus Averni /ˌfasɪlɪs deɪˌsɛnsəs aˈvəːnʌɪ/ *noun phrase* E17 **Latin** (= easy (is) the descent to Avernus). The descent to hell is easy.

■ A quotation from Virgil's *Aeneid* (vi.126); Avernus was the name of a deep lake near Puteoli in Italy, reputed to be one of the entrances to the underworld. The subsequent lines state that the difficulty lies in retracing one's steps to the upper air; hence *facilis descensus Averni* is a metaphor for the ease with which one can slide into bad ways, with the implication that it is very hard to recover. The phrase is sometimes abbreviated to simply *facilis descensus*.

façon de parler /fasɔ̃ də parle/ *noun phrase* plural **façons de parler** (pronounced same) E19 **French** (= way of speaking). A manner of speaking; a mere phrase or formula.

façon de Venise /fasɔ̃ də vəniz/ *adjective & noun phrase* L20 **French** (= manner of Venice). (Designating) glassware made according to the technically demanding method and decorative style developed first at Venice during the later Middle Ages.

façonné /fasɔne/ *adjective & noun* (also **faconne**) plural of noun pronounced same L19 **French** (past participial adjective of *façonner* to fashion). (Designating) a fabric into which a design has been woven.

façons de parler plural of FAÇON DE PARLER.

factotum /fakˈtəʊtəm/ *noun* M16 **Medieval Latin** (from *fac* imperative of *facere* to do, make + *totum* the whole). A person who does all kinds of work; a servant or other employee who manages all the employer's affairs.

■ Originally in the now obsolete phrases *dominus factotum* or *magister factotum* (Latin = master) or *Johannes factotum* (Latin = John), now most often in the phrase *general factotum*.

fado /ˈfaduː/, /ˈfɑːdəʊ/ *noun* plural **fados** /ˈfaduːʃ/, /ˈfɑːdəʊz/ E20 **Portuguese** (literally, 'fate'). A type of popular, frequently melancholy Portuguese song and dance, with a guitar accompaniment.

faena /faˈena/ *noun* E20 **Spanish** (literally, 'task'). *Bullfighting* A series of passes made by a matador with cape and sword, preparatory to the kill.

faenza /fɑːˈɛntsə/ *noun* (also **Faenza**) M19 **Italian** (*Faenza*, city in the northern Italian province of Emilia-Romagna). (Designating) the type of decorated, tin-glazed pottery made in Faenza, especially between *c.*1450 and 1520. See also FAÏENCE.

fagotto /fa'gɔtto/, /fə'gɒtəʊ/ *noun* plural **fagotti** /fa'gɔtti/, **fagottos** /fə'gɒtəʊz/ E18 **Italian**. A bassoon.

1982 G. Jacob *Orchestral Technique* This instrument is usually designated in scores by the abbreviation Fag., its Italian name being Fagotto.

faïence /fʌɪ'ɒ̃s/, /feɪ'ɒ̃s/, /fʌɪ'ɑːns/ *noun & adjective* (also **faience**, **fayence**) L17 **French** (from Faïence, Faenza). *Ceramics* (Designating) tin-glazed pottery (MAJOLICA), usually with elaborate and colourful painted decoration, of a type originally manufactured at the northern Italian town of Faenza; *generally*, any glazed ceramic. See also FAENZA.

1980 J. Baines and J. Málek *Atlas of Ancient Egypt* [caption] Small polychrome faience tiles representing lotus flowers, probably from the temple palace of Ramesses III at Tell el-Yahudiya.

faille /feɪl/ *noun* M19 **French**. A ribbed silk fabric.

■ When originally introduced (M16) it denoted a kind of head-covering worn by women.

fainéant /'feɪneɪɒ̃/, *foreign* /fɛneɑ̃/ (*plural of noun same*) *noun & adjective* (also **faineant**) E17 **French** (from *fait* 3rd person singular of *faire* to do + *néant* nothing). **A** *noun* E17 A person who does nothing; an idler. **B** *adjective* E19 Indolent, inactive.

fainéantise /feneɑ̃tiz/, /ˌfeɪneɪɒ̃'tiːz/ *noun* (also **faineantise**) E17 **French**. The state or quality of being a FAINÉANT; inactivity.

■ Also (L19) *fainéantism(e)*.

faisandé /fəzɑ̃de/ *adjective* E20 **French** (past participle of *faisander* hang (game) until it is high). Affected, artificial; piquant, improper.

1958 *Observer* He plays the part in a *faisandé* Cockney accent straight out of Bruce Bairnsfather's Old Bill cartoons.

fait accompli /fɛt akɔ̃pli/, /ˌfeɪt ə'kɒ̃pli/, /ˌfeɪt ə'kɒmpli/ *noun phrase* plural **faits accomplis** (pronounced same) M19 **French** (= accomplished fact). A thing done and irreversible before those affected know of it.

1996 *Spectator* He [sc. Konrad Adenauer] governed . . . by a mixture of persuasion, accusation, *faits accomplis* and pressure.

faits divers /ˌfeɪt diː'vɛː/ *noun phrase plural* L20 **French** (literally, 'sundry facts'). Short news items, usually trivial in character.

1993 *New Yorker* The month of June, 1993, was a good one for those who scrutinize the *faits divers* for clues to this nation's moral state.

faja /'faxa/ *noun* M19 **Spanish** (cf. FAJITA). A sash.

fajita /fə'hiːtə/, *foreign* /fa'xita/ *noun* plural **fajitas** /fə'hiːtəz/, *foreign* /fa'xitas/ L20 **Mexican Spanish** (literally, 'little belt'). *Cookery* A small strip of grilled spiced beef or chicken; *plural* a dish made by rolling such strips of meat in a tortilla with vegetables, grated cheese, and other garnishings, topped with sour cream.

faki /'feɪki/, /'faki/ *noun* L16 **Arabic**. An expert in Islamic law; in parts of Africa, a teacher in a Koran school.

■ Not to be confused with FAKIR.

fakir /'feɪkɪə/; *in sense 1 also* /'fakɪə/ *noun* (also formerly **faquir**) E17 **Arabic** (= poor (man); partly through French *faquir*). **1** E17 A Muslim (or *loosely* Hindu) religious mendicant or ascetic. **2** L19 A faker. *United States* (by popular etymology).

falafel /fə'lɑːf(ə)l/ *noun* (also **felafel**) plural same M20 **Arabic** (colloquial Egyptian). *Cookery* A small ball of spiced minced pulses, fried and usually eaten in bread.

falsetto /fɔːl'sɛtəʊ/, /fɒl'sɛtəʊ/ *noun & adjective* L18 **Italian**. *Music* **A** *noun* L18 A voice pitched above its natural register; also, a person who sings in such a voice. **B** *attributive* or as *adjective* E19 Above the natural register; high-pitched.

falsobordone /ˌfalsobor'doːne/ *noun* (also **falso bordone**) plural **falsobordoni** /ˌfalsobor'doːni/ M18 **Italian** (from *falso* false + bordone BOURDON; cf. French FAUXBOURDON). *Music* A technique of singing psalms in harmony, following simple chord progressions.

famille de robe /famij də rɔb/ *noun phrase* plural **familles de robe** (pronounced same) M19 **French** (literally, 'family of the robe'). In France: a family with a legal tradition or one founded by a lawyer.

famille jaune /famij ʒon/ *noun phrase* L19 **French** (literally, 'yellow family'). A type of Chinese enamelled porcelain of which the predominant colour is yellow, dating from the eighteenth century.

famille noire /famij nwar/ *noun phrase* L19 **French** (literally, 'black family'). A type of Chinese enamelled porcelain of which the predominant colour is black, dating from the eighteenth century.

famille rose /famij roz/ *noun phrase* L19 **French** (literally, 'pink family'). A type of Chinese enamelled porcelain of which the predominant colour is pink, dating from the reign of Yongzheng (1723–35).

famille verte /famij vɛrt/ *noun phrase* L19 **French** (literally, 'green family'). A type of Chinese enamelled porcelain of which the predominant colour is green, dating from the reign of Kangxi (1662–1722).

famulus /'famjʊləs/ *noun* plural **famuli** /'famjʊlʌɪ/, /'famjʊliː/ L19 **Latin** (= servant). A servant, especially a youth attendant upon a scholar or magician.

fana /fə'nɑː/ *noun* M19 **Arabic** (= annihilation). *Islam* In Sufism, the obliteration of all human concerns and of consciousness of self and their replacement by pure consciousness of God.

fandango /fan'daŋgəʊ/ *noun* plural **fandangos** or **fandangoes** M18 **Spanish**. A lively Spanish dance for two in 3/4 or 6/8 time, usually accompanied by guitars and castanets; a piece of music for this dance.

fanfaronade /ˌfanfarə'neɪd/, /ˌfanfarə'nɑːd/ *noun* (also **fanfaronnade**) M17 **French** (*fanfaronnade* from *fanfaron* a braggart). Ostentation; arrogant, swaggering talk; bluster.

fantaisiste /ˌfantə'ziːst/ *noun* E20 **French**. A person who indulges in extravagant fancies, especially an artist who creates elaborately fantastic works of art.

fantasia /fan'teɪzɪə/, /fantə'ziːə/ *noun* E18 **Italian**. A musical or other composition in which form is comparatively unimportant; a piece of music based on a familiar tune or tunes.

fantoccini /ˌfantot'ʧiːni/, /ˌfantə'ʧiːni/ *noun* L18 **Italian** (plural of *fantoccino*, diminutive of *fantoccio* puppet, from *fante* boy). **1** L18 *plural* Mechanically worked puppets; marionettes. **2** L18 *singular* A marionette show.

faquir variant of FAKIR.

farandole /ˌfar(ə)n'dəʊl/, /'far(ə)ndəʊl/ *noun* M19 **French** (from modern Provençal *farandoulo*. A lively Provençal communal dance, usually in 6/8 time; a piece of music for this dance.

farce /fɑːs/ *noun* E18 **French**. *Cookery* Forcemeat, stuffing.

■ In medieval cookbooks the word appears in the form *fars*. It was reintroduced into English in its modern form in Richard Bradley's *Family Dictionary* (1725), which was a translation of Chomel's *Dictionaire oeconomique*.

farceur /farsœr/ (*plural same*), /fɑː'səː/ *noun* (feminine **farceuse**) plural pronounced same L17 **French**. **1** L17 A joker or buffoon; someone who is not to be taken seriously. **2** L19 A writer or actor of farces.

2 1996 *Country Life* . . . it is more than a little odd for British culture to be represented by a detective writer, an actor-producer, a TV mogul, a violinist and a Whitehall *farceur*.

farci /fɑː'si/ *adjective* M20 **French** (from *farcir* to stuff. *Cookery* Stuffed; filled with forcemeat.

■ Always used postpositively.

farfalle /'farfɑlle/ *noun plural* L20 **Italian** (plural of *farfalla* butterfly). Pasta in the form of butterflies.

farfel /'fɑːf(ə)l/ *noun* (also **farfal**, **ferfel**) plural same or **farfels** L19 **Yiddish** (*farfal*, *farfil*, *ferfel* (*plural*), from Middle High German *varveln* noodles, noodle soup). *Cookery* Ground or granulated noodle dough; in *plural* granules of this.

far niente /ˌfar nɪ'ɛnte/ *noun phrase* E19 **Italian** (= doing nothing). Idleness; DOLCE FAR NIENTE.

farouche /fə'ruːʃ/ *adjective* M18 **French** (ultimately from Latin *foras* out-of-doors). Unused to company; sullen, shy, ill at ease.

1996 *Country Life* The farouche and unintentionally dangerous colt . . . has become a biddable, lovable and, when handled firmly, quite gentle creature.

farrago /fə'rɑːgəʊ/, /fə'reɪgəʊ/ *noun* plural **farragos**, (chiefly United States) **farragoes** M17 **Latin** (= mixed fodder for cattle, hence *figurative*, a medley). A jumble; a hotchpotch; a confused situation.

1995 *Spectator* Only one man, in this entire farrago, appears to have been corrupt in the word's fullest sense, in that he broke the law for the sake of personal financial gain.

farrash /fə'raʃ/ *noun* (also **ferash**) E17 **Persian and Urdu** (*farrāš* from Arabic = a person who spreads out bedding, carpets, etc.). A servant in some Muslim countries, especially one who performs heavy domestic tasks.

farruca /fə'ruːkə/ *noun* E20 **Spanish** (feminine of *farruco* Galician or Asturian, from *Farruco* pet form of male forename *Francisco*). A type of flamenco dance.

fartlek /ˈfɑːtlɛk/ *noun* M20 **Swedish** (from *fart* speed + *lek* play). A method of training used by middle- and long-distance runners, alternating fast and slow work in a run across country.

fasces /ˈfasiːz/ *noun plural* L16 **Latin** (plural of *fascis* bundle). **1** L16 In ancient Rome, rods tied in a bundle with an axe, carried before the leading magistrates as a symbol of power. **2** E17 (Emblems of) power or authority.

2 1996 *Times* And our VIPs are at heart no more eager than the Italians to give up their fasces of authority.

Fasching /ˈfaʃɪŋ/ *noun* E20 **German**. In southern Germany and Austria: the carnival season extending from Epiphany to Shrove Tuesday; a carnival.

fascia /ˈfaʃɪə/, /ˈfeɪʃɪə/, /ˈfaʃə/ *noun* (also (senses 4, 5) **facia**) plural **fasciae** /ˈfeɪʃɪiː/, **fascias** M16 **Latin** (= band, fillet, casing of a door, etc.). **1** M16 *Architecture* A horizontal band of wood, brick, etc., esp. as used in an architrave. **2** E18 Any object, or arrangement of objects, that gives the appearance of a stripe or band, **3** L18 *Anatomy* Connective tissue; a thin sheet of this enclosing a muscle or other organ. **4** E20 The board or strip over a shop front on which is written the trader's name and line of business. **5** E20 The instrument panel of a motor vehicle; dashboard.

fata morgana /ˌfɑːtə mɔːˈgɑːnə/ *noun* E19 **Italian** (= fairy Morgan (Morgan le Fay)). A kind of mirage often seen in the Strait of Messina between Italy and Sicily, formerly attributed to supernatural agency; an illusion.

■ According to the northern European Arthurian legends, Morgan le Fay was the sister of Britain's King Arthur and possessed magical powers. Her legend was taken to Sicily by the Normans when they conquered the island in the eleventh century.

fatwa /ˈfatwɑː/ *noun* (also **Fatwa**, **fetwa**, or **fatwah**) E17 **Arabic**. A ruling on a point of Islamic law given by a Muslim religious expert (MUFTI).

■ Although it was first used in English in the seventeenth century (in the form *fetfa*), the word came into general currency in the English-language media after February 1989, when Ayatollah Khomeini of Iran issued a *fatwa* condemning the Indian-born British writer Salman Rushdie and his publishers to death on account of Rushdie's novel *The Satanic Verses* (1988), which many Muslims held to be blasphemous and deeply objectionable in its treatment of the Koran. Because of the circumstances of the *fatwa* on Rushdie, the word is sometimes wrongly thought to mean 'a death sentence'. Since its revitalization in English, *fatwa* has moved far beyond its original Islamic context and is often used figuratively to indicate any strong denunciation (see quotation 1995).

1989 *Bookseller* The . . . International Committee . . . have capitalized on the outrage felt at the notorious *fatwa* to drive forward . . . the long-nurtured campaign for total abolition of blasphemy laws in this country.
1989 *Independent* This Fatwa . . . was written and signed by the Grand Ayatollah of Shia in Iraq, explaining his position regarding the executions of 16 Kuwaiti Pilgrims . . .
1995 *Times* That the bishops should choose to intone on a subject as morally trivial as the lottery is itself indicative of that order of priorities which so often flummoxes the Christian on the Clapham omnibus. *Fatwas* against the lottery reveal once more the confusion.

faubourg /fobur/ (*plural same*), /ˈfəʊbʊəg/ *noun* L15 **French** (cf. medieval Latin *falsus burgus* not the city proper). A suburb, especially a suburb of Paris; formerly that part of a town or city lying just outside the walls.

fauna /ˈfɔːnə/ *noun* plural **faunae** /ˈfɔːniː/, **faunas** L18 **Modern Latin** (application of *Fauna*, an ancient Italian rural goddess, sister of the god *Faunus*, who was equated with the Greek god Pan). **1** *collective singular and in plural* L18 The animals and animal life of a particular area, habitat, or epoch; cf. FLORA. **2** L19 A list of or treatise on these.

faute de mieux /fot də mjø/ *adjective & adverb phrase* M18 **French**. (Used or done) only for want of a more satisfactory alternative.

1995 *Times* The dinner party is dead. Enter, *faute de mieux*, the age of the supper party.

fauteuil /fotœj/ *noun* plural pronounced same M18 **French**. An armchair; hence, any seat, especially one in a theatre, resembling an armchair.

fauve /fəʊv/ *noun & adjective* (also **Fauve**) plural pronounced same E20 **French** (literally, 'wild animal'). **A** *noun* E20 An adherent of fauvism, a style of painting notable for its use of brilliant colour, originating in the early twentieth century with the work of Henri Matisse (1869–1954) and his followers; a fauvist(e). **B** *adjective* M20

Of or pertaining to fauvism(e) or fauvist(e)s.

■ The term was coined by the French art critic Louis Vauxcelles at the Autumn Salon in Paris in 1905, who, seeing a traditional Renaissance-type statue exhibited amidst the works of Matisse and his adherents, exclaimed, *'Donatello au milieu des fauves!'*

1984 A. G. Lehmann *The European Heritage* Matisse, even if called a '*fauve*', can convey a wonderful serenity . . .

fauvisme, fauviste see under FAUVE.

faux /fəʊ/ *adjective* L20 **French** (= false). *Fashion* and *Interior design* Imitation, fake.

■ Also *faux-* as first element in combinations, as in *faux-soul, faux-painted*, etc.

1993 W. Self *My Idea of Fun* I ran the length of the new hallway, with its Wilton carpeting, faux hunting prints and brocaded wallpaper. *transferred* **1996** *Spectator* The *faux* egalitarianism of Gap matches the *faux* illusion of the age of Clinton.

faux amis /ˌfəʊz 'əmi:/ *noun phrase plural* M20 **French** (literally, 'false friends'). Pairs of words in two different languages (especially French and English) that appear the same but which have entirely different meanings.

■ The term derives from *Les Faux Amis ou les Trahisons du vocabulaire anglais*, the title of a book with a collection of such terms made in 1928 by M. Koessler and J. Derocquigny. An example is English *defiance* and French *défiance* 'distrust'.

faux bonhomme /fo bɔnɔm/ *noun phrase* (also **faux-bonhomme**) plural **faux bonshommes** /fo bɔ̃zɔm/ E20 **French** (= false good-natured man). A malicious or devious person who pretends to be openhearted and good-natured.

faux-bourdon /foburdɔ̃/ *noun* plural pronounced same L19 **French** (= faburden, literally, 'false hum'). A type of improvised polyphony, popular in England from the fifteenth to the mid sixteenth century.

faux marbre /ˌfo 'marbrə/ *noun phrase* L20 **French** (= false marble). *Interior design* Fake marble; a finish imitating marble.

faux-naïf /fonaif/, /ˌfəʊnʌɪ'i:f/ *noun & adjective* (also **faux-naif**) plural pronounced same M20 **French** (from *faux* false + *naïf* ingenuous). **A** *noun* M20 A person who pretends to be naive. **B** *adjective* M20 Of a work of art, self-consciously or meretriciously simple; of a person, self-consciously artless.

1996 *Times* When she attempts the old, cheerful faux-naïf trick, it doesn't work.

faux pas /fo pa/, /fəʊ 'pɑ:/ *noun phrase* plural same L17 **French** (from *faux* false + *pas* step). An act that offends against social convention; an indiscreet remark or action; a slip.

1995 *Times* I never gave formal dinner parties and never liked them with their implications that they were to do with somehow showing off at the same time as being a minefield of *faux pas*.

favela /fa'vela/ *noun* M20 **Portuguese**. In Brazil: a shack or shanty.

■ Usually in plural *favelas* 'a slum'.

1961 G. Mikes *Tango* In the midst of all this beauty and elegance, you discover the *favelas* . . . A *favela* is a wretched, ramshackle, filthy hut run up out of sticks, rotting planks, dirty rags and cardboard, as a rule in less than twenty-four hours.

favelado /ˌfavə'lɑ:dəʊ/ *noun* M20 **Portuguese**. A person who lives in a FAVELA.

1961 G. Mikes *Tango* The *favelas* have no electricity (unless, as frequently happens, an enterprising favelado manages to tap an electric cable).

fazenda /fə'zɛndə/ *noun* E19 **Portuguese**. In Portugal, Brazil, and Portuguese-speaking countries: a large farm or estate; the homestead belonging to such an estate.

■ The equivalent in Spanish-speaking countries is a HACIENDA.

fazendeiro /ˌfazɛn'dɛ:rəʊ/ *noun* E19 **Portuguese**. A person who owns or lives on a FAZENDA.

fec. abbreviation of FECIT.

fecit /'feɪkɪt/ *verb & noun* 19 **Latin** (3rd person perfect singular of *facere* to make). *Art* (A statement:) he (or she) made (it).

■ Always preceded by a personal name, *fecit* is found inscribed on works of art. *Pinxit* 'he (or she) painted (it)' and *sculpsit* 'he (or she) sculpted (it)' are more specific alternatives. *Fecit* is sometimes abbreviated to *fec.*

fedai /fə'dɑ:i:/ *noun* plural (in sense 1) same, **fedais**; (in sense 2) **fedayeen** /ˌfɛdʌɪ'ji:n/ L19 **Arabic** ((or Persian) = one who sacrifices his life for another, from *fada* ransom). **1** L19 An assassin belonging to the Muslim Ismaili sect. **2** M20 (*in plural*) Guerrillas in Arab Muslim countries, especially Arab guerrillas operating against the Israelis.

feijão /feɪ'(d)ʒãu:/ *noun* M19 **Portuguese** (from Latin *phaseolus* bean). Any edible bean; especially a variety of haricot bean

(*Phaseolus vulgaris*) used as a staple item of diet in Brazil.

feijoada /feɪ'(d)ʒwada/, /feɪ'(d)ʒwadə/ *noun* M20 **Portuguese** (from FEIJÃO). A Brazilian stew made with black beans, pork, and sausage and served with rice.

feis /fɛʃ/, /feɪʃ/ *noun* (in sense 1 also **fes(s)**) plural **feiseanna** /fɛʃənə/ L18 **Irish** (= wedding feast, festival). **1** L18 An assembly of kings and chieftains, formerly believed to be a kind of early Celtic parliament. **2** L19 An Irish or Scottish arts festival, similar to the Welsh EISTEDDFOD.

felafel variant of FALAFEL.

feldgrau /'fɛltgraʊ/ *noun & adjective* M20 **German** (= field-grey). (Of) a dark grey; hence, a German soldier in a uniform of this colour.

feldsher /'fɛldʃə/ *noun* (also **feldscher**) L19 **Russian** (*fel'dsher* from German *Feldscher* a field surgeon). In Russia and the former USSR: a person with practical training in medicine and surgery, but lacking professional medical qualifications; an assistant to a physician or surgeon; a medical auxiliary.

felix culpa /ˌfiːlɪks 'kʌlpə/, /ˌfeɪlɪks 'kʊlpɑː/ *noun phrase* M20 **Latin** (literally, 'happy fault'). *Theology* The Fall of Man through the sin of Adam understood as having the blessed outcome of the redemption of mankind by Jesus Christ; *transferred* any fault or disaster with ultimately beneficial consequences.

■ The phrase is taken from the Exultet, which forms part of the Roman Catholic liturgy for Holy Saturday (Easter Eve).

1987 D. Hall *Seasons at Eagle Pond* And, *felix culpa*, Fall is the most beautiful season—at least in New Hampshire.

fellah /'fɛlə/ *noun* plural **fellaheen, fellahin** /'fɛləhiːn/, **fellahs** M18 **Arabic** (*fallah* colloquial plural *fallahin* tiller of the soil). A peasant in Egypt and other Arabic-speaking countries.

felo de se /ˌfiːləʊ dɪ 'siː/, /ˌfɛləʊ də 'seɪ/ *noun phrase* plural **felones de se** /fɪˌləʊniːz dɪ 'siː/, **felos de se** /ˌfɛləʊz də 'seɪ/ E17 **(Anglo-)Latin** (literally, 'felon of himself'). **1** E17 A person who commits suicide (formerly in the UK a criminal act) or intentionally brings about his or her own death. **2** L18 Suicide.

felsenmeer /'fɛlzənmiːr/ *noun* plural **felsenmeere** /'fɛlzənmiːrə/ E20 **German** (literally, 'rock-sea'). *Physical Geography* An expanse of angular, frost-riven rocks which may develop on level terrain in arctic or alpine climates; a boulder-field.

felucca /fɛ'lʌkə/ *noun* E17 **Italian** (*feluc(c)a* perhaps from an Arabic word via Spanish). A small sailing vessel with lateen sails and oars, formerly widely used in the Mediterranean area and still used on the River Nile.

feme covert /fiːm 'kʌvət/ *noun phrase* (also **femme couverte**) plural **femes coverts** (pronounced same) M16 **Old French**. *Law* A married woman.

■ The technical spelling is *feme*, but the Modern French *femme* is also found.

feme sole /fiːm 'səʊl/ *noun phrase* plural **femes soles** (pronounced same) M16 **Old French**. *Law* An unmarried woman, especially a divorcée; *historical* a married woman who carries on a business in her own right, independently of her husband.

femme couverte see FEME COVERT.

femme de chambre /fam də ʃɑ̃br/, /ˌfɛm də 'ʃɑːmbrə/ *noun phrase* plural **femmes de chambre** (pronounced same) M18 **French** (literally, 'woman of the (bed-)room'). **1** M18 A lady's maid. **2** E19 A chambermaid.

femme de ménage /fam də menaʒ/, /ˌfɛm də meɪ'nɑːʒ/ *noun phrase* (also **femme de menage**) plural **femmes de ménage** (pronounced same) L19 **French** (literally, 'woman of the household'). A domestic help; a charwoman.

femme de trent ans /fam də trɑ̃t ɑ̃/ *noun phrase* plural **femmes de trent ans** (pronounced same) **French** (literally, 'a woman of thirty'). A woman who has passed the age at which romantic affairs are easily enjoyed.

■ The phrase alludes to the title of a novel published by Balzac in 1834.

femme du monde /fam dy mɔd/, /ˌfɛm duː 'mɒnd/ *noun phrase* plural **femmes du monde** (pronounced same) L19 **French**. A woman of the world; a sophisticated woman.

femme fatale /fam fatal/, /ˌfɛm fa'tɑːl/ *noun phrase* plural **femmes fatales** (pronounced same) E20 **French** (literally, 'fatal woman'). A dangerously or irresistibly attractive woman.

1995 *Big Issue* Furthermore, the entrance of the femme fatale—embodied by such cat-like sirens as Lauren Bacall and Barbara Stanwyck—exposed male fears of the newly empowered woman . . .

femme incomprise /fɛm ɛ̃kɔ̃priz/ *noun phrase* plural **femmes incomprises** /fɛmz ɛ̃kɔ̃priz/ M19 French. A woman who is misunderstood or unappreciated.

femme savante /fam savɑ̃t/ *noun phrase* plural **femmes savantes** (pronounced same) L19 French. A learned woman.

■ Usually with an implied derogatory allusion to Molière's play *Les Femmes savantes* (1672).

1995 *Times* If the noble art of painting refused to lower itself to the caricaturist's level, it could simply, and decorously, choose to ignore the phenomenon of the *femme savante*.

fenestella /fɛnɪˈstɛlə/ *noun* LME Latin (diminutive of *fenestra* window). **1** LME *Architecture* A small opening in a wall, especially one in the side of an altar that enables relics inside to be seen. **2** L18 A niche in an interior wall of a church, usually on the south side of the altar and containing the PISCINA.

feng-shui /ˌfɛŋ ˈʃuːi/, /ˌfʌŋ ˈʃuːi/ *noun* L18 Chinese (from *feng* wind + *shui* water). *Chinese Mythology* A system of spirit influences, both benign and malignant, which inhabit the natural features of the landscape; a kind of geomancy for dealing with these spirits, employed particularly when selecting the site for a dwelling or a grave.

ferae naturae /ˌfɪəriː nəˈtʃʊəriː/, /ˌfɛrʌɪ nə ˈtʃʊərʌɪ/ *predicative & postpositive adjective & noun phrase* M17 Latin (= of wild nature). Chiefly *Law* Undomesticated or wild (animals).

ferash variant of FARRASH.

fer-de-lance /ˌfɛː də ˈlɑːns/ *noun* plural **fers-de-lance** (pronounced same), fer-de-lances L19 French (= iron (head) of lance). A highly venomous tropical American pit viper, *Bothrops atrox*.

ferfel variant of FARFEL.

feria /ˈfɪərɪə/, /ˈfɛrɪə/ *noun* LME Latin (= holiday; in sense 2 through Spanish). **1** LME *Ecclesiastical* A weekday, especially one on which no festival falls. **2** M19 In Spain and Spanish-speaking countries: a fair.

2 1996 *Spectator* . . . live television coverage of the [bull]fights at the major *ferias* has become commonplace.

fermata /fəːˈmɑːtə/ *noun* plural **fermatas**, **fermate** /fəːˈmɑːteɪ/ L19 Italian. *Music* (A sign indicating) an unspecified prolongation of a note or rest.

ferme ornée see under ORNÉ.

ferronnerie /fɛrɔnri/, /fɛˈrɒnəri/ *noun & adjective* (also **ferronerie**) E20 French (= (wrought) iron work). (Designating) decoration with motifs of arabesques and scrolls as used in wrought iron work.

ferronnière /fɛrɔnjɛr/ (*plural same*), /fɛ ˌrɒnɪˈɛː/ *noun* (also **ferronière**) M19 French (literally, 'blacksmith's wife'; a frontlet). A piece of jewellery comprising a decorative chain worn around the head with a pendant on the centre of the forehead; a frontlet.

■ The name derives from Leonardo da Vinci's portrait known as *La Belle Ferronnière*, which shows a woman wearing this sort of ornament.

fest /fɛst/ *noun* (also **Fest**) M19 German (= festival). A special occasion; a celebration, a celebratory gathering.

■ Originally United States, it is chiefly used as the second element in a combination, as in *filmfest*, *gabfest* (a gathering for talk; a conference), *glamfest* (= glamourfest), *songfest*, *talkfest*, etc.

1995 *Times* The elegance of the *ancien régime* is taken further in M Saint Laurent's own office, a glamfest of mirrors, gilt and velvet.

1995 *Times* By dawn the *mediafest* which had been gathering outside Westminster on College Green was already setting up its cameras.

festina lente /fɛsˈtiːnə ˌlɛnteɪ/ *interjection & noun phrase* L17 Latin (= make haste slowly (imperative singular of *festinare* to hasten + *lente* slowly)). (An expression) urging caution; more haste, less speed!

■ According to Suetonius (*Life of Augustus Caesar* xxv), the Greek form of this tag was a favourite with Augustus with reference to military operations and the qualities he looked for in a commnader.

1996 *Times* Why so long? Must *festina lente* always be the exchange's watchword?

Festschrift /ˈfɛs(t)ʃrɪft/ *noun* (also **festschrift**) plural **Festschriften** /ˈfɛs(t)ʃrɪftən/, **Festschrifts** E20 German (literally, 'celebration-writing'). A volume of writings collected in honour of a scholar, usually presented to mark an occasion in his or her life.

1994 W. D. Hackmann and A. J. Turner *Learning, Language and Invention* The mere existence of a *festschrift* is evidence of esteem for its recipient as it is for his stature in his profession.

figurative **1995** *Spectator* Charm is an underrated quality in public life, as is humour. Goodman had both, as this week's *festschrift* of Goodman stories has indicated.

feta /'fɛtə/ *noun* (also **fetta**) M20 **Modern Greek**. A white salty ewe's milk cheese originally made in Greece.

figurative **1996** *Economist* He should get on well with New York's big fettas, whom he will entertain in the archdiocese's grand building off Fifth Avenue.

fête /feɪt/, /fɛt/ *noun & verb* (also **fete**) LME **French** (from Old French *feste*). **A** *noun* **1** LME A festival, a fair. **2** L19 A sale or bazaar, often held out of doors, with the object of raising money for charity. **3** E19 A saint's day, a religious festival. **B** *transitive verb* E17 Entertain (a person) with a fête or feast, make much of (a person); give a fête in honour of.

fête champêtre /fɛt ʃɑ̃pɛtr/ *noun phrase* plural **fêtes champêtres** (pronounced same) L18 **French** (= a rural fête). An outdoor or pastoral entertainment, a rural festival.

1996 *Spectator* . . . no one before had painted prostitutes instead of goddesses, drunks and urban café scenes in the place of *fêtes champêtres*.

fête galante /fɛt galɑ̃t/ *noun phrase* plural **fêtes galantes** (pronounced same) E20 **French**. A rural entertainment, especially as depicted in an eighteenth-century French genre of painting, a fête champêtre; a painting in this genre.

■ The subject matter of young ladies and gentlemen in elaborate or theatrical dress making music, flirting, and dancing in Arcadian surroundings is particularly associated with Jean Antoine Watteau (1684–1721).

1996 *Country Life* It is surprising that rather than call on the talents of the two great animal painters Oudry and Desportes, the artists chosen were history painters or painters of *fêtes galantes*.

fêtes champêtres, **fêtes galantes** plural of FÊTE CHAMPÊTRE, FÊTE GALANTE.

fetta variant of FETA.

fettucine /fɛtʊ'tʃiːni/ *noun plural* (also **fettucine**) E20 **Italian** (plural of *fettuccina*, diminutive of *fetta* slice, ribbon). *Cookery* Pasta in the form of ribbons; an Italian dish consisting mainly of this, usually with a sauce.

fetus see FOETUS.

fetwa variant of FATWA.

feu /fø/ *adjective* E19 **French**. Of a person: deceased, late.

feu d'artifice /fø dartifis/ *noun phrase* plural **feux d'artifice** (pronounced same) L17 **French** (literally, 'fire of artifice'). A firework show; a firework.

feu de joie /fø də ʒwa/ *noun phrase* plural **feux de joie** (pronounced same) E17 **French** (literally, 'fire of joy'). **1** E18 A ceremonial or celebratory salute fired with rifles or other small arms. **2** M17 *figurative* A joyful occasion; a celebration.

feu follet /fø fɔlɛ/ *noun phrase* plural **feux follets** (pronounced same) M19 **French** (literally, 'frolicsome fire'). A will-o'-the-wisp, an IGNIS FATUUS. Usually *figurative*.

feuillemorte /fœjmɔrt/ *adjective* L16 **French** (= dead leaf). Of the colour of a dead leaf; yellowish brown.

feuilleton /'fəːɪtɒ̃/, *foreign* /fœjtɔ̃/ *noun* M19 **French** (from *feuillet*, diminutive of *feuille* leaf). A section of a newspaper etc. devoted to) fiction, criticism, light reading, etc.; an article or story suitable for or printed in that section.

fez /fɛz/ *noun* plural **fezzes** E19 **Turkish** (*fes*, perhaps through French *fez*). A flat-topped conical brimless red hat with a tassel, worn by men in some Muslim countries.

■ Named after *Fez* (now *Fès*) in Morocco, once the principal place of manufacture, the fez was the national headgear of the Turks until the reforms of Kemal Atatürk in the 1920s.

ff abbreviation of FORTISSIMO (*musical direction*).

fiancé /fɪ'ɒnseɪ/, /fɪ'ɑːnseɪ/, /fɪ'ɒ̃seɪ/ *noun* (feminine **fiancée**) M19 **French** (from (Old) French *fiancer* to betroth). A man engaged to be married; the person to whom one is engaged.

fianchetto /fɪən'tʃɛtəʊ/, /fɪən'kɛtəʊ/ *noun & verb* M19 **Italian** (diminutive of *fianco* flank). *Chess* **A** *noun* plural **fianchettoes** M19 The development of a bishop by moving it one square to a long diagonal of the board. **B** *transitive verb* E20 Develop (a bishop) in this way.

fiasco /fɪ'askəʊ/ *noun* plural **fiascos** M19 **Italian** (from phrase *far fiasco*, literally, 'make a bottle'). A complete and ignominious failure, originally of a theatrical or musical performance; an ignominious outcome.

■ The allusion in the Italian phrase is unexplained.

fiat /'fʌɪat/ *noun & verb* LME **Latin** (3rd person singular present subjunctive of *fieri* = let it be done, let there be made). **A** *noun*

1 LME A formal authorization for a proposed arrangement, etc.; generally, any authoritative pronouncement, decree. **2** L16 A command by which something is brought into being. **B** *transitive verb* M19 Sanction by (official) pronouncement.

■ In sense A.2 *fiat* is short for or an allusion to *fiat lux* = let there be light (Vulgate Genesis 1:3).

ficelle /fisɛl/ (*plural same*), /fɪ'sɛl/ *noun* L19 **French** (= string). **1** L19 The off-white colour of undyed string. **2** L19 A (stage) device, an artifice.

■ In sense 1 *ficelle* is used only attributively or in combination as *ficelle-colour(ed)*.

2 1968 *Listener* No Pucelle, Candy's a ficelle; and . . . her fate is to be briefly grabbed by a series of stereotypes.

fiche /fiʃ/ (*plural same*), /fi:ʃ/ *noun* M20 **French** (short for *fiche de voyageur*). The registration form on which foreign guests must record details of passport etc. when booking into a French hotel.

fichu /'fi:ʃu:/ *noun* M18 **French** (origin unknown). A triangular piece of lace or fine fabric worn by women round the neck or shoulders, and formerly also over the head.

fidalgo /fɪ'dalgəʊ/ *noun* plural **fidalgos** M17 **Portuguese** (contraction of *filho de algo* son of something). A Portuguese nobleman.

■ The word is now obsolete except when used historically; cf. HIDALGO.

fides Punica /ˌfɪdeɪs 'pju:nɪkə/ *noun phrase* (also **Punica fides**) 19 **Latin** (literally, 'Punic faith'). Treachery.

■ The phrase *Punica fide* 'with Punic (i.e. Carthaginian) faith' occurs in Sallust *Jugurthine War* cviii. It is one of several tags expressing the deep Roman distrust of the Carthaginians, their deadly rivals for control of the Mediterranean world during the initial phase of Roman overseas expansion in the third and second centuries BC.

fidus Achates /ˌfʌɪdəs ə'keɪti:z/ *noun phrase* L16 **Latin** (= faithful Achates). A trusted friend.

■ Quotation from Virgil *Aeneid* vi.158. Achates was the loyal and trusted companion of the poem's hero, Aeneas.

fiesta /fɪ'ɛstə/ *noun* M19 **Spanish** (= feast). In Spain or Spanish America: a religious festival; *generally*, any festivity or holiday.

figura /fɪ'gjʊərə/ *noun* plural **figurae** /fɪ'gjʊəri:/ M20 **Latin** (= figure). **1** M20 *Theology* A type of a person. **2** M20 In literary use, a person who represents a higher or supervening reality. **b** An act that is representative or symbolic.

figurant /figyrɑ̃/ (*plural same*), /'fɪgjʊr(ə)nt/ *noun* (feminine **figurante**) L18 **French** (present participial adjective of *figurer* to figure). A supernumerary actor with a walk-on role in a theatrical performance.

■ A *figurant* was originally a ballet dancer; in the context of ballet now the term usually denotes a non-dancing performer with a supporting role.

filé /'fi:leɪ/ *noun* M19 **French** (past participle of *filer* twist). In the United States: powdered or pounded sassafras leaves used to flavour and thicken soup, especially gumbo.

■ Earliest use in *gumbo filé*.

1996 *Times Magazine* If you can get powdered *file*, so much the better. This dried and powdered sassafras is what gives the gumbo its thick and shiny texture.

filet /'fi:leɪ/, /fɪlɪt/, *foreign* /filɛ/ (*plural same*) *noun* L19 **French** (= net). A kind of net or lace with a square mesh.

filet de boeuf /ˌfi:leɪ də 'bə:f/, *foreign* /filɛ də bœf/ *noun phrase* M19 **French**. *Cookery* A fillet of beef; *United States* a tenderloin.

filet mignon /ˌfi:leɪ 'mi:njɒ̃/, *foreign* /filɛ miɲɔ̃/ *noun phrase* plural **filet mignons** (pronounced same) E20 **French** (= small fillet). *Cookery* A slice cut from the small end of a fillet of beef.

1995 *Times* Succulent as *filet mignon* but low in fat and cholesterol . . .

filioque /fɪlɪ'əʊkweɪ/ *noun* (also **Filioque**) M19 **Latin** (= and from the Son). *Christian Church* The statement in the Nicene Creed that the Holy Spirit proceeds not only from God the Father but also from the Son.

■ *Filioque* appeared as an addition to the Creed in the Western Church in the sixth century, possibly originating in Spain. It gradually became a source of contention between the theologians of Rome and Constantinople, since it was accepted in the West but rejected by the Eastern Orthodox Churches. After the failure of attempts to resolve the issue in the period immediately before the conquest of Constantinople by the Ottoman Turks, it remains an issue between Eastern and Western Christendom.

filius nullius /ˌfɪlɪəs 'nʊlɪəs/ *noun phrase* plural **filii nullius** /ˌfɪlɪi: 'nʊlɪəs/ M20 **Latin**

(= son of nobody). An illegitimate son whose paternity is unacknowledged.

1963 S. M. Brewer *Design for a Gentleman* [Lord Chesterfield's] natural son by Elisabeth du Bouchet . . . was in law *filius nullius* (nobody's son) and was in fact utterly dependent upon his father for everything.

fille de joie /fij də ʒwa/ *noun phrase* plural **filles de joie** (pronounced same) E18 **French** (literally, 'girl of pleasure'). A prostitute.

fillette /fijɛt/ *noun* plural pronounced same M19 **French**. A young girl.

film noir /film nwar/, /fɪlm 'nwɑː/ *noun phrase* plural **films noirs** (pronounced same) M20 **French** (literally, 'black film'). A genre of cinematographic film of a pessimistic, cynical, and sombre character; a film of this type.

■ The typical *film noir* was a black-and-white Hollywood movie of the late 1940s or early 1950s with gloomy lighting, a menacing urban setting, and a fatalistic loner as the anti-hero. The phrase is sometimes abbreviated to simply *noir*, with examples of the revival of the genre in the 1990s being dubbed *neo noir*.

1995 *Big Issue* Film noir was a particular, time-specific genre, a shock antidote to the Technicolor musicals and 'aw-shucks' family dramas that dominated Forties Hollywood.

filo /'fiːləʊ/ *noun* (also **phyllo**) M20 **Modern Greek** (*phullo* leaf). Dough that can be stretched into very thin sheets and layered; pastry made from this dough and used in sweet and savoury pastries.

fils /fis/ *noun* L19 **French** (= the son). The son, the younger, junior.

■ *Fils* is appended to a name to distinguish between father and son of the same name; cf. PÈRE.

1996 *Bookseller* Amis *fils* was believed to have been unhappy about the . . . serialisation of a diary Mr Jacobs had kept of his last meetings with Amis *père*.

filtre /filtr/ *noun* plural pronounced same M20 **French**. A filtering appliance for making coffee, which allows boiling water to pass through ground coffee beans into a cup or pot; coffee made by this method.

1940 'M. Innes' *Secret Vanguard* Orchard was . . . measuring coffee into a *filtre*.

fin (de) see FIN DE SIÈCLE.

finale /fɪ'nɑːli/ *noun* M18 **Italian** (use as noun of adjective from Latin *finalis* from *finis* end). **1** M18 The closing section of a musical, operatic, or dramatic performance. **2** L18 The conclusion.

1 **1996** *Country Life* By now, the orchestra in the pit had reached its finale, rending the air with thundering timpani.

finca /'fiŋka/, /'fɪŋkə/ *noun* E20 **Spanish** (from *fincar* to cultivate). In Spain and Spanish America: a country estate; a ranch.

fin de guerre /fɛ̃ də gɛr/ *noun & adjective phrase* **French** (= end of war). (Designating or characteristic of) the end of a war.

fin de saison /fɛ̃ də sɛzɔ̃/ *noun & adjective phrase* M20 **French** (= end of season). (Designating or characteristic of) the end of a season.

1996 *Spectator* There is a *fin de saison* kind of feeling around here, with many friends having returned to London and points elsewhere.

fin de siècle /fɛ̃ də sjɛkl/ *noun phrase* (also **fin-de-siècle**) plural **fins de siècle** (pronounced same) L19 **French** (= end of century). (Designating or characteristic of) the final years of a century, especially the nineteenth century; decadent. Also *attributive* or as *adjective phrase*.

■ 'Fin de' is sometimes used jocularly in combination with an English word to make a phrase modelled on *fin de siècle*.

1995 *Spectator* *Fins de siècle* don't have too good a reputation.

attributive **1995** *Spectator* [Isaiah] Berlin is acutely aware of the pathology of nationalism, of the distortions of *fin-de-siècle* Romantic voluntarism that lie at the root of Nazi paganism.

fine /fɪn/ *noun* plural pronounced same E20 **French** (abbreviation of FINE CHAMPAGNE). (A) French brandy; specifically, FINE CHAMPAGNE.

fine champagne /fin ʃɑ̃paɲ/ *noun phrase* M19 **French** (= fine (brandy from) Champagne). Old liqueur brandy from the Grande Champagne and Petite Champagne vineyards in the Charente, France; an example, glass, or drink of this.

■ The abbreviation FINE is also found in English.

fines herbes /finz ɛrb/, /fiːnz 'ɛːb/ *noun phrase plural* M19 **French** (= fine herbs). Fresh mixed herbs (usually parsley, tarragon, chervil, and chives) chopped and used in cooking.

■ Frequently used in adjective phrase with *aux*, as in *omelette aux fines herbes*.

finesse /fɪ'nɛs/ *noun & verb* LME **French**. **A** *noun* **1** LME Clarity, purity (especially of metals). **2** M16 Delicacy of manipulation or discrimination; refinement. **3** M16

Artfulness; cunning. **4** An artful stratagem; a ruse, a trick. **b** M19 *Cards* An attempt to take a trick with a card lower than but not in sequence with a card of the same suit also held. **B** *verb* **1** M18 *Cards* **a** *intransitive* Attempt to take a trick by a finesse. **b** *transitive* Play (a card) in a finesse. **2** *intransitive* L18 Use artifice or stratagem. **b** *transitive* Achieve by stratagem; bring about or manage by artful handling.

Fingerspitzengefühl /ˈfɪŋgəʃpɪtz(ə)ngəˌfuːl/ *noun* L20 **German** (= fingertip feeling). Intuition; tact, deftness in handling a task or situation.

1996 *Spectator* ... it showed an absurd ... thickness in, [Sir Anthony] Eden to make a point of wearing a dinner jacket to entertain the khaki-clad Egyptian leader. Not too much *Fingerspitzengefühl* there ... .

finis /ˈfiːnɪs/, /ˈfɪnɪs/, /ˈfʌɪnɪs/ *noun* LME **Latin** (= end). **1** LME At the end of a book: the end. **2** L17 The finish, the conclusion; the end of life, death.

■ In the Latin tag *finis coronat opus* 'the end crowns the work', *finis* is used in sense 2.

fino /ˈfiːnəʊ/ *noun* plural **finos** M19 **Spanish** (= fine *adjective*). A type of pale-coloured dry sherry; an example, glass, or drink of this.

finocchio /fɪˈnɒkɪəʊ/ *noun* (also **finochio**) E18 **Italian** (from a popular Latin variant of *faeniculum* fennel). A form of fennel with swollen leaf-bases eaten as a vegetable.

fiord /fjɔːd/, /ˈfiːɔːd/ *noun* (also **fjord**) L17 **Norwegian**. A long, narrow, deep inlet of the sea between steep cliffs, as on the Norwegian coast.

fioritura /fɪˌɔːrɪˈtʊərə/ *noun* plural **fioriture** /fɪˌɔːrɪˈtʊəri/, /fɪˌɔːrɪˈtʊəreɪ/ M19 **Italian** (from *fiorire* to flower). *Music* An elaboration or decoration of a melody.

firn /fɪən/ *noun* M19 **German** ('(snow) of the previous year', from Old High German *firni* old, related to Old Saxon *fern* past, *forn* formerly, Old Norse *forn* ancient). The granular snow on the upper part of a glacier which is in the process of being compressed into ice. Also called NÉVÉ.

fiumara /fjuːˈmɑːrə/ *noun* E19 **Italian**. (The dried bed of) a mountain torrent.

fjeld /fjɛld/ *noun* M19 **Norwegian** (Bokmål) (from Old Norse *fjall*). A high barren rocky plateau, especially in Scandinavia.

fjord variant of FIORD.

fl. abbreviation of FLORUIT.

flacon /flakɔ̃/ *noun* plural pronounced same. E19 **French**. A small stoppered bottle, *especially* one used to contain perfume.

flagellum /fləˈdʒɛləm/ *noun* plural **flagella** /fləˈdʒɛlə/ E19 **Latin** (diminutive of *flagrum* scourge). **1** E19 A whip. **2** M19 *Biology* A motile whiplike projection from a cell; also, in botany, a runner, a creeping shoot.

flageolet /fladʒəˈlɛt/, /ˈfladʒəlɪt/ *noun 1* M17 **French**. *Music* **1** M17 A small wind instrument resembling a recorder, having six principal holes, including two for the thumb, and sometimes keys. **2** M19 An organ-stop having a tone similar to that of this wind instrument.

flageolet /fladʒəˈlɛt/, /flaʒɔlɛ/ (*plural same*) *noun 2* L19 **French** (ultimately from Latin *phaseolus* bean). *Cookery* A small kind of (especially French) kidney bean, dried and used in cassoulets. Also *flageolet bean*.

flagrante delicto /fləˌgrantɪ dɪˈlɪktəʊ/ *adverb phrase* E19 **Latin**. IN FLAGRANTE DELICTO.

flambé /flɑ̃be/, /ˈflɒmbeɪ/ *adjective & verb* L19 **French** (past participle of *flamber* singe, pass through flame). **A** *adjective* **1** L19 (Of a copper-based glaze) iridescent from the effects of a special firing process; (of a type of Chinese porcelain) characterized by such a glaze. **2** E20 *Cookery* Of food, set alight after being drenched in brandy or other spirit and served while still flaming. **B** *transitive verb* M20 Drench (food) in spirit and set alight.

flambeau /ˈflambəʊ/ *noun* plural **flambeaus**, **flambeaux** /ˈflambəʊz/ M17 **French** (diminutive of *flambe*, from Latin *flammula*, diminutive of *flamma* flame). **1** M17 A flaming torch. **2** L19 A large (branched) candlestick.

1996 *Times* A decade or more ago ... all the traffic-lights in London used to have *flambeaux*—flaming beacons in cast iron—proudly mounted on top.

flamenco /fləˈmɛŋkəʊ/ *noun & adjective* plural **flamencos** L19 **Spanish** (= Fleming). (Designating or pertaining to) a style of music played (especially on a guitar) and sung by Spanish gypsies; (a song or dance) to music in this style.

flâneur /flɑnœr/ *noun* (also **flaneur**) plural pronounced same. M19 **French** (from *flâner* to lounge, saunter idly). An idler.

1995 *Times* The more Vidal tries to tell us that he is only a *flaneur*, the more real and thorough is his work and life.

flautando /flaʊˈtandəʊ/ *noun & adverb* E19 **Italian** (present participle of *flautare* to play the flute). *Music* (A direction: with) a flutelike violin tone.

flautato /flaʊˈtɑːtəʊ/ *noun & adverb* M19 **Italian** (literally, 'fluted'). FLAUTANDO.

flautino /flaʊˈtiːnəʊ/ *noun* plural **flautinos**; in sense 2 also **flautina** E18 **Italian** (diminutive of *flauto* flute). **1** E18 A small flute or flageolet. **2** M19 A gemshorn organ-stop of 2-ft length and pitch.

flauto /ˈflauto/, /ˈflaʊtəʊ/ *noun* plural **flauti** /ˈflauti/, **flautos** /ˈflaʊtəʊz/ E18 **Italian** (= flute). **1** E18 Originally, a recorder; later, a flute; also, the part played by such an instrument. **2** L19 An organ-stop of flute scale.

■ The *flauto piccolo* was likewise formerly a small recorder, now a PICCOLO. Another instrument sometimes known under its Italian name is the side-blown flute, the *flauto traverso*.

flebile /ˈfleɪbɪleɪ/ *adjective* E17 **Italian** (from Latin *flebilis* that is to be wept for; plaintive). *Music* Mournful.

flèche /flɛʃ/, /fleɪʃ/ *noun* (also **fleche**) ME **French** (= arrow). **1** E18 *Fortification* A work in communication with the covered way, placed at the salient angle of the GLACIS. **2** M19 *Architecture* A slender spire, often of wood and rising from a roof. **3** M19 Any of the twenty-four points on a backgammon board. **4** E20 *Fencing* A running attack. In full *flèche attack*.

■ First (ME only) in its original French sense; reintroduced in the specialist applications above.

fléchette /fleɪˈʃɛt/ *noun* (also **flechette**) E20 **French** (diminutive of *flèhe* arrow). *Military* A missile resembling a dart, dropped from an aircraft.

fleur-de-coin /flœrdəkwɛ̃/ *noun phrase* L19 **French** (= bloom of the minting-die). *Numismatics* Mint or perfect condition of a coin.

fleur-de-lis /ˌfləːdəˈliː/ *noun phrase* (also **fleur-de-lys**) plural **fleurs-de-lis** (pronounced same) ME **French** (Old French *flour de lys*, literally, 'flower of the lily'). (The flower of) any of various plants of the iris family; hence, the heraldic lily composed of three petals bound together near their bases and traditionally supposed to have represented an iris, especially as used as a device on the former royal arms of France.

fleuron /ˈflʊərɒn/, /ˈfləːrɒn/, *foreign* /flœrɔ̃/ (*plural same*) *noun* LME **French**. A decorative motif in the form of a stylized flower, used especially in printing, architecture, or coinage.

flic /flɪk/, *foreign* /flik/ (*plural same*) *noun* L19 **French**. A French police officer. *slang*.

flicflac /ˈflɪkflak/ *noun* M19 **French** (imitative of a succession of sharp sounds). *Ballet* A lashing movement of the leg related to the FOUETTÉ.

flor. abbreviation of FLORUIT.

flora /ˈflɔːrə/ *noun* plural **floras**, **florae** /ˈflɔːriː/ E16 **Latin** (*flos* flower, plural *flora*; *Flora*, an ancient Italian goddess of fertility and flowers). **1** E16 The personification of nature's power to produce flowers. **2** L18 A catalogue of the plants of a given area, with descriptions. **3** L18 The plants or plant life of a particular area, habitat, or epoch; cf. FAUNA.

floreat /ˈflɒrɪat/, /ˈflɔːreɪat/ *noun* **Latin** (= may he/she/it flourish (3rd person singular present subjunctive of *florere* to flourish)). The expressed wish that someone or something may thrive and prosper; hence, a thriving and prospering.

■ Often used as an interjection, followed by the name of a person, institution, etc., as in *Floreat Etona!* 'May Eton flourish!'

1996 *Bookseller* Why should certain periods produce a floreat of great writers and others be barren for long periods?

flore pleno /ˌflɔːrɪ ˈpleɪnəʊ/, /ˌflɔːrɪ ˈpliːnəʊ/ *adjective phrase* L19 **Latin** (literally, 'with full flower'). Double-flowered.

■ Used after the names of certain garden flowers that exist in both single- and double-flowered versions.

florilegium /flɒrɪˈliːdʒɪəm/, /flɔːrɪˈliːdʒɪəm/ *noun* plural **florilegia** /flɒrɪˈliːdʒɪə/, **florilegiums** E17 **Modern Latin** (literally, 'bouquet', from Latin *flori-* combining form of *flos* flower + *legere* to gather, translating Greek *anthologion* anthology). A collection of choice extracts from literature; an anthology.

floruit /ˈflɒrʊɪt/, /ˈflɔːrʊɪt/ *noun* M19 **Latin** (= he/she/it flourished (3rd person singular perfect indicative of *florere* to flourish)). The period during which a person flourished; heyday, period of greatest activity or prosperity.

■ Often abbreviated to *fl.* or *flor.* and used in cases where a person's birth and death dates are unknown or uncertain.

flota /'fləʊtə/ *noun* L17 **Spanish** (= fleet). *History* The Spanish fleet which used regularly to cross the Atlantic during the colonial period to bring back the products of America and the West Indies.

flotilla /flə'tɪlə/ *noun* E18 **Spanish** (diminutive of *flota* fleet). A small fleet; a fleet of small vessels.

flügelhorn /'flu:g(ə)lhɔ:n/ *noun* (also **flugelhorn, flugel horn**) M19 **German** (*Flügelhorn*, from *Flügel* wing + *horn* horn). A brass wind instrument with a cup-shaped mouthpiece and a wide conical bore.

■ Also abbreviated to *flugel*.

focaccia /fɒ'katʃa/ *noun* plural **focacce** /fɒ'katʃe/ L20 **Italian**. Italian bread made with olive oil and sometimes herbs.

1996 *Times* Rivals include olive and tomato breads, focaccia and the more established baguette.

focus /'fəʊkəs/ *noun & verb* plural **foci** /'fəʊsʌɪ/, /'fəʊki/, **focuses** M17 **Latin** (= domestic hearth). **A** *noun* **1** L17 *Physics* The adjustment (of a lens, the eye, etc.) to produce a well-defined image; the state of producing a well-defined image thus. **2** M18 The centre of greatest interest, attraction, activity, or energy. **B1** *transitive verb* L18 Make converge to or as to a focus; bring into focus; concentrate *on*. **2** *intransitive verb* M19 Converge to or as to a focus; come into focus; concentrate *on*.

■ *Focus* was apparently first used in this Modern Latin sense by Kepler in his *Astronomia pars optica*, written in 1604, and it is conjectured that the technical sense of *focus* as 'the burning point of a lens or mirror' (which is easily derived from the literal one) was already current in technical Latin. It was introduced into English in similar technical contexts, first as a term in plane geometry by Hobbes, and then into physics by Boyle in its 'burning point' sense. The plural form *foci* is generally confined to the noun's more technical senses.

foetus /'fi:təs/ *noun* (also **fetus**) LME **Latin** (*fetus*, *foetus* pregnancy, giving birth, young offspring). An unborn viviparous animal in the womb, especially an unborn human more than eight weeks after conception; an unhatched oviparous animal in the egg.

■ The American form *fetus* has etymological correctness on its side, but *foetus* is still in general use in British English.

föhn /fə:n/ *noun* (also **foehn**) M19 **German** (in Old High German *phonno*, Middle High German *foenne*, ultimately from Latin (*ventus*) *Favonius* mild west wind). **1** M19 A warm dry south wind which blows down valleys on the north side of the Alps. **2** L19 *Meteorology* A warm dry katabatic wind developing on the lee side of a mountain range as a result of air moving across the range. Also *föhn wind*.

foie gras /fwɑ: 'grɑ:/ *noun phrase* (also **foie-gras**) E19 **French**. Abbreviation of PÂTÉ DE FOIE GRAS.

folie /'fɒli/, *foreign* /fɔli/ (*plural same*) *noun* E19 **French** (= madness). Mental illness, mania.

■ Now chiefly in names of pathological mental states (see following entries).

folie à deux /ˌfɒli ɑ: 'də:/, *foreign* /fɔli a dø/ *noun phrase* E20 **French**. An identical mental disorder or illusion affecting two closely associated people; *loosely* a shared act of folly between two people.

folie de grandeur /ˌfɒli də grɒ̃'də:/, *foreign* /fɔli də grɑ̃dœr/ *noun phrase* (also **folie des grandeurs**) L19 **French**. Delusions of grandeur or importance.

1995 *Times* . . . either this comet is vast and about to obliterate us; or it is a small comet that has suddenly brightened . . . All experts admit that a diminutive comet with *folie de grandeur* is the likeliest explanation.

folie du doute /ˌfɒli du: 'du:t/, *foreign* /fɔli dy dut/ *noun phrase* L19 **French**. Obsessive self-doubt.

fonctionnaire /fɔ̃ksjɔnɛr/ *noun* L20 **French**. In France: a state or local authority employee; a civil servant.

1995 *Spectator* 'Brussels can stay at home, thank you very much,' said Virginia, and how the *fonctionnaires* must have trembled in the Rue de la Loi.

fondant /'fɒnd(ə)nt/ *noun* L19 **French** (use as noun of present participle of *fondre* to melt). *Cookery* A sweet made of a soft paste of flavoured (and usually coloured) sugar; such a paste used in sweets and icings.

fondue /'fɒnd(j)u:/ *noun* M19 **French** (feminine past participle of *fondre*; cf. FONDANT). *Cookery* A dish of flavoured melted cheese, a speciality in the Swiss Alpine region; any dish in which small pieces of food are cooked, usually at table, by being dipped into boiling oil or liquid.

fons et origo /ˌfɒnz ɛt ˈɒrɪgəʊ/, /ˌfɒnz ɛt ɒˈrʌɪgəʊ/ *noun phrase* E19 **Latin**. The source and origin *of*.

■ Earliest use is in the phrase *fons et origo mali* the source and origin of evil.

1996 *Times Magazine* Half a mile northwest we come to Bedford Park . . . the *fons et origo* of every planned suburb between its inception in 1875 and the First World War.

foo yong variant of FU YUNG.

force de frappe /fɔrs də frap/ *noun phrase* plural **forces de frappe** (pronounced same) M20 **French**. *Military* A striking force; especially, the French independent nuclear capability.

1995 *Times* The French these days seem much more interested in jobs and taxes than in the *force de frappe*.

force majeure /fɔrs maʒœr/ *noun phrase* L19 **French** (= superior strength). Irresistible force, overwhelming circumstances or opposition; in *Law* or *Commerce* an unforeseeable sequence of events excusing the fulfilment of a contract.

1995 *Times* The oil companies . . . realised that their position was untenable. Therefore, they invoked *force majeure* and agreed new contracts with their customers . . .

forma pauperis /ˌfɔːmə ˈpɔːpərɪs/ *noun phrase* L16 **Latin** (literally, 'the form of a poor person'). *Law* (The condition of) a poor person in respect of being able to bring a legal action without payment; *figuratively* humbly, in supplication.

■ Also frequently in *in forma pauperis* or *sub forma pauperis* as a poor person.

Formgeschichte /ˈfɔːmgəʃɪxtə/ *noun* E20 **German** (from *Form* form + *Geschichte* history). Textual analysis, especially of the Bible, by tracing the history of its content of proverbs, myths, and other forms; form-criticism.

forte /ˈfɔːteɪ/, /ˈfɔːti/, /fɔːt/ *noun 1* M17 **French** (use as noun of feminine of *fort* strong). **1** M17 *Fencing* The stronger part of a sword-blade, from the hilt to the middle. **2** L17 The strong point of a person; the thing in which one excels.

■ The word entered English in its masculine form *fort*, but the feminine form *forte* was later substituted. The modern pronunciation has been influenced by Italian *forte* (see next).

forte /ˈfɔːti/ *adverb, adjective, & noun 2* E18 **Italian** (= strong, loud, from Latin *fortis* strong). *Music* **A** *adverb & adjective* E18 (A direction:) loud(ly). **B** *noun* M18 A loud tone or passage.

■ As a direction, usually abbreviated to *f*.

forte-piano /ˌfɔːtɪprˈanəʊ/ *noun, adverb, & adjective* M18 **Italian**. *Music* **A** *noun* M18 An early form of the pianoforte. **B** *adverb & adjective* L19 (A direction:) loud(ly) and then immediately soft(ly).

■ As a musical instrument often aphetized to PIANO (*noun* 2); as a musical direction, usually abbreviated to *fp*.

fortissimo /fɔːˈtɪsɪməʊ/ *adverb, adjective, & noun* E18 **Italian** (superlative of FORTE loud(ly)). *Music* **A** *adverb & adjective* E18 (A direction:) very loud(ly). **B** *noun* plural **fortissimos, fortissimi** /fɔːˈtɪsɪmi/ M19 A very loud tone or passage.

■ As direction, usually abbreviated to *ff*.

A *transferred* **1995** *Times* Defending himself yesterday, Mr Portillo conceded that his speech had been a 'fortissimo' expression of the Government's newly-sceptical European policy.

forum /ˈfɔːrəm/ *noun* plural **forums, fora**/ˈfɔːrə/ LME **Latin** (related to *fores* (outside) door, originally an enclosure surrounding a house). **1** LME *Roman Antiquity* The public place or market-place of a city; the place of assembly for judicial and civic business. **b** M18 A place of or meeting for public discussion; a periodical etc. which provides an opportunity for conducting a debate. **2** L17 A court, a tribunal. Also *figurative*.

forzando /fɔːtˈsandəʊ/ *adverb & adjective* E19 **Italian** (from *forzare* to force). *Music* (A direction:) with force or emphasis; SFORZANDO.

foudroyant /fuːˈdrɔɪənt/, /fudrwajɑ̃/ *adjective* M19 **French** (present participle of *foudroyer* to strike (as) with lightning, from *foudre* from Latin *fulgur* lightning). **1** M19 Thunderous, noisy. Also, dazzling. **2** L19 Of a disease, beginning suddenly and in a very severe form.

fouetté /fwete/ (*plural same*), /ˈfwɛteɪ/ *noun* M19 **French** (past participle of *fouetter* to whip). *Ballet* A movement in which a dancer pivots on one *pointe* and executes a rapid whip-like movement with the lower part of free leg.

foulard /ˈfuːlɑː/, /ˈfuːlɑːd/ *noun* M19 **French**. **1** M19 A lightweight printed or checked material of silk or silk and cotton. **2** L19 A headscarf or neckerchief made from this.

foulé /fule/ *noun* L19 **French** (= pressed (cloth), past participle of *fouler* to full). A light woollen dress material with a fibrous appearance.

fourchette /fʊəˈʃɛt/ *noun* M18 **French.** **1** M18 Something forked or resembling a fork. **2** M19 A forked object, device, or instrument; the forked piece between two adjacent fingers of a glove. **3** L19 In any of several card-games, a combination of cards immediately above and immediately below the card led.

fou rire /fu rir/ *noun phrase* E20 **French** (literally, 'mad laughter'). (A fit of) wild or uncontrollable laughter.

fourreau /ˈfʊərəʊ/ *noun* plural **fourreaux** (pronounced same) L19 **French** (literally, 'sheath, scabbard'). A close-fitting dress; an underskirt forming part of a dress.

foyer /ˈfɔɪeɪ/, *foreign* /fwaje/ (*plural same*) *noun* L18 **French** (= hearth, home, ultimately from Latin *focus* hearth). **1** L18 A centre of activity; a focus. **2** M19 A large room in a theatre, concert hall, etc., for the use of the audience during intervals; also, the entrance hall of a hotel or other public building.

■ Sense 1 is now uncommon, with *foyer* having been generally superseded by FOCUS in this sense.

fp abbreviation of FORTE-PIANO (musical direction).

fracas /ˈfrakɑː/ *noun* plural same /ˈfrakɑːz/ E18 **French** (from *fracasser* from Italian *fracassare* to make an uproar). A disturbance, an uproar, a row.

Fraktur /ˈfraktʊə/ *noun* (also **fraktur**) L19 **German.** *Typography* A German style of black-letter type, the normal type used for printing German from the sixteenth to the mid twentieth century.

framboise /frɒmˈbwɑːz/ *noun & adjective* L16 **French** (ultimately from a conflation of Latin *fraga ambrosia* ambrosian strawberry). **A** *adjective* E20 Of raspberry colour. **B** *noun* M20 A shade of pink; raspberry colour.

■ *Framboise* in its original sense of 'raspberry' was current in English only in the sixteenth and seventeenth centuries.

franc fort /frɑ̃ fɔr/ *noun phrase* L20 **French** (= strong franc). *Economics* The French monetary policy devoted to maintaining the value of the French franc at a high level among international currencies.

1995 *Spectator* Unemployment is, of course, a price paid for the *franc fort*.

franco /ˈfraŋko/ *adjective & adverb* L19 **Italian** ((*porto*) *franco* free carriage). Of a foreign business transaction, free of any postal or delivery charge.

franc tireur /frɑ̃ tirœr/ *noun phrase* plural **francs tireurs** (pronounced same) E19 **French** (= free shooter). An irregular soldier, a guerrilla fighter; *historically* a member of an irregular French light-infantry corps, originating in the Revolutionary wars.

franglais /frɑ̃glɛ/ *noun* (also **Franglais**) M20 **French** (blend of *français* French + *anglais* English). A non-standard version of the French language characterized by indiscriminate use of words and phrases taken from British and American English.

■ The problem, as perceived by the French, of their language being sullied by the influx of Anglo-Saxon words was aired under this name in R. Etiemble's *Parlez-vous Franglais* (1964). Despite various campaigns to exclude them, interlopers such as *le week-end* appear firmly entrenched and likely to remain.

frankfurter /ˈfraŋkfəːtə/ *noun* (also (chiefly *United States*) **frankfurt**) L19 **German** (*Frankfurter Wurst* Frankfurt sausage). A seasoned sausage made of smoked beef and pork, originally made at Frankfurt am Main in Germany.

frappé /frape/, /ˈfrapeɪ/ *adjective & noun* M19 **French** (past participle of *frapper* in the sense of 'to ice (drinks)'). **A** *adjective* M19 (Chiefly of wine) iced, chilled; (of a drink) served with crushed ice. **B** *noun* E20 A drink (especially coffee) served with crushed ice or partially frozen to a slushy consistency.

Frau /fraʊ/ *noun* (also **frau**) plural **Frauen** /fraʊən/, **Fraus** E19 **German.** A German or Austrian woman.

■ Also used as a title, corresponding to *Mrs.*

Frauendienst /ˈfraʊəndiːnst/ *noun* M20 **German** (*frauen* women + *dienst* service). Exaggerated chivalry towards women.

■ The word derives from the medieval tradition of courtly love, specifically the title of the mid thirteenth century *Frauendienst* of Ulrich von Lichtenstein (d. *c.*1275), in which the writer describes the extraordinary tasks required of him by his mistress.

1963 W. H. Auden *Dyer's Hand* We find neither outright sexual passion nor sentimental *Frauendienst*.

Fräulein /'frɔɪlʌɪn/, *foreign* /'frɔɪlaɪn/ *noun* (also **fraulein**) L17 **German** (diminutive of FRAU). An unmarried German woman; a German governess.

■ Also used as a title, corresponding to *Miss*.

frazil /'freɪz(ə)l/, /frə'zil/ *noun* L19 **Canadian French** (*frasil* = snow floating on water; cf. French *fraisil* cinders). Slush consisting of small ice crystals formed in water too turbulent to freeze solid. Also *frazil ice*.

fresco /'frɛskəʊ/ *noun & verb* L16 **Italian** (= cool, fresh). **A** *noun* plural **frescos, frescoes** L16 A method of painting by which watercolour is applied to damp, freshly laid plaster, so that the colours penetrate and become fixed as the plaster dries. **2** L17 A painting produced by this method. **B** *transitive verb* E19 Paint in fresco.

■ Earliest English use in the phrase *in fresco*, representing Italian *affresco* or *al fresco* 'on the fresh (plaster)'.

fresco buono /ˌfresko 'bwɔ:no/ *noun phrase* M19 **Italian** (= good fresco). FRESCO sense A. Also *buon fresco* (L19).

fresco secco /ˌfresko 'sekko/ *noun phrase* M19 **Italian** (= dry fresco). The process or technique of painting on dry plaster with colours mixed with water.

■ Sometimes abbreviated to *secco* (M19).

fricandeau /'frɪkandəʊ/ *noun & verb* E18 **French**. **A** *noun* plural **fricandeaux** /'frɪkandəʊz/ E18 *Cookery* (A slice of) veal or other meat fried or stewed and served with sauce; an escalope; a fricassee of veal. **B** *transitive verb* M18 Make into fricandeaux.

fricassee /'frɪkəsi:/, /frɪkə'si:/ *noun & verb* M16 **French** (*fricassée* feminine past participle of *fricasser* to cut up and stew in sauce). **A** *noun* M16 *Cookery* Meat sliced and fried or stewed and served with sauce, especially a ragout of game. **B** *transitive verb* M17 Make a fricassee of.

frigidarium /frɪdʒɪ'dɛrɪəm/ *noun* plural **frigidariums, frigidaria** /frɪdʒɪ'dɛrɪə/ E18 **Latin** (from *frigidus*, from *frigere* to be cold, from *frigus* cold). The room in Roman baths containing the final, cold bath.

frijoles /fri'xoles/, /frɪ'həʊlɛs/ *noun plural* L16 **Spanish** (plural of *frijol* bean, ultimately from Latin *phaseolus*). *Cookery* Especially in Mexico, a dish of beans.

frisé /'fri:zeɪ/ *adjective* L19 **French** (past participle of *friser* to curl). Of or designating a pile fabric with cut and uncut loops forming a pattern, chiefly used in upholstery.

frisée /'fri:zeɪ/ *noun* L20 **French** ((feminine) past participle of *friser* to curl). Curly endive.

■ Abbreviation of French *chicorée frisée*.

frisson /frisɔ̃/, /'frɪsɒn/ *noun* plural pronounced same L18 **French** (= shiver, thrill. An emotional thrill; a shiver of excitement.

1995 *Country Life* In the 18th century, some followers of the Picturesque movement used to enjoy the frisson of terror experienced when they beheld an unusually 'horrid' landscape; their fear became pleasurable from the knowledge that they were only going to look at the bleak scene before them, not live in it.

frittata /frɪ'tɑ:tə/ *noun* L20 **Italian**. An omelette.

fritto misto /ˌfritto 'misto/ *noun phrase* E20 **Italian** (= mixed fry). *Cookery* A dish of mixed foods, especially seafood, deep-fried in batter.

froideur /frwadœr/ *noun* L20 **French** (from *froid* cold). Coldness; lack of warmth.

■ Only in figurative use.

1995 *Times* When one interviewer . . . suggested that she [sc. Catherine Deneuve] seemed a little over-controlled herself, her response was a flash of ironic *froideur* that might have been scripted by Buñuel himself.

fromage blanc /ˌfrɒmɑ:ʒ 'blɒ̃/, *foreign* /frɔmaʒ blɑ̃/ *noun phrase* L20 **French** (= white cheese). *Cookery* A fresh soft white cheese.

fromage frais /ˌfrɒma:ʒ 'freɪ/, *foreign* /frɔmaʒ frɛ/ *noun phrase* L20 **French** (= fresh cheese). *Cookery* A soft curd cheese, often used as a basis for desserts.

■ In France this type of cheese is generally known as PETIT SUISSE.

fronde /frɔ̃d/ *noun* (usually **Fronde** in sense 1) plural pronounced same L18 **French** (literally, 'sling'). **1** L18 *French History* A political party in France during the mid seventeenth century, which initiated violent uprisings against the administration of Cardinal Mazarin during the minority of Louis XIV. **2** E19 *transferred* A malcontent or disaffected party; violent political opposition.

frondeur /frɔdœr/ *noun* (usually **Frondeur** in sense 1) plural pronounced same L18 **French** (from FRONDE). **1** L18 *French*

History A participant in the Fronde. **2** M19 *transferred* A malcontent; a political rebel.

fronton /ˈfrʌnt(ə)n/ *noun* L17 **French** (from Italian *frontone*, augmentative of *fronte* forehead; in sense 2 Spanish *frontón*). **1** L17 *Architecture* A pediment. **2** L19 A building in which pelota is played.

froom variant of FRUM.

frottage /ˈfrɒtɑːʒ/, *foreign* /frɔtaʒ/ *noun* M20 **French** (= rubbing, friction). **1** M20 The practice of rubbing against or touching the (clothed) body of another person (usually in a crowd) as a means of obtaining sexual gratification. **2** M20 *Art* The technique or process of taking a rubbing from an uneven surface, such as grained wood, as a basis for a work of art.

frotteur /frɒˈtəː/, *foreign* /frɔtœr/ *plural same noun* plural pronounced same L19 **French**. A person who indulges in FROTTAGE (sense 1).

frottola /ˈfrɒtələ/, *foreign* /ˈfrɔttola/ *noun* plural **frottole** /ˈfrɒtəleɪ/, *foreign* /ˈfrɔttole/ M19 **Italian** (literally, 'fib, tall story'). *Music* A form of Italian comic or amorous song, especially from the fifteenth and sixteenth centuries.

frou-frou /ˈfruːfruː/ *noun* L19 **French** (imitative). A continuous soft rustling sound, esp. of skirts; hence, frills and frippery. *verb* E20 Move with a rustle of fabric. Also *attributive*.

attributive **1946** B. Spencer *Aegean Islands 'Yachts on the Nile'* [Yachts] . . . fresh as a girl at her rendezvous, and wearing frou-frou names, Suzy, Yvette or Gaby.

fruits de mer /ˌfrwiːdəˈmɛː/ *noun phrase* M20 **French** (= fruits of the sea). *Cookery* Seafood, especially a dish made up of mixed shellfish.

frum /fruːm/ *adjective* (also **froom**) L19 **Yiddish** (from Middle High German *vrum* zealous; cf. German *fromm* pious). Pious, religious (used especially of an orthodox Jew).

frustum /ˈfrʌstəm/ *noun* (also **frustrum**) plural **frustums**, **frusta** /ˈfrʌstə/ M17 **Latin** (= piece cut off). *Mathematics* The portion of a solid figure, such as a cone, which remains after the upper part has been cut off by a plane parallel to the base.

fuehrer variant of FÜHRER.

fugato /fjuːˈgɑːtəʊ/ *adverb, adjective, & noun* M19 **Italian** (= fugued, from *fuga* FUGUE). *Music* **A** *adverb & adjective* M19 In the fugue style, but not in strict or complete fugue form. **B** *noun* plural **fugatos** L19 A passage in this style.

fughetta /fjuːˈgɛtə/ *noun* L19 **Italian** (diminutive of *fuga* fugue). *Music* A short condensed fugue.

fugu /ˈfuːguː/ *noun* M20 **Japanese**. A type of puffer fish, renowned as a Japanese delicacy.

fugue /fjuːg/ *noun* L16 **French** (or, its source, Italian *fuga*, from Latin *fuga* flight). **1** L16 *Music* A polyphonic composition in which a short melodic theme, the subject, is introduced by one part or voice, and successively taken up by the others and developed by their interweaving. **2** E20 *Psychiatry* A flight from or loss of awareness of one's own identity, sometimes involving wandering away from home, and often occurring as a reaction to shock or emotional distress.

führer /ˈfjʊərə/ *noun* (also **fuehrer**) M20 **German** (= leader). A (ruthless or tyrannical) leader; a dictator.

■ Hitler, in his role as leader of the Third Reich, is often alluded to under his assumed title of *the* (or) *die Führer*, and the transferred use of the word in English usually has strongly negative implications.

führerprinzip /ˈfjʊərəprɪnˌzɪp/ *noun* M20 **German** (literally, 'leader principle'). The doctrine that a FÜHRER has a right to command and the people a duty to obey.

■ Also partially Anglicized as *führer principle*.

1995 *Spectator* Vainly they [sc. the Tories] scan the Labour benches for vocal resentment of Mr Blair's *führerprinzip*.

fulcrum /ˈfʊlkrəm/ *noun* plural **fulcra** /ˈfʊlkrə/, **fulcrums** L17 **Latin** (= post or foot of couch, from base of *fulcire* to prop up, support). **1** A prop or support; now specifically, the point against which a lever is placed to get purchase or on which it turns or is supported. **2** L17 *figurative* The means by which or source from which influence etc. is brought to bear.

functus officio /ˌfʌŋktəs əˈfɪʃɪəʊ/ *predicative adjective phrase* plural **functi officio** /ˌfʌŋktʌɪ əˈfɪʃɪəʊ/ M19 **Latin** (= having discharged an office). *Law* Free from further obligations, having discharged its (or their) duty.

fungus /ˈfʌŋgəs/ *noun* plural **fungi** /ˈfʌŋgi/, /ˈfʌŋgʌɪ/, /ˈfʌndʒi/, /ˈfʌndʒʌɪ/ **fun-**

guses LME **Latin** (probably from Greek *sphoggos, spoggos* sponge). **1** LME Any of a large division of organisms including mushrooms, which lack chlorophyll and grow on, or obtain nutrients from, organic matter. **b** M18 *figurative* Something growing or spreading rapidly. **2** L17 Soft or spongy diseased tissue. **3** E20 *slang* A growth of facial hair, a beard.

furioso /ˌfjʊərɪˈəʊzəʊ/, *foreign* /furiˈo:so/ *noun, adjective, & adverb* M17 **Italian** (from Latin *furiosus* enraged, furious). **A** *noun* plural **furiosos** M17 A furious person. **B** *adjective & adverb* E19 *Music* (A direction:) furious(ly), wild(ly).

furor academicus /ˌfjʊərɔ: akəˈdɛmɪkəs/ *noun phrase* M20 **Latin**. Academic frenzy; excessive excitement provoked by or over an intellectual issue.

furore /fjʊəˈrɔ:ri/, /fjʊəˈrɔ:/ *noun* L18 **Italian** (from Latin *furor*, from *furere* to rage). **1** L18 Enthusiastic admiration; a craze. **2** M20 (An) uproar, (a) fuss.

furor poeticus /ˌfjʊərɔ: pəʊˈɛtɪkəs/ *noun phrase* E20 **Latin**. Poetic frenzy; emotional over-enthusiasm.

furor scribendi /ˌfjʊərɔ: skrɪˈbɛndi/ *noun phrase* M19 **Latin** (= frenzy of writing). An irresistible urge to write.

1975 S. Perelman *Vinegar Puss* The all-consuming urge to create, the *furor scribendi*, is upon him and will not be stilled.

fusain /ˈfju:zeɪn/, *also foreign* /fyzɛ/ (*plural same*) *noun* L19 **French** (= spindle tree, charcoal). *Art* Artists' charcoal (made from the wood of the spindle tree); a charcoal drawing.

fusee /fju:ˈzi:/ *noun* L16 **French** (*fusée* spindleful, ultimately from Latin *fusus* spindle). **1** E17 *Horology* A conical pulley onto which a chain is wound so as to equalize the power of the mainspring in a mechanical watch or clock. **2** M17 A detonating device; a fuse. **3** M19 A large-headed match for lighting a cigar or pipe.

fuselage /ˈfju:zəlɑ:ʒ/, /ˈfju:zəlɪdʒ/ *noun* E20 **French** (from *fuseler* to shape like spindle, from *fuseau* spindle). The elongated body section of an aircraft in which the crew and passengers or cargo are carried.

fusillade /fju:zɪˈleɪd/, /fju:zɪˈlɑ:d/ *noun & verb* E19 **French** (from *fusiller* to shoot). **A** *noun* E19 (Wholesale slaughter by) simultaneous or successive discharge of firearms; *figurative* a sustained barrage of criticism, etc. **B** *transitive verb* E19 Assault or shoot down with a fusillade.

fusilli /ˈfusɪli/ *noun plural* L20 **Italian**. Pasta in the shape of small twists or spirals.

fustanella /fʌstəˈnɛlə/ *noun* M19 **Italian** (from Modern Greek *phoustani, phoustanela*, Albanian *fustan*, probably from Italian *fustagno* fustian). A stiff white kilt formerly worn by men in Albania and Greece and still part of Greek ceremonial military dress.

futon /ˈfu:tɒn/ *noun* (also **futong**) L19 **Japanese**. In Japan: a cotton-stuffed mattress rolled out over a mat on the floor for use as a bed; more generally, a low-slung Japanese-style bed or mattress.

■ The word has occurred in accounts of Japanese culture since the nineteenth century, but its introduction as a fashionable item of Western furniture dates from the 1980s. In modern Western furnishing the futon often includes a slatted wooden base capable of conversion into a seat by day.

1996 *Times* Minimalists believe they will be redeemed by the futon, that they can meditate in the kitchen and create the metaphysical from the hygienic.

fu yung /fu: ˈjʌŋ/ *noun phrase* (also **foo yong**) /fu: ˈjɒŋ/ M20 **Chinese** (Cantonese *foo yung*, literally, 'hibiscus'). *Cookery* A Chinese dish made with eggs mixed and cooked with vegetables and other ingredients.

G

gabelle /ga'bɛl/ *noun* LME **French** (from Italian *gabella* corresponding to Spanish *alcavala*). Chiefly *History* A tax, *especially* a foreign tax; *specifically* the salt-tax imposed in France before the Revolution.

gabion /'geɪbɪən/ *noun* M16 **French** (from Italian *gabbione* augmentative of *gabbia* cage). A cylinder of wicker or woven metal bands to be filled with earth or stones for use in engineering or (*historical*) fortification.

gaffe /gaf/ *noun* (also **gaff**) E20 **French**. A blunder, a clumsy or indiscreet act or remark.

1996 *Times* It's not that Bottomley is alone in making such photographic gaffes—remember John Gummer stuffing a hamburger down his daughter in 1990 to allay fears of mad cow disease affecting humans?

gaga /'gɑ:gɑ:/, /'gagə/ *adjective & noun* (also **ga-ga**) E20 **French**. **A** *adjective* E20 Senile; mad, crazy; foolish, fatuous. **B** *noun* M20 A senile or foolish person. *slang*.

gagaku /'gagaku:/ *noun* M20 **Japanese** (from *ga* refined, graceful, noble + *gaku* music). A traditional type of (chiefly ceremonial) Japanese music.

gage d'amour /gaʒ damur/ *noun phrase* plural **gages d'amour** (pronounced same) M18 **French**. A pledge of love; a love-token.

gaieté de coeur /gete də kœr/ *noun phrase* E18 **French**. Light-heartedness, playfulness.

gaijin /gʌɪ'dʒɪn/ *noun & adjective* M20 **Japanese** (contraction of *gaikoku-jin*, from *gaikaku* foreign country + *jin* person). **A** *noun* M20 plural same. In Japan: a foreigner, an alien. **B** M20 *attributive* or as *adjective* Foreign, alien (to the Japanese).

A 1995 *Times* The dollars-for-bonds deal is designed to insure both against a collapse, but it is hard to say who is most put out—the Americans, forced to shore up their biggest economic competitor, or the Japanese, coming cap-in-hand to the *gaijin* for financial help.

gala /'gɑ:lə/, /'geɪlə/ *noun* E17 **French** (or its source in Italian from Spanish from Old French *gale* merrymaking). **1** E17 Fine or showy dress. Now only in *in gala*. **2** E18–E19 Festivity, rejoicing. **3** M18 A festive occasion; a festival characterized by finery and display; a special theatrical or other performance.

3 1996 *Spectator* Lovers of *Bohème*, those who already know the opera and want a definitive recording, as well as those won over to it by the Gubbay galas, should secure this set.

galabiya /gə'lɑ:bɪjə/, /galə'bi:jə/ *noun* (also **galabieh**, **gallabiya**, and many other variants) E18 **Arabic** (Egyptian variant of Arabic *jallābiyya*). A long loose garment worn in Arabic-speaking Mediterranean countries, especially in Egypt.

galant /galɑ̃/, /gə'lɑ:nt/ *adjective* L19 **French and German**. **1** L19 *Music* Designating or pertaining to a light and elegant style of eighteenth-century music. **2** L20 Courteous, attentive to women.

2 1995 D. Lodge *Therapy* Laurence remains wonderfully *galant*.

galanterie /galɑ̃tri/, (*in sense 1 also*) /ˌgal(ə)ntə'ri:/ *noun* plural **galanteries** (pronounced same), (*in sense 1 also with German plural*) **galanterien** /ˌgal(ə)ntə'ri:ən/ E20 **French** (or (sense 1) German). **1** E20 *Music* A light non-essential movement in an early eighteenth-century classical suite. **2** E20 Courtesy, politeness, especially to women.

■ *Galanterie* in its obsolete sense of 'splendour' or 'a display of magnificence' was introduced earlier (E17), but it did not displace the Anglicized form *gallantry* which was also formerly (L16–E19) used in this sense. The current senses represent a reintroduction.

galère /galɛr/ *noun* plural pronounced same M18 **French** (= galley). A coterie; a (usually undesirable) group of people; an unpleasant situation.

■ The primary literal sense of *galère* as 'a ship powered by oars' in which criminals were condemned to be rowers explains its use as a metaphor for a disagreeable situation or bad company. The figurative use is a reference to Molière's *Scapin* (II xi) *'Que diable allait-il faire dans cette galère?'*

1995 *Bookseller* I grow a-weary of . . . the whole *galère* of head honchos, smart-alec agents, insanely overpaid writers, etc.

galette /gə'lɛt/ *noun* L18 **French**. A broad thin cake usually of pastry.

Galgenhumor /ˈgalgən,hu:mɔr/ *noun* (also **galgenhumor**) E20 **German** (from *Galgen* gallows + *Humor* humour). Grim, ironical humour.

■ Also (E20) in the English form *gallows-humour.*

1963 W. H. Auden *Dyer's Hand* The gravedigger's song in Hamlet is . . . an expression of the *galgenhumor* which suits his particular mystery.

galipot /ˈgalɪpɒt/ *noun* L18 **French** (*galipot, garipot*: cf. Provençal *garapot* pine-tree resin). A kind of hardened turpentine formed on the stem of the cluster pine.

gallabiya variant of GALABIYA.

galleria /galəˈri:ə/ *noun* L19 **Italian**. A shopping arcade in an Italian city or designed in imitation of one of these.

■ The idea of the shopping arcade on the Italian *galleria* principle became fashionable among urban architects in the English-speaking world during the 1960s, but the word *galleria* only became a fashionable synonym for 'arcade' in the 1980s. The term is also applied to shops-within-a-shop.

1990 *Times* The winning scheme . . . incorporated the inevitable 'galleria'.

gallinazo /galɪˈneɪzəʊ/ *noun* plural **gallinazos** M18 **Spanish** (from Latin *gallina* hen). In Latin America: a turkey buzzard or other vulture.

galop /ˈgaləp/, /gəˈlɒp/ *noun* M19 **French**. A lively ballroom dance in 2/4 time; a piece of music for this dance.

galpon /galˈpəʊn/ *noun* L19 **American Spanish** (*galpón* from Nahuatl *calpulli* large hall). A large building like a barn on a South American farm.

gamba /ˈgambə/ *noun 1* (also **gambo**) L16 **Italian** (= leg; short for VIOLA DA GAMBA). **1** L16 A VIOLA DA GAMBA. **2** M19 An organ-stop resembling a violin or cello in tone. Also *gamba stop*.

gamba /ˈgambə/ *noun 2* M20 **Spanish**. A kind of prawn, *Palaemon serratus*, as an article of food.

gamelan /ˈgamәlan/ *noun* E19 **Javanese**. An Indonesian, especially Javanese or Balinese, orchestra consisting mainly of percussion instruments.

gamin /ˈgamɪn/, /ˈgamã/, *foreign* /gamɛ̃/ (*plural same*) *noun & adjective* M19 **French**. **A** *noun* M19 A street urchin, a waif; a street-wise or impudent child. **B** *adjective* M19 Of, pertaining to, resembling, or characteristic of a gamin.

gamine /gaˈmi:n/, *foreign* /gamin/ (*plural same*) *noun & adjective* L19 **French**. **A** *noun* L19 A female gamin; a small, attractively informal, mischievous, or elfish young woman. **B** *adjective* E20 Of, pertaining to, resembling, or characteristic of a gamine.

1984 A. Brookner *Hotel du Lac* In her navy linen trousers and her, perhaps too tight, white jersey, Jennifer was determinedly *gamine*.

gaminerie /gaminri/ *noun* E20 **French**. The behaviour or characteristics of a gamin or gamine.

gamma /ˈgamə/ *noun* LME **Latin** (from Greek). **1** LME The third letter (Γ, γ) of the Greek alphabet. **2** E17–E19 *Music* Gamut. **3** L17 Denoting the third in a numerical sequence: *attributively Science* Frequently written γ, as in *Astronomy* (preceding the genitive of the Latin name of the constellation) denoting the third brightest star in a constellation; *Chemistry* denoting the third of a number of isomeric forms of a compound, or of allotropes of an element, etc.; *Physics* designating high-energy electromagnetic radiation which consists of photons of wavelengths shorter than those of X-rays. **4** M20 A third-class mark in an examination etc. **5** M19 The silver Y, *Plusia gamma*. More fully *gamma moth*. **6** E20 A unit of magnetic field strength equal to 10^{-5} oersted. **b** M20 A unit of mass equal to 10^{-6} gram. **7** E20 *Photography* and *Television* A measure of the contrast of an image compared with that of the scene represented.

gammadion /gaˈmeɪdɪən/ *noun* M19 **Late Greek** (from GAMMA). An arrangement of shapes of capital gamma (Γ), especially of four, as a swastika or a hollow Greek cross.

ganbei /ganˈbeɪ/ *interjection* (also **kan-pei**) M20 **Chinese** (*gānbēi*, from *gān* empty, dry + *bēi* glass, cup). (A Chinese toast:) a call to drain one's glass.

ganbu /ˈganbu:/ *noun* (also **kanpu** /ˈkanpu:/) M20 **Chinese** (*gànbù*). In the People's Republic of China: an office-holder in a military or governmental organization; a CADRE.

gandharva /ganˈdɑ:və/ *noun* (also **gandharba** /ganˈdɑ:bə/) L18 **Sanskrit** (*gandharvās*; perhaps connected with Greek *kentauros* centaur). *Hindu Mythology* Any of a class of minor deities or genii of the sky, often represented as celestial musicians.

gandoura /gan'dʊərə/ *noun* (also **gandourah, gandura(h)**) M19 **Arabic** (Algerian *gandūra*, variant of classical Arabic *kandūra*). A long loose gown worn mainly in the Near East and North Africa.

gangue /gaŋ/ *noun* E19 **French** (from German *Gang* way, course, vein or lode of metal). The valueless or unwanted components of an ore deposit.

ganja /'ganʤə/, /'gɑːnʤə/ *noun* (also **ganga**) E19 **Hindi** (*gājā*). A strong preparation of marijuana, used chiefly for smoking.

ganosis /gə'nəʊsɪs/ *noun* E20 **Greek** (*ganōsis*, from *ganos* brightness, from *ganoun* to polish). The process of applying a wax polish to the white marble surface of a statue or occasionally to some other surface in order to give warmth to its appearance.

gaon /'gɑːəʊn/ *noun* plural **gaons, geonim** /geɪ'əʊnɪm/ L18 **Hebrew** (*gā'ōn* excellence, pride). (An honorific for) a head of a Jewish academy in Babylonia, Palestine, Syria, or Egypt, from the sixth to the eleventh centuries. Later, especially in Spain, France, Italy, and Lithuania, an outstanding Talmudic scholar. Also *generally*, a genius, a prodigy.

garam masala /ˌgʌrəm mə'sɑːlə/ *noun phrase* M20 **Urdu** (*garam maṣāla*). A spice mixture used in Indian cookery.

garbanzo /gɑː'banzəʊ/ *noun* plural **garbanzos** M18 **Spanish**. A chick-pea.

garçon /garsɔ̃/ *noun* plural pronounced same E17 **French**. A waiter, a male servant, especially in a French hotel or restaurant.

garconnière /garsɔnjɛr/ *noun* plural pronounced same E20 **French**. A bachelor's set of rooms or flat.

garde champêtre /gard ʃɑ̃pɛtr/ *noun phrase* plural **gardes champêtres** (pronounced same) E19 **French** (literally, 'rural guard'). In France: a rural police officer; a gamekeeper.

gare /gar/ *noun* plural pronounced same M19 **French**. **1** M19 A dock-basin on a river or canal. Also, a pier, a wharf. **2** L19 In France and French-speaking countries: a railway station.

gare /gar/ *intransitive verb* (*imperative*) M17 **French** (imperative of *garer* to shelter). Look out! Beware! Take care.

gargouillade /gargujad/ *noun* plural pronounced same M20 **French** (from *gargouiller* to bubble, gurgle). *Ballet* A series of steps in which the left leg describes two circular movements in the air, before the left foot is drawn up to the right knee.

garigue /garig/ *noun* (also **garrigue**) plural pronounced same L19 **French**. In the south of France: uncultivated land of a calcareous soil overgrown with low scrub; the vegetation found on such land.

garimpeiro /garim'peiru/ *noun* M19 **Portuguese**. In Brazil: an independent prospector for diamonds, gold, etc.

garrigue variant of GARIGUE.

garrocha /ga'rrotʃa/ *noun* M19 **Spanish**. A goad, *especially* (in bullfighting) a short-pointed spear.

garuda /'garʊdə/ *noun* L19 **Sanskrit** (*garuḍa*). *Indian Mythology* A fabulous bird, half-eagle, half-man, ridden by the god Vishnu.

garum /'gɛːrəm/ *noun* L16 **Latin** (from Greek *garon*, earlier *garos*). *History* A sauce made from fermented fish, popular in ancient Rome; this sauce used as a medicine for horses.

gaseosa /gase'osa/, /gasɪ'əʊsə/ *noun* E20 **Spanish**. A fizzy drink; (a drink of) carbonated (mineral) water.

gaspacho variant of GAZPACHO.

Gastarbeiter /'gastˌɑːrbaɪtər/ *noun* plural **Gastarbeiters**, same M20 **German** (from *Gast* guest + *Arbeiter* worker). A person with temporary permission to work in another (especially western European) country.

Gasthaus /'gasthaʊs/ *noun* plural **Gasthäuser** /'gasthɔyzər/ M19 **German** (from *Gast* guest + *Haus* house). A small inn or hotel in a German-speaking country.

Gasthof /'gasthoːf/ *noun* plural **gasthofs, Gasthöfe** /'gasthəːfə/ M19 **German** (from *Gast* guest + *Hof* hotel, large house). A German hotel, usually larger than a GASTHAUS.

gateau /'gatəʊ/ *noun* (also **gâteau**) plural **gateaux** /'gatəʊ(z)/, **gateaus** M19 **French** (*gâteau* cake). A large rich cake, *especially* one with layers of cream or fruit eaten as a dessert.

■ The word also applies to other recipes, such as a *gâteau de riz* /ˌgatəʊ də 'riːz/ (= of rice) (M19) a rich rice dessert in the shape of a cake, or to meat or fish baked and served in the form of a cake (L19); both usages are now rare.

gauche /gəʊʃ/ *adjective* M18 **French** (literally, 'left(-handed)'). **1** M18 Lacking in tact or ease of manner, awkward, blundering; lacking in subtlety or skill, crude, unsophisticated. **2** L19 *Mathematics* Skew, not plane. *archaic*. **b** M20 *Chemistry* Of a molecular conformation: skew, having two groups staggered along a central axis by (about) 60 degrees.

1 1995 *Country Life* It was an astounding performance from someone who had once been so gauche as to be an embarrassment before the television cameras.

gaucherie /'gəʊʃ(ə)ri/ *noun* L18 **French** (from *gauche*; see preceding). Gauche or awkward manner; a gauche action.

gaucho /'gaʊtʃəʊ/ *noun* plural **gauchos** E19 **American Spanish** (probably from Araucanian *kauču*). A mounted herdsman of the South American pampas, usually of mixed European and American Indian descent.

1996 *Oldie* The hotel bars would have been lined with gauchos with moustaches and bad teeth much as they are today.

gavotte /gə'vɒt/ *noun* L17 **French** (from modern Provençal *gavoto*, from *Gavot* an inhabitant of the Alps). **1** L17 A medium-paced dance popular in the eighteenth century. **2** E18 A piece of music for this dance, composed in common time with each phrase beginning on the third beat of the bar; a piece of music in this rhythm, *especially* one which forms a movement of a suite.

gazette /gə'zɛt/ *noun & verb* (also **Gazette**) E17 **French** (or its source Italian *gazzetta*, originally Venetian *gazeta de la novità* i.e. a 'halfpennyworth of news', so called because sold for a *gazeta*, a Venetian coin of small value). **A** *noun* **1** E17 Originally, a news-sheet; a periodical publication giving an account of current events. Now, a newspaper, *especially* (the title of) the official newspaper of an organization or institution. **2** M17 *specifically* (The title of) an official journal in Britain containing lists of government appointments, bankruptcies, and other public notices; an official journal of any government. **B** *transitive verb* L17 Publish in a gazette. Usually in *passive*, be the subject of an announcement in an official gazette, *especially* be named as appointed *to* a post, command, etc.

gazon coupé /gazɔ̃ kupe/ *noun phrase* L20 **French** (= cut lawn, cut turf). A garden feature comprising an area of grass out of which a design is cut and filled with a contrasting material such as coloured gravel.

1995 *Country Life* One such garden owner, aching to make a new flowerbed to please next year's pay-at-the-gate visitors, but fearful of the extra maintenance thereafter, has succumbed to the creation of a *gazon coupé*.

gazpacho /gəs'pɑːtʃəʊ/, *foreign* /gaθ'patʃo/, /gas'patʃo/ *noun* (also **gaspacho**) plural **gazpachos**, /gəs'pɑːtʃəʊz/, *foreign* /gaθ 'patʃos/, /gas'patʃos/ E19 **Spanish**. A Spanish soup made from tomatoes, peppers, cucumber, garlic, etc., and served cold.

Gebrauchsmusik /gə'braʊksmʊˌziːk/ *noun* M20 **German** (from *Gebrauch* use + *Musik* music). Music intended primarily for practical use and performance; *especially* music considered suitable for amateur groups and domestic playing.

Gedankenexperiment /gə'daŋk(ə)n ɛksˌpɛrɪm(ə)nt/ *noun* M20 **German** (from *Gedanken* thought + *Experiment* experiment). An experiment conducted in the imagination only; a thought-experiment.

gefilte fish /gə'fɪltə fɪʃ/ *noun phrase* (also **gefüllte fish**) L19 **Yiddish** (= stuffed fish, from *gefilte* inflected past participle of *filn* to fill). A dish either of stewed or baked stuffed fish or of fish cakes boiled in a fish or vegetable broth.

gelato /dʒə'lɑːtəʊ/ *noun* (also) plural **gelati** /dʒə'lɑːti/, **gelatos** L20 **Italian**. An ice-cream.

■ Originally in Italy and Italian-speaking countries and now also United States.

Gelehrte /gə'leːrtə/, /gə'lɛːtə/ *noun* (also **Gelehrter** /gə'leːrtə(r)/) plural **Gelehrten** /gə'leːrtən/, /gə'lɛːt(ə)n/ M19 **German** (from *gelehrt* learned, *lehren* to instruct). A learned (German) person; a scholar; a savant.

Gemeinschaft /gə'maɪnʃaft/ *noun* M20 **German** (from *gemein* common, general + *-schaft* -ship). *Sociology* A form of social integration based on personal ties; community. Cf. GESELLSCHAFT.

gemshorn /'gɛmzhɔːn/ *noun* E19 **German** (literally, 'chamois horn'). *Music* A light-toned organ-stop.

gemütlich /gə'myːtlɪç/, /gə'muːtlɪʃ/ *adjective* (also **gemutlich**) M19 **German**. Pleasant, cheerful; cosy, snug, homely; genial, good-natured.

1996 *Spectator* Austria wins hands down. The people are nicer, the villages more 'gemutlich' . . .

Gemütlichkeit /gə'myːtlɪçkaɪt/, /gə 'muːtlɪʃkʌɪt/ *noun* M19 **German** (cf. preceding). The quality of being *gemütlich*; geniality; cosiness; cheerfulness.

gendarme /'ʒɒndɑːm/, *foreign* /ʒɑ̃darm/ (*plural same*) *noun* plural **gendarmes**, (now *historical*) **gens d'armes** /ʒɑ̃ darm/ M16 **French** (a singular from the plural (now *historical*) *gens d'armes* men of arms). **1** M16 In the older French army, a horseman in full armour, having several others under his command; later, a mounted trooper, especially of the royal companies. Usually in *plural; obsolete* except *historical*. **2** L18 In France and French-speaking countries: a police officer; originally a member of a military force employed in policing. **b** E20 *generally* A police officer. *slang*.

gendarmerie /ʒɒn'dɑːməri/, *foreign* /ʒɑ̃darməri/ (*plural same*) *noun* (also **gendarmery**) M16 **French** (from *gendarme*; see preceding). **1** M16 *History* A body of cavalry, especially in the older French army. **2** L18 In France and French-speaking countries: a body of police officers, a police force. **b** M20 A police station.

gêne /ʒɛn/ *noun* E19 **French** (from Old French *gehine* torture). Constraint, embarrassment, discomfort.

gêné /ʒɛne/ *adjective* (feminine **gênée**) E19 **French** (past participial adjective of *gêner* to embarrass: related to preceding). Constrained, embarrassed, discomforted.

genera plural of GENUS.

generalia /ˌdʒɛn(ə)'reɪlɪə/ *noun plural* M19 **Latin** (neuter plural of *generalis* general). General principles.

generalissimo /ˌdʒɛn(ə)rə'lɪsɪməʊ/ *noun* plural **generalissimos** E17 **Italian** (superlative of *generale* general). The commander of a combined military, naval, and air force, or of several armies.

genesis /'dʒɛnɪsɪs/ *noun* LOE **Latin** (from Greek = generation, creation, nativity, horoscope, from base of *gignesthai* to be born or produced). **1** LOE (**Genesis**) (The name of) the first book of the Bible. **2** E17 Origin, mode of formation or generation.

■ *Genesis* is the name given in the Septuagint to the first book of the Old Testament, dealing with the creation of the world; from there it was adopted by the Vulgate and vernacular Bibles. It was formerly (LME–M17) also an astrological term for 'nativity, horoscope'.

genie /'dʒiːni/ *noun* plural **genii** /'dʒiːnɪʌɪ/, **genis** M17 **French** (*génie* from Latin GENIUS). **1** M17–E18 A GENIUS (sense 1). **2** M18 A spirit or jinnee (in Arabian stories), especially one inhabiting a bottle, lamp, etc., and capable of granting wishes.

genitor /'dʒɛnɪtə/ *noun* LME **Latin** (*genitor* (Old French *géniteur*) from base of *gignere* to beget. **1** LME A male parent. **2** M20 *Anthropology* A person's biological as opposed to legal father.

■ Long archaic in the general sense 1, *genitor* in sense 2 was revived in the specific context of the distinction between biological and legal fatherhood; cf. PATER sense 3b.

genius /'dʒiːnɪəs/ *noun* plural **genii** /'dʒiːnɪʌɪ/, **geniuses** LME **Latin** (from base of *gignere* to beget, Greek *gignesthai* to be born, come into being). **1** LME The tutelary or attendant spirit in classical pagan belief allotted to every person at their birth, or to a place, institution, etc. **b** L16 Especially as *good* or *evil genius*. Either of the two mutually opposed spirits or angels supposed to attend each person. Hence a person who or thing which for good or bad powerfully influences another. **2** L16 A demon or spirit. **3 a** L16–E19 Characteristic disposition, bent, or inclination. **b** M17 Prevalent feeling, opinion, taste, or character (of a nation, age, etc.). **c** M17 The prevailing character or spirit, or characteristic method (of a law, language, etc.). **d** E19 The body of associations connected with or inspirations derived from a place; the GENIUS LOCI. **4** E17 Natural ability or tendency; attributes which fit a person for a particular activity. (Passing into sense 5.) **b** M17 Natural aptitude, talent, or inclination *for, to* (something). **5** M17 Inborn exalted intellectual power; instinctive and extraordinary imaginative, creative, or inventive capacity, frequently opposed to *talent*; a person having this.

genius loci /ˌdʒiːnɪəs 'ləʊsʌɪ/, /'lɒkiː/ *noun phrase* E17 **Latin** (= genius of the place). The presiding god or spirit of a place. Also = sense 3d above.

1995 *Oldie* Betjeman was a genius in the popular literary sense of the word, but he was also a *genius loci*—a sort of tutelary deity who looked after a particular bit of earth, in his case these poor old islands of ours.

1996 *Spectator* At best, it [sc. a picnic] is as much the product of *genius loci* as the food, drink and company. The best one I have ever had was in Russia on the sprawling meadows of Tolstoy's Yasnaya Polyana estate.

genizah /gɛ'ni:zə/ *noun* (also **geniza**) L19 **Hebrew** (literally, 'a hiding, hiding place', from *gānaz* to set aside, hide). (The contents of) a storeroom for damaged, discarded, or heretical manuscripts and sacred relics, usually attached to a synagogue.

genre /'ʒɑ̃rə/, /'ʒɒnrə/ *noun* E19 **French** (= kind). Kind, type; *especially* a style or category of painting, novel, film, etc., characterized by a particular form or purpose; *specifically* a style of painting depicting scenes of ordinary life.

gens /dʒɛnz/ *noun* plural **gentes** /'dʒɛnti:z/, /'dʒɛnteɪz/ M19 **Latin** (from base of *gignere* to beget). **1** M19 In ancient Rome: a group of families with a supposed common origin, a common name, and common religious rites. Also, a similar group of families in other cultures. **2** L19 *Anthropology* A kinship group composed of people related through their male ancestors.

gens de la robe /ʒɑ̃ də la rɔb/ *noun phrase* (also **gens de robe**) L17 **French** (literally, 'folk of the long robe'). Lawyers.

genus /'dʒɛnəs/, /'dʒi:nəs/ *noun* plural **genera** /'dʒɛn(ə)rə/, **genuses** M16 **Latin** (= birth, family, nation). **1** M16 *Logic* A class of things containing a number of subordinate classes (called species) with certain common attributes. **2** E17 *Biology* A basic taxonomic grouping ranking below family and subfamily. Formerly also used in the classification of minerals, chemical substances, etc. **b** M17 *generally* A category, a kind. **3** M18 In ancient Greek music, each of the three kinds of tetrachord.

georgette /dʒɔ:'dʒɛt/ *noun & adjective* E20 **French** (from Mme *Georgette* de la Plante (flourished *c.*1900), French modiste). (Made of) a thin plain-woven crêpe dress-material, usually of silk.

germen /'dʒə:mən/ *noun* E17 **Latin** (= seed, sprout). **1** E17 The rudiment of an organism. Now only *figurative*. **2** E17–L18 A shoot, a sprout. **3** M18 *Botany* The rudiment of a seed-vessel.

Gesamtkunstwerk /gə'zamtkʊnstˌvɛrk/ *noun* plural **Gesamtkunstwerke** /gə'zamtkʊnstˌvɛrkə/ M20 **German** (from *gesamt* total + *Kunstwerk* work of art). An ideal work of art in which drama, music, and other performing arts are integrated and each is subservient to the whole.

1996 *Spectator* Diaghilev and his friends . . . were fascinated by the notion of the *Gesamtkunstwerk*—total work of art—integrating drama, music and spectacle.

Gesellschaft /gə'zɛlʃaft/ *noun* (also **gesellschaft**) L19 **German** (from *Gesell(e)* companion + *-schaft* -ship). *Sociology* A form of social integration based on impersonal ties; association. Cf. GEMEINSCHAFT.

gesso /'dʒɛsəʊ/ *noun* plural **gessoes** L16 **Italian** (from Latin GYPSUM; cf. YESO). Gypsum, plaster of Paris, now only as prepared for use in painting and sculpture; any white substance that can be mixed with water to make a ground.

gestalt /gə'ʃtɑ:lt/, /gə'ʃtalt/ *noun* (also **Gestalt**) E20 **German** (= form, shape). Chiefly *Psychology*. An integrated perceptual structure or unity conceived as functionally more than the sum of its parts.

Gestapo /gə'stɑ:pəʊ/ *noun* plural **Gestapos** M20 **German** (acronym, from *Geheime Staatspolizei* Secret State Police). *History* (An officer of) the secret police of the Nazi regime in Germany; also *transferred*.

1995 *Country Life* . . . one expects nothing better than charred raw meat and discomfort at barbecues. Why the environmental health officers, our wonderful germ gestapo, have not stamped them out long since is a mystery.

gett /gɛt/ *noun* (also **get**) L19 **Hebrew**. A Jewish bill of divorce, in prescribed form; a divorce by such a bill.

gharana /gə'rɑ:nə/ *noun* M20 **Hindustani** (*gharānā* family). *Indian Music* A school of players who practise a particular style of interpretation.

ghat /gɑ:t/, /gɔ:t/ *noun* (also **ghaut**) E17 **Hindustani** (*ghāṭ*). **1** E17 *The Ghats* Either of two mountain chains running parallel to the east and west coasts of southern India. **2** L17 In India: a mountain pass. **3** L18 In India: a flight of steps leading to a river-bank; a landing-place. **4** L19 A level place at the top of a river-bank ghat where Hindus cremate their dead. In full *burning-ghat*.

ghazal /'gazal/ *noun* (also **ghazel**) L18 **Persian** (from Arabic *ġazal*). A usually amatory Arabic, Turkish, Urdu, or (especially) Persian lyric poem or song characterized by a limited number of stanzas and the recurrence of the same rhyme.

ghazi /ˈgɑːzi/ *noun* (also (as a title) **Ghazi**) plural **ghazis** M18 **Arabic** (*al-ġāzī* active participle of *ġazā* to braid, invade, foray). In the Middle East: a champion, especially of Muslims against non-Muslims; a dedicated Muslim fighter. Frequently as an honorific title.

ghee /giː/ *noun* (also **ghi**) M17 **Hindustani** (*ghī*, from Sanskrit *ghṛta* past participle of *ghṛ-* to sprinkle). Indian clarified butter made from the milk of a buffalo or cow.

gherao /gɛˈraʊ/ *noun & verb* M20 **Hindi** (from *ghernā* to surround, besiege). **A** *noun* M20 plural **gheraos**. In India and Pakistan: a form of protest or harassment in labour disputes whereby employers etc. are prevented by workers from leaving the place of work until their claims have been granted. **B** *transitive verb* M20 Detain (a person) in this manner.

ghetto /ˈgɛtəʊ/ *noun & verb* E17 **Italian** (origin uncertain: perhaps abbreviation of Italian *borghetto* diminutive of *borgo* borough, or from Italian *getto* foundry, where the first ghetto established in Venice, in 1516, was sited). **A** *noun* plural **ghetto(e)s**. **1** E17 *History* The quarter in a city, originally in Italy, to which Jews were restricted. **2** L19 A densely populated slum area occupied by a minority group or groups, usually as a result of social or economic pressures; an isolated or segregated social group or area.

2 1996 *Spectator* They did a deal, but Mr Hume has been unable to sell it in the ghetto. The Bogside Residents' Association is an unlovely body.

ghi variant of GHEE.

ghibli /ˈgɪbli/ *noun* (also **gibli**, **qibli**) E19 **Arabic** (*ḳiblī* southern). A hot dry southerly wind of North Africa.

ghilgai variant of GILGAI.

giallo antico /ˌdʒallo anˈtiːko/, /ˌdʒaləʊ an ˈtiːkəʊ/ *noun & adjective phrase* M18 **Italian** (literally, 'ancient yellow'). (Made of) a rich yellow marble found among ruins in Italy, and used as a decoration.

gibber /ˈgɪbə/ *noun* L18 **Aboriginal**. In Australia: a boulder, a (large) stone.

gibli variant of GHIBLI.

gigolo /ˈʒɪgələʊ/, /ˈdʒɪgələʊ/ *noun* plural **gigolos** E20 **French** (formed as masculine of *gigole* dancehall woman). A professional male dancing-partner or escort; a (usually young) man supported by a (usually older) woman in return for his attentions.

gigot /ˈdʒɪgət/ *noun* E16 **French** (diminutive of dialect *gigue* leg, from *giguer* to hop, jump, of unknown origin). **1** E16 A leg of mutton etc. **2** M16–M17 A dish made from minced meat, a sausage. **3** E19 A leg-of-mutton sleeve. More fully *gigot sleeve*.

gigue /ʒiːg/ *noun* L17 **French**. A lively piece of music in duple or triple time, often with dotted rhythms and forming the last movement of a suite; a jig.

gilet /ʒilɛ/ *noun* plural pronounced same L19 **French**. A light often padded waistcoat, usually worn for warmth by women.

gilgai /ˈgɪlgʌɪ/ *noun* (also **ghilgai**) M19 **Aboriginal** ((Kamilaroi) *gilgaay*). In Australia: a shallow depression between mounds or ridges, in which rainwater collects.

gimbri /ˈgɪmbri/ *noun* (also **gunibri** /ˈguːnɪbri/) L19 **Arabic** (dialectal variant of *ḳunbura* pomegranate). A small Moorish guitar; a player of this instrument.

ginseng /ˈdʒɪnsɛŋ/ *noun* M17 **Chinese** (*rénshēn* (Wade–Giles *jên shên*), from *rén* man + *shēn* kind of herb). **1** M17 A tuberous root credited, especially in the Far East, with valuable tonic properties. **2** L17 The source of this root, any of several plants of the genus *Panax* (family Araliaceae), with palmate leaves and umbels of small greenish flowers.

giocoso /dʒəˈkəʊsəʊ/ *adverb & adjective* E19 **Italian** (= merry). *Music* (A direction:) merr(il)y, joyous(ly).

girandole /ˈdʒɪr(ə)ndəʊl/ *noun* (also **girandola** in senses 1 and 2) M17 **French** (from Italian *girandola*, from *girare* from late Latin *gyrare* to gyrate). **I 1** M17 A kind of revolving firework; a discharge of rockets etc. from a revolving wheel. **2** E19 A revolving jet of water; a series of jets in an ornamental fountain. **II 3** M18 A branched support for candles or other lights which either stands on a surface or projects from a wall. **4** E19 An earring, a pendant, *especially* one which has a large central stone surrounded by smaller ones.

girasol /ˈdʒɪrəsɒl/, /ˈdʒɪrəsəʊl/ *noun* (also **girasole** /ˈdʒɪrəsəʊl/) L16 **French** (or Italian *girasole*, from *girare* to gyrate + *sole* sun). **1** A sunflower. *rare*. Only in L16. **2** L16 A variety of opal which reflects a reddish glow, a fire-opal.

giro /ˈdʒiːro/ *noun 1* plural **giri** /ˈdʒiːri/ L17 **Italian** (= round, circuit). A tour, a circuit; a turn.

giro /ˈdʒʌɪrəʊ/ *noun 2 & verb* L19 **German** (from Italian = circulation (of money)). **A** *noun* plural **giros**. **1** L19 A system of credit transfer between banks, post offices, etc.; *specifically* (frequently **Giro**) a system run by the British Post Office for the banking and transfer of money. Also *giro system*. **2** L20 A cheque or money order issued through the giro system; *specifically* in Britain, such a cheque used for unemployment benefit or social security payments. In full *giro cheque*, *giro order*. **B** *transitive verb* L20 Pay by giro.

girouette /ʒirwɛt/ *noun* plural pronounced same E19 **French**. A weathercock.

gitana /dʒɪˈtɑːnə/, *foreign* /xiˈtana/ *noun* M19 **Spanish** (feminine of next). A female (Spanish) Gypsy.

gitano /dʒɪˈtɑːnəʊ/, *foreign* /xiˈtano/ *noun* plural **gitanos** /dʒɪˈtɑːnəʊz/, *foreign* /xiˈtanos/ M19 **Spanish** (representation of popular Latin = Egyptian, from Latin *Aegyptus* Egypt + *-anus*). A male (Spanish) Gypsy.

gîte /ʒit/ *noun* (also **gite**) plural pronounced same L18 **French**. **1** L18 A stopping-place, a lodging. Now *rare*. **2** M20 In France and French-speaking countries: a furnished holiday home usually in a rural district.

Giuoco Piano /dʒʊˌəʊkəʊ pɪˈɑːnəʊ/ *noun phrase* E19 **Italian** (= quiet game). *Chess* An initially quiet opening in chess.

gjetost /ˈjɛtɒst/ *noun* E20 **Norwegian** (from *gjet*, *geit* goat + *ost* cheese). A Norwegian cheese made from goat's milk.

glacé /ˈglaseɪ/ *adjective & noun* M19 **French** (past participle of *glacer* to ice, give a gloss to, from *glace* ice). **A** *adjective* **1** M19 Of cloth, leather, etc.: smooth, highly polished, glossy. **2** L19 Of fruit: covered with icing or sugar. Of icing: made with icing sugar and water. **B** *noun* M19 Glacé silk, glacé leather.

glacis /ˈglasɪs/, /ˈglasi/ *noun* plural same /ˈglasɪz/, /ˈglasiːz/ L17 **French** (from Old French *glacier* to slip, slide, from *glace* ice, from Proto-Romance alteration of Latin *glacies* ice). **1** L17 A gently sloping bank; *specifically* in *Fortification*, a natural or artificial bank sloping down from the covered way of a fort so as to expose attackers to the defenders' missiles etc. **b** M20 *figurative* A zone or area acting as a protective barrier or buffer between two (potential) enemies. **2** L19 A sloping armour-plate protecting an opening etc. in a ship. In full *glacis-plate*.

glaistig /ˈglastɪk/ *noun* (also **glastick**) E20 **Gaelic**. A fairy with a variety of forms and characters, frequently appearing in the shape of a goat or as half-woman, half-goat, but also as a beautiful water-sprite.

glasnost /ˈglaznɒst/, /ˈglɑːsnɒst/ *noun* L20 **Russian** (*glasnost'* the fact of being public). In the former USSR: the policy or practice of more open consultative government and wider dissemination of information. Also *transferred*.

■ *Glasnost* is an old Russian word, but its connotation of 'freedom of information' only evolved in the latter years of the Soviet regime. A debate on the subject started by the state newspaper *Izvestiya* in January 1985 was taken up by Mikhail Gorbachev in his speech in March the same year accepting the post of General Secretary of the Communist Party and expressing his commitment to reform. *Glasnost* was one of the key concepts in the Gorbachev reform programme (see also PERESTROIKA), and English-speaking political commentators, finding that there was no English word exactly equivalent to *glasnost*, opted to use the Russian one. It became widely current in the late 1980s and was soon applied to mean 'openness', in particular 'openness in government', in a variety of situations quite outside its original context.

1986 *New York Times* Exposés of corruption, shortages and economic problems appear virtually daily in the [Soviet] press. It is a change that became evident after Mikhail S. Gorbachev came to office last March and called for more 'glasnost', or openness, in covering domestic affairs.
transferred **1996** *Guardian 2* For royal correspondents, used to being fobbed off, lied to, and told off like naughty boys, Atkinson and Vulliamy represented a new *glasnost* in Palace PR.

glastick variant of GLAISTIG.

glaucoma /glɔːˈkəʊmə/ *noun* M17 **Greek** (*glaukōma*, from *glaukos* bluish-green, bluish-grey). *Medicine* An eye condition characterized by increased pressure within the eyeball and a gradual impairment or loss of sight.

Gleichschaltung /ˈglaɪçˌʃaltʊŋ/ *noun* (also **gleichschaltung**) M20 **German**. The standardization of political, economic, and cultural institutions in authoritarian States.

glissade /glɪ'sɑ:d/, /glɪ'seɪd/ *noun & verb* M19 **French** (from *glisser* to slip, slide). **A** *noun* **1** M19 *Dancing* A step consisting of a glide or slide in any direction, usually a joining step. **2** M19 *Mountaineering* The action or an act of sliding down a steep slope especially of snow, usually on the feet with the support of an ice-axe etc. **B** *verb* **1** *intransitive & transitive verb* M19 *Dancing* Perform a glissade; progress by glissades. **2** M19 *Mountaineering* Slide down a steep slope especially of snow by means of a glissade.

glissando /glɪ'sandəʊ/ *noun* plural **glissandi** /glɪ'sandi/, **glissandos** L19 **Italian** (from French *glissant* present participle of *glisser* to slip, slide). *Music* A continuous slide of adjacent notes upwards or downwards.

1996 *Times* The hour was late; the booze was strong; the notes on my trombone part seemed very small . . . I felt my *glissandi* getting limper and limper.

glissé /glise/ *noun* plural pronounced same E20 **French** (past participle of *glisser* to slip, slide). *Ballet* A sliding step in which the flat of the foot is often used. More fully *pas glissé* /pa glise/.

globule /'glɒbju:l/ *noun* M17 **French** (or Latin *globulus* diminutive of *globus* globe). **1** M17 A small spherical body or globe; a round drop (of liquid). **2** M19 A small pill.

glockenspiel /'glɒk(ə)nʃpi:l/, /'glɒk(ə)n spi:l/, *noun* E19 **German** (= bell-play). *Music* 1 E19 An organ-stop imitating the sound of bells. **2** M19 Any of several percussion instruments, *especially* (**a**) a series of tuned metal bars mounted on a horizontal frame; (**b**) a series of bells or metal bars in a lyre-shaped frame carried in marching bands (also *lyra glockenspiel*).

glögg /glœg/, /glɒg/ *noun* (also **glugg** /glʌg/) E20 **Swedish**. A Scandinavian winter drink, consisting of hot sweetened red wine with brandy, almonds, raisins, and spices.

gloire /glwar/ *noun* M19 **French**. Glory; *specifically* the national glory and prestige of France. In full *la gloire* /la glwar/.

gloria /'glɔ:rɪə/ *noun & adjective* (in sense 1 **Gloria**) ME **Latin** (= glory). **A** *noun* **1** ME Any of several Christian liturgical formulae, as *Gloria* (*Patri*) the doxology 'Glory be to the Father', *Gloria* (*tibi*) the response 'Glory be to thee', *Gloria* (*in excelsis*) the hymn 'Glory be to God on high', forming part of the Mass etc. **b** L16 The music to which any of these is set. **2** L18 An aureole, a nimbus. **3** M19 In France: (a drink of) coffee mixed with brandy or rum. **4** L19 A closely-woven fabric of silk and wool or cotton etc.; a garment made of this. **B** *adjective* E20 Made of the fabric gloria.

gloriette /ˌglɔ:rɪ'ɛt/ *noun* M19 **French**. A highly decorated chamber in a castle or other building.

glugg variant of GLÖGG.

glühwein /'gly:vaɪn/, /'glu:vʌɪn/ *noun* (also **gluhwein**) L19 **German** (from *glühen* to mull, glow + *wein* wine). Mulled wine.

gneiss /nʌɪs/ *noun* (also (earlier) **kneiss**) M18 **German** (from Old High German *gneisto* (= Old English *gnāst*, Old Norse *gneisti*) spark). A foliated usually coarse-grained metamorphic rock in which bands of granular minerals alternate with bands of flaky or prismatic ones, and typically consisting of feldspar, quartz, and mica.

gnocchi /'n(j)ɒki/, /'gnɒki/, *foreign* /'ɲokki/ *noun plural* L19 **Italian** (plural of *gnocco*, from *nocchio* knot in wood). Small dumplings made with flour, semolina, or potato.

gnomon /'nəʊmɒn/ *noun* M16 **French** (or Latin *gnomon*, from Greek *gnōmōn* inspector, indicator, carpenter's square). **1** M16 A pillar, rod, etc., which shows the time of day by casting its shadow on a marked surface; *especially* the pin or triangular plate of a sundial. **b** E17 A column etc. used in observing the meridian altitude of the sun. **2** L16 *Geometry* The part of a parallelogram left after a similar parallelogram is taken away from one of its corners.

■ Various other technical and general uses are now no longer current.

gnosis /'nəʊsɪs/ *noun* plural **gnoses** /'nəʊsi:z/ L16 **Greek** (*gnōsis* investigation, knowledge, from *gno-* base of *gignōskein* to know). A special knowledge of spiritual mysteries; *specifically* in *Theology*, the redemptive knowledge that the Gnostics claimed to possess.

go /gəʊ/ *noun* L19 **Japanese**. A Japanese board game of territorial possession and capture. Cf. WEI CH'I.

gobang /gəʊ'baŋ/ *noun* L19 **Japanese** (*goban* board for playing the game of go). A simplified form of the game of GO played on a board marked with squares, each player seeking to place five counters in a row.

godet /gəʊ'dɛt/, /'gəʊdeɪ/ *noun* ME **Old and Modern French**. **1** ME–E17 A drinking-cup. **2** L19 A triangular piece of material inserted into a dress, glove, or other garment. **3** E20 A driven roller or wheel around which the filaments of any of various man-made fibres are drawn during manufacture.

goitre /'gɔɪtə/ *noun* (also **goiter**) E17 **French** (either (i) from Old French *goitron* from Provençal from Proto-Romance, from Latin *guttur* throat, or (ii) back-formation from French *goitreux* goitred, from Latin adjective from *guttur*). *Medicine* A swelling of the neck due to enlargement of the thyroid gland, as caused by disease of the gland, iodine deficiency, etc.

goldwasser /'gəʊldvasə/, *foreign* /'gɔltvasər/ *noun* E20 **German** (= gold water). A liqueur containing particles of gold leaf, originally made at Gdańsk in Poland.

golem /'gəʊləm/, /'gɔɪləm/ *noun* L19 **Yiddish** (*goylem* from Hebrew *gōlem* shapeless mass). A human figure of clay etc. supernaturally brought to life; an automaton, a robot.

golgotha /'gɒlgəθə/ *noun* E17 **Late Latin** ((Vulgate), from Greek by metathesis from Aramaic *gōgoltâ*, perhaps under influence of Hebrew *gulgōleṯ* skull). A place of interment; a graveyard, a charnel-house.

■ From the explanation in Matthew 27:33 and elsewhere of the name of the site of the Crucifixion as 'a place of a skull', wits at the universities of Oxford and Cambridge formerly (E18–E19) gave the nickname of Golgotha to the meeting place of the heads ('skulls') of university colleges or halls.

gompa /'gɒmpə/ *noun* E20 **Tibetan** (*gōn-pa*, *gōm-pa* a solitary place, a hermitage). A Tibetan temple or monastery.

gondola /'gɒndələ/ *noun* M16 **Italian** ((Venetian) from Rhaeto-Romance *gondolà* to rock). **1** M16 A light asymmetric flat-bottomed boat used on the Venetian canals, having a high pointed prow and stern and usually propelled by a single oar at the stern. **2** L17 A large light flat-bottomed riverboat; a lighter, used also as a gunboat. *United States*. **3** M19 A car or nacelle attached to the underside of a dirigible or airship; something resembling this. **4** L19 An open railway goods wagon with low sides. More fully *gondola-car*, *gondola-wagon*. *United States*. **5** M20 A car attached to a ski-lift. **6** M20 An island display counter in a self-service shop.

gondolier /ˌgɒndə'lɪə/ *noun* E17 **French** (from Italian *gondoliere*, from GONDOLA). A person who rows a Venetian gondola.

gonfalonier /ˌgɒnf(ə)lə'nɪə/ *noun* L16 **French** (Old French *gonfanonier*). A standard-bearer; *specifically* (**a**) the Pope's standard-bearer; (**b**) *History* any of various officials or magistrates in the Italian city-states.

gonzo /'gɒnzəʊ/ *adjective & noun* L20 **Italian** (= foolish, or perhaps Spanish *ganso* goose, fool). **A** *adjective* L20 Of, pertaining to, or designating a style of subjective journalism characterized by factual distortion and exaggerated rhetoric; *generally* bizarre, crazy. **B** *noun* plural **gonzos** L20 Gonzo journalism; a journalist writing in this style; *generally* a crazy or foolish person.

■ Originally and chiefly United States slang.

goombah /'gu:mbɑ:/ *noun* (also **goombay** /'gu:mbeɪ/) L18 **West Indian creole** (cf. Kikongo [*n*]*kumbi* a kind of drum, Twi *gumbe* drum music). In the West Indies: any of various types of drum played with the fingers (rather than with sticks).

goonda /'gu:ndə/ *noun* (also **goondah**) E20 **Hindi** (*guṇḍā* rascal). In the Indian subcontinent: a hired bully.

goondie /'gu:ndi/ *noun* (also **gundy**) L19 **Aboriginal** ((Kamilaroi) *gunday* stringy-bark). In Australia: an Aboriginal hut; a GUNYAH.

gooroo variant of GURU.

gopi /'gəʊpi:/ *noun* (also **Gopi**) L18 **Sanskrit**. *Hindu Mythology* Any of the milkmaids of Brindavan, companions of Krishna.

gopura /'gəʊpʊrə/ *noun* (also **gopuram** /'gəʊpʊrəm/) M19 **Sanskrit** (*gopura* city gate, from *go* cow, cattle + *pura* city, quarter). In southern India: the great pyramidal tower over the entrance-gate to a temple precinct.

Gorsedd /'gɔ:sɛð/ *noun* L18 **Welsh** (= mound, throne, assembly). A meeting of

Welsh bards and druids; *especially* the assembly that meets to announce the next Royal National Eisteddfod and at certain times during this festival.

Götterdämmerung /ˈgœtərˌdɛmərʊŋ/, /gɒtəˈdamərʊŋ/ *noun* E20 **German** (literally, 'twilight of the gods'). *Germanic mythology* The downfall of the gods; *generally* a cataclysmic collapse of a regime, institution, etc. Cf. RAGNAROK.

■ *Götterdämmerung* is the title of the final opera in Wagner's Ring cycle.

gouache /guːˈɑːʃ/, *foreign* /gwaʃ/ *noun* L19 **French** (from Italian *guazzo*). A method of opaque watercolour painting, in which the pigments are bound by a glue to form a sort of paste; a painting executed in this way; the pigments thus used.

goujon /ˈgudʒ(ə)n/, *in sense 2 foreign* /guʒɔ̃/ (*plural same*) *noun* L19 **Old and Modern French** (from Latin *gobio(n)-*, from *gobius* goby). **1** L19 In the United States: the flathead catfish, *Pylodictis olivaris*. **2** M20 *Cookery* In *plural*. Narrow strips of fish, especially sole, or of chicken, usually for deep-frying.

goulash /ˈguːlaʃ/ *noun* M19 **Hungarian** (*gulyás(hús)*, from *gulyás* herdsman + *hús* meat). **1** M19 A highly seasoned stew or ragout of meat and vegetables. **2** E20 *Bridge* A fresh deal of unshuffled cards, usually three or more at a time, after the hands have been thrown in without bidding.

gourmand /ˈgʊəmənd/, /ˈgɔːmənd/, *foreign* /gurmɑ̃/ (*plural same*) *noun & adjective* (occasionally feminine **gourmande** /ˈgʊəmɒnd/, /ˈgɔːmɑːnd/, *foreign* /gurmɑ̃ːd/, (*plural same*)) LME **Old and Modern French** (of unknown origin). **A** *noun* **1** LME A person who is overfond of eating; a glutton. **2** M18 A person who is fond of, or a judge of, good food; a GOURMET. **B** *adjective* M16 Gluttonous, greedy; fond of eating.

gourmet /ˈgʊəmeɪ/, /ˈgɔːmeɪ/, *foreign* /gurmɛ/ (*plural same*) *noun & adjective* E19 **French** (formerly = wine-merchant's assistant, wine-taster, influenced in sense by GOURMAND). **A** *noun* E19 A connoisseur in eating and drinking; a judge of good food. **B** *attributive* or as *adjective* E20 Of the nature of a gourmet; of a kind or standard suitable for gourmets.

goût /guː/ *noun* (also **gout**) L16 **French** (earlier *goust* from Latin *gustus* taste). **1** L16 Liking, relish, fondness (*for*). **2** E18 The ability to perceive and discriminate between flavours, smells, etc.; the faculty of aesthetic appreciation or judgement; (good) taste. **3** E18 Style or manner; *especially* a prevailing or fashionable style. **4** M18 Flavour, savour, taste.

goy /gɔɪ/ *noun* plural **goyim** /ˈgɔɪɪm/, **goys** M19 **Hebrew** (*gōy* people, nation). Among Jews: a non-Jew, a Gentile.

gradus /ˈgreɪdəs/ *noun* M18 **Latin** (*gradus* step(s)). *History* A manual of classical prosody used in schools to help in writing Greek and Latin verse.

■ This category of schoolbook took its name from the title of a manual of Latin prosody, the *Gradus ad Parnassum* 'Step(s) to Parnassus', which appeared in England in many editions from the late seventeenth century onwards and inspired a *Greek Gradus* and other imitations.

Graf /grɑːf/ *noun* M17 **German**. A German nobleman corresponding in rank to a European count or British earl.

■ Chiefly in titles. The feminine equivalent is *Gräfin*.

graffiti /grəˈfiːti/ *transitive verb* L20 **Italian** (from plural of next). Apply graffiti to; write as graffiti.

graffito /grəˈfiːtəʊ/ *noun* plural (frequently used as *singular*) **graffiti** /grəˈfiːti/ M19 **Italian** (from *graffio* scratching). **1** M19 A drawing, writing, or scribbling on a wall etc., originally *specific* on an ancient wall, as at Rome and Pompeii. Usually in *plural*. **2** L19 A method of decoration or design produced by scratching through a plaster layer to reveal a different colour below.

gramdan /ˈgrɑːmdɑːn/ *noun* M20 **Sanskrit** (*grāma* village + *dāna* gift). In India: the pooling by villagers of their land for the collective good, especially as advocated by Vinoba Bhave (1895–1982).

grand battement /grɑ̃ batmɑ̃/, /ˈgrɒ̃ ˈbatmɒ̃/ *noun phrase* plural **grands battements** (pronounced same) M19 **French**. *Ballet* A BATTEMENT executed with the moving leg stretched out as it is raised.

grand coup /grɑ̃ ku/, /grɒ̃ ˈkuː/ plural **grands coups** (pronounced same) E19 **French**. **1** E19 A bold or important stroke or effort. **2** L19 *Whist* and *Bridge* The deliberate disposal of a superfluous trump by ruffing a winning card from the opposite hand.

grand cru /grɑ̃ kry/, /grɒ̃d 'kru:/ *noun & adjective phrase* plural **grands crus** /grɑ̃ kry/, **grand crus** /grɒ̃d 'kru:z/ E20 **French** (= great growth). *Wine* (Designating) a wine of superior quality.

1996 *Times Magazine* At the top of the pyramid are those glorious grands crus wines that dreams are made of.

grande amoureuse /grɑ̃d amurøz/ plural **grandes amoureuses** /grɑ̃dz amurøz/ E20 **French**. A passionate or amorous woman; a woman skilled in the arts of love.

grande dame /grɑ̃d dam/ plural **grandes dames** (pronounced same) M18 **French**. A woman of high rank or eminence and dignified bearing.

1995 *Times* The latest lifestyle tip from the grandes dames of chic: take your dog to work. The offices of *Tatler* are overrun . . .

grande horizontale /grɑ̃d ɔrizɔ̃tal/ *noun phrase* plural **grandes horizontales** (pronounced same) L19 **French**. A courtesan or prostitute.

1970 *New Yorker* He is overshadowed throughout by Aunt Augusta, the still unretired *grande horizontale* of seventy-three.

grande passion /grɑ̃d pasjɔ̃/ plural **grandes passions** (pronounced same) E19 **French** (= grand passion). An overmastering passion for another person; an engrossing love affair.

grande sonnerie /grɑ̃d sɔnri/, /grɒ̃d 'sɒnəri/ M20 **French**. *Horology* A system of chiming in which the hour and the quarter is struck each quarter on different toned bells.

grande tenue see EN GRANDE TENUE.

Grand Guignol /ˌgrɒ̃ gi:'njɒl/, *foreign* /grɑ̃ giɲɔl/ *noun phrase* E20 **French** (= Great Punch). A dramatic entertainment in which short horrific or sensational pieces are played successively; a literary work with similar characteristics.

■ In France *Guignol* is a marionette drama equivalent to the English Punch and Judy show. *Grand Guignol* takes its name from a theatre in Paris.

1996 *Spectator* Many novelists who specialise in *grand guignol* . . . might just as well be writing love stories, or crime stories, or something else without the gratuitous details of blood and gore.

grandioso /grandi'o:so/ *adverb, adjective & noun* L19 **Italian**. *Music* **A** *adverb & adjective* L19 (A direction:) in a grand or imposing manner. **B** *noun* plural **grandiosi** /grandi'o:si/ L20 A movement or passage played in this way.

grand jeté /grɑ̃ ʒəte/, /grɒ̃ 'ʒəteɪ/ *noun phrase* plural **grands jetés** (pronounced same) M20 **French**. *Ballet* A JETÉ achieving a high elevation.

grand mal /grɒ̃ 'mal/, *foreign* /grɑ̃ mal/ *noun phrase* L19 **French** (literally, 'great sickness'). General convulsive epilepsy, with loss of consciousness. Cf. PETIT MAL.

grand monarque /grɑ̃ mənark/, /ˌgrɒ̃ mɔ 'nɑ:k/ plural **grands monarques** (pronounced same) L17 **French**. A supreme and absolute ruler; *specifically* an epithet of Louis XIV of France (reigned 1643–1715).

grand monde /grɑ̃ mɔ̃d/, /'grɒ̃ 'mɒnd/ E18 **French**. The BEAU MONDE.

Grand Prix /grɒ̃ 'pri:/ *noun phrase* plural **Grands Prix** (pronounced same) M19 **French** (= great prize). **1** M19 An international horse race for three-year-olds run annually in June at Longchamps, Paris. In full *Grand Prix de Paris* /də pa'ri:/. **2** L19 The highest prize awarded in a competition or exhibition. **3** E20 Any of a series of motor or motorcycle races forming the World Championship, held in various countries under international rules. Also, a very important competitive event in various other sports.

grand seigneur /grɑ̃ sɛɲœr/, /ˌgrɒ̃ seɪn'jə:/ plural **grands seigneurs** (pronounced same) E17 **French**. A great nobleman.

grand siècle /grɑ̃ sjɛkl/, /ˌgrɒ̃ sɪ'ɛk(ə)l/ M19 **French** (literally, 'great century *or* age'). A classical or golden age; *especially* the reign of Louis XIV (1643–1715) in France.

granita /gra'ni:tə/, *foreign* /gra'nita/ *noun* plural **granite** /gra'ni:ti/, *foreign* /gra'nite/ M19 **Italian**. A coarse water-ice or sherbet; a drink made with crushed ice.

gran turismo /gran tu'rizmo/, /ˌgran tʊə 'rɪzməʊ/ *noun & adjective phrase* M20 **Italian** (literally, 'great touring'). (Designating) a comfortable high-performance model of motor car.

■ Abbreviated to *GT*.

grappa /'grapə/ *noun* L19 **Italian**. A brandy distilled from the refuse of grapes after wine-making.

graticule /'gratɪkju:l/ *noun* L19 **French** (from medieval Latin *graticula* for (also classical Latin) *craticula* small gridiron, diminutive of Latin *cratis* hurdle). **1** L19 A network of lines representing meridians and parallels, on which a map or plan can be represented. **2** E20 A series of fine lines or fibres incorporated in a telescope or other optical instrument as a measuring scale or an aid in locating objects; a plate etc. bearing this.

gratin /gratɛ̃/, /ˈgratã/ *noun* M17 **French** (from *gratter*, earlier *grater* to grate). **1** M17 A method of cooking, or a dish cooked, with a crisp brown crust, usually of grated cheese or breadcrumbs. Cf. AU GRATIN. **2** M20 The highest class of society.

■ For sense 2, cf. the English metaphorical phrase 'the upper crust'.

2 1959 *Sunday Times* She belonged to the Edwardo-Georgian *gratin*.

gratiné /gratine/ (*plural same*), /gratɪˈneɪ/ *noun & adjective* (also **gratinée**) E20 **French** (past participial adjective of *gratiner* to cook *au gratin*). *Cookery* (A dish) cooked with a crisp topping or stuffing of breadcrumbs or grated cheese.

gratis /ˈgratɪs/, /ˈgrɑːtɪs/, /ˈgreɪtɪs/ *adverb & adjective* LME **Latin** (*gratis* contraction of *gratiis* out of favour or kindness, ablative plural of *gratia* grace, favour). **A** *adverb* **1** LME Freely, for nothing, without return made or expected; without charge, cost, or pay. **2** L16–E19 Without a reason; gratuitously, unjustifiably. **B** *adjective* M17 Given or done for nothing; free; gratuitous.

graupel /ˈgraʊp(ə)l/ *noun* L19 **German**. *Meteorology* Soft hail, small snow pellets with a fragile ice crust.

gravadlax variant of GRAVLAX.

gravamen /grəˈveɪmɛn/ *noun* plural **gravamens**, **gravamina** /grəˈveɪmɪnə/ E17 **Late Latin** (*gravamen* physical inconvenience, (in medieval Latin) grievance, from Latin *gravare* to weigh on, oppress, from *gravis* heavy, grave). **1** E17 In the Anglican Church: a memorial from the Lower House of Convocation to the Upper House representing the existence of disorders and grievances within the Church. **b** M17–L19 A formal complaint or accusation. **2** M17 A grievance. **3** M19 The essential or most serious part of an accusation; the part that bears most heavily on the accused.

gravida /ˈgravɪdə/ *noun* M20 **Latin** (use as noun of feminine of *gravidus* gravid). *Medicine* A woman who is pregnant; (with preceding or following numeral) a woman who had had the specified number of pregnancies, including a present one.

gravitas /ˈgravɪtɑːs/, /ˈgravɪtas/ *noun* E20 **Latin**. Solemn demeanour; seriousness.

1996 *Times* It [sc. the appointment of a lord to a directorship] may well give added gravitas to the board, but gravitas does not equal competence.

gravlax /gravˈlaks/ *noun* (also **gravlaks**, **gravadlax** /ˌgravadˈlaks/) M20 **Swedish** (from *grav* grave, trench +*lax* salmon (because the process was originally carried out in a hole in the ground)). Raw salmon cured with salt, spices, and especially dill.

grazioso /gratsiˈoːzo/ *adjective & adverb* E19 **Italian** (= gracious, graceful). *Music* (A direction:) graceful(ly).

grecque /grɛk/ *noun* M19 **French** (feminine of *grec* Greek). *Architecture* A Greek fret.

grège /grɛʒ/ *adjective & noun* (also **greige** /greɪʒ/) E20 **French** (in *soie grège* raw silk, from Italian *greggio* raw, crude, unprocessed). (Of) a colour between beige and grey.

grenadine /ˈgrɛnədiːn/ *noun* L19 **French** ((*sirop de*) *grenadine* from *grenade* pomegranate). A cordial syrup made from pomegranates; a drink of this.

Grenzbegriff /ˈgrɛntsbəˌgrɪf/ *noun* L19 **German** (from *Grenze* limit, boundary + *Begriff* concept). In Kantian philosophy, a concept showing the limitation of sense-experience, a limiting concept; *generally* a conception of an unattained ideal.

grès /grɛ/ *noun* L19 **French**. Stoneware.

■ Chiefly in *grès de Flandres* /grɛ də flɑ̃dr/, Flemish ware.

grillade /grɪˈleɪd/, /grɪˈjɑːd/, /ˈgriːɑːd/ *noun* M17 **French** (from *griller* to cook on a grill). (A dish of) grilled food; a grill.

grimoire /grɪmˈwɑː/ *noun* M19 **French** (alteration of *grammaire* grammar). A manual of black magic supposedly used to cast spells, invoke demons, etc.

gringo /ˈgrɪŋgəʊ/ *noun & adjective* plural **gringos** M19 **Spanish** (= foreign, foreigner, gibberish). **A** *noun* M19 A (male) foreigner, especially British or American, in a Spanish-speaking country. **B** *adjective* L19 Of or pertaining to a gringo or gringos; foreign.

■ Usually derogatory.

griot /ˈgriːəʊ/ *noun* E19 **French**. In North and West Africa: a member of a class of travelling poets, musicians, and folk-historians; a praise-singer.

grippe /grɪp/, *foreign* /grip/ *noun* L18 **French**. Influenza.

grisaille /grɪˈzeɪl/, /grɪˈzeɪli/, *foreign* /gri zɑj/ (*plural same*) *noun & adjective* M19 **French** (from *gris* grey). **A** *noun* M19 A method of painting in grey monochrome, used to represent objects in relief or to decorate stained glass; a stained-glass window or other work of this kind. **B** *adjective* M19 Executed in grisaille.

grisette /grɪˈzɛt/ *noun & adjective* E18 **French** (from *gris* grey). **A** *noun* **1** E18 A cheap grey dress fabric, formerly worn by working girls in France. **2** E18 A young working-class Frenchwoman. **B** *adjective* E18 Made of grisette.

grissino /grisˈsiːno/, /grɪˈsiːnəʊ/ *noun* plural **grissini** /grisˈsiːni/ M19 **Italian**. A long thin stick of crisp bread.

■ Usually in plural.

grognard /grɔɲar/ *noun* plural pronounced same E20 **French** (literally, 'grumbler'). A member of Napoleon's Old Guard; *transferred* a veteran soldier.

gros /gro/ *noun* plural same M18 **French** (use as noun of *gros* gross). **1** A heavy silk fabric (*gros du soie*). Only in M18. **2** L18 A silk fabric originally from or associated with a specified city etc., as *gros de Londres* /də lɔ̃dr/, *gros de Lyons* /də ljɔ̃/, *gros de Naples* /də napl/, etc.

gros bleu /gro blø/ *noun & adjective phrase* L19 **French** (= dark blue). (Of) a deep blue used to paint china.

grosgrain /ˈgrəʊgreɪn/, *foreign* /grogrɛ̃/ (*plural same*) *noun & adjective* M19 **French**. (Made of) any of various heavy ribbed fabrics, especially silk or rayon.

gros point /gro pwɛ̃/ *noun phrase* M19 **French** (= large stitch). **1** M19 A type of lace, originally from Venice, worked in bold relief. More fully *gros point de Venise* /də vəniz/. **2** M20 Any of various embroidery stitches worked over two or more horizontal and vertical threads of the canvas.

grosso modo /ˌgrosso ˈmoːdo/, /ˌgrɒsəʊ ˈməʊdəʊ/ *adverb phrase* M20 **Italian**. Roughly, approximately.

Grübelsucht /ˈgryːbəlzʊxt/ *noun* L19 **German** (from *grübeln* to brood + *Sucht* mania). A form of obsession in which even the simplest facts are compulsively queried.

gruppetto /grupˈpetto/, /grʊˈpɛtəʊ/ *noun* plural **gruppetti** /grupˈpetti/, **gruppettos** M19 **Italian** (diminutive of *gruppo* group). *Music* A melodic ornament consisting of a group of three, four, or five notes, comprising the principal note and the notes one degree above and below it; a turn.

GT abbreviation of GRAN TURISMO.

guaca, **guaco** variants of HUACA, HUACO.

guacamole /gwɑːkəˈməʊli/ *noun* (also **guacomole**) E20 **American Spanish** (from Nahuatl *ahuacamolli*, from *ahuacatl* avocado + *molli* sauce). A Mexican dish made from mashed avocados, onions, tomatoes, chillies, and seasoning.

guaiacum /ˈgwʌɪəkəm/ *noun* M16 **Modern Latin** (from Spanish *guayaco*, *guayacan*, from Taino *guayacan*). **1** M16 Any of various trees and shrubs of the genus *Guaiacum* native to the West Indies and tropical America. **2** M16 The hard very heavy wood of such a tree; lignum vitae. **3** M16 A resin obtained from such a tree, formerly used to treat gout and rheumatism, now as a flavouring; a drug prepared from it. Also more fully *gum guaiacum*.

guajira /gwaˈxira/ *noun* E20 **Cuban Spanish** (feminine of next). A Cuban song and dance tune whose rhythm shifts from 6/8 to 3/4 time.

guajiro /gwaˈxiro/ *noun* plural **guajiros** /gwaˈxiros/ M19 **Cuban Spanish** (= rustic, rural). A Cuban agricultural worker.

guano /ˈgwɑːnəʊ/ *noun* plural **guanos** E17 **Spanish** (or South American Spanish *huano*, from Quechua *huanu* dung). **1** E17 The excrement of sea birds as found especially on the islands off Peru and Chile and used as fertilizer. **2** M19 More fully *fish guano*. An artificial fertilizer resembling natural guano, *especially* one made from fish.

guaracha /gwaˈratʃa/ *noun* M19 **Spanish**. A lively Cuban song and dance in 3/4 and 6/8, or 2/4, time; a ballroom dance resembling this.

guarache variant of HUARACHE.

guarana /gwəˈrɑːnə/, /ˈgwɑːrənə/ *noun* M19 **Portuguese** (from Tupi *guaraná*). A Brazilian liana, *Paullinia cupana*, of the soapberry family; a paste prepared from the seeds of this shrub, used as a food or medicine and especially to make a drink resembling coffee.

guardia civil /ˌgwardia θiˈbil/, /siˈbil/ *noun phrase* plural **guardias civiles** /ˌgwardias θiˈbiles/, /siˈbiles/ M19 **Spanish** (= civil guard). (A member of) a police force in Spain organized on military lines.

guêpière /gɛpjɛr/ *noun* M20 **French** (from *guêpe* wasp). A corset designed to emphasize the slenderness of the waist.

1995 *Oldie* All model girls wore stays—tiny ones called guêpières (wasp-waists).

guéridon /ˈgɛrɪd(ə)n/, *foreign* /gerɪdɔ̃/ *noun* M19 **French**. A small ornamental table or stand, usually round, with a single central pedestal, and ornately carved.

guerrilla /gəˈrɪlə/ *noun & adjective* (also **guerilla**) E19 **Spanish** (diminutive of *guerra* war). **A** *noun* **1** E19 A person taking part in an irregular war waged by small bands operating independently (frequently against a stronger more organized force) with surprise attacks etc. **2** E19 A war waged by guerrillas. Now *rare*. **B** E19 *attributive* or as *adjective* Of fighting: carried on by small irregular bands. Of a person: taking part in such fighting.

■ Introduced into France and England during the Peninsular War (1808–14), when the Spaniards fought such campaigns against the vastly superior invading forces of Napoleon.

gueule de bois /gœl də bwa/ *noun phrase* plural **gueules de bois** (*pronounced same*) L20 **French** (literally, 'mouth of wood'). A hangover.

■ Colloquial in both French and English.

1995 *Times* As every single drinker who has surged over the alcoholic Maginot Line at a pub or party knows, the thud-thud-thud-thud of the *gueule de bois* is one of the most disagreeable experiences the human head can aspire to.

gueux /gø/ *noun plural* E17 **French** (plural of *gueux* ragamuffin, beggar). *History* The Dutch nobles who in 1566 petitioned Margaret of Parma on behalf of Protestants; the Dutch and Flemish Protestant partisans who subsequently fought against Spain in the wars of the sixteenth century.

■ Four hundred nobles assembled in Brussels in April 1566 to present a petition to the Habsburg Governess of the Netherlands, Margaret of Parma, against the intolerant edicts being enforced by her administration in the provinces that she was ruling as deputy for her half-brother, the Spanish king Philip II. The president of her council of finance, the Count of Berlaymont, contemptuously dismissed them as *gueux* 'beggars', a sobriquet gleefully seized upon by the disaffected Dutch, who transformed it into a rallying cry for the subsequent revolt against the Habsburgs.

gugelhupf /ˈguːgəlhʊpf/ *noun* (also **guglhupf**, **kugelhupf** /ˈkuːgəlhʊpf/) plural **gugelhupfe** /ˈguːgəlhʊpfə/ L19 **German** (the form with *k* is from dialect). A light Austrian cake baked in a ring-shaped mould.

guichet /ˈgiːʃeɪ/ *noun* M19 **French**. A wicket, a hatch; *especially* one through which tickets are sold.

guidon /ˈgʌɪd(ə)n/ *noun* M16 **French** (from Italian *guidone*, from *guida* guide). **1** M16 A pennant narrowing to a point or fork at the free end, especially as used as the standard of a regiment or (*United States*) a troop of cavalry. **2** L16 An officer who carries a guidon.

guilloche /gɪˈləʊʃ/, /gɪˈlɒʃ/ *noun* M19 **French** (*guillochis* guilloche, or *guilloche* the tool used in making it). An architectural or metalwork ornament imitating braided or twisted ribbons.

1996 *Country Life* . . . the guilloche has a clarity that recalls the appearance of that ornament in borders to the plates in D'Hancarville's *Collection of Etruscan, Greek and Roman Antiquities* . . .

guillotine /ˈgɪlətiːn/, /gɪləˈtiːn/ *noun & verb* L18 **French** (from Joseph-Ignace *Guillotin* (1738–1814)). **A** *noun* **1** L18 An instrument for beheading consisting of a heavy blade with a diagonal cutting edge that is allowed to drop between two tall grooved uprights, used in France during the Revolution. **b** M19 *the guillotine* Execution by means of a guillotine. **2** M19 A surgical instrument with a blade that slides in a long groove. **3** L19 A machine with a long blade used for cutting paper etc. **4** L19 A method used in a legislative assembly for preventing obstruction of a bill by fixing times at which its different parts must be voted on. **B** *transitive verb* **1** L18 Behead by means of a guillotine. **2** L19 Cut with a guillotine; *figuratively* cut short.

■ Guillotin suggested the use of this instrument as a means of capital punishment in 1789 on the grounds that executions should be as swift and painless as possible. Such devices had been in operation earlier in England, Scotland (where it was called a 'maiden'), Germany (called a *Diele* or *Hobel*), and Italy (called a *mannaia*), but by the eighteenth century they seem to have fallen out of use until Guillotin's recommendation aroused new interest. There was a period of experimentation using dead bodies, during which the machine was referred to as *La Petite Louison* or the *Louisette*, but after its first public use in April 1792 it speedily and universally became known as *la guillotine*.

guimpe /gɪmp/, *foreign* /gɛ̃p/ *noun* (also **guimp**) M19 **French**. A high-necked CHEMISETTE; a blouse designed for wearing under a low-necked dress.

guipure /gɪˈpjʊə/ *noun* M19 **French** (from *guiper* to cover with silk, wool, etc., from Germanic base meaning 'wind round'). A kind of openwork lace in which the motifs are connected by threads.

guiro /ˈgwʌɪrəʊ/ *noun* L19 **Spanish** (= gourd). A gourd with an artificially serrated surface which gives a rasping sound when scraped with a stick, used (originally in Latin America) as a musical instrument.

gul /gʊl/ *noun* E19 **Persian**. **1** E19 A flower; *especially* a rose. **2** E20 A large geometrical motif derived from the shape of the rose that forms part of the design of a Turkoman rug.

■ Sense 1 is poetical, as in the phrase *gardens of gul*.

Gulag /ˈguːlag/, *foreign* /guˈlak/ *noun* (also **gulag**) M20 **Russian** (acronym, from *Glavnoe upravlenie ispravitel'no-trudovykh lagereĭ* Chief Administration for Corrective Labour Camps). **1** M20 A department of the Soviet secret police that administered corrective labour camps and prisons between 1934 and 1955. *rare*. **2** L20 The Soviet network of labour camps; a camp or prison within it; *figurative* a coercive institution, an oppressive environment.

2 1996 *New Scientist* He [sc. Lysenko] was a shrewd political manipulator, gradually rising in communist circles as his opponents were exiled to the gulags.

gundy variant of GOONDIE.

gung-ho /gʌŋˈhəʊ/ *adjective* M20 **Chinese** (*gōnghé*, taken as 'work together'). Enthusiastic, eager.

■ Adopted as a slogan in the war of 1939–45 by the United States Marines.

1996 *Country Life* . . . the banished Duke is neatly played by Robert Demeger as a gung-ho figure cheering up his fellow-exiles during an Arctic winter . . .

gunibri variant of GIMBRI.

gunyah /ˈgʌnjə/ *noun* E19 **Aboriginal**. In Australia: an Aboriginal hut; a bush hut.

gurdwara /gʊəˈdwɑːrə/, /gəːˈdwɑːrə/ *noun* E20 **Panjabi** (*gurduārā*, from Sanskrit GURU + *dvāra* door). A Sikh temple.

guru /ˈgʊruː/, /ˈguːruː/ *noun* (also **gooroo**) E17 **Sanskrit** (*guru* elder, teacher). **1** E17 A (Hindu) spiritual teacher. **2** M20 Anyone looked up to as a source of wisdom or knowledge; an influential leader or pundit.

2 1995 *Country Life* Some guru—in Yorkshire, maybe—has warned that we are to have a hard winter.

gusto /ˈgʌstəʊ/ *noun* plural **gusto(e)s** E17 **Italian** (from Latin *gustus* taste). Keen enjoyment displayed in action or speech, especially in eating or drinking; relish, zest.

■ Often in the phrase *with (great) gusto* (see quotation). The other early (E17) sense of *gusto* as 'an individual fondness or preference' and the art critical sense (M17) of 'the style in which a work of art etc. is executed' (especially in *great* or *grand gusto* (= Italian *gran gusto*)) are both now archaic.

1996 *Spectator* He is not a wild, untempered spirit; he cooks with gusto, but not without formality.

gutta /ˈgʌtə/ *noun* plural **guttae** /ˈgʌtiː/ LME **Latin** (= drop (of any liquid)). **1** LME–E18 Gum; gum resin, *especially* gamboge. **2** M16 *Architecture* Each of a row of usually conical projections resembling drops underneath the triglyph (and sometimes the mutule) of a Doric capital. **3** M16 *Pharmacology* and *Medicine* A drop of liquid. Now *rare* or *obsolete*. **4** E19 A roundish coloured dot on an insect's wing, *especially* one of a light colour.

gutta-percha /gʌtəˈpəːtʃə/ *noun* M19 **Malay** (*getah perca*, from *getah* gum + *perca* strips of cloth (which it resembles); assimilated to GUTTA). **1** M19 The coagulated latex of certain Malaysian trees, a hard tough thermoplastic substance consisting chiefly of a hydrocarbon isomeric with rubber and now used especially in dentistry and for electrical insulation. **2** M19 Any of the trees, of the sapote family, which yield gutta-percha.

gymnasium /dʒɪm'neɪzɪəm/ *noun* plural **gymnasiums**, **gymnasia** /dʒɪm'neɪzɪə/ L16 **Latin** (from Greek *gumnasion*, from *gumnazein* to exercise naked, from *gumnos* naked). **1** L16 A place, room, or building, equipped for gymnastics or for indoor sports. **2** L17 Formerly, a high school, college, or academy in Continental Europe. Now *specifically* in Germany and some other Continental countries, a school of the highest grade, preparing pupils for universities.

gypsum /'dʒɪpsəm/ *noun & verb* LME **Latin** (from Greek *gupsos* chalk, gypsum). **A** *noun* LME Hydrated calcium sulphate, a soft mineral that occurs as colourless, white, or grey monoclinic prismatic crystals in many sedimentary rocks and is used for making plaster of Paris and as a fertilizer. **B** *transitive verb* E19 *Agriculture* Dress with gypsum.

gyro /'dʒʌɪrəʊ/, /'dʒɪərəʊ/ *noun* plural **gyros** L20 **Modern Greek** (*guros* turning). A sandwich of pitta bread filled with slices of spiced meat cooked on a spit, tomatoes, onions, etc.

■ Mainly United States.

habanera /habəˈnɛːrə/, /ɑːbəˈnɛːrə/ *noun* L19 **Spanish** (short for *danza habanera* Havanan dance, feminine of *habanero* of Havana the capital of Cuba). A slow Cuban dance and song in duple time.

habeas corpora /ˌheɪbɪəs ˈkɔːpərə/ *noun phrase* LME **Latin** (= thou (shalt) have the bodies (sc. in court)). *Law* (now *historical*). A process formerly issued from the Court of Common Pleas, directing the sheriff to compel the attendance of reluctant jurors.

habeas corpus /ˌheɪbɪəs ˈkɔːpəs/ *noun phrase* LME **Latin** (= thou (shalt) have the body (sc. in court)). *Law* A writ requiring a person to be brought before a judge or into a court; *specifically* such a writ requiring the investigation of the legitimacy of a person's detention, by which his or her release may be secured.

1996 *Times* It is ironic that the American President who was most influenced by . . . the values of legalism was compelled by civil war to suspend the writ of habeas corpus and defy Chief Justice Taney.

habitat /ˈhabɪtat/ *noun* L18 **Latin** (literally, 'it inhabits', 3rd person singular present of *habitare* to dwell in). **1** L18 The natural environment characteristically occupied by a particular organism; an area distinguished by the set of organisms which occupy it. Also, such areas collectively. **2** M19 *generally* One's dwelling-place; a habitation; usual surroundings.

habitué /abitɥe/ (*plural same*); /həˈbɪtjʊeɪ/ *noun* E19 **French** (past participle of *habituer* from Latin *habituare* to frequent). A habitual visitor or resident (*of* a place).

1996 *Spectator* John became a habitué and, quite literally, sang its praises.

habutai /ˈhɑːbʊtʌɪ/ *noun* L19 **Japanese** (*habutae*). Fine soft silk of a type originally made in Japan. Also called *Japanese* (or *Jap*) *silk*.

háček /ˈhɑːtʃɛk/, /ˈhatʃɛk/ *noun* M20 **Czech** (diminutive of *hák* hook). A diacritic mark (ˇ) used chiefly in Baltic and Slavonic languages, especially to indicate various types of palatalization.

hacendado /asɛnˈdɑːdəʊ/, *foreign* /aθenˈdado/, /asenˈdado/ *noun* (also **haciendado** /ˌasɪɛnˈdɑːdəʊ/, *foreign* /aθienˈdado/, /asjenˈdaðo/ plural **hacendados** /asɛnˈdɑːdəʊz/, *foreign* /aθenˈdaðos/ M19 **Spanish**. The owner of a HACIENDA.

hachure /haˈʃjʊə/ *noun & verb* M19 **French** (from *hacher* to hatch). *Cartography* **A** *noun* M19 Any of a number of short lines of shading on a map running in the direction of a slope and indicating steepness by their closeness and thickness. Also *hachure line*. Usually in *plural*. **B** *transitive verb* M19 Shade (a map) with hachures.

hacienda /hasɪˈɛndə/, *foreign* /aθiˈenda/, /asiˈenda/ *noun* M18 **Spanish** (from Latin *facienda* things to be done, from *facere* to do). In Spain and Spanish-speaking countries: an estate including a house; a large farm, a plantation; a rural factory.

haciendado variant of HACENDADO.

Hadith /haˈdiːθ/ *noun* E18 **Arabic** (*ḥadīṯ* statement, tradition). The body of tradition concerning the sayings and doings of the Prophet Muhammad, now considered to be second in authority to the Koran and to embody the Sunna; a single such saying.

hadj, **hadji** variants of HAJJ, HAJJI.

haff /haf/ *noun* M19 **German** (from Middle and Modern Low German *haf* sea, corresponding to Old Norse *haf*, Old English *hæf* sea). A shallow freshwater lagoon found at a river mouth, especially on the Baltic coast.

hafiz /ˈhɑːfɪz/ *noun* M17 **Persian** (from Arabic *ḥāfiẓ* present participle of *ḥafiẓa* to guard, know by heart). A Muslim who knows the Koran by heart.

ha-ha /ˈhɑːhɑː/ *noun* (also **haw-haw** /ˈhɔːhɔː/) E18 **French** (perhaps from the cry of surprise on discovering the obstacle). A ditch with a wall on its inner side below ground level, forming a boundary to a garden or park without interrupting the view from within.

haham /ˈhɑːhəm/ *noun* (also **chacham** /ˈxɑːxəm/ and other variants) L17 **Hebrew** (*ḥāḵām* wise). A person learned in Jewish law; a wise man; *specifically* among Sephardic Jews, a rabbi; the spiritual head of a Sephardic community.

haiku /ˈhʌɪkuː/ *noun* plural same, **haikus** L19 **Japanese** (abbreviation of *haikai no ku* unserious or comic verse). A short Japanese poem in three parts and usually having seventeen syllables; an English imitation of such a poem. Cf. HOKKU.

hajj /hadʒ/ *noun* (also **hadj**, **haj**) E18 **Arabic** ((*al-*) *ḥajj* (the Great) Pilgrimage). The pilgrimage to the Sacred Mosque at Mecca undertaken in the twelfth month of the Muslim year and constituting one of the religious duties of Islam.

figurative **1995** *Times* The international conference has become a modern form of world pilgrimage, the haj of the leisure classes.

hajji /ˈhadʒiː/ *noun* (also (feminine) **hajja** /ˈhadʒə/; **hadji**) E17 **Persian** (Turkish *ḥājjī*, *ḥājī* pilgrim, from as preceding). (The title given to) a person who has undertaken the hajj. Cf. ALHAJI.

haka /ˈhɑːkə/ *noun* M19 **Maori**. A ceremonial Maori dance accompanied by chanting.

■ Best known through its adoption by New Zealand international rugby teams as a pre-match ritual.

hakama /ˈhakəmə/, /ˈhɑːkəmə/ *noun* M19 **Japanese**. Japanese loose trousers with many pleats in the front.

hakeem variant of HAKIM 2.

Hakenkreuz /ˈhɑːkənkrɔyts/ *noun* (also **hakenkreuz**) plural **Hakenkreuze** /ˈhɑːkənkrɔytsə/ M20 **German** (from *Haken* hook + *Kreuz* cross). A swastika, especially as a Nazi symbol.

hakim /ˈhɑːkɪm/ *noun 1* E17 **Arabic** (*ḥākim* ruler, governor, judge from *ḥakama* to pass judgement). A judge, ruler, or governor in a Muslim country.

hakim /haˈkiːm/ *noun 2* (also **hakeem**) M17 **Arabic** (*ḥakīm* wise man, philosopher, physician, from as preceding). A physician in a Muslim country.

halal /həˈlɑːl/ *adjective, verb, & noun* (also **hallal**) M19 **Arabic** (*ḥalāl* according to religious law). **A** *adjective* M19 Killed or prepared in the manner prescribed by Islamic law. **B** *transitive verb* M19 Kill (an animal) in this manner. **C** *noun* M20 An animal killed, or meat prepared, in this manner.

halcyon /ˈhalsɪən/, /ˈhalʃ(ə)n/ *noun & adjective* LME **Latin** ((*h*)*alcyon* from Greek *alkuōn* kingfisher (also *halkuōn* by association with *hals* sea and *kuōn* conceiving), related to Latin *alcedo* kingfisher). **A** *noun* **1** LME A bird said by the ancients to breed in a nest floating on the sea around the time of the winter solstice, and to charm the wind and waves so that the sea was calm for this purpose; *poetical* a kingfisher. **b** L18 Any of various brightly coloured tropical kingfishers of the genus *Halcyon*. **2** M17–L18 Calm, quietude. **B** *adjective* **1** L16 Calm, peaceful; happy, prosperous, idyllic. **2** E17 Of or pertaining to the halcyon or kingfisher.

haldi /ˈhʌldi/ *noun* (also **huldee**) M19 **Hindustani** (from Sanskrit *haridrā*). The plant *Curcuma longa*, of the ginger family, whose powdered tubers yield turmeric. Also, turmeric itself.

hallal variant of HALAL.

halling /ˈhalɪŋ/ *noun* M19 **Norwegian** (from *Hallingdal* a valley in southern Norway). A Norwegian country dance in duple rhythm; a piece of music for this dance.

halma /ˈhalmə/ *noun* L19 **Greek** (= leap). A game played by two or four people on a chequer-board of 256 squares, with pieces advancing from one corner to the opposite corner by being moved over other pieces into vacant squares.

haltere /halˈtɪə/ *noun* plural **halteres** /halˈtɪəriːz/ M16 **Greek** (*haltēres* plural (sense 1), from *hallesthai* to jump). **1** M16 In *plural*. Weights, like dumb-bells, held in the hand to give an impetus in jumping. **2** E19 *Entomology* Either of the two knobbed filaments which in dipteran insects take the place of posterior wings. Also called *balancer, poiser*. Usually in *plural*.

halutzim /hɑːluːtsɪm/, /xɑːluːtsɪm/ *noun plural* (also **haluzim**, **chalutzim**) E20 **Hebrew** (*ḥălūṣīm*). *History* Jewish pioneers who entered Palestine from 1917 onwards to build it up as a Jewish State.

halva /ˈhalvɑː/, /ˈhalvə/ *noun* (also **halvah**, (earlier) **hulwa**) M17 **Yiddish** (*hal(a)va*, modern Hebrew *ḥalḇāh*, modern Greek *khalbas*, Turkish *helva*, etc., from) Arabic (and Persian) *ḥalwā* sweetmeat). A Middle Eastern sweet confection made of sesame flour and honey.

■ Later (M19) also found in its Arabic form *halawi* /həˈlɑːwi/.

hamada variant of HAMMADA.

hamartia /həˈmɑːtɪə/ *noun* L18 **Greek** (= fault, failure, guilt). The fault or error leading to the destruction of the tragic hero or heroine of a play, novel, etc.

hamel /'hɑːm(ə)l/ *noun* M19 **Afrikaans** (= Dutch *hamel*, German *Hammel*, from Old High German *hamal* mutilated). In South Africa: a castrated ram, a wether.

hametz /hɑː'mɛts/, /'xɑːmɛts/ *noun* (also **chametz**, **chometz**) M19 **Hebrew** (*ḥāmēṣ*). Leaven or food mixed with leaven, prohibited during the Passover.

hammada /hə'mɑːdə/ *noun* (also **hamada**) M19 **Arabic** (*ḥammāda*). A flat rocky area of desert blown free of sand by the wind, typical of the Sahara.

hammam /'hamam/, /hə'mɑːm/, /'hʌmʌm/ *noun* (also **hummum** /'hʌmʌm/) E17 **Turkish** (or its source Arabic *ḥammām* bath, from *ḥamma* to heat). An establishment where one may take a Turkish bath.

hamsin variant of KHAMSIN.

hamza /'hamzə/ *noun* E19 **Arabic** (literally, 'compression'). (A symbol in Arabic script representing) the glottal stop.

han variant of KHAN.

haneef variant of HANIF.

hanepoot /'hɑːnəpʊət/ *noun* L18 **Afrikaans** (from Dutch *haan* cock + *poot* foot). **1** L18 A variety of sweet muscat grape, grown in South Africa and used for making wine or raisins. **2** E19 The sweet white wine made from these grapes.

hangi /'haŋi/, /'hɑːŋi/ *noun* M19 **Maori**. An earth-oven in which food is cooked on heated stones; the food cooked in such an oven.

■ Chiefly New Zealand.

hanif /ha'niːf/ *noun* (also **haneef**) M18 **Arabic** (*ḥanīf*, an epithet applied to Abraham in the Koran). Among Muslims, a follower of the original and true (monotheistic) religion.

haniwa /'hanɪwə/ *noun* plural same M20 **Japanese** (literally, 'rings of clay'). *Archaeology* A clay image based on a cylindrical shape of a type placed outside Japanese tombs of the fifth to seventh century.

Hanse /hans/ *noun* (also **hanse**) ME **Middle Low German** (*hanshūs* and medieval Latin *hansa* from Old High German *hansa*, Middle and Modern High German *hanse* (whence Middle Low German *hanse*) Gothic *hansa* company, crowd, from Germanic, whence also Finnish *kansa* people, company). *History* **1** ME A merchant guild. **b** LME *specifically* (A merchant, citizen, or town of) the Hanseatic League. **2** ME A membership fee payable to a merchant guild; a trading fee imposed on non-members of the guild.

haoma variant of HOM.

hapax legomenon /ˌhapaks lɛ'gɒmənɒn/ *noun phrase* plural **hapax legomena** /ˌhapaks lɛ'gɒmənə/ M17 **Greek** (= (a thing) said only once). A word, form, etc., of which only one recorded instance is known.

■ Used in Greek characters until L19 and sometimes abbreviated *hapax*.

harai-goshi /harʌɪ'gɒʃi/ *noun* M20 **Japanese** (from *harai* sweep + *koshi* waist, hips). *Judo* A type of sweeping hip throw.

hara-kiri /harə'kɪri/ *noun* (also (corruptly) **hari-kiri** /harɪ'kɪri/) M19 **Japanese** (from *hara* belly + *kiri* cutting). In Japan: a ritual form of suicide by disembowelling, formerly prescribed by a feudal superior to disgraced members of the samurai class as an alternative to execution. Also, suicide practised voluntarily from a sense of shame, as a protest, etc.

haram /hɑː'rɑːm/ *noun & adjective* E17 **Arabic** (*ḥarām* forbidden; cf. HAREM). **A** *noun* E17 A Muslim sacred place, forbidden to non-Muslims. **B** *adjective* E17 Of food; forbidden under Islamic law. Opposed to HALAL.

haras /'arɑː/ *noun* plural same ME **Old and Modern French** (of unknown origin). An enclosure or establishment in which horses are kept for breeding. Formerly, a herd of such horses.

harem /'hɑːriːm/, /hɑː'riːm/, /'hɛːrəm/ *noun* M17 **Turkish and Arabic** (originally from Turkish *harem*) from Arabic *ḥaram* (that which is) prohibited, (hence) sacred or inviolable place, sanctuary, women's apartments, wives, women; later also from Arabic *ḥarīm* with same meaning, both from *ḥaruma* to be prohibited or unlawful). **1** M17 Separate women's quarters in a Muslim house, designed for the privacy and seclusion of the occupants. **2** L18 The occupants of such quarters collectively; *specifically* a Muslim's wives and concubines. **b** L19 A group of female animals of a single species sharing a mate.

haricot /'harɪkəʊ/ *noun* M17 **French** (in sense 1 in *febves de haricot*, perhaps from Aztec *ayacotli*; in sense 2 Old French *hericoq*, *hericot* (*de mouton*), probably related to *harigoter* to cut up). **1** M17 A leguminous plant, *Phaseolus vulgaris*, native to tropical America but having numerous widely cultivated varieties; the edible pod or seed of this plant; *especially* white varieties of the dried seed. More fully *haricot bean*. **2** M17 A ragout, especially of mutton or lamb.

hari-kiri variant of HARA-KIRI.

harka /'hɑːkə/ *noun* E20 **Moroccan Arabic** (*ḥarka*: cf. literary Arabic *ḥaraka* movement, action, military operation). A body of Moroccan irregular troops.

harmattan /hɑː'mat(ə)n/ *noun* L17 **Twi** (*haramata*). A parching dusty land-wind on the West African coast from December to February. Also *harmattan wind*.

haroseth /hə'rəʊsɛθ/ *noun* (also **charoseth** /xə'rəʊsɛθ/, **haroset** /hə'rəʊsɛt/) L19 **Hebrew** (*ḥărōseṯ* from *ḥeres* earthware). A mixture of apples, nuts, spices, etc., eaten at the Passover Seder service to symbolize the clay mixed by the Israelites during their slavery in Egypt.

hartal /'hɑːtɑːl/, /'həːtɑːl/ *noun* E20 **Hindustani** (*haṛtāl*, *hartāl*, for *haṭṭal*, literally, 'locking of shops' (Sanskrit *haṭṭa* shop, *tāla* lock, bolt)). In the Indian subcontinent: the organized closing of shops and offices as a mark of protest or as an act of mourning.

1920 *Blackwood's Magazine* What I had seen there of the crowds at the Hartal . . . had made me nervous.

hashish /'haʃiːʃ/, /'haʃɪʃ/, /ha'ʃiːʃ/ *noun* L16 **Arabic** (*ḥašīš* dry herb, hay, powdered hemp-leaves, intoxicant made from this). Cannabis.

hasid /'hasɪd/ *noun* (also **cha(s)sid** /'xasɪd/, **hassid**, and with initial capital) plural **hasidim** /'hasɪdɪm/ E19 **Hebrew** (*ḥāsîḏ* pious, pietist). A member of a Jewish sect founded in the eighteenth century by Israel Baal Shem Tov and emphasizing joy in the service of God.

hasta la vista /ˌasta la 'vista/ *interjection* M20 **Spanish**. In Spain: goodbye, *au revoir*.

hatha yoga /ˌhʌtə 'jəʊgə/, /ˌhatə/ *noun phrase* E20 **Sanskrit** (from *haṭha* force + *yoga*). A system of physical exercises and breathing control used in YOGA.

hatha yogi /ˌhʌtə 'jəʊgi/, /'hatə/ *noun phrase* M20 **Sanskrit** (from *haṭha* force + *yogi*). A person who practises HATHA YOGA.

hausfrau /'haʊsfraʊ/ *noun* plural **hausfraus**, **hausfrauen** /'haʊsfraʊən/ L18 **German** (from *Haus* house + *Frau* wife, woman). A (German) housewife; a person who embodies housewifely qualities.

1995 *Times* If you saw her on the street she could be a *hausfrau*. It's very hard to relate her to the terrible things you are hearing about.

hausmaler /'haʊsmɑːlə/ *noun* M20 **German** (from *Haus* house + *Maler* painter). A person who paints undecorated china at home or in a private workshop.

haute Bohème /ot bɔɛm/, /ˌəʊt bəʊ'ɛm/ *noun phrase* E20 **French** (literally, 'high Bohemia'). A fast or upper-class Bohemian set of people.

■ The phrase was apparently coined by the English writer Maurice Baring in *Cat's Cradle* (1925) on the model of HAUTE BOURGEOISIE.

haute bourgeoisie /ot burʒwazi/, /ˌəʊt bʊəʒwɑː'ziː/ *noun phrase* L19 **French** (literally, 'high bourgeoisie'). The upper middle class.

1996 *Spectator* There is a thesis to be written on why all crime stories devised for the haute bourgeoisie have to present their viewers' class in a generally unfavourable light.

haute couture /ot kutyr/, /ˌəʊt kʊ'tjʊə/ *noun phrase* E20 **French** (literally, 'high dressmaking'). High fashion; the leading dressmakers and fashion houses or their products collectively.

1995 *Times* Here, at the office of Yves Saint Laurent, is the genuine article, the haute couture attainable by almost no one, where the likes of Catherine Deneuve and Elizabeth Taylor are fitted for dresses which will cost £25,000.

haute cuisine /ot kɥizin/, /ˌəʊt kwɪ'ziːn/ *noun phrase* E20 **French** (literally, 'high cooking'). High-class (French) cooking.

1996 *Times Haute cuisine* was followed by *nouvelle cuisine* . . .

haute école /ot ekɔl/, /ˌəʊt eɪ'kɒl/ *noun & adjective phrase* M19 **French** (literally, 'high school'). (Of or pertaining to) the more difficult feats of horsemanship, or *transferred* of music or other arts.

haute-luxe /ot lyks/, /əʊt 'lʊks/ *adjective* M20 **French** (literally, 'high luxury'). Luxurious, opulent.

1995 *Spectator* [A] play demanding incredible chic and a *haute-luxe* setting has been thrown onto a studio-stage set which looks as though it was run up by the cast during a brief break in rehearsals.

haute noblesse /ot nɔblɛs/, /ˌəʊt nəʊ'blɛs/ *noun phrase* L18 **French** (literally, 'high nobility'). The upper stratum of the aristocracy. Cf. PETITE NOBLESSE.

hauteur /əʊ'təː/, *foreign* /otœr/ *noun* E17 **French** (from *haut* high). Haughtiness of manner.

> **1996** *Times* To the dismay of her mother—who held out with an old-fashioned hauteur against her daughter's taking to the stage—Helene Cordot decided to embark upon a career as a cabaret artiste . . .

haute vulgarisation /ot vylgarizasjɔ̃/, /ˌəʊt vʌlgərʌɪ'zeɪʃ(ə)n/ *noun phrase* M20 **French** (literally, 'high vulgarization'). The popularization of abstruse or complex matters.

> **1995** *Times* This branch of *haute vulgarisation* takes patience, love of getting things shipshape and a tolerance of being thought a spoilsport.

haut-goût /ogu/, /'əʊguː/ *noun* M16 **French** (literally, 'high flavour'). **1** M16 A strong flavour or relish, seasoning (*literally* and *figuratively*). **2** M17–E19 A highly flavoured or seasoned dish. **3** L17 A slightly rotten flavour; a taint.

haut monde /o mɔ̃d/, /əʊ 'mɒnd/ *noun phrase* M19 **French** (literally, 'high world'). The fashionable world. Cf. BEAU MONDE.

haut-pas /opa/ *noun* plural same LME **French** (literally, 'high step'). A dais raised one or more steps above the level of the rest of the floor.

haut-relief /orəljɛf/, /əʊrɪ'liːf/ *noun* M19 **French** (literally, 'high relief'). ALTO-RELIEVO.

haut ton /o tɔ̃/ *noun phrase* E19 **French** (literally, 'high tone'). (People of) high fashion.

■ Now less common than just 'the TON' in the sense of 'fashionable society'.

havildar /'hạvɪldɑː/ *noun* L17 **Urdu** (*hawildār* from Persian *ḥawāl(a)dār* charge holder, from *ḥawāl*, from Arabic *ḥawāl(a)* charge, assignment + Persian *hawāl(a)dār* holding, holder). An Indian non-commissioned officer equivalent to a sergeant.

haw-haw variant of HA-HA.

hazzan /xə'zɑːn/, /'hɑːz(ə)n/ *noun* (also **chaz(z)an**, **hazan**) plural **hazzanim** /xə 'zɑːnim/ M17 **Hebrew** (*ḥazzān* beadle, cantor, probably from Assyrian *hazannu* overseer or governor). A CANTOR in a synagogue.

Hebe /'hiːbi/ *noun* E17 **Greek** (*hēbē* youthful beauty, *Hēbē* the Greek goddess of youth and spring, daughter of Zeus and Hera, and cupbearer of Olympus). **1** E17 A young woman resembling Hebe; a waitress. **2** M20 (**hebe**) Any of numerous New Zealand evergreen shrubs constituting the genus *Hebe* (formerly included in *Veronica*), with spikes of blue, white, mauve, etc., flowers.

hebra /'hɛbrə/ *noun* (also **chevra** /'xɛvrə/) plural **hebras**, **hebroth** /'hɛbrəʊt/ L19 **Hebrew** (*ḥeḇrāh* association, society). A small group formed by members of a Jewish community for religious and charitable purposes.

heder /'hɛdə/, /'xɛdə/ *noun* (also **cheder**) plural **hedarim** /hɛ'dɑːrɪm/, **heders** L19 **Hebrew** (*ḥēḏer* room). A school for Jewish children in which Hebrew and religious knowledge are taught.

Heft /hɛft/ *noun* plural **Hefte** /'hɛftə/ L19 **German**. A number of sheets of paper fastened together to form a book; *specifically* a part of a serial publication, a fascicle.

hegemon /'hɛgɪmɒn/, /'hiːgɪmɒn/, /'hɛdʒɪmɒn/ *noun* E20 **Greek** (*hēgemōn* leader, from *hēgeisthai* to lead). A leading or paramount power; a dominant state or person.

hegira /'hɛdʒɪrə/ *noun* (also **Hegira**, **hejira**, **hijra** /'hɪdʒrə/) L16 **Medieval Latin** (from Arabic *hijra* departure from one's home and friends, from *hajara* to separate, emigrate). **1** L16 The emigration of Muhammad from Mecca to Medina in 622; the Muslim era reckoned from this. **2** M18 Any exodus or departure.

■ The abbreviation AH (for *anno Hegirae*) is used in Islamic dates.

Heilsgeschichte /'haɪlsgəˌʃɪçtə/ *noun* M20 **German**. *Theology* Sacred history; *specifically* the history of the salvation of humankind by God; history seen as the working out of this salvation.

heimisch /'heɪmɪʃ/ *adjective* M20 **Yiddish** (*heymish* domestic, homelike). In Jewish speech: homely, unpretentious.

Heimweh /'haɪmveː/ *noun* E18 **German**. Homesickness.

hejira variant of HEGIRA.

hélas /e'lɑːs/ *interjection* LME **French** (later form of *ha las*, *a las* alas). Expressing grief, sadness, regret, etc.

Heldentenor /ˌhɛldənte'noːr/ *noun* plural **Heldentenöre** /ˌhɛldənte'nørə/ E20 **German** (= hero tenor). A singer with a powerful tenor voice suited to heroic roles, especially in Wagnerian opera.

helix /ˈhiːlɪks/ *noun* plural **helices** /ˈhɛlɪsiːz/, /ˈhiːlɪsiːz/, **helixes** M16 **Latin** (*helix, helicis* from Greek *helix*). **1** M16 Chiefly *Architecture*. A spiral ornament, a volute; *specifically* each of the eight smaller volutes under the abacus of a Corinthian capital. **2** E17 An object of coiled form, either round an axis (like a corkscrew) or, less usually, in one plane (like a watchspring); *Geometry* a three-dimensional curve on a (notional) conical or cylindrical surface which becomes a straight line when the surface is unrolled into a plane. **3** L17 *Anatomy* The curved fold which forms the rim of the exterior ear. **4** E19 *Zoology* Any spiral-shelled mollusc of the genus *Helix*.

helot /ˈhɛlət/ *noun* L16 **Latin** (*Helotes* plural from Greek *Heilōtes* (plural of *Heilōs*), also *Hilotae* from Greek *Heilōtai* (plural of *Heilōtēs*): usually derived from *Helos* a town in Laconia whose inhabitants were enslaved). *Greek History* **1** L16 (*Helot*) A member of a class of serfs in ancient Sparta, intermediate in status between slaves and citizens. **2** E19 *transferred* and *figurative* A serf, a slave.

hendiadys /hɛnˈdʌɪədɪs/ *noun* L16 **Medieval Latin** (from Greek *hen dia duoin* 'one through two'). A figure of speech in which a single complex idea is expressed by two words usually connected by *and*.

■ An example of *hendiadys* is *nice and warm* for *nicely warm*.

herbarium /həːˈbɛːrɪəm/ *noun* L18 **Late Latin** (*herbarium*, use as noun of adjective represented by Latin *herbarius* botanist, *herbaria* (sc. *ars*) botany). A collection of dried botanical specimens systematically arranged for reference. Also, a room or building housing such a collection.

herem variant of CHEREM.

hermandad /ˌermanˈdad/ *noun* plural **hermandades** /ˌermanˈdades/ M18 **Spanish** (= brotherhood). *History* In Spain: a resistance group against oppression by the nobility; *specifically* a voluntary organization later reorganized as regular national police.

heroon /hɪˈrəʊɒn/ *noun* plural **heroa** /hɪˈrəʊə/ (also (earlier) **heroum** /hɪˈrəʊəm/) L18 **Latin** (*heroum* from Greek *hērōon*, from *hērōios* of a hero, from *hērōs* hero). Originally, a temple dedicated to a hero, often over his supposed tomb. Now, a sepulchral monument in the form of a small temple.

herpes /ˈhəːpiːz/ *noun* LME **Latin** (= shingles, from Greek, literally, 'creeping', from *herpein* to creep). Originally, any skin disease characterized by the formation of groups of vesicles. Now, (infection with) any of a small group of viruses affecting the skin and nervous system.

Herrenvolk /ˈhɛːrənfɒlk/, /ˈhɛr(ə)nfɒlk/, /ˈhɛːrənfəʊk/ *noun* M20 **German** (= master-race, from *Herren*, plural of *Herr*, from Old High German *hērro*, comparative of *hēr* exalted + *volk* race). The German nation, viewed (especially by the Nazis) as a race born to mastery; in extended usage, a group regarding itself as innately superior.

hetaera /hɪˈtɪərə/ *noun* (also **hetaira** /hɪˈtʌɪrə/, plural **hetairas**, **hetairai** /hɪˈtʌɪrʌɪ/) plural **hetaeras**, **hetaerae** /hɪˈtɪəriː/ E19 **Greek** (*hetaira* feminine of *hetairos* companion). Especially in ancient Greece: a mistress, a concubine; a courtesan, a prostitute.

hetman /ˈhɛtmən/ *noun* M18 **Polish** (probably from German *Hauptmann* (earlier *Heubtman*) headman, captain). A Cossack military commander. Cf. ATAMAN.

Heurige /ˈhɔyrɪɡə/ *noun* (also **Heuriger** /ˈhɔyrɪɡər/) plural **Heurigen** /ˈhɔyrɪɡən/ M20 **German** ((southern and Austrian) = new (wine); vintner's establishment). **1** M20 Especially in Austria: wine from the latest harvest. **2** M20 An establishment where such wine is served.

hexapla /ˈhɛksəplə/ *noun* (also **hexaple** /ˈhɛksəp(ə)l/) E17 **Greek** ((*ta*) *hexapla* (title of Origen's work) neuter plural of *hexaplous* sixfold). A sixfold text in parallel columns, especially of the Old or New Testament.

hiatus /hʌɪˈeɪtəs/ *noun* plural same, **hiatuses** M16 **Latin** (= gaping, opening, from *hiare* to gape). **1** M16 A physical break in continuity; a gaping chasm; an opening, an aperture. *rare* in *general* sense. **b** L19 *Anatomy* Any of various natural openings or gaps. Usually with specifying word. **2** E17 A gap or break in continuity, especially in a series or an account; a missing link in a chain of events; *especially* in *Geology* (the time value of) a break or unconformity in the stratigraphic sequence. **b** M19 *Logic* A missing link in a chain of argument. **3** E18 *Grammar* and *Prosody* A break between two vowels which come together without an intervening consonant in successive words or syllables.

hibachi /hɪ'batʃi/, /'hɪbətʃi/ *noun* M19 **Japanese** (from *hi* fire + *hachi* bowl, pot). **1** M19 In Japan: a large earthenware pan or brazier in which charcoal is burnt to provide indoor heating. **2** M20 A type of especially outdoor cooking apparatus similar to a barbecue.

hibakusha /'hɪbəkuːʃə/ *noun* plural same M20 **Japanese** (from *hi* suffer + *baku* explosion + *sha* person). A survivor of an atomic explosion, *especially* in *plural*, the survivors of the atomic explosions at Hiroshima and Nagasaki in 1945.

hic jacet /hɪk 'dʒeɪsɛt/, /'jakɛt/ *noun phrase* E17 **Latin** (literally, 'here lies', the first two words of a Latin epitaph). An epitaph.

hidalgo /hɪ'dalgəʊ/ *noun* plural **hidalgos** L16 **Spanish** (formerly also *hijo dalgo* contraction of *hijo de algo*, literally, 'son of something'; cf. FIDALGO). **1** L16 In Spain: a member of the lower nobility. **2** E19 *transferred* A person resembling a hidalgo; *specifically* one who is suited to be or aspires to be a member of the nobility.

hiera picra /ˌhʌɪrə 'pɪkrə/ *noun phrase* LME **Medieval Latin** (from Greek, from *hiera* sacred (name of many medicines) + *pikra* feminine of *pikros* bitter). *Pharmacology* A purgative drug composed mainly of aloes and canella bark.

■ Also altered to *hickery-pickery*.

hijab /'hɪdʒab/ *noun* L20 **Arabic**. The headscarf worn by Muslim women.

1995 *Times* Western women observing this rush for the *hijab* (headscarf) tend to stare in disbelief, broadcasting the worst excesses of 'Muslim chauvinism'.

hijra variant of HEGIRA.

hilo /'hiːləʊ/ *noun* plural **hilos** M19 **Spanish** (= thread, from Latin *filum*). A thin vein of ore.

hippocampus /ˌhɪpə(ʊ)'kampəs/ *noun* plural **hippocampi** /ˌhɪpə(ʊ)'kampʌɪ/ L16 **Latin** (from Greek *hippokampos*, from *hippos* horse + *kampos* sea-monster). **1** L16 A fish of the genus *Hippocampus*; a sea horse. **2** E17 A mythical sea-monster, half horse and half fish or dolphin, represented as drawing the chariot of Neptune etc.; a representation of this. **3** E18 *Anatomy* A swelling on the floor of each lateral ventricle of the brain.

hippodrome /'hɪpədrəʊm/ *noun & verb* L16 **Old and Modern French** (Latin *hippodromus* from Greek *hippodromos*, from *hippos* horse + *dromos* race, course). **A** *noun* **1** L16 In ancient Greece and Rome, a course for chariot- or horse-races. Also, a modern circus. **2** L19 (*Hippodrome*) (The name of) a theatre used for various stage entertainments. **3** L19 A race or contest in which the result is prearranged or fixed. *United States slang*. **B** M19 *intransitive verb* Prearrange or fix the result of a race or contest. Chiefly as *hippodroming* verbal noun, *United States slang*.

hiragana /hɪrə'gɑːnə/ *noun* (also **hirakana** /hɪrə'kɑːnə/) E19 **Japanese** (from *hira* plain + KANA). The form of kana normally used in Japanese, derived from the cursive style of writing. Cf. KATAKANA.

hochgeboren /'hoːxgəˌboːrən/ *noun & adjective* plural of noun same E20 **German**. (A person who is) high-born.

hogan /'həʊg(ə)n/ *noun* L19 **Navajo**. An American Indian (especially Navajo) hut made from logs, earth, etc.

hoi polloi /hɔɪ 'pɒlɔɪ/, /hɔɪ pɒ'lɔɪ/ *noun phrase* M17 **Greek** (= the many). The majority, the masses; the rabble.

■ Frequently with *the* in English, unnecessarily duplicating the Greek definite article *hoi*.

1996 *Spectator* Why do people who can afford to run their businesses from anywhere . . . rush . . . to join city hoi polloi once the Ides of March approach.

hokku /'hɒkuː/ *noun* plural same, **hokkus** L19 **Japanese** (= 'opening verse (of a linked sequence of comic verses)'). A HAIKU.

hollandaise /hɒlən'deɪz/, *attributively also* /'hɒləndeɪz/ *noun & adjective* M19 **French** (feminine of *hollandais* Dutch, from *Hollande* Holland). (Designating) a sauce made with butter, egg-yolks, vinegar or white wine, and lemon juice, usually served with fish.

hom /həʊm/ *noun* (also **haoma**, **homa** /'həʊmə/) M19 **Persian** (obsolete *hōm* (modern *hūm*), Avestan *haoma* = Sanskrit *soma* SOMA). (The juice of) the sacred plant of the ancient Persians and Parsees.

hombre /'ɒmbreɪ/ *noun* M19 **Spanish** (= man, from Latin *homo*, *homin-* human being). In Spain and Spanish-speaking countries: a man.

■ Also in more general use, chiefly in United States slang.

1996 *Spectator* All newspapers periodically put tough hombres into the accounts department.

homme d'affaires /ɔm dafɛr/ *noun phrase* plural **hommes d'affaires** (*pronounced same*) E18 **French**. A businessman, an agent.

homme moyen sensuel /ɔm mwajɛ̃ sɑ̃sɥɛl/ *noun phrase* (also **homme sensuel moyen**) E20 **French.** The average man; the man in the street.

homo /ˈhəʊməʊ/, /ˈhɒməʊ/ *noun* plural **homos** L16 **Latin** (= man). **1** L16 A human being. **2** L18 (**Homo**) The genus to which human beings (HOMO SAPIENS) and certain of their fossil ancestors belong. Also with Latin specific epithets in names of (proposed) species, and with Latin or mock-Latin adjectives (in imitation of zoology nomenclature) in names intended to personify some aspects of human life or behaviour.

2 1961 *Times* Symbolizing . . . this concept of *homo turisticus*, the new Hilton hotel . . . will have 500 rooms—all with a view of the Parthenon.

2 1996 *Times* But as for homo *loquens* [speaking] we seem to be little closer to knowing when, where, why, or how this stage was reached.

homoeoteleuton /hɒˌmiːətɪˈljuːt(ə)n/ *noun* (also **homoioteleuton** /hɒˌmɔɪətɪˈljuːt(ə)n/) L16 **Late Latin** (from Greek *homoioteleuton* (sc. *rhēma* word), from *homoios* like + *teleutē* ending). **1** L16 A rhetorical figure consisting in the use of a series of words with the same or similar endings. *rare*. **2** M19 (An error in copying caused by) the occurrence of similar endings in two neighbouring words, lines, etc.

Homoiousion /hɒmɔɪˈuːsɪən/, /hɒmˈaʊuːsɪən/, /hɒmɔɪˈuːzɪən/ *noun* M19 **ecclesiastical Greek** (neuter of *homoiousios* of like essence, from *homoios* like, similar + *ousia* essence, substance). *Christian Theology The* doctrine that the first and second persons of the Trinity are of like but not identical essence or substance. Cf. HOMOOUSION.

Homoousion /hɒməʊˈuːsɪən/, /hɒmˈaʊuːsɪən/, /hɒməʊˈuːzɪən/; /həʊməʊˈuːsɪən/ *noun* L18 **ecclesiastical Greek** (neuter of *homoousios*, from *homos* same + *ousia* essence, substance). *Christian Theology The* doctrine that the first and second persons of the Trinity are of identical essence or substance. Cf. HOMOIOUSION.

■ After a long period of theological and philosophical discussion in the early centuries of the Christian era, this view prevailed at the Council of Chalcedon in 451 against that of the Homoiousian party.

Homo sapiens /ˌhəʊməʊ ˈsapɪɛnz/, /ˌhɒməʊ ˈsapɪɛnz/ *noun phrase* (also **homo sapiens**) E19 **Modern Latin** (= wise man). Modern human beings regarded as a species.

■ Term introduced in Linnaeus' *Systema Naturae* (10th edn. 1758), and thence into English via the translation of Linnaeus' book.

1996 *Times* She valuably reviews the anthropological, archaeological, and palaeontological evidence for the emergence of homo sapiens in the Rift Valley.

homunculus /hɒˈmʌŋkjʊləs/ *noun* plural **homunculi** /hɒˈmʌŋkjʊlʌɪ/, /hɒˈmʌŋkjʊliː/ M17 **Latin** (diminutive of *homo* man). A diminutive person, a dwarf.

■ Formerly also applied to a foetus considered as a fully formed human being.

honcho /ˈhɒntʃəʊ/ *noun & verb* M20 **Japanese** (*hanchō* group leader). **A** *noun* M20 plural **honchos**. The leader of a small group or squad; a person who is in a position of power; a strong leader. **B** *transitive verb* M20 Oversee; be in charge of (a situation).

■ Chiefly North American slang. See quotation at GALÈRE.

honda /ˈhɒndə/ *noun* (also **hondo** /ˈhɒndəʊ/, plural **hondos**, **hondu** /ˈhɒnduː/) L19 **Spanish** (probably from *hondón* eyelet, influenced by Spanish *honda* sling). The eye at the end of a lasso through which the rope passes to form a loop. *United States.*

hong /hɒŋ/ *noun* E18 **Chinese** (*háng*, (Cantonese) *hòhng* row, trade). **1** E18 In China: a series of rooms or buildings used as a warehouse, factory, etc. *especially* one of the foreign factories formerly maintained at Canton. Also in Hong Kong, a trading establishment. **2** L18 *History* The corporation of Chinese merchants at Canton who had a monopoly of trade with Europeans.

honnête homme /ɔnɛt ɔm/ *noun phrase* plural **honnêtes hommes** (pronounced same) M17 **French.** A decent, cultivated man of the world.

1960 J. Bayley *Characters of Love* Iago . . . is in many ways a terrible parody of the Augustan *honnête homme*.

honorarium /ɒnəˈrɛːrɪəm/ *noun* plural **honorariums**, **honoraria** /ɒnəˈrɛːrɪə/ M17 **Latin** (*honorarium* gift made on being admitted to a post of honour, use as noun of neuter of *honorarius* honorary). A (voluntary) fee, especially for professional services nominally rendered without payment.

1996 *Country Life* Mrs Young radiates enjoyment of her job, for which she is paid a reasonable honorarium . . .

honoris causa /ɒˌnɔːrɪs ˈkaʊzə/ *adverb phrase* E17 **Latin** (= for the sake of honour). As a mark of esteem, especially in reference to an honorary degree at a university.

hookah /ˈhʊkə/ *noun* M18 **Urdu** (from Arabic *ḥuḳḳa* small box, container, pot, jar). A pipe of oriental origin for smoking tobacco, marijuana, etc., with a long flexible tube connected to a container of water, through which the smoke is drawn from the tobacco etc.

hoop-la variant of HOUP-LA.

horae /ˈhɔːriː/ *noun* L19 **Latin** (*horae* plural of *hora* hour). A book of hours.

horchata /orˈtʃata/, /ɔːˈtʃɑːtə/ *noun* (also **orchata**) M19 **Spanish**. An almond-flavoured soft drink in Spain and Latin American countries.

horizontale /ɔrizɔ̃tal/ *noun slang* plural pronounced same L19 **French**. A prostitute. More fully GRANDE HORIZONTALE.

horme /ˈhɔːmi/ *noun* (also **hormé**) L17 **Greek** (*hormē* impulse). **1** L17 A passion, an impulse. *rare*. Only in L17. **2** E20 *Psychology* Vital or purposeful energy.

■ *Horme* was first used in English in the writings of the Cambridge Platonist philosopher Ralph Cudworth (1617–88) but did not achieve currency until its reintroduction as a term in Jungian psychology.

hornito /hɔːˈniːtəʊ/ *noun* plural **hornitos** M19 **American Spanish** (diminutive of *horno* (from Latin *furnus*) oven, furnace). *Geology* A driblet cone formed by successive ejections through a vent in a lava flow.

horresco referens /hɒˌrɛskəʊ rɛ ˈfəːrɛnz/ L17 **Latin** (= I shudder to relate, from *horrescere* to stand on end (of hair) + *referens*, present participle of *referre* to relate). Expressing horror at a memory.

■ The expression comes from Virgil's *Aeneid* (ii. 204), at the point when the hero Aeneas is relating how giant sea serpents killed the priest Laocoon for attempting to warn the Trojans against taking the Greeks' wooden horse into their city.

1995 *Spectator* I ended up bolting down a bowl of spaghetti bolognese the nastiness of which *horresco referens*.

horribile dictu /hɒˌrɪbɪleɪ ˈdɪktuː/, /hɒ ˌriːbɪli/ *adverb phrase* M19 **Modern Latin** (by analogy with MIRABILE DICTU). Horrible to relate.

horror vacui /ˌhɒrə ˈvakjuːʌɪ/ *noun phrase* M19 **Modern Latin** (= the horror of a vacuum). (A) fear or dislike of leaving empty spaces in an artistic composition etc.

1972 E. Lucie-Smith *Eroticism in Western Art* Nudes . . . fill the whole picture-space as if the artist suffered from *horror vacui*.

hors concours /ɔr kɔ̃kur/ *adverb & predicate adjective phrase* L19 **French** (= out of the competition). Not competing for a prize; *figurative* without a rival, in a class of its own.

■ Both the literal and the figurative senses are also present in modern French.

1941 V. Nabokov *Real Life of Sebastian Knight* Most husbands are fools, but that one was *hors concours*.

hors de combat /ɔr də kɔ̃bɑ/ *adverb & predicate adjective phrase* M18 **French** (= out of the fight). Out of the fight; out of the running; in an injured or disabled condition.

hors de question /ɔr də kɛstjɔ̃/ *adverb phrase* L20 **French**. Out of the question.

1995 *Spectator* As to her father, it was *hors de question* even to ask, enquiries about paternal parents being the modern age's highest form of indelicacy.

hors d'oeuvre /ɔr dœvr/, /ɔː ˈdəːvr(ə)/ *noun phrase* plural same, **hors d'oeuvres** M18 **French** (literally, 'outside the work'). An extra dish served as an appetizer before or (occasionally) during a meal; a starter; in *plural* also, (usually mixed) items of food served as such a dish. Also *figurative* a preliminary.

horst /hɔːst/ *noun* L19 **German** (= heap, mass). *Geology* A block of the earth's surface bounded by faults on some or all sides and raised relative to the surrounding land.

horti conclusi, horti sicci plurals of HORTUS CONCLUSUS, HORTUS SICCUS.

hortus conclusus /ˌhɔːtəs kənˈkluːsəs/ *noun phrase* plural **horti conclusi** /ˌhɔːtʌɪ kənˈkluːsʌɪ/, /ˌhɔːtiː kənˈkluːsiː/ E17 **Latin** (= enclosed garden). **1** E17 An enclosed inviolate garden; frequently, in spiritual and exegetical tradition, as symbolic of the soul, the Christian Church, or the virginity of Mary. **2** M19 A painting of the Madonna and Child in an enclosed garden.

1 1996 *Country Life* At the close of the 16th century, it [sc. the garden] is architecturally related to the house, a series of rooms continuing the tradition of the medieval *hortus conclusus* but multiplied . . . .

hortus siccus /ˌhɔːtəs ˈsɪkəs/ *noun phrase* plural **horti sicci** /ˌhɔːtʌɪ ˈsɪkʌɪ/, /ˌhɔːtiː ˈsɪkiː/ L17 **Latin** (= dry garden). An arranged collection of dried plants; *figurative* a collection of uninteresting facts etc.

hôtel de ville /otɛl də vil/ *noun phrase* plural **hôtels de ville** (pronounced same) M18 **French**. In France and French-speaking countries: a town-hall.

hôtel-Dieu /otɛl djø/ *noun* plural **hôtels-Dieu** (pronounced same) M17 **French**. In France and French-speaking countries: a hospital.

hôtel garni /otɛl garni/ *noun phrase* plural **hôtels garnis** (pronounced same) L18 **French**. In France and French-speaking countries: a lodging-house providing bed and breakfast only; also, a furnished apartment.

hotelier /həʊˈtɛlɪeɪ/, /həʊˈtɛlɪə/ *noun* E20 **French** (*hôtelier*). A person who owns or runs a hotel or group of hotels.

hotel particulier /otɛl partikylje/ *noun phrase* plural **hotels particuliers** (pronounced same) M20 **French**. In France and French-speaking countries: a large privately owned town house or block of flats.

hoummos, houmous variants of HUMMUS.

houp-la /ˈhuːplɑː/ *interjection & noun* (also **hoop-la**) L19 **French** (*houp-là!*, from *houp* interjection + *là* there). **A** *interjection* L19 Accompanying or drawing attention to a quick or sudden movement. **B** *noun* L19 An exclamation of 'houp-la!'; *slang* a commotion, ballyhoo, pretentious nonsense.

houri /ˈhʊəri/ *noun* M18 **French** (from Persian *ḥūrī* from Arabic *ḥūr* plural of *'aḥwar*, feminine *ḥawrā'* having eyes with marked contrast of white and black). Any of the virgins of the Muslim paradise, promised as wives to believers; *transferred* a voluptuously beautiful woman.

howdah /ˈhaʊdə/ *noun* L18 **Urdu** (*haudah* from Arabic *hawdaj* a litter carried by a camel). A seat for two or more, usually with a canopy, carried on an elephant's back.

huaca /ˈwɑːkə/ *noun* (also (earlier) **guaca**) E17 **Spanish** (*huaca, guaca* from Quechua *waca* god of the house). **1** E17 The all-pervading spirit thought by some Peruvian Indians to be disseminated through the whole world; any material object thought to be the abode of such a spirit. **2** M19 A prehistoric Peruvian tomb or temple.

huaco /ˈwɑːkəʊ/ *noun* (also **guaco** /ˈgwɑːkəʊ/) plural **huacos** M20 **Spanish** (alteration of preceding). In Peru, Bolivia, and Chile: a piece of ancient Indian pottery.

huarache /waˈrɑːtʃi/ *noun* (also **guarache** /gwaˈrɑːtʃi/) L19 **Mexican Spanish**. A leather-thonged sandal, originally worn by Mexican Indians.

hubris /ˈhjuːbrɪs/ *noun* (also **hybris** /ˈhʌɪbrɪs/) L19 **Greek**. Presumption, insolence; pride, excessive self-confidence.

■ The earliest instance of *hubris* in a non-specialist English text, a newspaper of 1884, refers to it as 'Academic slang' and defines it as 'a kind of high-flown insolence'. In its original context in ancient Greek literary texts it indicated insolence towards the gods, manifested either in spiritual pride or by behaviour that flouted divine or social law; thus the arrogant and riotous conduct of Penelope's suitors in Homer's *Odyssey* is an instance of hubris that met its due when they were almost all slaughtered by the returned Odysseus. The spelling *hybris* is a slightly later (E20) alternative transliteration of the Greek; both transliterations are current, but *hubris* is marginally more common in general contexts.

1996 *Spectator* Winning is success, and success brings *hybris*, and *hybris* brings disaster.

huerta /ˈhwɛːtə/ *noun* M19 **Spanish**. In Spain and Spanish-speaking countries: a piece of irrigated land; an orchard.

huevos rancheros /ˌwɛvɒs ranˈtʃɛːrɒs/ *noun phrase* L20 (Mexican) Spanish. A Mexican dish of fried eggs served on tortillas with a spicy sauce.

hui /ˈhuːi/ *noun* M19 **Maori and Hawaiian**. In New Zealand: a large social or ceremonial gathering; in Hawaii: a formal club or association.

hula /ˈhuːlə/ *noun & intransitive verb* (also **hula-hula**) E19 **Hawaiian**. (Perform) a Hawaiian dance with six basic steps and gestures symbolizing or imitating natural phenomena, historical events, etc. (See quotation at LEI *noun* 1.)

hulan variant of UHLAN.

huldee variant of HALDI.

hulwa variant of HALVA.

hum /hʌm/ *noun* E20 **Serbo-Croat.** *Physical Geography* A steep-sided hill, of roughly circular cross-section, characteristic of karst topography. Cf. MOGOTE.

huma /ˈhu:mə/ *noun* M19 **Persian and Urdu** (*humā* phoenix). A mythical bird similar to the phoenix, supposed to bring luck to any person over whom it hovers on its restless flights.

humanitas /hjʊˈmanɪtɑ:s/ *noun* M20 **Latin.** Humanity.

hummum variant of HAMMAM.

hummus /ˈhʊməs/ *noun* (also **hoummos, h(o)umous**) M20 **Arabic** (*ḥummuṣ*). Ground chick-peas mixed with tahini, garlic, and lemon juice, frequently served as an hors d'oeuvre or dip.

humus /ˈhju:məs/ *noun* L18 **Latin** (= soil). The organic constituent of soil, formed by the decomposition of plant materials.

hybris variant of HUBRIS.

hydra /ˈhʌɪdrə/ *noun & adjective* LME **Old French** (((*h*)*ydre, idre* from) Latin *hydra* from Greek *hudra* water snake). **A** *noun* **1** LME *Greek Mythology* (also **Hydra**) A monster with many heads, which grew again as fast as they were cut off. **2** LME (usually **Hydra**) (The name of) a long faint constellation; the Sea Serpent. **3** L15 A thing or person likened to the mythological hydra in its baneful character, its multifarious aspects, or the difficulty of its extirpation. **4** M16 Any terrible serpent or reptile. *rhetorical.* **5** E17 A water snake. **6** L18 Any of several hydrozoans of the genus *Hydra* that live as solitary polyps attached to pond plants.

3 1996 *Oldie* ... conspiracy mania is a hydra with many heads, and when one is lopped off others appear, even more fantastical.

hydria /ˈhʌɪdrɪə/, /ˈhɪdrɪə/ *noun* plural **hydriae** /ˈhʌɪdrii:/ ME **Old French** (*idr*(*i*)*e*, from Latin *hydria*, from Greek *hudria*). Formerly, a water-pot. Now (*Archaeology*), a three-handled pitcher of ancient Greece.

hydrophobia /ˌhʌɪdrə(ʊ)ˈfəʊbɪə/ *noun* LME **Late Latin** (*hydrophobia* from Greek *hudrophobia*, from *hudrophobos* water-fearing). **1** LME A strong aversion to or fear of water arising from the spasms that a rabid person suffers when attempting to drink; rabies itself. **2** M18 *generally* A fear or dislike of water; *figurative* madness.

hyle /ˈhʌɪli:/ *noun* LME **Late Latin** (from Greek *hulē* wood, timber, material, matter). Matter, substance; *specifically* the primordial matter of the universe.

hyperbaton /hʌɪˈpə:bətɒn/ *noun* M16 **Latin** (from Greek *huperbaton* overstepping, from *huperbainein*, from as *hyper-* beyond, over + *bainein* to walk). *Grammar* and *Rhetoric* A figure of speech in which the logical order of words or phrases is inverted, especially for the sake of emphasis.

hyperbole /hʌɪˈpə:bəli/ *noun* LME **Latin** (from Greek *huperbolē* excess, exaggeration, from as *hyper-* beyond, over + *ballein* to throw). A figure of speech consisting in exaggerated or extravagant statement, used to express strong feeling or produce a strong impression and not meant to be taken literally; an instance of this; *generally* overstatement.

1996 *New Scientist* Hyperbole seems to be the order of the day: this phenomenon is called colossal magnetoresistance.

hyperdulia /ˌhʌɪpədjʊˈlʌɪə/ *noun* M16 **Medieval Latin** (*hyperdulia*, from as *hyper-* beyond + *dulia*). *Roman Catholic Church* The veneration properly given to the Virgin Mary (higher than DULIA but less than LATRIA).

hypogeum /ˌhʌɪpə(ʊ)ˈdʒi:əm/ *noun* (also **hypogaeum**) plural **hypog(a)ea** /ˌhʌɪpə(ʊ)ˈdʒi:ə/ M17 **Latin** (*hypogeum, hypogaeum* from Greek *hupogeion, hupogaion* use as noun of neuter singular of *hupogeios* underground). An underground chamber or vault.

hypostasis /hʌɪˈpɒstəsɪs/ *noun* plural **hypostases** /hʌɪˈpɒstəsi:z/ E16 **ecclesiastical Latin** (from Greek *hupostasis* sediment, foundation, subject-matter, (later) substance, existence, essence, personality, from as *hypo-* below + *stasis* standing). **1** E16 *Theology* A person; *specifically* **a** the single person of Christ, as opposed to his two natures, human and divine; **b** each of the three persons of the Trinity. **2** M16 *Medicine* **a** A sediment, especially in urine. Long *rare* or *obsolete.* **b** M19 The accumulation of blood or other fluid in a dependent part of the body. **3 a** L16–E17 A base or foundation on which something abstract rests. **b** *Philosophy* E17 An underlying reality, substance, as opposed to attributes ('accidents') or as distinguished from what is unsubstantial. **c** L17 Essence, essential principle. **4** E20 *Genetics* (Back-formation from *hypostatic.*) Inhibition of the expression of a gene by another at a different locus. **5** M20 *Linguistics* The citing of a word, element, etc., as an example or model; the word etc. so cited.

■ The Anglicized form *hypostasy* is rare.

hypothesis /hʌɪˈpɒθɪsɪs/ *noun* plural **hypotheses** /hʌɪˈpɒθɪsiːz/ L16 **Late Latin** (from Greek *hupothesis* foundation, base, from as *hypo-* + *thesis* placing). **1** L16 A proposition put forward merely as a basis for reasoning or argument, without any assumption of its truth. **2** L16–E18 A subordinate thesis forming part of a more general one; a particular case of a general proposition; a detailed statement. **3** E17 A supposition, an assumption; *especially* one made as a starting-point for further investigation or research from known facts. **4** E17 A groundless assumption; a guess. **5** L18 An actual or possible situation considered as a basis for action.

hysterica passio /hɪˌstɛrɪkə ˈpasɪəʊ/ *noun phrase* E17 **Latin** (feminine of *hystericus* (from Greek *husterikos* belonging to the uterus) + *passio* passion). Hysteria.

■ Hysteria was formerly held to be a disorder peculiar to women resulting from a disturbance of the uterus.

hysteron proteron /ˌhɪstərɒn ˈprɒtərɒn/ *noun, adverb, & adjective phrase* M16 **Late Latin** (from Greek *husteron proteron* latter (put in place of) former). **A** *noun phrase* **1** M16 *Rhetoric* A figure of speech in which what should come last is put first. **2** L16 *generally* Position or arrangement of things in the reverse of their natural or rational order. **B** *adverb phrase* In a topsy-turvy way. Only in E17. **C** *adjective phrase* M17 Involving or employing hysteron proteron.

I

iambus /ʌɪ'ambəs/ *noun* plural **iambuses, iambi** /ʌɪ'ambʌɪ/ L16 **Latin** (from Greek *iambos* iambus, lampoon, from *iaptein* to assail in words). *Prosody* A metrical foot consisting of one short followed by one long syllable or (in English etc.) of one unstressed followed by one stressed syllable.

■ The metre known as the iambic trimeter was first used by the ancient Greek satirists, hence the connection with lampoons.

ibid /'ɪbɪd/ *adverb* M17 **Latin** (abbreviation of next). IBIDEM.

ibidem /'ɪbɪdɛm/, /ɪ'bʌɪdɛm/ *adverb* M18 **Latin** (= in the same place, from *ibi* there + demonstrative suffix *-dem*, as in *idem*, *tandem*, etc). In the same book, chapter, passage, etc.

■ The abbreviated form *ibid* is in more general use in bibliographies etc.

ichor /'ʌɪkɔː/ *noun* M17 **Greek** (*ikhōr*). **1** M17 Blood; a liquid likened to the blood of animals. Now *literary*. **2** M17 *Medicine* A watery discharge from a wound or sore. *archaic*. **3** L17 *Greek Mythology* A fluid supposed to flow like blood in the veins of the gods. **4** E20 *Geology* An emanation from magma supposed by some to cause granitization.

icon /'ʌɪkɒn/, /'ʌɪk(ə)n/ *noun* (also **ikon**) M16 **Latin** (from Greek *eikōn* likeness, image, similitude). **1** M16–L17 *Rhetoric* A simile. **2 a** L16–E18 A portrait, a picture; *especially* one of an animal or plant in a book of natural history. **b** M19 *Ecclesiastical* An image in traditional Byzantine style of Christ or a holy person that is used ceremonially and venerated in the Orthodox Church. **c** L20 *Computing* A small symbolic picture on a VDU screen, *especially* one that may be selected with a cursor to exercise an option that it represents. **3** L16 A statue. **4** L16 A realistic description in writing. *rare*. **5** E20 *Philosophy* A sign with some factor in common with the object it represents.

iconostasis /ʌɪkə'nɒstəsɪs/ *noun* plural **iconostases** /ʌɪkə'nɒstəsiːz/ M19 **Modern Greek** (*eikonostasis*, from as *icono-* (combining form of) icon + *stasis*, literally, 'standing'). A screen separating the sanctuary or altar from the nave in most Orthodox churches and used to display icons.

id /ɪd/ *noun* E20 **Latin** (= it, translating German *es*). *Psychoanalysis* The inherited instinctive impulses of the individual, forming part of the unconscious and, in Freudian theory, interacting in the psyche with the ego and the superego.

1996 *Spectator* . . . talk of leaving Europe is the politics of the id: a regression to infantile fantasy.

id al-fitr variant of ID UL-FITR.

idée fixe /ide fiks/, /ˌiːdeɪ 'fiːks/ *noun phrase* plural **idées fixes** (pronounced same) M19 **French** (= fixed idea). An idea that dominates the mind, an obsession.

1995 *Spectator* I had not realised that Cézanne's numerous bathers were such an *idée fixe*.

idée reçue /ide rəsy/, /ˌiːdeɪ rə'sjuː/ *noun phrase* plural **idées reçues** (pronounced same) M20 **French** (= received idea). A generally accepted notion or opinion.

idem /'ɪdɛm/, /'ʌɪdɛm/ *noun & adverb* LME **Latin**. (In) the same author, work, etc.

idem sonans /ˌʌɪdɛm 'səʊnanz/ *noun & adjective phrase* M19 **Latin** (= sounding the same). *Law* chiefly *United States*. **A** *noun* M19 The occurrence in a document of a material word or name misspelt but having the sound of the word or name intended. **B** *adjective* M19 Homophonous *with*.

Identitätsphilosophie /iˌdɛnti'tɛːts filozoˌfiː/ *noun* M19 **German** (= identity-philosophy). *Philosophy* A system or doctrine that assumes the fundamental identity of spirit and nature.

id est /ɪd 'ɛst/ *adverb phrase* L16 **Latin** (= that is). That is (to say).

■ Usually abbreviated to i.e.

idioticon /ɪdɪ'əʊtɪk(ə)n/ *noun* M19 **German** (from Greek *idiōtikon* use as noun of neuter singular of *idiōtikos* uneducated). A dictionary, word-list, etc., of words and phrases peculiar to a dialect, a particular group of people, etc.

idiot savant /idjo savɑ̃/ *noun phrase* plural **idiots savants** (*pronounced same*) L20 **French** (= learned idiot). A person who in many respects is ignorant or uneducated, but who has an exceptional mastery of one subject or (usually mental) skill.

1995 *New Scientist* She is no idiot savant like the Dustin Hoffman character in *Rain Man* who could memorise a casino-full of cards but could do nothing with the information . . .

idolum /ʌɪˈdəʊləm/ *noun* plural **idola** /ʌɪˈdəʊlə/ E17 **Latin** (from Greek *eidōlon* idol). **1** E17 An image without substance; a phantom; a mental image, an idea. **2** M17 *Philosophy* (now *historical*) A false mental image.

id ul-fitr /ˈiːdʊlfɪtrə/ *noun* (also **id al-fitr** /ˈiːdalfɪtrə/) M18 **Arabic** (*ʿīd al-fiṭr*; cf. EID). *Islam* The major festival to celebrate the ending of the Ramadan fast.

i.e. abbreviation of ID EST.

igloo /ˈɪgluː/ *noun* (in sense 2 also **agloo**, **aglu**, /ˈagluː/) M19 **Eskimo** ((Inuit) *iglu* house). **1** M19 An Eskimo dome-shaped hut, usually one built from blocks of snow. **b** *transferred* M20 Any similarly shaped building or structure used for storage, shelter, etc. **2** M19 A cavity in the snow above a seal's breathing-hole.

ignis fatuus /ˌɪgnɪs ˈfatjʊəs/ *noun phrase* plural **ignes fatui** /ˌɪgniːz ˈfatjʊʌɪ/, /ˌɪgneɪz ˈfatjʊiː/ M16 **Modern Latin** (= foolish fire, so called from its erratic flitting from place to place). **1** M16 A phosphorescent light seen hovering or floating over marshy ground, perhaps due to the combustion of methane; a will-o'-the-wisp. **2** L16 *figurative* A delusive guiding principle, hope, or aim.

ignoramus /ɪgnəˈreɪməs/ *noun* L16 **Latin** (= we do not know, (in legal use) we take no notice of (it)). **1** L16 The endorsement formerly made by a grand jury on an indictment which they rejected as not being backed by sufficient evidence. *obsolete* except *historical*. **2** E17 An ignorant person.

■ In sense 2 very probably from *Ignoramus*, a comedy by George Ruggle satirizing lawyers, produced before James I in 1615.

ignoratio elenchi /ɪgnəˌreɪʃɪəʊ ɪˈlɛŋkʌɪ/ *noun phrase* plural **ignorationes elenchi** /ˌɪgnəreɪʃɪˈəʊniːz/ L16 **Medieval Latin** (translation of Greek *hē tou elegkou agnoia* ignorance of the conditions of valid proof). A logical fallacy which consists in apparently refuting an opponent while actually disproving something not asserted; *generally* any argument which is irrelevant to its professed purpose.

ignotum per ignotius /ɪgˌnəʊtəm pər ɪgˈnəʊtɪəs/ *noun phrase* LME **Late Latin** (literally, 'the unknown by means of the more unknown'). An explanation which is harder to understand than what it is meant to explain.

ihram /ɪxˈrɑːm/, /ɪˈrɑːm/ *noun* E18 **Arabic** (*'iḥrām*, ultimately from *ḥarama* forbid; cf. HAREM). **1** E18 The sacred state into which a Muslim must enter before performing a pilgrimage, during which sexual intercourse, shaving, and several other actions are forbidden. **2** E18 The costume worn by a Muslim in this state, consisting of two lengths of seamless usually white fabric.

ikat /ˈiːkɑːt/ *noun* M20 **Malay** (literally, 'tie, fasten'). (A fabric made using) an Indonesian technique of textile decoration in which warp or weft threads, or both, are tied at intervals and dyed before weaving.

ikebana /ɪkɪˈbɑːnə/ *noun* E20 **Japanese**. The art of Japanese flower arrangement, with formal display according to strict rules.

ikon variant of ICON.

ilang-ilang variant of YLANG-YLANG.

illuminato /ɪˌluːmɪˈnɑːtəʊ/, /ɪˌljuːmɪˈnɑːtəʊ/ *noun* (also **Illuminato**) usually in plural **illuminati** /ɪˌluːmɪˈnɑːti/ L16 **Italian** (= enlightened; plural partly from Latin *illuminati* plural of *illuminatus*, but in German context translating German *Illuminaten*). A member of any of various sects or societies claiming special enlightenment. Also *generally*, a person claiming special knowledge on any subject.

illuminé /ilymine/ (*plural same*), /ɪˈluːmmeɪ/, /ɪˈljuːmmeɪ/ *noun* (also **Illuminé**) L18 **French** (= enlightened). An ILLUMINATO.

imago /ɪˈmeɪgəʊ/ *noun* plural **imagines** /ɪˈmeɪdʒɪniːz/, **imagos** L18 **Latin**. **1** L18 *Entomology* The final, fully developed form of an insect after passing through all stages of metamorphosis. **2** E20 *Psychoanalysis* An unconscious image of an archetype or of someone (especially a parent) which influences a person's behaviour etc.

imam /ɪˈmɑːm/ *noun* E17 **Arabic** (*'imām* leader, from *'amma* to lead the way). **1** E17 The leader of prayers in a mosque. **2** M17 (**Imam**) (A title of) any of various Muslim leaders, especially one succeeding Muhammad as the leader of Shiite Islam.

imam bayildi /ɪˌmɑːm ˈbɑːjɪldi/ *noun phrase* (also **Imam Bayildi**) M20 **Turkish** (*imam bayıldı*, literally, 'the imam fainted'). A dish, originating in Turkey, consisting of aubergines stuffed with a garlic-flavoured onion-and-tomato mixture and cooked in oil.

■ Whether the *imam* fainted from pleasure and repletion or because he was overcome by horror at the cost of the dish seems to be a moot point.

imbrex /ˈɪmbrɛks/ *noun* plural **imbrices** /ˈɪmbrɪsiːz/ M19 **Latin** (from *imber* rain-shower). *Archaeology* A curved roof-tile used to cover joints in a Roman tiled roof. Cf. TEGULA sense 2.

imbroglio /ɪmˈbrəʊlɪəʊ/ *noun* (also **embroglio**) plural **imbroglios** M18 **Italian** (from *imbrogliare* to confuse, corresponding to French *embrouiller* to embroil). **1** M18 A confused heap. *archaic*. **2** E19 A state of great confusion; a complicated or difficult (especially political or dramatic) situation; a confused misunderstanding.

2 1996 *Spectator* If the royal imbroglio does end in a tragedy, Major will have blood on his hands.

immortelle /ɪmɔːˈtɛl/ *noun* M19 **French** (from *fleur immortelle* everlasting flower). An everlasting flower, especially *Xeranthemum annuum*.

immram /ˈɪmrɑːm/ *noun* (also **imram**, **imrama**) plural **immra** /ˈɪmrɑː/ L19 **Old Irish** (*imram* (modern *iomramh*), from *imm-rá* to row around). Any of various stories of fabulous sea voyages written in Ireland between the late eighth and eleventh centuries.

impair /ˈɪmpɛː/; *in senses A.2, B.1 foreign* /ɛ̃pɛr/ (*plural same*) *adjective & noun* M19 **French** (= unequal, from negative *im-* un- + *pair* equal). **A** *adjective* **1** M19 Not paired; not forming one of a pair. **2** M20 *Roulette* Of or pertaining to an odd number or the odd numbers collectively. **B** *noun* M19 *Roulette* An odd number; the odd numbers collectively. Cf. PAIR.

■ In the early seventeenth century Shakespeare may have used *impair* in *Troilus and Cressida* in the sense of 'unfit, inferior', but the reading is doubtful.

impasse /amˈpɑːs/, /ˈampɑːs/, *foreign* /ɛ̃pɑs/ *noun* M19 **French** (from negative *im-* not + stem of *passer* to pass). **1** M19 A position from which there is no escape, a deadlock. **2** L19 *literal* A road etc. without an outlet, a blind alley.

1 1996 *New Scientist* . . . the only thing that can help developing countries escape this impasse is a second revolution.

impasto /ɪmˈpastəʊ/ *noun* L18 **Italian** (from *impastare*, from *im-* in + *pasta* paste). **1** L18 The action of painting by laying colour on thickly; this manner of painting. **2** E20 *Ceramics* Enamel etc. colours standing out in relief on a surface.

1 *transferred* **1996** *Spectator* As the swirling impasto of adjectives, similes and metaphors becomes increasingly thick and clotted, so the picture becomes less and less distinct.

impayable /ɪmˈpeɪəb(ə)l/; *in sense 3 foreign* /ɛ̃pɛjabl/ *adjective* ME **French** (from as *im-* not + *payer* to pay). **1** Implacable, unappeasable. Only in ME. **2** L18 Impossible to pay or discharge. **3** E19 Priceless, invaluable; extraordinary, absurd.

impedimenta /ɪmˌpɛdɪˈmɛntə/ *noun plural* E17 **Latin**. Travelling equipment, especially of an army etc.; encumbrances; bulky equipment in general.

1996 *Times* On the walls and hanging from the ceiling were the impedimenta of many sports: stuffed baseball players in New York Mets shirts, hang gliders, surf boards, caps, bats and gloves.

imperium /ɪmˈpɪərɪəm/ *noun* M17 **Latin**. Command; absolute power; supreme or imperial power; empire.

■ Used especially of the rule of the Roman emperors.

impetus /ˈɪmpɪtəs/ *noun* M17 **Latin** (= assault, force, from *impetere* to assail). **1** M17 The force or energy with which a body moves; impulsion. **2** M17 *figurative* Moving force, (an) impulse, a stimulus.

impi /ˈɪmpi/ *noun* M19 **Zulu**. Chiefly *South African History*. A body of Zulu warriors or armed tribesmen.

impluvium /ɪmˈpluːvɪəm/ *noun* plural **impluvia** /ɪmˈpluːvɪə/ E19 **Latin** (from *impluere* to rain into). *Roman Antiquities* The square basin in the centre of the atrium of a Roman house, which received rain-water from an opening in the roof.

imponderabilia /ɪmˌpɒnd(ə)rəˈbɪlɪə/ *noun plural* E20 **Modern Latin** (neuter plural of *imponderabilis* that cannot be weighed). Imponderables, imponderable factors.

impresa /ɪmˈpreɪzə/ *noun* L16 **Italian** (= undertaking, device, from Proto-Romance verb, from Latin *em-* on + *prendere* to take). **1** L16 An emblem, a device; *especially* one accompanied by a motto. **2** E17 A sentence accompanying an emblem; a motto, a maxim, a proverb. Long *rare*.

impresario /ˌɪmprɪˈsɑːrɪəʊ/ *noun* plural **impresarios** M18 **Italian** (from as preceding). An organizer or sponsor of public entertainments; a manager of an operatic or a concert company.

1996 *Spectator* [Diaghilev] became an impresario, inspirer and explainer—of Russia to the West and the West to Russia.

imprévu /ɛ̃prevy/ *noun* M19 **French** (from as *im-* + *prévu* past participle of *prévoir* foresee). *The* unexpected, *the* unforeseen.

imprimatur /ˌɪmprɪˈmeɪtə/, /ˌɪmprɪˈmɑːtə/, /ˌɪmprɪˈmɑːtʊə/ *noun* M17 **Latin** (= let it be printed, 3rd person singular present subjunctive passive of *imprimere* to imprint). In the Roman Catholic Church: an official licence authorizing the printing of an ecclesiastical or religious work etc.; *generally* official approval, an official sanction.

figurative **1995** *Times* Without America's imprimatur, inward investment to Northern Ireland would wither away.

imprimatura /ˌɪmpriːməˈtʊərə/, *foreign* /ˌimprimaˈtuːra/ *noun* M20 **Italian** (*imprimitura*). A usually coloured transparent primer or glaze applied to an artist's canvas or panel.

impromptu /ɪmˈprɒm(p)tjuː/ *adverb, noun, adjective, & verb* M17 **French** (from Latin *in promptu* at hand, in readiness, from *promptus* readiness). **A** *adverb* M17 Without preparation; on the spur of the moment; extempore. **B** *noun* L17 Something composed, uttered, or done impromptu; an improvisation; *specifically* a musical composition having the character of an improvisation. **C** *adjective* M18 Composed, uttered, or done impromptu; improvised; makeshift. **D** *transitive and intransitive verb* E19 Improvise; extemporize.

imram(a) variants of IMMRAM.

imshi /ˈɪmʃi/ *transitive verb* (*imperative*) (also **imshee**) E20 **Arabic** ((from colloquial) *ʼmšī* imperative of *miši* to go). Go away!

■ Military slang, recorded (1916) during World War I as being used to street hawkers in Cairo by the Australasian Corps.

in absentia /ɪn abˈsɛntɪə/, /ɪn abˈsɛnʃɪə/ *adverb phrase* L19 **Latin**. In his, her, or their absence.

■ Almost always in a legal context modifying the verbs 'try' or 'convict' (see quotation).

1996 *Times* The court is trying 71 members of the Dergue, of whom 25 . . . are being tried in absentia.

in abstracto /ɪn abˈstraktəʊ/ *adverb phrase* E17 **Latin** (= in the abstract). As an abstract thing. Cf. IN CONCRETO.

inamorata /ɪˌnaməˈrɑːtə/ *noun* (also **enamorata**) M17 **Italian** ((now *innamorata*), feminine of INAMORATO). A female lover.

1996 *Spectator* Paula Yates . . . estranged wife of Bob Geldof, inamorata of rock star has-been Michael Hutchence . . .

inamorato /ɪˌnaməˈrɑːtəʊ/ *noun* (also **enamorato**) plural **inamoratos** L16 **Italian** (now *innamorato*, past participle of *innamorare* to fall in love with). A male lover.

in antis /ɪn ˈantɪs/ *adjective phrase* M19 **Latin**. *Classical Architecture* (Of columns) positioned between two antas; (of a building) having walls prolonged beyond the front, with terminating pilasters in line with columns of a façade.

in articulo mortis /ɪn ɑːˌtɪkjʊləʊ ˈmɔːtɪs/ *adverb phrase* L16 **Latin** (= in the article of death). At the point or moment of death.

in camera /ɪn ˈkam(ə)rə/ *adverb phrase* E19 **Late Latin** (= in the chamber). In a judge's private chambers, not in open court; *generally* in secret or private session, not in public.

incipit /ˈɪnsɪpɪt/ *noun* L19 **Latin** (3rd person singular present indicative of *incipere* to begin). The opening words of a manuscript, a printed book (usually an early one), a chanted liturgical text, etc.

■ The word used by medieval scribes to indicate the beginning of a new treatise, poem, division, etc. Cf. EXPLICIT.

incisor /ɪnˈsʌɪzə/ *noun* L17 **Medieval Latin** (in *dens incisor* incisor tooth, from Latin, literally, 'cutter', from *incis-*, past participial stem of *incidere* to cut). A narrow-edged tooth adapted for cutting; in humans, any of the front four teeth in each jaw. Also *incisor tooth*.

incognita /ˌɪnˈkɒgnɪtə/ *noun plural* M19 **Latin** (neuter plural of *incognitus* unknown, from as INCOGNITO). Unknown things or places.

incognita /ˌɪnkɒgˈniːtə/, *foreign* /in ˈkoːɲita/ *adjective & noun* L17 **Italian** (feminine of *incognito* unknown). **A** *adjective*

L17 Of a woman: disguised; unknown. **B** *noun* E18 plural **incognitas**, **incognite** /ınkɒg'niːte/. A disguised or unknown woman, especially one's lover.

incognito /ˌınkɒg'niːtəʊ/, /ın'kɒgnıtəʊ/ *adjective, adverb, & noun* M17 **Italian** (from Latin *incognitus* unknown, from as *in-* un- + *cognitus*, past participle of *cognoscere* to know). **A** *adjective* M17 Of a person: concealed under a disguised or assumed identity; unknown. **B** *adverb* M17 Under a disguised or assumed identity. **C** *noun* plural **incognitos** **1** M17 A person who conceals his or her identity; an anonymous or unknown person. **2** E19 The condition of being unknown, anonymity; assumed or pretended identity.

B 1996 *Spectator* Surely anyone could see it is my duty [as a restaurant critic] to travel incognito.

incommunicado /ˌınkəmjuːnı'kɑːdəʊ/ *adjective & adverb* (also in Spanish form **incomunicado** *also foreign* /ˌinkomuni 'kado/) M19 **Spanish** (*incomunicado* past participle of *incomunicar* to deprive of communication). **A** *adjective* M19 Having no means of communication with others; *especially* (of a prisoner) held in solitary confinement. **B** *adverb* M20 Without means of communication with others.

in concreto /ın kɒn'kriːtəʊ/ *adverb phrase* E17 **Latin**. As a concrete thing. Cf. IN ABSTRACTO.

inconnu /'ıŋkənuː/, *foreign* /ɛ̃kɔny/ (*plural same*) *noun* (in sense 1 feminine **inconnue**, plural (in sense 1) **inconnu(e)s**, (in sense 2) same) E19 **French** (= unknown). **1** E19 An unknown person, a stranger. **2** E19 A predatory freshwater salmonid game-fish, *Stenodus leucichthys*, of the Arctic. Originally *Canadian*.

in contumaciam /ın ˌkɒntjʊ'meısıəm/ *adverb phrase* L19 **Latin**. While in contempt of court.

in corpore /ın 'kɔːpəreı/ *adjective & adverb phrase* E20 **Latin** (literally, 'in the body'). *Biology* IN VIVO.

incubus /'ıŋkjʊbəs/ *noun* plural **incubuses**, **incubi** /'ıŋkjʊbʌı/ ME **Late Latin** (= Latin *incubo* nightmare, from *incubare* to lie on). **1** ME An evil spirit supposed to descend upon sleeping people and especially to have sexual intercourse with sleeping women. **2** M16 An oppressive nightmare; a person who or thing which oppresses or troubles like a nightmare.

2 1996 *Times* She has no incubus of accumulated policies and attitudes.

incunabulum /ˌınkjʊ'nabjʊləm/ *noun* plural (earlier) **incunabula** /ınkjʊ 'nabjʊlə/ E19 **Latin** (*incunabula* neuter plural swaddling-clothes, cradle, from as *in-* in + *cunae* cradle). **1** E19 In *plural* The early stages of development of a thing. **2** M19 A book printed at an early date; *specifically* one printed before 1501.

indaba /ın'dɑːbə/ *noun* E19 **Zulu** (= discussion). **1** E19 A conference between or with members of southern African Black peoples. **2** L20 A person's business, problem, or concern. *South African colloquial.*

indecorum /ındı'kɔːrəm/ *noun* L16 **Latin** (use as noun of neuter singular of *indecorus* unseemly). **1** L16 An indecorous action or proceeding; an offence against recognized standards of behaviour. **2** M17 The quality of being indecorous; lack of decorum; improper behaviour.

index /'ındɛks/ *noun* plural **indexes**, (especially *in technical use*) **indices** /'ındısiːz/ LME **Latin** (*index*, *indic-* forefinger, informer, etc., from base represented by *dicere* to say, Greek *deiknunai* to show). **1** LME The finger used in pointing, the forefinger. Now usually *index finger.* **b** L19 *Ornithology* The second (occasionally the first) digit of the manus in a bird's wing. **2** L16 A piece of wood, metal, etc., which serves as a pointer; *specifically* (in a scientific instrument) a pointer which moves along a graduated scale so as to show movements or quantities. **b** L16 The arm of a surveying instrument; an alidade. **3** L16 A thing which serves to point *to* a fact or conclusion; a sign or indication *of*. **4** L16 A list of things in (usually alphabetical) order; *especially* a list, usually at the end of a book, giving the names, topics, etc., mentioned in the book and the places where they occur. Formerly also, a table of contents. **5 a** L16–M19 *Music* A sign placed on the stave at the end of a page or line to indicate the position of the next note. **b** E18 *Typography* A hand-shaped symbol with a pointing finger used to draw attention to a note etc. Also called *fist.* **6** L17 *Mathematics* A subscript or superscript symbol denoting some characteristic of a quantity or function, as the exponent in x^2, etc. **7** E19 A number or formula expressing a specific property, especially a ratio; *especially* in *Anatomy*, a formula expressing the ratio between two dimensions (especially of the skull). **8** L19 *Economics* (A number in) a scale relating (usually in the form of a percentage) the level of prices, wages, etc., at a particular time to those at a date taken as a base.

■ There are also a number of other specialist technical uses of *index* in mathematics, computing, and engineering. In sense 4 the Latin names of various types of index may be used: *index locorum* (index of the passages cited or discussed), *index nominum* (index of the names of people discussed), *index rerum* (index of the subjects and matters treated), *index verborum* (index of the significant words discussed).

index librorum prohibitorum /ˌɪndɛks lɪˌbrɔːrəm prəʊˌhɪbɪˈtɔːrəm/ *noun phrase* (also **Index Librorum Prohibitorum**) M17 **Latin** (= index of prohibited books). *Roman Catholic Church* The official list of books that Roman Catholics were forbidden to read.

■ The first *Index Librorum Prohibitorum* was published in 1564 as part of the Counter-Reformation programme instituted at the Council of Trent, and the list was not abolished until 1966. It was also referred to simply as *the Index*.

indicium /ɪnˈdɪsɪəm/ *noun* plural **indicia** /ɪnˈdɪsɪə/ E17 **Latin** (from as INDEX). An indication, a sign; a distinguishing mark. Usually in *plural*.

in dictione /ˌɪn dɪktɪˈəʊni/ *adjective phrase* E19 **Latin** (translation of Greek *para tēn lexin* in relation to the wording). Of a logical fallacy: arising from the wording used to express it.

■ One of the subdivisions of logical fallacy noted by Aristotle in his *Sophistici Elenchi* (ch. 4), also sometimes referred to in Latin as *in voce* in the voice. Opposed to EXTRA DICTIONEM.

indumentum /ˌɪndjʊˈmɛntəm/ *noun* plural **indumenta** /ˌɪndjʊˈmɛntə/ M19 **Latin** (= garment, from *induere* to put on). *Botany* The covering of hairs, scales, etc., on (part of) a plant, especially when dense.

induna /ɪnˈduːnə/ *noun* M19 **Zulu** (from nominal prefix *in-* + *duna* councillor, headman, overseer, captain). **1** M19 A tribal councillor or headman among the Nguni peoples of southern Africa. **2** M20 *transferred* A person, especially a Black person, in authority; a foreman.

inédit /inedi/ *noun* plural pronounced same E20 **French** (cf. next). An unpublished work; *figurative* something secret or unrevealed.

inedita /ɪnˈɛdɪtə/ *noun plural* L19 **Modern Latin** (use as noun of neuter plural of Latin *ineditus*, from *in-* not + *editus* past participle of *edere* to give out, edit). Unpublished writings.

inertia /ɪˈnəːʃə/ *noun* E18 **Latin** (= inactivity). **1** E18 *Physics* The property of a body, proportional to its mass, by virtue of which it continues in a state of rest or uniform straight motion in the absence of an external force. **b** L19 In other physical properties: the tendency to continue in some state, to resist change. **2** E19 *transferred* Inactivity; disinclination to act or exert oneself; sloth; apathy.

in esse /ɪn ˈɛsi/ *adjective phrase* L16 **Latin**. In actual existence.

■ Opposed to IN POSSE.

in excelsis /ɪn ɛkˈselsɪs/, /ɛksˈtʃɛlsɪs/ *adverb phrase* LME **Latin** (= in the highest (places); cf. EXCELSIOR). In the highest.

■ Often in the phrase *Gloria in excelsis Deo* 'Glory to God in the highest!'

in extenso /ɪn ɪkˈstɛnsəʊ/ *adverb phrase* E19 **Latin** (from *in* in + *extenso* ablative of *extensus* past participle of *extendere* to stretch out). In full, at length.

in extremis /ɪn ɛkˈstriːmɪs/, /ɪn ɪk ˈstriːmɪs/ *adverb phrase* M16 **Latin** (from *in* in + *extremis* ablative plural of *extremus* last, uttermost). At the point of death; in great difficulty; in a painful or awkward situation.

1996 *Spectator* I can still recall the glorious sight of his headlong dive to the ground and the altogether unexpected knowledge of English he revealed *in extremis*.

infanta /ɪnˈfantə/ *noun* L16 **Spanish** (Portuguese feminine of INFANTE). *History* A daughter of the King and Queen of Spain or Portugal; *specifically* the eldest daughter who is not heir to the throne. Formerly also *generally*, a girl, a princess.

infante /ɪnˈfanteɪ/ *noun* M16 **Spanish and Portuguese** (from Latin *infans*, *infant-* child). *History* A son of the King and Queen of Spain or Portugal other than the heir to the throne; *specifically* the second son.

inferno /ɪnˈfəːnəʊ/ *noun* plural **infernos** M19 **Italian** (from Christian Latin *infernus* below, subterranean). Hell; *transferred* a scene of horror or distress; *especially* a raging fire.

■ Reference to hell as *the inferno* is generally in allusion to Dante's *Divine Comedy*.

in fine /ɪn ˈfʌɪni/, /ˈfiːni/ *adverb phrase* M16 **Latin**. Finally, in short, to sum up.

1996 *Spectator* Alfred, *in fine*, created a wellspring of instinctive Tory-voting monarchists.

infinitum /ɪnfɪˈnʌɪtəm/ *noun* L16 **Latin** (use as noun of neuter of *infinitus* unlimited). Infinity; an infinitude, an endless amount or number.

■ Often in the phrase AD INFINITUM.

in flagrante /ɪn fləˈgranti/ *adverb phrase* E17 **Latin** (abbreviation of next or similar Latin phrase). In the very act. *colloquial.*

1996 *Oldie* Abby herself attempts to commit suicide on finding her agent *in flagrante* with his secretary.

in flagrante delicto /ɪn fləˌgrantɪ dɪˈlɪktəʊ/ *adverb phrase* L18 **Latin** (= in the heat of the crime: cf. preceding). In the very act of committing an offence; *specifically* in the act of adultery or other sexual misconduct.

1996 *Spectator* . . . his sacking as editor . . . was more abrupt since he was caught *in flagrante delicto* with his pretty secretary . . .

influenza /ˌɪnflʊˈɛnzə/ *noun* M18 **Italian** (literally, 'influence', from medieval Latin *influentia* influence). A highly contagious viral infection of the lining of the trachea and bronchi, often epidemic, and usually marked by fever, weakness, muscular aches, coughing, and watery catarrh. Frequent loosely, any acute respiratory infection accompanied by fever.

■ Generally abbreviated to *flu* in all but the most formal usage.

infra /ˈɪnfrə/ *adverb* L19 **Latin**. Later, further on (in a book or article); below.

infra dig /ˌɪnfrə ˈdɪg/ *adjective phrase* E19 **Latin** (abbreviation of Latin *infra dignitatem* beneath (one's) dignity). Beneath the dignity of one's position; undignified. *colloquial.*

1996 *Times* Hoping that this didn't look too infra dig, I duly grasped the mane on our final attempt, all but letting go of the reins . . .

ingenium /ɪnˈdʒiːnɪəm/ *noun* plural **ingenia** /ɪnˈdʒiːnɪə/ L19 **Latin** (= mind, intellect). Mental ability, talent; a person possessing this. Also, mental inclination, disposition.

1921 *Glasgow Herald* His scientific ingenium was as keen as ever.

ingénue /ˌanʒeɪˈnjuː/; *foreign* /ɛ̃ʒeny/ (*plural same*) *noun* (also **ingenue**) M19 **French** (feminine of *ingénu* ingenuous). An artless innocent young woman, especially as a stage role; an actress playing such a role.

1995 *Times* She is 60, that awkward age, too old for ingenues, too young for crones.

ingesta /ɪnˈdʒɛstə/ *noun plural* E18 **Latin** (neuter plural of *ingestus* past participle of *ingerere* to carry in, pour in). Substances introduced into the body as nourishment; food and drink.

in infinitum /ɪn ɪnfɪˈnʌɪtəm/ *adverb phrase* M16 **Latin**. To infinity, without end.

■ Cf. AD INFINITUM.

injuria /ɪnˈdʒʊərɪə/ *noun* plural **injuriae** /ɪnˈdʒʊərɪiː/ L19 **Latin**. *Law* An invasion of another's rights; an actionable wrong.

inkosi /ɪŋˈkəʊsi/ *noun* M19 **Nguni**. In South Africa: (the title of) a Zulu ruler, chief, or high official.

in limine /ɪn ˈlɪmɪni/ *adverb phrase* E19 **Latin**. On the threshold; at the outset.

in loco parentis /ɪn ˌləʊkəʊ pəˈrɛntɪs/ *prepositional phrase* E19 **Latin** (= in place of a parent). Assuming the responsibilities of a parent.

1995 *Spectator* One of us was in agony and one of us was *in loco parentis*, so it was a very sticky wait.

in medias res /ɪn ˌmɛdɪɑːs ˈreɪz/, /ˌmiːdɪɑːs/ *adverb phrase* L18 **Latin**. Into the midst of things; *especially* into the middle of a narrative, without preamble.

in medio /ɪn ˈmiːdɪəʊ/, /ˈmɛdɪəʊ/ *adverb phrase* E17 **Latin**. In the middle; in an undecided state.

in memoriam /ɪn mɪˈmɔːrɪam/ *prepositional & noun phrase* M19 **Latin**. **A** *prepositional phrase* M19 To the memory of, in memory of. **B** *noun phrase* L19 A poem, notice, etc., in memory of a dead person.

■ The fashion for poems with this title was set by Tennyson's sequence of poems (1850), written in memory of his friend A. H. Hallam, who died in 1833.

in nomine /ɪn ˈnəʊmɪneɪ/, /ɪn ˈnɒmɪneɪ/ *noun phrase* M17 **Latin** (= in the name (of)). An instrumental composition in fugal style (probably originally one set to a Latin text including the words *in nomine*); a free fugue in which the answer does not exactly correspond with the subject.

in nubibus /ɪn ˈnjuːbɪbəs/ *adverb & adjective phrase* L16 **Latin**. In the clouds; as yet unsettled; undecided; incapable of being carried out.

in nuce /ɪn ˈnuːkeɪ/ *adverb phrase* M19 **Latin**. In a nutshell; in a condensed form.

innuendo /ɪnjʊˈɛndəʊ/ *adverb & noun* M16 Latin (= by nodding at, pointing to, intimating, ablative gerund of *innuere* to nod to, signify, from as *in-* + *nuere* to nod). **A** *adverb* M16 Meaning, that is to say, to wit, (especially in legal documents, introducing a parenthetical explanation of the precise reference of a preceding noun or pronoun). **B** *noun* plural **innuendo(e)s**. **1** L17 A parenthetical explanation of, or construction put upon, a word or expression; *especially* in an action for libel or slander, the injurious meaning alleged to be conveyed by a word or expression not in itself actionable. **2** L17 An allusive or oblique remark, hint, or suggestion, usually disparaging; a remark with a (usually suggestive) double meaning; allusion, hinting, suggestion.

in ovo /ɪn ˈəʊvəʊ/ *adverb phrase* M19 **Latin** (= in the egg). In embryo. Also *figurative*.

in pari materia /ɪn ˌpɑːri məˈtɛːrɪə/, /mə ˈtɪərɪə/ *adverb phrase* M19 **Latin**. In an equivalent case or position.

in partibus /ɪn ˈpɑːtɪbəs/ *adverb phrase* L17 **Latin** (*in partibus* (*infidelium*) in the regions (of the infidels)). *Roman Catholic Church* In full *in partibus infidelium* /ɪnfɪ ˈdeɪlɪəm/, /ɪnfɪˈdiːlɪəm/. In heretical territory (with reference to a titular bishop etc., especially in a Muslim country).

in parvo /ɪn ˈpɑːvəʊ/ *adverb phrase* E20 **Latin**. In little, in miniature, on a small scale.

in pectore /ɪn ˈpɛktəri/ *adverb phrase* M19 **Latin** (= in one's breast). Secretly; IN PETTO sense 1.

in perpetuum /ɪn pəˈpɛtjʊəm/ *adverb phrase* M17 **Latin**. For all time, in perpetuity.

in personam /ɪn pəˈsəʊnam/ *adjective phrase* L18 **Latin** (= against a person). *Law* Made or availing against or affecting a specific person only; imposing a personal liability. Frequently *postpositive*. Cf. IN REM.

in petto /ɪn ˈpɛtəʊ/ *adverb phrase* L17 **Italian** (= in the breast). **1** L17 In contemplation; undisclosed, secretly (especially of the appointment of cardinals not named as such). **2** M19 (By confusion with *petty* (adjective)). In miniature, on a small scale; in short.

in pontificalibus /ɪn ˌpɒntɪfɪˈkeɪlɪbəs/, /ɪn ˌpɒntɪfɪˈkɑːlɪbəs/ *adverb phrase* LME **Latin**. In the full vestments of a cardinal, archbishop, etc.; in pontificals.

in posse /ɪn ˈpɒsi/ *adjective phrase* L16 **Latin**. In the condition of being possible. Opposed to IN ESSE.

in potentia /ɪn pəˈtɛnʃɪə/ *adverb phrase* E17 **Latin**. In potentiality.

in propria persona /ɪn ˌprəʊprɪə pə ˈsəʊnə/ *adverb phrase* M17 **Latin**. In one's own person.

in puris naturalibus /ɪn ˌpjʊərɪs natjʊ ˈrɑːlɪbəs/, /natjʊˈreɪlɪbəs/ *adverb phrase* E17 **Latin** (cf. PURIS NATURALIBUS). In one's natural state; stark naked.

in re /ɪn ˈreɪ/ *adverb, adjective, & preposition phrase* E17 **Latin**. **A** *adverb phrase* E17 In reality. **B** *adjective phrase* **1** M19 *Logic* EXTRA DICTIONEM. **2** L19 *Philosophy* Of a universal: existing only in the particulars that instantiate it. Cf. ANTE REM, POST REM. **C** *preposition phrase* L19 In the (legal) case of; with regard to. Cf. RE.

> **C 1996** *Times Magazine* . . . there are plenty of fathers around who feel they've been handed the post-marital short straw by the judiciary *in re* who gets to keep the children and who gets to pay for same.

in rem /ɪn ˈrɛm/ *adjective phrase* M18 **Latin** (= against a thing). *Law* Made or availing against or affecting a thing, and therefore other people generally; imposing a general liability. Frequently *postpositive*. Cf. IN PERSONAM.

in rerum natura /ɪn ˌreɪrəm nəˈtjʊərə/ *adverb phrase* L16 **Latin**. In nature, in the physical world.

inro /ˈɪnrəʊ/ *noun* plural **inros**, same E17 **Japanese** (*inrō*, from *in* seal + *rō* basket). An ornamental box with compartments for seals, medicines, etc., formerly worn by Japanese on a girdle.

in saecula saeculorum /ɪn ˌsʌɪkjʊlə sʌɪkjʊˈlɔːrəm/, /ɪn ˌseɪkjʊlə seɪkjʊˈlɔːrəm/ *adverb phrase* L16 **Late Latin** (= to the ages of ages). To all eternity; for ever.

in se /ɪn ˈseɪ/ *adverb phrase* M19 **Latin**. *Philosophy* In itself.

inselberg /ˈɪnsəlbəːg/ *noun* plural **inselbergs**, **inselberge** /ˈɪnsəlbəːgə/ E20 **German** (from *Insel* island + *Berg* mountain). *Physical Geography* An isolated hill or mountain which rises abruptly from the surrounding landscape, especially from an arid plain.

inshallah /ɪnˈʃalɑː/ *interjection* M19 **Arabic** (in *šā' Allāh*). If God wills it.

■ The Muslim equivalent of DEO VOLENTE.

insignia /ɪn'sɪgnɪə/ *noun* M17 **Latin** (plural of *insigne* mark, sign, badge of office, use as noun of neuter of *insignis* distinguished (as by a mark)). **1** *plural* M17 Badges or distinguishing marks (*of* office, honour, etc.); emblems (*of* a nation, person, etc.). **2** *singular* L18 (plural **insignias**) A badge or distinguishing mark (*of* office, honour, etc.); an emblem (*of* a nation, person, etc.). **3** L18 Usually as *plural*. Marks or tokens indicative of something.

in situ /ɪn 'sɪtjuː/ *adverb phrase* M18 **Latin**. In its (original) place; in position.

1996 *Country Life* Among these are sundry cranesbills . . . whose ends of root, accidentally left *in situ* when a plant is moved, will often sprout and grow anew.

insomnia /ɪn'sɒmnɪə/ *noun* (also (earlier) **insomnie**, **insomnium** /ɪn'sɒmnɪəm/) E17 **Latin** (from *insomnis* sleepless (from as negative *in-* + *somnus* sleep)). Chronic inability to sleep; sleeplessness.

insouciance /ɪn'suːsɪəns/, *foreign* /ɛ̃susjɑ̃s/ *noun* L18 **French** (from as next). Carefreeness, lack of concern.

1995 *Times* With each tightening of the regulations to prevent the spread of BSE, it [sc. the British government] has been forced into an almost furtive admission that earlier scare stories had more substance to them than its studied insouciance admitted.

insouciant /ɪn'suːsɪənt/, *foreign* /ɛ̃susjɑ̃/ *adjective* E19 **French** (from as negative *in-* + *souciant* present participle of *soucier* to care, from Latin *sollicitare* to disturb). Carefree, undisturbed.

inspan /ɪn'span/ *transitive verb* E19 **Afrikaans** (from Dutch *inspannen*, from *in-* + *spannen* to span, fasten). **1** E19 Yoke (oxen, horses, etc.) in a team to a vehicle; harness (a wagon). **2** E20 *figurative* Persuade (a person) to give assistance or service; use as a makeshift. *South African*.

2 1971 *Rand Daily Mail* Mrs Barton often gets on the telephone and inspans private householders to help out.

instanter /ɪn'stantə/ *adverb* L17 **Latin**. Immediately, at once.

■ Now archaic or jocular.

in statu pupillari /ɪn ˌstatjuː pjuːpɪ'lɑːriː/ *adjective phrase* M19 **Latin**. Under guardianship; of junior status at a university; not having a master's degree.

in statu quo /ɪn ˌstatjuː 'kwəʊ/ *adjective phrase* E17 **Latin**. In the same state as formerly. More fully *in statu quo ante*.

insurrecto /ɪnsə'rɛktəʊ/ *noun* plural **insurrectos** E20 **Spanish** (from Latin *insurrectus* past participle of *insurgere* to rise up). Especially in Spain and Spanish-speaking countries: an insurgent, a rebel; an insurrectionist.

intacta /ɪn'taktə/ *adjective* M20 **Latin** (feminine of *intactus*, extracted from VIRGO INTACTA). Inviolate, unaffected; not spoiled or sullied.

intaglio /ɪn'talɪəʊ/, /ɪn'tɑːlɪəʊ/ *noun & verb* (also **intaglia**) M17 **Italian** (from *intagliare* to engrave). **A** *noun* plural **intaglios**. **1** M17 A figure or design incised or engraved; a cutting or engraving in a hard material. **2** M17 A thing ornamented with incised work; *especially* a precious stone having a figure or design cut on its surface. **b** E19 A mould of something to be cast or struck in relief. **3** M18 The process or art of engraving or carving in a hard material; printing in which the image is engraved or etched into a metal plate or cylinder so that it lies below the non-printing areas. Also, the condition of being incised. **B** *transitive verb* M19 Engrave with a sunken pattern; execute in intaglio.

intarsia /ɪn'tɑːsɪə/ *noun* (in senses 1 and 2 also **intarsio** /ɪn'tɑːsɪəʊ/, plural **intarsios**) M19 **Italian** (*intarsio*). **1** M19 (A piece of) mosaic woodwork, especially made in fifteenth-century Italy; the art of making this. Also called *tarsia*. **2** M19 (A piece of) similar inlaid work in stone, metal, or glass. **3** M20 A method of knitting with a number of colours in which a separate length or ball of yarn is used for each area of colour (as opposed to the different yarns being carried at the back of the work). Frequently *attributive*.

intelligentsia /ɪnˌtɛlɪ'dʒɛntsɪə/ *noun* E20 **Russian** (*intelligentsiya*, from Polish *inteligencja*, from Latin *intelligentia* intelligence). The part of a nation (originally in pre-revolutionary Russia) having aspirations to intellectual activity, a section of society regarded as possessing culture and political initiative; *plural* the members of this section of a nation or society, intellectuals.

1996 *Country Life* The view that what happens on the screen can influence what happens in life—so long resisted by the liberal intelligentsia—is gaining ground.

intendant /ɪn'tɛnd(ə)nt/ *noun* (also **intendent**) M17 **French** (from Latin *intendent-* present participial stem of *intendere* to direst, promote). **1** M17 Chiefly as the title of certain officials: a superintendent, a director; *especially* (in seventeenth- and eighteenth-century France) any of certain agents of the King appointed to supervise the administration of justice, finance, etc., in the provinces on behalf of central government. **2** L19 The administrator of an opera-house or theatre. Also, a musical director, a conductor.

2 1996 *Spectator* He seems incapable of the smarmy two-facedness of the majority of opera house *Intendants* . . .

inter alia /ˌɪntə(r) ˈeɪlɪə/, /ˈalɪə/ *adverb phrase* M17 **Latin** (from *inter* among + *alia* accusative neuter plural of *alius* another). Among other things.

1996 *Times: Weekend* He recommends, *inter alia*, that sumps should be drained and refilled, fuel tanks should be drained . . . that the spark plug is removed and 'an eggspoon of oil' is dropped on the piston head.

inter alios /ˌɪntə(r) ˈeɪlɪəʊs/, /ˈalɪəʊs/ *adverb phrase* M17 **Latin** (from *inter* among + *alios* accusative masculine plural of *alius* another). Among other people.

interim /ˈɪnt(ə)rɪm/ *noun, adverb, & adjective* M16 **Latin** ((adverb), from *inter* between + adverbial ending *-im*). **A** *noun* **1** M16 *Ecclesiastical History* (usually *Interim*) A provisional arrangement for the adjustment of religious differences between the German Protestants and the Roman Catholic Church in the mid sixteenth century. **b** M16 *generally* A temporary or provisional arrangement. **2** L16–M17 A thing done in an interval; an interlude. **3** E17 An intervening time; *the* meantime. **4** M20 An interim dividend. **B** *adverb* L16 In the meantime; meanwhile. Now *rare*. **C** *adjective* E17 Done, made, provided, etc., in or for the meantime; provisional, temporary. Formerly (of time), intervening.

Interimsethik /ˈɪnterɪmzˌeːtɪk/ *noun* (also Anglicized as **interim-ethic** /ˈɪntərɪm ˌɛθɪk/) E20 **German** (from as INTERIM + *Ethik* ethics). *Theology* The moral principles of Jesus interpreted as meant for people expecting the imminent end of the world; *transferred* a code of behaviour for use in a specific temporary situation.

intermed(i)i plural of INTERMEDIO.

intermedia plural of INTERMEDIUM.

intermedio /ɪntəˈmɛdɪəʊ/ *noun* plural **intermed(i)i** /ɪntəˈmɛdiː/ L19 **Italian** (from as INTERMEDIUM). A musical interlude between the acts of a play or an opera. Cf. INTERMEZZO.

intermedium /ɪntəˈmiːdɪəm/ *noun* plural **intermedia** /ɪntəˈmiːdɪə/, **intermediums** L16 **Late Latin** (use as noun of neuter singular of Latin *intermedius* intermediate). **1** L16 An intervening action or performance. Now only *specifically* (*Music*), an INTERMEDIO. **2** E17 An interval of time or space. Now *rare* or *obsolete*. **3** M17 An intermediate agent, an intermediary. **4** L19 *Zoology* (modern Latin *os intermedium*). In tetrapods: a carpal in the centre of the wrist joint; a tarsal in the centre of the ankle joint.

intermezzo /ɪntəˈmɛtsəʊ/ *noun* plural **intermezzi** /ɪntəˈmɛtsi/, **intermezzos** L18 **Italian** (from as INTERMEDIUM; cf. MEZZO). **1** L18 A short light dramatic, musical, or other performance inserted between the acts of a play or (formerly) an opera. **2** M19 A short connecting instrumental movement in an opera or other musical work; a similar piece performed independently; a short piece for a solo instrument.

internuncio /ɪntəˈnʌnsɪəʊ/ *noun* plural **internuncios** M17 **Italian** (*internunzio* from Latin *internuntius*, from as *inter-* + *nuntius* messenger). **1** M17 A messenger between two parties; a go-between. **2** L17 An official papal representative or ambassador at a foreign court, ranking below a nuncio. **3** E18 *History* A minister representing a government (especially of Austria) at Constantinople (Istanbul).

inter partes /ˌɪntə ˈpɑːtiːz/ *adjective phrase* E19 **Latin**. *Law* (Of an action) relevant only to the two parties in a particular case; (of a deed etc.) made between two parties.

interreges plural of INTERREX.

interregnum /ɪntəˈrɛgnəm/ *noun* plural **interregnums**, **interregna** /ɪntəˈrɛgnə/ L16 **Latin** (from as *inter-* between + *regnum* reign). **1** L16–L18 Temporary authority or rule exercised during a vacancy of the throne or a suspension of the normal government. **2** L16 An interval during which the normal government is suspended, especially during the period between the end of a monarch's rule and the accession of his or her successor; any period of cessation or suspension of rule, authority, etc. **3** M17 An interval, a pause, a break.

interrex /ˈɪntərɛks/ *noun* plural **interreges** /ɪntəˈriːdʒiːz/ L16 **Latin** (from as *inter-* between + *rex* king). A person holding the supreme authority in a State during an interregnum.

in terrorem /ɪn tɛ'rɔːrəm/ *adverb & adjective phrase* E17 **Latin** (= into a state of terror). (Done) as a warning or to deter.

inter se /ˌɪntə 'seɪ/ *adverb phrase* M19 **Latin**. Between or among themselves.

interstitium /ɪntə'stɪʃɪəm/ *noun* plural **interstitiums**, **interstitia** /ɪntə'stɪʃɪə/ L16 **Latin** (from *intersistere* to stand between). **1** L16–E18 An intervening (usually empty) space, an interstice. **b** L16–E18 An intervening space. **2** M20 *Anatomy* and *Zoology* The tissue or region lying between the principal cells, tissues, etc., of a part of the body.

inter vivos /ˌɪntə 'viːvəʊs/ *adverb & adjective phrase* M19 **Latin**. (Made) between living people (especially of a gift as opposed to a legacy).

intifada /ɪntɪ'fɑːdə/ *noun* L20 **Arabic** (*intifāḍa* shaking off). An uprising by Arabs; *specifically* that begun by Palestinians in 1987 against Israeli authority.

■ The word had earlier been current among Islamic groups, for instance in Lebanon, but only began to appear in English-language reports of events on the West Bank in the late 1980s.

1988 *Independent* The Palestinians have succeeded for the first time in bringing the *intifada* in the occupied territories within Israel's pre-1967 boundaries.

1995 *Spectator* Such patterns are common in wars of national liberation, as exemplified . . . by the very high proportion of Palestinian casualties inflicted by their compatriots during the *Intifada*.

intime /ɛ̃tim/ *adjective* E17 **French** (from Latin *intimus* innermost). Intimate. Now only *specifically* friendly, familiar, cosy.

intimism /'ɪntɪmɪz(ə)m/ *noun* (also **intimisme** /ɛ̃timism/) E20 **French** (*intimisme*, from as INTIME). A style of intimate domestic genre painting using impressionist techniques.

intimist /'ɪntɪmɪst/ *noun & adjective* (also **intimiste** /ɛ̃timist/ (*plural same*)) E20 **French** (from *intimisme*, from as INTIME). **A** *noun* E20 A painter following the principles of intimism. **B** *adjective* M20 Of or pertaining to intimism.

intombi /ɪn'tɒmbi/ *noun* E19 **Xhosa and Zulu**. In southern Africa: a young Black woman who has been ritually prepared for marriage.

intonaco /ɪn'təʊnəkəʊ/ *noun* (also **intonico** /ɪn'təʊnɪkəʊ/) plural **intonacos** E19 **Italian** (*intonico*, *intonaco*, from *intonicare* to cover with plaster, ultimately from Latin *tunica* coat, tunic). The final coating of plaster spread upon a wall or other surface, especially for fresco painting.

in toto /ɪn 'təʊtəʊ/ *adverb phrase* L18 **Latin**. Completely, without exception; altogether, in all.

1995 *Spectator* This does not mean, however, that what the feminists said, *in toto*, was wrong—just as the theory of pure communism contained some benevolent and pertinent points.

intrados /ɪn'treɪdɒs/ *noun* L18 **French** (from as *intra-* inside + *dos* back). *Architecture* The lower or inner curve of an arch; *especially* the lower curve of the voussoirs which form the arch. Cf. EXTRADOS.

intra vires /ˌɪntrə 'vʌɪriːz/ *adverb phrase* L19 **Latin** (= within the powers). Chiefly *Law*. Within the powers or legal authority (*of* a corporation or person).

■ Opposed to ULTRA VIRES.

intra vitam /ˌɪntrə 'viːtam/, /'vʌɪtam/ *adjective phrase* L19 **Latin**. *Biology* Taking place during life; while still living. Cf. IN VIVO.

intriguant /'ɪntrɪg(ə)nt/, *foreign* /ɛ̃trigɑ̃/ (*plural same*) *noun & adjective* (also **intrigant**) L18 **French** (present participle of *intriguer* to scheme). **A** *noun* L18 An intriguer. **B** *adjective* E19 Intriguing; scheming.

intriguante /ɛ̃trigɑ̃t/ *noun* (also **intrigante**) plural pronounced same E19 **French** (feminine of *intriguant*: see preceding). A woman who intrigues.

introit /'ɪntrɔɪt/ *noun* LME **Old and Modern French** (*introït* from Latin *introitus* entrance, from *introire* to enter, from as *intro-* + *ire* to go). **1** LME The action or an act of going in; (an) entrance. Long *rare*. **2** L15 *Ecclesiastical* An antiphon or psalm sung while the priest approaches the altar to celebrate the Eucharist. Also, the first two or three words of the office of a particular day.

introuvable /ɛ̃truvabl/ *adjective* E19 **French** (from as negative *in-* + *trouver* to find). Unfindable, undiscoverable.

in utero /ɪn 'juːtərəʊ/ *adverb & adjective phrase* E18 **Latin**. In the womb; before birth.

1996 *Times* . . . the study tells us nothing about the route of maternal transmission, which could be *in utero*, at birth or soon after birth.

in vacuo /ɪn 'vakjʊəʊ/ *adverb phrase* M17 **Latin**. In a vacuum.

invita Minerva /ɪn,vʌɪtɑː mɪ'nəːvɑː/, /ɪn'vɪːta/ *adverb phrase* L16 **Latin** (= Minerva (being) unwilling). When one is not in the mood; without inspiration.

■ Minerva was the Roman goddess of learning and patroness of arts and handicrafts, so her blessing was considered essential to enterprises in these fields.

1954 M. Cost *Invitation from Minerva* It is always a mistake to do anything invita Minerva . . . Briefly, against the grain.

in vitro /ɪn 'viːtrəʊ/ *adjective & adverb phrase* L19 **Latin** (literally, 'in glass'). *Biology* (Performed, obtained, or occurring) in a test-tube or elsewhere outside a living organism.

attributive **1995** *New Scientist* A couple from the north of England are hoping that their embryos, conceived by in vitro fertilisation, will be the first to be screened for a gene that could cause cancer in later life.

in vivo /ɪn 'viːvəʊ/ *adjective & adverb phrase* E20 **Latin**. *Biology* (Performed, obtained, or occurring) within a living organism.

■ Opposed to EX VIVO; cf. INTRA VITAM.

1996 *New Scientist* . . . it is not possible, at present, to determine directly the impact, in vivo, of Prozac on a particular individual's serotonin receptors.

involucrum /ɪnvə'l(j)uːkrəm/ *noun* plural **involucra** /ɪnvə'l(j)uːkrə/ L17 **Latin** (from *involvere* to involve). **1** L17 An outer covering, an envelope; a covering membrane. **2** M18 *Botany* A whorl or rosette of bracts surrounding an inflorescence or at the base of an umbel; an involucre.

inyanga /ɪn'jɑːŋə/ *noun* M19 **Zulu**. In South Africa: a traditional herbalist and medicine man, sometimes acting as diviner or magician.

ion /'ʌɪən/ *noun* M19 **Greek** (neuter present participle of *ienai* to go). *Physics* and *Chemistry* Originally, either of the constituents which pass to the electrodes during electrolysis. Now *generally*, any individual atom, molecule, or group having a net electric charge (either positive or negative) due to loss or gain of one or more electrons.

iota /ʌɪ'əʊtə/ *noun* LME **Greek** (*iōta*, of Phoenician origin; cf. Hebrew *yod*). **1** LME The ninth (and smallest) letter (Ι, ι) of the Greek alphabet. **2** M17 *figurative* The smallest or a very small part or quantity.

■ The English noun *jot* (from Latin *iota*) is a doublet of *iota* in sense 2.

2 1996 *Spectator* In fact, I have never known him change his mind one iota.

ipecacuanha /,ɪpɪkakjʊ'anə/ *noun* E17 **Portuguese** (from Tupi-Guarani *ipekaaguéne*, from *ipe* small + *kaa* leaves + *guíne* vomit). **1** E17 The root of *Cephaelis ipecacuanha*, a Brazilian plant of the madder family; an extract or preparation of this, formerly much used as an emetic and expectorant. Also, the plant itself. **2** E18 Any of various other plants with emetic roots; a preparation of such a root.

ippon /'ɪpɒn/ *noun* M20 **Japanese**. A score of one full point in judo, karate, etc.

ipse dixit /,ɪpsiː 'dɪksɪt/, /,ɪpseɪ/ *noun* plural **ipse dixits** L16 **Latin** (literally, 'he himself said (it)', translation of Greek *autos epha*). An unproved assertion resting only on the authority of a speaker; a dogmatic statement; a dictum.

■ The Greek expression was used of their master's sayings by the followers of the sage Pythagoras.

ipsissima verba /ɪp,sɪsɪmə 'vəːbə/ *noun phrase* E19 **Latin** (= the very words themselves). The precise words used by a writer or speaker.

ipso facto /,ɪpsəʊ 'faktəʊ/ *adverb phrase* M16 **Latin**. By that very fact or act; by the fact itself; thereby. Cf. EO IPSO.

ipso jure /,ɪpsəʊ 'dʒʊəreɪ/, /'dʒʊəriː/ *adverb phrase* L16 **Latin**. By the operation of the law itself.

irredenta /irre'denta/, /ɪrɪ'dɛntə/ *noun* plural **irredente** /irre'dente/, **irredentas** /ɪrɪ'dɛntəz/ E20 **Italian**. A region containing people ethnically related to the inhabitants of one State but politically subject to another.

■ Also used postpositively as an adjective (see quotation 1967). Also in TERRA IRREDENTA.

1934 A. Huxley *Beyond Mexique Bay* British Honduras still is regarded by the Guatemalans as an *irredenta*.

1967 *Punch* They annexed Tibet, but they had argued themselves into the belief that this was ancient Chinese territory, China *irredenta*.

isangoma variant of SANGOMA.

isba /iz'ba/ *noun* (also **izba**) L18 **Russia** (*izba* (related to Old High German *stuba* from the Germanic base of which modern English *stove* is also ultimately derived)). A Russian hut or log-house.

isblink /ˈiːsblɪŋk/ *noun* L18 Swedish (or from corresponding words in Danish, German, Dutch). A luminous appearance on the horizon caused by the reflection from ice.

■ Also in Anglicized form as *iceblink*.

ishan /ˈiːʃɑːn/ *noun* E20 Arabic (perhaps from Arabic dialect *īšān* from Persian *nīšān* mark). A prehistoric mound in Iraq.

isolato /iːsəˈlɑːtəʊ/ *noun* plural **isolati** /iːsəˈlɑːti/, **isolatos** M19 Italian. An isolated person, an outcast.

item /ˈʌɪtəm/ *adverb* LME Latin (= just so, similarly, moreover, from *ita* thus, so). Likewise, also.

■ Chiefly used to introduce and draw attention to a new statement, particular, or entry, especially in a list or formal document. From this is derived the fully Anglicized noun meaning 'an individual thing, article, or unit included in a set, list, computation, etc.'.

ius cogens, **ius gentium**, **ius naturae**, **ius primae noctis** variants of JUS COGENS, JUS GENTIUM, JUS NATURAE, JUS PRIMAE NOCTIS.

izar /ɪˈzɑː/ *noun* M19 Arabic (*'zār*). An enveloping outer garment worn by Muslim women (and, in some countries, Muslim men). Also, the lower garment of the IHRAM (sense 2).

izba variant of ISBA.

izzat /ˈɪzʌt/ *noun* (also **izzut**) M19 Persian (Urdu *'izzat*, from Arabic *'izza* glory). Honour, reputation, credit, prestige.

1953 E. M. Forster *Hill of Devi* In every remark and gesture, does not the Indian prince either decrease his own 'izzat' or that of his interlocutor?

J

jabot /'ʒabəʊ/ *noun* plural pronounced same E19 **French** (= bird's crop, shirt-frill, probably from a Proto-Romance base meaning 'crop, maw, gullet'). **1** E19 A frill on the front of a man's shirt, edging the opening. Now chiefly *historical*. **2** L19 An ornamental frill on a woman's bodice.

jacal /hə'kɑːl/ *noun* M19 **Mexican Spanish** (from Nahuatl *xacalli* contraction of *xamitl calli* adobe house). A hut built of erect stakes filled in with wattle and mud, common in Mexico and the south-western United States; an adobe house. Also, the material or method used in building such a hut.

j'accuse /ʒakyz/ *noun* M20 **French** (= I accuse). An accusation, particularly one of injustice against an authority.

■ The opening words of Emile Zola's famous letter to the newspaper *L'Aurore* (13 Jan 1898) denouncing the French military establishment for wrongly condemning the Jewish army officer Alfred Dreyfus for treason in 1894 and then attempting to suppress the facts that proved that a miscarriage of justice had taken place.

1996 *Times* . . . this comes as something of a surprise . . . an authorial disclaimer designed to retract at the last minute what a few pages earlier looked like becoming a grandiloquent *j'accuse*.

jacquard /'dʒakɑːd/, /'dʒakəd/ *adjective & noun* (also **Jacquard**) M19 **French**. **A** *adjective* **1** M19 Designating an attachment to a loom which enables the pattern in the cloth to be produced automatically by means of punched cards. **2** M19 Designating a fabric, article, or pattern made with the aid of this; of an intricate variegated design. **B** *noun* **1** M19 A jacquard fabric, pattern, or article. **2** L19 A jacquard attachment or loom.

■ The loom attachment is called after its inventor, Joseph-Marie Jacquard (1752–1834).

jacquerie /'dʒeɪk(ə)ri/, *foreign* /ʒakri/ (*plural same*) *noun* E16 **Old and Modern French** (from male forename *Jacques*). A popular rising of the peasantry.

■ The original *jacquerie* was the revolt of the peasants of northern France against the nobles in 1357–8. *Jacques* was the former French name for a villein or peasant.

jadam /'dʒadam/ *noun* E20 **Malay**. A type of silver or brass niello ware from the Malay peninsula and Sumatra, used especially for decorating belt buckles.

j'adoube /ʒadub/ *interjection* E19 **French** (from *je, j'* I + 1st person singular of *adouber* to repair, mend (ultimate origin unknown)). *Chess* Indicating that a player wishes to touch a piece without making a move.

jäger /'jeɪgə/ *noun* (also **jaeger**) L18 **German** (from *jagen* to hunt, pursue). **1** L18 Originally, a marksman in the German or Austrian infantry. Later, a member of a battalion of riflemen in these armies. Now, a member of a regiment using the name as an official title. **2** E19 A (German or Swiss) huntsman or hunter. **3** E19 An attendant wearing a huntsman's costume. Cf. CHASSEUR sense 2a.

■ *Yager* /'jeɪgə/ (or *yager rifle*) (E19), meaning 'a type of short-barrelled large-bore rifle formerly used in the southern United States', is apparently an Anglicized form of *Jäger*.

jai alai /ˌhʌɪ ə'lʌɪ/ *noun phrase* E20 **Spanish** (from Basque *jai* festival + *alai* merry). The game of PELOTA.

jalap /'dʒaləp/, /'dʒɒləp/ *noun* M17 **French** (from Spanish *jalapa*, in full *purga de Jalapa*, from *Jalapa, Xalapa* a Mexican city). **1** M17 A purgative drug obtained from the tuberous roots of a Mexican climbing plant, *Ipomoea purga*, and from certain other plants of the bindweed family. **2** L17 The plant yielding this drug; (with specifying word) any of certain other plants yielding a similar drug.

jalapeño /halə'peɪnjəʊ/, /halə'piːnəʊ/ *noun* plural **jalapeños** M20 **Mexican Spanish**. A very hot green chilli pepper. Also *jalapeño pepper*.

jalebi /dʒə'leɪbi/ *noun* M19 **Hindustani** (*jalebī*). An Indian sweet made by frying a coil of batter and then soaking it in syrup.

jaleo /xa'leo/ *noun* M19 **Spanish** (literally, 'halloo'). Clapping to accompany Andalusian dancing; a lively Andalusian dance.

jalousie /ˌdʒalʊˈziː/ *noun* M18 **French** (literally, 'jealousy'; also, a type of blind or shutter). A blind or shutter made from a row of angled slats to exclude sun and rain and control the entry of air and light.

1961 I. Fleming *Thunderball* Inside the small room, the jalousies threw bands of light and shadow over the bed.

jambalaya /ˌdʒambəˈleɪə/, /ˌdʒambəˈlʌɪə/ *noun* L19 **Louisiana French** (from Provençal *jambalaia*). A dish composed of rice mixed with shrimps, ham, chicken, turkey, etc.; *figurative* a mixture, a jumble. Originally *United States*.

janitor /ˈdʒanɪtə/ *noun* M16 **Latin** (from *janua* door, entrance). **1** M16 A doorkeeper, a porter; *historically* an ostler. **2** E18 A caretaker of a building, especially a school, responsible for its cleaning, heating, etc.

janken /ˈdʒaŋk(ə)n/ *noun* M20 **Japanese**. A children's game played by using the hands to represent one of three things, paper, scissors, or stone.

japonaiserie /ʒapɔnezri/ *noun* L19 **French**. Japanese characteristics or fashion; in *plural*, Japanese ornaments or knick-knacks.

■ Cf. CHINOISERIE. The Anglicized form *Japanesery* also dates from the same period (L19) of enthusiasm for Japanese art and artefacts in the West.

jarabe /xaˈrabe/ *noun* (also **jarave**) M19 **American Spanish** (from Spanish = syrup). A Mexican pair dance in which the man dances the ZAPATEADO steps, performed especially as an exhibition dance in national costume.

jardinière /ˌdʒɑːdɪˈnjɛː/ *noun* M19 **French** (literally, 'female gardener'). **1** M19 An ornamental receptacle, pot, or stand for the display of growing or cut flowers. **2** M19 *Cookery* A garnish made with cooked vegetables.

jargonelle /ˌdʒɑːgəˈnɛl/ *noun* (also **jargonel**) L17 **French** (diminutive of *jargon* from Italian *giargone*, usually identified ultimately with zircon). An early-ripening (originally inferior) variety of pear.

jaspé /ˈdʒaspeɪ/, *foreign* /ʒaspe/ *noun* M19 **French** (past participle of *jasper* to marble). Marbled, mottled, variegated.

jat /dʒɑːt/ *noun* (also **jati** /ˈdʒɑːti/) L19 **Hindustani** (*jāt*, *jāti* from Sanskrit *jāti* birth). In the Indian subcontinent: a caste, a tribe, a class.

jatha /dʒəˈtɑː/ *noun* E20 **Panjabi and Hindustani** (*jāthā*). In the Indian subcontinent: an armed or organized band of Sikhs.

jati variant of JAT.

jaune /ʒon/ *adjective* LME **French** (from Latin *galbinum* greenish-yellow). Yellow.

■ Although formerly fully naturalized, *jaune* is now obsolete in English except in the names of pigments, such as *jaune brilliant* cadmium yellow.

jebel /ˈdʒɛbɛl/ *noun* M19 **Arabic** (*jabal*, (colloquial) *jebel*, plural *jibāl*, mountain). In the Middle East and North Africa: a mountain, a range of hills.

■ Frequently in place names.

jehad variant of JIHAD.

jellaba /ˈdʒɛləbə/ *noun* (also **djellaba**, **jellabah**, **jelab** /ˈdʒɛləb/, and other variants) E19 **Arabic** ((Moroccan) *jellāb(a)*, *jellābiyya*: cf. GALABIYA). A loose hooded long-sleeved usually woollen cloak of a kind worn originally by Arab men in North Africa.

je ne sais quoi /ʒənsɛkwa/, /ˌdʒə nə seɪ ˈkwɑː/ *noun phrase* M17 **French** (literally, 'I do not know what'). An indefinable quality, something indescribable or inexpressible.

1996 *Times* Of course, computer-generated images have been a part of movies for several years now . . . But it had always been thought . . . that human actors possessed a certain *je ne sais quoi* that would save them from being consigned to the scrapheap by the relentless advance of the techno-bores.

jet d'eau /ʒedo/ *noun* plural **jets d'eau** (pronounced same) L17 **French** (= jet of water). An ornamental jet of water rising from a fountain or pipe; a fountain or pipe from which such a jet rises.

jeté /ʒɛˈteɪ/, *foreign* /ʒəte/ (*plural same*) *noun* M19 **French** (past participle (sc. *pas* step) of *jeter* to throw). *Ballet* A step in which a spring is made from one foot to land on the other, especially with one leg extended forwards and the other backwards. Cf. GRAND JETÉ.

jeté en tournant /ʒɛˈteɪ ɒn ˈtʊənɒ̃/, *foreign* /ʒəte ɑ̃ turnɑ̃/ *noun phrase* plural **jetés en tournant** /ʒɛˈteɪz ɒn ˈtʊənɒ̃/, *foreign* /ʒətez ɑ̃ turnɑ̃/ M20 **French**. *Ballet* A jeté executed with a turning movement. Also called *tour jeté*.

jeton /ˈdʒɛtən/, *in sense 2 foreign* /ʒətɔ̃/ (*plural same*) *noun* (also in sense 1 **jetton**) M20 **Old and Modern French** (from *jeter* to cast up (accounts), calculate). **1** M20 A counter or token used to operate a slot machine. **2** M20 A metal disc used instead of a coin for insertion in a public telephone box, especially in France.

jets d'eau plural of JET D'EAU.

jetton variant of JETON.

jeu /ʒø/ *noun* plural **jeux** /ʒø/ L18 **French** (from Latin *jocus* joke). Play, game.

■ In English occurs only in various phrases.

jeu de mots /ʒø də mo/ *noun phrase* plural **jeux de mots** /ʒø də mo/ M18 **French** (literally, 'play of words'). A play on words, a pun.

jeu de paume /ʒø də pom/ *noun phrase* L18 **French** (literally, 'game of the palm (of the hand)'). Real tennis; a court where this is played.

jeu de société /ʒø də sɔsjete/ *noun phrase* plural **jeux de société** /ʒø də sɔsjete/ E19 **French** (literally, 'game of society'). A party game or amusement.

■ Used especially in the plural.

jeu d'esprit /ʒø dɛspri/ *noun phrase* plural **jeux d'esprit** /ʒø dɛspri/ E18 **French** (literally, 'game of wit'). A playful action in which some cleverness is displayed; (now usually) a humorous literary trifle.

1995 *Spectator* When the Stone of Scone was stolen from Westminster Abbey in the 1950s, E. V. Knox in *Punch* in a *jeu d'esprit* confessed that Inspector Lestrade was baffled and injected Sherlock Holmes into the case . . .

jeune fille /ʒœn fij/ *noun & adjective phrase* M19 **French**. **A** *noun phrase* M19 plural **jeunes filles** (pronounced same). A young girl, an ingénue. **B** *attributive* or as *adjective phrase* L19 Characteristic of an ingénue.

jeune fille bien élevée /ʒœn fij bjɛ̃n ɛlve/ *noun phrase* plural **jeunes filles bien élevées** (*pronounced same*) L20 **French**. A young girl brought up in a genteel way.

1995 G. Tindall *Célestine* Monsieur Allorent's composition seems redolent of the self-conscious world just being born: that of the *rentier* and the white-collar workers, of the ladylike wife and the *jeune fille bien élevée* . . .

jeune premier /ʒœn prəmje/ *noun phrase* plural **jeunes premiers** (pronounced same) feminine **jeune première** /prəmjɛr/) M19 **French** (literally, 'first young man (woman)'). An actor who plays the part of a principal lover or young hero (or heroine).

jeunes filles, jeunes filles bien élevées plurals of JEUNE FILLE, JEUNE FILLE BIEN ÉLEVÉE.

jeunes premiers plural of JEUNE PREMIER.

jeunesse /ʒœnɛs/ *noun* L18 **French**. Young people; the young.

jeunesse dorée /ʒœnɛs dɔre/ *noun phrase* M19 **French** (literally, 'gilded youth'). Young people of wealth and fashion.

■ The original *jeunesse dorée* was a group of fashionable counter-revolutionaries in France during the Revolution, following the fall of Robespierre.

1996 *Spectator* Sadly, neither *jeunesse dorée*, nor even golden oldies, still flock there.

jheel /dʒiːl/ *noun* (also **jhil**) E19 **Hindi** (*jhīl*). In the Indian subcontinent: a (large) pool or lake left after a flood.

jibba variant of JUBBA.

jigotai /dʒɪgəˈtʌɪ/ *noun* M20 **Japanese** (from *ji* self + *go* defence + *tai* posture). A defensive posture in judo.

jihad /dʒɪˈhɑːd/, /dʒɪˈhad/ *noun* (also **jehad**) M19 **Arabic** (*jihād*, literally, 'effort'). Religious warfare or a war for the propagation or defence of Islam; *transferred* a fervent campaign in some cause.

1995 *Spectator* The religious impulse, which can no longer attach itself to traditional religions, is satisfied by the taking up of a cause . . . The jihad against the export of veal calves is a case in point.

Jina /ˈdʒɪnə/ *noun* E19 **Sanskrit** (*jina*). *Jainism* A great Jain teacher who has attained liberation from KARMA; a sculptured representation of such a teacher.

jinnee /ˈdʒɪniː/ *noun* plural **jinn** (also **jinn**, **djinn**, /dʒɪn/, plural **jinnees**, same) E19 **Arabic** (*jinnī* masculine singular, plural *jinn*). In Arabian stories and Muslim mythology: a spirit of an order lower than the angels, able to appear in human or animal form and to exercise supernatural influence.

jinricksha /dʒɪnˈrɪkʃə/ *noun* (also **jinrikisha** /dʒɪnˈrɪkɪʃə/) L19 **Japanese** (*jin-rikisha*, from *jin* man + *riki* strength, power + *sha* vehicle). A rickshaw.

jiu-jitsu, jiu-jutsu variants of JU-JITSU.

jiva /ˈdʒiːvə/ *noun* E19 **Sanskrit** (*jīva*). *Hindu and Jain Philosophy* The soul; the embodied self; the vital principle.

joie de vivre /ʒwadəvivr/, /ˌʒwɑː də ˈviːvrə/ *noun phrase* L19 **French** (= joy of living). A feeling of healthy enjoyment of life; exuberance, high spirits.

1996 *Times Magazine* ' . . . Is she as proud as she says she is of being a spinster?' It is hard to judge beneath the joie de vivre.

jojoba /həˈhəʊbə/, /həʊˈhəʊbə/ *noun* E20 **Mexican Spanish**. A desert shrub, *Simmondsia chinensis* (family Simmondsiaceae), of Mexico and the south-western United States, whose seeds yield an oil used as a lubricant and in cosmetics.

■ The word was familiar in the United States long before it became current in British English, which happened only from the mid 1970s onwards, when its value as a substitute for sperm whale oil and its properties as an ingredient in cosmetics and soaps became more widely appreciated.

jolie laide /ʒɔli lɛd/ *noun & adjective phrase* plural **jolies laides** (pronounced same) L19 **French** (from feminine adjectives *jolie* pretty + *laide* ugly). (An) attractively or fascinatingly ugly (woman).

■ The masculine form *joli laid* is also occasionally found.

1996 *Spectator* We passed through unrecommendable, dull Downham Market, whose only points are a Victorian town clock and squat 100-year-old outlying houses in yellow stone which could be called *jolie laide*.

jong /jɒŋ/ *noun* E17 **Afrikaans** (= young (man)). Originally (*History*), a Coloured male slave or servant. Now, a form of address to a young man or woman.

■ South African colloquial, used especially among young people.

jongleur /ʒɔ̃glœr/ *noun* plural pronounced same L18 **French** (alteration of *jougleur* (Old French *jogleor* accusative of *joglere*) from Latin *joculator* jester). *History* An itinerant minstrel.

jornada /xorˈnada/, /hɔːˈnɑːdə/ *noun* plural **jornadas** /xorˈnadas/, /hɔːˈnɑːdəz/ M17 **Spanish** (= Italian *giornata*, French *journée* journey). **1** M17–M19 An act of a play; a book or canto of a poem. **2** E19 In Mexico etc.: a day's journey; *specifically* one across a waterless desert tract with no place to halt.

joruri /ˈdʒoːruri/ *noun* L19 **Japanese** (*jōruri*, from the name of a character in a popular recitation). **1** L19 A dramatic recitation to music, accompanying a Japanese puppet performance. **2** M20 Japanese puppet drama.

jota /ˈxota/ *noun* M19 **Spanish**. A northern Spanish folk-dance performed by one or more couples in rapid triple time; a piece of music for this dance.

jotun /ˈjəʊt(ə)n/ *noun* M19 **Old Norse** (*jǫtunn* = Old English *eoten*, from Germanic). In Scandinavian mythology: a member of a supernatural race of giants.

joual /ʒwal/, /ʒuːˈɑːl/ *noun* M20 **Canadian French** (dialect form of French *cheval* horse). Demotic Canadian French characterized by non-standard pronunciations and grammar, and influenced by English vocabulary and syntax.

jour /ʒur/ *noun* plural pronounced same LME **Old and Modern French** (from Latin *diurnum* neuter singular (used as noun in popular Latin) of *diurnus* diurnal). **1** LME–M16 A day. **2** M19 A kind of open stitch used in lace-making. Usually in *plural*.

■ In sense 1 now occurs only in certain phrases used in English, e.g. BONHEUR DU JOUR, PLAT DU JOUR.

jubba /ˈdʒʌbə/, /ˈdʒʊbə/ *noun* (also **jibba(h)** /ˈdʒɪbə/, **jubbah**) M16 **Arabic** (whence also French JUPE). A type of long open cloth coat with wide sleeves, worn especially by Muslims.

jubilate /ˌdʒuːbɪˈleɪti/, /ˌjuːbɪˈlɑːteɪ/ *noun* (also **Jubilate**) ME **Latin** (imperative of *jubilare* to call, halloo, (in Christian writers) shout for joy). **1** ME Psalm 100 (90 in the Vulgate) used as a canticle; a musical setting of this. More fully *Jubilate Deo* (the first two words of this psalm). **2** M18 A call to rejoice; an outburst of joyous triumph.

Judenrat /ˈjuːd(ə)nˌrɑːt/ *noun* plural **Judenrate** /ˈjuːd(ə)nˌrɑːtə/ M20 **German** (= Jewish council). A council representing a Jewish community in a locality controlled by the Germans during the war of 1939–45.

judenrein /ˈjuːd(ə)nˌraɪn/ *adjective* M20 **German** (= free from Jews). Of a society, organization, etc., *specifically* in Nazi Germany: without Jewish members, out of which Jews have been expelled.

1951 H. Arendt *Origins of Totalitarianism* When Hitler came to power, the German banks were already almost *judenrein*.

judo /ˈdʒuːdəʊ/ *noun* L19 **Japanese** (from *jū* gentle + *dō* way). A refined form of ju-jitsu using principles of movement and balance, practised as a sport or a form of physical exercise.

juge d'instruction /ʒyʒ dɛ̃stryksjɔ̃/ *noun phrase* plural **juges d'instruction** (pronounced same) L19 **French**. In France: an examining magistrate, a police magistrate.

Jugendstil /'ju:gəntˌʃti:l/ *noun & adjective* E20 **German** (from *Jugend* youth + *Stil* style). (Of, pertaining to, or designating) German ART NOUVEAU.

■ *Die Jugend* was the name of an influential German magazine started in 1896 in Munich.

ju-jitsu /dʒu:'dʒɪtsu:/ *noun* (also **jiu-jitsu**, **ju-jutsu** /dʒu:'dʒʌtsu:/) L19 **Japanese** (*jūjutsu*, from *jū* gentle + *jutsu* skill). A Japanese system of unarmed combat using an opponent's strength and weight to his or her disadvantage, now also practised as physical training. Cf. JUDO.

juju /'dʒu:dʒu:/ *noun* (also **ju-ju**) E17 **West African** (probably from French *joujou* plaything, reduplicated form from *jouer* to play from Latin *jocare*). A charm, amulet, or cult object in some West African belief systems; the supernatural force believed to be associated with such objects. Also, the system of observances associated with such objects.

jujube /'dʒu:dʒu:b/ *noun* LME **French** (or medieval Latin *jujuba*, ultimately from Latin *zizyphum* from Greek *zizuphos*, *zizuphon* zizyphus (tree)). **1** LME An edible berry-like drupe, the fruit of various trees of the genus *Ziziphus*, of the buckthorn family. **b** M16 Any of the trees which produce this fruit, especially *Ziziphus jujuba*, extending from the Mediterranean to China, and *Z. lotus* of North Africa. Also *jujube tree*. **2** M19 A sweet or confection made of gum arabic, gelatin, etc., originally one flavoured with or tasting like this fruit.

jukskei /'jœkskeɪ/ *noun* E19 **Afrikaans** (from *juk* yoke + *skei* pin, peg). **1** E19 A wooden peg on an ox-yoke. **2** M20 A game resembling quoits, originally played with yoke-pins; the bottle-shaped peg used in this game.

juku /'dʒu:ku:/ *noun* L20 **Japanese**. In Japan: a cramming school.

1992 *Economist* The best Japanese *juku* are so hard to get into that there is a booming secondary industry of cramming people to get into cramming schools.

julienne /ˌdʒu:lɪ'ɛn/, *foreign* /ʒyljen/ (*plural same*) *adjective & noun* E18 **French** (from male forename *Jules* or *Julien*). **A** *adjective* **1** E18 Designating soup made of various vegetables (especially carrots), chopped and cooked in meat stock. **2** L19 Designating a small thin strip of a vegetable etc.; (of a vegetable etc.) cut into such strips; (of a dish or garnish) consisting of or containing such strips. **B** *noun* **1** M19 Julienne soup. **2** E20 A julienne strip; a dish of julienne vegetables etc.

jumar /'dʒu:mə/ *noun* M20 **Origin unknown** (originally Swiss). *Mountaineering* A clamp which when attached to a fixed rope automatically tightens when weight is applied and relaxes when it is removed, thus facilitating the climbing of the rope; a climb using such clips.

jumby /'dʒʌmbi/ *noun* (also **jumbie**) E19 **Kikongo** (*zumbi* fetish; cf. *zombie*). A ghost, an evil spirit. Chiefly *West Indies*.

jumelle /ʒu:'mɛl/ *adjective* L15 **French** (feminine (masculine *jumeau*), from Latin *gemellus* diminutive of *geminus* twin). Twinned, paired; made or shaped in couples or pairs, double.

junker /'jʊŋkə/ *noun* M16 **German** (earlier *Junkher(r)*, from Middle High German *junc* young + *herre* (modern *Herr*) lord). A young German noble; *specifically* a member of the reactionary party of the Prussian aristocracy who aimed to maintain the exclusive privileges of their class; a narrow-minded, overbearing (younger) member of the German aristocracy.

■ Obsolete except in historical contexts.

junta /'dʒʌntə/, /'hʊntə/ *noun* E17 **Spanish and Portuguese** (*junta* (whence French *junte*) from Italian *giunta* from Proto-Romance use as noun of Latin *juncta* feminine past participle of *jungere* to join). **1** E17 A Spanish or Italian deliberative or administrative council or committee. **2** E18 *generally* A body of people combined for a common (especially political) purpose; a self-elected committee or council, a cabal. Now frequently *specifically*, a political or military clique or faction taking power after a revolution or *coup d'état*.

■ The alternative form *junto*, modelled on Spanish nouns in *-o*, has also been current in English in sense 2 from the same period and briefly (E–M18) in sense 1.

jupe /dʒu:p/, *foreign* /ʒyp/ (*plural same*) *noun* ME **Old and Modern French** (from Arabic JUBBA). **1** ME A man's loose jacket, tunic, or jerkin. Now only *Scottish*. **2** E18–E20 A woman's jacket, gown, or bodice. In *plural* also, a kind of bodice or stays. *Scottish.* **3** E19 A woman's skirt.

jupon /ˈdʒuːpɒn/, /dʒuːˈpɒn/ *noun* LME Old French (*juppon*, (also modern) *jupon*, from JUPE). *History* A close-fitting tunic or doublet; *especially* one worn under a hauberk, sometimes of thick material and padded. Also, a sleeveless surcoat worn outside armour, of rich material and emblazoned with arms.

jure divino /ˌdʒʊəri dɪˈviːnəʊ/ *adverb phrase* L16 Latin. By divine right or authority.

jus /ʒy/ *noun* M20 French (= juice). A thin broth or gravy.

1996 *Country Life* Smooth, creamy bread sauce . . . and a thin *jus*-like gravy flavoured with a little red Burgundy are the classic accompaniments.

jus cogens /ˌdʒʌs ˈkəʊdʒɛnz/ *noun phrase* (also **ius cogens**) L19 Latin (= compelling law). A principle of international law which cannot be set aside by agreement or acquiescence; a peremptory norm of general international law.

1996 T. Alexander *Unravelling Global Apartheid* There is no definitive list of laws covered by *jus cogens*, but aggression by one state against another, piracy, war crimes, slavery and genocide are generally accepted as illegal.

jus gentium /ˌdʒʌs ˈdʒɛnʃɪəm/ *noun phrase* (also **ius gentium**) M16 Latin (= law of nations). International law.

jus naturae /ˌdʒʌs nəˈtʃʊəriː/, /ˌdʒʌs nə ˈtʃʊərʌɪ/ *noun phrase* (also **ius naturae**) M17 Latin (= law of nature). Natural law.

1996 *Spectator* . . . it is in his prosecution of Warren Hastings that he appears as the really determined upholder of the *ius naturae*, precisely because there was no other law—Indian or British—under which Hastings could be condemned.

jus primae noctis /ˌdʒʌs ˌprʌɪmiː ˈnɒktɪs/ *noun* (also **ius primae noctis**) L19 Latin (= right of the first night). DROIT DU SEIGNEUR.

jusqu'au bout /ʒysko bu/ *adverb phrase* E20 French (= up to the end). To the bitter end; until a conclusive victory has been gained.

■ The policy of *jusqu'auboutisme* applied originally in the context of the war of 1914–18.

juste milieu /ʒyst miljø/ *noun phrase* M19 French (literally, 'the right mean'). A happy medium, the golden mean; judicious moderation, especially in politics.

juvenilia /ˌdʒuːvəˈnɪlɪə/ *noun plural* E17 Latin (neuter plural of *juvenilis* juvenile). Literary or artistic works produced in an author's or artist's youth.

kabbala variant of CABBALA.

kabloona /kə'blu:nə/ *noun* L18 **Eskimo** ((Inuit) *kabluna* big eyebrow). Among Canadian Eskimos: a person who is not an Eskimo; a White person.

kabuki /kə'bu:ki/ *noun & adjective* L19 **Japanese** (originally (as verb) to act dissolutely; later interpreted as from *ka* song + *bu* dance + *ki* art, skill). (Of, pertaining to, or characteristic of) a traditional and popular form of Japanese drama with highly stylized song, mime, and dance, performed by male actors only.

kacha variant of KUTCHA.

kachina /kə'tʃi:nə/ *noun* L19 **Hopi** (*kacína* supernatural, from Keresan). A deified ancestral spirit in North American Pueblo Indian mythology.

Kaddish /'kadɪʃ/ *noun* E17 **Aramaic** (*qaddīš* holy). An ancient Jewish doxology regularly recited in the synagogue, including brief prayers for the welfare of Israel and concluding with a prayer for universal peace.

kadi variant of CADI.

kafenion /kafə'ni:ən/ *noun* M20 **Greek** (*kafeneio(n)*). A Greek coffee-house.

Kaffeeklatsch /'kafeklatʃ/ *noun* (also **kaffee-klatch** /'kafɪklatʃ/) L19 **German** (from *Kaffee* coffee + *Klatsch* gossip; cf. KLATCH). Gossip over coffee cups; a coffee party.

kaffiyeh variant of KEFFIYEH.

kaftan variant of CAFTAN.

kagoule variant of CAGOULE.

kagura /'kɑ:gʊrə/ *noun* L19 **Japanese**. A form of traditional sacred music and dance performed at Shinto festivals.

Kahal /'kɑ:hal/ *noun* E20 **Hebrew** (*qāhāl* assembly, community). (The governing body of) any of the former localized Jewish communities in Europe.

kahuna /kə'hu:nə/ *noun* L19 **Hawaiian**. In Hawaii: a priest, a wise man; a minister; a sorcerer.

kai /kʌɪ/ *noun* M19 **Maori**. Food.

■ New Zealand colloquial. Also in reduplicated form *kaikai* or *kai-kai*, meaning the same or 'feasting'.

kaid /kɑ:'i:d/ *noun* (also (*archaic*) **caid**) E19 **Arabic** (*ḳā'id* leader). An ALCAIDE.

kaikai variant of KAI.

kain /'kʌɪn/ *noun* plural **kains**, same L18 **Malay**. In Malaysia and Indonesia: (a piece of) cloth, especially for use as clothing; a sarong.

■ Frequently with postpositive adjective (see quotation).

1963 J. Kirkup *Tropic Temper* There are many ways of folding the big starched kerchief in a form of head-dress . . . On the East Coast it is called kain satangan.

kairos /'kʌɪrɒs/ *noun* M20 **Greek** (= right or proper time). Fullness of time; the propitious moment, especially for decision or action.

■ The word became current in English through the writings of the German-born American theologian Paul Tillich (1886–1965).

Kaiser /'kʌɪzə/ *noun* M19 **German** (in modern use and in this form; ultimately from Latin *Caesar*, but cf. Old English *cāsere*, Old Frisian *keisar*, Old Saxon *kēsur*, *kēsar*, Old Norse *keisari*, Gothic *kaisar*, Dutch *keizer*). (The title of) an emperor: *specifically* an Austrian or German emperor.

■ Current in various spellings from the OE period, the word in its modern form reflects a Bavarian spelling which supplanted the more usual *keiser* in the seventeenth century. Its use in modern English appears to be because it was the form favoured by the nineteenth-century historian Thomas Carlyle.

k'ai shu /'kʌɪ ʃu:/ *noun phrase* L19 **Chinese** (*kǎishu*, from *kǎi* model + *shū* write). The usual script used for the Chinese language, suitable for everyday purposes.

kaizen /kʌɪ'zɛn/ *noun* L20 **Japanese** (= improvement). Continuous improvement of working practices, personal efficiency, etc., as a business philosophy.

1996 *Times* Standard Chartered Bank has decided to teach its executives Japanese *kaizen* teamwork and continuous self-appraisal.

kakemono /kakɪ'məʊnəʊ/ *noun* plural **kakemonos** L19 **Japanese** (from *kake-*

hang + *mono* thing). A Japanese unframed wall-picture, usually painted or inscribed on silk or paper.

kalimba /kəˈlɪmbə/ *noun* M20 **Bantu.** A musical instrument played with the thumbs, consisting of metal strips mounted on a small hollow piece of wood.

kalpa /ˈkalpə/ *noun* L18 **Sanskrit.** In Indian cosmology: an aeon, a great age of the world, a cycle of YUGAS; *specifically* in *Hinduism*, a period of 4,320 million years.

Kama Sutra /ˌkɑːmə ˈsuːtrə/ *noun & adjective phrase* L19 **Sanskrit** (from *kāma* love, desire + *sūtra* SUTRA). **A** *noun phrase* L19 (The title of) an ancient Sanskrit treatise on the art of love and sexual technique; a sex manual. **B** *adjective phrase* M20 Sexually explicit; sensual.

B 1972 R. Quilty *Tenth Session* He'll be bursting in any minute. Kama Sutra lips—ready for the last waltz.

kameez /kəˈmiːz/ *noun* (also **kameeze**) E19 **Arabic** (*ḳamīṣ*, perhaps from late Latin *camisia* shirt, nightgown). A loose long-sleeved shirt or tunic worn, especially by Muslims, in the Indian subcontinent, and by some Muslims elsewhere. Cf. SHALWAR.

kamerad /ˈkamərɑːd/, *foreign* /kaməˈrɑːt/ *interjection* E20 **German** (literally, 'comrade', from French *camerade*, *camarade*). (Expression used by a German-speaking soldier:) notifying to an enemy a wish to surrender.

■ The word was current between combatants in this situation during the 1914–18 war and became a cliché of war films.

kami /ˈkami/ *noun* plural same E17 **Japanese.** A Shinto god or deity. Also, the Japanese emperor.

kamikaze /kamɪˈkɑːzi/ *noun & adjective* L19 **Japanese** (= divine wind, from as KAMI + *kaze* wind). **A** *noun* **1** L19 In Japanese tradition, the gale that destroyed the fleet of the invading Mongols in 1281. **2** M20 In the war of 1939–45, (a crewman of) a Japanese aircraft, usually loaded with explosives, making a deliberate suicidal crash on an enemy target; a suicide pilot or plane; also *transferred*. **3** M20 *Surfing* A deliberately taken wipe-out. **B** M20 *adjective* Of, pertaining to, or characteristic of a kamikaze; reckless, potentially self-destructive.

A.2 *transferred* **1971** *Observer* The stand of the *kamikazes* means that in any critical division the Government is assured of a working majority.

B 1996 *Times Magazine* While these long odds will attract the odd kamikaze punter, . . . the horse cannot be considered a plausible contender for the big race.

kana /ˈkɑːnə/ *noun* plural same E18 **Japanese.** (A character or syllabary in) Japanese syllabic writing. Cf. HIRAGANA, KATAKANA.

kanat variant of QANAT.

kanban /ˈkanban/ *noun* L20 **Japanese** (= billboard, sign). **1** L20 A card used for ordering parts etc. in a just-in-time manufacturing system evolved in Japan. **2** L20 A just-in-time manufacturing system in which parts etc. are ordered on cards. In full *kanban-system*.

2 1993 *New Scientist* Like most other Japanese businesses, Asahi operates on the Kanban—or just-in-time—principle of stock control, which reduces stockholding to an absolute minimum.

kanga variant of KHANGA.

kanji /ˈkandʒi/, /ˈkɑːndʒi/ *noun* plural same E20 **Japanese** (from *kan* Chinese + *ji* letter, character). (Any of) the set of borrowed and adapted Chinese ideographs used in the Japanese writing system. Cf. KANA.

kanoon /kəˈnuːn/ *noun* E19 **Persian** (*ḳānūn* from Arabic, ultimately from Greek *kanōn*). A plucked musical instrument of the dulcimer or psaltery type, in the classic form with seventy-two strings, now with fifty to sixty.

kan-pei variant of GANBEI.

kanpu variant of GANBU.

kantele /ˈkantɪli/ *noun* E20 **Finnish.** A form of zither used in Finland and the adjoining part of Russia.

kanzu /ˈkanzuː/ *noun* E20 **Kiswahili.** A long white cotton or linen robe worn by East African men.

kaolin /ˈkeɪəlɪn/ *noun* E18 **French** (from Chinese *gāolǐng*, literally 'high hill', a place in Jiangxi province where it is found). A fine white clay resulting from the decomposition of feldspar, used to make porcelain and china, as a filler in paper and textiles, and in medicinal adsorbents and poultices. Also (*Mineralogy*), any of a group of clay minerals which typically occur in such clay, *especially* kaolinite.

kapai /ˈkɑːpʌɪ/ *adjective & adverb* M19 **Maori** (*ka pai*). Good; well, fine.

■ New Zealand. Also used as interjection, expressing pleasure or approval.

kapellmeister /kəˈpɛlmʌɪstə/ *noun* M19 **German** (from *Kapelle* court orchestra, from medieval Latin *capella* chapel + *Meister* master). Chiefly *History* The leader or conductor of a court orchestra, an opera, a choir, etc.

kappa /ˈkapə/ *noun* LME **Greek**. **1** LME The tenth letter (Κ, κ) of the Greek alphabet. **2** M20 *Biology* An infective and independently reproducing particle (now usually regarded as a commensal bacterium) which occurs within cells of some strains of the ciliate *Paramecium aurelia*. Also, such particles collectively.

kappie /ˈkapi/ *noun* M19 **Afrikaans** (from Dutch *kapje* diminutive of *kap* hood). In South Africa: a sun-bonnet with a large brim to protect the face.

kapu /ˈkapu/ *adjective & noun* M20 **Hawaiian**. TABOO.

kaput /kəˈpʊt/ *adjective* (also **kaputt**) L19 **German** (*kaputt* from French (*être*) *capot* (to be) without tricks in piquet etc.; cf. CAPOT). Finished, worn out; dead, destroyed; rendered useless or unable to function; broken.

■ Slang. The allusion by an English writer in 1914 to *kaputt* as 'the Germans' favourite word about their foe, meaning "done" ' (Duchess of Sutherland *Six Weeks at the War*) indicates the historical background to the word's entrance into the English-speaking consciousness.

karabiner /karəˈbiːnə/ *noun* M20 **German** (abbreviation of German *Karabiner-haken* spring-hook). A metal oval or D-shaped coupling link with a closure protected against accidental opening, used in mountaineering.

■ Often further contracted to *krab* in colloquial use.

karaburan /ˌkarəˈbjʊər(ə)n/, /ˌkarabʊˈran/ *noun* E20 **Turkish** (from *kara* black + *buran* whirlwind). A hot dusty wind which blows in central Asia.

karakul /ˈkarəkʊl/ *noun & adjective* (also **caracul**) M19 **Russian** (*karakul'*, from the name of an oasis in Uzbekistan and of two lakes in Tadzhikistan, apparently ultimate from Turkic). **A** *noun* **1** M19 (An animal of) a breed of sheep with a coarse wiry fleece. **2** L19 (Cloth or fur resembling) the glossy curled fleece of a young lamb of this breed. Also called *Persian lamb*. **B** L19 *attributive* or as *adjective* Of or pertaining to the karakul or karakul.

karamat variant of KRAMAT.

karana /ˈkʌrənə/ *noun* M20 **Sanskrit** (*karaṇa* action, posture). Any of the 108 basic postures in Indian dance.

karanga /ˈkarəŋə/ *noun* E20 **Maori**. A (Maori) ritual chant of welcome. *New Zealand*.

karaoke /karəˈəʊki/, /karɪˈəʊki/ *noun* L20 **Japanese** (from *kara* empty + *oke* abbreviation of *ōkesutora* orchestra). A form of entertainment (originating in Japan) in which one or more people sing popular songs as soloists against pre-recorded backing music; (in full *karaoke music*) such pre-recorded backing music.

■ Introduced in both the United States and Britain during the 1980s, *karaoke* became hugely popular. The word is often used attributively, as in *karaoke bar*, an establishment in which the management provides the *karaoke machine* or jukebox that plays the backing music.

1986 J. Melville *Go Gently Gaijin* The hotel people had provided a *karaoke* kit: a microphone and amplifier with backing tapes for amateur songsters.

karate /kəˈrɑːti/ *noun* M20 **Japanese** (from *kara* empty + *te* hand). A Japanese system of unarmed combat using the hands and feet as weapons.

karezza /kəˈrɛtsə/ *noun* (also **carezza**) L19 **Italian** (*carezza* caress). Sexual intercourse in which ejaculation is avoided.

karma /ˈkɑːmə/, /ˈkəːmə/ *noun* E19 **Sanskrit** (*karman* action, effect, fate). Fate or destiny following as effect from cause.

■ *Karma* has specific meanings within the religions of the Indian subcontinent: in Buddhism and Hinduism, it is the sum of a person's actions, especially intentional actions, regarded as determining that person's future states of existence; in Jainism it is subtle physical matter which binds the soul as a result of bad actions.

1996 *Times Magazine* The whole complex will, Spielberg hopes, be imbued with world-beating creative karma.

karoshi /kəˈrəʊʃi/ *noun* L20 **Japanese**. Death through overwork.

1991 *New Age* Thousands of workers have become victims of *karoshi*, or death by overwork.

kaross /kəˈrɒs/ *noun* (also **kross**) M18 **Afrikaans** (*karos*, perhaps from Nama). A cloak or sleeveless jacket like a blanket made of hairy animal skins, worn by the indigenous peoples of southern Africa. Also, a rug of sewn skins used on a bed or on the floor.

Karren /'kar(ə)n/ *noun plural* L19 **German.** *Physical Geography* The furrows or fissures of a KARRENFELD; terrain characterized by these. Cf. LAPIÉS.

Karrenfeld /'kar(ə)nfɛlt/, /'kar(ə)nfɛld/ *noun* plural **Karrenfelder** /'kar(ə)nfɛldə/, **Karrenfelds** /'kar(ə)nfɛldz/ L19 **German** (from preceding + *Feld* field). *Physical Geography* An area or landscape, usually of limestone bare of soil, which has been eroded by solution so as to have an extremely dissected surface with conspicuous furrows and fissures, often separated by knifelike ridges. Cf. LAPIÉS.

karst /kɑ:st/ *noun* L19 **German** (*der Karst* (perhaps related to Slovene *Krâs*) a limestone plateau region in Slovenia). *Physical Geography* A kind of topography characteristic of areas of relatively soluble rock (usually limestone) and mainly underground drainage, marked by numerous abrupt ridges, gorges, fissures, swallowholes, and caverns; a region dominated by such topography.

kasbah /'kazbɑ:/ *noun* (also **casbah**) M18 **French** (*casbah* from Maghribi pronunciation of Arab *ḳaṣaba* fortress). (The Arab quarter surrounding) a North African castle or fortress-citadel.

kasha /'kaʃə/ *noun* (also (earlier) **casha**) E19 **Russian.** **1** E19 A porridge made from cooked buckwheat or other grains. **2** M20 A beige colour resembling that of buckwheat groats.

Kashrut /kaʃ'ru:t/ *noun* (also **Kashruth** /kaʃ'ru:θ/) E20 **Hebrew** (= legitimacy (in religion), from as KOSHER *adjective*). The body of Jewish religious laws relating to the suitability of food, ritual objects, etc.; the observance of these laws.

kat variant of KHAT.

kata /'kɑ:tɑ:/ *noun* M20 **Japanese.** A system of basic exercises or postures and movements used to teach and improve the execution of techniques in judo and other martial arts.

katabothron see KATAVOTHRON.

katakana /katə'kɑ:nə/ *noun* (also **katagana**) E18 **Japanese** (from *kata* side + KANA). An angular form of kana, used in modern Japanese mainly for writing words of foreign origin and for emphasis. Cf. HIRAGANA.

katavothron /katə'vɒθrən/ *noun* (also **catavothron**, **katabothron** /katə'bɒθrən/, **katavothra** /katə'vɒθrə/) plural **katavothra** /katə'vɒθrə/, **katavothrai** /katə'vɒθrʌɪ/, **katavothrons** E19 **Modern Greek** (*katabothra*, plural *katabothrai*, *katabothres*, from Greek *kata* down + *bothros* hole (*katavothron* representing modern Greek pronunciation, *katavothron* from misunderstanding singular as neuter plural)). A subterranean channel or deep hole formed by the action of water; a swallowhole.

■ A feature of the landscape in certain parts of mainland Greece. In general use the word is now usually replaced by *swallow-hole*.

katel /'kɑ:t(ə)l/ *noun* (also **kartel**) M19 **Afrikaans** (apparently from Portuguese *catel*, *catle* little bed, from Malay *katil* from Tamil *kaṭṭil* bedstead). A lightweight portable bed or hammock, used in an oxwagon.

■ South African. The Malay word *katil* is used in the Cape Malay community to denote the bier used in funeral ceremonies.

katharevousa /ˌkaθərə'vu:sə/, /ˌkaθə'rɛvʊsə/ *noun* E20 **Modern Greek** (*kathareuousa* feminine of *kathareuōn* present participle of Greek *kathareuein* to be pure, from *katharos* pure). The purist form of modern Greek.

■ At one time (but not since 1976), the archaizing literary version of Greek officially used by the State, as opposed to the popular and spoken demotic.

kathi /'kɑ:ði/ *noun* M20 **Malay** (*kadi* from Arabic *ḳāḍī* CADI). A judge in Islamic law, who also functions as a registrar of Muslim marriages, divorces, etc.

katsuo /'katswo/ *noun* E18 **Japanese.** A bonito, *Katsuwonus pelamis*, important as a food fish in Japan, fresh or dried.

katsura /kat'sʊərə/ *noun* E20 **Japanese.** **1** E20 A type of Japanese wig worn mainly by women. **2** E20 A type of romantic Noh play with a woman as the central character. In full *katsuramono* /katˌsʊərə'məʊnəʊ/ (*mono* piece, play).

katzenjammer /'kats(ə)njamə/ *noun* M19 **German** (from *Katzen* (combining form of *Katze* cat) + *Jammer* distress, wailing). **1** M19 A hangover; a severe headache. **2** L19 *transferred* and *figurative* Confusion, disorder; clamour, uproar.

■ United States colloquial. The currency of the word has been promoted by the comic strip called *The Katzenjammer Kids*, first drawn in 1897 by Rudolph Dirks for the *New York Journal*.

kava /ˈkɑːvə/ *noun* L18 **Tongan**. A shrub, *Piper methysticum*, of the West Pacific islands; a narcotic fermented drink made especially in Fiji from its macerated roots. Cf. YANGGONA.

kavadi /ˈkɑːvədi/ *noun* M20 **Tamil** (*kāvaṭi*). In Hindu religious practice, a decorated arch carried on the shoulders as an act of penance or in fulfilment of a vow. Also the festival at which this act is performed.

1993 A. Diesel & P. Maxwell *Hinduism in Natal* For those Hindus who 'carry kavadi' today, self-inflicted pain is believed to be another sign of devotion to Maruga.

kayak /ˈkʌɪak/ *noun* M18 **Eskimo** ((Inuit) *qayaq*). **A** *noun* **1** M18 An Eskimo canoe, made of a framework of light wood covered with sealskins, and having a small watertight opening in the top to admit a single man. **2** M20 A small covered canoe modelled on this, used for touring or sport. **B** *intransitive verb* L19 Travel by kayak, paddle a kayak.

kazachoc /kazəˈtʃɒk/ *noun* (also **kozatchok** and other variants) E20 **Russian** (diminutive of *kazak* cossack). A Slavonic, chiefly Ukrainian, dance with a fast and usually quickening tempo, and employing the step PRISIADKA.

kebab /kɪˈbab/, /kəˈbab/, /kɪˈbɑːb/ *noun* (also (earlier) **cabob** /kəˈbɒb/) L17 **Arabic** (*kabāb* (perhaps ultimately from Persian), partly through Urdu, Persian, and Turkish). A dish consisting of pieces of meat (occasionally with vegetables) grilled or roasted on a skewer or spit.

■ The arrangement of the meat pieces on the skewer has given rise (L20) to the use of *kebab* for components of a similar polymer structure in physical chemistry.

kebaya /kəˈbɑːjə/ *noun* (also (earlier) **cabaia** and other variants) L16 **Arabic** (*ḳabāya* representing colloquial pronunciation of *ḳbā'a* feminine of *ḳbā'* tunic, gown, shirt; in early use through Portuguese *cabaya* or Persian, in modern use through Malay *kebaya*). **1** L16 A light loose tunic of a type worn in South-East Asia by women or (formerly) by men. **2** M20 A short tight-fitting long-sleeved jacket, together with a sarong the traditional dress of Malay and Indonesian women.

kef variant of KIEF.

keffiyeh /kəˈfiː(j)ə/ *noun* (also **kaffiyeh**, **kuffiyeh** and other variants) E19 **Arabic** (*kūfiyya*, (colloquial) *keffiyya*). A kerchief worn as a head-dress by Bedouin Arabs.

keftedes /kɛfˈtɛdiːz/ *noun plural* (also **keftedhes**) E20 **Modern Greek** (*kephtes*, plural *kephtedes* from Turkish *köfte* from Persian KOFTA). In Greek cookery, small meatballs made with herbs and onions.

kehilla /kəˈhɪlə/, /kɛhɪˈlɑː/ *noun* plural **kehillot(h)** /kɛhɪˈləʊt/ L19 **Yiddish** (*kĕhilĕ* from Hebrew *qĕhillāh* community). The Jewish community in a town or village.

keif variant of KIEF.

keiretsu /ˈkeɪrɛtsu/ *noun* L20 **Japanese**. A group of closely associated Japanese business companies linked especially by cross-shareholding.

1993 *Seattle Times* Some companies seem to be trying to join whatever *keiretsu* is forming just out of fear that they won't back the right horse.

kelebe /ˈkɛləbi/ *noun* M19 **Greek** (*kelebē*). *Greek Antiquities* A wide-mouthed vessel with a broad flat rim and two handles connecting this to the body but not extending above the rim.

Kelim variant of KILIM.

keller /ˈkɛlə(r)/ *noun* (also **Keller**) E20 **German** (= cellar). A beer-cellar in Austria or Germany.

Kempeitai /ˈkɛmpeɪtʌɪ/ *noun* M20 **Japanese** (*kenpeitai*). The Japanese military secret service in the period 1931–45.

ken /kɛn/ *noun* L19 **Japanese**. A Japanese game of forfeits played with the hands and with gestures.

kenaf /kəˈnaf/ *noun* L19 **Persian** (variant of *kanab* hemp). The brown fibre of the *Hibiscus cannabinus* plant used to make rope and coarse cloth; ambari hemp.

kendo /ˈkɛndəʊ/ *noun* E20 **Japanese** (from *ken* sword + *dō* way). A Japanese sport of fencing with two-handed bamboo staves.

kenosis /kɪˈnəʊsɪs/ *noun* L19 **Greek** (*kenōsis* an emptying). *Christian Theology* Christ's full or partial renunciation of his divine nature or powers in his Incarnation.

■ The reference is to the Greek New Testament text of Philippians 2:7 *heauton ekenōse*, literally, 'he emptied himself'.

kente /ˈkɛntə/ *noun* (also **Kente**) M20 **Twi** (= cloth). In Ghana: a brightly coloured banded material; a long garment made from this material, loosely draped on or worn around the shoulders and waist. More fully *kente cloth*.

kepi /ˈkɛpi/, /ˈkeɪpi/ *noun* M19 **French** (*képi* from Swiss German *Käppi* diminutive of *Kappe* capital). A French military cap with a flat circular top which slopes towards the front and a horizontal peak.

kêrel /ˈkɛːr(ə)l/ *noun* (also **kerel**) L19 **Afrikaans** (from Dutch from Old High German *kar(a)l* man). A fellow, a chap, a young man; a boyfriend. *South African colloquial.*

kermes /ˈkəːmɪz/ *noun* L16 **French** (*kermès* from Arabic *ḳirmiz* (= sense 2 below)). **1** L16 A small evergreen oak, *Quercus coccifera*, of the Mediterranean region. More fully *kermes oak*. **2** E17 (The dried bodies of) adult females of the scale insect *Kermes ilicis*, which form hard berry-like galls on the kermes oak, used to make dye and (formerly) medicines; the scarlet dye made from these.

kermesse /kəˈmɛs/ *noun* L19 **French** (from as next). **1** L19 A KERMIS. **2** M20 *Cycling* A circuit race.

kermis /ˈkəːmɪs/ *noun* (also **kirmess**) L16 **Dutch** (*kermis, kermisse*, from *kerk* church + *misse* mass). In the Low Countries, parts of Germany, etc.: an annual fair or carnival. Also (*United States*), a similar fair or bazaar, usually for charitable purposes.

■ Originally a *kermis* was a mass held annually on the anniversary of the dedication of a church, when a fair was also held.

kernos /ˈkəːnɒs/ *noun* plural **kernoi** /ˈkəːnɔɪ/ E20 **Greek**. *Archaeology* An ancient Mediterranean and Near Eastern baked clay vessel having small cups around the rim or fixed in a circle to a central stem.

ketubah /ˌkətuːˈbɑː/ *noun* M19 **Hebrew** (*kĕṯubbāh* written statement). A formal Jewish marriage contract which includes financial provisions for the wife in the event of the husband's death or of divorce.

khaddar /ˈkadə/ *noun & adjective* (also **khadi** /ˈkadi/) E20 **Panjabi** (*khaddar*, Hindustani *khādar, khādī*). (Made of) handspun hand-woven cotton (or silk) cloth of the Indian subcontinent.

khaki /ˈkɑːki/ *adjective & noun* M19 **Urdu** (*ḵākī* dust-coloured, from *ḵāk* dust from Persian). **A** *adjective* M19 Dust-coloured; dull brownish yellow. Also, made of khaki. **B** *noun* **1** M19 Dust-colour; dull brownish yellow. **2** M19 A dull yellowish-brown fabric, originally of stout twilled cotton, later also of wool, etc., used especially for army uniforms. **3** L19 A soldier dressed in khaki; *specifically* (*South African slang*) a British soldier in the Boer War of 1899–1902. **4** M20 In *plural* Khaki trousers; khaki clothes.

khalifa /kəˈliːfə/ *noun* (in sense 2 also **chalifa**) E18 **Arabic** (*ḵalīfa*). **1** E18 Chiefly *History* The chief civil and religious ruler of the Muslim community, a caliph. **2** M19 A Malay ceremony in which a dancer pierces his person with swords, originally as a demonstration of Islamic faith. *South African.*

khalsa /ˈkɑːlsə/ *noun* (also **khalsah**) L18 **Urdu** (from Persian *ḵāl(i)ṣa* crown land, revenue department, from feminine of Arabic *ḵāliṣ* pure, free (from), belonging (to)). **1** L18 The governmental revenue department in a State in the Indian subcontinent. **2** L18 The fraternity of warriors into which Sikh males are initiated at puberty.

khamsin /ˈkamsɪn/ *noun* (also **hamsin** /ˈhamsɪn/) L17 **Arabic** (*ḵamāsīn*, from *ḵamsīn, ḵamsūn* fifty (from the number of days on which it blows)). An oppressive hot southerly wind, which blows in Egypt at intervals for about fifty days in March, April, and May, and fills the air with sand from the desert.

khan /kɑːn/, /kan/ *noun* (also **han** /hɑːn/) LME **Persian** (*ḵān*). A caravanserai.

khanga /ˈkaŋgə/ *noun* (also **kanga**) M20 **Kiswahili**. In East Africa: a fabric printed in various colours and designs with borders, used especially for women's clothing.

khanum /ˈkɑːnəm/ *noun* M17 **Persian** (*ḵānum* from Turkish *hanim*, from *hān* lord + *-im* 1st person singular possessive suffix). In certain parts of the Middle East and the Indian subcontinent: a lady of high rank, *historically* the wife of a khan. Now also used as a polite form of address affixed to a Muslim woman's name.

khat /kɑːt/ *noun* (also **kat, qat**) M19 **Arabic** (*ḵāt*). A shrub, *Catha edulis*, of the spindle tree family, cultivated in Arabia for its leaves, which are chewed or infused as a stimulant; the narcotic drug obtained from these leaves.

1996 *Oldie* Our own cook was a wild-eyed northerner whose cheeks bulged night and day with qat.

khatun /'kɑːtuːn/ *noun* M19 **Turkic** (*ḳatūn*, Persian *ḳātūn* perhaps from Sogdian *ḳwa-t'yn* queen). In certain parts of the Middle East: a lady of high rank; *historically* a queen. Also used as an honorific title affixed to a Muslim woman's name.

khidmutgar /'kɪdmʌtgɑː/ *noun* (also **khitmutgar** /'kɪtmʌtgɑː/) M18 **Urdu** (from Persian *ḳidmatgār*, from Arabic *ḳidma(t)* service + Persian agent-suffix *-gār*). In the Indian subcontinent: a male servant who waits at table.

khoja /'kəʊdʒə/ *noun* E17 **Turkish** ((*hoca* from) Persian *kʷāja*). **1** E17 A teacher in a Muslim school; a Muslim scribe or clerk. **2** L19 (*Khoja*) A member of a Muslim sect found mainly in western India.

khutbah /'kʊtbə/ *noun* E19 **Arabic** (*ḳuṭba*). A form of sermon, consisting of homily and supplication, delivered in mosques before the midday Friday prayer, at the time of the two main Muslim festivals, and on other exceptional occasions.

ki /kiː/ *noun* M19 **Hawaiian**. A shrub of the agave family, *Cordyline fruticosa*, found in China and the Pacific islands, the fermented root of which yields an alcoholic drink.

kibbutz /kɪ'bʊts/ *noun* plural **kibbutzim** /kɪ'bʊtsɪm/, (occasionally) **kibbutzes** M20 **Modern Hebrew** (*qibbūṣ* gathering). A collective (especially farming) settlement in Israel, owned communally by its members, and organized on cooperative principles.

kibbutznik /kɪ'bʊtsnɪk/ *noun* M20 **Yiddish** (from as KIBBUTZ + Polish and Russian noun suffix *-nik* person connected with (something)). A member of a kibbutz.

kibitz /'kɪbɪts/ *intransitive verb* E20 **Yiddish** (from German *kiebitzen*, from *Kiebitz* lapwing, pewit, interfering onlooker at cards). Look on at cards, or some other activity, especially offering unwanted advice.

■ Slang, chiefly in North American use.

kiblah /'kɪblə/ *noun* (also **qibla(h)**, **kibla**) M17 **Arabic** (*ḳibla* that which is opposite). **1** M17 (The direction of) the place to which Muslims must turn for prayer, now the Kaaba at Mecca. **2** L18 The MIHRAB on an oriental rug.

kiboko /kɪ'bəʊkəʊ/ *noun* plural **kibokos** E20 **Kiswahili** (= hippopotamus). A strong heavy whip made of hippopotamus hide.

kiddush /'kɪdʊʃ/ *noun* (also **Kiddush**) M18 **Hebrew** (*qiddūš* sanctification). A ceremony of prayer and blessing over wine, performed by the head of a Jewish household at the meal ushering in the Sabbath (on a Friday night) or a holy day or at the lunch preceding it.

kiddushin /kɪ'duːʃiːn/ *noun* (also **Kiddushin**) L19 **Aramaic** (*qiddūshīn*). *Judaism* The section of the Mishnah dealing with betrothal and marriage. Also, the Jewish ceremony of betrothal; the gift given by a Jewish groom to effect a betrothal.

kief /kiːf/ *noun* (in sense 1 also **kef** /kɛf/, **keif** /keɪf/; in sense 2 also **kif**) E19 **Arabic** (representing colloquial pronunciation of *kayf*). **1** E19 A state of drowsiness or dreamy intoxication produced by the use of cannabis etc. Also, the enjoyment of idleness. **2** L19 In Morocco and Algeria: cannabis or some other substance smoked to produce dreamy intoxication.

kielbasa /kiːl'basə/, /kjɛl'basə/ *noun* M20 **Polish** (*kiełbasa* sausage). A type of highly seasoned Polish sausage, usually containing garlic.

kierie /'kɪri/ *noun* (also (earlier) **kirri**) M18 **Nama**. A short club or knobbed stick used as a club or missile by indigenous peoples of South Africa.

■ The South African English word *knobkerrie*, by which this weapon is also known, is from Afrikaans *knop* knob + *kierie*.

kif variant of KIEF.

kikoi /kɪ'kɔɪ/ *noun* M20 **Kiswahili**. In East Africa: a distinctive striped cloth with an end fringe, worn round the waist.

kilim /kɪ'liːm/ *adjective & noun* (also **Kilim**, **Kelim**) L19 **Turkish** (*Kılım* from Persian *gelīm*). (Designating) a pileless woven carpet, rug, etc., made in Turkey, Kurdistan, and neighbouring areas, and now a fashionable furnishing item in the West.

kimchi /'kɪmtʃi/ *noun* L19 **Korean**. A raw strongly-flavoured cabbage pickle, the Korean national dish.

kimono /kɪ'məʊnəʊ/ *noun & adjective* M17 **Japanese** (from *ki* wearing + *mono* thing). **A** *noun* M17 plural **kimonos**. A long Japanese robe with wide sleeves, tied with a sash. Now also, in Western countries, a garment (especially a dressing-gown) modelled on this. **B** *attributive* or as *adjective* E20 Resembling or characteristic of a kimono.

kinder, kirche, küche /ˌkɪndər ˌkɪrçə ˈkyːçə/ *noun phrase plural* L19 **German** (literally, 'children, church, kitchen'). The domestic and religious concerns traditionally regarded as appropriate for a woman.

■ Doubly discredited by its association with the Nazi ideal of womanhood and by the agenda of modern feminism, *kinder, kirche, küche* is now most frequently used ironically.

1996 *Times Magazine* But theirs is also the quaintly strident *kinder, kirche, küche* voice of Alf Garnett . . .

kindergarten /ˈkɪndəgɑːt(ə)n/ *noun* M19 **German** (literally, 'children's garden'). **1** M19 A nursery school. **2** E20 *History* The group of young men with imperialist ideals recruited by Lord Milner, High Commissioner of South Africa, to help with reconstruction work after the second Boer War of 1899–1902.

■ The term *kindergarten* was coined in 1840 by Friedrich Fröbel (1782–1852) for a school for teaching young children according to his method of stimulating their intelligence by means of interesting objects, exercises with toys, games, singing, etc.

kinderspiel /ˈkɪndəʃpiːl/ *noun* E20 **German** (literally, 'children's play'). A dramatic piece performed by children.

kinesis /kɪˈniːsɪs/, /kʌɪˈniːsɪs/ *noun* plural **kineses** /kɪˈniːsiːz/ E17 **Greek** (*kinēsis* movement). **1** E17 *generally* Motion; a kind of movement. *rare*. **2** E20 *Biology* An undirected movement of an organism that occurs in response to a particular kind of stimulus. **3** M20 *Zoology* Mobility of the bones of the skull, as in some birds and reptiles.

kippa /kɪˈpɑː/ *noun* (also **kipa(h)**, **kippah**) M20 **Modern Hebrew** (*kippāh*). A skullcap, usually of crocheted thread, worn by Orthodox male Jews.

kir /kɪə/, /kəː/ *noun* (also **Kir**) M20 **French** (personal name). (Proprietary name for) a drink made from dry white wine and cassis.

■ Called after Canon Félix *Kir* (1876–1968), mayor of Dijon in France, who is said to have invented the recipe.

kirin /ˈkɪərɪn/ *noun* (also **Kirin**) E18 **Japanese** (from as KYLIN). A mythical beast of composite form resembling a unicorn, frequently portrayed in Japanese pottery and art.

kirmess variant of KERMIS.

kirpan /kəːˈpɑːn/ *noun* E20 **Panjabi and Hindustani** (*kirpān* from Sanskrit *kṛpāṇa* sword). The dagger or sword worn by Sikhs as a religious symbol.

kirri variant of KIERIE.

kirsch /kɪəʃ/ *noun* M19 **German** (abbreviation of *Kirsch(en)wasser* from *Kirsche* cherry + *Wasser* water). An alcoholic spirit distilled, chiefly in Germany and Switzerland, from the fermented juice of cherries.

■ Earlier (E19) in English in the fuller form *Kirschenwasser*.

kisan /kɪˈsɑːn/ *noun* M20 **Hindustani** (*kisān* from Sanskrit *kṛṣāṇa* person who ploughs). In the Indian subcontinent: a peasant, an agricultural worker.

kishke /ˈkɪʃkə/ *noun* (also **kishka**, **kishkeh**) M20 **Yiddish** (from Polish *kiszka* or Ukrainian *kishka*: cf. Russian *kishka*). **1** M20 Beef intestine casing stuffed with a savoury filling. **2** M20 *singular* and in *plural* The guts. *slang*.

kismet /ˈkɪzmɛt/, /ˈkɪzmɪt/, /ˈkɪsmɛt/ *noun* E19 **Turkish** (*kısmet* from Arabic *ḳisma(t)* division, portion, lot, fate). Destiny, fate.

kissel /ˈkɪs(ə)l/, /kɪˈsjɛl/ *noun* E20 **Russian** (*kisel'*, from same base as *kislyĭ* sour). A dessert dish made from fruit juice or purée boiled with sugar and water and thickened with potato or cornflour.

kist /kɪst/ *noun* ME **Old Norse** (*kista*; cf. Dutch *kist*). **A** *noun* **1** ME A chest, a trunk, a coffer. **2** ME A coffin; *especially* a stone coffin, a sarcophagus. **b** M19 *Archaeology* A prehistoric burial chamber lined with stone slabs, a cist.

■ The early use of *kist*, mainly in the north of England and Scotland, derives from Old Norse, but its use in South African English in the sense of 'chest' or 'coffer' is derived through Dutch and Afrikaans.

Kitab /kɪˈtɑːb/ *noun* L19 **Arabic** (*kitāb* piece of writing, record, book). The Koran. Also, among Muslims, the sacred book of any of certain other revealed religions, as Judaism or Christianity.

kithara variant of CITHARA.

kitsch /kɪtʃ/ *noun & adjective* (also **Kitsch**) E20 **German**. **A** *noun* E20 Art or artefacts perceived as being of poor quality, especially when garish or sentimental; these enjoyed in a perverse or self-conscious way; the qualities associated with such art or artefacts. **B** *adjective* Of the nature of or pertaining to kitsch; garish, tasteless.

A **1995** *Country Life* I'm sorry, but at Christmas I want maximum kitsch, not ghastly good taste.

kittel /ˈkɪt(ə)l/ *noun* L19 **Yiddish** ((German = overall, smock), from Middle High German *ki(e)tel* cotton or hempen outer garment). A white cotton or linen robe worn by orthodox Jews on certain holy days; such a robe used as a shroud.

kiva /ˈkiːvə/ *noun* L19 **Hopi** (*kíva*). A chamber, built wholly or partly underground, used by male Pueblo Indians for religious rites etc. Cf. ESTUFA.

klaberjass /ˈklabəjas/ *noun* (also **clobiosh** /ˈklɒbɪjɒʃ/ and other variants) L19 **German** (from Dutch *klaverjas*). *Cards* A two-handed card-game distantly related to bezique, in which points are scored for winning value cards in tricks and for declaring combinations.

klatch /klatʃ/ *noun* (also **Klatsch**) M20 **German** (*Klatsch* gossip). A social gathering. Cf. KAFFEEKLATSCH.

kletterschuh /ˈklɛtəʃuː/ *noun* plural **kletterschuhe** /ˈklɛtəʃuːə/ E20 **German** (literally, 'climbing-shoe'). A cloth- or felt-soled light boot worn especially for rock-climbing. Usually in *plural*.

klezmer /ˈklɛzmə/ *noun* plural same, **klezmorim** /ˈklɛzmərɪm/ M20 **Yiddish** (contraction of Hebrew *kělēy zemer* musical instruments). A member of a group of musicians playing traditional eastern European Jewish music; this type of music (in full *klezmer music*).

klippe /ˈklɪpə/ *noun* E20 **German** (= partly submerged or buried rock). *Geology* A part of a nappe which has become detached from its parent mass by sliding or by erosion of intervening parts.

klister /ˈklɪstə/ *noun* M20 **Norwegian** (= paste). *Skiing* A soft wax for applying to the running surface of skis to facilitate movement, used especially when the temperature is above freezing.

klompie /ˈklɒmpi/ *noun* (also **klompje**) M19 **Afrikaans** (from Dutch *klompje* diminutive of *klomp* clump). **1** M19 A group, a cluster, especially of animals or of shrubs or trees. *South African colloquial.* **2** E20 A type of hard yellow brick, originally imported into South Africa from the Netherlands.

klonkie /ˈklɒŋki/ *noun* M20 **Afrikaans** (blend of *klein* small, *jong* boy + diminutive suffix *-kie*). In South Africa: a young Black or Coloured boy.

kloof /kluːf/ *noun* M18 **Dutch** (= cleft). A deep valley, a ravine, a gorge. *South African.*

klops /klɒps/ *noun* plural same **klopse** /ˈklɒpsə/ M20 **German**. A type of meatball or meat loaf.

klutz /klʌts/ *noun & verb* (also **klotz**) M20 **Yiddish** (from German *Klotz* wooden block, from Middle High German *kloz*; cf. Old English *clot(t)*, whence modern English *clot* (in derogatory sense) stupid or awkward person). **A** *noun* M20 A clumsy awkward person, *especially* one considered socially inept; a fool. **B** *intransitive verb* L20 Followed by *about, around*: behave awkwardly or foolishly, move clumsily.

■ North American slang.

1970 *Time* Basically I'm the klutz who makes a terrific entrance to the party and then trips and falls and walks around with food in her hair.

knaidel /ˈkneɪd(ə)l/ *noun* (also **kneidel**) plural **knaidlach** /ˈkneɪdlax/ M20 **Yiddish** (*kneydel* from Middle High German, German KNÖDEL). A type of dumpling eaten especially in Jewish households during Passover. Usually in *plural*.

knallgas /ˈknalgas/ *noun* L19 **German** (from *Knall* bang, detonation + *Gas* gas). *Chemistry* An explosive mixture of gases, especially one of two volumes of hydrogen with one of oxygen.

kneidel variant of KNAIDEL.

Kneipe /ˈknaɪpə/ *noun* plural **Kneipen** /ˈknaɪpən/, **Kneipes** M19 **German**. In Germany: a lively social gathering of young people, especially students, in a bar or restaurant; a public house, a bar.

knish /knɪʃ/ *noun* M20 **Yiddish** (from Russian (also *knysh*) kind of bun or dumpling). A baked or fried dumpling made of flaky dough filled with chopped liver, potato, or cheese.

knödel /ˈknəːd(ə)l/ *noun* (also **knoedel**) E19 **German**. In South Germany and Austria: a type of dumpling.

knout /naʊt/, /nuːt/ *noun* M17 **French** (from Russian *knut* from Old Norse *knútr* related to 'knot'). *History* A scourge or whip used in imperial Russia, often causing death.

ko /kəʊ/ *noun* plural **kos** M20 **Chinese** (*gē* (Wade-Giles *ko*) spear, lance). *Chinese Antiquities* A dagger, a halberd.

koan /'kəʊɑːn/ *noun* M20 **Japanese** (*kōan*, from Chinese *gōngàn* official business). *Zen Buddhism* A riddle without a solution, used to demonstrate the inadequacy of logical reasoning and provoke sudden enlightenment.

1972 *Times Literary Supplement* What he comes up with—his runes and enigmas and impromptu koans—builds gradually into a supplementary creation.

kobold /'kəʊbəld/ *noun* M19 **German**. In German folklore, a familiar spirit, supposed to haunt houses and help the occupants; a brownie. Also, an underground spirit; a goblin, a gnome.

koeksister /'kʊksɪstə/ *noun* (also **koesister** /'kʊəsɪstə/) E20 **Afrikaans** (*koe(k)sister*, perhaps from *koek* cake + *sissen* sizzle). In South Africa: a plaited doughnut dipped in syrup, a traditional South African confection.

kofta /'kɒftə/, /'kəʊftə/ *noun* L19 **Urdu and Persian** (*koftah* pounded meat). A kind of meat or fish rissole, popular in Eastern cookery.

kohl /kəʊl/ *noun* L18 **Arabic** (*kuḥl*). A powder, usually consisting of antimony sulphide or lead sulphide, used as eye make-up and as eye ointment, especially in Eastern countries.

kohlrabi /kəʊl'rɑːbi/ *noun* E19 **German** (*Kohlrabi* from (with assimilation to *Kohl* cole) Italian *cauli* or *cavoli rape*, plural of *cavolo rapa* (whence French *chou-rave*), representing medieval Latin *caulorapa*). A variety of cabbage, *Brassica oleracea* var. *gongylodes*, with an edible turnip-shaped base to its stem.

koi /kɔɪ/ *noun* plural same E18 **Japanese**. A carp (in Japan). Now *especially* a carp of a large ornamental variety bred in Japan. Also *koi carp*.

koine /'kɔɪniː/ *noun* L19 **Greek** (*koinē* feminine singular of *koinos* common, ordinary). **1** L19 The common literary language of the Greeks from the close of classical Attic to the Byzantine era. **2** L19 *Linguistics* and *Philology* A language or dialect common to a wide area in which different languages or dialects are, or were, used locally; a lingua franca. **3** E20 A set of cultural or other attributes common to various groups.

koinonia /kɔɪ'nəʊnɪə/ *noun* E20 **Greek** (*koinōnia* communion, fellowship). *Theology* Christian fellowship or communion, with God or, more commonly, with fellow Christians.

kolach /'kɒlətʃ/ *noun* plural **kolache** /'kɒlətʃiː/, **kolaches** /'kɒlətʃɪz/ E20 **Czech** (*koláč*, from *kolo* wheel, circle). A small tart or pie popular in the Czech Republic and Slovakia, topped or filled with fruit.

kolkhoz /'kɒlkɒz/, /kʌlk'hɔːz/ *noun* plural same, **kolkhozes** /'kɒlkɒzɪz/, **kolkhozy** /kʌlk'hɔːzi/ E20 **Russian** (from *kol(lektivnoe khoz(yaĭstvo* collective farm). In countries of the former USSR: a collective farm.

Kol Nidre /kɒl 'niːdreɪ/ *noun* L19 **Aramaic** (*kol nidrē* all the vows (the opening words of the prayer)). An Aramaic prayer annulling vows made before God, sung by Jews at the opening of the Day of Atonement service on the eve of Yom Kippur. Also, the service or the melody at or to which this prayer is sung.

kolo /'kəʊləʊ/ *noun* plural **kolos** L18 **Serbo-Croat** (= wheel). A Slavonic dance performed in a circle.

kombu /'kɒmbuː/ *noun* L19 **Japanese**. A brown seaweed of the genus *Laminaria*, used in Japanese cooking, especially as a base for stock.

Kommers /kɔ'mɛrs/ *noun* plural **Kommerse** /kɔ'mɛrsə/ M19 **German** (from Latin *commercium* communication). A social gathering of German students.

konak /kəʊ'nɑːk/ *noun* M19 **Turkish** (= halting-place, inn). A large house, palace, or official residence, in Turkey or the former Ottoman Empire.

Konditorei /ˌkɔndɪto'raɪ/ *noun* plural same, **Konditoren** /ˌkɔndɪ'torən/ M20 **German** (from *Konditor* confectioner). Confectionery; a shop selling confectionery or rich pastries.

konfyt /kɒn'feɪt/ *noun* M19 **Afrikaans** (= Dutch *konfijt*, probably from French *confiture*). Fruit preserved in sugar; preserve, jam. *South African*.

kop /kɒp/ *noun* M19 **Afrikaans** (from Dutch *kop* head). **1** M19 A prominent hill or peak. Frequently in place-names. *South African*. **2** E20 *Soccer* (*the Kop*) A high bank of terracing for standing spectators, usually supporting the home side, originally and especially at the ground of Liverpool Football Club; the spectators massed on such terracing.

■ In sense 2, also more fully *Spion Kop* /ˈspʌɪən kɒp/, after a mountain in Natal which was the site of a battle in 1900 during the South African Boer War.

kopje variant of KOPPIE.

koppel /ˈkʌp(ə)l/, /ˈkɒp(ə)l/ *noun* L19 **Yiddish.** A skullcap worn by male Jews.

koppie /ˈkɒpi/ *noun* (also **kopje**) M19 **Afrikaans** (from Dutch *kopje* diminutive of *kop* head; cf. KOP). In South Africa: a small hill, *especially* any of the flat-topped or pointed hillocks characteristic of the veld.

koradji /ˈkɒrədʒi/, /kəˈradʒi/ *noun* (also (earlier) **coradgee** and other variants) L18 **Aboriginal.** In Australia: an Aboriginal medicine man.

kore /ˈkɔːreɪ/ *noun* E20 **Greek** (*korē* = maiden). *Greek Antiquities* A statue of a clothed young woman. Cf. KOUROS.

korero /ˈkɔːrərəʊ/ *noun* plural **koreros** E19 **Maori.** In New Zealand: talk, conversation, discussion; a conference.

korma /ˈkɔːmə/ *noun* L19 **Urdu** (*ḳormā*, *ḳormah* from Turkish *kavurma*). A mildly spiced Indian dish of meat or fish marinaded in yoghurt or curds.

koro /ˈkɔːrəʊ/ *noun* E19 **Japanese** (*kōro* incense-pot, censer). An elaborate Japanese vase, usually of bronze, jade, or porcelain, in which incense is burned.

korrigan /ˈkɒrɪg(ə)n/ *noun* M19 **Breton** ((Vannes dialect) feminine of *korrig* gnome, diminutive of *korr* dwarf). In Breton folklore, a fairy or witch noted especially for stealing children.

kosher /ˈkəʊʃə/ *adjective & noun* M19 **Hebrew** (*kāšēr* fit, proper). **A** *adjective* **1** M19 Of food: prepared according to the Jewish law. **2** L19 That sells or prepares such food; where such food is cooked or eaten. **3** L19 Correct, genuine, legitimate. *colloquial.* **B** *noun* **1** L19 *elliptical* Kosher food; a kosher shop. **2** M20 The Jewish law regarding food. Chiefly in *keep kosher.*

koto /ˈkəʊtəʊ/ *noun* plural **kotos** L18 **Japanese.** A long Japanese zither, now usually having thirteen silk strings, usually played on the floor.

kotow variant of KOWTOW.

koumiss variant of KUMIS.

kouros /ˈkuːrɒs/ *noun* plural **kouroi** /ˈkuːrɔɪ/ E20 **Greek** (Ionic form of *koros* boy). *Greek Antiquities* A sculptured representation of a naked youth. Cf. KORE.

kowtow /kaʊˈtaʊ/ *noun & verb* (also **kotow** /kəʊˈtaʊ/) E19 **Chinese** (*kētóu* (Wade–Giles *k'ot'ou*), from *kē* knock, strike + *tóu* head). **A** *noun* E19 The action or practice, formerly customary in China, of touching the ground with the forehead as a sign of extreme respect, submission, or worship; *figuratively* an act of obsequious respect. **B** *intransitive verb* M19 Perform the kowtow; *figurative* act in an obsequious manner.

kozatchok variant of KAZACHOC.

kraak porselein /ˌkrɑːk ˈpɔːsəleɪn/ *noun phrase* (also **kraak porcelain** /ˈpɔːs(ə)lɪn/) M20 **Dutch** (from *kraak* carrack (the type of Portuguese ship from which the porcelain was first captured in 1603) + *porselein* porcelain). Blue and white Chinese porcelain of the Wan-li period (1573–1619) or later in the seventeenth century; a European imitation of this.

kraal /krɑːl/ *noun* M18 **Afrikaans** (from Portuguese *curral* from Nama). **1** M18 In southern Africa: a village of huts enclosed by a fence or stockade, and often having a central space for cattle etc.; the community of such a village. **2** L18 In southern Africa: an enclosure for cattle or sheep, a stockade, a pen, a fold. **3** L19 In Sri Lanka (Ceylon): an enclosure into which wild elephants are driven; the process of capturing elephants by driving them into an enclosure.

krab see KARABINER.

kragdadig /kraxˈdɑːdɪx/ *adjective* (also (in attributive use) **kragdadige**) M20 **Afrikaans** (= Dutch *krachtdadig*). Forceful, vigorous in wielding power, unyielding. *South African.*

kraken /ˈkrɑːk(ə)n/ *noun* M18 **Norwegian.** A mythical sea-monster of enormous size, said to appear off the coast of Norway.

kramat /kraˈmɑːt/, /ˈkrɑːmət/ *noun & adjective* (also **karamat** /kəˈrɑːmət/) L18 **Malay** (*keramat* (adjective) sacred, holy, (noun) holy place, holy person, from Arabic *karāma* miracle worked by a saint other than a prophet). **A** *noun* L18 A Muslim holy place or place of pilgrimage. **B** *adjective* M20 Sacred to Muslims.

krans /krɑːns/ *noun* (also **krantz** /krants/) L18 **Afrikaans** (from Dutch = coronet, chaplet from Old High German, Middle High German, German *Kranz* coronet, circle, encircling ring of mountains, from a base meaning 'ring'). In South Africa: a wall of rock encircling a mountain or summit; a precipitous or overhanging cliff above a river, valley, etc.

kraut /kraʊt/ *noun* M19 **German** (= vegetable, cabbage; cf. earlier SAUERKRAUT). **1** M19 Sauerkraut. **2** E20 (usually **Kraut**) A German, *especially* a German soldier. *derogatory slang.*

kremlin /'krɛmlɪn/ *noun* M17 **French** (from Russian *kreml'* citadel). A citadel or fortified enclosure within a Russian town or city, *especially* (*Kremlin*) that of Moscow; (*the Kremlin*) *the* government of the former USSR.

kreplach /'krɛplɑːx/ *noun plural* L19 **Yiddish** (*kreplech* plural of *krepel* from dialect German *Kräppel* fritter). Triangular noodles filled with chopped meat or cheese and served with soup.

kriegspiel /'kriːgʃpiːl/ *noun* L19 **German** (from *Krieg* war + *Spiel* game). **1** L19 A war-game in which blocks representing troops etc. are moved about on maps. **2** L19 A form of chess with an umpire and two players, in which each player plays at a separate board and has only limited information about the other's moves.

kril /krɪl/ *noun* (also **krill**) plural same E20 **Norwegian** (*kril* small fish fry). A small shrimplike planktonic crustacean of the order Euphausiacea, important as food for fish, and for some whales and seals.

■ Chiefly used as collective plural.

krimmer /'krɪmə/ *noun* (also **crimmer**) M19 **German** (from *Krim* (Russian *Krym*) Crimea). The grey or black furry fleece of young lambs from the Crimean area; a cloth resembling this. Cf. KARAKUL.

kris /kriːs/ *noun* (also **creese**) L16 **Malay** (*keris*, partly through Dutch *kris*, German *Kris*, Spanish, Portuguese *cris*, French *criss*, etc.). A Malay or Indonesian dagger with a straight or wavy blade.

kross variant of KAROSS.

krug /krʊg/ *noun* M19 **German**. In Germany and German-speaking countries: a beer-mug, a tankard.

krummholz /'krʌmhɒlts/ *noun* E20 **German** (= elfin-tree, literally, 'crooked wood'). A wood composed of dwarfed and deformed trees, such as is found in alpine regions, an elfin-wood.

krummhorn /'krʌmhɔːn/, /'krʊmhɔːn/ *noun* (also **crumhorn**) L17 **German** (from *krumm* crooked, curved + *Horn* horn). *Music* **1** L17 A medieval and Renaissance wind instrument with a double reed and a curved end. **2** L19 An organ reed-stop, usually of 8-ft pitch, suggestive of a krummhorn or clarinet in tone; a CROMORNE.

kuchen /'kuːxən/ *noun* plural **kuchens** M19 **German** (= cake). In Germany or among German- or Yiddish-speaking people: a cake; *especially* a cake taken with coffee.

kudos /'kjuːdɒs/ *noun* L18 **Greek** (= praise, renown). Glory, renown. *colloquial.*

> **1996** *Times* . . . the video company ends up with the product, the TV company with first broadcast rights, the opera company with kudos and 'accessibility' brownie points.

kudzu /'kʊdzuː/ *noun* L19 **Japanese** (*kuzu*). A climbing leguminous plant, *Pueraria lobata*, of China and Japan, cultivated elsewhere for fodder, as an ornamental, and to prevent soil erosion. In full *kudzu vine*.

kuei /'kuːeɪ/ *noun* M20 **Chinese** (*gūi* (Wade–Giles *kūei*)). *Chinese Antiquities* A bronze food-vessel, usually with two handles and often surmounted by animal heads.

kuffiyeh variant of KEFFIYEH.

kugel /'kuːg(ə)l/ *noun* M19 **Yiddish** (= ball, from Middle High German *kugel(e)* ball, globe). In Jewish cookery: a kind of pudding; *especially* a savoury pudding, usually of potatoes or other vegetables, served as a separate course or as a side dish.

kugelhupf variant of GUGELHUPF.

kukri /'kʊkri/ *noun* E19 **Nepali** (*khukuri*). A curved knife broadening towards the point and usually with the sharp edge on the concave side, used by Gurkhas.

kula /'kuːlə/ *noun* E20 **Melanesian**. In some Pacific communities, especially in the Trobriand Islands: an inter-island system of ceremonial exchange of items as a prelude to or concomitant of regular trading.

kulah /'kuːlə/ *noun* E20 **Persian** (*kulāh* cap). A conical cap of felt or lambskin worn by Muslims in the Middle East.

kulak /'kuːlak/ *noun* L19 **Russian** (literally, 'fist, tight-fisted person' from Turkic *ḳol* hand). Originally, a well-to-do Russian farmer or trader. Later, a peasant-proprietor working for his own profit in the Soviet Union.

1996 *Times* To suggest that wealthier taxpayers should plan for the worst does not imply that Labour is studying Stalin's treatment of the kulaks as a post-election model.

Kultur /kʊl'tu:r/ *noun* (also **kultur**) E20 **German** (*Kultur* from Latin *cultura* or French *culture* culture). German civilization and culture.

■ Often used in the aftermath of the Nazi era in a derogatory sense to suggest authoritarianism and militarism but also used neutrally as a component in words such as those below.

Kulturgeschichte /kʊl'tu:rgə,ʃɪçtə/ *noun* (also **kulturgeschichte**) L19 **German** (*Kultur* culture + *Geschichte* history). The history of the cultural development of a country; history of civilization.

Kulturkampf /kʊl'tu:r,kampf/ *noun* (also **kulturkampf**) L19 **German** (*Kultur* culture + *Kampf* struggle). The conflict in Germany (1872–87) between the government and the Church for control of schools and ecclesiastical appointments; *transferred* a conflict of moral or social issues and ideas.

1996 *Spectator* The great North American *kulturkampf* between classes, between moral codes and between visions of the future has chosen as its latest battlefield a city that was once known, ironically, as Toronto the Good.

kulturny /kʊlj'turnɪj/, /kʊl'tə:ni/ *adjective* M20 **Russian** (*kul'turnyĭ*, from *kul'tur* from Latin *cultura* or French *culture* culture). In countries of the former USSR: cultured, civilized; good mannered, well behaved. Cf. NEKULTURNY.

kumis /'ku:mɪs/ *noun* (also **koumiss, kumiss**) L16 **French** (*koumis*, German *Kumiss*, Polish *kumys*, Russian *kumys* from Tartar *kumiz*). A fermented liquor prepared from mare's or other milk, used as a beverage and medicinally especially by central Asian nomadic tribes; a spirituous liquor distilled from this.

kumkum /'kʊmkʊm/ *noun* M20 **Sanskrit** (*kuṅkuma* saffron). A red powder used ceremonially, especially by Hindu women to make a small distinctive mark on the forehead; the mark so made.

kümmel /'kʊm(ə)l/ *noun* M19 **German** (representative of Middle High German, Old High German *kumil* variant of *kumîn* cumin). A sweet liqueur flavoured with caraway and cumin seeds.

kundalini /'kʊndəlɪni:/ *noun* L19 **Sanskrit** (*kuṇḍalinī* literally 'snake'). *Yoga* **1** L19 The latent (female) energy which lies coiled at the base of the spine. **2** M20 A type of meditation which aims to direct and release this energy. In full *Kundalini yoga*.

kung fu /kʊŋ'fu:/, /kʌŋ'fu:/ *noun* L19 **Chinese** (*gongfu* (Wade–Giles *kung fu*), from *gong* (*kung*) merit + *fu* master). The Chinese form of KARATE.

Kunstforscher /'kʊnst,fɔrʃər/ *noun* plural same L19 **Greek** (from *Kunst* art + *Forscher* researcher). An art historian.

Kunstgeschichte /'kʊnstgə,ʃɪçtə/ *noun* L19 **German** (from *Kunst* art + *Geschichte* history). The history of art, art history.

Kunsthistoriker /'kʊnsthɪ,sto:rikər/ *noun* plural same M20 **German** (from *Kunst* art + *Historiker* historian). An art historian.

Künstlerroman /'kynstlərо,mɑ:n/ *noun* plural **Künstlerromane** /'kynstlərо,mɑ:nə/ M20 **German** (from *Künstler* artist + *Roman* novel). A BILDUNGSROMAN about an artist.

Kunstprosa /'kʊnstpro:za/ *noun* M20 **German** (from *Kunst* art + *Prosa* prose). Literary prose, ornate and stylized prose.

Kur /ku:r/ *noun* plural **Kuren** /'ku:rən/ L19 **German** (= a cure). A cure, a medicinal drinking of the waters at a spa in Germany or a German-speaking country; a spa.

kurgan /kʊə'gɑ:n/ *noun* L19 **Russian** (of Turkic origin: cf. Turkish *kurgan* castle, fortress). A prehistoric sepulchral tumulus or barrow such as is found in Siberia and central Asia.

Kurhaus /'ku:rhaʊs/ *noun* plural **Kurhäuser** /'ku:rhɔyzər/ M19 **German** (from *Kur* cure + *Haus* house). In Germany and German-speaking countries: a building at a health resort where medicinal water is dispensed; a pump room.

kuri /'kʊri/ *noun* M19 **Maori** (= dog). In New Zealand: a Maori dog. Also, a mongrel; *slang* an unpleasant or disliked person.

Kurort /'ku:r,ɔrt/ *noun* plural **Kurorte** /'ku:r,ɔrtə/ M19 **German** (from *Kur* cure + *Ort* place). In Germany and German-speaking countries: a health-resort, a spa, a watering-place.

kursaal /'ku:rsɑ:l/ *noun* plural **kursäle** /'ku:rsɛ:lə/, **kursaals**, /'ku:rsɑ:lz/ M19 **German** (from as *Kur* cure + *Saal* hall, room).

Especially in Germany and German-speaking countries: a public building at a health resort, provided for the use and entertainment of visitors.

kurta /ˈkəːtə/ *noun* E20 **Urdu and Persian** (*kurtah*). A loose shirt or tunic worn by especially Hindu men and women.

kurtosis /kəːˈtəʊsɪs/ *noun* E20 **Greek** (*kurtōsis* a bulging, convexity, from *kurtos* bulging, convex). *Statistics* The degree of sharpness of the peak of a frequency-distribution curve.

kuru /ˈkʊruː/ *noun* M20 **New Guinea**. *Medicine* A fatal viral brain disease found among certain peoples of New Guinea.

■ *Kuru* was formerly of mainly anthropological interest as a disease found amongst peoples of New Guinea who practised ritual cannibalism of human brain tissue. It became of interest to the wider medical establishment on account of its similarities to BSE (bovine spongiform encephalopathy) or *mad cow disease* which was identified in cattle in the UK in 1986. In 1990 it was discovered that cats could also contract the disease, maybe as the result of eating contaminated cattle brain or other tissue in pet foods, and the possibility that BSE could be transmitted to humans through cattle offal became the subject of urgent investigations.

kutcha /ˈkʌtʃə/ *adjective & noun* (also **cutcha**, **kacha**) E19 **Hindustani** (*kaccā* raw, crude, uncooked). **A** *adjective* E19 In the Indian subcontinent: slight, makeshift, unfinished; built of dried mud. **B** *noun* M19 Dried mud used as a building material in the Indian subcontinent.

kuzushi /kʊˈzʊʃi/ *noun* M20 **Japanese**. *Judo* The fact or state of being unbalanced by one's opponent; a loss of the initiative.

kvass /kvɑːs/ *noun* (also **kvas**, **quass**) M16 **Russian** (*kvas*). In Russia and some neighbouring countries: a fermented beverage, low in alcohol, made from rye flour or bread with malt; rye beer.

kvell /kvɛl/ *intransitive verb* M20 **Yiddish** (*kveln* from German *quellen* gush, well up). Boast; feel proud or happy; gloat.

■ United States slang.

kvetch /kvɛtʃ/ *noun & verb* M20 **Yiddish** (as noun from Yiddish *kvetsh*, as verb from Yiddish *kvetshn*, from German *Quetsche* crusher, presser, *quetschen*, crush, press). **A** *noun* M20 An objectionable person; *specifically* someone who complains a great deal, a fault-finder. **B** *intransitive verb* M20 Complain, whine. Chiefly as *kvetching* verbal noun.

■ North American slang.

kvutza /ˈkvʊtsɑː/, /kvʊtˈsɑː/ *noun* E20 **Modern Hebrew** (*qĕbhūṣāh* from Hebrew = group). In Israel: a communal and cooperative settlement, which, with others, may form a kibbutz.

kwai-lo /ˈkwʌɪləʊ/ *noun* M20 **Chinese** ((Cantonese) (*faan*) *kwaí ló*, literally, '(foreign) devil fellow'). In China, a foreigner, *especially* a European.

■ A derogatory Chinese expression for all non-Chinese.

kwashiorkor /ˌkwɒʃɪˈɔːkɔː/, /ˌkwaʃɪˈɔːkɔː/ *noun* M20 **Ghanaian** (local name). A form of malnutrition caused by severe protein and energy deficiency, chiefly affecting young (especially newly weaned) children in tropical Africa, and producing apathy, oedema, loss of pigmentation, diarrhoea, and other symptoms.

kwela /ˈkweɪlə/ *noun* M20 **Afrikaans** (perhaps from Zulu *khwela* climb, mount). A popular dance, and its accompanying music, resembling jazz, of central and southern Africa.

1958 *Time* In the dusty streets, urchins rock to the penny-whistle's fast *kwela* beat.

kya /ˈkʌɪə/ *noun* E20 **Zulu** (*-khaya* place of abode). In South Africa, Zimbabwe, etc.: an African's hut; the living accommodation of an African servant.

kylin /ˈkiːlɪn/ *noun* M19 **Chinese** (*qílín*, from *qí* male + *lín* female). A mythical animal of composite form figured on Chinese and Japanese pottery, a Chinese unicorn. Cf. KIRIN.

kylix /ˈkʌɪlɪks/, /ˈkɪlɪks/ *noun* (also **cylix**, plural **cylices** /ˈkʌɪlɪsiːz/) plural **kylikes** /ˈkʌɪlɪkiːz/ M19 **Greek** (*kulix*). *Greek Antiquities* A shallow cup with a tall stem, a tazza.

kyogen /ˈkjəʊgɛn/ *noun* plural same L19 **Japanese** (*kyōgen*). A comic interlude presented between performances of Noh plays.

Kyrie eleison /ˌkɪrɪeɪ ɪˈleɪɪzɒn/, /ˌkɪrɪeɪ ɪˈleɪɪsɒn/ *noun phrase* ME **Medieval Latin** (from Greek *Kuriē eleēson* Lord, have mercy). The words ('Lord, have mercy') of a short repeated invocation or response used in the Roman Catholic, Greek Orthodox, and Anglican Churches, especially at the beginning of the Eucharist. Also, a musical setting of these words, especially as the first movement of a mass.

kyu /kju:/ *noun* M20 **Japanese** (*kyū* class). Each of the (numbered) grades of the less advanced level of proficiency in judo, karate, and other martial (or originally martial) arts, (also *kyu grade*); a person who has reached (a specified grade of) this level. Cf. DAN.

L

La /lɑ/, /lɑː/ *adjective* (*definite article*) (also **la**) M19 **French** (or Italian feminine definite article, from Latin *illa*, feminine of *ille* that). Used preceding the name of a prima donna, or (frequently *jocular* or *ironical*) the name of any woman.

1996 *Times* The doughty girl has a touch of the Katharine Hepburns about her. *La* Hepburn, 88, still goes swimming in the lake by her house, even if she has to break the ice . . .

laager /ˈlɑːgə/ *noun* M19 **Afrikaans** (= German *Lager*, Dutch *leger*). A camp, an encampment; *South African History* a Boer camp marked out and protected by a circle of wagons; *transferred* and *figurative* a defensive position, *especially* one protected by armoured vehicles; an entrenched policy, viewpoint, etc., under attack from opponents.

■ In its figurative sense *laager* was often used attributively in the phrase *laager mentality* to denote the intransigent defensiveness of Afrikaners in their dealings with the outside world during the apartheid era. The noun gave rise (L19) to both transitive and intransitive verbal uses of *laager*, sometimes followed by *up*.

figurative **1996** *Times* The stage appeared to be too big for his four-piece band, whose equipment was drawn up into a laager in the middle.

laban /ˈlaban/ *noun* (also **leban** /ˈlɛban/, **leben** /ˈlɛbən/) L17 **Arabic** (= milk). A drink consisting of coagulated sour milk.

labarum /ˈlabərəm/ *noun* E17 **Late Latin** (whence Byzantine Greek *labaron*). The imperial standard of Constantine the Great (306–337), with Christian symbols added to Roman military symbols; *generally* a symbolic banner.

labrys /ˈlabrɪs/ *noun* E20 **Greek** (*labrus*). *Greek Antiquities* The sacred double-headed axe of ancient Crete; a representation of this.

lac /lak/ *noun* (also **lack**, (earlier) **lacca**) LME **Medieval Latin** (*lac*, *lac(c)a* from Portuguese *lac(c)a* from Hindustani *lākh*, Persian *lāk*). LME The dark-red resinous incrustation secreted as a protective covering by the females of certain homopteran insects (especially *Laccifer lacca*) parasitic on South-East Asian trees, used (especially in the Indian subcontinent) to make shellac and dye.

■ Formerly (L16–E18) used also for the varnish made from lac or various other resinous wood varnishes (*lacquer*) and (L17–M18) for the crimson colour or pigment derived from lac (*lake*).

lacet /lasɛ/ *noun* plural pronounced same L19 **French** (= lace, hairpin bend). A hairpin bend in a road.

lachryma Christi /ˌlakrɪmə ˈkrɪstʌɪ/, /ˌlakrɪmə ˈkrɪstiː/ *noun phrase* L17 **Modern Latin** (literally, 'Christ's tear(s)', in Italian *lagrima* (or *-me*) *di Cristo*). A white, red, or pink Italian wine originally from grapes grown near Mount Vesuvius, now also produced elsewhere in Italy.

lachsschinken /ˈlaxsˌʃɪŋkən/ *noun* E20 **German** (from *Lachs* salmon + *Schinken* ham). Cured and smoked loin of pork.

lacrimae rerum /ˌlakrɪmʌɪ ˈreɪrəm/, /ˌlakrɪmiː ˈrɪərəm/ *noun* (also **lachrymae rerum**) E20 **Latin** (literally, 'tears (for the nature) of things'). The sadness of life; tears for the sorrows of life.

■ A quotation from Virgil's *Aeneid* (i.462). The etymologically incorrect spelling *lachrymae* is also frequent.

1995 *Oldie* [Critics] wrote off Betjeman as a phoney and a doggerel rhymester. They had not sensed the *lachrymae rerum* in the poems.

lacuna /ləˈkjuːnə/ *noun* plural **lacunae** /ləˈkjuːniː/, **lacunas** M17 **Latin** (from *lacus* lake). **1** M17 A hiatus, a blank, a missing portion, especially in a manuscript or text. **2** E18 *in technical use* A gap, a depression; a space or cavity.

ladanum /ˈladənəm/ *noun* M16 **Latin** (*ladanum*, *ledanum* from Greek *ladanon*, *lēdanon*, from *lēdon* mastic). A gum resin which exudes from plants of the genus *Cistus*, much used in perfumery and for fumigation.

ladino /ləˈdiːnəʊ/ *noun* E20 **Italian**. A large fast-growing variety of white clover (*Trifolium repens*), native to northern Italy and cultivated elsewhere, especially in the United States, as a fodder crop. In full *ladino clover*.

la dolce vita see DOLCE VITA.

l'affaire see AFFAIRE.

lager /ˈlɑːgə/ *noun* M19 **German** (*Lager-Bier* beer brewed for keeping, from *Lager* storehouse). A light kind of beer, originally

German or Bohemian, which is stored to mature before use; a drink of this.

lahar /'lɑ:hɑ:/ *noun* E20 **Javanese**. *Geology* A mud-flow of volcanic ash mixed with water.

laissez-aller /ˌlɛseɪ'aleɪ/, *foreign* /lɛseale/ *noun* (also **laisser-aller**) E19 **French** (literally, 'allow to go'). Absence of restraint; unconstrained ease and freedom.

laissez-faire /ˌlɛseɪ'fɛ:/, *foreign* /lɛsefɛr/ *noun* (also **laisser-faire**) E19 **French** (literally, 'allow to do'). Government abstention from interference in the actions of individuals, especially in commerce; *generally* non-interference or indifference.

■ The maxim *laissez faire et laissez passer* is associated particularly with the French free-trade economists of the eighteenth century. See also quotation at DIRIGISME.

1996 *Country Life* The professor's *laissez-faire* philosophy is quite clearly presiding over an impoverishment of English, which is losing not simply its richness but also its comprehensibility.

laissez-passer /ˌlɛseɪ'pɑ:seɪ/, *foreign* /lɛspɑse/ (*plural same*) *noun* (also **laisser-passer**) E20 **French** (literally, 'allow to pass'). A permit to travel or to enter a particular place, a pass.

1955 *Times* He has been granted by the Greek Foreign Ministry a laisser-passer to the Greek military zone of the Greek–Bulgarian frontier.

lakh /lak/ *noun* (also **lac**) E17 **Hindustani** (*lākh* from Sanskrit *lakṣa* mark, token, 100,000). In the Indian subcontinent: one hundred thousand; occasionally, an indefinite large number.

lakoum, **lakum** variants of LOKUM.

lama /'lɑ:mə/ *noun* M17 **Tibetan** (*bla-ma* (the *b* is silent)). A Buddhist religious teacher of Tibet or Mongolia.

lambada /lam'bɑ:də/ *noun* L20 **Brazilian Portuguese** (literally, 'beating, lashing'). A fast and erotic dance of Brazilian origin, in which couples dance with their stomachs touching each other; the music for this dance.

■ The *lambada*, danced in Brazil for many years, became a craze in the United States in the late 1980s, and media hype helped spread it to the United Kingdom and Australia. The speed and thoroughness with which this ethnic dance was marketed in the West gave rise to the coinage *lambadazation* for the whole process of taking up and marketing elements of ethnic culture for Western consumers.

1990 *Sun* We danced the lambada face to face and sort of going up and down against each other.

lambda /'lamdə/ *noun* E17 **Greek**. **I 1** E17 The eleventh letter (Λ, λ) of the Greek alphabet. **II 2** M20 *Chemistry* A millionth of a litre. Usually written λ. **3** M20 *Nuclear Physics* A neutral hyperon (or its antiparticle) with a mass 2183 times that of the electron; originally also, any of several similar charged hyperons. Frequently written Λ. More fully *lambda particle*. **4** M20 *Microbiology* A bacteriophage originally isolated from *Escherichia coli*, used in genetic research. Frequently written λ.

lamdan /'lʌmdən/ *noun* E20 **Hebrew** (*lamdān*, literally, 'a person who has learned', from *lāmaḏ* learn). A person learned in Jewish law; a Talmudic scholar.

lamé /'lɑ:meɪ/ *noun & adjective* E20 **French** (from Old French *lame* from Latin *lamina*, *lamna* thin plate, especially of metal). (Made of) a brocaded fabric consisting of silk or other yarns interwoven with metallic threads.

lamento /la'mento/ *noun* plural **lamenti** /la'menti/ M20 **Italian**. *Music* An elegiac or mourning song; in Italian opera, a tragic aria.

lamentoso /ˌlamen'to:so/ *adverb & adjective* L19 **Italian**. *Music* (A direction:) in a mournful style.

lamia /'leɪmɪə/ *noun* plural **lamias**, **lamiae** /'leɪmɪi:/ LME **Latin** (from Greek = mythical monster, carnivorous fish). A mythical monster supposed to have the body of a woman, and to prey on human beings and suck the blood of children. Also, a witch, a she-demon.

lamina /'lamɪnə/ *noun* plural **laminae** /'lamɪni:/ M17 **Latin** (*la(m)mina*). A thin plate or layer of a metal or other material.

■ Also with technical senses in Anatomy and Biology, Botany (M18), Geology (M19), and Mathematics (M19).

lammergeyer /'laməgʌɪə/ *noun* (also **lammergeier**) E19 **German** (*Lämmergeier*, from *Lämmer* plural of *Lamm* lamb + *Geier* vulture). A long-winged, long-tailed vulture, *Gypaetus barbatus*, inhabiting lofty mountains in southern Europe, Asia, and Africa. Also called *bearded vulture*.

lammervanger /'laməvaŋə/, /'laməfaŋə/ *noun* M19 **Afrikaans** (from *lam* lamb + *vanger* catcher). In South Africa: an eagle, especially one believed to prey on lambs. Also, = preceding.

lanai /lə'nʌɪ/ *noun* (also (earlier) **ranai**) E19 **Hawaiian**. A porch or veranda, originally in Hawaii; a roofed structure with open sides near a house.

Land /lant/, /land/ *noun* plural **Länder** /'lɛndər/, **Lands** /landz/ E20 **German**. A semi-autonomous unit of local government in Germany and Austria.

> **1996** *Bookseller* The location was chosen to attract booksellers in the reunified Germany's eastern *Länder*, although this did not deter those from Munich and Stuttgart.

landau /'landɔː/, /'landaʊ/ *noun* M18 **German** (from *Landau* name of town in Germany, where first made). Chiefly *History* A four-wheeled horse-drawn carriage, with folding front and rear hoods enabling it to travel open, half-open, or closed. Also *landau carriage*.

lande /lɑ̃d/ *noun* plural pronounced same L18 **French**. A tract of wild land, a moor, especially in south-west France.

Länder plural of LAND.

ländler /'lɛndlə/ *noun* L19 **German**. An Austrian peasant dance, similar to a slow waltz; a piece of music for this dance.

landnam /'landnəm/ *noun* M20 **Danish** (= occupation of land). *Archaeology* The clearance of forested land for (usually short-term) agricultural purposes; evidence of this provided by sudden changes in pollen spectra.

landrace /'landreɪs/ *noun* M20 **Danish** (= national breed). A breed of large white pig, originally developed in Denmark; an animal of this breed.

landsknecht see LANSQUENET.

landsman /'lɒntsmɒn/ *noun* plural **landsleit** /'lɒntslʌɪt/ M20 **Yiddish** (from Middle High German *lantsman*, *lantman* a native). Among Jews: a fellow Jew; a compatriot.

Landsturm /'lant,ʃtʊrm/ *noun* plural **Landstürme** /'lant,ʃtyrmə/ E19 **German** (literally, 'land-storm'). *History* In Germany and German-speaking countries: a general levy in time of war; an auxiliary militia force.

Landwehr /'lantveːr/ *noun* E19 **German** (literally, 'land-defence'). *Military* In Germany and some other countries: that part of the organized land forces of which continuous service is required only in time of war; the army reserve.

langeleik /'laŋəlʌɪk/ *noun* plural **langeleiken** /'laŋəlʌɪkən/ (also **langleik** /'laŋlʌɪk/) E20 **Norwegian**. An early Norwegian stringed instrument, resembling the zither.

langlauf /'laŋlaʊf/ *noun* (also **Langlauf**) E20 **German** (literally, 'long run'). Cross-country skiing; a cross-country skiing race.

langleik variant of LANGELEIK.

langosta /laŋ'gɒstə/ *noun* L19 **Spanish** (from popular Latin alteration of Latin *locusta* locust). **1** L19 A locust. Now *rare* or *obsolete*. **2** E20 A LANGOUSTE.

■ Chiefly United States.

langostino /lango'stino/, /laŋgə'stiːnəʊ/ *noun* plural **langostinos** /lango'stinos/, /laŋgə'stiːnəʊz/ E20 **Spanish** (from as preceding). A LANGOUSTINE.

langouste /'lɒŋguːst/, *foreign* /lɑ̃gust/ (*plural same*) *noun* M19 **French** (from Old Provençal *lagosta* from popular Latin alteration of Latin *locusta* locust). A lobster; *especially* the spiny lobster, *Palinurus vulgaris*.

langoustine /'lɒŋgʊstiːn/, *foreign* /lɑ̃gustin/ (*plural same*) *noun* M20 **French** (from as preceding). The Norway lobster, especially as food.

langue /lɑ̃g/ *noun* plural pronounced same ME **French** (from Latin *lingua* tongue, language). **1** ME–M17 A language. *rare*. **2** L18 A national division or branch of a religious and military Order. Long *rare* except *historical*. **3** E20 *Linguistics* A language viewed as an abstract system used by a speech-community, in contrast to the actual linguistic behaviour of individuals. Opposed to PAROLE sense 3.

langue de chat /lɑ̃g də ʃa/, /ˌlɑːŋ də 'ʃɑː/ *noun phrase* plural **langues de chat** (pronounced same) L19 **French** (literally, 'cat's tongue'). A long thin piece of chocolate; a long finger-shaped biscuit.

langue d'oc /lɑ̃g dɔk/ *noun phrase* E18 **Old and Modern French** (from as LANGUE + *de* of + *oc* yes (from Latin *hoc*)). The language of medieval France south of the Loire, generally characterized by the use of *oc* to mean 'yes', and the basis of modern Provençal. Cf. LANGUE D'OÏL.

langue d'oïl /lɑ̃g dɔi/ *noun phrase* (also **langue d'oui** /lɑ̃g dwi/) E18 **Old and Modern French** (from as LANGUE + *de* of + *oïl* (now *oui*) yes (from Latin *hoc ille*)). The language of medieval France north of the

Loire, generally characterized by the use of *oïl* to mean 'yes', and the basis of standard modern French. Cf. LANGUE D'OC.

langues de chat plural of LANGUE DE CHAT.

lansquenet /'lɑːnskənɛt/, /'lanskənɛt/ *noun* (also (in sense 1 now the usual form) **landsknecht** /'lan(d)sknɛkt/) E17 **French** (from German *Landsknecht*, from genitive of *Land* land + *Knecht* soldier). **1** E17 *History* A member of a class of mercenary soldiers in the German and other Continental armies in the sixteenth and seventeenth centuries. **2** L17 A gambling card-game of German origin.

lanx /laŋks/ *noun* plural **lances** /'lansiːz/ LME **Latin**. *Antiquities* A large dish or bowl.

lapiés /'lapjez/, /'lapɪeɪz/ *noun plural* (also **lapies**) E20 **French** (dialectal *lapiaz, lapiés* (singular *lapié*) ultimately from Latin *lapis* stone). *Physical Geography* KARREN. Also (treated as *singular*) KARRENFELD.

lapillus /lə'pɪləs/ *noun* plural **lapilli** /lə'pɪlʌɪ/, /lə'pɪliː/ M18 **Latin** (diminutive of *lapis* stone; in plural also from Italian *lapilli*, plural of *lapillo*). Originally, a small stone or pebble. Now (*Geology*), a fragment of rock or lava ejected from a volcano, *specifically* one between 2 and 64 mm in size. Usually in *plural*.

lapis /'lapɪs/ *noun* LME **Latin**. **1** LME Stone; *specifically* the philosopher's stone. *rare* except in phrases. **2** E19 (Abbreviated form of) LAPIS LAZULI.

lapis lazuli /ˌlapɪs 'lazjʊlʌɪ/, /ˌlapɪs 'lazjʊli/ *noun phrase* LME **Latin** (from Latin *lapis* stone + medieval Latin *lazuli* genitive of *lazulum*, varying with *lazur, lazurius*, from Persian *lāžward* lapis lazuli). A blue semiprecious stone composed chiefly of a sulphur-containing silicate of sodium and aluminium; *History* a pigment consisting of crushed grains of this, the original ultramarine; the colour ultramarine.

lappa /'lapə/ *noun* M20 **Hausa** (from Arabic *laffa* to wrap up, cover). In West Africa: a woman's shawl, wrap, or skirt.

lapsus /'lapsəs/ *noun* plural same E17 **Latin**. A lapse, a slip, an error.

■ Chiefly in phrases below.

lapsus calami /ˌlapsəs 'kaləmʌɪ/ *noun phrase* L19 **Latin**. A slip of the pen.

lapsus linguae /ˌlapsəs 'lɪŋgwiː/ *noun phrase* M17 **Latin**. A slip of the tongue.

laquear /'lakwɪɑː/ *noun* plural **laquearia** /ˌlakwɪ'ɑːrɪə/ E18 **Latin** (*laqueare* panelled ceiling). *Architecture* A ceiling consisting of panelled recessed compartments, with bands between the panels.

lar /lɑː/ *noun* (in sense 1 also **Lar**) plural **lars, lares** /'lɑːriːz/ L16 **Latin**. **1** L16 *Roman History* A household or ancestral god. Frequently in *plural*, the protective gods of a house; household gods; also, the home. Cf. PENATES. **2** E19 The common or white-handed gibbon, *Hylobates lar*, of Thailand and Malaysia. More fully *lar gibbon*.

■ The phrase *lares et penates* (or *lares and penates*) is used figuratively of those components of a household that the owner holds dearest; thus in 1775 Horace Walpole wrote in a letter 'I am returned to my own Lares and Penates—to my dogs and cats'.

lardon /'lɑːdən/ *noun* (also **lardoon** /lɑː'duːn/) LME **French** (from Old French *lard* bacon, from Latin *lar(i)dum* related to Greek *larinos* fat). *Cookery* A strip of bacon or pork inserted into other meat before cooking to give it flavour and keep it moist.

la recherche du temps perdu see RECHERCHE DU TEMPS PERDU.

lares plural of LAR.

largamente /lɑːgə'mɛnti/ *adverb & adjective* M19 **Italian** (= broadly). *Music* (A direction:) in a slow dignified style.

largesse /lɑː'ʒɛs/, /lɑː'dʒɛs/ *noun* (also **largess**) ME **Old and Modern French** (from Proto-Romance, from Latin *largus* liberal in giving). **1** ME Liberality, generosity, munificence. Long *obsolete* except *historical*. **2** ME Liberal bestowal of gifts, especially by a person in a high position on some special occasion. **b** M16 An act of such giving; a free gift of money etc. **3** LME–L16 Freedom, liberty.

2.b 1995 D. Lodge *Therapy* The youth came back soon afterwards, hoping for more *largesse*.

larghetto /lɑː'gɛtəʊ/ *adverb, adjective, & noun* E18 **Italian** (diminutive of LARGO). *Music* **A** *adverb & adjective* E18 (A direction:) in fairly slow time. **B** *noun* plural **larghettos** L19 A movement or passage (to be) played in this way.

largo /'lɑːgəʊ/ *adverb, adjective, & noun* L17 **Italian** (= broad). *Music* **A** *adverb & adjective* L17 (A direction:) in slow time and with a broad dignified treatment. **B** *noun* plural **largos** M18 A movement or passage (to be) played in this way.

larmoyant /lɑːˈmɔɪənt/ *adjective* E19 **French** (present participle of *larmoyer* to be tearful). Given to tears, lachrymose.

> **1972** P. Porter *'Preaching to the Converted'* Calling down the funnel of your mind News the charnel chords make *larmoyant*, The Pretenders come . . .

larnax /ˈlɑːnaks/ *noun* plural **larnakes** /ˈlɑːnəkiːz/ L19 **Greek.** *Greek Antiquities* A chest, ossuary, urn, or coffin, usually of terracotta and frequently ornamented with designs.

larva /ˈlɑːvə/ *noun* plural **larvae** /ˈlɑːviː/ M17 **Latin** (= ghost, mask). **1** M17 A disembodied spirit; a ghost, a spectre. *obsolete* except *historical.* **2** M18 An insect in a state of development (displaying little or no similarity to the adult) lasting from the time of its leaving the egg until its transformation into a pupa; a grub, a caterpillar. Also, an immature form in other animals that undergo some sort of metamorphosis, e.g. amphibians, tapeworms, etc.

larynx /ˈlarɪŋks/ *noun* plural **larynges** /ləˈrɪndʒiːz/, **larynxes** L16 **Modern Latin** (from Greek *larugx, larugg-*). *Anatomy* and *Zoology* A hollow cartilaginous and muscular organ forming the upper part of the trachea or windpipe, and holding the vocal cords in humans and most mammals.

lasagne /ləˈzanjə/, /ləˈsanjə/, /ləˈsɑːnjə/, /ləˈzɑːnjə/ *noun* (also **lasagna**) M19 **Italian** (plural of *lasagna*, ultimately from Latin *lasanum* chamber-pot, perhaps also cooking-pot). Pasta in the form of long wide strips; an Italian dish consisting largely of this, usually with a sauce.

lassi /ˈlʌsi/, /ˈlasi/ *noun* L19 **Hindustani** (*lassī*). In the Indian subcontinent: a drink made from a buttermilk or yoghurt base with water.

lasya /ˈlɑːsjə/ *noun* M20 **Sanskrit** (*lāsya*). A graceful Indian style of female dancing.

latex /ˈleɪtɛks/ *noun* plural **latexes, latices** /ˈleɪtɪsiːz/ M17 **Latin** (= liquid, fluid). **1** M17–M18 *Medicine* Any of various body fluids. **2** M19 *Botany* A milky liquid found in many plants; *specifically* that of *Hevea brasiliensis* or other plants used to produce rubber. **3** M20 A dispersion in water of particles of a polymer that is formed during polymerization and is used to make paints, coatings, etc.

lathi /ˈlɑːtiː/ *noun* (also **lathee**) M19 **Hindustani** (*lāṭhī*). In the Indian subcontinent: a long heavy iron-bound stick, usually of bamboo, used as a weapon.

latifundium /lɑːtɪˈfʌndɪəm/, /latɪˈfʌndɪəm/, /leɪtɪˈfʌndɪəm/ *noun* plural **latifundia** /lɑːtɪˈfʌndɪə/ M19 **Latin** (from *latus* broad + *fundus* landed estate; partly from Spanish *latifundio* from Latin). A large landed estate or ranch, frequently worked by slaves or people of semiservile status; *especially* one in Spain or Latin America or in ancient Rome.

■ Now usually occurring in the plural, *latifundium* was originally (M17) Anglicized as *latifund*. Its opposite is a MINIFUNDIUM.

latigo /ˈlatɪɡəʊ/ *noun* plural **latigo(e)s** L19 **Spanish.** A strap for tightening a cinch. *United States.*

Latino sine flexione /ˌlatɪnəʊ ˌsɪnɪ flɛksɪˈəʊni/ *noun phrase* E20 **Latin** ((*Latino* ablative of adjective *Latinus* Latin) = in Latin without inflection). The language Interlingua, in which nouns are taken from the ablative case of Latin nouns.

latke /ˈlʌtkə/ *noun* E20 **Yiddish** (from Russian *latka* earthenware cooking vessel, (dialect) dish cooked in such a vessel). In Jewish cookery: a pancake, *especially* one made with grated potato.

latria /ləˈtrʌɪə/ *noun* E16 **Late Latin** (from Greek *latreia*, from *latreuein* to wait on, serve with prayer). *Roman Catholic Church* The highest form of worship, due to God alone; the veneration properly given to God. Cf. DULIA, HYPERDULIA.

latticinio /lattiˈtʃiːnjo/, /latɪˈtʃiːnjəʊ/ *noun* Also written **latticino** /lattiˈtʃiːno/, /latɪˈtʃiːnəʊ/ M19 **Italian** (literally, 'dairy produce', from medieval Latin *lacticinium*). An opaque white glass used in threads to decorate clear Venetian glass.

laúd /laˈud/ *noun* plural **laúdes** /laˈudes/ L19 **Spanish** (*laúd* from Arabic *al-ʿūd*). A Spanish lute.

laudator temporis acti /lɔːˌdeɪtə ˌtɛmp(ə)rɪs ˈaktʌɪ/ *noun phrase* plural **laudatores temporis acti** /lɔːdəˌtɔːriːz/ M18 **Latin** (= a praiser of times past). A person who holds up the past as a golden age.

■ *Laudator temporis acti se puero* 'a praiser of former times when he himself was a boy' is a quotation from a passage in Horace's *Ars*

Poetica (173–4) on the tiresome traits that tend to accompany old age.

laulau /ˈlaʊlaʊ/ *noun* M20 **Hawaiian** (reduplication of *lau* leaf). A portion of a Hawaiian dish of meat or fish wrapped in leaves and steamed or baked. Also, the wrapping of leaves for this dish.

laura /ˈlɔːrə/ *noun* (also **lavra** /ˈlavrə/) E18 **Greek** (= lane, passage, alley). *Christian Church* A group of huts or cells inhabited by reclusive monks in Egypt and the Middle East. In the Orthodox Church, a monastery consisting of separate cells; a large monastery.

lavabo /ləˈveɪbəʊ/, *in sense 2* /ˈlavəbəʊ/ *noun* plural **lavabo(e)s** M18 **Latin** (= I will wash). **1** M18 *Ecclesiastical* In the Eucharist, the ritual washing of a celebrant's hands at the offertory; also the small towel or the basin used for the washing. **2 a** L19 A washing-trough used in some medieval monasteries. **b** E20 A wash-hand basin. **c** M20 A lavatory; washroom.

lavage /ˈlavɪʤ/, /laˈvɑːʒ/ *noun & verb* L18 **French** (from *laver* to wash). **A** *noun* **1** L18 An act of washing, a wash. **2** L19 *Medicine* The irrigation of an organ, either to cleanse it or to allow its contents to be examined. **B** *transitive verb* M20 *Medicine* Cleanse, irrigate, (an organ).

lava-lava /ˈlɑːvəlɑːvə/ *noun* L19 **Samoan**. In Samoa and some other Pacific islands: a wrap-around skirtlike garment worn by either sex.

lavaliere /ləˈvaljɛː/ *noun* (also **lava(l)lière**, **lavalier** /ləˈvalɪə/, **Lavaliere**) L19 **French** (proper name). **1** L19 Used *attributively* to designate any of various items of women's clothing in styles associated with the reign of Louis XIV of France. **2** E20 A pendent necklace. **3** M20 A loosely tied cravat. **4** M20 A small microphone worn hanging around the neck. Also *lavaliere microphone*.

■ Louise de *la Vallière* (1644–1710) was mistress to the French king Louis XIV. In French the most frequent context is *une cravate lavallière*.

lavolta /ləˈvɒltə/ *noun* L16 **Italian** (from *la* the + *volta* turn). *History* A lively dance for couples in 3/4 time, in which each partner lifts the other clear of the ground in turn.

lavra variant of LAURA.

layette /leɪˈjɛt/ *noun* M19 **French** (diminutive of Old French *laie* drawer, box, from Middle Dutch *laege*). A set of clothing, toilet articles, and bedclothing for a newborn child.

lazaretto /lazəˈrɛtəʊ/ *noun* plural **lazarettos** M16 **Italian** (diminutive of LAZZARO). **1** M16 A hospital for diseased people, especially those with leprosy. **2** E17 A building or ship for quarantine. **3** E18 *Nautical* The after part of a ship's hold, used for stores.

■ Less common, but also used in all three senses, is the French word *lazaret* (E17 in sense 1), derived from the Italian.

lazzaro /ˈlazərəʊ/ *noun* (also plural **lazzari** /ˈlazəri/) M17 **Italian**. A LAZZARONE.

lazzarone /lazəˈrəʊneɪ/ *noun* plural **lazzaroni** /lazəˈrəʊni/ L18 **Italian** (augmentative of LAZZARO). In Naples and other Italian cities: a person who subsists on the proceeds of odd jobs, an idler, a beggar.

leban, **leben** variants of LABAN.

Lebensform /ˈleːbənsfɔrm/, /ˈleɪbənz fɔːm/ *noun* plural **Lebensformen** /ˈleːbəns fɔrmən/ M20 **German** (literally, 'form of life'). A sphere of human social activity involving values; a style or aspect of life.

Lebenslust /ˈleːbənslʊst/, /ˈleɪbənzlʊst/ *noun* L19 **German**. Zest for life, *joie de vivre*.

1958 P. De Vries *Mackeral Plaza* Security he could give her, yes, but not, I'm afraid, something else demanded by her *Lebenslust*.

lebensraum /ˈleːbənsraʊm/, /ˈleɪbənz raʊm/ *noun* Also written **Lebensraum** E20 **German** (= living room). Space for living, room to exist and function freely; *specifically* territory which many German nationalists in the mid twentieth century claimed was needed for the survival and healthy development of the nation.

■ Originally the biological concept of a space inhabited, or habitable, by a particular organism, *Lebensraum* was developed by the nineteenth-century German geographer Friedrich Ratzel to mean the space sufficient both for a people's material needs and for the evolution of its particular social and cultural identity. The concept was subsequently hijacked by the Nazis to justify the racist and expansionist policies of the Third Reich.

1995 *Spectator* The sub-text is that if the united Germany . . . can be closely bound into the Community she will never again be tempted to fight for *lebensraum*.

transferred **1996** *Spectator* My liver obviously needed *lebensraum* and was heavily leaning on its neighbours.

lebensspur /ˈleːbənsˌʃpuːr/, /ˈleɪbənz ˌʃpʊə/ *noun* plural **lebensspuren** /ˈleːbəns ˌʃpuːrən/ (also **Lebensspur**) M20 **German** (from *Leben* life + *Spur* trace, track). *Geology* A small track, burrow, cast, etc., left in sediment by a living organism; *especially* one preserved in fossil form in sedimentary rock, a trace fossil.

■ Usually in the plural, the term was apparently first used in German by O. Abel in 1912.

1973 *Nature* In a recently completed series of laboratory studies, lebensspuren were produced by individual macrobenthic organisms on a variety of marine sand and mud substrates . . .

Lebenswelt /ˈleːbənsvɛlt/, /ˈleɪbənzvɛlt/ *noun* plural **Lebenswelten** /ˈleːbəns vɛltən/ M20 **German**. *Philosophy* All the immediate experiences, activities, and contacts that make up the world of an individual, or of a corporate, life.

■ A term particularly associated with the German philosopher E. G. A. Husserl (1859–1938), it is often translated into English as 'life-world'.

leberwurst /ˈleɪbəwəːst/, /ˈleɪbəvʊəst/ *noun* M19 **German**. (A) liver sausage.

lebes /ˈlɛbiːz/ *noun* M19 **Greek** (*lebēs*). *Greek Antiquities* A deep round-bottomed bowl for holding wine.

lechayim /ləˈxajim/ *interjection* (also **lechaim** /ləˈxʌɪm/ and other variants) M20 **Hebrew** (*lĕ-ḥayyīm*). (A drinking toast:) to life!

lectio difficilior /ˌlɛktɪəʊ dɪfɪˈkɪlɪɔː/ *noun phrase* plural **lectiones difficiliores** /lɛktɪ ˌəʊneɪz dɪfɪkɪlɪˈɔːreɪz/ M20 **Latin**. (Word-order variant of) DIFFICILIOR LECTIO.

lector /ˈlɛktɔː/ *noun* LME **Latin** (from *lect-* past participial stem of *legere* to read). **1** LME *Ecclesiastical* A person commissioned as, or ordained to the office of, a liturgical reader. **2** LME A person who reads; *specifically* a reader or lecturer in a college or university, now especially one in a Continental country, as Germany or France, or in a foreign country teaching his or her native language.

lectrice /lɛkˈtriːs/, /ˈlɛktriːs/ *noun* L19 **French** (from Latin *lectrix* feminine of Latin LECTOR). **1** L19 A woman engaged as an attendant or companion to read aloud. **2** M20 A female lecturer.

lecythus see LEKYTHOS.

lederhosen /ˈleɪdəhəʊz(ə)n/ *noun plural* M20 **German** (from *Leder* leather + *Hosen* plural of *Hose* trouser). Leather shorts, especially as traditionally worn in Alpine regions of Bavaria etc.

legato /lɪˈgɑːtəʊ/ *adjective, adverb, & noun* M18 **Italian** (past participle of *legare* to bind, from Latin *ligare*). *Music* **A** *adjective & adverb* M18 (A direction:) smooth(ly) and connected(ly), with no breaks between successive notes. **B** *noun* L19 A legato style of performance; a piece or passage (to be) played legato.

legator /lɪˈgeɪtə/ *noun* M17 **Latin** (from *legat-* past participial stem of *legare* to bequeath). A person who gives something by will, a testator.

legerdemain /ˌlɛdʒədəˈmeɪn/ *noun* LME **French** (*léger de main*, from *léger* light + *de* of + *main* hand). **1** LME Sleight of hand; juggling; conjuring. **2** M16 *transferred* and *figurative* Trickery, deception. **3** M16–M17 An instance of legerdemain.

leggiero /lɛˈdʒɛːrəʊ/, *foreign* /lɛdˈdʒɛːro/ *adjective & adverb* (also **leggero**) L19 **Italian**. *Music* (A direction:) light(ly) and graceful(ly).

legionnaire /ˌliːdʒəˈnɛː/ *noun* (also **legionaire**) E19 **French** (*légionnaire*, from *légion* legion). A member of a legion; *especially* (usually *Legionnaire*) a member of a named legion, as the American Legion, the Royal British Legion, or the French Foreign Legion.

legong /lɛˈgɒŋ/ *noun* E20 **Indonesian**. (A participant in) a stylized Balinese dance performed especially by young girls.

legume /ˈlɛgjuːm/ *noun* M17 **French** (*légume* from Latin *legumen*, from *legere* to gather: so called because the fruit may be gathered by hand). **1** M17 The fruit or edible portion of any leguminous plant (bean, pea, etc.) grown for food; any vegetable used as food. Usually in *plural*. **2** L17 A leguminous plant. **3** L18 The pod or seed-vessel of a leguminous plant.

■ The Latin word *legumen* was used earlier (LME) in English and is found, though not so commonly, in all three senses above.

Lehrjahr /ˈleːrjaːr/ *noun* plural **Lehrjahre** /ˈleːrjaːrə/ M19 **German** (from *lehr(en)* teach + *Jahr* years). A year of apprenticeship or learning.

■ Usually in the plural, the word is also often used figuratively for one's apprenticeship to life. Cf. WANDERJAHR.

lei /leɪ/ *noun 1* M19 **Hawaiian**. A Polynesian garland made of flowers, feathers, shells, etc., often given as a symbol of affection.

1996 *Times* The lure of the lei, that garland of welcome traditionally bestowed on visitors by bare-bosomed young hula dancers, is considerable.

lei /leɪ/ *noun 2* E20 **Chinese** (*léi*). *Chinese Antiquities* An urn-shaped bronze wine-vessel of the Shang period (*c.* 250 BC).

leitmotiv /ˈlʌɪtməʊtiːf/ *noun* (also **leitmotif**) L19 **German** (from *leit-* leading + *Motiv* motive). **1** L19 *Music* A theme associated throughout a work with a particular person, situation, or sentiment. **2** L19 *generally* A recurrent idea or image in a literary work etc.

1995 *Spectator* Gray finds in Berlin's 'value pluralism' the *leitmotif* of all his writings.

lekach /ˈlɛkax/ *noun* M20 **Yiddish**. A Jewish cake traditionally made with honey.

lekane /lɛˈkɑːni/ *noun* E20 **Greek** (*lekanē* a bowl, a dish). *Greek Antiquities* A shallow bowl, usually with handles and a cover.

lekker /ˈlɛkə/ *adjective* E20 **Afrikaans** (from Dutch (cf. German *lecker*) related to Dutch *likken* to lick). Pleasant, sweet, nice; good, excellent.

■ South African colloquial, used as a general term of approbation.

lekythos /ˈliːkɪθɒs/, /ˈlɛkɪθɒs/ *noun* plural **lekythoi** /ˈliːkɪθɔɪ/ M19 **Greek** (*lēkuthos*). *Greek Antiquities* A vase or flask with a narrow neck.

■ Also in the Late Latin form *lecythus* (M19).

lemma /ˈlɛmə/ *noun* plural **lemmas, lemmata** /ˈlɛmətə/ L16 **Latin** (from Greek *lēmma*, plural *lēmmata*, something taken for granted or assumed, theme, argument, title, from base also of *lambanein* to take). **1** L16 An axiom or demonstrated proposition used in an argument or proof. **2** E17 The argument or subject of a literary work, prefixed as a heading. Also, a motto attached to a picture etc. **3** M20 A word or phrase defined in a dictionary, glossed in a glossary, entered in a word-list, etc.

lemur /ˈliːmə/ *noun* plural (in sense 1) **lemures** /ˈlɛmjʊriːz/, (in sense 2) **lemurs** M16 **Modern Latin** (from Latin *lemures* (plural) shades of the dead). **1** M16 Chiefly *Roman Mythology* In *plural*, the spirits of the dead, ghosts. Now occasionally *singular*, a ghost. **2** L18 *Zoology* Any mammal of the prosimian family Lemuridae, comprising long-tailed, sharp-muzzled, arboreal animals found chiefly in Madagascar. Also, any related primate, as the indri and the loris.

lentamente /lɛntəˈmɛnti/ *adverb* M18 **Italian** (from *lento* from Latin *lentus* slow). *Music* Slowly, in slow time.

lente /ˈlɛnti/ *adjective* M20 **Latin** (= slowly). *Medicine* Of a substance, especially insulin: that is metabolized or absorbed gradually when introduced into the body.

lento /ˈlɛntəʊ/ *adverb & adjective* E18 **Italian**. **1** *adverb & adjective* E18 *Music* (A direction:) in slow time, slower than adagio. **2** *adjective* M20 Pronounced more slowly than in normal speech.

leprechaun /ˈlɛprəkɔːn/ *noun* E17 **Irish** (*leipreachán* alteration of Middle Irish *luchrupán* alteration of Old Irish *luchorpán*, from *lu* small + *corp* body). In Irish folklore, a small, usually mischievous being of human form, often associated with shoemaking or buried treasure.

lèse-majesté /lɛzmaʒɛste/ *noun* (also **lese-majesty** /liːzˈmadʒɪsti/) LME **French** (from Latin *laesa majestas* hurt or violated majesty (i.e. of the sovereign people), from *laesa* feminine past participle of *laedere* to injure, hurt, *majestas* majesty). **1** LME The insulting of a monarch or other ruler. Also, treason. **2** M17 *transferred* Presumptuous behaviour, disrespect.

■ *Lese-* or *lèse-* is also used with other French or English words in jocular imitation of *lese-majesty* or *lèse-majesté* (see quotation 1995 (2)).

1 1995 *Times* [Wei Jingsheng] was brazen enough to write to Mr Deng and denounce him as a man 'who will be laughed at and condemned by history'. Such lèse-majesté is deeply wounding.

2 1996 *Times Les Enfants [du Paradis]* really is one of the best movies ever made ... So the stage version got a panning for *lèse-majesté* ...

2 1995 *Spectator* To suppress or control such emotions is to be guilty of absurd and psychologically unhealthy stiff-upper-lippism; it is to commit the terrible crime of *lese-psychotherapie*.

le tout /lə tu/ *adjective phrase* E20 **French**. The whole of, everyone in, all, (a place).

■ Frequently used in a context of making fun of social pretensions. The word(s) defined by *le tout* may be French, on the analogy of (*le*) *tout Paris* all Paris (meaning 'Parisian society') or, in jocular use, more often English (see quotations). Cf. TOUT.

1995 *Spectator* I look forward to the day when *le tout Londres* goes to a lecture once a week as a matter of course . . .
1996 *Oldie* When *Cav* and *Pag* were given by the Moldavian State Opera, *le tout* gentrified Hackney and Islington attended.

lettre /lɛtr/ *noun* plural pronounced same E18 **French** (from Latin *littera* letter of the alphabet, (*in plural*) epistle, document). A letter.

■ Occurs in English only in various phrases mainly designating styles of handwriting: e.g. *lettre bâtard* a kind of cursive Gothic script originating in France in the late Middle Ages (also known as *bastarda*), *lettre de forme* a kind of formal, angular handwriting on which some typefaces for early printed books were based (also known as *textura*), and *lettre de somme* a kind of rounded Gothic script originating in thirteenth-century Italy on which some typefaces for early printed books were based (also known as *rotunda*).

lettre de cachet /lɛtr də kaʃe/ *noun phrase* plural **lettres de cachet** (pronounced same) E18 **French** (literally, 'letter of seal'). **1** *History* In France under the *ancien régime*, a warrant for the imprisonment of a person without trial at the pleasure of the monarch. **2** An (arbitrary) official order for imprisonment, exile, etc.

lettrisme /lɛtrism/ *noun* (also in Anglicized form **lettrism** /'lɛtrɪz(ə)m/) M20 **French** (from as LETTRE). A movement in French art and literature characterized by a repudiation of meaning and the use of letters (sometimes invented) as isolated units.

levade /lə'vɑːd/ *noun* M20 **French** (from *lever* to raise). A dressage movement (superseding the *pesade*) in which the horse raises its forequarters with the forelegs drawn up, and balances on its hind legs which are placed well forward under the body and deeply bent.

levee /'lɛvi/, /'lɛveɪ/ *noun 1* L17 **French** (*levé* variant of *lever* rising, use as noun of *lever* to rise). **1 a** L17 *History* A reception of visitors on rising from bed; a morning assembly held by a person of distinction. **b** M18 *History* An afternoon assembly for men only held by (a representative of) the British monarch. **c** M18 A reception or assembly at any time of day. Now *archaic* except in *North America*. **2** The company assembled at a levee. Only in 18. **3** E18–E19 The action of rising, *specifically* from one's bed.

■ The less fashionable evening equivalent of sense 1 was the COUCHEE.

levee /'lɛvi/, /lɪ'viː/ *noun 2 & verb* E18 **French** (*levée* feminine of *levé* past participle of *lever* to raise). **A** *noun* **1** E18 An embankment to prevent the overflow of a river. **b** L19 *Physical Geography* A low broad ridge of sediment running alongside a river channel. Also, any similar natural embankment, as one formed by a mud flow, lava flow, or submarine current. **2** M19 A landing-place, a pier, a quay. **B** *transitive verb* M19 Raise a levee or embankment along (a river) or in (a district). Also, shut or keep *off* by means of a levee.

levée en masse /ləve ɑ̃ mas/ *noun phrase* plural **levées en masse** (pronounced same) E19 **French**. A mass mobilization (originally in Revolutionary France) in response to the threat of invasion.

lever de rideau /ləve də rido/ *noun phrase* plural **levers de rideau** (pronounced same) M19 **French** (= curtain-raiser). A short opening piece before the main perfomance; a preliminary event.

lex domicilii /ˌlɛks dɒmɪ'sɪlɪʌɪ/ *noun phrase* E19 **Latin** (= law of the domicile). *Law* The law of the country in which a person is domiciled, as determining the right to make a will, succeed to property, etc.

lex fori /lɛks 'fɔːrʌɪ/ *noun phrase* E19 **Latin** (= law of the court). *Law* The law of the country in which an action is brought, as regulating procedure, evidence, execution of judgements, etc.

lexis /'lɛksɪs/ *noun* M20 **Greek** (= a word, phrase, from *legein* to speak). **1** M20 The diction or wording, in contrast to other elements, of a piece of writing. **2** M20 *Linguistics* Items of lexical, as opposed especially to grammatical, meaning; the total word-stock of a language. Also, the branch of knowledge that deals with words as lexical items.

lex loci /lɛks 'ləʊsʌɪ/ *noun phrase* L18 **Latin** (= law of the place). *Law* The law of the country in which some event material to a case took place.

■ Frequently followed by a defining word or phrase, as in *lex loci contractus* the law of the country in which a contract was made or *lex loci delicti* the law of the country in which an offence was committed.

lex talionis /ˌlɛks talɪˈəʊnɪs/ *noun phrase* M17 **Latin** (from *lex* law + *talionis* genitive of *talio(n)* recompense). The (supposed) law of retaliation; the retributive theory of punishment, based on the Mosaic principle 'an eye for an eye, a tooth for a tooth'.

li /liː/ *noun 1* L17 **Chinese** (*lǐ*). In Neo-Confucianism: correct observance of the rules governing behaviour to others, regarded as needed to maintain a person's harmony with the moral principles of nature.

li /liː/ *noun 2* plural same M20 **Chinese** (*lǐ*). *Chinese Antiquities* A bronze or pottery cooking vessel, with (usually three) hollow legs.

liaison /lɪˈeɪz(ə)n/, /lɪˈeɪzɒn/, /lɪˈeɪzɒ̃/ *noun* M17 **French** (from *lier* to bind, from Latin *ligare*). **1** M17 *Cookery* A binding or thickening agent for sauces, consisting chiefly of the yolks of eggs. Formerly, the process of binding or thickening. **2** E19 An intimate relation or connection; *specifically* an illicit sexual relationship, especially between a man and a married woman. **3** E19 Communication and cooperation, original *specifically* between military forces or units, especially during a battle or campaign. **4** L19 *Phonetics* The pronunciation of a normally silent final consonant before a vowel (or mute *h*) beginning the following word, especially in French.

■ In sense 2 sometimes in the phrase *liaison dangereuse* (literally, 'dangerous acquaintance'), an allusion to the brilliant and scandalous epistolary novel *Les Liaisons dangereuses* (1782) by Pierre Laclos.

1996 *Times* The Auld Alliance is the Sunday name for the long flirtation between France and Scotland which, like all *liaisons dangereuses*, has provided the spice to keep the main marriage successful.

libero /ˈliːbero/ *noun* plural **liberi** /ˈliːberi/ M20 **Italian** (literally, 'free'). *Soccer* A defending player positioned near the goal, a sweeper.

liberum arbitrium /ˌliːbərʊm ɑːˈbɪtrɪəm/, /ˌlʌɪbərəm/ *noun phrase* M17 **Latin** (= free judgement, free will). Full power to decide; freedom of action.

■ A quotation from Livy's history of Rome (iv.43.5).

libido /lɪˈbiːdəʊ/, /lɪˈbʌɪdəʊ/ *noun* E20 **Latin** (= desire, lust). *Psychoanalysis* Psychic drive or energy, *especially* that associated with the sexual instinct.

1996 *Times* Loss of libido is only one cause of failing potency. More often the spirit is willing but the mechanism has failed naturally.

libretto /lɪˈbrɛtəʊ/ *noun* plural **librettos**, **libretti** /lɪˈbrɛti/ M18 **Italian** (diminutive of *libro* book). The text of an opera or other long vocal composition.

lidia /ˈlidja/ *noun* L19 **Spanish** (literally, 'fight'). A bullfight, especially the earlier stages in which the CUADRILLA prepares the bull for the FAENA.

lidiador /ˌlidjaˈdor/ *noun* plural **lidiadores** /ˌlidjaˈdores/ L19 **Spanish**. A bullfighter.

lido /ˈliːdəʊ/, /ˈlʌɪdəʊ/ *noun* plural **lidos** L17 **Italian** (= shore, beach, from Latin *litus*). A bathing beach; a resort; a public open-air swimming pool.

■ Originally specifically *the Lido*, a bathing beach near Venice.

lié /lje/, /ˈliːeɪ/ *predicative adjective* M19 **French** (past participle of *lier* to bind). Connected (*with*), intimately acquainted (*with*).

liebchen /ˈliːpçən/, /ˈliːbtʃ(ə)n/ *noun* (also **Liebchen**) L19 **German**. A person who is very dear to another; a sweetheart, a pet, a darling.

■ Frequently used as a term of endearment.

Liebestod /ˈliːbəstoːt/ *noun* (also **liebestod**) L19 **German** (literally, 'love's death'). An aria or a duet in an opera etc. proclaiming the suicide of lovers; such a suicide.

liebling /ˈliːplɪŋ/, /ˈliːblɪŋ/ *noun* (also **Liebling**) M19 **German**. A sweetheart. Cf. LIEBCHEN.

lied /liːd/, /liːt/ *noun* plural **lieder** /ˈliːdə/ (also **Lied**) M19 **German**. A song; *especially* a song characteristic of the German Romantic period, usually for solo voice with piano accompaniment.

lien /liːn/, /ˈliːən/, /ˈlʌɪən/ *noun* M16 **French** (from Old French *loien* from Latin *ligamen* bond, from *ligare* to tie). *Law* A right to retain possession of property belonging to another person until a debt due by that person is discharged.

■ Often in the expression *have a lien on (something)*, used both literally and figuratively.

lierne /lɪ'əːn/ *noun* LME **French** (perhaps transferred use of *lierne* clematis, dialectal variant of *liane*). *Architecture* A short rib connecting the bosses and intersections of vaulting-ribs.

lieu /ljuː/, /luː/ *noun* ME **French** (from Latin *locus* place). Place, stead.

■ Only in *in lieu* 'in the place, instead, (*of*)'.

lignum vitae /ˌlɪgnəm 'vʌɪtiː/, /'viːtʌɪ/ *noun* L16 **Latin** (= wood of life). GUAIACUM (senses 1–3).

limaçon /'lɪməsɒn/ *noun* (also **limacon**) L16 **French** (= snail shell, spiral staircase, etc., from Old and modern French *limace* from Latin *limax, limac-* slug, snail). **1** A kind of spiral military manoeuvre. Only in L16. **2** L19 *Mathematics* A type of heart-shaped curve.

limbo /'lɪmbəʊ/ *noun* plural **limbos** LME **Latin** (ablative singular of *limbus* edge, border (in medieval Latin, border of Hell), in phrases like *in limbo*, *e* (= out of) *limbo*). **1** LME *Christian Church* A region supposed in some beliefs to exist on the border of Hell as the abode of the just who died before Christ's coming and of unbaptized infants. **b** L16–M17 Hell, Hades. **2** L16 Prison, confinement. *slang*. **3** M17 An unfavourable place or condition, likened to limbo; *especially* a condition of neglect or oblivion to which people or things are consigned when regarded as superseded, useless, or absurd; an intermediate or indeterminate condition; a state of inaction or inattention pending some future event.

limes /'lʌɪmiːz/ *noun* plural **limites** /'lʌɪmɪtiːz/ M16 **Latin** (= limit). Now *Archaeology* A boundary; *specifically* the boundary of the Roman Empire, especially in the north of Europe.

linctus /'lɪŋktəs/ *noun* L17 **Medieval Latin** ((classical Latin = licking, from *lingere* to lick), after late Latin *electuarium* electuary). A syrupy liquid medicine, now *especially* a soothing cough mixture.

linga /'lɪŋgə/ *noun* (also **lingam** /'lɪŋgam/) E18 **Sanskrit** (*liṅga* sign, (sexual) characteristic; variant influenced by Tamil *iliṅkam*). A Hindu sacred object constituting a symbol of the god Siva, *specifically* (the representation of) a phallus.

ling chih /'lɪŋ dʒə/ *noun phrase* E20 **Chinese** (*língzhī* (Wade–Giles *ling chih*), from *ling* divine + *zhī* fungus). A motif on Chinese ceramic ware, especially a representation of the fungus *Polyporus lucidus*, symbolizing longevity or immortality.

lingerie /lãʒ(ə)ri/, *foreign* /lɛ̃ʒri/ *noun* M19 **French** (from *linge* linen). Originally, linen articles collectively; all the articles of linen, lace, etc., in a woman's wardrobe or trousseau. Now, women's underwear and nightclothes.

lingoa geral variant of LINGUA GERAL.

lingua franca /ˌlɪŋgwə 'fraŋkə/ *noun phrase* plural **lingua francas**, **lingue franche** /ˌlɪŋgwɪ 'fraŋki/ L17 **Italian** (= Frankish tongue). A mixture of Italian with French, Greek, Arabic, Turkish, and Spanish, used in the Levant (now *historical*). Also, any language serving as a medium between different nations etc. whose own languages are not the same; a system of communication providing mutual understanding.

■ 'Frank', in many local variants, was the word generally used by the inhabitants of the eastern Mediterranean region for a person of western or northern European origin—not only a Frenchman.

lingua geral /ˌlɪŋgwə dʒə'rɑːl/ *noun phrase* (also **lingoa geral**) M19 **Portuguese** (*língua geral* general language). A trade language based on Tupi and used as a LINGUA FRANCA in Brazil.

lingue franche plural of LINGUA FRANCA.

linguine /lɪŋ'gwiːni/ *noun plural* M20 **Italian** (plural of *linguina* diminutive of *lingua* tongue, from Latin). Pasta in the form of tongue-shaped ribbons; an Italian dish consisting largely of this and usually a sauce.

Linzertorte /'lɪntsərtɔrtə/, /'lɪntsətɔːtə/ *noun* plural **Linzertorten** /'lɪntsərtɔrt(ə)n/ E20 **German** (from *Linzer* adjective of the Austrian city *Linz* + *Torte* tart, pastry, cake). A kind of pastry with a jam filling, decorated on top with strips of pastry in a lattice pattern.

liqueur /lɪ'kjʊə/ *noun* M18 **French** (= liquor). **1** M18 Any of various strong sweet alcoholic spirits flavoured with aromatic substances, usually drunk after a meal.

Also, a glass of such a drink. **2** E20 *elliptically* A liqueur-glass; a liqueur chocolate.

lisse /li:s/ (*plural same*) *noun & adjective* M19 **French** (= smooth (in *crêpe lisse*)). (Of) a kind of silk or cotton gauze.

lissoir /'li:swɑ:/, *foreign* /liswar/ (*plural same*) *noun* E20 **French** (from *lisser* to smooth). *Archaeology* A smoothing, polishing tool.

literae humaniores /ˌlɪtərʌɪ hju:ˌmanɪ'ɔ:ri:z/ *noun phrase* (also **litterae humaniores**) M18 **Latin** (= more humane letters). The humanities, secular learning as opposed to divinity; *especially* at Oxford University, the school or subject of Greek and Roman classical literature, philosophy, and ancient history.

■ Abbreviated as *lit. hum.*

litera scripta /ˌlɪtərə 'skrɪptə/ *noun phrase* M19 **Latin**. The written word.

literati /lɪtə'rɑ:ti:/ *noun plural* E17 **Latin** (*lit(t)erati* plural of *lit(t)eratus* literate). Men of letters; the learned class as a whole.

1996 *Spectator* . . : much of his [sc. Larbaud's] best writing is taken up with the subject of getting away from France, a variant on the theme currently much canvassed by American campus literati under the label 'otherness'.

literatim /lɪtə'reɪtɪm/, /lɪtə'rɑ:tɪm/ *adverb* M17 **Medieval Latin** (*lit(t)eratim*, from *lit(t)era* letter, after *gradatim* step by step; cf. VERBATIM). Letter for letter; literally.

literato /lɪtə'rɑ:təʊ/ *noun singular* (corresponding plural LITERATI) E18 **Italian** (*litterato* (now usually *letterati*) from as Latin *lit(t)eratus* literate). A member of the literati; a man of letters.

litotes /lʌɪ'təʊti:z/ *noun* L16 **Late Latin** (from Greek *litotēs*, from *litos* single, simple, meagre). *Rhetoric* Ironical understatement, *specifically* in which an affirmative is expressed by the negative of the contrary.

■ Examples of this figure of speech are 'no small amount' and 'no mean feat'. It is also called, less commonly, MEIOSIS.

litterae humaniores variant of LITERAE HUMANIORES.

littérateur /ˌlɪtərɑ:'tə:/, *foreign* /literatœr/ (*plural same*) *noun* E19 **French** (from Latin *litterator*). A writer of literary or critical works, a literary person.

litzendraht /'lɪtsəndrɑ:t/ *noun* E20 **German** (from *Litze* braid, cord, lace, strand + *Draht* wire). Wire composed of many fine strands twisted together and individually insulated.

■ Also partially translated as Litz wire.

livraison /livrɛzɔ̃/ *noun* plural pronounced same E19 **French** (from Latin *liberatio(n-)* liberation). A part, number, or fascicle of a work published by instalments.

livre de chevet /livrə də ʃəvɛ/ *noun phrase* plural **livres de chevet** (pronounced same) E20 **French** (literally, 'book of the bed-head'). A bedside book; a favourite book.

1958 L. Durrell *Mountolive* It was Darley . . . who introduced me to the current Alexandrian *livre de chevet* which is a French novel called *Moeurs*.

livre de circonstance /livrə də sirkɔ̃stɑ̃s/ *noun phrase* plural **livres de circonstance** (pronounced same) M20 **French**. A book composed or adapted for the occasion.

1957 C. Vereker *Development of Political Theory* Begun as a *livre de circonstance*, Hooker's great work raised most of the abiding problems of political authority.

llanero /(l)ja'nero/, /ljɑ:'nɛ:rəʊ/ *noun* plural **llaneros** E19 **South American Spanish** (from next). An inhabitant of a llano.

llano /'(l)jano/, /'ljɑ:nəʊ/ *noun* plural **llanos** E17 **Spanish** (from Latin *planum* level ground). A level treeless plain in the south-western United States and the northern parts of South America.

loa /'ləʊə/ *noun* plural same, **loas** M20 **Haitian** (creole *lwa*, from Yoruba *oluwa* lord, owner). A god in the voodoo cult of Haiti.

lobo /'ləʊbəʊ/ *noun* plural **lobos** M19 **Spanish** (from Latin *lupus* wolf). A large grey wolf of the south-western United States. Also called *loafer* (*wolf*).

lobola /lə'bəʊlə/ *noun* (also **lobolo** /lə'bəʊləʊ/) M19 **Bantu** (cf. Xhosa *lobola* to give a bride-price). The bride-price, usually in cattle, given by many Black grooms in southern Africa to the parent or guardian of the bride; the custom of paying such a bride-price.

locale /ləʊ'kɑ:l/ *noun* (also **local**) L18 **French** (*local* (noun), respelt to indicate stress; cf. MORALE). A place, a locality, especially with reference to some event or circumstances connected with it; a venue.

loc. cit. /ˌlɒk 'sɪt/ *adverb phrase* M19 **Latin** (abbreviation of Latin *loco citato* or *locus citatus* (in) the place cited). In the book etc. that has previously been quoted, in the passage already cited.

loch /lɒk/, /lɒx/ *noun* LME **Gaelic**. In Scotland: a lake; (more fully *sea loch*) an arm of the sea, especially when narrow or partially land-locked.

loci classici, **loci desperati** etc. plurals of LOCUS CLASSICUS, LOCUS DESPERATUS, etc.

loco /'ləʊkəʊ/ *noun & adjective* L19 **Spanish** (= insane). **A** *noun* plural **loco(e)s**. **1** L19 Any of several leguminous plants (chiefly species of *Astragalus*) found in the western and south-western United States which cause loco disease when eaten by cattle, horses, etc. **2** L19 Loco disease.

loco citato see LOC. CIT.

locoum variant of LOKUM.

locum /'ləʊkəm/ *noun 1* E20 **Latin** (abbreviation of medieval Latin *locum tenens* from Latin *locum* accusative of *locus* place + *tenens* present participle of *tenere* to hold). **1** E20 A person (especially a physician or priest) who undertakes the professional duties of someone else or stands in for someone else during his or her absence. **2** E20 The situation of a locum; a post as a locum.

■ *Locum tenens*, now entirely superseded in everyday English usage, antedated *locum* in both sense 1 (from M17) and sense 2 (from L19).

locum noun 2 variant of LOKUM.

locus /'ləʊkəs/, /'lɒkəs/ *noun* plural **loci** /'ləʊsʌɪ/, /'lɒkiː/ E18 **Latin** (= place). **1** E18 A place, a site; a position, a point, especially in a text. **b** E20 *Genetics* A position on a chromosome at which a particular gene is located; a gene. **2** E18 *Mathematics* The curve or other figure composed of all the points which satisfy a particular equation or are generated by a point, line, or surface moving in accordance with defined conditions. **3** M18 A subject, a topic. **4** E20 LOCUS STANDI.

locus citatus see LOC. CIT.

locus classicus /ˌləʊkəs 'klasɪkəs/, /ˌlɒkəs/ *noun phrase* plural **loci classici** /ˌləʊsʌɪ 'klasɪsʌɪ/, /ˌlɒkiː 'klasɪkiː/ M19 **Latin** (= classical place). A passage regarded as the principal authority on a subject or the origin of a quotation or saying; the best-known occurrence of an idea or theme.

1996 *Times* You would certainly not suspect from this . . . production . . . that Strindberg's preface to *Miss Julie* is a *locus classicus* of naturalist theory.

locus desperatus /ˌləʊkəs dɛspə'reɪtəs/, /ˌlɒkəs dɛspə'rɑːtəs/ *noun phrase* plural **loci desperati** /ˌləʊsʌɪ dɛspə'reɪtʌɪ/, /ˌlɒkiː dɛspə'rɑːtiː/ E20 **Latin** (= hopeless place). A corrupt manuscript reading that defies interpretation.

1969 R. Renehan *Greek Textual Criticism* The textual critic . . . must decide in each case whether the original reading . . . has been or can be recovered by modern conjecture or whether the passage is a *locus desperatus*.

locus poenitentiae /ˌləʊkəs piːnɪ'tɛnʃiː/, /ˌlɒkəs piːnɪ'tɛnʃɪʌɪ/ *noun phrase* plural **loci poenitentiae** /ˌləʊsʌɪ piːnɪ'tɛnʃiː/, /ˌlɒkiː piːnɪ'tɛnʃɪʌɪ/ M18 **Latin** (= place of penitence). A place of repentance; *Law* an opportunity for a person to withdraw from a commitment or contract, especially an illegal one, so long as some particular step has not been taken.

locus standi /ˌləʊkəs 'standʌɪ/, /ˌlɒkəs 'standiː/ *noun phrase* plural **loci standi** /ˌləʊsʌɪ 'standʌɪ/, /ˌlɒkiː 'standiː/ E19 **Latin** (= place of standing). A recognized or identifiable status, especially in law; the right to be heard in a court of law.

1974 *Times* The power of the Department [sc. of Trade and Industry] should of course be discretionary but the Panel should be given a *locus standi* with the Department.

loden /'ləʊd(ə)n/ *noun & adjective* (also **Loden**) E20 **German**. **A** *noun* **1** E20 A heavy waterproof woollen cloth. **2** M20 A coat or cloak made of this. **3** M20 A dark green colour in which the cloth is often made. **B** *adjective* E20 Made of this cloth.

loess /'ləʊɪs/, /lɜːs/ *noun* M19 **German** (*Löss* from Swiss German *lösch* loose, from *lösen* to loosen). *Geology* A fine yellowish-grey loam composed of material transported by the wind during and after the glacial period which forms extensive deposits from north central Europe to eastern China, in the American Midwest, and elsewhere.

loge /lɔʒ/ (*plural same*), /ləʊʒ/ *noun* M18 **French**. **1 a** M18 A booth, a stall. **b** M20 A concierge's lodge. **2** M18 A box in a theatre, opera-house, etc.

loggia /ˈləʊdʒə/, /ˈlɒdʒə/, /ˈləʊdʒɪə/ *noun* M18 **Italian** (= lodge). **1** M18 A gallery or arcade having one or both of its sides open to the air. **2** E20 An open-sided extension to a house, a veranda.

Logos /ˈlɒgɒs/ *noun* L16 **Greek** (= account, relation, ratio, reason(ing), argument, discourse, saying, speech, word, related to *legein* to choose, collect, gather, say). **1** L16 *Philosophy* and *Christian Theology* The Word of God, the second person of the Trinity. **2** M17 A pervading cosmic idea or spirit of creativity or rationality.

■ Used in a mystic sense by Hellenistic and Neoplatonist philosophers, *Logos* entered Christian discourse primarily through its use in the opening passage of St John's Gospel.

Lohan /ˈləʊhɑːn/ *noun* M19 **Chinese** (*luóhàn* (Wade–Giles *Lo-han*)). An ARHAT.

lokoum variant of LOKUM.

lokshen /ˈlɒkʃ(ə)n/ *noun plural* L19 **Yiddish** (plural of *loksh* noodle). Noodles (in Jewish cookery).

lokum /lɒˈkuːm/ *noun* (also **lokoum**, **loc(o)um**, **lakum** /ləˈkuːm/) E20 **Turkish** (abbreviation of Turkish RAHAT *lokum*). Turkish delight.

loma /ˈləʊmə/ *noun* M19 **Spanish** (from *lomo* back, loin, ridge). In the south-western United States: a broad-topped hill or ridge.

longeron /ˈlɒndʒərɒn/ *noun* E20 **French**. *Aeronautics* A frame member running lengthways along a fuselage.

longo intervallo /ˌlɒŋgəʊ ɪntəˈvaləʊ/ *adverb phrase* L17 **Latin** (= at a distance). At some remove; in spite of the gulf between.

■ Virgil uses the phrase in the spatial sense (*Aeneid* v.320), but other Roman writers (e.g. Cicero) also used it in the temporal sense 'after a long time'.

1935 J. C. Masterman *Fate Cannot Harm Me* I remember asking him once . . . who were his literary idols among the moderns. 'Well,' he said, 'Max Beerbohm of course . . . and then, but *longo intervallo* P. G. Wodehouse.'

longueur /lɔ̃gœr/ (*plural same*), /lɔ̃(ŋ)ˈgəː/ *noun* L18 **French** (= length). A lengthy or tedious passage of writing, music, etc.; a tedious stretch of time.

1995 *Spectator* Looking back, *The Name of the Rose* bears up pretty well, although the longueurs seem much more like inexperience in pacing a novel than an engaging, wacky academic wanting to share an odd bit of information with the reader.

loofah /ˈluːfə/ *noun* (also **luffa** /ˈlʌfə/) L19 **Arabic** (*lūfa* the plant, *lūf* the species). A coarse sponge made from the bleached vascular system of the fruit of a tropical gourd, *Luffa aegyptiaca*, used to cleanse and scrub the skin. Also, the gourd itself.

loquitur /ˈlɒkwɪtə/ *intransitive verb* M19 **Latin** (3rd person singular present of *loquor* to speak). Speaks.

■ Used with the speaker's name added, as a stage-direction or to inform a reader. Abbreviated as *loq*.

lorgnette /lɔːnˈjɛt/, *foreign* /lɔrɲɛt/ (*plural same*) *noun* E19 **French** (from *lorgner* to squint, ogle). *singular* and in *plural* A pair of eyeglasses to be held in the hand, usually by a long handle. Also, a pair of opera-glasses.

■ *Lorgnon(s)* (M19), meaning 'a single eyeglass' as well as the above, is rather less common.

louche /luʃ/, /luːʃ/ *adjective* E19 **French** (= cross-eyed, squinting). Not straightforward. Now usually, dubious, shifty, disreputable.

1996 *Times* Enter that figure so beloved of late-Victorian dramatists, the siren with the louche past.

loup /lu/ *noun* plural pronounced same. M18 **French** (= wolf, from Latin *lupus*). **1** M18 The sea-bass, *Dicentrachus labrax*, found off the western European coast and in the Mediterranean. **2** M19 A light mask or half-mask for a woman's face.

■ In sense 2 the word was known earlier (L17) in the form *loo* or more fully *loo-mask*.

loup-garou /ˈluːgəruː/ *noun* L16 **French** (from *loup* wolf + *garou* (from Old High German antecedent of Middle High German *werwolf*) werewolf). A werewolf.

luau /ˈluːaʊ/ *noun* M19 **Hawaiian** (*lūʻau*). A Hawaiian party or feast usually accompanied by some form of entertainment.

lucus a non lucendo /ˌluːkʊs ɑː nɒn luːˈkɛndəʊ/, /ˌl(j)uːkʊs eɪ nɒnl(j)uːˈsɛndəʊ/ *noun phrase* E18 **Latin** (literally, 'a grove from its not shining', i.e. *lucus* (a grove) is derived from *lucere* (to shine) because there is no light there). A paradoxical or otherwise absurd derivation; something of which the qualities are the opposite of what its name suggests.

■ Also abbreviated *lucus a non*. The phrase is discussed by the Roman rhetorician Quintilian in his *Institutio Oratoria* (i.6.34).

1958 R. Liddell *Morea* Was its name Hydraea (watery), a *lucus a non lucendo*—it is singularly waterless today.

ludo /ˈluːdəʊ/, /ˈljuːdəʊ/ *noun* L19 **Latin** (= I play). A simple board game played with dice and counters.

lues /ˈluːiːz/, /ˈljuːiːz/ *noun* M17 **Latin** (= plague). Syphilis (also more fully *lues venerea* /vəˈnɪərɪə/). Formerly also, a plague, a pestilence.

■ *Lues* also appears in a modern Latin phrase apparently coined by Macaulay who in 1834 wrote in the *Edinburgh Review* of the *Lues Boswellianae* or 'disease of admiration' that tends to afflict biographers writing uncritically about their subjects—as James Boswell did in his life of Dr Johnson.

luffa variant of LOOFAH.

luftmensch /ˈlʊftmɛnʃ/ *noun* (also **luftmensh**) plural **luftmens(c)hen** /ˈlʊft mɛnʃ(ə)n/ E20 **Yiddish** (*luftmensh*, from *luft* (German *Luft*) air + *mensh* (German *Mensch*) person). An impractical visionary.

1966 *New Society* Americans, children of the soil, have become traders in air, advertising men, *luftmenschen*.

luge /luːʒ/ *verb & noun* L19 **Swiss French**. **A** *intransitive verb* L19 Toboggan; ride or race on a luge. **B** *noun* E20 A light toboggan for one or two people usually ridden in a supine position; the sport in which these are raced.

lulav /ˈluːlɑːv/, /ˈlʊləv/ *noun* (also **lulab**) plural **lulavs**, **lulavim** /ˈluːlɑːvɪm/ L19 **Hebrew** (*lūlāḇ* branch). A palm branch traditionally carried at the Jewish festival of Succoth.

lumbago /lʌmˈbeɪgəʊ/ *noun* L17 **Latin** (*lumbago*, *lumbagino*, from *lumbus* loin). Rheumatic pain in the lower muscles of the back.

lumen siccum /ˌluːmɛn ˈsɪkəm/, /ˌljuːmɛn ˈsɪkəm/ *noun phrase* E17 **Latin** (literally, 'dry light'). The objective light of rational knowledge or thought.

■ Francis Bacon characterized rational knowledge as *lumen siccum* in 1605 in his *Advancement of Learning* (II.f.48), and the metaphor has been in intermittent use, especially among English philosophers, since then.

lumpenproletariat /ˌlʌmpənprəʊlɪˈtɛːrɪət/ *noun derogatory* E20 **German** (from *Lumpen* rag + PROLETARIAT). The poorest and least cohesive section of the proletariat, making no contribution to the workers' cause; the ignorantly contented lower orders of society uninterested in revolutionary advancement. *derogatory*.

■ Originally used by Karl Marx in *Die Klassenkämpfe in Frankreich* (1850).

1995 *Times* Which is preferable, to patronise 'ordinary people' with string quartets, or exploit them, treat them as a lumpenproletariat and ensure that they remain lumpen by depriving them of anything better?

lundum /ˈlʊndəm/ *noun* M20 **Portuguese**. A simple Portuguese song and dance originating from Africa, probably one of the sources from which the FADO developed.

lunette /luːˈnɛt/, /ljuːˈnɛt/ *noun* L16 **French** (diminutive of *lune* moon, from Latin *luna*). **1** L16 *Farriery* A semicircular horseshoe for the front of the hoof only. Also *lunette-shoe*. **2** E17 *Architecture* **a** An arched aperture in a concave ceiling for the admission of light. **b** E18 A crescent-shaped or semicircular space in a ceiling, dome, etc., decorated with paintings or sculptures; a piece of decoration filling such a space. **3** M17 A blinker for a horse. **4** L17 In *plural* Spectacles. Now *rare*. **5** E18 *Fortification* A work larger than a redan, consisting of two faces forming a salient angle and two flanks. **6** L18 The figure or shape of a crescent moon. **7** M19 A watch-glass of flattened shape. Also *lunette (watch-)glass*. **8** M19 In the guillotine, the circular hole which receives the neck of the victim. **9** M19 Any of the flues connecting a glass furnace and its arch. (Earlier in the form *linnet-hole*.) **10** M19 A crescent-shaped ornament. **11** L19 A ring or forked plate to or by which a field-gun carriage or other vehicle for towing is attached. **12** L19 *Roman Catholic Church* A circular case, fitting into an aperture in a monstrance, for holding the consecrated host. **13** M20 *Physical Geography* A broad shallow mound of wind-blown material along the leeward side of a lake or dry lake basin, especially in arid parts of Australia, and typically crescent-shaped with the concave edge along the lake shore.

lunula /ˈluːnjʊlə/ *noun* plural **lunulae** /ˈluːnjʊliː/ L16 **Latin** (diminutive of *luna* moon). **1** L16 *Geometry* A figure formed on a plane by arcs of two circles intersecting at two points, a lune. **2** E18 *Archaeology* A gold crescent-shaped neck ornament of the early Bronze Age. **3** E19 *Anatomy, Zoology,* and *Botany* A crescent-shaped mark or spot, *specifically* the pale area at the base of a fingernail, a lunule. **b** M19 *Anatomy* A crescent-shaped region of thin tissue on each side of the nodule on each cusp of a valve in the heart or aorta. **4** M19 *Conchology* The crescent-shaped depression in front of the umbo of a shell, a lunule.

lupara /lu'pɑ:ra/, /lu:'pɑ:rə/ *noun* M20 **Italian** ((slang), from *lupa* she-wolf). A sawn-off shotgun as used by the Mafia.

lustrum /'lʌstrəm/ *noun* plural **lustra** /'lʌstrə/, **lustrums** L16 **Latin** (originally, a purificatory sacrifice after a quinquennial census, later also, a period of five years: ultimate origin unknown). A period of five years.

lusus /'lu:səs/, /'lju:səs/ *noun* plural same /'lu:su:s/, **lususes** E17 **Latin** (*lusus naturae* a sport of nature). A freak of nature, an abnormal formation, a natural curiosity. In full *lusus naturae* /nə'tjʊəri:/, /nə 'tjʊərʌɪ/.

luthier /'lu:tɪə/, /'lju:tɪə/ *noun* L19 **French** (from *luth* lute). A maker of stringed instruments, *specifically* of the violin family.

luxe /lʌks/, /lʊks/ *noun* M16 **French** (from Latin *luxus* luxury). (A) luxury. Cf. DE LUXE.

lycée /lise/ (*plural same*), /'li:seɪ/ *noun* M19 **French** (from Latin LYCEUM). A State secondary school in France.

Lyceum /lʌɪ'si:əm/ *noun* L16 **Latin** (from Greek *Lukeion* (sc. *gumnasion* gymnasium) neuter of *Lukeios* epithet of Apollo (from whose neighbouring temple the Lyceum was named)). **1** L16 The garden at Athens in which Aristotle taught his philosophy; Aristotelian philosophy and its adherents. **2** E19 A LYCÉE. **3** E19 *United States History* (**lyceum**) An institution in which popular lectures were delivered on literary and scientific subjects. **4** L19 *Theatre* A theatre near the Strand in London, England. Used *attributively* to denote a melodramatic performance or style, formerly characteristic of this theatre.

Lyonnais /li:ə'neɪ/, *foreign* /ljɔnɛ/ *adjective* (feminine **Lyonnaise** /li:ə'neɪz/, *foreign* /ljɔnɛz/) E19 **French** (from *Lyon* the name of a city in south-east France). Of, pertaining to, or characteristic of the city of Lyons (Lyon) or the former province of Lyonnais, in France; *specifically* (*Lyonnaise*) in *Cookery*, designating food, especially sliced potatoes, cooked with onions or with white wine and onion sauce.

maar /mɑː/ *noun* plural **maars**, **maare** /ˈmɑːrə/ E19 **German** (dialect). **1** E19 (Usually **Maar**) A crater-lake in the Eifel district of Germany. **2** L19 *Geology* A broad low-rimmed usually lake-filled volcanic crater of a kind exemplified by the Eifel Maars.

maas /mɑːs/ *noun* (also in Zulu form **amasi** /əˈmɑːsi/) E19 **Afrikaans** (from Zulu (plural) *amasi* curdled milk). In South Africa: thick sour milk.

mabele /məˈbiːli/ *noun* E19 **Bantu** (cf. Zulu, Xhosa *ibele*, plural *amabele*). In South Africa: kaffir corn, *Sorghum bicolor* var. *caffrorum*; meal or porridge made from this.

macabre /məˈkɑːbr(ə)/, *foreign* /makabr/ *adjective* M19 **French** (Old French *macabré* adjective (modern *macabre*), perhaps alteration of *Macabé* Maccabaeus, Maccabee, with reference to a miracle play containing the slaughter of the Maccabees). Grim, gruesome.

■ In early use perhaps regarded as a proper name and introduced into English as a noun; the earliest (LME) instance of the phrase *daunce of Machabree* is in the title of one of Lydgate's works, but this usage has long been obsolete. The modern adjectival sense likewise originated in the phrase *dance macabre*, an Anglicized version of the French DANSE MACABRE. The deaths of seven Jewish brothers and their mother, tortured to death for their religion under Hellenistic rule in the second century BC, are narrated in the Apocrypha (2 Maccabees 7); the Western Christian Church honoured them as martyrs, with a feast day celebrated on 1 August.

macaroni /makəˈrəʊni/ *noun* plural **macaronies** L16 **Italian** (*mac(c)aroni*, later *maccheroni*, plural of *mac(c)arone*, *maccherone* from late Greek *makaria* barley food). **1** L16 Pasta in the form of tubes. **2** M18 A fop, a dandy. *obsolete* except *historical*. **3** E19 *History* A West Indian coin worth a quarter of a dollar or (later) one shilling. **4** M19 In full *macaroni penguin*. A penguin, *Eudyptes chrysolophus*, apparently so called from its orange crest. **5** M19 An Italian. *slang*. *derogatory*. **6** E20 Nonsense, meaningless talk. *slang* (chiefly *Australian*).

macchia /ˈmɑːkɪə/ *noun* E20 **Corsican Italian** (from Latin *macula* spot). **1** E20 MAQUIS vegetation. **2** *Art* In painting, a fleck or touch of paint. (See quotation.)

2 1988 K. Adler *Unknown Impressionists* The Macchiaoli were so named because of the extensive use they made of '*macchia*' (or, in French, the '*tache*'), the patch or touch which was seen in France in the 1860s to be a distinguishing feature of anti-academic painting.

macédoine /ˈmasɪdwɑːn/ *noun* E19 **French** (from *Macédoine* Macedonia, with reference to the diversity of peoples in the empire of Alexander the Great, King of Macedon). Mixed fruit or vegetables cut up into small pieces; *figurative* a medley, a mixture.

machair /ˈmakə/, /ˈmaxə/ *noun* L17 **Gaelic**. In Scotland: a flat or low-lying coastal strip of arable or grassland; land of this nature.

1996 *Country Life* Stand with your back to the sea on South Uist, where the most spectacular machair is to be found, and look inland across the vast, fenceless expanses . . .

mâche /mɑːʃ/ *noun* L17 **French**. Lamb's lettuce, corn-salad.

■ Originally Anglicized (only in plural) in the now obsolete form of *maches*.

macher /ˈmaxə/ *noun* M20 **Yiddish** (from German = maker, doer). A man of importance, a bigwig; a braggart. *United States*, frequently *derogatory*.

machete /məˈtʃɛti/, /məˈʃɛti/ *noun* (also **matchet** /ˈmatʃɪt/ and other variants) L16 **Spanish** (from *macho* hammer, from Latin *marcus*). A broad and heavy knife or cutlass, used, especially in Central America and the West Indies, as a tool or a weapon.

■ *Machete* has gained general currency in English in the twentieth century, superseding the Anglicized *matchet* and the other variants.

machismo /məˈtʃɪzməʊ/, /məˈkɪzməʊ/ *noun* M20 **Mexican Spanish** (from as MACHO). The quality of being macho; male virility, masculine pride; a show of this.

1996 *Times* Spanish Man seems to have changed as well, at a pace remarkable for a society which was once so steeped in *machismo*.

macho /ˈmatʃəʊ/ *noun & adjective* E20 **Mexican Spanish** (= male animal or plant, (as adjective) masculine, vigorous). **A** *noun* plural **machos** **1** E20 A man; *specifically* an assertively vigorous man. **2** M20 MACHISMO. **B** *adjective* Ostentatiously masculine, virile.

■ Originally United States.

B 1996 *Times* There is no merit in adopting a macho attitude regardless of its efficacy.

Macht-politik /ˈmaxtpɔlɪˌtiːk/ *noun* E20 **German** (from *Macht* power, strength + *Politik* policy, politics). Power politics; strength as a potential factor to use in gaining a desired result.

macramé /məˈkrɑːmi/ *noun & adjective* M19 **Turkish** (*makrama* handkerchief, tablecloth, towel from Arabic *miḳrama* bedcover, bedspread). **A** *noun* M19 A fringe, trimming, or lace of knotted thread or cord; knotted-work; the art of making this. **B** *attributive* or as *adjective* L19 Made of or by macramé.

macro /ˈmakrəʊ/ *noun & adjective* M20 **Greek** (*makro-* combining form of *makros* large, long). **A** *noun* plural **macros**. **1** M20 *Computing* A macro-instruction. **2** M20 *Photography* Macrophotography; a macro lens. **B** *adjective* M20 Macroscopic, large-scale; overall, comprehensive; *Chemistry* of macroanalysis; *Photography* pertaining to or used in macrophotography.

■ An independent use of the combining form found in numerous English words derived from Greek, particularly in scientific terminology; cf. MEGA. *Macro* is frequently contrasted, either explicitly or implicitly, with MICRO.

macron /ˈmakrɒn/ *noun* M19 **Greek** (*makron* neuter of *makros* long). A straight horizontal line (¯) written or printed over a vowel to indicate length or stress.

macula /ˈmakjʊlə/ *noun* plural **maculae** /ˈmakjʊliː/, **maculas** LME **Latin**. **1** LME Chiefly *Science* A spot, a stain; *Medicine* a permanent spot or stain in the skin. **2** M19 *Anatomy* Any of various structures which have the appearance of a spot.

■ The French word *macule* deriving from *macula* was also found in English in sense 1 (from L15).

Madame /madam/, /məˈdɑːm/, /ˈmadəm/ *noun* (also **madame, madam**) plural **Mesdames** /medam/, /mɛˈdam/, /meɪˈdam/ ME Old French. **I 1** ME Madam, my lady. **II 2 a** M16 Used as a title (preceding the surname) of or as a respectful form of address to a French married woman or (more widely) a married woman of any non-British nationality (corresponding to English *Mrs, Lady*, etc.), or in literal renderings of French speech. **b** L16 *French History* (A title of) a female member of the French royal family, *specifically* the eldest daughter of the French king or the dauphin (cf. MADEMOISELLE 3). **c** M19 Used as a title (preceding a name) by a businesswoman, fortune-teller, etc., especially to imply skill and sophistication, or foreign origin. **3** L16–M18 A woman usually addressed or referred to as 'Madame'; a French married woman; a Frenchman's wife.

■ As a title, usually abbreviated to *Mme*. The plural *Mesdames* (abbreviation *Mmes*) is also used as the plural of *Mrs*. The usual Anglicized version *madam* has also been current since the Middle Ages and is most generally used as a respectful form of address to a woman, although it has also evolved some derogatory associations (e.g. 'a spoilt or affected woman' (L16), 'a female brothel-keeper' (L19)).

madeleine /ˈmadleɪn/ *noun* M19 **French** (probably from *Madeleine* Paulmier, nineteenth-century French pastry-cook). A (kind of) small rich cake, in French cookery baked in a fluted tin, and in English cookery usually baked in a dariole mould and decorated with coconut and jam.

Mademoiselle /madmwazɛl/, /ˌmadəm wəˈzɛl/ *noun* (also **mademoiselle**) plural **Mesdemoiselles** /medmwazɛl/, /ˌmɛdm waˈzɛl/, /ˌmeɪdəmwəˈzɛl/, **Mademoiselles** /madmwazɛl/, /ˌmadəmwəˈzɛlz/ LME **Old French**. **1** LME Used as a title (preceding a name) of or as a respectful form of address to an unmarried Frenchwoman or (more widely) an unmarried woman of any non-British nationality (corresponding to English *Miss*), or in literal renderings of French speech. Also used as a respectful form of address to a French governess or a female French teacher in an English-speaking school. **2** M17 A woman usually addressed or referred to as '*Mademoiselle*'; an unmarried Frenchwoman; a French governess. **3** L17 *French History* (A title of) the eldest daughter of the eldest brother (known as '*Monsieur*') of the French king. Later, (a title of) the French king's eldest daughter or (if he had no daughter) the unmarried princess most closely related to him (cf. MADAME 2b). **4** L19 A croaker (fish), *Bairdiella chrysoura*, of the southern United States. Also called *silver perch, yellowtail*. *United States*.

■ As a title, usually abbreviated to *Mlle*.

madérisé /maderize/ *adjective* M20 **French** (past participle of *madériser*). Of wine: affected with the brown discoloration that afflicts white wines that have been stored too long or under unsuitable conditions.

Madonna /mə'dɒnə/ *noun* (also **madonna**) L16 **Italian** (from *ma* old unstressed form of *mia* my (from Latin *mea*) + *donna* lady (from Latin *domina*)). **1 a** L16 Used as a respectful form of address to an Italian woman, or in literal renderings of Italian speech. **b** E17 An Italian woman. *rare*. **2** M17 The or *the* Virgin Mary; a picture or statue of the Virgin Mary. **3** M19 A hairstyle in which the hair is parted in the centre and arranged smoothly on either side of the face, as in certain Italian representations of the Virgin Mary. More fully *Madonna braid*.

madrasah /mə'drasə/ *noun* (also **medresseh** /mɛ'drɛseɪ/ and other variants) M17 **Arabian** (*madrasa*, noun of place from *darasa* to study). A Muslim college.

madrigal /'madrɪg(ə)l/ *noun* L16 **Italian** (from medieval Latin *matricalis* mother: cf. medieval Latin *ecclesia matrix* mother church). **1** L16 A short lyrical love poem. **2** L16 *Music* A part-song for several voices, *specifically* one of a sixteenth- or seventeenth-century Italian style, arranged in elaborate counterpoint, and sung without instrumental accompaniment. Also, a fourteenth-century Italian pastoral song of several stanzas. **3** L16 *generally* A song, a ditty.

madrilene /madrɪ'li:n/, /madrɪ'lɛn/ *noun* E20 **French** ((*consommé à la*) *madrilène*, of or pertaining to Madrid). A clear soup usually served cold.

maelstrom /'meɪlstrəm/ *noun* L17 **Early Modern Dutch** ((now *maalstroom*), from *maalen* to grind, whirl round + *stroom* stream whence the Scandinavian forms (e.g. Swedish *malström*, Danish *malstrøm*). **1** L17 A great whirlpool, originally one in the Arctic Ocean off the west coast of Norway, formerly supposed to suck in and destroy all vessels that ventured near it. **2** M19 *figurative* A state of turbulence or confusion.

maestoso /mʌɪ'stəʊsəʊ/ *adverb, adjective, & noun* E18 **Italian** (= majestic, from *maestà* from Latin *majestas, majestatis* majesty). *Music* **A** *adverb & adjective* E18 (A direction:) majestic(ally). **B** *noun* plural **maestosos** L19 A majestic piece or movement.

maestrale /mʌɪ'strɑ:leɪ/ *noun* M18 **Italian** (from Latin *magistralis* (sc. *ventus* wind) from *magister* master; cf. MISTRAL). Any of several mainly north-westerly winds which blow in the Mediterranean, especially a summer wind in the Adriatic, and a winter wind, milder than a mistral, in the west.

maestria /mʌɪ'stri:ə/ *noun* L19 **Italian** (from Latin *magisterium*, from *magister* master). Skill, mastery.

maestro /'mʌɪstrəʊ/, *foreign* /ma'ɛstro/ *noun* plural **maestri** /'mʌɪstri:/, *foreign* /ma'ɛstri/, **maestros** E18 **Italian** (from Latin *magister* master). **1 a** E18 An expert in music; a great musical composer, teacher, or conductor. **b** M20 *transferred* A great performer or leader in any art, profession, etc. **2** E20 The MAESTRALE.

1.a 1996 *Spectator* I had some reservations about Bernard Haitink's conducting—unusually for him (normally the most cushioning of maestros) he seemed at times to be pushing too hard . . .

Mafia /'mafɪə/ *noun* (also **mafia**, **maffia**) M19 **Italian** ((Sicilian) = bragging, specifically hostility towards the law and its upholders, frequently as manifested in vindictive crimes). **1** M19 *the Mafia*, an organized secret society of criminals, originating in Sicily but now operating internationally, especially in the United States. **2** M20 *generally* Any group regarded as exerting a secret and often sinister influence.

2 1995 *Private Eye* Crofton himself is now in trouble with the council's race relations mafia having accused a black colleague . . . of failing to deal with these allegations.

Mafioso /mafɪ'əʊsəʊ/ *noun* plural **Mafiosi** /mafɪ'əʊsi/, **Mafiosos** feminine **Mafiosa** /mafɪ'əʊsə/ (also **mafioso**, **maffioso**) L19 **Italian** (from as MAFIA). A member or supporter of the Mafia or a mafia.

1996 *Times: Weekend* Adams's new thriller . . . is heavily laced with all the paraphernalia of the genre in the new world order, including post-Soviet Russian female mafiosi, a few mad generals . . .

Magen David /mɑ:ˌgɛn dɑ:'vi:d/ *noun phrase* E20 **Hebrew** (literally, 'shield of David' (king of Israel from *c.*1000 BC)). The Star of David, a six-pointed figure consisting of two interlaced equilateral triangles, used as a Jewish and Israeli symbol.

magi plural of MAGUS.

magma /ˈmagmə/ *noun* LME Latin (from Greek, from base of *massein* to knead). **1** LME–M19 The dregs remaining after a semi-liquid substance has been pressed or evaporated. **2** L17 A mixture of mineral or organic substances having the consistency of paste. Now *rare*. **3** M19 *Geology* A hot fluid or semifluid material beneath the crust of the earth or other planet, from which igneous rocks are formed by cooling and which erupts as lava.

Magna Carta /ˌmagnə ˈkɑːtə/ *noun phrase* (also **Magna Charta**) L15 Medieval Latin (literally, 'great charter'). The charter of English personal and political liberty obtained from King John in 1215; *transferred* any similar document establishing rights.

magna cum laude /ˌmagnə kʌm ˈlɔːdiː/, /ˌmagnɑː kʊm ˈlaʊdeɪ/ *adverb & adjective phrase* L19 Latin (literally, 'with great praise'). With or of great distinction; *specifically* (of a degree, diploma, etc.) of a higher standard than the average (though not the highest).

■ Chiefly North American; cf. CUM LAUDE, SUMMA CUM LAUDE.

magna mater /ˌmagnə ˈmeɪtə/, /ˈmɑːtə/ *noun phrase* plural **magnae matres** /ˌmagniː ˈmeɪtriːz/, /ˌmagnʌɪ ˈmɑːtreɪz/ E18 Latin (literally, 'great mother'). A mother-goddess; a fertility goddess.

magna opera see MAGNUM OPUS.

magnificat /magˈnɪfɪkat/ *noun* ME Latin (2nd person singular present indicative of *magnificare* to magnify. **1** ME (the *Magnificat*) A canticle forming part of the Christian liturgy at evensong and vespers, and comprising the hymn of the Virgin Mary in Luke 1:46–55 (in the Vulgate beginning *Magnificat anima mea Dominum*). Also, the music to which this is set. **2** E17 *transferred* A song of praise.

magnifico /magˈnɪfɪkəʊ/ *noun* plural **magnifico(e)s** L16 Italian ((adjective) = magnificent). A magnate (originally a Venetian one); a grandee.

magnum /ˈmagnəm/ *noun & adjective* L18 Latin (use as noun of neuter singular of *magnus* large). **A** *noun* **1** L18 A bottle for wine, spirits, etc., twice the standard size, now usually containing 1.5 litres; the quantity of liquor held by such a bottle. **2** M20 (Also *Magnum*) A Magnum revolver or cartridge (see sense **B** below). **3** M20 *Zoology* The section of a bird's oviduct which secretes albumen. **B** *attributively* or as *adjective* **1** M20 (Also *Magnum*) Of a cartridge: adapted so as to be more powerful than its calibre suggests. Of a gun: designed to fire such cartridges. **2** L20 Large, oversized.

■ In the United States, senses A.2 and B.1 are proprietary names.

B.2 1996 *New Scientist* All this, and much more, Lord Justice Scott relates in his magnum Arms-to-Iraq report published last month.

magnum opus /ˌmagnəm ˈəʊpəs/, /ˈɒpəs/ *noun phrase* (also **opus magnum**) plural **magnum opuses, magna opera** /ˌmagnə ˈəʊpərə/, /ˌmagnə ˈɒpərə/ L18 Latin (= great work). A great and usually large work of art, literature, etc.; *specifically* the most important work of an artist, writer, etc.

magus /ˈmeɪgəs/ *noun* (also **Magus**) plural **magi** /ˈmeɪdʒʌɪ/ ME Latin (from Greek *magos* from Old Persian *maguš*). **1** ME *History* A member of an ancient Persian priestly caste; *transferred* a magician, a sorcerer. **2** LME *the* (*three*) *Magi*, the three 'wise men' from the East who brought gifts to the infant Jesus (Matthew 2:1), a representation of these.

maharaja /ˌmɑː(h)əˈrɑːdʒə/, /ˌməhɑːˈrɑːdʒə/ *noun* (also **maharajah, maharaj** /ˌmɑː(h)əˈrɑːdʒ/, **Maharaja**) L17 Sanskrit (*mahārājā*, from *mahā* great + *rājan* RAJA). (The title of) an Indian prince of high rank.

maharani /ˌmɑː(h)əˈrɑːni/, /ˌməhɑːˈrɑːniː/ *noun* (also **maharanee, Maharani**) M19 Hindustani (*mahārāṇī*, from Sanskrit *mahā* great + *rājñī* RANEE). (The title of) the wife or widow of a maharaja.

maharishi /ˌmɑː(h)əˈrɪʃi/ *noun* (also **Maharishi**) L18 Sanskrit (alteration of Sanskrit *maharṣi*, from *mahā* great + *ṛṣi* holy man). (The title of) a Hindu sage; *generally* (the title of) a popular leader of spiritual thought. Cf. GURU.

mahatma /məˈhatmə/, /məˈhɑːtmə/ *noun* L19 Sanskrit *mahātman*, from *mahā* great + *ātman* soul). **1** L19 In the Esoteric Buddhism of members of the Theosophical Society: any of a class of people with preternatural powers, supposed to exist in the Indian subcontinent and Tibet; *transferred* a sage, an adept. **2** M20 (*Mahatma*) In the Indian subcontinent: (the title of) a revered person regarded with love and respect.

Mahdi /ˈmɑːdi/ *noun* E19 Arabic ((*al-*)*mahdī*, literally, 'he who is rightly guided', from passive participle of *hadā* to lead on the right way, guide aright). In Muslim belief:

the restorer of religion and justice who will rule before the end of the world; a claimant of this title.

■ The *Mahdi* best known to history was Muhammad Ahmad of Dongola in Sudan who proclaimed himself such in 1881 and launched a political and revolutionary movement which overthrew the Turco-Egyptian regime.

mah-jong /mɑːˈdʒɒŋ/ *noun* (also **mah-jongg**) E20 **Chinese** (dialect *ma jiang* sparrows). A game (originally Chinese) for four, played with 136 or 144 pieces called tiles, divided into five or six suits.

maillot /majo/ *noun* plural pronounced same L19 **French**. **1** L19 Tights. **2** E20 A tight-fitting, usually one-piece, swimsuit. **3** M20 A jersey, a top.

maiolica variant of MAJOLICA.

maison /mɛzɔ̃/ *noun* plural pronounced same M16 **French**. In France and French-speaking countries: a house; now usually a business (especially a fashion) house or firm.

■ See phrases below and PÂTÉ MAISON.

maison clos /mɛzɔ̃ kloz/ *noun phrase* M20 **French** (literally, 'closed house'). A brothel.

1939 E. Ambler *Mask of Dimitrios* Your *maison close* must have proved disappointing. The inevitable Armenian girls, of course.

maison de couture /mɛzɔ̃ də kutyr/ *noun phrase* E20 **French**. A fashion house.

1970 S. J. Perelman *Baby, it's Cold Inside* The rigors of squiring her through a score of *maisons de couture*, jewelers', and millinery shops were . . . unimaginable.

maison de passe /mɛzɔ̃ də pas/ *noun phrase* (also **maison-de-passe**) M20 **French** (literally, 'house of passage'). A house to which prostitutes can take clients.

1960 B. Marshall *Divided Lady* The hotel we drew up at eventually reminded me of a *maison-de-passe* I used to know in Barcelona.

maison de santé /mɛzɔ̃ də sɑ̃te/ *noun phrase* M19 **French** (literally, 'house of health'). A nursing home, *especially* one for the mentally ill.

1942 A. Bridge *Frontier Passage* We don't want him shut up in a *maison de santé* for spy mania.

maisonette /meɪzəˈnɛt/ *noun* L18 **French** (*maisonnette* diminutive of *maison* house). **1** L18 A small house. **2** E20 A part of a residential building which is occupied separately, usually on more than one floor.

maison tolérée /mɛzɔ̃ tɔlere/ *noun phrase* L19 **French** (literally, 'tolerated house'). A licensed brothel.

1970 K. Chesney *Victorian Underworld* Conditioned by her existence in a *maison tolérée*, . . . she was very much in the hands of the bawd to whom she was consigned.

maître /mɛːtr(ə)/ *noun* plural pronounced same L19 **French** (literally, 'master'). The title of or form of address to a French lawyer.

■ Also with the sense of 'instructor' in the phrases MAÎTRE D'ARMES and MAÎTRE DE BALLET; see also CHER MAÎTRE, MAÎTRE D'HÔTEL.

maître d' /mɛtr(ə) də/; /ˌmeɪtrə ˈdə/, /ˈdiː/ *noun phrase* (also **maître de**, /ˈdə/) plural **maîtres d'**, **maîtres de**, (pronounced same) L19 **French** (colloquial abbreviation of MAÎTRE D'HÔTEL). The manager of a hotel dining-room or restaurant, a head waiter.

1996 *Times* [Flowers] conducted with small, effete waves of his baton, like the maître d' of an upmarket restaurant waving his clients towards their table.

maître d'armes /mɛtr(ə) darm/ *noun phrase* L19 **French** (literally, 'master of arms'). A fencing instructor.

maître de ballet /mɛtr(ə) də balɛ/ *noun phrase* E19 **French**. *Ballet* Originally, the composer of a ballet who superintended its production and performance; now, a trainer of ballet dancers.

maître d'hôtel /mɛtr(ə) dotɛl/, /ˌmeɪtrə dəʊˈtɛl/ *noun phrase* plural **maîtres d'hôtel** (pronounced same) M16 **French** (literally, 'master of house'). **1** M16 A major-domo, a steward, a butler. **2** L19 A hotel manager. Now usually the manager of a hotel dining-room or restaurant, a head waiter.

maîtres d', **maîtres d'armes**, etc. plurals of MAÎTRE D', MAÎTRE D'ARMES, etc.

maîtresse en titre /mɛtrɛs ɑ̃ titr/ *noun phrase* (also **maîtresse-en-titre**, **maitresse en titre**) plural **maîtresses en titre** (*pronounced same*) M19 **French** (literally, 'mistress in name'). An official or acknowledged mistress.

1973 D. Chandler *Marlborough* Arabella [Churchill] was . . . combining the roles of maid-of-honour to the Duchess and *maîtresse-en-titre* to the Duke, to whom she bore several children.

maîtresse femme /mɛtrɛs fam/ *noun phrase* M19 **French**. A strong-willed or domineering woman.

1973 E. Hyams *Final Agenda* The widow was a *maîtresse femme* whose place in the hierarchy was three steps higher than that of her . . . husband.

maja /'maxa/ *noun* M19 **Spanish**. In Spain and Spanish-speaking countries: a woman who dresses gaily.

■ Best known in English in the titles of two of Goya's paintings, the *Naked Maja* and the *Clothed Maja*. The equivalent male term *majo* (M19) is less common.

Majlis /madʒ'lɪs/ *noun* (also **majlis**) E19 **Arabic** (= place of session, from *jalasa* to be seated). An assembly for discussion, a council; *specifically* the Parliament of any of various North African or Middle Eastern countries, especially Iran. Also, a reception room.

majolica /mə'jɒlɪkə/, /mə'dʒɒlɪkə/ *noun & adjective* (also **maiolica** /mə'jɒlɪkə/) M16 **Italian** (from the former name of the island of Majorca). **A** *noun* M16 A fine kind of Renaissance Italian earthenware with coloured decoration on an opaque white glaze; any of various other kinds of glazed Italian ware. Also, a modern imitation of this. **B** *attributive* or as *adjective* M19 Made of majolica.

majuscule /'madʒəskju:l/ *adjective & noun* E18 **French** (from Latin *majuscula* (*littera*) diminutive of *major* major). **A** *adjective* **1** E18 *Typography* Of a letter: capital. *rare*. **2** M19 *Palaeography* Of a letter: large (whether capital or uncial); pertaining to, of, or written in large lettering; designating or pertaining to a script having every letter bounded by the same two (imaginary) lines. **B** *noun* **1** E19 *Typography* A capital letter. *rare*. **2** M19 *Palaeography* A large letter, whether capital or uncial; (a manuscript in) large lettering or majuscule script.

makai /mə'kʌɪ/ *adverb & adjective* M20 **Hawaiian** (from *ma* toward + *kai* the sea). In Hawaii: in the direction of the sea, seaward.

makimono /makɪ'mono/, /makɪ'məʊnəʊ/ *noun* plural same, **makimonos** L19 **Japanese** (= something rolled up, a scroll). A Japanese scroll containing a narrative, usually in pictures with explanatory writing, designed to be examined progressively from right to left as it is unrolled. Cf. EMAKIMONO.

malade imaginaire /malad imaʒinɛr/ *noun phrase* plural **malades imaginaires** (pronounced same) E19 **French**. A person with an imaginary illness.

■ After the title of a play by Molière (1673).

maladif /maladif/ *adjective* M19 **French** (from *malade* sick, ill, from Proto-Romance, from Latin *male* badly + *habitus*, past participle of *habere* to have, hold). Sickly.

maladresse /maladrɛs/, /malə'drɛs/ *noun* E19 **French** (from *mal-* bad, ill + *adresse* skill, dexterity). Lack of dexterity or tact; awkwardness.

maladroit /'malədrɔɪt/ *adjective* L17 **French** (from *mal-* bad(ly) + *adroit* skilful). Lacking in adroitness or dexterity; awkward, bungling, clumsy.

1996 *Spectator* He has tried to introduce a sense of fun, though sometimes the tone is childishly maladroit . . .

mala fide /ˌmeɪlə 'fʌɪdi:/, /ˌmalə 'fi:deɪ/ *adverb & adjective phrase* E17 **Latin** (= with bad faith (ablative of next)). (Acting or done) in bad faith; insincere(ly), not genuine(ly).

mala fides /ˌmeɪlə 'fʌɪdi:z/, /ˌmalə 'fi:deɪz/ *noun phrase* L17 **Latin** (= bad faith). Chiefly *Law* Bad faith, intent to deceive.

mala in se plural of MALUM IN SE.

malaise /ma'leɪz/ *noun* M18 **French** (from Old French *mal* bad, ill (from Latin *malus*) + *aise* ease). A condition of bodily discomfort, *especially* one without the development of specific disease; a feeling of uneasiness. Frequently *figurative*.

1996 *Country Life* In his opening analysis of the Grecian malaise he describes how their cause is ruined by 'so many factions' . . .

malapropos /ˌmalaprə'pəʊ/ *adverb, adjective, & noun* (also **mal-à-propos** and other variants) M17 **French** (*mal à propos*, from *mal* ill + *à* to + *propos* purpose). **A** *adverb* M17 In an inopportune or awkward manner; at an inopportune or awkward time; inappropriately. **B** *adjective* E18 Inopportune, inappropriate. **C** *noun* M19 An inopportune or inappropriate thing.

malaria /mə'lɛ:rɪə/ *noun* M18 **Italian** (*mal' aria* = *mala aria* bad air). Originally, an unwholesome condition of the atmosphere in hot countries due to the exhalations of marshes, to which fevers were ascribed. Now (also *malaria fever*), any of a class of intermittent and remittent febrile diseases formerly supposed to result from this cause, but now known to be due to infection with parasitic protozoans of the genus *Plasmodium*, transmitted by the bite of a mosquito of the genus *Anopheles*.

mal de mer /mal də mɛr/ *noun phrase* L18 **French**. Seasickness.

mal du siècle /mal dy sjɛkl/ *noun phrase* E20 **French**. World-weariness, weariness of life, deep melancholy because of the condition of the world.

malebolge /malɪ'bɒldʒeɪ/, *foreign* /male 'bɒldʒe/ *noun* M19 **Italian** (*Malebolge*, from *male* feminine plural of *malo* evil + *bolge* plural of *bolgia* literally 'sack, bag'). A pool of filth; a hellish place or condition.

■ In literary use only. Malebolge was the name given in Dante's *Inferno* to the eighth circle in hell, consisting of ten rock-bound concentric circular trenches (see especially Canto xviii).

maleesh /'mɑːliːʃ/ *interjection & noun* E20 **Arabic** (colloquial) (*mā 'alē-š* never mind). **A** *interjection* E20 No matter! never mind! **B** *noun* M20 Indifference, slackness.

mal élevé /mal el(ə)ve/ *adjective phrase* (feminine **mal élevée**) L19 **French** (= badly brought up). Bad-mannered, ill-bred.

mal-entendu /malɑ̃tɑ̃dy/ *adjective & noun* E17 **French** (from *mal* ill + *entendu* past participle of *entendre* to hear, understand). **A** *adjective* Mistaken, misapprehended. Only in E17. **B** *noun* (plural pronounced same) L18 A misunderstanding.

malerisch /'mɑːlərɪʃ/ *adjective* M20 **German** (= painterly, from *Maler* painter). (Of painting) characterized more by the merging of colours than by a formal linear style; painterly.

■ A term used by Heinrich Wölfflin in his *Kunstgeschichtliche Grundbegriffe* (1915).

1955 *Times* This is . . . a resuscitation of the great malerisch tradition, which was rejected by those who thought they were following Cézanne.

malgré /malgre/ *preposition* E16 **French**. In spite of, notwithstanding.

mallee /'maliː/ *noun* M19 **Aboriginal**. Any of various low-growing eucalypts which have many slender stems rising from a large underground stock; scrub or thicket formed by such trees, typical of some arid parts of Australia.

malpais /ˌmalpɑː'iːs/ *noun* M19 **Spanish** (from *malo* bad + *país* country, region). Rugged or difficult country of volcanic origin. *United States*.

malum in se /ˌmaləm ɪn 'siː/, /'seɪ/ *noun & adjective phrase* plural of noun **mala in se** /'malə/ E17 **Medieval Latin** (= bad in itself). (A thing) intrinsically evil or wicked. *especially in legal contexts*.

mal vu /mal vy/ *adjective phrase* E20 **French** (literally, 'badly seen'). Held in low esteem, looked down on.

1958 L. Durrell *Mountolive* He is . . . rather an old-fashioned reactionary in his outlook, and is consequently rather *mal vu* by his brother craftsmen.

mamaloi /'mam(ə)lwɑː/ *noun* plural **mamalois**, same L19 **Haitian** (creole *mamalwa*, from *mama* mother + *lwa* LOA). A voodoo priestess. Cf. PAPALOI.

mama-san /'maməsan/ *noun* plural **mama-sans**, same M20 **Japanese** (from *mama* mother + SAN). In Japan and the Far East: a woman in a position of authority, *specifically* one in charge of a geisha-house; the mistress of a bar.

mambo /'mambəʊ/ *noun* plural **mambos** M20 **American Spanish** (probably from Haitian creole, from Yoruba, literally, 'to talk'). **1** M20 A kind of rumba, a ballroom dance of Latin American origin; a piece of music for this dance. **2** M20 A voodoo priestess.

mamzer /'mʌmzə/ *noun* (also **momser**, **momzer**, /'mɒmzə/) plural **mamzerim** /'mʌmzərɪm/, **mamzers** M16 **Late Latin** (from Hebrew *mamzēr*). A person conceived in a forbidden sexual union, especially as defined by rabbinical tradition.

■ In contemporary colloquial speech often used, like 'bastard', as a term of abuse or familiarity.

mana /'mɑːnə/ *noun* M19 **Maori**. Power, authority, prestige; *Anthropology* an impersonal supernatural power which can be associated with people or with objects and which can be transmitted or inherited.

■ Originally New Zealand.

1995 D. Lodge *Therapy* Actresses and production assistants and publicity girls and secretaries—all susceptible to the *mana* of a successful writer.

mañana /ma'ɲana/, /man'jɑːnə/ *adverb & noun* M19 **Spanish** (= morning, tomorrow (in this sense from Old Spanish *cras mañana*, literally, 'tomorrow early') ultimately from Latin *mane* in the morning). Tomorrow, (on) the day after today; (in) the indefinite future (from the supposed easy-going procrastination of Spain and Spanish-speaking countries).

1995 *Oldie* And . . . of course the damage would be paid for . . . *mañana*.

mancala /man'kɑːlə/ *noun* M19 **Arabic** ((colloquial) *mankala*, from *nakala* to remove, take away). A board game for two players, originally Arabic but now common throughout Africa and Asia, played on a special board with rows of holes or hollows.

mancando /man'kando/, /man'kandəʊ/ *adjective & adverb* E19 **Italian** (= lacking, failing). *Music* (A direction:) becoming even softer, dying away.

mandala /'mandələ/, /'mʌndələ/ *noun* M19 **Sanskrit** (*máṇḍala* disc, circle). A symbolic circular figure, usually with symmetrical divisions and figures of deities, etc., in the centre, used in Buddhism and other religions as a representation of the universe; *Jungian Psychology* an archetype of a similar circle, held to symbolize a striving for unity of self and completeness.

mandat /mɑ̃da/ (*plural same*), /'mandat/ *noun* M19 **French** (from Latin *mandatum* use as noun of neuter past participle of *mandare* to command, enjoin, entrust, from *manus* hand). **1** M19 *History* A paper money issued by the revolutionary government of France from 1796 to 1797. **2** L19 In France: a money order.

1939 E. Ambler *Mask of Dimitrios* I received here a letter from him enclosing a *mandat* for the three thousand francs.

mandolin /'mandəlɪn/ *noun* (also (the usual form in sense 2) **mandoline**) E18 **French** (*mandoline* from Italian *mandolino* diminutive of *mandola*). **1** E18 A musical instrument of the lute kind having from four to six paired metal strings stretched on a deeply-rounded body, usually played with a plectrum. **2** M20 A kitchen utensil fitted with cutting blades and used for slicing vegetables.

mandorla /man'dɔːlə/ *noun* L19 **Italian** (= almond). An almond-shaped panel or decorative space in religious art.

manège /ma'neɪʒ/ *noun* (also **manege**) M17 **French** (from Italian *maneggio* from *maneggiare* from Proto-Romance from Latin *manus* hand). **1** M17 A riding-school. **2** L18 The movements in which a horse is trained in a riding-school; the art or practice of training and managing horses; horsemanship.

manes /'mɑːneɪz/, /'meiniːz/ *noun* LME **Latin**. **1** LME *plural* The deified souls of dead ancestors (as beneficent spirits). **2** L17 *singular* The spirit or shade of a dead person, considered as an object of reverence or as demanding to be propitiated.

manga /'maŋgə/ *noun 1* E19 **Spanish** (literally, 'sleeve', from Latin *manica*). A Mexican and Spanish-American cloak or poncho.

manga /'maŋgə/ *noun 2* L20 **Japanese**. A Japanese comic book or strip.

1996 *Independent* The biggest trend, though, is the continual advance of the Japanese manga, and lately, the first co-operations between Japanese publishers and western artists.

mange-tout /'mɑ̃ʒtuː/, /mɑ̃ʒ'tuː/ *noun* plural same, **mange-touts** (pronounced same) E19 **French** (literally, 'eat-all'). A variety of pea of which the pods are eaten whole with the seeds they contain. Also *mange-tout pea*. Also called *sugar pea* or *sugar snap*.

manicotti /manɪ'kɒti/ *noun plural* M20 **Italian** (plural of *manicotto* sleeve, muff). Large tubular pasta shells; an Italian dish consisting largely of these and usually a sauce.

maniéré /manjere/ *adjective* M18 **French**. Affected or characterized by mannerism, mannered.

manière criblée /manjɛr krible/ *noun phrase* E20 **French**. CRIBLÉ engraving.

manifesto /manɪ'fɛstəʊ/ *noun* plural **manifestos**, **manifestoes** M17 **Italian** (from *manifestare* to show, display, from Latin *manifestus* from *manus* hand + *-festus* struck). A public declaration or proclamation; *especially* a printed declaration or explanation of policy (past, present, or future) issued by a monarch, State, political party or candidate, or any other individual or body of individuals of public relevance.

manna /'manə/ *noun* OE **Late Latin** (from Hellenistic Greek from Aramaic *mannā* from Hebrew *mān* corresponding to Arabic *mann* exudation of the tamarisk *Tamarix mannifera*). **I 1** OE The edible substance described as miraculously supplied to the Israelites in the wilderness (Exodus 16). **2** ME Spiritual nourishment, *especially* the Eucharist; something beneficial provided unexpectedly (frequently *manna from heaven*). **II 3** LME A sweet hardened flaky exudation obtained from the manna-ash and used as a mild laxative. Also, a similar exudation from other plants and certain insects. **4** LME–M18 (A grain of) frankincense. **5** L17–E18 *Chemistry* A fine white precipitate. **6** L18 The seeds of the floating sweet-grass, *Glyceria* *fluitans*, used as food. In full *Polish manna*.

mannequin /'manɪkɪn/, /'manɪkwɪn/ *noun* M18 **French** (from Dutch *manneken* diminutive of *man* man). **1** M18 A model of a human figure; an artist's lay figure; a dummy for the display of clothes etc. **2** E20 A woman (or occasionally a man) employed by a dressmaker, costumier, etc., to display clothes by wearing them; a model.

mano /'mano/, /'mɑːnəʊ/ *noun* plural **manos** /'manos/, /'mɑːnəʊz/ E20 **Spanish** (= hand). *Anthropology* A primitive hand-held stone implement, used in the Americas for grinding cereals etc.

mano a mano /ˌmɑːnəʊ ə 'mɑːnəʊ/ *foreign* /ˌmano a 'mano/ *adjective, adverb, & noun phrase* (also **mano-a-mano**) L20 **Spanish** (= hand to hand). **A** *adjective & adverb phrase* L20 Hand to hand; one to one; face to face. **B** *noun phrase* L20 A confrontation, a duel.

manoir /manwɑr/ *noun* plural pronounced same M19 **French**. A French manor-house; a country house built in the style of a French manor-house.

manqué /mɑ̃ke/, /'mɒŋkeɪ/ *adjective* (feminine **manquée**) L18 **French** (past participial adjective of *manquer* to lack). **1** *postpositive* L18 That might have been but is not, that has missed being. **2** *predicative* L18 Defective, spoilt, missing, lacking.

1 1996 *Times Magazine* The subway genius is probably . . . a writer manqué, since many of his chosen citations deal with creating literature.

manso /'manso/ *noun & adjective* plural **mansos** /'mansos/ M19 **Spanish**. (A person who or animal which is) meek, tame, or cowardly.

■ Especially in the context of bullfighting.

manta /'mantə/ *noun* L17 **Spanish** (= blanket). **1** L17 In Spain and Spanish-speaking countries: a wrap, a cloak. **2** M18 A very large tropical ray of the genus *Manta* or the family Mobulidae. More fully *manta ray*. Also called *devilfish*.

mantelletta /mantɪ'lɛtə/ *noun* plural **mantellettas**, **mantellette** /mantɪ'lɛti/ M19 **Italian** (probably from medieval Latin *mantelletum* from Latin *mantellum* mantle). *Roman Catholic Church* A sleeveless vestment reaching to the knees, worn by cardinals, bishops, and other high-ranking ecclesiastics.

mantilla /man'tɪlə/ *noun* E18 **Spanish** (diminutive of *manta* mantle). **1** E18 A light scarf, frequently of black lace, worn over the head and shoulders, especially by Spanish women. **2** M19 A small cape or mantle.

mantra /'mantrə/ *noun* (also (*rare*) **mantram** /'mantrəm/) L18 **Sanskrit** (literally, 'thought', from *man* to think). A sacred Hindu text or passage, *especially* one from the Vedas used as a prayer or incantation; in Hinduism and Buddhism, a holy name or word, for inward meditation; *transferred* and *figurative* a repeated phrase or sentence, a formula, a refrain.

1995 *Spectator* The Princess 'just wants to be happy'. She wants everyone to be happy. We know this because she has said it time and time again, like a mantra.

manyatta /man'jatə/ *noun* E20 **Masai**. Among certain African peoples, especially the Masai: a group of huts forming a unit within a common fence.

manzanilla /manzə'nɪlə/, /manzə'niːljə/; *foreign* /manθa'ni(l)ja/, /mansa'ni(l)ja/ *noun* M19 **Spanish** (literally, 'camomile'). **1** M19 A kind of pale very dry sherry; a drink or glass of this. **2** E20 A variety of olive, distinguished by small thin-skinned fruit.

maquereau /makro/ *noun* plural **maquereaux** /makro/ L19 **French** (literally, 'mackerel'). A pimp.

■ Colloquial, also used as a term of abuse.

1971 D. Wallis *Bad Luck Girl* No girl . . . goes on ship these days. They . . . lead you to some place where her *maquer[e]au* can slug you.

maquette /ma'kɛt/ *noun* E20 **French** (from Italian *macchietta* speck, diminutive of *macchia* spot, from *macchiare* to spot, from Latin *maculare* to stain). A small preliminary sketch or wax or clay model from which a sculpture is elaborated.

maquiladora /ˌmakila'dora/ *noun* L20 **Mexican Spanish** (from *maquilar* to assemble). A factory in Mexico run by a foreign company and exporting its products to the country of that company.

attributive **1996** M. Anderson *Frontiers* The 1965 *maquiladora* programme to attract US industry into the frontier region of Mexico explicitly stated that in northern Mexico US firms would face both lower labour costs and less exacting health and environmental regulations.

maquillage /makijaʒ/ *noun* L19 **French** (from *maquiller* to make up one's face, from Old French *masquiller* to stain, alteration of *mascurer* to darken). Make-up, cosmetics; the application of this.

1959 R. Graves *Collected Poems* Confirming hazardous relationships By kindly maquillage of Truth's pale lips.

maquillé /makije/ *adjective* (feminine **maquillée**) E20 **French**. Wearing cosmetics, made up.

maquis /ˈmɑːkiː/ *noun* plural same M19 **French** (from as MACCHIA). **1** M19 The dense scrub characteristic of certain Mediterranean coastal regions, especially in Corsica. **2** M20 *History* (usually **Maquis**) A member of the French resistance movement during the German occupation (1940–5). **b** M20 A member of any resistance group or army.

■ The maquis scrub was the traditional hiding place for fugitives, hence the connection between senses 1 and 2.

maquisard /ˌmɑːkiːˈsɑː/ *noun* M20 **French**. A member of the Maquis.

marabou /ˈmarəbuː/ *noun & adjective* (also **maribou** /ˈmarɪbuː/, **marabout**) E19 **French** (from Arabic *murābiṭ* holy man (see next), the stork being regarded as holy). **A** *noun* **1** E19 A tropical African stork, *Leptoptilus crumeniferus*. Also *marabou stork*. **2** E19 A tuft of soft white down from the wings or tail of this stork, used for trimming hats etc.; *collectively* trimming made of this down. **3** M19 An exceptionally white kind of raw silk which can be dyed without first removing the natural gum and is used in crêpe weaving. **B** *adjective* E19 Made of marabou.

marabout /ˈmarəbuːt/ *noun* E17 **French** (from Portuguese *marabuto* from Arabic *murābiṭ*, from *ribāṭ* frontier station, where merit could be acquired by combat against the infidel). **1** E17 A Muslim holy man or mystic, especially in North Africa. **2** M19 A shrine marking the burial place of a marabout.

maraca /məˈrakə/ *noun* (also **maracca**) E17 **Portuguese** (*maracá* from Tupi *maráka*). A Latin American percussion instrument made from a hollow gourd or gourd-shaped container filled with beans etc., and usually shaken in pairs. Usually in *plural*.

maranatha /marəˈnaθə/ *adverb, noun, & interjection* (also **Maranatha**) LME **Greek** (from Aramaic *māran ʼṯā* our Lord has come, or *māranā ṯā* O Lord, come). **A** *adverb* LME In translations of 1 Corinthians 16:22: at the coming of the Lord. **B** *noun* M17 (By a misunderstanding of 1 Corinthians 16:22:) a portentously intensified anathema; a terrible curse. More fully *anathema maranatha*. **C** *interjection* L19 In the early Church: expressing a deep longing for the coming of the Lord.

maraschino /marəˈskiːnəʊ/, /marəˈʃiːnəʊ/ *noun* plural **maraschinos** L18 **Italian**. A strong sweet red liqueur distilled from the marasca cherry.

figurative **1995** *Times* God, what would those of us cursed with wen and crow's-foot and blackhead and the maraschino mappings of bust capillaries not give for the secrets of Douglas's posset-pot!

marc /mɑːk/ *noun* E17 **French** (from *marcher* to walk (originally, to tread, trample, ultimately from late Latin *marcus* hammer)). **1** E17 The refuse of processed grapes etc. **2** M19 A brandy made from this. Also *marc brandy*.

marcato /mɑːˈkɑːtəʊ/ *adverb & adjective* M19 **Italian** (past participle of *marcare* to mark, accent, of Germanic origin). *Music* (With each note) emphasized.

Märchen /ˈmɛːrçən/ *noun* plural same (also **märchen**) L19 **German** (= fairy tale from Middle High German *merechyn* short verse narrative, from Middle High German *mære* (Old High German *mārī*) news, famous, ultimately from Germanic). A folk-tale, a fairy tale.

marcottage /mɑːkɒˈtɑːʒ/, /mɑːˈkɒtɪdʒ/ *noun* E20 **French** (= layering). *Horticulture* A method of propagating plants in which an incision is made below a joint or node and covered with a thick layer of moss etc., into which new roots grow.

Mardi gras /ˌmɑːdɪ ˈgrɑː/ *noun phrase* L17 **French** (literally, 'fat Tuesday'). Shrove Tuesday, celebrated in some Roman Catholic countries with a carnival; the last day of a carnival etc., especially in France; *Australia* a carnival or fair at any time.

maréchaussée /mareʃose/ *noun* (also **Maréchaussée**) plural pronounced same L18 **French** (from Old French *mareschaucie*). *History* A French military force under the command of a marshal. Now (*jocular* and *colloquial*), the French police, the gendarmerie.

mare clausum /ˌmɑːreɪ ˈklaʊsʊm/, /ˌmɛːrɪ ˈklɔːzəm/ *noun phrase* plural **maria clausa** /ˌmɑːrɪə ˈklaʊsə/, /ˌmɛːrɪə ˈklɔːzə/

M17 **Latin** (= closed sea). A sea under the jurisdiction of a particular country.

■ The title of a work published in 1635 by the English jurist John Selden (1584–1654), in answer to Grotius (see MARE LIBERUM). The terms *mare clausum* and *mare liberum* both originated in the struggle between the Dutch and English maritime empires in the seventeenth century.

mare liberum /ˌmɑːreɪ ˈliːbərʊm/, /ˌmɛːrɪ ˈlʌɪbərəm/ *noun phrase* plural **maria libera** /ˌmɑːrɪə ˈliːbərə/, /ˌmɛːrɪə ˈlʌɪbərə/ M17 **Latin** (= free sea). A sea open to all nations. Cf. MARE CLAUSUM.

■ The title of a treatise (1609) by Hugo Grotius (1583–1645), Dutch jurist.

maremma /məˈrɛmə/ *noun* plural **maremme** /məˈrɛmi/ M19 **Italian** (from Latin *maritima* feminine of *maritimus* maritime). In Italy: low marshy unhealthy country by the seashore; an area of this.

mariachi /marɪˈɑːtʃi/ *noun* M20 **Mexican Spanish** (*mariache*, *mariachi*). An itinerant Mexican folk band (also *mariachi band*); a member of such a band.

maria clausa plural of MARE CLAUSUM.

mariage blanc /marjaʒ blɑ̃/ *noun phrase* plural **mariages blancs** (pronounced same) E20 **French** (literally, 'white marriage'). An unconsummated marriage.

1975 *Listener* Opal . . . suggested a *mariage blanc* between Natalie and Bosie that would enable Opal and Bosie to have a lasting liaison.

mariage de convenance /marjaʒ də kɔ̃vnɑ̃s/ *noun phrase* plural **mariages de convenance** (pronounced same) M19 **French**. A marriage of convenience.

1995 *Country Life* The following year, she [sc. Sonia Delaunay] entered a brief *mariage de convenance* with the homosexual art dealer Wilhelm Uhde . . .

maria libera plural of MARE LIBERUM.

maribou(t) variant of MARABOU.

mari complaisant /mari kɔ̃plɛzɑ̃/ *noun phrase* plural **maris complaisants** (pronounced same) L19 **French**. A husband tolerant of his wife's adultery.

1958 L. Durrell *Justine* She was reputed to have had many lovers, and Nessim was regarded as a *mari complaisant*.

marijuana /marɪˈhwɑːnə/, /ˌmarjʊˈɑːnə/ *noun* (also **marihuana**) L19 **American Spanish**. **1** L19 Cannabis, *especially* in a form for smoking. **2** E20 Indian hemp, cannabis plant.

marimba /məˈrɪmbə/ *noun* E18 **Congolese**. A kind of deep-toned xylophone, originating in Africa and consisting of wooden keys on a frame with a tuned resonator beneath each key.

marina /məˈriːnə/ *noun* E19 **Italian and Spanish** (feminine of *marino* from Latin *marinus* marine). A harbour, usually specially designed or located, with moorings for yachts and other small craft.

marinade /marɪˈneɪd/ *noun* E18 **French** (from Spanish *marinada*, from *marinar* to pickle in brine (= Italian *marinare*, French *mariner*), from *marino*, from Latin *marinus* marine). A flavouring and tenderizing mixture of wine, vinegar or other acidic liquid, with oil, herbs, spices, etc., in which meat, fish, etc., may be soaked before cooking; the meat, fish, etc., thus soaked.

marinara /mɑːrɪˈnɑːrə/, /marɪˈnɑːrə/ *adjective* M20 **Italian** (*alla marinara* sailor-fashion, from feminine of *marinero* seafaring). Designating a sauce made from tomatoes, onions, herbs, etc., usually served with pasta.

marinera /mariˈnera/ *noun* E20 **Spanish** (feminine of *marinero* marine, seafaring). A lively South American dance. Also called *cueca*.

marionette /ˌmarɪəˈnɛt/ *noun* E17 **French** (*marionnette*, from *Marion* diminutive of *Marie* Mary). A puppet with jointed limbs operated by strings.

maris complaisants plural of MARI COMPLAISANT.

marivaudage /marivodaʒ/ *noun* M18 **French** (from P. C. de *Marivaux* (1688–1763), French novelist and dramatist). Exaggeratedly sentimental or affected style, language, etc., characteristic of Marivaux.

1969 *Observer* It [sc. lesbianism] is a tricky subject, poised on the brink of either tiresome *marivaudage* or tasteless titillation.

marmite /ˈmɑːmʌɪt/, *in sense 1 also foreign* /marmit/ (*plural same*) *noun* E19 **French**. **1** E19 An earthenware cooking-vessel. **2** E20 (also **Marmite**) (Proprietary name for) a savoury extract made from fresh brewer's yeast, used especially in sandwiches and for flavouring.

marocain /marəˈkeɪn/ *noun & adjective* E20 **French** (from *Maroc* Morocco). **A** *noun* E20 (A garment made from) a crêpe fabric of silk or wool or both. **B** *adjective* L20 Made of marocain.

maror /mɑːˈrɔː/ *noun* L19 **Hebrew** (*mārōr*). Bitter herbs eaten at the Passover Seder service as a reminder of the bitterness of the Israelites' captivity in Egypt.

marque /mɑːk/ *noun* E20 **French** (back-formation from *marquer* to mark or brand, alteration of Old French *merchier*, from *merc* limit, of Scandinavian origin (cf. Old High German *marc(h)a* mark)). A make or brand of something, especially a motor vehicle.

1996 *Country Life* All this might give the impression that Rafael Gonzalez is an ancient and noble marque . . .

marquise /mɑːˈkiːz/, *foreign* /markiz/ (*plural same*) *noun* E17 **French** (feminine of *marquis* marquess, from Old French *marchis* (later altered to *marquis* after Provençal *marques*, Spanish *marqués*) from Proto-Romance base of *march* border). **1** E17 (The title of) a marchioness in Continental Europe or (formerly) Britain. **2** E18 A variety of pear. **3a** L18 A marquee. Now *rare* or *obsolete*. **b** L19 A permanent canopy projecting over the entrance to a hotel, theatre, etc. Also called *marquee*. **4** L19 A finger-ring set with a pointed oval gem or cluster of gems. Also more fully *marquise ring*.

marquisette /mɑːkɪˈzɛt/ *noun & adjective* E20 **French** (diminutive of MARQUISE). (Of) a plain gauze dress fabric originally made from silk, later from cotton.

marron /ˈmarɒn/, *foreign* /marɔ̃/ *noun* L16 **French**. A large and particularly sweet kind of chestnut.

■ Now chiefly in MARRON GLACÉ.

marron glacé /ˌmarɒn ˈglaseɪ/, *foreign* /marɔ̃ glase/ *noun phrase* plural **marrons glacés** (pronounced same) L19 **French**. A chestnut preserved in syrup as a sweet.

martelé /ˈmɑːt(ə)leɪ/ *adjective, adverb, & noun* L19 **French** (past participle of *marteler* to hammer). *Music* Martellato.

■ Used only with reference to bowed stringed instruments (cf. MARTELLATO).

martellato /mɑːtɪˈlɑːtəʊ/ *adjective, adverb, & noun* L19 **Italian** (past participle of *martellare* to hammer). *Music* **A** *adjective & adverb* L19 (Played) with notes heavily accented and left before their full time has expired. **B** *noun* E20 Martellato playing.

martyrion /mɑːˈtɪrɪən/ *noun* (also in Latin form **martyrium** /mɑːˈtɪrɪəm/) plural of both **martyria** /mɑːˈtɪrɪə/ E18 **Greek**. A shrine, oratory, or church built in memory of a martyr; a building marking the place of a martyrdom or the site of a martyr's relics.

Marxisant /marksizɑ̃/ *adjective* (also **marxisant**) M20 **French** (from *Marxiste* Marxist). Having Marxist leanings.

marzacotto /mɑːtsəˈkɒtəʊ/, /mɑːzəˈkɒtəʊ/ *noun* plural **marzacottos** L19 **Italian**. A transparent glaze used by Italian majolica workers.

mas /mɑ/ *noun* plural same E20 **Provençal**. A farm, house, or cottage in the south of France.

1996 *Times Magazine* . . . the houses themselves, no longer dilapidated, but restored through lavish investment of care and understanding—centuries-old village houses, abandoned *mas* or farmhouses, grand *bastides*, dressed up for today's tastes but retaining their nobility.

masa /ˈmasa/ *noun* E20 **Spanish**. In Central and South American cuisine, a type of dough made from cornmeal and used to make tortillas etc.

masala /məˈsɑːlə/ *noun* L18 **Urdu** (*maṣālaḥ* from Persian and Urdu *masāliḥ* from Arabic *maṣāliḥ*). Any of various spice mixtures ground into a paste or powder for use in Indian cookery; a dish flavoured with this. Cf. GARAM MASALA.

mascara /maˈskɑːrə/ *noun & verb* L19 **Italian** (*mascara, maschera* mask). **A** *noun* L19 A cosmetic for darkening and colouring the eyelashes. **B** *transitive verb* M20 Put mascara on.

mascaron /maskarɔ̃/ (*plural same*), /ˈmaskər(ə)n/ *noun* M17 **French** (from Italian *mascherone*, from *maschera* mask). *Decorative Arts* A grotesque face or mask.

mascarpone /ˌmaskarˈpoːne/ *noun* M20 **Italian**. A soft mild Italian cream cheese.

mashallah /maˈʃalə/, /ˌmɑːʃɑːˈlɑː/ *interjection* E19 **Arabic** (*mā šāʼllāh*). (This is) what God wills.

■ Used as an expression of praise or resignation.

masjid /ˈmʌsdʒɪd/, /ˈmasdʒɪd/ *noun* M19 **Arabic**. A mosque.

Masorah /masəˈrɑː/, /məˈsɔːrə/ *noun* (also **Massorah**, **Masora**) E17 **Hebrew** (variant of *māsōreṯ* bond (Ezekiel 20:37), from *ʼāsar* to bind (later interpreted as 'tradition' as if from *māsar* to hand down)). The body of traditional information and comment relating to the text of the Hebrew Scriptures, compiled by Jewish scholars in the tenth century and earlier; the collection of critical notes in which this information is preserved.

massage /ˈmasɑːʒ/, /maˈsɑːʒ/, /ˈmasɑːdʒ/ *noun & verb* L19 **French** (from *masser* to apply massage to, perhaps from Portuguese *amassar* to knead). **A** *noun* **1** L19 The application (usually with the hands) of pressure and strain on the muscles and joints of the body by rubbing, kneading, etc., in order to stimulate their action and increase their suppleness; an instance or spell of such manipulation. **2** E20 *euphemistic* The services of prostitutes. Chiefly in *massage parlour*. **B** *transitive verb* **1** L19 Apply massage to; treat by means of massage. **b** L20 Rub (lotion etc.) *into* by means of massage. **2** M20 Manipulate (data, figures, etc.), especially in order to give a more acceptable result.

massé /ˈmaseɪ/ *adjective & noun* L19 **French** (past participle of *masser* to play a massé stroke, from *masse* mace). *Billiards* etc. (Designating) a stroke made with the cue more or less vertical, so as to impart extra swerve to the cue-ball.

massecuite /masˈkwiːt/ *noun* L19 **French** (literally, 'cooked mass'). The juice of sugar cane after concentration by boiling.

masseur /maˈsəː/ *noun* (feminine **masseuse** /maˈsəːz/) L19 **French** (from *masser* to apply massage to). A person who provides massage (professionally).

massif /ˈmasɪf/, /maˈsiːf/, *foreign* /masif/ (*plural same*) *noun* E16 **French** (use as noun of *massif* massive). **1** E16 A block of building. Passing into *figurative* use of sense 2. **2** L19 A large mountain-mass; a compact group of mountain heights. **3** L19 *Horticulture* A mass or clump of plants.

Massorah variant of MASORAH.

mastaba /ˈmastəbə/ *noun* (also **mastabah**) E17 **Arabic** (*miṣṭaba, maṣ-*). **1** E17 In Islamic countries: a (stone) bench or seat attached to a house. **2** L19 *Archaeology* An ancient Egyptian flat-topped tomb, rectangular or square in plan and with sides sloping outward to the base. Also *mastaba tomb*.

mastika /maˈstiːkə/ *noun* E20 **Modern Greek** (*mastikha*). A liquor flavoured with mastic gum.

matador /ˈmatədɔː/ *noun* (also (especially senses 2, 3) **matadore**) L17 **Spanish** (from *matar* to kill). **1** L17 A bullfighter whose task is to kill the bull. **2** L17 In some card-games (as quadrille, ombre, solo): any of the highest trumps so designated by the rules of the game. **3** M19 A domino game in which halves are matched so as to make a total of seven; any of the dominoes which have seven spots altogether, together with the double blank.

matchet variant of MACHETE.

maté /ˈmateɪ/ *noun* E18 **Spanish** (*mate* from Quechua *mati*). **1** E18 A gourd, calabash, etc., in which the leaves of the shrub maté are infused. Also *maté-cup*. **2** M18 (An infusion of) the leaves of a South American shrub, *Ilex paraguariensis*; the shrub itself. Also more fully *yerba maté*.

matelassé /mat(ə)ˈlaseɪ/, *foreign* /matlase/ (*plural same*) *noun & adjective* (also **matelasse**) L19 **French** (past participle of *matelasser* to quilt, from *matelas* mattress). **A** *noun* L19 A silk or wool fabric with a raised design. **B** *adjective* L19 Having a raised design like quilting.

matelot /ˈmatləʊ/ *noun* E20 **French** (= sailor). **1** E20 A sailor. *nautical slang*. **2** E20 A shade of blue.

> **1 1995** *Spectator* When Floyd cooks for, say, a crew of matelots, you never know whether they really enjoyed his bouillabaisse or whether they are just doing it to please him.

matelote /ˈmat(ə)ləʊt/, *foreign* /matlɔt/ (*plural same*) *noun* E18 **French** (from as preceding). A dish of fish etc. served in a sauce of wine, onions, etc.

mater /ˈmeɪtə/ *noun* L16 **Latin** (literally, 'mother'). **1** L16 The thickest plate of an astrolabe. **2** M19 Mother.

■ Sense 2 is chiefly jocular or in school slang; cf. PATER.

Mater Dolorosa /ˌmeɪtə dɒləˈrəʊsə/ *noun phrase* plural **Matres Dolorosae** /ˌmeɪtriːz dɒləˈrəʊsiː/ E19 **Medieval Latin** (literally, 'sorrowful mother'). (A title of) the Virgin Mary, as having a role in the Passion of Christ; a representation, in painting or sculpture, of the Virgin Mary sorrowing; *transferred* a woman resembling the sorrowful Virgin in appearance, manner, etc.

materfamilias /ˌmeɪtəfəˈmɪlɪəs/ *noun* M18 **Latin** (from MATER + *familias* old genitive of *familia* family). The female head of a family or household.

materia medica /məˌtɪərɪə ˈmɛdɪkə/ *noun phrase plural* L17 **Modern Latin** (translation of Greek *hulē iatrikē* healing material). The remedial substances used in the practice of medicine; (treated as *singular*) the branch of medicine that deals with their origins and properties.

materia prima /məˌtɪərɪə ˈprʌɪmə/ *noun phrase* M16 **Latin** (= first matter). The primordial substance formerly considered to be the original material of the universe.

matériel /materjɛl/, /məˌtɪərɪˈɛl/ *noun* E19 **French** (use as noun of adjective). **1** E19 Available means or resources. Also (*rare*), technique. **2** E19 The equipment, supplies, etc., used in an army, navy, or business. Opposed to *personnel*.

matière /matjɛr/ *noun* E20 **French**. The quality an artist gives to the pigment used.

matinée /ˈmatɪneɪ/, *foreign* /matine/ (*plural same*) *noun* (also **matinee**) M19 **French** (= morning, what occupies a morning, from *matin*). **1** M19 An afternoon performance at a theatre, cinema, or concert hall. **2** L19 A woman's lingerie jacket.

matje /ˈmatjə/ *noun* (also **matjes** /ˈmatjəs/) L19 **Dutch** (*maatjes*). A young herring, especially salted or pickled. More fully *matje herring*.

■ In the form *matie*, *mattie* or other variants the word was known much earlier (E18), chiefly in Scotland. The form with 'j' represents a reintroduction from Dutch.

matraca /məˈtrɑːkə/ *noun* E20 **Spanish**. In Spain: a mechanical wooden rattle used instead of church bells on Good Friday.

Matres Dolorosae plural of MATER DOLOROSA.

matrix /ˈmeɪtrɪks/ *noun* plural **matrixes**, **matrices** /ˈmeɪtrɪsiːz/ LME **Latin** (= breeding-female, register, (in Late Latin) womb, from *mater*, *matr-* mother). **1** LME The uterus, the womb. *archaic* **2** M16 A place or medium in which something is bred, produced, or developed; a setting or environment in which a particular activity or process occurs or develops; a place or point of origin and growth. **3** L16 A mould in which something is cast or shaped. **4** M17 The rock material in which a fossil, gem, etc., is embedded.

■ *Matrix* has also been adopted as a specialist technical term in a whole range of disciplines including Anatomy and Zoology (M19), Botany (M19), Mathematics (M19), and Computing (M20).

matzo /ˈmʌtsə/, /ˈmatsəʊ/ *noun* (also **matzah** /ˈmʌtsə/) plural **matzos**, **matzoth** /ˈmʌtsəʊt/ M19 **Yiddish** (*matse* from Hebrew *maṣṣāh*). (A wafer of) unleavened bread for Passover.

maudit /modi/ *noun & adjective* M20 **French** (literally, 'cursed', from *maudire* to curse). **A** *noun* M20 plural pronounced same. A person who is cursed; a despicable or deeply unpleasant person. **B** *adjective* L20 Cursed; (of an artist etc.) insufficiently appreciated, forgotten.

■ The adjective is usually postpositive. Cf. POÈTE MAUDIT.

Maulana /maʊˈlɑːnə/ *noun* M19 **Arabic** (*mawlānā* our master). (A title given to) a Muslim man revered for his religious learning or piety.

maulvi variant of MOULVI.

mau-mau /ˈmaʊmaʊ/ *transitive verb* L20 **Kikuyu** (*Mau Mau*, a secret society dedicated to the expulsion of British settlers from Kenya in the 1950s). Terrorize, threaten.

■ United States slang.

mausoleum /mɔːsəˈlɪəm/ *noun* plural **mausolea** /mɔːsəˈlɪə/, **mausoleums** LME **Latin** (from Greek *Mausōleion*, from *Mausōlos* Mausolos). **1** LME The magnificent tomb of Mausolus, King of Caria, erected in the 4th century BC at Halicarnassus by his queen Artemisia. **2** LME *generally* A large and magnificent place of burial.

mauvais /mɔvɛ/ *adjective* E18 **French**. Bad.

■ In English only in the following French phrases.

mauvais coucheur /mɔvɛ kuʃœr/ *noun phrase* plural **mauvais coucheurs** (pronounced same) M20 **French** (literally, 'bad bedfellow'). A difficult, uncooperative, or unsociable person.

1963 *Times Literary Supplement* Goddard was a man of talent but he was obviously a *mauvais coucheur*.

mauvaise foi /mɔvɛz fwa/ *noun phrase* M20 **French**. Bad faith.

1995 *Spectator* They accept the general futility of life and take corruption and *mauvaise foi* in anyone 'important' for granted.

mauvaise langue /mɔvɛz lɑ̃g/ *noun phrase* plural **mauvaises langues** (pronounced same) L19 **French** (literally, 'bad tongue'). A venomous tongue; a scandalmonger.

1936 R. West *Thinking Reed* In another moment that couple of *mauvaises langues* would have something to wag about.

mauvais pas /mɔvɛ pa/ *noun phrase* plural same E19 **French** (literally, 'bad step'). *Mountaineering* A place that is difficult or dangerous to negotiate.

1940 F. S. Chapman *Helvellyn to Himalaya* We decided to return once more to the couloir . . . thus short-circuiting the *mauvais pas* we had seen in our reconnaisance.

mauvais quart d'heure /mɔvɛ kar dœr/ *noun phrase* plural **mauvais quarts d'heure** (pronounced same) M19 **French** (literally, 'bad quarter of an hour'). An unpleasant but brief period of time; an unnerving experience.

1965 *Economist* John Kennedy had his *mauvais quart d'heure* between April and June, 1961.

mauvais sujet /mɔvɛ syʒɛ/ *noun phrase* plural **mauvais sujets** (pronounced same) L18 **French** (literally, 'bad subject'). A worthless person, a scoundrel.

1975 A. Christie *Curtain* The *mauvais sujet*—always women are attracted to him.

maven /'meɪv(ə)n/ *noun* M20 **Hebrew** (*mēḇīn* understanding). An expert, a connoisseur. *North American.*

1975 *New York Times* Mama, who had managed to support herself by becoming a local real estate *maven*, negotiated the purchase.

mavrodaphne /ˌmavrə'dafni/ *noun* E20 **Modern Greek** (from late Greek *mauros* dark (Greek *amauros*) + *daphnē* laurel). A dark-red sweet Greek wine; the grape from which this is made.

maxixe /mak'si:ks/, *foreign* /mə'ʃiʃə/ *noun* E20 **Portuguese**. A dance for couples, of Brazilian origin, resembling the polka and the local tango.

1995 *Spectator* From Brazil in the 20s there came a dance called the maxixe—a challenge to those not confident of their Portuguese pronunciation—followed by the samba and the more primitive baiao.

maya /'mɑ:jə/ *noun* L18 **Sanskrit** (*māyā*, from *mā* create). In *Hindu Philosophy*, illusion, magic, the supernatural power wielded by gods and demons. In *Hindu and Buddhist Philosophy*, the power by which the universe becomes manifest, the illusion or appearance of the phenomenal world.

mayonnaise /meɪə'neɪz/ *noun* E19 **French** (also *magnonaise*, *mahonnaise*, perhaps feminine of *mahonnais* adjective, from *Mahon* capital of Minorca). A thick sauce consisting of yolk of egg beaten up with oil and vinegar and seasoned with salt etc., used as a dressing especially for salad, eggs, cold meat, or fish; a dish (of meat etc.) having this sauce as a dressing.

mazar /mə'zɑ:/ *noun* E20 **Arabic** (*mazār* place visited, from *zāra* to visit). A Muslim tomb revered as a shrine.

mazel tov /'maz(ə)l to:v/, /tɒf/ *interjection* M19 **Modern Hebrew** (*mazzāl ṭōḇ*, literally, 'good star', from Hebrew *mazzāl* star). Among Jews: good luck, congratulations.

mazout variant of MAZUT.

mazuma /mə'zu:mə/ *noun* E20 **Yiddish** (from Hebrew *mĕzummān*, from *zimmēn* to prepare). Money, cash; *especially* betting money. *United States and Australian slang.*

mazurka /mə'zə:kə/, /mə'zʊəkə/ *noun* E19 **French** (or from German *masurka* from Polish *mazurka* woman of the province Mazovia). **1** E19 A Polish dance in triple time, usually with a slide and hop. **2** M19 A piece of music for this dance or composed in its rhythm, usually with accentuation of the second or third beat.

mazut /mə'zu:t/ *noun* (also **mazout**) L19 **Russian**. A viscous liquid left as residue after the distillation of petroleum, used in Russia as a fuel oil and coarse lubricant.

mbira /(ə)m'bɪərə/ *noun* L19 **Bantu**. A musical instrument of southern Africa consisting of a set of keys or tongues attached to a resonator, which are plucked with the thumb and forefingers. Also called *sansa*.

mea culpa /ˌmeɪə 'kʊlpə/, /ˌmi:ə 'kʌlpə/ *interjection & noun phrase* LME **Latin** (literally, '(through) my own fault'). **A** *interjection* LME Acknowledging one's guilt or responsibility for an error. **B** *noun phrase* E19 An utterance of '*mea culpa*'; an acknowledgement of one's guilt or responsibility for an error.

■ Taken from the prayer of confession in the Latin liturgy of the Church. Also sometimes *mea maxima culpa* '(through) my own great fault'. As an interjection, now often jocular.

B 1996 *Times* In fact, Mr de Klerk's statement was far from the *mea culpa* many had hoped for and was a masterfully bland performance.

mealie /'mi:li/ *noun* (also **mielie**) E19 **Afrikaans** (*mielie* from Portuguese *milho* maize, millet, from Latin *milium*). In

South Africa: maize; a corn-cob (usually in *plural*).

mebos /'mi:bɒs/, *foreign* /'me:bɔs/ *noun* L18 **Afrikaans** (probably from Japanese *umeboshi* dried and salted plums). A South African confection made from dried flattened apricots, preserved in salt and sugar.

mecate /meɪ'kɑ:teɪ/ *noun* M19 **Mexican Spanish** (from Nahuatl *mecatl*). A rope made of horsehair or of maguey fibre, used especially to tether or lead a horse. Chiefly *United States*.

méchant /meʃɑ̃/ *adjective* (feminine **méchante** /meʃɑ̃t/) E19 **French**. Malicious, spiteful.

médaillon /medajɔ̃/ *noun* plural pronounced same E20 **French** (from Italian *medaglione*, augmentative of *medaglia* medal). A small, flat, round or oval cut of meat or fish.

■ The cognate *medallion*, in the sense of 'large medal', was established in English much earlier (M17).

media /'mi:dɪə/ *noun* E20 **Latin** (plural of MEDIUM (noun)). **1** E20 *plural* and *collective singular* The main means of mass communication (also *mass media*), *especially* newspapers, radio, and television; the reporters, journalists, etc., working for organizations engaged in such communication. **2** E20 *singular* A means of mass communication, a MEDIUM.

medina /mɪ'di:nə/ *noun* (also **Medina**) E20 **Arabic** (literally, 'town'). The old Arab or non-European quarter of a North African town.

medium /'mi:dɪəm/ *noun & adjective* plural of noun **media** /'mi:dɪə/, **mediums** (see also MEDIA) L16 **Latin** (literally, 'middle, midst', medieval Latin 'means', use as noun of *medius* mid). **A** *noun* **1** L16 A middle quality, degree, or condition; something intermediate in nature or degree. **2** L16 An intervening substance through which a force acts on objects at a distance or through which impressions are conveyed to the senses, as air, water, etc. **b** M19 A pervading or enveloping substance; the substance in which an organism lives or is cultured; *figurative* one's environment, one's usual social setting. **3** E17 An intermediate agency, instrument, or channel; a means; *specifically* a channel of mass communication, as newspapers, radio, television, etc. See also MEDIA. **4 a** E19 A person acting as an intermediary, a mediator. *rare*. **b** M19 (plural **mediums**) A person thought to be in contact with the spirits of the dead and to communicate between the living and the dead. **5** M19 A liquid substance with which a pigment is mixed for use in painting. Also, anything used as a raw material by an artist etc.; a style or variety of art, as determined by the materials or artistic form used. **B** *adjective* **1** L17–E19 Average, mean. **2** E18 Intermediate between two or more degrees in size, character, amount, quality, etc.

■ There also are or have been numerous technical applications of the noun *medium*, as in Logic (L16–E19) 'the middle term of a syllogism', Geometry and Arithmetic (E17–E19) 'a mean; an average', and Photography (L19) 'a varnish used in retouching'.

medresseh variant of MADRASAH.

medusa /mɪ'dju:zə/, /mɪ'dju:sə/ *noun* (in sense 1 usually **Medusa**) plural **medusae** /mɪ'dju:zi:/, /mɪ'dju:si:/, **medusas** LME **Latin** (from Greek *Medousa* the only mortal one of the three Gorgons in Greek mythology, with snakes for hair and a gaze which turned any beholder to stone: in sense 2 originally as modern Latin genus name). **1** LME A terrifying or ugly woman, a gorgon. **2** M18 A jellyfish; *specifically* in *Zoology*, a coelenterate in the medusoid stage of its life cycle.

mee /mi:/ *noun* M20 **Chinese** (*miàn* (Wade–Giles *mien*) flour). A Chinese dish made with noodles and other ingredients, popular in Malaysia.

meerschaum /'mɪəʃɔ:m/, /'mɪəʃəm/ *noun* L18 **German** (from *Meer* sea + *Schaum* foam, translation of Persian *kef-i-daryā* foam of sea, with reference to its frothiness). A tobacco-pipe with a bowl made from speiolite or hydrated magnesium silicate occurring as a soft white or yellowish claylike mineral.

méfiance /mefjɑ̃s/ *noun* L19 **French**. Mistrust.

mega /'mɛgə/ *adjective* L20 **Greek** (*mega-* combining form of *megas* great) Large, great. Also, brilliant, excellent.

■ Originating in the United States, this is an independent colloquial use of a combining form, similar to that of MACRO.

megaron /'mɛgər(ə)n/ *noun* L19 **Greek**. In ancient Greece: the great central hall of a type of house characteristic especially of the Mycenaean period.

Megillah /mə'gɪlə/ *noun* (also **megillah**) M17 **Hebrew** (*mĕgillāh*, literally, 'roll, scroll'). **1** M17 Each of five books of the Hebrew Scriptures (the Song of Solomon, Ruth, Lamentations, Ecclesiastes, and Esther) appointed to be read on certain Jewish notable days; *especially* the Book of Esther, read at the festival of Purim. Also, a copy of all, or any, of these books. **2** M20 A long, tedious, or complicated story. Frequently in *a* or *the whole megillah*. *slang*.

1970 S. Sheldon *Naked Face* 'Do you know the most peculiar thing about this whole megillah?' queried Moody thoughtfully.

meiosis /mʌɪ'əʊsɪs/ *noun* plural **meioses**, /mʌɪ'əʊsiːz/ M16 **Modern Latin** (from Greek *meiōsis*, from *meioun* to lessen, from *meiōn* less). **1** M16 *Rhetoric* **a** A figure of speech by which something is intentionally presented as smaller, less important, etc., than it really is. Now *rare*. **b** M17 LITOTES. **2** E20 *Biology* A particular kind of cell division.

mei ping /ˌmeɪ 'pɪŋ/ *noun phrase* E20 **Chinese** (*méi píng* prunus vase). A kind of Chinese porcelain vase with a narrow neck designed to hold a single spray of flowers.

meisie /'meɪsi/ *noun* L19 **Afrikaans** (from Dutch *meisje*). In South Africa: a girl, a young woman.

melamed /mɪ'lɑːməd/ *noun* L19 **Hebrew** (*mĕlammēḏ*). A teacher of elementary Hebrew.

melancholia /mɛlən'kəʊlɪə/ *noun* L17 **late Latin** (from Greek *melankholia* from *melan-*, *melas* black + *kholē* bile). *Medicine* A pathological state of depression. Also (*generally*), melancholy, depression.

mélange /melɑ̃ʒ/ (*plural same*), /meɪ'lɒ̃ʒ/ *noun* M17 **French** (from *mêler* to mix). **1** M17 A mixture; a collection of heterogeneous items or elements, a medley. **2** L19 Yarn, especially woollen yarn, to which dye has been applied unevenly so as to leave some areas undyed; a fabric of such a yarn. **3** E20 Coffee made with sugar and whipped cream; a drink of this.

1 1995 *Times* Davenport-Hines denounces the usual biographical *mélange* of gossip, scandal and 'sexual tale-telling'.

mêlée /'mɛleɪ/ *noun* (also **melée**, **melee**) M17 **French** (from Old French *mellée* past participial adjective of *meller* variant of *mesler* to meddle; sense 2 probably a different word). **1** M17 A battle at close quarters, a hand-to-hand fight; a confused struggle or skirmish, especially involving many people; a crush, turmoil; a muddle. **2** E20 *collectively* Small diamonds less than about a carat in weight.

1 1996 *Times* He continued to kick and punch at officers as he was led away after the two-minute mêlée.

melisma /mɪ'lɪzmə/ *noun* plural **melismata**, /mɪ'lɪzmətə/, **melismas** L19 **Greek** (literally, 'song'). *Music* Originally, a melodic tune, melodic music. Now, in singing, the prolongation of one syllable over a number of notes.

1996 *Times* Ray Charles is the name that invariably comes to mind in any discussion of Feliciano—not simply for the trite reason that they are both blind and fond of gospel melismata . . .

melktert /'mɛlkteːt/ *noun* M20 **Afrikaans** (from *melk* milk + *tert* tart, pie). In South Africa: a kind of open tart with a custard filling sprinkled with cinnamon.

melos /'mɛlɒs/, /'miːlɒs/ *noun* M18 **Greek** (= song, music). *Music* Song, melody; *specifically* the succession of tones considered apart from rhythm; an uninterrupted flow of melody.

meltemi /mɛl'tɛmi/ *noun* E20 **Modern Greek** (*meltémi*, Turkish *meltem*). A dry north wind blowing over the eastern Mediterranean region in summer; an Etesian wind.

melusine /ˌmɛl(j)ʊ'siːn/ *noun & adjective* (also **Melusine**) E20 **French** (*mélusine*, perhaps connected with *Mélusine*, a fairy in French folklore). **A** *noun* E20 A silky long-haired felt, used for making hats. **B** *attributive* or as *adjective* M20 Made of this material.

membra disiecta, **membra disjecta** variants of DISJECTA MEMBRA.

membrillo /mem'bri(l)jo/, /mɛm'briːljəʊ/ *noun* E20 **Spanish** (= quince). A Spanish preserve of quinces.

membrum virile /ˌmɛmbrəm vɪ'riːli/ *noun phrase* M19 **Latin** (= male member). The penis. *Archaic* or *euphemistic*.

memento /mɪ'mɛntəʊ/ *noun* plural **memento(e)s** LME **Latin** (imperative of *meminisse* to remember). **1** LME *Christian Church* Either of the two prayers (beginning with *Memento*) in the canon of the Mass, in which the living and the dead are respectively commemorated; the commemoration of the living or the dead in these prayers. **2** L16 A reminder, warning, or hint as to future conduct or events. Now *especially* an object serving as such a reminder or warning. Cf. MEMENTO MORI, MEMENTO VIVERE. **3** M18 A reminder of a past event or condition, of an absent person, or something that once existed. Now *especially* an object kept as a memorial of some person or event, a souvenir.

memento mori /mɪˌmɛntəʊ 'mɔːrʌɪ/, /mɪ ˌmɛntəʊ 'mɔːri/ *noun phrase* **Latin** (= remember that you have to die). A warning or reminder of death, *especially* a skull or other symbolical object.

1996 *Country Life* . . . it explores the theme of life among the ruins . . . a powerful memento mori of departed grandeur.

memento vivere /mɪˌmɛntəʊ 'viːvəri/ *noun phrase* E20 **Latin** (= remember that you have to live). A reminder of (the pleasures of) life.

■ Formed as the opposite of MEMENTO MORI.

1928 E. Blunden *Undertones of War* Sitting in the headquarters dugout with 'La Vie Parisienne' as a *memento vivere.*

memo abbreviation of MEMORANDUM.

memorabilia /ˌmɛm(ə)rə'bɪlɪə/ *noun plural* L18 **Latin** (use as noun of neuter plural of *memorabilis* from *memorare* to bring to mind). **1** L18 Memorable or noteworthy things. **2** L19 Souvenirs.

1 1996 D. Chambers *Stonyground* As the museum of the house, this parlour of my childhood was filled with memorabilia: a loon, now stuffed, that my grandmother had rescued from a ditch and nursed to tameness; my great-uncle Hugh's bayonet from the First World War . . .

memorandum /mɛmə'randəm/ *noun* plural **memoranda** /mɛmə'randə/, **memorandums** L15 **Latin** (neuter singular of *memorandus* gerundive of *memorare* to bring to mind, from *memor* mindful). **1** L15 A note to help the memory, a record of events or of observations on a particular subject, especially for future consideration or use. **2** L16 *Law* A writing or document summarizing or embodying the terms of a transaction, contract, agreement, establishment of a company etc. **3** E17 A record of a money transaction. **4** M17 An informal diplomatic message, especially summarizing the state of a question or justifying a decision. **5** L19 An informal written communication of a kind conventionally not requiring a signature, as within a business or organization, usually written on paper headed 'Memorandum' or 'Memo'.

■ *Memorandum* was first introduced (LME) as an adjective meaning 'to be remembered' and placed at the beginning of a note of something to be remembered or a record (for future reference) of something done, but this usage is now confined to legal contexts. In sense 5 *memorandum* is now generally abbreviated to *memo*, which also functions attributively (as in *memo pad*) and as a transitive verb meaning 'to make a memorandum of'.

memoria technica /mɪˌmɔːrɪə 'tɛknɪkə/ *noun phrase* M18 **Modern Latin** ((= technical memory) represented Greek *to mnēmonikon tekhnēma*). A method of assisting the memory by artificial contrivances; a system of mnemonics, a mnemonic aid.

memsahib /'mɛmsɑːb/ *noun* M19 **Anglo-Indian** (from *mem* representing a pronunciation of 'ma'am' + SAHIB). A European married woman as spoken of or to by Indians.

ménage /meɪ'nɑːʒ/, *foreign* /menaʒ/ (*plural same*) *noun* (also **menage**) ME **French** (Old French *menaige*, *manaige* (modern *ménage*) from Proto-Romance, from Latin *mansio* station, abiding-place, from *mans-* past participial stem of *manere* to stay, remain). **1** ME A domestic establishment, a household. Formerly also, the members of a household. **b** M20 A sexual relationship; an affair. **2** E19 The management of a household, housekeeping. **3** E19 A benefit society or savings club of which every member pays in a fixed sum weekly; an arrangement for paying for goods by instalments. *Scottish and northern dialect.*

■ In sense 1 also occasionally found in the phrases *ménage à deux* 'household of two' and *ménage à quatre* 'household of four', but by far the most frequent is MÉNAGE À TROIS. The related French word *menagerie* (introduced L17) meaning 'a collection of wild animals kept in cages' is now completely Anglicized in pronunciation (/mə 'nadʒ(ə)ri/).

ménage à trois /menaʒ a trwɑ/, /meɪ ˌnɑːʒ a trwɑː/ (*plural same*) *noun phrase* (also **ménage-à-trois**) L19 **French** (= household of three). An arrangement or relationship in which three people live together, usually consisting of a husband and wife and the lover of one of them.

1996 *Spectator* He seemed saddened by some people's view that 'I might be having my cake and eating it', referring to his *ménage-à-trois* with wife Rosie and mistress Morrigan.

menhaden /mɛn'heɪd(ə)n/ *noun* L18 **Algonquian** (perhaps from a base meaning 'fertilize'). A fish of the herring family, *Brevoortia tyrannus*, of the Atlantic coast of North America, an important source of fish guano and oil.

menhir /'mɛnhɪə/ *noun* M19 **Breton** (*maenhir* (*maen* stone, *hir* long) = Welsh *maen hir*, Cornish *mênhere*). *Archaeology* A single tall upright monumental stone, especially of prehistoric times.

meniscus /mɪ'nɪskəs/ *noun* plural **menisci** /mɪ'nɪskʌɪ/ L17 **Modern Latin** (from Greek *mēniskos* crescent, diminutive of *mēnē* moon). **1** L17 A lens convex on one side and concave on the other; *especially* a convexo-concave lens (i.e. one thickest in the middle, with a crescent-shaped section). **2** E18 A crescent moon. *rare*. **3** E19 The convex or concave upper surface of a column of liquid in a tube, caused by surface tension or capillarity. **4** M19 *Anatomy* A disclike fibrocartilage situated between the articular surfaces of certain joints, as those of the wrist and knee. **5** L19 A figure in the form of a crescent.

meno /'mɛnəʊ/, /'meməʊ/ *adverb* L19 **Italian**. *Music* Less.

■ Used in directions, as *meno mosso* 'less rapidly'.

menologium /ˌmɛnə(ʊ)'ləʊdʒɪəm/ *noun* (also **menology** /mɪ'nɒlədʒi/) plural **menologia** /ˌmɛnə(ʊ)'ləʊdʒɪə/, **menologiums** E18 **Modern Latin** (from ecclesiastical Greek *mēnologion*, from *mēn* month + *logos* account). An ecclesiastical calendar of the months.

■ The English form *menology* was introduced earlier (E17), but the form *menologium* is used in parallel with it, in particular with reference to the Old English metrical church calendar first published in 1705. The Greek form is also used specifically to mean a calendar of the Orthodox Church containing biographies of the saints in the order of the dates on which they are commemorated.

menorah /mɪ'nɔːrə/ *noun* L19 **Hebrew** (*mĕnōrāh* candlestick). A holy candelabrum with seven branches that was used in the temple in Jerusalem; a candelabrum having any number of branches, but usually eight, used in Jewish worship, especially during Hanukkah; a representation of either as a symbol of Judaism.

mensch /mɛnʃ/ *noun* M20 **Yiddish** (from German = person). A person of integrity or rectitude; a just, honest, or honourable person.

1972 *New Yorker* What is a *mensch*? . . . It means you're a substantial human being.

menses /'mɛnsiːz/ *noun plural* L16 **Latin** (plural of *mensis* month). The menstrual discharge. Also, the time of menstruation.

mens rea /ˌmɛnz 'riːə/ *noun phrase* M19 **Latin** (= guilty mind). *Law* The state of mind accompanying an illegal act which makes the act a crime; criminal state of mind.

1992 P. Manning *Erving Goffman and Modern Sociology* The law encourages this defense strategy by requiring prosecution lawyers to demonstrate *mens rea* on the part of the accused; that is, it requires proof that the accused intended to commit the crime.

mens sana in corpore sano /mɛns ˌsɑːnə ɪn ˌkɔːpəreɪ 'sɑːnəʊ/ *noun phrase* E17 **Latin**. A sound mind in a sound body, especially regarded as the ideal of education.

■ Also elliptical as *mens sana* (see quotation 1967). The quotation is from the *Satires* (x.356) of the Roman poet Juvenal.

1967 S. Johnson *Gold Drain* 'They' accused him of suffering from the effects of a public-school education, from the *mens sana* approach.

mensur /mɛn'zuːr/, /mɛn'sʊə/ *noun* plural **mensuren** /mɛn'zuːrən/, **mensurs** E20 **German** (literally, 'measure'). Chiefly *History* In Germany: a fencing duel between students fought with partially blunted weapons.

1970 M. Hebden *Mask of Violence* Anarchical young men of . . . the older universities . . . were already shouting the old *Mensur* wish before the commencement of a fight: '*Waffenschein!*'

mentor /'mɛntɔː/ *noun* M18 **French** (from Latin *Mentor* from Greek *Mentōr* the guide and adviser of Odysseus' son Telemachus (probably chosen as a name as from base meaning 'remember, think, counsel')). An experienced and trusted adviser or guide; a teacher, a tutor.

menudo /mɪ'n(j)uːdəʊ/ *noun* M20 **Mexican Spanish** (use as noun of adjective = small from Latin *minutus* very small). A spicy Mexican soup made from tripe.

menus plaisirs /məny plɛzir/ *noun phrase plural* L17 **French** (= small pleasures). Simple pleasures; small personal expenses or gratifications; fanciful or trifling objects bought with pocket money.

1966 M. Innes *Change of Heir* 'It's in her letter. The bit about . . . *menus frais*.' 'What's that?'

'The same as *menus plaisirs*. Pocket-money on the scale appropriate to an English gentleman.'

mercado /mə:ˈkɑ:dəʊ/, *foreign* /merˈkado/ *noun* plural **mercados** /mə:ˈkɑ:dəʊz/, *foreign* /merˈkados/ M19 **Spanish** (from Latin *mercatus* market). In Spain and Spanish-speaking countries: a market.

merde /mɛrd/ *noun* M20 **French** (from Latin *merda*). Excrement, dung.

■ Also in slang use as an interjection, expressing annoyance, exasperation, surprise, etc. Cf. MOT DE CAMBRONNE.

merdeka /mə:ˈdeɪkə/ *noun* M20 **Malay**. In Malaysia and Indonesia: freedom, independence.

mère /mɛr/, /mɛ:/ *noun* M19 **French** (= mother). The mother, elder.

■ *Mère* is appended to a name especially to distinguish between a mother and daughter of the same name (see quotation).

1968 J. Haythorne *None of Us Cared for Kate* Prentice *mère* has been bombarding the Secretary of State with letters.

merengue /məˈrɛŋgeɪ/ *noun* (also **meringue** /məˈraŋ/) M20 **American Spanish** (from Haitian creole *méringue* literally, 'meringue' from French). A dance of Dominican and Haitian origin, with alternating long and short stiff-legged steps; a piece of music for this dance, usually in duple and triple time.

meridional /məˈrɪdɪən(ə)l/ *adjective* & *noun* (also **meridianal**) LME **Old and Modern French** (*méridional* from late Latin *meridionalis*, irregularly from *meridies* after *septentrionalis* septentrional). **A** *adjective* **1** LME Of or pertaining to the south; situated in the south; southern, southerly. **b** M19 *specifically* Pertaining to or characteristic of the inhabitants of southern Europe. **2** LME–M19 Of or pertaining to the position of the sun at midday; pertaining to or characteristic of midday. **3** M16 Of, pertaining to, or aligned with a meridian. **4** M17 Of a marking or structure on a roundish body: lying in a plane with the axis of the body. **B** *noun* L16 A native or inhabitant of the south. Now *specifically* a native or inhabitant of the south of France.

meringue /məˈraŋ/, *foreign* /mərɛ̃g/ (*plural same*) *noun* E18 **French** (of unknown origin). A confection made chiefly of sugar and whites of eggs whipped together and baked crisp; a small cake or shell of this, usually decorated or filled with cream.

merino /məˈri:nəʊ/ *noun & adjective* plural of noun **merinos** L18 **Spanish** (of unknown origin). **1** L18 (Designating or pertaining to) a breed of sheep prized for the fineness of its wool, originating in Spain; (designating) a sheep of this breed. **b** E19 *pure merino*, (*i*) an early immigrant to Australia with no convict origins, a member of a leading family in Australian society, a person of fine breeding or good character; (*ii*) *attributively* first-class, well-bred, excellent. *Australian slang*. **2** E19 (Of) a soft fine material resembling cashmere, made of wool (originally merino wool) or wool and cotton. **b** M19 A garment, especially a dress or shawl, made of this; *West Indies* a vest. **3** L19 (Of) a fine woollen yarn used in the manufacture of hosiery and knitwear.

mesa /ˈmeɪsə/ *noun* M18 **Spanish** (= table, from Latin *mensa*). A high rocky tableland or plateau; a flat-topped hill with precipitous sides.

■ The earliest occurrences are in the names of particular plateaux or hills in the United States.

mésalliance /mezaljɑ̃s/ (*plural same*), /mɛˈzalɪəns/ *noun* L18 **French** (from *més-* mis- + *alliance* alliance). A marriage with a person thought to be of inferior social position; an unsuitable union.

■ The English form *misalliance* (M18) is also current for an inappropriate marital or sexual union, but it is also used more generally.

mes ami(e)s plural of MON AMI(E).

mescal /ˈmɛskal/, /mɛˈskal/ *noun* E18 **Spanish** (*mezcal* from Nahuatl *mexcalli*). **1** E18 Any of several plants of the genus *Agave* found in Mexico and the south-western United States, used as sources of fermented liquor, food, or fibre. **2** E19 A strong intoxicating spirit distilled from the fermented sap of the American aloe or allied species. Cf. TEQUILA. **3** L19 A small desert cactus, *Lophophora williamsii*, of Mexico and Texas; a preparation of this used as a hallucinogenic drug. Cf. PEYOTE.

Mesdames plural of MADAME.

Mesdemoiselles plural of MADEMOISELLE.

meseta /meˈseta/ *noun* E20 **Spanish** (diminutive of MESA). In Spain and Spanish-speaking countries: a plateau; specifically *the* high plateau of central Spain.

meshuga /mɪˈʃʊɡə/ *adjective* (also **meshugga(h)** and other variants) L19 **Yiddish** (*meshuge* from Hebrew *mĕshuggā‘*; cf. German *meschugge* crazy). Mad, crazy; stupid.

■ Slang. *Meshuga* is chiefly used predicatively, in contrast to MESHUGENER.

meshugaas /mɪˈʃʊɡɑːs/ *noun* (also **mishugas** and other variants) E20 **Yiddish** (from Hebrew *mĕshuggā‘*: see MESHUGA). Madness, craziness; nonsense, foolishness. *slang*.

meshugener /mɪˈʃʊɡənə/ *attributive adjective & noun slang* (also **meshuggener**, **meshugenah**, and other variants) E20 **Yiddish** (from Hebrew *mĕshuggā‘*: see MESHUGA). (A person who is) mad, crazy, or stupid.

■ Slang. It is a positional variant of *meshuga* in that it precedes its noun.

meshugga(h) variant of MESHUGA.

meshuggenah, **meshuggener** variants of MESHUGENER.

meshumad /mɪˈʃʊmad/ *noun* (also **meshummad**) plural **meshumadim** /mɪˈʃʊmadɪm/ L19 **Yiddish** (from Hebrew *mĕšhummāḏ*, literally, ‘a person who is destroyed’, or *mĕšu‘māḏ* baptized, from Aramaic *‘maḏ* to be baptized). An apostate from Judaism.

meson /meɪˈsɒn/ *noun* E19 **Spanish** (*mesón*). In Mexico or the south-western United States: an inn or lodging-house.

messa di voce /ˌmessa di ˈvotʃe/, /ˌmɛsə dɪ ˈvəʊtʃi/ *noun phrase* plural **messe di voce** /ˌmesse/, /ˌmɛseɪ/ L18 **Italian** (literally, ‘placing of the voice’). In singing, a gradual crescendo and diminuendo on a long-held note.

messagerie /mesaʒri/ *noun* plural pronounced same L18 **French**. The transportation or delivery of goods, messages, or people; a conveyance for these. In *plural* also, goods, messages, or people for transportation or delivery.

messaline /ˈmɛsəliːn/ *noun & adjective* E20 French. (Made of) a soft lightweight and lustrous silk or rayon fabric.

messe di voce plural of MESSA DI VOCE.

Messiah /mɪˈsʌɪə/ *noun* (also **messiah**, (earlier) **Messias**) ME **Old and Modern French** (*Messie* from popular Latin *Messias* from Greek *Messias* from Aramaic *mĕšīḥā*, Hebrew *māšhīāḥ* anointed, from *māšhaḥ* to anoint). The promised deliverer of the Jewish nation prophesied in the Hebrew Scriptures; Jesus regarded as the saviour of humankind. Also (*transferred*), an actual or expected liberator of an oppressed people or country etc.; a leader or saviour of a specified group, cause, etc.

■ The modern form *Messiah* was created by the Geneva translators of the Bible of 1560 as looking more Hebraic than *Messias*.

transferred **1996** *New Scientist* Shoko Asahara, the self-styled messiah who convinced his followers that Armageddon was coming . . . , is accused of masterminding a nerve-gas attack in the Tokyo underground . . .

mestizo /mɛˈstiːzəʊ/ *noun & adjective* plural of noun **mestizos** (feminine **mestiza** /mɛˈstiːzə/) L16 **Spanish** (from Proto-Romance from Latin *mixtus* past participle of *miscere* to mix). **A** *noun* L16 A Spanish or Portuguese person with parents of different races, *specifically* one with a Spaniard as one parent and an American Indian as the other; *generally* any person of mixed blood. Also, a Central or South American Indian who has adopted European culture. **B** *attributive* or as *adjective* E17 That is a mestizo or mestiza.

mesto /ˈmɛsto/ *adverb & adjective* E19 **Italian** (from Latin *maestus* sad). *Music* (A direction:) sad(ly), mournful(ly).

métairie /meteri/ *noun* plural pronounced same E19 **French** (from as MÉTAYER). A farm held on the MÉTAYAGE system.

metamorphosis /mɛtəˈmɔːfəsɪs/, /ˌmɛtə mɔːˈfəʊsɪs/ *noun* plural **metamorphoses** /mɛtəˈmɔːfəsiːz/, /ˌmɛtəmɔːˈfəʊsiːz/ M16 **Latin** (from Greek *metamorphōsis*, from *metamorphoun* to transform, from as *meta-* + *morphē* a form). **1** M16 The action or process of changing in form, shape, or substance; *especially* transformation by supernatural means. **b** L16 A metamorphosed form. **2** M16 A complete change in appearance, circumstances, condition, or character. **3** M17 *Biology* Normal change of form of a living organism, part, or tissue; *specifically* the transformation that some animals undergo in the course of becoming adult (e.g. from tadpole to frog), in which there is a complete alteration of form and habit.

metanoia /mɛtəˈnɔɪə/ *noun* L19 **Greek** (from *metanoein* to change one's mind, repent). Penitence; reorientation of one's way of life, spiritual conversion.

metastasis /mɪˈtastəsɪs/ *noun* plural **metastases** /mɪˈtastəsiːz/ L16 **Late Latin** (from Greek = removal, change, from *methistanai* to remove, change). **1** L16 *Rhetoric* A rapid transition from one point to another. Long *rare*. **2** M17 *Medicine* The transference of a bodily function, pain, or disease, or of diseased matter, from one site to another; *specifically* the occurrence or development of secondary foci of disease at a distance from the primary site, as in many cancers.

metate /məˈtɑːteɪ/ *noun* E17 **American Spanish** (from Nahuatl *métatl*). In Central America: a flat or somewhat hollowed oblong stone on which grain, cocoa, etc., are ground by means of a smaller stone. Also *metate-stone*.

metathesis /mɛˈtaθɪsɪs/, /mɪˈtaθɪsɪs/ *noun* plural **metatheses** /mɛˈtaθɪsiːz/ L16 **Late Latin** (from Greek, from *metatithenai* transpose, change, from as *meta-* + *tithenai* to put, place). **1** L16 *Linguistics* The transposition of sounds or letters in a word; the result of such a transposition. Formerly also, the transposition of words. **2** L17–M19 *Medicine* Spread of a disease within the body, METASTASIS; movement of diseased matter to another part of the body. **3** E18 *generally* Change or reversal of condition. **4** L19 *Chemistry* (An) interchange of an atom or atoms between two different molecules; *especially* double decomposition.

métayage /metɛjɑʒ/ (*plural same*) *noun* (also **metayage**) L19 **French** (from as MÉTAYER). A system of land tenure in Europe and the United States, in which the farmer pays the owner a proportion (usually half) of the produce as rent, and the owner normally provides the stock and seeds.

métayer /metɛje/ *noun* plural pronounced same L18 **French** (from medieval Latin *medietarius*, from *medietas* half). A farmer who holds land on the MÉTAYAGE system.

metempsychosis /ˌmɛtɛm(p)sʌɪˈkəʊsɪs/ *noun* plural **metempsychoses** /ˌmɛtɛm(p)sʌɪˈkəʊsiːz/ L16 **Late Latin** (from Greek *metempsukhōsis*, from as *meta-* + *en* in + *psukhē* soul). Transmigration of the soul; *especially* the passage of the soul of a person or animal at or after death into a new body of the same or a different species.

■ Belief in *metempsychosis* was a feature of the ancient sect of Pythagoreans and is also a tenet in some Eastern religions.

méthode champenoise /metɔd ʃɑ̃pənwaz/ *noun phrase* E20 **French** (literally, 'champagne method'). The method of introducing a sparkle into wine by allowing the last stage of fermentation to take place in the bottle; a sparkling wine made in this way.

1995 *Country Life* And, thanks to Napoleon's sister and the introduction of the *méthode champenoise*, bottles of the modest, local, sparkling brew, Malvasia.

Methodenstreit /meˈtoːdənˌʃtraɪt/ *noun* plural **Methodenstreite** /meˈtoːdən ˌʃtraɪtə/ M20 **German** (literally, 'methods struggle'). (A) discussion or dispute concerning the methodology of a field of study.

Methuselah /mɪˈθ(j)uːz(ə)lə/ *noun* (also **Methuselem** /mɪˈθ(j)uːz(ə)ləm/) LME **Hebrew** (*mĕṯūšelaḥ*, a pre-Noachian patriarch, stated to have lived 969 years (Genesis 5:27)). **1** LME A very old person or thing, especially as a type or representation of extreme longevity. **2** M20 (Usually **methuselah**) A very large wine bottle, equivalent to eight ordinary bottles.

métier /metje/, /ˈmeɪtɪeɪ/ *noun* L18 **French** (from Proto-Romance alteration of Latin *ministerium* service, ministry, probably influenced by *mysterium* mystery). One's occupation or department of activity. Now usually, a field in which one has special skill or ability; one's forte.

1995 *Spectator* Louisa Alcott was to find her true métier as a chronicler of family life . . . .

metif /meɪˈtiːf/ *noun* E19 **French** (*métif*, alteration of *métis*: see METIS). A person with one White and one quarter Black parent.

metis /meɪˈtiːs/ *Canadian* /meɪˈtiː/, /ˈmeɪti/ *noun* plural same /meɪˈtiː(s)/, /ˈmeɪti/, /ˈmeɪtɪz/ (feminine **métisse** /meɪˈtiːs/, *Canadian also* /ˈmeɪtiːs/, plural **métisses**) E19 **French** (*métis* from Old French *mestis* from Proto-Romance, from Latin *mixtus* past participle of *miscere* to mix). A person of mixed descent; *especially* (in Canada) a person with one White and one American Indian parent.

metope /ˈmɛtəʊp/, /ˈmɛtəpi/ *noun* M16 **Latin** (*metopa* from Greek *metopē*, from *meta* between + *opē* hole in a frieze for a beam-end). *Architecture* A square space between triglyphs in a Doric frieze.

metro /ˈmɛtrəʊ/, /ˈmeɪtrəʊ/ *noun colloquial* (also **Metro**) plural **metros** E20 **French** (*métro* abbreviation of (*Chemin de Fer*) *Métropolitain* Metropolitan (Railway)). An underground railway system in a city, *especially* that in Paris.

metteur en scène /mɛtœr ɑ̃ sɛn/ *noun phrase* plural **metteurs en scène** (pronounced same) E20 **French** (literally, 'a person who puts on the stage'; cf. MISE EN SCÈNE). A producer of a play; a director of a film.

Mettwurst /ˈmɛtvʊrst/ *noun* L19 **German**. A type of smoked German sausage.

meum /ˈmiːəm/, /ˈmeɪəm/ *noun archaic* L16 **Latin** (neuter of *meus* mine). The principle that a person has sole rights to his or her own property and no rights to another's.

■ Chiefly in *meum and tuum*, '(the distinction between) what is mine or one's own and what is yours or another's'.

meunière /məːˈnjɛː/, *foreign* /mønjɛr/ *adjective* M19 **French** ((*à la*) *meunière*, literally, '(in the manner of) a miller's wife'). *Cookery* Especially of fish: cooked or served in lightly browned butter with lemon juice and parsley.

■ Usually postpositive, as in *trout meunière*.

mézair /meɪˈzɛː/, *foreign* /mezɛr/ (*plural same*) *noun* M18 **French** (from Italian *mezzaria* middle gait). *Horsemanship* A movement involving a series of levades with a short step between each.

meze /ˈmeɪzeɪ/ *noun* (also **mezé**) plural same, **mezes** E20 **Turkish** (= snack, appetizer, from Persian *maza* to taste, relish). (Any of) a selection of hot and cold dishes served as an hors d'oeuvre in the Middle East and eastern Mediterranean region.

mezuza /məˈzuːzə/ *noun* (also **mezuzah**) plural **mezuzoth** /məˈzuːzəʊt/ M17 **Hebrew** (*mĕzūzāh*, literally 'doorpost'). A piece of parchment inscribed with Pentateuchal texts enclosed in a case and attached to the doorpost of a Jewish house in fulfilment of religious law.

■ The practice is based upon the injunction in Deuteronomy 6:9.

mezzani /mɛtˈsɑːni/ *noun* L19 **Italian** (plural of *mezzano*: see next). Pasta in the form of medium-sized tubes; an Italian dish consisting largely of this and usually a sauce.

mezzanine /ˈmɛzəniːn/ *noun & adjective* E18 **French** (from Italian *mezzanino* diminutive of *mezzano* middle, medium, from Latin *medianus* median). **A** *noun* **1** E18 A low storey between two others in a building, usually between the ground floor and the floor above. **b** M19 *Theatre* A floor beneath the stage, from which the traps are worked. **c** E20 The lowest gallery in a theatre or cinema; a dress circle. *North American*. **2** M18 A small window at the level of a mezzanine or attic. **B** *adjective* **1** M19 Designating an intermediate floor, storey, etc. **2** L20 *Commerce* Designating unsecured, higher-yielding loans that are subordinate to bank loans and secured loans but rank above equity.

B 1 1996 *Times Magazine* Even when the overall area is divided into smaller units, the tall ceilings provide an opportunity for horizontal divisions such as mezzanine floors.

mezza voce /ˌmɛtsə ˈvɒtʃi/ *adverb, noun, & adjective phrase* L18 **Italian** (*mezza* feminine of *mezzo* middle, half, *voce* voice). *Music* (With) half of the possible vocal or instrumental power; restrained.

mezzo /ˈmɛtsəʊ/ *adverb* M18 **Italian** (= middle, half, from Latin *medius* medium). *Music* (Qualifying a direction:) half, moderately, fairly.

mezzo noun abbreviation of MEZZO-SOPRANO.

mezzo-relievo /ˌmɛtsəʊrɪˈliːvəʊ/ *noun* (also **mezzo-rilievo** /ˌmɛtsəʊrɪˈljeɪvəʊ/) plural **mezzo-relievos** L16 **Italian** (*mezzo* half + *relievo* relief). (A sculpture, moulding, carving, etc., in) half-relief.

mezzo-soprano /ˌmɛtsəʊsəˈprɑːnəʊ/ *noun & adjective* M18 **Italian** (*mezzo* middle + SOPRANO). *Music* **A** *noun* M18 plural **mezzo-sopranos**. A female voice intermediate in compass between soprano and contralto; a singer with such a voice; a part written for such a voice. **B** *adjective* E19 Designating, pertaining to, or intended for a mezzo-soprano.

■ In informal contexts often abbreviated to *mezzo*.

mezzo termine /ˌmɛttso ˈtɛrmine/ *noun phrase* plural **mezzo termini** /ˈtɛrmini/ M18 **Italian** (*mezzo* half, *termine* term). A middle term, measure, or period.

miasma /mɪˈazmə/, /mʌɪˈazmə/ *noun* plural **miasmas, miasmata** /mɪˈazmətə/ M17 **Greek** (*miasma(t-)* defilement, pollution, related to *miainein* to pollute). **1** M17 (An) infectious or noxious vapour, especially from putrescent organic matter, which pollutes the atmosphere. **2** M19 *figurative* A polluting, oppressive, or foreboding atmosphere; a polluting or oppressive influence.

micro /ˈmʌɪkrəʊ/ *noun & adjective* M19 **Greek** (combining form *mikr-* from *mikros* small) **A** *noun* plural **micros**. **1** M19 *Entomology* A moth belonging to the Microlepidoptera. **2** M20 A microskirt. **3** L20 A microcomputer; a microprocessor. **4** L20 A microwave oven. **B** *adjective* **1** E20 Microscopic; very small; small-scale; *Chemistry* of microanalysis. **2** M20 Microeconomic.

■ A colloquial, independent use of the combining form found in many English words derived from Greek and other sources, particularly in technical terminology; cf. MEGA. *Micro*, particularly in its chemical sense, is often contrasted, either explicitly or implicitly, with MACRO.

midinette /mɪdɪˈnɛt/, *foreign* /midinɛt/ (*plural same*) *noun* E20 **French** (from *midi* midday + *dînette* light dinner). A French, especially a Parisian, shop-girl; *especially* a milliner's assistant.

mielie variant of MEALIE.

migma /ˈmɪgmə/ *noun* M20 **Greek** (= mixture). *Geology* (A) MAGMA containing solid material.

mignon /ˈmiːnjɒn/, *foreign* /miɲɔ̃/ (*plural same*) *adjective & noun* (feminine **mignonne** /ˈmiːnjɒn/, *foreign* /miɲɔn/) M16 **French**. **A** *adjective* M16 Delicately formed; prettily small or delicate. **B** *noun* E19 A pretty child or young person.

mignonette /mɪnjəˈnɛt/ *noun* E18 **French** (*mignonnette* diminutive of MIGNON). **1** E18 A kind of light fine narrow pillow-lace. Also *mignonette lace*. **2** L18 Any of several plants of the genus *Reseda*, with small greenish or whitish flowers; specifically *R. odorata*, cultivated for its fragrant flowers. **b** L19 A colour resembling that of the flowers of the mignonette; greyish green or greenish white. **c** L19 A perfume derived from or resembling that of the flowers of the mignonette.

migraine /ˈmiːgreɪn/, /ˈmʌɪgreɪn/ *noun* LME **Old and Modern French** (from late Latin *hemicrania* from Greek *hēmikrania*, from *hēmi-* half + *kranion* skull). A recurrent throbbing headache, usually affecting one side of the head, often accompanied by nausea or disturbed vision; the illness or condition characterized by such headaches.

mihrab /ˈmiːrɑːb/ *noun* E19 **Arabic** (*miḥrāb*). **1** E19 A niche, chamber, or slab in a mosque, indicating the direction of Mecca. **2** E20 A niche motif on an oriental prayer rug, resembling the shape of a mihrab in a mosque.

mikva /ˈmɪkvə/ *noun* (also **mikvah**, **mikveh**) M19 **Yiddish** (*mikve* from Hebrew *miqweh*, literally, 'collection, mass, especially of water'). A bath in which certain Jewish ritual purifications are performed; the action of taking such a bath.

miles gloriosus /ˌmiːleɪz glɔːrɪˈəʊsəs/, /ˌmʌɪliːz/ *noun* plural **milites gloriosi** /ˌmiːlɪteɪz glɔːrɪˈəʊsiː/, /ˌmʌɪlɪtiːz glɔːrɪˈəʊsʌɪ/ E20 **Latin** (= boastful soldier). A vainglorious soldier who boasts about his military exploits.

■ *Miles gloriosus* is the title of a comedy by the Roman playwright Plautus (*c.*250–184 BC). The *miles gloriosus* became a stock character of Renaissance comedy—Shakespeare's Parolles in *All's Well That Ends Well* is an example—and the phrase generally occurs in literary contexts.

milieu /ˈmiːljəː/, /mɪˈljəː/, *foreign* /miljø/ *noun* plural **milieus**, **milieux** /ˈmiːljəːz/, *foreign* /miljø/ M19 **French** (from *mi* (from Latin *medius* mid) + *lieu* place). **1** M19 An environment; (especially social) surroundings. **2** M20 *transferred* A group of people with a shared (cultural) outlook; a social class or set. **b** L20 (also **Milieu**) In France: (a group or organization belonging to) the criminal underworld.

1 1996 *Spectator* She sketches in the Surrealist milieu of Twenties Paris.

milites gloriosi plural of MILES GLORIOSUS.

militia /mɪˈlɪʃə/ *noun* L16 **Latin** (= military service, warfare, war, from *miles*, *milit-* soldier). **1** L16–L17 A system of military discipline, organization, and tactics; a manner or means of conducting warfare. **2** L16 A military force, a body of soldiers; *specifically* a military force raised from the civilian population, as distinguished from mercenaries or professional soldiers; an auxiliary military force drawn from the civilian population in order to supplement the regular forces in an emergency; *collectively* the members of such a militia. **3** L18 The body of people, usually men, legally liable to military service, without enlistment. *United States*.

millefeuille /milfœj/, /ˈmiːlfəːj/ *noun* plural pronounced same L19 **French** (literally, 'a thousand leaves'). A rich confection of thin layers of puff pastry and a filling of jam, cream, etc.

millefiore /ˌmiːlɪfrˈɔːri/ *noun* M19 **Italian** (from *mille* thousand + *fiore* flowers). A kind of ornamental glass made by fusing together a number of glass rods of different sizes and colours and cutting the mass into sections which exhibit ornamental figures of varying pattern. Also *millefiore glass*.

mille-fleurs /milflœr/ *noun* M19 **French** (literally, 'a thousand flowers'). **1** M19 A perfume distilled from flowers of different kinds. **2** E20 A pattern of flowers and leaves used in tapestry, on porcelain, etc.

■ Usually attributive (see quotation).

2 1996 *Country Life* The enclosed garden in which she is sitting is chequered with tiny daisies and small birds like a *mille-fleurs* tapestry.

millegrain /ˈmɪlɪgreɪn/ *noun & adjective* (also **milligrain**) M20 **French** (*mille* thousand + *grain* grain). (Designating) a gem setting of beaded or crenellated metal.

millennium /mɪˈlɛnɪəm/ *noun* plural **millenniums**, **millennia** /mɪˈlɛnɪə/ M17 **Modern Latin** (from Latin *mille* thousand, after BIENNIUM). **1** M17 A period of one thousand years. Also, a thousandth anniversary. **2** M17 *Christian Church The* period of one thousand years during which (according to one interpretation of Revelation 20:1–5) Christ will reign in person on earth. **3** E19 A period of peace, happiness, prosperity, and ideal government.

millet /ˈmɪlɛt/ *noun* E20 **Turkish** (= nation, group of co-religionists, from Arabic *milla(t)* religion). *History* A part of the population of the Ottoman Empire that owed allegiance to a particular religious leader, especially a non-Muslim one.

milpa /ˈmɪlpə/ *noun* M19 **Mexican Spanish**. In Central America and Mexico: a small cultivated field, usually of corn or maize.

mimbar /ˈmɪmbɑː/ *noun* (also **minbar** /ˈmɪnbɑː/) M19 **Arabic** (*minbar*, from *nabara* to raise). A small set of steps in a mosque from which the KHUTBAH is delivered.

mimesis /mɪˈmiːsɪs/, /mɪˈmʌɪsɪs/ *noun* M16 **Greek** (*mimēsis*, from *mimeisthai* to imitate, from *mimos* mime). **1** M16 Chiefly *Rhetoric* Imitation of another person's words or actions. **b** M20 The representation of the real world in art, poetry, etc. **2** M19 *Biology* Mimicry by one organism of another. Now *rare*. **3** M20 *Sociology* The deliberate imitation of the behaviour of one group of people by another as a factor in social change.

minaret /ˈmɪnərɛt/, /mɪnəˈrɛt/ *noun* L17 **French** (or Spanish *minarete*, Italian *minaretto*, from Turkish *mināre* from Arabic *manāra* lighthouse, minaret, from *nāra* to shine). **1** L17 A tall tower or turret connected with a mosque and surrounded by one or more projecting balconies from which a muezzin calls at hours of prayer. **2** M19 *transferred* An object or structure shaped like this.

minaudière /minodjɛr/ *noun* plural pronounced same E18 **French** (from *minauder* to simper, flirt, from *mine* mien). **1** E18–E19 A coquettish woman. **2** M20 A small handbag without a handle, a clutch-bag.

minbar variant of MIMBAR.

minerval /mɪˈnəːv(ə)l/ *noun* E17 **Latin** (from *Minerva* (earlier *Menerva*) the Roman goddess of handicrafts, wisdom (cf. Sanskrit *manasvin* wise), and later also of war, from earlier form related to Sanskrit *manas* mind, Greek *menos* courage, fury). A gift given in gratitude by a pupil to a teacher.

minestra /mɪˈnɛstrə/ *noun* L17 **Italian**. In Italy: soup, *especially* MINESTRONE.

minestrone /mɪnɪˈstrəʊni/ *noun* L19 **Italian**. A thick soup containing vegetables, beans, and pasta.

mingei /mɪŋˈgeɪ/ *noun* M20 **Japanese** (from *min* people + *gei* arts). Japanese folk-art; traditional Japanese handicraft.

minifundium /mɪnɪˈfʌndɪəm/ *noun* plural **minifundia** /mɪnɪˈfʌndɪə/ (also **minifundio** /mɪnɪˈfʌndɪəʊ/, plural **minifundios**) M20 **Modern Latin** (or Spanish *minifundio* smallholding: cf. LATIFUNDIUM). In Latin America: a small farm or property, *especially* one that is too small to support a single family. Usually in *plural*.

minimus /ˈmɪnɪməs/ *noun & adjective* L16 **Latin**. **A** *noun* plural **minimi** /ˈmɪnɪmʌɪ/, /ˈmɪnɪmiː/. L16 A very small or insignificant creature. **B** *adjective* L18 Designating the youngest of several pupils with the same surname or the last to enter a school.

■ As an adjective appended to a surname, the usage is found especially in public schools; thus the eldest and middle brothers of the three of which Smith *minimus* was the youngest would be known respectively as Smith *major* and Smith *minor*. Cf. PRIMUS.

Minnelied /ˈmɪnəliːd/ *noun* plural **Minnelieder** /ˈmɪnəliːdə(r)/ L19 **German** (from *Minne* love + *Lied* song). A love-song written by a minnesinger, or in the style of the minnesingers.

Minnesinger /ˈmɪnəsɪŋə/ *noun* (also **minnesinger**) E19 **German** (from *Minne* love + *Singer* (modern *Sänger*) singer). A German lyric poet or singer of the twelfth to fourteenth centuries.

minuetto /minuˈetto/, /mɪnjʊˈɛtəʊ/ *noun* plural **minuetti** /minuˈetti/, **minuettos** /mɪnjʊˈɛtəʊz/ E18 **Italian**. A minuet.

minuterie /mɪˈnjuːt(ə)ri/ *noun* M20 **French** (= clockwork, timing mechanism, from *minute* minute). (An electric light controlled by) a light switch incorporating a timing mechanism to turn it off automatically after a short time.

1955 W. Gaddis *Recognitions* Crémer opened the door, and the light of the minuterie threw his flat shadow across the sill.

minutia /mɪˈnjuːʃɪə/, /mʌɪˈnjuːʃɪə/ *noun* plural **minutiae** /mɪˈnjuːʃɪiː/, /mɪˈnjuːʃɪʌɪ/ M18 **Latin** (= smallness (in plural, trifles), from *minutus* small). A precise detail; a small or trivial matter or object.

■ Almost always used in the plural.

minyan /ˈmɪnjan/ *noun* plural **minyanim** /ˈmɪnjanɪm/ M18 **Hebrew** (*minyān*, literally, 'count, reckoning'). The quorum of ten males over thirteen years of age required for traditional Jewish public worship.

mirabelle /ˈmɪrəbɛl/ *noun* E18 **French**. **1** E18 (A fruit from) a European variety of plum tree. **2** M20 (A) liqueur distilled from mirabelles, especially those grown in Alsace, France.

mirabile dictu /mɪˌrɑːbɪleɪ ˈdɪktuː/ *interjection* M19 **Latin** (*mirabile* neuter of *mirabilis* wonderful + *dictu* supine of *dicere* to say). Wonderful to relate.

■ Generally used sarcastically (see quotation).

1996 *New Scientist* '*Mirabile dictu!*' one might exclaim, though few people did. Most used an Anglo-Saxon term: hogwash.

mirabilia /mɪrəˈbɪlɪə/ *noun plural* M20 **Latin** (use as noun of neuter plural of *mirabilis* wonderful). Wonders, marvels, miracles.

mirador /miraˈdor/ *noun* L17 **Spanish** (from *mirar* to look, observe). In Spain: a watch-tower. Also, a turret or belvedere on the top of a Spanish house.

mirage /ˈmɪrɑːz/, /mɪˈrɑːz/ *noun & adjective* E19 **French** (from *se mirer* to be reflected or mirrored, from Latin *mirare*). **A** *noun* **1** E19 An optical illusion caused by atmospheric conditions (usually the refraction of light in heated air); *especially* the false appearance of a distant sheet of water in a desert or on a hot road. Also, the appearance in the sky of a reflected image of a distant object, a wavelike appearance of warmed air just above the ground. **2** E19 *figuratively* An illusion, a fantasy. **3** E20 Any of various pale fashion colours; *especially* pale blue, grey, or turquoise. **B** *adjective* **1** E20 Resembling a mirage. **2** M20 Of a pale colour, especially blue, grey, or turquoise.

mirepoix /mirpwa/ *noun* plural same L19 **French** (from the Duc de *Mirepoix* (1699–1757), French diplomat and general). *Cookery* A mixture of sautéed diced vegetables used in sauces etc. or served as a separate dish.

mirliton /ˈməːlɪtɒn/ *noun* E19 **French** (= reed pipe, of imitative origin). **1** E19 A musical instrument resembling a kazoo; any instrument in which a sound is given a nasal quality by means of a vibrating membrane. **2** E20 A CHAYOTE. *United States*.

miscellanea /mɪsəˈleɪnɪə/ *noun* L16 **Latin** (neuter plural of Latin *miscellaneus* from *miscellus* mixed). As *plural*, miscellaneous items, especially literary compositions, collected together. As *singular*, a miscellaneous collection, especially of literary compositions; a miscellany.

Mischsprache /ˈmɪʃˌʃpraːxə/ *noun* plural **Mischsprachen** /ˈmɪʃˌʃpraːxən/ M20 **German** (= mixed language). A language made up of elements of two or more languages.

mise au point /miz o pwɛ̃/ *noun phrase* plural **mises au point** (pronounced same) M20 **French**. A focusing or clarification of an obscure subject or problem.

1946 *Word* A general *mise au point* of the linguistic side of semantic problems is thus overdue.

mise-en-page /mizɑ̃paʒ/ *noun* plural **mises-en-page** (pronounced same) E20 **French** (*mise en pages* page-setting, imposition). The design of a printed page etc., including the layout of text and illustrations. Also, the composition of a picture.

1968 *Listener* Television cannot emphasise in the manner of a newspaper's *mise-en-page*.

mise en scène /miz ɑ̃ sɛn/ *noun phrase* (also **mise-en-scène**) plural **mises en scène** (pronounced same) M19 **French** (cf. METTEUR EN SCÈNE). **1** M19 The staging of a play; the scenery and properties of a stage production. **2** L19 The setting or surroundings of an event or action.

1 1996 *Spectator* Covent Garden has really done it proud, . . . with a stupendously gorgeous staging by that genius of *mise-en-scène* Philip Prowse . . .

2 1995 *Observer Review* . . . the way the book imports real-life VIPs . . . and restaurants . . . into its narrative suggests the *mise en scène* isn't to be taken as entirely fantastical.

misère /mɪˈzɛː/, *foreign* /mizɛr/ (*plural same*) *noun* E19 **French** (= poverty, misery). **1** E19 *Cards* A declaration by which the caller undertakes not to win any tricks. **2** L19 Misery; a miserable condition or circumstance.

1 1995 *New Scientist* Many games exist in a 'misère' version, where the aim is to lose, not win. The misère version of dividing economic goods is dividing economic 'bads' such as unemployment, responsibility for pollution or responsibility for crime.

miserere /mɪzəˈrɪəri/, /mɪzəˈrɛːri/ *noun* ME **Latin** (imperative singular of *misereri* to have pity, have mercy, from *miser* wretched). **1 a** ME Psalm 51 (50 in the Vulgate), beginning *Miserere mei Deus* 'Have mercy upon me, O God', one of the penitential psalms. **b** L18 A musical setting of this psalm. **2** E17 *transferred* A cry for mercy; a prayer in which mercy is sought. **3** L18 A misericord seat.

mises au point plural of MISE AU POINT.

mises-en-page, **mises en scène** plurals of MISE-EN-PAGE, MISE EN SCÈNE.

miso /ˈmiːsəʊ/ *noun* E18 **Japanese**. Paste made from fermented soya beans and barley or rice malt, used in Japanese cookery.

mistral /ˈmɪstr(ə)l/, /mɪˈstrɑːl/ *noun* E17 **French** (from Provençal from Latin *magistralis* (sc. *ventus* wind)). A strong cold north-west wind which blows through the Rhône valley and southern France into the Mediterranean, mainly in winter.

1996 *Times Magazine* Overtones of Africa must be cheering in mid-winter when the *mistral* sweeps down the Rhône Valley from Siberia.

mit /mɪt/ *preposition & adverb* L19 **German** (= with). With (me, us, etc.). *jocular* and *colloquial*.

Mitbestimmung /ˈmɪtbəˌʃtɪmʊŋ/ *noun* M20 **German** (= co-determination). In Germany: the policy in industry of involving both workers and management in decision-making.

1996 *Independent* And the other way round: no Ernest Bevin, no *Mitbestimmung*—the great postwar understanding between German unions and the bosses which still, just about, lasts.

Mitnagged /mɪtˈnagɛd/ *noun* plural **Mitnaggim** /mɪtˈnagɪm/ E20 **Hebrew** (*mitnaggēḏ* opponent). A religious opponent of the Hasidim; any Jew who is not a Hasid.

Mitsein /ˈmɪtzʌɪn/ *noun* M20 **German** (use as noun of infinitive *mitsein*, from *mit* with + *sein* to be). *Philosophy* The concept of a person's being in its relationship with others.

1966 A. Manser *Sartre* The essence of relations between consciousnesses is not Mitsein (being together), it is conflict.

Mittelschmerz /ˈmɪtəlˌʃmɛrts/ *noun* L19 **German** (= middle pain). *Medicine* Pain in the lower abdomen regularly experienced by some women midway between successive menstrual periods and often thought to coincide with ovulation.

Mittelstand /ˈmɪtəlstand/ *noun* L20 **German** (= middle class). Something between extremes of size; middling size range.

1994 *Guardian* The problems facing smaller firms in growing into the Mittelstand are also highlighted . . .

mittimus /ˈmɪtɪməs/ *noun & verb* LME **Latin** (literally, 'we send', the first word of the writ in Latin). **A** *noun* **1** *Law* **a** LME–E18 A writ to transfer records from one court to another. **b** L16 A warrant committing a person to prison. **2** L16 A dismissal from office; a notice to quit.

■ Sense 2 is chiefly used colloquially and in dialect in *get one's mittimus*, that is, 'be dismissed'.

mitzvah /ˈmɪtsvə/ *noun* plural **mitzvoth** /ˈmɪtsvəʊt/ M17 **Hebrew** (*miṣwāh* commandment). *Judaism* A precept; a duty, an obligation. Also, a good deed. Cf. BAR MITZVAH, BAT MITZVAH.

mixte /mikst/ *adjective & noun* plural of noun pronounced same L20 **French** (= mixed). (Designating) a bicycle or bicycle frame having no crossbar but instead two thin tubes running from the head of the steering column to either side of the rear axle.

Mizpah /ˈmɪzpə/ *adjective* L19 **Hebrew** (*Miṣpah* place-name in ancient Palestine). Designating a ring, locket, etc., given as an expression or token of association or remembrance, originally and especially one with 'Mizpah' inscribed on it.

■ The allusion is to the cairn of stones made in token of the covenant between Jacob and Laban (Genesis 31:43–55), which was called Mizpah 'for he said, The Lord watch between me and thee, when we are absent one from another' (verse 49).

moccasin /ˈmɒkəsɪn/ *noun* E17 **Virginia Algonquian** (*mockasin*, and in other North American Indian languages). **1 a** E17 A kind of soft leather shoe, worn by North American Indians, trappers, etc. **b** L19 A soft informal shoe resembling this. **2** L18 A venomous North American snake.

mochi /ˈmɒtʃi/ *noun* plural same E17 **Japanese**. A cake made from glutinous rice, steamed and pounded.

modello /mɒˈdɛləʊ/, *foreign* /moˈdɛllo/ *noun* plural **modelli** /moˈdɛlli/, **modellos** M20 **Italian**. A detailed sketch for a larger painting, prepared for a patron's approval. Also, a small model for a larger sculpture.

moderato /mɒdəˈrɑːtəʊ/ *adverb* E18 **Italian** (= moderate). *Music* (A direction:) at a moderate pace or tempo.

moderne /məˈdəːn/, *foreign* /mɔdɛrn/ *adjective & noun* M20 **French** (= modern). (Designating or characterized by) a popularization of the art deco style marked by bright colours and austere geometric shapes, or (frequently *derogatory*) any ultra-modern style.

Modernismus /modɛrˈnɪsmʊs/, /mɒdəˈnɪzməs/ *noun* M20 **German** (= modernism). Modernism in architecture, art, etc.

■ Frequently derogatory.

modi plural of MODUS.

modicum /ˈmɒdɪkəm/ *noun* L15 **Latin** (= little way, short time, neuter singular of *modicus* moderate, from *modus* mode). A small quantity or portion; a limited amount.

■ Usually followed by *of* in contexts in which *modicum* means 'a decent or necessary minimum amount' (see quotation).

1996 *Spectator* . . . there seems no reason why an editor, if he has to be sacked, cannot be despatched with a modicum of courtesy.

modiste /mɒˈdiːst/, *foreign* /mɔdist/ (*plural same*) *noun* M19 **French** (from *mode* fashion, mode). A person who makes, designs, or deals in articles of fashion; *especially* a fashionable milliner or dressmaker.

1996 *Spectator* The result can be seen in the glorious 'Milliner's Shop' . . . in which the *modiste* can be seen nestling behind her stock as if sheltering beneath brilliantly coloured tropical flowers.

modulus /ˈmɒdjʊləs/ *noun* plural **moduli** /ˈmɒdjʊlʌɪ/, /ˈmɒdjʊliː/, **moduluses** M16 **Latin** (diminutive of *modus* mode). **1** M16–M17 *Architecture* A unit of length by which proportions are expressed. **2** *Mathematics* **a** M18 A number by which logarithms to one base must be multiplied in order to obtain the corresponding logarithms to another base. **b** M19 A constant multiplier, coefficient, or parameter. **c** M19 A measure of a quantity which depends on two or more other quantities. **d** M19 A number by which another number may be divided leaving a remainder. **3** E19 *Physics* and *Engineering* A numerical quantity representing some property of a substance, and equal to the ratio of the magnitude of a (usually mechanical) cause to the magnitude of its effect on the substance; *specifically* = modulus of elasticity.

modus /ˈməʊdəs/ *noun* plural **modi** /ˈməʊdʌɪ/, **moduses** L16 **Latin**. A mode; *especially* the way in which something is done; a mode or manner of operation.

■ Now chiefly in Latin phrases (see following entries) or used elliptically for MODUS OPERANDI.

modus operandi /ˌməʊdəs ɒpəˈrandiː/, /ˌməʊdəs ɒpəˈrandʌɪ/ *noun phrase* M17 **Modern Latin** (= mode of operating). **1** M17 The way in which something operates. **2** L19 The way in which a person sets about a task.

2 1995 *Spectator* Certainly, as the last *NoW* editor to benefit from the narks, Mr Morgan would be familiar with their *modus operandi*.

modus vivendi /ˌməʊdəs vɪˈvɛndiː/, /ˌməʊdəs vɪˈvɛndʌɪ/ *noun phrase* L19 **Modern Latin** (= mode of living). A way of living or coping; *especially* a working arrangement between parties in dispute pending a final settlement.

1996 *Times* It is the *modus vivendi* of Christianity which underpins European thought.

moellon /ˈmwɛlɒn/ *noun* L19 **French**. DEGRAS sense 1.

moeurs /məːz/, /mœr/ *noun plural* E20 **French** (from Latin MORES, plural of *mos* custom). The behaviour, customs, or habits of a people or a group of people.

1996 *Spectator* The director Stefano Vizioli and his designer Susanna Rossi Just present this sharp satire of marital *moeurs* with a light touch . . .

mofette /mɒˈfɛt/ *noun* E19 **French** (from Neapolitan Italian *mofetta* = Spanish *mofeta*). (An exhalation of gas from) a fumarole.

mofussil /məʊˈfʌsɪl/ *noun & adjective* (also **Mofussil**, **mofusil**) L18 **Urdu** (*mufassil* from Persian and Urdu *mufassal* from Arabic *mufaṣṣal* passive participle of *faṣṣala* to divide, separate). **A** *noun* L18 In the Indian subcontinent: the rural localities of a district as distinguished from the chief station or the town. **B** *attributive* or as *adjective* Of the mofussil; remote, provincial.

1996 *Spectator* Whether from across the sea or the Indian *mofusil*, immigrants come to these island cities to escape not only from poverty but also from the social constraints that held them back in their old worlds.

mogote /məˈɡəʊti/ *noun* E20 **Spanish** (= hillock, heap, haystack). *Physical Geography* A steep-sided hill of roughly circular cross-section characteristic of karst topography, especially in Cuba. Cf. HUM.

mohel /ˈməʊ(h)(ə)l/ *noun* M17 **Hebrew** (*mōhēl*). A Jew who performs the rite of circumcision.

moi /mwa/ *personal pronoun* L20 **French** (= me). Me; I, myself.

■ Since the late 1970s in jocular use as a pretentious reference to oneself. Chief popularizer of the expression was the character Miss Piggy in the television series *The Muppets*, the children's puppet show created by Jim Henson, and it was then also taken up by adult shows.

1996 *Times: Weekend* But naturally. Why do anything by halves? Cynical, moi? Not at all.

moire /mwɑː/ *noun* M17 **French** (later form of *mouaire* mohair). A watered fabric (originally mohair, now usually silk). Also *moire antique*.

moiré /ˈmwɑːreɪ/ *adjective & noun* E19 **French** (past participle of *moirer* to give a watered appearance to, from as preceding). **A** *adjective* **1** E19 Of silk: watered. Also, (of metal etc.) having a clouded appearance like watered silk. **2** M20 Designating or pertaining to a pattern of light and dark fringes observed when a pattern of lines, dots, etc., is visually superimposed on another similar pattern, or on an identical one slightly out of alignment with the first. **B** *noun* **1** E19 A variegated or clouded appearance like that of watered silk, especially as an ornamental finish applied to metal; a moiré pattern or effect. **2** M19 MOIRE.

A.1 *figurative* **1995** *Spectator* . . . it is very long, at times a shade too fluid, too gorgeously *moiré*.

moksha /ˈmɒkʃə/ *noun* L18 **Sanskrit** (*mokṣa*, from *muc* to set free, release). *Hinduism* and *Jainism* The final release of the soul from a cycle of incarnations; the bliss so attained. Also called *mukti*.

mola /ˈməʊlə/ *noun* M20 **Cuna**. A square of brightly coloured appliquéd cloth worn as a blouse by Cuna Indian women of the San Blas Islands, Panama.

1977 A. Jeffs (ed.) *Creative Crafts* Originally, when the Indians moved to the islands in the mid-19th century, these molas were simple garments made from dark blue fabric with just a narrow single band of color around the bottom.

molcajete /molkaˈxete/, /mɒlkəˈheɪteɪ/ *noun* L20 **Mexican Spanish** (from Spanish *moler* to grind + *cajete* pot, bowl). A mortar for grinding spices and small seeds in.

mole /ˈmoli/, /ˈməʊli/ *noun* M20 **Mexican Spanish** (from Nahuatl *molli* sauce, stew). A highly spiced Mexican sauce made chiefly from chilli and chocolate, served with meat.

molleton /ˈmɒlɪtɒn/ *noun* L18 **French** (from *mollet* diminutive of *mol* soft). Swanskin (flannel).

moloch /ˈməʊlɒk/ *noun* (in sense 1 usually **Moloch**) E17 **Late Latin** (from Greek *Molokh* from Hebrew *mōleḵ*, a Canaanite idol to whom children were sacrificed as burnt offerings (Leviticus 18:21), held to be alteration of *meleḵ* king, by substitution of the vowels of *bōšeṯ* shame). **1** E17 An object to which horrible sacrifices are made. **2** M19 A slow-moving spiny Australian lizard, *Moloch horridus*, of grotesque appearance. Also called *mountain devil*, *spiny lizard*, *thorny devil*. **3** L19 A forest monkey of tropical America, a dusky titi.

molossus /məˈlɒsəs/ *noun* plural **molossi** /məˈlɒsʌɪ/ L16 **Latin** (= Greek *Molossos*). **1** L16 *Prosody* A metrical foot consisting of three long syllables. **2** E17 *History* A mastiff dog from the region of ancient Molossia, in north-western Greece. More fully *molossus dog*.

molto /ˈmɒltəʊ/ *adverb* E19 **Italian** (from Latin *multus* much). *Music* Very.

■ Usually in directions modifying adjectives from Italian.

momentum /məˈmɛntəm/ *noun* plural **momenta** /məˈmɛntə/ E17 **Latin** (see MOMENT). **1** E17–M19 A turning motion. **2 a** L17 *Physics* The quantity of motion of a moving body, equal to the product of the mass and the velocity of the body. **b** L18 The effect of inertia in the continuance of motion; impetus gained by movement; *figuratively* strength or continuity derived from an initial effort. **3** *Mathematics* An infinitesimal increment. Only in M18. **4** M18–E19 Force of movement. **5** E19 An element of a complex conceptual identity, a moment.

mompei /ˈmɒmpeɪ/ *noun plural* (also **mompe**) M20 **Japanese** (*monpe*). Baggy working trousers worn in Japan.

momser, **momzer** variants of MAMZER.

monad /ˈmɒnad/, /ˈməʊnad/ *noun & adjective* (in sense 1 also (earlier) in Latin form **monas** /ˈmɒnas/, plural **monades** /ˈmɒnədiːz/ M16 **French** (*monade* or its source late Latin *monas*, *monad-* from Greek, from *monos* alone). **1** M16 (**Monad**) The Deity, God. **b** E17 The number one, unity; a unit. Now chiefly *Historical*, with reference to ancient Greek philosophy, in which the numbers were regarded as being generated from the unitary one. **2** M18 *Philosophy* Especially in the philosophy of Leibniz: an indivisible unit of being (as a soul, an atom); an absolutely simple entity. **3** M19 *Biology* A hypothetical simple organism, *especially* one assumed as the first term in the genealogy of living beings, or regarded as associated with others to form an animal or vegetable body.

mon ami /mɔn ami/ *noun phrase* (also (feminine) **mon amie**) plural **mes amis** (feminine **mes amies**) /mez ami/ L18 **French**. (As a form of address:) my friend.

monas see MONAD.

mon cher /mɔ̃ ʃɛr/ *noun phrase* L17 **French**. (As a form of address to a male:) my dear, my dear fellow.

mondain /mɔ̃dɛ̃/ *noun & adjective* (feminine **mondaine** /mɔ̃dɛn/) L19 **French**. **A** *noun* L19 plural pronounced same. A worldly or fashionable person. Cf. DEMIMONDAINE. **B** *adjective* L19 Of the fashionable world; worldly.

monde /mɔ̃d/, /mɒnd/ *noun* M18 **French** (= world). The world of fashionable or aristocratic people; such people collectively. Also, a person's particular circle or set.

■ Earlier in BEAU MONDE.

mondo /ˈmɒndəʊ/ *noun* plural **mondos** E20 **Japanese** (from *mon* asking + *dō* answering). An instructional technique of Zen Buddhism consisting of rapid dialogue of questions and answers between teacher and pupil.

mondo /ˈmɒndəʊ/ *adjective & adverb* M20 **Italian** (= world). **A** *adjective* **1** M20 Anarchic and tasteless. **2** L20 As an intensifier: considerable, much; huge. **B** *adverb* L20 Very, extremely.

■ Slang use of *mondo* derives ultimately from *Mondo Cane*, the title of an Italian film (1961) showing bizarre behaviour (released in 1963 in the English-speaking world as *A Dog's Life*). The film became a cult and was imitated in similar titles such as *Mondo Bizarro* (1966). The adjectival and adverbial uses arose through the interpretation of, for instance, *mondo bizarro* as 'very bizarre'. In the 1980s *mondo* became simply an intensifier in American slang. It was taken up in this way by the children's comic-book characters the Teenage Mutant Ninja Turtles (in Britain, the Teenage Mutant Hero Turtles) in phrases such as *mondo cool* to express approval, and the usage spread to Britain during the Turtlemania of 1989–90.

mondongo /mɒnˈdɒŋgəʊ/ *noun* plural **mondongos** E17 **Spanish** (= tripe, black pudding). A Latin American or West Indian dish composed of tripe.

monocoque /ˈmɒnə(ʊ)kɒk/ *noun & adjective* E20 **French** (from *mono-* mono- + *coque* eggshell). **A** *noun* **1** E20 An aircraft fuselage or other structure having an outer covering in the form of a rigid load-bearing shell, usually without longerons or stringers. **2** M20 A motor vehicle underframe and body built as a single rigid structure (or in racing cars as a number of boxlike sections) throughout which the stresses are distributed. **B** *attributive* or as *adjective* E20 Designating or based on a structure of this type.

monosabio /mono'sabjo/, /mɒnəʊ'sabɪəʊ/ *noun* plural **monosabios** /mono'sabjos/, /mɒnəʊ'sabɪəʊz/ L19 **Spanish** (from *mono* monkey + *sabio* wise, trained). *Bullfighting* A picador's assistant in the ring.

monsoon /mɒn'su:n/ *noun* L16 **Early Modern Dutch** (*monssoen* (modern *moesson*, influenced by French forms) from Portuguese *monção* (cf. Old Spanish *monzon*) from Arabic *mawsim* season, fixed period, from *wasama* to brand, mark). **1** L16 A seasonal wind which blows in southern Asia, especially in the Indian Ocean, approximately from the south-west from April to October (in full *south-west, summer, wet*, or *rainy monsoon*), and from the north-east from October to April (in full *north-east, winter*, or *dry monsoon*). **b** M18 The rainfall which accompanies the south-west or summer monsoon; the rainy season. **2** L17 Any wind which reverses its direction seasonally, as the temperature varies between two areas, especially between land and ocean.

mons pubis /mɒnz 'pju:bɪs/ *noun phrase* L19 **Latin** (= mount of the pubes). *Anatomy* The rounded mass of fatty tissue on the lower abdomen, over the joint of the pubic bones; *especially* that of a female (= MONS VENERIS sense 2).

monstre sacré /mɔ̃str sakre/ *noun phrase* plural **monstres sacrés** (pronounced same) M20 **French** (literally, 'sacred monster'). A striking, eccentric, or controversial public figure.

1995 *Spectator* Since Scruton was demolishing the claims of much of the painting and sculpture featured in the Tate, its director, Nicholas Serota, the *monstre sacré* of London's modern art establishment, found it convenient to be in New York.

mons Veneris /mɒnz 'vɛnərɪs/ *noun phrase* E17 **Latin** (= mount of Venus). **1** E17 *Palmistry* The ball of the thumb. **2** L17 *Anatomy* The rounded mass of fatty tissue on a female's lower abdomen, above the vulva. Cf. MONS PUBIS.

montage /mɒn'tɑ:ʒ/, /'mɒntɑ:ʒ/ *noun* E20 **French** (from *monter* to mount). **1** E20 *Cinematography* and *Television* The selection and arrangement of separate sections of film as a consecutive whole; the blending (by superimposition) of separate shots to form a single picture; a sequence or picture resulting from such a process. **2** *generally* M20 The process or technique of producing a composite whole by combining several different pictures, pieces of music, or other elements, so that they blend with or into one another; the result of such a process.

montagnard /mɔ̃taɲar/, /mɒntə'njɑ:d/ (*plural same*) *adjective & noun* M19 **French** (from *montagne* mountain). **A** *adjective* M19 Inhabiting a mountain region; of or pertaining to montagnards. **B** *noun* M20 A native or inhabitant of a mountain region; a highlander.

montagne russe /mɔ̃taɲ rys/ *noun phrase* plural **montagnes russes** (pronounced same) M19 **French** (literally, 'Russian mountain'). A switchback, a scenic railway, a roller coaster. *Canadian*.

Montaña /mon'taɲa/ *noun* M19 **Spanish** (= mountain). In Spanish-American countries: a forest of considerable extent; *specifically* the forested eastern foothills of the Andes in Peru etc.

mont de piété /mɔ̃ də pjete/ *noun phrase* plural **monts de piété** (pronounced same) M19 **French** (= mount of piety). A State pawnbroking organization in France providing loans to the poor at low rates of interest.

■ The term 'mount' for a financial institution was formerly (E17–M18) current in English. Cf. Italian MONTE DI PIETÀ.

monte /'mɒnti/ *noun* (in branch I (especially sense 2) also **monty** E19 **Spanish** (= mountain, pile of cards left after dealing). **I 1** E19 A Spanish and Spanish-American gambling game usually played with a pack of forty cards. Also (in full *three-card monte*), a form of three-card trick. **2** L19 A certainty; *specifically* a horse considered a safe bet to win a race. *Australian and New Zealand colloquial*. **II 3** M19 In Spanish-American countries: a small wooded tract; (a region of) chaparral or scrub.

monte di pietà /ˌmonte di pje'tɑ:/ *noun phrase* plural **monti di pietà** /ˌmonti/ M17 **Italian** (= mount of piety). A State pawnbroking organization in Italy providing loans to the poor at low rates of interest. Cf. French MONT DE PIÉTÉ.

montera /mon'tera/ *noun* (also (now *rare*) **montero** /mon'tero/, plural **monteros** /mon'teros/) E17 **Spanish** (from *montero* mountaineer, hunter, from *monte* mount). A Spanish cap, originally worn for hunting, with a spherical crown and flaps able to be drawn over the ears. Now usually *specifically*, the black hat worn by a bullfighter.

monti di pietà, monts de piété plurals of MONTE DI PIETÀ, MONT DE PIÉTÉ.

montuno /mɒn'tu:nəʊ/ *noun* plural **montunos** M20 **American Spanish** (= native to mountains, wild, untamed). **1** M20 A traditional male costume worn in Panama, consisting of white cotton short trousers and an embroidered shirt. **2** M20 An improvised passage in a rumba.

mon vieux /mɔ̃ vjø/ *noun phrase* L19 **French**. (As an affectionate form of address:) old friend, old man.

moolvi(e) variant of MOULVI.

moquette /mɒ'kɛt/ *noun* M19 **French** (perhaps from obsolete Italian *mocaiardo* mohair). A heavy piled fabric used for carpets and upholstery.

1996 *Times The Virgin in the Garden* supplies the interior decor of a Fifties lower middle-class home in such evocative detail that you can feel the texture of the uncut moquette.

mor /mɔ:/ *noun* M20 **Danish** (= humus). *Soil Science* Humus forming a discrete layer on top of the soil with little mineral soil mixed with it, characteristic of coniferous forests and generally strongly acid.

moraine /mə'reɪn/ *noun* L18 **French** (from Savoyard Italian *morena*, from southern French *mor(re)* muzzle, snout, from Proto-Romance word). **1** L18 An area or bank of debris that a glacier or ice sheet has carried down and deposited; the material forming such a deposit. **2** E20 *Gardening* A bed made largely of stones covered with fine chippings, designed to produce suitable conditions for alpine plants.

morale /mə'rɑ:l/ *noun* M18 **French** (*moral*, respelt to indicate stress; cf. LOCALE). **1** M18 Morality; moral teaching. Now *rare*. **2** M19 The mental and emotional attitude of a group or individual with regard to confidence, willingness, hope, etc.; degree of contentment with one's lot or situation.

moratorium /mɒrə'tɔ:rɪəm/ *noun* plural **moratoriums, moratoria** /mɒrə'tɔ:rɪə/ L19 **Modern Latin** (use as noun of neuter singular of late Latin *moratorius* that delays, from *morat-* past participial stem of *morari* to delay). **1** L19 *Law* A legal authorization to a debtor to postpone payment for a certain time; the period of such a postponement. **2** M20 A postponement or deliberate temporary suspension of some activity etc.

2 1995 *New Scientist* . . . there are plenty of grey whales migrating past Vancouver Island these days, after a decade-long moratorium on commercial whaling.

morbidezza /morbi'dɛddza/, /mɔ:bɪ'dɛtsə/ *noun* E17 **Italian** (from *morbido* morbid). **1** E17 *Painting* Lifelike delicacy in flesh tints. **2** L19 Delicacy, softness, especially in musical performance; sensibility, smoothness; sickliness.

morbilli /mɔ:'bɪlʌɪ/ *noun plural* M16 **Medieval Latin** (plural of *morbillus* pustule, spot characteristic of measles, diminutive of Latin *morbus* disease). *Medicine* (The spots characteristic of) measles.

morceau /mɔ:'səʊ/, *foreign* /mɔrso/ *noun* plural **morceaux** /mɔ:'səʊz/, *foreign* /mɔrso/ M18 **French** (Old French *morsel*, *morcel* diminutive of *mors* from Latin *morsus* bite, from *mors-* past participial stem of *mordere* to bite). A short literary or musical composition.

mordent /'mɔ:d(ə)nt/ *noun* E19 **German** (from Italian *mordente* use as noun of verbal adjective from *mordere* to bite, from Proto-Romance alteration of Latin *mordere*). *Music* An ornament consisting of the rapid alternation of the note written with the one immediately below it. Cf. PRALLTRILLER.

mordida /mor'dida/ *noun* M20 **Central American and Mexican Spanish**. In Mexico and Central America: a bribe, an illegal exaction.

mordoré /mɔrdɔre/ *noun* L18 **French** (from Old French *More* (modern *Maure*) Moor + *doré* past participle of *dorer* to gild). A colour between brown and red; russet.

more /'mɔ:reɪ/ *noun* E17 **Latin** (ablative of *mos*, *mor-* custom). In the fashion *of*, according to the custom *of*.

■ Only in Latin adverbial phrases (see following entries).

more hispanico /ˌmɔ:reɪ hɪ'spanɪkəʊ/ *adverb phrase* M20 **Latin**. In accordance with Spanish custom.

more majorum /ˌmɔ:reɪ mə'dʒɔ:rəm/ *adverb phrase* E17 **Latin** (*majorum*, genitive plural of *majores* ancestors). In traditional manner.

more meo /ˌmɔ:reɪ 'meɪəʊ/ *adverb phrase* E19 **Latin**. In my own fashion.

mores /'mɔ:reɪz/, /'mɔ:ri:z/ *noun plural* L19 **Latin** (plural of *mos* manner, custom). **1** L19 The acquired customs and moral assumptions which give cohesion to a community, social group, or period. Cf. O TEMPORA, O MORES. **2** E20 *Zoology* The habits, behaviour, etc., of a group of animals of the same kind.

1 1996 *Times* By posthumously according his official and unofficial families equal status, the former President held up a strange mirror to French *mores*.

Moresca /mə'rɛskə/ *noun* M19 **Italian** (feminine of *Moresco* from *Moro* Moor; cf. MORISCA). An Italian folk-dance related to the English morris dance.

more suo /ˌmɔːreɪ 'suːəʊ/ *adverb phrase* M19 **Latin**. In his own fashion.

morgue /mɔːg/ *noun* M19 **French** (proper name of a Paris mortuary). **1** M19 A mortuary. **2a** E20 In a newspaper office, the collection of material assembled for the future obituaries of people still living. *colloquial*. **b** E20 A repository of cuttings, photographs, and information in a newspaper office, film studio, etc. *colloquial*.

Morisca /mə'rɪskə/ *noun* M20 **Spanish** (feminine of next; cf. MORESCA). A Spanish folk-dance related to the English morris dance.

Morisco /mə'rɪskəʊ/ *adjective & noun* M16 **Spanish** (from *Moro* Moor). **A** *adjective* M16 Of or pertaining to the Moors; Moorish. **B** *noun* plural **Morisco(e)s**. **1** M16 A Moor, especially in Spain. **2** M16 Originally, a dance with Moorish elements and sharing some features with the morris dance. Now usually = MORISCA. **3** E18 Arabesque art, ornament, etc.

morituri te salutamus /mɒrɪˌtʊri teɪ salʊ'tɑːməs/ *interjection* (also **morituri te salutant** and other variants) E18 **Latin** (= we who are about to die salute you). *Roman History* The words addressed by gladiators to the Roman emperor as they entered the arena.

■ Quoted from Suetonius *Life of Claudius* xxi.6. Used allusively in English in many variant forms by people facing danger or difficulty.

moron /'mɔːrɒn/ *noun* E20 **Greek** (*mōron* neuter of *mōros* foolish). **1** E20 *Medicine* An adult with a mental age of between about eight and twelve. **2** E20 A stupid or slow-witted person; a fool. *colloquial*.

mortadella /mɔːtə'dɛlə/ *noun* plural **mortadellas, mortadelle** /mɔːtə'dɛli/ E17 **Italian** (irregular from Latin *murtatum* (sausage) seasoned with myrtle berries). A large spiced pork sausage; Bologna sausage.

moscato /mə'skɑːtəʊ/ *noun* plural **moscatos** E20 **Italian**. A sweet Italian dessert wine.

moshav /'məʊʃɑːv/ *noun* plural **moshavim** /'məʊʃɑːvɪm/ M20 **Modern Hebrew** (*mōšāḇ* dwelling, colony). In Israel: a group of agricultural smallholdings worked partly on a cooperative and partly on an individual basis.

mosso /'mɒsəʊ/ *adverb* L19 **Italian** (past participle of *muovere* to move). *Music* (A direction:) rapidly, with animation.

mot /mo/, /məʊ/, (*plural same*), *in sense 1* /mɒt/ *noun* L16 **French** (= word, saying, from Proto-Gallo-Romance alteration of popular Latin *muttum* related to Latin *muttire* to murmur; cf. MOTTO). **1** L16 Originally, a motto. Later (now *dialectal*) a word, an opinion. **2** E19 A witty saying. Cf. BON MOT.

2 1996 *Country Life* If I should leave my notebook open on the kitchen seat, I may find that some priceless thought, some *mot*, or maybe merely some item on a shopping list, has been eaten off the page.

motard /mɔtar/ *noun* plural pronounced same M20 **French** (from *moto-* combining form of *moteur*). A member of the French motor cycle police.

1963 B. Abro *July 14 Assassination* Two motards were by the door . . . They . . . kicked their machines into life.

mot de Cambronne /mo də kambrɔn/, /ˌməʊ də kam'brɒn/, *noun phrase* **French** (literally, 'Cambronne's word'). The French expletive *merde!*

■ The reputed reply of General Pierre Cambronne (1770–1842) when called upon to surrender at the Battle of Waterloo. The official version of what he said—*La garde meurt mais ne se rend pas* 'The Guard dies, but does not surrender'—seems to have been a happy journalistic invention, since the general himself denied saying it.

mot d'ordre /mo dɔrdr/, /məʊ 'dɔːdrə/, *noun phrase* plural **mots d'ordres** (*pronounced same*) M19 **French** (= word of command). A political slogan; a statement of policy; an oral directive.

1930 *Observer* The official *mot d'ordre* is that Mr. Gandhi's salt campaign must be treated with a sense of humour.

motif /məʊ'tiːf/ *noun* M19 **French**. **1** M19 A distinctive, significant, or dominant idea or theme; *specifically* (**a**) *Art* a distinctive feature, subject, or structural principle in a composition or design; (**b**) in literature or folklore, a particular or recurrent event, situation, theme, character, etc.; (**c**) *Music* a figure, a leitmotiv. **2** L19 An ornamental design or piece of decoration; *specifically* (**a**) an ornament of lace, braid, etc., sewn separately on a garment; (**b**) an ornament on a vehicle identifying the maker, model, etc. **3** L19 A motivation, a basis, (for an idea etc.).

motivi plural of MOTIVO.

motiviert /moti'vi:rt/ *adjective* E19 **German**. Motivated.

motivo /mo'ti:vo/ *noun* plural **motivi** /mo 'ti:vi/ M18 **Italian**. *Music* A motif.

mot juste /mo ʒyst/, /məʊ 'ʒu:st/ *noun phrase* plural **mots justes** (*pronounced same*) E20 **French** (= exact word). The precisely appropriate expression.

moto /'məʊtəʊ/ *noun* M18 **Italian**. *Music* Movement, pace.

■ In various musical directions; cf. CON MOTO.

moto perpetuo /ˌməʊtəʊ pə'pɛtjʊəʊ/ *noun phrase* plural **moti perpetui** /ˌməʊti: pə'pɛtjʊi:/ L19 **Italian** (= perpetual motion). A rapid instrumental composition consisting mainly of notes of equal value.

motte /mɒt/ *noun* L19 **French** (= mound). *Antiquities* A large man-made earthen mound with a flattened top, usually surmounted by a fort, castle, etc.

motto /'mɒtəʊ/ *noun* plural **mottos, mottoes** L16 **Italian** (from Proto-Gallo-Romance word whence also MOT). **1** L16 Originally, a sentence or phrase attached to an emblematical design to explain its significance. Later, a short sentence or phrase inscribed on an object, expressing a reflection or sentiment considered appropriate to its purpose or destination. Also, a maxim adopted as a rule of conduct. **b** E17 *Heraldry* A significant word or sentence usually placed on a scroll, either below an achievement of arms or above the crest. **c** M19 A verse or saying in a paper cracker etc. **2** E18 A short quotation or epigram placed at the beginning of a book, chapter, etc.; an epigraph. **3** M19 A sweet wrapped in fancy paper together with a saying or scrap of verse. Also *motto-kiss*. *United States*. **4** L19 *Music* A recurrent phrase having some symbolical significance.

motu proprio /ˌməʊtu: 'prəʊprɪəʊ/, /ˌməʊtu: 'prɒprɪəʊ/ *adverb & noun phrase* E17 **Latin**. **A** *adverb phrase* E17 Of one's own volition, on one's own initiative, spontaneously. **B** *noun phrase* plural **motu proprios**. M19 An edict issued by the Pope personally to the Roman Catholic Church, or to a part of it.

mouche /mu:ʃ/ *noun* L17 **French** (literally, 'a fly', from Latin *musca*). **1** L17 *History* A small patch of black plaster worn on the face as an ornament or to conceal a blemish. **2** M19 A natural mark on the face resembling such a patch; a beauty spot.

mouchette /mu:'ʃɛt/ *noun* E20 **French**. *Architecture* A motif in curvilinear tracery shaped like a curved dagger.

moue /mu:/ *noun* M19 **French**. A pouting expression, a pout.

moujik variant of MUZHIK.

moulage /'mu:lɑ:ʒ/ *noun* E20 **French** (= moulding, moulded reproduction, from *mouler* to mould). A cast or impression of a (part of a) person or thing; the material used for or the process of making a cast or taking an impression.

moule /mul/ *noun* plural pronounced same L19 **French**. *Cookery* A mussel.

■ Usually in plural in names of dishes, as in *moules marinières*.

moulin /'mu:lɪn/, *foreign* /mulɛ̃/ (*plural same*) *noun* M19 **French** (literally, 'mill'). **1** M19 A deep, nearly vertical shaft in a glacier, formed by falling water. Also called *glacier mill*. **2** M20 A type of kitchen utensil for grinding or puréeing food.

moulvi /'mu:lvi/ *noun* (also **maulvi** /'maʊlvi/, **moolvi(e)**) E17 **Urdu** (*maulvī* from Arabic *mawlawī* judicial (used as noun), from *mawlā* mullah). A Muslim doctor of the law, an imam; *generally* (especially in the Indian subcontinent, used as a form of address to) a learned person or teacher.

mousaka variant of MOUSSAKA.

mousquetaire /ˌmu:skə'tɛ:/ *noun & adjective* E18 **French** (= musketeer, from *mousquet* musket). **A** *noun* **1** E18 *History* A French musketeer. **2** L19 A glove with a long loose wrist. More fully *mousquetaire glove*. **B** *attributive* or as *adjective* M19 Of an article of clothing: in the style of that of a French musketeer.

moussaka /mu:'sɑ:kə/, /mu:sə'kɑ:/ *noun* (also **mousaka**) M20 **Turkish** (*musakka*, ultimately from Arabic *musakkā*; cf. modern Greek *mousakas*, Romanian *musaca*, Albanian, Bulgarian *musaka*, etc.). An eastern

Mediterranean dish made with minced beef or lamb, aubergine, etc., with a cheese sauce.

mousse /mu:s/ *noun* M19 **French** (= moss, froth). **1** M19 The aggregation of tiny bubbles in sparkling wine, as champagne etc. **2** L19 *Cookery* A sweet or savoury dish made from a purée or other base stiffened with whipped cream, gelatin, egg whites, etc., and usually served chilled. Frequently with specifying word. **3** M20 A brown emulsion of seawater and oil produced by the weathering of oil spills and resistant to dispersal; a mass of this substance. More fully *chocolate mousse*. **4** L20 *Hairdressing* A frothy preparation for applying to the hair to facilitate setting or colouring.

mousseline /'mu:sli:n/ *noun* L17 **French**. **1** L17 French muslin; a dress of this material. Also *mousseline-de-laine*. **2** M19 (A wineglass of) a very thin blown glassware with ornamentation resembling muslin or lace. More fully *mousseline glass*. **3** E20 *Cookery* A rich frothy sauce of seasoned or sweetened eggs or cream. More fully *mousseline sauce*. **b** E20 Any of various dishes with a light frothy texture and usually prepared by whipping or beating; a mousse.

mousseux /musø/, /mu:'sə:/ *adjective & noun* E19 **French** (from as MOUSSE). **A** *adjective* E19 Of wine: sparkling. **B** *noun* M20 plural same. A sparkling wine, a VIN MOUSSEUX.

moustache /mə'stɑ:ʃ/ *noun* (also **mustache**) L16 **French** (from Italian *mostaccio*, *mostacchio* from medieval Latin *mustacia*, ultimately from Greek *mustax*, *mustak-* upper lip, moustache). **1** L16 A (cultivated) growth of hair above the whole or either half (frequently in *plural*, especially in *pair of moustaches*) of a man's lip or extending from this on either side of the lip; a growth of hair above a woman's lip. Also, an artificial strip of hair worn in imitation of this. **2** E17 A growth of hairs or bristles, or a marking resembling a man's moustache, round the mouth of certain animals or birds.

mouton enragé /mutɔ̃ ɑ̃raʒe/ *noun phrase* plural **moutons enragés** (pronounced same) M20 **French** (literally, 'angry sheep'). A normally placid person who has become suddenly enraged or violent.

moutonné(e) see ROCHE MOUTONNÉE.

mouvementé /muvmɑ̃te/ *adjective* E20 **French**. Animated, agitated, bustling, full of variety; *specifically* (of music) lively.

1965 *Guardian* Her life has been unusually mouvementé—and erratic.

moyen-âge /ˌmwɑ:jən'ɑ:ʒ/ *adjective* (also **moyen-age** and with capital initials) M19 **French** (= the Middle Ages). Of or pertaining to the Middle Ages, medieval.

moyen sensuel /mwajɛ̃ sɑ̃sɥɛl/ *adjective phrase* (also **moyen-sensuel**) E20 **French**. Of an average sensual and materialistic character.

■ Generally in the phrase HOMME MOYEN SENSUEL.

1996 *Spectator* He is told to 'go and sell that thou hast, and give to the poor', but with the proviso: 'If thou wilt be perfect . . . and . . . have treasure in heaven'—to which the *moyen sensuel* capitalist could reply: 'who is talking about perfection, and surely any place in Heaven is treasure?'

mozetta variant of MOZZETTA.

mozzarella /mɒtsə'rɛlə/ *noun* E20 **Italian** (diminutive of *mozza* a kind of cheese, from *mozzare* to cut off). A white Italian cheese originally made in the Naples area from buffalo milk. More fully *mozzarella cheese*.

mozzetta /məʊ'zɛtə/, /məʊ'tsɛtə/ *noun* (also **mozetta**) L18 **Italian** (aphetized from *almozzetta*, from medieval Latin *almucia* amice). *Roman Catholic Church* A short cape with a hood, worn by the Pope, cardinals, and some other ecclesiastics.

mu /mju:/ *noun* ME **Greek**. **1** ME The twelfth letter (Μ, μ) of the Greek alphabet. **2** L19 Plural same. One micrometre (micron). Usually denoted by μ. **3** E20 *Electronics* The amplification factor of a valve.

muchacha /mʊ'tʃɑ:tʃə/ *noun* L19 **Spanish** (feminine of next). In Spain and Spanish-speaking countries: a girl, a young woman; a female servant.

muchacho /mʊ'tʃɑ:tʃəʊ/ *noun* plural **muchachos** L16 **Spanish**. In Spain and Spanish-speaking countries: a boy, a young man; a male servant.

mudra /'mʌdrə/, /'mu:drə/ *noun* E19 **Sanskrit** (*mudrā* seal, sign, token). Any of a large number of symbolic hand gestures used in Hindu religious ceremonies and in Indian dance. Also, a movement or pose in yoga.

muesli /ˈmuːzli/, /ˈmjuːzli/ *noun* M20 **Swiss German.** A dish, originating in Switzerland, consisting of a cereal (usually oats), fruit, nuts, etc., eaten with milk or cream, especially for breakfast.

muezzin /muːˈɛzɪn/ *noun* L16 **Arabic** (dialectal variant of Arabic *mu'aḏḏin* active participle of *'aḏḏana* to call to prayer, from *'uḏn* ear). A Muslim crier who proclaims the hours of prayer from a minaret or the roof of a mosque.

mufti /ˈmʌfti/ *noun* L16 **Arabic** (*muftī* active participle of *'aftā* to decide a point of law (related to FATWA)). A Muslim cleric or legal expert empowered to give rulings on religious matters; in the Ottoman Empire, a chief legal authority, especially of a large city (also *Grand Mufti*).

■ *Mufti* in the sense of 'plain or informal clothes worn by a person who has the right to wear a uniform of some kind' (E19) may be a facetious use of this word, but its origins are uncertain.

muguet /mygɛ/ *noun* L16 **French** (from medieval Latin *muscatum* musk-scented, from *muscus* musk). **1** L16–M17 Any of certain fragrant plants; *specifically* woodruff, *Galium odoratum*. **2** L16 Lily of the valley, *Convallaria majalis*; a scent made from or resembling it.

mukhtar /ˈmʊktɑː/ *noun* E20 **Turkish** (*muhtar* from Arabic *muḵtār* passive participle of *iḵtāra* to choose, elect). In Turkey and some Arab countries: the head of the local government of a town or village; a minor provincial official.

mukti /ˈmʌkti/, /ˈmʊkti/ *noun* L18 **Sanskrit** (= release, from *muc* to set free, release). *Hinduism* and *Jainism* MOKSHA.

mulatta /mjuːˈlatə/ *noun* E17 **Spanish** (*mulata* feminine of *mulato* mulatto). A female mulatto.

mulatto /mjuːˈlatəʊ/ *noun & adjective* plural **mulatto(e)s** L16 **Spanish and Portuguese** (*mulato* young mule, mulatto, irregularly from *mulo* mule). **A** *noun* L16 A person having one White and one Black parent; a person of mixed White and Black parentage. **B** *adjective* **1** E17 Of the colour of the skin of a mulatto; tawny. **2** L17 That is a mulatto; of or pertaining to mulattos. **3** M18 Designating a kind of mid-brown fertile soil. *United States.*

muleta /məˈleɪtə/ *noun* M19 **Spanish.** *Bullfighting* A red cloth fixed to a stick used by a matador during the FAENA.

1996 *Spectator* Because some of the bulls tired quickly, opportunities for assessing performances with the *muleta* were limited.

mulga /ˈmʌlgə/ *noun* M19 **Aboriginal.** **1** M19 Any of several small acacia, forming dense scrub in dry inland areas of Australia and sometimes used for fodder (also *mulga tree*); the land covered with such vegetation, (*colloquial*) the outback. **2** M19 A thing made of the wood of a mulga tree, *especially* a club or shield. **3** L19 A rumour, a message, a (false) report; *the* grapevine. In full *mulga wire. Australian slang.*

mullah /ˈmʌlə/, /ˈmʊlə/ *noun* E17 **Persian** (Urdu *mullā*, Turkish *molla* from Arabic *mawlā*). (A title given to) a Muslim learned in Islamic theology and sacred law.

multum in parvo /ˌmʌltəm ɪn ˈpɑːvəʊ/ *noun phrase* M18 **Latin** (= much in little). A great deal in a small compass.

mumpsimus /ˈmʌmpsɪməs/ *noun* M16 **pseudo-Latin** (erroneously for Latin *sumpsimus* in the passage in the Eucharistic service that runs *quod in ore sumpsimus* 'which we have taken into the mouth'). **1** M16 An obstinate adherent of old ways, in spite of clear evidence of their error; an ignorant and bigoted opponent of reform. Formerly also *loosely*, an old fogey. **2** M16 A traditional custom or notion obstinately adhered to although shown to be unreasonable.

■ The origin is Richard Pace's anecdote in *De Fructu* (1517) of an illiterate English priest who garbled the passage in the Mass quoted above by substituting the nonsense word *mumpsimus*. When corrected, he replied 'I will not change my old mumpsimus for your new sumpsimus'. Now only in literary use. Cf. SUMPSIMUS.

mu-mu variant of MUU-MUU.

mung /mʌŋ/, /muːŋ/ *noun* E19 **Hindi** (*mūng*). (The seed of) either of two widely cultivated tropical legumes.

municipio /mjuːnɪˈsɪpɪəʊ/, /mjuːnɪˈʧɪpɪəʊ/ *noun* plural **municipios** L19 **Spanish and Italian** (from Latin *municipium*). A Spanish, Latin American, or Italian municipality.

munshi /ˈmuːnʃiː/ *noun* (also **moonshee**) L18 **Persian and Urdu** (*munšī* from Arabic *munšī'* writer, author, active participle of *'anša'a* to write (a book)). In the Indian subcontinent: a secretary, an assistant; a language-teacher.

murex /'mjʊərɛks/ *noun* plural **murices** /'mjʊərɪsi:z/, **murexes** L16 **Latin** (perhaps related to Greek *muax* sea-mussel). Any of various spiny-shelled predatory gastropod molluscs of the genus *Murex* and related genera, of tropical and temperate seas, from some of which the dye Tyrian purple was formerly obtained. Also *murex shell*.

murus gallicus /ˌmjʊərəs 'galɪkəs/ *noun phrase* plural **muri gallici** /ˌmjʊəri: 'galɪki:/ M20 **Latin** (from *murus* wall + *gallicus* Gallic). *Archaeology* A type of late Iron Age Celtic fort having stone walls bound by horizontally placed timber frames.

muscadel variant of MUSCATEL.

muscae /'mʌsi:/ *noun plural* M18 **Latin** (plural of *musca* fly). Chiefly *Medicine* Specks which appear to float before the eyes, frequently due to particles in the vitreous humour of the eye. In full *muscae volitantes* /vɒlɪ'tanti:z/ (present participle of *volitare* to fly about).

muscat /'mʌskat/ *noun* M16 **Old and Modern French** (from Provençal (= Italian MOSCATO), from *musc* musk). **1** M16 MUSCATEL wine. In full *muscat wine*. **2** M17 Any of several varieties of grape with a musky taste or smell; a vine bearing a variety of such a grape. In full *muscat grape*. **3** M17–M18 A kind of peach or pear with a musky taste or smell.

muscatel /mʌskə'tɛl/ *noun* (also **muscadel** /mʌskə'dɛl/) LME **Old French** (*muscadel*, *muscatel* (= Italian *moscatello*) from Provençal diminutive of MUSCAT). **1** LME (A) strong sweet wine made from the muscat or similar grape; a drink of this. **2** E16 A muscat grape. In full *muscatel grape*. **3** M16–M18 A variety of pear with a musky taste or smell. **4** M17 A raisin from the muscatel grape. In full *muscatel raisin*. Usually in *plural*.

museau /myzo/ *noun* plural **museaux** /myzo/ E19 **French** (colloquial, literally, 'muzzle, snout'). A person's face.

musée /myze/ (*plural same*), /'mju:zeɪ/ *noun* M17 **French** (from Latin *mus(a)eum* library, study, from Greek *mouseion* seat of the Muses). In France and French-speaking countries: a museum.

musette /mju:'zɛt/ *noun* LME **Old and Modern French** (diminutive of *muse* bagpipe). **1** LME A kind of small bagpipe, *especially* a small French bagpipe of the eighteenth century with a soft tone. **2** E18 A soft pastoral air imitating the sound of the musette; a dance performed to such music. **3** E19 A reed-stop in an organ producing a soft tone resembling that of the musette. **4** L19 A small and simple variety of oboe without a reed-cap. **5** E20 A type of lightweight knapsack used especially by the military and by racing cyclists. More fully *musette bag*.

> **5 1965** *Sun* The musette, or featherweight knapsack from the Continent, has largely replaced the saddlebag.

musica /'mju:zɪkə/ *noun* **Latin** (= music). Occurring in various phrases used in English, especially with reference to early music (see entries below).

musica ficta /ˌmju:zɪkə 'fɪktə/ *noun phrase* E19 **Latin** (literally, 'feigned music'). (Early contrapuntal music characterized by) the introduction by a singer of conventional chromatically altered tones to avoid unacceptable intervals.

musica figurata /ˌmju:zɪkə fɪgjʊ'rɑ:tə/ *noun phrase* M18 **Latin** (literally, 'figured music'). **1** Contrapuntal music in which the different melodic strands move more or less independently. **2** M20 Plainsong with decorated melody.

musica plana /ˌmju:zɪkə 'plɑ:nə/ *noun phrase* M20 **Latin** (literally, 'plain music'). Plainsong, canto fermo.

musica reservata /ˌmju:zɪkə rɛzə'vɑ:tə/ *nounb phrase* M20 **Latin** (literally, 'reserved music'). Early music characterized by clarity, balance, restraint, and expressiveness.

musicale /mju:zɪ'kɑ:l/ *noun* L19 **French** ((*soirée*) *musicale* musical evening). A musical party; a concert, especially at a private address.

■ United States; cf. SOIRÉE MUSICALE.

musique concrète /myzik kɔ̃krɛt/, /mju:ˌzi:k kɒn'krɛt/ *noun phrase* M20 **French** (= concrete music). Electronic music constructed by the rearrangement of recorded natural sounds.

mustache variant of MOUSTACHE.

mustafina /mʌstə'fi:nə/ *noun* E19 **Spanish** (apparently from *mustee*, abbreviation of Spanish MESTIZO). A person with one parent a mestizo and the other a White.

muta /'mju:tə/ *intransitive verb* L19 **Italian** (imperative of *mutare* to change). *Music* (A direction:) change instrument or tuning.

mutatis mutandis /mju:ˌtɑ:tɪs mju:'tandɪs/, /mu:ˌtɑ:tɪs/, /mju:'tandi:s/ *adverb* *phrase* L15 **Latin** (literally, 'things being changed that have to be changed'). Making the necessary changes; with due alteration of details.

1962 S. E. Finer *Man on Horseback* What is said of the army here is to be taken also to apply, *mutatis mutandis*, to the air force and the navy.

mutato nomine /mjuːˌtɑːtəʊ 'nəʊmmeɪ/, /muːˌtɑːtəʊ 'nɒmmeɪ/ *adverb phrase* E17 **Latin**. The name being changed, with a change of name or names.

■ Earliest in English as a quotation from Horace's *Satires* (I.i.69): *Quid rides? mutato nomine de te / Fabula narratur* 'Laughing are you? Just change the name and the tale is told about you.'

mutuel /'mjuːʧʊəl/, /'mjuːtjʊəl/, *foreign* /mytɥɛl/ (*plural same*) *noun* E20 **French** (abbreviation of PARI-MUTUEL). A totalizator, a *pari-mutuel*. Chiefly *North American*.

muu-muu /'muːmuː/ *noun* (also **mu-mu**) E20 **Hawaiian** (*mu'u mu'u*, literally, 'cut off' from the original absence of a yoke). A woman's usually brightly coloured and patterned loose-fitting dress, (as) worn in Hawaii.

muzhik /muː'ʒɪk/ *noun* (also **moujik**) M16 **Russian**. *History* A Russian peasant.

mystae plural of MYSTES.

mystagogue /'mɪstəgɒg/ *noun* M16 **French** (Latin *mystagogus* from Greek *mustagōgos*, from *mustēs* MYSTES + *agōgos* leading, from *agein* to lead). In ancient Greece, a person who gave preparatory instruction to candidates for initiation into the Eleusinian or other mysteries; *generally* a person who introduces others to religious mysteries, a teacher of mystical doctrines, a creator or disseminator of mystical doctrines.

mysterioso /mɪˌstɪərɪ'əʊzəʊ/ *adjective* M20 **Italian** (= mysterious). *Music* Executed in a mysterious manner.

mysterium tremendum /mɪˌstɪərɪəm trɪ'mɛndəm/ *noun phrase* E20 **Latin** (= tremendous mystery). A great or overwhelming mystery, *especially* the great or overwhelming mystery of God or of existence.

mystes /'mɪstiːz/ *noun* plural **mystae** /'mɪstiː/ L17 **Latin** (from Greek *mustēs*). A person initiated into mysteries.

mystique /mɪ'stiːk/ *noun* L19 **French**. The atmosphere of mystery and veneration investing some doctrines, arts, professions, or people; a mysterious attraction; any professional skill or technique designed or able to mystify and impress the lay person.

mythoi plural of MYTHOS.

mythopoeia /ˌmɪθə(ʊ)'piːə/ *noun* M20 **Greek** (*muthopoiia*). The creation of a myth or myths.

mythos /'mʌɪθɒs/ *noun* plural **mythoi** /'mʌɪθɔɪ/ M18 **Greek** (*muthos* myth). **1** M18 A traditional story, either wholly or partly fictitious, a myth; a body of myths. **2** M20 A traditional or recurrent narrative theme or pattern; a standard plot in literature.

■ *Mythos* and its Latin derivative *mythus* (E19), both now used solely in literary contexts, were current before the Anglicized *myth* (M19), which is now the form used in all general contexts for sense 1.

N

naan variant of NAN.

naartjie /ˈnɑːtʃi/, /ˈnɑːki/ *noun* (also **naartje** and other variants) L18 **Afrikaans** (from Tamil *nārattai* citrus). In South Africa: a soft loose-skinned tangerine or mandarin orange.

naat /nɑːt/ *noun* M20 **Afrikaans** (= seam, from Dutch *naad*). An irregularity in the structure of a diamond caused by a change in direction in the grain; a diamond containing such an irregularity.

nabi /ˈnɑːbiː/ *noun* plural (in sense 1) **nebiᶜim** /nɛˈbiːɪm/, (in sense 2) **nabis** (also **Nabi**) L19 **Hebrew** (*nābī* prophet). **1** L19 *Theology* A person inspired to speak the word of God; a prophet; *specifically* a prophetical writer of the Old Testament and Hebrew Scriptures. Also (in *plural*) = *the Prophets*. **2** M20 A member of a group of late nineteenth-century French post-impressionists following the artistic theories of the French painter Paul Gauguin (1848–1903).

nabla /ˈnablə/ *noun* L19 **Greek** (= a kind of harp, probably of Semitic origin). *Mathematics* The symbolic differential operator in the shape of the inverted Greek capital letter delta Δ (hence often known under the abbreviation *del*).

nabob /ˈneɪbɒb/ *noun* E17 **Portuguese** (*nababo* or Spanish *nabab* from Urdu *nawwāb*, *nawāb* deputy governor: cf. NAWAB). **1** E17 *History* (The title of) any of certain Muslim officials acting as deputy governors of provinces or districts in the Mughal Empire; a governor of an Indian town or district. **2** M18 A person of great wealth or (formerly) high rank; *specifically* a European returning from India with a large fortune acquired there.

nacarat /ˈnakərat/ *noun* M18 **French** (perhaps from Spanish and Portuguese *nacarado*, from *nacar* nacre). **1** M18 A bright orange-red colour. **2** M19 A fine linen fabric dyed in this colour.

nacelle /nəˈsɛl/ *noun* E20 **French** (from late Latin *navicella*, diminutive of Latin *navis* ship). **1** E20 The basket or car of a balloon or airship. **2** E20 Originally, the cockpit of an aeroplane. Now, a streamlined bulge on an aircraft's wing or fuselage enclosing an engine etc. **3** M20 A similarly shaped structure on or in a motor vehicle.

■ In the core sense of 'a small boat', *nacelle* appears in Caxton's *Golden Legend* (1483), but it never achieved much currency in this sense, and seems not to have been used in English between the late fifteenth century and its modern reintroduction.

naches /ˈnʌxəs/ *noun* (also **nachas**) E20 **Yiddish** (*nakhes* from Hebrew *naḳaṯ* contentment). A sense of pleasure or pride, especially at the achievements of one's children; joy, gratification. *United States*.

Nachlass /ˈnɑːxlas/ *noun* plural **Nachlasse** /ˈnɑːxlasə/, **Nachlässe** /ˈnɑːxlɛsə/ M19 **German**. *singular* and (*rare*) in *plural*. Unpublished material left by an author after his or her death.

nacho /ˈnatʃəʊ/ *noun* plural **nachos** M20 **(Mexican) Spanish** (origin uncertain: perhaps from Mexican Spanish *Nacho* pet-form of male forename *Ignacio*, but cf. Spanish *nacho* flat-nosed). A snack or appetizer consisting of fried tortilla chips covered in melted cheese, peppers, spices, etc.

■ Perhaps the invention of a Mexican chef, Ignacio Anaya, who worked in the Piedras Niegras area in the 1940s, the dish was originally found only in the northern Mexico–Texas area and did not spread much beyond there until the 1970s. Taken up by the fast-food chains in the 1980s, it is now a popular food item in Europe too. *Nacho* is always used in the plural except when attributive (see quotation).

1983 *Fortune* The chain of Mexican fast-food restaurants is busily expanding its product line to include . . . a nacho side dish, and a salad.

Nachschlag /ˈnɑːxʃlɑːk/ *noun* plural **Nachschläge** /ˈnɑːxʃlɛːgə/ L19 **German** (from *nach* after + *Schlag* blow, note). *Music* A grace-note taking its value from that of the note preceding it.

Nachtmaal variant of NAGMAAL.

Nacht und Nebel /ˌnaxt ʊnt ˈneːb(ə)l/ *noun phrase* M20 **German** (literally, 'night and fog'). A situation characterized by mystery or obscurity, especially as associated with Nazi Germany between 1941 and 1945.

nacre /'neɪkə/ *noun* L16 **French** (probably ultimately of oriental origin). Mother-of-pearl.

nada /'nɑ:da/ *noun 1* E20 **Sanskrit** (*nāda* sound). *Hinduism* Inchoate or elemental sound considered as the source of all sounds and as a source of creation.

nada /'nada/, /'nadə/ *noun 2* M20 **Spanish** (= nothing, from Latin (*res*) *nata* thing born, insignificant thing). Nothing; nothingness, non-existence.

nadir /'neɪdɪə/ *noun* LME **Old and Modern French** ((also Spanish, Italian) from Arabic *naẓīr* (*as-samt*) opposite (the zenith)). **1** LME–E18 *Astronomy* A point in the heavens diametrically opposite to some other point, especially to the sun. Followed by *of, to*. **2** L15 *Astronomy* The point of the heavens diametrically opposite to the zenith; the point directly below an observer. **3** L18 The lowest point (*of* something); the place or time of greatest depression or degradation.

naevus /'ni:vəs/ *noun* (also **nevus**) plural **naevi** /'ni:vʌɪ/ M19 **Latin**. *Medicine* A congenital reddish or brown mark or (usually) raised blemish on the skin, *especially* a haemangiona; a birthmark, a mole.

naga /'nɑ:gə/ *noun* L18 **Sanskrit** (*nāga* serpent, snake). *Indian Mythology* A member of a race of semi-divine creatures, half-snake and half-human, that are the genii of rain, rivers, etc.

nagana /nə'gɑ:nə/ *noun* L19 **Zulu** (*nakane*). A disease of cattle, antelope, etc., in southern Africa, characterized by fever, lethargy, and oedema caused by trypanosomes transmitted by tsetse-flies.

Nagmaal /'naxmɑ:l/ *noun* (also (earlier) **Nachtmaal** /'naxtmɑ:l/) M19 **Afrikaans** (*nagmaal* (Dutch *nachtmaal*), from *nag* (Dutch *nacht*) night + *maal* meal). In South Africa: the usually quarterly celebration of the Eucharist in the Dutch Reformed Church (an occasion of family reunions and celebration).

nahal /nə'hɑ:l/ *noun* M20 **Hebrew** (from initials of the name of the organization, *Nōʿar Ḥălūtzī Lōḥēm* Pioneer Military Youth). A military youth organization in Israel; an agricultural settlement manned by members of this organization.

naïf /nʌɪ'i:f/, /nɑ:'i:f/ *adjective & noun* plural of noun pronounced same L16 **French** (see NAIVE). **A** *adjective* **1** L16 NAIVE sense 1. **b** M20 NAIVE sense 1b. **2** M–L17 Of a diamond: without an imperfection, flawless. *rare*. **B** *noun* L19 A naive person.

naive /nʌɪ'i:v/, /nɑ:'i:v/ *adjective* (also **naïve**) M17 **Old and Modern French** (*naïve*, feminine of *naïf* from Latin *nativus* native; cf. NAÏF). **1** M17 Unaffected, unconsciously artless. Also, foolishly credulous, simple. **b** M20 Of art etc.: straightforward in style, eschewing subtlety or conventional technique. **2** M20 *Biology* and *Psychology* Not having had a particular experience before, or been the subject of a particular experiment; lacking the knowledge to guess the purpose of an experiment; *especially* not having taken or received a particular drug. (Followed by *to*.)

naïveté /naivte/, /nʌɪ'i:vteɪ/ *noun* plural pronounced same L17 **French** (from as preceding). **1** L17 A naive action, remark, etc. **2** E18 The state or quality of being naive.

namaskar /ˌnʌməs'kɑ:/ *noun* M20 **Hindi** (from Sanskrit *namaskāra*, from *namas* (see next) + *kāra* action). A traditional Hindu gesture of greeting made by bringing the palms together before the face or chest and bowing.

■ In Thailand a similar gesture is called *wai*.

namaste /'nʌməsteɪ/ *noun, interjection, & verb* M20 **Hindi** (from Sanskrit *namas* bowing, obeisance + *te* dative of *tvam* you (singular)). **A** *noun* M20 A traditional Hindu greeting, a NAMASKAR. **B** *interjection* M20 Expressing respectful greeting (said when giving a namaskar). **C** *intransitive verb* M20 Give a namaskar.

nan /nɑ:n/ *noun* (also **naan**) E20 **Persian and Urdu** (*nān*). In Indian cookery, a type of leavened bread cooked especially in a clay oven.

naos /'neɪɒs/ *noun* L18 **Greek** (= temple). (The inner cell or sanctuary of) a temple; also *Christian Church*, the main part of an Orthodox church where the congregation assembles (cf. BEMA, NARTHEX).

nappe /nap/ *noun* L19 **French** (literally, 'tablecloth'). **1** L19 A sheet of water falling over a weir or similar surface. **2** E20 *Geology* A sheet of rock which has moved horizontally over neighbouring strata, as a result of overthrusting or recumbent folding.

narcosis /nɑ:'kəʊsɪs/ *noun* plural **narcoses** /nɑ:'kəʊsi:z/ L17 **Greek** (*narkōsis*, from *narkoun* to make numb). *Medicine* The operation or effects of narcotics on the body; a state of insensibility or stupor, especially as induced by a drug; the production of this state. Also, therapeutic sleep artificially prolonged by the use of drugs.

narghile /ˈnɑːgɪleɪ/ *noun* (also **narghileh**) M18 **Persian** (*nārgīl* coconut, hookah, from Sanskrit *nārikela* coconut; partly through French *nargileh*, *narguilé* from Turkish *nargile* from Persian *nārgīl*). A hookah.

narikin /ˈnarɪkɪn/ *noun* E20 **Japanese**. In Japan: a wealthy parvenu.

narod /naˈrod/ *noun* M20 **Russian**. In countries of the former USSR: the people; *specifically* the common people seen (in some ideologies) as the bearers of national culture.

■ The Narodnik movement was a type of socialism originating among the Russian intelligentsia in the nineteenth century which looked on the peasants and intelligentsia as revolutionary forces, rather than the urban working class. Supporters (*Narodniki*) endeavoured to give political education to a community of rural or urban poor while sharing its living conditions.

narrischkeit /ˈnɑːrɪʃkʌɪt/ *noun slang* L19 **Yiddish** (*naarishkeit*, *narrishkeit* from German *Närrischkeit*, from *närrisch* foolish, from *Narr* fool). Foolishness, nonsense.

narthex /ˈnɑːθɛks/ *noun* L17 **Latin** (from Greek *narthēx* giant fennel, stick, casket, narthex). An antechamber at the western end of some (especially early and Orthodox) churches, separate from the NAOS.

nasi /ˈnɑːsi/ *noun* L19 **Malay**. In Malaysian and Indonesian cookery: cooked rice.

naskhi /ˈnaski/ *noun & adjective* (also **neskhi** /ˈnɛski/) L18 **Arabic** (*naskī* (plural), from *nasaka* to copy). (Designating) the standard Arabic script.

natatorium /ˌneɪtəˈtɔːrɪəm/ *noun* L19 **Late Latin** (use as noun of *natatorius* of a swimmer). A swimming pool, *especially* an indoor swimming pool. *North American*.

natura naturans /naˌtjʊərə ˈnatjʊranz/ *noun phrase* E19 **Latin** (Latin *natura* nature + medieval Latin *naturans* (present participle) creating, from *naturare*). *Philosophy* Nature as creative; the essential creative power or act. Cf. next.

natura naturata /naˌtjʊərə natjʊˈrɑːtə/ *noun phrase* E19 **Latin** (Latin *natura* nature + medieval Latin *naturata* (past participle) created, from *naturare*). *Philosophy* Nature as created; the natural phenomena and forces in which creation is manifested. Cf. preceding.

naturelle /ˌnatʃʊˈrɛl/, *foreign* /natyrɛl/ *adjective & noun* L19 **French** (feminine of *naturel* natural). (Of) a pale pink or beige colour; skin-colour(ed).

nature morte /natyr mɔrt/ *noun phrase* plural **natures mortes** (pronounced same) E20 **French**. A still life.

■ Used as a descriptive term in French art since the eighteenth century.

Naturphilosophie /naˈtuːrfɪlozoˌfiː/ *noun* E19 **German** (from *Natur* nature + *Philosophie* philosophy). The theory put forward, especially by Schelling (1775–1854) and other German philosophers, that there is an eternal and unchanging law of nature, proceeding from the absolute, from which all laws governing natural phenomena and forces derive.

naumachia /nɔːˈmeɪkɪə/ *noun* plural **naumachiae** /nɔːˈmeɪkɪiː/, **naumachias** L16 **Latin** (from Greek *naumakhia*, from *naus* ship + *makhē* fight). *Roman History* An imitation sea battle staged for entertainment; a place, especially a building enclosing a stretch of water, specially constructed for such a battle.

navarin /ˈnav(ə)rɪn/, *foreign* /navarɛ̃/ (*plural same*) *noun* L19 **French**. A casserole of mutton or lamb with (especially root) vegetables.

navarin printanier /navarɛ̃ prɛ̃tanje/ *noun phrase* plural **navarins printaniers** (pronounced same) E20 **French** (= spring navarin). A navarin made with spring vegetables.

navette /naˈvɛt/ *noun* E20 **French** (= little boat, shuttle, from medieval Latin *naveta* diminutive of Latin *navis* ship). **1** E20 A cut of jewel in the shape of a pointed oval; a jewel cut in such a shape. **2** L20 A railway truck designed to shuttle cars through a tunnel under the sea, *specifically* through the Channel Tunnel.

navicula /nəˈvɪkjʊlə/ *noun* plural **naviculae** /nəˈvɪkjʊliː/, /nəˈvɪkjʊlʌɪ/, **naviculas** M19 **Latin** (diminutive of *navis* ship). *Ecclesiastical* An incense-holder shaped like a boat.

nawab /nəˈwɑːb/, /nəˈwɔːb/ *noun* (also (as a title) **Nawab**) M18 **Urdu** (*nawāb* from Urdu, Persian *nawwāb* variant of *nuwwāb* plural (used as singular) of (Arabic) *nā'ib* deputy; cf. NABOB). (The title of) a governor or nobleman in the Indian subcontinent (*historical*); (the title of) a distinguished Muslim in the Indian subcontinent.

NB abbreviation of NOTA BENE.

né /neɪ/, *foreign* /ne/ *adjective* **M20 French** (= born, masculine past participle of *naître* to be born). Born with the name, originally called: placed before the name by which a man was originally known.

■ Much more usual in the feminine NÉE.

nebbish /ˈnɛbɪʃ/ *noun & adjective* (also **nebbich**) **L19 Yiddish** (*nebech* poor thing). **A** *noun* L19 A nobody, a nonentity, a submissive timid person. Also as *interjection*, expressing commiseration, dismay, etc. **B** *adjective* M20 Of a person: innocuous, ineffectual; timid, submissive. *colloquial.*

nebelwerfer /ˈnɛːb(ə)lˈvɛrfər/, /ˈnɛb(ə)l ˌwəːfə/ *noun* **M20 German** (from *Nebel* mist, fog + *Werfer* thrower, mortar, from *werfen* to throw). A six-barrelled rocket mortar used by the German forces in the war of 1939–45.

nebula /ˈnɛbjʊlə/ *noun* plural **nebulae** /ˈnɛbjʊliː/, **nebulas** **M17 Latin** (= mist, vapour). **1 a** M17 A film or clouded spot on or over the cornea of the eye. Now only *Medicine*. **b** M18 A cloud, (a) cloudlike appearance; an indistinct, insubstantial, or nebulous thing or (*figurative*) person. **2** E18 *Astronomy* A hazy or indistinct luminous area in the night sky representing a distant cluster of stars. Now usually *specifically*, a cloud of gas, dust, etc., in deep space.

nebulé /ˈnɛbjʊleɪ/ *adjective* (also **nebuly** /ˈnɛbjʊli/) **M16 French** (*nébulé* from medieval Latin *nebulatus* past participle of *nebulare* to cloud). **1** M16 *Heraldry* Of a particular wavy form, used to represent clouds. **2** M19 *Architecture* Of a moulding: of a wavy form.

nécessaire /nesɛsɛr/ *noun* plural pronounced same **E19 French**. A small usually ornamental case for pencils, scissors, tweezers, etc.

necessarium /nɛsəˈsɛːrɪəm/ *noun* plural **necessaria** /nɛsəˈsɛːrɪə/, **necessariums** **M19 Medieval Latin** (use as noun of neuter singular of *necessarius* (probably after accusative (*locum*) *necessarium* necessary (place)) from Latin *necessarius*). A privy, a lavatory, especially in a monastic building.

necrosis /nɛˈkrəʊsɪs/ *noun* plural **necroses** /nɛˈkrəʊsiːz/ **M17 Modern Latin** (from Greek *nekrōsis* state of death, from *nekroun* to kill, mortify). *Medicine* and *Biology* The death or decay of (part of) an organ or tissue due to disease, injury, or deficiency of nutrients; mortification.

née /neɪ/, *foreign* /ne/ *adjective* (also **nee**) **M18 French** (= born, feminine past participle of *naître* be born; cf. NÉ). **1** M18 Born with the name. **2** M20 *transferred* Formerly called.

■ Normally follows a woman's married name to indicate her family name before she married, as in 'Julia Smith *née* Jones'.

negligée /ˈnɛglɪʒeɪ/ *noun* (also **negligee**, **néglígé** *also foreign* /neglіʒe/ (*plural same*)) **M18 French** (*négligé* past participle of *négliger* neglect). **1** M18 *History* A kind of loose gown worn by women in the eighteenth century. **2** M19 Informal, unceremonious, or incomplete attire. **3** E20 A shroud. *United States.* **4** M20 A woman's light dressing-gown, *especially* one of flimsy semi-transparent fabric trimmed with ruffles, lace, etc.

4 1996 *Times* There were crocheted tops suited to a chilly English summer worn over ankle-length négligés.

négociant /negɔsjɑ̃/ *noun* plural pronounced same **E20 French** (= merchant (sc. *des vins*), from *négoce*, from Latin *negotium* business). A wine merchant.

1995 *Country Life* We put this to the test . . . recently, with a tasting of growers' and small *négociant's* champagnes compared with three non-vintage, benchmark *grandes marques* . . .

Negritude /ˈnɛgrɪtjuːd/ *noun* (also **Négritude** /negrityd/, **negritude**) **M20 French** (*négritude* from Latin *nigritudo*, from *niger*, *nigr-* black). The quality or characteristic of being a Negro (Black); affirmation of the value of Black or African culture, identity, etc.

nekulturny /nikʊljˈturnɪj/, /nɛkʊlˈtəːni/ *adjective* **M20 Russian** (*nekul'turnyĭ* uncivilized, from *ne-* not + KULTURNY). In countries of the former USSR: not having cultured manners, uncivilized, boorish.

nembutsu /nɛmˈbʊtsuː/ *noun* **M20 Japanese** (from *nen* thought + *butsu* Buddha). In Japanese Buddhism, the invocation and repetition of the name of the Buddha Amida for the purpose of salvation and spiritual unity; this invocation.

nem. con. /nɛm ˈkɒn/ *adverb phrase* **L16 Latin** (abbreviation of *nemine contradicente*). With no one contradicting.

■ *Nemine contradicente* (M17) is very seldom found in English.

nem. diss. /nɛm 'dɪs/ *adverb phrase* L18 **Latin** (abbreviation of *nemine dissentiente*). With no one dissenting.

■ *Nemine dissentiente* is not used in English in its full form.

nemesis /'nɛmɪsɪs/ *noun* (also **Nemesis**) plural **nemeses** /'nɛmɪsi:z/ L16 **Greek** (= righteous indignation, personified as the goddess of retribution or vengeance, from *nemein* to deal out what is due, related to *nomos* custom, law). **1** L16 An agent of retribution; a person who avenges or punishes. **b** M20 A persistent tormentor; a long-standing rival or enemy. *United States.* **2** L16 (An instance of) retributive justice.

1.b 1996 *New Scientist* . . . Mallon's nemeses, Dr George Soper and S. Josephine Baker, were reasonable and humane public health officials who took the actions they and their colleagues felt were best . . .

nemine contradicente see NEM. CON.

nemine dissentiente see NEM. DISS.

nepenthes /nɪ'pɛnθi:z/ *noun* L16 **Latin** (from Greek *nēpenthes* neuter of *nēpenthēs* banishing pain (qualifying *pharmakon* drug), from *nē-* not + *penthos* grief). **1** L16 A drug mentioned in Homer's *Odyssey* (iv.221) as liberating the mind from grief or trouble; any drug or potion bringing welcome forgetfulness. Also, a plant yielding such a drug. **2** M18 Any of various frequently climbing pitcher plants of the genus *Nepenthes*, chiefly of South East Asia.

ne plus ultra /ˌni: plʌs 'ʌltrə/, /ˌneɪ plʊs 'ʊltrɑ:/ *noun phrase* M17 **Latin** (= not further beyond). **1** M17 A prohibition of further advance or action; an impassable obstacle or limitation. **2** L17 The furthest limit reached or attainable; *especially* the point of highest attainment, the acme or highest point *of* a quality etc.

■ The inscription imagined by the inhabitants of the ancient Mediterranean world to be on the Pillars of Hercules (Strait of Gibraltar), prohibiting further westward passage by ships.

2 1996 *Country Life* . . . in the United States, where Cuban cigars are not available, Davidoff cigars are regarded as the *ne plus ultra*.

neroli /'nɪərəli/ *noun* L17 **French** (*néroli*, from Italian *neroli* after an Italian princess of that name, to whom its discovery is attributed). An essential oil distilled from the flowers of the Seville orange and used in perfumery. Also *neroli oil*, *oil of neroli*.

neskhi variant of NASKHI.

netsuke /'nɛtski/, /'nɛtsʊki/ *noun* plural **netsukes**, same. L19 **Japanese**. A small piece of ivory, wood, or other material, carved or otherwise decorated, formerly worn by Japanese on a cord suspending articles from a girdle.

Neue Sachlichkeit /ˌnɔyə 'zaxlɪçkʌɪt/ *noun phrase* E20 **German** (literally, 'new objectivity'). A movement in the fine arts, music, and literature, which developed in Germany during the 1920s and was characterized by realism and a deliberate rejection of romantic attitudes. Cf. SACHLICHKEIT.

neurosis /njʊə'rəʊsɪs/ *noun* plural **neuroses** /njʊə'rəʊsi:z/ M18 **Modern Latin** (from Greek *neuron* nerve). **1** M18 *Psychology* (A) mild mental illness, not attributable to organic disease, characterized by symptoms of stress such as anxiety, depression, obsessive behaviour, hypochondria, etc., without loss of contact with reality. **2** E20 Any more or less specific anxiety or malaise experienced by an individual, group, nation, etc.

névé /neve/ *noun* plural pronounced same M19 **Swiss French** (from Latin *nix*, *niv-* snow). The crystalline or granular snow on the upper part of a glacier, which has not yet been compressed into ice. Also, a field or bed of this. Also called FIRN.

nevus variant of NAEVUS.

nexus /'nɛksəs/ *noun* plural same, **nexes** /'nɛksi:z/ M17 **Latin** (from *nex-* past participial stem of *nectere* to bind). **1** M17 A connection; a bond, a link. **b** E20 *Grammar* A group of words (with or without a verb) expressing a predicative relation. **2** M19 A connected group or series; a network.

2 1996 *Spectator* But most of their successes were due to social control: the nexus of family life, religion and working-class self-help groups which enabled bourgeois values to permeate society.

ngoma /(ə)ŋ'gəʊmə/ *noun* E20 **Kiswahili** ((also *goma*) drum, dance, music). In East Africa: a dance; a night of dancing.

nibbana /nɪˈbɑːnə/ *noun* E20 **Pali** (*nibbāna*, Sanskrit *nirvāṇa* nirvana). *Buddhism* NIRVANA.

niche /nɪtʃ/, /niːʃ/ *noun* E17 **Old and Modern French** (from Old French *nichier* (modern *nicher*) to make a nest, nestle, from Proto-Romance from Latin *nidus* nest). **1** E17 An artificially constructed wall recess; *specifically* a shallow ornamental recess for a statue, urn, etc. **b** M19 A natural hollow in a rock or hill. **c** E20 A MIHRAB motif on an oriental prayer rug. More fully *prayer niche*. **2** *figurative* **a** E18 A place or position suited to or intended for a person's capabilities, occupation, or status. **b** E18 A place of safety or retreat. **c** E20 *Ecology* A position or role taken by a kind of organism within its community. **d** M20 *Commerce* A position from which an opening in a market etc. can be exploited; *especially* a specialized but profitable segment of a commercial market.

nicht wahr /nɪçt vɑːr/ *interjection* E20 **German** (literally, 'not true'). Is it not true? Isn't that so?

Niçois /niswa/, /niːˈswɑː/ *adjective* (feminine **Niçoise** /niswaz/, /niˈswɑːz/) L19 **French** (= of Nice, a city in southern France). Of, pertaining to, or characteristic of Nice or its inhabitants; *specifically* in *Cookery*, designating food, especially garnished with tomatoes, capers, anchovies, etc., characteristic of Nice or the surrounding region.

■ Generally postpositive, as in *salade Niçoise*.

niello /nɪˈɛləʊ/ *noun* plural **nielli** /nɪˈɛli/, **niellos** E19 **Italian** (from Latin *nigellus* diminutive of *niger* black). **1** A black composition of sulphur with silver, lead, or copper, for filling engraved designs on silver or other metals. **2** M19 (A specimen of) such ornamental work; an article decorated with niello. **3** M19 An impression on paper of a design to be filled with niello. **b** *transitive verb* M19 Inlay with niello. Chiefly as *nielloed* participial adjective.

nien hao /nɪən haʊ/ *noun* plural same, **nien haos** L19 **Chinese** (*niánhào*, literally, 'reign year'). A title given to (part of) the reign of a Chinese emperor, used in imperial China as a system of dating. Also, a mark (signifying the reign of a particular emperor) used on Chinese pottery or porcelain to indicate an object's period of manufacture.

niente /niˈɛnte/, /nɪˈenti/ *noun, adverb, & adjective* E19 **Italian**. **A** *noun* E19 Nothing. **B** *adverb & adjective* E20 *Music* (A direction:) with gradual fading away of the sound or tone to nothing.

■ In nineteenth-century use the noun apparently existed in English only in the phrase (DOLCE) FAR NIENTE.

niet /ˈnjɛt/ *adverb & noun* (also **nyet**) E20 **Russian** (*net* no). **A** *adverb* E20 In Russian: no, *especially* expressing a blunt refusal. **B** *noun* E20 An utterance of 'niet'.

nihil obstat /ˌnʌɪhɪl ˈɒbstat/, /ˌnɪhɪl/ *noun phrase* M20 **Latin** (literally, 'nothing hinders' (the censor's formula of approval)). A certificate or statement recording that a work has been approved by the Roman Catholic Church as free of doctrinal or moral error; a statement of official approval, authorization.

nil admirari /ˌnɪl admɪˈrɑːri/ *noun* M18 **Latin** (= to wonder at nothing). An attitude of imperturbability or indifference to the distractions of the outside world.

■ A stance advocated by the Roman poet Horace in the opening lines of one of his *Epistles* (I.vi.1): *nil admirari prope res est una ... solaque quae possit facere et servare beatum* 'to wonder at nothing is just about the only way a man can become contented and remain so.'

nilas /ˈniːlas/ *noun* M20 **Russian**. Partly refrozen ice forming a thin flexible layer on the surface of water.

nil desperandum /ˌnɪl dɛspəˈrandəm/ *interjection* E17 **Latin** (= no need to despair). Do not despair, never despair.

■ From Horace *Odes* I.vii.27: *nil desperandum Teucro duce et auspice Teucro*) 'no need to despair with Teucer as your leader and Teucer to protect you'.

nimbi plural of NIMBUS.

nimbu-pani /ˈnɪmbuːˌpɑːni/ *noun* M20 **Hindustani** (*nimbū* lime, lemon + *pānī* water). A drink of the Indian subcontinent consisting of lemon juice or lime juice with sugar and ice or water.

nimbus /ˈnɪmbəs/ *noun* plural **nimbi** /ˈnɪmbʌɪ/, /ˈnɪmbiː/, **nimbuses** E17 **Latin** (= cloud, rain, aureole). **1** E17 A bright or luminous cloud or cloudlike formation investing a god etc.; *transferred* a cloud of fine particles or other matter surrounding a person or thing. **2** E18 (A representation of) a halo surrounding the head of Jesus, a saint, etc. **3** E19 *Meteorology* A rain-cloud. Now *rare*.

ninja /ˈnɪndʒə/ *noun* plural same M20 **Japanese** (= spy). A person, especially a Japanese samurai, expert in NINJUTSU.

■ The word was little known in the West until the rise of interest in oriental martial arts in 1970s. *Ninjas* then began to play a role in fantasy and computer games but it was the huge popular and commercial success of the children's comic-book characters the Teenage Mutant Ninja Turtles in the United States at the end of the 1980s that brought the word into a wider circulation.

ninjutsu /nɪnˈdʒʌtsuː/ *noun* M20 **Japanese** (from *nin* stealth, invisibility + *jutsu* art, science). The traditional Japanese technique of espionage, developed in feudal times for military purposes and subsequently used in the training of samurai.

Niño, el see EL NIÑO.

ninon /ˈniːnɒn/, *foreign* /ninɔ̃/ *noun & adjective* E20 **French**. **A** *noun* E20 A lightweight dress fabric of silk, nylon, etc. **B** *attributive* or as *adjective* E20 Made of ninon.

nirvana /nɪəˈvɑːnə/ *noun* M19 **Sanskrit** (*nirvāṇa* use as noun of past participle of *nirvā-* to be extinguished, from *nis-* out + *vā-* to blow). In *Buddhism*, the experience that comes to a person in life when greed, hatred, and delusion are extinguished and enlightenment gained; the release from the effects of KARMA and the cycle of death and rebirth that comes when an enlightened person dies. In *Hinduism* and *Jainism*, liberation of the soul from the effects of karma and from bodily existence. Also *figurative* a state of bliss, an ideal state.

figurative **1996** *New Scientist* Without patents on extracted human material, . . . investment in biotechnology will drain out of Europe and into the patent nirvanas of the US and Japan . . .

nisei /ˈniːseɪ/ *noun* plural same M20 **Japanese** (from *ni-* second + *sei* generation). An American whose parents were immigrants from Japan. Cf. SANSEI.

nisi /ˈnʌɪsʌɪ/ *postpositive adjective* M19 **Latin** (= unless). *Law* That takes effect only on certain conditions, not final.

■ Generally in the phrase *decree nisi* 'a provisional order for divorce that will be made absolute unless cause to the contrary can be shown within a fixed period'.

nitchevo /ˌniːtʃɪˈvəʊ/ *interjection & noun* E20 **Russian** (*nichego*). **A** *interjection* E20 In Russian: Never mind! It does not matter! **B** *noun* M20 The use of the word 'nitchevo'; an attitude of resignation or fatalism.

noblesse /nəʊˈblɛs/, *foreign* /nɔblɛs/ *noun* ME **Old and Modern French** (from Latin *nobilis*). **1** ME Noble birth or rank; nobility, nobleness. **2** L15 *The* nobility; a class of people of noble rank, now especially in a foreign country.

■ The most usual occurrence in English is of sense 1 in NOBLESSE OBLIGE; *petite noblesse* (sense 2) is used of the minor nobility of France.

noblesse oblige /nɔblɛs ɔbliʒ/, /nəʊˌblɛs ɒˈbliːʒ/ *noun phrase* M19 **French**. (The principle that) noble ancestry and privilege entail responsibility.

1995 *Spectator* But then I decided they were victims of *noblesse oblige*, considering it incumbent upon themselves as dukes to supply any reasonable favour requested of them.

noceur /nɔsœr/ *noun* plural pronounced same E20 **French**. A reveller, a rake, a libertine; a person who stays up late at night.

nockerl /ˈnɔkərl/ *noun* plural **nockerln** /ˈnɔkərln/ M19 **Austrian German** (= little dumpling). A small light Austrian and Bavarian dumpling, made with a batter including eggs, and usually semolina.

■ A *Salzburger nockerl* is a sweetened version eaten as a pudding.

nocturne /ˈnɒktəːn/ *noun* M19 **French**. **1** M19 A musical composition of a dreamy character. **2** L19 A painting of a night scene, a night-piece.

noel /nəʊˈɛl/ *noun* (also **noël**) E19 **French** (*noël*). A Christmas carol.

noema /nəʊˈiːmə/, /nəʊˈeɪmə/ *noun* plural **noemata** /nəʊˈiːmətə/ E20 **Greek** (*noēma* thought). *Philosophy* An object of perception or thought, as opposed to a process or aspect of perceiving or thinking. Cf. NOESIS 3.

noesis /nəʊˈiːsɪs/ *noun* plural **noeses** /nəʊˈiːsiːz/ L19 **Greek** (*noēsis*, from *noein* to think, perceive). **1** L19 Mental capacity or action. *rare*. **2** L19 An intellectual view of the moral and physical world. *rare*. **3** M20 *Philosophy*. A process or aspect of perceiving or thinking, as opposed to an object of perception or thought. Cf. NOEMA.

nogaku /ˈnɔːgaku/, /ˈnəʊgakuː/ *noun* E20 **Japanese** (*nōgaku*, from *nō* Noh + *gaku* music). Noh as a dramatic form or genre.

Noh /nəʊ/ *noun* (also **No**) L19 **Japanese** (*nō* (also = talent, accomplishment)). The traditional Japanese masked drama with dance and song, evolved from Shinto rites.

noia /'nɔɪə/ *noun* M20 **Italian** (ultimately from Latin *in odio*; cf. ENNUI). Boredom, weariness, ennui.

noir /nwɑː/ *adjective & noun* LME **French**. **1** LME Black. **2** L18 Black as one of the two colours of divisions in rouge-et-noir and roulette. Earliest in *rouge-et-noir*.

■ Sense 1 is rare in English except in or with reference to the cinematic genre of FILM NOIR or, by extension, black humour in other media (see quotations below and ROMAN NOIR). It occurs in its literal meaning in a few phrases such as *pinot noir* (a variety of black grape) and figuratively in EN NOIR.

1996 *Times Magazine* More noir than knockabout, thriller than caper, it is an effort to transport the [Dr Who] series in time and imbue it with the values of a new television era. **1996** *Bookseller* Higson . . . says that he is more conscious of the influence of the American *noir* writer Jim Thompson.

noisette /nwɑː'zɛt/ *noun* L19 **French** (diminutive of NOIX nut). A small round piece of meat.

noix /nwa/ *noun* plural same M19 **French** (literally, 'nut'; cf. NOISETTE). A piece of veal cut from the rump. Also *noix de veau* /nwa də vo/.

nolens volens /ˌnəʊlɛnz 'vəʊlɛnz/ *adverb phrase* L16 **Latin** (present participles of *nolo, nolle* to be unwilling, and *volo, velle* to be willing). Willing or unwilling, whether willing or not, willy-nilly.

noli me tangere /ˌnəʊlʌɪ miː 'tan(d)ʒəri/, /ˌnəʊlɪ meɪ 'taŋg(ə)ri/ *noun* LME **Latin** (= do not touch me). **1** LME *Medicine* An ulcerous condition attacking bone and soft tissues especially of the face: *specifically* lupus. Now *rare* or *obsolete*. **2** LME A person who or thing which must not be touched or interfered with. **3** M16–M18 *Botany* A balsam or impatiens the seed capsules of which burst open on a touch; *specifically Impatiens noli-tangere*, touch-me-not. **4** M17 A warning or prohibition against meddling or interference. **5** L17 A painting representing the appearance of Jesus to Mary Magdalen at the sepulchre (John 20:17).

■ The original injunction is the Vulgate version of the risen Christ's warning to Mary Magdalen when He appears to her outside the sepulchre (John 20:17).

nolle prosequi /ˌnɒlɪ 'prɒsɪkwʌɪ/ *noun* L17 **Latin** (= be unwilling to pursue). *Law* (Originally, now *United States*) the relinquishment by a plaintiff or prosecutor of part or all of his or her suit or prosecution; (later) a procedure by which the Attorney General can terminate criminal proceedings. Also, an entry of this in a court record.

■ Also abbreviated to *nolle* in the United States (L19).

nolo contendere /ˌnəʊləʊ kɒn'tɛndəri/ *noun* L19 **Latin** (= I do not wish to contend). *United States Law* A plea by which a defendant in a criminal prosecution accepts conviction as in the case of a plea of guilty but does not admit guilt.

nom de guerre /nɔ̃ də gɛr/, /ˌnɒm də 'gɛː/ *noun phrase* plural **noms de guerre** (pronounced same) L17 **French** (= war-name). An assumed name under which a person fights or engages in some other action or enterprise.

1995 *Spectator* . . . Avraham Stern of the eponymous gang took the *nom de guerre* 'Yair' after the commander of the Sicarii garrison at Masada.

nom de plume /ˌnɒm də 'pluːm/, *foreign* /nɔ̃ də plym/ *noun phrase* plural **noms de plume** (pronounced same) E19 **pseudo-French** (formed from *nom* name, *de* of, *plume* pen, after *nom de guerre*). An assumed name under which a person writes, a pen-name.

1996 *Times* . . . Elytis was the *nom de plume* he chose to use in place of his family name . . .

nom de théâtre /nɔ̃ də teɑtr/, /ˌnɒm də teɪ'ɑːtrə/ *noun phrase* plural **noms de théâtre** (pronounced same) L19 **French** (= theatre-name). An assumed name under which a person performs on stage.

nomen dubium /ˌnəʊmən 'djuːbɪəm/ *noun phrase* plural **nomina dubia** /ˌnɒmɪnə 'djuːbɪə/ E20 **Latin** (= doubtful name). *Taxonomy* A Latin name the correct application of which is vague or uncertain.

nomenklatura /naˌmjɛnkla'tura/, /nɒ ˌmɛnklə'tjʊərə/ *noun* M20 **Russian** (from Latin *nomenclatura* list of names). In the former Soviet Union: a list of influential posts in government and industry to be filled by Party appointees; *collectively* the holders of these posts, the Soviet élite; also *transferred*.

1995 *Spectator* Naturally, the BBC's higher *nomenklatura*—all those Controllers and Heads of This and That—will reply that the two [sc., high ratings and public service broadcasting] are not incompatible.

nomen nudum /ˌnəʊmən ˈnjuːdəm/ *noun phrase* plural **nomina nuda** /ˌnɒmmə ˈnjuːdə/ E20 **Latin** (= naked name). *Taxonomy* A Latin name which has no standing because it was not validly published.

nominata plural of NOMINATUM.

nominatim /nɒmɪˈneɪtɪm/ *adverb* M19 **Latin** (from *nomen, nomin-* name). Chiefly *Law* By name; particularly, expressly.

nominatum /nɒmɪˈnɑːtəm/, /nɒmɪ ˈneɪtəm/ *noun* plural **nominata** /nɒmɪ ˈnɑːtə/ M20 **Latin** (neuter of *nominatus*). The thing named by a sign or expression.

nominis umbra /ˌnɒmɪnɪs ˈʌmbrə/ *noun phrase* M19 **Latin** (literally, 'the shadow or appearance of a name'). A name without substance; a thing which is not what the name implies.

■ The phrase comes from Lucan's *Pharsalia* (i. 135): *Stat magni nominis umbra* 'he stands the mere shadow of a mighty name'.

nomos /ˈnɒmɒs/ *noun* M20 **Greek** (= usage, custom, law). *Theology* The law; the law of life.

noms de guerre, **noms de plume**, etc. plurals of NOM DE GUERRE, NOM DE PLUME, etc.

non /nɔ̃/ *noun* plural pronounced same L20 **French** (= no). In France and French-speaking countries: an utterance of 'non', an absolute refusal or veto.

nonchalance /ˈnɒnʃ(ə)l(ə)ns/ *noun* L17 **Old and Modern French** (see next). The state of being nonchalant; lack of enthusiasm or interest; casual indifference, unconcern.

nonchalant /ˈnɒnʃ(ə)l(ə)nt/ *adjective* M18 **Old and Modern French** (from *non* + *chalant* present participle of *chaloir* to be concerned). Calm and casual; lacking or showing no enthusiasm or interest.

non compos mentis /nɒn ˌkɒmpɒs ˈmɛntɪs/ *adjective phrase* E17 **Latin**. Not in one's right mind. Cf. COMPOS MENTIS.

■ Almost always predicative and often shortened to *non compos* (also E17).

non est /nɒn ˈɛst/ *adjective phrase* L19 **Latin** (abbreviated from *non est inventus* he was not found). Non-existent, absent.

■ *Non est inventus* (L15) was the legal name formerly given to a sheriff's statement in returning a writ, to the effect that the defendant was not to be found within the sheriff's jurisdiction.

non est factum /ˌnɒn ɛst ˈfaktəm/ *noun phrase* E17 **Latin** (= it was not done). *Law* A plea that a written agreement is invalid because the defendant was mistaken about its character when signing it. Long chiefly *United States*.

non nobis /nɒn ˈnəʊbɪs/ *interjection* E19 **Latin** (= not to us). Expressing humble gratitude or thanksgiving; disclaiming credit for a success or benefit.

■ In the Vulgate *Non nobis, Domine, non nobis* 'Not to us, O Lord, not to us' is part of a verse of Psalm 113; in the English Bible the words form the opening of Psalm 115.

non-obstante /ˌnɒnɒbˈstanti/ *noun* (also **non obstante**) LME **Medieval Latin** (*non obstante* not being in the way, from *non* not + *obstante* ablative present participle of *obstare* to be in the way (originally in ablative absolute, as *non obstante veredicto* notwithstanding the verdict)). **1** LME *History* A clause in a statute or letter patent, beginning 'non obstante', and conveying a dispensation from a monarch to perform an action despite any statute to the contrary. Also, a similar clause issued by the Pope. In full *clause of non-obstante*. **2** E17–M18 *generally* A dispensation from or relaxation of a law or rule (followed by *on, of, to*). Also, an exception to a rule.

nonpareil /ˌnɒnpəˈreɪl/ *adjective & noun* LME **French** (from *non-* + *pareil* like, equal, from popular Latin *pariculus* diminutive of Latin *par*). **A** *adjective* LME Having no equal; unrivalled, unique. **B** *noun* **1** L15 A person or thing having no equal; an unrivalled or unique person or thing. **2** M18 An old variety of apple. **3 a** M18 The painted bunting, *Passerina ciris*. **b** M18 The eastern rosella, *Platycercus eximius*. More fully *nonpareil parrot*. Chiefly *Australian*. **4** M18 Any of several attractively patterned moths.

■ Formerly also a size of type roughly equivalent to modern 6 point (L17) and a kind of sweet (L17).

B 1 1996 *Spectator* She's a genius, an inspirational revolutionary, a great designer, a nonpareil . . .

non placet /ˌnɒn ˈpleɪsɛt/ *noun & verb phrase* (as verb also **non-placet**) L16 **Latin** (= it does not please). **A** *noun* L16 Originally, an expression of dissent or disapproval. Later, a negative vote in a university or Church assembly. **B** *transitive verb* E19 Give a negative vote on (a proposition); reject (a measure).

■ A formula used especially in university and Church assemblies in giving a negative vote on a proposition.

nonplus /nɒn'plʌs/ *noun & verb* L16 **Latin** (from *non plus* not more, no further). **A** *noun* L16 A state in which no more can be said or done; inability to proceed in speech or action; a state of perplexity; a standstill. Chiefly in *at a nonplus, bring* or *reduce to a nonplus.* **B** *transitive verb* L16 (inflected *-ss-*) Bring (a person etc.) to a nonplus; perplex; make (a thing) ineffective or inoperative. Frequently as *nonplussed* participial adjective.

non plus ultra /ˌnɒn plʌs 'ʌltrə/ *noun phrase* L17 **Latin** (= not more beyond). A NE PLUS ULTRA, the highest point or culmination *of*.

non sequitur /nɒn 'sɛkwɪtə/ *noun* M16 **Latin** (literally, 'it does not follow'). An inference or conclusion not logically following from the premisses; a response, remark, etc., not logically following from what has gone before.

■ Earliest in a rare and obsolete use (only LME) for part of the collar of a shirt etc.; an unfastened collar.

1996 *Spectator* There are one or two odd slips and non sequiturs in the book, which may be attributed to inexpert editing . . .

nori /'nɔːri/ *noun* L19 **Japanese**. Edible seaweed of the genus *Porphyra*, eaten especially by the Japanese either fresh or dried in sheets.

noria /'nɔːrɪə/ *noun* L18 **Spanish** (from Arabic *nāy'ūra*). Especially in Spain and the East: a device for raising water from a stream etc., consisting of a chain of pots or buckets, revolving round a wheel driven by the water current.

norte /'norte/ *noun* M19 **Spanish** (= north). Any of the violent gales from the north prevailing in the Gulf of Mexico from September to March. Usually in *plural*.

norteamericano /ˌnorteameri'kano/ *noun & adjective* plural of noun **norteamericanos** /ˌnorteameri'kanos/ (also **Norteamericano**, feminine **norteamericana** /ˌnorteameri'kana/) E20 **Spanish and Portuguese** (from *norte* north + *americano* American). Especially in Latin America, (a native or inhabitant) of North America, a North American.

nosh /nɒʃ/ *noun & verb* E20 **Yiddish** (cf. German *naschen* to nibble). **A** *noun* **1** E20 A restaurant; a snack bar. More fully *nosh bar, nosh-house.* **2** M20 Food, a meal. **3** M20 A snack eaten between meals, a titbit. Chiefly *North American.* **B** *transitive and intransitive verb* **1** M20 Nibble or eat (a snack) (chiefly *North American*); eat (food), especially heartily or greedily. **2** M20 Practise fellatio (with). *slang.*

nostalgie de la boue /nɔstalʒi də la bu/ *noun phrase* L19 **French** (literally, 'yearning for mud'). A desire for degradation and depravity.

1995 *Spectator* Feinstein allows Mellors' inherent misogyny, fascism and *nostalgie de la boue* to overwhelm him, and permits Connie to be reclaimed by her own well-heeled bohemian class.

nostos /'nɒstɒs/ *noun* plural **nostoi** /'nɒstɔɪ/ L19 **Greek**. A homecoming, a homeward journey, *specifically* of Odysseus and the other heroes from Troy. Also, an account of such a homecoming or homeward journey, especially as the conclusion of a literary work. *literary.*

■ *Nost(o)i* was the title of an ancient Greek poem, now lost, dealing with the homecomings of the Greek heroes after the Trojan War.

nostrum /'nɒstrəm/ *noun* plural **nostrums**, **nostra** /'nɒstrə/ E17 **Latin** (neuter singular of *noster* our). **1** E17 A quack remedy, a patent medicine, *especially* one prepared by the person recommending it. **2** M18 A pet scheme, a favourite remedy, especially for bringing about social or political reform or improvement.

2 1995 *Times* Every age has its prevailing fallacies, and most of them from a similar origin: the insensitive overuse of an apparently commonsense nostrum.

nota bene /ˌnəʊtə 'bɛneɪ/ *verb phrase transitive & intransitive* (*imperative*) E18 **Latin** (from *nota* note + *bene* well). Mark well, observe particularly (usually drawing attention to a following qualification of what has preceded).

■ In general use in the abbreviated form *NB*.

notabilia /nəʊtə'bɪlɪə/ *noun plural* M19 **Latin** (neuter plural of *notabilis* notable, after MEMORABILIA). Things worthy of note.

notes inégales /nɔts inegal/ *noun phrase plural* E20 **French** (literally, 'unequal notes'). *Music* In baroque music, notes performed by convention in a rhythm different from that shown in the score.

note verbale /nɔt vɛrbal/ *noun phrase* plural **notes verbales** (pronounced same) M19 **French** (literally, 'verbal note').

An unsigned diplomatic note, of the nature of a memorandum, written in the third person.

notitia /nəʊˈtɪʃɪə/, /nəʊˈtɪʃə/ *noun* E18 **Latin** (= knowledge, (in late Latin) list, account, etc., from *notus* known). **1** Knowledge, detailed information. *rare*. Only in E18. **2** L18 An account, a list; *specifically* a register or list of ecclesiastical sees or districts.

nougat /ˈnuːgɑː/, /ˈnʌgət/ *noun* (also (earlier) **nogat**) E19 **French** (from Provençal *nogat*, from *noga* nut, from Latin *nux*). (A sweet made from) egg-white sweetened with sugar or honey and mixed with nuts and sometimes pieces of fruit.

nouille /nuːj/ *noun* plural pronounced same M19 **French**. Noodle. Usually in *plural*.

noumenon /ˈnaʊmənɒn/, /ˈnuːmənɒn/ *noun* plural **noumena** /ˈnaʊmənə/ L18 **German** (from Greek, use as noun of neuter present participle passive of *noien* to apprehend, conceive). An object of purely intellectual intuition, devoid of all phenomenal attributes.

■ Chiefly in the philosophy of Immanuel Kant (1724–1804); cf. DING AN SICH.

nous /naʊs/ *noun* (also **nouse**) L17 **Greek**. **1** L17 *Greek Philosophy* Intuitive apprehension, intelligence; mind, intellect. **2** E18 Common sense, practical intelligence, gumption. *colloquial*.

2 1996 *Times* Taxpayers who follow them blindly, without using their nous, are fools.

nous autres /nuz otr/ *personal pronoun* (*1st plural*) M19 **French** (literally 'we others'). We as opposed to somebody or anybody else.

nouveau /ˈnuːvəʊ/, /nuːˈvəʊ/, *foreign* /nuvo/ *adjective & noun* E20 **French** (= new). **A** *adjective* **1** E20 *Nouveau art* = ART NOUVEAU. **2** M20 Of a person: possessing recently acquired wealth, NOUVEAU RICHE; ostentatiously displaying such wealth. Of wealth etc.: recently acquired. **b** L20 *Nouveau poor* = NOUVEAU PAUVRE. **3** L20 Modern, up to date. **B** *noun* plural **nouveaus**, **nouveaux** /ˈnuːvəʊ/, /ˈnuːvəʊz/, *foreign* /nuvo/. **1** L20 A *nouveau riche*. Usually in *plural*. **2** L20 BEAUJOLAIS NOUVEAU. *colloquial*.

■ *Nouveau* seldom occurs independently in English, but is used elliptically and colloquially for such phrases as *Beaujolais nouveau* etc., the context making plain the meaning intended.

nouveau pauvre /nuvo povr/, /ˌnuːvəʊ ˈpɔːvrə/ *adjective & noun phrase* plural **nouveaux pauvres** (pronounced same) M20 **French** (literally, 'new poor', after NOUVEAU RICHE). **A** *adjective* M20 Of a person: newly impoverished. **B** *noun* L20 A person who has recently become poor.

A 1995 *Times* Far better, for a *nouveau pauvre* hostess, to take advantage of the national mood of exhaustion among thirty-to-forty somethings . . . and issue instead a more casual invitation.

nouveau riche /nuvo riʃ/, /ˌnuːvəʊ ˈriːʃ/ *noun & adjective phrase* plural **nouveaux riches** (pronounced same) E19 **French** (literally, 'new rich'). **A** *noun* E19 A person who has recently acquired wealth, *especially* one who displays the fact ostentatiously or vulgarly. **B** *attributive* or as *adjective* L19 Of, pertaining to, or characteristic of a *nouveau riche*; that has recently acquired wealth.

B 1995 *Spectator* Throughout last week I had to endure the roar of *nouveaux riches* engines as their hideous-looking children gunned them to impress.

nouveau roman /nuvo rɔmɑ̃/ *noun phrase* M20 **French** (literally, 'new novel'). A type of (especially French) novel characterized by precise descriptions of characters' mental states and absence of interpretation of or comment on them.

1974 *Times Literary Supplement* The sources of Mr Gordon's off-the-peg technique are fairly clear: some Kafka; the Burroughs scissors; but mostly the *nouveau roman*. The novel, so this modish dogma asserts, is a 'vision of things', and the universe no more than the sum of the author's sensations.

nouveaux plural of NOUVEAU.

nouveaux arrivés /nuvoz arive/ *noun phrase plural* L19 **French** (literally, 'new arrivals'). People who have recently acquired a higher financial and social standing.

nouveaux pauvres, nouveaux riches plurals of NOUVEAU PAUVRE, NOUVEAU RICHE.

nouvelle /nuvɛl/ *noun* plural pronounced same L17 **French**. A short fictitious narrative, a short novel, *especially* one dealing with a single situation or a single aspect of a character or characters.

nouvelle /nuːˈvɛl/, *foreign* /nuvɛl/ *adjective* L18 **French** (feminine of NOUVEAU; in sense 2 elliptical for NOUVELLE CUISINE). **1** L18 *generally* New, novel. Now *rare*. **2** L20

Of, pertaining to, or characteristic of *nouvelle cuisine*.

nouvelle cuisine /nuvɛl kɥizin/, /ˌnuːvɛl kwɪˈziːn/ *noun phrase* L20 **French** (literally, 'new cooking'). A style of (especially French) cooking that avoids traditional rich sauces and emphasizes the freshness of the ingredients and attractive presentation.

■ The fashion for *nouvelle cuisine* spread beyond France in the 1970s and early 1980s, and its characteristics of lightness, short cooking times, and small helpings continued to endear it to the healthy eating lobby. In the hands of pretentious practitioners, however, the fashionable extremes of artistic presentation and meagreness of quantity have incurred considerable ridicule (see quotation).

1990 *Country Living* One establishment we visited served every dish flanked by the same ludicrously inappropriate clutter: a frilly lettuce leaf pinned down by a couple of hefty spring onions, a pallid slice of kiwi fruit and a strawberry. Oh nouvelle cuisine, what have you spawned!

nouvelles plural of NOUVELLE.

nouvelle vague /nuvɛl vag/ *noun phrase* M20 **French** (literally, 'new wave'; cf. VAGUE). A new movement or trend; *specifically* that in film-making originating in France in the late 1950s.

attributive **1996** *Times* As a young man at the Amsterdam Film Academy in the early Sixties, Jan De Bont . . . would make a regular pilgrimage to Paris to sit at the feet of the *nouvelle vague* guru Jean-Luc Goddard.

nova /ˈnəʊvə/ *noun* plural **novae** /ˈnəʊviː/, **novas** L19 **Latin** (feminine singular of *novus* new). *Astronomy* Originally, a new star or nebula. Now *specifically* a star whose brightness suddenly increases by several magnitudes, with violent ejection of gaseous material, and then decreases more or less gradually. Formerly also, a supernova.

■ The present astronomical term is a reintroduction, as *nova* was originally (L17) used in the rare and obsolete sense of 'a thick ring or roll of tobacco'.

novella /nə(ʊ)ˈvɛlə/ *noun* E20 **Italian**. A short fictitious prose narrative, a short novel, a long short story.

■ The word was particularly applied to the tales in Boccaccio's *Decameron* and its Italian imitators before being transferred to a work in any language midway in length between a full-scale novel and a short story.

novena /nə(ʊ)ˈviːnə/ *noun* plural **novenae** /nə(ʊ)ˈviːniː/, **novenas** M19 **Medieval Latin** (from *novem* nine, after Latin *novenarius* of nine days). *Roman Catholic Church* A devotion consisting of special prayers or services on nine successive days.

novi homines plural of NOVUS HOMO.

novillada /noviˈ(l)jada/, /nɒvɪˈljɑːdə/ *noun* plural **novilladas** /noviˈ(l)jadas/, /nɒvɪˈljɑːdəz/ L19 **Spanish** (from NOVILLO). A bullfight in which three-year-old bulls are fought by novice matadors.

novillero /noviˈ(l)jero/, /nɒvɪˈljɛːrəʊ/ *noun* plural **novilleros** /noviˈ(l)jeros/, /nɒvɪˈljerəʊz/ E20 **Spanish** (from NOVILLO). An apprentice matador who has fought only in NOVILLADAS.

novillo /noˈvi(l)jo/, /nɒˈviːljəʊ/ *noun* plural **novillos** /noˈvi(l)jos/, /noˈviːljəʊz/ M19 **Spanish** (from Latin *novellus* new). A young bull; *specifically* a fighting bull not more than three years old.

novio /ˈnovjo/ *noun* plural **novios** /ˈnovjos/ E20 **Spanish**. In Spain and Spanish-speaking countries: a boyfriend, a lover.

novus homo /ˌnəʊvəs ˈhɒməʊ/ *noun phrase* plural **novi homines** /ˌnəʊvʌɪ ˈhɒmɪniːz/ L16 **Latin** (literally, 'new man'). A man who has recently risen to a position of importance from insignificance; an upstart.

■ In ancient Rome, the phrase was specifically applied to the first man in a particular family to rise to the office of a magistrate.

noxa /ˈnɒksə/ *noun* plural **noxae** /ˈnɒksiː/ L19 **Latin** (= hurt, damage). *Medicine* A thing harmful to the body.

noyade /nwɑːˈjɑːd/, *foreign* /nwajad/ *noun* plural **noyades** /nwɑːˈjɑːdz/, *foreign* /nwajad/) E19 **French** (from *noyer* to drown, from Latin *necare* kill without a weapon, (later) drown, from *nex*, *nec-* slaughter). An execution carried out by drowning, especially a mass one as in France in 1794.

noyau /nwɑːˈjəʊ/, *foreign* /nwajo/ *noun* plural **noyaux** /nwɑːˈjəʊz/, *foreign* /nwajo/ L18 **French** (earlier *noiel* kernel, from Proto-Romance use as noun of neuter of late Latin *nucalis*, from *nux*, *nuc-* nut). **1** L18 A liqueur made of brandy flavoured with the kernels of certain fruits. **2** E20 A type of sweet similar to nougat.

nritta /ˈ(ə)nrɪtə/ *noun* E20 **Sanskrit** (*nṛtta* dancing). A type of Indian dance with abstract patterns of movement and neutral facial expressions.

nritya /'(ə)nrɪtjə/ *noun* L19 **Sanskrit** (*nṛtya* dance, mime). A type of Indian dance through which ideas or emotions are expressed.

nuance /'nju:ɑ:ns/ *noun & verb* L18 **French** (from *nuer*to show cloudlike variations in colour, from *nue* cloud, from popular Latin variant of Latin *nubes*). **A** *noun* L18 A slight or subtle variation in or shade of meaning, expression, colour, etc. **B** *transitive verb* L19 Give a nuance or nuances to.

nuancé /nɥɑ̃se/ *adjective* M20 **French** (from as preceding). Having or characterized by nuances.

nucleus /'nju:klɪəs/ *noun* plural **nuclei** /'nju:klɪʌɪ/, **nucleuses** E18 **Latin** (= nut, kernel, inner part, variant of *nuculeus*, from *nucula* diminutive of *nux*, *nuc-* nut). **1** E18 *Astronomy* The dense core of the head of a comet. **b** L18 A dense, usually bright, central part in a galaxy or nebula. **2** M18 The central part or thing around which others are grouped or collected; the centre or kernel of an aggregate or mass; an initial part or collection of things to which others may be added.

■ Besides its initial astronomical sense, *nucleus* has acquired a large number of specialist senses in a variety of subject fields: Anatomy (E19), Archaeology (M19), Biology (M19), Chemistry (M19), Bee-keeping (L19), Physics (E20), and Linguistics (E20).

nudnik /'nʊdnɪk/ *noun* (also **nudnick**) M20 **Yiddish** (from Russian *nudnyĭ* tedious, boring + noun suffix *-nik* person connected with (something)). A pestering, nagging, or irritating person; a bore. *United States slang.*

attributive **1972** *New York* Too many of our nudnik moviegoers . . . dread the prospect of sharing their pleasures with the plain folks.

nuée ardente /nɥe ardɑ̃t/ *noun phrase* plural **nuées ardentes** (pronounced same) E20 **French** (literally, 'burning cloud'). *Geology* A hot dense cloud of ash and fragmented lava suspended in a mass of gas, typically ejected from the side of the dome of certain volcanoes and flowing downhill like an avalanche.

■ The phrase was introduced into formal vulcanology in 1903 by A. Lacroix, who subsequently observed (in *La Montagne Pelée et ses eruptions* (1904)) that the expression had earlier been in use amongst the inhabitants of San Jorge in the Azores. While Lacroix said that by *nuée ardente* he meant *brulant* 'burning' rather than *incandescent* 'glowing', the phrase is nonetheless usually rendered in English as 'glowing cloud'.

nugae /'nju:ʤi:/, /'nu:gʌɪ/ *noun plural* E18 **Latin**. Trifles.

■ Chiefly in NUGAE DIFFICILES.

nugae difficiles /ˌnju:dʒi: 'dɪfɪkɪleɪz/ *noun plural phrase* E18 **Latin** (= difficult trifles). *Philosophy* Matters of trifling importance occupying a disproportionate amount of time owing to their difficulty.

nuit blanche /nɥi blɑ̃ʃ/ *noun phrase* plural **nuits blanches** (pronounced same) M19 **French** (literally, 'white night'). A sleepless night.

nulla bona /ˌnʌlə 'bəʊnə/ *noun phrase* E19 **Latin** (= no goods). The return made by a sheriff upon an execution when the party has no goods to be distrained.

nulli secundus /ˌnʌlɪ sɪ'kʌndəs/ *adjective phrase* (also **nulli secundum** /ˌnʌlɪ sɪ 'kʌndəm/) M19 **Latin**. Second to none.

numdah /'nʌmdə/ *noun* E19 **Urdu** (*namdā* from Persian *namad* felt, carpet, rug). **1** E19 In the Indian subcontinent and the Middle East: a kind of felt or coarse woollen cloth, frequently embroidered; a rug or carpet made from this (also *numdah rug*). **2** L19 A NUMNAH.

numen /'nju:mən/ *noun* plural **numina** /'nju:mɪnə/ E17 **Latin** (related to *nuere* to nod, Greek *neuein* to incline the head). Divinity; a local or presiding god.

numéro /nymero/ *noun* plural **numéros** /nymero/ E20 **French**. A person or thing having a place in a series, a number. Also, a remarkable or strange person.

numero uno /ˌnju:mərəʊ 'u:nəʊ/ *noun phrase* plural **numero unos** L20 **Italian and Spanish** (= number one). The best or most important person.

1996 *Spectator* Then there is Enrique Ponce, acclaimed as *numero uno* and already being spoken of as the matador of the century.

numerus clausus /ˌnju:mərəs 'klaʊsəs/ *noun phrase* E20 **Latin** (literally, 'closed number'). A fixed maximum number of entrants admissible to an academic institution.

numina plural of NUMEN.

numnah /'nʌmnə/ *noun* M19 **Urdu** (*namdā* from Persian *namad* felt, carpet, rug; a variant of NUMDAH). A saddle-cloth; a pad placed under a saddle to prevent soreness.

nunatak /ˈnʌnətak/ *noun* L19 **Eskimo** ((Greenlandic) *nunataq*). An isolated peak of rock projecting above a surface of inland ice or snow in Greenland, Norway, etc.

nunc dimittis /ˌnʌŋk dɪˈmɪtɪs/ *noun phrase* M16 **Latin** (= now you let (your servant) depart). **1** M16 A canticle forming part of the Christian liturgy at evensong and compline, comprising the song of Simeon in Luke 2:29–32 (in the Vulgate beginning *Nunc dimittis, Domine*). **2** L16 Permission to depart; dismissal.

nunchaku /nʌnˈtʃaku:/ *noun* L20 **Japanese** (from Okinawa dialect). A Japanese martial arts weapon consisting of two hardwood sticks joined together by a strap, chain, etc. More fully *nunchaku stick*. Usually in *plural*.

nuncio /ˈnʌnsɪəʊ/, /ˈnʌnʃɪəʊ/ *noun* plural **nuncios** E16 **Italian** (*nuncio*, *nuntio* (now *nunzio*) from Latin *nuncius*, *nuntius* messenger). **1** E16 *Roman Catholic Church* A papal ambassador to a foreign court or government. **2** E17 A person bearing a message; a messenger. **3** L17 *History* A member of the Polish diet.

nuntius /ˈnʌnʃɪəs/, /ˈnʌnʃəs/ *noun* plural **nuntii** /ˈnʌnʃɪʌɪ/ E17 **Latin** (variant of *nuncius* messenger). A NUNCIO.

nuoc mam /nwɒk ˈmɑ:m/ *noun phrase* E20 **Vietnamese**. A spicy Vietnamese fish sauce.

nuragh /ˈnʊərag/ *noun* plural **nuraghi** /ˈnʊəragi/ E19 **Sardinian**. *Archaeology* A type of massive stone tower found in Sardinia, dating from the Bronze and Iron Ages. Cf. TALAYOT.

nux vomica /ˌnʌks ˈvɒmɪkə/ *noun phrase* LME **Medieval Latin** (literally, 'emetic nut', from Latin *nux* nut + adjective from *vomere* to vomit). The highly poisonous seeds of the tree *Strychnos nux-vomica*, used as a major source of strychnine and in homoeopathic remedies; this tree, a native of southern Asia.

nyet variant of NIET.

nymphaeum /nɪmˈfi:əm/ *noun archaic* plural **nymphaea** /nɪmˈfi:ə/ (also **nympheum**, plural **nymphea**) L18 **Latin** (from Greek *numphaion*, *-eion* temple or shrine of the nymphs, neuter of *numphaios*, *-eios* sacred to the nymphs, from *numphē* nymph). *Classical Antiquities* A grotto or shrine dedicated to a nymph or nymphs; (a part of) a building built to represent this.

ob. abbreviation of OBIIT.

obbligato /ɒblɪˈɡɑːtəʊ/ *adjective and noun* (also **obligato**) L18 **Italian** (= obliged, obligatory). *Music* **A** *adjective* L18 Indispensable; that cannot be omitted: designating a part or accompaniment forming an integral part of a composition, and the instrument on which it is played. **B** *noun* M19 plural **obbligatos**. An obbligato part or accompaniment, *especially* one of particular prominence in a piece.

obelus /ˈɒb(ə)ləs/ *noun* plural **obeli** /ˈɒb(ə)lʌɪ/, /ˈɒb(ə)liː/ LME **Latin** (= spit, critical obelus, from Greek *obelos*). A straight horizontal stroke (-), sometimes with a dot above and below (÷), used in ancient manuscripts to mark a word, passage, etc., especially as spurious. Also, a dagger-shaped reference mark (†) used in printed matter as a reference to a footnote etc., and in some dictionaries to denote obsoleteness. Also called *obelisk*.

oberek /ə(ʊ)ˈbɛrɪk/ *noun* M20 **Polish**. A lively Polish dance in triple time, related to the mazurka but usually faster.

obi /ˈəʊbi/ *noun* E19 **Japanese** (= belt). A sash worn round the waist with Japanese clothing.

obiit /ˈɒbɪɪt/ *verb* **Latin**. He, she, or it died.

■ Frequently on epitaphs, followed by the date of death; also abbreviated to *ob*.

obiit sine prole /ˌɒbɪɪt ˌsmeɪ ˈprəʊleɪ/ *phrase* L19 **Latin**. He, she, or it died without offspring.

■ Frequently in genealogies, usually abbreviated to *ob.s.p.* or *o.s.p.*

obit /ˈɒbɪt/, /ˈəʊbɪt/ *noun* LME **Old and Modern French** (from Latin *obitus* going down, setting, death, from *obit-* past participial stem of *obire* to perish, die (from *mortem obire* to meet death); in sense 3 partly abbreviation of *obituary*). **1** LME–L17 Departure from life, death, decease. **2 a** LME–E18 A ceremony performed at the burial of a deceased person; a funeral service. **b** LME *History* A ceremony (usually a mass) commemorating, or commending to God, a deceased person, especially a founder or benefactor of an institution on the anniversary of his or her death; an annual or other regular memorial service. **3** LME Originally, a record or notice of (the date of) a person's death. Later (*colloquial*), an obituary.

obiter /ˈɒbɪtə/ *adverb, noun, & adjective* L16 **Latin** (originally two words, *ob itur* by the way). **A** *adverb* L16 By the way, in passing, incidentally. **B** *noun* E17 A thing said, done, or occurring by the way; an incidental matter. Also, an OBITER DICTUM. **C** *adjective* M18 Made or said by the way; incidental.

obiter dictum /ˌɒbɪtə ˈdɪktəm/ *noun phrase* plural **obiter dicta** /ˌɒbɪtə ˈdɪktə/ E19 **Latin** (from as preceding + DICTUM). A judge's expression of opinion uttered in discussing a point of law or in giving judgement, but not essential to the decision and so without binding authority; *generally* an incidental remark.

1996 *Spectator* The *obiter dicta* of earlier scientific materialists, all of them in their own day at least as eminent and confident as Dawkins, make hilarious reading today.

objet /ɔbʒɛ/, /ˈɒbʒeɪ/ *noun* plural pronounced same M19 **French**. **1** M19 An object displayed as an ornament. **2** M19 A person forming the object of another's attentions or affection. *rare*.

1 1996 *Country Life* Occasionally, a composition is enriched by other *objets* such as shells, a jewel, even a skull.

objet d'art /ɔbʒɛ dar/, /ˌɒbʒeɪ ˈdɑː/ *noun phrase* plural **objets d'art** (pronounced same) M19 **French** (literally, 'object of art'; cf. preceding). A small decorative object.

oblietjie /ɒˈbliːki/ *noun* L19 **Afrikaans** (from French *oublie* (from ecclesiastical Latin *oblata* use as noun of feminine of past participle of *offerre* to offer) + diminutive suffix *-tjie*). In South Africa: a rolled wafer-thin teacake.

obligato variant of OBBLIGATO.

oboe da caccia /ˌəʊbəʊ da ˈkatʃa/ *noun phrase* plural **oboi da caccia** /ˈəʊbɔɪ/ L19 **Italian** (literally, 'hunting oboe'). Chiefly *History* An obsolete type of tenor oboe with a pitch a fifth lower than the ordinary oboe.

oboe d'amore /ˌəʊbəʊ daˈmɔːreɪ/ *noun phrase* plural **oboes d'amore, oboi d'amore** /ˈəʊbɔɪ/ L19 **Italian** (literally, 'oboe of love'). A type of alto oboe with a pear-shaped bell and a pitch a minor third below that of the ordinary oboe, now used especially in baroque music.

oboi da caccia, **oboi d'amore** plurals of OBOE DA CACCIA, OBOE D'AMORE.

obscurum per obscurius /əbˌskjʊərəm pər əbˈskjʊərɪəs/ *noun phrase* L19 **Late Latin** (literally, 'the obscure by the still more obscure'). An explanation that is more difficult to understand than that which it purports to explain. Cf. IGNOTUM PER IGNOTIUS.

ob.s.p. abbreviation of OBIIT SINE PROLE.

ocarina /ɒkəˈriːnə/ *noun* L19 **Italian** (from *oca* goose (with reference to its shape)). A simple wind instrument in the form of a hollow egg-shaped body with finger-holes and a hole to blow at.

occupatio /ɒkjʊˈpeɪʃɪəʊ/, /ɒkjʊˈpɑːtɪəʊ/ *noun* L16 **Latin**. *Rhetoric* (The device of making) mention of a thing by pretending to omit to mention it.

octapla /ˈɒktəplə/ *noun* (also **octaple** /ˈɒktəp(ə)l/) L17 **Greek** (*oktapla* neuter plural of *oktaplous* eightfold, after HEXAPLA). A text consisting of eight versions in parallel columns, especially of the Old or New Testament.

octli /ˈəʊktli/ *noun* M19 **Mexican Spanish**. PULQUE.

oculus /ˈɒkjʊləs/ *noun* plural **oculi** /ˈɒkjʊlʌɪ/, /ˈɒkjʊliː/ M19 **Latin** (= eye). *Architecture* A round or eyelike opening or design; *specifically* a circular window (especially in a church); the central boss of a volute; an opening at the apex of a dome.

■ Prevously also in the phrases *oculus Christi* (literally, 'of Christ'), wild clary (a plant reputed to be good for the eyes) (LME–M17), and *oculus mundi* (literally, 'of the world') a white variety of opal, hydrophane (L17–L18).

odalisque /ˈəʊd(ə)lɪsk/ *noun* L17 **French** (from Turkish *ōdalık*, from *ōda* chamber + *lık* suffix expressing function). A female slave or concubine in an Eastern harem, especially in the seraglio of the Sultan of Turkey (now *historical*); *transferred* an exotic sexually attractive woman.

odeon /ˈəʊdɪən/ *noun* (also in sense 1 **odeion**; in sense 2 **Odeon**) M19 **Greek** (*ōdeion*; see ODEUM). **1** M19 An ODEUM. **2** M20 Any of a chain of large, lavish cinemas in a chain built by Oscar Deutsch in the 1930s; *generally* a luxurious cinema.

odeum /ˈəʊdɪəm/ *noun* plural **odeums**, **odea** /ˈəʊdɪə/ E17 **French** (*odéum* or Latin *odeum* from Greek *ōideion* from *ōidē* Attic form of *aoidē* song, singing, from *aeidein* to sing). A building for the performance of vocal and instrumental music, especially among the ancient Greeks and Romans.

odium /ˈəʊdɪəm/ *noun* E17 **Latin** (= hatred, from *odi* I hate). The fact or state of being hated; general or widespread unpopularity or opprobrium.

oedema /ɪˈdiːmə/ *noun* plural **oedemata** /ɪˈdiːmətə/, **oedemas** LME **Late Latin** (from Greek *oidēma*, from *oidein* to swell). *Medicine* (A) local or general swelling produced by the accumulation of fluid in the body tissues or cavities; dropsy.

oeil-de-boeuf /œjdəbœf/ *noun* plural **oeils-de-boeuf** (pronounced same) M18 **French** (literally, 'ox-eye'). **1** M18 A small round window. **2** L18 A small vestibule or antechamber in a palace (*specifically* one in Versailles lighted by a small round window); *transferred* (a part of) a monarch's court.

■ Sense 1 appears later (M19) in English form as 'bull's-eye'.

1 1996 *Country Life* He added a new range of three rooms . . . , with a symmetrical, Classical façade, the pediment containing an *œil-de-bœuf* window. . . . They [sc. the stables] have old-fashioned mullion and transom windows and an *œil-de-bœuf* in the east façade.

oeil-de-perdrix /œjdəpɛrdri/ *noun* M19 **French** (literally, 'partridge-eye'). **1** M19 In French pottery and porcelain, a design of dotted circles, usually on a coloured background, frequently used on Sèvres porcelain. Also *oeil-de-perdrix pattern* etc. **b** L19 A similar design used as a ground in lace-making. **2** L19 Pink or pale red wine or champagne. In full *oeil-de-perdrix wine*, *champagne*.

oeils-de-boeuf plural of OEIL-DE-BOEUF.

oenochoe /iːˈnɒkəʊi/ *noun* (also **oinochoe** /iːˈnɒkəʊi/, /ɔɪˈnɒkəʊi/) L19 **Greek** (*oinokhoē*, from *oeno-* combining form of *oinos* wine + *khoas*, *khoē* pouring). *Greek Antiquities* A vessel used for ladling wine from a bowl into a cup.

oesophagus /ɪˈsɒfəgəs/ *noun* (also **esophagus**) LME **Medieval Latin** (*ysophagus*, *iso-* from Greek *oisophagos*, from obscure first element + (apparently) *-phagos* eating, eater; current spelling after modern Latin). *Anatomy* and *Zoology* The canal leading from the back of the mouth, through which food and drink pass to the stomach; the gullet.

oestrus /'iːstrəs/, /'ɛstrəs/ *noun* (also **estrus**) L17 **Latin** (from Greek *oistros* gadfly, breeze, sting, frenzy). **1** L17 A parasitic insect; now *specifically* a biting fly of the genus *Oestrus* or the family Oestridae whose larvae are parasitic on various animals; a botfly. Now chiefly as modern Latin genus name. **2** E19 *figurative* A sharp stimulus; a passion, a frenzy. Now *rare*. **3** L19 *Zoology* and *Physiology* (The period of) a female animal's readiness to mate, accompanied by certain physiological changes; the rut, heat.

oeufs en cocotte /øf ɑ̃ kɔkɔt/ *noun phrase plural* E20 **French** (= eggs in a cocotte). A French dish of eggs in butter baked and served in individual cocottes or ramekins.

œuvre /œvr/, /'əːvrə/ *noun* (also **oeuvre**) plural pronounced same L19 **French** (= work). A work of art, music, literature, etc.; the whole body of work produced by an artist, composer, etc. Cf. CHEF-D'ŒUVRE.

> **1996** *Oldie* . . . that he has been able to keep both aspects of his oeuvre alive and developing with such élan is in itself remarkable.

œvre de vulgarisation /œvr də vylgarizasjɔ̃/, /'əːvrə də ˌvʊlgarɪ'zasjɔ̃(ŋ)/ *noun phrase* (also **oeuvre de vulgarisation**) M20 **French** (= work of popularization). A work which attempts to make an academic or esoteric subject accessible to the general public.

officina /ɒfɪ'sʌɪnə/, /ɒfɪ'siːnə/ *noun* plural **officinae** /ɒfɪ'sʌɪniː/, /ɒfɪ'sʌɪnʌɪ/ E19 **Latin** (= workshop etc., contraction of *opificina*, from *opifex* workman). A workshop; a place of production, (frequently *figurative*).

oficina /ɒfɪ'siːnə/ *noun* L19 **Spanish** (from Latin OFFICINA). In Spanish-speaking South America or Mexico: a factory.

ogham /'ɒgəm/ *noun* (also **ogam**, **Ogham**) E18 **Old Irish** (*ogam*, *ogum* (genitive *oguim*), modern Irish *ogham*, plural **oghaim**, Gaelic *oghum*, connected with its mythical inventor *Ogma*). An ancient British and Irish system of writing using an alphabet of twenty or twenty-five characters; any of these characters, consisting of a line or stroke, or a group of two to five parallel strokes, arranged alongside or across a continuous line or the edge of a stone (usually in *plural*). Also, an inscription in this alphabet.

oinochoe variant of OENOCHOE.

ojime /'əʊdʒɪmeɪ/, *foreign* /'ɔːdʒime/ *noun* plural same, **ojimes** L19 **Japanese** (from *o* string + *shime* fastening, fastener). A bead or beadlike object, often very elaborate, used in Japan as a sliding fastener on the strings of a bag, pouch, or INRO.

ole /'ole/ *noun* M19 **Spanish**. A Spanish folk-dance which is accompanied by castanets and singing.

olé /o'le/, /əʊ'leɪ/ *interjection & noun* E20 **Spanish**. **A** *interjection* E20 Bravo! **B** *noun* M20 A cry of '*olé!*'

olim /əʊ'lɪm/ *noun plural* M20 **Hebrew** ('*ōlīm* plural of '*ōleh* person who ascends). Jewish immigrants who settle in the State of Israel.

olim /'əʊlɪm/ *adverb* M17 **Latin**. At one time; formerly.

olla /'ɒlə/ *noun* plural **ollas**, (in sense 3) **ollae** /'ɒliː/, /'ɒlʌɪ/ E17 **Spanish** ((Portuguese *olha*) from Proto-Romance variant of Latin *olla* pot, jar; in sense 3, from Latin). **1** E17 In Spain and Spanish-speaking countries: an earthen jar or pot used for cooking etc.; a dish of (especially stewed) meat and vegetables cooked in this. Cf. OLLA PODRIDA sense 1. **2** M19 In Spanish America: a large porous earthen jar for keeping drinking-water cool by evaporation from its outer surface. **3** M19 An ancient cinerary urn.

■ *Olio* (M17) is an alteration of *olla* used in sense 1 and also figuratively for a hotchpotch, medley, or miscellany.

olla podrida /ˌɒlə pə(ʊ)'driːdə/ *noun phrase* L16 **Spanish** (literally 'rotten pot', from as OLLA *noun* + *podrida* putrid). **1** L16 A highly spiced stew of various meats and vegetables, of Spanish and Portuguese origin; *generally* any dish containing a great variety of ingredients. **2** M17 *figurative* Any mixture of heterogeneous things or elements; a hotchpotch, a medley.

> **2 1996** *Spectator* . . . the RSC, so careful of Shakespeare on our behalf, long ago decided to commit this *olla podrida* of Bardic tricks [sc. *Cymbeline*] to the scrapheap for scholars to pick over . . .

oloroso /ɒlə'rəʊsəʊ/ *noun* plural **olorosos** L19 **Spanish** (= fragrant). A heavy, dark, medium-sweet sherry; a glass of this.

olpe /'ɒlpeɪ/ *noun* L19 **Greek** (*olpē*). *Greek Antiquities* A leather flask for oil, wine, etc. Also, a pear-shaped jug with a handle.

om /əʊm/ *interjection & noun* L18 **Sanskrit** (*oṃ, om*, sometimes regarded as composed of three sounds, *a-u-m*, symbolizing the three major Hindu deities: see also OM MANI PADME HUM). *Hinduism* and *Tibetan Buddhism* **A** *interjection* L18 Used as a mantra or auspicious formula at the beginning of prayers etc. **B** *noun* L19 An utterance of 'om'.

ombré /ɔ̃bre/ *noun & adjective* L19 **French** (past participle of *ombrer* to shade). (A fabric or design) having gradual shading of colour from light to dark.

ombrellino /ˌombrel'liːno/, /ˌɒmbrɛ 'liːnəʊ/ *noun* plural **ombrellini** /ˌombrel 'liːni/, **ombrellinos** /ˌɒmbrɛ'liːnəʊz/ M19 **Italian**. *Roman Catholic Church* A small umbrella-like canopy held over the sacraments when they are moved from one place to another.

ombres chinoises /ɔ̃br ʃinwaz/ *noun phrase plural* L18 **French** (= Chinese shadows). *History* A European version of Chinese shadow-puppets, used in a galanty show.

ombudsman /'ɒmbʊdzmən/ *noun* plural **ombudsmen** M20 **Swedish** (from *ombud* commissioner, agent, representing Old Norse *umboð* charge, commission, *umboðsmaðr* commissary, manager). An official appointed to investigate complaints by individuals against maladministration by public authorities; *especially* a British official of this kind (officially called the Parliamentary Commissioner for Administration), first appointed in 1967.

omega /'əʊmɪgə/ *noun* E16 **Greek** (*ō mega*, literally, 'great O', opposed to *o mikron* omicron). **1** E16 The last letter (Ω, ω) of the Greek alphabet, having originally the value of a long open *o*; *figurative* the last of a series; the last word, the final development. **2** M20 *Particle Physics* Either of two subatomic particles: *omega meson* and *omega minus*.

■ In the figurative use of sense 1, often in the phrase 'the alpha and the omega' (see under ALPHA).

omertà /omer'taː/ *noun* L19 **Italian** (dialectal variant of *umiltà* humility). A code of silence observed by members or associates of the Mafia or (*transferred*) others engaged in clandestine activities.

■ The Italian sense of 'humility' originally referred to the Mafia code which enjoins submission of the group to its leader.

1996 *Times* Pressed time and again on quarantine by baffled Members of Parliament, she preserved the ministry *omertà* towards the kennel owners and referred only to her 'veterinary advisers'.

om mani padme hum /əʊm ˌmʌni pʌdmeɪ 'huːm/ *noun phrase & interjection* L18 **Sanskrit** (*Oṃ maṇipadme hūṃ* literally, 'oh (goddess) Manipadma', reinterpreted as 'oh jewel in the lotus', from *maṇi* jewel, *padma* lotus; cf. OM). *Tibetan Buddhism* (Used as) a mantra or auspicious formula in prayer and meditation.

omnium /'ɒmnɪəm/ *noun* M18 **Latin** (literally, 'of all (things, sorts)', genitive plural of *omnis* all: cf. next). **1** *Stock Exchange* **a** M18 *History* The total value of the stock and other interests offered by the Government to each subscriber when raising a loan. **b** L19 Any combined stock the constituents of which can be dealt with separately. *colloquial*. **2** M18 The sum of what one values; one's all. **3** M19 A piece of furniture with open shelves for ornaments; a whatnot.

omnium gatherum /ˌɒmnɪəm 'gaðərəm/ *noun phrase* plural **omnium gatherums**, (*rare*) **omnium gathera** /ˌɒmnɪəm 'gaðərə/ M16 **pseudo-Latin** (from Latin OMNIUM + English *gather*). A gathering or collection of all sorts of persons or things; a confused medley. *colloquial*.

omphalos /'ɒmfəlɒs/ *noun* M19 **Greek** (literally, 'navel'). **1** M19 *Greek Antiquities* **a** A boss on a shield etc. **b** M19 A stone, in the temple of Apollo at Delphi, reputed to mark the central point of the earth. **2** M19 *figurative* A central point, a centre.

on dit /ɔ̃ di/ *noun* plural **on dits** (pronounced same) E19 **French** (= they say). An item of gossip; something reported on hearsay.

onnagata /ɒnə'gɑːtə/ *noun* plural same E20 **Japanese** (from *onna* woman + *kata* figure). In Japanese kabuki theatre, a man who plays female roles. Also called *oyama*.

onomasticon /ɒnə(ʊ)'mastɪkɒn/ *noun* E18 **Greek** (use as noun (sc. *biblion* book) of neuter of *onomastikos* pertaining to naming, from *onoma* name). A vocabulary or alphabetic list of (especially personal) proper names. Also, a vocabulary of nouns; a general lexicon.

onomatopoeia /ˌɒnə(ʊ)matəˈpiːə/ *noun* L16 **Late Latin** (from Greek *onomatopoiia* making of words, from *onomatopoios*, from *onomato-* combining form of *onoma* name + *-poios* making, from *poiein* to make, create). **1** L16 The formation of a word by an imitation of the sound associated with the thing or action designated; the principle or practice of forming words by this process. **2** M19 A word formed by this process. **3** M19 *Rhetoric* The use of naturally suggestive language for rhetorical effect.

onus /ˈəʊnəs/ *noun* M17 **Latin** (= load, burden). A burden, a responsibility, a duty.

1996 *Times* The onus will now be on the many producers who make some claim to eco-friendly status . . . to prove to consumers that their products really are all that they claim.

oom /ʊəm/ *noun* E19 **Afrikaans** (from Dutch *oom*). Uncle.

■ Frequently used by children or young people in South Africa as a respectful form of address to any older or elderly man.

oomiak variant of UMIAK.

op. abbreviation of OPUS.

op. cit. /ɒp ˈsɪt/ *noun & adverb phrase* L19 **Latin** (abbreviation of *opus citatum* the work quoted, or *opere citato* in the work quoted). (In) the work already quoted.

opera plural of OPUS.

opéra bouffe /ɔpera buf/, /ˌɒp(ə)rə ˈbuːf/ *noun phrase* plural **opéras bouffe(s)** (pronounced same) L19 **French** (from as next). OPERA BUFFA; (an example of) French comic opera.

figurative **1995** *Times* Eventually their relationship turned into an *opera bouffe* of the most debilitating, if diverting, kind.

opera buffa /ˌɒp(ə)rə ˈbuːfə/, *foreign* /ˌopera ˈbuffa/ *noun phrase* plural **operas buffa, opere buffe** /ˈopere ˈbuffe/ E19 **Italian** (= comic opera). (Italian) comic opera, with dialogue in recitative and characters drawn from everyday life; an example of this.

1995 *Spectator* Yet much of this power is dissipated by the preceding *opera buffa* with the disguises. Those who wear Armani suits must behave like Armani suit-wearers.

opéra comique /ɔpera kɔmik/, /ˌɒp(ə)rə kɒˈmiːk/ *noun phrase* plural **opéras comiques** (pronounced same) M18 **French** (= comic opera). A type of opera (originally humorous, later romantic) characterized by spoken dialogue; an example of this.

opéras bouffe(s), operas buffa, etc. plurals of OPÉRA BOUFFE, OPERA BUFFA, etc.

opera seria /ˌɒp(ə)rə ˈsɪərɪə/, *foreign* /ˌopera ˈsɛːrja/ *noun phrase* plural **operas seria, opere serie** /ˌopere ˈsɛːrje/ L19 **Italian** (= serious opera). A type of opera prevalent in the eighteenth century, with elaborate arias and usually based on mythological themes; an example of this. Cf. TRAGÉDIE LYRIQUE.

opere buffe, opere serie plurals of OPERA BUFFA, OPERA SERIA.

operetta /ɒpəˈrɛtə/ *noun* L18 **Italian** (diminutive of *opera*). A short, originally one-act, opera on a light or humorous theme.

■ *Opérette*, the French word derived from *operetta* and Anglicized as *operette*, is a more recent introduction (L19), but *operetta* remains the more generally used term.

opprobrium /əˈprəʊbrɪəm/ *noun* plural **opprobria** /əˈprəʊbrɪə/ M17 **Latin** (= infamy, reproach, from *ob-* towards + *probrum* shameful deed, disgrace, use as noun of neuter of *probus* disgraceful). **1** M17 An occasion or cause of reproach; shameful conduct; something that brings disgrace. **2** L17 Disgrace attached to conduct considered shameful; the expression of this disgrace; shame, reproach.

2 1996 *Spectator* The German translation has not yet been published here, but it has already managed to attract relentless opprobrium.

optime /ˈɒptɪmeɪ/ *noun* M18 **Latin** (= best, very well, from *optime disputasti* you have disputed very well). In the mathematical tripos at Cambridge University, a student placed in the second or third division. Also (respectively) *senior, junior optime*.

optimum /ˈɒptɪməm/ *noun & adjective* L19 **Latin** (use as noun of neuter of *optimus* best). Originally *Biology*. **A** *noun* L19 The conditions most favourable for growth, reproduction, or other vital process; *generally* the best, a level, condition, etc., regarded as the best or most favourable. Opposed to PESSIMUM. **B** *adjective* L19 Best, most favourable, especially under a particular set of circumstances; optimal.

opus /ˈəʊpəs/, /ˈɒpəs/ *noun* plural **opuses** /ˈəʊpəsɪz/, /ˈɒpəsɪz/, **opera** /ˈɒp(ə)rə/ E18 **Latin** (= work). An artistic work, a composition; *especially* a musical composition or set of compositions as numbered among the works of a composer in order of publication.

■ In bibliographies and catalogues usually abbreviated to *op.* Cf. OP. CIT.

opus Alexandrinum /ˌɒpəs ˌalɛksɑːn ˈdriːnəm/ *noun phrase* M19 **Medieval Latin** (literally, 'Alexandrian work'). A pavement mosaic work widely used in Byzantium in the ninth century and later in Italy, consisting of coloured stone, glass, and semiprecious stones arranged in intricate geometric patterns.

opus anglicanum /ˌɒpəs aŋglɪˈkɑːnəm/ *noun phrase* (also **opus Anglicanum**) M19 **Medieval Latin** (literally, 'English work'). Fine pictorial embroidery produced in England in the Middle Ages and used especially on ecclesiastical vestments.

opus araneum /ˌɒpəs aˈrɑːnɪəm/ *noun phrase* M19 **Medieval Latin** (literally, 'spider's work'). Darned netting; delicate embroidery done on a net and resembling a spider's web. Also called *spider-work*.

opus citatum see OP. CIT.

opus consutum /ˌɒpəs kɒnˈsuːtəm/ *noun phrase* L19 **Medieval Latin** (literally, 'work sewn together'). APPLIQUÉ work.

opuscule /əˈpʌskjuːl/ *noun* plural **opuscules** (also in Latin form **opusculum** /əˈpʌskjʊləm/, plural **opuscula** /əˈpʌskjuːlə/) M17 **Old and Modern French** (from Latin *opusculum* diminutive of *opus* work). A minor (especially literary or musical) work.

opus Dei /ˌɒpəs ˈdeɪiː/ *noun phrase* L19 **Medieval Latin.** **1** L19 *Ecclesiastical* The work of God; *specifically* liturgical worship regarded as man's primary duty to God. **2** L19 (*Opus Dei*) A Roman Catholic organization of priests and lay people founded in Spain in 1928 with the aim of re-establishing Christian ideals in society.

opus magnum variant of MAGNUM OPUS.

opus sectile /ˌɒpəs ˈsɛktɪleɪ/ *noun phrase* M19 **Latin** (literally, 'cut work'). An originally Roman floor decoration made up of pieces shaped individually to fit the pattern or design, as distinct from mosaic which uses regularly shaped pieces.

opus signinum /ˌɒpəs sɪgˈniːnəm/ *noun phrase* M18 **Latin** (literally, 'work of Signia'). An originally Roman flooring material consisting of broken tiles etc. mixed with lime mortar.

■ The town of Signia (now Segni) in Central Italy was famous for its tiles.

or /ɔː/ *noun* LME **Old and Modern French** (ultimately from Latin *aurum* gold). Originally, gold. Later (*Heraldry*), the tincture gold or yellow in armorial bearings.

orangerie /ˈɒrɪnʤ(ə)ri/ *noun* (also **orangery**) M17 **French** (from French *oranger* orange tree). A place, especially a special protective structure, where orange trees are cultivated.

orans /ˈɔːrənz/ *noun* E20 **Latin** (*orans, orantem* present participle of *orare* to pray). *Art* A representation of a person in a kneeling or praying position.

■ Often postpositive, as in *Virgin orans.*

oratio obliqua /ɒˌrɑːtɪəʊ ɒˈbliːkwə/, /ɒˌreɪʃ(ɪ)əʊ əˈblʌɪkwə/ *noun phrase* M19 **Latin** (*oratio* speech + *obliqua* feminine of *obliquus* oblique). Indirect speech.

oratio recta /ɒˌrɑːtɪəʊ ˈrɛktə/, /ɒˌreɪʃ(ɪ)əʊ ˈrɛktə/ *noun phrase* M19 **Latin** (from *oratio* speech + *recta* feminine of *rectus* straight, direct). Direct speech.

oratorio /ɒrəˈtɔːrɪəʊ/ *noun* plural **oratorios** E18 **Italian** (from ecclesiastical Latin *oratorium* oratory). **1** E18 A semi-dramatic extended musical composition, usually based on a Scriptural theme, performed by a choir with soloists and a full orchestra, without costume, action, or scenery. **2** L19 The genre of musical composition or drama characterized by such a theme and such performance.

■ Originally (M17) in English in its more literal sense of 'a pulpit', but this is rare and became obsolete before its reintroduction in its modern senses, which derive from the musical services in the church of the Oratory of St Philip Neri in Rome.

orchata variant of HORCHATA.

ordinaire abbreviation of VIN ORDINAIRE.

ordonnance /ˈɔːdənəns/, *foreign* /ɔrdɔnɑ̃s/ (*plural same*) *noun* M17 **French** (alteration of Old French *ordenance* after Old and Modern French *ordonner* to arrange). **1** M17 Systematic arrangement, especially of literary material or architectural parts; a plan or method of literary or artistic composition; an architectural order. **2** M18 In various European countries, especially France, an ordinance, a decree, a law. **3** M18 *French History* Any of those organized companies of men-at-arms who formed the beginnings of a standing army in France. In full *company of ordonnance.*

oregano /ɒrɪˈɡɑːnəʊ/, /əˈrɛɡənəʊ/ *noun* L18 **Spanish and American Spanish** (variant of ORIGANUM). A seasoning prepared from the (usually dried) leaves of wild marjoram, *Origanum vulgare*, or, especially in Central and South America, of shrubs of the genus *Lippia*, especially *Lippia graveolens*.

ore rotundo /ˌɔːrɪ rəˈtʌndəʊ/ *adverb phrase* E18 **Latin** (literally, 'with round mouth', from ablative of *os* mouth + ablative of *rotundus* round). With round, well-turned speech.

orfèvrerie /ɔrfɛvrəri/ *noun* ME **French** (from *orfèvre* from popular Latin *aurifabrum* worker in gold, goldsmith). Goldsmiths' work.

■ Formerly also the goldsmiths' quarter in London.

organon /ˈɔːɡ(ə)nɒn/ *noun* L16 **Greek** (= instrument, organ). **1** L16–E17 A bodily organ, especially as an instrument of the soul. **2** E17 An instrument of thought or knowledge; a means of reasoning; *specifically* a system of logical rules of investigation or demonstration.

■ The *Organon* is the collective title of the logical treatises of Aristotle.

orgeat /ˈɔːdʒɪət/ *foreign* /ɔrʒa/ (*plural same*) *noun* LME **French** (from Provençal *orjat*, from *ordi* barley from Latin *hordeum*). A syrup or cooling drink made from barley (later from almonds) and orange-flower water.

orientalia /ˌɔːrɪɛnˈteɪlɪə/, /ˌɒrɪɛnˈteɪlɪə/ *noun plural* E20 **Latin** (neuter plural of *orientalis* oriental). Things, especially books, relating to or characteristic of the Orient.

oriflamme /ˈɒrɪflam/ *noun* LME **Old and Modern French** (*oriflambe*, *oriflamme*, in medieval Latin *auriflamma*, from *aurum* gold + *flamma* flame). **1** LME *History* The sacred red or orange-red silk banner of St Denis, given to early kings of France by the abbot of St Denis on setting out for war. **2** E17 *transferred* and *figurative* **a** A banner, principle, ideal, etc., that serves as a rallying point in a struggle. **b** M19 A bright conspicuous object, colour, etc.

origami /ɒrɪˈɡɑːmi/ *noun* M20 **Japanese** (from *oru*, *-ori* fold + *kami* paper). The Japanese art of folding paper into decorative shapes and objects. Also *figurative*.

figurative **1996** *Spectator* . . . any information about the songs has been left to rot in the unfathomable origami of CD booklets.

origanum /ɒˈrɪɡ(ə)nəm/ *noun* ME **Latin** (from Greek *origanon*, perhaps from *oros* mountain + *ganos* brightness, joy; cf. OREGANO). Any of various aromatic labiate plants of the genus *Origanum*, much grown as herbs; *especially* wild marjoram, *O. vulgare*.

orihon /ˈɒrɪhɒn/ *noun* E20 **Japanese** (from *ori* fold + *hon* book). A book formed by folding a printed roll alternately backwards and forwards between the columns, and usually fastening it with cord down one side.

orlo /ˈɔːləʊ/ *noun* plural **orlos** M17 **Italian** (= border, hem, etc., from Latin *ora* edge, border). *Architecture* **1** M17 The fillet under the ovolo of a capital. **2** E18 The plinth under the base of a column.

orné /ˈɔːneɪ/ *adjective* (feminine **ornée**) L18 **French** (= ornate, past participle of *orner* from Latin *ornare* to adorn). Decorated, ornate.

■ Usually in English in the noun phrases *cottage orné* and *ferme ornée* (see quotations). Despite its appearance, *cottage orné* ('a rural dwelling in the form of a cottage with a decorative appearance') is an Anglo-French hybrid, as *cottage* derives from Old English *cot*, via Anglo-Latin *cotagium* and Anglo-Norman *cotage*. *Cottage*, identified in the *Encyclopédie* in 1754 as a *mot anglais* was indeed borrowed into French in the nineteenth century, but the English phrase (L18) antedates this borrowing. A *ferme ornée* is 'a farm designed for aesthetic pleasure as well as practical purposes'.

1995 G. Tindall *Célestine* A handyman, he had embellished the classic French exterior with a veranda and a blue-painted trellis, so that it now resembled an English *cottage orné* of the Edwardian era.

1996 D. Chambers *Stonyground* . . . Philip Southcote . . . first created . . . what came to be known as a *ferme ornée*—Wooburn Farm in Surrey: a modest farm around and through which went walks planted with trees and shrubs and flowers, so that one could stroll through a farm in a garden and enjoy the beauties of horticulture and agriculture together.

orterde /ˈɔːtɛːdə/ *noun* M20 **German** (from *Ort* place + *Erde* earth). *Soil Science* A dark sandy layer in soil containing redeposited materials from the upper layers, but not cemented into a hardpan. Cf. ORTSTEIN.

orthosis /ɔːˈθəʊsɪs/ *noun* plural **orthoses** /ɔːˈθəʊsiːz/ M20 **Greek** (*orthōsis* making straight, from *orthoun* to set straight). *Medicine* An artificial external device, as a brace or splint, serving to prevent or assist relative movement in the limbs or the spine.

ortolan /'ɔ:t(ə)lən/ *noun* M17 **French** (from Provençal = gardener, from Latin *hortulanus*, from *hortulus* diminutive of *hortus* garden). A bunting, *Emberiza hortulana*, found throughout much of the western Palaearctic, formerly esteemed as a delicacy (also *ortolan bunting*). Also (*United States* and *West Indies*, *rare*) any of certain other birds of similar gastronomic reputation.

■ Earlier (but only E16) in its original sense of 'gardener'.

ortstein /'ɔ:tstʌɪm/ *noun* E20 **German** (from *Ort* place + *Stein* stone). *Soil Science* A hardpan; *especially* an iron pan in a podzol. Cf. ORTERDE.

orzo /'ordzo/ *noun* L20 **Italian** (= barley). Pasta in the shape of grains of rice.

o.s.p. abbreviation of OBIIT SINE PROLE.

ossia /ɒ'si:ə/, /'ɒsjə/ *conjunction* L19 **Italian**. *Music* In directions: or, alternatively.

■ Indicating an alternative and usually easier way of playing a passage.

osso bucco /ˌɒsəʊ 'bu:kəʊ/ *noun phrase* M20 **Italian** (= marrowbone). (An Italian dish of) shin of veal containing marrowbone stewed in wine with vegetables.

ostinato /ɒstɪ'nɑ:təʊ/ *adjective & noun* L19 **Italian** (= obstinate, persistent). *Music* **A** *adjective* L19 Recurring; frequently repeated. **B** *noun* E20 plural **ostinati** /ɒstɪ'nɑ:ti/, **ostinatos**. A melodic phrase repeated through all or part of a piece.

B 1996 *Country Life* Matthew Richardson's short film, which told of the beginning of Lulu's downfall, was perfectly tailored to the catastrophic progress of the central orchestral *ostinato*.

Ostpolitik /'ɒstpɒlɪˌti:k/ *noun* M20 **German** (from *Ost* east + *Politik* policy). *History* The foreign policy of a western country (*specifically* of the Federal Republic of Germany) with reference to the Communist States. Cf. WESTPOLITIK.

ostracon /'ɒstrəkɒn/ *noun* plural **ostraca** /'ɒstrəkə/ (also **ostrakon**, plural **ostraka**) L19 **Greek** (*ostrakon* hard shell, potsherd). *Archaeology* A potsherd used as a writing surface. Usually in *plural*.

o tempora, o mores! /əʊ 'tɛmpərə əʊ ˌmɔ:reɪz/ *interjection* M16 **Latin** (= o times, o manners!). What times, what ways!

■ Originally quoted from the Roman orator Cicero's impeachment of the conspirator Catiline (*In Catilinam* I.1) in 63 BC; now a general expression of alarm, contempt, amusement, etc., about behaviour in contemporary society.

1996 *Times* 'Even in the age of Aids, . . . self-styled vampires drink blood—but from monogamous donors.' Sexually responsible vampires? *O tempora! O mores!*

otium /'əʊʃɪəm/ *noun* E18 **Latin**. Leisure, ease, idleness.

■ Chiefly in *otium cum dignitate* or *cum dignitate otium* 'dignified leisure', quoting from one of Cicero's letters *Ad Familiares* (I.ix.21).

ottava rima /otˌta:va 'ri:ma/, /ɒˌtɑ:və 'ri:mə/ *noun* L18 **Italian** (= eighth rhyme). A stanza of eight lines, 11-syllabled in Italian, 10-syllabled in English, rhyming as *abababcc*.

ottocento /ɒtəʊ'ʧɛntəʊ/ *noun* (also **Ottocento**) E20 **Italian** (= eight hundred). The nineteenth century in Italy; the style of Italian art, architecture, music, etc., of this period.

ou /əʊ/ *adjective & noun* M19 **Afrikaans** (from Dutch *oud* old). **A** *adjective* M19 Old, elder. **B** *noun* plural **ouens** /'əʊənz/, **ous** M20 A man, a fellow. Cf. OUTJIE.

■ In South African colloquial speech, frequently used in terms of affection or casual reference.

oubaas /'əʊbɑ:s/ *noun* M19 **Afrikaans** (from OU + BAAS). A head of a family; an elderly man.

■ In South Africa, a colloquial form of address to an older man.

oubliette /u:blɪ'ɛt/ *noun* L18 **French** (from *oublier* to forget). A secret dungeon accessible only through a trapdoor.

oudstryder /'əʊtstreɪdə/ *noun* M20 **Afrikaans** (= ex-soldier). In South Africa: a veteran of the South African War (1899–1902) who fought on the side of the Boer republics; *generally* any war veteran.

oued see under WADI.

ouens plural of OU.

oukha variant of UKHA.

ouma /'əʊmə/ *noun* E20 **Afrikaans** (= grandmother, from OU old + *ma* mother). A grandmother; an elderly woman.

■ In South Africa, chiefly as a respectful or affectionate form of address or reference.

oupa /'əʊpə/ *noun* E20 **Afrikaans** (= grandfather, from OU old + *pa* father). A grandfather; an elderly man.

■ In South Africa, chiefly as a respectful or affectionate form of address or reference.

oursin /'ɔ:san/, *foreign* /ursɛ̃/ *noun* E20 **French**. A sea urchin, *especially* an edible one.

outjie /'əʊki/, /'əʊtʃi/ *noun* M20 **Afrikaans** (from as OU + diminutive suffix *-tjie*). A child, a little fellow.

■ In South African colloquial speech can also be used jocularly or derogatively of an adult.

outré /utre/, /'u:treɪ/ *adjective* E18 **French** (past participle of *outrer* to exaggerate). Beyond the bounds of what is usual or proper; eccentric, unusual, out-of-the-way.

1996 *Country Life* Peter York celebrates some of the artefacts which still shine forth as emblems of the British soul, be they as conservative as the Bath Oliver biscuit or as outré as a Vivienne Westwood frock.

ouvert /uvɛr/ *noun* plural pronounced same E20 **French** (= open). *Ballet* An open position of the feet.

ouvrier /uvrije/ *noun* (feminine **ouvrière** /uvrijɛr/) plural pronounced same M19 **French**. In France: a manual or industrial worker; a labourer.

1996 *Times Magazine* Most of this non-village comprises formerly humble *ouvrier* dwellings of two storeys plus semi-basement for burglar access.

ouzo /'u:zəʊ/ *noun* plural **ouzos** L19 **Modern Greek**. (A glass of) an aniseed-flavoured spirit from Greece.

ova plural of OVUM.

ovolo /'əʊvələʊ/ *noun* plural **ovoli** /'əʊvəli/ M17 **Italian** (diminutive of *uovo*, *ovo* from Latin *ovum* egg). *Architecture* A rounded convex moulding.

ovum /'əʊvəm/ *noun* plural **ova** /'əʊvə/ E17 **Latin** (= egg). **1** E17 *Roman History* Any of a number of egg-shaped objects used in the circus to indicate the number of laps in a race. Usually in *plural*. **2** E18 *Biology* The female gamete or reproductive cell in animals; an egg, an egg cell. **b** M18 *Botany* Originally (*rare*), the ovule or seed of a plant. Now, the egg cell in the nucellus of an ovule. **3** E18 *Architecture* An egg-shaped ornament or carving.

oy /ɔɪ/ *interjection* (also **oi**) L19 **Yiddish**. Used by Yiddish-speakers as an exclamation of dismay, grief, etc.

■ Also in *oy vay, oy vey* /ɔɪ veɪ/ (Yiddish *vey* = woe).

oyama /əʊ'jɑ:mə/ *noun* plural same M20 **Japanese**. An ONNAGATA.

oyer /'ɔɪə/ *noun* LME **Anglo-Norman** (= Old French *oïr*: see next). *Law* **1** LME The hearing of a case. **2** LME A criminal trial held under the commission of oyer and terminer. **3** E17 *History* The hearing of a document read in court, especially an instrument in writing pleaded by one party in a suit.

■ Sense 1 exists only in the phrase *oyer and terminer* (formerly also *oyer (and) determiner*) 'a commission authorizing a judge on circuit to hold courts'.

oyez /əʊ'jɛs/, /əʊ'jɛz/, /əʊ'jeɪ/ *verb* & *noun* (also **oyes** /əʊ'jɛs/) LME **Anglo-Norman** (Old French (also *oiez*) imperative plural of *oïr* (modern *ouïr*) from Latin *audire* to hear). **A** *intransitive verb* LME (*imperative*) Listen! **B** *noun* LME plural same **oyesses**. A call or cry of 'oyez!'.

■ Uttered (usually three times) by a public crier or a court officer to command silence and attention.

p.a. abbreviation of PER ANNUM.

pabulum /'pabjələm/ *noun* M17 **Latin** (from stem of *pascere* to feed). **1** M17 Food, nutriment, especially for plants or animals or their tissues. **2** L17 That which feeds a fire. **3** M18 That which nourishes and sustains the mind or soul. **4** L20 Bland intellectual fare; an insipid or undemanding diet of words, entertainment, etc.

> **4 1996** *Spectator* The dons who supply these masses with pabulum are not allowed to feel job-secure unless they are also engaged upon their own 'work'.

pace /'pɑːtʃeɪ/, /'peɪsi/ *preposition* L18 **Latin** (ablative singular of *pax* peace, as in *pace tua* by your leave). With due deference to (a person named).

■ Used especially as a courteous or ironical apology for a contradiction or difference of opinion (see quotation). Normally italicized to distinguish it from the English verb or noun 'pace'.

> **1996** *Spectator* Had he read the magnificent Turing biography by Andrew Hodges, which remains the best work on Bletchley Park to date (*pace* Robert Harris and his marvellous book), the hapless Volkman could have provided us with the theologically resonant denouement.

pacha variant of PASHA.

pachalic variant of PASHALIC.

pachinko /pə'tʃɪŋkəʊ/ *noun* M20 **Japanese.** A variety of pinball popular in Japan.

pachisi /pə'tʃiːzi/ *noun* (also **parcheesi** /pɑː'tʃiːzi/, **Pachisi**) E19 **Hindustani** (*pac(c.)īsī* (throw of) twenty-five (the highest in the game), ultimately from Sanskrit *pañcaviṃśati* twenty-five). A four-handed Indian board game with six cowries for dice.

pachuco /pə'tʃʊkəʊ/, *foreign* /pa'tʃuko/ *noun* plural **pachucos** /pə'tʃʊkəʊz/, *foreign* /pa'tʃukos/ M20 **Mexican Spanish** (literally, 'flashily dressed'). A juvenile delinquent of Mexican-American descent, especially in the Los Angeles area; *derogatory* any Mexican-American. Also the argot spoken by pachucos.

> **1972** J. Wambaugh *Blue Knight* '*Órale, panzón*,' he said, like a pachuco, which he put on for me. He spoke beautiful Spanish . . . but the barrios of El Paso Texas died hard.

pacifico /pə'sɪfɪkəʊ/ *noun* plural **pacificos** L19 **Spanish.** A person of peaceful character; *specifically* (*historical*) a native or inhabitant of Cuba or the Philippines who submitted without active opposition to Spanish occupation.

paco /'pɑːkəʊ/, *foreign* /'pako/ *noun* plural **pacos** /'pɑːkəʊz/, *foreign* /'pakos/ E17 **Spanish** ((in sense 2 with reference to the brown and white colour) from Quechua *pako* red, reddish yellow). **1** E17 An alpaca. **2** M19 *Mineralogy* An earthy brown oxide of iron, containing particles of silver.

padma /'pʌdmə/ *noun* M19 **Sanskrit** (= lotus). (The flower of) the lotus-plant; an emblematic representation of this.

padmasana /pʌd'mɑːsənə/ *noun* L19 **Sanskrit** (*padmāsana*, from *padma* lotus + *āsana* seat, posture). *Yoga* A bodily position with legs crossed and feet resting on the opposite thighs, said to resemble the flower of a lotus.

padre /'pɑːdri/, /'pɑːdreɪ/ *noun* L16 **Italian** ((also Spanish, Portuguese) from Latin *pater, patr-* father). In Italy, Spain, Portugal, Latin America, and other areas of Spanish influence: (a title of) a Christian clergyman, especially a Roman Catholic priest. Now chiefly (*colloquial*), a chaplain in the armed services.

padrone /pa'drəʊni/, *foreign* /pa'drone/ *noun* plural **padrones** /pa'drəʊnɪz/, **padroni** /pa'droni/ (feminine (especially in sense (b)) **padrona** /pa'drəʊnə/, *foreign* /pa 'drona/, plural **padronas** /pa'drəʊnəz/, **padrone** /pa'drone/) L17 **Italian.** A patron, a master; *specifically* (*a*) (now chiefly *United States colloquial*) an employer, a manager; *especially* an exploitative employer of unskilled immigrant workers; (*b*) the proprietor of an inn or hotel in Italy.

paedeia variant of PAIDEIA.

paella /pʌɪ'ɛlə/, /pa'e(l)ja/ *noun* L19 **Catalan** (from Old French *paele* (modern *paêle*), from Latin *patella* pan, dish). A Spanish dish of rice, saffron, chicken, seafood, vegetables, etc., cooked and served in a large shallow pan.

> *figurative* **1996** *Times* He is a full 20 seats short [of a parliamentary majority], compelling

him to rely for survival . . . on a *paella* of regional parties.

pagoda /pə'gəʊdə/ *noun* L16 **Portuguese** (*pagode*, probably ultimately from Persian *butkada* idol temple, from *but* idol + *kada* habitation, alteration by association with Prakrit *bhagodī* divine, holy). **1** A Hindu or Buddhist temple or sacred building, usually in the form of a many-tiered tower with storeys of diminishing size, each with an ornamented projecting roof, in China, India, Japan, and elsewhere in the Far East. **2** L18 An ornamental structure built in imitation of such a temple.

pagri variant of PUGGAREE.

pahit /'pɑːhɪt/ *noun* E20 **Malay** (= bitter). In South East Asia: gin and bitters. More fully *gin pahit*.

pahoehoe /pə'həʊɪhəʊi/ *noun* M19 **Hawaiian.** *Geology* Smooth, undulating or corded lava. Cf. AA.

paideia /pʌɪ'dʌɪə/ *noun* (also **paedeia**) M20 **Greek.** *Greek History* Education, upbringing; the ideal result of this; a society's culture.

pai-hua /'pʌɪhwɑː/ *noun* E20 **Chinese** (*báihuà* (Wade–Giles *pai-hua*), from *bái* white, clear, plain + *huà* language, speech). The standard written form of modern Chinese, based on the northern dialects, especially that of Peking (Beijing). Cf. PUTONGHUA.

paillette /pal'jɛt/, /pʌɪ'jɛt/ *noun* M19 **French** (diminutive of *paille* straw, chaff). **1** M19 A small piece of glittering foil, shell, etc., used to decorate a garment; a spangle. **2** L19 A decorative piece of coloured foil or bright metal used in enamel painting.

pain /pɛ̃/ *noun* LME **Old and Modern French** (from Latin *panis*, *pan-*). Bread, *specifically* in French bakery.

■ Formerly naturalized, it now occurs only in *pain perdu* (toasted stale bread, usually sweetened and flavoured with cinnamon) and in names of specialty breads.

pair /pɛr/ *noun & adjective* plural of noun same M19 **French** (= equal). *Roulette* (Of) an even number; (of) the even numbers collectively.

paisano /pʌɪ'sɑːnəʊ/, *foreign* /pai'sano/ *noun* plural **paisanos** /pʌɪ'sɑːnəʊz/, *foreign* /pai'sanos/ M19 **Spanish** (= peasant, rustic). **1** M19 In Spain and Spanish-speaking areas, especially in the south-western United States: a fellow-countryman; a peasant. **2** L19 In Mexico and the south-western United States: a road-runner.

pakapoo /'pakəpuː/, /pakə'puː/ *noun* (also **pakapu** and other variants) E20 **Chinese** (*bái gē piào* (Wade–Giles *pai ko p'iao*) literally, 'white pigeon ticket', perhaps referring to a Cantonese competition which involved releasing pigeons and predicting the distance they would fly and the numbers expected to return). A Chinese form of lottery played with slips of paper marked with columns of characters.

■ Chiefly Australian, and in the phrase *like a pakapoo ticket*, meaning 'disordered, unintelligible'.

pak-choi /pak'tʃɔɪ/ *noun* M19 **Chinese** ((Cantonese) *paâk ts' oì* white vegetable: cf. PE-TSAI). Chinese cabbage.

pakeha /'pɑːkɪhɑː/ *noun & adjective* E19 **Maori. A** *noun* E19 A White person (as opposed to a Maori). **B** *adjective* M19 Of, pertaining to, or designating a pakeha. *New Zealand.*

pakora /pə'kɔːrə/ *noun* M20 **Hindustani** (*pakoṛā* a dish of vegetables in gram-flour). A savoury Indian dish consisting of diced or chopped vegetables coated in batter and deep fried.

pa-kua /pɑː'kwɑː/ *noun* L19 **Chinese** (*bāguà* (Wade–Giles *pà-kua*), from *bā* eight + *guà* divinatory symbols). **1** L19 *Art* Any of various decorative and religious motifs incorporating the eight trigrams of *I Ching*; *specifically* an arrangement of these trigrams in a circle round the yin-yang symbol. **2** M20 A Chinese martial art in which fighters are arranged around a circle according to the trigram sequence in positions which they must defend.

palacio /pa'laθjo/, /pa'lasjo/, /pə'lasɪəʊ/ *noun* plural **palacios** /pa'laθjos/, /pa'lasjos/, /pə'lasɪəʊz/ M19 **Spanish** (from Latin *palatium*). In Spain and Spanish-speaking countries: a palace, a country seat, an imposing official building.

paladin /'palədɪn/ *noun* L16 **French** (from Italian *paladino*, from Latin *palatinus* officer of the palace). Each of the twelve bravest and most famous warriors of Charlemagne's court. Also, a knight errant, a champion.

palaestra /pə'liːstrə/, /pə'lʌɪstrə/ *noun* (also **palestra** /pə'liːstrə/, /pə'lɛstrə/) LME **Latin** (from Greek *palaistra*, from *palaiein* wrestle). *Classical History* **1** LME A place devoted to the public teaching and practice of wrestling and athletics. **2** LME Wrestling, athletics.

palais /ˈpaleɪ/ *noun* plural same /ˈpaleɪz/ E20 **French** (literally, 'palace') Abbreviation of PALAIS DE DANSE.

■ Frequently used attributively, as in *palais glide* a form of ballroom dance.

palais de danse /ˌpaleɪ də ˈdɒ̃s/ *noun phrase* plural same E20 **French**. A public hall for dancing.

Palais Royal /ˌpaleɪ ˈrɔ(ə)l/, *foreign* /palɛ rwajal/ *adjective phrase* L19 **French** Designating a type of indelicate farce said to be typical of the Palais Royal theatre, Paris.

palapa /pəˈlapə/ *noun* L20 **Mexican Spanish** (= (the leaves and branches of) the palm *Orbignya cohune*). A traditional Mexican shelter roofed with palm leaves or branches. Also, any structure imitating this, especially on a beach. *United States*.

palatschinken /ˌpalatˈʃɪŋkən/ *noun plural* E20 **Austrian German** (from Hungarian *palacsinta* from Proto-Romance *placinta* from Latin *placenta* cake). Austrian (stuffed) pancakes.

palazzo /pəˈlatsəʊ/ *noun & adjective* M17 **Italian** (from Latin *palatium* palace). **A** *noun* plural **palazzos**, (in sense 1) **palazzi** /pəˈlatsi/. **1** M17 A palatial mansion; a large imposing building. **2** L20 *singular* and (usually) in *plural* Loose wide-legged trousers worn by women. **B** *attributive* or as *adjective* M20 Designating a loose wide-legged garment, outfit, etc.

1 1996 *Spectator* Of course, not everyone could afford imitation *palazzi* of their own.

palestra variant of PALAESTRA.

paletot /ˈpalətəʊ/ *noun* M19 **French** (of unknown origin). A short loose outer garment, coat, or cloak. Also, a fitted jacket worn by women in the nineteenth century.

palette /ˈpalɪt/ *noun* L18 **French**. **1** L18 A thin (oval) board or slab, usually with a hole for the thumb, on which an artist lays and mixes colours. **b** L19 *transferred* The range of colours used by a particular artist or in a particular picture. **c** M20 The range or variety of tonal or instrumental colour in a musical piece, composer's work, etc.; the verbal range of a writer etc. **d** L20 *Computing* In computer graphics, the range of colours or shapes available to the user. **2** M19 *Zoology* A disc-like structure. **3** M20 A device used by the banker in certain card-games to move cards and money.

pali /ˈpɑːli/ *noun* E19 **Hawaiian**. In Hawaii: a steep cliff.

■ *The Pali* is a precipice on the island of Oahu.

palio /ˈpɑːlio/, /ˈpalɪəʊ/ *noun* L17 **Italian** (from Latin *pallium* covering, cover). A traditional horse-race held in Italy, especially in Siena, every July and August. Also, the cloth or banner of velvet, silk, etc., given as the prize for winning this race.

paliotto /paliˈɔtto/, /palɪˈɒtəʊ/ *noun* plural **paliotti** /paliˈɔt(t)i/, **paliottos** /palɪˈɒtəʊz/ M20 **Italian**. The frontal painting on an altarpiece.

palladium /pəˈleɪdɪəm/ *noun* plural **palladia** /pəˈleɪdɪə/ LME **Latin** (from Greek *palladion*, from *Pallas*, *Pallad-* epithet of the goddess Athene). **1** LME *Classical Mythology* An image of the goddess Pallas (Athene), in the citadel of Troy, on which the safety of the city was supposed to depend, later reputed to have been taken to Rome. **2** E17 *transferred* and *figurative* A thing on which the safety of a nation, institution, etc., is believed to depend; a safeguard.

2 1989 R. Milner-Gulland *Cultural Atlas of Russia* The icon of the 'Virgin of Vladimir,' the palladium of Vladimir and Moscow Grand Principalities, is of the iconographic type known as 'Tenderness' . . .

pallium /ˈpalɪəm/ *noun* plural **pallia** /ˈpalɪə/, **palliums** ME **Latin** (= covering, mantle). **1** ME *Ecclesiastical* A woollen vestment conferred by the Pope on an archbishop in the Latin Church, consisting of a narrow circular band placed round the shoulders with a short lappet hanging from front and back. Also (*transferred*), the office or dignity of an archbishop. **2** M16 *Antiquities* A man's large rectangular cloak, worn especially by Greek philosophical and religious teachers. **3a** L19 *Zoology* The mantle of a mollusc or brachiopod. **b** L19 *Anatomy* and *Zoology* The outer wall of the cerebrum.

pallone /palˈlone/ *noun* L19 **Italian** (augmentative of *palla* ball). An Italian game, partially resembling tennis, in which a large ball is struck with a cylindrical wooden guard, worn over the hand and wrist.

palmette /palˈmɛt/ *noun* M19 **French** (diminutive of *palme* palm leaf). *Archaeology*

An ornament (in sculpture or painting) with radiating petals like a palm leaf.

palmier /palmje/ *noun* plural pronounced same. E20 **French** (literally, 'palm tree'). A small crisp cake shaped like a palm leaf, made from puff pastry and sugar.

palomino /palə'mi:nəʊ/ *noun* plural **palominos** E20 **American Spanish** (from Spanish from Latin *palumbinus* of or resembling a dove). **1** E20 A horse with light golden-brown coat and white or pale mane and tail. Also *palomino horse*. **2** M20 A pale golden-brown colour.

■ Originally United States.

palsa /'palsə/ *noun* M20 **Swedish** (*palse*, *pals* (plural *palsar*) from Finnish and Lappish *palsa*). A landform of subarctic regions, consisting of a mound or ridge of peat covered with vegetation and containing a core of frozen peat or mineral soil in which are numerous ice lenses.

pampas /'pampəs/, /'pampəz/ *noun plural*, also used as *singular* (also in singular form **pampa**) E18 **Spanish** (plural of *pampa* from Quechua = a plain). **1** E18 *plural* (treated as *singular* or *plural*). The extensive treeless plains of South America south of the Amazon. Also in *singular*, these plains considered collectively; any one of these plains. **2** L20 *plural* (treated as *singular*). A yellowy-green colour. Usually *attributive*.

pan /pɑ:n/ *noun* E17 **Hindustani** (*pān* betel leaf, from Sanskrit *parṇa* feather, leaf). In the Indian subcontinent: the leaf of the betel, especially as used to enclose slices of areca nut mixed with lime for chewing; the mixture for chewing so formed.

p'an /pan/ *noun* M20 **Chinese** (*pán*). *Chinese Antiquities* A kind of shallow dish-shaped ritual vessel.

panacea /panə'si:ə/ *noun* M16 **Latin** (from Greek *panakeia*, from *panakēs* all-healing, from *pan-* all + base of *akos* remedy). A remedy for all diseases; a thing for solving all difficulties or adopted in every case of difficulty.

panache /pə'naʃ/ *noun* M16 **French** (from Italian *pennacchio* from late Latin *pinnaculum* diminutive of *pinna* feather). **1** M16 A tuft or plume of feathers, especially as a head-dress or a decoration for a helmet. Formerly also, a decoration like a plume of feathers, e.g. a tassel. **2** L19 Flamboyantly or stylishly confident behaviour; a manner marked by this.

2 1996 *Country Life* Lord Petersham drove his Cumberland cobs with considerable panache through the marathon obstacles in the horse pairs class . . .

panada /pə'nɑ:də/ *noun* (also **panade** /pə'neɪd/) L16 **Spanish** ((also Portuguese) = Italian *panata*, represented a Proto-Romance derivation of Latin *panis* bread). Bread boiled in water to a pulp and flavoured. Also, a paste of flour, water, etc., used for thickening.

panatela /panə'tɛlə/ *noun* M19 **American Spanish** (= long thin biscuit, sponge cake from Spanish from Italian *panatello* small loaf, diminutive of *panata* (as PANADA)). **1** M19 A long slender cigar, *especially* one tapering at the sealed end. Also more fully *panatela cigar*. **2** M20 *transferred* A cigarette made of Central or South American marijuana. *slang*.

pancetta /pan'(t)ʃɛtə/, *foreign* /pan'tʃetta/ *noun* M20 **Italian** (diminutive of *pancio* belly from Proto-Romance word (whence also 'paunch'). Italian cured belly of pork.

panchshila /pɑ:n'ʃi:lə/, /pan'ʃi:lə/ *noun* M20 **Sanskrit** (*pañcaśīla*, from *pañca* five + *śīla* moral principle). The five principles of peaceful relations formulated between India and China (and, by extension, other Communist countries) and set out in the preamble of a treaty signed in April 1954.

pancratium /pan'kreɪʃɪəm/ *noun* (also in Greek form **pancration** /pan'kreɪʃɪən/, /pan'kreɪtɪən/) E17 **Latin** (from Greek *pagkration*, from *pan-* all + *kratos* strength). **1** E17 *Greek History* An athletic contest combining both wrestling and boxing. **2** M17 *Botany* Any of various bulbous African and Mediterranean plants; *especially* the sea daffodil, *P. maritimum*.

panem et circenses /ˌpanɛm ɛt sə:'kɛnzi:z/, /kə:'kɛnseɪz/ *noun phrase* L18 **Latin** (= bread and circuses). State provision of popular entertainment and distribution of food to win popularity with the people.

■ Originally, the hand-outs and gladiatorial games provided by Roman statesmen and emperors in the Circus of ancient Rome to assuage the city's notoriously volatile populace.

1961 D. L. Munby *God and Rich Society* Leaders . . . win votes by offering *panem et circenses* to those they despise.

panettone /panɪ'təʊni/, *foreign* /panet'toni/ *noun* (also **panetone** /panɪ'təʊni/, *foreign* /pane'tone/) plural **panettoni** /panet'toni/ E20 **Italian** (from *panetto* cake, bar, diminutive of *pane* bread, from Latin *panis*). A rich Italian bread made with eggs, fruit, and butter.

panforte /pan'fɔ:ti/, *foreign* /pan'forte/ *noun* L19 **Italian** (from *pane* bread + *forte* strong). A hard spicy Sienese cake containing nuts, candied peel, and honey.

panga /'pɑ:ŋgə/ *noun 1* (also **ponga**) E20 **American Spanish**. A flat-bottomed boat with rising stem and stern used especially in Latin America.

panga /'paŋgə/ *noun 2* M20 **Kiswahili**. In East Africa: a large knife used either as a tool or a weapon.

panier de crabes /panje də krab/ *noun phrase* plural **paniers de crabes** (pronounced same) M20 **French** (literally, 'basket of crabs'). A competitive struggle.

1963 *Economist* The visitor is . . . not able to move around in this communist *panier de crabes*.

panino /pa'ni:no/ *noun* plural **panini** /pa 'ni:ni/ M20 **Italian**. An Italian bread roll or sandwich.

panne /pan/ *noun* L18 **French** (of unknown origin). A soft silk or rayon fabric with a flattened pile, resembling velvet. Also *panne velvet*.

panocha, **panoche** variants of PENUCHE.

pansala /'pʌnsələ/ *noun* M19 **Sinhalese** (from *pan* leaf + *sala* dwelling) from Sanskrit *parṇaśālā*, Pali *pannasālā*). A Buddhist temple or monastery; the home of a Buddhist religious teacher.

panthea see SIGNUM PANTHEUM.

panzanella /ˌpantsə'nɛlə/ *noun* L20 **Italian**. Bread salad made with olive oil and chopped vegetables.

panzer /'panzə/, *foreign* /'pantsər/ *noun & adjective* (also **Panzer**) M20 **German** (= mail, coat of mail). **A** *noun* M20 (A member of) a German armoured unit. Also, a German tank. **B** *attributive* or as *adjective* M20 Of, pertaining to, or designating a panzer; *transferred* heavily armoured.

A *figurative* **1996** *Times Magazine* . . . the story was also swiftly turned into a television comedy, . . . the starring role being given to 'Wanda', a panzer among other cheerleader moms.
B 1995 *Spectator* [The opposition's informants] were subsequently invited to leave instantly, unless they wanted their departures assisted by the steel-capped boot of a management which has proved over the past three years that it can make a panzer division look positively benign.

papabile /papa'bi:le/, /pə'pɑ:bɪli/ *adjective & noun* (also (as adjective) **papabili** /papa 'bi:li/) M20 **Italian** (from *papa* Pope). **A** *adjective* M20 (Of a prelate) worthy of or eligible to be elected Pope; *generally* suitable for high office. **B** M20 *absolutely* as *noun* plural **papabili** /papa'bi:li/. A prelate regarded as eligible to be elected Pope; *generally* one regarded as suitable for high office. Usually in *plural*.

A 1964 *Spectator* He [sc. Harold Macmillan] thought that three of the members of his Cabinet who were in the House of Commons, apart from Butler, were *papabile* and of sufficient seniority to be considered: Maudling, Heath and myself [sc. Iain Macleod].

papaloi /'pap(ə)lwɑ:/ *noun* plural **papalois**, same L19 **Haitian** (creole *papalwa*, from *papa* father + *lwa* LOA). A voodoo priest. Cf. MAMALOI.

paparazzo /papə'ratsəʊ/ *noun* plural **paparazzi** /papə'ratsi/ M20 **Italian**. A (freelance) photographer who pursues celebrities in order to take their pictures.

1995 *Times* Video paparazzi, who sell their film to downmarket television shows, are viewed as the vultures of the celebrity market, sometimes seeking to pick fights with the famous to secure pictures.

paperasserie /paprasri/ *noun* E20 **French**. Excessive official paperwork or routine; bureaucracy.

papeterie /pap(ə)tri/ (*plural same*), /'papətri/ *noun* M19 **French** (= paper manufacture, stationer's shop, writing-case, from *papetier* paper-maker). A (usually ornamental) case or box for paper and other writing materials.

papier collé /papje kɔle/ *noun phrase* plural **papiers collés** (*pronounced same*) M20 **French** (= glued paper). A collage made from paper; the use of paper for collage.

papier déchiré /papje deʃire/ *noun phrase* plural **papiers déchirés** (*pronounced same*) M20 **French** (= torn paper). Paper torn haphazardly for use in collage; a collage made of such paper.

papier mâché /ˌpapɪeɪ 'maʃeɪ/, *foreign* /papje mɑʃe/ *noun & adjective phrase* M18 **French** (*papier* paper + *mâché* past participle of *mâcher* to chew, from Latin *masticare*). **A** *noun* M18 Material made from pulped paper; paper reduced to a pulp mixed with glue etc. or (for fine work) sheets of paper pasted together, used for making moulded boxes, jars, trays, etc. **B** *adjective* M18 Made of papier mâché.

B 1996 *Times Magazine* A visit to the set of *Dr Who* conjures up images of papier-mâché monstrosities, nightmares in latex.

papier poudré /papje pudre/ *noun phrase* plural **papiers poudrés** (*pronounced same*) E20 **French** (= powdered paper). A paper impregnated with face-powder.

papillote /ˈpapɪləʊt/, /ˈpapɪlɒt/, *in sense 2 usually* /ˈpapɪjɒt/ *noun* M18 **French**. **1** M18 A curl-paper. *obsolete* except *historical*. **2** E19 A usually greased paper wrapper in which a fillet etc. of meat or fish is cooked.

■ Frequently in *en papillote* /ɒ̃/, in a paper wrapper.

1996 *Times* Usually it comes between the aubergine caviar and the salmon *en papillote*, though sometimes it can be staved off until the moment of decision between coffee and camomile tea.

pappardelle /papɑːˈdɛli/ *noun plural* L20 **Italian**. Pasta made in wider strips than TAGLIATELLE and served especially with meat sauces.

1996 *Spectator* Pappardelle with tender little broad beans and dark shards of rocket were good as well . . .

paprika /ˈraprɪkə/, /pəˈpriːkə/ *noun & adjective* L19 **Hungarian**. **A** *noun* **1** L19 A condiment made from the dried ground fruits of certain (especially red) varieties of the sweet pepper, *Capsicum annuum*. **b** M20 The bright orange-red colour of this. **2** E20 Any of several European varieties of the sweet pepper bearing mildly flavoured fruits. **B** *adjective* **1** M20 Of a dish: flavoured with (especially the condiment) paprika. Often *postpositive*. **2** M20 Of the colour of paprika.

papyrus /pəˈpʌɪrəs/ *noun* plural **papyri** /pəˈpʌɪrʌɪ/, /pəˈpʌɪriː/ LME **Latin** (from Greek *papuros* paper reed, of unknown origin). **1** LME An aquatic plant of the sedge family, formerly abundant in Egypt and the source of the writing material papyrus. **2** E18 Material in the forms of fine strips of the stem of the papyrus plant, soaked in water, pressed together, and dried, to form a writing surface, used by the ancient Egyptians, Romans, etc. **3** E19 A manuscript or document written on this.

par /par/, /pɑː/ *preposition* ME **Old and Modern French** (from Proto-Romance combination of Latin *per* through + *ad* to). Through, by.

■ Occurring in various phrases used in English: see PAR ÉMINENCE, PAR EXCELLENCE, PAR EXEMPLE.

parador /ˈparədɔː/ *noun* plural **paradores** /ˈparədɔːrɛz/, **paradors** M19 **Spanish**. In Spain: a hotel owned and administered by the government. Formerly, any Spanish hotel or inn.

1995 D. Lodge *Therapy* It's now a five-star *parador*, one of the grandest hotels in Spain.

parados /ˈparədɒs/, *foreign* /parado/ *noun* plural **paradoses** /ˈparədɒsɪz/, same M19 **French** (from *para-* protector of + *dos* back). An elevation of earth behind a defended place as a protection against attack from the rear; the mound along the back of a trench.

paramo /ˈparəməʊ/ *noun* plural **paramos** M18 **Spanish** ((also Portuguese) *páramo* from Spanish Latin *paramus* bare plain). A high plateau in the tropical parts of South America, bare of trees and exposed to wind and thick cold fogs.

parang /ˈpɑːraŋ/ *noun* M19 **Malay**. A large heavy knife used in Malaysia for clearing vegetation etc.

paraphernalia /ˌparəfəˈneɪlɪə/ *noun plural* M17 **Medieval Latin** (use as noun of neuter plural of *paraphernalis*, from Latin *parapherna* from Greek, from *para-* beside, beyond + *phernē* dowry). **1** M17 *History* Those articles of personal property which the law allowed a married woman to keep and deal with as her own, when most of her personal or movable property vested in her husband. **2** M18 Personal belongings, especially of dress or adornment; the miscellaneous objects that go to make up a thing or are associated with it; trappings, bits and pieces. Also treated as *singular*.

paratha /pəˈrɑːtə/ *noun* M20 **Hindustani** (*parāṭhā*). In Indian cookery, a flat piece of unleavened bread fried in butter, ghee, etc., on a griddle.

paratonnerre /paratɔnɛr/ *noun* plural pronounced same E19 **French** (from *para-* protection against + *tonnerre* thunder). A lightning-conductor.

parc fermé /ˌpɑːk ˈfɛːmeɪ/ *noun phrase* (also **parc ferme**) M20 **French** (literally, 'enclosed area'). In motor sports, an enclosure or paddock used by vehicles before or after a race.

parcheesi variant of PACHISI.

par éminence /par eminɑ̃s/, /pɑː(r) 'ɛmɪnəns/ *adverb phrase* L19 **French**. Pre-eminently.

parens patriae /ˌparɛnz 'patriiː/ *noun phrase* M18 **Modern Latin** (literally, 'parent of the country'). *Law* The monarch, or any other authority, regarded as the legal protector of citizens unable to protect themselves.

parergon /pə'rəːgɒn/ *noun* plural **parerga** /pə'rəːgə/ E17 **Latin** (from Greek, from *para-* beyond, beside + *ergon* work). **1** E17–E18 An ornamental accessory or addition, especially in a painting; an embellishment. **2** E17 Subsidiary work or business, apart from one's ordinary employment. Also, a work, composition, etc., that is supplementary to or a by-product of a larger work.

par excellence /par ɛkslɑ̃s/, /pɑː(r) 'ɛks(ə)ləns/ *adverb phrase* L17 **French** (from Latin *per excellentiam* by virtue of excellence). Pre-eminently; supremely, above all.

1996 *Country Life* Miss Guest is an Edwards pasticheur *par excellence* . . .

par exemple /par əgzɑ̃pl/, /pɑːr əg 'zɒmp(ə)l/ *adverb phrase* M19 **French**. For example.

parfait /'pɑːfeɪ/ *noun* L19 **French** (literally, 'perfect'). A rich iced pudding of whipped cream, eggs, etc. Also, a sweet consisting of layers of ice-cream, fruit, syrup, whipped cream, etc., served in a tall glass.

parfleche /'pɑːflɛʃ/ *noun & adjective* E19 **Canadian French** (*parflèche*, from French *parer* + *flèche* arrow). **A** *noun* E19 (A) depilated (especially buffalo's) hide dried by stretching on a frame; an article made from this. **B** *attributive* or as *adjective* M19 Made of parfleche.

parfumerie /parfymri/ *noun* plural pronounced same M19 **French**. A shop or department which sells perfume. Also, a perfume factory.

pariah /pə'rʌɪə/ *noun* E17 **Tamil** (*paṛaiyar* plural of *paṛaiyan*, literally, 'hereditary drummer', from *paṛai* drum). **1** E17 Originally, a member of a very extensive low caste in southern India. Later, a member of a low caste or of no Hindu caste. *obsolete* except *historical*. **2** E19 *transferred* A member of a despised social class; an outcast. **3** E19 A half-wild stray dog. Also *pariah-dog* or *pye-dog*.

2 1996 *Times* Nothing seems to boost a dictator so much as to be . . . ostracised. The world's longest established rulers—Castro, Gaddafi, Assad, Saddam Hussein, the Ayatollahs—have all benefited from such pariah status.

pari-mutuel /parimytɥɛl/ (*plural same*); /ˌpɑːrɪ'mjuːtʃʊəl/ *noun* L19 **French** (= mutual stake or wager). **1** L19 A form of betting in which those backing the first three places divide the losers' stakes. **2** E20 A booth for placing bets under this system; a totalizator.

■ Often abbreviated to MUTUEL.

pari passu /ˌpɑːriː 'pasuː/, /'pari/ *adverb phrase* M16 **Latin** (literally, 'with equal step'). With equal speed; side by side; simultaneously and equally. Also, on an equal footing, without preference.

1997 *Spectator* . . . these blunders in public relations moved *pari passu* with the growth of the media . . .

parka /'pɑːkə/ *noun* L18 **Aleut** (from Russian = skin jacket). A long hooded skin jacket worn by Eskimos; a similar garment, usually of windproof fabric, worn especially by mountaineers.

parlando /pɑː'landəʊ/ *adverb, adjective, & noun* L19 **Italian**. *Music* **A** *adverb & adjective* L19 (A direction:) in an expressive or declamatory manner, as if speaking. **B** *noun* M20 plural **parlandos, parlandi** /pɑː'landi/ An expressive or declamatory passage or piece.

parlementaire /ˌpɑːləmɛn'tɛː/ *noun* E20 **French** (from *parlementer* to discuss terms, parley). A person deputed to parley with an enemy.

parloir /parlwar/ *noun* plural pronounced same E18 **French**. A conversation room in a monastery or convent; a parlour. Also, a similar room in a prison.

parmigiana /ˌpɑːmɪ'dʒɑːnə/ *adjective* L19 **Italian** (feminine of *parmigiano* of or pertaining to the city and province of Parma in northern Italy). *Cookery* Made or served with Parmesan cheese.

■ Chiefly used postpositively in names of dishes, as in *veal parmigiana*.

parnas /pɑː'nas/ *noun* (also **parnass**) plural **parnassim** /pɑː'nəsɪm/ M19 **Hebrew** (from Greek *pronous* provident). The lay leader of the congregation of a synagogue.

parochet /pa'roxet/ *noun* (also **parocheth** and other variants) plural **parochot** /pa'roxɒt/ L19 **Hebrew** (*pārōḵeṯ* curtain; cf. Akkadian *parāku* to shut off). A richly decorated curtain which hangs in front of the Ark in a synagogue.

parole /pə'rəʊl/, *in sense 3 usually foreign* /parɔl/ *noun & verb* L15 **Old and Modern French** (from Proto-Romance, from Latin *parabola* parable, from Greek *parabolē* comparison, analogy, proverb, from *paraballein* to put alongside, compare). **A** *noun* **1** L15 A person's word of honour; *specifically* (*a*) a prisoner of war's promise to abide by the specific terms of a conditional release; (*b*) a prisoner's promise of good behaviour in return for release before the expiry of a custodial sentence. Also, the granting to or acceptance by a prisoner of a conditional release on the basis of such a promise; the system or practice of granting or accepting such a conditional release. **2** L18 *Military* The password used by an officer or inspector of the guard. **3** M20 *Linguistics* The actual linguistic behaviour or performance of an individual, in contrast to the linguistic system. Opposed to LANGUE sense 3. **B** *transitive verb* M17 Put on parole; release on parole.

paroli /'pɑːrəli/ *noun* E18 **French** (from Italian, from *paro* like, from Latin *par* equality). In a gambling card-game (especially faro), the staking of double the sum previously staked.

paronomasia /ˌparənə'meɪzɪə/ *noun* L16 **Latin** (from Greek, from as *para-* beside, beyond + *onomasia* naming). A play on words, a pun; punning.

parquet /'pɑːki/, /'pɑːkeɪ/, *in sense 3 foreign* /parkɛ/ *noun* E19 **Old and Modern French** (= small marked-off space etc., diminutive of *parc* park). **1** E19 A flooring, *especially* one composed of blocks of various woods arranged in a geometric pattern. Also *parquet floor*. **2** M19 (The front part of) the ground floor of a theatre or auditorium. Chiefly *United States*. **3** L19 In France and French-speaking countries: the branch of the administration of the law that deals with the prosecution of crime.

parroco /'parɒkəʊ/ *noun* plural **parrocos** M19 **Italian** (*parroco*, Spanish *párroco* = parish priest). In Italian- and Spanish-speaking countries: a priest, *especially* a parish priest.

parsemé /parsəme/, /'pɑːsəmeɪ/ *adjective* E19 **French** (past participle of *parsemer* to sprinkle, strew). Especially of a fabric, garment, etc.: decorated with embroidered motifs, beads, etc., sprinkled over a background.

■ Usually postpositive.

pars pro toto /ˌpɑːz prəʊ 'təʊtəʊ/ *noun phrase* E18 **Latin**. A part taken as representative of the whole.

■ Frequently attributive.

parterre /pɑː'tɛː/ *noun* E17 **French** (use as noun of *parterre* on or along the ground). **1** E17 A level space in a garden occupied by an ornamental arrangement of flowerbeds. **2** L17 A level space on which a house or village stands. **3** E18 The part of the ground-floor of the auditorium of a theatre behind the orchestra; *United States* the part beneath the galleries; the occupants of this.

parti /parti/ (*plural same*) *noun* L18 **French** (= choice, from Old French *partie* part, share, side in a contest, from Proto-Romance use as noun of Latin *partita* feminine past participle of *partiri* to part). A person (especially a man) considered in terms of eligibility for marriage on grounds of wealth, social status, etc.

partie /parti/ *noun* plural pronounced same L17 **French** (cf. PARTI). A match in a game; a game.

partie carrée /parti kare/ *noun phrase* plural **parties carrées** (pronounced same) M18 **French** (from as PARTI + *carrée* square). A party of four, especially comprising two men and two women.

partigiano /ˌparti'dʒiano/ *noun* (also **Partigiano**) plural **partigiani** /ˌparti'dʒiani/ M20 **Italian** (Tuscan). *History* A member of the Italian resistance during the war of 1939–45, an Italian partisan.

parti pris /parti pri/, /ˌpɑːtɪ 'priː/ *noun & adjective phrase* M19 **French** (literally, 'side taken', from as PARTI + *pris* past participle of *prendre* to take). **A** *noun phrase* M19 plural **partis pris** (pronounced same). A preconceived view, a prejudice; bias. **B** *adjective phrase* E20 Prejudiced, biased; on the side of a particular party.

B 1995 *Spectator* He doesn't attempt to hide the fact that he is *parti pris*.

partita /pɑː'tiːtə/ *noun* plural **partite** /pɑː'tiːteɪ/, **partitas** L19 **Italian** (feminine past participle of *partire* to divide from Latin *partiri* to part). *Music* A suite, *especially* one for a solo instrument or a chamber ensemble; a variation in early modern music.

partouse /partuz/ *noun* (also **partouze**) plural pronounced same M20 **French** (from as *parti* party + pejorative slang suffix *-ouse*). **1** M20 A party at which there is indiscriminate and collective sexual activity. **2** L20 A nightclub etc. noted for the licentiousness of its entertainment.

parure /pəˈrʊə/ *noun* ME **Old and Modern French** (from *parer* to adorn, arrange, peel (fruit), from Latin *parare* to prepare). **1** ME–E16 An ornament for an alb or amice. **2** LME–L16 A paring, a peeling. **3** E19 A set of jewels or other ornaments intended to be worn together.

parvenu /ˈpɑːvənuː/, /ˈpɑːvənjuː/ *noun & adjective* E19 **French** (use as noun of past participle of *parvenir* to arrive from Latin *pervenire*, from *per-* through + *venire* to come). **A** *noun* E19 (feminine **parvenue**) A person of humble origin who has gained wealth or position and risen in society, *especially* one regarded as unfitted for the position achieved in this way, or as lacking the accomplishments appropriate to it; an upstart. **B** *adjective* E19 That has recently risen to wealth or position; resembling or characteristic of a parvenu.

A 1996 *Spectator* There are also several female whores . . . , a witch, and the famous *parvenu*, Trimalchio, who gives a Lucullan banquet with perverse and ingenious cookery . . .

B 1996 *Spectator* As a rule, though, the [Jockey] club has been happier cracking down on some flat-hatted trainer or parvenu owner who would never be allowed in.

pas /pa/, /pɑː/ *noun* plural same E18 **French**. **1** E18 The right of going first; precedence. **2** L18 A step in dancing; a kind of dance, especially in classical ballet.

■ In sense 2 chiefly with qualifying word or phrase.

pas ciseaux variant of PAS DE CISEAUX.

pas d'action /padaksjɔ̃/ *noun phrase* M20 **French**. *Ballet* A dance expressing a theme or narrative.

pas d'âne /padan/ *noun* L19 **French** (literally, 'donkey's step'). *Fencing* Two rings below the cross-guard of some old swords for protecting the fingers.

pas de basque /pa də bask/ *noun phrase* E19 **French**. A dance step in three beats similar to a waltz step, but with a circular movement of the right leg on the second beat.

pas de bourrée /pa də bure/ *noun phrase* E20 **French**. A BOURRÉE step.

pas de chat /pa də ʃa/ *noun phrase* E20 **French** (literally, 'step of cat'). *Ballet* A springing step in which each foot in turn is raised to the opposite knee.

pas de cheval /pa də ʃəval/ *noun phrase* E20 **French** (literaly, 'step of horse'). *Ballet* A step in which a pawing movement is executed with one foot.

pas de ciseaux /pa də sizo/ *noun phrase* (also **pas ciseaux**) L19 **French** (literally, 'step of scissors'). *Ballet* A jump in which the legs are opened wide apart in the air.

pas de deux /pa də dø/, /ˌpa də ˈdəː/ *noun phrase* M18 **French**. A dance for two people, especially in classical ballet.

1995 *Times* Stuart Cassidy and Muriel Valtat, dressed in vaporous white, . . . swirl and float through their romantic pas de deux.

pas de quatre /pa də katr/ *noun phrase* L19 **French**. A dance for four people, especially in classical ballet.

pas de trois /pa də trwɑ/ *noun phrase* M18 **French**. A dance for three people, especially in classical ballet.

pas devant /pa dəvɑ̃/ *interjection* M20 **French** (= not in front of). Of a statement, action, etc.: not appropriate or proper for the present company.

■ *Pas devant* is an elliptical version of the warning expression *pas devant les enfants* /lɛz ɑ̃fɑ̃/ 'not in front of the children'. The assumption is that the children will not understand a warning given in French. Other nouns are substituted, as appropriate, for *les enfants*.

pas du tout /pa dy tu/ E19 **French**. Not at all.

pasear /paseɪˈɑː/ *intransitive verb & noun* M19 **Spanish** (= to take a walk; cf. PASEO). (Take) a walk. *United States slang* and *dialect*.

paseo /paˈseɪəʊ/, *foreign* /paˈseo/ *noun* plural **paseos** /paˈseɪəʊz/, *foreign* /paˈseos/ M19 **Spanish**. In Spain, Spanish-speaking parts of America, and the south-western United States: a leisurely walk or stroll; a parade or procession, *especially* at a bullfight; also, a road, an avenue.

pasha /ˈpɑːʃə/ *noun* (also **pacha**) M17 **Turkish** (*paşa*, from Persian *pād(i)šāh*, Pahlavi *pati* lord + SHAH). *History* (The title of) a Turkish officer of high rank, as a military commander, provincial governor, etc.

pashalic /ˈpɑːʃəlɪk/, /pəˈʃɑːlɪk/ *noun & adjective* (also **pachalic**) L17 **Turkish** (*paşalık*, from as PASHA + suffix indicating quality or condition *-lık*). *History* **A** *noun* L17 The jurisdiction of a pasha; the district governed by a pasha. **B** *adjective* M19 Of or pertaining to a pasha.

paskha /ˈpasxə/, /ˈpaskə/ *noun* (also **paska**) E20 **Russian** (= Easter). A rich Russian dessert made with curd cheese, dried fruit, nuts, spices, etc., set in a mould and traditionally eaten at Easter.

paso /ˈpaso/, /ˈpasəʊ/ *noun* plural **pasos** /ˈpasos/, /ˈpasəʊz/ E20 **Spanish**. An image or group of images representing Passion scenes, carried in procession as part of Holy Week observances in Spain.

paso doble /ˌpasə(ʊ) ˈdəʊbleɪ/ *noun phrase* plural **paso dobles** E20 **Spanish** (= double step). A quick ballroom dance based on a Latin American style of marching; a piece of music for this dance, usually in 2/4 time.

■ See quotation at CHA-CHA.

pasquinade /ˌpaskwɪˈneɪd/ *noun & verb* (originally **pasquinadata**) L16 **Italian** (*pasquinata*, French *pasquinade*, from *Pasquin* the name of a statue in Rome on which abusive Latin verses were annually posted during the sixteenth century). **A** *noun* L16 A lampoon, a satire, originally one exhibited in a public place. **B** *transitive verb* L18 Satirize or libel in a pasquinade.

passacaglia /pasəˈkɑːlɪə/ *noun* M17 **Italian** (from Spanish *pasacalle*, from *pasar* to pass + *calle* street (originally often played in the streets)). A slow musical composition usually with a ground bass and in triple time; an early kind of dance to this music.

passacaille /pasəˈkʌɪ/ *noun* (also **passecaille**) E18 **French** (from Spanish *pasacalle*). A PASSACAGLIA.

passade /pəˈseɪd/, *in sense 2* /paˈsɑːd/, *foreign* /pasad/ (*plural same*) *noun* M17 **French** (from Italian *passata* or Provençal *passada*, from medieval Latin *passare* to pass). **1** M17 *Horsemanship* A forwards or backwards turn performed on the spot. *rare*. **2** E19 A transitory love affair; a passing romance.

passe /pɑs/ *noun* M19 **French** (from *passer* to pass). In roulette: the section of the cloth covering the numbers 19 to 36; a bet placed on this section.

passé /ˈpaseɪ/, *foreign* /pɑse/ *adjective & noun* (feminine **passée**) L18 **French** (past participial adjective of *passer* to pass). **A** *adjective* **1** L18 Past one's prime. *archaic*. **2** E19 No longer fashionable; out of date, behind the times. **B** *noun* M20 *Ballet* The transitional movement of the leg from one position to the next.

A.2 1996 *Bookseller* European publishers who went to Milia last week to display their latest CD-ROM products with pride must have been more than a little put out to hear American visitors saying that CD-ROMs are passé.

passecaille variant of PASSACAILLE.

passée see PASSÉ.

passeggiata /ˌpassedˈdʒiata/ *noun* plural **passeggiate** /ˌpassedˈdʒiate/ M20 **Italian**. A stroll, a promenade.

■ Usually referring to the evening stroll for relaxation and socializing habitually taken by citizens of many Mediterranean countries (see quotation); the equivalent of the Greek *volta*.

1971 N. Fisher *Rise at Dawn* We drove into Viareggio one evening. It was the hour of the *passeggiata* . . . The pavements thronged with strolling families.

passéisme /pɑseism/ *noun* M20 **French**. Adherence to and regard for the traditions and values of the past, especially in the arts.

passementerie /ˈpasm(ə)ntri/, *foreign* /pɑsmɑ̃tri/ *noun* E17 **French** (from *passement* from *passer* to pass; the connection with Spanish and Italian *passamano* (apparently from *passare* to pass + *mano* hand) and the reason for this name are both obscure). Decorative trimming consisting of gold or silver lace, gimp, or braid.

passe-partout /ˌpaspɑːˈtuː/, /ˌpɑːspɑːˈtuː/ *noun* L17 **French** (from *passer* to pass + *partout* everywhere). **1** L17 A thing which goes or provides a means of going everywhere; *specifically* a master-key. **2** M19 A frame or border into which a picture of suitable size may be inserted for display; a frame for displaying mounted photographs etc., consisting of two sheets of transparent material (or one sheet with a card backing) stuck together at the edges with adhesive tape. Also, adhesive tape used in such framing.

pas seul /pa sœl/ *noun phrase* plural **pas seuls** (*pronounced same*) E19 **French**. A dance for one person, especially in classical ballet.

passim /ˈpasɪm/ *adverb & adjective* E19 Latin (literally, 'scatteredly', from *passus* scattered, past participle of *pandere* to spread out). Of an allusion or reference in a published work: (to be found) at various places throughout the text. Also *transferred* and *figurative*.

1996 *Country Life* . . . a minister's life—see Tristan Garel-Jones *passim*—can and does include a certain salty lack of political correctness when it comes to dealing with foreigners.

passus /ˈpasəs/ *noun* plural same L16 **Latin** (= step, pace). A section, division, or canto of a (medieval) story or poem.

pasta /ˈpastə/ *noun* L19 **Italian** (from late Latin *pasta* a small square piece of medicinal preparation, from Greek *pastē*). **1** L19 A type of dough made from durum wheat flour and water and extruded or stamped into particular shapes (and often dried if not for immediate use). Also, an Italian dish consisting largely of this and usually a sauce. **2** L20 Marijuana. *slang*.

pasticcio /paˈstɪtʃɪəʊ/ *noun* plural **pasticcios** M18 **Italian** (= pie, pasty, from Proto-Romance, from late Latin *pasta* paste). A PASTICHE.

pastiche /paˈstiːʃ/ *noun & verb* L19 **French** (from as PASTICCIO). **A** *noun* L19 A medley of various things; *specifically* (*a*) a picture or a musical composition made up of pieces derived from or imitating various sources; (*b*) a literary or other work of art composed in the style of a well-known author, artist, etc. **B** *transitive & intransitive verb* M20 Copy or imitate the style of (an artist, author, etc.).

A.b *transferred* **1996** *Times Magazine* It's a pastiche of a fashionable London restaurant of the moment.

pasticheur /ˌpastiːˈʃəː/ *noun* E20 **French** (from PASTICHE). An artist who imitates the style of another artist.

1996 *Country Life* Miss Guest is an Edwards pasticheur . . . , creating wide-screen images of hounds in full cry and horses streaming across open country.

pastiglia /paˈstiːlja/, /paˈstiːlɪə/ *noun* E20 Italian (= paste). Intricately moulded gesso used in the decoration of furniture, caskets, etc., in Renaissance Italy.

pastille /ˈpast(ə)l/, /ˈpastɪl/ *noun* (also **pastil**) M17 **French** (from Latin *pastillus* little loaf or roll, lozenge, diminutive of *panis* loaf). **1** M17 A small pellet of aromatic paste burnt as a perfume or as a fumigator, deodorizer, or disinfectant. **2** M17 A small flat, usually round, sweet, often coated with sugar and sometimes medicated; a lozenge. **b** E20 *Medicine* A small disc of barium platinocyanide whose gradual change of colour when exposed to X-rays was formerly used as an indication of the dose delivered.

pastis /ˈpastɪs/, /paˈstiːs/ *noun* E20 **French**. (A drink of) a liqueur flavoured with aniseed.

pastorale /pastəˈrɑːl/, /pastəˈrɑːleɪ/ *noun* plural **pastorales**, **pastorali** /pastəˈrɑːli/ E18 **Italian** (use as noun of *pastorale* pastoral, from Latin *pastoralis* from *pastor* shepherd, from *past-* past participial stem of *pascere* to feed, graze). *Music* **1** E18 A slow instrumental composition in compound time, often with drone notes in the bass suggestive of a shepherd's bagpipes. **2** L19 A simple musical play with a rural subject.

pastoralia /pɑːstəˈreɪlɪə/ *noun plural* E18 **Latin** (neuter plural of *pastoralis* pastoral). Spiritual care or guidance as a subject of theological study; the duties of a pastor.

pastourelle /pasturɛl/ (*plural same*), /pastʊˈrɛl/ *noun* L19 **French** (feminine of *pastoureau* shepherd). A medieval lyric whose theme is love for a shepherdess.

■ The Provençal or Portuguese word *pastorela* (L19) is also used.

pastrami /paˈstrɑːmi/ *noun* M20 **Yiddish** (from Romanian *pastramă*, probably of Turkish origin). Highly seasoned smoked beef, usually, served in thin slices.

pata /ˈpʌtə/ *noun* M20 **Sanskrit** (*paṭa*). Cloth, canvas; *especially* (an example of) an ancient form of Indian painting typically executed on a strip of cloth or scroll of canvas.

patchouli /ˈpatʃʊli/, /pəˈtʃuːli/ *noun* (also **patchouly**) M19 **Tamil** (*pacçuli*). **1** M19 Either of two Indo-Malayan labiate shrubs, *Pogostemon cablin* and *P. heyneanus*, whose leaves yield an essential oil much used in perfumery. **2** M19 Perfume prepared from this plant.

pâte /pɑt/ *noun* M19 **French**. Paste.

■ Occurs in English with a defining word or phrase, usually indicating a substance or process.

pâte brisée /pɑt brize/ *noun phrase* M19 **French** (literally, 'broken paste'). *Cookery* A type of sweet shortcrust pastry.

pâte de verre /pɑt də vɛr/ *noun phrase* E20 **French** (literally, 'paste of glass'). Powdered glass that has been fired a second time.

pâte dure /pɑt dyr/ *noun phrase* M19 **French** (literally, 'hard paste'). (Porcelain made from) hard clay.

pâte-sur-pâte /pɑtsyrpɑt/ *noun phrase* L19 **French** (literally, 'paste on paste'). A method of relief decoration formed by applying layers of white slip on unfired porcelain.

pâte tendre /pɑt tɑ̃dr/ *noun phrase* M19 **French** (literally, 'tender paste'). (Porcelain made from) soft clay.

pâté /'pateɪ/ *noun* E18 **French** (from Old French *pasté*). **1** E18 A pie, a pasty. Now *rare*. **2** L19 A rich paste or spread made from finely minced or pounded meat, fish, herbs, etc.

■ In sense 2 often with a qualifying word or phrase indicating a particular recipe, such as *rough pâté, Strasbourg pâté* (see also phrases below).

pâté de campagne /ˌpateɪ də kɒm 'pɑːnjə/ *noun phrase* M20 **French** (= country pâté). A coarse pork and liver pâté.

pâté de foie gras /'pateɪ də fwɑː ˌgrɑː/ *noun phrase* E19 **French**. A smooth rich pâté of fatted goose liver.

■ Originally a pie filled with this paste, also known as a 'Strasbourg pie'; now applied just to the filling served as a separate dish.

pâté en croûte /ˌpateɪ ɑ̃ 'kruːt/ *noun phrase* M20 **French**. Pâté baked in a pastry case.

pâté maison /'pateɪ ˌmɛzɔ̃ː/ *noun phrase* M20 **French** (= house pâté). Pâté made to the recipe of a particular restaurant.

patella /pə'tɛlə/ *noun* plural **patellae** /pə 'tɛliː/ (originally Anglicized as **patel**) L15 **Latin** (diminutive of PATERA). **1 a** *generally* A pan. Only in L15. **b** M19 *Archaeology* A small pan or shallow vessel, *especially* a Roman one. **2** L16 *Anatomy* The kneecap. **3** L17 A natural structure in the form of a shallow cup or pan. **4** L17 *Zoology* A univalve mollusc of the genus *Patella*, which includes the common limpet. Chiefly as modern Latin genus name.

pater /'peɪtə/, *in sense 1 also* /'pɑːtə/ *noun* ME **Latin**. **1** ME The Lord's Prayer, the PATERNOSTER. **2** E17–M19 An ecclesiastical or spiritual father. **3** E18 Father. Cf. MATER sense 2. Chiefly *jocular* and *school slang*. **b** M20 *Anthropology* A person's legal as opposed to biological father. Cf. GENITOR.

patera /'pat(ə)rə/ *noun* plural **paterae** /'pat(ə)riː/ M17 **Latin** (from *patere* to be open). **1** M17 *Roman Antiquities* A broad shallow dish used especially for pouring libations. **2** L18 *Architecture* An ornament resembling a shallow dish; any flat round ornament in bas-relief.

paterfamilias /ˌpeɪtəfə'mɪlɪas/, /ˌpatəfə 'mɪlɪas/ *noun* plural **patresfamilias** /ˌpeɪtriːzfə'mɪlɪas/, /ˌpatriːzfə'mɪlɪas/ L15 **Latin** (from *pater* father + archaic genitive of *familia* family). **1** L15 A male head of a family or household. **2** M19 *Roman Law* The male head of a family or household having authority over its members. Also, any male legally independent and free from parental control.

paternoster /patə'nɒstə/, /pɑːtə'nɒstə/ *noun* OE **Latin** (*paternoster* literally, 'our father', the first two words of the Lord's Prayer in Latin). **1** OE The Lord's Prayer, especially in the Latin version. **b** ME A repetition or recital of this as an act of worship. **c** LME *transferred* A form of words repeated as or like a prayer, imprecation, or charm. Also, a nonsensical or tedious recital. **2** ME Any of several special beads occurring at regular intervals in a rosary to indicate that a paternoster is to be said. Also, the whole rosary. **3** M19 A fishing line with hooks or weights attached at intervals. More fully *paternoster line*. **4** E20 A lift consisting of a series of doorless compartments moving continuously on an endless belt. Also more fully *paternoster elevator, paternoster lift*.

patha patha /ˌpatə 'patə/ *noun phrase* M20 **Xhosa** (*phathphatha* to feel with the hands). **1** M20 In South Africa: a sensuous Black African dance; music for this dance. **2** L20 Sexual intercourse. *South African slang*.

pathos /'peɪθɒs/ *noun* L16 **Greek** (= suffering, feeling, related to *paskhein* to suffer, *penthos* grief). **1** L16 A pathetic expression or utterance. *rare*. **2** M17 A quality in speech, writing, events, persons, etc., which excites pity or sadness; the power of stirring tender or melancholy emotion. **3** L17 Physical or mental suffering. *rare*.

2 1996 *Country Life* . . . the work's humour served deeply serious ends and was flecked with darker moments and a touchingly lyrical pathos.

patina /'patɪnə/ *noun* M18 **Italian** (from Latin = shallow dish or pan). A usually green film produced by oxidation on the surface of old bronze; a similar alteration of the surface of coins, flint, etc. Also, a gloss on wooden furniture produced by age, polishing, etc; an acquired change in the appearance of a surface, *especially* one suggestive of age.

transferred **1996** *Country Life* In keeping with this patina of elder statesmanship, the tone is disconcertingly formal by today's standards . . .

patio /'patɪəʊ/ *noun* plural **patios** E19 **Spanish** (= court of a house). **1** E19 Originally, an inner court, open to the sky, in a Spanish or Spanish-American house. Now also, a usually roofless paved area adjoining and belonging to a house. **2** M19 *Mining* A yard or floor where ores are cleaned, sorted, or amalgamated.

patisserie /pə'ti:s(ə)ri/ *noun* (also **pâtisserie**) L16 **French** (*pâtisserie* from medieval Latin *pasticium*, from *pasta* paste). **1** L16 *singular* and in *plural* Articles of food made by a pastry-cook, pastries collectively. **2** E20 A shop which sells pastries.

patissier /pə'ti:sɪə/, *foreign* /pɑtisje/ *noun* (also **pâtissier**, feminine **patissiere**, **pâtissière** /pə'ti:sɪɛ:/, *foreign* /pɑtisjɛr/) E20 **French**. A pastry-cook.

1995 *Times Magazine* If I were seriously rich and had a large kitchen, I sometimes think I would like to employ a pâtissier.

patois /'patwɑ:/ *noun & adjective* M17 **Old and Modern French** (= rough speech, perhaps from Old French *patoier* to handle roughly, trample, from *patte* paw, of unknown origin). **A** *noun* plural same /'patwɑ:z/. **1** M17 A dialect (originally in France) of the common people in a particular area, differing fundamentally from the literary language; any non-standard local dialect. **2** L18 *transferred* A social dialect; jargon. **3** M20 The creole of the English-speaking Caribbean, especially Jamaica. **B** *attributive* or as *adjective* L18 Of, pertaining to, or of the nature of a patois.

A.1 1995 G. Tindall *Célestine* In . . . age he had become hard of hearing and had reverted in his own speech to the *patois* of long ago.

B 1996 *Spectator* One needs to speak Swahili or Urdu to be understood, although at times *patois* French will do.

patresfamilias plural of PATERFAMILIAS.

patria /'patrɪə/, /'peɪtrɪə/ *noun* E20 **Latin**. One's native country; one's homeland.

patrin /'patrɪn/ *noun* M19 **Romany**. A trail left by Gypsies, using arrangements of grass, leaves, twigs, etc., to indicate the direction taken.

patron /pa'trɒn/, *foreign* /patrɔ̃/, *foreign* /pa'tron/ *noun* ME **Old and Modern French** (from Latin *patronus* protector of clients, advocate, defender, from *pater*, *patr-* father). **1** LME The captain or master of a Mediterranean galley or coaster (now *rare* or *obsolete*); in North American waters, the captain or steersman of a long-boat, barge, etc. **2** M16 A case for pistol cartridges; a cartridge. Now *obsolete* except *historical*. **3** E17–E18 A master or owner of slaves in countries bordering the eastern and southern Mediterranean. **4** M19 A manager or boss of a hacienda; in New Mexico, the master or head of a family. (From *Spanish*). **5** L19 The proprietor of an inn or restaurant, especially in France and Spain. Cf. Italian PADRONE.

■ The above senses represent only modern Romance uses, as *patron*, with the pronunciation /'peɪtr(ə)n/, has also been fully Anglicized (ME onwards), in senses derived from ecclesiastical and classical Latin.

patronat /patrɔna/ *noun* M20 **French**. An organization of industrial employers in France; French employers collectively.

patronne /patrɔn/ *noun* plural pronounced same L18 **French** (feminine of PATRON). A woman who is the owner, or the wife of the owner, of a business, especially a café, hotel, or restaurant.

patte /pat/ *noun* L18 **French** (of unknown origin). **1** L18 A paw; *jocularly* a hand. Now only in PATTE DE VELOURS. **2** M19 A short band or strap sewn on a dress as a trimming, or used to fasten a coat, hold a belt in place, etc.

patte de velours /pat də vlur/ *noun phrase* M19 **French** (= paw of velvet). A cat's paw with the claws retracted, as symbolic of ruthlessness or inflexibility hidden beneath apparent softness.

paupiette /pɔ:p'jɛt/ *noun* (originally **poupiets**) E18 **French** (perhaps from Italian *polpetta*, from Latin *pulpa* pulp). *Cookery* A long thin slice of fish, meat, etc., especially rolled and stuffed with a filling.

■ Usually in plural in names of dishes, as in *paupiettes de veau*. A dish of this sort is also sometimes called *alouettes sans tête* '(sky)larks without heads'. An alternative etymology perhaps connects with French *poupée* 'doll'; cf. the minced-meat dish called in modern Greek *koukla*, also meaning 'doll'.

pavane /pə'van/, /pə'vɑ:n/ *noun* (also **pavan**, /'pav(ə)n/) M16 **French** (probably from Italian dialect *pavana* feminine of *pavano* of Padua, from *Pavo* dialect name of Padua (Italian *Padova*)). **1** M16 *History* A grave and stately dance in slow duple time, performed in elaborate clothing and popular in the sixteenth century. **2** M16 A piece of music for this dance or in its rhythm.

pavé /'paveɪ/, *foreign* /pave/ (*plural same*) *noun* (also (earlier) Anglicized as **pave** /peɪv/) LME **French** (use as noun of past participle of *paver* to pave). **1** LME A paved road or path. **2** L19 A setting of jewels placed close together so that no metal is visible.

2 1996 *Country Life* The brooch . . . is a geometric platinum-set design of baguette and brilliant cut diamonds with *pavé*-set terminals . . .

pavillon /pavijɔ̃/ *noun* L19 **French** (literally 'pavilion'). **1** L19 The bell-shaped mouth of a trumpet or similar musical instrument. **2** L19 A percussion instrument similar to a Turkish crescent, consisting of a stick having transverse brass plates from which hang a number of small bells which jingle. More fully *pavillon chinois* /pavijɔ̃ ʃinwa/ 'Chinese pavillon'. Also called *jingling Johnny*.

pax /paks/ *noun* LME **Latin** (= peace). **1** LME *Ecclesiastical* (also **Pax**) The ceremonial exchange of greetings as part of a church service to signify Christian concord. **2** LME *Ecclesiastical History* A tablet of gold, silver, ivory, glass, etc., with a projecting handle, depicting the Crucifixion or other sacred subject, which was kissed by all participants at mass. Also called *osculatory*. **3** L15 Peace, tranquillity, concord; *especially* peace between nations. Cf. PAX ROMANA. **4** L18 A friend; good friends. *School slang*. **5** M19 As *interjection* A call for quiet or (a) truce. *school slang*.

pax Romana /ˌpaks rəʊ'mɑ:nə/ *noun phrase* L19 **Latin** (= Roman peace). The peace which existed between nationalities under the Roman Empire.

■ Originally from Pliny's *Natural History* (xxvii.3), *pax Romana* has been the model for other phrases with a Latin or modern Latin adjective referring to the dominant influence of a State, empire, etc. (see quotation 1996).

1993 G. Fowden *Empire to Commonwealth* They [sc. the Jews] benefited from the *pax Romana* to develop their communities, build impressive synagogues, and assert a claim to social esteem.

1996 *Times* They [sc. the Serbs] will fight, fight and fight again for this, long after the Americans lose interest in their *pax Americana*, as it becomes a desert . . .

paysage /peizaʒ/ *noun* plural pronounced same E17 **French** (from *pays* country). (A representation of) a rural scene or landscape.

paysan /peizɑ̃/ *noun & adjective* E19 **French** (from Old French *païsant*, *païsent*, alteration of earlier *païsenc*, from *païs* (modern *pays*) country, from Proto-Romance alteration of Latin *pagus* rural district). **A** *noun* E19 plural pronounced same. A peasant, a countryman, especially in France. **B** *adjective* L19 Of a style of art, dress, etc: resembling that of peasants.

paysanne /peizan/ *noun* plural pronounced same M18 **French** (feminine of PAYSAN). A peasant-woman, a countrywoman, especially in France.

peag /pi:g/ *noun* (also **peak** /pi:k/) M17 **American Indian.** WAMPUM.

péage /'peɪɑ:ʒ/, *in sense 2 also foreign* /peaʒ/ (*plural same*) *noun* (in sense 1 also **payage**) LME **Old and Modern French** (from medieval Latin *pedaticum*, from Latin *pes*, *ped-* foot; in sense 2 from modern French). **1** LME Toll paid for passing through a place or country. *obsolete* in *general* sense. **2** L20 Toll paid to travel on a French motorway; a gate or barrier where this is paid.

peau-de-soie /podəswa/, /ˌpəʊdə'swɑ:/ *noun* M19 **French** (literally, 'silk skin'). A close-woven heavy satin silk; an (especially rayon) imitation of this.

peau d'Espagne /po dɛspaɲ/ *noun phrase* (also **Peau d'Espagne**) M19 **French** (literally, 'skin of Spain'). **1** M19 Perfumed leather. **2** L19 A scent suggestive of the aroma of this leather.

peccadillo /pɛkə'dɪləʊ/ *noun* plural **peccadilloes**, **peccadillos** L16 **Spanish** (*pecadillo* diminutive of *pecado* sin). A small fault, a venial sin; a trifling offence.

peccavi /pɛ'kɑ:vi:/ *interjection & noun* E16 **Latin** (= I have sinned). **A** *interjection* E16 Acknowledging guilt. **B** *noun* L16 An acknowledgement or confession of guilt.

■ As an interjection, now usually jocular; cf. MEA CULPA.

pecorino /pɛkəˈriːnəʊ/ *noun* M20 **Italian** (from *pecora* sheep). A hard Italian cheese made from ewe's milk.

pedregal /pɛdrɪˈɡɑːl/, /ˈpɛdrɪɡ(ə)l/ *noun* M19 **Spanish** (from *piedra* stone, from Latin *petra*). In Mexico and the south-western United States: a rocky tract, especially in a volcanic region; an old lava-field.

peignoir /ˈpeɪnwɑː/ *noun* M19 **French** (from *peigner* to comb). A woman's loose dressing-gown or bathrobe.

peineta /peiˈneta/ *noun* M20 **Spanish**. A woman's ornamental comb traditionally worn with a mantilla.

pelmeny /pɛlˈmɛni/ *noun plural* M20 **Russian** (*pel'meni*). Small pasta cases stuffed with seasoned meat etc. as a Russian dish.

pelota /pɪˈlɒtə/, /pɪˈləʊtə/ *noun* E19 **Spanish** (= ball, augmentative of *pella* from Latin *pila* ball). **1** E19 A Basque or Spanish ball game played in a walled court using basket-like wicker rackets attached to gloves. **2** E20 The ball used in pelota.

peloton /ˈpɛlətɒn/ *noun* M20 **French** (from *pelote* from Proto-Romance diminutive of Latin *pila* ball). *Cycling* The main field, group, or pack of cyclists in a race.

■ The original senses in which *peloton* was introduced (both E18) are now rare or obsolete: 'a small ball or pellet' and (its modern French sense) 'a platoon'.

1996 *Times* Riis . . . has grown up in the peloton, the toughest school of all, and has no time for niceties.

pelouse /pəluz/ *noun* plural pronounced same E20 **French**. Especially in France: an area of grass; *specifically* a public enclosure at a racecourse.

pelta /ˈpɛltə/ *noun* plural **peltae** /ˈpɛltiː/ (also Anglicized as **pelt**) E17 **Latin** (from Greek *peltē* a small light leather shield). **1** E17 *Classical Antiquities* A small light shield; a buckler. **2** M18 *Botany* Any of various shieldlike structures. **3** E20 An ornamental motif resembling a shield in architecture, metalwork, etc.

pelure /ˈpɛljʊə/ *noun* L19 **French** (literally, 'peeling', from *peler* to peel). Especially *Philately*. A kind of very thin paper. Also *pelure-paper*.

pelure d'oignon /p(ə)lyr dɔɲɔ̃/ *noun & adjective phrase* M20 **French** (literally, 'onion peel'). **A** *noun phrase* M20 plural **pelures d'oignons** (pronounced same). A tawny colour characteristic of some aged red wines; a wine of this colour. **B** *adjective phrase* M20 (Designating a wine) of this colour.

pemmican /ˈpɛmɪk(ə)n/ *noun* L18 **Cree** (pimihkan, from *pimiy* grease). A lightweight, highly nutritious food of pounded dried meat mixed to a paste with melted fat and berries, used originally by North American Indians, now also by explorers, hikers, etc.

penates /pɪˈnɑːtiːz/, /pɪˈneɪtiːz/ *noun plural* E16 **Latin** (*Penates* (plural), from *penus* provision of food, related to *penes* within). *Roman History* The protective gods of a house, especially of its storeroom; household gods. Cf. LAR.

■ Often in English in the phrase *lares and penates*.

penchant /ˈpɒ̃ʃɒ̃/ *noun* L17 **French** (use as noun of present participle of *pencher* to incline, lean). An inclination, a (strong or habitual) liking.

1996 *Spectator* She had a *penchant* for younger men, on whom she squandered much of her money . . .

penchée /pɑ̃ʃe/, /ˈpɒnʃeɪ/ *adjective* M20 **French** (feminine of *penché* past participle of *pencher* to lean, incline). *Ballet* Especially of an arabesque: performed while leaning forward.

■ Usually postpositive.

pendeloque /ˈpɒnd(ə)lɒk/, *foreign* /pɑ̃dlɔk/ (*plural of noun same*) *adjective & noun* M19 **French** (from Old French *pendeler* to dangle). (A gem, especially a diamond) cut in the shape of a drop.

pendente lite /pɛnˌdɛntɪ ˈlʌɪti/ *adverb phrase* E18 **Latin** (literally, 'with the lawsuit pending'). *Law* During the progress of a suit; during litigation.

penetralia /pɛnɪˈtreɪlɪə/ *noun plural* M17 **Latin** (use as noun of *penetralia* neuter plural of *penetrālis* innermost). The innermost parts of a building etc.; *especially* the sanctuary or innermost shrine of a temple; *figurative* secret parts, mysteries.

penne /ˈpɛneɪ/ *noun plural* L20 **Italian** (literally, 'quills, pens'). Pasta in the form of short tubes cut diagonally at both ends.

pensée /pɑ̃se/ *noun* (also (in sense 1) **pensee**) plural pronounced same LME **Old French** (*pensee*; in sense 2 reintroduced from French). **1** LME–L15 Thoughtfulness, anxiety, care; a thought, an idea. **2** L19 A poem or prose composition expressing a single thought or reflection. Also, an aphorism.

penseroso /pɛnsəˈrəʊsəʊ/, *foreign* /penseˈrozo/ *noun & adjective* L18 **Italian** (obsolete form of *pensieroso*, from (obsolete) *pensiere* thought, from Provençal *pensier*, from Proto-Romance variant of Latin *pensare* to weigh, ponder, consider). **A** *noun* L18 plural **penserosos** /pɛnsəˈrəʊsəʊz/, **penserosi** /penseˈrozi/. (A person having) a brooding or melancholy character. **B** *adjective* E19 Pensive, brooding, melancholy.

■ John Milton's classic depiction of the melancholy character in his poem 'Il Penseroso' (1632) was responsible for the wider use of the word in English.

pensiero /penˈsjɛːro/ *noun* plural **pensieri** /penˈsjɛːri/ E20 **Italian**. **1** E20 A thought, an idea; an anxiety. **2** M20 *Art* A sketch.

pension /pɑ̃sjɔ̃/ (*plural same*) *noun* M17 **French** (Old French *pension* from Latin *pensio(n-)* payment, rent, from *pens-* past participial stem of *pendere* to weigh, pay). A usually fixed-rate boarding-house or (formerly) a boarding-school in France or another European country. Cf. EN PENSION.

■ *Pension* was first introduced in the LME period and, with the pronunciation /ˈpɛnʃ(ə)n/, is now wholly Anglicized in its numerous senses deriving from Old French and Latin, almost all of which contain the idea of 'a fixed regular payment'. The sense above was also formerly Anglicized.

pensionnaire /pɑ̃sjɔnɛr/ *noun* plural pronounced same L16 **French** (from medieval Latin *pensionarius*). **1** L16 A person receiving a pension; a pensioner, a paid retainer. *rare*. **2** L18 A person who boards in a French lodging-house or institution, or with a French family.

pentathlon /pɛnˈtaθlɒn/, /pɛnˈtaθlən/ *noun* (also formerly in Latin form **pentathlum**) E17 **Greek** (from *penta-* five + *athlon* contest). **1** E17 *Classical History* An athletic contest in which competitors engaged in five different events (leaping, running, discus-throwing, spear-throwing, and wrestling). **2** E20 An athletic or sporting contest in which competitors engage in five different events (especially (in full *modern pentathlon*) fencing, shooting, swimming, riding, and cross-country running).

pentimento /pɛntɪˈmɛntəʊ/ *noun* plural **pentimenti** /pɛntɪˈmɛnti/ E20 **Italian** (literally, 'repentance'). *Art* A visible trace of (an) earlier painting beneath a layer or layers of paint; (a) painting revealed by such traces.

penuche /pɛˈnuːtʃi/ *noun* (also **panocha** /paˈnɒtʃə/, **panoche** /paˈnɒtʃi/, and other variants) M19 **American Spanish** (*panoche*). **1** M19 A kind of coarse brown sugar used in Mexico. **2** L19 A kind of sweet resembling fudge, made with brown sugar, butter, milk or cream, and often nuts. *North American*.

peon /ˈpiːən/, *in branch I also* /pjuːn/, *in branch II also* /peɪˈɒn/, *foreign* /peˈon/ *noun* plural **peons**, (*in sense 3 also*) **peones** /ˈpiːənɪz/, *foreign* /peˈones/ E17 **Portuguese and Spanish** (in sense 1 from Portuguese *peão*; in senses 2 and 3 from Spanish *peón* peasant, from medieval Latin *pedo(n-)* foot-soldier). **I 1** E17 In the Indian subcontinent and South East Asia: a person of low rank; *specifically* (*a*) a foot-soldier; (*b*) an orderly; (*c*) an office boy. **II 2** E19 A Spanish-American day labourer or farm worker, *especially* one in poor circumstances. Also (*historical*), a debtor held in servitude by a creditor, especially in the southern United States and Mexico. **3** M20 A BANDERILLERO.

peperoni variant of PEPPERONI.

peplos /ˈpɛplɒs/ *noun* L18 **Greek**. *Greek Antiquities* A (usually rich) outer robe or shawl worn by women in ancient Greece, hanging in loose folds and sometimes drawn over the head; *specifically* the one woven for the statue of the goddess Athene at Athens, and carried in procession to her temple at the greater Panathenaea.

peplum /ˈpɛpləm/ *noun* L17 **Latin** (from Greek PEPLOS). **1** L17 A PEPLOS. **2** M19 Formerly, a kind of overskirt, in supposed imitation of the ancient peplum. Now also, a usually short flounce on a jacket, blouse, or tunic, hanging from the waist over a skirt; a jacket etc. incorporating this.

pepperoni /pɛpəˈrəʊni/ *noun* (also **peperoni**) M20 **Italian** (*peperone* chilli, from *peper-*, *pepe* pepper, from Latin *piper* + augmentative suffix *-one*). Beef and pork sausage seasoned with pepper.

per /pəː/ *preposition* LME **Latin** (whence Old French and Italian *per*, French *par* through). **1** LME Through, by; by means of: (*a*) in Latin and modern Latin (also medieval Latin and Italian) phrases, as PER SE; (*b*) in Old French phrases and words derived therefrom. **2** M16 *Heraldry* In the direction of (a specified ordinary). **3** L16 By means of, by the instrumentality of; in accordance with (usually *as per*); *Law* as laid down by (a judge) in a specified case. **4** L16 For each, for every, as *per cent*, *per mil*, etc. **b** L19 With ellipsis of following noun: per hour, per cent, etc. Chiefly *United States*.

per accidens /pəː(r) 'aksɪdɛnz/ *adverb phrase* E16 **Modern Latin** (from as PER + Latin *accidens*, *accident-* present participial stem of *accidere* to happen). **1** E16 By virtue of some non-essential circumstance; contingently, indirectly. Opposed to PER SE. **2** L16 *Logic* By which the quantity of the proposition is changed from universal to particular in a conversion. Opposed to *simply*.

per annum /pə(r) 'anəm/ *adverb phrase* E17 **Modern Latin** (from as PER + accusative of Latin *annus* year). For or in each year.

■ Abbreviated to *p.a.*

percale /pə'keɪl/, *foreign* /pɛrkal/ *noun* E17 **French** (in modern use, but origin unknown (= Spanish *percal*, Italian *percalle*)). Originally, a fabric imported from India in the seventeenth and eighteenth centuries. Later, a light fine cotton fabric without gloss.

per capita /pə 'kapɪtə/ *adverb & adjective phrase* L17 **Modern Latin** (from as PER + accusative plural of Latin *caput* head). **A** *adverb phrase* **1** L17 *Law* (Divided, shared, etc.) equally among or by individuals, on an individual basis. Opposed to PER STIRPES. **2** E20 For each person or head of population. **B** *adjective phrase* M20 Possessed, performed, etc., by each person when averaged over a population etc.

A.2 1996 *Times* Government expenditure in Scotland is nearly one-third higher *per capita* than that for England.

per centum /pə 'sɛntəm/ *adverb phrase* M17 **Modern Latin** (Latinized form of *per cent*). Per cent.

■ Frequently in legal contexts.

perceptum /pə'sɛptəm/ *noun* plural **percepta** /pə'sɛptə/ L19 **Latin** (neuter of *perceptus* past participle of *percipere* to perceive). An object of perception, a percept.

per contra /pəː 'kɒntrə/ *adverb & noun phrase* M16 **Italian**. **A** *adverb phrase* M16 On the opposite side (of an account, assessment, etc.); on the other hand. **B** *noun phrase* E19 The opposite side.

1996 *Times* . . . a mass exit by the City herd would make AIM shares even more volatile than they are by nature. *Per contra*, AIM could become too respectable.

per diem /pəː 'diːɛm/, /'dʌɪɛm/ *adverb, noun, & adjective phrase* E16 **Modern Latin** (from as PER + accusative of Latin *dies* day). **A** *adverb phrase* E16 For or in each day. **B** *noun phrase* E19 An amount or allowance of so much each day. Chiefly *North American*. **C** *adjective phrase* E19 Daily. Chiefly *North American*.

B 1996 *Spectator* . . . Hollywood doesn't help at all and he goes crackers *con brio* with vanishing agents, certifiable producers, grotty hotels, stingy *per diems* and lurking rewrite men.

perdu /pəː'djuː/, *foreign* /pɛrdy/ *adjective* (also **perdue**) L16 **Old and Modern French** (past participle of *perdre* to lose, from Latin *perdere*). **A** *adjective* **1** L16–L17 Posted in, or designating, a sentinel's position that is so dangerous that death is almost inevitable. Only in *sentinel perdue*, *perdue sentinel*. **b** E–M17 Placed in a very hazardous situation; (of a case) desperate. **2** E17 Hidden and on the watch; lying in ambush. Chiefly in *lie*, *set*, *stand*, etc., *perdu*. **3** E18 Concealed, hidden; out of sight; disguised.

■ Also formerly a noun (E17–M18), meaning principally 'soldier(s) posted in a very hazardous situation', but now obsolete in all nominal senses.

père /pɛr/, /pɛː/ *noun* E17 **French** (= father). **1** E17 Father: used in France and French-speaking countries as a title preceding the name of a priest. **2** E19 The father, senior.

■ *Père* in sense 2 is appended to a name to distinguish between a father and son of the same name (see quotations). Cf. FILS; also in phrase *père et fils* 'father and son'.

1995 *Spectator* And yet—another irony—Forte *père* remained, well beyond normal retirement age, a fiercely combative entrepreneur . . .

père de famille /pɛ də famij/, /ˌpɛː də fa 'miː/ *noun phrase* E19 **French**. A father of a family, a family man.

perestroika /pɛrɪ'strɔɪkə/ *noun* L20 **Russian** (*perestroĭka* restructuring). The reform of the economic and political system of the former USSR, first proposed by Leonid Brezhnev in 1979 and actively promoted under the leadership of Mikhail Gorbachev from 1985; *transferred* any programme of fundamental reform.

1996 *Spectator* Ostensibly, it's to pay for digital technology in radio and television, . . . but I don't accept that this is the main reason for such *perestroika*.

perfecta /pəˈfɛktə/ *noun* L20 **American Spanish** (shortened from *quiniela perfecta* perfect quinella). *Betting* A bet in which the first and second finishers of a race must be predicted in the correct order.

perfecto /pəˈfɛktəʊ/ *noun* plural **perfectos** L19 **Spanish** (= perfect). A large thick cigar tapered at each end.

perfide Albion /pɛrfid albjɔ̃/ *noun phrase* M19 **French** (= perfidious Albion). England (with reference to its alleged habitual treachery towards other nations); an (untrustworthy) Englishman.

pergola /ˈpəːɡələ/ *noun* L17 **Italian** (from Latin *pergula* projecting roof, vine arbour, from *pergere* to come or go forward). An arbour or covered walk, formed of growing plants trained over trellis-work.

■ First (M17 only) in the sense of 'an elevated stand or balcony', but this never passed into general currency.

peri /ˈpɪəri/ *noun* L18 **Persian** (*perī*). In Iranian mythology, one of a race of superhuman beings, originally represented as evil but subsequently as good and graceful; *transferred* a graceful or beautiful person.

peridot /ˈpɛrɪdɒt/ *noun* ME **Old French** (*peritot* (modern *peridot*) = medieval Latin *peridotus*, of unknown origin; in sense 2 readopted from French). **1** A green gemstone. Only in ME. **2** E18 Olivine (chrysolite), especially as used as gem.

periegesis /ˌpɛrɪɪˈdʒiːsɪs/ *noun* plural **periegeses** /ˌpɛrɪɪˈdʒiːsiːz/ E17 **Greek** (*periēgēsis* from *peri-* around + *hēgēsis*, from *hēgeisthai* to lead, guide). A description of a place or region.

per impossibile /ˌpəː(r) ɪmpɒˈsɪbɪli/ *adverb phrase* M19 **Latin**. As is impossible.

1995 *Spectator* Una Woodruff . . . will go to infinite trouble to choose brushes for a particular task, and then soak them in warm water so that she can identify and pull out any slightly loose single hair which might, *per impossibile*, threaten a perfectly smooth wash.

peripeteia /ˌpɛrɪpɪˈtʌɪə/, /ˌpɛrɪpɪˈtiːə/ *noun* (also **peripetia** /ˌpɛrɪpɪˈtiːə/) L16 **Greek** (ultimately from *peri-* around + stem *pet-* of *piptein* to fall). A sudden change of fortune or reverse of circumstances (fictional or real).

■ Used by Aristotle in his *Poetics* as a technical term for the sequence of events in the plot of a drama which, in the case of a tragic hero, takes the protagonist from happiness to misfortune.

1984 A.G. Lehmann *European Heritage* The insidious flatteries of the 'mirror' stage—the symmetrical throne-room scenes, the hero revolving great dilemmas, the god descending, the wonderful *peripeteia*—become lessons in style to haunt the prince's dream and shape his acts.

periphrasis /pəˈrɪfrəsɪs/ *noun* plural **periphrases** /pəˈrɪfrəsiːz/ M16 **Latin** (from Greek, from *periphrazein*, from *peri-* + *phrazein* to declare). The figure of speech which consists in expressing a meaning by many or several words instead of by few or one; a roundabout way of speaking or writing; (a) circumlocution.

periplus /ˈpɛrɪplʌs/ *noun* L18 **Latin** (from Greek *periplous*, from *peri-* around + *plous* voyage). (A) circumnavigation; a voyage (or journey) round a coastline etc.; a narrative of such a voyage.

peristyle /ˈpɛrɪstʌɪl/ *noun* E17 **French** (*péristyle* from Latin *peristylum* from Greek *peristulon* use as noun of neuter of *peristulos* having pillars all round, from *peri-* + *stulos* column). *Architecture* **1** E17 A row of columns surrounding a building, court, cloister, etc.; the court etc. surrounded by the columns. **2** L17 The columned porch of a church or other large building; a pillared verandah.

per mensem /pəː ˈmɛnsɛm/ *adverb phrase* M17 **Modern Latin** (from as PER + accusative singular of Latin *mensis* month). For or in each month.

permis de séjour /pɛrmi də seʒur/ *noun phrase* plural same L19 **French**. Permission to stay in a country; a residence permit.

perpetuum mobile /pəːˌpɛtjʊəm ˈməʊbɪli/, /pəːˌpɛtjʊʊm/, /ˈməʊbɪleɪ/ *noun phrase* L17 **Latin** (from *perpetuus* perpetual + *mobilis* movable, mobile, after PRIMUM MOBILE). **1** L17 Motion that continues forever; *specifically* that of a hypothetical machine that runs forever; such a machine. **2** L19 *Music* A MOTO PERPETUO.

perruquier /pɛˈruːkɪeɪ/ *noun* M18 **French** (from *perruque* peruke). A person who makes, dresses, or sells wigs.

per se /pəː seɪ/ *adverb phrase* L16 **Latin**. By or in itself; intrinsically. Opposed to PER ACCIDENS 1.

1995 *Times* Knives—beyond a small variety such as flick-knives—are not 'offensive weapons' per se.

persiennes /pəːsɪ'ɛnz/ *noun plural* M19 **French** (use as noun of feminine plural of *persien* Persian). Window-shutters or outside blinds made of light movable slats fastened horizontally in a frame.

persiflage /'pəːsɪflɑːʒ/ *noun* M18 **French** (from *persifler* to banter, from as PER- + *siffler* to whistle). Light banter or raillery; frivolous talk.

persona /pə'səʊnə/ *noun* plural **personas, personae** /pə'səʊniː/ E20 **Latin** (originally = the mask worn by actors in ancient Greek and Roman drama). **1** E20 A character assumed by an author, performer, etc., in his or her writing, work, etc. **2** E20 An aspect of the personality as displayed to others. Cf. ANIMA.

1 1996 *Times* She [sc. Aliki Vouyouklaki] combined two apparently contradictory types in her screen persona, the unspoiled girl-next-door and the sex bomb, wrapped up in one alluring package.
2 1996 *Times Magazine* He has finally moved into a new flat, which was decorated by someone else, and he has been totally sucked in by the persona imposed on him by the soft furnishings.

persona designata /pə,səʊnə dɛzɪg 'nɑːtə/ *noun phrase* plural **personae designatae** /pə,səʊniː dɛzɪg'nɑːtiː/ L19 **Law Latin** (from as PERSONA + Latin *designata* feminine of *designatus* past participle of *designare* to mark out, elect). A person individually specified in a legal action, as opposed to one included in a category.

personae gratae, personae non gratae plurals of PERSONA GRATA, PERSONA NON GRATA.

persona grata /pə,səʊnə 'grɑːtə/ *noun phrase* plural **personae gratae** /pə,səʊniː 'grɑːtiː/ L19 **Late Latin** (from as PERSONA + Latin *grata* feminine of *gratus* pleasing). A person, especially a diplomat, acceptable to certain others.

personalia /pəːsə'neɪlɪə/ *noun plural* E20 **Latin** (neuter plural of *personalis* personal). Personal matters; personal mementoes.

persona non grata /pə,səʊnə nɒn 'grɑːtə/, /nəʊn/ *noun phrase* plural **personae non gratae** /pə,səʊniː/, /'grɑːtiː/ E20 **Late Latin** (from as PERSONA GRATA + Latin *non* not). An unacceptable or unwelcome person.

1996 *Times* ... in a tit-for-tat expulsion ..., four Russian 'diplomats' had been expelled from London as four British 'spies' had been declared *personae non gratae*.

personnel /pəːsə'nɛl/ *noun* E19 **French** (use as noun of adjective, as contrasted with MATÉRIEL). **1** E19 The body of people employed in an organization etc. or engaged in a service or undertaking, especially a military one. Opposed to *matériel*. **2** M20 *specifically* The members of an orchestra or band. **3** M20 The department in an organization etc. concerned with the appointment, welfare, records, etc., of employees. Also more fully *personnel department*.

per stirpes /pəː 'stəːpiːz/ *adverb phrase* L17 **Modern Latin** (from as PER + accusative plural of Latin *stirps* family, stem). *Law* (Divided, shared, etc.) equally among the branches of a family (and then each share among the members of one branch). Opposed to PER CAPITA sense A.1.

pervenche /pɛː'vɑːnʃ/ *noun* L19 **French** (= periwinkle). A shade of light blue resembling the colour of the flowers of the periwinkle. More fully *pervenche blue*.

peshmerga /pɛʃ'məːgə/ *noun* plural **peshmergas**, same M20 **Kurdish** (*pêshmerge* from *pêsh* before, in front of + *merg* death). A member of a Kurdish nationalist guerrilla organization.

pessimum /'pɛsɪməm/ *noun* M20 **Latin** (neuter singular of *pessimus* worst). The most unfavourable condition (original especially, in the habitat of an animal or plant). Frequently *attributive*. Opposed to OPTIMUM.

pesto /'pɛstəʊ/ *noun* M20 **Italian** (contraction of *pestato* past participle of *pestare* to pound, crush). A sauce of crushed basil, nuts (especially pine nuts), cheese, garlic, and olive oil, served with pasta and other foods. Cf. PISTOU.

pétanque /petɑ̃k/, /pə'taŋk/ *noun* M20 **French**. A game similar to BOULE noun 2 sense 2.

pétillant /petijɑ̃/, /'peɪtɪjɒ̃/ *adjective* L19 **French**. Sparkling, lively. Of wine: slightly sparkling.

petit /pəti/, /pə'tiː/, /'pɛti/; *same in plural collocations adjective* LME **French** (cf. feminine PETITE). Little, small.

■ Occurs in various phrases used in English, and until the seventeenth century was in common use alongside the English form *petty*.

petit battement /pəti batmɑ̃/ *noun phrase* plural **petits battements** (*pronounced same*) E20 **French**. *Ballet* A BATTEMENT executed with the moving leg bent.

petit beurre /pəti bœr/ *noun phrase* plural **petits beurres** (*pronounced same*) E20 **French**. A sweet butter biscuit.

petit bourgeois /ˌpɛtɪ ˈbʊəʒwɑː/, /pəˌtiː/; *foreign* /pəti burʒwa/ *noun & adjective phrase* plural **petits bourgeois** (pronounced same); (feminine **petite bourgeoise** /pəˌtiːt ˈbʊəʒwɑːz/, *foreign* /pətit burʒwaz/, plural **petites bourgeoises** (pronounced same)) M19 **French** (literally, 'little citizen'). **A** *noun phrase* M19 A member of the lower middle classes; *derogatory* a person judged to have conventional or conservative attitudes. **B** *adjective phrase* L19 Pertaining to or characteristic of the PETITE BOURGEOISIE; lower middle class; conventional.

■ Also partially Anglicized (L19 onwards) as *petty bourgeois*.

B 1996 *Spectator* Mr Volkman rails about the CIA's petit bourgeois ignorance of foreign cultures in his account of a disastrous operation in Cuba . . .

petite /pəˈtiːt/, *foreign* /pətit/ *adjective & noun* M16 **French** (feminine of PETIT). **A** *adjective* **1 a** M16–L17 Of a small size or importance. **b** L18 Of small stature. Now chiefly of a woman or girl. **c** E20 Designating a small size in women's clothing. **2** E18 The French (feminine) for 'little, small', occurring in various phrases used in English. **3** M20 *Microbiology* Designating mutant strains of yeast that are characterized by defective mitochondrial DNA and tend to form small colonies. **B** *noun* **1** M20 A petite woman or girl. **2** M20 A petite size in women's clothing. **3** M20 A petite strain of yeast.

A.b 1996 *Country Life* She is as bright and charming as she is petite and beautiful.

petite amie /pətit ami/ *noun phrase* plural **petites amies** M20 **French** (= little (female) friend). A young mistress.

1978 W. Garner *Möbius Trip* His *petite amie* . . . had raised the subject of marriage.

petite bourgeoise see PETIT BOURGEOIS.

petite bourgeoisie /pəˌtiːt bʊəʒwɑːziː/, *foreign* /pətit burʒwazi/ *noun phrase* E20 **French**. The lower middle classes collectively.

■ Also partially Anglicized (M19, but mainly 20) as *petty bourgeoisie*.

1995 *Spectator* Lack of a belief in the social explanation of crime is thought to be a failing of the petite bourgeoisie.

petite noblesse /pətit nɔblɛs/ *noun phrase* L19 **French**. The lesser nobility in France. Cf. HAUTE NOBLESSE.

petites amies, petites marmites, etc. plurals of PETITE AMIE, PETITE MARMITE, etc.

petit four /ˌpɛtɪ ˈfɔː/, *foreign* /pəti fur/ *noun phrase* plural **petits fours** /ˌpɛtɪ ˈfɔːz/, *foreign* /pəti fur/ L19 **French** (literally, 'little oven'). A small cake or biscuit usually served with the coffee after a meal.

petitio principii /pɪˌtɪʃɪəʊ prɪnˈsɪpɪʌɪ/, /prɪŋˈkɪpɪʌɪ/ *noun phrase* M16 **Latin** (= assuming a principle, from *petitio* laying claim to + genitive of PRINCIPIUM). *Logic* A fallacy in which a conclusion is taken for granted in a premiss; begging the question.

petit-maître /pətimɛtr/ *noun phrase* plural **petits-maîtres** (*pronounced same*) E18 **French** (literally, 'little master'). **1** E18 A dandy, a fop. **2** M19 An artist, writer, etc., of minor importance.

■ In sense 2 sometimes translated as *little masters* with reference to practitioners of the minor arts, such as the engravers of late medieval Germany.

1996 *Spectator* These are the pictures that have earned him [sc. William Nicholson] the title of *petit maître*, a French expression for a rather English virtue of recognising one's limits and sticking within them.

petit mal /ˌpɛtɪ ˈmal/, /pəti mal/ *noun phrase* L19 **French** (literally, 'little sickness'). Mild epilepsy, with only momentary loss of consciousness. Cf. GRAND MAL.

petit marmite /pətit marmit/ *noun phrase* plural **petits marmites** (*pronounced same*) E20 **French**. Soup served in the (individual serving sized) MARMITE in which it has been cooked.

petit pain /pəti pɛ̃/ *noun phrase* plural **petits pains** (*pronounced same*) M18 **French**. A small bread roll.

petit point /pəti pwɛ̃/, /ˌpɛtɪ ˈpɔɪnt/ *noun phrase* L19 **French**. **1** L19 Embroidery on canvas using small stitches. **2** L19 Tent-stitch.

petit poussin /pəti pusɛ̃/ *noun phrase* plural **petits poussins** (*pronounced same*) E20 **French**. A young chicken for eating.

■ Now rare, being almost entirely superseded by POUSSIN.

petits battements, **petits beurres**, etc. plurals of PETIT BATTEMENT, PETIT BEURRE, etc.

petits chevaux /pəti ʃəvo/ *noun phrase plural* L19 **French** (literally, 'little horses'). A gambling game in which bets are placed on mechanical horses made to spin round a flag at the centre of a special table.

petits fours, **petits pains** plurals of PETIT FOUR, PETIT PAIN.

petits pois /ˌpɛtɪ ˈpwɑː/, *foreign* /pəti pwa/ *noun phrase plural* E19 **French** (literally, 'small peas'). Small young green peas.

petits poussins plural of PETIT POUSSIN.

petits soins /pəti swɛ̃/ *noun phrase plural* E19 **French**. Small attentions or services.

petit suisse /pəti sɥis/, /ˌpɛtɪ ˈswiːs/ *noun phrase* E20 **French**. A small round cream cheese. Cf. FROMAGE FRAIS.

petit tranchet /pəti trɑ̃ʃɛ/, /ˌpɛtɪ ˈtrɑːnʃɪt/ *noun phrase* M20 **French** (= little knife). *Archaeology* A small stone artefact of mesolithic and neolithic cultures with the end made into a broad cutting edge.

petit verre /pəti vɛr/ *noun phrase* plural **petits verres** (*pronounced same*) M19 **French**. A glass of liqueur.

1995 *Spectator* Instead of some monumental goddess at the dawn of time, . . . you see only a sagging model of the *quartier*, longing for a *petit verre* and the regained dignity of her corsets.

pétrissage /petrisaʒ/ *noun* L19 **French** (from *pétrir*, *pétriss-* to knead). A kneading process used in massage.

pétroleur /pɛtrɔlœr/ *noun* (feminine **pétroleuse** /pɛtrɔløz/) plural pronounced same L19 **French** (from *pétrole* petrol). An arsonist who uses petrol.

pe-tsai /peɪˈtsʌɪ/ *noun* L18 **Chinese** ((Pekingese) *báicài* (Wade–Giles *pê ts'ai*), literally, 'white vegetable': cf. PAK-CHOI). A kind of Chinese cabbage, *Brassica pekinensis*, with leaves in a loose head, grown as a winter vegetable.

peyote /peɪˈəʊti/ *noun* M19 **American Spanish** (from Nahuatl *peyotl*). MESCAL sense 3.

phaeton /ˈfeɪt(ə)n/ *noun* L16 **French** (*phaéton* from Latin *Phaethon* from Greek *Phaethōn* (*phaethōn* shining), in Greek mythology the son of Helios and Clymene, who was allowed to drive the sun's chariot for a day, with disastrous results). **1** L16–M18 A rash or adventurous charioteer like Phaethon; any charioteer; a thing that, like Phaethon, sets the world on fire. **2** M18 Chiefly *History* A light four-wheeled open carriage, usually drawn by a pair of horses, and with one or two forward-facing seats. **3** E20 A touring car. *United States*.

phallus /ˈfaləs/ *noun* plural **phalli** /ˈfalʌɪ/, /ˈfaliː/, **phalluses** E17 **Late Latin** (from Greek *phallos*). **1** E17 An image of the erect penis, symbolizing the generative power in nature; *specifically* that carried in solemn procession in the Dionysiac festivals in ancient Greece. **2** E20 The penis, especially as an organ of symbolic significance; an erect penis.

phantasma /fanˈtazmə/ *noun* plural **phantasmas**, **phantasmata** /fanˈtazmətə/ L16 **Italian** (*fantasma* from Latin *phantasma* from Greek, from *phantazein* to make visible). An illusion, a vision, a dream; an apparition, a ghost.

pharmacopoeia /ˌfɑːməkəˈpiːə/ *noun* (also **pharmacopeia**) E17 **Modern Latin** (from Greek *pharmakopoiia* art of preparing drugs, from *pharmakopoios* preparer of drugs, from *pharmaco-* combining form of *pharmakon* drug + *-poios* making, maker). **1** E17 A book containing a list of drugs with their effects and directions for their use (and, formerly, their preparation and identification); *specifically* such a book officially published and revised periodically. **2** E18 A collection or stock of drugs.

phenomenon /fɪˈnɒmɪnən/ *noun* (also **phaenomenon**, **phainomenon**) plural **phenomena** /fɪˈnɒmɪnə/, also (*non-standard*) used as singular, **phenomenas** L16 **Late Latin** (*phaenomenon* from Greek *phainomenon* use as noun of neuter present participle passive of *phainein* to show, (in passive) be seen, appear). **1** L16 A fact or event that appears or is perceived by one of the senses or by the mind; *especially* one whose cause or explanation is in question. **2** L17 *Philosophy* An immediate object of perception (as distinguished from substance, or a thing in itself). **3** E18 A very notable, extraordinary, or exceptional fact or occurrence; *colloquial* a thing, person, or animal remarkable for some unusual quality.

Phi Beta Kappa /ˌfʌɪ ˌbiːtə ˈkapə/ *noun phrase* M19 **Greek** (from the initial letters *phi, beta, kappa*, of *philosophia biou kubernētēs* philosophy the guide of life). (A member of) an intercollegiate society to which distinguished (usually undergraduate) scholars may be elected as an honour. Frequently *attributive. United States.*

philia /ˈfɪlɪə/ *noun* M20 **Greek**. Amity, friendship, liking.

philosophe /ˌfɪlə(ʊ)ˈzɒf/ *noun* OE **French** (from Latin *philosophus* from Greek *philosophos* lover of wisdom, from *philo-* from *philein* to love + *sophos* wise). A (sceptical) philosopher, *specifically* a member of the French rationalist group associated with the production of the *Encyclopédie* in the mid eighteenth century.

■ *Philosophe*, which was also occasionally found in Anglicized form as *philosoph*, appears in Old English in the general sense of *philosopher*, and during the Middle Ages the form *philosophe* was reinforced by Old French *philosophe* or *filosophe*. Since the Enlightenment, the word is mainly used in English for the French Encyclopedists or, derogatively, for those who emulate their sceptical stance or fall into similar errors.

1995 *Spectator* Diderot once complained to David Hume that *philosophes* 'preach wisdom to the deaf'.

philosophia perennis /fɪləˌsɒfɪə pəˈrɛnɪs/ *noun phrase* M19 **Latin** (= perennial philosophy). A posited core of philosophical truths independent of and unaffected by time or place, frequently taken to be exemplified in the writings of Aristotle and St Thomas Aquinas.

philosophia prima /fɪləˌsɒfɪə ˈpriːmə/ *noun phrase* E17 **Latin** (= first philosophy). (The branch of inquiry that deals with) the most general truths of philosophy; *specifically* (the branch of inquiry that deals with) the divine and the eternal.

phobia /ˈfəʊbɪə/ *noun* L18 **Latin** (independent use of the Latin suffix *-phobia* from Greek *-phobos* fearing, from *phobos* fear). (A) fear, (a) horror, (an) aversion; *especially* an abnormal and irrational fear or dread aroused by a particular object or circumstance.

■ *Phobia* as a suffix also appears in numerous abstract nouns, especially in modern coinages after the Greek denoting states in clinical psychology, such as AGORAPHOBIA, *arachnophobia* (E20) 'fear of spiders', etc., and in other (often jocular or nonce) formations such as *Anglophobia* (L18), *Francophobia* (L19), etc.

physique /fɪˈziːk/ *noun* E19 **French** (use as noun of adjective = physical). The form, size, and development of a person's body.

pi /pʌɪ/ *noun* LME **Greek** (in sense 2 representative of initial letter of Greek *peripheria* periphery; in sense 3 from the shape; in sense 4 after *pi-orbital* etc.). **1** LME The sixteenth letter (Π, π) of the Greek alphabet. **2** E18 *Mathematics* The ratio of the circumference of a circle to its diameter. Usually written π.

■ More recently (E20) pi (generally written π or Π and used attributively) has also become part of the technical vocabulary of Electricity (as *pi-network* etc.) and Physics and Chemistry (as π electron or Π molecule).

piaffe /piaf/ *verb & noun* M18 **French** (*piaffer* to strut, make a show). *Horsemanship* **A** *intransitive verb* M18 Move (especially on the spot) with a high slow trotting step. **B** *noun* L19 An act of piaffing.

pianissimo /pɪəˈnɪsɪməʊ/ *adverb, adjective, & noun* E18 **Italian** (superlative of PIANO). *Music* **A** *adverb & adjective* E18 (A direction:) very soft(ly). **B** *noun* L19 plural **pianissimos, pianissimi** /pɪəˈnɪsɪmi/ A very soft passage.

■ As a musical direction abbreviated to *pp* or *ppp*.

B 1996 *Times* And on top is that 'brilliant technique', . . . and floating pianissimos to melt the sternest critical heart.

piano /ˈpjɑːnəʊ/ *noun 1* plural **pianos, piani** /ˈpjɑːni/ M18 **Italian** (from Latin *planus* flat, (later of sound) soft, low). **1** M18 *Music* A soft or quiet passage. **2** M19 A flat or storey in an Italian building. Cf. PIANO NOBILE.

piano /pɪˈanəʊ/ *noun 2* plural **pianos** E19 **Italian** (abbreviation of PIANOFORTE or aphetized from FORTE-PIANO). **1** E19 A large keyboard musical instrument having metal strings struck by hammers and stopped by dampers, with two or three pedals to regulate the volume or length of the notes. **2** M20 The playing of this instrument.

piano /ˈpjɑːnəʊ/ *adverb & adjective* L17 **Italian** (from Latin *planus* flat, (later of sound) soft, low). **1** *adverb & adjective* L17 *Music* (A direction:) soft(ly), quiet(ly). **2** *adjective* E19 Of a person: quiet, subdued.

■ As a musical direction usually abbreviated to *p*.

pianoforte /pɪˌanəʊˈfɔːti/ *noun* M18 **Italian** (earlier *pian(o) e forte*, literally, 'soft and loud' (with reference to its capacity for gradation of tone); cf. FORTE-PIANO). A PIANO noun 2 sense 1.

piano nobile /ˌpjano ˈnobile/ *noun* L19 **Italian** (from *piano* floor, storey + *nobile* noble, great). *Architecture* The main (usually first-floor) storey of a large house, containing the principal rooms.

1995 *Spectator* To let in Bishopsgate is the lavish modern mansion built for Standard Chartered, complete with *piano nobile*.

piano piano /ˈpjano ˈpjano/ *adverb phrase* (also (earlier) **pian piano**) E17 **Italian** (= softly, softly). In a quiet leisurely manner; little by little.

piazza /pɪˈatsə/ *noun* L16 **Italian** (= French *place* (town) square). **1** L16 A public square or market-place, *especially* one in an Italian town. Formerly also, any open space surrounded by buildings. **2 a** M17 A covered gallery or walk surrounding an open square; a single such gallery or walk in front of a building. Now *rare*. **b** E18 The veranda of a house. Chiefly *United States*.

pibroch /ˈpiːbrɒk/, /ˈpiːbrɒx/ *noun* E18 **Gaelic** (*piobaireachd* the art of playing the bagpipe, from *pìobair* piper (from *pìob* pipe, from English *pipe*) + suffix of function *-achd*). A series of variations on a theme for the bagpipes, usually of a martial or funerary character.

picador /ˈpɪkədɔː/ *noun* L18 **Spanish** (from *picar* to prick, pierce). *Bullfighting* A person mounted on horseback who goads the bull with a lance.

picaresque /pɪkəˈrɛsk/ *adjective & noun* E19 **French** (from Spanish *picaresco*, from *pícaro* roguish, knavish, (noun) rogue; cf. next). **A** *adjective* **1** E19 Of or pertaining to rogues, knaves, or urchins; *especially* (of a style of especially Spanish fiction) dealing with the episodic adventures of such characters. **2** M20 Drifting; wandering.

picaro /ˈpɪkərəʊ/ *noun* plural **picaros** E17 **Spanish** (see PICARESQUE). A rogue, a scoundrel.

picayune /pɪkəˈjuːn/ *noun & adjective* E19 **French** (*picaillon* old copper coin of Piedmont, halfpence, cash from Provençal *picaioun*, of unknown origin). **A** *noun* E19 Originally (in the southern United States), a Spanish half-real, worth 6¼ cents. Now, a five-cent piece or other coin of small value; *colloquial* an insignificant or mean person or thing. **B** *adjective* E19 Mean, contemptible, insignificant. *North American colloquial*.

piccolo /ˈpɪkələʊ/ *noun & adjective* M19 **Italian** (= small). **A** *noun* plural **piccolos** **1** M19 A small flute sounding an octave higher than the ordinary flute; a player on this in an orchestra etc. **b** L19 An organ-stop having the tone of a piccolo. **2** M19 A small upright piano. **3** E20 A waiter's assistant in a hotel, restaurant, etc.; a page at a hotel. **4** M20 A jukebox. *United States slang*. **B** *adjective* M19 Designating the highest-pitched member of a family of musical instruments.

pickelhaube /ˈpɪk(ə)lˌ(h)aʊbə/ *noun* plural **pickelhaubes, pickelhauben** /ˈpɪk(ə)lˌ(h)aʊbən/ L19 **German**. *History* A spiked helmet worn by German soldiers, especially before and during the war of 1914–18.

1996 *Times* Their [sc. British policemen's] helmets were modelled on the Prussian pickelhaube . . .

picot /ˈpiːkəʊ/ *noun* E17 **French** (diminutive of *pic* peak, point, prick). Any of a series of small loops worked in lace or embroidery, used to form an ornamental edging, buttonhole, etc.

picotee /pɪkəˈtiː/ *noun & adjective* E18 **French** (*picoté(e)* past participle of *picoter* to mark with points, prick, from as PICOT). **A** *noun* E18 A variety of carnation, having light petals marked or edged with a darker colour. **B** *adjective* L19 Of a colour, pattern, etc.: resembling that of the picotee.

B 1996 *Country Life* The last variant [of busy lizzie] was the picotee type . . . and the next will have speckled flowers.

picquet variant of PIQUET.

pièce à thèse /pjɛs a tɛz/ *noun phrase* plural **pièces à thèse** (pronounced same) M20 **French**. A play written with the aim of supporting a thesis or proposition. Also called *thesis-play*.

pièce de circonstance /pjɛs də sirkɔ̃stɑ̃s/ *noun phrase* plural **pièces de circonstance** (pronounced same) M19 **French**. A literary composition, theory, etc., arising out of a particular situation.

pièce de résistance /pjɛs də rezistɑ̃s/, /pɪˌɛs də rɛˈzɪstɒ̃s/, /ˈrɛzɪstɒ̃s/ *noun phrase* plural **pièces de résistance** (pronounced same) L18 **French**. **1** L18 The most important or outstanding item. **2** M19 The main dish of a meal.

1 1996 *Country Life* The *pièce de résistance* was Thomas Cooper's enormous canvas, *The Monarch of the Meadows* . . .

pièce d'occasion /pjɛs dɔ̃kazjɔ̃/ *noun phrase* plural **pièces d'occasion** (pronounced same) L19 **French**. A literary or musical work written for a special occasion.

1996 *Country Life* Another *pièce d'occasion*, created for San Francisco's United We Dance festival which, in 1995, celebrated the 50th anniversary of the United Nations Charter, Bruce's *Meeting Point* overcomes its Nyman score . . . with far greater success.

pièce noire /pjɛs nwar/ *noun phrase* plural **pièces noires** (pronounced same) M20 **French** (literally, 'black play'). A play or film with a tragic or macabre theme.

■ The phrase originated with French dramatist Jean Anouilh (1910–87); see PIÈCE ROSE.

pièce rose /pjɛs roz/ *noun phrase* plural **pièces roses** (pronounced same) M20 **French** (literally, 'pink play'). A play or film with a pleasantly entertaining theme; a comedy.

■ *Pièces roses* and *Pièces noires* were the titles given by Anouilh to collections of his plays published in 1942, roughly analogous to George Bernard Shaw's *Plays: Pleasant and Unpleasant*.

pièces à thèse, **pièces de circonstance** etc. plurals of PIÈCE À THÈSE, PIÈCE DE CIRCONSTANCE, etc.

pied-à-terre /ˌpjeɪdɑːˈtɛː/ *noun* plural **pieds-à-terre** (pronounced same) E19 **French** (literally, 'foot to earth'). A small town house, flat, or room used for short periods of residence; a home base.

1995 *Country Life* The ideal pied-à-terre should be compact, easy and economical to run, well placed for the City, the West End or escape routes to the country, and secure without being claustrophobic.

pied d'éléphant /pje delefɑ̃/ *noun phrase* plural **pieds d'éléphant** (pronounced same) M20 **French** (literally, 'elephant's foot'). A padded sack used to protect the lower part of the body on a bivouac when mountaineering etc.

pied noir /pje nwar/ *noun phrase* plural **pieds noirs** (pronounced same) M20 **French** (literally, 'black foot'). A person of European origin who lived in Algeria during French rule.

■ Competing explanations of the sobriquet are based either on the black shoes worn by Europeans but not by native Algerians or on the traditional employment of barefooted Algerians as stokers on French steamers.

pieds-à-terre, **pieds d'éléphant**, etc. plurals of PIED-À-TERRE, PIED D'ÉLÉPHANT, etc.

pierrette /pɪəˈrɛt/, /pjɛˈrɛt/ *noun* L19 **French** (feminine diminutive of *Pierre* Peter, corresponding to next). A female member of a company of pierrots.

pierrot /ˈpɪərəʊ/, /ˈpjɛrəʊ/ *noun* (also **Pierrot**) M18 **French** (appellative use of pet-form of *Pierre* Peter). A typical character in French pantomime. Now also, a musical entertainer with a whitened face and a loose white costume.

Pietà /pɪeɪˈtɑː/, *foreign* /pjeˈtɑː/ *noun* M17 **Italian** (from Latin *pietas* piety). A painting or sculpture representing the Virgin Mary holding the dead body of Jesus on her lap or in her arms.

pietas /piːˈeɪtɑːs/ *noun* E20 **Latin**. An attitude of respect towards an ancestor, institution, etc.

pietra commessa /piˌetra komˈmessa/ *noun phrase* plural **pietre commesse** /pi ˌetre komˈmesse/ M17 **Italian** (literally, 'stone fitted together'). (An example of) mosaic work.

pietra dura /piˌetra ˈdura/ *noun phrase* plural **pietre dure** /piˌetre ˈdure/ E19 **Italian** (literally, 'hard stone'). Semiprecious stones; *singular* and in *plural*, mosaic work of such stones.

pietre commesse, **pietre dure** plurals of PIETRA COMMESSA, PIETRA DURA.

pignon /piŋɔ̃/ *noun* plural pronounced same E17 **French** (= Spanish *piñon*, Portuguese *pinhão*, all from late Latin derivation of Latin *pinea* pine cone). The edible seed of the stone pine, *Pinus pinea*, of southern Europe.

pikau /ˈpiːkaʊ/ *noun & verb* M19 **Maori**. **A** *noun* M19 A pack for carrying on the back, a knapsack. **B** *transitive verb* L19 Carry (a load or pack) on the back. *New Zealand*.

piki /ˈpiːki/ *noun* L19 **Hopi** (*pí:ki*). Maize-meal bread in the form of very thin sheets, made by the Hopi Indians of the south-western United States.

pilau /pɪˈlaʊ/, /ˈpiːlaʊ/ *noun* (also **pilaff** /pɪˈlaf/, **pilaw** /pɪˈlɔː/, **pulao** /pəˈlaʊ/, and other variants) E17 **Turkish** (*pilâv* cooked rice = Persian *pīlaw* boiled rice and meat). An Indian or Middle Eastern dish of rice (or occasionally other grain) cooked in stock with spices and often meat, fish, vegetables, etc.

pileus /ˈpʌɪlɪəs/ *noun* plural **pilei** /ˈpʌɪlɪʌɪ/ M18 **Latin** (= felt cap). **1** M18 *Botany* The spore-bearing circular structure surmounting the stipe in a mushroom or toadstool, which has an undersurface composed of radiating plates or gills. Also called *cap*. **2** L18 *Classical Antiquities* L18 A felt cap without a brim.

pilón /piˈlon/, /piːˈləʊn/ *noun* plural **pilones** /piˈlones/, /piːˈləʊnɪz/ L19 **Mexican Spanish** (from Spanish = sugar loaf, pillar, post). In Mexico and the south-western United States: a small gift given to a customer making a purchase etc.

pilotis /pilɔti/ *noun plural* M20 **French**. *Architecture* A series of columns or piles, used to raise the base of a building above ground level.

pilpul /ˈpɪlp(ə)l/ *noun* L19 **Hebrew** (from *pilpēl* to search, debate hotly). (An instance of) subtle or keen rabbinical disputation; *transferred* unprofitable argument, hair-splitting.

pimento /pɪˈmɛntəʊ/ *noun & adjective* L17 **Spanish** (PIMIENTO). **A** *noun* plural **pimentos** **1** Cayenne pepper. Only in L17. **2** L17 The spice allspice; (more fully *pimento tree*) the West Indian tree, *Pimenta dioica*, of the myrtle family, from which allspice is obtained. Now *West Indies*. **3** E20 A sweet (especially a red) pepper, a capsicum. **B** *adjective* M20 Pimento red.

pimiento /pɪmɪˈɛntəʊ/, /pɪmˈjɛntəʊ/ *noun* plural **pimientos** (also written **pimienta** /pɪmɪˈɛntə/) M17 **Spanish** (from Latin *pigmentum* paint, colour). **1** M17 PIMENTO sense 2. *West Indies*. **2** M19 PIMENTO sense 3.

pina colada /ˌpiːnə kəˈlɑːdə/ *noun* (also **piña colada** /ˌpiːnjə kəˈlɑːdə/, *foreign* /ˌpiɲa koˈlaa/ E20 **South American Spanish** (literally, 'strained pineapple' from *piña* (Portuguese *pinha*) pineapple, (originally pine cone, from Latin *pinea* pine cone). A drink made with pineapple juice, rum, and coconut (milk).

1975 P. Moyes *Black Widower* In the bar itself, ice tinkled merrily into tall glasses of rum punch and *pina colada* . . .

pinard /pinar/ *noun* (also **Pinard**) plural pronounced same E20 **French**. Rough red wine; *generally* any wine; a glass of this.

piñata /pɪˈnjɑːtə/ *noun* L19 **Spanish** (= jug, pot). In Mexico and the south-western United States: a decorated container filled with sweets or small gifts, which is opened (especially by breaking) by a blindfolded person at a festive celebration.

pinax /ˈpɪnaks/ *noun* plural **pinaces** /ˈpɪnəsiːz/ L17 **Latin** (from Greek = board, plank, tablet, picture). **1** L17 A tablet; a list inscribed on this; a catalogue, an index. Now *rare* or *obsolete*. **2** M19 *Antiquities* A (painted or engraved) plate, platter, or dish.

pince-nez /pansˈneɪ/, *foreign* /pɛ̃sne/ *noun* (treated as *singular* or *plural*) L19 **French** (from *pincer* to pinch + *nez* nose). A pair of eyeglasses kept in position by a spring clipping the nose rather than by ear-pieces.

pinetum /pʌɪˈniːtəm/ *noun* plural **pineta**, /pʌɪˈniːtə/ M19 **Latin** (from *pinus* pine). A plantation or collection of pines or other conifers, for scientific or ornamental purposes.

pinga /ˈpiŋa/ *noun* M20 **Portuguese** (literally, 'drop (of water)'). A raw white rum distilled from sugar cane in Brazil; a drink of this.

pingo /ˈpɪŋgəʊ/ *noun* plural **pingo(e)s** M20 **Eskimo** ((Inuit) *pinguq* NUNATAK). *Physical Geography* A persistent low conical or dome-shaped mound, often with a crater on top, formed in regions with thin or discontinuous permafrost; a round depression in temperate regions thought to be the remains of such a mound.

pinole /pɪˈnəʊleɪ/ *noun* M19 **American Spanish** (from Aztec *pinolli*). Parched cornflour mixed with the flour of mesquite beans, sugar, and spice. *United States*.

piñon /pɪˈnjɒn/, /ˈpɪnjən/ *noun* plural **piñons**, **piñones** /pɪˈnjəʊnɪz/ M19 **Spanish** (cf. French PIGNON). (The edible seed of) any of a group of small pines of south-western North America. Also, the wood of these trees.

pinto /ˈpɪntəʊ/ *adjective & noun* plural **pintos** M19 **Spanish** (= painted, mottled, from Proto-Romance). **A** *adjective*. **1** M19 Of a horse: piebald; skewbald. **2** E20 *pinto bean*, a variety of kidney bean with mottled seeds, widely cultivated in Central America and the south-western United States; the seed of this. **B** *noun* M19 A piebald horse.

■ With reference to horses, chiefly North American.

piob mhor /piːp ˈvɔːr/, /piːəb/ *noun phrase* M19 **Gaelic** (*piob mhòr*, literally, 'big pipe'). A kind of bagpipes traditionally played in the Scottish Highlands.

piolet /pjəʊˈleɪ/ *noun* M19 **French** ((Savoy dialect) diminutive of *piolo*, apparently cognate with *pioche*, *pic* pickaxe). A two-headed ice-axe used by mountaineers.

piperade /pɪpəˈrɑːd/, *foreign* /pipərad/ (*plural same*) *noun* M20 **French**. A dish originating in the Basque country, consisting of eggs scrambled with tomatoes and peppers.

pipette /pɪˈpɛt/ *noun & verb* (also **pipet**) M19 **French** (diminutive of *pipe* pipe). **A** *noun* M19 A frequently tubular device for transferring or measuring small quantities of a liquid or gas by means of aspiration and dispensation, used especially in scientific laboratories. **B** M19 *transitive verb* inflected *pipette*, **pipete**. Transfer, measure, draw *off* or *out*, (a liquid or gas) with a pipette.

pipkrake /ˈpɪpkreɪk/, /ˈpɪpkrɑːkə/ *noun* plural **pipkrakes**, **pipkraker** /ˈpɪpkrɑːkə/ M20 **Swedish** ((dialect) from *pip* pipe + *krake* variant of *klake* frozen ground). *Physical Geography* An ice-needle; needle ice.

piquant /ˈpiːk(ə)nt/, /ˈpiːkɑːnt/ *adjective* (in senses 2 and 3 also **piquante** /pɪˈkɑːnt/) E16 **French** (present participial adjective of *piquer* to prick, sting). **1** E16 Sharp or stinging to the feelings; severe, bitter. Long *archaic*. **2** M17 Of food etc.: agreeably pungent, sharp-tasting, spicy; savoury, appetizing. **3** M17 Pleasantly stimulating to the mind; racy, spicy; fascinating, charming.

pique /piːk/ *noun* M16 **French** (literally, 'pike', figuratively, 'cutting remark', from *piquer* to prick, pierce, sting, irritate, *se piquer* take offence, from Proto-Romance, origin uncertain). **1** M16 A quarrel or feeling of enmity between two or more people; ill feeling, animosity. **2** L16 (A feeling of) anger or resentment resulting from a slight or injury, especially to one's pride; offence taken.

■ Also early (M17) in English use as verb.

piqué /ˈpiːkeɪ/ *noun, adjective, & verb* (also **pique** M19 **French** (use as noun of past participle of *piquer* to backstitch). **A** *noun* **1** M19 A stiff fabric woven in a strongly ribbed or raised pattern (originally in imitation of hand quilting); the raised pattern (characteristic) of such a fabric. **2** L19 Work inlaid with gold etc. dots. **3** M20 *Ballet* A step directly on to the point of the leading foot without bending the knee. **B** *adjective* **1** M19 *Cookery* Larded. *rare*. **2** L19 Made of piqué; having the pattern of piqué. **3** L19 Inlaid with gold etc. dots. **4** *Ballet* E20 Stepping directly on to the point of the leading foot without bending the knee. **C** *transitive verb* M19 *Cookery* Lard.

piquet /pɪˈkɛt/ *noun* (also **picquet**) M17 **French** (of unknown origin). A card-game for two players with a pack of 32 cards, the cards from the two to the six being excluded.

piqûre /pikyr/ *noun* (also **piqure**) plural pronounced same E20 **French** (from *piquer*; see PIQUE). A hypodermic injection; a puncture made in the skin by such an injection.

piranha /pɪˈrɑːnə/, /pɪˈrɑːnjə/ *noun* M18 **Portuguese** (from Tupi *pirán*ʸ*e*, *piráya*, from *pirá* fish + *sainha* tooth). Any of several gregarious predatory freshwater fishes of South America, noted for their aggressiveness and voracity.

piri-piri /ˈpɪrɪpɪri/ *noun* M20 **Ronga** (= pepper). A sauce made with red peppers. Also *piri-piri sauce*.

pirog /pɪˈrɒg/ *noun* plural **pirogi** /pɪˈrɒgi/, **pirogen** /pɪˈrɒgən/ M19 **Russian**. A large Russian pie. Cf. PIROSHKI.

pirogue /pɪˈrəʊg/ *noun* E17 **French** (probably from Carib). A long narrow canoe. Also, any canoe or open boat.

piroshki /pɪˈrɒʃki/ *noun plural* (also **pirotchki** /pɪˈrɒtʃki/, **pirozhki** /pɪˈrɒzki/) E20 **Russian** (*pirozhki* plural of *pirozhok* diminutive of PIROG). Small Russian pastries or patties filled with meat, fish, rice, etc.

pirouette /pɪrʊˈɛt/ *noun & verb* M17 **French** (ultimate origin unknown). **A** *noun* **1** M17 *Horsemanship* A full circle made by pivoting on a hind leg while walking or cantering. **2** E18 An act of spinning round on one foot or on the points of the toes by a ballet dancer etc.; *generally* a rapid whirl of the body. **3** L19 *Music* A form of mouthpiece used with a shawm, rackett, etc. **B** *intransitive verb* E19 Perform a pirouette.

pirozhki variant of PIROSHKI.

pis aller /pizale/ (*plural same*), /piːz ˈaleɪ/ *noun* L17 **French** (from *pis* worse + *aller* to go). The worst that can be or happen; a last resort.

piscina /pɪ'siːnə/, /pɪ'sʌɪnə/ *noun* plural **piscinas**, **piscinae** /pɪ'siːniː/ L16 **Latin** (= fish-pond, in medieval Latin in sense 2, from *piscis* fish). **1** L16 A fish-pond. Also (*historical*), a pool or pond for bathing or swimming. **2** L18 *Ecclesiastical* A stone basin for draining water used in the Mass.

pisé /pize/, /'piːzeɪ/ *noun & adjective* (also **pisée**) L18 **French** (use as noun of past participle of *piser* to beat, pound, stamp (earth), from Latin *pinsere*). **A** *noun* L18 A building material of stiff clay or earth, sometimes mixed with gravel, forced between boards which are removed as it hardens; building with this material. Also *pisé de terre* /də tɛr/, /də tɛː/ (= of earth). Also called *terre pisée*. **B** *attributive* or as *adjective* M19 Made with or using *pisé*.

pissaladière /pisaladjɛr/ *noun* (also **pissaladiera** /pisaladjera/) M20 **French** (from Provençal *pissaladiero*, from *pissala* salt fish). A Provençal open tart similar to pizza, usually with onions, anchovies, and black olives.

pissoir /piswar/ (*plural same*), /piː'swɑː/, /'pɪswɑː/ *noun* E20 **French**. A public urinal, especially in France.

> **1996** *Bookseller* If I call this *pissoir* a great work of art and sign it, who are you to disprove that?

piste /piːst/ *noun* E18 **French** (= track, from Latin *pista* (sc. *via*) beaten track, from feminine past participle of *pinsere* to pound, stamp). **1** E18 A trail or track beaten by a horse or other animal; the track of a racecourse or training ground. **2** E20 The specially marked-out rectangular playing area in fencing. **3** E20 A specially prepared or marked slope or trail of compacted snow used as a ski-run.

pistou /pistu/, /'piːstuː/ *noun* M20 **Provençal** (= Italian PESTO). A sauce or paste made from crushed basil, garlic, cheese, etc., used especially in Provençal dishes; a thick vegetable soup made with this.

pita variant of PITTA.

pithos /'pɪθɒs/ *noun* plural **pithoi** /'pɪθɔɪ/ L19 **Greek**. *Archaeology* A large spherical wide-mouthed earthenware jar used for holding wine, oil, food, etc.

piton /'piːtɒn/ *noun* L19 **French** (= eye-bolt). **1** L19 *Mountaineering* A metal spike which is hammered into rock or ice and used to secure a rope through an eye at one end. **2** E20 A (steep-sided) volcanic peak, especially in the West Indies.

pitta /'pɪtə/ *noun* (also **pita**) M20 **Modern Greek** (*pētta*, *pit(t)a* bread, cake, pie; cf. Turkish *pide*, Aramaic *pittā* in similar sense). A flat unleavened bread of Mediterranean and Arab countries, which can be cut open to receive a filling.

più /pjuː/ *adverb* E18 **Italian**. *Music* More.

■ Used in directions, as in *più mosso* more animated(ly).

pizza /'piːtsə/ *noun* L19 **Italian** (= pie). A flat usually round base of dough baked with a topping of tomatoes, cheese, meat, olives, etc.

pizzeria /ˌpiːtsə'riːə/ *noun* M20 **Italian**. A place where pizzas are made or sold.

pizzicato /ˌpɪtsɪ'kɑːtəʊ/ *noun, adjective, & adverb* M19 **Italian** (past participle of *pizzicare* to pinch, twitch, from *pizzare*, from Old and Modern Italian *pizza* point, edge). *Music* **A** *noun* plural **pizzicati** /ˌpɪtsɪ'kɑːti/, **pizzicatos**. M19 A note or passage played on a violin, cello, etc., by plucking a string with the finger instead of bowing. **B** *adjective & adverb* L19 (Played) by plucking a string instead of bowing.

placebo /plə'siːbəʊ/ *noun* plural **placebo(e)s** ME **Latin** (= I shall please or be acceptable (first word of Psalm 114:9), 1st person singular future indicative of *placere* to please). **1** ME *Roman Catholic Church* The vespers for the dead, from the initial word of the antiphon formerly used to open the office. **2** LME–L18 A flatterer, a sycophant. **3** L18 A pill, medicine, procedure, etc., prescribed more for the psychological benefit to the patient of being given a prescription than for any physiological effect. Also, a substance with no therapeutic effect used as a control in testing new drugs etc.; a blank sample in a test.

> **3 1996** *New Scientist* However, the day when the placebo effect becomes a respectable medical tool is still some way off.

place d'armes /plas darm/ *noun phrase* plural **places d'armes** (pronounced same) E18 **French** (= place of arms). An assembly point for troops, weapons, or ammunition; a parade ground; an arsenal.

placement /plasmɑ̃/ *noun* M19 **French** (from *placer* to place, seat (guests)). The allocation of places to people at a dining-table etc. Also *place à table*.

■ Also fully naturalized, with pronunciation /'pleɪsm(ə)nt/, in the sense of 'the action or an act of placing or positioning a thing or person', especially '(a period of) attachment to a workplace or educational establishment other than one's own'.

1962 J. Le Carré *Murder of Quality* If you . . . make a fault in the *placement* of your dinner guests . . . D'Arcy will find you out.

places d'armes plural of PLACE D'ARMES.

placet /'pleɪsɛt/, /'plakɛt/ *interjection & noun* L16 **Latin** (= it pleases, 3rd person singular present indicative of *placere* to please). **A** *interjection* L16 Expressing assent to a vote in a council or assembly of a university, Church, etc. **B** *noun* L16 Assent or sanction (as) by an utterance of '*placet*'.

plafond /plafɔ̃/ (*plural same*) *noun* **M17 French** (from *plat* flat + *fond* bottom). **1** M17 *Architecture* An ornately decorated ceiling, either flat or vaulted; painting or decoration on a ceiling. Also, a soffit. **2** M20 *Cards* An early form of contract bridge.

plage /plaʒ/, *in sense 4* /pleɪdʒ/ *noun* **LME Old French** (= region, (modern) beach (from Italian *piaggia*) from medieval Latin *plaga* open space). **1** LME–E17 A region, a district; a zone. **2** LME–M17 Each of the four principal directions or quarters of the compass; a direction, a side. **3** L19 A beach or promenade at a seaside resort, especially at a fashionable one; a seaside resort. **4** M20 *Astronomy* A bright region of the sun's chromosphere, usually associated with sunspots. Also *plage region*.

planche /plɑːnʃ/ *noun* **E20 French** (literally, 'plank'). *Gymnastics* A position in which the body is held parallel to the ground, especially by the arms (as on the parallel bars etc.).

planchette /plɑːn'ʃɛt/ *noun* **M19 French** (diminutive of *planche* plank, (wooden) board). **1** M19 A small usually heart-shaped board, supported by two castors and a vertical pencil, which, when one or more people rest their fingers lightly on the board, supposedly writes automatic messages under spirit guidance. **2** M20 A small shallow dish used to hold a sample while its radioactivity is measured.

planctus /'plaŋktəs/ *noun* plural same /'plaŋktuːs/ **E20 Latin** (= beating of the breast, lamentation). A medieval poem or song of lament.

plastique /pla'stiːk/, *foreign* /plastik/ (*plural same*) *noun* **L19 French** (use as noun of adjective = plastic, from Latin *plasticus* from Greek *plastikos* from *plastos* past participle of *plassein* to mould, form). **1** L19 *Dance* Statuesque poses or slow graceful movements; the art or technique of performing these. **2** E20 A plastic substance used for modelling. **3** M20 Plastic explosive; a plastic bomb.

plastiqueur /plastikœr/, /'plastɪkə/ (*plural same*) *noun* **M20 French** (from as PLASTIQUE). A person who plants or detonates a plastic bomb.

plat /pla/ *noun* plural pronounced same **M18 French**. A dish of food.

plat du jour /pla dy ʒur/ *noun phrase* plural pronounced same **E20 French** (= dish of the day). A dish specially featured on a restaurant's menu for a particular day.

1996 *Spectator* Another *plat du jour* was breast of pheasant in a port wine sauce . . .

plateau /'platəʊ/ *noun & adjective* plural **plateaux** /'platəʊz/, **plateaus** **L18 French** (Old French *platel*, from *plat* wide, flat, from popular Latin, from Greek *platus* broad, flat). **A** *noun* **1** L18 *Physical Geography* An elevated tract of comparatively flat or level land; a tableland. **b** L19 *transferred* A more or less level portion of a graph or trace (originally, of the pulse) adjacent to a lower sloping portion; a stage, condition, or period when there is neither an increase nor a decrease in something. **2** L18 An ornamented tray or dish for table-service. **B** E20 *attributive* or as *adjective* Of the nature of or pertaining to a plateau.

platteland /'platəland/ *noun* **M20 Afrikaans** (from Dutch *plat* flat + *land* country). The remote rural inland part of South Africa.

■ In South Africa often used attributively with derogatory connotations of backwardness and reaction, as in 'platteland mentality'.

platzel /'plats(ə)l/ *noun* **M20 Yiddish** (perhaps related to German *Plätzchen* fancy biscuit). A flat crisp bread roll.

playa /'plʌɪə/ *noun* **M19 Spanish** (= shore, beach, coast, from late Latin *plagia* open space). **1** M19 A flat area of silt or sand, free of vegetation and usually salty, lying at the bottom of a desert basin and dry except after rain; (more fully *playa lake*) a temporary lake formed in such an area. **2** M19 In Spain and Spanish-speaking countries: a beach. **3** L19 *Geography* Flat alluvial coastland.

■ Originally United States.

plaza /'plɑːzə/ *noun* L17 **Spanish** (from Proto-Romance source of *place*). A marketplace, square, or open public space, originally in Spain and Spanish-speaking countries; (chiefly *North America*) a large paved area surrounded by or adjacent to buildings, especially as a feature of a shopping complex.

plectrum /'plɛktrəm/ *noun* plural **plectrums, plectra** /'plɛktrə/ LME **Latin** (from Greek *plēktron* anything to strike with, from *plēssein* to strike). **1** LME Originally (*rare*), a device for tightening the strings of a harp. Now, a thin flat piece of horn, metal, plastic, etc., held in the hand and used to pluck the strings of a guitar, lyre, etc. Also, the corresponding mechanical part of a harpsichord etc. **2** E19 *Anatomy* and *Zoology* A small process, a single thick bristle.

plein-air /plɛnɛr/ *adjective* L19 **French** (from EN PLEIN AIR (literally, 'in full air')). Designating a style or school of impressionist painting originating in France during the late 1860s, which sought to represent the transient effects of atmosphere and light by direct observation from nature. Also, designating a work painted out of doors or representing an outdoor scene and painted with a spontaneous technique.

■ Also as a noun phrase *plein air.*

1995 *Spectator* . . . most of the Impressionist canvases on show smell of lamp-oil rather than *plein air.*

plein-airisme /plɛnɛrism/ *noun* M20 **French** (from as PLEIN-AIR). The theories and practices of the *plein-air* school of painters.

plein-airiste /plɛnɛrist/ *noun* L19 **French** (from as PLEIN-AIR). A painter of the *plein-air* school.

plein jeu /plɛ̃ ʒø/ *adverb, adjective, & noun phrase* M19 **French** (= full play). *Music* **A** *adverb & adjective phrase* M19 (A direction:) with full power; *specifically* without reeds in organ playing. **B** *noun* M19 A type of mixture stop in an organ; music written for the full organ.

plenum /'pliːnəm/ *noun & adjective* L17 **Latin** (neuter of *plenus* full (sc. *spatium* space); in sense 2 later influenced by Russian *plenum* plenary session). **A** *noun* **1** L17 *Physics* A space completely filled with matter; *specifically* the whole of space regarded as being so filled. **b** L18 *transferred* A condition of fullness; a full place. **2** L18 A full assembly; a meeting of a legislative body, conference, association, etc., at which all the members are expected to be present; *specifically* a meeting of all the members of a Communist Party committee. **3** M20 (The air in) a plenum chamber in a ventilation system etc. **B** *attributive* or as *adjective* E20 Pertaining to or designating an artificial ventilation system in which fresh air is forced into a building and drives out the stale air.

pleroma /plə'rəʊmə/ *noun* M18 **Greek** (*plērōma* that which fills, from *plēroun* to make full, from *plērēs* full). *Theology* **1** M18 In Gnosticism, the spiritual universe as the abode of God and of the totality of the divine powers and emanations. **2** E19 The totality of the Godhead which dwells in Christ; completeness, fullness (with allusion to Colossians 2:9).

plethora /'plɛθ(ə)rə/ *noun* M16 **Late Latin** (from Greek *plēthōrē* fullness, repletion, from *plēthein* to be full). **1** M16 *Medicine* Originally a condition characterized by an excess of blood or a bodily humour; later, an excess of red blood cells. **2** E18 Overfullness, oversupply; a glut.

■ Sense 2 is now the only current sense, as sense 1, except in historical contexts, is rare or obsolete.

2 1996 *Times Magazine* . . . I read the plethora of faxes detailing where and whither I am to be sent . . .

plié /plije/ *noun* plural pronounced same L19 **French** (past participle of *plier* to bend). *Ballet* A movement in which the knees are bent outwards in line with the out-turned feet.

plique à jour /plik a ʒur/ *noun* L19 **French** (literally, 'braid that lets in the daylight'). A technique in enamelling in which small areas of translucent enamel are fused into the spaces of a wire framework to give an effect similar to stained glass.

plissé /'pliːseɪ/, *foreign* /plise/, (*plural of noun same*) *noun & adjective* L19 **French** (past participle of *plisser* to pleat). **A** *noun* L19 Originally, a piece of fabric shirred or gathered into narrow pleats; a gathering of pleats. Now usually, fabric with a wrinkled or puckered finish produced by chemical treatment. **B** *adjective* L19 Formed into small pleats; treated so as to give a wrinkled or puckered effect.

plombière /ˌplɒmbɪˈɛː/ *noun* M19 **French** (*Plombières*-les-Bains, a village in the Vosges department of eastern France). A kind of dessert made with ice-cream and glacé fruits.

plongeur /plɔ̃ʒœr/ *noun* plural pronounced same M20 **French** (from *plonger* to plunge, immerse in liquid). A person employed as a menial in a restaurant or hotel, especially to wash dishes.

■ The word entered English via George Orwell's account of menial labour in *Down and Out in Paris and London* (1933).

plumeau /plymo/ *noun* plural **plumeaux** /plymo/ L19 **French** (from *plume* from Latin *pluma* small soft feather). A duvet.

plus ça change /ply sa ʃɑ̃ʒ/ *interjection & noun phrase* E20 **French** (shortened form of *plus ça change, plus c'est la même chose*). The more things change, the more they remain the same.

■ The observation was originally made by the French author and satirical journalist Alphonse Karr (1808–90) writing in *Les Guêpes* (January 1849).

1995 *Times* Both have printed reams of photographs through the decades. The pictures are shockingly similar—a serious case of *plus ça change.*

Pluvius /ˈpluːvɪəs/ *adjective* E20 **Latin** (= rainy, causing or bringing rain). Designating the insurance of holidays, outdoor sports and events, etc., against disruption by bad weather.

■ Frequently in the phrase *Pluvius policy.*

p.m. abbreviation of POST MERIDIEM.

pneuma /ˈnjuːmə/ *noun* L19 **Greek** (= wind, breath, spirit, that which is blown or breathed, from *pneein, pnein* to blow, breathe). The spirit of a person, as opposed to the soul; the breath of life.

■ In Stoic and Epicurean philosophy the *pneuma* was a person's vital force or energy, but modern usage takes its cue from the New Testament distinction between the spirit and the soul or PSYCHE (cf. 1 Thessalonians 5.23).

poblador /ˌpoblaˈdor/ *noun* plural **pobladores** /ˌpoblaˈdores/ M20 **Spanish.** In Spanish America: a settler, a colonist; *specifically* a country person who moves to settle or squat in a town.

pochade /pɔʃad/ (*plural same*), /pɒˈʃɑːd/ *noun* L19 **French** (from *pocher* to sketch (roughly), blur). A rough, smudgy, or blurred sketch.

poché /ˈpɒʃeɪ/, *foreign* /pɔʃe/ *noun* E20 **French** (use as noun of past participle of *pocher* to sketch). *Architecture* Shading on an architectural plan representing the solid parts of a building; the use of such shading.

pochette /pɒˈʃɛt/ *noun* L19 **French. 1** L19 A small violin, as used by French dancing-masters. **2** E20 A small pocket. **3** E20 A handbag shaped like an envelope. Also *pochette bag.*

pochismo /poˈtʃizmo/ *noun* plural **pochismos** /poˈtʃizmos/ M20 **Mexican Spanish** (from as POCHO). A form of slang consisting of English words given a Mexican Spanish form or pronunciation; a word of this sort.

■ An example of a *pochismo* is *lonche* for 'lunch'.

pocho /ˈpotʃo/ *noun & adjective* plural of noun **pochos** /ˈpotʃos/ M20 **Mexican Spanish** (= Spanish *pocho* discoloured, pale, faded). (Designating or pertaining to) a citizen of the United States of Mexican origin or a culturally Americanized Mexican. Often *derogatory.*

pochoir /pɔʃwar/ *noun* plural pronounced same M20 **French** (= stencil). A process used in book illustration, especially for limited editions, in which a monochrome print is coloured by hand, using a series of stencils; a print made by this process.

pococurante /ˌpəʊkəʊkjʊˈranteɪ/ *noun & adjective* M18 **Italian** (from *poco* little + *curante* caring). **A** *noun* M18 A careless, indifferent, or nonchalant person. Now *rare.* **B** *adjective* E19 Caring little; careless, indifferent, nonchalant.

pocosin /pəˈkəʊsɪn/ *noun* (also **poquosin**) M17 **Algonquian** (probably from Algonquian *poquosin*). In the southern United States: a tract of low swampy ground, usually wooded; a marsh, a swamp.

podium /ˈpəʊdɪəm/ *noun* plural **podia** /ˈpəʊdɪə/, (in branch I also) **podiums** M18 **Latin** (= elevated place, balcony from Greek *podion* diminutive of *pous, pod-* foot). **I 1** M18 A raised platform surrounding the arena in an ancient amphitheatre. **2** L18 *Architecture* **a** A continuous projecting base or pedestal, a stylobate. **b** M20 A projecting lower structure around the base of a tower block. **3** M20 A raised platform or dais at the front of a hall or stage; *specifically* one occupied by the conductor of an orchestra. **II 4** M19 *Zoology* A foot; an organ acting as a foot.

podzol /ˈpɒdzɒl/ *noun* (also **podsol** /ˈpɒdsɒl/) E20 **Russian** (from *pod-* under + *zola* ash; variant altered after *-sol* from Latin *solum* soil). *Soil Science* An acidic, generally infertile soil characterized by a white or grey subsurface layer resembling ash, and occurring especially under coniferous woods or heaths in moist, usually temperate climates.

poêlée /pwale/ *noun* M19 **French** (literally, 'panful', from *poêler* to cook in a pan). A broth or stock made with bacon and vegetables.

poète maudit /pɔɛt modi/ *noun phrase* plural **poètes maudits** (pronounced same) M20 **French** (literally, 'cursed poet'). A poet or other creative artist who is insufficiently appreciated by his or her contemporaries.

■ *Les Poètes maudits* (1884) was the title of a study of several such poets by the French Symbolist poet Paul Verlaine (1844–96).

1977 *Time* Once the ignored art, photography now stands robed in puffery, and . . . like painting, . . . has acquired its cast of heroes and *poètes maudits*.

poffertje /ˈpɔfərtjə/ *noun* (also **poffertjie** /ˈpɔfərtʃə/) L19 **Dutch** (*poffertje*, Afrikaans *poffertjie*, from French *pouffer* to blow up). A small light doughnut or fritter dusted with sugar, as made in the Low Countries and South Africa.

pogrom /ˈpɒgrəm/, /ˈpɒgrɒm/, /pəˈgrɒm/ *noun & verb* E20 **Russian** (= devastation, from *gromit'* to destroy by violent means). **A** *noun* **1** E20 An organized massacre in Russia, originally and especially of Jews. **2** E20 *generally* An organized, officially tolerated, attack on any community or group. **B** *transitive verb* E20 Massacre or destroy in a pogrom.

poi /pɔɪ/ *noun* E19 **Polynesian** (cf. POIPOI). A Hawaiian dish made from the fermented root of the taro. Also = POIPOI.

poilu /ˈpwɑːluː/, *foreign* /pwaly/ (*plural same*) *noun* E20 **French** (= hairy, virile, from Latin *pilus* hair). A soldier in the French army. *especially* one who fought in the war of 1914–18.

■ Slang, alluding to the unkempt appearance.

point /pwɛ̃/ *noun* plural pronounced same M17 **French** (= stitch). Needle-lace.)

■ Chiefly in *point de* (or *d'*) /d(ə)/ (of), specifying a real or supposed place of manufacture, as *point d'Alençon*, *point d'Angleterre*, *point de France*, *point de Paris*, *point de Venise*, etc. Cf. PETIT POINT.

point d'appui /pwɛ̃ dapɥi/ *noun phrase* E19 **French** (= point of support). A fulcrum; a strategic point.

point de départ /pwɛ̃ də depar/ *noun phrase* E20 **French**. A point of departure.

point de repère /pwɛ̃ də rəpɛr/ *noun phrase* L19 **French**. A point of reference.

point d'orgue /pwɛ̃ dɔrg/ *noun phrase* L19 **French**. An organ-point, a pedal-point.

pointe /pwɛ̃t/ *noun* plural pronounced same M19 **French**. *Dancing* The tip of the toe. Also, a dance movement executed on the tips of the toes.

pointillé /pwɛ̃tije/ *adjective* E20 **French** (past participle of *pointiller* to mark with dots). Ornamented with designs engraved or drawn with a sharp-pointed tool or style.

pointillisme /pwɛ̃tijism/ *noun* (also **pointillism** /ˈpwantɪlɪz(ə)m/) E20 **French** (*pointillisme*, from *pointiller* to mark with dots, from *pointille* from Italian *puntiglio* diminutive of *punto* point). **1** E20 A technique of impressionist painting in which luminous effects are produced by tiny dots of various pure colours, which become blended in the viewer's eye. **2** M20 *Music* The breaking up of musical texture into thematic, rhythmic, and tonal fragments.

poipoi /ˈpɔɪpɔɪ/ *noun* E19 **Polynesian** (reduplication of POI). A Polynesian dish made from fermented fruit, especially breadfruit.

poivrade /pwavrad/ *noun* L17 **French** (from *poivre* pepper). Pepper sauce.

polder /ˈpəʊldə/ *noun* E17 **Dutch** (from Middle Dutch *polre*). A piece of low-lying land reclaimed from the sea, a lake, etc., and protected by dykes, originally and especially in the Netherlands.

polenta /pə(ʊ)ˈlɛntə/, *foreign* /poˈlenta/ *noun* OE **Latin** (in later use directly from Italian from Latin = pearl barley). Originally, pearl barley, (porridge made from) barley meal. Later, maize flour as used in Italian cookery; a paste or dough made from this boiled and then often fried or baked.

policier /pɔlisje/ *noun* plural pronounced same L20 **French** (literally, 'detective novel'). A film based on a police novel. Cf. ROMAN POLICIER.

1977 *Time* Not so in *Man on the Roof*, the Swedish-made *policier* based on one of the Martin Beck novels.

polis /ˈpɒlɪs/ *noun* plural **poleis** /ˈpɒleɪs/ L19 **Greek** (= city). *History* A city-State, especially in ancient Greece; *specifically* such a State considered in its ideal form.

1996 *Spectator* We are also political in that nearly everything that happens is looked at for the effect it is likely to have on the *polis*—or what politics graduates call 'the political process'.

polisson /pɔlisɔ̃/ *noun* plural pronounced same M19 **French**. An urchin, a scamp; an ill-bred and uncouth person.

Politbureau /ˈpɒlɪtˌbjʊərəʊ/ *noun* (also **politburo**, plural **politburos**) E20 **Russian** (*politbyuro*, from *polit(icheskiĭ* political + *byuro* bureau). The highest policy-making committee of a Communist country or party, especially of the former USSR. Also *transferred* and *figurative*.

politesse /pɔlitɛs/ *noun* E18 **French** (from Italian *politezza*, *pulitezza*, from *pulito* from Latin *politus* past participle of *polire* to smooth, polish). Formal politeness.

politique /pɔlitik/ *noun* plural pronounced same E17 **French** (use as noun of adjective = political). **1** *History* E17 A member or supporter of a French opportunist and moderate party, founded in *c.*1573, which regarded peace and reform as more important than the continuing civil war between Catholics and Huguenots. Also, an indifferentist, a temporizer. **2** M20 A political concept or doctrine; an expression of political ideas.

polka /ˈpəʊlkə/ *noun & verb* M19 **German** (French from Czech, perhaps related to *Polka* feminine of *Polák* a Pole). **A** *noun* **1** M19 A lively dance of Bohemian origin in duple time. **2** M19 A piece of music for this dance or in its rhythm. **3** M19 A woman's tight-fitting jacket, usually knitted. Now *rare*. **B** *intransitive verb* M19 Dance the polka.

■ The nineteenth-century craze for the *polka* led to the word's being attached a variety of commercial articles; hence *polka dot* for a pattern of dots of uniform size and distribution.

pollo /ˈpɒləʊ/ *noun* plural **pollos** M19 **Spanish** (Italian = chicken). *Cookery* Chicken, a chicken dish, *especially* one cooked in an Italian or (Mexican-)Spanish fashion.

polloi /pɒˈlɔɪ/ *noun* M20 **Greek** (= many). A crowd, a mob.

■ Slang, shortened from HOI POLLOI.

polonaise /pɒləˈneɪz/ *noun, adjective, & verb* M18 **French** (use as noun of feminine of *polonais* Polish, from medieval Latin *Polonia* Poland). **A** *noun* **1** M18 A slow dance of Polish origin, consisting chiefly of an intricate march or procession, in triple time; a piece of music for this dance or in its time or rhythm. **2** L18 A kind of dress or overdress, with the skirt open at the front and looped up at the back, originally resembling a garment worn by Polish women. **b** L19 A fabric made from a silk and cotton mixture. **3** L19 *Cookery* A dish cooked in a Polish style. **4** M20 A polonaise rug or carpet. **B** *adjective* **1** E20 Designating a kind of rug or carpet made in Persia during the sixteenth and seventeenth centuries, using silver and gold warp threads. **2** *Cookery* M20 Of a dish: cooked in a Polish style. **C** *intransitive verb* E19 Dance a polonaise; move in a stately manner.

polska /ˈpɒlskə/ *noun* L19 **Swedish** (from *Polsk* Polish). A processional Scandinavian folk-dance of Polish origin, usually in 3/4 time; a piece of music for this dance.

poltergeist /ˈpɒltəgʌɪst/ *noun* M19 **German** (from *poltern* to make a noise, create a disturbance + *Geist* ghost). A spirit believed to manifest itself by making noises and moving physical objects.

polynya /pəʊˈlɪnjə/ *noun* (also **polynia**) M19 **Russian** (from base of *pole*, *polyana* field). A space of open water in the midst of ice, especially in Arctic seas.

pomade /pəˈmeɪd/, /pəˈmɑːd/ *noun & verb* M16 **French** (*pommade* from Italian *pomata* from modern Latin POMATUM). **A** *noun* M16 A scented ointment (in which apples were perhaps originally an ingredient) for the skin, now especially for the skin of the head and for the hair. **B** *transitive verb* L19 Anoint with pomade. Chiefly as *pomaded* participial adjective.

pomatum /pə(ʊ)ˈmeɪtəm/ *noun & verb* M16 **Modern Latin** (from Latin *pomum* apple). **A** *noun* M16 Hair ointment, pomade. **B** *transitive verb* M17 Anoint with pomatum. Chiefly as *pomatumed* participial adjective.

pomme /pɔm/ *noun* plural pronounced same E20 **French** (short for POMME DE TERRE). *Cookery* A potato.

■ Chiefly plural and in phrases designating ways of cooking potatoes, as in *pommes allumettes* (matchstick-thin potato chips) and *pommes frites* (fried potato chips).

pomme de terre /pɔm də tɛr/ *noun* plural **pommes de terre** (pronounced same) E19 **French** (literally, 'apple of the earth'). *Cookery* A potato.

pompadour /ˈpɒmpədʊə/ *noun & adjective* M18 **French** (Jeanne-Antoinette Poisson, Marquise de *Pompadour* (1721–64), mistress of Louis XV of France). **A** *noun* **1** M18 Any of various items of costume fashionable in the time of the Marquise de Pompadour or resembling these. **2** M18 A shade of crimson or pink; a fabric of this colour. **3** M18 A South American cotinga with brilliant crimson-purple plumage. Also *pompadour cotinga*. **4a** L19 A style of dressing men's hair, in which it is combed back from the forehead without a parting. *United States*. **b** L19 A style of arranging women's hair, in which it is turned back off the forehead in a roll, sometimes over a pad. **B** *attributive* or as *adjective* M18 (Of dress, furniture, etc.) in the style prevalent in the time of the Marquise de Pompadour; *specifically* (*a*) of a crimson colour or fabric; (*b*) patterned with sprigs of (usually pink and blue) flowers on a white ground; (*c*) (of hair) arranged in a pompadour.

pompier /pɔ̃pje/ (*plural same*), /ˈpɒmpɪə/ *noun* M19 **French** (from *pompe* pump). **1** M19 In France, a fireman. **2** E20 An artist regarded as painting in an academic, imitative, vulgarly neoclassical style.

■ The designation of late nineteenth-century French academic artists as *pompiers* is probably based on their fondness for showing the Greek and Roman heroes in their pictures wearing helmets that put the viewer in mind of the helmets worn by Parisian firefighters.

pompon /ˈpɒmpɒn/, *foreign* /pɔ̃pɔ̃/ (*plural same*) *noun* (also (in senses 2 and 3) **pompom** /ˈpɒmpɒm/, (in sense 1) **pompoon**) M18 **French** (of unknown origin). **1** M18 A bunch of ribbon, feathers, flowers, silk threads, etc., formerly worn by women in the hair, or on the cap or dress. *obsolete* except *historical*. **2** M19 A variety of chrysanthemum, dahlia, or cabbage rose, bearing small globular flowers. **3** L19 An ornamental ball of wool, silk, ribbons, etc., on a woman's hat, a slipper, etc.; the round tuft on a sailor's cap, on the front of a shako, etc.

pomposo /pɒmˈpəʊzəʊ/ *adverb & noun* E19 **Italian** (from Latin *pomposus* from *pompa* solemn procession, from Greek *pompē* from *pempein* to send). **A** *adverb* E19 *Music* A direction:) in a stately manner. **B** *noun* **1** M20 An affected, self-important person. **2** M20 *Music* A stately movement or passage.

poncho /ˈpɒntʃəʊ/ *noun* plural **ponchos** E18 **South American Spanish** (from Araucanian). A South American cloak made of a piece of cloth like a blanket with a slit in the middle for the head; any garment in this style.

poncif /pɔ̃sif/ *noun* E20 **French** (literally, 'pounced design'). Stereotyped literary ideas, plot, character, etc.

pondok /ˈpɒndɒk/ *noun* (also **pondokkie** /pɒnˈdɒki/) E19 **Afrikaans** (probably from Malay, ultimately from Arabic *funduq* hotel). A shack or shanty made of oddments of wood, corrugated iron, etc.; *transferred* a house etc. in a poor state of repair. *South African*.

pons asinorum /ˌpɒnz asɪˈnɔːrəm/ *noun phrase* M18 **Latin** (= bridge of asses). The fifth proposition of the first book of Euclid, so called from the difficulty which beginners find in 'getting over' it.

ponticello /ˌpɒntɪˈtʃɛləʊ/ *noun, adverb, & adjective* M18 **Italian** (= little bridge). *Music* **A** *noun* plural **ponticellos**. M18 The bridge of a stringed instrument. **B** *adverb & adjective* M19 (A direction:) with the bowing close to the bridge.

pontifex /ˈpɒntɪfɛks/ *noun* (also **Pontifex**) plural **pontifices** /pɒnˈtɪfɪsiːz/ L16 **Latin** (from *pons, pontis* bridge + *-fex* from *facere* to make). **1** L16 *Roman History* A member of the principal college of priests in ancient Rome. **2** M17 The Pope.

pontificalia /ˌpɒntɪfɪˈkeɪlɪə/, /ˌpɒntɪfɪˈkɑːlɪə/ *noun plural* L16 **Latin** (use as noun of neuter plural of *pontificalis* pontifical). The vestments and insignia of a bishop, cardinal, or abbot; pontificals.

pontil /ˈpɒntɪl/ *noun* M19 **French** (apparently from Italian *pontello, puntello* diminutive of *punto* point). *Glass-making* An iron rod used to hold or shape soft glass (also *pontil rod*). Also called *punty*.

pooja variant of PUJA.

poort /pʊət/ *noun* L18 **Dutch** (*poort* gate, port). In South Africa: a narrow mountain pass, *especially* one cut by a stream or river.

popadam variant of POPPADAM.

popote /pɔpɔt/ *noun* plural pronounced same E20 **French**. A French military kitchen or canteen.

poppadam /ˈpɒpədəm/ *noun* (also **popadam**, **poppadom**, and other variants) E19 **Tamil** (*pappaṭam*, perhaps from *paruppa aṭam* lentil cake). A (flat cake of) thin crisp spiced bread usually eaten with curry or other Indian food.

poquosin variant of POCOSIN.

port-a-beul /ˌpɔːʃtəˈbiːəl/ *noun* (also **puirt-a-beul** /ˌpʊəʃtəˈbiːəl/) plural **puirt-a-beul** E20 **Gaelic** (literally, 'music from mouth'). A quick lively tune of Lowland Scottish origin to which Gaelic words of a quick repetitive nature have been added.

portail /ˈpɔːteɪl/ *noun* L15 **French** (literally, 'façade of a church', alteration of Old French *portal* from medieval Latin *portale*). A door or gateway.

■ Confused with *portal* in both French and English.

portamento /pɔːtəˈmɛntəʊ/ *noun* plural **portamenti** /pɔːtəˈmɛnti/ L18 **Italian** (literally, 'a carrying'). *Music* Gliding or moving from one note to another without a break in singing or in playing a trombone or a bowed stringed instrument, as a violin. Also, piano-playing of a style between legato and staccato.

port-crayon /pɔːtˈkreɪən/ *noun* (also **porte-crayon** /pɔrt(ə)krɛjɔ̃/ (*plural same*)) E18 **French** (*porte-crayon*, from *porte-* stem of *porter* to carry + *crayon* crayon). An instrument used to hold a crayon for drawing, usually a metal tube split at the end with a sliding ring so as to secure the crayon.

port de bras /pɔr də bra/ *noun phrase* plural **ports de bras** (pronounced same) E20 **French** (literally, 'carriage of the arms'). *Ballet* The action or manner of moving and posing the arms; any of a series of exercises designed to develop graceful movement and disposition of the arms.

port de voix /pɔr də vwa/ *noun* plural **ports de voix** (pronounced same) M18 **French** (literally, 'carrying of the voice'). *Music* Originally, a kind of APPOGGIATURA. Now, a vocal PORTAMENTO.

porte-bouquet /ˈpɔːtbʊkeɪ/, /ˈpɔːtbəʊkeɪ/ *noun* M19 **French** (from *porte-* stem of *porter* to carry + *bouquet* bouquet). A device for holding a bouquet.

porte-cochère /ˌpɔːtkəʊˈʃɛː/, *foreign* /pɔrtkɔʃɛr/ (*plural same*) *noun* (originally **port-cocher**; also **porte cochère**) L17 **French** (from *porte* port + *cochère* feminine adjective from *coche* coach). **1** L17 A gateway for carriages, leading into a courtyard. **2** L19 A covered area at the entrance to a building into which vehicles can be driven. Chiefly *United States*.

2 1996 *Times Magazine* . . . the view from the west corner is lost, as is something of the drama and excitement of being dropped off under the glittering lights of the porte cochère.

porte-crayon variant of PORT-CRAYON.

portée /ˈpɔːteɪ/, *foreign* /pɔrte/ (*plural same*) *noun* (also **portee** /ˈpɔːtiː/) L19 **French** (from *porter* to carry, from Latin *portare*). **1** L19 The importance or weight of a theory, an argument, etc.; the (far-reaching) consequences of an action or event. **2** E20 In handloom weaving, a specified number of threads grouped together to form the warp. **3** M20 *Military* A self-propelled vehicle on which an anti-tank gun can be mounted.

porte-monnaie /ˈpɔːtmɒneɪ/ *noun* M19 **French** (from *porte-* stem of *porter* to carry + *monnaie* money). A flat purse or pocket-book, especially of leather.

porteur /pɔrtœr/ *noun* plural pronounced same M20 **French** (literally, 'a person who carries'). *Ballet* A male dancer whose role is (only) to lift and support a ballerina when she performs leaping or jumping movements.

portico /ˈpɔːtɪkəʊ/ *noun* plural **portico(e)s** E17 **Italian** (from Latin *porticus* porch). *Architecture* A formal entrance to a classical temple, church, or other building, consisting of columns at regular intervals supporting a roof often in the form of a pediment; a covered walkway in this style; a colonnade.

portière /pɔrtjɛr/ *noun* plural pronounced same M19 **French** (from *porte* door). A curtain hung over a door or doorway, as a screen or for ornament, or to prevent draughts.

portmanteau /pɔːtˈmantəʊ/ *noun & adjective* M16 **French** (*portemanteau* from *porte-* stem of *porter* to carry + *manteau* mantle). **A** *noun* plural **portmanteaus**, **portmanteaux** /pɔːtˈmantəʊz/ **1** M16 A case or bag for carrying clothing etc. when travelling, *especially* one made of stiff leather and hinged at the back so as to open into two equal parts. **2** E18 A rack or arrangement of pegs for hanging clothes on. Now *rare.* **B** *attributive* or as *adjective* L19 Of a word, expression, etc.: consisting of a blend, both in spelling and meaning, of two other words. Of a description, expression, etc.: of general or widespread application.

portrait parlé /pɔrtrɛ parle/ *noun phrase* plural **portraits parlés** (pronounced same) E20 **French** (= spoken portrait). A detailed chiefly anthropometric description of a person's physical characteristics, especially of the type invented by Bertillon and used in the identification of criminals.

ports de bras, ports de voix plurals of PORT DE BRAS, PORT DE VOIX.

posada /pəˈsɑːdə/, *foreign* /poˈsada/ *noun* M18 **Spanish** (from *posar* to lodge). **1** M18 In Spain and Spanish-speaking countries: an inn or place of accommodation for travellers. **2** M20 In Mexico: each of a series of visits traditionally paid to different friends before Christmas, representing Mary's and Joseph's search for a lodging in Bethlehem.

posaune /pəˈzaʊnə/ *noun* plural **posaunen** /pəˈzaʊnən/, **posaunes** /pəˈzaʊnɪz/ E18 **German** (ultimately from Old French *buisine* from Latin *buccina* trumpet). *Music* **1** E18 A trombone. **2** M19 An organ reed-stop resembling a trombone in tone.

posé /ˈpəʊzeɪ/, *foreign* /poze/ (*plural same*) *adjective & noun* E18 **French** (past participle of *poser* to place, pose). **A** *adjective* **1** E18 *Heraldry* Of an animal: standing still. **2** M19 Composed, poised, self-possessed. **3** M20 *Ballet* Of a position: held, prolonged. **4** M20 Adopted as a pose. *rare.* **B** *noun* **1** E20 *Ballet* A movement in which a dancer steps with a straight leg on to the full or half point. **2** M20 *North American History* A resting-place on a portage.

pose plastique /poz plastik/ *noun phrase* plural **poses plastiques** (pronounced same) M19 **French** (literally, 'flexible pose'). A type of *tableau vivant*, usually one featuring near-naked women.

1969 V. G. Kiernan *Lords of Human Kind* There was a vogue of *poses plastiques*, and tableaux such as 'The Sultan's favourite returning from the bath' were popular.

poseur /pəʊˈzəː/ *noun* (feminine **poseuse** /pəʊˈzəːz/) L19 **French** (from *poser* to pose). A person who poses for effect or attitudinizes; one who adopts an affected style or demeanour.

1996 *Times* His full, florid voice, face, wig and cravat all seem designed to evoke Wilde himself; but, as it turns out, less Wilde the poseur and paradoxist than Wilde the enemy of the rigid and frigid.

post-bellum /pəʊs(t)ˈbɛləm/ *adjective* (also **Post-bellum, post-Bellum**) L19 **Latin** (from *post* after + *bellum* war). Existing, occurring, etc., after a (particular) war, especially (*United States*) the American Civil War. Opposed to ANTE-BELLUM.

1996 *Spectator* . . . it was for the rural post-Bellum Virginia of her birth and her innate American roots she . . . yearned.

post coitum /pəʊs(t) ˈkəʊɪtəm/ *adjective, adverb & noun phrase* E20 **Latin** (from *post* after + *coitum* accusative of COITUS). (Condition) following sexual intercourse; post-coital(ly) (state).

■ Used especially with reference to the saying *post coitum omne animal triste est* 'after sexual intercourse every animal is sad'. The saying itself is not known from classical Latin, although the idea can be traced back to passages in Aristotle and Pliny.

transferred **1975** M. Bradbury *History Man* He is in that flat state of literary post coitum that affects those who spend too much time with their own lonely structures and plots.

poste restante /pəʊst ˈrɛstɒt/, *foreign* /pɔst rɛstɑ̃t/ *adverb & noun phrase* M18 **French** (= letter(s) remaining). **1** *adverb & noun phrase* M18 (A direction written on a letter indicating that it is) to remain at the post office specified until called for by the addressee. **2** *noun* M19 The department in a post office where such letters are kept.

post eventum /pəʊst ɪˈvɛntəm/ *adverb phrase* M19 **Latin** (= after the event). POST FACTUM.

post factum /pəʊs(t) ˈfaktəm/ *adverb phrase* L17 **Latin** (= after the fact). After the event; with hindsight.

post festum /pəʊs(t) ˈfɛstəm/ *adverb phrase* L19 **Latin** (= after the festival). After the event.

post hoc /pəʊst ˈhɒk/ *adverb & adjective phrase* M19 **Latin**. After this; after the event; consequent(ly).

■ Chiefly with reference to the fallacy *post hoc, ergo propter hoc* 'after this, therefore because of this'.

postiche /pɒˈstiːʃ/ *adjective & noun* (as adjective also (earlier) **postique**) E18 **French** (from Italian *posticcio* counterfeit, feigned). **A** *adjective* E18 Artificial; (of a decoration in architecture etc.) added to a finished work, especially inappropriately or superfluously. *rare*. **B** *noun* **1** L19 An imitation substituted for the real thing; *especially* a piece of false hair worn as an adornment. **2** L19 Imitation, pretence. *rare*.

post meridiem /pəʊs(t) məˈrɪdɪəm/ *adjective & adverb phrase* M17 **Latin**. After mid-day; between noon and midnight.

■ Abbreviated to *p.m.*

post-mortem /pəʊs(t)ˈmɔːtəm/ *adverb, adjective, noun, & verb* (also (especially as adverb) **post mortem**) M18 **Latin**. **A** *adverb* M18 After death. **B** *adjective* M18 Taking place, formed, or done after death or (*colloquial*) after the conclusion of a matter (cf. sense C.2 below). **C** *noun* **1** M19 An examination of a body performed after death especially in order to determine the cause of death; an autopsy. **2** E20 An analysis or discussion conducted after the conclusion of a game, examination, or other event. *colloquial*. **D** *transitive verb* L19 Conduct a post-mortem examination of.

post-partum /pəʊs(t)ˈpɑːtəm/ *adjective & adverb* M19 **Latin** (*post partum* after childbirth). *Medicine* (Occurring, existing, etc.) after childbirth; postnatal(ly).

post rem /pəʊst ˈrɛm/ *adjective & adverb phrase* E20 **Medieval Latin** (= after the thing). *Philosophy* Subsequent to the existence of something else; (of a universal) existing only as a mental concept or as an abstract word after the fact of being experienced from particulars. Cf. ANTE REM, IN RE.

postscriptum /pəʊs(t)ˈskrɪptəm/ *noun* plural **postscripta** /pəʊs(t)ˈskrɪptə/ E16 **Latin** (use as noun of neuter past participle of *postscribere* to write after, from *post* after + *scribere* to write). Additional matter appended to any text, a postscript.

potage /pɔtaʒ/ (*plural same*), /pɒˈtɑːʒ/ *noun* ME **Old and Modern French** (literally, 'what is put in a pot', from *pot* pot). (A) soup, *especially* (a) thick (vegetable) soup.

■ Originally from Old French, the word was Anglicized in the form *pottage*; it was later reintroduced from French first in Scotland and later (M17) in England with reference to dishes of French provenance.

potager /ˈpɒtədʒə/, *foreign* /pɔtaʒe/ (*plural same*) (also **potagère**) *noun* M17 **French** (in (*jardin*) *potager* (garden) for the kitchen). A kitchen garden.

■ The original sense of *potager* as 'one who makes pot(t)ages' is long obsolete. The seventeenth-century garden writer John Evelyn introduced the word with its present sense in the form *potagere*.

1996 *Country Life* Chinese chives . . . are worthy of a prominent place in a perennial border or potager.

pot-au-feu /pɔtofø/ *noun* plural **pot-au-feux** /pɔtofø/ L18 **French** (literally, 'pot on the fire'). A large cooking pot of a kind common in France; the (traditional) soup cooked in this.

pot de chambre /po də ʃɑ̃br/ *noun phrase* plural **pots de chambre** (pronounced same) L18 **French**. A chamber-pot.

1995 *Spectator* [He] mainly reviews films made by Americans, who luckily do not refer to *pots de chambre* as 'chambers', 'jerries', 'goesunders' or—when placed on dreaming spires—'articles'.

pot-et-fleur /pɔteflœr/ (*plural same*), /ˌpɒteɪˈfləː/ *noun* M20 **French** (literally, 'pot and flower'). A style of floral decoration using pot plants together with cut flowers.

potiche /pɔtiʃ/ *noun* plural pronounced same L19 **French**. A large (especially Chinese) porcelain jar or vase with a rounded bulging shape and a wide mouth, frequently having a lid.

pot-pourri /pəʊˈpʊəri/, /pəʊˈpʊəriː/, /pɒt ˈpʊəri/ *noun* (also **potpourri**) E17 **French** (literally, 'rotten pot', from *pot* pot + *pourri* past participle of *pourrir* to rot (translating Spanish OLLA PODRIDA). **1** E17–E18 A stew made of different kinds of meat. **2** M18 Dried flower petals, leaves, etc., mixed with spices and kept in a jar or bowl to scent the air. Also, a container for holding this. **3** M19 *figurative* A medley, *especially* a musical or literary one.

potrero /pɒˈtrɛːrəʊ/ *noun* plural **potreros** M19 **Spanish** (from as next). **1** M19 In South America and the south-western United States, a paddock or pasture for horses or cattle. **2** L19 In the south-western United States, a narrow steep-sided plateau.

potro /ˈpɒtrəʊ/ *noun* plural **potros** L19 **Spanish**. A colt, a pony. *United States*.

pots de chambre plural of POT DE CHAMBRE.

poudre /'pu:drə/ *noun* L18 French (= powder, earlier *pol(d)re* from Latin *pulvis, pulver-* dust). Light powdery snow. *Canadian.*

poudré /pudre/, /pu:'dreɪ/ *adjective* (feminine **poudrée**) E19 French (past participial adjective of *poudrer* to powder). Of the hair, a wig, etc.: powdered.

poudreuse /pudrøz/ *noun* plural pronounced same E20 French (from as POUDRE). A lady's dressing table of a kind made in France in the time of Louis XV.

pouf /pu:f/ *noun* (in sense 3 usually **pouffe**) E19 French (ultimately imitative). **1** E19 An elaborate female head-dress fashionable in the late eighteenth century; (*History*) a high roll or pad of hair worn by women. **2** M19 *Dressmaking* A part of a dress gathered up to form a soft projecting mass of material. **3** L19 A large firm cushion with a stable base, used as a low seat or footstool. Also, a soft stuffed ottoman or couch.

poule /pul/ *noun* plural pronounced same E20 French (literally, 'hen'). A young woman, *especially* a promiscuous one. *slang.*

1955 D. Barton *Glorious Life* 'If I had thought she would have understood,' said Swindlehurst, 'I would have called her to her face "the typing *poule*".'

poule au pot /pul o po/ *noun phrase* plural **poules au pot** (pronounced same) L19 French. A boiled chicken.

poule de luxe /pul də lyks/ *noun phrase* plural **poules de luxe** (pronounced same) M20 French (= 'poule' of luxury). A prostitute.

1976 *Times Literary Supplement* . . . his wife has remarried and . . . his daughter is in business as a *poule de luxe* and doing very well.

poulet /pulɛ/ (*plural same*), /'pu:leɪ/ *noun* M19 French. **1** M19 A chicken; a chicken dish. **2** M19 A (neatly-folded) billet-doux.

■ In sense 1 especially with reference to French cooking, usually with a qualifying adjective, as in *poulet Provençal* (Provençal chicken), *poulet rôti* (roast chicken), etc.

poulette /'pu:lɛt/ *noun* E19 French. *Cookery* A (French) sauce made with butter, cream, and egg-yolks. More fully *poulette sauce.*

poult-de-soie /pu:də'swɑ:/ *noun & adjective* M19 French (alteration of *pou-de-soie* of unknown origin). (Made of) a fine corded silk or taffeta, usually coloured.

poupée /pupe/ *noun* plural pronounced same L18 French (= doll, puppet, wax figure). A figure used in making and displaying dresses, wigs, and other items of dress.

pourboire /purbwar/ *noun* plural pronounced same E19 French (literally, 'for drinking'). A gratuity, a tip.

pour encourager les autres /pur ɑ̃kuraʒe lez otr/ *adverb phrase* E19 French (literally, 'to encourage the others'). As an example to others; to encourage others.

■ The source is a witticism of Voltaire's in *Candide* (1759) concerning the execution in 1757 of Admiral John Byng for failing to relieve Minorca when the island came under attack by the French in 1756: *Dans ce pays-ci il est bon de tuer de temps en temps un amiral pour encourager les autres* (In this country [sc. England] it is thought a good idea to kill an admiral from time to time to encourage the others).

1995 *Spectator* The only thing that could be said in its [sc. the hospital's] favour was that it was better than Addenbrookes [Hospital], in Cambridge, with its giant crematorium chimney next to the entrance, *pour encourager les autres*, I suppose.

pour le sport /pur lə spɔr/ *adverb phrase* E20 French. For fun, amusement, or sport.

1973 L. Meynell *Thirteen Trumpeters* Lucian had automatically made tentative exploratory investigations as to her readiness *pour le sport* and bedworthiness.

pourparler /purparle/ *noun* plural pronounced same E18 French (use as noun of Old French *po(u)rparler* discuss, from *po(u)r-* pro- + *parler* to speak). An informal discussion or conference preliminary to actual negotiation.

pour passer le temps /pur pɑse lə tɑ̃/ *adverb phrase* L17 French. To pass the time; to amuse oneself.

1976 M. Birmingham *Heat of the Sun* Cynthia asked if she could go too: 'Pour passer le temps,' she said . . . 'I love riding in cars at night.'

pour rire /pur rir/ *adjective & adverb phrase* L19 French (literally, 'in order to laugh'). (In a manner) that causes amusement or suggests jocular pretence; not serious(ly).

1980 *Country Life* The jokes about such jargon . . . have long ceased to be *pour rire*.

pourriture noble /purityr nɔbl/ *noun phrase* E20 French (= noble rot). A common grey mould, *Botrytis cinerea*, as deliberately cultivated on grapes to perfect certain French and German wines and Tokay; the condition of being affected by this mould; noble rot.

pour-soi /purswa/ *noun* M20 **French** (literally, 'for itself, for oneself'). *Philosophy* In the thought of J.-P. Sartre, the spontaneous free being of consciousness; being for itself.

■ Contrasted with *en-soi* ((being) in itself) in Sartre's *L'Être et le néant* (1943).

pousada /pəʊ'sɑːdə/ *noun* M20 **Portuguese** (literally, 'resting-place', from *pausar* to rest). An inn or hotel in Portugal, *especially* one of a chain of hotels administered by the State.

pousse-café /puskafe/ *noun* plural pronounced same L19 **French** (literally, 'push coffee'). A glass of various liqueurs or cordials poured in successive layers, taken immediately after coffee.

poussin /'puːsɑ̃/, *foreign* /pusɛ̃/ (*plural same*) *noun* M20 **French**. A young chicken for eating.

■ Earlier in PETIT POUSSIN.

pou sto /paʊ 'stəʊ/, /puː 'stɔː/ *noun* M19 **Greek** (*pou stō* where I may stand). A place to stand on, a standing-place; *figuratively* a basis of operation.

■ *Dos moi pou stō kai kinō tēn gēn* (Give me a place where I may stand and I will move the earth), a saying attributed to the ancient Greek sage Archimedes (died *c.*212 BC).

powwow /'paʊwaʊ/ *noun & verb* (also **pow-wow**) E17 **Narragansett** (*powah, powwaw* shaman). **A** *noun* **1** E17 A North American Indian priest, sorcerer, or medicine man, a shaman. **b** M19 The art of a powwow, especially as used in healing. **2** E17 A North American Indian ceremony, *especially* one involving magic, feasting, and dancing. Also, a council or conference of or with Indians. **3** E19 *transferred* Any meeting for discussion; a conference, congress, or consultation, especially among friends or colleagues. Also, noisy bustle or activity. Originally *United States*. **B** *verb* **1** *intransitive verb* M17 Of North American Indians: practise powwow; hold a powwow. **2** *transitive verb* E18 Treat with powwow. **3** *intransitive verb* L18 *transferred* Confer, discuss, deliberate. Chiefly *North American*.

praecognitum /priː'kɒgnɪtəm/ *noun* plural **praecognita** /priː'kɒgnɪtə/ E17 **Latin** (neuter past participle of *praecognoscere* to know beforehand). A thing known beforehand; *especially* a thing needed or assumed to be known in order to infer or ascertain something else. Usually in *plural*.

praenomen /priː'nəʊmɛn/ *noun* E17 **Latin** (= forename, from *prae* pre- + *nomen* name). An ancient Roman's first or personal name preceding the nomen and cognomen (as *Marcus* Tullius Cicero); *generally* a first name, a forename.

Praesidium variant of PRESIDIUM.

praetorium /priː'tɔːrɪəm/ *noun* (also **pretorium**) plural **praetoria** /priː'tɔːrɪə/ E17 **Latin** (use as noun of adjective *praetorius* belonging to a praetor). *Roman History* **1** E17 The tent of the commanding general in a Roman camp; the space where this was placed. **2** E17 The court or palace of the governor of a Roman province; *transferred* an official building, *especially* the court or palace of an ancient king. **3** L17 The quarters of the praetorian guard in Rome.

Prägnanz /prɛg'nants/ *noun* E20 **German** (= conciseness, definiteness). *Psychology* In gestalt theory, the tendency of every perceptual or mental form to be integrated into a whole and become coherent and simple.

■ Also Anglicized as *pregnance* (M20).

praire /prɛr/ *noun* plural pronounced same E20 **French**. The European clam or the North American hard-shell clam especially as an item of food.

praline /'prɑːliːn/ *noun* E18 **French** (from Marshal de Plessis-*Praslin* (1598–1675), the French general whose cook invented the technique). A confection made by heating together chopped almonds or other nuts with sugar until the sugar liquefies and turns brown and then letting the mixture cool, used especially as a filling for chocolates.

1996 *Spectator* A real plantsman's border is as bitty as a chocolate praline.

pralltriller /'praltrɪlə/ *noun* plural same, **pralltrillers** M19 **German** (from *prallen* to bounce + *Triller* trill). *Music* An ornament consisting of rapid alternation of the note written with the one immediately above it. Cf. MORDENT.

pratiquant /pratikɑ̃/ *adjective* E20 **French**. Observant of religious duties or practices.

1965 *New Statesman* After lapsing for 15 years, she had recently tried to become *pratiquant* again.

pratique /ˈpratiːk/, *foreign* /pratik/ *noun* E17 **Old and Modern French** (= practice, intercourse, corresponding to or from Italian *pratica* from medieval Latin *practica* use as noun (sc. *ars* art) of *practicus* from Greek *praktikos* from *prattein* to do). Permission granted to a ship to use a port after quarantine or on showing a clean bill of health.

praxis /ˈpraksɪs/ *noun* L16 **Medieval Latin** (from Greek, from *prattein* to do). **1 a** L16 Action, practice; *specifically* the practice of a technical subject or art, as opposed to or arising out of the theory of it. **b** L19 Habitual action, accepted practice, custom. **c** M20 In Marxism, the willed action by which a theory or philosophy becomes a practical social activity. **2** E17 An example or collection of examples used for practice in a subject, especially in grammar; a practical specimen.

1.a 1996 *Oldie* He recalls that the lecturing, as opposed to praxis, was deficient and that most students went over to the Architectural Association for intellectual stimulus.

précieux /presjø/ *noun & adjective* (feminine **précieuse** /presjøz/) E18 **French** (= precious). **A** *noun* E18 plural same /presjøz/ A person affecting an over-refined delicacy of language and taste. **B** *adjective* L18 Overrefined, affectedly fastidious in taste etc.

■ Use of *précieux* (or *précieuse*) in English is under the influence of *Les Précieuses ridicules* (1659), Molière's famous comedy of manners satirizing the circle of people surrounding the Marquise de Rambouillet; thus the feminine form of the French noun and adjective was current in English earlier than the masculine (M20 and L19 respectively). The English word 'precious' as an adjective had long been in use (LME onwards) in the sense of 'overrefined', 'affected'. However, as a noun (L16) it is used only as an endearment and the derogatory sense is confined to the French word.

precipitato /preˌtʃipiˈtato/, /prɪˌtʃɪpɪˈtɑːtəʊ/ *adjective & adverb* L19 **Italian**. *Music* (A direction:) in a hurried or headlong manner; (to be) played in this manner.

précis /ˈpreɪsi/ *noun & verb* M18 **French** (use as noun of *précis*). **A** *noun* plural same /ˈpreɪsiːz/. **1** M18 A summary or abstract, especially of a text or speech. **2** L19 The action or practice of précis-writing. **B** *transitive verb* M19 Make a précis of; summarize.

B 1996 *Times* A glance at the subtitles which every few seconds précis the disorder in question . . . will testify to that . . .

predella /prɪˈdɛlə/ *noun* M19 **Italian** (= stool). **1** M19 A step or platform on which an altar is placed, an altar-step; a painting or sculpture on the vertical face of this. **2** M19 A raised shelf at the back of an altar; a painting or sculpture on the front of this, forming an appendage to an altarpiece above; any painting that is subsidiary to another painting.

premier cru /prəmje kry/, /ˌprɛmɪə ˈkruː/ *noun phrase* plural **premiers crus** (pronounced same) M19 **French** (literally, 'first growth'). A wine of the best quality.

premier danseur /prəmje dɑ̃sœr/ *noun phrase* plural **premiers danseurs** (pronounced same) E19 **French** (literally, 'first dancer'). A leading male dancer in a ballet company. Cf. PREMIÈRE DANSEUSE.

première /ˈprɛmɪɛː/, *foreign* /prəmjɛr/ (*plural same*) *noun & adjective* (also **premiere**) L19 **French** (feminine of *premier*; as noun short for *première représentation* first representation). **A** *noun* L19 A first performance or showing of a play, film, etc.; a first night. **B** *adjective* L19 First in order or importance; leading, foremost.

■ *Première* as a transitive and intransitive verb is a more recent (M20) development.

A 1996 *Spectator La Bohème* was not an instant success . . . at its Turin première on 1 February 1896 . . .

première danseuse /prəmjɛr dɑ̃søz/ *noun phrase* plural **premières danseuses** (pronounced same) E19 **French** (feminine of PREMIER DANSEUR). A leading female dancer in a ballet company; a ballerina.

premiers crus, **premiers danseurs** plurals of PREMIER CRU, PREMIER DANSEUR.

pre-mortem /priːˈmɔːtəm/ *adjective & noun* L19 **Latin** (*prae mortem* before death). **A** *adjective* L19 Taking place or performed before death (opposed to *post-mortem*). **B** *noun* L20 A discussion or analysis of a presumed future death. Chiefly *figurative*.

pré-salé /presale/ *noun* M19 **French** (= salt meadow). In France: seashore meadow or marshland, *especially* one on which sheep are reared; the flesh of sheep reared on such a meadow.

presidio /prɪˈsɪdɪəʊ/, *foreign* /preˈsidjo/ *noun* plural **presidios** /prɪˈsɪdɪəʊz/, *foreign* /preˈsidjos/ M18 **Spanish** (from Latin *praesidium* garrison, fort). In Spain and Spanish America: a fort, a fortified settlement, a garrison town. Also, a Spanish penal settlement in a foreign country.

Presidium /prɪˈsɪdɪʌm/, /prɪˈzɪdɪʌm/ *noun* (also **Praesidium**) plural **Presidia** /prɪˈsɪdɪə/, **Presidiums** E20 **Russian** (*prezidium* from Latin *praesidium*). The presiding body or standing committee in a Communist organization, *especially* (*historical*) that in the Supreme Soviet.

prestissimo /prɛˈstɪsɪməʊ/ *adverb, adjective, & noun* E18 **Italian** (superlative of PRESTO). *Music* **A** *adverb & adjective* E18 (A direction:) very rapid(ly). **B** *noun* E20 plural **prestissimos**, **prestissimi** /prɛˈstɪsɪmi/ A very rapid movement or passage.

presto /ˈprɛstəʊ/ *adverb, interjection, noun, & adjective* L16 **Italian** (= quick, quickly, from late Latin *praestus* ready, for Latin *praesto* at hand). **A** *adverb & interjection* **1** L16 In various commands used by conjurors: quickly, at once. Also as *interjection*, announcing the climax of a trick or a surprising dénouement. Frequently in *hey presto*. **2** L17 *Music* (A direction:) rapidly. **B** *noun* plural **prestos** **1** E17 An exclamation of 'presto!' **2** M19 *Music* A rapid movement or passage. **C** *attributive* or as *adjective* **1** M17 Originally, in readiness. Now, rapid, instantaneous; of the nature of a magical transformation. **2** M20 *Music* In a rapid tempo.

A.1 1996 *Spectator* A ghetto upbringing, a broken home, an abusive parent and, presto, the criminal is 'emoting his feelings' as he maims, robs or even kills his victim.

prêt-à-porter /prɛtəˈpɔːteɪ/, *foreign* /prɛtapɔrte/ *adjective & noun* M20 **French**. **A** *adjective* M20 Of clothes: sold ready to wear. **B** *noun* M20 Ready-to-wear clothes.

A 1996 *Times Magazine* No Anglo-Saxon squeamishness here—animals are either prêt-à-manger or prêt-à-porter.

B 1995 *Times* Paris, in October, goes *prêt à porter* mad.

pretorium variant of PRAETORIUM.

pretzel /ˈprɛts(ə)l/ *noun* (also (now *rare* or *obsolete*) **bretzel** /ˈbrɛts(ə)l/) M19 **German** (South German dialect form of *Brezel* from Old High German *brizzilla* (Italian *bracciello* usually taken as adaptation of medieval Latin *bracellus* bracelet). A hard salted biscuit usually in the form of a knot, eaten originally in Germany.

preux chevalier /prø ʃəvalje/ *noun phrase* L18 **French**. A gallant knight, *especially* a man who behaves chivalrously towards women.

■ The Old French adjective *preu*, from which the modern *preux* derives, was current in the Middle English period but became obsolete in the sixteenth century. Revived in the phrase *preux chevalier*, *preux* now exists in English only in this context.

Priapus /prʌɪˈeɪpəs/ *noun* (also **priapus**) plural **Priapi** /prʌɪˈeɪpʌɪ/, /prʌɪˈeɪpiː/, **Priapuses** LME **Latin** (from Greek *Priapos*, the Greek and Roman god of procreation whose symbol was the phallus, later adopted as a god of gardens). **1** LME A statue or image of the god Priapus, especially characterized by having large genitals. **2** L16 *transferred* (A representation of) the penis, especially when erect.

prie-dieu /priːˈdjəː/, *foreign* /pridjø/ *noun* plural **prie-dieux** (pronounced same), same M18 **French** (literally, 'pray God'). A desk for prayer consisting of a kneeling surface and a narrow upright front surmounted by a ledge for books etc. Also, (more fully *prie-dieu chair*) a chair with a low seat and a tall sloping back, used especially as a prayer seat or stool and fashionable in the mid nineteenth century.

prima /ˈpriːmə/ *noun* M18 **Italian** (feminine of PRIMO). A first or most important female; a prima donna, a prima ballerina.

prima ballerina /ˌpriːmə baləˈriːnə/ *noun phrase* L19 **Italian** (from as PRIMA + BALLERINA). The principal female dancer in a ballet or ballet company; a ballerina of the highest accomplishment or rank.

prima donna /ˌpriːmə ˈdɒnə/ *noun phrase* L18 **Italian** (from as PRIMA + *donna* lady). **1** L18 The principal female singer in an opera or opera company; a female opera singer of the highest accomplishment or rank. **2** M19 Originally, *transferred* a person of high standing in a particular field of activity. Now chiefly, a temperamentally self-important person.

prima facie /ˌprʌɪmə ˈfeɪʃiː/ *adverb & adjective phrase* L15 **Latin** (= at first sight, from feminine ablative of *primus* first and of *facies* face). **A** *adverb* L15 At first sight; from a first impression. **B** *adjective* E19

Arising at first sight; based on a first impression.

adjective phrase **1996** *Spectator* . . . the widespread acceptance of the phrase 'couch potato' is good *prima facie* evidence of the direction of that influence [of commercial television].

prima inter pares see PRIMUS INTER PARES.

prima materia /ˌprʌɪmə məˈtɪərɪə/ *noun phrase* E20 **Latin** (literally, 'first matter'). A supposed formless primordial matter out of which the universe was created.

prima vista /ˌprima ˈvista/ *adverb phrase* M19 **Italian** (literally, 'first sight'). *Music* At first sight.

primeur /primœr/ *noun* plural pronounced same L19 **French** (= newness, something quite new, from as *prime* first). A new or early thing; *specifically* (*a*) in *plural*, fruit or vegetables grown to be available very early in the season; (*b*) new wine. Cf. EN PRIMEUR.

primo /ˈpriːməʊ/ *adjective & noun* plural (in senses A.1, B) **primi** /ˈpriːmi/, (in sense B) **primos** M18 **Italian** (= first; cf. PRIMA). **A** *adjective* **1** M18 *Music* Of a musician, performer, role, etc.: principal, chief; of highest quality or importance. **2** L20 First-class, first-rate; of top quality. *slang* (chiefly *United States*). **B** *noun* L18 *Music* (The pianist who plays) the upper part in a piano duet.

primum mobile /ˌpriːməm ˈməʊbɪli/, /ˌprʌɪməm ˈməʊbɪliː/ *noun phrase* plural **primum mobiles** L15 **Medieval Latin** (literally, 'first moving thing', from Latin neuter of *primus* first + *mobilis* mobile). **1** L15 In the medieval version of the Ptolemaic system, an outermost sphere supposed to revolve round the earth in twenty-four hours, carrying with it the inner spheres. **2** E17 *transferred* An initiator of a course of action, events, etc.

primus /ˈpriːməs/, /ˈprʌɪməs/ *adjective* L16 **Latin** (= first). **1** L16 First, original, principal. Originally and chiefly in Latin phrases. **2** L18 Designating the first of several pupils with the same surname to enter a school. Cf. SECUNDUS, TERTIUS.

primus inter pares /ˌpriːməs ɪntə ˈpɑːriːz/, /ˌprʌɪməs/ *adjective & noun phrase* (feminine **prima inter pares** /ˌpriːmə/, /ˌprʌɪmə/) E19 **Latin**. (The) first among equals, (the) senior in a group.

1996 *Economist* A predecessor who made the mistake of behaving too much like an ordinary boss . . . and too little as *primus inter pares* did not last long.

princesse lointaine /prɛ̃sɛs lwɛ̃tɛn/ *noun phrase* plural **princesses lointaines** (pronounced same) E20 **French** (literally, 'distant princess'). An idealized unattainable woman.

■ The title of a play (1895) by Edmond Rostand (1868–1918), based on the theme of the love of the twelfth-century troubadour poet Rudel for the Lady of Tripoli.

principium /prɪnˈkɪpɪəm/, /prɪnˈsɪpɪəm/ *noun* plural **principia** /prɪnˈkɪpɪə/ L16 **Latin** (from *princip-*). **1** L16 *Roman History* In *plural* The general's quarters in an army camp. **2** E17 A fundamental cause or basis of something; a principle.

■ In scholastic philosophy the *principium individuationis* ('principle of individuation') was the criterion by which any individual was uniquely distinguished from any other. In sense 2 *Principia* occurs as the abbreviated title of either of two major works by English philosophers: the *Philosophiae Naturalis Principia Mathematica* (1687) of Isaac Newton and the *Principia Mathematica* (1910–13) of Bertrand Russell and A. N. Whitehead.

printanier /prɛ̃tanje/ *adjective & noun* (feminine **printanière** /prɛ̃tanjɛr/) M19 **French** (literally, 'of springtime', from *printemps* spring, from Latin *primus* first + *tempus* time). (A soup) made from or garnished with spring vegetables.

prisiadka /prjiˈsjatkə/ *noun* M20 **Russian** (*prisyadka*). A dance step in which a squatting male dancer kicks out each leg alternately to the front; the dance which uses this step. Cf. KAZACHOC.

prix fixe /pri fiks/ *noun phrase* L19 **French** (literally, 'fixed price'). A meal consisting of several courses served at a total fixed price. Cf. À LA CARTE.

1996 *Spectator* Thus, taramasalata is there, and moussaka on the lunchtime *prix fixe* . . .

pro /prəʊ/ *preposition, adverb, noun & adjective* LME **Latin** (= before, in front of, for, on behalf of, in return for). **A** *preposition* **1** LME For. In Latin phrases (cf. PRO BONO PUBLICO, PRO FORMA). **2** M19 In favour of. **B** *adverb* LME In favour (of a proposition etc.). **C** *noun* **pros** LME A reason, argument, or arguer in favour of something. **D** *adjective* E18 Favourable, supportive.

■ As an adverb, chiefly in the phrase *pro and contra* or *pro and con* ('for and against'), and as a noun chiefly in the phrase *pros and cons* ('(the points) for and against').

B 1996 *Times* . . . the famous Christian name eggs on a studio audience to put in its frenzied two penn'orth, pro and con, until some kind of conclusion is arrived at . . .

problematique /ˌprɒbləmə'tiːk/, *foreign* /prɔbləmatik/ *noun* (also **problématique** /prɔblematik/) L20 **French**. The problematic area of a subject etc.; *specifically* environmental and other global problems collectively.

■ Earlier in sociological terminology in Anglicized form *problematic* (M20).

pro bono publico /prəʊ ˌbɒnəʊ 'pʊblɪkəʊ/, /prəʊ ˌbəʊnəʊ 'pʌblɪkəʊ/ *adverb & adjective phrase* E18 **Latin**. For the public good.

■ In colloquial use often shortened to *pro bono*. This has given rise, originally in United States usage, to the adjective *pro-bono* (or *pro bono*), designating legal work undertaken at no charge for a person unable to pay legal fees, also a lawyer who undertakes such work (see quotation 1995 (2)).

1995 *Times* Mr Goldsmith made his promise as he launched a Bar Council *pro bono publico* scheme . . . to co-ordinate the provision of free services by barristers.

1995 *Times* It is hoped that it may prompt lawyers to dig into their pockets or do more *pro bono* work.

procédé /prɔsede/ *noun* plural pronounced same L19 **French**. Manner of proceeding; a method, a procedure, a process.

1962 *Listener All the familiar procédés* of opera have vanished, whether set numbers or Wagnerian leading-motives.

procès-verbal /prɔsɛvɛrbal/, /ˌprɒseɪvəː'bɑːl/ *noun* plural **procès-verbaux** /prɔsɛvɛrbo/, /ˌprɒseɪvəː'bəʊ/ M17 **French**. A detailed written report of proceedings; minutes; an authenticated written statement of facts in support of a charge.

proconsul /prəʊ'kɒns(ə)l/ *noun* LME **Latin** (from earlier *pro consule* (person acting) for the consul). **1** LME *History* In the Roman Republic, an officer, usually an ex-consul, who acted as governor or military commander of a province; in the Roman Empire, the governor of a senatorial province. **2** L17 A governor of a modern dependency, colony, or province.

proferens /prə'fɛrɛnz/ *noun* plural **proferentes** /prɒfə'rɛntiːz/ M20 **Latin** (present participle of *proferre* to bring forth). *Law* The party which proposes or adduces a contract or a condition in a contract.

profil perdu /profil pɛrdy/ *noun phrase* plural **profils perdus** (pronounced same) M20 **French** (literally, 'lost profile'). A profile in which the head is more than half turned away from the onlooker.

1967 E. Wymark *As Good as Gold* She . . . stood gazing down the street, her figure a *profil perdu* against a grey sky.

profiterole /prə'fɪtərəʊl/ *noun* L19 **French** (diminutive of *profit* profit). A small hollow case of choux pastry usually filled with cream and covered with chocolate sauce.

■ Earlier (E16–E18) evidence exists in English for the word in the sense of some kind of cooked food; the literal etymological sense of 'small gains', meaning the gratuities or tips that a servant can pick up, is attested in Cotgrave's French–English dictionary of 1611.

pro forma /prəʊ 'fɔːmə/ *adverb, adjective, & noun phrase* E16 **Latin**. **A** *adverb phrase* E16 As a matter of form. **B** *adjective phrase* M19 Done or produced as a matter of form; designating a model or standard document or form; *specifically* (of an invoice) sent in advance of goods supplied or with goods sent on approval. **C** *noun* plural **pro formas** E20 A pro forma invoice or form.

B 1996 *Times* Somerfield is now being sold on a multiple of only 6.5 times its pro forma earnings to the end of April.

prognosis /prɒg'nəʊsɪs/ *noun* plural **prognoses** /prɒg'nəʊsiːz/ M17 **Late Latin** (from Greek *prognōsis*, from *progignōskein* to know beforehand, from *pro-* before + *gignōskein* to know). **1** M17 *Medicine* (A prediction of) the likely outcome of a disease (in general or in a particular case). **2** E18 *generally* (A) prognostication.

projet /prɔʒɛ/ *noun* plural pronounced same E19 **French** (from Latin from *projectum* from *project-* past participial stem of *pro(j)icere*) to throw out). A proposal or a draft, especially of a treaty.

prolegomenon /prəʊlɪ'gɒmɪnən/ *noun* plural **prolegomena** /prəʊlɪ'gɒmɪnə/ M17 **Latin** (from Greek, use as noun of neuter present participle of *prolegein* to say beforehand). A critical or discursive introduction prefaced to a literary work; *transferred* a preliminary remark; *figurative* an event, action, etc., serving as an introduction *to* something. Frequently in *plural* (treated as *singular* or *plural*).

proletariat /ˌprəʊlɪ'tɛːrɪət/ *noun* M19 **French** (*prolétariat*, from Latin *proletarius* a Roman citizen of the lowest class, from *proles* offspring (since such citizens were considered capable of serving the State only by producing offspring)). **1** M19 The lowest classs of any community, especially when regarded as uncultured. **2** M19 The working class(es); wage-earners collectively.

proletkult /prəʊ'lɛtkʊlt/ *noun* (also **proletcult**) E20 **Russian** (contraction of *proletarskaya kul'tura* proletarian culture). Especially in the former USSR, (the advocacy of) cultural activities designed to reflect or encourage a purely proletarian ethos.

prominenti /prɒmɪ'nɛnti/ *noun plural* M20 **Italian** (plural of noun from *prominente* adjective, from Latin *prominent-* present participial stem of *prominere* to jut out). Prominent or eminent people; leading personages.

pronaos /prəʊ'neɪɒs/ *noun* plural **pronaoi** /prəʊ'neɪɔɪ/ E17 **Latin** (from Greek, from *pro-* before + NAOS). *Classical Antiquities* The space in front of the body of a temple, enclosed by a portico and projecting sidewalls. Also, a narthex.

prononcé /prɔnɔ̃se/ *adjective* M19 **French** (past participle of *prononcer* to pronounce, from Latin *pronuntiare* to proclaim, narrate). Pronounced; strongly marked; conspicuous.

pronto /'prɒntəʊ/ *adverb 1 & adjective* M18 **Italian** (from Latin *promptus* prompt; cf. next). *Music* (A direction:) quick(ly), prompt(ly).

pronto /'prɒntəʊ/ *adverb 2* E20 **Spanish** (from Latin *promptus* prompt; cf. preceding). Quickly; promptly, at once.

■ Colloquial, originally United States.

1976 P. Cave *High Flying Birds* You tell that bastard to come and see me . . . Pronto.

pronunciamento /prəˌnʌnsɪə'mɛntəʊ/ *noun* plural **pronunciamentos** M19 **Spanish** (*pronunciamiento*, from *pronunciar* (from Latin *pronuntiare* to pronounce). Especially in Spain and Spanish-speaking countries: a pronouncement, proclamation, or manifesto, *especially* a political one.

1995 *Oldie* The book keeps trumpeting such pseudo-omniscient *pronunciamentos* as that 'there is no reciprocity in love, harmony is not the human condition, and the thing sung will always be the unenjoyed ideal'.

pro-nuncio /prəʊ'nʌnsɪəʊ/, /prəʊ 'nʌnʃɪəʊ/ *noun* M20 **Italian** (*pro-nunzio*, from *pro-* + *nunzio* nuncio). *Roman Catholic Church* A papal ambassador to a country which does not accord the Pope's ambassador automatic precedence over other ambassadors.

propaganda /prɒpə'gandə/ *noun* E18 **Italian** (from modern Latin *congregatio de propaganda fide* congregation for propagating the faith). **1** E18 *Roman Catholic Church* (Also **Propaganda**) A committee of cardinals responsible for foreign missions, founded in 1622 by Pope Gregory XV. Also more fully *Congregation* or *College of the Propaganda*. **2** L18 An organization or concerted movement for the propagation of a particular doctrine, practice, etc. Now *rare*. **3** E20 The systematic dissemination of doctrine, rumour, or selected information to propagate or promote a particular doctrine, view, practice, etc.; ideas, information, etc., disseminated thus (frequently *derogatory*).

proprium /'prəʊprɪəm/ *noun* plural **propria** /'prəʊprɪə/ M16 **Latin** (use as noun of neuter singular of *proprius* proper). **1** M16 *Logic* A non-essential characteristic common to all, and only, the members of a class, a property. **2** L18 Chiefly *Theology*. An essential attribute of something, a distinctive characteristic; essential nature, selfhood.

propugnaculum /ˌprəʊpʌg'nakjʊləm/ *noun* L18 **Latin**. A bulwark, a rampart; *figurative* a defence, a protection.

propylaeum /prɒpɪ'li:əm/ *noun* plural **propylaea** /prɒpɪ'li:ə/ E18 **Latin** (from Greek *propulaion* use as noun of neuter of adjective *propulaios* before the gate, from *pro-* before + *pulē* gate). The entrance to a temple or other sacred enclosure; *specifically* (**Propylaeum**) *the* entrance to the Acropolis at Athens; *generally* a gateway, a porch.

■ The Greek word is represented in English in the form *propylon* (M19); both are current, although the Latin word is perhaps more common.

pro rata /prəʊ 'rɑ:tə/, /'reɪtə/ *adverb & adjective phrase* L16 **Latin** (= according to the rate). **A** *adverb* L16 In proportion, proportionally. **B** *adjective* M19 Proportional.

proscenium /prə'si:nɪəm/, /prəʊ'si:nɪəm/ *noun* plural **prosceniums**, **proscenia** /prə'si:nɪə/ E17 **Latin** (from Greek *proskēnion*, from *pro-* before + *skēnē* scene). **1** E17 *Classical Antiquities* The performance area between the background and the orchestra of a theatre; the stage. **b** E19 The part of the stage of a modern theatre between the curtain or drop-scene and the auditorium, often including the curtain itself and the enclosing arch. Frequently *attributive*. **2** *transferred* and *figurative* M17 The front, the foreground.

prosciutto /prɒˈʃuːtəʊ/ *noun* M20 **Italian** (= ham). Italian cured ham, usually served raw and thinly sliced as an hors d'oeuvre.

prosit /ˈproːzɪt/ *interjection & noun* (also **prost** /proːst/, (as noun) **Prosit**) M19 **German** (from Latin = may it benefit). (An utterance of the exclamation) wishing a person good health, success, etc., especially in drinking a toast.

prospectus /prəˈspɛktəs/ *noun* M18 **Latin** (= view, prospect, use as noun of past participle of *prospicere* to look forward). A printed document giving advance notification of the chief features of a forthcoming publication, issue of shares for a commercial enterprise, etc. Also, a brochure or pamphlet detailing the courses, facilities, etc., of an educational institution.

prosthesis /ˈprɒsθɪsɪs/, *in sense 2 usually* /prɒsˈθiːsɪs/ *noun* plural **prostheses** /ˈprɒsθɪsiːz/, *in sense 2 usually* /prɒsˈθiːsiːz/ M16 **Late Latin** (from Greek, from *prostithenai* to add, from *pros* to + *tithenai* to place). **1** M16 *Grammar* The addition of a letter or syllable at the beginning of a word. **2 a** E18 The branch of surgery that deals with artificial replacements for defective or absent parts of the body. Now *rare*. **b** E20 An artificial replacement for a part of the body.

protégé /ˈprɒtɪʒeɪ/, /ˈprɒtɛʒeɪ/, /ˈprəʊtɪʒeɪ/ *noun* (feminine **protégée**) L18 **French** (past participial adjective of *protéger* from Latin *protegere* to protect). A person under the protection, care, or patronage of another, especially of a person of superior position or influence.

> **1996** *Spectator* I do so with [sc. doff my cap to] Mr Preston, even though he was rather rude about me . . . after I had elsewhere written some disobliging comments about his newly appointed protégé, Mr Jaspan.

pro tem abbreviation of PRO TEMPORE.

pro tempore /prəʊ ˈtɛmpəri/ *adverb & adjective phrase* LME **Latin** (= for the time). **A** *adverb phrase* LME For the time being, temporarily. **B** *adjective phrase* M18 Temporary.

■ Also colloquially in abbreviated form *pro tem* (E19).

protocolaire /prɔtɔkɔlɛr/ *adjective* M20 **French** (from *protocole* protocol). Characterized by a strict regard for protocol; formal, ceremonial.

> **1979** H. Wilson *Final Term* Duncan Sandys . . . said that even in pre-Amin days he had always insisted on the title 'Britain' despite protocolaire objections.

protome /ˈprɒtəmi/ *noun* M18 **Greek** (*protomē* the foremost or upper part of a thing, from *protoenein* to cut off in front). Chiefly *Classical Antiquities*. A bust; a piece of sculpture representing the forepart of an animal.

proviso /prəˈvʌɪzəʊ/ *noun* plural **proviso(e)s** LME **Latin** (neuter ablative singular of past participle of *providere* to provide, as in medieval Latin *proviso quod* (or *ut*) it being provided that). A clause in a legal or formal document, making some condition, stipulation, exception; or limitation, or on the observance of which the operation or validity of the instrument depends; *generally* a condition, a qualification, a stipulation, a provision.

provocateur /prɔvɔkatœr/ *noun* plural pronounced same E20 **French** (= provoker). A person who provokes a disturbance; an agitator. Cf. AGENT PROVOCATEUR.

provolone /prɒvəˈləʊni/ *noun* M20 **Italian** (from *provola* buffalo's milk cheese). An Italian smoked cheese, often made in a variety of shapes. Also *provolone cheese*.

prox. abbreviation of PROXIMO.

proxime accessit /ˌprɒksɪmeɪ akˈsɛsɪt/ *noun phrase* L19 **Latin** (literally, '(he or she) came very near'). Second place in merit to the actual winner of a prize, scholarship, etc.; a person gaining this.

> **1995** *Spectator* As Herbert Morrison found out, to be *proxime accessit* in Labour's class list is not much fun.

proximo /ˈprɒksɪməʊ/ *adjective* M19 **Latin** (= in the next (sc. *mense* month)). Chiefly *Commerce* Of next month.

■ Often abbreviated to *prox.*, it is used following the ordinal number denoting the day, as in *1st proximo*.

prunelle /prynɛl/ *noun* E20 **French** (literally, 'sloe', diminutive of *prune* ultimately from Latin *prunum* plum; cf. PRUNELLO). A French brandy-based liqueur flavoured with sloes.

prunello /prʊˈnɛləʊ/ *noun* plural **prunello(e)s** E17 **Italian** (alteration of obsolete Italian *prunella* diminutive of *pruna* (now *prugna*) plum, prune). Originally, a variety of plum or prune. Now, a fine kind of prune, *especially* one made from a greengage.

pruritus /prʊəˈrʌɪtəs/ *noun* M17 **Latin** (from *prurire* to itch). Itching of the skin, with or (especially) without visible eruption.

■ Frequently with modern Latin specifying word.

pseudepigrapha /ˌsjuːdɪˈpɪgrəfə/ *noun plural* L17 **Greek** (use as noun of neuter plural of *pseudepigraphos* with false title, from *pseudo-* false + *epigraphein* to inscribe). Books or writings collectively wrongly titled or attributed; spurious writings; *specifically* Jewish writings ascribed to various biblical patriarchs and prophets but composed *c.*200 BC–AD 200.

pseudo /ˈsjuːdəʊ/ *adjective & noun* LME **Greek** (independent use of *pseudo-* false). **A** *adjective* **1** LME False, counterfeit, pretended, spurious. **2** M20 Intellectually or socially pretentious; insincere, affected; meaningless. **B** *noun* plural **pseudo(e)s**. **1** LME–M19 A false person, a pretender. **2** M20 An intellectually or socially pretentious person; an insincere person. Abbreviated to *pseud* (*slang*).

psi /psʌɪ/, /sʌɪ/ *noun* LME **Greek** (*psei*). **1** LME The twenty-third letter (Ψ, ψ) of the Greek alphabet. **2** M20 Paranormal phenomena or faculties collectively; the psychic force supposed to be manifested by these. Frequently *attributive*, as *psi powers* etc. **3** L20 *Nuclear Physics* A neutral, relatively long-lived strongly interacting particle, produced by high-energy collisions.

psyche /ˈsʌɪki/ *noun* M17 **Latin** (from Greek *psukhē* breath, life, soul, mind (also butterfly, moth), related to *psukhein* to breathe; in some uses with allusion to *Psukhē* Psyche, in Greek mythology the beloved of Eros (Cupid), the god of love). **I** **1** M17 The soul, the spirit. Formerly also (*rare*), the animating principle of the universe. Now chiefly *historical*. **2** E20 The mind, especially in its spiritual, emotional, and motivational aspects; the collective mental or psychological characteristics of a nation, people, etc. **II** **3** E19 (After Greek). A butterfly, a moth. *rare*. **III** **4** M19 (Said to be after Raphael's painting of Psyche.) A cheval-glass. Also *psyche-glass*. *archaic*.

psychomachia /ˌsʌɪkə(ʊ)ˈmeɪkɪə/ *noun* (also occasionally Anglicized as **psychomachy** /sʌɪˈkɒməki/) E17 **Late Latin** ((title of a poem by Prudentius *c.* 400) from Greek *psukhē* psyche + *makhē* fight). Conflict of the soul; the battle between spirit and flesh, or virtue and vice.

psychopompos /ˌsʌɪkə(ʊ)ˈpɒmpɒs/ *noun* (also in English form **psychopomp** /ˈsʌɪkə(ʊ)pɒmp/) M19 **Greek** (*psukhopompos*, from *psukhē* psyche + *pompos* conductor). A mythical conductor of souls to the place of the dead. Also, the spiritual guide of a (living) person's soul.

pteroma /təˈrəʊmə/ *noun* plural **pteromata** /təˈrəʊmətə/ M19 **Latin** (from Greek *pterōma*). *Architecture* The space between the cella of a Greek temple and the surrounding colonnade (peristyle).

pubes /ˈpjuːbiːz/, /ˈpjuːbz/ *noun* plural same L16 **Latin** (= the pubic hair, the groin, the genitals). **1** L16 The pubic hair. Now *colloquial*. **2** L17 The lower part of the abdomen at the front of the pelvis, which becomes covered with hair from the time of puberty.

puchero /pʊˈʧɛrəʊ/ *noun* plural **pucheros** M19 **Spanish** (= pot, from Latin *pultarius* cooking- or drinking-vessel, from *puls*, *pult-* a kind of thick porridge). **1** M19 A glazed earthenware cooking-pot. *rare*. **2** M19 A Latin American stew of beef, sausage, bacon, and various vegetables.

pucka variant of PUKKA.

pudendum /pjʊˈdɛndəm/ *noun* plural **pudenda** /pjʊˈdɛndə/ M17 **Latin** (*pudenda* use as noun of neuter plural of *pudendus* gerundive of *pudere* to be ashamed). In *plural* and (occasionally) *singular*. The genitals, *especially* the female external genitals.

pudeur /pydœr/ *noun* M20 **French** (from Latin PUDOR). A sense of shame or embarrassment, especially with regard to matters of a sexual or personal nature; modesty.

1995 D. Lodge *Therapy* A kind of *pudeur* restrained me.

pudor /ˈpjuːdɔː/ *noun* E17 **Latin** (= shame, modesty, from *pudere* to be ashamed). Due sense of shame; bashfulness, modesty.

pueblo /ˈpwɛbləʊ/ *noun & adjective* plural **pueblos** E19 **Spanish** (from Latin *populus* people). **A** *noun* **1** E19 A town or village in Latin America or the south-western United States; *especially* an Indian settlement. **2** M19 (**Pueblo**) A member of the Pueblo Indians. **B** *attributive* or as *adjec-*

tive M19 Of or pertaining to a pueblo; (usually **Pueblo**) designating or pertaining to a group of North American Indians living in pueblos chiefly in New Mexico and Arizona.

puggaree /ˈpʌg(ə)riː/ *noun* (also **pagri** /ˈpagri/, **puggree** /ˈpʌgriː/) M17 **Hindustani** (*pagṛī* turban). **1** M17 A turban, as worn in the Indian subcontinent. **2** M19 A thin scarf wound round the crown of a sun-helmet or hat so that the ends of the scarf form a shade for the neck.

2 1996 *Spectator* We are shown, above a wood engraving . . . of the two explorers doffing their headgear to one another at Ujiji, Stanley's helmet with its red check pagri and Livingstone's cap.

puisne /ˈpjuːni/ *noun & adjective* L16 **Old French** ((modern *puîne*), from *puis* (from Latin *postea* afterwards) + *né* (from Latin *natus* born)). **A** *noun* **1** L16–M17 A junior; an inferior; a novice. **2** E19 A puisne judge (see sense B.1 below). **B** *adjective* **1** E17 Younger, junior. Now *rare* or *obsolete* except in *Law*, designating an ordinary judge of the High Court. **2** E17–L18 Small, insignificant, petty. **3** M17 Later, more recent, of subsequent date. Now chiefly in *puisne mortgage*.

puissance /ˈpjuːɪs(ə)ns/, /ˈpwiːs(ə)ns/, /ˈpwɪs(ə)ns/, (*especially in sense 1b*) /ˈpwiːsɒ̃s/ *noun* LME **Old and Modern French** (from Proto-Gallo-Romance from Latin *posse* to be able). **1** LME Power, strength, force, might; influence. Chiefly *archaic* and *poetical*. **b** M20 A showjumping competition testing a horse's ability to jump large obstacles. **2** LME–L16 An armed force. Also, a number or crowd of people.

puja /ˈpuːdʒə/ *noun* (also **pooja**, **pujah**) L17 **Sanskrit** (*pūjā* worship). A Hindu religious ceremony or rite.

pukka /ˈpʌkə/ *adjective* (also **pukkah**, **pucka**) L17 **Hindi** (*pakkā* cooked, ripe, substantial). **1** L17 Of full weight, full; genuine. **2** L18 Certain, reliable; authentic, true; proper, socially acceptable. **3** L18 Permanent; (of a building) solidly built. Cf. KUTCHA.

■ Originally Anglo-Indian, often in phrases such as *pukka sahib*, a true gentleman; now colloquial or slang. The spelling *pucka* was the one in most frequent use prior to the twentieth century. *Pukka* was also formerly used in nominal and other adjectival senses that are now rare or obsolete.

2 1996 *Times Magazine* . . . foreign literature, nevertheless, dominates—the study of indigenous Indian-language writers is not regarded as pukka by renowned institutions of learning.

pulao variant of PILAU.

pullus /ˈpʊləs/ *noun* plural **pulli** /ˈpʊlʌɪ/ L18 **Latin** (= young chick). A young bird or nestling prior to fledging (especially with reference to ringed birds and museum specimens).

pulperia /ˌpʊlpəˈriːə/, *foreign* /ˌpulpeˈria/ *noun* E19 **American Spanish**. In Spanish-speaking America: a grocery; a tavern.

pulpitum /ˈpʊlpɪtəm/ *noun* M19 **Latin**. A stone screen in a church separating the choir from the nave, frequently surmounted by an organ-loft.

pulque /ˈpʊlkeɪ/, /ˈpʊlki/ *noun* L17 **American Spanish** (from Nahuatl *puliúhki* decomposed). A Mexican and Central American fermented drink made from the sap of any of several agaves.

pulvino /pʌlˈviːnəʊ/ *noun* plural **pulvini** /pʌlˈviːni/, **pulvinos** E20 **Italian** (from Latin *pulvinus* cushion, pillow). *Architecture* A dosseret resembling a cushion pressed down by a weight.

pumpernickel /ˈpʊmpəˌnɪk(ə)l/, /ˈpʌmpəˌnɪk(ə)l/ *noun* M18 **German** (transferred use of earlier sense 'lout', ultimate origin unknown). Dark German bread made from coarsely ground wholemeal rye.

puna /ˈpuːnə/ *noun* E17 **American Spanish** (from Quechua). **1** E17 A high bleak plateau in the Peruvian Andes. **2** M19 Difficulty of breathing, nausea, etc., caused by climbing to high altitudes; mountain sickness.

punctum /ˈpʌŋ(k)təm/ *noun* plural **puncta** /ˈpʌŋ(k)tə/ L16 **Latin** (originally neuter of *punctus* past participle of *pungere* to prick). **1** L16 A point. *obsolete* except in phrases; cf. PUNCTUM INDIFFERENS. **2** M17 *Zoology, Botany, Medicine*, etc. A minute rounded speck, dot, or spot of colour, or a small elevation or depression on a surface. **3** L18 *Anatomy* The orifice of either of the two lacrimal canals, at the corner of the eye. More fully *punctum lachrymale*. **4** M20 *Palaeography* A punctuation mark consisting of a point in a medieval manuscript.

punctum indifferens /ˌpʌŋ(k)təm ɪn ˈdɪfərɛnz/ *noun phrase* E20 **Latin** (= not differing point). A neutral point.

1976 J. Davey *Treasury Alarm* Things may rearrange themselves around me just because I'm there—as a *punctum indifferens*.

punctus /ˈpʌŋktəs/ *noun* plural **puncti** /ˈpʌŋktʌɪ/, /ˈpʌŋktiː/ M20 **Latin** (see PUNCTUM). *Palaeography* A punctuation mark in a medieval manuscript.

pundonor /ˌpundoˈnor/ *noun* plural **pundonores** M17 **Spanish** (contraction of *punto de honor* point of honour). In Spain: (originally, with *plural*) a point of honour; (now) one's sense of honour, dignity, self-respect, pride.

Punica fides variant of FIDES PUNICA.

punkah /ˈpʌŋkə/, /ˈpʌŋkɑː/ *noun* (also **punka**) L17 **Hindustani** (*paṅkhā* fan, from Sanskrit *pakṣaka*, from *pakṣa* wing). In the Indian subcontinent: a large fan to cool a room etc.; *specifically* (*a*) a large portable fan made especially from a palmyra leaf; (*b*) a large swinging cloth fan on a frame worked manually by a cord operated by a punkah-WALLAH or by electricity.

punto /ˈpʌntəʊ/, *foreign* /ˈpunto/ *noun* (in sense 3 also **ponto** /ˈpɒntəʊ/) plural **puntos** /ˈpʌntəʊz/, *foreign* /ˈpuntos/ L16 **Italian or Spanish** (= Latin *punctum* point). **1** L16–E18 A small point or detail; a particle, a jot. Also, a moment, an instant. **b** L16–M18 A small point of behaviour, (a) punctilio. **2** L16–E17 *Fencing* A stroke or thrust with the point of the sword or foil. **3** L17 *Cards* In quadrille, the ace of trumps when trumps are either diamonds or hearts. **4** M19 *Lace-making* Lace, embroidery. Only in phrases *punto a rilievo*, a type of lace worked in bold relief, and *punto in aria*, an early form of needlepoint lace originally made in Venice.

punto banco /ˌpʊntəʊ ˈbaŋkəʊ/ *noun phrase* L20 **Italian or Spanish** (probably from as PUNTO + BANCO). A form of baccarat.

purdah /ˈpəːdə/ *noun* E19 **Persian and Urdu** (*parda* veil, curtain). **1** E19 In the Indian subcontinent and South East Asia, a curtain, a veil; *especially* one used to screen women from men or strangers. **2** M19 A system in certain Muslim and Hindu societies, especially in the Indian subcontinent, of screening women from men or strangers by means of a veil or curtain. **b** E20 *transferred* Seclusion; (medical) isolation or quarantine; secrecy. Chiefly in *in, into, out of, purdah*.

> **1977** D. Bagley *Enemy* When I came out of purdah, but before I was discharged, I went to see her.

purée /ˈpjʊəreɪ/, *as noun also foreign* /pyre/ (*plural same*) *noun & verb* E18 **Old and Modern French** (in form feminine past participle of *purer* from medieval Latin *purare* to refine (metal), from *purus* pure). **A** *noun* E18 A pulp of vegetables, fruit, etc., reduced to the consistency of cream. **B** *transitive verb* M20 Reduce (food) to a purée.

pur et simple /pyr e sɛ̃pl/ *adjective phrase* M19 **French** (= pure and simple). Taken absolutely by itself, nothing short of.

> ■ Follows a noun, as does its much more common English equivalent 'pure and simple'.

puri /ˈpuːri/ *noun* M20 **Hindustani** (*pūrī* from Sanskrit *pūrikā*). In Indian cookery, a small round cake of unleavened wheat flour deep-fried in ghee or oil.

puris naturalibus /ˌpjʊərɪs natjʊˈrɑːlɪbəs/, /ˌpjʊərɪs natjʊˈreɪlɪbəs/ *adverb phrase* E20 **Latin** (cf. earlier IN PURIS NATURALIBUS). In one's natural state; stark naked.

puro /ˈpuro/ *noun* plural **puros** /ˈpuros/ M19 **Spanish** (literally, 'pure'). In Spain and Spanish-speaking countries: a cigar.

pur sang /pyr sɑ̃/ *adjective & adverb phrase* M19 **French** (*pur-sang* thoroughbred animal, from *pur* pure + *sang* blood). Without admixture, genuine(ly).

purusha /ˈpʊrʊʃə/ *noun* L18 **Sanskrit** (*puruṣa* literally 'man', plural 'mankind'; in Hindu mythology, a being sacrificed by the gods in order to create the universe). *Hinduism* The universal spirit or soul; spirit or consciousness as opposed to matter; *specifically* in Sankya philosophy, the active or animating principle (personified as male) which with the passive (female) principle produces the universe.

puta /ˈputa/ *noun* M20 **Spanish**. A prostitute, a slut. *slang*.

putonghua /puːˈtʊŋhwɑː/ *noun* M20 **Chinese** (*pǔtōnghuà*, from *pǔtōng* common + *huà* spoken language; cf. PAI-HUA). The standard spoken form of modern Chinese, based on the northern dialects, especially that of Peking (Beijing).

putsch /pʊtʃ/ *noun* E20 **Swiss German** (= thrust, blow). **1** E20 An attempt at (political) revolution; a violent uprising. **2** M20 A sudden vigorous effort or campaign. *colloquial*.

> *transferred* **1 1996** *Times* [Chris Evans] boasts about how he is famous enough to leave for six

weeks in Barbados while wimpier DJs clutch their headphones for fear of a putsch.

putto /ˈpʊtəʊ/, *foreign* /ˈputto/ *noun* plural **putti** /ˈpʊti/, *foreign* /ˈputti/ M17 **Italian** (from Latin *putus* boy). A representation of a (boy) child, naked or in swaddling clothes, in (especially Renaissance and baroque) art, a cherub, a cupid.

putz /pʊts/, /pʌts/ *noun* E20 **German** (= decoration, finery; in sense 2 from Yiddish). **1** E20 In Pennsylvanian Dutch homes, a representation of the Nativity scene traditionally placed under a Christmas tree. *United States.* **2** M20 The penis. *United States slang.* **b** M20 A fool; a stupid or objectionable person. *North American slang.*

puy /pwiː/ *noun* plural pronounced same M19 **French** (= hill, from Latin PODIUM). A small extinct volcanic cone; originally and *specifically* any of those in the Auvergne, France.

qadi variant of CADI.

qanat /kə'nɑːt/ *noun* (also **kanat**) M19 Persian (from Arabic *ḳanāt* reed, lance, pipe, channel). A gently sloping underground channel or tunnel, *especially* one constructed to lead water from the interior of a hill to a village below.

qat variant of KHAT.

QED abbreviation of QUOD ERAT DEMONSTRANDUM.

QEF abbreviation of QUOD ERAT FACIENDUM.

qibla(h) variants of KIBLAH.

qinghaosu /ˌtʃɪŋhaʊ'suː/ *noun* L20 Chinese (*qīmghāosū*, from *qinghao* artemisia (plant) + suffix *-su* 'active principle'). *Medicine* A naturally occurring compound extracted from the Chinese plant *Artemisia annua* for use against malaria, artemisium.

■ Used for centuries against fever in traditional Chinese medicine, *qinghaosu* became an object of study by Western researchers seeking for a compound with which to treat strains of malaria that were resistant to standard anti-malarial drugs.

qiviut /'kɪvɪət/ *noun* M20 Eskimo ((Inuit) plural of *qiviuq*). The underwool of the musk ox; fibre made from this.

qq.v. see QUOD VIDE.

qua /kweɪ/, /kwɑː/ *adverb* M17 Latin (ablative singular feminine of *qui* who). In so far as; in the capacity of.

1996 *Spectator* So can the historian *qua* historian give any sort of credence to *any* of this?

quadra /'kwɒdrə/ *noun* M17 Latin (= a square). *Architecture* The plinth of a podium. Also, a platband, a fillet, *especially* one above or below the scotia in an Ionic base.

quadrennium /kwɒ'drɛnɪəm/ *noun* (also (earlier) **quadriennium** /kwɒdrɪ'ɛnɪəm/) plural **quadrenniums**, **quadrennia** /kwɒ'drɛnɪə/ E19 Latin (*quadriennium*, from *quadri-* combining form of *quottuor* four + *annus* year). A period of four years.

quadriga /kwɒd'riːgə/, /kwɒd'rʌɪgə/ *noun* plural **quadrigae** /kwɒd'riːgiː/ E17 Latin (singular form of plural *quadrigae* contraction of *quadrijugae*, from *quadri-* combining form of *quottuor* four + *jugum* yoke). *Roman Antiquities* A chariot drawn by four horses harnessed abreast; *especially* a representation of this in sculpture or on a coin.

quadrille /kwə'drɪl/ *noun 1* M18 French (from Spanish *cuadrilla*, Italian *quadriglia* troop, company, from *cuadro*, *quadro* square). **1** M18 Each of four groups of riders taking part in a tournament or carousel; *generally* a riding display. **2** L18 A square dance usually performed by four couples and containing five figures, each of which is a complete dance in itself; a piece of music for such a dance.

quadrille /kwə'drɪl/ *adjective & noun 2* (also **quadrillé** /kwɒ'drɪleɪ/) L19 French *quadrillé*, from *quadrille* small square from Spanish *cuadrillo* square block). (Something, especially paper) marked with small squares.

quadrivium /kwɒ'drɪʌɪəm/ *noun* E19 Latin (= place where four ways meet, from *quadri-* combining form of *quottuor* four + *via* way). In the Middle Ages, the higher division of a course of study of seven sciences, comprising arithmetic, geometry, astronomy, and music. Cf. TRIVIUM.

quaere /'kwɪəri/ *verb & noun* (also (earlier) **quere**) M16 Latin (imperative singular of *quaerere* to inquire, seek). **1** *transitive verb* M16 (in *imperative* now also interpreted as *noun*) Ask, inquire, query. Chiefly and now only in *imperative* introducing a question. **2** *noun* L16 A question, a query.

quaesitum /kwiː'sʌɪtəm/ *noun* plural **quaesita** /kwiː'sʌɪtə/ M18 Latin (neuter singular of *quaesitus* past participle of *quaerere* to inquire, seek). That which is sought; the answer to a problem.

quae vide plural of QUOD VIDE.

quai /keɪ/, *foreign* /ke/ (*plural same*) *noun* L19 French. **1** L19 A public street or path along the embankment of a stretch of navigable water, usually having buildings on the land side; *specifically* such a street on either bank of the Seine in Paris. **2** E20 The French Foreign Office. In full *Quai d'Orsay* /'dɔːseɪ/, *foreign* /dɔrsɛ/ (the quai on the south bank of the Seine where the French Foreign Office is situated).

quaich /kweɪk/, /kweɪx/ *noun* (also **quaigh**) M16 **Gaelic** (*cuach* cup, perhaps from *cua* hollow; cf. Latin *caucus* (Greek *kauka*), Welsh *caurg* bowl). In Scotland: a shallow cup, usually made of wooden staves hooped together and having two handles, but sometimes made of silver or fitted with a silver rim.

quand même /kɑ̃ mɛm/ *adverb phrase* E19 **French**. All the same, even so, nevertheless.

quanta see QUANTUM.

quantité négligeable /kɑ̃tite negliʒabl/ *noun phrase* plural **quantités négligeables** (pronounced same) L19 **French** (= negligible quantity). A factor of no account, something insignificant.

quantum /ˈkwɒntəm/ *noun & adjective* M16 **Latin** (neuter of *quantus* how much). **A** *noun* plural **quanta** /ˈkwɒntə/, **quantums**. **1** M16 Quantity; a quantity. Now *especially* in *Law*, an amount of or *of* money payable in damages etc. **2** M17 One's (required or allowed) share or portion. **3** E20 *Physics* A discrete quantity of electromagnetic energy proportional in magnitude to the frequency of the radiation it represents. **b** M20 *transferred* and *figurative* A small discrete amount of anything. **4** M20 *Physiology* The unit quantity of acetylcholine which is released at a neuromuscular junction by each single synaptic vesicle, corresponding to a certain small voltage. **B** *attributive* or as *adjective* E20 *Physics* etc. Involving quanta or quantum theory; quantized.

quantum meruit /ˌkwɒntəm ˈmɛrʊɪt/ *noun phrase* M17 **Latin** (= as much as he has deserved). *Law* A reasonable sum of money to be paid for services rendered or work done, when the amount due is not stipulated in a legally enforceable contract.

quantum sufficit /ˌkwɒntəm ˈsʌfɪsɪt/ *adverb & noun phrase* L17 **Latin**. As much as suffices; (in) a sufficient quantity; (to) a sufficient extent.

quark /kwɑːk/, /kvɑːk/ *noun* M20 **German** (= curd(s), cottage or curd cheese). A low-fat soft cheese of German origin.

quartier /kartje/ *noun* plural pronounced same E19 **French** (from Latin *quartarius* fourth part of a measure, from *quartus* fourth). A district or area, originally of a French city; *elliptical* for *Quartier Latin* the Latin Quarter of Paris on the left bank of the Seine, where students and artists live.

1995 *Spectator* Twenty years ago, Covent Garden was a deserted no-man's-land at weekends. On Saturday night, a quarter of a million people must have been carousing through this now gilded *quartier*.

quasi in rem /ˌkweɪzʌɪ ɪn ˈrɛm/, /ˈkweɪsʌɪ ɪn ˈrɛm/ *adjective phrase* L19 **Latin** (literally, 'as if against a thing'). *United States Law* Brought against a person in respect of his or her interest in a property within the jurisdiction of the court. Frequently *postpositive*.

quatorze /kəˈtɔːz/ *noun* E18 **French** (from Latin *quattuordecim* fourteen). **1** E18 In piquet, a set of four aces, kings, queens, or jacks held by one player, scoring fourteen. **2** M20 In full *Quatorze Juillet* /ˈʒwiːjeɪ/. In France, Bastille Day (14 July).

quatre-couleur /ˌkatrəkuːˈləː/ *adjective* (also **quatre-couleurs** /ˌkatrəkuːˈləː/) M20 **French** (*quatre-couleurs*, from *quatre* four + *couleurs* colours). Of an *objet d'art*: made of or decorated with carved gold of several (especially four) different colours.

quatsch /kvatʃ/ *noun* E20 **German**. Nonsense, rubbish.

■ Frequently used as an interjection.

1979 N. Freeling *Widow* 'Oh Quatsch,' she said. 'I . . . know how to look after myself.'

quattrocento /ˌkwatrə(ʊ)ˈtʃɛntəʊ/ *noun & adjective* L19 **Italian** (= four hundred). **A** *noun* L19 The fifteenth century in Italy; the Italian style of art, architecture, etc., of this period. **B** *attributive* or as *adjective* E20 Of or pertaining to the quattrocento.

quebrada /keˈbrada/, /kɪˈbrɑːdə/ *noun* plural **quebradas** /keˈbradas/, /kɪˈbrɑːdəz/ M19 **Spanish** (feminine of *quebrado* past participle of *quebrar* to break). A mountain stream or ravine in South America.

quel /kɛl/ *adjective* plural **quels** (feminine **quelle**, plural **quelles**) L19 **French**. What (a) (with following noun).

■ Only in French phrases and in English phrases imitating them.

1996 *Spectator* 'Arnie! *Quelle surprise!* What are you doing here?'

Quellenforschung /ˈkvɛlənˌfɔrʃʊŋ/ *noun* M20 **German** (from *Quelle* source + *Forschung* research). The investigation of the sources of, or influences on, a literary work.

quenelle /kə'nɛl/ *noun* M19 **French** (of unknown origin). A seasoned ball or roll of meat or fish ground to a paste.

quere variant of QUAERE.

querencia /ke'renθja/, /ke'rensia/ *noun* M20 **Spanish** (= lair, haunt, home ground, from *querer* to desire, love). **1** M20 *Bullfighting* The part of the arena where the bull takes its stand. **2** M20 *figurative* A person's home ground, a refuge.

2 1952 R. Campbell *Lorca* Andalusia is Lorca's *querencia*.

quesadilla /kesa'di(l)ja/, /keɪsə'di:ljə/ *noun* plural **quesadillas** /kesa'di(l)jas/, /keɪsə'di:ljəz/ M20 **Spanish**. A tortilla stuffed with cheese (or occasionally other filling) and heated.

questionnaire /kwɛstʃə'nɛ:/, /kɛstjə'nɛ:/ *noun* L19 **French** (from *questionner* to question). A formulated series of questions by which information is sought from a selected group, usually for statistical analysis; a document containing these.

quête /kɛt/ *noun* E20 **French** (= quest). The traditional act of begging for food or alms to the accompaniment of folksong.

quia timet /ˌkwi:ə 'tɪmɛt/ *adverb & adjective phrase* E17 **Latin** (literally, 'because he or she fears'). *Law* **A** *adverb phrase* E17 So as to prevent a possible future injury. **B** *adjective phrase* L17 Of an injunction: brought for this purpose.

quiche /ki:ʃ/ *noun* M20 **French** (from Alsatian dialect *Küchen* (German *Kuchen* cake)). An open flan consisting of a pastry case filled with a savoury mixture of milk, eggs, and other ingredients, and baked until firm.

quid /kwɪd/ *noun* L16 **Latin** (= what, anything, something, neuter singular of *quis* who, anyone, etc.; in sense 3 abbreviation of TERTIUM QUID). **1** A nicety in argument, a quibble. *rare*. Only in L16. **2** E17 The nature of something; that which a thing is. **3** E19 *United States History* A section formed within the Republican Party, 1805–11.

quid pro quo /ˌkwɪd prəʊ 'kwəʊ/ *noun phrase* M16 **Latin** (= something for something). **1** M16 A thing (originally a medicine) given or used in place of another; a substitute. **b** L17 The action or fact of substituting one thing for another. Also, a mistake or blunder arising from such substitution. **2** L16 An action performed or thing given in return or exchange for another.

2 1996 *Spectator* Mr Major's error was to let the Chancellor pocket a concession without extracting a quid pro quo.

quieta non movere /kwi:ˌeɪtə nəʊn məʊ 'vɛ:ri:/ *verb phrase* L18 **Latin** (literally, 'not to move settled things'). Let sleeping dogs lie.

1960 *Encounter Quieta non movere* is the motto of many once aggressive . . . radicals.

quietus /kwʌɪ'i:təs/ *noun* LME **Latin** (abbreviation of medieval Latin *quietus est*, literally, 'he is quit'). **1 a** LME An acquittance granted on payment of a debt; a receipt. Originally more fully *quietus est*. **b** L16–L18 A discharge or release from office or duty. **2** M16 *figurative* Death regarded as a release from life; something which causes death. **b** E19 A final settlement, an ending. **3** M18 (By association with *quiet*). A sedative, a salve; a state of quiet or repose, a lull.

quincaillerie /kɛ̃kajri/ *noun* plural pronounced same L19 **French**. **1** L19 Metalwork; metal artefacts. *rare*. **2** M20 In France: a hardware or ironmonger's shop.

quinella /kwɪ'nɛlə/ *noun* (also (earlier) **quiniela** /kwɪnɪ'ɛlə/) E20 **American Spanish** (*quiniela*). A form of betting in which the punter must select the first two placewinners in a race etc., not necessarily in the correct order. Originally *United States*.

quinquennium /kwɪŋ'kwɛnɪəm/ *noun* plural **quinquenniums**, **quinquennia** /kwɪŋ'kwɛnɪə/ E17 **Latin** (from *quinque* five + *annus* year). **1** E17 A fifth anniversary. **2** M17 A period of five years.

quinta /'kinta/, /'kwɪntə/ *noun* M18 **Spanish and Portuguese** (from *quinta parte* fifth part, originally the amount of a farm's produce paid as rent). In Spain, Portugal, and Latin America: a large house or villa in the country or on the outskirts of a town; a country estate; *specifically* a wine-growing estate in Portugal.

quipu /'ki:pu:/, /'kwɪpu:/ *noun* (also **quipo**) E18 **Quechua** (*khípu* knot). An ancient Peruvian device for recording information, events, etc., consisting of variously coloured cords arranged and knotted in different ways.

qui vive /ki: 'vi:v/, *foreign* /ki viv/ *noun phrase* L16 **French** (literally, '(long) live who?'). An alert or watchful state or condition. Chiefly in *on the qui vive*, on the alert or lookout.

■ Originating in a sentry's challenge to a person approaching his post in order to ascertain to whom that person is loyal.

1996 *Spectator* Ever on the *qui vive* for the bore of the party, when sheep replace cows in the fields nearby he comments approvingly: 'Sheep have a more active, at least more interesting, social life than cows.'

quoad /'kwəʊad/ *preposition* E17 **Latin** (= so far as, as much as, as to, from *quo* where, whither + *ad* to). To the extent of, as regards, with respect to.

quod erat demonstrandum /kwɒd ə ˌrat dɛmən'strandəm/ *noun phrase* M17 **Latin** (translating Greek *hoti edei deixai*). (Which is) what it was necessary to prove.

■ Generally abbreviated to QED and used to emphasize the clinching point in an argument or to conclude a mathematical proof. Like the less widely used QUOD ERAT FACIENDUM, the phrase and its use are derived from the Greek mathematician Euclid (early 3rd century BC).

quod erat faciendum /kwɒd əˌrat faʃɪ'ɛndəm/, /kwɒd əˌrat fakɪ'ɛndəm/ *noun phrase* L17 **Latin** (translating *hoti edei poiein*). (Which is) what it was necessary to construct.

■ Abbreviated to QEF and appended to a geometrical proof.

quodlibet /'kwɒdlɪbɛt/ *noun* LME **Medieval Latin** (*quodlibet(um)* from Latin *quodlibet*, from *quod* what + *libet* it pleases). **1** LME *History* A question proposed as an exercise in philosophical or theological debate; a scholastic debate, thesis, or exercise. **2** E19 *Music* A light-hearted combination of several tunes; a medley.

quod vide /kwɒd 'viːdeɪ/ *noun phrase* plural **quae vide** /kwʌɪ 'viːdeɪ/ M18 **Latin** (*quod* which + imperative singular of *videre* to see). Which see.

■ Abbreviated to *q.v.* (plural *qq.v.*) and used to direct a reader to further information under the reference cited.

quondam /'kwɒndəm/, /'kwɒndam/ *adverb, noun, & adjective* M16 **Latin** (= formerly). **A** *adverb* M16 At one time, formerly. *rare*. **B** *noun* M16 The former holder of an office or position; *derogatory* a person who has been deposed or ejected. **C** *adjective* L16 That once was or existed; former.

quorum /'kwɔːrəm/ *noun* LME **Latin** (literally, 'of whom (we wish that you be one, two, etc.)' in the wording of commissions for members of bodies, committees, etc.). **1** LME Originally, certain (usually eminent) justices of the peace whose presence was necessary to constitute a deciding body. Later *generally*, all justices collectively. **b** L16 *transferred* Distinguished or essential members of any body; a select company. **2** E17 A fixed minimum number of members whose presence is necessary to make the proceedings of an assembly, society, etc., valid.

quota /'kwəʊtə/ *noun* E17 **Medieval Latin** (*quota* (sc. *pars*) how great (a part), feminine of *quotus*, from Latin *quot* how many). **1** E17 The share which an individual or group is obliged to contribute to a total; the minimum number or quantity of a particular product which under official regulations must be produced, exported, imported, etc. **b** M19 In a system of proportional representation, the minimum number of votes required to elect a candidate. **2** L17 The share of a total or the maximum number or quantity belonging, due, given, or permitted to an individual or group. **b** E20 The maximum number (of immigrants or imports) allowed to enter a country within a set period; (a) regulation imposing such a restriction on entry to a country. Also, the number of students allowed to enrol for a course, at a college, etc.

quot homines, tot sententiae /kwɒt ˌhɒmɪneɪz tɒt sɛn'tɛntɪʌɪ/ *noun phrase & interjection* M16 **Latin**. (There are) as many opinions as (there are) men.

■ From the comedy *Phormio* (line 454) by the Roman playwright Plautus (died 184 BC).

1996 *Oldie* As then, so now: *quot homines, tot sententiae*, there are as many opinions as there are people.

quotum /'kwəʊtəm/ *noun* M17 **Latin** (neuter singular of *quotus*). A number or quantity considered in proportion to a larger number or amount of which it forms part; a quota.

q.v. abbreviation of QUOD VIDE.

rabat /ra'bat/ *noun* M20 **French** (= collar). A false shirt-front, a stock.

■ Earlier (L16–M17) a *rabat* (also called a *rabato*) was a stiff collar but the word has long been obsolete in this sense.

rabbi /'rabʌɪ/ *noun* LOE **ecclesiastical Latin and Greek** (from Hebrew *rabbī* my master, from *raḇ* master). **1** LOE A Jewish scholar or teacher having authority on law and doctrine; now *specifically* one authorized by ordination to deal with questions of law and ritual and to perform certain functions. Also as a title of respect and form of address (usually with following personal name). **2** M16 *transferred* A person whose learning, authority, or status is comparable to that of a Jewish rabbi; *specifically* (*United States slang*) a senior official who exerts influence or patronage on behalf of a person.

■ The French word *rabbin* is now rare in English but was formerly used in both senses (sense 1 from L16, sense 2 M16–M17). The ending *-n* may be due to a Semitic plural form.

raccourci /rakursi/ *noun* plural pronounced same M20 **French** (use as noun of past participle of *raccourcir* to shorten). *Ballet* A movement in which the toe is made to touch the bent knee of the other leg.

rackett /'rakɪt/ *noun* (also **racket**, **ranket** /'raŋkɪt/) L19 **German** (*Rackett*, *Rankett*). *Music* A Renaissance wind instrument related to the oboe.

raclette *in sense 1* /ra'klɛt/, *in sense 2 foreign* /raklɛt/ (*plural same*) *noun* M20 **French** (= small scraper). **1** M20 *Archaeology* A stone tool of the scraper type discovered in the valley of the Vézère in south-west France, dating from the early Magdalenian period. **2** M20 A dish of cheese melted before an open fire, scraped on to a plate, and served with potatoes.

racloir /'raklwɑː/ *noun* L19 **French** (= scraper). *Archaeology* A prehistoric flint instrument with one broad side shaped for scraping.

raconteur /ˌrakɒn'təː/ *noun* E19 **French** (from *raconter* to relate). A (usually skilled) teller of anecdotes.

raconteuse /ˌrakɒn'təːz/ *noun* M19 **French** (feminine of RACONTEUR). A female teller of anecdotes.

1995 *Spectator* Freely is not an incisive polemicist, but she's an excellent raconteuse, and one who has knocked around enough to have a good fund of stories.

radeau /ra'dəʊ/ *noun* M18 **French** (from Provençal *radel*, from Latin diminutive of *ratis* raft). A raft; *specifically* (*Military*) a floating battery.

radicchio /ra'diːkɪəʊ/ *noun* plural **radicchios** L20 **Italian** (= chicory). A variety of chicory from Italy, with reddish-purple white-veined leaves.

radius /'reɪdɪəs/ *noun* plural **radii** /'reɪdɪʌɪ/ L16 **Latin** (= staff, spoke, ray). **1** L16–M18 A straight object such as a staff or bar. **2** L16 *Anatomy* and *Zoology* One of the two bones of the forearm; the corresponding bone of a tetrapod's foreleg or a bird's wing. **3** E17 A straight line from the centre of a circle or sphere to the circumference. **4** E18 Any of a set of lines, rods, spokes, etc., diverging from a point like the radii of a circle; a radiating part. **5** M19 A circular area of which the extent is measured by the length of the radius of the circle which bounds it.

radix /'radɪks/, /'reɪdɪks/ *noun* plural **radices** /'radɪsiːz/, **radixes** L16 **Latin** (*radix*, *radic-* root of a plant). **1 a** L16–E18 *Mathematics* A root of a number. **b** L18 *Mathematics* and *Computing* The number from whose various powers a system of counting, logarithms, etc., proceeds, a base. **2** E17–L18 *Astrology* and *Astronomy* A fact used as a basis of calculation. **3** E17 A thing in which something originates; a source.

■ Sometimes in the phrase *radix malorum* 'the root of evil', with allusion to 1 Timothy 6:10 (Vulgate version). In the Bible it is 'love of money' (*cupiditas*) which is 'the root of all evil', while in popular use it is frequently just 'money'.

rafale /rafal/ *noun* plural pronounced same E20 **French** (literally, 'gust of wind'). Repeated bursts of gunfire; a drum roll.

raffia /'rafɪə/ *noun* (in sense 1 also **raphia**, (earliest) **rofia**) E18 **Malagasy**. **1** E18 A palm of the African genus *Raphia*, especially *R. farinifera* of Madagascar. **2** L19 The soft fibre from the leaves of such a palm, used as garden twine, in basketwork, etc.

raffiné /rafine/ *adjective* L19 **French**. Of manners or judgement: refined.

raga /'rɑːɡə/ *noun* (also **rag** /rɑːg/) L18 **Sanskrit** (*rāga* colour, passion, melody). In Indian music: a pattern of notes used as a basis for melodies and improvisations; a piece of music based on a particular raga.

Ragnarok /'ragnarɒk/ *noun* (also **Ragnarök**) L18 **Old Norse** (*ragnarǫk, ragnarøkkr* (Icelandic *Ragnarök*), from *ragna* genitive of *regin* the gods + *rǫk* destined end or (later) *røkr, røkkr* twilight). *Scandinavian Mythology* The destruction of the gods; *specifically* the defeat of gods and men by monsters in a final battle. Cf. GÖTTERDÄMMERUNG.

ragout /ra'guː/ *noun* M17 **French** (*ragoût*, from *ragoûter* to revive the taste of, from as GOÛT). **1** M17 A highly seasoned dish of meat cut into small pieces and stewed with vegetables. **2** L17–M18 A sauce, a relish.

rahat /'rɑːhat/ *noun* M19 **Turkish** (*rahat (lokum)* from Arabic *rāḥat (al-ḥulḳūm)* ease (of the throat); cf. LOKUM). Turkish delight. In full *rahat lokum* /lɒ'kuːm/.

rais variant of REIS.

raison d'état /rɛzɔ̃ deta/ *noun phrase* plural **raisons d'état** (pronounced same) M19 **French** (= reason of State). A reason having to do with the security or interests of a State.

> **1996** *Spectator* This must be conducted on the basis of *raison d'état*, which includes secrecy.

raison d'être /rɛzɔ̃ dɛtr/, /'reɪzɔ̃ ˌdɛtrə/ *noun* plural **raisons d'être** (pronounced same) M19 **French** (= reason for being). A purpose or reason accounting for or justifying the existence of a thing.

> **1996** *Spectator* . . . it had the bad luck to be the first big British company to become caught up in a lurching shift in society's perceptions of the rights, responsibilities and *raison d'être* of business.

raisonné /rɛzɔne/ *adjective* L18 **French** (past participle of *raisonner* to reason, from *raison* reason). Reasoned out, systematic. Chiefly in CATALOGUE RAISONNÉ.

raisonneur /rɛzɔnœr/ *noun* plural pronounced same E20 **French** (literally 'a person who reasons or argues'). A character in a play etc. who expresses the author's message or standpoint.

raisons d'état, raisons d'être plurals of RAISON D'ÉTAT, RAISON D'ÊTRE.

raita /rɑː'iːtə/ *noun* M20 **Hindustani** (*rāytā*). An Indian dish consisting of chopped vegetables (or fruit) in curd or yoghurt.

raj /rɑː(d)ʒ/ *noun* E19 **Hindustani** (*rāj* from Sanskrit *rājya*; cf. RAJA). **1** E19 Sovereignty, rule; kingdom. **2** M19 *History* (*the Raj*) (The period of) British rule in the Indian subcontinent before 1947. In full *British Raj*.

raja /'rɑːdʒə/ *noun* (also **rajah**, (as a title) **Raja**) M16 **Sanskrit** (*rājan* king, from *rāj* to reign or rule; probably through Portuguese and related to Latin *rex, regis*, Old Irish *rí, ríg* king). *History* Originally, an Indian king or prince. Later also, a petty dignitary or noble in India; a Malay or Javanese ruler or chief.

raja yoga /ˌrɑːdʒə 'jəʊɡə/ *noun phrase* L19 **Sanskrit** (from *rājan* king + YOGA). A form of yoga aimed at gaining control over the mind and emotions.

raki /rə'kiː/, /'raki/ *noun* L17 **Turkish** (*rāqī* (now *rakı* whence also modern Greek *rhakē, rhaki*) brandy, spirits). Originally, an aromatic liquor made from grain-spirit or grape juice in Greece, Turkey, and the Middle East. Now also, a liquor made from various other ingredients in eastern Europe and the Middle East; a drink of this.

rakshasa /'rɑːkʃasa/ *noun* (also **raksasa**) M19 **Sanskrit** (*rākṣasa* demon). *Hindu Mythology* A malignant demon, *especially* any of a band at war with Rama and Hanuman; a representation of such a demon.

raku /'rɑːkuː/ *noun & adjective* L19 **Japanese** (literally 'ease, relaxed state, enjoyment'). (Designating) a kind of usually lead-glazed Japanese pottery, often used as tea-bowls and similar utensils.

rallentando /ˌralən'tandəʊ/ *adverb, adjective, & noun* E19 **Italian** (present participle of *rallentare* to slow down). *Music* **A** *adverb & adjective* E19 (A direction:) with gradual decrease of speed. **B** *noun* M19 plural **rallentandos, rallentandi** /ˌralən'tandi/. A gradual decrease of speed; a passage (to be) played with a gradual decrease of speed.

ramada /rə'mɑːdə/ *noun* M19 **Spanish**. An arbour, a porch. *United States*.

rambutan /ram'bu:t(ə)n/ *noun* (also **rambootan**) E18 **Malay** (from *rambut* hair, in reference to the covering of the fruit). A Malaysian tree, *Nephelium lappaceum* (family Sapindaceae); the fruit of this tree, resembling a lychee and covered with soft bright red spines or prickles.

ramen /'rɑ:mɛn/ *noun* (treated as *singular* or *plural*) L20 **Japanese** (from Chinese *lā* to pull + *miàn* noodles). Quick-cooking Chinese noodles, usually served in a broth with meat and vegetables.

rancheria /ˌrɑ:n(t)ʃə'ri:ə/ *noun* E17 **Spanish** (*ranchería*, from as RANCHO). In Spanish America and the western United States: a collection of Indian huts; a place or house where a number of rancheros live.

ranchero /rɑ:n'tʃɛ:rəʊ/ *noun* plural **rancheros** E19 **Spanish** (from as RANCHO). A rancher or ranchman, especially in Mexico.

ranchito /rɑ:n'tʃi:təʊ/ *noun* plural **ranchitos** M19 **Spanish** (diminutive of RANCHO). In the western United States: a small ranch or farm.

rancho /'rɑ:n(t)ʃəʊ/ *noun* plural **ranchos** E19 **Spanish** (= a group of people who eat together). **1** E19 In Latin America: a hut, a hovel, a very simple building; a group of these, a small village; *especially* one put up to accommodate travellers. Later also, a roadhouse, an inn; a meal at such a place. **2** M19 In the western United States: a cattle-farm, a ranch.

rancio /'rɑnsɪəʊ/ *adjective & noun* M19 **Spanish** (literally, 'rancid', from Latin *rancidus* stinking). **A** *adjective* M19 Of wine: having the distinctive bouquet, nutty flavour, or tawny colour characteristic of certain well-matured, fortified, or dessert wines. **B** *noun* M20 plural **rancios** /'rɑnsɪəʊz/. A rancio wine.

rand /rand/, /rant/ *noun* plural **rands**, (in sense 2 also) same M19 **Afrikaans** (from Dutch *rand* edge). **1** M19 In South Africa: a rocky ridge or area of high sloping ground, especially overlooking a river-valley; *specifically* (*the Rand*), the Witwatersrand, the chief gold-mining area of the Transvaal. **2** M20 The basic monetary unit of South Africa since 1961.

randkluft /'rantklʊft/ *noun* plural **randklufts**, **randklüfte** /'rantklyftə/ E20 **German** (literally, 'edge, crevice'). A crevasse between the head of a glacier and a surrounding rock wall.

randori /ran'dɔ:ri/ *noun* E20 **Japanese** (from *ran* disorder + *tori* bout, participation). Free or informal judo practice.

ranee /'rɑ:ni:/ *noun* (also **rani**, (as a title) **Ranee**) L17 **Hindustani** (*rānī* from Prakrit from Sanskrit *rājñī* feminine of *rājan* RAJA). *History* A Hindu queen; a raja's wife or widow.

rangé /rɑ̃ʒe/ *adjective* (feminine **rangée**) L19 **French** (past participial adjective of *ranger* to range). Of a person, lifestyle, etc.: orderly, regular, settled.

■ Earlier (L18) in dictionaries in a heraldic sense describing charges 'placed in a row' or 'set within a band', but this sense seems never to have gained wider circulation.

rangoli /raŋ'gəʊli/ *noun* M20 **Marathi** (*rā̃golī*). A Hindu symbolic design painted in coloured powdered stone, rice, etc.

rani variant of RANEE.

ranz-des-vaches /rɑ̃devaʃ/ *noun* plural same L18 **Swiss French dialect** (from unknown first element + 'of the cows'). A melody played especially by Swiss cowherds, consisting of irregular phrases formed from the harmonic notes of the Alpine horn.

rapide /rapid/, /ra'pi:d/ *noun* plural pronounced same E20 **French**. In France: an express train.

rapido /'rapɪdəʊ/, *foreign* /'rapido/ *adverb, adjective, & noun* L19 **Italian**. **A** *adverb and adjective* L19 *Music* (A direction:) in rapid time. **B** *noun* M20 plural **rapidi** /'rapɪdi/, **rapidos** /'rapɪdəʊz/. In Italy: an express train.

rappel /ra'pɛl/ *noun* M19 **French** (from *rappeler* to recall). **1** M19 A drum roll calling soldiers to arms. *rare*. **2** M20 *Mountaineering*. An abseil.

rapport /ra'pɔ:/ *noun* M17 **French** (from *rapporter* to bring back). **1** M17 Relationship, *especially* a relationship characterized by harmonious accord. **2** M19 A posited state of deep spiritual, emotional, or mental connection between people.

■ Originally (M16) introduced in the sense of 'report' or 'talk', but this was never widely current and has been totally ousted by the current sense. Cf. EN RAPPORT.

1 1996 *Times* The 'jungle fighter' boss, who rules by fear and manipulation, gets less out of the workforce than the manager who sets out to establish a close rapport with the employees.

rapportage /rapɔrtaʒ/, /ˌrapɔːˈtɑːʒ/ *noun* E20 **French** (literally, 'tale-telling', influenced by *reportage*). The reporting or describing of events in writing; mere description, uncreative recounting.

rapporteur /ˌrapɔːˈtəː/ *noun* L18 **French** (from *rapporter* to bring back). A person who makes a report of the proceedings of a committee etc. for a higher body.

■ Introduced earlier (but used only L15) from Old French in the general sense of 'a reporter, a recounter', *rapporteur* is now used in English only in the very specific sense above.

1996 *Times* How many emuwonks does it take to change a light-bulb? Five hundred and one. One to hold the bulb, 250 to revolve the room around him, and another 250 to act as *rapporteurs* for the ghastly documentation with 94 subsections.

rapprochement /raprɔʃmɑ̃/, /raˈprɒʃmɑ̃/ *noun* E19 **French** (from *rapprocher* to bring closer together, from *re-* + *approcher* to approach). (An) establishment or resumption of harmonious relations, especially between foreign States.

1996 *Country Life* . . . the shooting down of two light planes by the Cuban airforce has reversed the rapprochement with the United States . . .

raptus /ˈraptəs/ *noun* M19 **Latin**. **1** M19 A state of rapture. **2** M19 *Medicine* A sudden violent attack. Usually with modern Latin specifying word.

rara avis /ˌrɛːrə ˈeɪvɪs/, /ˌrɑːrə ˈavɪs/ *noun phrase* plural **rarae aves** /ˌrɛːriː ˈeɪviːz/, /ˌrɑːriː/, /ˌrɑːreɪ ˈaviːz/ E17 **Latin** (= rare bird). **1** E17 A kind of person rarely encountered; an unusual or exceptional person. **2** L19 A rarity; an unusual or exceptional occurrence or thing.

rariora /rɛːrɪˈɔːrə/, /rarɪˈɔːrə/ *noun plural* M19 **Latin** (neuter plural comparative of *rarus* rare *adjective*). Rare books.

rarissime /rɛːˈrɪsɪmeɪ/, /raˈrɪsɪmeɪ/ *adjective* E20 **Latin** (literally, 'very rarely (sc. found)'). Extremely rare.

rasa /ˈrʌsə/ *noun 1* (also **ras** /rʌs/) L18 **Sanskrit** (literally, 'juice, essence, flavour'). The mood or aesthetic impression of an artistic work.

rasa /ˈrɑːsə/ *noun 2* (also **ras** /rɑːs/) E19 **Sanskrit** (*rāsa*). A traditional Indian dance (commemorating that) performed by Krishna and the gopis in Hindu mythology; a festival celebrating this.

rasant /ˈreɪz(ə)nt/ *adjective* (also **razant**) L17 **Old and Modern French** (present participle of *raser* to shave close). *Military* Of a line of defence: sweeping; long and curving (originally so that the shot would graze the target).

rasgado /rasˈgado/, /razˈgɑːdəʊ/ *noun* plural **rasgados** /rasˈgados/, /razˈgɑːdəʊz/ M19 **Spanish** (past participle of *rasgar* to strum, make a flourish). *Music* (An arpeggio produced by) the act of sweeping the strings of a guitar with the fingertips.

Raskolnik /rʌˈskɒlnɪk/ *noun* (also **raskolnik**) E18 **Russian** (*raskol'nik*, from *raskol* separation, schism + noun suffix *-nik* person connected with (something)). *Ecclesiastical History* A member of a Russian Orthodox group which refused to accept the liturgical reforms of the patriarch Nikon (1605–81); an Old Believer.

rassolnik /rʌsˈsoljnjik/ *noun* (also **rasolnik**) E20 **Russian** (*rassol'nik* from *rassol* brine + *-nik*). A Russian soup of brine, salted dill cucumbers, and pickled vegetables, meat, or fish, served chilled.

rasta /rasta/ *noun* plural pronounced same E20 **French**. Abbreviation of RASTAQUOUÈRE.

rastaquouère /rastakwɛr/ *noun & adjective* plural pronounced same L19 **French** (from South American Spanish *rastacuero* tycoon in the hide trade, upstart). **A** *noun* L19 A person (especially from a Mediterranean or South American country) intruding into a particular social group and having an exaggerated manner or style of dress; a dashing but untrustworthy foreigner. **B** *attributive* or as *adjective* E20 Of, pertaining to, or characteristic of *rastaquouères*; of the nature of a *rastaquouère*.

ratafia /ratəˈfɪə/ *noun* L17 **French**. **1** L17 A liqueur flavoured with almonds or kernels of peach, apricot, or cherry. **2** M19 A kind of small macaroon.

rataplan /ratəˈplan/ *noun* M19 **French** (of imitative origin). A drumming or beating noise; a tattoo.

ratatouille /ratəˈtuːi/, /ratəˈtwiː/ *noun* L19 **French** ((dialect) cf. French *touiller* to stir up). **1** A ragout. Only in L19. **2** M20 A vegetable dish of aubergines, courgettes, tomatoes, onions, and peppers fried and stewed in oil.

raté /rate/ *adjective & noun* plural pronounced same E20 **French**. **A** *adjective* E20

Ineffective; unsuccessful. **B** *noun* E20 A person who has failed in his or her vocation.

A 1977 *Times* They are failures . . . They will all be *ratés* and hopeless when they are 30.

ratelier /rɑtəlje/ *noun* plural pronounced same M17 **French** (*râtelier*). **1** A stand for arms. *rare*. Only in M17. **2** M19 A set of (especially false) teeth.

ratine /rə'tiːn/ *noun & adjective* (also **ratiné** /rə'tiːneɪ/) E20 **French** (*ratiné* past participle of *ratiner* to put a nap on (cloth), from *ratine* ratteen). (Made of) a plain-woven (usually cotton) fabric with a loose open weave and rough surface, used for linings, furniture covers, etc.

rauschpfeife /'raʊʃˌ(p)fʌɪfə/ *noun* plural **rauschpfeifen** /'raʊʃˌ(p)fʌɪf(ə)n/ L19 **German** (= reed-pipe; cf. SCHREIERPFEIFE). *Music* **1** L19 A low-pitched mixture stop in an organ. **2** M20 A reed-cap shawm of the Renaissance period.

ravalement /ravalmɑ̃/ *noun* plural pronounced same M20 **French** (from *ravaler* to bring down, reduce). *Music* The action or an instance of modifying and extending the range of a keyboard instrument by rebuilding; an instrument modified in this way.

ravelin /'ravlɪn/ *noun* L16 **French** (from Italian *ravellina* (now *rivellino*), of unknown origin). *History* An outwork of fortifications, consisting of two faces forming a salient angle, constructed beyond the main ditch and in front of the curtain.

ravigote /ravigɔt/ *noun* M19 **French** (from *ravigoter* to invigorate). A mixture of chopped chervil, chives, tarragon, and shallots, used to give piquancy to a sauce, as a base for a herb butter, etc.; a vinaigrette dressing containing capers and chopped hard-boiled egg flavoured with such a mixture; a velouté sauce containing such a herb butter.

ravinement /rə'viːnm(ə)nt/ *noun* E20 **French** (from *raviner* to furrow). *Physical Geography* Erosion of ravines or gullies in soil or soft rock by running water. Also, an unconformity in river or shallow marine sediments caused by interruption of deposition by erosion.

ravioli /ravɪ'əʊli/ *noun* M19 **Italian** (plural of *raviolo*). Pasta in the form of small square cases filled with minced meat, vegetables, etc.

ravissant /ravisɑ̃/ *adjective* (also (feminine) **ravissante** /ravisɑ̃t/) M17 **French** (present participial adjective of *ravir* (formerly) to seize, carry off, (now) to enchant). Ravishing, delightful.

■ Originally (ME–M16) used in English of an animal and reflecting the older French sense of *ravir*, hence 'ravening'; it also had a specific heraldic sense (E18) meaning 'in the half-raised posture of a wolf beginning to spring on its prey'.

rayah /'rʌɪə/ *noun* E19 **Turkish** (*râya* from Arabic *ra'āyā* plural of *ra'iyya(t)*). Under the Ottoman Empire, a non-Muslim subject of the Sultan of Turkey, liable to a poll tax.

rayonnant /rɛjɔnɑ̃/ *adjective* (feminine **rayonnante** /rɛjɔnɑ̃t/) E19 **French** (present participial adjective of *rayonner* to shine forth). Of a person: beaming, radiant.

razant variant of RASANT.

razet /razɛ/ *noun* plural pronounced same M20 **French** (from Provençal *raset*). *Bullfighting* In southern France, a contest in which teams compete to snatch a rosette from between the bull's horns.

razeteur /razətœr/ *noun* M20 **French**. A member of a team competing in a *razet*.

razzia /'razɪə/ *noun* M19 **French** (from Algerian Arabic *ġāziya* raid, from Arabic *ġazā* to go forth to fight, make a raid). A raid, a foray; *specifically* (*historical*) a hostile Moorish incursion for purposes of conquest, plunder, capture of slaves, etc.

re /reɪ/, /riː/ *preposition* E18 **Latin** (ablative of *res* thing). In the matter of, concerning, about.

realia /reɪ'ɑːlɪə/, /rɪ'eɪlɪə/ *noun plural* M20 **Late Latin** (use as noun of neuter plural of *realis* real). **1** M20 Objects which may be used as teaching aids but were not made for the purpose. *North American*. **2** M20 Real things, actual facts, especially as distinct from theories about them.

realpolitik /reˌɑːlpɒli'tiːk/, /reɪ'ɑːlpɒlɪtiːk/ *noun* E20 **German** (*real* real + *Politik* politics). Politics based on practical, rather than moral or ideological, considerations; practical politics.

1995 *Spectator* The Defence Secretary, Michael Portillo, was at last moved by the spectacle of the Balkan tragedy to go beyond considerations of *realpolitik* to true moral indignation.

Realpolitiker /reˌɑːlpɒ'litiːkə/, /reɪ'ɑːlpɒˌlɪtiːkə/ *noun* M20 **German**. A person who believes in, advocates, or practises REALPOLITIK.

1995 *Spectator* Machiavelli . . . is not a mere *realpolitiker* writing a handbook counselling princes how to achieve and maintain themselves in power.

reata variant of RIATA.

reb /rɛb/ *noun* L19 **Yiddish** (from as REBBE). A traditional Jewish courtesy title used preceding a man's forename or surname.

rebab /rɪˈbab/ *noun* M18 **Arabic** (*rabāb*). A bowed or (occasionally) plucked stringed instrument of Arab origin, used especially in North Africa, the Middle East, and the Indian subcontinent.

rebbe /ˈrɛbə/ *noun* L19 **Yiddish** (from Hebrew *rabbī* rabbi). A rabbi; *specifically* a Hasidic religious leader.

rebbitzin /ˈrɛbɪtsɪn/ *noun* L19 **Yiddish** (feminine of REBBE). The wife of a rabbi.

rebec /ˈriːbɛk/ *noun* (also **rebeck**) LME **French** (alteration of Old French *rebebe*, *rubebe*). Chiefly *History* A medieval musical instrument with usually three strings and played with a bow; a player on this in an orchestra etc.

reblochon /rəblɔʃɔ̃/ *noun* E20 **French**. A soft French cheese made originally and chiefly in Savoy.

reboso variant of REBOZO.

rebours see À REBOURS.

rebozo /rɪˈbəʊzəʊ/, /rɪˈbəʊsəʊ/ *noun* (also **reboso**) plural **rebozos** E19 **Spanish**. A long scarf covering the head and shoulders, traditionally worn by Spanish-American women.

rebus /ˈriːbəs/ *noun* E17 **French** (*rébus* from Latin *rebus* ablative plural of *res* thing). A representation of a word or phrase by pictures, symbols, arrangement of letters, etc., which suggest the word or phrase, or the syllables of which it is made up; *specifically* a device, often of heraldic appearance, suggesting the name of its bearer.

■ This usage originated in *De rebus quae geruntur* (literally, 'concerning the things that are taking place'), the title given in sixteenth-century Picardy to satirical pieces containing riddles in picture form.

rebus sic stantibus /ˌreɪbəs sɪk ˈstantɪbəs/ *noun & adverb phrase* E17 **Modern Latin** (literally, 'things standing thus'). *International Law* (According to) the principle that a treaty is subject to an implied condition that if circumstances are substantially different from those obtaining when it was concluded, then a party to the treaty is entitled to be released from it.

recado /reˈkado/, /rɪˈkɑːdəʊ/ *noun* plural **recados** /reˈkados/, /rɪˈkɑːdəʊz/ E17 **Spanish and Portuguese** (= gift, of unknown origin). **1** A present; a message of goodwill. Only in 17. **2** E19 A South American saddle or saddle-cloth.

Récamier /reɪˈkamjeɪ/, *foreign* /rekamje/ (*plural same*) *noun & adjective* (also **récamier**) E20 **French** (from the name of Jeanne *Récamier* (1777–1849), society hostess, depicted reclining on a chaise longue in a famous portrait by Jacques Louis David). (Designating) a style of chaise longue.

1979 *New York Times Magazine* The smaller studio . . . is more formal, primarily because of the major furnishings—a matching pair of *récamiers* (Empire-style lounges).

réchaud /reʃo/ *noun* plural pronounced same E20 **French** (from *réchauffer* to reheat, warm up again). A dish in which food is warmed or kept warm.

réchauffé /reʃofe/, /reɪˈʃəʊfeɪ/ *noun & adjective* E19 **French** (past participle of *réchauffer* to reheat, from *re-* again + *échauffer* to warm (up), from Proto-Romance variation of Latin *cal(e)facere* to make warm, from *calere* to be warm + *facere* to make). **A** *noun* E19 A warmed-up dish; *figurative* a rehash. **B** *adjective* E20 (Of food) reheated; *figurative* rehashed.

recherché /rəˈʃɛːʃeɪ/ *adjective* L17 **French** (past participle of *rechercher* to seek out, look for). Carefully sought out; rare, exotic; far-fetched, obscure.

1995 *Observer Review* Now there's nothing wrong with using *recherché* words—Nabokov did it all the time—and the inquisitive need only consult a dictionary.

recherche du temps perdu /rəʃɛrʃ dy tɑ̃ pɛrdy/ *noun phrase* M20 **French** (*à la recherche du temps perdu*, literally, 'in search of the lost time', title of novel by Marcel Proust (1871–1922)). A narration or evocation of one's early life.

1996 *Spectator* Marcel Proust was never one of the great rugby players, but the entire impetus of the French rugby union team springs from *la recherche du temps perdu*.

Rechtsstaat /ˈrɛçtsˌʃtɑːt/ *noun* M20 **German** (from *Recht* right + genitive suffix *-s* +

Staat State). A country in which the rule of law prevails.

récit /resi/ *noun* plural pronounced same L19 **French**. **1** L19 *Music* A passage or composition for a solo voice or instrument. Also, a division of the classical French organ. **2** M20 The narrative of a book as opposed to the dialogue; a book or passage consisting largely of this.

recitativo /ˌretʃita'ti:vo/, /ˌrɛsɪtə'ti:vəʊ/ *noun* plural **recitativi** /ˌretʃita'ti:vi/, **recitativos** /ˌrɛsɪtə'ti:vəʊz/ M17 **Italian** (from Latin *recitat-* past participial stem of *recitare* to recite). *Music* A style of musical declamation between singing and ordinary speech; a passage in a musical score or libretto (intended to be) delivered in this style; (a) recitative.

■ *Recitativo* may be accompanied either by the full orchestra (*recitativo accompagnato* or *recitativo stromentato* (literally, 'instrumented')) or by continuo instruments only (*recitativo secco*).

réclame /reklam/ *noun* plural pronounced same L19 **French** (from *réclamer* to ask for). (An) advertisement; self-publicity; public acclaim or notoriety.

1996 *Spectator* It is difficult for people today to realise the extraordinary *réclame* that T. E. Lawrence . . . had in those years between the wars.

récolte /rekɔlt/ *noun* plural pronounced same (also (earlier) **recolt**) L18 **French**. In France: a harvest, a crop.

recta plural of RECTUM.

recte /'rɛkteɪ/ *adverb* M19 **Latin** (literally, 'in a straight line, rightly'). Correctly.

■ Used when introducing a word or phrase as a correct version of that just given, as in 'Jane Blundell *recte* Blunden'.

recti plural of RECTUS.

rectius /'rɛktɪəs/ *adverb* M20 **Latin** (comparative of RECTE). More correctly: introducing a word or phrase as a more correct version of that just given.

recto /'rɛktəʊ/ *noun* plural **rectos** E19 **Latin** ((sc. *folio*) ablative of *rectus* right). The right-hand page of an open book; the front of a leaf in a manuscript or printed book, as opposed to the back or VERSO.

rectum /'rɛktəm/ *noun* plural **rectums**, **recta** /'rɛktə/ M16 **Latin** (neuter of *rectus* straight, short for *intestinum rectum* straight gut). The final section of the large intestine leading to the anus.

rectus /'rɛktəs/ *noun* plural **recti** /'rɛktʌɪ/ E18 **Latin** ((sc. *musculus* muscle) see preceding). **1** E18 *Anatomy* Any of several straight muscles, especially of the abdomen, thigh, neck, and eye. Frequently with modern Latin specifying word. Also *rectus muscle*. **2** M20 *Music* In a fugal composition, the version of a theme performed in the original, as opposed to the reversed or inverted, order.

recueil /rəkœj/ *noun* L15 **Old and Modern French** (from *recueillir* to gather up, from Latin *recolligere*, from as *re-* + *colligere* to collect). **1** L15 A literary compilation. **2** L15–L16 Reception, welcome; succour.

recueillement /rəkœjmɑ̃/ *noun* M19 **French** (from as RECUEIL). Serious concentration of thought.

reculer pour mieux sauter /rəkyle pur mjø sote/ *noun phrase* E19 **French** (literally, 'to draw back in order to leap better'). The use of a withdrawal or setback as a basis for further advance or success.

1996 *Country Life* Hostility towards mobiles runs high in the world of commuters for the train has traditionally provided a brief capsule of immunity from the real world, an opportunity to *reculer pour mieux sauter*.

redingote /'rɛdɪŋgəʊt/ *noun* L18 **French** (from English *riding-coat*). Originally, a man's double-breasted greatcoat with long plain skirts not cut away in the front. Now usually, a woman's long coat with a cut-away front or a contrasting piece on the front.

redivivus /rɛdɪ'vi:vəs/ *postpositive adjective* (feminine **rediviva** /rɛdɪ'vi:və/; occasionally (earlier) Anglicized as **redivive** /rɛdɪ'vʌɪv/) L16 **Latin** (from *re-* again + *vivus* living, alive). Come back to life; reborn, renewed.

■ Always postpositive (see quotation). The Latin form first appeared (L17) in book titles, e.g. R. Head's *Proteus redivivus: or the art of wheedling* (1675). Cf. REDUX.

1975 *Times* Some still believe in Stormont Redivivus.

redowa /'rɛdəvə/ *noun* M19 **French** (or German, from Czech *rejdovák*, from *rejdovat* to turn or whirl round). A Bohemian folk-dance; a ballroom dance in relatively quick triple time resembling this; a piece of music for such a dance.

reductio ad absurdum /rɪˌdʌktɪəʊ ad əb'sə:dəm/ *noun phrase* M18 **Latin** (literally, 'reduction to the absurd'). *Logic* A method of proving the falsity of a premiss by showing that the logical consequence is absurd.

1995 *Times* Making criminal the carrying of all knives in public places could—and this is the *reductio ad absurdum*—lead to the prosecution of people going on a picnic.

reductio ad impossibile /rɪˌdʌktɪəʊ ad ɪmpɒˈsɪbɪliː/ *noun phrase* M16 **Latin** (literally, 'reduction to the impossible'). A method of proving a proposition by drawing an absurd or impossible conclusion from its contradictory.

redux /ˈriːdʌks/ *adjective* L19 **Latin** (from *reducere* to bring back). **1** L19 *Medicine* Of crepitation etc.: indicating the return of the lungs to a healthy state. Now *rare*. **2** L19 Brought back, revived, restored.

■ Usually postpositive and often in titles, from John Dryden's poem on the restoration of King Charles II *Astraea Redux* (1662) to John Updike's novel *Rabbit Redux* (1971); cf. REDIVIVUS.

Reeperbahn /ˈriːpəbɑːn/ *noun* L20 **German** (a street in Hamburg, Germany, literally, 'rope-walk', from *Reeper* rope-maker + *Bahn* road, way). (The principal street in) the red-light district of a city etc.

referendum /rɛfəˈrɛndəm/ *noun* plural **referendums**, **referenda** /rɛfəˈrɛndə/ M19 **Latin** (gerund or neuter gerundive of *referre* to refer). The process or principle of referring an important political question, e.g. a proposed constitutional change, to the entire electorate to be decided by a general vote; a vote taken by referendum.

reflet /rəflɛ/ *noun* plural pronounced same M19 **French**. Colour due to reflection; lustre, iridescence; *specifically* a metallic lustre on pottery.

refugium /rɪˈfjuːdʒɪəm/ *noun* plural **refugia** /rɪˈfjuːdʒɪə/ M20 **Latin** (= place of refuge). *Biology* A refuge, *specifically* one in which a species survived a period of glaciation.

1996 *New Scientist* . . . during the last ice ages . . . less rain fell over Amazonia. As a result, the rainforest shrunk into isolated pockets, or refugia, in the wettest parts of the region.

reg /rɛg/ *noun* E20 **Arabic** (colloquial). *Physical Geography* A desert plain covered with small rounded pebbles; a stony desert.

1976 L. Deighton *Twinkle, Twinkle, Little Spy* The going changed to the gravelly surface of the 'reg' and then to rough 'washboard'.

regalia /rɪˈgeɪlɪə/ *noun 1 plural and collective singular* M16 **Medieval Latin** (= royal residence, royal rights, use as noun of neuter plural of *regalis* regal). **1** M16 Rights belonging to a king or queen; royal powers or privileges. **2** The emblems or insignia of royalty. Also *transferred*, the decorations or insignia of an order; any distinctive or elaborate clothes.

2 1996 *Times Magazine* Just as no one who lives in London has ever been . . . to see the crown jewels, so I had never been to Edinburgh Castle to see the Scottish regalia.

regalia /rɪˈgeɪlɪə/ *noun 2* E19 **Spanish** (= royal privilege). A Cuban or other large high-quality cigar.

regardant /rɪˈgɑːd(ə)nt/ *adjective & noun* LME **Old and Modern French** ((also Anglo-Norman) present participle of *regarder* to look at). **1** LME *Heraldry* Usually of a lion: looking backwards over the shoulder. Usually *postpositive*. **2** L16 Observant, watchful, contemplative.

■ In feudal usage also with reference to a serf attached to a manor, as in *villein regardant*.

regatta /rɪˈgatə/ *noun* E17 **Italian** (Venetian dialect *regatta*, *rigatta*, *regata* a fight, a struggle, a contest). **1** E17 Any of certain boat races held on the Grand Canal in Venice. **2** L18 An organized series of boat or yacht races. **3** M19 A cotton fabric, usually made in twill; a striped garment made in this fabric.

régie /reʒi/ *noun* plural pronounced same L18 **French** (feminine past participle of *régir* to rule). In some European countries, a government department that controls an industry or service; *specifically* (*historical*) one with complete control of the importation, manufacture, and taxation of tobacco, salt, etc.

regime /reɪˈʒiːm/ *noun* (also **régime**) L15 **French** (*régime* from Latin REGIMEN). **1** L15 A lifestyle adopted for health reasons; a REGIMEN 2. **2** L18 A method or system of rule or government; a system or institution having widespread influence or prevalence. Now frequently (usually *derogatory*), a particular government. **3** *Physical Geography* **a** M19 The condition of a watercourse with regard to changes in its form or bed; *especially* an equilibrium between erosion and deposition. **b** L19 The condition of a body of water with regard to the rates at which water enters and leaves it. **4** L19 *Science* and *Engineering* The set of conditions under which a system occurs or is maintained.

regimen /ˈrɛdʒɪmən/ *noun* LME **Latin** (from *regere* to rule). **1** LME The action of governing; government, rule. Later also, a particular system of government; a regime. *archaic*. **2** LME Chiefly *Medicine* A prescribed course of exercise, way of life, or diet, especially for the promotion or restoration of one's health. **3** M16 *Grammar* The government of one word by another; the relationship between one word and another dependent word. Now *rare*. **4** E19 *Physical Geography* REGIME sense 3a.

régisseur /reʒisœr/ *noun* plural pronounced same E19 **French**. *Theatre* and *Ballet* A stage-manager, an artistic director.

Regius /ˈriːdʒɪəs/ *adjective* E17 **Latin** (= royal, from *rex, reg-* king). Designating (a professor holding) a university chair founded by a monarch or filled by Crown appointment.

reglement /rɛgləmɑ̃/ *noun* plural pronounced same L16 **French** (*règlement, reiglement*, from Old and Modern French *regler, reigler* to rule, from late Latin *regulare* to regulate). **1** L16–M18 The action of regulating or controlling something. **2** M17 A regulation.

règlement de compte /rɛgləmɑ̃ də kɔ̃t/ *noun phrase* L20 **French**. Settlement of an account; the settling of a score.

1995 *Spectator* The summer of dirt and treachery will be followed by a *règlement des comptes* in the autumn.

Reich /rʌɪk/, /rʌɪx/ *noun* plural **Reiche** /rʌɪkə/ E20 **German** (= kingdom, empire, State). Chiefly *History* The former German State or commonwealth, *especially* the Third Reich (the Nazi regime 1933–45).

reine /rɛn/ *noun* M19 **French** (= queen). *Cookery* Chiefly in *à la reine* (literally, 'in the fashion of a queen'), designating a dish prepared in some special way.

reinette /reɪˈnɛt/ *noun* LME **French** (*reinette, rainette*, perhaps from *raine* tree frog (from Latin *rana* frog), from the spots in certain varieties). Any of several eating apples of French origin, chiefly small and late-ripening, with dry skin and firm juicy flesh.

reis /reɪs/ *noun* (also **rais** /rʌɪs/) L16 **Arabic** (*raʾīs* chief from *raʾs* head). **1** L16 The captain of a boat or ship. **2** L17 A chief, a governor.

2 1996 *Times* On January 20, the Palestinian people will vote to elect their *rais*, or 'leader', and an 88-member national council.

reja /ˈrexa/ *noun* M19 **Spanish**. In Spain: a wrought-iron screen or grille used to protect windows, chapel tombs, etc.

relâche /rəlɑʃ/ *noun* plural pronounced same M19 **French**. A period of rest, an interval; a break *from* something.

relais /rəlɛ/ *noun* plural pronounced same M20 **French**. In France: a café, a restaurant, sometimes also providing overnight accommodation.

relance /rəlɑ̃s/ *noun* plural pronounced same L20 **French**. *Politics* A relaunch, a revival, especially of a policy.

relevé /rələˈveɪ/ *noun* E19 **French** (= raised up). **1** E19 A course of a meal; a remove. *archaic*. **2** M20 *Ballet* A step in which the body is raised on half or full point. **3** M20 *Ecology* An enumeration of the species and environmental factors in a small stand of vegetation, taken as a sample of a wider area; the stand of vegetation itself.

relievo /rɪˈliːvəʊ/ *noun* plural **relievos** (also **rilievo** /rɪˈljeɪvəʊ/) E17 **Italian** (*rilievo* from *rilevare* to raise, ultimately from Latin *relevare* to raise again). **1** A method of moulding, carving, etc., in which the design stands out from the plane surface. Cf. ALTO-RELIEVO, BASSO-RELIEVO, MEZZO-RELIEVO. **2** The appearance of solidity given to a composition on a plane surface; *figurative* vividness or distinctness due to artistic presentation.

religieuse /rəliʒjøz/ *noun* plural pronounced same L17 **French** (feminine of next). **1** L17 A woman bound by religious vows; a nun. **2** M20 A confection consisting of two round cakes of choux pastry sandwiched together with cream and decorated with icing.

religieux /rəliʒjø/ *noun* plural same M17 **French**. A man bound by religious vows; a monk.

religioso /reˌlidʒiˈoːzo/, /rɪˌlɪdʒɪˈəʊzəʊ/ *adverb & adjective* M19 **Italian** (= religious). *Music* (A direction:) with a devotional quality.

reliquiae /rɪˈlɪkwiː/ *noun plural* M17 **Latin** (use as noun of feminine plural of *reliquus* remaining, from as *re* + *liq-* stem of *linquere* to leave). Remains; *specifically* (*a*) *Geology* fossilized remains of animals or plants; (*b*) literary remains, unpublished or uncollected writings.

relleno abbreviation of CHILLI RELLENO.

remanié /rəmanje/ *adjective* L19 **French** (past participle of *remanier* to rehandle, reshape). *Geology* Derived from an older stratum or structure.

remaniement /rəmanimɑ̃/ *noun* plural pronounced same E20 **French** (from as preceding). A rearrangement, a reconstruction.

remarque /rɪˈmɑːk/, *foreign* /rəmark/ (*plural same*) *noun* (also **remark**) L19 **French**. *Engraving* A distinguishing feature indicating the state of the plate, frequently taking the form of a sketch in the margin.

remboîtage /rɑ̃bwataʒ/ *noun* plural pronounced same M20 **French** (from *remboîter* to re-case (a book)). The action or an act of transferring a book into new binding, especially of superior quality.

remittitur /rɪˈmɪtɪtəː/ *noun* L18 **Latin** (3rd person singular passive of *remittere* to remit). *Law* **1** L18 The remission of excessive damages awarded to a plaintiff; a formal statement of this. **2** L18 The action of sending the transcript of a case back from an appellate to a trial court; a formal notice of this.

remontoir /ˌrɛmənˈtwɑː/ *noun* (also **remontoire**) E19 **French** (from *remonter* to remount). *Horology* A device by which a uniform impulse is given to the pendulum or balance at regular intervals.

remora /ˈrɛmərə/ *noun* M16 **Latin** (= delay, hindrance, from *re-* + *mora* delay). **1** M16 Any of various slender marine fishes of the family Echeneidae, with the dorsal fin modified to form a large sucker for attachment to sharks etc., formerly believed to hinder the progress of any sailing ship to which it attached itself. **2** E17 An obstacle, a hindrance, an impediment.

rémoulade /ˈrɛmʊlɑːd/, *foreign* /remulad/ (*plural same*) *noun* (also **remoulade**) M19 **French** (from Italian *remolata*, of unknown origin). A salad dressing made with hard-boiled egg-yolks, oil, vinegar, herbs, etc.

remplaçant /rɑ̃plasɑ̃/ *noun* (feminine **remplaçante** /rɑ̃plasɑ̃t/) plural pronounced same M19 **French** (present participial adjective of *remplacer* to replace). A person who replaces another.

remskoen /ˈrɛmskʊn/ *noun* (also **riemskoen** /riːmskʊn/ and other variants) plural **remskoene** /ˈrɛmskʊnə/ E19 **Afrikaans** (from Dutch *remschoen*, from *rem* brake + *schoen* shoe). *South African History* A wooden or metal shoe used to prevent a wheel from revolving; *figurative* an impediment to progress.

remuage /rəmɥaʒ/, /ˌrɛmjʊˈɑːʒ/ *noun* E20 **French** (literally, 'moving about'). The periodic turning or shaking of bottled wine, especially champagne, to move sediment towards the cork.

remuda /rəˈmuːdə/ *noun* L19 **American Spanish** (from Spanish = exchange, replacement). A collection of saddle-horses kept for remounts.

remueur /rəmɥœr/ *noun* plural pronounced same E20 **French** (literally, 'mover'). A person who engages in REMUAGE.

Renaissance /rɪˈneɪs(ə)ns/, *foreign* /rənɛsɑ̃s/ *noun* (also (especially in sense 2) **renaissance**) M19 **French** ((in specific use short for *renaissance des arts*, *renaissance des lettres*), from as *re-* + *naissance* birth from Latin *nascentia*, from *nasci* be born, or from French *naiss-* present stem of *naître* from Proto-Romance). **1 a** M19 The revival of art and literature under the influence of classical models between the fourteenth and sixteenth centuries, begun in Italy; the period of this movement. **b** M19 The style of art, architecture, etc., developed in and characteristic of this period. **2** L19 Any revival or period of significant improvement and new life in cultural, scientific, economic, or other areas of activity.

rendezvous /ˈrɒndɪvuː/, /ˈrɒndeɪvuː/ *noun* (also **rendez-vous**) plural same /ˈrɒndɪvuːz/ L16 **French** (use as noun of imperative *rendez-vous* 'present yourselves', from *rendre* from Proto-Romance alteration of Latin *reddere* to give back). **1** *Military* **a** L16 A place appointed for the assembling of troops or armed forces. **b** E17 A place or port used or suitable for the assembling of a fleet or number of ships. Also, instructions concerning such a place. **2** L16 *generally* Any appointed or habitual meeting-place. **3** E17 A meeting or assembly held by appointment or arrangement. Formerly also, a group of people thus assembled. **b** M–L17 An assemblage of things. **c** M20 The prearranged meeting in space between a spacecraft and another spacecraft or a celestial body; an instance of this.

2 1996 *Spectator* . . . we had both been the recipients of mysterious notes from Richard, establishing the rendez-vous for lunch and insisting upon the most absolute secrecy.

rendu /rɑ̃dy/ *adjective* M20 **French** (= rendered, delivered). Designating a price on imported goods which includes tariffs and delivery costs.

rendzina /rɛnd'ziːnə/ *noun* E20 **Russian** (from Polish *rędzina*). *Soil Science* A fertile lime-rich soil characterized by a dark friable humus-rich surface layer above a softer pale calcareous layer.

renga /'rɛŋgə/ *noun* plural same, **rengas** L19 **Japanese** (from *ren* linking + *ga* from *ka* poetry). A Japanese poem consisting of a series of half-tanka contributed by different poets in turn.

renseignement /rɑ̃sɛɲəmɑ̃/ *noun* plural pronounced same M19 **French**. (A piece of) information. Also, a letter of introduction.

rente /rɑ̃t/ *noun* plural pronounced same L19 **French**. Stock, *especially* French government stock; the interest or income accruing from such stock.

rentier /rɑ̃tje/, /'rɒntɪeɪ/ *noun* plural pronounced same M19 **French** (from RENTE). A person who makes an income from property or investment.

1995 G. Tindall *Célestine* [The] composition seems redolent of the self-conscious world just being born: that of the *rentier* and the white-collar workers, . . . of trains and newspapers and morning coffee . . .

rentrée /'rɒntreɪ/, *foreign* /rɑ̃tre/ (*plural same*) *noun* L19 **French**. A return, *especially* a return home after an annual holiday.

renvers /rɑ̃vɛrs/, /'rɛnvəs/ *noun* plural same L19 **French** (from *renverser*, from as *re-* + *enverser* to overturn). *Horsemanship* A movement in which a horse walks parallel to a wall with its head and neck facing forward and its hindquarters curved towards the wall.

renversement /rɑ̃vɛrsəmɑ̃/ (*plural same*), /rɒn'vəːs(ə)m(ə)nt/ *noun* E17 **French** (from as RENVERS). Originally, the action of reversing or inverting; the result of this. Now usually *specifically*, an aeroplane manoeuvre consisting of a half-loop effected simultaneously with a half-turn.

repêchage /'rɛpəʃɑːʒ/ *noun* E20 **French** (from *repêcher*, literally, 'to fish out, rescue'). An extra contest, especially in rowing and cycling, in which the runners-up in the eliminating heats compete for a place in the final.

1996 *Times* . . . an unsettlingly sportless lull between the recorded highlights of, as I recall, the men's synchronised triple frisbee and the repechage of the women's 80m coxless egg-and spoon . . .

répétiteur /repetitœr/ (*plural same*), /rɛˌpɛtɪ'təː/ *noun* M20 **French** (= tutor, coach). **1** M20 A person who teaches musicians and singers, especially opera singers, their parts. **2** M20 A person who supervises ballet rehearsals etc.

1 1996 *Times* Maybe Savonlinna should beef up its team of répétiteurs; the raw material is marvellous, and could be further refined.

réplique /replik/ *noun* (also **replique**) plural pronounced same L15 **French** (from *répliquer* from Latin *replicare* to unfold, (later) reply). A reply, a rejoinder.

■ Formerly fully Anglicized.

repoussé /rə'puːseɪ/ *adjective & noun* M19 **French** (past participle of *repousser*, from *re-* + *pousser* to push). **A** *adjective* M19 Of metalwork: raised into or ornamented in relief by means of hammering from the reverse side. **B** *noun* M19 Ornamental metalwork fashioned by the repoussé method; the process of hammering into relief.

repoussoir /rəpuswar/ *noun* plural pronounced same L19 **French** (from REPOUSSÉ). An object in the foreground of a painting serving to emphasize the principal figure or scene.

reprise /rɪ'prʌɪz/, *chiefly in sense 6* /rɪ'priːz/ *noun* LME **Old and Modern French** (use as noun of past participle feminine of *reprendre* to take back, take again). **I 1** The fact of taking back something for one's own advantage; an amount taken back; loss, expense, cost. Only in LME. **2** LME A charge or payment falling due annually from a manor or estate. Usually in *plural*. **3a** M16–M18 Compensation. **b** M17–E18 The action of taking something by way of retaliation. **4** L17 A renewal or repetition of an action; a separate occasion of doing something. **II 5** E16 *Architecture* A return of mouldings etc. in an internal angle. **6a** E18 *Music* The repetition of the first theme of a movement after the close of the development. Formerly also, a refrain. **b** M20 *Linguistics* The repetition of a word or word group occurring in a preceding phrase. **c** M20 A repetition of a theatrical performance; a restaging or rewriting of a play; a replay. Also more widely, a further performance of any kind.

requiem /'rɛkwɪəm/, /'rɛkwɪɛm/ *noun* ME Latin (accusative of *requies* rest, first word of the introit in the mass for the dead, *Requiem aeternam dona eis, Domine* Give them eternal rest, O Lord). **1** ME (frequently **Requiem**) *Roman Catholic Church* A special mass said or sung for the repose of the soul of a dead person. Also *mass of requiem, requiem mass*. **b** L18 A musical setting of a mass for the dead. **2** E17 Any dirge, solemn chant, etc., for the repose of the dead; *figurative* a memorial, a commemoration. **3** E17 Rest, peace, quiet; a period of this. Now *rare*.

requiescat /rɛkwɪ'ɛskat/ *noun* E19 Latin (from *requiescat in pace* may he or she rest in peace). A wish for the repose of a dead person.

res /reɪz/ *noun* plural same E17 Latin (= thing). A thing, a matter.

■ Originally in legal terminology and still chiefly in Latin legal phrases, e.g. *res communis* 'common property', *res integra* 'a matter that has not been covered', *res judicata* 'a matter that has been adjudicated', *res nullius* 'no one's property'. Used alone, *res* can now also have the more general senses of 'the condition of something; the matter in hand, the point at issue, the crux' (see quotation).

1966 P. G. Wodehouse *Plum Pie* I saw that I had better come to the *res* without delay.

res cogitans /reɪz 'kɒgɪtanz/, /reɪz 'kɒdʒɪtanz/ *noun phrase* E20 Latin (= thinking thing). *Philosophy* The concept of a human as a thinking being.

■ The concept originated with Descartes in his *Meditationes* (1641): *Sed quid igitur sum? res cogitans* 'But what therefore am I? A thinking being' (ii.23).

réseau /'reɪzəʊ/, *foreign* /rezo/ *noun* plural **réseaux** /'reɪzəʊ/, *foreign* /rezo/ (also **rézel** /'reɪzɛl/, *foreign* /rezɛl/ (*plural same*)) L16 French (= net, web) **1** L16 A plain net ground used in lace-making. **2** E20 A network, a grid, *especially* one superimposed as a reference marking on a photograph in astronomy, surveying, etc. **3** M20 A spy or intelligence network, especially in the French resistance movement during the German occupation (1940–5).

res extensa /reɪz ɪk'stɛnsə/ *noun phrase* plural **res extensae** /reɪz 'ɪkstɛnsi:/ M20 Latin (= extended thing). *Philosophy* A material thing considered as material substance.

res gestae /reɪz 'gɛstʌɪ/, /reɪz 'dʒɛsti:/ *noun phrase plural* E17 Latin (= things done). (An account of) things done; (a person's) achievements; events in the past; in *Law* the facts of the case.

1969 *North Dakota Law Review* What they [sc. children] say when pressures of emotion and strangeness are absent is more apt to be true, somewhat analogous to *res gestae*.

residentura /ˌrɪzɪdɛn'turə/, /ˌrɛzɪdɛn 'tʊərə/ *noun* M20 Russian (*rezidentura*). A group or organization of intelligence agents in a foreign country.

residuum /rɪ'zɪdjʊəm/ *noun* plural **residua** /rɪ'zɪdjʊə/ L17 Latin (use as noun of neuter of *residuus* remaining, from *residere* to reside). **1** L17 That which remains; a residue. **b** M19 The masses; the poor. **2** M18 *Law* The residue of an estate. **3** M18 *Chemistry* etc. A substance left after combustion, evaporation, etc., a residue.

résistant /rezistɑ̃/ *noun* plural pronounced same M20 French. A member of the French Resistance movement in the war of 1939–45.

1996 *Spectator* In 1994, the then President Mitterand, whilst claiming to have been a *résistant*, under the patronage of Marshal Pétain, stated that in 1942 he knew nothing about the anti-Jewish laws that Pétain's government had passed in 1940 and 1941.

res non verba /ˌreɪz nɒn 'və:bə/ *noun phrase plural* M20 Latin (= things not words). Action rather than talk.

■ Also as a motto, sometimes with the addition *crux non vis* 'the Cross not force'.

respondentia /ˌrɪspɒn'dɛnʃə/ *noun* E18 Modern Latin (from *respondent-* present participial stem of Latin *respondere* from *re-* + *spondere* to pledge). A loan on the cargo of a vessel, to be repaid (with maritime interest) only if the goods arrive safe at their destination.

responsum /rɪ'spɒnsəm/ *noun* plural **responsa** /rɪ'spɒnsə/ L19 Latin (= reply). A written reply by a rabbi or Talmudic scholar to an inquiry on some matter of Jewish law.

ressentiment /rəsɑ̃timɑ̃/ *noun* M20 German (*Ressentiment* from French *ressentiment*, from *ressentir* to feel). *Social Psychology* A negative attitude towards society or authority arising from repressed hostility, feelings of inadequacy, etc.

■ The term is particularly associated with the philosophy of Friedrich Nietzsche (1844–1900) (see quotation).

1994 I. M. Zeitlin *Nietzche Ressentiment* entails a negation and repudiation of the master's values, a saying of No!, which eventually becomes the creative act of inverting those values and substituting new ones for them.

restaurant /'rɛst(ə)rɒnt/, /'rɛst(ə)r(ə)nt/, /'rɛst(ə)rɔ̃:/, /'rɛst(ə)rɒ̃/, /'rɛst(ə)rɑ̃:/ *noun* E19 **French** (use as noun of present participle of *restaurer* to restore). A public establishment where meals or refreshments may be obtained.

restaurateur /rɛst(ə)rə'tə:/, /ˌrɛstɒrə'tə:/ *noun* L18 **French** (from *restaurer* to restore). A keeper of a restaurant.

restitutio in integrum /rɛstɪˌtju:tɪəʊ ɪn ɪn'tɛgrəm/ *noun phrase* E18 **Latin** (= restoration to the uninjured state). *Law* Placement of an injured party in the situation which would have prevailed had no injury been sustained; restoration of the STATUS QUO ANTE.

résumé /'rɛzjʊmeɪ/ *noun* (also **resumé**, in sense 2 **resume**) E19 **French** (past participle of *résumer* to resume). **1** E19 A summary, an epitome. **2** M20 A CURRICULUM VITAE. Chiefly *North American*.

1 1996 *Times* His 'quest' is in reality a literary convention: what Johnson has written is an excellent résumé of a traditional Catholic's faith.

2 1996 *Spectator* Only incidentals on the résumé are different—Stanton missed Vietnam because of a crocked knee.

resurgam /rɪ'sə:gam/ *interjection* M17 **Latin** (literally, 'I shall rise again'). Proclaiming one's Christian faith in the resurrection of the dead. Usually *transferred* and *figurative*.

retable /rɪ'teɪb(ə)l/ *noun* E19 **French** (*rétable, retable* from Spanish *retablo* from medieval Latin *retrotabulum*, from Latin *retro-* behind + *tabula* table). A frame enclosing painted or decorated panels or a shelf or ledge for ornaments, raised above the back of an altar.

retablo /rɪ'tɑ:bləʊ/ *noun* plural **retablos** M19 **Spanish** (see preceding). A RETABLE. Also, a votive picture displayed in a church.

retardataire /rətardatɛr/ *noun & adjective* plural of noun pronounced same E20 **French**. Chiefly *Art*. **A** *noun* E20 A work of art executed in the style of an earlier period. **B** *adjective* M20 Behind the times; characterized by the style of an earlier period.

B 1977 *Times Literary Supplement* The *retardataire* appearance of much colonial architecture is derived from the poor, often secondhand knowledge of contemporary architectectual practice as well as from a conservatism in patrons' tastes.

retiarius /rɛtɪ'ɑ:rɪəs/, /rɛtɪ'ɛ:rɪəs/ *noun* plural **retiarii** /rɛtɪ'ɑ:rɪʌɪ/, /rɛtɪ'ɛ:rɪi:/ M17 **Latin** (from *rete* net). *Roman History* A gladiator who fought using a net with which to entangle his adversary.

reticella /rɛtɪ'ʧɛlə/ *noun & adjective* M19 **Italian** (diminutive of *rete* net). **A** *noun* M19 A lacelike fabric with a characteristic geometric pattern produced especially in Venice from the fifteenth to the seventeenth century. **B** M20 *attributive* or as *adjective* Of, pertaining to, or characteristic of reticella.

reticello /rɛtɪ'ʧɛləʊ/ *noun* plural **reticelli** /rɛtɪ'ʧɛli/ L19 **Italian** (from as preceding). A network of fine glass threads embedded in some Venetian glass. Also (more fully *reticello glass*), glass made with this type of decoration.

reticule /'rɛtɪkju:l/ *noun* E18 **French** (*réticule* from Latin *reticulum* diminutive of *rete* net). **1** E18 A grid of fine lines or threads set in the focal plane or eyepiece of an optical instrument, a reticle. **2** E19 A woman's small netted or other bag, especially with a drawstring, carried or worn to serve the purpose of a pocket.

retina /'rɛtɪnə/ *noun* LME **Medieval Latin** (from Latin *rete* net). The light-sensitive layer which lines much of the inside of the eyeball, in which nerve impulses are triggered and pass via the optic nerve to the brain where a visual image is formed.

retiré /rətire/ *noun* plural pronounced same M20 **French** (past participle of *retirer* to withdraw). *Ballet* A movement in which one leg is raised at right angles to the body until the toe is in line with the knee of the supporting leg.

retornado /ˌretur'nadu/ *noun* plural **retornados** /ˌretur'naduʃ/ L20 **Portuguese** (from past participle of *retornar* to return). A Portuguese citizen returning to settle in Portugal after living in a Portuguese colony.

retraite /rətrɛt/ *noun* plural pronounced same M19 **French** (from Old French *retraite* retreat). **1** M19 Retirement, seclusion, retreat. **2** L19 *Military* The signal for retreating.

retroussage /rətrusaʒ/ *noun* M20 **French** (from as *retroussé*: see next). In etching, the action of drawing a fine cloth across an inked plate to draw out some ink and smear it irregularly across the plate.

retroussé /rə'tru:seɪ/, *foreign* /rətruse/ *adjective* E19 **French** (past participle of *retrousser* to turn up, from *re-* + *trousser* from Old French *trusser*, medieval Latin *trossare*, probably from late Latin *tors-* past participial stem of *torquere* to twist). Usually of the nose: turned up at the tip.

retsina /rɛt'si:nə/ *noun* E20 **Modern Greek** (from *retsini* from Greek *rētinē* pine resin). A Greek white wine flavoured with resin.

réussi /reysi/ *adjective* M20 **French** (past participle of *réuss* to turn out, result, succeed). Fine, excellent, successful.

revanche /rəvɑ̃ʃ/ *noun* M19 **French** (earlier *revenche*, from Old French *revencher* from late Latin *revindicare* to avenge, claim). Revenge; retaliation; *specifically* a nation's policy of seeking the return of lost territory.

■ The policy of *revanchisme* was particularly associated with France's determination to recover Alsace-Lorraine after losing the territory to Germany in the Franco-Prussian War of 1870, but in other contexts the word is now generally Anglicized as *revanchism*.

reveille /rɪ'vali/ *noun* (also (now *rare*) **reveillé** /rɪ'valeɪ/) M17 **French** (*réveillez* imperative plural of *réveiller* to awaken, from *ré-* + *veiller* from Latin *vigilare* to keep watch). A signal given in the morning, usually on a drum or bugle, to waken soldiers and indicate that it is time to rise; (the time of) the sounding of this signal.

réveillon /revɛjɔ̃/ *noun* plural pronounced same E19 **French** (from *réveiller* (see preceding)). In France: a night-time feast or celebration, originally one after midnight on Christmas morning.

revenant /'rɛv(ə)nənt/, *foreign* /rəvənɑ̃/ (*plural of noun same*) *noun & adjective* E19 **French** (present participle of *revenir* to return). **A** *noun* E19 A person who has returned, especially supposedly from the dead; a ghost. **B** *adjective* E20 Returned, especially supposedly from the dead.

B 1996 *Spectator* Evidently a revenant, a returning spirit, . . . really wants only to be allowed to die and stay dead.

reverdie /rəvɛrdi/ *noun* plural pronounced same M20 **French** (use as noun of feminine past participle of *reverdir* to grow, turn green again). A medieval French song celebrating the return of spring.

reverie /'rɛv(ə)ri/ *noun* (also **revery**) ME **French** (in branch I from Old French *reverie* rejoicing, revelry, from *rever* to be delirious (modern *rêver* to dream), of unknown origin; in branch II from later French *resverie* (now *rêverie*)). **I 1** ME–M16 Joy, delight; revelry; wantonness, wildness. *rare*. **II 2** E17 A fantastic, fanciful, or unpractical notion; a delusion. *archaic*. **3** M17 A fit of abstracted musing; a daydream. **b** L19 *Music* An instrumental composition suggestive of a dreamy or musing state. **4** M18 The fact, state, or condition of being lost in thought or engaged in musing.

revers /rɪ'vɪə/ *noun* plural same /rɪ'vɪəz/ M19 **French**. A turned-back edge of a garment revealing the undersurface; the material covering such an edge. Usually *plural*.

revirement /rəvirmɑ̃/ *noun* plural pronounced same E20 **French**. An alteration of one's plans; a complete change of attitude or opinion.

revolte /reɪ'vəʊlteɪ/ *noun* (also **révolté**, (feminine) **révoltée**, /revolte/ (*plural same*)) L19 **French**. A person who revolts; a rebel; a nonconformist.

revue /rɪ'vju:/ *noun* L19 **French** (= review). A light theatrical entertainment consisting of a series of short (usually satirical) sketches, comic turns, songs, etc. Also, the genre comprising such entertainments.

rezident /rɛzɪ'dɛnt/ *noun* plural **rezidenty** /rɛzɪ'dɛnti/ M20 **Russian**. An intelligence agent in a foreign country.

rhagades /'ragədi:z/ *noun plural* OE **Latin** (from Greek, plural of *rhagas* fissure). *Medicine* Cracks, fissures, or thin scars in the skin, especially around the mouth or anus.

rho /rəʊ/ *noun* LME **Greek** (*rhō*). **1** LME The seventeenth letter (Ρ, ρ) of the Greek alphabet. **2** M20 *Statistics* A correlation coefficient. **3** M20 *Physics* A meson with isospin and spin of one and a mass of 770 MeV. In full *rho meson*.

rhodomontade variant of RODOMONTADE.

rhombus /'rɒmbəs/ *noun* plural **rhombuses**, **rhombi** /'rɒmbʌɪ/ M16 **Latin** (from

Greek *rhombos*). **1** M16 *Geometry* A plane figure having four equal sides and equal opposite angles (two acute and two obtuse); an oblique equilateral parallelogram. **2** E17 A lozenge-shaped object, part, marking, etc.

rhumba variant of RUMBA.

rhyton /ˈrʌɪtɒn/, /ˈrɪtɒn/ *noun* plural **rhytons**, **rhyta** /ˈrʌɪtə/ M19 **Greek** (*rhuton* neuter of *rhutos* flowing, related to *rhein* to flow). *Greek Antiquities* A type of drinking-vessel, often in the form of an animal's head, with one or more holes at the bottom through which liquid can flow.

ria /ˈriːə/ *noun* L19 **Spanish** (*ría* estuary). *Physical Geography* A long narrow inlet of the sea formed by partial submergence of an unglaciated river valley.

Rialto /rɪˈaltəʊ/ *noun* (also **rialto**) M16 **Italian** (name of district of Venice in which the Exchange was situated). A market, an exchange.

riata /rɪˈɑːtə/ *noun* (also **reata**) M19 **Spanish** (*reata*). A lariat.

richesse /riːˈʃɛs/, /ˈrɪtʃɛs/ *noun* ME **Old French** (*richeise*, *richesce* (modern *richesse*), from *riche* rich). **1** ME–L17 *singular* and in *plural* Wealth; richness; riches. **2** L15 A number or group of martens.

■ Long archaic, but cf. EMBARRAS DE RICHESSE.

ricochet /ˈrɪkəʃeɪ/, /ˈrɪkəʃɛt/ *noun* M18 **French** (= the skipping of a shot or of a flat stone on water, of unknown origin). Originally *Military* The action of a projectile, especially a bullet or shell, in rebounding at an angle off a surface or surfaces after being fired; a hit made after such a rebound.

1996 *New Scientist* The fax messages are sent by someone living in 2024. Because of some ricochet of the arrow of time they are received by a present-day and startled Brazilian.

ricordo /riˈkordo/ *noun* plural **ricordi** /riˈkordi/ E20 **Italian** (literally, 'memory'). A token of remembrance, a souvenir; *Art* a copy made by a painter of another's composition.

ricotta /rɪˈkɒtə/ *noun* L19 **Italian** (= recooked, from Latin *recocta* feminine past participle of *recoquere*, from as *re-* + *coquere* cook). A kind of soft white unsalted Italian cheese. Also *ricotta cheese*.

rictus /ˈrɪktəs/ *noun* M18 **Latin** (literally, 'open mouth', from *rict-* past participial stem of *ringi* to gape). **1** M18 *Botany* The throat of a two-lipped corolla. **2** E19 The expanse or gape of the mouth, or of the beak or jaws of a bird, fish, etc.; *transferred* a fixed grin or grimace.

riegel /ˈriːg(ə)l/ *noun* E20 **German** (from Middle High German *rigel* crossbar, Old High German *rigil* bar). *Physical Geography* A low transverse ridge of resistant bedrock on the floor of a glacial valley, a rock bar.

riem /rɪm/, /riːm/ *noun* E19 **Dutch** (from Middle Dutch *rieme*). A long strip or thong of dressed softened leather. *South African*.

riempie /ˈrɪmpi/, /ˈriːmpi/ *noun & adjective* (also **riempje**) M19 **Dutch** (*riempje*, from as RIEM + Afrikaans diminutive suffix *-ie*). **A** *noun* M19 A fine narrow *riem* or leather thong. **B** E20 *attributive* or as *adjective* Of furniture: having a seat or bottom of criss-crossed fine narrow leather thongs, as a *riempie chair* (Afrikaans *riempiestoel*). *South African*.

rien ne va plus /rjɛ̃ nə va ply/ *interjection* (also **rien n'va plus**) L19 **French**. In roulette, the call made by the croupier while the wheel is spinning: no more bets!

rifacimento /rɪˌfatʃɪˈmɛntəʊ/, *foreign* /rifatʃiˈmento/ *noun* plural **rifacimenti** /rɪˌfatʃɪˈmɛnti/ L18 **Italian** (from *rifacimento* stem of *rifare* to remake). A remodelling or recasting of a literary work.

rigadoon /rɪgəˈduːn/ *noun* (also **rigaudon** /rigɔdɔ̃/ (*plural same*)) L17 **French** (*rigodon*, *rigaudon* said to be from *Rigaud* a dancing-master who devised it). **1** L17 A lively dance for couples, in duple or quadruple time, of Provençal origin. **2** M18 A piece of music for this dance.

rigatoni /rɪgəˈtəʊni/ *noun* M20 **Italian** (from *rigato* past participle of *rigare* to draw a line, make fluting, from *riga* a line). Pasta in the form of short hollow fluted tubes; an Italian dish consisting largely of this and usually a sauce.

rijsttafel /ˈrʌɪsˌtɑːf(ə)l/ *noun* L19 **Dutch** (from *rijst* rice + *tafel* table). A South East Asian meal consisting of a selection of different foods (such as eggs, meat, fish, fruit, curry, etc.) mixed with rice and served in separate dishes.

rikka /ˈrika/ *noun* L19 **Japanese** (literally, 'standing flowers', from *ritsu* stand + *ka* flower(s)). A traditional and formal style of Japanese flower arrangement, used especially to decorate Buddhist temples.

rillettes /'ri:jɛt/ *noun* (treated as *singular* or *plural*) L19 **French**. Pâté made of minced pork, chicken, etc., seasoned and combined with fat.

rimaye /ri:'meɪ/ *noun* E20 **French** (from Latin *rima* fissure + French collective suffix *-aye*). A BERGSCHRUND.

rimmon /ri'mo:n/ *noun* (also **rimon**) plural **rimmonim** /ri'mo:nɪm/ M20 **Hebrew** (*rimmōn*, literally, 'pomegranate'). A pomegranate-shaped ornament or decorative cover for each of the bars at either end of a Jewish law-scroll.

rinceau /rɛ̃so/ *noun* plural **rinceaux** /rɛ̃so/ L18 **French**. A moulded, carved, or painted decoration on furniture etc., often in the form of scrolls or acanthus leaves.

rinderpest /'rɪndəpɛst/ *noun* M19 **German** (from *Rinder* cattle (plural of *Rind*) + *Pest* plague). An infectious disease of ruminants, especially oxen; cattle-plague.

rinforzando /ˌrɪnfɔ:t'sandəʊ/ *adverb, adjective, & noun* E19 **Italian** (present participle of *rinforzare* to strengthen). *Music* **A** *adverb & adjective* E19 (A direction:) with a sudden stress or crescendo. **B** *noun* M19 plural **rinforzandos**, **rinforzandi** /ˌrɪnfɔ:t'sandi/ A sudden stress or crescendo made on a short phrase.

ripieno /rɪpɪ'eməʊ/ *adjective & noun* E18 **Italian** (from *ri-* re- + *pieno* full). *Music* **A** *attributive adjective* E18 Originally, supplementary, re-enforcing. Now chiefly, of or pertaining to a ripieno. **B** *noun* M18 plural **ripienos**, **ripieni** /rɪpɪ'emi/ Originally, a supplementary player or instrument. Now chiefly, the body of instruments accompanying the concertino in baroque concerto music.

riposte /rɪ'pɒst/ *noun* E18 **French** ((earlier *risposte*) from Italian *risposta* use as noun of feminine past participle of *rispondere*, from Latin *respondere* from *re-* + *spondere* to pledge). **1** E18 *Fencing* A quick thrust given after parrying a lunge; a return thrust. **2** M19 A retaliatory action; a quick sharp reply or retort.

2 1996 *Spectator* Unfortunately, a witty riposte invariably escaped me.

ripresa /ri'presa/ *noun* plural **riprese** /ri'prese/ M18 **Italian**. *Music* A repeat; a refrain.

ris de veau /ri də vo/ *noun phrase* E19 **French**. Sweetbread of veal prepared as a dish.

risoluto /rɪzə'lu:təʊ/ *adjective & adverb* M18 **Italian**. *Music* **A** *adjective* Resolved into a concord. Only in M18. **B** *adverb* M19 (A direction:) with resolution or emphasis.

Risorgimento /rɪˌsɔ:dʒɪ'mɛntəʊ/ *noun* plural **Risorgimenti** /rɪˌsɔ:dʒɪ'mɛnti/, **Risorgimentos** L19 **Italian** (= renewal, renaissance). **1** L19 *History* The movement which led to the unification of Italy as an independent State in 1870. **2** M20 A revitalization or renewal of activity in any sphere.

risotto /rɪ'zɒtəʊ/ *noun* plural **risottos** M19 **Italian** (from *riso* rice). An Italian dish of rice cooked in stock with various other ingredients, as meat, onions, etc.

risqué /'ri:skeɪ/ /'rɪskeɪ/, /rɪ'skeɪ/ *adjective* (feminine **risquée**) M19 **French** (past participle of *risquer* to risk). Slightly indecent, liable to shock slightly.

1996 *Spectator* The erotic poetry of the 17th and 18th centuries and the libertinism of Restoration drama, however risqué, lead you down a garden path with carefully laid out grassy borders.
1996 *Times* Nowadays, Vivienne [Westwood] is still considered *risquée*.

rissole /'rɪsəʊl/ *noun* E18 **French** (later form of Old French *ruissole* dialectal variant of *roisole*, *roussole* from Proto-Romance use as noun of feminine of late Latin *russeolus* reddish, from Latin *russus* red). A ball or small cake of chopped meat etc. coated with breadcrumbs, cooked by frying.

risus sardonicus /ˌrʌɪsəs sɑ:'dɒnɪkəs/ *noun phrase* L17 **Modern Latin** (from Latin *risus* laugh (from *ridere* to laugh) + medieval or modern Latin *sardonicus* sardonic). *Medicine* An involuntary grinning expression resulting from chronic abnormal contraction of the facial muscles, as in tetanus.

ritardando /rɪtɑ:'dandəʊ/ *adverb, adjective, & noun* plural of noun **ritardandos**, **ritardandi** /rɪtɑ:'dandi/ E19 **Italian** (present participle of *ritardare* to slow down). *Music* RALLENTANDO.

rite de passage /rit də pɑsaʒ/, /ˌri:t də pa'sɑ:ʒ/ *noun phrase* plural **rites de passage** (pronounced same) E20 **French**. *Anthropology* A formal procedure or act marking the beginning of a new defined stage in a person's life, a rite of passage.

■ The phrase was coined by Arnold van Gennep in the title of his book *Les Rites de passage* (1909). In English use, the translation *rite of passage* appeared in the same year as van Gennep's book; the 1960 translators of *Les Rites de passage* suggested that *rites of transition* would have been a better rendering, but acknowledged that *rites of passage* had become too firmly established in general usage to dislodge. Although less frequent than the English version, *rite de passage* is still found.

1977 *Times* The [Newfoundland] seal hunt is . . . a necessary *rite de passage* for all young men.

ritenuto /rɪtəˈnuːtəʊ/ *adverb, adjective, & noun* E19 **Italian** (past participle of *ritenere* from Latin *retinere* to hold back). *Music* **A** *adverb & adjective* E19 (A direction:) with immediate reduction of speed, restrained, held back in tempo. **B** *noun* E19 plural **ritenuti** /rɪtəˈnuːti/, **ritenutos** A ritenuto phrase or passage.

rites de passage plural of RITE DE PASSAGE.

ritornello /rɪtɔːˈnɛləʊ/ *noun* plural **ritornellos, ritornelli** /rɪtɔːˈnɛli/ L17 **Italian** (diminutive of *ritorno* return). *Music* An instrumental refrain, interlude, or prelude, especially in a vocal work.

ritournelle /ˌrɪtʊəˈnɛl/ *noun* M19 **French** (from as preceding). *Music* A RITORNELLO.

ritter /ˈrɪtə/ *noun* E19 **German** (variant of *reiter* rider). A German or Austrian knight or mounted warrior; a member of the German or Austrian minor nobility.

■ Obsolete except in historical contexts.

riu variant of RYU.

riverain /ˈrɪvərem/ *adjective & noun* M19 **French** (from *rivière* river). **A** *adjective* M19 Riverine. **B** *noun* M19 A person who lives beside or near a river.

riviera /rɪvɪˈɛːrə/ *noun* (also **Riviera**) M18 **Italian** (= seashore, coast). A coastal region with a warm climate and popularity as a holiday resort, originally *specifically* one around Genoa in Italy, later also the Mediterranean coast from Marseilles in France to La Spezia in Italy.

rivière /rivjɛr/ (*plural same*), /ˌrɪvɪˈɛː/ *noun* M19 **French**. **1** M19 *Needlework* A row of openwork. **2** L19 A necklace of diamonds or other gems, *especially* one consisting of more than one string.

riza /ˈriːzə/ *noun* E20 **Russian** (from Old Church Slavonic = garment). A metal shield or plaque framing the painted face and other features of a Russian icon, and engraved with the lines of the completed picture.

robe de chambre /rɔb də ʃɑ̃br/ *noun phrase* plural **robes de chambre** (pronounced same) M18 **French**. A dressing-gown, a negligée.

robe de nuit /rɔb də nɥi/ *noun phrase* plural **robes de nuit** (pronounced same) M19 **French**. A nightdress.

robe de style /rɔb də stil/ *noun phrase* plural **robes de style** (pronounced same) E20 **French**. A woman's formal dress with a tight bodice and a long bouffant skirt.

robes de chambre, robes de nuit, etc. plurals of ROBE DE CHAMBRE, ROBE DE NUIT, etc.

rocaille /rə(ʊ)ˈkʌɪ/, *foreign* /rɔkaj/ *noun* M19 **French**. An artistic or architectural style of decoration characterized by ornate rock- and shell-work; a rococo style.

roche moutonnée /rɔʃ mutɔne/, /ˌrɒʃ muːtɒˈneɪ/ *noun phrase* plural **roches moutonnées** (pronounced same) M19 **French** (*roche* rock (from medieval Latin *rocca, rocha* of unknown origin) + *moutonnée* (from *mouton* sheep, from medieval Latin *multo(n-)*, probably of Gaulish origin). *Physical Geography* A bare rock outcrop which has been shaped by glacial erosion, characteristically smoothed and rounded by abrasion but often displaying one side which is rougher and steeper.

1977 A. Hallam *Planet Earth* Many valleys are very deeply incised, with U-shaped cross-profiles and floors composed of smoothed, striated and streamlined rock hummocks (called roches moutonées).

rococo /rəˈkəʊkəʊ/ *adjective & noun* M19 **French** (fanciful alteration of *rocaille* pebble- or shell-work from *roc* rock). **A** *adjective* **1** M19 Old-fashioned, antiquated. **2** M19 (Of furniture or architecture) of or characterized by an elaborately ornamental late baroque style of decoration prevalent in eighteenth-century Continental Europe, with asymmetrical patterns involving motifs, scroll-work, etc.; (of music, literature, etc.) highly ornamented, florid; *generally* extravagantly or excessively ornate. **B** *noun* M19 The rococo style of art, decoration, etc.

rodeo /ˈrəʊdɪəʊ/, /rəˈdeɪəʊ/ *noun* plural **rodeos** M19 **Spanish** (from *rodear* to go round, based on Latin *rotare* to rotate). **1** M19 A round-up of cattle for counting, inspecting, branding, etc.; a place where cattle are rounded up. **2** E20 A display or competition exhibiting the skills of riding broncos, roping calves, wrestling steers, etc. **b** E20 *transferred* A similar (usually competitive) exhibition of other skills, as motorcycle riding, fishing, etc.

■ Originally United States.

rodomontade /ˌrɒdə(ʊ)mɒnˈteɪd/ *noun, verb, & adjective* (also **rhodomontade**) E17 **French** (from Italian *rodomontada, rodomontata*, from *Rodomonte* the name of a boastful character in the Renaissance *Orlando* epics). **A** *noun* **1** E17 A brag, a boast; an extravagantly boastful or arrogant remark or speech. **2** M17 Boastful or inflated language or behaviour; extravagant bragging. **B** *intransitive verb* L17 Boast, brag; rant. **C** *adjective* M18 Bragging, boastful; ranting.

roemer /ˈrømə/ *noun* L19 **Dutch** (or German *Römer*). A type of decorated German or Dutch wineglass with knobs or prunts on the stem.

■ The English *rummer* or *rummer-glass* is cognate with *roemer* and its other Continental variants and has nothing to do with the liquor rum. The ultimate origin may be 'Roman glass'.

roesti /ˈrøsti/ *noun plural* (treated as *singular* or *plural*) (also **rösti**) M20 **Swiss German**. A Swiss dish of grated potatoes, formed into a pancake and fried.

rofia see RAFFIA.

rogan josh /ˌrəʊg(ə)n ˈdʒəʊʃ/ *noun phrase* (also **roghan josh**) M20 **Urdu** (*roġan još, rauġan-još* (preparation of mutton) stewed in ghee, from Urdu *roġan, rauġan* from Persian *rauġan* oil, ghee + Urdu, Persian *roġan još* act of braising or stewing). A dish of curried meat (usually lamb) cooked in a rich sauce.

rognon /rəɲɔ̃/ *noun* plural pronounced same E19 **French**. **1** E19 A kidney, used as food. Usually in *plural*. **2** M20 *Mountaineering* A rounded outcrop of rock or stones surrounded by a glacier or an icefield.

roi fainéant /rwa fɛneɑ̃/ *noun phrase* plural **rois fainéants** (pronounced same) M19 **French** (literally, 'sluggard king'; cf. FAINÉANT). Any person with merely nominal power.

■ Originally applied to any of the later Merovingian kings of France, whose power was merely nominal.

1966 *Economist* The launching of the Sputnik in 1957, in the reign of the *roi fainéant*, President Eisenhower, seemed to justify Khrushchevian boasts that America's days of . . . supremacy were numbered.

roi soleil /rwa sɔlɛj/ *noun phrase* plural **rois soleils** (pronounced same) L19 **French** (literally, 'sun king', (the heraldic device of) Louis XIV of France). A pre-eminent person or thing.

romaine /rə(ʊ)ˈmeɪn/ *noun* E20 **French** (feminine of *romain* Roman). **1** E20 A cos lettuce. Also more fully *romaine lettuce*. Chiefly *North American*. **2** E20 Any of various crêpe fabrics.

■ *Romaine crêpe* (a proprietary name in the United States) is a semi-sheer crêpe fabric of silk, rayon, or acetate.

roman-à-clef /rɔmɑ̃ a kle/, /rəʊˌmɑːn ɑː ˈkleɪ/ *noun phrase* (also **roman à clef**) plural **romans-à-clef** (pronounced same) L19 **French** (literally, 'novel with a key'). A novel in which actual people or events appear under fictitious names.

1996 *Times: Weekend* Anonymous's novel is more than a political *roman à clef* . . .

roman à thèse /rɔmɑ̃ a tɛz/ *noun phrase* plural **romans à thèse** (pronounced same) M19 **French** (literally, 'novel with a thesis'). A novel that seeks to expound or promote a theory.

romancé /rɔmɑ̃se/ *adjective* M20 **French** (from *romancer* to fictionalize). Especially of a biography: fictionalized, written in the form of a novel.

roman de geste /rɔmɑ̃ də ʒɛst/ *noun phrase* plural **romans de geste** (pronounced same) M19 **French** (literally, 'romance of heroic deeds'). A CHANSON DE GESTE.

roman-fleuve /rɔmɑ̃ flœv/ *noun phrase* plural **romans-fleuves** (pronounced same) M20 **French** (literally, 'river novel'). A novel featuring the leisurely description of the lives and members of a family; a sequence of self-contained novels.

1996 *Times* The *roman fleuve* is a courageous undertaking.

romanità /roˌmaniˈtɑː/ *noun* E20 **Italian** (from next). **1** E20 ROMANITAS. **2** M20 The spirit or influence of the central Roman Catholic authorities; acceptance of papal policy.

romanitas /rəʊˈmɑːnɪtɑːs/, /rəʊˈmanɪtɑːs/ *noun* M20 **Late Latin** (from Latin *Romanus*). The spirit or ideals of ancient Rome.

roman noir /rɔmɑ̃ nwar/ *noun phrase* plural **romans noirs** (pronounced same) M20 French (literally, 'black novel'). A Gothic novel, a thriller.

■ See quotation 1996(2) at NOIR.

roman policier /rɔmɑ̃ pɔlisje/ *noun phrase* plural **romans policiers** (pronounced same) E20 **French**. A detective novel or story.

1995 *Times* French *romans policiers*, and crime procedural novels from John Creasey to Nicholas Freeling, have brought in chippy police heroes instead of private detectives.

romanza /ro'mansa/, /ro'mantsa/, /ro 'manza/ *noun* M19 **Spanish** (or Italian, from popular Latin adverb formed on Latin *Romanicus* from *Romanus* Roman). *Music* A romantic song or melody; a lyrical piece of music; a romance.

Romanze /ro'mantsə/ *noun* plural **Romanzen** /ro'mantsən/ L19 **German** (literally, 'romance'). *Music* A composition of a tender or lyrical character; *specifically* a slow romantic instrumental piece or movement.

rondavel /rɒn'dɑːv(ə)l/ *noun* L19 **Afrikaans** (*rondawel*). A round tribal hut usually with a thatched conical roof. Also, a similar building used especially as a holiday cottage or an outbuilding on a farm. *South African*.

rond de cuir /rɔ̃ də kɥir/ *noun phrase* plural **ronds de cuir** (pronounced same) E20 French (literally, 'circle of leather'). A round leather cushion, often used on office chairs in France. Also *transferred*, a bureaucrat.

ronde /rɒnd/ *noun* M19 **French** (feminine of *rond* round). **1** M19 A style of script with gothic characteristics used in France from the eighteenth century; printing type imitating or based on this writing. **2** M20 A dance in which the participants move in a circle or ring. **3** M20 A round or course of talk, activity, etc.; *figurative* a treadmill.

3 1977 *Times Literary Supplement* Heinz already represented the first step away from what was ultimately unbearable about the homosexual *ronde*.

rondeau /'rɒndəʊ/ *noun* plural **rondeaux** /'rɒndəʊ/, /'rɒndəʊz/ E16 **Old and Modern French** (later form of *rondel* from *rond* round). **1** E16 A poem of ten or thirteen lines with only two rhymes throughout and with the opening words used twice as a refrain. **2** L18 *Music* A RONDO sense 1.

rondelle /rɒn'dɛl/ *noun* M19 **French** (from *rond* round). A circular piece of something.

rondo /'rɒndəʊ/ *noun* plural **rondos** L18 **Italian** (from French RONDEAU). **1** L18 A piece of music with a recurring leading theme, often as the final movement of a concerto, sonata, etc. **2** M19 A game of chance played with balls on a table.

rond-point /rɔ̃pwɛ̃/ *noun* plural **ronds-points** (pronounced same) L19 **French** (from *rond* round + *point* centre). A circular space in a garden whence paths radiate; a roundabout where roads converge.

ronds de cuir plural of ROND DE CUIR.

rongeur /rɔ̃ʒœr/ *noun* L19 **French** (= gnawing, a rodent, from *ronger* to gnaw). *Surgery* Strong surgical forceps with a biting action, used for removing small pieces from bone. Also *rongeur forceps*.

ronin /'rəʊnɪn/ *noun* plural same, **ronins** L19 **Japanese**. In feudal Japan: a lordless wandering samurai; an outlaw. Now also *transferred*, a Japanese student who has failed and is permitted to retake a university (entrance) examination.

rooinek /'rɔɪnɛk/ *noun* L19 **Afrikaans** (from *rooi* red + *nek* neck). A British or English-speaking South African.

■ In derogatory or jocular use in South African slang, the term was especially associated with the British troops in South Africa during the Boer War (1899–1902).

roquette /rɒ'kɛt/ *noun* E20 **French**. A cruciferous plant eaten as a salad, rocket.

rosalia /rəʊ'zɑːlɪə/ *noun* E19 **Italian** (female forename in *Rosalia, mia cara* title of an Italian song using this device). *Music* The repetition of a phrase or melody one note higher, with the retention of the same intervals and a consequent change of key.

rosé /'rəʊzeɪ/, *foreign* /roze/ *noun & adjective* L19 **French** (= pink). (Designating) any light red or pink wine, coloured by brief contact with red grape skins.

rosemaling /'rəʊsəˌmɑːlɪŋ/, /'rəʊsə ˌmɔːlɪŋ/ *noun* M20 **Norwegian** (= rose-painting). The art of painting (wooden objects) with flower motifs; flower motifs, especially painted on wood.

rosolio /rəʊ'zəʊlɪəʊ/ *noun* (also **rosoglio**) plural **rosolios** E19 **Italian** (variant of *ro-*

soli, from Latin *ros* dew + *solis* genitive of *sol* sun). A sweet cordial made especially in Italy from alcohol, raisins, sugar, rose-petals, cloves, cinnamon, etc.

rosso antico /ˌrɒsəʊ anˈtiːkəʊ/ *noun phrase* L18 **Italian** (literally, 'ancient red'). **1** L18 A red stoneware produced at Josiah Wedgwood's Staffordshire factories. **2** L19 A rich red Italian marble used for decoration.

rösti variant of ROESTI.

rostrum /ˈrɒstrəm/ *noun* plural **rostra** /ˈrɒstrə/, (*rare*) **rostrums** M16 **Latin** (= beak, beak-head, from *rodere* to gnaw). **1** M16 *Roman Antiquities* A platform or stand for speakers in the Forum of ancient Rome, decorated with the beak-heads of captured warships. **b** M18 *transferred* A platform, stage, stand, etc., especially for public speaking; *specifically* (*a*) a pulpit; (*b*) a conductor's platform facing the orchestra; (*c*) a platform for supporting a film or television camera. **2** E17 *Roman Antiquities* A beaklike projection from the prow of a warship. **3** *Anatomy* and *Zoology* **a** M18 A beak, a snout; an anterior prolongation of the head, as in a weevil. **b** E19 A process or formation resembling a beak. **4** M19 *Botany* A beaklike process.

rota /ˈrəʊtə/ *noun* L17 **Latin** (= wheel). A rotational order of people, duties to be done; a list of these.

■ *Rota* occurs first (E17) as the name of the supreme court of the Roman Catholic Church, then (M17) as the name of a political club. The above is the only sense generally used in English.

roti /ˈrəʊtiː/ *noun* E20 **Hindustani** (*roṭī*). A type of unleavened bread originally from the Indian subcontinent.

rôti /roti/ *noun & postpositive adjective* plural of noun pronounced same L18 **French** (from *rôtir* to roast). *Cookery* **A** *noun* L18 A dish or main course of roasted meat. **B** *postpositive adjective* M19 Of food: roasted.

rotisserie /rə(ʊ)ˈtɪs(ə)ri/ *noun* M19 **French** (*rôtisserie*, from *rôtir* to roast). **1** M19 A restaurant or shop specializing in roasted or barbecued meat etc. **2** M20 A type of roasting oven with a power-driven rotating spit. Also *rotisserie oven*.

2 1996 *Times: Weekend* A few weeks ago I wrote that the demise of the spit (or rotisserie, if you prefer) had robbed us of roast meat . . .

rôtisseur /rotisœr/ *noun* plural pronounced same M18 **French** (from *rôtir* to roast). A chef in charge of all roasting, and usually grilling and frying, in a restaurant etc.

roué /ˈruːeɪ/ *noun* E19 **French** (use as noun of past participle of *rouer* to break on the wheel (the punishment said to be deserved by such a person)). A debauchee, a rake.

1996 *Times* . . . I got hopelessly lost in the Casanova papers themselves, mainly because they assumed some knowledge of the old roué's life.

rouge /ruːʒ/ *noun & adjective* LME **Old and Modern French** (from Latin *rubeus* red). **A** *adjective* LME Red. *obsolete* except in certain heraldic contexts. **B** *noun* **1** The colour red. *rare*. Only in LME. **2** M18 A red powder or cream used as a cosmetic to add colour to the lips or especially the cheeks. **3** L18 Red as one of the two colours of divisions in rouge-et-noir and roulette. Earliest in ROUGE-ET-NOIR. **4** E19 A radical; a republican; a socialist. Now chiefly (*Canadian*), a member of the Quebec Liberal Party. **5** M19 Any of various metallic oxides etc. used as polishing powders; *especially* (in full *jeweller's rouge*) a fine preparation of ferric oxide used as a metal polish. Usually with specifying word. **6** M20 French red wine.

rouge de fer /ˌruːʒ də ˈfɛː/ *noun phrase* E20 **French** (literally, 'red of iron'). An orange-red enamel used on Chinese porcelain, made from a ferric oxide base.

rouge-et-noir /ˌruːʒeɪˈnwɑː/ *noun phrase* L18 **French** (= red and black). A gambling game in which stakes are placed on a table marked with red and black diamonds.

rouge flambé /ruːʒ ˈflɒmbeɪ/ *noun phrase* E20 **French**. A bright red Chinese porcelain glaze, made from copper oxide.

rouget /ruʒɛ/ *noun* plural pronounced same L19 **French**. A red mullet, especially as used in cooking.

rouille /ruj/ *noun* M20 **French** (literally, 'rust'). A Provençal sauce made from pounded red chillies, garlic, breadcrumbs, etc., blended with stock, frequently added to bouillabaisse.

roulade /rʊˈlɑːd/ *noun* E18 **French** (from *rouler* to roll). **1** E18 *Music* A florid passage of runs etc. in solo vocal music, *especially* one sung to one syllable. **2** L19 Any of various dishes prepared by spreading a filling on to a base of meat, sponge, etc., which is then rolled up and frequently served sliced.

rouleau /rʊ'ləʊ/ *noun* plural **rouleaux** /rʊ 'ləʊ/, **rouleaus** L17 **French** (from *rôle*, originally, a roll or paper containing an actor's part). **1** L17 A cylindrical packet of gold coins. **b** M19 A stack of disc-shaped objects, especially red blood cells. **2** L18 A roll or a coil *of* something, especially hair. **3** E19 A turned tube or length of rolled fabric used as trimming or to form a belt on a garment etc. **4** E20 A type of narrow-necked cylindrical vase originally made in China in the late seventeenth century. In full *rouleau vase*.

roulement /rulmɑ̃/ *noun* plural pronounced same E20 **French** (literally, 'roll, roster'). *Military* (A) movement of troops or equipment, especially from a reserve force to provide relief.

roulette /rʊ'lɛt/ *noun* M18 **French** (diminutive of *rouelle* wheel, from late Latin *rotella* diminutive of *rota* wheel). **1** *generally* A small wheel. *rare*. Only in M18. **2** M18 A gambling game in which a ball is dropped on to a revolving wheel with numbered compartments in the centre of a table, players betting on (the colour, height, or parity of) the number at which the ball comes to rest. **3** M19 A revolving toothed wheel; *specifically* (*a*) one for making dotted lines in etching and engraving; (*b*) one for perforating a sheet of paper.

■ Other senses are now rare or obsolete. A transferred use of sense 2 is in the phrase 'Russian roulette' (the act of bravado involving spinning the cylinder of a revolver, one chamber of which is loaded, and then pulling the trigger while pointing it at one's head); hence figuratively, *playing Russian roulette* means taking dangerous risks.

routier /rutje/ *noun* plural pronounced same M17 **French** (from Old French *rute* from Proto-Romance use as noun (sc. *via* way) of feminine of Latin *ruptus* past participle of *rumpere* to break). **1** M17 *History* A mariner's guide to sea routes, a rutter. **2** M19 *History* A member of any of numerous bands of mercenaries active in France during the later Middle Ages. **3** M20 In France: a long-distance lorry driver.

routinier /rutinje/ *noun* plural pronounced same E19 **French**. A person who adheres to (a) routine; *especially* (*Music*) a conductor who performs in a mechanically correct but uninspiring way.

roux /ru:/ *noun* E19 **French** (= browned (sc. butter)). *Cookery* A blend of melted fat (especially butter) and flour used as a thickener in making sauces.

ruana /rʊ'ɑ:nə/ *noun* M20 **American Spanish** (from Spanish (*manta*) *ruana*, literally, 'poor man's cloak', from *rúa* street, from late Latin *ruga* furrow, street, from Latin *ruga* wrinkle). A South American cape or poncho, worn especially in Colombia and Peru.

rubato /rʊ'bɑ:təʊ/ *adjective & noun* L18 **Italian** (literally, 'robbed'). *Music* **A** *adjective* L18 *tempo rubato*, rubato. **B** *noun* plural **rubatos**, **rubati** /rʊ'bɑ:ti/ L19 The action or practice of temporarily disregarding strict tempo during performance; an instance of this.

rubella /rʊ'bɛlə/ *noun* L19 **Latin** (use as noun of neuter plural of Latin *rubellus* reddish, from *rubeus* red). German measles.

ruche /ru:ʃ/ *noun* E19 **Old and Modern French** (from medieval Latin *rusca* tree bark, of Celtic origin). A frill of gathered ribbon, lace, etc., used especially as a trimming on a garment.

rucola /'rʊkəʊlə/ *noun* L20 **Italian**. A vegetable the leaves of which are used for salads.

rumba /'rʌmbə/ *noun* (also **rhumba**) E20 **American Spanish**. An Afro-Cuban dance; a ballroom dance imitative of this, danced on the spot with a pronounced movement of the hips; the dance rhythm of this, usually in 2/4 time; a piece of music with this rhythm.

rusé /ryze/ *adjective* (feminine **rusée**) M18 **French**. Inclined to use ruses; deceitful, sly, cunning.

1973 C. M. Woodhouse *Capodistria* They constantly used of him [sc. Capodistria] the conventional epithets which seemed to fit his nationality—wily, *rusé*, supple, crafty.

ruse de guerre /ryz də gɛr/ *noun phrase* plural **ruses de guerre** (pronounced same) E19 **French** (literally, 'ruse of war'). A stratagem intended to deceive an enemy in war; *transferred* a justifiable trick.

rusée see RUSÉ.

ruses de guerre plural of RUSE DE GUERRE.

rus in urbe /ˌruːs ɪn ˈəːbeɪ/ *noun phrase* M18 **Latin** (literally, 'country in city'). An illusion of countryside created by a building, garden, etc., within a city; an urban building etc. which has this effect.

1976 *Times* Two foxes . . . live in a corner of the allotments—which seems to be taking *rus in urbe* too far.

rya /ˈriːə/ *noun* M20 **Swedish**. A Scandinavian type of knotted pile rug. In full *rya rug*.

ryu /rɪˈuː/ *noun* (also **riu**) plural same L19 **Japanese** (*-ryū* school, style, system). Any Japanese school or style of art.

S

sabayon /'sabʌɪjɒn/ *noun* E20 **French** (from Italian *zabaione* variant of ZABAGLIONE). Zabaglione.

sabha /sə'bɑː/ *noun* E20 **Sanskrit** (*sabhā*). In the Indian subcontinent: an assembly; a council; a society.

■ Hence the *Lok Sabha* and the *Rajya Sabha* are respectively the lower and the upper houses of the Indian parliament.

sabi /'sabi/ *noun* M20 **Japanese** (literally, 'loneliness'). In Japanese art, a quality of simple and mellow beauty expressing a mood of spiritual solitude recognized in Zen Buddhist philosophy. Cf. WABI.

sabkha /'sabkə/, /'sabxə/ *noun* (also **sebkha** /'sɛbkə/) L19 **Arabic** (*sabḵa* a saline infiltration, salt flat). *Geography* An area of coastal flats subject to periodic flooding and evaporation, found especially in North Africa and Arabia.

sabot /'sabəʊ/ *noun* E17 **French** (from Old French *çabot* blend of *çavate* (modern SAVATE) and *bote* (modern *botte*) boot). **1 a** E17 A shoe made of a single piece of wood shaped and hollowed out to fit the foot. **b** M19 A heavy shoe with a thick wooden sole. **c** M20 A decorative metal foot-cover for a piece of wooden furniture. **2** *Military* **a** M19 A wooden disc attached to a spherical projectile to keep it in place in the bore when discharged. **b** M19 A metal cup or ring fixed to a conical projectile to make it conform to the grooves of the rifling. **c** M20 A device fitted inside the muzzle of a gun to hold the projectile to be fired. **3** M20 In baccarat and chemin de fer, a box for dealing the cards, a shoe. **4** M20 A small snub-nosed yacht. *Australian*.

sabotage /'sabətɑːʒ/ *noun & verb* E20 **French** (from *saboter* to make a noise with sabots, execute badly, destroy, from as preceding). **A** *noun* E20 Deliberate damage to or destruction of property, especially in order to disrupt the production of goods or as a political or military act. **B** *transitive verb* E20 Commit sabotage on; destroy; make useless.

saboteur /ˌsabə'təː/ *noun* E20 **French** (from *saboter* (see SABOTAGE)). A person who commits sabotage.

sabra /'sabrə/ *noun* (also **Sabra**) M20 **Modern Hebrew** (*ṣabbār* or its source Arabic *ṣabr* prickly pear). A Jew born in the region of the modern State of Israel.

attributive **1995** *Times* Yitzhak Rabin was . . . the first *sabra*, or native-born, leader of his country.

sabreur /sa'brəː/ *noun* M19 **French** (from *sabrer* to sabre). **1** M19 A person, especially a cavalry soldier, who fights with a sabre. **2** E20 A person who fences using a sabre.

saccade /sə'kɑːd/ *noun* E18 **French.** **1** E18 A jerking movement. Now *rare* except as passing into sense 2. **2** M20 A brief rapid movement of the eye from one position of rest to another, whether voluntary or involuntary.

Sachertorte /'zaxərˌtɔrtə/ *noun* plural **Sachertorten** /'zaxərˌtɔrt(ə)n/ E20 **German** (from Franz *Sacher* Viennese pastry-chef, its creator + *Torte* tart, pastry, cake). A chocolate gateau with apricot jam filling and chocolate icing.

sachet /'saʃeɪ/ *noun* L15 **Old and Modern French** (diminutive of *sac*). **1** A small carrying bag. *rare* Only in L15. **2 a** M19 A small scented bag, especially for holding handkerchiefs. **b** M19 (A small bag or packet containing) dry perfume for placing among clothing etc. **3** E20 A small sealed bag or packet, now frequently of plastic, containing a small portion of a substance, especially shampoo.

Sachlichkeit /'zaxlɪçkaɪt/ *noun* M20 **German** (literally, 'objectivity'). Objectivism, realism. Also *specifically* NEUE SACHLICHKEIT.

1984 A. G. Lehmann *European Heritage* George Lukács calls *Sachlichkeit* 'mere reportage', instead of an interpretation of reality.

sacro egoismo /ˌsakro ego'izmo/ *noun phrase* M20 **Italian** (literally, 'sacred egoism'). Egocentric nationalism, especially in dealing with foreign States.

■ Usually derogatory, the phrase was coined (1914) by the Italian statesman Antonio Salandra (1853–1931) who, on the outbreak of World War I, first proclaimed Italy's neutrality in defiance of treaty obligations to Germany and Austria-Hungary and then brought Italy into the war on the side of the Allies.

1996 *Spectator* It is the law of nations that countries are driven by *sacro egoismo*—each one, naturally, wishes to defend its own interests.

sacrum /'seɪkrəm/ *noun* plural **sacrums, sacra** /'seɪkrə/ M18 **Latin** (short for late Latin *os sacrum*, translation of Greek *hieron osteon* sacred bone (from the belief that the soul resides in it)). *Anatomy* A triangular bone which is wedged between the two hip-bones, forming the back of the pelvis and resulting from the fusing of (usually five) vertebrae.

sadhu /'sɑ:dhu:/ *noun* (also **Sadhu**) M19 **Sanskrit** (*sādhu* adjective, good, (as noun) good man, holy man). *Hinduism* A holy man, a sage.

saeva indignatio /ˌsʌɪvə ɪndɪg'nɑ:tɪəʊ/ *noun phrase* M19 **Latin** (literally, 'savage indignation'). An intense feeling of contemptuous anger at human folly.

■ The phrase is particularly associated with the satirist Jonathan Swift (1667–1745), appearing in the epitaph that he composed for his tomb in St Patrick's, Dublin.

1969 *Punch* Solzhenitsyn's *The First Circle* . . . fell short of greatness because it was too docile. It lacked *saeva indignatio*.

safari /sə'fɑ:ri/ *noun, verb, & adjective* L19 **Kiswahili** (from Arabic *safar* journey, trip, tour). **A** *noun* **1** L19 A hunter's or traveller's party or caravan, especially in East Africa. **2** E20 A journey; a cross-country expedition on foot or in vehicles, originally and especially in East Africa, for hunting, tourism, or scientific investigation. Frequently in *on safari*. **B** *intransitive verb* E20 Go on safari. **C** *attributive* or as *adjective* L20 Sandy brown or beige; of the colour of clothes traditionally worn on safari.

saga /'sɑ:gə/ *noun* E18 **Old Norse** ((Icelandic); cf. Old English *sagu* (modern *saw*), German *Sage*). **1** E18 An Old Norse prose narrative of Iceland or Norway, *especially* one which recounts the traditional history of Icelandic families or of the kings of Norway. **b** *transferred* M19 A narrative regarded as having the traditional characteristics of the Icelandic sagas; a story of heroic achievement. Also, a novel or series of novels recounting the history of a family through several generations; *loosely* a long and complicated account of a series of events. **2** M19 (partly after German *Sage*) A story which has been handed down by oral tradition and added to or adapted in the course of time; historical or heroic legend.

sagamité /səˌgɑ:mɪ'teɪ/ *noun* M17 **French** (representing Cree *kisa:kamite:w*, literally, 'it is a hot liquid'). Gruel or porridge made from coarse hominy.

saganaki /sagə'nɑ:ki/ *noun* M20 **Modern Greek** (= small two-handled frying-pan (traditionally used to prepare the dish)). A Greek dish consisting of breaded or floured cheese fried in butter, often with lemon juice, served as an appetiser.

sahib /'sɑ:(h)ɪb/, /sɑ:b/ *noun* (also **saab** /sɑ:b/) L17 **Urdu** (through Persian from Arabic *ṣāḥib* friend, lord, master). **1** L17 An Englishman or other European as addressed or spoken of by Indians. **2** E20 *transferred* A gentleman; a person considered socially acceptable. See also PUKKA.

■ Anglo-Indian. Also as a title affixed to a person's name or office, as in *Malarao Sahib*, *the inspector sahib*.

sainfoin /'seɪnfɔɪn/, /'sanfɔɪn/ *noun* (also **sanfoin**) M17 **French** (*saintfoin* (modern *sainfoin*), originally 'lucerne', from modern Latin *sanctum foenum*, literally, 'holy hay', alteration of *sanum foenum* wholesome hay, which was based on Latin *herba medica* erroneous alteration of *herba Medica*, literally, 'Median grass', translation of Greek *Mēdikē poa*). A leguminous plant, *Onobrychis viciifolia*, with pinnate leaves and bright pink flowers in dense racemes, formerly much grown for fodder.

sais variant of SYCE.

sake /'sɑ:ki/, /'sakeɪ/ *noun* (also **saké, saki**) L17 **Japanese**. A Japanese alcoholic drink made from fermented rice.

sakia /'sɑ:kɪə/ *noun* L17 **Arabic** (*sāḳiya* use as noun of feminine active participle of *saḳā* to irrigate). A machine for drawing water for irrigation, consisting of a large vertical wheel to which earthen pots are attached and moved by means of a horizontal wheel turned by oxen or asses.

salaam /sə'lɑ:m/ *noun* E17 **Arabic** (*salām* = Hebrew *šālōm*). **1** E17 An oriental greeting, meaning 'Peace', used chiefly in Muslim countries; a ceremonial obeisance sometimes accompanying this salutation, consisting in the Indian subcontinent of a low bow with the right palm on the forehead. **2** L18 In *plural* Respectful compliments.

salade niçoise /salad niswaz/ *noun phrase* plural **salades niçoises** (pronounced same) E20 **French** (= salad from Nice (in southern France)). A salad usually made from hard-boiled eggs, anchovies, black olives, tomatoes, etc.

saladero /salə'dɛːrəʊ/ *foreign* /sala'dero/ *noun* plural **saladeros** /salə'dɛːrəʊz/, *foreign* /sala'deros/ L19 **Spanish**. In Spain and Latin America: a slaughterhouse where meat is also prepared by drying or salting.

salades niçoises plural of SALADE NIÇOISE.

salami /sə'lɑːmi/ *noun* M19 **Italian** (plural of *salame*, representing popular Latin word from verb meaning 'to salt'). **1** M19 An original Italian variety of sausage, highly seasoned and often flavoured with garlic. **2** L20 A way of carrying out a plan by means of a series of small or imperceptible steps; *specifically* computer fraud in which small amounts of money are transferred from numerous customer accounts into another account. In full *salami technique* or *salami tactics*.

salariat /sə'lɛːrɪət/ *noun* E20 **French** (from *salaire* salary, after *prolétariat* PROLETARIAT). *The* salaried class; salary-earners collectively.

salaud /salo/ *noun* plural pronounced same M20 **French** (from *sale* dirty). As a term of abuse: a contemptible or objectionable person.

salep /'saləp/ *noun* M18 **French** (from Turkish *sālep* from Arabic *ṯa'lab* fox, shortening of *ḵuṣā 'ṯ-ṯa'lab* orchid (literally, 'fox's testicles')). A starchy preparation of the dried tubers of various orchids, used in cookery and formerly as a tonic.

salina /sə'lʌɪnə/ *noun* L16 **Spanish** (from medieval Latin = salt pit; in Latin only as plural *salinae* salt-pans). A salt lake, spring, or marsh; a salt-pan, a salt-works. Also (originally *Jamaican*), a low marshy area of land near the coast.

salle /sal/ *noun* plural pronounced same M18 **French**. A hall; a large room

■ Generally as an element in one of the following phrases, but also sometimes as the abbreviation of one of them.

salle-à-manger /salamɑ̃ʒe/ *noun phrase* M18 **French**. A dining-hall, a dining-room.

salle d'armes /sal darm/ *noun phrase* L19 **French**. A fencing hall or school.

salle d'attente /sal datɑ̃t/ *noun* M19 **French**. A waiting-room, especially at a station.

salle d'eau /sal do/ *noun phrase* M20 **French**. A washroom, a shower-room.

salle de jeux /sal də ʒø/ *noun phrase* M20 **French**. A gambling house or room.

salle des pas perdus /sal de pa pɛrdy/ *noun phrase* M19 **French** (literally, 'of the lost footsteps'). A waiting-hall at a court of law, station, etc.; a lobby.

salle privée /sal prive/ *noun phrase* M20 **French**. A private gambling room in a casino.

salmi /'salmi/ *noun* (also **salmis**) plural pronounced same M18 **French** (abbreviation of French *salmigondis* salmagundi). A game stew with a rich sauce.

salon /'salɒn/, *foreign* /salɔ̃/ (*plural same*) *noun & adjective* L17 **French** (from Italian *salone* augmentative of *sala* hall). **A** *noun* **1** L17 A reception room in a palace or large house, especially in France or other Continental country; a drawing-room. **2** E19 *specifically* The reception room of a lady of fashion, especially in Paris; a social gathering of eminent people in such a room. **3** E20 An establishment in which the business of hairdresser, beautician, etc., is conducted.

salon des refusés /salɔ̃ de rəfyze/ *noun phrase* L19 **French** (= exhibition of rejected works). An exhibition ordered by Napoleon III in 1863 to display pictures rejected by the Salon; also *transferred*.

■ The Salon, the annual exhibition in Paris of painting, sculpture, etc., by living artists, was notoriously hostile to the works of impressionist artists.

salonnière /sə,lɒnɪ'ɛː/ *noun* (also **salonière**) E20 **French** (from as SALON). A woman who holds a salon; a society hostess.

1995 *Times* . . . apart from the ever-present George Sand, Flaubert's mistress Louise Colet and a few *salonières*, the thinking-woman-in-oils is striking by her absence.

salopette /salə'pɛt/ *noun* L20 **French**. *singular* and (usually) in *plural* Trousers with a high waist and shoulder-straps, worn especially as a skiing garment and as a Frenchman's overalls.

salpicon /'salpɪkɒn/ *noun* E18 **French** (from Spanish, from *salpicar* to sprinkle (with salt)). *Cookery* A stuffing for veal, beef, or mutton, also used as a garnish.

salsa /'salsə/ *noun* M19 **Spanish** (= sauce; in sense 2 American Spanish). **1** M19 *Cookery* A sauce served with meat. **2** L20 Contemporary dance music of Caribbean origin which incorporates jazz and rock elements; a dance to this music.

2 1996 *Country Life* Over the road, a salsa band blared out in raunchy competition.

saltarello /saltə'rɛləʊ/ *noun* plural **saltarellos**, **saltarelli** /saltə'rɛli/ L16 **Italian** (*salterello*, Spanish *salterelo* related to Italian *saltare*, Spanish *saltar* to leap, dance, from Latin *saltare*). **1** L16 The jack of a spinet or harpischord. *rare*. **2** E18 *History* An animated Italian and Spanish dance for a couple involving numerous sudden skips or jumps; a piece of music for this dance or in its rhythm.

salti plural of SALTO.

saltimbocca /ˌsaltɪm'bɒkə/ *noun* M20 **Italian** (from *saltare* to leap + *in* in, into + *bocca* mouth). *Cookery* A dish consisting of rolled pieces of veal and ham cooked with herbs.

salto /'saltəʊ/, /'sɔːltəʊ/, *in sense 1 also foreign* /'salto/ *noun* plural **saltos**, (in sense 1) **salti** /'salti/ L19 **Italian** (= leap, from Latin *saltus*). **1** L19 *salto mortale* /mɔː'tɑːleɪ/, *foreign* /mor'tɑːle/ (= fatal leap), a daring or flying leap; *figurative* a risky step, an unjustified inference, a leap of faith. **2** L20 A somersault.

salumeria /ˌsalume'riːa/, /ˌsal(j)ʊmə'riːə/ *noun* E20 **Italian** (= grocer's, or pork-butcher's shop, from *salume* salted meat, from *sale* from Latin *sal* salt). A delicatessen.

salve /'salveɪ/, /'salviː/ *noun* LME **Latin** (= hail, greetings, imperative of *salvere* be well; in sense 1 from the opening words of the antiphon *salve regina* hail (holy) queen). **1** LME *Roman Catholic Church* (usually **Salve**) More fully *Salve Regina* /rə'ʤiːnə/. A popular Marian antiphon, now said or sung especially after compline. Also, a musical setting for this. **2** L16 An utterance of 'salve'; a greeting or salutation on meeting. Now *rare* or *obsolete*.

salvo /'salvəʊ/ *noun* plural **salvos** E17 **Latin** (ablative neuter singular of *salvus* safe, as in medieval Latin law phrases like *salvo jure* without prejudice to the right of (a specified person) etc.). **1** E17 A saving clause; a provision that a certain ordinance shall not be binding where it would interfere with a specified right or duty; a reservation, a qualification. (Followed by *of*, *for*, *to*.) **2** M17 A dishonest mental reservation; an evasion, an excuse. Now *rare*. **3** M17–L18 A solution of a difficulty, an answer to an objection. **4** M18 A thing intended to save a person's reputation or soothe offended pride or conscience.

sal volatile /ˌsal və'latɪli/ *noun phrase* M17 **Modern Latin** (= volatile salt). Ammonium carbonate, especially in the form of an aromatic solution in alcohol to be sniffed as a restorative in faintness etc.; smelling-salts.

salwar variant of SHALWAR.

samadhi /sə'mɑːdi/ *noun* L18 **Sanskrit** (*samādhi* contemplation, literally, 'a putting together, joining'). *Hinduism* and *Buddhism* **1** L18 The state of union with creation into which a perfected yogi or holy man is said to pass at the time of apparent death. **2** E19 A state of intense concentration induced by meditation, in which union with creation is attained; the last stage of yoga.

samba /'sambə/ *noun* L19 **Portuguese** (of African origin). A Brazilian dance of African origin; a Latin American and ballroom dance imitative of this; a piece of music for this dance, usually in 2/4 or 4/4 time.

sambal /'sambal/ *noun* E19 **Malay**. In Malayan and Indonesian cookery, a relish consisting of raw vegetables or fruit prepared with spices and vinegar.

sambar /'sambɑː/ *noun* M20 **Tamil** (*cāmpār* from Marathi *sā̃b(h)ar* from Sanskrit *sambhāra* collection, materials). In southern Indian cookery, a highly seasoned lentil and vegetable dish.

sambo /'sambəʊ/ *noun* M20 **Russian** (acronym, from *samozashchita bez oruzhiya*, literally, 'unarmed self-defence'). A type of wrestling resembling judo, originating in the former USSR. Also more fully *sambo wrestling*.

sambok variant of SJAMBOK.

samfu /'samfuː/ *noun* M20 **Chinese** ((Cantonese) *shaam foò*, from *shaam* coat + *foò* trousers). A suit consisting of jacket and trousers worn by Chinese women and occasionally men.

samisen /'samɪsɛn/ *noun* (also **shamisen** /'ʃamɪsɛn/) E17 **Japanese** (from Chinese *sānxián* (Wade–Giles *sān-hsien*), from *sān* three + *xián* string). A long-necked three-stringed Japanese lute, played with a plectrum. Cf. SAN-HSIEN.

samizdat /'samɪzdat/, /ˌsamɪz'dat/ *noun* (also **Samizdat**) M20 **Russian** (from *sam(o-* self + *izdat(el'stvo* publishing house). The clandestine or illegal copying and distribution of literature, especially in the former USSR; an underground press; a text or texts produced by this.

> **1980** *Times Literary Supplement* The strongest works to have come out since 1962 . . . have appeared, and could only appear, in *samizdat*.

samosa /sə'məʊsə/ *noun* M20 **Persian and Urdu** (*samosa(h)*). A triangular pastry fried in ghee or oil, containing spiced vegetables or meat.

samovar /'saməvɑː/, /samə'vɑː/ *noun* M19 **Russian** (from *samo-* self + *varit'* to boil). A Russian tea urn, with an internal heating device to keep the water at boiling point.

sampan /'sampan/ *noun* E17 **Chinese** (*sānban* (Wade–Giles *san-pan*) boat, from *sān* three + *bǎn* board). A small boat used in the Far East, usually with a stern-oar or stern-oars.

samsara /səm'sɑːrə/ *noun* L19 **Sanskrit** (*saṃsāra* a wandering through). *Hinduism* and *Buddhism* The endless cycle of death and rebirth to which life in the material world is bound.

samskara /səm'skɑːrə/ *noun* E19 **Sanskrit** (*saṃskāra* preparation, a making perfect). **1** E19 *Hinduism* A purificatory ceremony or rite marking a stage or an event in life. **2** E19 *Buddhism* A mental impression, instinct, or memory.

samurai /'samʊrʌɪ/, /'samjʊrʌɪ/ *noun & adjective* E18 **Japanese**. **A** *noun* E18 plural same. In feudal Japan, a member of a military caste, *especially* a member of the class of military retainers of the daimyos. Now also more widely, a Japanese army officer. **B** *attributive* or as *adjective* **1** L19 Of or pertaining to the samurai. **2** L20 *Samurai bond*, a bond in yen in the Japanese market, issued by a foreigner.

samyama /'samjəmə/ *noun* E19 **Sanskrit** (*saṃyama* restraint, control of the senses). *Hinduism* and *Buddhism* Collectively, the three final stages of meditation in yoga, which lead to SAMADHI.

san /san/ *noun* L19 **Japanese** (contraction of more formal *sama*). In Japan: an honorific title used after a personal or family name as a mark of politeness. Also (*colloquially*), used after other names or titles (cf. MAMA-SAN).

sanatarium /sanə'tɛːrɪəm/ *noun* plural **sanataria** /sanə'tɛːrɪə/, **sanatariums** M19 **Modern Latin** (from as SANATORIUM). A SANATORIUM senses 1, 2. Chiefly *United States*.

sanatorium /sanə'tɔːrɪəm/ *noun* plural **sanatoriums**, **sanatoria** /sanə'tɔːrɪə/ M19 **Modern Latin** (from *sanat-* past participial stem of *sanare* to heal). **1** M19 An establishment for the medical treatment and recuperation of invalids, especially convalescents or the chronically sick. **2** M19 A health resort. **3** M19 A room or building for sick people in a school etc. Often abbreviated in school slang to *san*.

sanbenito /ˌsanbə'niːtəʊ/ *noun* plural **sanbenitos** M16 **Spanish** (*sambenito*, from *San Benito* St Benedict, so called ironically from its resemblance to the Benedictine scapular). In the Spanish Inquisition, a yellow scapular-shaped garment, with a red St Andrew's cross before and behind, worn by a confessed and penitent heretic. Also, a similar black garment with flames, devils, and other devices, worn by an impenitent confessed heretic at an auto-da-fé.

sancocho /san'kotʃo/ *noun* M20 **American Spanish** (from Spanish = half-cooked meal, from *sancochar* to parboil). In South America and the Caribbean: a rich soup or stew of meat, fish, and vegetables.

sancta plural of SANCTUM.

sancta sanctorum plural of SANCTUM SANCTORUM.

sancta simplicitas /ˌsaŋ(k)tə sɪm'plɪsɪtɑːs/ *interjection* M19 **Latin** (literally, 'holy simplicity'). Expressing astonishment at a person's naivety.

■ These are said to have been the last words of the Bohemian religious reformer John Huss, burnt at the stake in 1415, on seeing a simple peasant bringing wood to add to the fire.

sanctum /'saŋ(k)təm/ *noun* plural **sanctums**, **sancta** /'saŋ(k)tə/ L16 **Latin** (neuter of *sanctus* holy; cf. next). **1** L16 A sacred place or shrine in a temple or church. **2** E19 A place where a person can be alone and free from intrusion; a private room, study, etc.

sanctum sanctorum /ˌsaŋ(k)təm saŋ(k)'tɔːrəm/ *noun phrase* plural **sancta sanctorum** /ˌsaŋ(k)tə/ LME **Latin** (neuter singular and neuter genitive plural of *sanctus* holy, translation of Hebrew *qōḏeš haqqōḏāšīm* holy of holies). **1** LME *Jewish Antiquities* The holy of holies in the Jewish Temple. **2** L16 A SANCTUM sense 1. **3** E18 A SANCTUM sense 2.

sanctus /ˈsaŋ(k)təs/ *noun* LME **Latin** (= holy, the first word of the hymn). *Christian Church* (also **Sanctus**) The hymn beginning *Sanctus, sanctus, sanctus* 'Holy, holy, holy', which forms the conclusion of the Eucharistic preface; a musical setting of this.

sandur /ˈsandə/, /ˈsandəː/ *noun* plural **sandar**, **sandurs** (also **sandr**, plural same, **sandurs**) L19 **Icelandic** (*sandur*, plural *sandar*, (Old Norse *sandr*), sand). *Physical Geography* A broad, flat or gently sloping plain of glacial outwash.

sanfoin variant of SAINFOIN.

sang-de-boeuf /sɑ̃dəbœf/ *noun* L19 **French** (literally, 'ox's blood'). A deep red colour found on old Chinese porcelain; (porcelain bearing) a ceramic glaze of this colour.

Sängerfest /ˈsɛŋərfɛst/ *noun* (also **Saengerfest**) M19 **German** (from *Sänger* singer + FEST). A choral festival. *United States*.

sang-froid /sɒŋˈfrwɑː/ *noun* M18 **French** (literally, 'cold blood'). Coolness, self-possession, especially in the face of danger or disturbing circumstances.

1996 *Spectator* Thanks to our sang-froid, we have only once fallen into the hands of idiotic optimists—the grim Puritans of the Commonwealth.

sangha /ˈsaŋgə/ *noun* M19 **Sanskrit** (*saṃgha*, from *sam* together + *han* to come in contact). *Buddhism* The Buddhist community, the Buddhist order of monks, nuns, and novices.

sanglier /sɑ̃glije/ *noun* plural pronounced same LME **Old French** (*sengler*, (also modern) *sanglier* from Latin *singularis* solitary, singular, used as noun in late Latin = a boar separated from the herd, in medieval Latin = wild boar). A wild boar. Formerly *specifically*, one that is fully grown.

sangoma /saŋˈgɔːma/ *noun* (also **isangoma** /ɪsaŋˈgɔːma/) L19 **Nguni**. In southern Africa: a witch-doctor, usually a woman, claiming supernatural powers of divination and healing.

sangre azul /ˌsangre aˈθul/, /aˈsul/ *noun phrase* M19 **Spanish** (= blue blood). The purity of blood claimed by certain ancient Castilian families, which professed to be free from Moorish or Jewish ancestry.

sangria /saŋˈgriːə/ *noun* (also **Sangria**) M20 **Spanish** (*sangría*, literally, 'bleeding'). A Spanish drink made of sweetened diluted red wine with spices and fruit.

san-hsien /sanˈʃjɛn/ *noun* (also **sanxian**) M19 **Chinese** (*sānxián* (Wade–Giles *sān-hsien*), from *sān* three + *xián* string). *Music* A Chinese three-stringed lute. Cf. SAMISEN.

sannyasi /sənˈjɑːsi/ *noun* (also **sanyasi**, **sannyasin** /sənˈjɑːsɪn/) E17 **Sanskrit** (*saṃnyāsī* nominative singular of *saṃnyāsin* laying aside, abandoning, ascetic, from *saṃ* together + *ni* down + *as* throw). A brahmin in the fourth stage of his life; a wandering Hindu fakir.

sanpaku /sanˈpaku/ *noun* M20 **Japanese** (literally, 'three white', from *san* three + *haku* white). Visibility of the white of the eye below the iris as well as on either side.

sans /sɑ̃(z)/, /san(z)/ *preposition* ME **Old French** (*san*, *sanz* (modern *sans*), earlier *sen(s)* from Proto-Romance variation of Latin *sine* without, partly influenced by Latin *absentia* absence). Without.

■ Although formerly fully naturalized, *sans* is now, apart from use in heraldic terminology, mainly literary and often jocular—especially with reference to Shakespeare's line on second childhood: 'Sans teeth, sans eyes, sans taste, sans everything' (*As You Like It* II.vii). It also occurs in a number of phrases borrowed from French.

1996 *Times* Ms Thompson is not allowed to leave her house in a track-suit *sans* make-up without being pilloried by the press.

sans blague /sɑ̃ blag/ *interjection* E20 **Old French** (literally, 'without joking'). You don't say! I don't believe it!

sans cérémonie /sɑ̃ seremɔni/ *adverb phrase* M17 **Old French**. Unceremoniously; without the usual ceremony or formality.

sansculotte /ˌsanzkjuːˈlɒt/, *foreign* /sɑ̃kylɔt/ (*plural same*) *noun* (also **sans culottes**) L18 **French** (from *sans* without + *culotte* knee-breeches). **1** L18 *History* A lower-class Parisian republican in the French Revolution; *generally* an extreme republican or revolutionary. **2** E19 *transferred* A shabbily dressed person, a ragamuffin.

1 1996 *Times* After my election . . . I warned my council colleagues that if I were seen to be obstructed, it would not be long before *sans culottes* to the left of me emerged.

sansei /ˈsanseɪ/ *noun* plural same M20 **Japanese** (from *san* three, third + *sei* generation). An American whose grandparents were immigrants from Japan. Cf. NISEI.

sanserif variant of SANS SERIF.

sans façon /sɑ̃ fasɔ̃/ *adverb phrase* L17 **Old French** (literally, 'without manner'). Without the customary formality; SANS CÉRÉMONIE.

sans-gêne /sɑ̃ ʒɛn/ *noun phrase* L19 **Old French** (literally, 'without embarrassment'). Disregard of the ordinary forms of civility or politeness.

sans pareil /sɑ̃ parɛj/ *adjective phrase* **Old French** (literally, 'not having its like'). Unique, unequalled.

■ Earlier (M18) current as a noun meaning 'smelling salts' or some other kind of perfume.

1996 *Times* Not for nothing is Mr Gordon considered an agent *sans pareil*.

sans peur /sɑ̃ pœr/ *adjective phrase* E19 **Old French**. Without fear, fearless.

■ Especially in the phrase *sans peur et sans reproche*, which was applied to the Chevalier de Bayard (1476–1524), a renowned soldier in the Italian wars of Charles VIII of France.

1995 *Spectator* Whether for religious reasons or because it hasn't got a licence, there's no alcohol in the place, though you can bring your own with you *sans peur et sans reprôche* [*sic*].

sans phrase /sanz ˈfrɑːz/ *adjective phrase* E19 **Old French**. Without more words, without exceptions or qualifications.

■ After *La mort sans phrase* ('death, without more words'), the expression allegedly used by the Abbé Sieyès (1748–1836) in giving his vote for the execution of Louis XVI.

sans recours /sɑ̃ r(ə)kur/, /ˌsanz rəˈkəː/ *noun phrase* L19 **Old French** (literally, 'without recourse'). *Law* An endorsement on a bill of exchange absolving the endorser or any other party from liability.

sans reproche /sanz rəˈprɔʃ/ *adjective phrase* M19 **Old French**. Without reproach, blameless.

■ Earlier (E19), and especially, in *sans peur et sans reproche*; cf. SANS PEUR.

sans serif /san ˈsɛrɪf/ *noun & adjective* (also **sanserif**) M19 **French** (apparently from SANS + *serif* cross-stroke of a letter (origin uncertain, but possibly from Dutch *schreef* dash, line)). *Typography* **A** *noun* M19 A letterform, especially a typeface, without serifs. **B** *adjective* L19 Having no serifs.

santeria /ˌsanteˈria/ *noun* M20 **Spanish** (*santería*, literally, 'holiness, sanctity'). An Afro-Cuban religious cult with many Yoruba elements.

santero /sanˈtero/ *noun* plural **santeros** /sanˈteros/ M20 **Spanish**. **1** M20 In Mexico and Spanish-speaking areas of the south-western United States: a maker of religious images. **2** M20 A priest of a religious cult, especially of *santeria*.

santir /sanˈtɪə/ *noun* (also **santoor**, **santour** /sanˈtʊə/) M19 **Arabic** (*sanṭīr*, *sinṭīr*, *sanṭūr* (Persian *santūr*, Turkish *santur*), alteration of Greek *psaltērion* psaltery). A dulcimer of Arab and Persian origin.

santo /ˈsantəʊ/ *noun* plural **santos** M17 **Spanish** (or Italian). **1** M17 A SANTON sense 1. **2** M19 A wooden representation of a saint or other religious symbol from Mexico or the south-western United States.

santon /ˈsantɒn/ *noun* L16 **French** (from Spanish, from *santo* saint). **1** L16 A Muslim hermit or holy man, a marabout. Formerly also, a yogi, a Hindu ascetic. **2** E20 Chiefly in Provence: a figurine adorning a representation of the manger in which Jesus was laid.

santoor, **santour** variants of SANTIR.

san ts'ai /ˈsan tsʌɪ/ *noun phrase* E20 **Chinese** (*sāncǎi* (Wade–Giles *sān-ts'ai*), from *sān* three + *cǎi* colour). Chinese pottery, especially of the Tang dynasty, decorated in three colours; decoration in three enamel colours applied to pottery and porcelain.

sanyasi variant of SANNYASI.

saphir d'eau /safir do/ *noun* E19 **French** (literally 'sapphire of water'). An intense blue variety of cordierite occurring mainly in Sri Lanka; a water sapphire.

sarabande /sarəˈbɑːnd/ *noun* (also **saraband** /ˈsarəband/) E17 **French** (from Spanish or Italian *zarabanda*). A slow and stately Spanish dance in triple time; a piece of music for this dance or in its rhythm.

sarang variant of SERANG.

sarangi /sə'raŋgi/, /sɑː'rʌŋgi/ *noun* M19 Sanskrit (*sāraṅgī*). An Indian bowed stringed instrument.

sarape variant of SERAPE.

sarcoma /sɑː'kəʊmə/ *noun* plural **sarcomas**, **sarcomata** /sɑː'kəʊmətə/ M17 **Modern Latin** (from Greek *sarkōma*, from *sarkoun* to become fleshy, from *sarx*, *sark*- flesh). *Medicine* **1** M17–M18 A fleshy excrescence. **2** E19 A malignant tumour of connective or other non-epithelial tissue.

sarcophagus /sɑː'kɒfəgəs/ *noun* plural **sarcophagi** /sɑː'kɒfəgʌɪ/, /sɑː'kɒfəʤʌɪ/ LME **Latin** (from Greek *sarkophagos* (adjective & noun), from *sarx*, *sark*- flesh + -*phagos* eating). **1** A stone coffin, *especially* one adorned with sculpture, an inscription, etc. **2** E17 *Greek Antiquities* A stone fabled to be able to consume the flesh of dead bodies deposited in it, and used for coffins. Now *rare*. **3** E17–M19 A flesh-eater; a cannibal. *rare*.

sardana /sar'ḍana/ *noun* E20 **Catalan and Spanish**. A Catalan dance performed to pipes and drum.

sari /'sɑːri/ *noun* (also **saree**) L18 **Hindi** (*sāṛī* from Sanskrit *śāṭikā*). A traditional garment of Indian women, worn over a CHOLI and an underskirt, consisting of a length of cotton, silk, or other cloth wrapped around the waist and draped over one shoulder.

sarmale /sar'male/ *noun plural* M20 **Romanian**. A Romanian dish of forcemeat and other ingredients wrapped in especially cabbage or vine leaves.

sarod /sə'rəʊd/ *noun* M19 **Urdu** (from Persian *surod* song, melody). An Indian stringed musical instrument.

saron /'sɑːrɒn/ *noun* E19 **Javanese**. An Indonesian musical instrument, normally having seven bronze bars which are struck with a mallet.

sarong /sə'rɒŋ/ *noun* M19 **Malay** (literally, 'sheath, quiver'). A traditional skirtlike garment of the Malay archipelago, Java, and some Pacific islands, consisting of a long strip of (often striped) cloth worn tucked round the waist or under the armpits by both sexes; a woman's garment resembling this, worn especially on the beach.

sarsaparilla /ˌsɑːs(ə)pə'rɪlə/ *noun* L16 **Spanish** (*zarzaparilla*, from *zarza* bramble + diminutive of Spanish *parra* vine, twining plant). **1** L16 Any of several tropical American kinds of smilax used medicinally; the dried root of such a plant, used to treat rheumatism, skin complaints, and formerly also syphilis. Also, a carbonated drink flavoured with this root. **2** M19 Any of several plants of other genera which resemble sarsaparilla or have a root used similarly. Chiefly with specifying word.

sartage /'sɑːtɪʤ/ *noun* L19 **French** (from *sarter* to clear ground). The clearing of woodland by setting fire to trees. *United States*.

sashimi /'saʃɪmi/ *noun* L19 **Japanese** (from *sashi* pierce + *mi* flesh). A Japanese dish of slices of raw fish served with grated horseradish and soy sauce.

sassafras /'sasəfras/ *noun* L16 **Spanish** (*sasafrás*, perhaps ultimately from Latin *saxifraga* saxifrage). **1** L16 A tree of the genus *Sassafras*, of the laurel family, especially *S. albidum* native to the eastern United States; also, the wood of this tree. **b** L16 The dried bark of this tree, used as a medicine and flavouring and for infusing. **c** M18 An oil extracted from (the bark of) the sassafras, used medicinally and in perfumery. In full *sassafras oil*, also *oil of sassafras*. **2** E19 Any of various similarly aromatic and medicinal trees of other genera and families; also, the wood or bark of such a tree.

sastruga /sa'struːgə/ *noun* (also **zastruga** /za'struːgə/) plural **sastrugi** /sa'struːgi/ M19 **German** (from Russian *zastruga* small ridge, furrow in snow, from *zastrugat'* to plane or smooth, from *strug* plane (the tool)). Any of a series of low irregular ridges formed on a level snow surface by wind erosion, often aligned parallel to the wind direction. Usually in *plural* (see quotation).

> **1975** E. Hillary *Nothing Venture, Nothing Win* The surface, which had appeared so smooth from above, was . . . liberally peppered with large sastrugi—some of them up to three feet in height.

satay /'sateɪ/ *noun* (also **satai**, **saté**) M20 **Malay** (*satai*, *sate*, Indonesian *sate*; cf. SOSATIE). An Indonesian and Malaysian dish consisting of small pieces of meat grilled on a skewer and usually served with a spiced peanut sauce.

sati variant of SUTTEE.

satori /sə'tɔːri/ *noun* E18 **Japanese** (= awakening). *Zen Buddhism* A sudden inner experience of enlightenment.

satranji /ʃə'trandʒi/ *noun* (also **sitringee** /sɪ'trɪndʒiː/ and other variants) E17 **Persian and Urdu** (*šhaṭranjī* from Persian *šaṭranj* chess, ultimately from Sanskrit *caturaṅga* army, chess, with reference to the original chequered pattern). A carpet or floor-rug made of coloured cotton, now usually with a striped pattern.

satsuma /sat'suːmə/, in sense 1 also /'satsjʊmə/ *noun* (also (especially in sense 1) **Satsuma**) L19 **Japanese** (name of a province in the island of Kiusiu, Japan). **1** L19 A kind of cream-coloured Japanese pottery. In full *Satsuma ware*. **2** L19 A variety of tangerine, originally from Japan, with a sharper taste and frequently seedless or with undeveloped seeds; the tree bearing this fruit.

Saturnalia /satə'neɪlɪə/ *noun* (treated as *singular* or *plural*) (in sense 2 also **saturnalia**) L16 **Latin** (use as noun of neuter plural of *Saturnalis* of or pertaining to *Saturnus* Saturn, the Roman god of agriculture and ruler of the gods until deposed by his son Jupiter). **1** L16 *Roman History* The festival of Saturn, held in mid December and characterized by general unrestrained merrymaking, the precursor of Christmas. **2** L18 *transferred* and *figurative* A period of unrestrained tumult and revelry; an orgy.

satyagraha /sʌ'tjɑːgrəhɑː/ *noun* E20 **Sanskrit** (*satyāgraha* force born of truth, from *satya* truth + *āgraha* pertinacity). **1** E20 *History* A policy of passive resistance to British rule in India formulated by M. K. Gandhi. **2** E20 *generally* Any policy of non-violent resistance.

saucier /sosje/ *noun* plural pronounced same M20 **French**. A sauce cook.

saucisson /sosisɔ̃/ *noun* plural pronounced same M17 **French** (augmentative of *saucisse* sausage). **1a** M17 A firework consisting of a tube packed with gunpowder. **b** E19 *History* A long tube packed with gunpowder, formerly used as a fuse for firing a mine. **2** E18 *Military* A large fascine. **3** M18 A large thick sausage.

saudade /sau'dadʒi/ *noun* E20 **Portuguese**. Longing, melancholy, nostalgia, as a supposed characteristic of the Portuguese or Brazilian temperament.

sauerbraten /'saʊəbrɑːt(ə)n/ *noun* L19 **German** (from *sauer* sour + *Braten* roast meat). A dish of German origin consisting of beef marinaded in vinegar with peppercorns, onions, and other seasonings and then cooked. *North American*.

sauerkraut /'saʊəkraʊt/ *noun* M17 **German** ((whence French *choucroute*), from *sauer* sour + *Kraut* vegetable, cabbage). Finely chopped pickled cabbage, a typical German dish.

■ In United States slang *Sauerkraut* was in use earlier (M19) as a derogatory word for 'a German' than its British equivalent KRAUT.

sauna /'sɔːnə/ *noun* L19 **Finnish**. A Finnish-style hot steam bath; a room or building in which such a bath is taken. Also *sauna bath*.

saut /so/ *noun* plural pronounced same L19 **French** (= leap). **1** L19 *Saut Basque*, a dance of the French Basque provinces. **2** L19 *Ballet* A leap in dancing. Especially in *saut de Basque*, a leap made while turning, holding one leg straight and the other at right angles to the body.

sauté /'səʊteɪ/ *noun, adjective, & verb* E19 **French** (past participle of *sauter* to leap). *Cookery* **A** *noun* E19 A dish cooked by frying quickly in a little hot fat. **B** *adjective* M19 Of meat, vegetables, etc.: fried quickly in a little hot fat. **C** *transitive verb* M19 (past tense and participle *sautéd*, *sautéed*) Fry (food) quickly in a little hot fat.

sautoir /'səʊtwɑː/ *noun* M20 **French** (Old French *saut(e)our*, *sau(l)toir* stirrup cord). A long necklace consisting of a fine gold chain usually set with jewels.

1980 *Times* Sautoirs, or long neckchains . . . were very popular at the beginning of the century.

sauve qui peut /sovkipø/ *noun & verb phrase* E19 **French** (literally, 'save-who-can'). **A** *noun phrase* E19 A general stampede, a complete rout; panic, disorder. **B** *verb phrase intransitive* M20 Stampede or scatter in flight.

A 1980 *Guardian* It is in those hallowed halls of the UN . . . that I feel most keenly the theatre of anarchy, of sauve-qui-peut.

savannah /sə'vanə/ *noun* (also **savanna**) M16 **Spanish** (*zavana*, *çavana*, (now *sabana*) from Taino *zavana*). **1** M16 Originally, a treeless plain, especially in tropical America. Now, an open grassy plain with few or no trees in a tropical or subtropical region; grassland or vegetation of this kind. **2** L17 A tract of low-lying damp or marshy ground. *United States*.

savant /ˈsav(ə)nt/, *foreign* /savɑ̃/ (*plural same*) *noun* E18 **French** (use as noun of adjective, originally present participle of *savoir* to know). A learned person, *especially* a distinguished scientist.

savante /ˈsav(ə)nt/, *foreign* /savɑ̃:t/ (*plural same*) *noun* M18 **French** (feminine of preceding). A learned (French) woman. Cf. FEMME SAVANTE.

savarin /ˈsavərɪn/, *foreign* /savarɛ̃/ (*plural same*) *noun* L19 **French** (Anthelme Brillat-*Savarin* (1755–1826), French gastronome). A light ring-shaped cake made with yeast and soaked in liqueur-flavoured syrup.

savate /səˈvɑ:t/, *foreign* /savat/ (*plural same*) *noun* M19 **French** (originally, a kind of shoe (cf. SABOT)). A form of boxing in which the feet and fists are used.

savoir /savwar/ *noun* E19 **French** (literally, 'know'). Knowledge.

■ Also used elliptically for SAVOIR FAIRE and SAVOIR VIVRE.

savoir faire /savwar fɛr/ *noun* (also **savoir-faire**) E19 **French** (literally, 'to know how to do'). The instinctive ability to act suitably in any situation; tact.

1996 *Spectator* Others who had some political savoir-faire (such as Fitzroy Maclean, who had been a diplomat in Moscow before the war) had no special knowledge of the Balkans.

savoir vivre /savwar vivr/ *noun* M18 **French** (literally, 'know how to live'). Knowledge of the world and the ways of society, ability to conduct oneself well; worldly wisdom, sophistication.

savonette /ˈsavɒnɛt/ *noun* E18 **French** ((now *savonnette*), diminutive of *savon* soap). Soap, especially in the form of a ball.

sayonara /sʌɪəˈnɑ:rə/ *interjection & noun* L19 **Japanese** (literally, 'if it be so'). (The Japanese word for) goodbye.

sayyid /ˈseɪjɪd/ *noun* (also **saiyid**, **syed**, and other variants, **Sayyid**) M17 **Arabic** (= lord, prince). (A title of respect for) a Muslim claiming descent from Muhammad through Husain, the prophet's elder grandson.

■ In Muslim countries, also as a respectful form of address.

sc. abbreviation of SCILICET.

scaglia /ˈskɑ:ljə/ *noun* L18 **Italian** (= scale, chip of marble, from Germanic base from which modern English *scale* (noun)). *Geology* A dark fine-grained shale found in the Alps and Apennines.

scagliola /skalˈjəʊlə/ *noun* L16 **Italian** *scagli(u)ola* diminutive of SCAGLIA). **1** L16–L18 SCAGLIA. **2** M18 Plasterwork of Italian origin, designed to imitate marble and other kinds of stone.

scala mobile /ˌskala ˈmo:bile/ *noun phrase* L20 **Italian** (literally, 'moving stair, escalator'). In Italy: a system of wage indexation by which earnings are linked by a sliding scale to the retail price index.

scald variant of SKALD.

scaloppine /ˌskalə(ʊ)ˈpi:neɪ/ *noun* (also Anglicized as **scallopini** /ˌskalə(ʊ)ˈpi:ni/) M20 **Italian** (plural of *scaloppina* diminutive of *scaloppa* escalope). A dish consisting of escalopes of meat (especially veal) sautéed or fried.

scampi /ˈskampi/ *noun plural* (also treated as *singular*; in sense 1 singular **scampo** /ˈskampəʊ/) E19 **Italian** (plural of *scampo*). **1** E19 Norway lobsters. Also (*rare*) *singular*, a Norway lobster. **2** M20 A dish of these lobsters, usually fried in breadcrumbs or in a sauce. Usually treated as *singular*.

■ In both senses also called *Dublin Bay prawn(s)*.

scandalon variant of SKANDALON.

scarabaeus /ˌskarəˈbi:əs/ *noun* plural **scarabaei** /ˌskarəˈbi:ʌɪ/ L16 **Latin** (= beetle: cf. Greek *karabos* horned beetle). **1** L16 *Entomology* A scarabaeid beetle. Now only as modern Latin genus name. **2** L18 *Antiquities* An ancient Egyptian amulet or seal in the form of a beetle with symbols on its flat underside, a scarab.

scarpetti /skɑ:ˈpɛti/ *noun plural* L19 **Italian** (plural of *scarpetto* small shoe, from *scarpa* shoe). Rope-soled shoes worn for rock-climbing, especially in the North Italian Alps.

scenario /sɪˈnɑ:rɪəʊ/ *noun & verb* L19 **Italian** (from Latin *scena* scene). **A** *noun* plural **scenarios**. **1a** L19 A sketch or outline of the plot of a play, ballet, novel, etc., with details of the scenes and situations. **b** E20 *Cinematography* A film script with all the details of scenes, stage-directions, etc., necessary for shooting the film. **2** M20 A description of an imagined situation or a postulated sequence of events; an outline of an intended course of action; *specifically* a scientific description or speculative model intended to account for observable facts. Also *loosely*, a situation, a sequence of events. **B** *transitive verb* M20 Make a scenario of (a book, idea, etc.); sketch *out*.

2 1996 *New Scientist* Once the current crisis is over, the most important question for the government will be why it never planned for a worst-case scenario when the risks of BSE were first raised in 1986.

scène à faire /sɛn a fɛr/ *noun phrase* plural **scènes à faire** (pronounced same) L19 **French** (literally, 'scene for action'). *Theatrical* The most important scene in a play or opera.

Schadenfreude /ˈʃɑːd(ə)nfrɔɪdə/ *noun* (also **schadenfreude**) L19 **German** (from *Schaden* harm + *Freude* joy). Malicious enjoyment of another's misfortune.

1995 *Times* In a lifelong personal effort not to become a sour old besom, I fight very hard against *Schadenfreude* and its complement, Saki's 'natural displeasure at the good fortune of a friend'.

schalet /ˈʃalɪt/, /ʃaˈlɛt/ *noun* M20 **Yiddish** (*shalent, shalet* variant of *tsholnt* cholent). **1** M20 CHOLENT. **2** M20 A Jewish baked fruit pudding.

schappe /ʃap/, /ˈʃapə/ *noun* L19 **German** (= silk waste). A fabric or yarn made from waste silk.

schema /ˈskiːmə/ *noun* plural **schemata** /ˈskiːmətə/, **schemas** L18 **German** (from Greek *skhēma, skhēmat-*). **1** L18 In Kantian philosophy, a rule or procedure of the imagination enabling the understanding to apply a concept, especially a category, to what is given in sense-perception. **2** M19 *Ecclesiastical* A draft canon or decree for discussion. **3** L19 A schematic representation of something; a hypothetical outline or plan; a draft, a synopsis, a design. **4** E20 *Psychology* An (unconscious) organized mental model of something in terms of which new information can be interpreted or an appropriate response made.

schemozzle variant of SHEMOZZLE.

scherzando /skɛːtˈsandəʊ/ *adverb, adjective, & noun* E19 **Italian** (from *scherzare* to joke, from SCHERZO). *Music* **A** *adverb & adjective* E19 (A direction:) playful(ly). **B** *noun* L19 plural **scherzandos, scherzandi** /skɛːtˈsandi/. A movement or passage (to be) played playfully.

scherzo /ˈskɛːtsəʊ/ *noun* plural **scherzos, scherzi** /ˈskɛːtsi/ M19 **Italian** (literally, 'sport, jest'). *Music* A vigorous, light, or playful composition, especially as a movement in a symphony or sonata.

attributive **1996** *Times* This is not to say that Ozick doesn't go at all her subjects with anything less energetic than a scherzo tempo . . .

schiacciato variant of STIACCIATO.

schiller /ˈʃɪlə/ *adjective & noun* E19 **German** (= play of colours). *Geology* **A** E19 *attributive adjective* Designating minerals or rocks having a shining surface. **B** *noun* M19 An iridescent lustre, *specifically* that characteristic of certain minerals.

Schimpfwort /ˈʃɪmpfˌvɔrt/ *noun* plural **Schimpfwörter** /ˈʃɪmpfˌvœrtər/ M20 **German** (from *Schimpf* insult + *Wort* word). An insulting epithet, a term of abuse.

schinken /ˈʃɪŋkən/ *noun* M19 **German**. German ham.

schlag /ʃlɑːk/ *noun* M20 **German** (abbreviation). **1** SCHLAGOBERS. **2** SCHLAGSAHNE.

Schlagobers /ʃlɑːkˈoːbərs/ *noun* M20 **German** ((dialect) from *schlagen* to beat + *Obers* cream). (Coffee with) whipped cream.

schlagsahne /ˈʃlɑːkzɑːnə/ *noun* E20 **German** (from *schlagen* to beat + *Sahne* cream). Whipped cream.

Schlamperei /ˈʃlampəraɪ/ *noun* M20 **German**. Indolent slovenliness, muddle-headedness.

■ In its original German context, used derogatorily to designate the supposed sloppiness of the south Germans and Austrians.

schlemiel /ʃləˈmiːl/ *noun* (also **schlemihl, Shlemihl**) L19 **German** (*Shlemihl*). An awkward or clumsy person; a foolish or unlucky person. *colloquial.*

■ The word may ultimately be connected with the biblical *Shelumiel*, head of the tribe of Simeon (Numbers 1:6), who, according to the Talmud, came to an unfortunate end. Modern use of *schlemiel* is influenced by Adelbert von Chamisso's famous tale *Peter Schlemihls wundersame Geschichte* (1814), the eponymous hero of which sells his shadow.

schlenter /ˈʃlɛntə/ *noun & adjective* (also (*Australia* and *New Zealand*) **slanter** /ˈslantə/ and other variants) M19 **Afrikaans** (or Dutch possibly from Dutch *slenter* knavery, trick). **A** *noun* **1** M19 A trick. *Australian* and *New Zealand colloquial.* **2** L19 A counterfeit diamond. *South African.* **B** *adjective* L19 Dishonest, crooked; counterfeit, fake. *Australian, New Zealand,* and *South African colloquial.*

■ The history of this word is obscure; the likelihood is that the Australian and New Zealand usages derive from South African English, but the route of the borrowing is uncertain. In Australia and New Zealand the most common spelling is now *slanter*, presumably under the influence of *slant* (i.e. crooked).

schlep /ʃlɛp/ *noun 1* **M20 Yiddish** (abbreviation). A SCHLEPPER. *United States colloquial.*

schlep /ʃlɛp/ *noun 2* **M20 Yiddish** (probably from German *schleppen* to drag). A troublesome business, (a piece of) hard work. Chiefly *United States colloquial.*

schlep /ʃlɛp/ *verb* (also **schlepp**; inflected *-pp-*) **E20 Yiddish** (*shelpn* from German *schleppen* to drag). **1** *transitive verb* E20 Haul, carry, drag. **2** *intransitive verb* M20 Toil; move or go slowly or awkwardly. *colloquial.*

schlepper /ˈʃlɛpə/ *noun* **M20 Yiddish** (as preceding). A person of little worth; a fool; a hanger-on. *United States colloquial.*

schlimazel /ʃlɪˈmɒz(ə)l/ *noun* (also **shlimazel**, **schlimazl**) **M20 Yiddish** (from Middle High German *slim* crooked + Hebrew *mazzāl* luck). A consistently unlucky and accident-prone person. Chiefly *United States colloquial.*

schlock /ʃlɒk/ *noun & adjective* **E20 Yiddish** (apparently from *shlak* apoplectic stroke, *shlog* wretch, untidy person, apoplectic stroke, from *shlogn* to strike). **A** *noun* E20 Cheap, shoddy, or defective goods; inferior material, trash. **B** *adjective* E20 Cheap, inferior, trashy.

■ Colloquial and chiefly North American (but see quotation).

A 1996 *Times Silver Lake* is a fascinating hybrid: certainly not an opera, but . . . not quite a musical either, at least not the escapist schlock that the term 'musical' so often suggests nowadays.

schlong /ʃlɒŋ/ *noun* **M20 Yiddish** (*shlang*, from Middle High German *slange* (German *Schlange*) snake). The penis. Also, a contemptible person. *United States slang.*

schloss /ʃlɒs/ *noun* **E19 German**. A castle, *especially*, one in Germany or Austria.

1995 *Spectator* On the way we had a glimpse of Glamis Castle . . . [a] charming *schloss*, turreted and stucco'd . . .

schlub variant of SHLUB.

schmaltz /ʃmɔːlts/, /ʃmalts/ *noun & verb* **M20 Yiddish** (from German *Schmalz* dripping, lard). **A** *noun* **1** M20 Melted chicken fat. Chiefly in *schmaltz herring*, a form of pickled herring. **2** M20 Sentimentality, emotionalism; excessively sentimental music, writing, drama, etc. *colloquial.* **B** *transitive verb* M20 Impart a sentimental atmosphere to; play (music) in a sentimental manner. Frequently followed by *up*. *colloquial.*

A.2 1995 *Spectator* This orgy of smug schmalz starts with Doris's dad dropping dead in church, presumably having seen the rest of the show in rehearsal . . .

schmatte variant of SHMATTE.

schmear, **schmeer** variants of SHMEAR.

schmelz /ʃmɛlts/ *noun* **M19 German** (= enamel). Any of several varieties of decorative glass; *especially* one coloured red with a metallic salt, used to flash white glass.

Schmelzglas /ˈʃmɛltsˌglɑːs/ *noun* **M20 German**. SCHMELZ.

Schmerz /ʃmɛrts/ *noun* **E20 German** (= pain). Grief, sorrow, regret, pain.

schmierkäse /ˈʃmiːrˌkɛːzə/ *noun* **E20 German** (from *schmieren* to smear + *Käse* cheese). A soft cheese, *specifically* cottage cheese.

schmooze /ʃmuːz/, /ʃmuːs/ *noun* **M20 Yiddish** (*schmues* chat, gossip from Hebrew *šĕmūʻōṯ* plural of *šĕmūʻāh* rumour). Chat; gossip; a long and intimate conversation. *North American colloquial.*

schmuck /ʃmʌk/ *noun* **L19 Yiddish** (*shmok* penis). A contemptible or objectionable person; an idiot.

■ North American slang. *Schmo* is a more recent (M20) alternative.

schmutz /ʃmʊts/ *noun* **M20 Yiddish or German**. Dirt, filth, rubbish. *slang.*

schnapps /ʃnaps/ *noun* (also **schnaps**) **E19 German** (*Schnaps* dram of drink, liquor (especially gin) from Low German, Dutch *snaps* gulp, mouthful, from *snappen* to seize, snatch, snap). Any of various strong spirits resembling genever.

■ The Dutch, Danish, and Swedish word *snaps* (M19) is less common in English.

schnitzel /ˈʃnɪtz(ə)l/ *noun* **M19 German**. A veal cutlet.

■ Especially in *Wiener* (or *Vienna*) *schnitzel*, a veal cutlet coated with egg and breadcrumbs and fried.

schnook /ʃnʊk/ *noun* **M20 German or Yiddish** (perhaps from German *Schnucke* a small sheep, or Yiddish *shnuk* snout). A dupe, a sucker; a simpleton. *North American colloquial.*

schnorrer /ˈʃnɒrə/ *noun* L19 **Yiddish** (variant of German *Schnurrer*, from *schnurren* (slang) go begging). Originally (*specifically*) a Jewish beggar. Now (*generally*), a beggar, a layabout, a scrounger. Chiefly *United States.*

schnozz /ʃnɒz/ *noun* M20 **Yiddish** (*shnoytz* from German *Schnauze* snout. The nose; a nostril.

■ North American slang. The Yiddish diminutive form of *shnoytz*, *shnoytzl*, has given rise to *schnozzle* /ˈʃnɒz(ə)l/ (M20), also a slang word for 'nose'.

schola cantorum /ˌskəʊlə kanˈtɔːrəm/ *noun phrase* plural **scholae cantorum** /ˌskəʊliː/, /ˌskəʊlʌɪ/ L18 **Medieval Latin** (= school of singers). **1** L18 A choir school attached to a cathedral or monastery; originally, the papal choir at Rome, established by Gregory the Great (*c.*540–604). **2** E20 *generally* A group of singers. Frequently as the title of such a group.

scholium /ˈskəʊlɪəm/ *noun* plural **scholia** /ˈskəʊlɪə/ M16 **Modern Latin** (from Greek *skholion* from *skholē* learned discussion). An explanatory note or comment, *especially* one made by an ancient commentator on a classical text.

■ Generally used in the plural, but in the singular the Greek ending *-ion* (L16) is also found.

schottische /ʃɒˈtiːʃ/, /ˈʃɒtɪʃ/ *noun* M19 **German** ((*der*) *Schottische*(*tanz*) (the) Scottish (dance)). **1** M19 A dance resembling a slow polka; a piece of music for this dance. **2** L19 (*Highland Schottische*) A lively dance resembling the Highland fling.

Schrecklichkeit /ˈʃrɛklɪçˌkaɪt/ *noun* (also **schrecklichkeit**) E20 **German** (= frightfulness). Originally *specific*, a deliberate military policy of terrorizing an enemy, especially the civilian population. Now *generally*, frightfulness, awfulness, an atmosphere of dread or fear.

1972 K. Bonfiglioli *Don't Point that Thing at Me* I embarked on the quotidian *schrecklichkeit* of getting up.

schreierpfeife /ˈʃrʌɪəˌ(p)fʌɪfə/ *noun* plural **schreierpfeifen** /ˈʃrʌɪəˌ(p)faɪf(ə)n/ M20 **German** (literally, 'screamer pipe'; cf. RAUSCHPFEIFE). *Music* A kind of shawm used in the sixteenth and seventeenth centuries.

■ This instrument is also called a *schryari* (M20), a word the origin of which is uncertain but which may be related to *schreierpfeife*.

schrund /ʃrʊnt/ *noun* L19 **German** (= cleft, crevice). A crevasse; *specifically* a BERGSCHRUND.

schtoom variant of SHTOOM.

Schuhplattler /ˈʃuːˌplatlər/ *noun* L19 **German** (from *Schuh* shoe + southern German dialect *Plattler* (from *platteln* to slap)). A lively Bavarian and Austrian folk-dance, characterized by the slapping of the thighs and heels.

schuss /ʃʊs/ *noun & verb* M20 **German** (literally, 'a shot'). **A** *noun* M20 A straight downhill run on skis; the slope on which such a run is executed. Also *transferred*, a rapid downward slide. **B** *verb* **1** *transitive verb* M20 Ski straight down (a slope etc.); cover (a certain distance) by means of a schuss. **2** *intransitive verb* M20 Ski straight down a slope. Also *transferred*, move rapidly (especially downwards).

schvartze, schvartzer see SCHWARTZE.

schwa /ʃwɑː/ *noun* (also **shwa**) L19 **German.** *Phonetics* The neutral central vowel sound /ə/, typically occurring in unstressed syllables, as the final syllable of 'sofa' and the first syllable of 'along'. Also, the symbol '/ə/' representing this sound, as in the International Phonetic Alphabet. Also called SHEVA.

schwarm /ʃvarm/ *noun* E20 **German.** An enthusiasm, a craze, an infatuation.

■ Followed by *for* (see quotation).

1968 N. Marsh *Clutch of Constables* The wretched woman . . . had developed a *schwarm* for Troy herself.

schwärmerei /ˌʃvɛrməˈraɪ/, /ˈʃvɛrməraɪ/ *noun* plural **schwärmereien** /ˌʃvɛrməˈraɪən/ M19 **German** (from *schwärmen* to swarm, display enthusiasm, rave). Enthusiastic or fervent devotion to a person or a cause; a juvenile attachment, especially to a person of the same sex; (an) infatuation, a crush.

schwartze /ˈʃvɑːtsə/ *noun* (also **schvartze, schwartzer**, and other variants) M20 **Yiddish** (*shvartser* (masculine), *shvartse* (feminine), from *shvarts* black, from German *schwarz* from Old High German *swarz* from Germanic). A Black person. *slang, generally derogatory.*

Schweinerei /ˌʃvaməˈraɪ/, /ˈʃvaməraɪ/ *noun* (also **schweinerei**) plural **Schweinereien** /ˌʃvaməˈraɪən/ E20 **German** (literally, 'piggishness'). Obnoxious behaviour, an instance of this; a repulsive incident or object, a scandal.

1965 *Economist* Some Japanese producers were recently discovered selling out of line at the recent Canton Fair. But this *schweinerei* was swiftly stamped on.

schwerpunkt /'ʃvɛːrpʊŋkt/ *noun* M20 **German** (= centre of gravity, focal point, from *schwer* hard, weighty + *Punkt* point). Focus, emphasis; strong point; area of concentrated (especially military) effort.

Schwung /ʃvʊŋ/ *noun* M20 **German** (literally, 'swinging motion'). Energy, verve, panache.

scilicet /'sʌɪlɪsɛt/, /'skiːlɪkɛt/ *adverb & noun* LME **Latin** (from *scire licet* one may understand or know; cf. VIDELICET). **A** *adverb* LME To wit; that is to say; namely. **B** *noun* M17 The word 'scilicet' or its equivalent, introducing a specifying clause.

■ As an adverb, used to introduce a word to be supplied or an explanation of an ambiguity and generally abbreviated to *scil.* or sc.

scintilla /sɪn'tɪlə/ *noun* L17 **Latin**. A spark; a trace, a tiny piece or amount.

1996 *Times* . . . serious thinkers in sharp suits . . . convene around shiny rosewood tables, on both sides of the Atlantic, to thrash out the last scintilla of marketing policy.

scirocco variant of SIROCCO.

scordatura /ˌskorda'tura/ *noun* plural **scordature** /ˌskorda'ture/ L19 **Italian** (from *scordare* to be out of tune). *Music* Alteration of the normal tuning of a stringed instrument so as to produce particular effects for certain pieces or passages; an instance of this.

scoria /'skɔːrɪə/ *noun* plural **scoriae** /'skɔːrɪiː/, (*rare*) **scorias** LME **Latin** (from Greek *skōria* refuse, from *skōr* dung). **1** LME The slag or dross remaining after the smelting out of a metal from its ore. **2** L18 *Geology* Rough masses resembling clinker, formed by the cooling of volcanic ejecta, and of a light aerated texture.

scorzonera /ˌskɔːzə(ʊ)'nɪərə/ *noun* E17 **Italian** (from *scorzone* from Proto-Romance alteration of medieval Latin *curtio(n)*- poisonous snake, against whose venom the plant may have been regarded as an antidote). Any of various plants constituting the genus *Scorzonera*; especially *S. hispanica*, cultivated in Europe for its tapering purple-brown root. Also, the root of *S. hispanica*, eaten as a vegetable.

scotia /'skəʊʃə/ *noun* M16 **Latin** (from Greek *skotia* from *skotos* darkness (with reference to the dark shadow within the cavity)). *Architecture* A concave moulding, especially at the base of a column; a casement.

scriptorium /skrɪp'tɔːrɪəm/ *noun* plural **scriptoria** /skrɪp'tɔːrɪə/, **scriptoriums** L18 **Medieval Latin** (from *script-* past participial stem of *scribere* to write). A room set apart for writing; *especially* a room in a monastery where manuscripts were copied.

scrutator /skruː'teɪtə/ *noun* L16 **Latin** (from *scrutat-* past participial stem of *scrutari*). **1** L16 A person who examines or investigates something or someone. **2** E17 A person whose official duty it is to examine or investigate something closely; *especially*, a scrutineer at an election.

scungille /skun'dʒille/ *noun* plural **scungilli** /skun'dʒilli/ M20 **Italian** (dialect *scunciglio*, probably alteration of Italian *conchiglia* seashell, shellfish). A mollusc, a conch; *especially* the meat of a mollusc eaten as a delicacy.

scuola /'skwola/ *noun* plural **scuole** /'skwole/ M19 **Italian** (= school). In Venice: any of the buildings in which the medieval religious confraternities or guilds used to meet, a guildhall; *History* any of these guilds.

sebkha variant of SABKHA.

sebum /'siːbəm/ *noun* L19 **Modern Latin** (use of Latin *sebum* suet, grease, tallow). *Physiology* The oily secretion of the sebaceous glands which lubricates and protects the hair and skin.

sec /sɛk/ *adjective & noun* ME **French** (from Latin *siccus*). Dry (wine); a drink of this.

secateur /sɛkə'təː/, /'sɛkətəː/ *noun* M19 **French** (*sécateur*, irregularly from Latin *secare* to cut + *-ateur*). *singular* and (usually) in *plural* A pair of pruning clippers with crossed blades, for use with one hand. Also *pair of secateurs*.

secco /'sɛko/ *noun & adjective* M19 **Italian** (from Latin *siccus* dry; in sense A.1 elliptical for *fresco secco*, literally, 'dry fresco'). **A** *noun* plural **seccos** **1** M19 The process or technique of painting on dry plaster with colours mixed with water. **2** M20 *Music* (A) RECITATIVO secco. **B** *adjective* L19

Music Of recitative: plain, lacking or having only sparse instrumental accompaniment.

secretaire /ˌsɛkrɪˈtɛː/ *noun* L18 **French** (*secrétaire* from late Latin *secretarius* confidential officer, use as noun of adjective from Latin *secretum* secret). A writing-desk with drawers and pigeon-holes; a bureau.

secretariat /ˌsɛkrəˈtɛːrɪət/ *noun* (also **Secretariat**) E19 **French** (*secrétariat* from medieval Latin *secretariatus*, from as SECRETAIRE). The official position of secretary; the place where a secretary works, preserves records, etc. Also, the administrative and executive department of a government or similar organization; such a department's staff or premises.

secret de Polichinelle /səkrɛ də pɔliʃinɛl/ *noun phrase* M19 **French** (= Punchinello's secret). An apparent secret which is generally known; an open secret.

secundus /sɪˈkʌndəs/ *adjective* E19 **Latin** (= second). Designating the second of two or more pupils of the same surname to enter the school. Cf. PRIMUS adjective 2, TERTIUS.

sederunt /sɪˈdɪərənt/ *noun* E17 **Latin** (= there were sitting (sc. the following persons), use as noun of 3rd person plural perfect indicative of *sedere* to sit). **1** E17 A sitting of a deliberative or judicial body, especially an ecclesiastical assembly. Also *generally* (now *rare*), a (period of) sitting, especially for discussion or talk. **2** E18 The list of people present at such a sitting. Also in *plural*, the people named on such a list.

sede vacante /ˌsiːdiː vəˈkantiː/, /ˌseɪdeɪ vəˈkantiː/ *adverb phrase* LME **Latin** (= the seat being vacant). *Ecclesiastical* During the vacancy of an episcopal see.

sedile /sɪˈdʌɪli/ *noun* plural **sedilia** /sɪˈdɪlɪə/ LME **Latin** (= seat, from *sedere* to sit). **1** *generally* A seat. Only in LME. **2** L18 *Ecclesiastical* Each of a series of usually canopied and decorated stone seats, usually three in number, placed on or recessed into the south side of the choir near the altar for use by the clergy. Usually in *plural*.

segue /ˈsɛgweɪ/ *adverb, verb, & noun* M18 **Italian** (3rd person singular present indicative of *seguire* to follow). *Music* **A** *adverb* M18 (A direction:) proceed to the next movement without a break; continue with an indicated formula. **B** *intransitive verb* M20 Of a person or music: move without interruption from one (live or prerecorded) song or melody to another. Frequently followed by *into*. **C** *noun* M20 An uninterrupted transition from one song or melody to another.

Sehnsucht /ˈzeːnzʊxt/ *noun* M19 **German**. Yearning, wistful longing.

seicento /seɪˈtʃɛntəʊ/ *noun* (also **Seicento**) E20 **Italian** (= six hundred). The seventeenth century in Italy; the Italian style of art, literature, etc., of this period.

seiche /seɪʃ/ *noun* M19 **Swiss French** (perhaps from German *Seiche* sinking (of water)). *Physical Geography* A short-lived standing oscillation of a lake or other body of water (as a bay or basin of the sea), resembling a tide, caused especially by abrupt changes in atmospheric conditions or by small earth tremors.

seif /siːf/, /seɪf/ *noun* (also **sif**) E20 **Arabic** (*sayf*, literally, 'sword'). *Physical Geography* A sand-dune in the form of a long narrow ridge parallel to the direction of the prevailing wind. Also *seif dune*.

seigneur /seɪˈnjəː/, *foreign* /sɛɲœr/ (*plural same*) *noun* (also **Seigneur**) L16 **Old and Modern French** (from Latin *senior* comparative of *senex* old). Especially in France and Canada, a feudal lord, the lord of a manor, (chiefly *historical* except in the Channel Islands, *specifically* Sark). Now *generally*, a lord, a person exercising (feudal) authority.

seigneurie /sɛɲœri/ *noun* (also **seigneury** /ˈseɪmjəri/) plural pronounced same L17 **French** ((Old French *seignorie*) from as preceding; cf. SIGNORIA). **1** L17 *History* Especially in France and Canada, a landed estate held by feudal tenure, the territory or domain of a seigneur. **2** L19 Especially in the Channel Islands and Canada, the residence or mansion of a seigneur.

Seilbahn /ˈzaɪlbɑːn/ *noun* M20 **German** (from *Seil* cable, rope + *Bahn* road, way). A cable railway, an aerial cableway.

seiza /ˈseɪzə/ *noun* M20 **Japanese** (from *sei* correct + *za* sitting). An upright kneeling position which is the Japanese traditional formal way of sitting and is used in meditation and as part of the preparation in martial arts.

séjour /seʒur/ *noun* plural pronounced same M18 **French** (from *séjourner* to sojourn). **1** M18 The action of staying or sojourning in a place. **2** M18 A place of sojourn or residence.

Sekt /zɛkt/ *noun* E20 **German**. A German sparkling white wine; a drink of this.

selon les règles /səlɔ̃ le rɛgl/ *adverb phrase* E19 **French**. According to the rules (of polite society).

selva /'sɛlvə/ *noun* M19 **Spanish or Portuguese** (from Latin *silva* wood). *Physical Geography* (A tract of land covered by) dense equatorial forest, especially in the Amazon basin. Usually in *plural*.

semiosis /ˌsiːmɪ'əʊsɪs/, /ˌsɛmɪ'əʊsɪs/ *noun* (also **semeiosis**) E20 **Greek** (*sēmeiosis* (inference from) a sign, from *sēmeion* sign, from *sēma* sign, mark). The process of signification, especially in language or literature.

semis /səmi/, /sə'miː/ *noun* E20 **French** (literally, 'sowing', from *semer* to sow). A form of decoration used in bookbinding, in which small ornaments are repeated regularly.

sempervivum /ˌsɛmpə'vʌɪvəm/ *noun* (formerly Anglicized as **sempervive**) L16 **Latin** (neuter of *sempervivus* ever-living). Any of various succulent plants constituting the genus Sempervivum, of the stonecrop family; *especially* houseleek, *S. tectorum*.

semplice /'sɛmplɪtʃi/ *adverb & adjective* M18 **Italian** (= simple). *Music* (A direction:) simply, simple.

sempre /'sɛmpreɪ/ *adverb* E19 **Italian**. *Music* (A direction:) always, still, throughout.

senex /'sɛnɛks/ *noun* plural **senes** /'sɛneɪs/ L19 **Latin** (= old man). In literature (especially comedy), an old man as a stock figure.

senhor /sɛn'jɔː/, *foreign* /se'ɲor/ *noun* L18 **Portuguese** (from Latin *senior* comparative of *senex* old). Used as a title (preceding the surname or other designation) of or as a respectful form of address to a Portuguese or Brazilian man (corresponding to English *Mr* or *Sir*); a Portuguese or Brazilian man.

senhora /sɛn'jɔːrə/, *foreign* /se'ɲora/ *noun* E19 **Portuguese** (feminine of SENHOR). Used as a title (preceding the surname or other designation) of or as a respectful form of address to a Portuguese or Brazilian woman, especially a married one (corresponding to English *Mrs* or *madam*); such a woman.

senhorita /sɛnjə'riːtə/, /seɲo'rita/ *noun* L19 **Portuguese** (diminutive of preceding). Used as a title (preceding the surname or other designation) of or as a respectful form of address to a young especially unmarried Portuguese or Brazilian woman (corresponding to English *Miss*); such a woman.

sennachie /'sɛnəxi/ *noun* (also **shenachie** /'ʃɛnəxi/ and other variants) LME **Gaelic** (*seanachaidh* (= Old Irish *senchaid*), from *sean* old (Old Irish *sen*)). In Ireland and the Scottish Highlands: a professional recorder and reciter of family or traditional history and genealogy, attached to the household of a clan chieftain or person of noble rank. Now, a teller of traditional Gaelic heroic tales (chiefly in Scotland).

sennin /'sɛnɪn/ *noun* (also **sennen**) plural same L19 **Japanese** (= wizard, sage, recluse, from Chinese *Xi'anren* immortal man). In oriental mythology (originally in Taoism): an elderly recluse who has achieved immortality through meditation and self-discipline; a human being with supernatural powers, a reclusive mystic or teacher.

señor /sɛn'jɔː/ *foreign* /se'ɲor/ *noun* plural **señores** /sɛn'jɔːrɪz/, *foreign* /se'ɲores/ **1** E17 **Spanish** (from Latin *senior* comparative of *senex* old). Used as a title (preceding the surname or other designation) of or as a respectful form of address to a Spanish or Spanish-speaking man (corresponding to English *Mr* or *Sir*). **2** M19 A Spanish or Spanish-speaking man.

señora /sɛn'jɔːrə/, *foreign* /se'ɲora/ *noun* L16 **Spanish** (feminine of SEÑOR). Used as a title (preceding the surname or other designation) of or as a respectful form of address to a Spanish or Spanish-speaking woman, especially a married one (corresponding to English *Mrs* or *madam*; such a woman.

señorita /sɛnjə'riːtə/, *foreign* /seɲo'rita/ *noun* E19 **Spanish** (diminutive of preceding). **1** E19 Used as a title (preceding the surname or other designating) of or as a respectful form of address to a young especially unmarried Spanish or Spanish-speaking woman (corresponding to English *Miss*); such a woman. **2** L19 A small labroid fish, *Oxyjulis californica*, of the eastern Pacific. Also *señorita-fish*.

señorito /seɲo'rito/ *noun* plural **señoritos** /seɲo'ritos/ E20 **Spanish** (diminutive of SEÑOR). Used as a title (preceding the surname or other designation) or as a respectful form of address to a young man; a young man, *especially* (frequently *derogative*) a noble or rich one regarded as leading an ostentatious or frivolous existence.

sensei /sɛn'seɪ/ *noun* L19 **Japanese** (from *sen* previous + *sei* birth). In Japan: a teacher, an instructor, frequently of martial or other arts; a professor, a scholar.

sensibile /sɛn'sɪbɪleɪ/ *noun* plural **sensibilia** /ˌsɛnsɪ'bɪlɪə/ M19 **Latin** (neuter of *sensibilis* sensible). *Philosophy* The kind of thing which, if sensed, is a sense-datum.

sensibilité /sɑ̃sibilite/ *noun* E20 **French**. Sensibility; sensitivity.

1995 *Times* Not since Ronald Reagan's Bonzo went to college have American chimpanzees been treated with such *sensibilité*.

sensiblerie /sɑ̃siblǝri/ *noun* M20 **French**. Sentimentality; exaggerated or superficial sensitivity.

sensorium /sɛn'sɔːrɪəm/ *noun* plural **sensoria** /sɛn'sɔːrɪə/, **sensoriums** M17 **Late Latin** (from Latin *sens-* past participial stem of *sentire* to feel). The seat of sensation in the brain of humans and animals; the percipient centre to which sensory impulses are transmitted by the nerves; the whole sensory apparatus (including the sensory nerves). Formerly also, the brain regarded as centre of consciousness and nervous energy. Also *common sensorium*.

sensu lato /ˌsɛnsuː 'lɑːtəʊ/ *adverb & adjective phrase* M20 **Latin**. (Of a scientific etc. term) In the broad sense. Opposite of SENSU STRICTO.

sensu stricto /ˌsɛnsuː 'strɪktəʊ/ *adverb & adjective phrase* M19 **Latin** (= in the restricted sense). (Of a scientific etc. term) Strictly speaking, in the narrow sense. Opposite of SENSU LATO.

■ Also latterly (M20) as STRICTO SENSU.

sententia /sɛn'tɛnʃɪə/ *noun* plural **sententiae** /sɛn'tɛnʃɪiː/ E20 **Latin** (= mental feeling, opinion, philosophical judgement, from *sentire* to feel). A pithy or memorable saying, a maxim, an aphorism, an epigram; a thought, a reflection.

senza /'sɛntsa/ *preposition* E18 **Italian** (probably from Latin *absentia* absence, with influence of Latin *sine* without; cf. SANS). *Music* (In directions:) without.

separatum /sɛpə'reɪtəm/ *noun* plural **separata** /sɛpə'reɪtə/ L19 **Latin** (use as noun of neuter, singular of *separatus* past participle of *separare* to separate). An offprint.

sephira /'sɛfɪrɑː/ *noun* plural **sephiroth** /'sɛfɪrəʊθ/ M16 **Hebrew** (*sĕpīrāh* (plural *sĕpīrōt*), from *sāpar* to number). In the philosophy of the Jewish cabbala, each of the ten hypostatized attributes or emanations surrounding the Infinite, by means of which the Infinite enters into relation with the finite. Usually in *plural*.

sepia /'siːpɪə/ *noun & adjective* LME **Latin** (from Greek *sēpia* cuttlefish; in sense 2 (as French *sépia*) probably immediately from Italian *seppia*). **A** *noun* **1** LME A cuttlefish. Now chiefly as modern Latin genus name. **2** E19 A rich brown pigment prepared from the black secretion of the cuttlefish, used in monochrome drawing and watercolour painting; the dark reddish-brown colour of this pigment. Also, a brown tint used in photography. **b** L19 The black secretion itself. **3** M19 *elliptical* A sepia photograph or drawing. **B** *adjective* E19 Of the colour of sepia; drawn or tinted in sepia.

■ The adjective was also used as an euphemism in the 1940s in the United States to denote skin colour amongst American Blacks.

seppuku /sɛ'puːkuː/ *noun* L19 **Japanese** (from *setsu* to cut + *fuku* abdomen). HARAKIRI.

sepsis /'sɛpsɪs/ *noun* L19 **Greek** (*sēpsis*, from *sēpein* to make rotten). *Medicine* The state of being septic; blood-poisoning, especially through infection of a wound.

septennium /sɛp'tɛnɪəm/ *noun* plural **septennia** /sɛp'tɛnɪə/, **septenniums** M19 **Late Latin** (for classical Latin *septuennium*, from Latin *septem* seven + *annus* year). A period of seven years.

septum /'sɛptəm/ *noun* plural **septa** /'sɛptə/ M17 **Latin** ((also *saeptum*), from *sepire*, *saepire* to enclose, from *sepes*, *saepes* hedge). **1** M17 *generally* A partition; a dividing wall, layer, membrane, etc., especially in a living organism. **2** L17 *specifically* in *Anatomy* A thin layer of tissue forming a partition in a cavity, organ, etc. **3** E18 *Geology* A thin sheet of material filling a crack. **4** M20 *Electronics* A metal plate placed transversely across a wave-guide and attached to the walls by conducting joints.

sequela /sɪ'kwi:lə/ *noun* plural **sequelae** /sɪ'kwi:lə/ L18 **Latin** (*sequel(l)ae*, from *sequi* to follow). **1** L18 *Medicine* A disease or condition occurring as the result of a previous disease or condition. Usually in *plural*. **2** L19 A consequence or result.

sequin /'si:kwɪn/ *noun* (in sense 1 also (earlier) **chequeen** /ʧɪ'ki:n/) L16 **French** (from Italian *zecchino*, from *zecca* mint, from Arabic *sikka* a die for coining, a coin). **1** L16 *History* Any of various Italian and Turkish gold coins. **2** L19 A small shiny usually circular piece of material for attaching to garments as a decoration.

sequitur /'sɛkwɪtə/ *noun* M19 **Latin** (= it follows). An inference or conclusion which follows logically from the premisses; a logical deduction, a logical remark. Cf. NON SEQUITUR.

sera plural of SERUM.

serac /'sɛrak/, /sə'rak/ *noun* M19 **Swiss French** (*sérac*, originally the name of a compact white cheese, probably from Latin *serum* whey). A pinnacle or ridge of ice on the surface of a glacier where crevasses intersect.

seraglio /sɛ'rɑ:lɪəʊ/, /sɪ'reɪlɪəʊ/ *noun* plural **seraglios** L16 **Italian** (*serraglio*, from Turkish *saray* palace, mansion, from Persian, with assimilation to Italian *serraglio* cage (from medieval Latin *serraculum* diminutive of Latin *sera* bolt)). **1** L16 A harem, *especially* one in a palace. **b** M17 The women of a harem. **c** M–L17 *generally* An enclosure; a place of confinement. **2** L16 *History* A Turkish palace, *especially* that of the Sultan in Istanbul.

serai /sə'rʌɪ/ *noun* E17 **Turkish** (*saray* palace, mansion, from Persian: cf. preceding). **1** E17 In various South West Asian countries: a building for the accommodation of travellers, a caravanserai. **2** E17 *History* A SERAGLIO sense 2.

serang /sə'raŋ/ *noun* (also **sarang**) L18 **Anglo-Indian** (Persian and Urdu *sar-hang* commander, from *sar* head + *hang* authority. **1** A headman among Lascars. **2** E20 A person in authority, a person in charge. More fully *head serang*. *Australian slang*.

serape /sɛ'rɑ:peɪ/, *foreign* /se'rape/ *noun* (also **sarape** /sa'rɑ:peɪ/, **zarape** /sa'rape/) E19 **Mexican Spanish**. A shawl or blanket worn as a cloak by Spanish-Americans.

serdab /sə:'dɑ:b/ *noun* M19 **Arabic** (*sirdāb* cellar, underground vault; or directly from Persian *sardāb* grotto, cellar for ice, from *sard* cold + *āb* water). **1** M19 In the Middle East: a cellar, an underground chamber. **2** L19 *Egyptology* A secret passage or chamber in an ancient tomb.

serein /sərɛ̃/ *noun* L19 **Old and Modern French** (from Proto-Gallo-Romance, from Latin *serum* evening, use as noun of *serus* late). *Meteorology* A fine rain (apparently) falling from a cloudless sky.

sereno /sɛ'reɪnəʊ/, *foreign* /se'reno/ *noun* plural **serenos** /sɛ'reɪnəʊz/, *foreign* /se'renos/ L19 **Spanish**. In Spain and Spanish-speaking parts of America: a night-watchman.

seriatim /ˌsɪərɪ'eɪtɪm/ *adverb & adjective* L15 **Medieval Latin** (from as Latin *series* chain, row, series (from *serere* to join, connect) + *-atim* after Latin *gradatim*, *literatim*). **A** *adverb* L15 One after another, one by one in succession. **B** *adjective* L19 Following one after the other. *rare*.

serin /'sɛrɪn/ *noun* M16 **French** (= canary, of unknown origin). Originally, a canary. Now, any bird of the same genus, *especially* (more fully *serin finch*) *Serinus serinus*, a small yellow European finch.

seron /'sɪərən/ *noun* (also **ceroon**, **seroon** /sɪ'ru:n/) M16 **Spanish** (= hamper, crate (from *sera* large basket), partly through French *serron*). A bale or package (especially of tropical plant products) bound with hide.

serra /'sɛrə/ *noun* M19 **Portuguese** (from Latin *serra* saw; cf. SIERRA). In Portuguese-speaking regions: a ridge of mountains or hills.

serré /sɛre/ *adjective* M19 **French**. Tightly compact; *figurative* constricted by grief or emotion.

sertão /'sɛ:tɑ̃:ʊ/ *noun* plural **sertãos** /'sɛ:tɑ̃:ʊʃ/ E19 **Portuguese**. *Geography* An arid barren region of Brazil; the remote interior of Brazil.

serum /'sɪərəm/ *noun* plural **sera** /'sɪərə/, **serums** L17 **Latin** (= whey, watery fluid). **1** L17 Watery fluid, as a normal or pathological constituent of animal tissues; *specifically* the yellowish protein-rich liquid which separates from coagulated blood.

2 L19 *Medicine* The blood serum of an animal used as a therapeutic or diagnostic agent.

servante /sɛrvɑ̃t/ *noun* plural pronounced same L19 **French** (= side-table). An extra table or concealed shelf used in conjuring tricks.

serviette /səːvɪ'ɛt/ *noun* L15 **Old and Modern French** (= towel, napkin, from *servir* to serve). A table-napkin, now *especially* a paper one.

sestina /sɛ'stiːnə/ *noun* M19 **Italian** (from *sesto* from Latin *sextus* sixth). A form of rhymed or unrhymed poem of six stanzas of six lines and a concluding triplet in which the same six words at the line-ends occur in each stanza in six different sequences.

se-tenant /sətənɑ̃/ *adjective* E20 **French** (literally, 'holding together'). *Philately* Of postage stamps, especially of different denominations or designs: joined together as when printed.

settecento /sɛtɪ'tʃɛntəʊ/ *noun* E20 **Italian** (= seven hundred). The eighteenth century in Italy; the style of Italian art, architecture, music, etc., of this period.

sève /sɛv/ *noun* M18 **French** (= sap). The quality and flavour appropriate to a specified wine; liveliness, savour.

seviche /sɛ'viːtʃeɪ/ *noun* (also **ceviche**) M20 **South American Spanish** (*seviche, cebiche*). A South American dish of marinaded raw fish or seafood, usually garnished and served as a starter.

sévigné /seviɲe/ *noun* (also **sevigné**) plural pronounced same E19 **French** (probably from Mme de *Sévigné* (1626–96), French letter-writer). *History* A kind of bandeau, especially for the hair; a jewel or ornament for decorating a head-dress.

sevruga /sɛv'ruːgə/ *noun* L16 **Russian** (*sevryuga*). (Caviar from) the sturgeon, of the Caspian and Black Seas.

Sezession /zeˌtsɛ'sioːn/ *noun* plural **Sezessien** /ze'tsɛsiən/ E20 **German**. *Art* A radical art movement that started in Vienna and was contemporaneous with and related to ART NOUVEAU; SEZESSIONSSTIL.

Sezessionsstil /zeˌtsɛsi'oːnsˌʃtiːl/ *noun* L20 **German**. *Art* The style of the SEZESSION.

sf abbreviation of SFORZANDO (*musical direction*).

sforzando /sfɔː'tsandəʊ/ *adjective, adverb, & noun* E19 **Italian** (present participle of *sforzare* to use force). *Music* **A** *adjective & adverb* E19 (A direction:) with special emphasis or sudden loudness. Abbreviated to *sf, sfz.* **B** *noun* M19 plural **sforzandi** /sfɔː'tsandi/, **sforzandos**. A note or group of notes specially emphasized; an increase in emphasis and loudness.

sforzato /sfɔː'tsɑːtəʊ/ *adjective, adverb, & noun* plural of noun **sforzati** /sfɔː'tsɑːti/, **sforzatos** E19 **Italian** (past participle of *sforzare* to use force). *Music* SFORZANDO.

sfumato /sfu'mato/, /sfʊ'mɑːtəʊ/ *adjective & noun* M19 **Italian** (past participle of *sfumare* to shade off, from *s-* ex- + *fumare* to smoke). *Painting* **A** *adjective* M19 Painted with or using indistinct outlines, depicting hazy forms. **B** *noun* E20 The technique of softening outlines and allowing tones and colours to shade gradually into one another; an indistinct outline or hazy form produced in this way.

sfz abbreviation of SFORZANDO (musical direction).

sgraffiato /zgraffi'ato/ *noun* plural **sgraffiati** /zgraffi'ati/ M19 **Italian** (past participle of *sgraffiare* to scratch away; see next). SGRAFFITO.

sgraffito /sgra'fiːtəʊ/ *noun* plural **sgraffiti** /sgra'fiːti/ M18 **Italian** (from *sgraffiare* to scratch away: *s-* representing Latin *ex-* ex- + (later) GRAFFITO). A form of decoration or design made by scratching through wet plaster on a wall or through slip on pottery to reveal a different colour below.

shabti /'ʃabti/ *noun* plural **shabtiu** /'ʃabtɪuː/, **shabtis** M19 **Egyptian** (*šbty*). *Egyptology* A USHABTI. Cf. SHAWABTI.

shabu-shabu /ˌʃabuː'ʃabuː/ *noun* L20 **Japanese**. A Japanese dish of pieces of thinly sliced beef or pork cooked quickly with vegetables in boiling water.

shadoof /ʃə'duːf/ *noun* (also **shaduf**) M19 **Arabic** ((Egyptian) *šādūf*). A device consisting of a pivoted rod or pole with a bucket at one end and a counterbalancing weight at the other, used especially in Egypt for raising water.

shaganappi /ˌʃagə'napi/ *noun & adjective* M18 **Ojibwa**. **A** *noun* M18 Thread, cord, or thong made from rawhide, rawhide cut into strips; a strip of rawhide. Also, a rough pony. **B** *adjective* E19 Made of a strip or strips of rawhide; *figurative* tough, rough; cheap, inferior, makeshift. *North American*.

shagetz, shagitz variants of SHEGETZ.

shah /ʃɑː/ *noun* (also (as title) **Shah**) M16 **Persian** (*šāh* from Old Persian *xšāyaθiya* king). *History* (A title of) the monarch of Iran (Persia).

shahada /ʃəˈhɑːdəʊ/ *noun* L19 **Arabic** (*šahāda* testimony, evidence). The Muslim profession of faith.

■ The *shahada*—*Lā ilāha illā (A)llāh, Muḥammadun rasūl Allāh* 'there is no God but Allah, [and] Muhammad is the messenger of Allah'—forms part of the regular call to prayer.

shahid /ʃəˈhiːd/ *noun* (also **shaheed**) L19 **Arabic** (*šahīd* witness, martyr). A Muslim martyr.

shaikh, Shaikha variants of SHEIKH, SHEIKHA.

shako /ˈʃeɪkəʊ/, /ˈʃakəʊ/ *noun* plural **shakos** E19 **French** (*schako* from Hungarian *csákó* probably from German *Zacken* peak, point, spike). A cylindrical military hat with a peak and a plume or pompon.

shakudo /ˈʃakudəʊ/ *noun & adjective* M19 **Japanese** (from *shaku* red + *dō* copper). (Made of) a Japanese alloy of copper and gold.

shakuhachi /ˌʃakuˈhɑːtʃi/ *noun* L19 **Japanese**. An end-blown Japanese flute, made of bamboo.

shalom /ʃəˈlɒm/, *foreign* /ʃaˈlɔm/ *interjection & noun* L19 **Hebrew** (*šālōm* peace). In Jewish society, used as a salutation at meeting or parting; an utterance of 'shalom'.

shalwar /ˈʃʌlvɑː/ *noun* (also **salwar, shalvar**) E19 **Persian and Urdu** (*šalwār*). *singular* and in *plural* Loose trousers worn in some South Asian countries and by some Muslims elsewhere, *especially* those worn by women together with a KAMEEZ.

■ Often in the combination *shalwar-kameez*, describing a woman's matching outfit.

1996 *Times* Shalwar kameez tunics were layered over tiered bloomers.

shaman /ˈʃamən/ *noun* L17 **German** (*Schamane*, Russian *shaman* from Tungusian *šaman*). A priest among certain peoples of northern Asia, regarded as one with healing and magical powers and influence over the spirits who bring about good and evil; a healer among North American Indians, regarded as possessing magical powers. Now also, a person regarded as having powers of spiritual guidance and healing through direct access to and influence in the spirit world.

shamba /ˈʃambə/ *noun* L19 **Kiswahili**. In East Africa: a cultivated plot of ground. Also, a farm, a plantation.

shambok variant of SJAMBOK.

shamisen variant of SAMISEN.

shanachie variant of SENNACHIE.

shanti /ˈʃɑːnti/ *interjection & noun* L19 **Sanskrit** (*śānti* peace, tranquillity). *Hinduism* (A prayer for) peace; peace be with you.

■ Usually repeated three times at the end of an Upanishad for the peace of the soul.

sharif /ʃəˈriːf/ *noun* (also **shareef, shereef, sherif**) L16 **Arabic** (*šarīf* noble, highborn). **1** L16 A descendant of Muhammad through his daughter Fatima. **2** E17 (frequently **Sharif**) (The title of) any of various Arab rulers, magistrates, or religious leaders; *specifically* (*a*) the ruler of Morocco; (*b*) the governor of Mecca.

sharifa /ʃəˈriːfə/ *noun* (also **shereefa, sherifa, Sharifa**) E20 **Arabic** (*šarīfa* feminine of *šarīf* SHARIF). The wife of a Moroccan sharif.

shashlik /ˈʃaʃlɪk/ *noun* E20 **Russian** (*shashlyk* from Crimean Turkish *şişlik* from *şiş* skewer; cf. SHISH KEBAB). An eastern European and Asian kebab of mutton and garnishings, frequently served on a skewer.

shauri /ˈʃaʊriː/ *noun* plural **shauri(e)s** E20 **Kiswahili** (from Arabic *šūrā* consultation, deliberation, counsel). In East Africa: counsel, debate; a problem.

1970 *Kenya Farmer* Often he can solve a problem by calling a meeting of the staff and obtaining their views and suggestions, not only on their personal *shauris*, but also on improvements in sales and service.

shawabti /ʃəˈwabti/ *noun* plural **shawabtiu** /ʃəˈwabtɪuː/, **shawabtis** E20 **Egyptian** (*šwɜbt(y)*, probably from *šwɜb* persea wood, perhaps the original material). *Egyptology* An USHABTI. Cf. SHABTI.

shchi /ʃtʃi/ *noun* E19 **Russian**. A Russian cabbage soup.

shebeen /ʃɪˈbiːn/ *noun* L18 **Irish** ((Anglo-Irish form of) *síbín*, of unknown origin).

An unlicensed house or shop selling alcoholic liquor; a disreputable public house.

■ Originally meaning an illicit liquor outlet in Ireland, *shebeen* is now commonly used in South African English for a Black-run establishment where alcohol is illegally brewed and sold.

shechita /ʃɛ'xita/ *noun* L19 **Hebrew** (*šĕḥīṭāh*, from *šāḥaṭ* to slaughter). The method of slaughtering animals that fulfils the requirements of Jewish law.

sheesh kebab variant of SHISH KEBAB.

shegetz /'ʃeɪgɪts/ *noun* (also **shagetz**, **shagitz**) plural **shkotsim** /'ʃkɔ:tsɪm/ E20 **Yiddish** (*sheygets*, *sheyhets* from Hebrew *sheqeṣ* detested thing; cf. SHIKSA). Among Jewish people, a Gentile boy; a Jewish boy not observing traditional Jewish behaviour.

■ Originally and chiefly United States, and usually derogatory.

sheikh /ʃeɪk/, /ʃi:k/ *noun* (also **shaikh**, **sheik**) L16 **Arabic** (ultimately from Arabic *šayḵ* sheikh, old man, elder, from *šāḵa* to be or grow old). **1a** L16 (also **Sheikh**) Originally, an Eastern governor, prince, or king. Later *especially*, a chief or head of an Arab family, people, or village. Also, a title of respect. **b** E20 A strong, romantic, or dashing male lover. **2** L16 A leader of a Muslim religious order or community; a great religious doctor or preacher; now *especially*, a saint with a localized cult. **3** L19 In the Indian subcontinent, a Hindu convert to Islam.

■ In sense 1b from *The Sheik*, a novel by E. M. Hull (1919) made into a film (1921) starring Rudolph Valentino.

sheikha /'ʃeɪkə/ *noun* (also **Sheik(h)a**, **Shaikha**) M19 **Arabic** (*šayḵa*). An Arab lady of good family; the (chief) wife of a sheikh. Also, a title of respect.

shekel /'ʃɛk(ə)l/ *noun* M16 **Hebrew** (*šeqel*, from *šāqal* to weigh). **1** *History* A unit of weight and silver coin used in the ancient Middle East. **2** In *plural* Money; riches. *colloquial.* **3** The basic unit of currency in modern Israel.

■ In sense 2 often in colloquial phrases such as *bringing* (or *raking*) *in the shekels* meaning 'making a lot of money quickly and easily' (see quotation).

2 1996 *Spectator* They [sc. oysters] are sold all year round for some reason, which I think is a mistake, but doubtless it brings in the shekels.

shemozzle /ʃɪ'mɒz(ə)l/ *noun & verb slang* (also **schemozzle**) L19 **Yiddish** (probably from as SCHLIMAZEL). **A** *noun* L19 A muddle, a complicated situation; a quarrel, a brawl, a mêlée. **B** *intransitive verb* E20 Make one's escape, leave hastily.

shenachie variant of SENNACHIE.

shenzi /'ʃɛnzi/ *noun* E20 **Kiswahili**. In East Africa: an uncivilized African; a barbarian, a person outside one's cultural group. Chiefly *derogatory*.

1970 K. Thackeray *Crownbird* The Chinese face was impassive . . . That he should be . . . involved with this bunch of shenzis . . . was very confusing.

sherbet /'ʃə:bət/ *noun* E17 **Turkish** (*şerbet*, Persian *šerbet* from Arabic *šarba(t)* draught, drink, from *šariba* to drink). **1** E17 A cooling drink made of sweetened and diluted fruit juice, drunk especially in Arab countries. Now also, an effervescing drink made of sherbet powder (see sense 2). **2** M19 A flavoured sweet powder containing bicarbonate of soda, tartaric acid, etc., eaten as a confection or used to make an effervescing drink. Also more fully *sherbet powder*. **3a** L19 A water-ice. *North American.* **b** L19 (A glass of) alcoholic liquor, especially (*specifically* in *Australia*) beer. *slang*.

shereef, **shereefa** variants of SHARIF, SHARIFA.

sherif, **sherifa** variants of SHARIF, SHARIFA.

sherpa /'ʃə:pə/ *noun, adjective, & verb* M19 **Tibetan** (*sharpa* inhabitant of an eastern country). **A** *noun* plural **sherpas**, same **1** M19 (*Sherpa*) A member of a Tibetan people inhabiting the southern slopes of the Himalayas, renowned for their skill in mountaineering. **2** M20 (*sherpa*) *transferred* and *figurative* A mountain guide or porter; an official making preparations for a summit conference. **B** E20 *attributive* or as *adjective* Of, pertaining to, or designating the Sherpas and their language. **C** L20 *intransitive verb* Act as or like a sherpa.

C 1996 *Spectator* In the weeks before their principals meet, hundreds of officials are sherpa-ing all over Europe.

sheshbesh /'ʃɛʃbɛʃ/ *noun* L20 **Turkish** (*şeşbeş*, from Persian *šaš* six + Turkish *beş* five). A variety of backgammon played in the Middle East.

sheva /ʃə'vɑ:/ *noun* (also **shewa**) L16 **Hebrew** *šĕwā'*, apparently arbitrary alteration of *šāw'* emptiness, vanity, spelt in German books *Schwa*, whence SCHWA). **1** L16 *Hebrew Grammar* The sign : placed under a consonant to express the absence of a following vowel sound, having in certain positions no sound (*quiescent sheva*) but in others sounding as a schwa /ə/ (*movable sheva*); the sound of movable sheva. **2** *Phonetics* E19 A SCHWA.

shiatsu /ʃɪ'atsu:/ *noun* **M20 Japanese** (literally, 'finger pressure'). A kind of therapy of Japanese origin, in which pressure is applied with the thumbs and palms to certain points of the body.

■ Imported under this name into the West in the 1960s, *shiatsu* has, since the late 1970s, become more generally referred to as *acupressure*.

shibboleth /'ʃɪbəlɛθ/ *noun* **M17 Hebrew** (*šibbōleṯ* ear of corn, stream in flood, used as a test of nationality for the difficulty for foreigners of pronouncing /θ/ (see Judges 12:4–6)). **1** M17 A word used as a test for detecting people from another district or country by their pronunciation; a word or sound very difficult for foreigners to pronounce correctly. **b** M17 A peculiarity of pronunciation or accent indicative of a person's origin; the distinctive mode of speech of a profession, class, etc. **c** E19 A custom, habit, style of dressing, etc., distinguishing a particular class or group of people. **2** M17 A longstanding formula, idea, phrase, etc., held (especially unreflectingly) by or associated with a group, class, etc.; a catchword, a slogan; a taboo. Also, a received wisdom; a truism, a platitude.

shibui /'ʃɪbui/ *adjective & noun* (also **shibu** /'ʃɪbʊ/) **M20 Japanese** (= astringent, from *shibu* an astringent substance). **A** M20 *adjective* Tasteful in a quiet, profound, or unostentatious way. **B** *noun* M20 Tastefulness, refinement; appreciation of elegant simplicity.

shidduch /'ʃɪdəx/ *noun* **L19 Yiddish** (from Hebrew *šiddūḵ* negotiation, especially of an arranged marriage). An arranged marriage, a (good) match.

shifta /'ʃɪftə/ *noun* plural same, **shiftas** **M20 Somali** (*shúfto* bandit, from Amharic). A Somali bandit or guerrilla, operating mainly in northern Kenya.

shiitake /ʃɪ'tɑ:keɪ/, /'ʃɪɪtɑ:keɪ/ *noun* **L19 Japanese** (from *shii* a kind of oak + *take* mushroom). An edible agaric (mushroom), *Lentinus edodes*, cultivated in Japan and China on logs of various oaks and allied trees. Also *shiitake mushroom*.

shikar /ʃɪ'kɑ:/ *noun & verb* **E17 Persian and Urdu** (*šikār*). **A** *noun* E17 Hunting, shooting; game. **B** *verb* Inflected *-rr-*. **1** *intransitive verb* L19 Hunt animals for sport. **2** *transitive verb* L19 Hunt (animals).

■ Originating and used almost solely in the Indian subcontinent, the word often occurs in the phrase *on shikar* 'on a hunting expedition'.

shikari /ʃɪ'kɑ:ri:/ *noun* **E19 Urdu** (from Persian *šikārī*: see SHIKAR). In the Indian subcontinent: a hunter (either European or Indian); an expert guide or tracker.

shikhara /'ʃɪkhərə/ *noun* (also **sikhara**) **E19 Sanskrit** (*śikhara* peak, spire). A pyramidal tower on a Hindu temple, sometimes having convexly curved sides.

shiksa /'ʃɪksə/ *noun & adjective* **L19 Yiddish** (*shikse* from Hebrew *šiqṣāh* from *šeqeṣ* detested thing + feminine suffix *-āh*). **A** *noun* L19 A Gentile girl or woman. **B** *attributive* or as *adjective* M20 Of a girl or woman: Gentile. *derogatory*.

shippo /'ʃi:pəʊ/ *noun & adjective* (also **shipo**) **L19 Japanese** (*shippō* seven precious things, from *shichi* seven + *hō* jewel). (Made of) Japanese cloisonné-enamel ware.

shisha /'ʃi:ʃə/ *noun* (also **shi-sha** **M20 Urdu** (*šīša(h)*, Persian *šīša* glass, mirror). (Used *attributively* to designate) mirror-work and items connected with it.

1977 A. Jeffs *Creative Crafts* Though India and Pakistan are known for many different forms of embroidery, the one style that is considered to be unique is the mirror embroidery known as 'Shishakari' or 'Shi-sha', which originated many centuries ago in the arid plateaux of Sind and Baluchistan in Pakistan.

shish kebab /ʃɪʃ kɪ'bab/ *noun* (also **sheesh kebab** /ʃi:ʃ/) **E20 Turkish** (*şiş kebab*, from *şiş* skewer + *kebab* roast meat; cf. SHASHLIK). A dish consisting of pieces of marinated meat (usually lamb) and vegetables grilled and served on skewers.

shiva /'ʃɪvə/ *noun* (also **shivah**) **L19 Hebrew** (*šiḇʻāh* seven). *Judaism* A period of seven days' formal mourning for the dead, beginning immediately after the funeral. Frequently in *sit shiva*, observe this period.

shivaree variant of CHARIVARI.

shkotsim plural of SHEGETZ.

shlub /ʃlʌb/ *noun* (also **schlub**) M20 **Yiddish** (perhaps from Poland *żłób* blockhead). A worthless person, an oaf. *United States slang.*

shmatte /ˈʃmatə/ *noun* (also **schmatte**) L20 **Yiddish** (*schmatte*, from Poland *szmata* rag). A rag; a garment, *especially* a ragged one. *United States colloquial.*

shmear /ʃmɪə/ *noun* (also **schmear, schmeer**) M20 **Yiddish** (*schmirn* to flatter, grease, smear: cf. German *schmieren* smear). Bribery, corruption, flattery.

■ North American colloquial. Often in the phrase *the whole shmear* meaning 'everything (possible)'.

1969 E. Stewart *Heads* Why couldn't you burrow around and ferret out the whole shmear yourself?

shochet /ˈʃɒxɛt/ *noun* plural **shochetim** /ˈʃɒxɛtɪm/ L19 **Hebrew** (*šōḥēṭ* present participle of *šāḥaṭ* to slaughter). A person officially certified as competent to kill cattle and poultry in the manner prescribed by Jewish law.

shofar /ˈʃəʊfə/ *noun* plural **shofroth** /ˈʃəʊfrəʊt/ M19 **Hebrew** (*šōpār*, plural *šōpārōṯ*). A ram's-horn trumpet used in Jewish religious services and in biblical times as a war-trumpet.

shogi /ˈʃəʊgi/ *noun* M19 **Japanese** (*shōgi*). A Japanese board game resembling chess.

shogun /ˈʃəʊgʊn/ *noun* E17 **Japanese** (*shōgun*, from Chinese *jiāng jūn* general). *History* Any of a succession of hereditary commanders-in-chief of the Japanese army, before 1868 the virtual rulers of Japan.

shomer /ˈʃəʊmə/ *noun* plural **shomerim** /ˈʃəʊmərɪm/ E20 **Hebrew** (*šōmēr* watchman). **1** E20 A watchman, a guard, now especially in Israel. **2** E20 An inspector who verifies that food is prepared in accordance with Jewish religious laws.

shonda /ˈʃɒndə/ *noun* M20 **Yiddish** (*shande* from Middle High German *schande*). A disgrace. *colloquial*, chiefly *United States.*

shosagoto /ˌʃɒsəˈgəʊtəʊ/ *noun* plural same E20 **Japanese** (from *shosa* acting, conduct + *koto* matter, affair). In Japanese kabuki theatre: a dance play, a mime performed to music.

shosha /ˈʃəʊʃə/ *noun* plural same L20 **Japanese** (*shōsha* business firm, from *shō* mercantile + *sha* society, company). A SOGO SHOSHA.

shott /ʃɒt/ *noun* (also **chott**) L19 **Arabic** (*šaṭṭ* shore, strand; (in North Africa) salt lake; (in Iraq) waterway, river). A shallow brackish lake or marsh especially in Algeria and southern Tunisia, usually dry in summer and covered with saline deposits. Cf. SABKHA.

shoyu /ˈʃəʊjuː/ *noun* E18 **Japanese** (*shōyu* from Chinese *jiàngyóu* (Wade-Giles *chiang-yu*) from *jiàng* bean paste + *yóu* oil). A sauce made from fermented soya beans; soy sauce. Also *shoyu sauce.*

shrikhand /ˈʃriːkand/ *noun* M20 **Sanskrit** (*śrīkhaṇḍa* sandalwood). An Indian sweet dish made from curd, sugar, almonds, and spices.

shtetl /ˈʃtɛt(ə)l/, /ˈʃteɪt(ə)l/ *noun* plural **shtetlach** /ˈʃtɛt(ə)lɑːx/, **shtetls** M20 **Yiddish** (= little town, from German *Stadt* town). *History* A small Jewish town or village in eastern Europe.

1996 *Times* Wiesenthal was born in a *shtetl* in Buczacz in Galicia.

shtibl /ˈʃtiːb(ə)l/ *noun* (also **shtiebel**) plural **shtiblach** /ˈʃtiːb(ə)lɑːx/ E20 **Yiddish** (diminutive of *shtub* room, house; cf. German dialect *Stüberl* small room). A small synagogue.

shtick /ʃtɪk/ *noun* (also **shtik**) M20 **Yiddish** (from German *Stück* piece, play). **1** M20 A (comedian's) stage routine; a joke; *transferred* a patter, a gimmick. **2** M20 A particular area of activity or interest. *slang*, chiefly *North American.*

1 1996 *Spectator* Yes, as critics have pointed out, a lot of Carrey's shtick dies even as he utters it . . .

shtiebel variant of SHTIBL.

shtik variant of SHTICK.

shtoom /ʃtʊm/ *adjective & verb* (also **s(h)tumm** /ʃtʌm/, **schtoom**) M20 **Yiddish** (from German *stumm* silent). **A** *adjective* M20 Silent, mute. Chiefly in *keep* (or *stay*) *shtoom*, refrain from disclosing information etc. **B** *intransitive verb* M20 Become silent, shut *up*.

shufti /ˈʃʊfti/ *noun* (also **shufty**) M20 **Arabic** (from colloquial Arabic *šuftī* have you seen?, from *šāfa* to see). A look; a glance.

■ Especially in *take* (or *have*) *a shufti*. Originally military slang, but also more generally used in dated colloquial speech (see quotation). The verbal use from which the noun derives is rare in English.

1980 R. Adams *Girl in a Swing* Good idea, old boy. I'm game. Let's 'ave a crafty shufti round with that in mind, shall we?

shul /ʃuːl/ *noun* L19 **Yiddish** (from German *Schule* school). A synagogue.

shunga /ˈʃuːŋɡɑː/ *noun* plural same M20 **Japanese** (from *shun* spring + *ga* picture). An example of Japanese erotic art.

shura /ˈʃʊərə/ *noun* M20 **Arabic** (*šūrā* consultation). The Islamic principle of (rule by) consultation; an Islamic consultative council.

shuriken /ˈʃʊərɪkɛn/ *noun* L20 **Japanese** (*shuri-ken*, literally, 'dagger in the hand', from *shu* hand + *ri* inside + *ken* sword, blade). A weapon in the form of a star with projecting blades or points, used in some martial arts.

sic /sɪk/ *adverb & noun* L19 **Latin** (= so, thus). **A** L19 *adverb* Used or spelt as written. **B** *noun* M20 An instance of using 'sic'.

■ As an adverb used parenthetically after a quoted word etc. to call attention to an anomalous or erroneous form or to prevent the supposition of misquotation.

sic et non /ˈsɪk ɛt ˌnɒn/ *noun phrase* E20 **Latin** (literally, 'yes and no'). *Theology* A method of argument used by medieval theologians, in which contradictory passages of scripture are presented without commentary in order to stimulate readers to resolve the contradictions themselves. Frequently *attributive*.

■ *Sic et non* was the title of a work by the twelfth-century French theologian and philosopher Peter Abelard, in which he employed this method, later imitated by other Scholastic philosophers.

Sicherheitsdienst /ˈzɪçərhaɪtsˌdiːnst/ *noun* M20 **German** (from *Sicherheit* security + *dienst* service). *History* The security branch of the Nazi Schutzstaffel (SS), set up in 1931–2. Abbreviated to *SD*.

siciliana /sitʃiˈljana/, /sɪˌtʃɪlɪˈɑːnə/ *noun* plural **siciliane** /sitʃiˈljane/, /sɪˌtʃɪlɪˈɑːneɪ/ (also **siciliano** /sitʃiˈljano/, /sɪˌtʃɪlɪˈɑːnəʊ/, plural **sicilianos** /sɪˌtʃɪlɪˈɑːnəʊz/, **siciliani** /sitʃiˈljani/) E18 **Italian** (feminine of *Siciliano* Sicilian). *Music* A piece of music for a Sicilian peasant dance, resembling a slow jig; *transferred* a composition in 6/8 or 12/8 time, frequently in a minor key and evoking a pastoral mood.

sicilienne /sɪˌsɪlɪˈɛn/ *noun* L19 **French** (feminine of *sicilien* Sicilian). **1** L19 A fine poplin of silk and wool. **2** L19 *Music* A SICILIANA.

siddha /ˈsɪdhə/ *noun* M19 **Sanskrit**. In Indian religions: a person who has attained perfection, a saint, a semi-divine being; *specifically* in *Jainism*, a perfected bodyless being freed from the cycle of rebirths.

Sieg Heil /ziːk ˈhaɪl/ *noun phrase & interjection* M20 **German** (literally, 'Hail victory'). (An exclamation of) a victory salute used especially at a political rally originally during the Nazi regime in Germany.

sierozem /ˈsɪərə(ʊ)zɛm/ *noun* M20 **Russian** (*serozëm*, from *seryĭ* grey + Slavonic base *zem-* (cf. Russian *zemlya*) earth, soil)). *Soil Science* A soil, usually calcareous and humus-poor, characterized by a brownish-grey surface and developed typically under mixed shrub vegetation in arid climates.

sierra /sɪˈɛrə/, /sɪˈɛːrə/ *noun* plural **sierras** M16 **Spanish** (from Latin *serra* saw; cf. SERRA). A long mountain range rising in jagged peaks, especially in Spain and Latin America.

siesta /sɪˈɛstə/ *noun & verb* M17 **Spanish** (from Latin *sexta (hora)* sixth hour of the day). **A** *noun* M17 An afternoon rest or nap; *especially* one taken during the hottest hours of the day in a hot country. **B** *intransitive verb* M19 Take a siesta.

siffleur /siːˈflɜː/ *noun* (feminine (sense 2) **si'ffleuse** /siːˈflɜːz/) E18 **French** (from *siffler* to whistle). **1** E18 Any of various animals that make a whistling noise. **2** E19 A person who entertains professionally by whistling.

sigilla plural of SIGILLUM.

sigillata /sɪdʒɪˈleɪtə/, /sɪɡɪˈlɑːtə/ *noun* E20 **Latin** (= sealed). *Archaeology* TERRA SIGILLATA sense 3.

sigillum /sɪˈdʒɪləm/ *noun* plural **sigilla** /sɪˈdʒɪlə/ M17 **Late Latin** (= sign, trace, impress, (in medieval Latin) seal (classical Latin *sigilla* (plural) little images, seal), diminutive of Latin *signum* sign). **1** In *plural* Small human images. *rare*. Only in M17. **2** E20 *Roman Catholic Church* The seal of confession. **3** M20 A sign, a symbol; an abbreviation.

siglum /ˈsɪɡləm/ *noun* plural **sigla** /ˈsɪɡlə/ E18 **Late Latin** (*sigla* plural, perhaps for *singula* neuter plural of *singulus* single). A letter (especially an initial) or other symbol used as an abbreviation for a word, proper name, etc., in a printed text; *Bibliography* such a letter or symbol used to designate a particular version of a literary text.

sigma /'sɪgmə/ *noun* LME **Latin** (from Greek). **1** LME The eighteenth letter (Σ, σ, or, when final, ς), of the Greek alphabet represented in English by *S, s.* **2** E20 *Physics* and *Chemistry* **a** Used *attributively* to designate an electron, orbital, molecular state, etc., possessing zero angular momentum about an internuclear axis. **b** M20 *Particle Physics* Used (usually *attributive*), to denote each of a triplet of hyperons (and their antiparticles). **3** L20 *Biochemistry* A component of RNA polymerase which determines where transcription begins. In full *sigma factor.* **4** L20 *Statistics* A (unit of) standard deviation.

signa, **signa panthea** plurals of SIGNUM, SIGNUM PANTHEUM.

significacio /sɪg,nɪfɪ'kɑːsɪəʊ/ *noun* (also **significatio** /sɪg,nɪfɪ'kɑːtɪəʊ/) plural **significaciones** /sɪg,nɪfɪ,kɑːsɪ'əʊniːz/ M20 **Medieval Latin** (from Latin *significatio(n)-*). A parallel or second meaning not directly stated in a text; the deeper or implied meaning of an allegory, emblem, symbol, etc.

signor /'siːnjɔː/ *noun* plural **signori** /siːn'jɔri/ L16 **Italian** (reduced form of *signore*, from Latin *senior*). **1** L16 Used as a title (preceding the surname or other designation) of or as a respectful form of address to an Italian or Italian-speaking man (corresponding to English *Mr* or *sir*). **b** L18 An Italian man, especially a singer. **2** L16 A man of distinction, rank, or authority; a gentleman or nobleman.

signora /siːn'jɔːrə/ *noun* M17 **Italian** (feminine of SIGNORE). Used as a title (preceding the surname or other designation) of or as a respectful form of address to an Italian or Italian-speaking (especially married) woman (corresponding to English *Mrs* or *madam*). Also, an Italian (especially married) woman.

signoria /,siːnjə'riːə/ *noun* M16 **Italian** (from as SIGNOR). *History* The governing body of any of various medieval Italian republics, especially Venice.

signorina /,siːnjə'riːnə/ *noun* E19 **Italian** (diminutive of SIGNORA). Used as a title (used preceding the surname or other designation) of or as a respectful form of address to a young (especially unmarried) Italian or Italian-speaking woman (corresponding to English *Miss*). Also, a young (especially unmarried) Italian woman.

signum /'sɪgnəm/ *noun* plural **signa** /'sɪgnə/ M19 **Latin**. A mark, a sign.

signum pantheum /,sɪgnəm pan'θiːəm/ *noun phrase* plural **signa panthea** /,sɪgnə pan'θiːə/ E18 **Latin** (= divine statue, from *signum* statue + *pantheus* from Greek *pantheios* dedicated to all the gods (from *pan-* all + *theios* divine)). *Classical Antiquities* A statue combining the figures, symbols, or attributes of several gods.

sikhara variant of SHIKHARA.

silenus /sʌɪ'liːnəs/ *noun* (also **Silenus**) plural **sileni** /sʌɪ'liːnʌɪ/ E17 **Latin** (*Silenus* from Greek *Seilēnos* foster-father of Bacchus and leader of the satyrs). *Greek Mythology* A wood-god, a satyr, *especially* one represented as a bearded old man with the tail and legs of a horse.

■ Earlier (L16) in the Anglicized form *silen.*

silhouette /sɪlʊ'ɛt/ *noun & verb* L18 **French** (from Étienne de *Silhouette* (1709–67), French author and politician). **A** *noun* **1** L18 A portrait obtained by tracing the outline of a profile, head, or figure, especially by means of its shadow, and filling in the whole with black or cutting the shape out of black paper; a figure or picture drawn or printed in solid black. **b** *figuratively* E19 A brief verbal description of a person etc. **2 a** M19 An object seen as a dark outline against a lighter background; a dark shadow of something. **b** E20 The contour or outline of a garment or a person's body. **B** *verb* **1** *transitive verb* L19 Represent in silhouette, throw up the outline of. Usually in *passive* (followed by *against, on*). **2** *intransitive verb* L19 Show up as a silhouette.

sillar /siː'ljɑː/ *noun* M20 **Spanish**. *Geology* A kind of volcanic tuff.

silo /'sʌɪləʊ/ *noun* plural **silos** M19 **Spanish** (from Latin *sirus* from Greek *siros* pit). **1** M19 A pit or underground chamber used for storing grain, roots, etc.; *specifically* one in which green crops are compressed and preserved for fodder as silage. Also, a cylindrical tower or other structure built above ground for the same purpose. **2** E20 *transferred* A large bin used for storing loose materials etc. **3** M20 An underground structure in which a guided missile is stored and from which it may be fired.

silva variant of SYLVA.

simba /ˈsɪmbə/ *noun* E20 **Kiswahili.** A lion; *figurative* a warrior. Chiefly *East African.*

simchah /ˈsɪmtʃə/, /ˈsɪmtʃxa/ *noun* M20 **Hebrew** (*śimḥāh* rejoicing). A Jewish private party or celebration.

simi /ˈsɪmi/ *noun* M20 **Kiswahili** (*sime*). In East Africa: a large two-edged knife.

simoom /sɪˈmuːm/ *noun* (also **simoon** /sɪˈmuːn/) L18 **Arabic** (*samūm*, from *samma* to poison). A hot dry dust-laden wind blowing at intervals in the African and Asian (especially Arabian) deserts.

simpatico /simˈpatiko/, /sɪmˈpatɪkəʊ/ *adjective* (feminine **simpatica** /simˈpatika/, /simˈpatɪkə/) M19 **Spanish** (*simpático*, from *simpatía*, or Italian *simpatico* from *simpatia*, both from Latin *sympathia* from Greek *sumpatheia* from *sumpathēs* having a fellow-feeling). Pleasing, likeable; congenial.

1995 *Oldie* And Fangio was so charming and so *simpatico*, and of course the damage would be paid for . . .

simplex /ˈsɪmplɛks/ *adjective & noun* L16 **Latin** (= single, variant of *simplus* simple, with second element as in *duplex*, *multiplex*, etc.). **A** *adjective* **1** L16 Composed of or characterized by a single part or structure. **2** *Telecommunications* and *Computing* L19 Designating a system, circuit, etc., along which signals can be sent in only one direction at a time. **3** *Genetics* E20 Of a polyploid individual: having the dominant allele of a particular gene represented once. **B** *noun* **1** L19 A word without an affix; a simple uncompounded word. **2** E20 *Geometry* The figure, in any given number of dimensions, that is bounded by the least possible number of hyperplanes (e.g. the simplex in two dimensions is a triangle). **3** M20 *Linguistics* In early transformational grammar, a basic or core sentence, a kernel sentence.

simplex munditiis /ˌsɪmplɛks mʊnˈdɪtiːs/ *noun & adjective phrase* M18 **Latin** (literally, 'simple in your adornments'). **A** *noun phrase* M18 Beauty without adornment or ostentation. **B** *adjective phrase* L19 Unostentatiously beautiful.

■ A quotation from Horace *Odes* I.v.

simulacrum /ˌsɪmjʊˈleɪkrəm/ *noun* plural **simulacrums**, **simulacra** /ˌsɪmjʊˈleɪkrə/ L16 **Latin** (from *simulare* to simulate). **1** L16 A material image or representation of a person or thing, *especially* a god. **2** E19 A thing having the appearance but not the substance or proper qualities of something; a deceptive imitation or substitute; a pretence.

2 1996 *Times* The effort to turn the whole continent into the economic simulacrum of Germany . . . has instilled pessimism and depression into the peoples of all Europe.

simurg /sɪˈməːg/ *noun* (also **simurgh**) L18 **Persian** (*sīmurġ*, from Pahlavi *sēn* eagle + *murġ* bird). *Iranian Mythology* A giant bird believed to have the power of speech and reasoning and to be of great age.

sindicato /sindiˈkato/ *noun* plural **sindicatos** /sindiˈkatos/ M20 **Spanish** (= syndicate, trade union). In Spain and Spanish-speaking countries: a trade union.

sine die /ˌsʌɪni ˈdʌɪiː/, /ˌsɪneɪ ˈdiːeɪ/ *adverb phrase* E17 **Latin** (= without day, from *sine* without + *die* ablative singular of *dies* day). With reference to adjourned business etc.: without any day being appointed for resumption; indefinitely.

sine qua non /ˌsʌɪnɪ kweɪ ˈnɒn/, /ˌsɪneɪ kwɑː ˈnəʊn/ *adjective & noun phrase* (also in Latin plural form **sine quibus non** /ˌsʌɪnɪ kwiːbəs ˈnɒn/, /ˌsɪneɪ kwiːbəs ˈnəʊn/, (chiefly *Scottish Law*) Latin masculine form **sine quo non** /ˌsʌɪnɪ kwəʊ ˈnɒn/, /ˌsɪneɪ kwəʊ ˈnəʊn/) E17 **Latin** ((*causa*) *sine qua non* literally, '(cause) without which not', from *sine* without + *qua* ablative singular feminine of *qui* which + *non* not). **A** *adjective phrase* E17 Indispensable, absolutely essential. Also *postpositive*. **B** *noun phrase* **1** E17 An indispensable person or thing; *especially* an essential condition or element. **2** L17 *Scottish Law* (*sine quo non*) A curator, a trustee, *archaic*.

B.1 1996 *Times* A merchant banker in London . . . told me that at one stage an Eton and Oxbridge education was almost a *sine qua non* in his organisation . . .

sinfonia /sɪnfəˈniːə/, /sɪnˈfəʊnɪə/ *noun* L18 **Italian** (from Latin *symphonia* instrumental harmony, voices in concert, from Greek *sumphōnia* from *sumphōnos* harmonious). *Music* **1** L18 In baroque music, an orchestral piece used as an introduction to an opera, cantata, or suite; an overture. **2** (*Sinfonia*) (The title of) a small symphony orchestra.

sinfonietta /ˌsɪnfəʊnɪˈɛtə/ *noun* E20 **Italian** (diminutive of SINFONIA). *Music* **1** E20 A short or simple symphony. **2** E20 (*Sinfonietta*) A SINFONIA sense 2.

singerie /sɛ̃ʒri/ *noun* plural pronounced same E20 **French** (from *singe* monkey). A painting depicting monkeys in human roles and attitudes; a piece of porcelain decorated with such paintings; work done in this style.

Singspiel /ˈzɪŋʃpiːl/ *noun* plural **Singspiele** /ˈzɪŋʃpiːlə/ L19 **German** (from *singen* to sing + *Spiel* play). *Music* A dramatic performance alternating between song and dialogue, popular especially in late eighteenth-century. Germany; (a) comic opera.

sinopia /sɪˈnəʊpɪə/ *noun* plural **sinopie** /sɪˈnəʊpɪeɪ/ M19 **Italian**. **1** M19 A red pigment containing sinopite or similar-coloured minerals. **2** M20 *transferred* A preliminary rough sketch for a fresco, covered by the final work.

sinter /ˈsɪntə/ *noun* L18 **German** (= cinder). **1** L18 A hard incrustation formed on rocks etc. by precipitation from mineral waters. **2** E20 Material which has been coalesced into a solid or porous mass under the influence of heat or pressure without liquefaction, especially after compression in a shaped die.

sirocco /sɪˈrɒkəʊ/ *noun* (also **scirocco**) plural **siroccos** E17 **Italian** (*scirocco* ultimately from Spanish Arabic *šalūķ*, *šulūķ*, *šalūk* south-east wind, perhaps of Romance origin). **1** E17 A hot, oppressive, and often dusty or rainy wind which blows from the north coast of Africa over the Mediterranean and parts of southern Europe; *generally* any hot southerly wind. **2** *figurative* M19 A blighting influence; a fiery storm. **3** L19 A machine or oven for drying hops or tea leaves by means of a hot, moist current of air. Also more fully *sirocco drying-machine*, *sirocco oven*.

sirop /siro/ *noun* plural pronounced same L19 **French**. (A drink made from) a syrupy preparation of sweetened fruit-juice.

sissonne /ˈsiːsɒn/, *foreign* /sisɔn/ (*plural same*) *noun* E18 **French**. *Ballet* A jump in the air from fifth position, landing on one foot with the other leg extended.

sistrum /ˈsɪstrəm/ *noun* plural **sistra** /ˈsɪstrə/, **sistrums** LME **Latin** (from Greek *seistron*, from *seiein* to shake). A musical instrument of ancient Egyptian origin, consisting of a metal frame with transverse metal rods which rattled when the instrument was shaken.

sitar /ˈsɪtɑː/, /sɪˈtɑː/ *noun* M19 **Persian and Urdu** (*sitār* from *sih* three + *tār* string). A stringed Indian musical instrument, resembling a lute, with a long neck and (usually) seven principal strings which the player plucks.

situla /ˈsɪtjʊlə/ *noun* plural **situlae** /ˈsɪtjʊliː/, **situlas** L19 **Latin** (= bucket). *Archaeology* A vessel resembling a bucket in shape.

situs /ˈsʌɪtəs/ *noun* E18 **Latin**. **1** E18 Situation, position *rare*. **2** *Law* **a** E19 The place to which for purposes of legal jurisdiction or taxation a property belongs. Chiefly *United States*. **b** M20 A work-site, *especially* (in full *common situs*) one occupied by two or more employers. *United States*.

Sitzfleisch /ˈzɪtsˌflaɪʃ/ *noun* (also written **sitzfleisch**) E20 **German** (from *sitzen* to sit + *Fleisch* flesh). The ability to persist in or endure an activity.

1975 *Harpers & Queen* Lenny hadn't got the patience, the concentration, the sitzfleisch.

Sitz im Leben /ˌzɪts ɪm ˈleːbən/ *noun phrase* M20 **German** (literally, 'place in life'). *Theology* In biblical criticism, the determining circumstances in which a tradition developed.

sitzkrieg /ˈsɪtskriːg/ *noun* M20 **pseudo-German** (after BLITZKRIEG, as if from German *sitzen* to sit + *krieg* war). (A part of) a war marked by a (relative) absence of active hostilities.

sjambok /ˈʃambɒk/ *noun* (also **sambok**, **shambok**) L18 **Afrikaans** (from Malay *sambuk*, *chambuk* from Persian and Urdu *chābuk* horsewhip). In South Africa: a heavy whip made of rhinoceros or hippopotamus hide.

skald /skɔːld/, /skald/ *noun* (also **scald**) M18 **Old Norse** (*skáld*, of unknown origin). *History* An (itinerant or court) oral poet, a bard, originally and especially in ancient Scandinavia.

skandalon /ˈskandəlɒn/ *noun* (also **scandalon**) M20 **Greek**. *Theology* A stumbling-block; a cause of offence; a scandal.

skat /skɑːt/ *noun* M19 **German** (from Italian *scarto* (= French *écart*) cards laid aside, from *scartare* to discard; cf. ÉCARTÉ). A three-handed card-game with bidding for contract, originating in Germany; *collective* the two cards dealt to the table in this game.

skaz /skaz/ *noun* E20 **Russian**. First-person narrative in which the author assumes a persona.

skene /ˈskiːni/ *noun* L19 **Greek** (*skēnē* hut, tent). *Theatre* In ancient Greek theatre, a three-dimensional structure forming part of the stage or set and able to be decorated according to the current play's theme.

skepsel /ˈskɛps(ə)l/ *noun* M19 **Afrikaans** (*skepsel*, Dutch *schepsel* creature, from *scheppen* to create). A creature, a villain, a rascal.

■ In South African colloquial speech frequently used as a derogatory and offensive form of address to a Black or Coloured person.

ski-joring /ˈskiːdʒɔːrɪŋ/, /ʃiːˈjəːrɪŋ/ *noun* (also **skikjøring** E20 **Norwegian** (*skikjøring*, from *ski* ski + *kjøring* driving). A winter sport in which a skier is towed by a horse or vehicle.

> **1996** *Country Life* Racing on ice has a long history in St Moritz, and skikjøring races started in 1906.

skoff /skɔf/ *noun* L18 **Afrikaans** (*skof* from Dutch *schoft* quarter of the day, each of the four meals of a day). A stage of a journey; a period of travel between outspans. Also, a period of work, a shift. *South African colloquial.*

slainte /ˈslɑːntʃə/ *interjection* E19 **Gaelic** (*slàinte* (*mhór*) = '(good) health'). Expressing good wishes, especially before drinking.

slalom /ˈslɑːləm/ *noun & verb* E20 **Norwegian** (*slalåm*, from *sla* sloping + *låm* track). **A** *noun* **1** E20 A downhill ski race on a zigzag course marked by artificial obstacles, usually flags, and descended singly by each competitor in turn. **2** M20 A similar obstacle race for canoeists, waterskiers, skateboarders, etc. **B** *intransitive verb* M20 Perform or compete in a slalom; make frequent sharp turns (as) in a slalom.

slivovitz /ˈslɪvəvɪts/ *noun* (also **slivovic**) L19 **Serbo-Croat** (*šljivovica* from *šljiva* plum). A plum brandy made chiefly in Romania, Serbia, and neighbouring States.

smetana /ˈsmɛtənə/ *noun* E20 **Russian** (from *smetat'* to sweep together, collect). Sour cream. Frequently in *smetana sauce.*

smørbrød /ˈsməːbrəːd/ *noun* M20 **Norwegian** (from *smøre* butter + *brød* bread: cf. next). In Norway: an open sandwich; food consisting of open sandwiches.

smorgasbord /ˈsmɔːgəsbɔːd/ *noun* L19 **Swedish** (*smörgåsbord*, from *smörgås* (slice of) bread and butter (from *smör* butter, *gås* goose, lump of butter) + *bord* board, table). **1** L19 Open sandwiches served with delicacies as hors d'oeuvres or a buffet, originally and especially in Scandinavia. **2** M20 *figurative* A medley, a miscellany, a variety.

> **2 1996** *Times* This being Dead Can Dance, there was a whole *smorgasbord* of musical styles on show . . .

smørrebrød /ˈsməːrəbrəːd/, /ˈsməːrə brəːð/ *noun* E20 **Danish** (from *smør* butter + *brød* bread: cf. preceding). In Denmark: an open sandwich; food consisting of open sandwiches.

smorzando /smɔːˈtsandəʊ/ *adverb, adjective, & noun* E19 **Italian** (present participle of *smorzare* to extinguish). *Music* **A** *adverb & adjective* E19 (A direction:) dying away. **B** *noun* E19 plural **smorzandos**, **smorzandi** /smɔːˈtsandi/. A smorzando passage.

snobisme /snobism/ *noun* E20 **French**. Snobbishness.

snoek /snuːk/, /snʊk/ *noun* plural same L18 **Dutch** (= pike). A long slender food fish of southern oceans, a barracouta. Chiefly *South African.*

soba /ˈsəʊbə/ *noun* (treated as *singular* or *plural*) L19 **Japanese**. Japanese noodles made from buckwheat flour.

sobornost /soˈbornost/ *noun* M20 **Russian** (*sobornost'* conciliarism, catholicity). *Theology* A unity of people in a loving fellowship in which each member retains freedom and integrity without excessive individualism.

sobriquet /ˈsəʊbrɪkeɪ/ *noun* M17 **French** (of unknown origin). An epithet, a nickname.

■ The older French form SOUBRIQUET is also found in English.

socle /ˈsəʊk(ə)l/, /ˈsɒk(ə)l/ *noun* E18 **French** (from Italian *zoccolo* wooden shoe, socle, representing Latin *socculus* diminutive of *soccus* sock). A low plinth serving as a pedestal for a statue, column, vase, etc.

sogo shosha /ˌsəʊgəʊ ˈʃəʊʃə/ *noun phrase* plural same, **sogo shoshas** M20 **Japanese** (*sōgō shōsha*, from *sōgō* comprehensive + SHOSHA). A very large Japanese company that trades internationally in a wide range of goods and services.

soi-disant /swadizɑ̃/ *adjective* (also **soi disant**) M18 **French** (from *soi* oneself + *disant* present participle of *dire* to say). **1** M18 Of a person: self-styled, would-be. **2** M19 Of a thing: so-called, pretended.

1 1995 *Times* A French *soi-disant* sexual scientist claims that women who are worried about being pestered by men on the beach this summer should go topless.

soigné /swaɲe/, /ˈswɑːnjeɪ/ *adjective* (feminine **soignée**) E19 **French** (past participial adjective of *soigner* to care for, from *soin* care). Meticulously dressed, prepared, or arranged; well-groomed.

1996 *Times* What could be more classic than a soigné tuxedo suit or an understated little black dress . . . ?

soigneur /swaɲœr/ *noun* plural pronounced same L20 **French** (from *soigner* to care for). In cycling, a person who gives training, massage, and other assistance to a team.

soirée /ˈswɑːreɪ/, *foreign* /sware/ (*plural same*) *noun* L18 **French** (from *soir* evening). An evening party, gathering, or social meeting, especially in a private house.

soirée dansante /sware dɑ̃sɑ̃t/ *noun phrase* plural **soirées dansantes** (pronounced same) M19 **French** (from as SOIRÉE + *dansante* feminine of present participle of *danser* to dance). An evening party with dancing.

soirée musicale /ˌswɑːreɪ mjuːzɪˈkɑːl/ *noun phrase* plural **soirées musicales** (pronounced same) M19 **French** (from as SOIRÉE + MUSICALE). An evening party to perform or listen to music.

soit /swa/ *interjection* L19 **French** (3rd person singular present subjunctive of *être* be). So be it.

soixante-neuf /swasɑ̃t nœf/ *noun* L19 **French** (= sixty-nine, after the position of the couple involved). Sexual activity between two people involving mutual oral stimulation of the genitals; a position enabling this.

1973 M. Amis *Rachel Papers* The other couple were writhing about still, now seemingly poised for a session of fully robed soixante-neuf.

sokaiya /ˈsəʊkʌɪjə/ *noun* plural same L20 **Japanese** (from *sōkai* general meeting + *-ya* dealer). A holder of shares in a company who tries to extort money from it by threatening to cause trouble for executives at a general meeting of the shareholders.

sola /ˈsəʊlə/ *adverb & adjective* M18 **Latin** (feminine of *solus* alone, or Italian, feminine of *solo* alone). **1** *adverb & predicative adjective* M18 Of a woman: solitary; alone. **2** *adjective* M18 *Commerce* Of a bill of exchange: single (as opposed to one of a set).

solarium /səˈlɛːrɪəm/ *noun* plural **solaria** /səˈlɛːrɪə/, **solariums** M19 **Latin** (from *sol* sun). **1** M19 A sundial. Now *rare* or *obsolete*. **2a** A room etc usually with large areas of glass designed to maximize exposure to the sun's rays. **2b** M20 A room equipped with sun-lamps for inducing an artificial suntan; an establishment providing sun-lamps.

solatium /səˈleɪʃɪəm/ *noun* plural **solatia** /səˈleɪʃɪə/ E19 **Latin**. A sum of money or other compensation given to a person to make up for loss, inconvenience, injured feelings, etc.; *specifically* in *Law*, such an amount awarded to a litigant over and above the actual loss.

sola topi see under TOPI.

solera /səˈlɛːrə/, *foreign* /soˈlera/ *noun* M19 **Spanish** (literally, 'crossbeam, stone base' from *suelo* ground, floor, dregs, from Latin *solum* soil). **1** M19 A blend of sherry or Malaga wine produced by the Spanish solera system (see sense 3 below). Also *solera wine*. **2** M19 A wine-cask, usually with a capacity of four hogsheads; a set of such casks arranged in tiers so as to produce wine by the solera system. **3** M20 (*solera system*) A method of producing wine, especially sherry and Madeira, whereby small amounts of younger wines stored in an upper tier of casks are systematically blended with the more mature wine in the casks below.

solfatara /sɒlfəˈtɑːrə/ *noun* (also earlier **solfaterra** /sɒlfəˈtɛrə/) L18 **Italian** (originally, a sulphurous volcano near Naples, from Italian *solfo* sulphur). *Geology* A fumarole which emits sulphurous gases, encrusting the edge with sulphur etc. Cf. SOUFRIÈRE.

solfège /sɔlfɛʒ/ *noun* plural pronounced same E20 **French**. *Music* SOLFEGGIO. Also (*generally*), rudimentary musical instruction, especially using textless exercises for the voice.

solfeggio /sɒlˈfɛdʒɪəʊ/ *noun* plural **solfeggi** /sɒlˈfɛdʒi/, **solfeggios** L18 **Italian** (from *sol-fa* sol-fa). *Music* An exercise for the voice (formerly also for a musical instrument), using the sol-fa syllables. Also, solmization.

solidus /ˈsɒlɪdəs/ *noun* plural **solidi** /ˈsɒlɪdʌɪ/ ME **Latin** (*solidus* solid used as noun; in branch I from Latin *solidus* (*nummus*) a gold coin). **I 1** ME *History* A gold coin of the later Roman Empire, originally worth about 25 denarii. Formerly also, in medieval England, a shilling. **2** L19 An oblique stroke formerly written to separate shillings from pence, and now used in writing fractions, to separate figures and letters, or to denote alternatives or ratios. Cf. VIRGULE sense 1. **II 3** E20 A line or surface in a binary or ternary phase diagram respectively, or a temperature (corresponding to a point on the line or surface), below which a mixture is entirely solid and above which it consists of solid and liquid in equilibrium.

solitaire /ˈsɒlɪtɛː/, /sɒlɪˈtɛː/ *noun* E18 **French** (from Latin *solitarius* solitary. **1** E18 A person who lives in solitude; a recluse. **2** E18 (A ring with) a diamond or other gem set by itself. **3** M18 A card or board game for one player. **4** M18 *History* A man's loose necktie of black silk or broad ribbon. **5** L18 Either of two extinct flightless birds related to the dodo.

solod /ˈsɒlət/ *noun* (also **soloth** /ˈsɒləθ/) plural **solodi** /ˈsɒlədi/, **soloti** /ˈsɒləti/, **solods** /ˈsɒləts/ E20 **Russian** (*solod'* from *sol'* salt). *Soil Science* A type of soil derived from a SOLONETZ by leaching of saline or alkaline constituents, occurring in arid regions.

solonchak /ˈsɒləntʃak/ *noun* E20 **Russian** (= salt-marsh, salt lake, from *sol'* salt). *Soil Science* A type of salty alkaline soil that has little or no structure, is typically pale in colour, and occurs in poorly drained regions.

solonetz /ˈsɒlənɛts/ *noun* E20 **Russian** (*solonets* salt-marsh, salt lake, from *sol'* salt). *Soil Science* A type of alkaline soil that is rich in carbonates, has a thin friable surface layer, and occurs in better-drained areas than a SOLONCHAK.

solus /ˈsəʊləs/ *adverb & adjective* L16 **Latin** (cf. SOLA). **1** *adverb & predicative adjective* L16 Of a male (occasionally a female) person: alone, by oneself. Frequently as a stage direction. **2** *adjective* **a** M20 Of an advertisement: standing alone on a page etc.; dealing with one item only. Also, pertaining to such an advertisement. **b** M20 *Commerce* Of a petrol station etc.: selling the products of one company only. Also, of or pertaining to such an arrangement.

solyanka /səˈljankə/ *noun* M20 **Russian**. A soup made of vegetables and meat or fish.

sol y sombra /ˌsol i ˈsombra/ *noun* M20 **Spanish** (literally, 'sun and shade'). A drink of brandy mixed with anisette or gin.

soma /ˈsəʊmə/ *noun* L18 **Sanskrit**. A plant the juice of which was used in India to prepare an intoxicating liquor; the liquor itself, used in Vedic ritual. Cf. HOM.

■ In his novel *Brave New World* (1932), Aldous Huxley gave the name *soma* to the narcotic drug distributed by the State to keep people happy and acquiescent.

sombrero /sɒmˈbrɛːrəʊ/ *noun* plural **sombreros** L16 **Spanish** (from *sombra* shade). **1** L16–E18 An oriental umbrella or parasol. **2** L18 A broad-brimmed hat of felt or other soft material, of a type common in Mexico and the south-western United States.

sommelier /ˈsɒm(ə)ljeɪ/, /səˈmɛljeɪ/; *foreign* /sɔməlje/ (*plural same*) *noun* E19 **French**. A wine waiter.

1996 *Times: Weekend* For fun, we asked for the wine list, and irritated the sommelier by pondering a Pétrus 1955 Pomerol at £1,307 before settling for a glass of house white.

sommité /sɔmite/ *noun* plural pronounced same M19 **French** (= summit, top, tip). A person of great eminence or influence.

son /səʊn/ *noun* M20 **Spanish** (= sound). A slow Cuban dance and song in 2/4 time.

sonata /səˈnɑːtə/ *noun* L17 **Italian** (feminine past participle of *sonare* to sound). A musical composition for one or two instruments (one usually being the piano), usually in several movements with one (especially the first) or more in sonata form.

■ Varieties of *sonata* popular in the seventeenth and eighteenth centuries were the *sonata da camera* (literally, 'chamber sonata'), for one or more solo instruments and continuo and usually consisting of a suite of dance movements, and the *sonata da chiesa* (literally, 'church sonata'), likewise for one or more solo instruments and continuo, but usually consisting of four alternately slow and fast movements. Both phrases were introduced into English somewhat later (E19).

sonatina /sɒnəˈtiːnə/ *noun* M18 **Italian** (diminutive of SONATA). A short or simple sonata.

sondage /sɒnˈdɑːʒ/ *noun* plural **sondages** /sɒnˈdɑːʒɪz/ M20 **French** (= sounding, borehole). *Archaeology* A trench dug to investigate the stratigraphy of a site.

sonde /sɒnd/ *noun* E20 **French** (= sounding-line, sounding). **1** E20 A radiosonde or similar device that is sent aloft to transmit or record information on conditions in the atmosphere. Originally only in combination with specifying word, as *ballon-sonde* etc. **2** M20 An instrument probe for transmitting information about its surroundings underground or under water.

son et lumière /ˌsɒn eɪ ˈluːmjɛː/, *foreign* /sɔn e lymjɛr/ *noun phrase* plural **son et lumières** /ˈluːmjɛːz/, *foreign* /lymjɛr/ M20 French (literally, 'sound and light'). **1** M20 An entertainment using recorded sound and lighting effects, usually presented at night at a historic building or other site to give a dramatic narrative of its history. **2** M20 *figurative* Writing or behaviour resembling a son et lumière presentation, especially in its dramatic qualities.

sons bouchés /sɔ̃ buʃe/ *noun plural* E20 French (literally, 'blocked sounds'). In horn-playing, notes stopped by the insertion of the hand into the bell of the instrument; a direction indicating this.

sopaipilla /sopaiˈpilja/, /ˌsəʊpʌɪˈpiːljə/ *noun* plural **sopaipillas** /sopaiˈpiljas/, /ˌsəʊpʌɪˈpiːljəz/ M20 **American Spanish** (diminutive of Spanish *sopaipa* a kind of sweet fritter). Especially in New Mexico, a deep-fried usually square pastry eaten with honey or sugar or as a bread.

sopra bianco /ˌsopra ˈbjanko/ *noun phrase* M19 **Italian** (elliptical for BIANCO SOPRA BIANCO). Bianco sopra bianco.

soprani see SOPRANO.

sopranino /sɒprəˈniːnəʊ/ *noun & adjective* plural **sopraninos** E20 **Italian** (diminutive of SOPRANO). (Designating) an instrument (usually wind) of higher pitch than a soprano instrument.

soprano /səˈprɑːnəʊ/ *noun & adjective* M18 **Italian** (from *sopra* above, from Latin *supra*). **A** *noun* plural **sopranos**, **soprani** /səˈprɑːni/. **1** M18 The highest singing voice; the quality or range of this voice. **b** E19 A part for or sung by such a voice. **2** M18 A female or boy singer having such a voice; a person singing a soprano part. **b** L19 (The player of) an instrument of a high pitch, *specifically* of the highest pitch in a family. **B** *attributive* or as *adjective* M18 Of, pertaining to, or designating the highest singing voice or instrumental pitch.

A.1 1996 *Spectator* Musetta and Mimì are both written for lyric sopranos, the commonest voices . . .

sorbet /ˈsɔːbeɪ/, /ˈsɔːbɪt/ *noun* L16 **French** (from Italian *sorbetto* from as SHERBET). Originally, an Eastern sherbet. Now usually, a water-ice.

sorbetière /sɔːˈbɛtɪɛː/, *foreign* /sɔrbətjɛr/ *noun* M20 **French** (from as SORBET). A domestic ice-cream-making machine, in which the mixture is stirred as it is being frozen.

sordino /sɔːˈdiːnəʊ/ *noun* plural **sordini** /sɔːˈdiːni/ (also **sordine** /sɔːˈdiːn/) L16 **Italian** (from *sordo*, from Latin *surdus* deaf, mute). A mute for a wind or bowed instrument; a damper for a piano. Cf. CON SORDINO.

sortes /ˈsɔːtiːz/, /ˈsɔːteɪz/ *noun plural* also treated as *singular* L16 **Latin** (plural of *sors* lot, chance). Divination, or the seeking of guidance, by chance selection of a passage in a book.

■ The authorities traditionally consulted in this way are Virgil (in full *sortes Virgilianae* /ˌvəːdʒɪlɪˈɑːniː/), Homer (in full *sortes Homericae* /həʊˈmɛrɪkiː/), and the Bible (in full *sortes Biblicae* /ˈbɪblɪkiː/).

sosatie /sɔˈsɑːti/, /səˈsɑːti/ *noun* M19 **Afrikaans** (ultimately from Malay *sesate*; cf. SATAY). In South Africa: marinaded spiced meat grilled on a skewer.

soshi /ˈsəʊʃi/ *noun* plural same L19 **Japanese** (*sōshi*, literally, 'strong man'). A mercenary political agitator.

sostenuto /ˌsɒstəˈn(j)uːtəʊ/ *adverb, adjective, & noun* E18 **Italian** (past participle of *sostenere* to sustain). *Music* **A** *adverb & adjective* E18 (A direction) in a sustained or prolonged manner. **B** *noun* M18 plural **sostenutos**. A passage (to be) played in a sustained or prolonged manner. Also, a sustained sound or note.

sottise /sɔˈtiːz/ *noun* plural pronounced same L17 **French** (from *sot* fool, from medieval Latin *sottus*). A foolish remark or action.

1977 *Times* The *Daily Mail* Diary . . . is not slow to criticize errors and *sottises* in rival newspapers.

sottisier /sɔtizje/ *noun* plural pronounced same E20 **French** (from as SOTTISE). A collection or (especially) a written list of *sottises*.

sottoportico /sottoˈportiko/, /ˌsɒtəʊ ˈpɔːtɪkəʊ/ *noun* plural **sottoportichi**

/sotto'portiki/, **sottoporticos** (also **sottoportego** /sotto'portego/, /sɒtəʊ'pɔːteɪgəʊ/, plural **sottoportighi** /sotto'portigi/, **sottoportigos**) E20 **Italian** (from *sotto* under + PORTICO). *Architecture* The passage formed by a portico.

sotto voce /ˌsotto 'votʃe/, /ˌsɒtəʊ 'vəʊtʃi/ *adverb & adjective phrase* M18 **Italian** (*sotto* under + *voce* voice). **A** *adverb* M18 In an undertone or aside. **B** *adjective* E19 Uttered in an undertone; *transferred* muted, understated.

B 1995 *Spectator* Sir Edward [Heath] is not so rude (at least to foreigners) as to suggest that he believes today's apologetic and democratic Germany is a potential threat to European peace, but that is the *sotto voce* message nonetheless.

sou /suː/ *noun* L15 **French** (singular form deduced from *sous, soux* plural of Old French *sout*, from Latin *solidus* (sc. *nummus* coin) use as noun of *solidus* solid). *History* A French coin, formerly a twentieth of a livre, later a five-centime piece.

■ In English mainly used in one or other form of the colloquial expression *haven't a sou*, i.e. 'have absolutely no money at all'. Cf. SOU MARKEE.

Soubise /subiz/ *noun* plural pronounced same L18 **French** (Charles de Rohan *Soubise* (1715–87), French general and courtier). **1** A kind of cravat. Only in L18. **2** E19 A white onion sauce. Also *sauce Soubise*.

soubresaut /subrəso/ *noun* plural pronounced same M19 **French**. **1** M19 A jumping motion seen in some liquids when boiling. Now *rare* or *obsolete*. **2** E20 *Ballet* A straight-legged jump from both feet with the toes pointed and feet together, one behind the other.

soubrette /suː'brɛt/ *noun* M18 **French** (from modern Provençal *soubreto* feminine of *soubret* coy, from *soubra* (Provençal *sobrar*) from Latin *superare* to be above). **1** M18 A maidservant or lady's maid as a character in a play or opera, *especially* one of a pert or coquettish character; an actress or singer playing the role of a pert or coquettish female in any light entertainment. **2** E19 A lady's maid; a maidservant.

1 1996 *Spectator* ... she ... can toss her auburn curls with the wily femininity of a soubrette from Offenbach.

soubriquet /'suːbrɪkeɪ/ *noun* E19 **French** (older variant of *sobriquet*). A nickname, a SOBRIQUET.

souchong /'suːʃɒŋ/ *noun* M18 **Chinese** ((Cantonese) *siú chúng* small sort). A fine black variety of China tea.

soucouyant /ˌsuːkuː'jɒ̃/ *noun West Indies* (also **soucriant** /ˌsuːkriː'jɒ̃/ and other variants) M20 **West Indian creole** (probably related to Fulah *sukunyadyo* sorcerer, witch). In eastern Caribbean folklore, a malignant witch believed to shed her skin by night and suck the blood of her victims.

soufflé /'suːfleɪ/, *foreign* /sufle/ (*plural same*) *noun & adjective* E19 **French** (past participle of *souffler* from Latin *sufflare*, from *sub* under + *flare* to blow). **A** *noun* E19 A light spongy dish made by mixing egg-yolks and other ingredients with stiffly beaten egg-whites, usually baked in an oven until puffy. **B** *adjective* L19 Of ceramic ware: having liquid colour applied by means of blowing.

souffrante /sufrɑ̃t/ *adjective* E19 **French** (feminine singular present participial adjective of *souffrir* to suffer). Of a woman: delicate; prone to illness, anxiety, or depression.

souffre-douleur /sufrədulœr/ *noun* plural pronounced same M19 **French** (literally, 'to suffer sorrow'). A person who is in a subservient position and must listen to or share another's troubles; *specifically* a woman who acts as a paid companion to an older woman.

soufrière /ˌsuːfrɪ'ɛː/ *noun* M19 **French** (from *soufre* sulphur). A SOLFATARA.

souk /suːk/ *noun* (also **suk**, **sukh**, **suq**) E19 **Arabic** (*sūḳ* market, probably through French *souk*). An Arab market or marketplace, a bazaar.

soukous /'suːkuːs/ *noun* L20 **African** (from French *secouer* to shake). Zairean popular dance music.

sou markee /ˌsuː mɑː'kiː/ *noun* M17 **French** (*sou marqué*, literally, 'marked sou'). A small eighteenth-century French coin issued for the colonies and circulating especially in the West Indies and North America (*historical*); *generally* something of little value.

soupçon /'suːpsɒn/, *foreign* /supsɔ̃/ *noun* M18 **French** (from Old French *sous(s)peçon*, from medieval Latin *suspectio(n-)*). A suspicion, a suggestion; a very small quantity, a trace.

1996 *Spectator* The bomb had had little effect on the markets—except for a *soupçon* of trouble for leisure groups with Northern Ireland interests.

soupe /sup/ *noun* M18 **French**. Soup, especially in French cooking.

■ Chiefly in phrases designating particular kinds of soup, as *soupe à l'oignon* onion soup.

soupirant /supirɑ̃/ *noun* M19 **French** (present participle of *soupirer* to sigh). A male admirer, a suitor.

souple /supl/ *noun* L19 **French**. A fabric made of partially degummed silk. More fully *souple silk*.

sous- /su/, /suz/ *prefix* ME **Old and Modern French** (*sous*, from Latin *subtus* under). Under-, sub-.

■ Used in words adopted from French such as *sous-chef*, *sous-lieutenant*, etc.

sous-entendu /suzɑ̃tɑ̃dy/ *noun* plural pronounced same M19 **French**. Something implied or understood but not expressed.

sous vide /su vid/, /suː ˈviːd/ *adjective & adverb phrase* L20 **French** (from *sous* under + *vide* vacuum). Of food: (prepared) by partial cooking followed by vacuum-sealing and chilling.

soutache /suːˈtaʃ/ *noun* M19 **French** (from Hungarian *sujtás*). A narrow flat ornamental braid used for decorative trimming. More fully *soutache braid*. Also called *Russia braid*.

soutane /suːˈtɑːn/ *noun* M19 **French** (from Italian *sottana*, from *sotto* from Latin *subtus* under). *Roman Catholic Church* A cassock, *especially* a cassock with scarf and cincture worn by a priest.

souteneur /sutənœr/ *noun* plural pronounced same E20 **French** (= protector, from *soutenir* to sustain). A pimp.

soutenu /sutəny/ *adjective & noun* M20 **French** (past participle of *soutenir* to sustain). *Ballet* **A** *adjective* M20 Of a movement: sustained, performed slowly. **B** *noun* M20 plural pronounced same. A sustained or slow movement; *especially* a complete turn on point or half point.

souterrain /ˈsuːtərem/ *noun* M18 **French** (from *sous* under + *terre* earth, after Latin *subterraneus*). Chiefly *Archaeology* An underground chamber or passage.

souvenir /ˌsuːvəˈnɪə/ *noun* L18 **French** (use as noun of verb = to remember, from Latin *subvenire* to come into the mind, from *sub-* + *venire* to come). **1** L18 A remembrance, a memory. Now *rare*. **2** L18 A token of remembrance; *especially* an article given or purchased as a reminder *of* a particular person, place, or event; a keepsake. **b** E19 *specifically* A usually illustrated publication designed to be purchased as a gift. **c** E20 In the war of 1914–18, a bullet, a shell. *Military slang*.

souvlaki /suːˈvlɑːki/ *noun* plural **souvlakia** /suːˈvlɑːkɪə/ M20 **Modern Greek** (*soublaki* from *soubla* skewer). A Greek dish of small pieces of meat grilled on a skewer.

sovkhoz /ˈsɒvkɒz/, /sʌvˈkɔːz/ *noun* plural same, **sovkhozes** /ˈsɒvkɒzɪz/, **sovkhozy** /ˈsɒvkɒzi/ E20 **Russian** (from *sov(etskoe khoz(yaĭstvo* Soviet farm). A State-owned farm in countries of the former USSR.

soya /ˈsɔɪə/ *noun* L17 **Dutch** (*soja* from Japanese *shōyu*; cf. SHOYU). Soy sauce.

■ Also used as short for *soya bean*, the leguminous plant grown as a vegetable or for its protein-rich seeds that yield an edible oil.

spaghetti /spəˈgɛti/ *noun* M19 **Italian** (plural of diminutive of *spago* string). **1** M19 Pasta in the form of long solid threads, between MACARONI and VERMICELLI in thickness. **2** M20 Complex roadways forming a multi-level junction, especially on a motorway. In full *spaghetti junction*. *colloquial*.

spaghettini /ˌspagɛˈtiːni/ *noun* M20 **Italian** (diminutive of preceding). Pasta in the form of strings of thin spaghetti.

Spätlese /ˈʃpɛtleːzə/ *noun* plural **Spätlesen** /ˈʃpɛtleːzən/, **Spätleses** M20 **German** (from *spät* late + *Lese* picking, vintage). A white wine made (especially in Germany) from grapes picked later than the general harvest.

Spätzle /ˈʃpɛtslə/, /ˈʃpɛts(ə)l/ *noun plural* L19 **German** ((dialect) literally, 'little sparrows'). Noodles of a type made in southern Germany.

spécialité /spesjalite/ *noun* (also **specialité**) M19 **French** (Old French *especialité* from late Latin *specialitas*, from Latin *specialis* special, particular). **1** M19 An article or service specially characteristic of, dealt in, or produced by, a particular place, firm, etc. **2** M19 An unusual or distinctive thing.

■ *Speciality* in the sense of 'the quality of being special, distinctive, or limited in some respect' was adopted from Old French in the late medieval period and quickly Anglicized, and the Anglicized version of *spécialité* (and of closely related (*e*)*specialté*) is used in most general senses. In sense 1, *spécialité* is often used in the phrase *spécialité de la maison* 'special(i)ty of the house', to mean a dish on which a particular restaurant prides itself.

specie /ˈspiːʃiː/, /ˈspiːʃi/ *noun* E17 **Latin** (ablative singular of *species* kind, originally (M16) in phrase *in specie* in the real, precise, or actual form). Coin money as opposed to paper money. Frequently *attributive*.

spectrum /ˈspɛktrəm/ *noun* plural **spectra** /ˈspɛktrə/, **spectrums** E17 **Latin** (= image of a thing, apparition). **1** E17 An apparition, a spectre. *archaic*. **2** L17 An image. *rare*. **3 a** L17 The coloured band into which a beam of light is split by means of a prism or diffraction grating. **b** L19 (Any part of) the entire range of wavelengths of electromagnetic radiation. **c** L19 An actual or notional arrangement of the component parts of any phenomenon according to frequency, energy, mass, etc. **d** M20 *figurative* The entire or a wide range of something arranged by degree, quality, etc.

speculum /ˈspɛkjʊləm/ *noun* plural **specula** /ˈspɛkjʊlə/, **speculums** LME **Latin** (from base of *specere* to look, see). **1** LME *Medicine* An instrument, usually of metal, used to dilate an orifice or canal in the body to allow inspection. **2** M17 Chiefly *Science* A mirror or reflector of glass or metal. **3** E19 *Ornithology* A bright patch of plumage on the wings of certain birds. **4** E20 An alloy of copper and tin in a ratio of around 2:1, formerly used to make mirrors for scientific instruments. Also more fully *speculum metal*.

spermaceti /ˌspəːməˈsiːti/, /ˌspəːməˈsɛti/ *noun* L15 **Medieval Latin** (from late Latin *sperma* (from Greek = sperm, seed, from base of *speirein* to sow) + *ceti* genitive of *cetus*, Greek *kētos* whale (from its appearance or the belief that it represents whale-spawn)). A soft white waxy substance used in the manufacture of candles, ointments, etc., found in the sperm whale and some other cetaceans, chiefly in a rounded organ in the head which focuses acoustic signals and aids control of buoyancy.

sphendone /ˈsfɛndəni/ *noun* M19 **Greek** (*sphendonē*). *Archaeology* **1** M19 A headband or fillet shaped like a form of sling, worn by women in ancient Greece. **2** M19 An area composed of elongated sloping sides with a rounded end.

sphincter /ˈsfɪŋ(k)tə/ *noun* L16 **Latin** (from Greek *sphigktēr* band, contractile muscle, from *sphiggein* to draw tight). *Anatomy* A contractile muscular ring by which an orifice of the body is normally kept closed.

■ Often with modern Latin specifying word, as *sphincter ani* 'sphincter of the anus'.

sphinx /sfɪŋks/ *noun* plural **sphinxes**, **sphinges** /ˈsfɪndʒiːz/ LME **Latin** (from Greek *Sphigx*, *Sphigg-*, apparently from *sphiggein* to draw tight). **1** LME *Greek Mythology* (*Sphinx*) A hybrid monster, usually described as having a woman's head and a (winged) lion's body, which plagued the Greek city of Thebes until Oedipus solved its riddle. Also, any monster resembling this. **b** E17 *figurative* An inscrutable or enigmatic person or thing; a mystery. **2** L16 Any of several ancient Greek or (especially) Egyptian stone figures of a creature with a human or animal head and a lion's body. **3** M18 A moth of the genus *Sphinx*, or of the family Sphingidae, so called from the typical attitude of the caterpillar; a hawkmoth. Also *sphinx-moth*. Chiefly *United States*.

spianato /spɪəˈnɑːtəʊ/ *adjective & adverb* L19 **Italian**. *Music* (Played) in a smooth, even, level-toned style.

spiccato /spɪˈkɑːtəʊ/ *adjective, adverb, & noun* E18 **Italian** (= detailed, distinct). *Music* **A** *adjective & adverb* E18 (Played) in a staccato style performed by bouncing the bow on the strings of a violin etc. **B** *noun* L19 Spiccato playing; a passage played in this style.

Spielraum /ˈʃpiːlraʊm/ *noun* plural **Spielräume** /ˈʃpiːlrɔymə/ E20 **German** (from *Spiel* game, play + *Raum* room). *Philosophy* The range of possibilities within which the probability of an outcome or likelihood of a hypothesis is to be assessed.

1969 P. Geach *God and Soul* There has to be this element of chance in things if human choices are to have any *Spielraum*.

spinto /ˈspɪntəʊ/ *noun & adjective* plural of noun **spintos** M20 **Italian** (past participle of *spingere* to push). *Music* (Designating) a lyric soprano or tenor voice of powerful dramatic quality; (designating) a singer with such a voice.

spirituel /spiritүɛl/, /ˌspɪrɪtjʊˈɛl/ *adjective* (also **spirituelle**) L17 **French**. Highly refined and lively; witty.

spiritus rector /ˌspɪrɪtʊs ˈrɛktɔː/ *noun phrase* E20 **Latin**. A ruling or directing spirit.

1980 *Encounter* More than fifteen years ago he was the *spiritus rector* of the *European Journal of Sociology.*

sporran /ˈspɒr(ə)n/ *noun* M18 **Gaelic** (*sporan* = Irish *sparán* purse, Middle Irish *sboran* from Latin *bursa* purse). A pouch or large purse usually made of leather or sealskin covered with fur and with ornamental tassels etc., worn by a Scottish Highlander in front of the kilt.

sportif /spɔrtif/ *adjective* M20 **French**. Sportive; active or interested in athletic sports; (of a garment) suitable for sport or informal wear.

1996 *Oldie* . . . her sneering references to his game attempts to take up water-skiing on their honeymoon when he was a mere sixty-two have proved equally irritating to more *sportif* oldies.

Sprechgesang /ˈʃprɛçgəˌzaŋ/ *noun* E20 **German** (literally, 'speech song'). *Music* A style of dramatic vocalization intermediate between speech and song.

Sprechstimme /ˈʃprɛçˌʃtɪmə/ *noun* E20 **German** (literally, 'speech voice'). *Music* SPRECHGESANG.

sprezzatura /ˌsprettsaˈtura/ *noun* M20 **Italian**. Ease of manner, studied carelessness, nonchalance, especially in art or literature.

1973 *Times Literary Supplement* Literary fashion and his own aristocratic *sprezzatura* demanded that he affect an unconcern.

springar /ˈsprɪŋə/ *noun* M20 **Norwegian**. (A piece of music for) a Norwegian country dance in 3/4 time.

springbok /ˈsprɪŋbɒk/ *noun* (in sense 2 also **Springbok**, in sense 1 also Anglicized as **springbuck** /ˈsprɪŋbʌk/) L18 **Afrikaans** (from Dutch *springen* to spring + *bok* goat, antelope). **1** L18 A common and gregarious southern African gazelle, characterized by the habit of leaping (pronking) when excited or disturbed. **2** E20 A South African.

■ *Springboks* (often abbreviated to *Boks*) was formerly the name given to South African national sporting (especially rugby) teams.

spritzer /ˈsprɪtsə/ *noun* M20 **German** (= a splash). A mixture of (usually white) wine and soda water; a drink or glass of this.

spritzig /ˈʃprɪtsɪç/ *adjective & noun* M20 **German** (from *spritzen* to squirt, splash). **A** *adjective* M20 Of wine: sparkling. **B** *noun* M20 Sparkle in wine.

spruit /spreɪt/, *foreign* /sprœyt/ *noun* M19 **Dutch** (= sprout). In South Africa: a small watercourse that is usually dry except in the rainy season.

spumante /spuːˈmanti/ *noun* E20 **Italian** (= sparkling). A sparkling white wine, especially from the Italian province of Asti (in full *Asti spumante*).

spumoni /spuːˈməʊni/ *noun* E20 **Italian** (*spumone*, from *spuma* foam). A rich dessert consisting of layered ice-cream with candied fruits, nuts, and sometimes brandy. *North American*.

spurlos /ˈʃpuːrloːs/ *adjective* E20 **German** (= (sunk) without trace). (Sunk) without trace. Chiefly *figurative*, lost from sight, ruined. In full *spurlos versenkt* /ˌʃpuːrloːs fərˈsɛŋkt/.

■ The phrase became widely used in English as the result of the publication of a notorious secret telegram sent in May 1917 by the German minister in Buenos Aires, Count Luxburg, to Berlin, in which he recommended that Argentine shipping should either be turned back or sunk without trace.

1963 *Oxford Medical School Gazette* Many distinguished research workers have ceased production when they have become professors and like submarines in dangerous waters have been *spurlos versenkt.*

sputa plural of SPUTUM.

sputnik /ˈspʊtnɪk/, /ˈspʌtnɪk/ *noun* (also **Sputnik**) M20 **Russian** (literally, 'travelling companion', from *s* with + *put*' way, journey + noun suffix *-nik* person connected with (something)). **1** M20 An unmanned artificial earth satellite, especially a Russian one; *specifically* each of a series of such satellites launched by the Soviet Union between 1957 and 1961. **2** M20 *Bridge* A take-out double of a suit overcall of one's partner's opening bid. In full *Sputnik double*.

sputum /ˈspjuːtəm/ *noun* plural **sputa** /ˈspjuːtə/ L17 **Latin** (use as noun of neuter past participle of *spuere* to spit). *Medicine* Thick mucus coughed up from the respiratory tract especially in certain diseases of the lungs, chest, or throat; a mass or quantity of this.

staccato /stəˈkɑːtəʊ/ *adjective, adverb, noun, & verb* E18 **Italian** (past participle of *staccare* aphetic from *distaccare* to detach). **A** *adjective & adverb* E18 With each note or sound sharply separated or detached from the next, with a clipped style. Opposed to LEGATO. **B** *noun* L18 A succession of disconnected notes or sounds; a staccato passage in music etc.; staccato delivery, playing, or speech. **C** *transitive verb* E19 Play or utter in a staccato manner.

stadium /ˈsteɪdɪəm/ *noun* plural **stadiums**; **stadia** /ˈsteɪdɪə/ LME **Latin** (from Greek *stadion*). **I 1** LME *Classical Antiquities* A unit of length, usually equal to 600 Greek or Roman feet, or one-eighth of a Roman mile (*c.*185 m.). **2** E17 *Classical Antiquities* A course (originally a stadium in length) for foot-racing or chariot-racing; a race on such a course. **3** M19 An athletic or sports ground or arena with tiered seats or terraces for spectators. **II 4** M17 A stage of a process, disease, etc. **b** L19 *Zoology* An interval between moults in the growth of an insect, crustacean, etc. **5** M19 Any of various instruments for measuring distance; a levelling rod.

Stadthaus /ˈʃtathaʊs/ *noun* plural **Stadthauser** /ˈʃtathɔyzər/ M19 **German** (from *Stadt* town + *Haus* house). A town hall in a German-speaking country.

■ The partially Anglicized form *stadthouse* derives either from *stadthaus* or from Dutch *stadhuis* and is used of a town hall in a German-speaking or (especially) a Dutch-speaking country.

staffage /stəˈfɑːʒ/ *noun* L19 **German** (pseudo-French form from *staffieren* to fit out, decorate, perhaps from Old French *estoffer*, from *estoffe* stuff). Accessory items in a painting, especially figures or animals in a landscape picture.

stagione /staˈdʒone/ *noun* plural **stagioni** /staˈdʒoni/ M20 **Italian** (= season). An opera or ballet season, *especially* an opera season in which one work is performed on several occasions in a limited period with no change of cast.

stanza /ˈstanzə/, (*in sense 2 also*) /ˈstantsə/ *noun* plural **stanzas**, (in sense 2 also) **stanze** /ˈstantsi/ L16 **Italian** (= standing, stopping-place, room, strophe, from Proto-Romance, from Latin *stant-* present participial stem of *stare* to stand). **1** L16 A group of (usually between four and twelve) lines of verse occurring as the basic metrical unit of a song or poem consisting of a series of such groups; a verse. **2** M17 In Italy: an apartment, a chamber, a room; *specifically* a room in the Vatican (usually in *plural*). **3** M20 A half or other session of a game or sporting contest.

starets /ˈstarjɛts/ *noun* (also **startz**) plural **startsy**, **startzy**, /ˈstartsi/ E20 **Russian** (= (venerable) old man, elder). A spiritual leader or counsellor in the Russian Orthodox Church.

starover /starəˈvjɛr/, /starəˈvjɛː/ *noun* plural **starovery** /starəˈvjɛri/, **starovers** E19 **Russian**. *Ecclesiastical History* An Old Believer, a RASKOLNIK.

startsy, **startz** see STARETS.

stasis /ˈsteɪsɪs/, /ˈstasɪs/ *noun* plural **stases** /ˈsteɪsiːz/, /ˈstasɪs/ M18 **Modern Latin** (from Greek, literally, 'standing, stoppage; party, faction', from *sta-* base of *histanai* to stand). **1** M18 *Medicine* A stagnation or stoppage of flow due usually to obstruction, as of the blood or lymph, or of the intestinal contents. **2** E20 *generally* Inactivity; stagnation; a state of equilibrium. **3** M20 *Psychoanalysis* The presence of high energy or excitement in the libido caused especially by repression and thought to produce neurosis. **4** M20 Party faction, civil strife.

status /ˈsteɪtəs/ *noun* plural **statuses**, (*rare*) same L17 **Latin** (from *stat-* past participial stem of *stare* to stand). **1** *Medicine* **a** The crisis of a disease. *rare*. Only in L17. **b** L19 A state, a condition. Only with modern Latin specifying word (e.g. *status epilepticus* a condition in which epileptic fits follow one another without pause). **2** L18 Chiefly *Law* A person's standing or position such as determines his or her legal rights or limitations; condition in respect of marriage or celibacy, minority or majority, etc. **3** E19 Position or standing in society; rank, profession; relative importance; *specifically* (a) superior social etc. position. Also *social status*. **4** M19 Condition or position of a thing, especially with regard to importance.

status quo /ˌsteɪtəs ˈkwəʊ/ *noun phrase* M19 **Latin** (= the state in which). The existing state of affairs.

1996 *Times* This was the *status quo*, and it was a brave Tory who dared to challenge it.

status quo ante /ˌsteɪtəs ˌkwəʊ ˈanti/ *noun phrase* L19 **Latin** (= the state in which before). The previously existing state of affairs.

1996 *Spectator* Those who framed the peace treaties had objectives far beyond restoring the *status quo ante*, which would in most cases have been impossible.

stela /'sti:lə/ *noun* plural **stelae** /'sti:li:/ L18 **Latin** (from as STELE). *Antiquities* An upright slab or pillar, usually bearing a commemorative inscription or sculptured design and often serving as a gravestone.

stele /sti:l/, /'sti:li/ *noun* plural **steles**, (especially in sense 1) **stelae** /'sti:li:/ E19 **Greek** (*stēlē* standing block; cf. STELA). **1** E19 *Antiquities* A stela. Also *loosely*, any prepared surface on the face of a building, rock, etc., bearing an inscription. **2** L19 *Botany* The central core of the stem and root of a vascular plant.

stelline /stɛ'li:ni/ *noun plural* (also **stellini**) M20 **Italian** (from *stellina* diminutive of *stella* star). Small star-shaped pieces of pasta.

stelling /'stɛlɪŋ/ *noun* M19 **Dutch** (from *stellen* to place). In Guyana and the Caribbean: a wooden pier or landing-stage.

stemma /'stɛmə/ *noun* plural **stemmata** /'stɛmətə/ M17 **Latin** (from Greek (= garland), from *stephein* to crown). **1a** M17 A recorded genealogy of a family, a family tree; a pedigree. **b** M20 A diagram representing a reconstruction of the interrelationships between surviving witnesses in the (especially manuscript) tradition of a text. **2** E19 *Zoology* In arthropods, a simple eye, an ocellus.

steppe /stɛp/ *noun* L17 **Russian** (*step'*). Any of the vast level grassy usually treeless plains of South East Europe and Siberia. Also, any similar plain elsewhere.

stet /stɛt/ *noun & verb* M18 **Latin** (3rd person singular present subjunctive of *stare* = let it stand). **A** *noun* M18 A direction in the margin of a proof-sheet etc. indicating that a correction or deletion should be ignored and that the original matter is to be retained. **B** *transitive verb* L19 (inflected *-tt*) Cancel the correction or deletion of; write 'stet' against (an accidental deletion, miscorrection, etc.).

stiacciato /stja'tʃɑ:təʊ/ *noun* (also **schiacciato** /skja'tʃɑ:təʊ/) M19 **Italian** (*schiacciato*, *stiacciato* past participle of *schiacciare*, *stiacciare* to flatten). *Sculpture* Very low relief. Also more fully *stiacciato-relievo*, *relievo stiacciato*.

stifado /stɪ'fɑ:dəʊ/ *noun* plural **stifados** M20 **Modern Greek** (*stiphado* probably from Italian *stufato*). A Greek dish of meat stewed with onions and sometimes tomatoes.

stigma /'stɪgmə/ *noun* plural **stigmas**, **stigmata** /'stɪgmətə/, /stɪg'mɑ:tə/ L16 **Latin** (from Greek *stigma*, *stigmat-*, from base of *stizein* to prick). **1** L16 A mark made on the skin by pricking, cutting, or (especially) branding, as a sign of disgrace or subjection. **b** M17 (in *plural*) Marks resembling the wounds on Jesus' crucified body, said to have appeared on the bodies of certain saints etc. **2a** E17 A mark or sign of disgrace or discredit, regarded as impressed on or carried by a person or thing. **b** M19 A visible or apparent characteristic indicative of some (especially undesirable or discreditable) quality, action, or circumstance (followed by *of*); *Medicine* a visible sign *of* a disease or condition. **3** M18 *Zoology* **a** A small external opening or pore. **b** E19 A natural spot or mark. **4** M18 *Botany* That part of the pistil in flowering plants which receives the pollen in impregnation.

2.a 1996 *Country Life* But generally it can be said that divorce has lost most, if not all, of its social stigma.

stile antico /ˌstile an'tiko/ *noun phrase* M20 **Italian** (= old style). *Music* The strict contrapuntal style of the sixteenth century, especially as exemplified in the works of Palestrina.

stile concitato /ˌstile kontʃi'tato/ *noun phrase* E20 **Italian** (= excited style). *Music* A baroque style developed by Monteverdi, emphasizing dramatic expression and excitement.

stile rappresentativo /ˌstile ˌrapprezenta'tivo/ *noun phrase* L19 **Italian** (= representative style). *Music* The vocal style of recitative used by Italian musicians of the early seventeenth century.

stiletto /stɪ'lɛtəʊ/ *noun* E17 **Italian** (diminutive of *stilo* dagger, ultimately from Latin *stilus* stylus). **A** *noun* plural **stiletto(e)s**. **1** E17 A short dagger with a thick blade. **2** E19 A small pointed instrument for making eyelet-holes. **3** M20 A very high tapering heel on a woman's shoe; a shoe with such a heel. In full *stiletto heel*.

Stimmung /'ʃtɪmʊŋ/ *noun* E20 **German**. Mood, spirit, atmosphere, feeling.

stimulus /'stɪmjʊləs/ *noun* plural **stimuli** /'stɪmjʊlʌɪ/, /'stɪmjʊli:/ L17 **Latin** (= goad, spur, incentive, probably from base also of *stilus* stylus). **1** L17 A thing that provokes, increases, or quickens bodily activity. **b** L18 *generally* An agency or influence that rouses or spurs something or someone to action or quickens an activity or process; a spur, an incentive (followed by *to* an action etc.) **c** L19 *Psychology* Any change or event which excites a nerve impulse and gives rise to a response or reaction. **2** L17 The effect or property of producing such a reaction; stimulation; an instance of this.

stoa /ˈstəʊə/ *noun* plural **stoas**, **stoai** /ˈstəʊʌɪ/ E17 **Greek**. **1** E17 (*the Stoa*) The great hall in ancient Athens in which the philosopher Zeno lectured; the Stoic school of philosophy. **2** L18 A portico, a roofed colonnade.

■ The followers of Zeno (335–263 BC) were accordingly called Stoics.

stoep /stuːp/ *noun* L18 **Afrikaans** (from Dutch, related to *step*, from West Germanic; cf. STOOP). In South Africa: a raised platform or veranda running along the front and sometimes round the sides of a house.

stollen /ˈstɒlən/, /ˈʃtɒlən/ *noun* E20 **German**. A rich fruit loaf, often with nuts added.

stoop /stuːp/ *noun* M18 **Dutch** (cf. STOEP). A small raised platform at the entrance door of a house; a set of steps approaching this; a small porch or veranda. *North American*.

stoss /stɒs/, *foreign* /ʃtoːs/ *adjective* L19 **German** (= thrust, push). *Geology* Designating the side of an object that faces a flow of ice or water.

strabismus /strəˈbɪzməs/ *noun* L17 **Modern Latin** (from Greek *strabismos*, from *strabizein* to squint, from *strabos* squinting). **1** L17 *Medicine* A disorder of the eye-muscles resulting in an inability to direct the gaze of both eyes to the same object simultaneously; squinting, a squint. **2** M19 *figurative* Perversity of intellectual perception.

stracchino /straˈkiːnəʊ/ *noun* M19 **Italian**. A variety of soft cheese made in the north of Italy. In full *stracchino cheese*.

stracciatella /ˌstratʃəˈtɛlə/ *noun* M20 **Italian**. An Italian soup made with stock, eggs, and cheese.

strapontin /strapɔ̃tɛ̃/ *noun* plural pronounced same E20 **French**. A tip-up seat, usually additional to the ordinary seating in a theatre, taxi, etc., especially in France.

strata plural of STRATUM.

strath /straθ/ *noun* M16 **Gaelic** (*Scottish s(t)rath* = Old Irish *srath* (modern *sraith*)). A broad river valley bounded by hills or high ground. Formerly also, a stretch of flat land by the waterside.

stratum /ˈstrɑːtəm/, /ˈstreɪtəm/ *noun* plural **strata** /ˈstrɑːtə/, /ˈstreɪtə/ L16 **Modern Latin** (use of Latin *stratum*, literally, 'something spread or laid down', neuter past participle of *sternere* to lay down, throw down). **1** L16 *generally* A quantity of a substance or material spread over a nearly horizontal surface to a more or less uniform thickness; *especially* each of two or more parallel layers or coats successively superposed one upon another. **2** L17 A bed of sedimentary rock, usually consisting of a series of layers of the same kind. **3** M18 *Anatomy* and *Biology* Each of a number of layers composing an animal or plant tissue or structure (frequently with modern Latin specifying word). Also *Ecology*, a layer of vegetation in a plant community. **4** L18 A region of the atmosphere, of the sea, or of a quantity of fluid, assumed for purposes of calculation to be bounded by horizontal planes. **5** E19 *figurative* **a** A portion of a body of institutions, a set of traditions, an artist's work, etc., originating from one historical period, or representing one stage of development or level of analysis. **b** M19 (Part of a population belonging to) a particular level or grade in social status, education, etc. **6** E20 *Statistics* Each of the groups into which a population is divided in the technique of stratified sampling.

strepitoso /strɛpɪˈtəʊsəʊ/ *adverb, adjective, & noun* E19 **Italian** (literally, 'noisy, loud'). *Music* **A** *adverb & adjective* E19 (A direction:) spirited(ly), boisterous(ly). **B** *noun* M20 A spirited or boisterous piece or passage.

stretta /ˈstrɛtə/ *noun* plural **strette** /ˈstrɛti/, **strettas** L19 **Italian** (feminine of STRETTO). *Music* A final passage played at a (gradually) faster tempo.

stretto /ˈstrɛtəʊ/ *adverb & noun* M18 **Italian** (literally, 'narrow'). *Music* **A** *adverb* M18 (A direction:) with gradually increasing speed (especially in a final passage). **B** *noun* M19 A fugal device in which subject entries follow closely in succession.

streusel /'strɔɪz(ə)l/, /'stru:z(ə)l/ *noun* E20 **German** (from *streuen* to sprinkle). (A cake or pastry with) a crumbly topping or filling made from fat, flour, cinnamon, and sugar.

■ Chiefly North American and frequently attributive as in *streusel cake*.

stria /'strʌɪə/ *noun* plural **striae** /'strʌɪi:/ M16 **Latin** (= furrow, grooving). **1** M16 *Architecture* A fillet between the flutes of a column, pilaster, etc. **2** L17 Chiefly *Science* A small groove, channel, or ridge; a narrow streak, stripe, or band of distinctive colour, structure, or texture; *especially* each of two or more.

stricto sensu /ˌstrɪktəʊ 'sɛnsu:/ *adverb & adjective phrase* M20 **Latin** (= in the restricted sense). SENSU STRICTO.

striges /'strʌɪdʒi:z/ *noun plural* M16 **Latin**. *Architecture* The fillets of a fluted column.

■ Deriving from the writings of the Roman architectural authority Vitruvius (*c*.50–26BC), *striges* is perhaps a misreading of *striae* (see STRIA) or *strigae* 'row, strip'.

stringendo /strɪn'dʒɛndəʊ/ *adverb, adjective, & noun* M19 **Italian** (present participle of *stringere* to press, squeeze, bind together, from Latin *stringere* to bind). *Music* **A** *adverb & adjective* M19 (*A direction:*) *with increasing speed and excitement.* **B** *noun* M20 plural **stringendos**, **stringendi** /strɪn'dʒɛndi/. An increase of speed and excitement; a passage (to be) played with such an increase.

strophe /'strəʊfi/ *noun* plural **strophes** /'strəʊfɪz/, **strophae** /'strəʊfi:/ E17 **Greek** (*strophē* (whence late Latin *stropha*), literally, 'turning', from *stroph-* ablaut variant of base of *strephein* to turn). Originally, a movement from right to left in Greek choruses and dances, answered by an ANTISTROPHE; the lines of choral song recited during this movement. Also (*Prosody*), a metrically structured section of a usually Greek choral ode or lyric verse, the structure of which is repeated in an antistrophe. More widely, a group of lines forming a section of a lyric poem.

strudel /'stru:d(ə)l/, /'ʃtru:d(ə)l/ *noun* L19 **German** (literally, 'eddy, whirlpool'). A confection of thin layers of flaky pastry rolled up round a usually fruit filling and baked.

Stube /'ʃtu:bə/ *noun* plural **Stuben** /'ʃtu:bən/ M20 **German** (= room). A BIERSTUBE.

stucco /'stʌkəʊ/ *noun* plural **stuccoes** L16 **Italian** (ultimately from Germanic). **1a** L16 A fine plaster, especially made from gypsum and pulverized marble, for covering walls, ceilings, etc., and making cornices and other architectural decorations. **b** M18 A coarse plaster or calcareous cement especially for covering a rough exterior surface to give the appearance of stone. **c** M19 Plaster of Paris. **2** L17 The process of ornamenting walls, ceilings, etc. with stucco; work or ornamentation produced by this process. **b** L20 A building plastered with stucco.

studiolo /studi'olo/ *noun* plural **studioli** /studi'oli/ E20 **Italian** (= small study). In Italy: a private study hung with paintings.

1996 *Country Life* . . . apart from the building's splendid chimneypieces, two overdoors in the Queen's apartment and the panelling in François I's *studiolo*, there was no original decoration left.

studium generale /ˌstju:dɪəm dʒɛnə'reɪleɪ/, /ˌstju:dɪəm dʒɛnə'rɑ:leɪ/ *noun phrase* plural **studia generalia** /ˌstju:dɪə dʒɛnə'reɪlɪə/, /ˌstju:dɪə dʒɛnə'rɑ:lɪə/ M19 **Latin** (*studium* zeal, application (to learning) + neuter singular of *generalis* general). *History* In the Middle Ages, a university attended by students from outside as well as within its own locality.

stupa /'stu:pə/ *noun* L19 **Sanskrit** (*stūpa*). A round usually domed structure erected as a Buddhist shrine.

Sturm und Drang /ˌʃtʊrm ʊnt 'draŋ/ *noun phrase* M19 **German** (literally, 'storm and stress'). (The period of) a radical movement in German literature in the late 1770s characterized by the violent expression of emotion and the rejection of neoclassical literary norms; *transferred* (a period of) emotion, stress, or turbulence.

■ *Sturm und Drang* was the title of a 1776 play by Friedrich Maximilian Klinger (1752–1831).

transferred **1996** *Times* There are effective supporting performances from Paul Jesson as an implacable Burleigh, Ben Miles as a *Sturm und Drang* hero who wants simultaneously to rape and rescue Mary . . .

stylus /'stʌɪləs/ *noun* plural **styli** /'stʌɪlʌɪ/, /'stʌɪli:/, **styluses** E18 **Latin** (erroneous spelling of Latin *stilus* writing implement (influenced by the spelling of Greek *stulos* column)). **1** E18 *Botany* A projection of the ovary bearing the stigma. Now *rare*. **2** E19 An ancient implement for incising letters on wax. **3** M19 *Zoology* A small slender pointed process or part. **4** L19 A tracing-point used to produce a written record in a chart recorder, telegraph receiver, etc. **b** L19 A hard (especially diamond or sapphire) point following a groove in a record and transmitting the recorded sound for reproduction; a similar point used to make such a groove when producing a record; a needle.

■ Senses 1–3 are also found in the English form *style*.

subbotnik /suːˈbɒtnɪk/ *noun* plural **subbotniki** /suːˈbɒtnɪki/, **subbotniks** E20 **Russian** (from *subbota* Saturday + noun suffix *-nik* person connected with (something)). In countries of the former USSR: the practice or an act of working voluntarily on a Saturday, for the benefit of the national economy.

subgum /ˈsʌbgʌm/ *noun* (also **sub gum**, **sup gum** /ˈsʌpgʌm/ E20 **Chinese** ((Cantonese) *shâp kám*, from *shâp* mixed + *kám* brocade). A Chinese dish of mixed vegetables, as water chestnuts, mushrooms, bean sprouts, etc.

subito /ˈsuːbɪtəʊ/ *adverb* E18 **Italian**. *Music* (A direction:) suddenly, quickly.

sub judice /sʌb ˈdʒuːdɪsi/, /sʊb ˈjuːdɪkeɪ/ *adjective phrase* E17 **Latin** (literally, 'under a judge'). *Law* Under the consideration of a judge or court and therefore prohibited from public discussion elsewhere.

sub rosa /sʌb ˈrəʊzə/ *adjective & adverb phrase* M17 **Latin** (literally, 'under the rose'). Of communication, consultation, etc.: (given, told, etc.) in secrecy or confidence.

■ The concept of the rose as a symbol of confidentiality or secrecy may have originated in Germany and is enshrined in the German phrase *unter der rose* (cf. Early Modern Dutch *onder de roose*).

sub silentio /sʌb sɪˈlɛntɪəʊ/, /sʌb sɪ ˈlɛnʃɪəʊ/ *adverb phrase* E17 **Latin** (literally, 'under silence'). In silence, without remark.

sub specie aeternitatis /sʌb ˈspiːʃiː ɪˌtəːnɪˈtɑːtɪs/ *adverb phrase* L19 **Latin** (literally, 'under the aspect of eternity'). Viewed in relation to the eternal; in a universal perspective.

■ In Spinoza's *Ethices* (*Posthuma Opera* (1677) V.xxix.254). The opposite of SUB SPECIE TEMPORIS.

sub specie temporis /sʌb ˌspiːʃiː tɛm ˈpɔːrɪs/ *adverb phrase* L19 **Latin** (literally 'under the aspect of time'). Viewed in relation to time rather than eternity.

1960 *Encounter Sub specie temporis* his Combination Rooms say more to us than Beckett's wet and windy plains.

substratum /sʌbˈstrɑːtəm/, /sʌb ˈstreɪtəm/ *noun* plural **substrata** /sʌb ˈstrɑːtə/, (*rare*) **substratums** M17 **Modern Latin** (use as noun of neuter past participle of Latin *substernere*, from *sub-* under + *sternere* to lay down, throw down). **1** M17 *Metaphysics* That which is regarded as supporting attributes or accidents; the substance in which qualities inhere. **2** M17 An underlying layer or substance; the basis or foundation of a structure, condition, activity, etc. **3** M18 An underlayer of soil or earth. **4** E20 *Linguistics* Elements or features of a language identified as being relics of, or due to the influence of, an earlier extinct language.

sub verbo /sʌb ˈvəːbəʊ/ *adverb phrase* E20 **Latin**. SUB VOCE.

sub voce /sʌb ˈvəʊsi/, /ˈvəʊtʃi/ *adverb phrase* M19 **Latin**. (As a direction in a text:) under the word or heading given; SUB VERBO.

■ Abbreviated to *s.v.*.

succah /ˈsʊkə/ *noun* **succoth** /ˈsʊkɒt/ L19 **Hebrew** (*sukkāh*, literally, 'hut'). Any of the booths in which a practising Jew spends part of the feast of Tabernacles (Succoth).

succedaneum /sʌksɪˈdemɪəm/ *noun* plural **succedanea** /sʌksɪˈdemɪə/, **succedaneums** E17 **Modern Latin** (neuter singular of Latin *succedaneus* from *succedere* to come close after). **1** E17 A thing which takes the place of another; a substitute; *specifically* a medicine or drug substituted for another. (Followed by *for*, *of*, *to*.) **2** M–L18 A remedy, a cure.

succès d'estime /syksɛ dɛstim/ *noun phrase* M19 **French** (= success of opinion or regard). A critical as opposed to a popular or commercial success.

1996 *Spectator* Being a *succès d'estime* is not enough for a mid-market newspaper which must rely on a much wider constituency than the chattering classes.

succès de scandale /syksɛ də skɑ̃dal/ *noun phrase* L19 **French** (= success of scandal). Success due to notoriety or scandalous character.

1996 *Spectator* His book had achieved a notable *succès de scandale* in this town, particularly amongst the Society's older members who remembered many of the characters mentioned.

succès fou /syksɛ fu/ *noun phrase* L19 **French** (= mad success). A success marked by wild enthusiasm.

1996 *Times* I picked Newell because he had used my drawing-room to shoot a scene of a previous *succès fou* of his, *Enchanted April*.

succi plural of SUCCUS.

succuba /'sʌkjʊbə/ *noun* plural **succubae** /'sʌkjʊbiː/ L16 **Late Latin** (= prostitute, from *succubare* from *sub-* under + *cubare* to lie. A SUCCUBUS.

succubus /'sʌkjʊbəs/ *noun* plural **succubi** /'sʌkjʊbʌɪ/ LME **Medieval Latin** (masculine form (with feminine meaning) corresponding to SUCCUBA, after INCUBUS). **1** LME A demon in female form supposed to have sexual intercourse with sleeping men. **b** E17 *generally* A demon, an evil spirit. **2** E17 A prostitute, a whore. *archaic* and *derogatory*.

succus /'sʌkəs/ *noun* plural **succi** /'sʌk(s)ʌɪ/, /'sʌk(s)iː/ L18 **Latin**. A juice; a fluid secretion in an animal or plant.

sucrier /'suːkrɪeɪ/, *foreign* /sykrie/ (*plural same*) *noun* M19 **French** (from *sucre* sugar). A sugar bowl, usually made of porcelain and with a cover.

sudarium /suː'dɛːrɪəm/, /sjuː'dɛːrɪəm/ *noun* plural **sudaria** /suː'dɛːrɪə/ E17 **Latin** (from *sudor* sweat). **1** E17 A cloth for wiping the face. **2** E17 A cloth with a likeness of Christ's face on it, a veronica. **3** M19 Chiefly *Roman Antiquities* A steam or hot air bath.

sudd /sʌd/ *noun* L19 **Arabic** (= obstruction, dam, from *sadda* to obstruct, block, congest). **1** L19 An area of floating vegetation which impedes navigation on the White Nile. **2** L19 *transferred* A temporary dam across a river.

suede /sweɪd/ *noun & adjective* (also **suède**) M17 **French** (*Suède* Sweden). **A** *noun* M17 Leather, originally especially kidskin, with the flesh side rubbed to make a velvety nap; a shoe or other article made of this. **B** *attributive or as adjective* L19 Made of suede.

■ The French phrase *gants de Suède* 'gloves of Sweden' was misunderstood as referring to the material rather than to the country of origin.

suggestio falsi /sə,dʒɛstɪəʊ 'falsʌɪ/ *noun phrase* plural **suggestiones falsi** /sə ,dʒɛstɪ,əʊniːz/ E19 **Modern Latin** (literally, 'suggestion of what is false'). A misrepresentation of the truth whereby something incorrect is implied to be true.

■ Often in contexts with the associated verbal stratagem of SUPPRESSIO VERI (see quotation).

1980 D. Newsome *On Edge of Paradise* There are undoubted cases of *suppressio veri*; on the other hand, he appears to eschew *suggestio falsi*.

suiboku /'suːɪbəʊkuː/ *noun* E20 **Japanese** (literally, 'liquid ink', from *sui* water + *boku* ink stick). A style of Japanese painting, using black ink on a white surface and characterized by bold brush-work and subtle tones.

sui generis /suːʌɪ 'dʒɛn(ə)rɪs/, /suːiː/; /sjuːɪ 'dʒɛn(ə)rɪs/ *adjective phrase* L18 **Latin**. Of its own kind; peculiar, unique.

1996 *Spectator* Major's rhinocerine obstinacy in putting his personal political survival before any other consideration is *sui generis* . . .

sui juris /suːʌɪ 'dʒʊərɪs/, /suːɪ 'dʒʊərɪs/, /sjuːɪ 'dʒʊərɪs/ *adjective phrase* E17 **Latin** (literally, 'of one's own right'). *Law* **1** E17 *Roman History* Of the status of a person who was not subject to paternal authority. **2** L17 Of full age and capacity.

suite /swiːt/ *noun* L17 **French**. **1** L17 A set of people in attendance; a retinue. **2** E18 A succession, a series; a set of things belonging together. **3** E18 *specifically* **a** A set of rooms in a hotel etc. for use by one person or group of people. **b** M18 *Music* Originally, a set or series of lessons etc. Later, a set of instrumental compositions, in dance style, to be played in succession; a set of selected pieces from an opera, ballet, etc., arranged to be played as one instrumental work. **c** E19 A set of furniture, especially a sofa and armchairs, of the same design. **d** M19 *Geology* A group of associated minerals, rocks, or fossils, especially from the same place; an associated sequence of strata etc. that is repeated at different localities.

suk, **sukh** variants of SOUK.

sukiya /sʊ'kiːyə/ *noun* E20 **Japanese** (literally, 'room of fantasy, room of refined taste'). **1** E20 A room in which the tea ceremony is held, a tea-house. **2** M20 *Archi-*

tecture A style of Japanese architecture inspired by a certain type of tea-house, characterized by functionality of design and the use of wood and other natural materials. Frequently *attributive*.

sukiyaki /sʊkɪˈjaki/, /sʊkɪˈjɑːki/ *noun* E20 **Japanese**. A Japanese dish consisting of thin slices of beef fried with vegetables in sugar, stock, and soy sauce.

sultan /ˈsʌlt(ə)n/ *noun* M16 **French** (or medieval Latin *sultanus*, from Arabic *sulṭān* power, ruler). **1** M16 The monarch or chief ruler of a Muslim country. **b** M17 An absolute ruler; a despot, a tyrant. **2** M17 A plant of the Near East grown for its sweet-scented purple, pink, white, or yellow flowers. Originally more fully *sultan's flower*; now usually *sweet sultan*. **3** M19 A small white-crested variety of domestic fowl, originally brought from Turkey.

sultana /sʌlˈtɑːnə/, *in sense 5 also* /s(ə)lˈtɑːnə/ *noun* L16 **Italian** (feminine of *sultano* sultan). **1** L16 A wife or concubine of a sultan; the queen mother or any other woman of a sultan's family. **2** E18 A mistress, a concubine. **3** E18 A Turkish warship. *obsolete* except *historical*. **4** M19 Any of various gallinules, *especially* the purple gallinule. Now *rare*. **5** M19 A kind of small seedless raisin used in puddings, cakes, etc. **6** M20 The plant Busy Lizzie, *Impatiens walleriana*.

sulu /ˈsuːluː/ *noun* M19 **Fijian**. In Fiji: a length of cotton or other light fabric wrapped about the body as a sarong; a type of sarong worn from the waist by men and full-length by women; a similar fashion garment worn by women.

sumi /ˈsuːmi/ *noun* E20 **Japanese** (= ink, blacking). A carbon-based pigment used for painting and writing.

summa /ˈsʊmə/, /ˈsʌmə/ *noun & adverb* plural **summae** /ˈsʊmiː/, **summa(e)s** LME **Latin**. **1** LME–L18 A sum total. **2** L15–E16 The quantity or number *of* something. **3** E18 A treatise, a manual; a compendium of knowledge. **4** L20 A degree SUMMA CUM LAUDE.

> **3 1996** *Country Life* Bach's artistic last will and testament, *The Art of Fugue*, is a musical *summa* which demonstrates the expressive power of his beloved counterpoint.

summa bona plural of SUMMUM BONUM.

summa cum laude /ˌsʌmə kʌm ˈlɔːdiː/, /ˌsʊmə kʊm ˈlaʊdeɪ/ *adverb & adjective phrase* L19 **Latin** (literally, 'with the highest praise'). With or of highest distinction; *specifically* (of a degree, diploma, etc.) of the highest standard.

■ Chiefly North American; cf. CUM LAUDE, MAGNA CUM LAUDE.

summae see SUMMA.

summa genera plural of SUMMUM GENUS.

summum bonum /ˌsʊməm ˈbɒnəm/, /ˌsʌməm ˈbəʊnəm/ *noun phrase* plural **summa bona** /ˌsʊmə ˈbɒnə, /ˌsʌmə ˈbəʊnə/ M16 **Latin** (= highest good). The chief or a supreme good; *specifically* (*Ethics*) the highest good as the end or determining principle in an ethical system.

summum genus /ˌsʊməm ˈdʒɛnəs/, /ˌsʌməm ˈdʒiːnəs/ *noun* plural **summa genera** /ˌsʊmə ˈdʒɛn(ə)rə/, /ˌsʌmə/ L16 **Latin** (= highest kind). The highest or most comprehensive class in a classification; *specifically* (*Logic*) a genus not considered as a species of a higher genus.

summum jus /ˌsʊməm ˈjuːs/, /ˌsʌməm ˈdʒʌs/ *noun* L16 **Latin** (= highest law). The utmost rigour of the law, extreme severity.

sumo /ˈsuːməʊ/ *noun* plural **sumos**, same L19 **Japanese** (*sūmo*). A Japanese form of heavyweight wrestling in which a wrestler wins a bout by forcing his opponent outside a circle or making him touch the ground with any part of the body except the soles of the feet. Also, a sumo wrestler.

sumotori /ˌsuːməʊˈtɔːri/ *noun* L20 **Japanese** (*sūmotori*, from as preceding + *tori* taking). A sumo wrestler.

sumpsimus /ˈsʌm(p)sɪməs/ *noun* M16 **Latin** (1st person plural perfect indicative of *sumere* to take). A correct expression taking the place of an incorrect but popular one.

■ Cf. MUMPSIMUS. The expressions usually occur together in contexts contrasting obtuse conservatism with a more enlightened attitude.

sunyata /ˈʃuːnjətɑː/, /ˈsuːnjətɑː/ *noun* E20 **Sanskrit** (*śūnyatā* emptiness, from *śūnya* empty, void). *Buddhism* The doctrine that phenomena are devoid of an immutable or determinate intrinsic nature, often regarded as a means of gaining an intuition of ultimate reality.

superficies /ˌsuːpəˈfɪʃɪiːz/, /ˌsjuːpəˈfɪʃɪiːz/ *noun* plural same M16 **Latin** (from *super-*

above + *facies* face). **1** M16 *Geometry* A magnitude of two dimensions, having only length and breadth; a surface. **2 a** L16 The outer surface of an object. **b** E17 A surface layer. Now *rare.* **3a** L16–L18 A thing likened to a surface; the outward form or aspect. **b** L16 The outward appearance as distinct from the real nature. **4** M17 Superficial area or extent. **5** M19 *Roman Law* A structure in or on the surface of a piece of land which is so closely connected with it as to form part of it.

suppositum /səˈpɒzɪtəm/ *noun* plural **supposita** /səˈpɒzɪtə/ M17 **Medieval Latin** (use as noun of neuter singular of *suppositus* past participle of *supponere* to place under). **1** M17 *Metaphysics* A being that subsists by itself, an individual thing or person; occasionally, a being in relation to its attributes. Long *rare* or *obsolete.* **2** M19 *Logic* An assumption.

suppressio veri /səˌprɛʃɪəʊ ˈvɪərʌɪ/ *noun phrase* plural **suppressiones veri** /səˌprɛʃɪˌəʊniːz/ M18 **Modern Latin** (literally, 'suppression of what is true'). A misrepresentation of the truth by concealing facts which ought to be made known.

■ In use often linked with SUGGESTIO FALSI (at which see quotation).

supra /ˈsuːprə/, /ˈsjuːprə/ *adverb & adjective* E16 **Latin.** **A** *adverb* **1** E16 Earlier in a book or article; above. Cf. UT SUPRA. **2** L16–L18 In addition, besides. **B** *adjective* L16–L18 Additional, extra.

suprême /syprɛm/, /suːˈprɛm/ *noun* E19 **French.** A rich cream sauce; a dish of especially chicken breasts cooked in this sauce.

■ Latterly (M20) often Anglicized as *supreme,* as in *chicken supreme.*

supremo /suːˈpriːməʊ/, /suːˈpreɪməʊ/, /sjuːˈpriːməʊ/ *noun* plural **supremos** M20 **Spanish** ((*generalísimo*) *supremo* supreme general). **1** M20 A supreme leader or ruler. **2** M20 *transferred* A person in overall charge of something.

■ *Supremo* was the nickname given to Earl Mountbatten of Burma during his time as Supreme Allied Commander, South East Asia.

2 1983 *Private Eye* A short list of possible replacements . . . included . . . the ruthless supremo of the Royal Philharmonic Orchestra.

suq variant of SOUK.

sura /ˈsʊərə/ *noun* E17 **Arabic** (*sūra*, (with definite article) *as-sūra*, probably from Syriac *ṣūrṭā* scripture). Any of the sections of the Koran.

■ *Sura* (M17) supplanted the now obsolete form *assura* (incorporating the Arabic definite article), in which the word was first used in English.

surah /ˈsʊərə/, /ˈsjʊərə/ *noun & adjective* L19 **French** (representing French pronunciation of *Surat* a port in India). (Of) a soft twilled silk fabric.

surbahar /ˈsʊəbəhɑː/ *noun* L19 **Bengali** (*surbāhār*). A mellow-toned Indian stringed instrument, a bass sitar.

surimono /ˌsʊərɪˈməʊnəʊ/ *noun* plural same L19 **Japanese** (from *suri* printing + *mono* thing). A print; *specifically* a small Japanese colour print used to convey greetings or to mark a special occasion.

sur place /syr plas/ *adverb phrase* E20 **French.** **1** E20 At the place in question; on the spot. **2** M20 *Ballet* Without leaving the place where one has been standing.

Sursum corda /ˌsəːs(ə)m ˈkɔːdə/ *noun phrase* M16 **Latin** (from *sursum* upwards + *corda* plural of *cor* heart). *Christian Church* In Latin Eucharistic liturgies, the words addressed by the celebrant to the congregation at the beginning of the Eucharistic Prayer; in English rites, the corresponding versicle, 'Lift up your hearts'.

surveillant /syrvɛjɑ̃/, /səːˈveɪl(ə)nt/ *noun & adjective* (also (feminine) **surveillante** /syrvɛjɑ̃t/, /ˌsəːveɪˈjɑːnt/) E19 **French** ((use as noun of) present participle of *surveiller* to watch over, from as *sur-* over + *veiller* to keep watch, from Latin *vigilare*). **A** *noun* **1** E19 A person who exercises surveillance. **2** M19 A teacher on non-teaching duty. **B** *adjective* M19 Exercising surveillance.

■ The corresponding noun *surveillance* (E19) is now fully Anglicized.

sushi /ˈsuːʃi/, /ˈsʊʃi/ *noun* L19 **Japanese.** A Japanese dish consisting of rolls of cold boiled rice flavoured with vinegar and garnished with raw fish.

1996 *Times* From the earliest records, fish have had a fried deal from chippers and a raw deal from sushi-eaters.

susurrus /sjuːˈsʌrəs/, /suːˈsʌrəs/ *noun* LME **Latin** (= a whisper, humming, muttering, of imitative origin). **1** Malicious whispering. Only in LME. **2** E19 A low soft whispering or rustling sound.

■ Only in literary use.

sutra /ˈsuːtrə/ *noun* E19 **Sanskrit** (*sūtra* thread, string, rule). **1** E19 In Sanskrit literature, a rule or aphorism, or a set of these, on grammar, or Hindu law or philosophy, expressed with maximum brevity. **2** L19 A Buddhist scripture, usually doctrinal in content. Also, the Jain scriptures.

suttee /sʌ'tiː/, /'sʌti/ *noun* (also **sati**) L18 **Sanskrit** (*satī* faithful wife, feminine of *sat* good). Chiefly *History* **1** L18 A Hindu widow who immolates herself on her husband's funeral pyre. **2** E19 The immolation of a Hindu widow in this way.

suzuribako /sə,zʊərɪ'bɑːkəʊ/ *noun* plural same M20 **Japanese** (from *suzuri* slab for ink + *hako* box). A box, often of finely-wrought lacquer-work, for holding Japanese writing implements.

s.v. abbreviation of SUB VOCE.

svelte /svɛlt/ *adjective* E19 **French** (from Italian *svelto*). **1** E19 Slender, willowy. **2** E20 *transferred* Elegant, graceful.

swami /'swɑːmi/ *noun* (also **swamy**) L18 **Sanskrit** (*svāmin*, nominative *svāmī*, master, prince). **1** L18 A Hindu image or temple. **2** E20 A male Hindu religious teacher.

swart gevaar /,swart xə'fɑːr/ *noun phrase* M20 **Afrikaans** (literally, 'black peril', from Dutch *zwart* black + *gevaar* danger). The threat to the Western way of life and White supremacy in South Africa believed by some to be posed by the Blacks. *South African*.

1996 T. Alexander *Unravelling Global Apartheid Die swart gevaar*—the black danger—united the white minority after their savage conflict in the Boer War.

swastika /'swɒstɪkə/ *noun* L19 **Sanskrit** (*svastika* from *svasti* well-being, luck, from *su* good + *asti* being). **1** L19 An ancient symbol in the form of a cross with equal arms with a limb of the same length projecting at right angles from the end of each arm, all in the same direction and (usually) clockwise. **2** M20 This symbol (with clockwise projecting limbs) used as the emblem of the German and other Nazi parties; a HAKENKREUZ. Also, a flag bearing this emblem.

syce /sʌɪs/ *noun* (also **sais**) M17 **Persian and Urdu** (*sā'is* from Arabic). In parts of Africa and Asia, and especially in the Indian subcontinent: a groom, a servant who attends to horses, drives carriages, etc.; a chauffeur. Also, an attendant following on foot a mounted rider or a carriage.

sylva /'sɪlvə/ *noun* (also **silva**) plural **sylvae** /'sɪlviː/, **sylvas** M17 **Latin** (*silva* a wood, woodland (misspelt *sylva* after synonymous Greek *hulē* wood); in sense 2, after the title (*Silvae*) of Statius' collection of occasional poems). **1** M17 A treatise on forest trees; (a descriptive catalogue of) the trees of a particular region. Cf. FLORA sense 2. **2** M17–L18 A collection of pieces, especially of poems.

■ The spelling *sylva* in English treatises on arboriculture is a tribute to the authority of John Evelyn's *Sylva; or a discourse of Forest Trees and the propagation of timber* (1664), which for many years remained the standard English text in its field.

symbiosis /,sɪmbɪ'əʊsɪs/, /,sɪmbʌɪ'əʊsɪs/ *noun* plural **symbioses** /,sɪmbɪ'əʊsiːz/ E17 **Modern Latin** (from Greek *sumbiōsis* a living together, from *sumbioun* to live together, from *sumbios* (adjective) living together, (noun) companion, partner, from *sym* together + *bios* life). **1** E17 Living together, communal living. *rare*. **2** L19 *Biology* An interaction between two dissimilar organisms living in close physical association; *especially* one in which each benefits the other. **3** E20 *transferred* and *figurative* A relationship or association of mutual advantage between people, organizations, etc.

sympathique /sɛ̃patik/ *adjective* M19 **French**. Of a thing, a place, etc.: agreeable, to one's taste, suitable. Of a person: likeable, in tune with or responsive to one's personality or moods.

1996 *Times Magazine* I answer sometimes indiscreetly, which I tend to do when I find the interviewer intelligent and *sympathique*.

sympathisch /zym'pɑːtɪʃ/ *adjective* E20 **German**. SYMPATHIQUE.

symposium /sɪm'pəʊzɪəm/ *noun* plural **symposia** /sɪm'pəʊzɪə/, **symposiums** L16 **Latin** (from Greek *sumposion*, from *sumpotēs* fellow-drinker, from *sym-* together + *potēs* drinker). **1** L16 A drinking-party; a convivial meeting, *especially* (*historical*) one held by the ancient Greeks for drinking, conversation, philosophical discussion, etc.; *History* an account of such a meeting or the conversation at it. **2a** L18 A meeting or conference for the discussion of a particular subject; a collection of opinions delivered or a series of articles contributed at such a meeting or conference. **b** L19 A collection of essays or papers on various aspects of a particular subject by a number of contributors.

syncope /ˈsɪŋkəpi/ *noun* LME **Late Latin** (from Greek *sugkopē*, from *sun-* with + *kop-* stem of *koptein* to strike, cut off). **1** LME Fainting; temporary loss of consciousness caused by an insufficient flow of blood to the brain, frequently due to blood loss, shock, long standing, overheating, etc. **2** M16 Shortening of a word by omission of one or more syllables or letters in the middle; a word so shortened. **3** M17–L18 *Music* Syncopation. **4** M17 *generally* A cutting short of something; sudden cessation or interruption. *rare*.

synecdoche /sɪˈnɛkdəki/ *noun* LME **Latin** (from Greek *sunekdokhē*, from *sunekdekhesthai*, literally, 'to take with something else', from *sun-* with + *ekdekhesthai* take, take up). *Grammar* and *Rhetoric* A figure of speech in which a more inclusive term is used for a less inclusive one or vice versa, as a whole for a part or a part for a whole.

1996 *Country Life* It is a remarkable thing that, now that the very synecdoche of these islands—Land's End and John o'Groats—have come up for sale, no national body . . . appears to be formulating a plan to buy them on behalf of the nation.

synthesis /ˈsɪnθɪsɪs/ *noun* plural **syntheses** /ˈsɪnθɪsiːz/ LME **Latin** (from Greek *sunthesis*, from *suntithenai*, from *sun-* with + *tithenai* to put, place). **I 1** *Grammar* **a** Apposition. Only in LME. **b** E17–E18 The construction of a sentence according to sense, in violation of strict syntax. **II 2** E17 *Logic* and *Philosophy* **a** The action of proceeding in thought from causes to effects, or from laws or principles to their consequences. **3** E18 *Medicine* The joining of divided parts in surgery. Now *rare* or *obsolete*. **4** M18 *Chemistry* Formation of a compound by combination of its elements or constituents. **b** M19 *Physics* Production of white or other compound light by combination of its constituent colours, or of a complex musical sound by combination of its component simple tones. **5** M19 *Linguistics* The tendency of a language to mark categories by inflections rather than by (groups of) distinct words. Also, the process of making compound and derivative words. **6** M19 *generally* The action or an act of putting together parts or elements to make up a complex whole. Also, a complex whole made up of a number of united parts or elements. **III 7** E17 *Roman Antiquities* A loose flowing robe worn at meals and festivities.

■ Sense 2 also occurs in specialized uses in Kantian and Hegelian philosophy.

système D /sistɛm de/ *noun phrase* L20 **French** (contraction of *système débrouillard* (or *système débrouiller*), literally, 'resourceful system'). A policy or practice for coping with difficult circumstances.

■ Apparently originating in France as a response to conditions during the 1939–45 war, the phrase returned to currency during the French public transport strikes of 1995.

1995 *Times* The French have a phrase for the survivalist spirit: *Système-D*, which stands for *débrouiller*—manage, sort yourself out, muddle through by making do.

T

taal /tɑːl/ *noun* (also **Taal**) L19 **Dutch** (= language, speech, from Middle Dutch *tāle* = Old English *talu* tale). Afrikaans.

■ In colloquial South African English *die* (or *the*) *taal* is often a mildly contemptuous way of referring to Afrikaans.

tabac /taba/ *noun* plural pronounced same E20 **French**. In French-speaking countries: a tobacconist's shop.

tabbouleh /təˈbuːleɪ/ *noun* M20 **Arabic** (*tabbūla*). A Syrian and Lebanese salad made with bulgur, parsley, onion, mint, lemon juice, oil, and spices.

tabi /ˈtɑːbi/ *noun* plural same **tabis** E17 **Japanese**. A thick-soled Japanese ankle sock with a separate stall for the big toe.

tabla /ˈtʌblə/, /ˈtʌblɑː/ *noun* M19 **Persian and Urdu** (*tabla(h)*, Hindustani *tablā* from Arabic *ṭabl*). A pair of small hand drums of unequal size used in Indian music; the smaller of these drums.

tableau /ˈtabləʊ/, *foreign* /tablo/ *noun* plural **tableaux** /ˈtabləʊz/, *foreign* /tablo/ L17 **French** (from Old French *tablel* diminutive of *table* from Latin *tabula* plank, tablet, list). **1** L17 A picture; *figurative* a picturesque presentation or description. **2** L18 A table, a schedule; an official list. **b** M20 *Mathematics* In full *simplex tableau*. A table displaying the constraints in problems of the type soluble by the simplex method. **3 a** E19 A group of people etc. forming a picturesque scene. **b** E19 A TABLEAU VIVANT. **c** M19 *Theatre* A motionless representation of the action at some (especially critical) stage in a play; a stage direction for this. Also (*transferred*), the sudden creation of a striking or dramatic situation. **4** L19 *Cards* The arrangement of the cards as laid out in a game of patience.

tableau vivant /ˌtabləʊ ˈviːvɒ̃/, *foreign* /tablo vivɑ̃/ *noun* plural **tableaux vivants** (pronounced same) E19 **French** (literally, 'living picture'). A silent and motionless representation of a character, scene, incident, etc., by a person or group of people; *transferred* a picturesque actual scene.

1996 *Spectator* But viewed as the sequence of one glittering plastic set after another, . . . and a series of fantastically elaborate, dizzying *tableaux vivants*, no one could resist its poisoned brilliant intensity.

table d'hôte /ˌtɑːb(ə)l ˈdəʊt/, *foreign* /tablə dot/ *noun phrase* E17 **French** (= host's table). Originally, a common table for guests at a hotel or eating-house. Now usually, a meal at a hotel, restaurant, etc., consisting of a set menu at a fixed price.

tablier /ˈtablɪeɪ/, *foreign* /tablje/ (*plural same*) *noun* (in sense 1 also (earlier) **tabler** ME **Old and Modern French** (ultimately from Latin *tabula* plank, tablet, list). **1** ME–L15 A backgammon board or chessboard. Also, backgammon. **2** M19 *History* A part of a woman's dress resembling an apron; the front of a skirt having the form of an apron. **3** L19 *Anthropology* An extension of the labia minora characteristic of Khoisan women.

taboo /təˈbuː/ *adjective & noun* (also **tabu**, (chiefly *New Zealand*) **tapu** /ˈtɑːpuː/) L18 **Tongan** (*tabu*). **A** *adjective* **1** L18 Set apart for or consecrated to a special use or purpose; forbidden to general use or to a particular person or class of people; sacred; forbidden. **2** E19 *transferred* and *figurative* Especially of a word, topic, or activity: avoided or prohibited, especially by social custom. **B** *noun* L18 The putting of a person or thing under temporary or permanent prohibition or interdict, especially as a social custom; the fact or condition of being taboo; a customary prohibition or interdict. **2** M19 *transferred* and *figurative* Prohibition or interdiction of the use or practice of anything; ostracism; *specifically* a prohibition of the use of certain words, topics, etc., especially in social conversation.

tabouret /ˈtabərɛt/, /ˈtabəreɪ/ *noun* M17 **French** (diminutive of Old French *tabour* (also *tanbor*, *tamb(o)ur*), apparently of oriental origin; cf. Persian *tabīra*, *tabūrāk* drum). **1** M17 A low backless seat or stool for one person. **2** E20 A small table, especially one used as a stand for houseplants; a bedside table. *United States*.

tabula gratulatoria /ˌtabjʊlə ˌgratjʊlə ˈtɔːrɪə/ **Late Latin** (*tabula* list + feminine of *gratulatorius* congratulatory). L20 A list in a FESTSCHRIFT of the people and institutions who have subscribed to the publication.

tabula rasa /ˌtabjʊlə ˈrɑːzə/ *noun phrase* **Latin** (literally, 'scraped tablet'). A tablet from which the writing has been erased, ready to be written on again; a blank tablet; *figurative* a clean slate; a mind having no innate ideas (as in some views of the human mind at birth).

1995 J. D. Barrow *Artful Universe* No mind was ever a *tabula rasa*. We enter the world with minds that possess an innate ability to learn.

tac-au-tac /ˈtakəʊtak/ *noun* E20 **French** (literally, 'clash for clash', from *tac* (imitative)). *Fencing* A parry combined with a riposte.

tacenda /təˈsɛndə/ *noun plural* M19 **Latin** (plural of *tacendum*, use as noun of neuter of gerundive of *tacere* to be silent). Things to be passed over in silence; matters not to be mentioned or made public, *especially* those of an embarrassing nature.

tacet /ˈteɪsɛt/, /ˈtasɪt/ *adverb & noun* E18 **Latin** (= is silent, from *tacere* to be silent). *Music* **A** *adverb* E18 (A direction:) be silent for a time; pause. **B** *noun* L18 A pause.

tache /tɑːʃ/, /taʃ/ *noun* ME **Old French** (*teche*, (also modern) *tache*, ultimately from Frankish = a token). **1 a** ME A spot, a blotch, a blot. *obsolete* except *Scottish*. **b** L19 *Medicine* A blemish on the skin, an organ, etc. Usually with French specifying word. **c** *Art* M20 A dab or dash of colour. **2** *figurative* **a** ME–E17 A moral spot or blemish. **b** E17 An imputation of fault or disgrace; a stain or blot on one's character. *Scottish*. **3** LME A distinctive mark, quality, or habit. *obsolete* except *dialect*.

1.c 1978 G. Greene *Human Factor* The simple precise words, with the single tache of colour reminded Castle of the local background so often to be found in primitive paintings.

taco /ˈtɑːkəʊ/, /ˈtakəʊ/ *noun* plural **tacos** M20 **Mexican Spanish**. A Mexican dish comprising a tortilla or cornmeal pancake rolled or folded and filled with various mixtures, such as seasoned mincemeat, chicken, beans, etc.

taedium vitae /ˌtʌɪdɪəm ˈviːtʌɪ/, /ˌtiːdɪəm ˈvʌɪtiː/ *noun phrase* M18 **Latin** (*taedium* weariness, disgust + *vitae* genitive of *vita* life). Weariness of life; extreme ennui or inertia, often as a pathological state with a tendency to suicide.

tae kwon do /ˌtʌɪ kwɒn ˈdəʊ/ /ˌteɪ kwɒn ˈdəʊ/ *noun phrase* M20 **Korean** (literally, 'art of hand and foot fighting'). A modern Korean system of unarmed combat developed chiefly in the mid twentieth century, combining elements of KARATE, ancient Korean martial art, and KUNG FU, differing from karate in its wide range of kicking techniques and its emphasis on different methods of breaking objects.

taele variant of TJAELE.

taenia /ˈtiːnɪə/ *noun* (also **tenia**) plural **taeniae** /ˈtiːnɪiː/, **taenias** M16 **Latin** (from Greek *tainia* band, fillet, ribbon). **1** M16 *Architecture* A fillet or band between a Doric architrave and frieze. **2** E18 *Zoology* A tapeworm. Now only as modern Latin genus name. **3** M19 *Greek Antiquities* A headband, ribbon, or fillet. **4** L19 *Anatomy* A ribbon-like structure. Usually with specifying word.

Tafelmusik /ˈtɑːfəlmuˌziːk/ *noun* L19 **German** (literally, 'table music'). **1** L19 Music so printed as to enable the same page to be read by two or more people seated on opposite sides of a table. **2** L19 Music intended to be performed at a banquet or a convivial meal, especially popular in the eighteenth century.

Tafelwein /ˈtɑːfəlvaɪn/ *noun* L20 **German** (literally, 'table wine'). Ordinary German wine of mediocre quality, suitable for drinking with a meal.

tafia /ˈtafɪə/ *noun* M18 **French** (from West Indian creole, alteration of RATAFIA). In the West Indies: a liquor resembling rum distilled from the lower grades of molasses, refuse brown sugar, etc.

tafone /taˈfəʊni/ *noun* plural **tafoni** /taˈfəʊni/ M20 **Corsican** (dialect *tafóne* hole, hollow). *Geology* A shallow rounded cavity in rock produced by weathering. Usually in *plural*.

tagliarini /taljəˈriːni/ *noun* M19 **Italian** (*taglierini* plural, from *tagliare* to cut). Pasta made in very narrow strips.

tagliatelle /taljəˈtɛli/ *noun* L19 **Italian** (from *tagliare* to cut; cf. preceding). Pasta made in narrow strips.

tahina /tɑːˈhiːnə/ *noun* (also **tahini** /tɑːˈhiːni/) M20 **Modern Greek** (*takhini* from Arabic *ṭaḥīnā* from *ṭaḥana* to grind, crush, pulverize). A Middle Eastern paste or sauce made from sesame seeds.

T'ai Chi /tʌɪ ˈtʃiː/ *noun* M18 **Chinese** (*tàijí* (Wade–Giles *t'ai chi*), from *tài* extreme + *jí* limit). **1** M18 In Taoism and Neo-Confucianism, the ultimate point, constituting both source and limit, of the life-force. Also, the symbol representing this.

2 M20 A Chinese martial art and system of callisthenics consisting of sequences of very slow controlled movements, believed to have been devised by a Taoist priest in the Song dynasty (960–1279). In full *T'ai Chi Ch'uan* /ˈtʃwɑːn/ (Chinese *quán* fist).

taiga /ˈtʌɪɡə/ *noun* L19 **Russian** (*taĭga* from Mongolian). The swampy coniferous forest of high northern latitudes, *especially* that between the tundra and steppes of Siberia.

taiglach variant of TEIGLACH.

taihoa /tʌɪˈhəʊə/ *interjection* M19 **Maori**. Wait a bit; by and by; presently. *New Zealand.*

taiko /ˈtʌɪkəʊ/ *noun* plural same, **taikos** L19 **Japanese**. A Japanese drum; *specifically* any of a class of barrel-shaped drums.

taille /tɑːj/, /taj/ *noun* plural pronounced same M16 **French** (from Old French *taillier* (modern *tailler* from Proto-Romance (medieval Latin *tailliare*) from Latin *talea* rod, twig, cutting). **1** M16 In France, a tax levied on the common people. *obsolete* except *historical.* **2** M17 Cut, shape, form; shape of the bust from the shoulders to the waist; figure, build. **3** M19 *Music* (now *historical*). The register of a tenor or similar voice; an instrument of this register.

taille-douce /tajdus/ *noun* M17 **French** (= soft cutting, from TAILLE + *douce* soft). Engraving on a metal plate with a graver or burin as opposed to a dry-point or etching needle.

tailleur /tajœr/ *noun* plural pronounced same E20 **French** (from TAILLE). A woman's tailor-made suit.

1982 T. Fitzgibbon *With Love* I pressed the black *tailleur*, bought a gay scarf . . . and went off to look for a job.

taipan /ˈtʌɪpan/ *noun* M19 **Chinese** ((Cantonese) *daaihbāan*). Originally, a foreign merchant or businessman in China. Now *especially*, the head of a foreign business in China.

taisch /tʌɪʃ/ *noun* (also **taish**) L18 **Gaelic** (*taibhse* from Old Irish *taidbse* phantasm). In Scottish folklore, the apparition of a living person who is about to die; *generally* something perceived by second sight.

takamakie /ˌtɑːkəmɑːkɪˈjɛ/ *noun* (also **takamakiye** and other variants) E20 **Japanese**. Decorative Japanese lacquer-work done in relief, especially in gold.

takhaar /ˈtakhɑː/ *noun* plural **takhare** /ˈtakhɑːri/, **takhaars** L19 **Afrikaans** (from Dutch *tak* branch + *haar* hair). In South Africa: an unkempt, unsophisticated person, especially from a rural area. *colloquial* and *derogatory.*

takht /tɑːkt/ *noun* L20 **Persian** (*takt*). In Eastern countries: a sofa, a bed.

talak /təˈlɑːk/ *noun* (also **talaq**) L18 **Arabic** (*ṭalāḳ*, from *ṭalaḳat*, *ṭaluḳat* be repudiated). In Islamic law: divorce, especially by the husband's verbal repudiation of his wife in the presence of witnesses.

talaq variant of TALAK.

talaria /təˈlɛːrɪə/ *noun plural* L16 **Latin** (neuter plural of *talaris* from *talus* ankle). *Roman Mythology* Winged sandals or small wings attached to the ankles of some gods and goddesses, especially Mercury.

talayot /təˈlɑːjɒt/ *noun* L19 **Catalan** (*talaiot* small watch-tower, from Arabic (Muslim Spain) *ṭāli'āt* plural of *ṭāli'a* watch-tower). *Archaeology* A Bronze Age stone tower characteristic of the Balearic Islands, usually circular with a large central pillar supporting the roof. Cf. NURAGH.

taleggio /taˈlɛdʒɪəʊ/ *noun* L20 **Italian**. A rinded semi-soft cheese.

talik /ˈtalɪk/ *noun* M20 **Russian** (from *tayat'* to melt). *Physical Geography* An area of unfrozen ground surrounded by permafrost.

talio /ˈtalɪəʊ/ *noun* E17 **Latin**. (A) retaliation.

tallith /ˈtalɪθ/ *noun* E17 **Hebrew** (rabbinical Hebrew *ṭallīt*, from biblical Hebrew *ṭillel* to cover). The shawl with fringed corners traditionally worn by male Jews at prayer.

talus /ˈteɪləs/ *noun* plural **taluses** M17 **French** (of unknown origin). **1** M17 A slope; *specifically* (*Fortification*) the sloping side of a wall or earthwork. **2** M19 *Geology* A scree slope, consisting of material which has fallen from the face of the cliff above. **b** *generally* M19 The slope of a mountain, hill, or iceberg. Now *rare.*

tamagotchi /ˌtaməˈɡɒtʃi/ *noun* (also **Tamagotchi, tamagocchi**) L20 **Japanese** (= lovable egg). (Proprietary name for) a small, portable electronic device which can be programmed to mimic the demands for food, attention, etc. of a pet bird or animal.

1997 *Weekend Telegraph* . . . the record Tamagotchi lifespan is less than a month . . .

tamale /tə'mɑːli/ *noun* L17 **Mexican Spanish** (*tamal*, plural *tamales*, from Nahuatl *tamalli*). A Mexican dish of seasoned meat and maize flour steamed or baked in maize husks.

tamari /tə'mɑːri/ *noun* L20 **Japanese**. A Japanese variety of rich wheat-free soy sauce. Also *tamari sauce*.

tamasha /tə'mɑːʃə/ *noun* (also (earlier) **tomasha**) E17 **Persian and Urdu** (*tamāšā* (for *tamāšī*) walking about for amusement, entertainment, from Arabic *tamāšā* walk about together, from *mašā* walk). **1** E17 In the Indian subcontinent: an entertainment, a show, a spectacle, a public function. **2** L19 A fuss, a commotion. *colloquial*.

2 1981 S. Rushdie *Midnight's Children* Enough of this tamasha! No more of this . . . tomfoolery!

tambour /'tambʊə/ *noun* L15 **French** (Old French *tabour* (also *tanbor*, *tamb(o)ur*), apparently of oriental origin (cf. Persian *tabīra*, *tabūrāk* drum), spelling perhaps influenced by Arabic *ṭunbūr* a kind of lute or lyre). **1** L15 A drum; now *especially* a small drum with a deep tone. **2** E18 *Architecture* **a** The part of a Corinthian or composite capital around which the foliage and volutes are arranged, a bell. **b** E18 Any of the courses forming the shaft of a cylindrical column. **c** E18 A lobby with a ceiling and folding doors serving to obviate draughts, especially in a church porch. **d** E19 A wall of circular plan, as one supporting a dome or surrounded by a colonnade. **3** E18 A projecting part of the main wall of a real tennis or fives court, with a sloping end face. **4 a** A circular frame formed of one hoop fitting inside another, in which fabric is held taut for embroidering. **b** M19 Material embroidered or embroidery done using such a frame. **5** M19 *Military* A small redan defending an entrance or passage. **6** L19 *Medicine* A stretched membrane forming part of an instrument for recording arterial pulsations, respiratory movements, etc., by slight changes in air pressure. **7** M20 A sliding flexible shutter or door on a desk, cabinet, etc., made of strips of wood attached to a canvas backing.

tameletjie /tamə'lɛki/, /tamə'lɛtʃi/ *noun* M19 **Afrikaans** (perhaps from *tabletje* small cake). In South Africa: (a piece of) hard toffee often containing almonds or pine nuts. Now also, a sweet consisting of a roll of compressed and sweetened dried fruit (also more fully *tameletjie-roll*).

tandoor /'tandʊə/, /tan'dʊə/ *noun* (also (in sense 1 usually) **tandour**, and other variants) M17 **French or Urdu** (sense 1 from French *tandour* from Turkish *tandır* variant of Persian, Arabic *tannūr* oven, furnace; sense 2 from Urdu, *tandūr*, Persian *tanūr* ultimately from Arabic *tannūr*). **1** M17 A square table with a brazier under it, round which people sit for warmth in cold weather in Persia, Turkey, and adjacent countries. Now *rare*. **2** M19 A clay oven of a kind used originally in northern India and Pakistan; a shop selling food cooked in such an oven.

tandoori /tan'dʊəri/ *adjective & noun* M20 **Persian and Urdu** (from *tandūr*: see preceding). **A** *adjective* M20 Designating, pertaining to, or using a style of Indian cooking based on the use of a tandoor. **B** *noun* M20 Tandoori cooking or food; a tandoori dish.

tandour see TANDOOR.

tanga /'taŋgə/ *noun* E20 **Portuguese** (ultimately of Bantu origin). **1** E20 *Anthropology* A triangular loincloth or pubic covering worn by indigenous peoples in tropical America. **2** L20 A very brief bikini made of triangles of material connected by thin ties.

tango /'taŋgəʊ/ *noun & verb* plural **tangos**, (now *rare*) **tangoes** L19 **American Spanish** (perhaps of African origin). **A** *noun* **1** L19 A kind of Spanish flamenco dance. **2** L19 A syncopated ballroom dance in 2/4 or 4/4 time, of South American origin, characterized by slow gliding movements and abrupt pauses; a piece of music intended to accompany or in the rhythm of this dance. **B** *intransitive verb* E20 Dance a tango.

tanka /'taŋkə/ *noun* plural same, **tankas** L19 **Japanese** (from *tan* short + *ka* song). A Japanese poem consisting of thirty-one syllables in five lines, the first and third lines having five and the others seven syllables. Also called *uta*.

tant bien que mal /tɑ̃ bjɛ̃ kə mal/ *adverb phrase* M18 **French** (literally, 'as well as badly'). With indifferent success; moderately well, after a fashion.

tant mieux /tɑ̃ mjø/ *interjection* M18 **French**. So much the better. Cf. TANT PIS.

1972 M. Kaye *Lively Game of Death* If your boss can pin his death on somebody, *tant mieux.*

tanto /ˈtantəʊ/ *adverb* L19 **Italian** (from Latin *tantum* so much). *Music* So, so much.

■ Used to modify adjectives from Italian, as in *allegro non tanto*, meaning 'fast, but not too much so'.

tant pis /tɑ̃ pi/ *interjection* L18 **French.** So much the worse. Cf. TANT MIEUX.

1995 D. Lodge *Therapy* I hope that Laurence and I can go back to our chaste, companionable relationship, but if we can't, *tant pis.*

tantra /ˈtantrə/ *noun* (also **Tantra**) L18 **Sanskrit** (= loom, warp, groundwork, system, doctrine). **1** L18 Any of a class of Hindu or Buddhist religious writings of the late medieval period, often of a magical, erotic, or mystical nature. **2** M20 Tantrism.

tapa /ˈtapa/ *noun* M20 **Spanish** (literally, 'cover, lid'). In a bar or café, especially one providing Spanish food, a savoury snack to accompany a glass of wine.

■ Usually in plural *tapas*, which is often treated as singular (see quotation).

1996 *Spectator Tapas* in the town square—*tortilla de patatas, rinones al Jerez, caracoles, albondigas, calamares*—was followed by a swim and a siesta.

tapadero /tapəˈdɛːrəʊ/ *noun* plural **tapaderos** (also **tapadera** /tapəˈdɛːrə/) M19 **Spanish** (= cover, lid, stopper, from *tapar* to stop up, cover). In the western United States: a leather hood for the front of a stirrup, to hold and protect the foot especially when riding through brush.

tapénade /tapenad/ *noun* M20 **French** (from Provençal *tapeno*). A Provençal dish, usually served as an hors d'oeuvre, made mainly from black olives, capers, and anchovies.

tapette /tapɛt/ *noun & adjective* M20 **French** ((slang) = pederast, homosexual, from *taper* hit, tap). **A** *noun* M20 Plural pronounced same. A passive male homosexual; an effeminate man. **B** *adjective* M20 Of a man: effeminate; like a *tapette*.

B 1978 J. Sherwood *Limericks of Lachasse* My mother . . . wondered if you were perhaps *tapette*, but my brothers assured her that . . . you were perfectly masculine.

tapia /ˈtapɪə/ *noun* M18 **Spanish** (= mud-wall). Clay or mud puddled, compressed, and dried, as a material for walls.

tapis /ˈtapi/ *noun* plural same L15 **French** (= carpet, tablecloth, from Old French *tapiz* (also modern *tapis*) from late Latin *tapetium* from Greek *tapētion* diminutive of *tapēs, tapēt-* tapestry). A cloth, especially of a decorated oriental fabric of a type exported to France in the eighteenth century, worked with artistic designs in colours, used as a curtain, tablecloth, etc.; a tapestry.

■ The phrase (*up*)*on the tapis* (L17) meaning 'under discussion (*or* consideration)', is a partial translation of French *sur le tapis* (literally, 'on the tablecloth'), also occasionally used in English.

tapis vert /tapi vɛr/ *noun phrase* plural **tapis verts** (pronounced same) M20 **French** (= green carpet). A long strip of grass.

1965 (Mrs) L. B. Johnson *White House Diary* He wants to . . . preserve the tapis vert, the long green ribbon that stretches . . . from the Capitol to the Lincoln Memorial.

tapotement /təˈpəʊtm(ə)nt/ *noun* L19 **French** (from *tapoter* to tap). A percussive technique used in massage, consisting of hacking, clapping, and pounding actions.

taqueria /ˌtɑːkəˈriːə/ *noun* L20 **Mexican Spanish** (from TACO). In the United States: a restaurant specializing in tacos.

taqueté /takte/ *adjective* M20 **French** (from *taquet* wedge, peg). *Ballet* Designating or pertaining to a style of point-work accentuated with quick precise short steps.

tarantella /ˌtar(ə)nˈtɛlə/ *noun* (also **tarantelle** /ˌtar(ə)nˈtɛl/) L18 **Italian** (diminutive of *Taranto* (Latin *Tarentum*), a town in southern Italy: popularly associated with *tarantola* tarantula). **1** L18 A rapid whirling South Italian dance popular since the fifteenth century, when it was supposed to be the most effective cure for tarantism. **2** M19 A piece of music for such a dance or composed in its triplet rhythm, with abrupt transitions from the major to the minor.

tarboosh /tɑːˈbuːʃ/ *noun* (also **tarbush**) E18 **Arabic** ((Egyptian) *ṭarbūš* from Ottoman Turkish *terpōş*, Turkish *tarbuş* from Persian *sarpūš*, from *sar* head + *pūš* cover). A cap similar to a fez, usually of red felt with a tassel at the top, worn by Muslim men either alone or as part of a turban.

targa /ˈtɑːgə/ *adjective & noun* L20 **Italian** (= plate, shield; the name of a model of Porsche motor car (introduced in 1965) with a detachable hood (see below), probably after the *Targa Florio* (= Florio Shield), a motor time-trial held annually in Sicily). **A** *adjective* L20 Designating a type of detachable roof hood or panelling on a convertible sports car, *especially* one which when removed leaves a central roll-bar for passenger safety. **B** *noun* L20 A car having this feature.

tarkashi /tɑːˈkaʃiː/ *noun* L19 **Urdu** ((and Persian) *tār-kašī*, literally, 'wire-drawing'). Especially in the Indian subcontinent: the craft of inlaying wood with brass wire; the artefacts so produced.

tarot /ˈtarəʊ/ *noun* L16 **French** (from Italian *tarocchi* plural of *tarocco*, of unknown origin). **1** L16 In *singular* or *plural* Any of various games played with a pack of tarot cards (see sense 2). **2** L19 Any of a pack of 78 playing-cards having five suits, the last of which is a set of permanent trumps, first used in Italy in the fifteenth century and now also used for fortune-telling. Also, any of the trump cards in such a pack. Also *tarot card*.

tarsia /ˈtɑːsɪə/ *noun* L17 **Italian**. INTARSIA.

tartine /tɑːˈtiːn/ *noun* E19 **French** (from *tarte* tart). A slice of (usually toasted) bread spread with butter or jam.

tasajo /təˈsɑːhəʊ/, *foreign* /taˈsaxo/ *noun* L18 **Spanish** (= slice of dried meat, of unknown origin). Buffalo meat cut into strips and dried in the sun.

■ Chiefly North American. The synonymous *tasso* is perhaps a derivation from *tasajo*, but cf. Louisiana French *tasseau* (jerked beef).

tastevin /tastəvɛ̃/ *noun* plural pronounced same M20 **French** (*tastevin*, *tâtevin* wine-taster). A small shallow (especially silver) cup for tasting wines, of a type used in France. Also (**Tastevin**), a member of a French order or guild of wine-tasters.

tasto /ˈtastəʊ/ *noun* plural **tastos** M18 **Italian** (= touch, key). *Music* A key of a piano or other keyboard instrument; the fingerboard of a stringed instrument.

tatami /təˈtɑːmi/ *noun* E17 **Japanese**. **1** E17 A rush-covered straw mat forming the standard floor-covering in Japan. Also *tatami mat*. **2** E20 A standard unit in room measurement in Japan, approximately 1.83 by 0.91 metres.

tathata /tatəˈtɑː/, /taθəˈtɑː/ *noun* M20 **Pali** (*tathatā* true state of things, from *tathā* in that manner, so). *Buddhism* The ultimate nature of all things, as expressed in phenomena but inexpressible in language.

tâtonnement /tɑtɔnmɑ̃/ *noun* plural pronounced same M19 **French** (from *tâtonner* feel one's way, proceed cautiously). Experimentation, tentative procedure; an instance of this.

tau /tɔː/, /taʊ/ *noun* (also **taw**) ME **Greek** (from Hebrew *tāw* final letter of Hebrew alphabet). **1** ME The nineteenth (originally the final) letter (T, τ) of the Greek alphabet, corresponding in form to the letter T. **2** ME A T-shaped mark, sign, or object; *specifically* (*a*) the sign of the cross as made with the hand; (*b*) (more fully *tau cross*) a cross in which the transverse piece surmounts the upright piece (also called *St Anthony's cross*); (*c*) An ANKH; (*d*) a T-shaped pastoral staff. (more fully *tau-staff*) **3** M20 *Particle Physics* Frequently written τ. **a** A meson that decays into three pions, now identified as a kaon. **b** L20 An unstable heavy charged lepton. Also *tau lepton*, *tau particle*.

taula /ˈtaʊlə/ *noun* L19 **Catalan** (from Latin *tabula* table). *Archaeology* A megalithic Bronze Age structure found on Minorca, consisting of two slabs forming a T-shaped column, frequently enclosed by a horseshoe-shaped wall.

taupe /təʊp/ *noun & adjective* E20 **French** (from Latin *talpa* mole). (Of) a brownish shade of grey resembling the colour of moleskin.

taverna /təˈvəːnə/ *noun* E20 **Modern Greek** (from Latin *taberna* tavern). A Greek eating-house.

taxe de séjour /taks də seʒur/ *noun phrase* plural **taxes de séjour** (pronounced same) E20 **French** (literally, 'tax of visit'). In France and French-speaking countries: a tax imposed on visitors to spas or tourist resorts.

tazia /taˈziːə/ *noun* E19 **Arabic** (*ta'ziya* consolation, mourning). *Islam* **1** E19 A representation, often made of paper and elaborately decorated, of the tomb of Husain (grandson of Muhammad) carried in procession during Muharram. **2** L19 A play commemorating the suffering and death of Husain, performed especially on the anniversary of the event each year.

tazza /ˈtatsə/ *noun* plural **tazze** /ˈtatseɪ/, **tazzas** E19 **Italian** (from Arabic *ṭasa*). A shallow ornamental wine-cup or vase, *especially* one mounted on a foot.

tchin /tʃɪn/ *noun* (also **chin**) M19 **Russian** (*chin* = rank). Rank; person or persons of quality.

tchotchke variant of TSATSKE.

te /teɪ/ *noun* L19 **Chinese** (*dé* virtue (Wade-Giles *te*)). (In Taoism) the essence of Tao inherent in all beings; (in Confucianism and in extended use) moral virtue.

tecbir variant of TEKBIR.

tedesco /te'desko/ *noun & adjective* plural **tedeschi** /te'deski/ E19 **Italian** (= German, from medieval Latin *theodiscus*, ultimately from Germanic base of *Dutch*). (An instance of) German influence in Italian art or literature; showing such influence.

Te Deum /tiː 'diːəm/, /teɪ 'deɪəm/ *noun phrase* OE **Latin**. **1** OE An ancient Latin hymn of praise beginning *Te deum laudamus* 'We praise you, O God', sung as an expression of thanksgiving on special occasions, and sung or recited regularly at Roman Catholic matins and (in translation) at Anglican matins. **2** L17 A recital of this; any (public) expression of thanksgiving or exultation. **3** M19 A musical setting of this hymn.

teepee variant of TEPEE.

tefillin /tiː'fɪliːn/ *noun plural* E17 **Aramaic** (*tĕpillīn* prayers). Jewish phylacteries; the texts inscribed on these.

tegula /'tɛgjʊlə/ *noun* plural **tegulae** /'tɛgjʊliː/ E19 **Latin** (= tile, from *tegere* to cover). **1** E19 *Entomology* A small scalelike sclerite covering the base of the forewing in the orders Lepidoptera, Hymenoptera, Diptera, etc. **2** L19 *Archaeology* A flat roof-tile, used especially in Roman roofs. Cf. IMBREX.

teiglach /'teɪgləx/ *noun plural* (also **taiglach** and other variants) E20 **Yiddish** (*teiglekh* plural of *teigl* dough pellet, from *teig* dough, ultimately from Old High German *teic* from Germanic from Indo-European base meaning 'smear, knead'). A Jewish confection made of pellets of dough boiled in honey.

tekbir /'tɛkbɪə/ *noun* (also **tecbir**) E18 **Arabic** (*tekbīr*, colloquial pronunciation of *takbīr* to proclaim the greatness of, from base also of *kabīr* great, *'akbar* greater, greatest). A cry of *Allāhu 'akbar* 'Allah is most great', uttered by Muslims.

tekke /'tɛkeɪ/ *noun* M17 **Turkish** (*tekke*, Arabic *takiyya*, Persian *takya* place of repose, pillow, abode of a dervish or fakir, perhaps ultimately from Arabic *ittaka'a* to lean on). A monastery of dervishes, especially in Ottoman Turkey.

telamon /'tɛləmən/, /'tɛləməʊn/ *noun* plural **telamones** /tɛlə'məʊniːz/ E17 **Latin** (*telamones* (plural) from Greek *telamōnes* plural of *Telamōn* Telamon, a mythical hero). *Architecture* A male figure used as a pillar to support an entablature or other structure.

■ The female equivalent is a *caryatid*.

téléphérique /teleferik/ *noun* (also **teleferic** /tɛlɪ'fɛrɪk/, **téléférique** /teleferik/ (*plural same*), **telepherique**, /ˌtɛlɪfɛ'riːk/) plural pronounced same E20 **French** (Italian *teleferica*, from Greek *tēle-* far + *pherein* to carry). A cableway.

telos /'tɛlɒs/ *noun* plural **teloi** /'tɛlɔɪ/ M16 **Greek** (= end). **1** M16 FINIS sense 1. *rare*. **2** L19 End, purpose, (an) ultimate object or aim.

2 1995 *Spectator* The *telos* of society became increasing amounts of health, wealth and happiness.

tel quel /tɛl 'kɛl/ *adjective phrase* L19 **French**. Just as it is; without improvement or modification.

temblor /tɛm'blɔː/ *noun* L19 **American Spanish**. An earthquake. *South-western United States*.

temenos /'tɛmənɒs/ *noun* plural **temene** /'tɛməniː/ E19 **Greek** (from stem of *temnein* to cut off, sever). Chiefly *Archaeology* A piece of ground surrounding or adjacent to a temple; a sacred enclosure or precinct.

temmoku /'tɛməʊkuː/ *noun* (also **tenmoku** /'tɛnməʊkuː/) L19 **Japanese** (from Chinese *tiān mù* eye of heaven). A type of Chinese porcelain or stoneware with lustrous black or dark brown glaze; the glaze used on such porcelain or stoneware.

témoignage /temwaɲaʒ/ *noun* M20 **French** (from *témoigner* to bear witness). Testimony, witness; *especially* testimony regarding the character or beliefs of a person.

tempeh /'tɛmpeɪ/ *noun* M20 **Indonesian** (*tempe*). An Indonesian dish made by deep-frying fermented soya beans.

tempera /'tɛmp(ə)rə/ *noun* M19 **Italian** (in *pingere a tempera* paint in distemper). A method of painting using especially an emulsion e.g. of pigment with egg, especially as a fine art technique on canvas.

Also, the emulsion etc. used in this method.

tempête /tɛm'pɛt/, *foreign* /tɑ̃pɛt/ *noun* L19 **French**. A country dance popular in England in the late nineteenth century; a piece of music for this dance.

tempi plural of TEMPO.

tempietto /ˌtɛmpɪ'ɛtəʊ/ *noun* plural **tempietti** /ˌtɛmpɪ'ɛti/ L19 **Italian** (literally, 'little temple'). A small usually circular building resembling a miniature temple.

tempo /'tɛmpəʊ/ *noun* plural **tempi** /'tɛmpi/, **tempos** M17 **Italian** (from Latin *tempus* time). **1** M17 The timing of an attack in fencing so that one's opponent is within reach. *rare*. **2** L17 *Music* Relative speed or rate of movement; pace; time; *specifically* the (especially characteristic) speed at which music for a dance etc. is or should be played. **3** L19 The rate of motion or activity (*of* someone or something).

tempo giusto /ˌtɛmpəʊ 'dʒu:stəʊ/ *noun phrase* M18 **Italian** (literally, 'strict time'). The speed at which a particular style of music is or should be played.

temporale /ˌtɛmpə'rɑ:l/ *noun* M19 **Spanish** (*temporal* storm, spell of rainy weather). A weather condition on the Pacific coast of Central America consisting of strong south-west winds bringing heavy rain.

tempo rubato /ˌtɛmpəʊ rʊ'bɑ:təʊ/ *noun phrase* L18 **Italian** (literally, 'stolen time'). Cf. RUBATO.

temps /tɑ̃/ *noun* plural same L19 **French** (literally, 'time'). *Ballet* **1** L19 A movement in which there is no transfer of weight from one foot to the other. **2** E20 A movement forming one part of a step.

temps perdu /tɑ̃ pɛrdy/ *noun phrase* M20 **French** (literally, 'time lost'). The past, contemplated with nostalgia and a sense of irretrievability. Cf. RECHERCHE DU TEMPS PERDU.

tempura /'tɛmpʊrə/ *noun* E20 **Japanese** (probably from Portuguese *tempêro* seasoning). A Japanese dish consisting of shellfish or whitefish and often vegetables, fried in batter.

temura /ˌtəmʊ'rɑ:/ *noun* (also **temurah**) E20 **Hebrew** (*tĕmūrāh* exchange). A cabbalistic method of interpreting the Hebrew scriptures by the systematic replacement of the letters of a word with other letters.

tendenz /tɛn'dɛnts/ *noun* L19 **German** (from English *tendence* or French *tendance*). Drift or aim of a story; purpose of a novel, etc.

Tendenzroman /tɛn'dɛntsrəˌmɑ:n/ *noun* M19 **German** (TENDENZ + *Roman* novel). A novel with a purpose; a ROMAN À THÈSE.

1975 *Listener* Humphrey House, the eminent Dickens critic, said that it [sc. *Oliver Twist*] was the closest thing to a *tendenzroman* that Dicken ever wrote . . .

tendido /ten'dido/ *noun* plural **tendidos** /ten'didos/ M19 **Spanish** (past participle of *tender* to stretch). An open tier of seats above the barrera in a bullring.

tendresse /tɑ̃drɛs/ *noun* plural pronounced same LME **French** (from *tendre* tender). (A) fondness, (an) affection.

1996 *Bookseller* . . . he played a shy landowner, struggling with the *tendresse* he felt for Ted . . . , his estate manager.

tendu /tɑ̃dy/ *adjective* E20 **French** (past participle of *tendre* to stretch). *Ballet* Stretched out or held tautly.

tenebroso /tene'broso/ *noun & adjective* L19 **Italian** (= dark, from Latin *tenebrosus* dark, gloomy). **A** *noun* L19 plural **tenebrosi** /tene'brosi/ A member of a group of early seventeenth-century Italian painters influenced by Caravaggio, whose work is characterized by dramatic contrasts of light and shade. **B** *adjective* L19 Designating the style of this group of painters.

tenendum /tɪ'nɛndəm/ *noun* E17 **Latin** (literally, 'to be held' neuter gerundive of *tenere* to hold). *Law* (now *historical* except *United States*) That part of a deed defining the tenure by which the things granted are to be held.

tenet /'tɛnɪt/, /'ti:nɛt/ *noun* L16 **Latin** (literally, 'he holds', 3rd person present singular of *tenere* to hold). A doctrine, dogma, principle, or opinion, in religion, philosophy, politics, etc., held by a group or person. Also *loosely*, any opinion held.

■ Since E18 has entirely superseded the earlier form *tenent* (M16).

teniente /te'njente/ *noun* L18 **Spanish**. A lieutenant.

tenmoku variant of TEMMOKU.

tenore /te'no:re/ *noun* M18 **Italian**. An adult male voice intermediate between a bass and counter-tenor or alto, a tenor voice; a singer having such a voice.

tenore di forza /teˌnoːre di̥ ˈfɔrtsa/ *noun phrase* L19 **Italian** (literally, 'tenor of power'). A singer with a powerful tenor voice.

> **1996** *Spectator* Unnecessarily pleading indulgence for a throat infection, he [sc. José Cura] sounded excitingly like a true *tenore di forza*, a Mario del Monaco for the Millennium, and an Otello in the making.

tenore di grazia /teˌnoːre di ˈgratsia/ *noun phrase* L19 **Italian** (literally, 'tenor of grace'). A light or lyric tenor.

tenore robusto /teˌnoːre roˈbusto/ *noun phrase* L19 **Italian** (= strong tenor). A dramatic tenor.

tenorino /tɛnəˈriːnəʊ/ *noun* plural **tenorini** /tɛnəˈriːni/ M19 **Italian** (diminutive of TENORE). A high tenor.

tenue /təny/ *noun* E19 **French** (use as noun of feminine past participle of *tenir* to hold, keep). Deportment, bearing; propriety, manners; dress.

> **1996** *Spectator* ... there is a photograph, taken in 1914, of Wallis wearing this bizarre *tenue* [sc. monocle and spats] in Michael Bloch's newest book on the Duchess.

tenuto /təˈnuːtəʊ/ *adverb, adjective & noun* M18 **Italian** (past participle of *tenere* to hold). *Music* **A** *adverb & adjective* M18 (A direction:) giving the note its full time-value; sustained(ly). Abbreviated to *ten.* **B** *noun* M20 plural **tenutos**, **tenuti** /təˈnuːti/ A note or chord played tenuto.

teocalli /tiːəˈkali/ *noun* E17 **American Spanish** (from Nahuatl *teo:kalli*, from *teo:tl* god + *kalli* house). An ancient Mexican or Central American place of worship, usually consisting of a truncated pyramid surmounted by a temple.

tepache /teˈpatʃe/ *noun* E20 **Mexican Spanish** (from Nahuatl *tepiatl*). Any of several Mexican drinks of varying degrees of fermentation, typically made with pineapple, water, and brown sugar.

tepee /ˈtiːpiː/ *noun* (also **teepee**, **tipi**) M18 **Sioux** (*tʰípi* dwelling). A conical tent of the North American Indians, made of skins, cloth, canvas, etc., stretched over a frame of poles fastened together at the top. Now also, a structure imitating or resembling such a tent.

tephra /ˈtɛfrə/ *noun* M20 **Greek** (= ashes). *Geology* Dust and rock fragments that have been ejected into the air by a volcanic eruption.

tepidarium /tɛpɪˈdɛːrɪəm/ *noun* plural **tepidaria** /tɛpɪˈdɛːrɪə/ E19 **Latin**. In an ancient Roman bath, the warm room between the frigidarium and the caldarium. Also, a similar room in a Turkish bath.

teppan-yaki /ˈtɛpanjaki/ *noun* L20 **Japanese** (from *teppan* steel plate + *yaki* fry). A Japanese dish of meat, fish, or both, fried with vegetables on a hot steel plate forming the centre of the dining-table.

tequila /tɛˈkiːlə/ *noun* M19 **Mexican Spanish** (from the name of a town producing the drink). A Mexican spirit made by distilling the fermented sap of a maguey, *Agave tequilana*. Cf. MESCAL sense 2.

terai /təˈrʌɪ/ *noun* L19 **Hindustani** (*tarāī* marshy lowlands). A wide-brimmed felt hat with a double-layered crown and a vent, worn by travellers etc. in subtropical regions. In full *terai hat*.

■ The *terai* is a belt of marshy jungle lying between the southern foothills of the Himalayas and the plains.

tercet /ˈtəːsɪt/ *noun* L16 **French** (from Italian *terzetto*, from *terzo* from Latin *tertius* third). *Prosody* A set or group of three lines rhyming together, or bound by double or triple rhyme with the adjacent triplet or triplets.

tercio /ˈtəːsɪəʊ/, /ˈtəːʃɪəʊ/ *noun* plural **tercios** /ˈtəːsɪəʊz/, /ˈtəːʃɪəʊz/ (in sense 1 also **tertio**) L16 **Spanish** (Italian *tertio*, *terzo*, Portuguese *têrço* a regiment, from Latin *tertium* a third). **1** L16 A regiment of Spanish (or, formerly, Italian) infantry, originally of the sixteenth and seventeenth centuries. Also *generally*, a body of infantry forming a main division of an army. **2** M20 Each of the three parts of a bullfight. **b** M20 Each of the three concentric circular areas into which a bullring is considered to be divided.

teriyaki /tɛrɪˈjɑːki/ *noun* M20 **Japanese** (from *teri* gloss, lustre + *yaki* grill). A Japanese dish consisting of fish or meat marinated in soy sauce and grilled.

terminus ad quem /ˌtəːmɪnəs ad ˈkwɛm/ *noun phrase* M16 **Latin** (= end to which; cf. TERMINUS A QUO). The finishing-point of an argument, policy, period, etc.

terminus ante quem /ˌtəːmɪnəs antɪ ˈkwɛm/ *noun phrase* M20 **Latin** (= end before which). The finishing-point of a period, the latest possible date for something.

■ Also elliptically as *terminus ante*.

terminus a quo /ˌtəːmɪnəs ɑː ˈkwəʊ/ *noun phrase* M16 **Latin** (= end from which). The starting-point of an argument, policy, period, etc.

■ Like TERMINUS AD QUEM, originally part of the technical vocabulary of the thirteenth-century scholastic philosophers (Albertus Magnus, Thomas Aquinas, etc.).

terminus post quem /ˌtəːmɪnəs pəʊst ˈkwɛm/ *noun phrase* M20 **Latin** (= end after which). The starting-point of a period, the earliest possible date for something.

■ Also elliptically as *terminus post.*

terra alba /ˌtɛrə ˈalbə/ *noun phrase* E20 **Latin** (*terra* earth + feminine of *albus* white). Any of various white earths, as pipeclay, kaolin, etc.; now *specifically* white pulverized gypsum used in the manufacture of paper, paint, etc.

terra cognita /ˌtɛrə kɒgˈniːtə/ *noun phrase* M20 **Latin** (*terra* land + feminine of *cognitus* known). *figurative* Familiar territory. Opposite of TERRA INCOGNITA.

1962 E. Snow *Other Side of River* My last remark had put them back on terra cognita and it would have been an appropriate moment to leave.

terracotta /tɛrəˈkɒtə/ *noun & adjective* E18 **Italian** (*terra cotta* baked earth from Latin *terra cocta*). **A** *noun* **1** E18 Hard unglazed usually brownish-red earthenware, used chiefly for decorative tiles and bricks and in modelling. **b** E19 A statuette or figurine made of this substance. **2** L19 The typical brownish-red colour of this earthenware. **B** *attributive* or as *adjective* M19 Of or pertaining to terracotta; made of terracotta; of the typical colour of terracotta, brownish red.

terrae filius /ˌtɛriː ˈfɪlɪəs/, /ˌtɛrʌɪ/ *noun phrase* plural **terrae filii** /ˈfɪlɪʌɪ/, /ˈfɪliː/ L16 **Latin** (= a son of the earth, a man of unknown origin). **1** L16 A person of doubtful or obscure parentage. **2** M17 At Oxford University, an orator who made a humorous and satirical speech during the Act or public defence of candidates' theses. *obsolete* except *historical.*

terra firma /ˌtɛrə ˈfəːmə/ *noun phrase* M17 **Latin** (= firm land). **1** M17–E18 A mainland or continent, as distinct from an island etc. **2** L17 The land as distinguished from the sea; dry land; firm ground. **3** L17–E18 Landed estate; land. *jocular* and *colloquial.*

■ Originally (E17) in English as the name of the territories on the Italian mainland which were subject to the State of Venice. Then later (M18–E19) used for the northern coastland of South America (Colombia), as distinguished from the West Indies. Also, the isthmus of Panama. Sense 2 is now the only one in common use.

terraglia /tɛrˈɑːlɪə/ *noun* M19 **Italian** (= earthenware, china, from Latin *terra* earth). *Ceramics* An Italian cream-coloured earthenware.

terra ignota /ˌtɛrə ɪgˈnəʊtə/ *noun phrase* E20 **Latin** (*terra* land + feminine of *ignotus* unknown). TERRA INCOGNITA.

terra incognita /ˌtɛrə ɪnˈkɒgnɪtə/, /ɪnkɒgˈniːtə/ *noun phrase* E17 **Latin** (= unknown land). An unknown or unexplored territory, land, or region; *figurative* an unknown or unexplored area of study, knowledge, or experience.

■ Frequently without article.

1996 *New Scientist* . . . sequencing the yeast genome has revealed a vast *terra incognita*. Biologists have no clue as to the function of 40 per cent of the genes they have identified . . .

terrain vague /tɛrɛ̃ vag/ *noun phrase* E20 **French** (colloquial, literally 'waste ground'). Wasteland, no man's land; a grey area.

1984 *Sunday Times* Alastair Reid occupies a *terrain vague* between reportage and *belles lettres*.

terra irredenta /ˌtɛrə ɪrɪˈdɛntə/ *noun phrase* M20 **Italian.** IRREDENTA.

terra rosa /ˌtɛrə ˈrəʊzə/ *noun phrase* L19 **Italian** (literally, 'rose-coloured earth'). A light red pigment produced from iron oxide and used in oil and watercolour painting; the light red colour of this pigment, similar to Venetian red.

terra rossa /ˌtɛrə ˈrɒsə/ *noun phrase* L19 **Italian** (*terra* earth + feminine of *rosso* red). *Soil Science* A reddish soil occurring on limestone in Mediterranean climates.

terra sigillata /ˌtɛrə sɪdʒɪˈleɪtə/ *noun phrase* LME **Medieval Latin** (= sealed earth). **1** LME An astringent bole, of fatty consistency and reddish colour, originally obtained from the Aegean island of Lemnos, formerly valued as a medicine and antidote. *obsolete* except *historical.* **2** M16–E17 Red pigment; ruddle. **3** E20 *Archaeology* A type of fine Roman earthenware, especially Samian ware, made from this or a similar earth from the first century BC to the third century AD in Gaul (also Italy and Germany), usually red in colour and sometimes decorated with stamped figures or patterns. **b** M20 A ware made in imitation of this.

terrasse /tɛras/ *noun* plural pronounced same L19 **French**. Originally in France, a flat, paved area outside a building, especially a café, where people sit to take refreshments.

terrazzo /təˈratsəʊ/ *noun* plural **terrazzos** E20 **Italian** (= terrace, balcony). A flooring-material made of chips of marble or granite set in concrete and polished to give a smooth surface.

terre-à-terre /tɛratɛr/ *adjective & adverb phrase* E18 **French** (from Italian *terra a terra* level with the ground). *Ballet* Of a step or manner of dancing: in which the feet remain on or close to the ground. Also *transferred*, without elevation of style; down-to-earth, realistic; pedestrian, unimaginative.

terre cuite /tɛr kɥit/ *noun phrase* M19 **French** (literally, 'baked (cooked) earth'). TERRACOTTA sense 1.

terre pisée /tɛr pize/ *noun phrase* M20 **French** (literally, 'beaten earth'). PISÉ.

terreplein /ˈtɛːpleɪn/, *foreign* /tɛrplɛ̃/ (*plural same*) *noun* L16 **French** (*terre-plein* from Italian *terrapieno*, from *terrapienare* to fill with earth, from *terra* earth + *pieno* (from Latin *plenus*) full). **1** L16 Originally, a talus or sloping bank of earth behind a wall or rampart. Later, the surface of a rampart behind a parapet. **2** M17 The level base (above, on, or below the natural surface of the ground) on which a battery of guns is mounted in field fortifications. Also, the natural surface of the ground around a fortification.

terre-verte /tɛːˈvɛːt/ *noun* M17 **French** (= green earth). A soft green earth of varying composition used as a pigment, *especially* a variety of glauconite obtained from Italy, Cyprus, and France; the colour of this pigment, a soft greyish green.

terribilità /ˌterribiliˈta/ *noun* (also **terribiltà** /terˌribilˈta/) L19 **Italian**. **1** L19 *Art* Awesomeness or emotional intensity of conception and execution in an artist or work of art; originally a quality attributed to Michelangelo by his contemporaries. **2** M20 *generally* Terrifying or awesome quality.

2 1975 *New Yorker* Fathers have voices, and each voice has a *terribilità* of its own.

terrine /təˈriːn/ *noun* E18 **French** (= large earthenware pot, feminine of Old French *terrin* earthen, from Latin *terra* earth). **1** E18 Originally a tureen. Now, an earthenware or similar fireproof vessel, *especially* one in which a terrine or pâté is cooked or sold. **2** E18 Originally, a dish of meat, game, poultry, etc., stewed in a tureen or covered earthenware vessel. Now, a kind of pâté, usually coarse-textured, cooked in and often served from a terrine or earthenware vessel.

terroir /tɛrwar/ *noun* L20 **French** (= soil). *Viticulture* The soil and other local conditions especially as seen as giving a particular character to a wine.

1995 *Country Life* The world of still wine continues to preach the 'small is beautiful' message, the importance of the individual grower and winemaker, the influence of *terroir* (that elusive mix of soil and climate) and the effect of both on wines.

tertium comparationis /ˈtəːʃɪəm ˌkɒmpareɪʃɪˈəʊnɪs/, /ˈtəːtɪəm ˌkɒmparɑːtɪˈəʊnɪs/ *noun phrase* E20 **Latin** (= the third element in comparison). The factor which links or is the common ground between two elements in comparison.

tertium quid /ˌtəːʃɪəm ˈkwɪd/, /ˌtəːtɪəm ˈkwɪd/ *noun phrase* E18 **Late Latin** (translation of Greek *triton ti* some third thing). Something indefinite or left undefined related in some way to two definite or known things, but distinct from both.

tertius /ˈtəːʃɪəs/, /ˈtəːtɪəs/ *adjective* E19 **Latin** (= third). Designating the youngest (in age or standing) of three people, especially pupils, with the same surname.

■ Appended to a surname and used especially in public schools. Cf. PRIMUS adjective 2, SECUNDUS.

tertius gaudens /ˌtəːʃɪəs ˈgaʊdɛnz/, /ˌtəːtɪəs/ *noun phrase* L19 **Latin** (from *tertius* third + *gaudens* present participle of *gaudere* rejoice). A third party benefiting by the conflict or estrangement of two others.

1980 D. Newsome *On Edge of Paradise* It would be better for them both to withdraw to allow the election of a *tertium gaudens*.

terza rima /ˌtɛːtsə ˈriːmə/ *noun phrase* E19 **Italian** (= third rhyme). *Prosody* A form of iambic verse of Italian origin, consisting of triplets in which the middle line of each triplet rhymes with the first and third of the next.

■ Best known as the metre of Dante's *Divina Commedia*.

terzetto /tɛːtˈsɛtəʊ/, /təːtˈsɛtəʊ/ *noun* plural **terzettos**, **terzetti** /tɛːtˈsɛti/ E18 **Italian**. *Music* A vocal or (occasionally) instrumental trio.

tessera /ˈtɛs(ə)rə/ *noun* plural **tesserae** /ˈtɛs(ə)riː/ M17 **Latin** (from Greek, neuter of *tesseres* variant of *tessares* four). **1a** M17 *Classical Antiquities* A small quadrilateral tablet of wood, bone, etc., used as a token, tally, ticket, etc. **b** M17 *figurative* A distinguishing sign or token; a watchword. **2** L18 A small square block of marble, glass, tile, etc., used in mosaic. **3** E20 *Zoology* Each of the plates of an armadillo's carapace.

tessitura /tɛsɪ'tʊərə/ *noun* L19 **Italian.** *Music* The range within which most tones of a voice part or melody lie.

1978 *Early Music* He chose singers for whom the resulting tessituras did not mean any strain.

teste /'tɛsti:/, /'tɛsteɪ/ *noun & preposition* LME **Latin** (ablative of *testis* witness, in the formula of authentication *teste meipso*, literally, 'I myself being a witness'). **A** *noun* LME *Law* (now *historical*). Originally, the final clause in a royal writ naming the person who authenticates the monarch's seal. Later, the concluding part of any duly attested writ, giving the date and place of issue. **B** *preposition* M19 On the authority or testimony of (a specified person).

testimonium /tɛstɪ'məʊnɪəm/ *noun* plural **testimonia** /tɛstɪ'məʊnɪə/ L17 **Latin** (from *testis* witness). **1** L17 A letter testifying to the suitability of a candidate for holy orders; a certificate of proficiency awarded by a university, college, etc. **2** M19 *Law* A concluding part of a document stating the manner of its execution. In full *testimonium clause*.

transferred **1996** *Spectator* The *testimonia* collected by his widow [sc. R. A. Butler's] . . . are further reminders of the loss.

testo /'tɛsto/ *noun* plural **testi** /'tɛsti/ E18 **Italian** (from Latin *textus* text). *Music* **1** E18 The words of a song; the libretto of an opera; the text or theme of a composition. **2** M20 The narrator in an oratorio or similar work.

tête-à-tête /ˌteɪtɑː'teɪt/, /ˌtɛta'tɛt/ *noun, adverb, adjective, & verb* (also **tête à tête**) L17 **French** (literally, 'head to head'). **A** *noun* **1** L17 A private conversation or interview, especially between two people. **2** M19 An S-shaped sofa, enabling two people to sit face to face. **B** *adverb* E18 Together in private; face to face. **C** *attributive* or as *adjective* E18 Private, confidential; involving or attended by only two people. **D** *intransitive verb* M19 Engage in private conversation (*with* another person).

A.1 1995 D. Lodge *Therapy* I knew I was in for a long, harrowing *tête à tête*.

tête-bêche /tɛtbɛʃ/; /tɛt'bɛʃ/, /teɪt'bɛʃ/ *noun & adjective* plural of noun pronounced same L19 **French** (from *tête* head + *bêche* (reduced from *béchevet*), literally, 'double bed-head'). *Philately* (A postage stamp) printed upside down relative to the next stamp in the same row or column.

tête de boeuf /tɛt də bœf/ *adjective phrase* L19 **French** (literally, 'ox's head'). *Embroidery* Designating an embroidery stitch involving two slanting stitches in the form of a vee.

tête de cuvée /tɛt də kyve/ *noun phrase* plural **têtes de cuvées** (pronounced same) E20 **French** (literally, 'head of the vatful'). (Wine from) a vineyard producing the best wine in the locality of a village.

tête de nègre /tɛt də nɛgr/ *adjective phrase* E20 **French** (literally, 'negro's head'). Of a dark brown colour approaching black.

tête montée /tɛt mɔ̃te/ *adjective & noun phrase* E19 **French** (literally, 'excited head'). **A** *adjective phrase* E19 Overexcited, agitated, worked up. **B** *noun phrase* M19 plural pronounced same. Such a state of mind.

têtes de cuvées plural of TÊTE DE CUVÉE.

textura /tɛk'stjʊərə/ *noun & adjective* E20 **German** ((also *Textur*) from Latin *textura* texture). (Designating or pertaining to) any of a group of typefaces first used in the earliest printed books, distinguished by narrow, angular letters and a strong vertical emphasis. Also, (designating or pertaining to) the formal manuscript hand on which these typefaces were based.

textus receptus /ˌtɛkstəs rɪ'sɛptəs/ *noun* plural same M19 **Latin** (literally, 'received text' (medieval Latin *textus* the Gospel)). A text accepted as authoritative; *specifically* (usually with capital initials) the received text of the Greek New Testament.

thali /'tɑːli/ *noun* M20 **Hindustani** (*thālī* from Sanskrit *sthālī*). A metal platter or flat dish on which Indian food is served; an Indian meal comprising a selection of assorted dishes, especially served on such a platter.

thalweg /'tɑːlvɛg/, /'θɑːlwɛg/ *noun* (also **talweg**) M19 **German** (from *thal* (now *Tal*) valley + *Weg* way). *Physical Geography* The line of fastest descent from any point on land; *especially* one connecting the deepest points along a river channel or the lowest points along a valley floor.

1996 M. Anderson *Frontiers* According to the 1913 Protocol of Constantinople, part of the frontier was to follow the *Thalweg*, but the waters of the lower part of the river and the estuary remained Turkish.

theatrum mundi /teɪˌɑːtrəm ˈmʌndʌɪ/, /teɪˌɑːtrəm ˈmʊndiː/ *noun phrase* M16 **Latin** (literally, 'theatre of the world'). The world thought of as a theatrical presentation of all aspects of human life.

thé complet /te kɔ̃plɛ/ *noun phrase* plural **thés complets** (pronounced same) M20 **French** (literally, 'complete tea'). A light meal including tea and usually bread and cake. Cf. CAFÉ COMPLET.

thé dansant /te dɑ̃sɑ̃/ *noun phrase* plural **thés dansants** (pronounced same) E19 **French** (literally, 'dancing tea'). An afternoon entertainment at which there is dancing and tea is served.

1995 *Spectator* One afternoon I went to Hatchett's to observe a typical afternoon *thé dansant*. What a strange thing to have done.

thermae /ˈθəːmiː/ *noun plural* M16 **Latin** (from Greek *thermai* hot baths). *Classical Antiquities* Public baths.

■ The Anglicized singular form, *therm*, is seldom found.

thesaurus /θɪˈsɔːrəs/ *noun* plural **thesauri** /θɪˈsɔːrʌɪ/, **thesauruses** L16 **Latin** (from Greek *thesauros* store, treasure, storehouse). **1** L16 A dictionary; an encyclopedia. **b** M19 A collection of words arranged in lists or groups according to sense. Also (chiefly *North American*), a dictionary of synonyms (and occasionally of antonyms). **c** M20 A classified list of terms, especially keywords, in a particular field, for use in indexing and information retrieval. **2** E19 A treasury, especially of a temple.

thesis /ˈθiːsɪs/; *in branch I also* /ˈθɛsɪs/ *noun* plural **theses** /ˈθiːsiːz/ LME **Late Latin** (from Greek = putting, placing; a proposition, an affirmation, from *the-* base of *tithenai* to put, place). **I 1** LME The syllable or part of a metrical foot that is unstressed (originally, *Classical Prosody*, by lowered pitch or volume); the stressed beat in barred music. Opposed to ARSIS. **II 2** L16 A proposition laid down or stated, *especially* one maintained or put forward as a premise in an argument, or to be proved; a statement, an assertion, a tenet. **3** L16 A dissertation to maintain and prove a thesis or proposition; *especially* one written or submitted by a candidate as the sole or principal requirement for a university degree.

theta /ˈθiːtə/ *noun* LME **Greek** (*thēta*). **1** LME The eighth letter (Θ, θ) of the Greek alphabet, also used in transliterating other languages. Also, the phonetic symbol θ, used *specifically* in the International Phonetic Alphabet to represent a voiceless dental fricative. **2** M20 *Chemistry* Used *attributively* to designate the temperature of a polymer solution at which it behaves ideally as regards its osmotic pressure (also θ, Θ *temperature*), and the conditions, solvent, etc., associated with such behaviour. **3** M20 *Particle Physics* A meson that decays into two pions, now identified as a kaon. Also *theta meson*, *θ-meson*.

■ In a transferred use of sense 1, *theta* is a sign of doom or a death sentence, in allusion to the custom of using θ as standing for *thanatos* 'death' on the ballots used in voting on a sentence of life or death in ancient Greece.

tholos /ˈθɒlɒs/ *noun* plural **tholoi** /ˈθɒlɔɪ/ (also (especially in sense 1) **tholus** /ˈθəʊləs/, plural **tholi** /ˈθəʊlʌɪ/) M17 **Latin** (*tholus*, Greek *tholos*). **1** M17 *Architecture* A circular domed building or structure; a dome, a cupola. **2** L19 *Greek Antiquities* A dome-shaped tomb, especially of the Mycenaean period. Also *tholos tomb*.

thorax /ˈθɔːraks/ *noun* plural **thoraces** /ˈθɔːrəsiːz/, **thoraxes** LME **Latin** (from Greek *thōrax*, *thōrak-*). **1** LME *Anatomy* and *Zoology* The part of the body of a mammal between the neck and the abdomen; the chest. Also, the corresponding part of a bird, reptile, amphibian, or fish. **2** M18 *Zoology* The middle section of the body of an arthropod, between the head and the abdomen. **3** M19 *Greek Antiquities* A breastplate, a cuirass.

threnos /ˈθriːnɒs/ plural **threnoi** /ˈθriːnɔɪ/ E17 **Greek** (*thrēnos* funeral lament). A song of lamentation; a dirge, a threnody.

■ The Anglicized form *threne* (cf. Old French *thrène*) was in use earlier (LME), but is now chiefly poetic. *Threnos* was the heading given by Shakespeare to the lament in his *Phoenix and Turtle* (1601), but in modern usage it is generally used with reference to a ritualized funeral lamentation as practised in the ancient Mediterranean world.

Thule /ˈθjuːli/, *in sense 2* /θuːl/, /θjuːl/ *noun* OE **Latin** (*Thule*, *Thyle* from Greek *Thoulē*,

Thulē, of unknown origin; in sense 2, from *Thule* (now Dundas), a settlement in North West Greenland). **1a** OE *Antiquities* A land (variously conjectured to be the Shetland Islands, Iceland, or part of Denmark or Norway) to the north of Britain, believed by ancient Greek and Roman geographers to be the most northerly region in the world. **b** L18 *transferred* ULTIMA THULE. **2** E20 *Archaeology* A prehistoric Eskimo culture. Frequently *attributive*.

Thummim /ˈθʌmɪm/ *noun* M16 **Hebrew** (*tummīm* plural of *tōm* completeness). One of the two objects of a now unknown nature worn on the breastplate of a Jewish high priest (Exodus 28:30). Chiefly in *Urim and Thummim*. See URIM.

thuringer /ˈθjʊərɪŋə/ *noun* M20 **German** (*Thüringer Wurst* Thuringian sausage). A mildly seasoned summer sausage. Chiefly *United States*.

thyrsus /ˈθəːsəs/ *noun* plural **thyrsi** /ˈθəːsʌɪ/, /ˈθəːsiː/ L16 **Latin** (from Greek *thursos* stalk of a plant, Bacchic staff). **1** L16 *Classical Antiquities* A staff or spear tipped with an ornament like a pine cone, carried by Bacchus and his followers. **2** E18 *Botany* Any of several forms of inflorescence.

tian /tjɑ̃/ *noun* plural pronounced same M20 **Provençal** (ultimately from Greek *tēganon* frying-pan, saucepan). A large oval earthenware cooking-pot traditionally used in Provence; a dish of finely chopped vegetables cooked in olive oil and then baked *au gratin*.

tiara /tɪˈɑːrə/ *noun* M16 **Latin** (from Greek, partly through Italian). **1** M16 *History* Any of various head-dresses formerly worn in (the region of) ancient Persia. **2** M17 A richly ornamental three-crowned diadem formerly worn by popes; *figurative* the office of pope. Also more fully *triple tiara*. **b** L18 *Heraldry* A charge in the form of a triple crown, representing the papal tiara. **3** E18 A woman's (usually jewelled) ornamental coronet or headband worn on the front of the hair. **4** M19 The head-dress of the Jewish high priest.

tic /tɪk/ *noun* E19 **French** (from Italian *ticchio*). **1** E19 (A disorder characterized by) a repeated habitual spasmodic twitching of one or more muscles, especially of the face, largely involuntary and accentuated under stress. **2** E19 TIC DOULOUREUX. **3** L19 A whim, a spontaneous reaction, an idiosyncrasy.

1978 C. P. Snow *Realists* He had the tic, common to many writers, of insisting that the table be kept pernicketily tidy.

tic douloureux /ˌtɪk duːləˈruː/, /ˌtɪk duːləˈrəː/ *noun phrase* E19 **French** (= painful tic). Trigeminal neuralgia, in which spasms of pain are frequently accompanied by twitching of the facial muscles.

tiens /tjɛ̃/ *interjection* M20 **French** (imperative singular of *tenir* hold). Expressing surprise.

tienta /ˈtjenta/ *noun* E20 **Spanish** (literally, 'probe'). In Spain: an occasion at which young bulls are tested for qualities suitable for stud and fighting bulls.

tiercé /ˈtjəːseɪ/, *foreign* /tjɛrse/ *noun* (also **tierce** /tɪəs/) M20 **French** (past participle of Old and Modern French *tiercer* to divide into three parts). Especially in France, a method of betting requiring the first three horses in a race to be named in the correct order; a horse-race at which this method prevails.

tierceron /ˈtɪəsərɒn/ *noun* M19 **French** (from *tiers* third). *Architecture* A subordinate rib springing from the point of intersection of two main ribs of a vault.

tiers état /tjɛrz eta/ *noun phrase* L18 **French**. Chiefly *History* The Third Estate, the commons in the National Assembly of pre-Revolutionary France.

tiers monde /tjɛr mɔ̃d/ *noun phrase* M20 **French**. The Third World; the developing nations.

tignon /ˈtiːjɒn/ *noun* L19 **Louisiana French** (from French *tigne* dialectal variant of *teigne* moth). A handkerchief worn as a turban head-dress especially in Louisiana by Creole women.

tika /ˈtiːkɑː/, /ˈtɪkɑː/ *noun* (also **tikka**) L19 **Hindustani** (*ṭīkā*, Panjabi *ṭikkā*). Among Hindus, a mark on the forehead (especially of a woman) indicating caste, status, etc., or worn by both sexes as an ornament. Also *tika dot*, *mark*. Cf. TILAK.

tiki /ˈtɪki/ *noun* L18 **Maori** (= image). A large wooden or small ornamental greenstone image of an ancestor or any human figure.

tikka /ˈtɪkə/, /ˈtiːkə/ *noun* M20 **Panjabi** (*ṭikkā*). *Indian Cookery* (A dish of) small pieces of meat or vegetable marinaded in spices and cooked on a skewer. Frequently with qualifying word, as *chicken tikka*, *lamb tikka*.

tilak /'tɪlək/ *noun* L19 **Sanskrit** (*tilaka*). Among Hindus, a mark or large symbol on the forehead indicating caste, status, etc., or worn as an ornament. Cf. TIKA.

tilde /'tɪldə/ *noun* M19 **Spanish** (from (with metathesis) Latin *titulus* title). **1** M19 The diacritic mark ˜ placed in Spanish above *n* to indicate the palatalized sound /ɲ/, as in *señor*; a similar mark in Portuguese above *a* and *o* and in some phonetic transcriptions to indicate nasality. **b** M20 *Palaeography* and *Printing* The diacritic mark ˜ placed above a letter to indicate contraction of a following *n* or *m*. **2** M20 This mark used as a symbol in mathematics and logic, chiefly to indicate negation.

tilleul /tɪ'jəːl/ *noun & adjective* M16 **French** (from Latin diminutive form from *tilia* linden). **A** *noun* **1** M16 A lime or linden tree. **2** L19 A pale yellowish-green colour. Also *tilleul green*. **B** *adjective* L19 Of a pale yellowish-green colour.

tilma /'tɪlmə/ *noun* M19 **Mexican Spanish** (from Nahuatl *tilmatli*). A simple cloak or blanket secured with a knot, worn by Mexican Indians.

timbale /tam'bɑːl/, /tẽbal/ (*plural same*); *in sense 3* /tɪm'bɑːli/ *noun* E19 **French** (in sense 3, perhaps from Spanish *timbal*, plural *timbales* of same origin). **1** E19 A drum-shaped dish made of finely minced meat, fish, etc., cooked in a pastry crust or a mould. Also (in full *timbale mould*), the mould or crust in which this dish is served. **2** M19 *Entomology* A membrane which forms part of the sound-producing organ in various insects, as the cicada. **3** E20 In *plural* Two single-headed drums played as a pair with drumsticks.

tinaja /tɪ'nɑːhə/, *foreign* /ti'naxa/ *noun* plural **tinajas** /tɪ'nɑːhəz/, *foreign* /ti'naxas/ L16 **Spanish** (augmentative of *tina*, *tino* vat from Latin *tina*). **1** L16 In Spain: a large earthenware jar for holding wine, oil, olives, or salted fish or meat. In parts of Latin America: such a jar used for storing water. **2** M19 In the south-western United States: a rock hollow where water is retained; any temporary or intermittent pool.

t'ing /tɪŋ/ *noun* M19 **Chinese** (*tíng* (Wade-Giles *t'ing*)). In China: a small open pavilion used as a place to rest or view the landscape.

tinnitus /tɪ'nʌɪtəs/, /'tɪnɪtəs/ *noun* M19 **Latin** (from *tinnire* to ring, tinkle, of imitative origin). *Medicine* A sensation of ringing or buzzing in the ears.

tinto /'tɪntəʊ/ *noun* L16 **Spanish** (= tinted, dark-coloured). A sweet deep-red wine. Now also *generally*, (a drink of) any red wine.

tiorba /'tjɔrba/ *noun* plural **tiorbe** /'tjɔrbe/ M20 **Italian**. A theorbo.

tipi variant of TEPEE.

tirade /tʌɪ'reɪd/, /tɪ'reɪd/ *noun & verb* E19 **French** (from Italian *tirata* volley, from *tirare* Proto-Romance verb meaning 'draw'). **A** *noun* **1** E19 A long vehement speech on some subject; a declamation, a denunciation. **2** E19 A passage of a poem dealing with a single theme or idea. **3** L19 *Music* An ornamental run or flourish filling an interval between two notes. **B** *intransitive verb* L19 Utter or write a tirade; declaim vehemently.

tirage /tɪ'rɑːʒ/, *foreign* /tiraʒ/ *noun* plural pronounced same L19 **French** (= drawing, bringing out, printing, from *tirer* to draw). A reprint of a book from the same type; an impression.

tirailleur /ˌtɪrʌɪ'jəː/ *noun* L18 **French** (from *tirailler* to fire in skirmishing order, from *tirer* to draw, shoot). *French History* Any of a body of skirmishers employed in the French Revolutionary War in 1792; a skirmisher, a sharpshooter.

tiramisu /ˌtiːrəmɪ'suː/ *noun* L20 **Italian** (from phrase *tira mi sù* pick me up). An Italian dessert consisting of layers of sponge cake soaked in coffee and brandy or liqueur with powdered chocolate and mascarpone cheese.

tiro /'tʌɪrəʊ/ *noun* (also **tyro**) plural **tiro(e)s** LME **Latin** (= young soldier, recruit). A beginner, a learner, a novice.

■ The medieval Latin spelling *tyro* is also very widely used.

1996 *Spectator* . . . all the business people . . . , whether tyros or managing directors of major corporations, were unanimous about their value.

tirocinium /ˌtʌɪrəʊ'sɪnɪəm/ *noun* (also **tyrocinium**) plural **tirocinia** /ˌtʌɪrəʊ'sɪnɪə/ E17 **Latin** (= first military service on campaign, young troops, from preceding). **1** E17 First experience of anything; training, apprenticeship; *transferred* inexperience, rawness. **2** M17 A band of novices or recruits.

tisane /tɪ'zan/ *noun* LME **Old and Modern French** (*tisane*, also formerly *ptisane*, from

Latin (*p*)*tisana* from Greek *ptisanē* peeled barley, barley-water, related to *ptissein* to peel). A wholesome or medicinal drink or infusion, originally *specifically* made with barley; now (*especially*), a herbal tea.

titre /'tʌɪtə/, /'tiːtə/ *noun* (also (*United States*) **titer**) M19 **French**. **1** M19 Originally, the fineness of gold or silver. Now (*Chemistry*), the concentration of a solution as determined by titration; *Medicine* the concentration of an antibody, as measured by the extent to which it can be diluted before ceasing to give a positive reaction with antigen. **2** L19 *Chemistry* The highest temperature reached during controlled crystallization of free insoluble fatty acids in an oil.

titulus /'tɪtjʊləs/ *noun* plural **tituli** /'tɪtjʊlʌɪ/, /'tɪtjʊliː/ E20 **Latin**. An inscription on or over something; *especially* the inscription on the Cross.

ti-tzu /'tiːtsuː/ *noun* L19 **Chinese** (*dízi* (Wade–Giles *ti-tzu*)). *Music* A Chinese bamboo transverse flute.

tjaele /'ʧeɪlə/, /'ʃeɪlə/ *noun* (also **taele** /'teɪlə/) E20 **Swedish** (*tjäle* ice in frozen ground). A frozen surface at the base of the active layer in a periglacial environment, which moves downwards as thaw occurs. Frequently *attributive*.

tjurunga /ʧə'rʊŋgə/ *noun* (also **churinga** /ʧə'rɪŋgə/) plural **tjurungas**, same L19 **Aranda** (*tywerrenge*). Among Australian Aborigines, a sacred object, *specifically* an amulet.

tmesis /'tmiːsɪs/ *noun* plural **tmeses** /'tmiːsiːz/ M16 **Greek** (*tmēsis* cutting, from *temnein* to cut). *Grammar* and *Rhetoric* The separation of the elements of a compound word by the interposition of another word or words.

toccata /tə'kɑːtə/ *noun* E18 **Italian** (use as noun of feminine past participle of *toccare* to touch). *Music* A composition for a keyboard instrument, intended to exhibit the performer's touch and technique and having the air of an improvisation. Also, a fanfare for brass instruments.

toccatina /tɒkə'tiːnə/ *noun* M18 **Italian** (diminutive of TOCCATA). *Music* A short toccata.

tochis variant of TOKUS.

tofu /'təʊfuː/ *noun* L18 **Japanese** (*tōfu* from Chinese *dòufu*, from *dòu* beans + *fǔ* rot, turn sour). A curd made from mashed soya beans; bean curd.

toga /'təʊgə/ *noun* E17 **Latin** (related to *tegere* to cover). **1** E17 *Roman History* A loose flowing outer garment worn by a Roman citizen, made of a single piece of cloth and covering the whole body apart from the right arm. **2** M18 *transferred* and *figurative* A robe of office; a professional gown; a mantle of responsibility etc.

togidashi /tɒgɪ'daʃi/ *noun & adjective* L19 **Japanese** (from *togu* whet, grind + *dasu* produce, let appear). (Made of) a kind of Japanese lacquer in which gold or silver designs are overlaid with several coats of lacquer which are then rubbed and ground down, revealing the underlying design as if floating below the lacquer surface.

togt /tɒxt/ *noun* M19 **Afrikaans** (from Dutch *tocht* expedition, journey). **1** A trading expedition or venture. Only in M19. **2** E20 In South Africa: casual labour, hired for a specific job.

tohu-bohu /ˌtəʊhuː'bəʊhuː/ *noun* E17 **Hebrew** (*thōhū wa-bhōhū* emptiness and desolation (Genesis 1:2)). That which is empty and formless; chaos; utter confusion.

toile /twɑːl/ *noun* LME **French**. **1 a** LME–L16 Cloth; cloth or canvas used for painting on. *rare*. **b** E20 A painting on canvas. **2** L18 Any of various linen or cotton fabrics. Frequently with French specifying word(s), as in *toile de Jouy*. **3** M20 A reproduction of a fashion garment made up in muslin or other cheap material so that fitting alterations or copies can be made.

3 1982 *Times* I spent seven months of a two-year couture course *just* making toiles for skirts.

toison d'or /twazɔ̃ dɔr/ *noun phrase* E17 **French** (= fleece of gold). *Heraldry* and *Greek Mythology* The Golden Fleece.

tokamak /'təʊkəmak/ *noun* M20 **Russian** (from *to*roidal'naya *ka*mera s *ma*gnitnym polem, toroidal chamber with magnetic field). *Physics* A toroidal apparatus for producing controlled fusion reactions in a hot plasma, in which the controlling magnetic field is the sum of a toroidal field and a poloidal field.

tokoloshe /tɒkə'lɒʃi/ *noun* M19 **Sesotho** (*thokolosi*, *t(h)koloshi*, Xhosa *uThikoloshe*, Zulu *utokoloshe*). In southern African folklore, a mischievous and lascivious hairy manlike creature of short stature.

tokus /'təʊkəs/ *noun* (also **tochis** /'təʊkɪs/, /'tɒkɪs/, **tuchis** /'tuːkɪs/) E20 **Yiddish**

(*tokhes* from Hebrew *taḥaṯ* beneath). The buttocks; the anus. *North American slang.*

toldo /'toldo/ *noun* plural **toldos** /'toldos/ M19 **Spanish** (= awning, canopy, penthouse). **1** M19 In Spanish-speaking countries: a canopy. **2** M19 A South American Indian tent, hut, or other simple dwelling.

tole /təʊl/ *noun & adjective* (also **tôle** /to:l/) M20 **French** (*tôle* sheet iron, from dialect *taule* table, from Latin *tabula* a flat board). **A** *noun* M20 Enamelled or lacquered tinplated sheet iron used for making decorative metalwork. Also *tôle peinte*. **B** *attributive* or as *adjective* M20 Made of tole.

1996 *Country Life* . . . a decorative feature was the use of locally made *tôle peinte*, or japanned tinware, in imitation of porcelain . . . a splendid pair of *tôle* vases on red lacquer, pagoda-shaped stands . . .

tolkach /'tolkatʃ/ *noun* plural **tolkachi** /'tolkatʃi/ M20 **Russian** (from *tolkat'* to push, jostle). In countries of the former USSR: a person who negotiates difficulties or arranges things, a fixer.

toman /'təʊmən/ *noun* E19 **Gaelic** (diminutive of *tom* hill). A hillock; a mound, *especially* one formed of glacial moraine.

tomatillo /'tɒmətɪləʊ/ *noun* L20 **Mexican Spanish** (= small tomato). A small green berry used in Mexican cooking.

tombac /'tɒmbak/ *noun* E17 **French** (from Portuguese *tambaca* from Malay *tembaga* copper, brass, perhaps from Sanskrit *tāmraka* copper; cf. TUMBAGA). *Metallurgy* A brittle brass alloy originally produced in Indo-China, containing from 72 to 99 per cent of copper and from 1 to 28 per cent of zinc, used in the east for gongs and bells, and in the west for cheap jewellery etc. Also called *red brass*.

tombarolo /tomba'ro:lo/ *noun* plural **tombaroli** /tomba'ro:li/ L20 **Italian** (from *tomba* tomb, grave). A grave-robber.

tombola /tɒm'bəʊlə/ *noun* L19 **French** (or Italian, from Italian *tombolare* to turn a somersault, tumble). A kind of lottery with tickets usually drawn from a turning drum-shaped container, especially at a fête or fair.

tombolo /'tɒmbələʊ/ *noun* plural **tombolos** L19 **Italian** (= sand-dune). *Physical Geography* A bar of shingle, sand, etc., joining an island to the mainland.

tomme /tɔm/ *noun* plural pronounced same M20 **French**. Any of various cheeses made in Savoy, a region of south-east France.

ton /tɔ̃/ *noun* M18 **French** (from Latin *tonus* tone). **1** M18 *The* fashion, *the* vogue; fashionableness, style. **2** M18 Fashionable people collectively; the fashionable world. Treated as *singular* or *plural*. Cf. HAUT TON.

2 1969 H. Elsna *Abbot's House* A waste, when all the *ton* will flock here for this event.

tonadilla /tona'di(l)ja/, /tɒnə'di:ljə/ *noun* plural **tonadillas** /tɒna'di(l)jas/, /tɒnə'di:ljəz/ M19 **Spanish** (diminutive of *tonada* tune, song). A light operatic interlude performed originally as an intermezzo but later independently.

tondi plural of TONDO.

tondino /ton'di:no/ *noun* plural **tondini** /ton'di:ni/ E18 **Italian** (diminutive of TONDO). **1** E18 *Architecture* A round moulding resembling a ring. **2** L19 *Ceramics* A majolica plate with a wide flat rim and deep centre.

tondo /'tɒndəʊ/ *noun* plural **tondi** /'tɒndi/, **tondos** L19 **Italian** (= a round, a circle, a compass, shortened from *rotondo* round). An easel painting of circular form; a carving in relief within a circular space.

tong /tɒŋ/ *noun* L19 **Chinese** ((Cantonese) *t'ōng* (= Mandarin *táng*) hall, meeting place). An association or secret society of Chinese in the United States, originally formed as a benevolent or protective society but frequently associated with underworld criminal activity.

tonneau /'tɒnəʊ/ *noun* plural **tonneaus**, in sense 1 also **tonneaux** L18 **French** (= barrel, cask). **1** L18 A unit of capacity for French (especially Bordeaux) wine, usually equal to 900 litres (198 gallons). **2** E20 The rounded rear body of some vintage motor-cars (originally with the door at the back); the rear part of a car with front and rear compartments, or of an open car or carriage. Also, a car having a tonneau.

tonnelle /tɔnɛl/ *noun* plural pronounced same M19 **French** (= tunnel). An arbour.

tontine /tɒn'ti:n/ *noun & adjective* M18 **French** (from Lorenzo *Tonti* (1630–95), Neapolitan banker, who started such a scheme to raise government loans in France around 1653). **A** *noun* **1** M18 A financial scheme by which subscribers to a loan or common fund each receive an annuity for life, the amount increasing as each dies, till the last survivor enjoys the whole income. Also, the share or right of each subscriber in such a scheme; the subscribers collectively; the fund so established. **2** L19 A scheme for life assurance in which the beneficiaries are those who survive and maintain a policy to the end of a given period. **B** *attributive* or as *adjective* L18 Of, pertaining to, or of the nature of a tontine.

tonto /ˈtɒntəʊ/ *noun & adjective* L20 **Spanish**. **A** *noun* L20 plural **tontos**. A foolish or stupid person. **B** *adjective* L20 Foolish, crazy; mad.

■ Colloquial, originally United States.

topi /ˈtəʊpi/ *noun* (also **topee**) M19 **Anglo-Indian** (Hindustani *ṭopī* hat). A hat; *specifically* a pith helmet, a sola topi.

■ *Sola topi* has no etymological connection with the sun or *solar*, but refers to the tropical Asian swamp plants (Bengali *solā*, Hindustani *śolā*) from the lightweight pith of which the sun-helmets were made.

topinambour /tɒpɪˈnambʊə/ *noun* (also (earlier) **topinambou**) M17 **French** (*topinambou*, now *topinambour*, from Portuguese *tupinambo(r)* alteration of *tupinamba* (sc. *batata* potato)). The Jerusalem artichoke, *Helianthus tuberosus*.

topos /ˈtɒpɒs/ *noun* plural **topoi** /ˈtɒpɔɪ/ M20 **Greek**. A traditional theme in a literary composition; a rhetorical or literary formula.

toque /təʊk/ *noun* E16 **French** (corresponding obscurely to Italian *tocca*, *tocco*, Spanish *toca*, Portuguese *touca* cap, woman's head-dress, of unknown origin). **1** E16 Originally, a type of hat with a full pouched crown and a narrow closely turned-up brim, fashionable amongst both sexes in the sixteenth century. Now, a small hat without a projecting brim, or with a very small or closely turned-up brim. **b** E19 *History* A pad used in hairdressing to give additional height. *rare*. **2** L19 A TUQUE. *Canadian*. **3** M20 A tall white hat with a full pouched crown, worn by chefs.

torana /ˈtɔːrana/ *noun* L19 **Sanskrit** (*toraṇa* gate, arched portal). In the Indian subcontinent: a sacred Buddhist gateway, consisting of a pair of uprights with one or more (usually three) crosspieces and elaborate carving.

torc variant of TORQUE.

torchère /tɔːˈʃɛː/, *foreign* /tɔrʃɛr/ *noun* plural pronounced same E20 **French** (from Old and Modern French *torche* torch, from Proto-Romance, from Latin *torqua* variant of *torques* necklace, wreath, from *torquere* to twist). A tall ornamental flat-topped stand for a candlestick.

1995 *Country Life* A detail of a painting of the interior . . . shows in the niches . . . gilt metal torchères in tripod form . . .

torchon /ˈtɔːʃ(ə)n/, *foreign* /tɔrʃɔ̃/ *noun* M19 **French** (= duster, dish-cloth, from *torcher* to wipe). A coarse loose-textured kind of bobbin lace with geometrical designs. In full *torchon lace*.

toreador /ˈtɒrɪədɔː/, /ˌtɒrɪəˈdɔː/ *noun* plural **toreadors**, **toreadores** /ˈtɒrɪədɔːrɪz/ E17 **Spanish** (from *torear* to fight bulls, from TORO). A bullfighter, *especially* one on horseback. Cf. TORERO.

torero /tɒˈrɛːrəʊ/, *foreign* /toˈrero/ *noun* plural **toreros** /tɒˈrɛːrəʊz/, *foreign* /toˈreros/ E18 **Spanish** (from TORO). A bullfighter, *especially* one on foot. Cf. TOREADOR.

tori plural of TORUS.

torii /ˈtɔːrɪiː/ *noun* plural same E18 **Japanese** (from *tori* bird + *i* sit, perch). A ceremonial gateway of a Japanese Shinto shrine, with two uprights and two crosspieces.

toril /toˈril/ *noun* plural **toriles** /toˈriles/ L19 **Spanish**. *Bull-fighting* Any of a series of pens confining the bull before a fight, *especially* the last pen leading to the ring.

toro /ˈtɔːrəʊ/, *foreign* /ˈtoro/ *noun* plural **toros** /ˈtɔːrəʊz/, *foreign* /ˈtoros/ M17 **Spanish** (from Latin *taurus* bull). A bull used in bullfighting.

torque /tɔːk/ *noun* (also **torc**) M19 **French** (from Latin *torques* necklace, wreath, from *torquere* to twist). *History* A neck ornament formed from a twisted band of (usually precious) metal, worn especially by the ancient Celts.

torsade /tɔːˈseɪd/ *noun* L19 **French** (from Latin *tors-* past participial stem of *torquere* to twist). A decorative twisted braid, ribbon, etc., used as trimming; an artificial plait of hair.

Torschlusspanik /ˈtoːrʃlʊsˌpɑːnɪk/ *noun* M20 **German** (= last-minute panic (literally, 'shut door (or gate) panic')). A sense of alarm or anxiety at the passing of life's opportunities, said to be experienced in middle age.

torso /ˈtɔːsəʊ/ *noun* plural **torsos** L18 **Italian** (= stalk, stump, trunk of a statue, from as THYRSUS). **1** L18 The trunk of a statue, without or considered independently of head and limbs. Also, the trunk of the human body. **2** E19 *figurative* An incomplete or mutilated thing.

torte /'tɔ:t/ *noun* plural **tortes**, **torten** /'tɔ:t(ə)n/ **M18 German** (*Torte* tart, pastry, cake, from Italian *torta* from late Latin; cf. TOURTE). An elaborate sweet cake or tart.

■ Originally (ME–M16) used in English in the sense of 'round loaf of bread', probably deriving directly from late Latin *torta* meaning 'round loaf or cake', but the sense derived from German is now the only one current. Cf. LINZERTORTE, SACHERTORTE.

tortellini /tɔ:tɪ'li:ni/ *noun plural* **M20 Italian** (plural of *tortellino* diminutive of *tortello* small cake, fritter). Small squares of pasta stuffed with meat, cheese, etc., rolled and shaped into rings; an Italian dish consisting largely of this and usually a sauce.

torticollis /tɔ:tɪ'kɒlɪs/ *noun* **E19 Modern Latin** (from Latin *tortus* crooked, twisted + *collum* neck). *Medicine* A condition in which the head is persistently or intermittently turned or twisted to one side.

tortilla /tɔ:'ti:jə/ *noun* **L17 Spanish** (diminutive of *torta* cake, from late Latin; see TORTE). Especially in Mexican cookery, a thin round cake made with either cornmeal or wheat flour and frequently filled with meat, cheese, beans, etc. Also, in Spanish cookery, a thick flat omelette frequently eaten cold in wedges.

tortillon /tɔ:'tɪljən/ *noun* **L19 French** (from *tortiller* to twist, twirl). An instrument with tapered ends used for softening the edges of a drawing and for making tints uniform, a stump.

torus /'tɔ:rəs/ *noun* plural **tori** /'tɔ:rʌɪ/, **toruses** **M16 Latin** (= swelling, bolster, round moulding). **1** M16 *Architecture* A large convex moulding, especially at the base of a column. **2** E19 *Botany* The receptacle of a flower. **3** L19 *Zoology* A protuberant part or organ; *Anatomy* a smooth rounded ridge. **4** L19 *Geometry* Originally, a surface or solid generated by the revolution of a circle or other conic about any axis. Now *specifically* a surface or solid generated by the circular motion of a circle about an axis outside itself but lying in its plane; a solid ring of circular cross-section; a body topologically equivalent to this, having one hole in it but not necessarily circular in form or cross-section.

tostada /tɒ'stɑ:də/ *noun* (also **tostado** /tɒ'stɑ:dəʊ/, plural **tostados**) **M20 Spanish** (past participle of *tostar* to toast). A deep-fried cornmeal pancake topped with a seasoned mixture of beans, mincemeat, and vegetables.

Totentanz /'totəntants/ *noun* plural **Totentänze** /'totəntɛntsə/ **L18 German** (literally, 'death dance'). A representation of Death leading people of all ranks in a dance towards the grave; the Dance of Death. Cf. DANSE MACABRE.

totidem verbis /ˌtɒtɪdɛm 'və:bi:s/ *adverb phrase* **M17 Latin**. In so many words.

toties quoties /ˌtɒtɪeɪz 'kwɒtɪeɪz/, /ˌtəʊʃɪi:z 'kwəʊʃɪi:z/ *adverb phrase* **LME Latin** (= so often as often). As often as something happens or occasion demands.

toto /'təʊtəʊ/ *noun* plural **totos** **E20 Kiswahili** (*mtoto* offspring, child). In East Africa: a child; a baby; a young animal; a young servant.

toto caelo /ˌtəʊtəʊ 'si:ləʊ/, /'kʌɪləʊ/ *adverb phrase* **L17 Latin** (literally, 'by the whole heaven'). Entirely, utterly.

tot siens /tɔt 'sɪns/, /tɒt 'si:ns/ *interjection & noun* **M20 Afrikaans** (*tot* (*weer*)*siens* until we meet again, from Dutch *tot* until + *zien* see). In South Africa: (goodbye) until we meet again; an utterance of this.

touché /'tu:ʃeɪ/ *interjection* **E20 French** (past participle of *toucher* to touch). **1** E20 *Fencing* Expressing acknowledgement of a hit by one's opponent. **2** E20 Expressing good-humoured acknowledgement of a valid point or justified accusation made by another person.

2 1981 A. Price *Soldier no More* '*Touché* . . . ' he nodded, accepting the rebuke.

toughra variant of TUGHRA.

toujours gai /tuʒur ge/ *adverb* **E18 French**. Always cheerful, cheerful under all circumstances.

■ Now generally with reference to its use as the slogan of mehitabel the cat in Don Marquis' *archy and mehitabel* (1927).

toujours perdrix /tuʒur pɛrdri/ *adverb* **E18 French** (literally, 'always partridge'). (Implying that one can have) too much of a good thing.

toupet /'tu:peɪ/, /'tu:pɪt/, *foreign* /tupɛ/ (*plural same*) *noun* **E18 French**. A patch of false hair or a small wig to cover a bald spot.

■ Originally, a curl or artificial lock of hair worn on the top of the head, especially as part of a wig, or a wig or natural hair dressed to create such a topknot. Formerly also, a wearer of a toupee or topknot, hence a fashionable person.

tourbillion /tʊəˈbɪljən/ *noun* (also (especially in sense 3) **tourbillon** /tʊəˈbɪlən/, /tʊəˈbɪjən/, *foreign* /turbijɔ̃/ (*plural same*)) L15 **French** (*tourbillon* from Old French *torbeillon*, from Latin *turbellae* bustle, stir, blended with *turbo* whirlwind). **1** L15 A whirlwind, a whirling storm. Now usually *transferred* and *figurative*, a vortex, a whirl; an eddy, a whirlpool. **2** M18 A kind of firework which spins as it rises. **3** L19 *Watchmaking* A revolving carriage in which the escapement is fitted to counteract position errors.

tour de force /ˌtʊə də ˈfɔːs/, *foreign* /turdəfɔrs/ *noun phrase* plural **tours de force** (pronounced same) E19 **French**. A feat of strength or skill; an impressive achievement or performance.

1995 *New Scientist* The book is a *tour de force* by nearly 40 contributing authors . . .

tour d'horizon /tur dɔrizɔ̃/ *noun phrase* plural **tours d'horizon** (pronounced same) M20 **French** (literally, 'tour of the horizon'). An extensive tour. Chiefly *figurative*, a broad general survey.

1995 *Times* His [sc. the Foreign Secretary's] aim, after a *tour d'horizon* of world affairs, was to press against the Opposition the charge of inconsistency and on Europe, abdication.

tour jeté see JETÉ EN TOURNANT.

tourmente /turmɑ̃t/ *noun* plural pronounced same M19 **French**. A whirling storm or eddy of snow.

tournasin /ˈtʊənəsɪn/ *noun* M19 **French** (*tournas(s)in*, from *tournas(s)er* to turn pottery on a wheel, from *tourner* to turn). A knife or spatula used to remove partially dried excess slip from decorated pottery.

tournedos /ˈtʊənədəʊ/, *foreign* /turnədo/ *noun* plural same /ˈtʊənədəʊz/, *foreign* /turnədo/ L19 **French** (from *tourner* to turn + *dos* back). A small round thick cut from a fillet of beef, with a surrounding strip of fat.

tournee /ˈtʊəni/ *noun* (also **tournée** /turne/ (*plural same*)) L18 **French**. A round, a circuit, a tour.

tournette /tʊəˈnɛt/ *noun* E20 **French** (from *tourner* to turn). *Archaeology* A rotating disc resembling a simple form of potter's wheel.

tourniquet /ˈtʊənɪkeɪ/ *noun* L17 **French** (perhaps alteration of Old French *tournicle* variant of *tounicle*, *tunicle* coat of mail, tunicle, by association with *tourner* to turn). A device for stopping or slowing the flow of blood through an artery by compression.

tournure /ˈtʊənjʊə/, *foreign* /turnyr/ (*plural same*) *noun* M18 **French** (from Old French *torneure* from popular Latin *tornatura*, from Latin *tornare* to turn). **1** M18 Graceful manner or bearing, deportment. **2** E19 The turning of a phrase, mode of expression. *rare*. **3** E19 The contour or shape of a limb etc. **4** M19 *History* A bustle. Also, a kind of corset.

tours de force, tours d'horizon plurals of TOUR DE FORCE, TOUR D'HORIZON.

tourte /tʊət/, *foreign* /turt/ (*plural same*) *noun* M17 **French** (from late Latin *torta* round loaf, cake; cf. TORTE). A pie, a tart, a flan.

tourtière /tʊətɪˈɛː/, *foreign* /turtjɛr/ (*plural same*) *noun* M20 **French** (from as TOURTE). **1** M20 A kind of meat pie traditionally eaten at Christmas in Canada. **2** M20 A tin or round baking-sheet for tarts and pies.

tout /tu/ *adjective, noun, & adverb* E18 **French**. All, everything; quite entirely.

■ Mainly in following phrases, but see also LE TOUT, which may be shortened to *tout*, with similar high society connotations, as in *tout Paris* 'all Paris'.

1996 *Country Life Tout* Shropshire (and Hereford) were invited to drinks . . .

tout au contraire /tut o kɔ̃trɛr/ *adverb phrase* E18 **French**. Quite the contrary. Cf. AU CONTRAIRE.

tout compris /tu kɔ̃pri/ *adverb & adjective phrase* E18 **French**. All included, inclusive.

tout court /tu kur/ *adverb phrase* E18 **French**. In short, simply, without qualification or addition.

1995 *Spectator* Unlike Selwyn Lloyd, who was sacked *tout court*, Mr Lamont was offered another job . . .

tout de suite /tu də sɥit/ *adverb phrase* E18 **French**. At once, immediately.

1995 D. Lodge *Therapy* I chipped in *tout de suite* to say that I quite understood.

tout ensemble /tut ɑ̃sɑ̃bl/ *noun phrase* E18 **French** (from TOUT + ENSEMBLE *noun*). (The parts of) a thing viewed as a whole.

■ Independent use of *ensemble* in this sense is slightly later (M18).

tout le monde /tu lə mɔ̃d/ *noun phrase* E18 French. All the world, everyone.

tout Paris see under LE TOUT, TOUT.

tou ts'ai /tuː 'tsʌɪ/ *noun & adjective* M20 Chinese (*dǒucǎi* (Wade–Giles *tou ts'ai*), literally, 'contrasting colours'). *Ceramics* (Designating) a kind of Chinese porcelain delicately decorated with a blue underglaze overlaid with coloured enamels, developed in the reign of Ch'êng Hua (1465–87); (of or designating) this style of decoration.

tout seul /tu sœl/ *adverb phrase* E18 French. Quite alone, on one's own.

tout simple /tu sɛ̃pl/ *adverb phrase* M20 French. Quite simply, just that.

tovarish /tɒ'vɑːrɪʃ/ *noun* (also **tovarich**) E20 Russian (*tovarishch* from Turkic, perhaps Tatar). In the former USSR: comrade.

■ Frequently as a form of address.

tracasserie /trə'kas(ə)ri/ *noun* M17 French (from *tracasser* to bustle, worry oneself). A state of disturbance or annoyance; a fuss; a petty quarrel.

■ Usually in plural.

tragédie lyrique /traʒedi lirik/ *noun phrase* plural **tragédies lyriques** (pronounced same) E20 French (literally, 'lyric tragedy'). A type of serious French opera of the seventeenth and eighteenth centuries making use of tragic mythological or epic subjects; an example of this. Cf. OPERA SERIA.

tragédienne /trəˌdʒiːdɪ'ɛn/ *noun* M19 French (feminine of *tragédien* tragedian). A tragic actress.

tragédies lyriques plural of TRAGÉDIE LYRIQUE.

tragedietta /trəˌdʒiːdɪ'ɛtə/ *noun* L19 Italian (from *tragedia* tragedy). A slight or short tragedy; a dramatic sketch of tragic character.

trahison des clercs /traizɔ̃ de klɛr/ *noun phrase* M20 French (literally, 'the treachery of the clerks'). A compromise of intellectual integrity or betrayal of standards by writers, artists, and thinkers.

■ From *La Trahison des Clercs*, the title of a work by Julien Benda (1927).

1978 *Listener* Look, they say, terrorism is a phenomenon of our times. Let us . . . acknowledge that a diplomat . . . is fair game . . . I find this *trahison des clercs*.

traineau /treɪ'nəʊ/, *foreign* /trɛno/ *noun* plural **traineaux** (pronounced same) M17 French (*traîneau*, from *traîner*). A sledge, a sleigh, *especially* one drawn by one or more horses or dogs over snow or ice.

trait d'union /trɛ dynjɔ̃/ *noun phrase* plural **traits d'union** (pronounced same) E20 French (literally, 'hyphen'). A link or point of contact between or amongst otherwise unconnected characteristics or parties.

traiteur /trɛtœr/ *noun* plural pronounced same M18 French (from *traiter* to treat, supply with food for money). Originally, (a person running) a restaurant in France, Italy, etc., supplying or sending out meals to order. Now, a caterer; (a person who runs) a delicatessen selling prepared meals.

traits d'union plural of TRAIT D'UNION.

trajet /'tradʒɪt/, *foreign* /traʒɛ/ (*plural same*) *noun* M18 French (from Latin *trajectus* place for crossing). **1** M18 A crossing, a passage. **2** M19 The course of a nerve, blood-vessel, etc. *rare*.

tramontana /ˌtramɒn'tɑːnə/ *adjective & noun* ME Italian (*tramontana* north wind, polestar, *tramontani* dwellers beyond the mountains, from Latin *transmontanus*, from *trans-* across + *mons*, *mont-* mount). **A** *noun* **1** ME–M17 The polestar (originally so called because visible beyond the Alps from Italy); *figurative* a guiding star. **2** L16 A person living or originating from beyond the mountains, especially the Alps as seen from Italy; (especially from the Italian point of view) a foreigner. **3** E17 In the Mediterranean and especially in Italy, the north wind (as coming from beyond the Alps). More widely, a cold wind from across a mountain range. **B** *adjective* **1** L16 Living, situated, or originating from beyond the mountains, especially the Alps as seen from Italy. Also (especially from the Italian point of view), foreign; barbarous. **2** E18 Of wind: coming across or from beyond the mountains (especially the Alps).

tranche /trɑːnʃ/, /trɑ̃ːʃ/ *noun* plural pronounced same or /trɑːnʃɪz/ L15 Old and Modern French (from *trancher* to cut, ultimately from Latin *truncare*). **1** L15 A cutting, a cut; a piece cut off, a slice. **2** M20 Chiefly *Economics* A portion of something, especially of income; an instalment of a loan; a block of shares or of government stock.

2 1995 *Spectator* The initial tranche of applications has been remarkably evenly spread.

tranche de vie /ˌtrɑːnʃ də ˈviː/ *noun phrase* M20 **French** (literally, 'slice of life'). A representation of daily life, especially in literature or painting.

tranchet /ˈtrɑːnʃɪt/, *foreign* /trɑ̃ʃɛ/ (*plural same*) *noun* M19 **French** (from *trancher* to cut: cf. TRANCHE). **1** A cobbler's knife. Only in M19. **2** L19 *Archaeology* A chisel-shaped flint implement of some mesolithic and neolithic cultures.

tranchette /trɑːnˈʃɛt/ *noun* L20 **French** (from as TRANCHE). *Economics* A small tranche; *especially* a limited issue of government stocks.

tranquillo /tranˈkwɪləʊ/ *adverb, adjective, & noun* M19 **Italian** (from Latin *tranquillus*). *Music* **A** *adverb & adjective* M19 (A direction:) in a tranquil style or tempo; tranquil(ly). **B** *noun* M19 plural **tranquillos, tranquilli** /tranˈkwɪli/. A movement or piece in a tranquil style or tempo.

transire /tranˈzʌɪə/, /trɑːnˈzʌɪə/, /tranˈsʌɪə/, /tranˈzʌɪri/ *noun* L16 **Latin** (= to go across). *Law* A customs permit for the passage of goods.

trapezium /trəˈpiːzɪəm/ *noun* plural **trapezia** /trəˈpiːzɪə/, **trapeziums** L16 **Late Latin** (from Greek *trapezion* from *trapeza* table). **1** *Geometry* **a** L16 Any quadrilateral that is not a parallelogram. Now *rare*. **b** L17 A quadrilateral having one pair of opposite sides parallel. **c** L18 An irregular quadrilateral having neither pair of opposite sides parallel, a trapezoid. Now chiefly *North American*. **2** M19 *Anatomy* and *Zoology* The first distal carpal bone of the wrist; the corresponding bone in other mammals. Also *trapezium bone*. **3** M19 *Astronomy* An asterism in the form of a trapezium; *specifically* the multiple star θ Orionis in the Great Nebula of Orion.

trapiche /traˈpitʃe/ *noun* M17 **American Spanish** (from Latin *trapetum* oil-press). A sugar cane mill.

trapunto /trəˈpʊntəʊ/, /trəˈpʌntəʊ/ *noun* E20 **Italian** (use as noun of past participle of *trapungere* to embroider). A kind of quilting in which the design is padded by pulling or cutting the threads of the underlying fabric to insert stuffing.

attributive **1977** A. Jeffs *Creative Crafts* Trapunto quilting lends itself particularly well to pictorial use because of its interesting three-dimensional effect.

trascinando /traʃɪˈnandəʊ/ *adverb & adjective* L19 **Italian** (present participle of *trascinare* to drag, pull). *Music* RALLENTANDO *adverb & adjective*.

trasformismo /ˌtrasforˈmizmo/ *noun* E20 **Italian** (from *trasformare* to change, transform). In Italy: a system of shifting political alliances to form a stable administration or a workable policy.

trauma /ˈtrɔːmə/, /ˈtraʊmə/ *noun* plural **traumas, traumata** /ˈtrɔːmətə/, /ˈtraʊmətə/ L17 **Greek** (= wound). **1** L17 *Medicine* Originally, physical wound. Now, external or internal injury; a state or condition resulting from this, e.g. shock. **2** L19 *Psychoanalysis* and *Psychiatry* A psychic injury, especially one caused by emotional shock; a state or condition resulting from this. **3** L20 *generally* Distress; (a) disturbance.

travaux préparatoires /travo prɛparatwar/ *noun phrase plural* M20 **French** (literally, 'preparatory works'). *Law* Drafts, records of discussions, etc., relating to legislation or a treaty under consideration.

travers /travɛr/, /ˈtravəs/ *noun* plural same L19 **French** (*pied de travers* foot askew, from *travers* breadth, irregularity, from *traverser* to traverse). *Horsemanship* A movement in which a horse walks parallel to a wall with its head and neck facing forward and its hindquarters curved out from the wall.

traverso /trəˈvəːsəʊ/ *noun* plural **traversos** E19 **Italian**. *Music* A transverse flute.

travois /trəˈvɔɪ/ *noun* plural same /trəˈvɔɪz/ M19 **North American French** (alteration of French *travail*). A traditional North American Indian vehicle consisting of two joined poles pulled by a horse etc.

trebuchet /ˈtrɛbjʊʃɛt/, /ˈtrɛbəʃɛt/, *foreign* /trebyʃɛ/ (*plural same*) *noun* (also **trebucket** /ˈtriːbʌkɪt/, /ˈtrɛbʌkɪt/) ME **Old and Modern French** (*trébuchet* (medieval Latin *trebuchetum, trabuchetum*), from *trébucher* to overturn, overthrow, stumble, fall, ultimately from *tra-, tres-* (from Latin *trans-* expressing displacement) + *buc* trunk (of the body), bulk, from Frankish *būk* belly). **1** ME *History* A medieval military machine used in siege warfare for hurling heavy stones and other missiles. **2** M16 A small delicately poised balance or pair of scales. **3** M17 *History* A ducking-stool.

trecento /treɪˈʧɛntəʊ/ *noun* M19 **Italian** (= three hundred). The fourteenth century as a period of Italian art, architecture, literature, etc.; the style of the art etc. of this period.

tre corde /ˌtreɪ ˈkɔːdeɪ/ *adverb & adjective phrase* M20 **Italian** (= three strings). (A direction in music for the piano:) with release of the soft pedal; (to be) played with such release. Cf. UNA CORDA.

trefa /ˈtreɪfə/ *noun & adjective* (also **trifa** /ˈtrʌɪfə/, **tref** /treɪf/, and other variants) M19 **Hebrew** (*ṭĕrēpāh* flesh of an animal torn or mauled, from *ṭārap* to tear, rend). **A** *noun* M19 Meat forbidden to Jews because of coming from an animal not slaughtered according to Jewish law; *generally* any food that is not kosher. **B** *attributive* or as *adjective* M19 Of food: not prepared according to Jewish law, forbidden to Jews, not kosher.

B 1966 H. Kemelman *Saturday the Rabbi went Hungry* When a utensil becomes tref, the way you cleanse it is to bury it in the earth.

treff /trɛf/ *noun* M20 **German** (*Treff* meeting(-place), *Treffpunkt* rendezvous, from *treffen* to meet, strike). In espionage, a secret meeting or meeting-place, especially for the transfer of goods or information. *slang*.

treillage /ˈtreɪlɪʤ/ *noun* L17 **French** (from Old French *treille* from Latin *trichila* arbour, bower). A trellis; trellis-work.

attributive **1996** *Country Life* The treillage obelisks are engulfed and obscured by climbers and hedges . . .

trek /trɛk/ *noun* M19 **Afrikaans** (from Dutch *trekken* to pull). **1** M19 Travel by ox-wagon; a journey, especially an organized migration or expedition, made in this way; a stage of such a journey. *South African*, chiefly *historical*. **2** L19 *generally* A long and arduous journey or expedition, *especially* one made on foot or by inconvenient means.

tremblement /ˈtrɛmb(ə)lm(ə)nt/, *in sense 3 foreign* /trɑ̃bləmɑ̃/ (*plural same*) *noun* L17 **French**. **1** L17 A tremor; the act of trembling. **2** L17 A cause of trembling; a terror. *rare*. **3** L19 *Music* A trill.

trembleuse /trɛmˈbləːz/ *noun* M19 **French** (feminine of *trembleur* trembler). A cup having a saucer with a well into which it fits. More fully *trembleuse cup*.

tremendum /trɪˈmɛndəm/ *noun* E20 **Latin** (neuter of *tremendus* fearful, terrible, from *tremere* to tremble). Elliptical form of MYSTERIUM TREMENDUM.

tremie /ˈtrɛmi/ *noun* E20 **French** (*trémie* from Old French *tremuie* (mill-)hopper, from Latin *trimodia* a three-peck measure, from *tri-* three + *modius* peck). *Engineering* A movable metal tube, widening at its upper end into a large hopper, for depositing concrete under water.

tremolando /trɛməˈlandəʊ/ *noun, adverb, & adjective* M19 **Italian** (present participle of *tremolare* to tremble). *Music* **A** *noun* M19 plural **tremolandos, tremolandi** /trɛməˈlandi/ A TREMOLO senses 1, 2a. **B** *adverb & adjective* M19 (A direction:) with tremolo.

tremolant /ˈtrɛm(ə)l(ə)nt/ *noun* M19 **German** (from Italian *tremolante* tremulant). A TREMOLO sense 2a.

tremolo /ˈtrɛm(ə)ləʊ/ *noun, adjective, & adverb* M18 **Italian** (from Latin *tremulus* from *tremere* to tremble). *Music* **A** *noun* plural **tremolos** **1** M18 A tremulous or vibrating effect produced on musical instruments or in singing by rapid reiteration of a single note (especially on a stringed instrument) or rapid alternation between two notes. Cf. VIBRATO. **2a** M19 A mechanical device fitted in an organ to produce such an effect; a tremulant. Also *tremolo stop*. **b** M20 A device, especially a lever, fitted to an electric guitar to produce a similar effect (also *tremolo arm*); an electrical device of similar effect in an amplifier etc. **B** *adjective & adverb* L19 (A musical direction:) with tremolo.

trente-et-quarante /trɑ̃tɛkarɑ̃t/, /trɑ̃t eɪkaˈrɑ̃t/ *noun* L17 **French** (literally, 'thirty-and-forty'). = ROUGE-ET-NOIR.

très /trɛ/, /treɪ/ *adverb* E19 **French**. Very.

■ Colloquial, usually with reference to a fashionable or modishly superior quality.

triage /ˈtrʌɪɪʤ/, *in senses A.2 and B also* /trɪˈɑːʒ/, *foreign* /trijaʒ/ *noun & verb* E18 **Old and Modern French** (from *trier* to sort out). **A** *noun* **1** E18 The action of sorting samples of a commodity according to quality. **2** M20 *Medicine* The assignment of degrees of urgency of need in order to decide the order of treatment of a large number of injured or ill patients. **b** L20 *generally* Prioritization. **B** *transitive & intransitive verb* L20 Assign a degree of urgency of need to (a casualty); separate *out* by triage.

2 1995 *Times Magazine* With so many girls arriving every week, only the strongest are put up for adoption, and the orphanages are forced to practise a sort of triage.

tribade /'trɪbəd/ *noun* E17 **French** (or its source Latin *tribas, tribad-* from Greek *tribas*, from *tribein* to rub). A lesbian.

triclinium /trʌɪ'klɪnɪəm/, /trʌɪ'klʌɪnɪəm/ *noun* plural **triclinia** /trʌɪ'klɪnɪə/ M17 **Latin** (from Greek *triklinion* diminutive of *triklinos* dining-room with three couches, from *tri-* combining form of *treis* three + *klinē* couch, bed). *Roman Antiquities* A couch, running round three sides of a table, on which to recline at meals. Also, a dining-room.

tricorne /'trʌɪkɔːn/ *adjective & noun* (also **tricorn**) M18 **French** (*tricorne* or Latin *tricornis* three-horned, from *tri-* combining form of *tris* three + *cornu* horn). **A** *noun* **1** M18 An imaginary creature with three horns. **2** L19 A hat with the brim turned up on three sides. **B** *adjective* M19 Having three horns; (of a cocked hat) having the brim turned up on three sides.

tricot /'trɪkəʊ/, /'triːkəʊ/ *noun* L18 **French** (from *tricoter* to knit). A fine warp knitted fabric made of a natural or man-made fibre, produced in any of various designs.

tricoteuse /trikɔtøz/ *noun* plural pronounced same M19 **French** (from *tricoter* knit). **1** M19 *History* A woman who, during the French Revolution, sat and knitted at meetings of the Convention or at executions by guillotine. **2** M20 A small table with a gallery used for sewing.

2 1996 *Country Life* Until about that date [1848], the term *tricoteuse* would presumably not have been popular in France for a lady's tray-top worktable. Marie Antoinette had had one, but after that, the word would have been painful to Royalists.

tric-trac /triktrak/ *noun* L17 **French** (from the clicking sound made by the pieces in the playing of the game). Chiefly *History* A form of backgammon.

triduo /'trɪdjʊəʊ/, /'trʌɪdjʊəʊ/ *noun* plural **triduos** M19 **Italian and Spanish** (from Latin TRIDUUM). *Roman Catholic Church* A three days' prayer or festal celebration.

triduum /'trɪdjʊəm/, /'trʌɪdjʊəm/ *noun* E18 **Latin** (use as noun of adjective (sc. *spatium* space), from *tri-* combining form of *tres* three + *dies* day). A period of three days; *especially* (*Roman Catholic Church*) the last three days of Lent.

triennium /trʌɪ'ɛnɪəm/ *noun* plural **trienniums, triennia** /trʌɪ'ɛnɪə/ M19 **Latin** (from *tri-* combining form of *tres* three + *annus* year). A space or period of three years.

trifa variant of TREFA.

triforium /trʌɪ'fɔːrɪəm/ *noun* plural **triforia** /trʌɪ'fɔːrɪə/ E18 **(Anglo-)Latin** (of unknown origin). *Architecture* A gallery or arcade above the arches at the sides of the nave, choir, and sometimes transepts of some large churches, originally *specifically* of Canterbury Cathedral.

Trinkhalle /'trɪŋkˌhalə/ *noun* L19 **German** (literally, 'drinking-hall'). In German-speaking countries: a place at a spa where medicinal water is dispensed for drinking; a pump room. Also, an establishment at which alcoholic drink is served.

trio /'triːəʊ/ *noun* E18 **Italian** (from Latin *tres, tria* three, after DUO). **1** *Music* **a** E18 A composition for three voices or instruments. Also, a group or company of three performers. **b** M19 The central section of a minuet, scherzo, or march, frequently in a different key and style from the preceding and following main division. **2** L18 A group or set of three things or people.

tripot /tripo/ *noun* plural pronounced same M19 **French**. In France: a gaming-house, a gambling-den.

tripotage /tripɔtaʒ/ *noun* L18 **French**. Underhand dealings, intrigue.

triptyque /trɪp'tiːk/, *foreign* /triptik/ (*plural same*) E20 **French**. A customs permit (originally in three sections) serving as a passport for a motor vehicle.

triquetra /trʌɪ'kwɛtrə/, /trʌɪ'kwiːtrə/ *noun* plural **triquetrae** /trʌɪ'kwɛtriː/, **triquetras** L16 **Latin** (feminine of *triquetrus* three-cornered). Originally, a triangle. Now *specifically* a symmetrical triangular ornament formed of three interlaced arcs or lobes.

triste /triːst/ *adjective* (originally Anglicized as **trist**) LME **Old and Modern French** (from Latin *tristis* sad). **1** LME Feeling or expressing sorrow; sad, melancholy; causing sorrow, lamentable. **2** M18 Not lively or cheerful; dull, dreary.

2 1996 *Country Life* When the photographs and descriptions are truly breath-taking . . . , I get the particulars. As my purchasing power is nil, this may seem a triste activity.

tristesse /trɪˈstɛs/ *noun* LME **Old French** (*tristesce* (modern *tristesse*) from Latin *tristitia*, from *tristis* sad). Sadness, sorrow; melancholy.

tristeza /trɪˈsteɪzə/ *noun* E20 **Portuguese** (and Spanish) literally, 'sadness', cognate with preceding). **1** E20 *Veterinary Medicine* In South America: Texas fever of cattle. Now *rare*. **2** M20 *Agriculture* A viral disease affecting some citrus plants, causing yellowing of the leaves, stunting, and death.

triumvir /trʌɪˈʌmvə/ *noun* plural **triumvirs**, **triumviri** /trʌɪˈʌmvɪrʌɪ/ LME **Latin** (from *triumviri* plural, back-form from *trium virorum* genitive plural of *tres viri* three men). **1** LME *Roman History* Each of three public officers forming a committee overseeing any of the administrative departments. Also *specifically*, each member of the first or second triumvirate. **2** E17 *transferred* In *plural* Any group of three persons or things in a joint position of power or authority.

trivia /ˈtrɪvɪə/ *noun plural* E20 **Modern Latin** (plural of TRIVIUM, influenced in sense by *trivial*). Trivialities, trifles; *specifically* unimportant factual information (as) used in the game of Trivial Pursuit.

> **1996** *Times* But the message is surely universal: lift your eyes to the hills, to the greater questions, away from the trivia that clutter our frantic modern lives.

trivium /ˈtrɪvɪəm/ *noun* E19 **Latin** (= place where three ways meet, from *tri-* combining form of *tres* three + *via* way). *History* In the Middle Ages, the lower division of a university course of study, comprising grammar, rhetoric, and logic. Cf. QUADRIVIUM.

trochilus /ˈtrɒkɪləs/ *noun* M16 **Latin** (apparently from Greek *trokhilos*, from *trekhein* to run). *Architecture* A SCOTIA.

Trockenbeerenauslese /ˈtrɔkənbeːrən ˌaʊsleːzə/ *noun* (also **trockenbeerenauslese**) plural **Trockenbeerenauslesen** /ˈtrɔkənbeːrənˌaʊsleːzən/, **Trockenbeerenausleses** M20 **German** (from *trocken* dry + AS BEERENAUSLESE). A sweet white wine of superior quality made (especially in Germany) from selected individual grapes picked later than the general harvest and affected by noble rot.

troika /ˈtrɔɪkə/ *noun* M19 **Russian** (*troĭka*, from *troe* a set of three). **1** M19 A Russian vehicle drawn by three horses abreast; the team of horses for such a vehicle. **2** M20 A group of three people or things working together, especially in an administrative or managerial capacity.

> **2 1996** *Spectator* . . . the terrible troika of Steven Spielberg, Jeffrey Katzenberg and David Geffen announced they were setting up a billion dollar entertainment company . . .

trombenik /ˈtrɒmb(ə)nɪk/ *noun* M20 **Yiddish** (from *tromba* trumpet, horn + noun suffix *-nik* person connected with (something)). A boaster, a bragger; an idle or dissolute person. *United States slang.*

trompe l'oeil /trɔ̃p lœj/ *noun phrase* plural **trompe l'oeils** (pronounced same) L19 **French** (literally, 'deceives the eye'). Deception of the eye; (an) optical illusion; *especially* a painting or object intended to give an illusion of reality.

> **1995** *Times Magazine* Barnes's most recent favourite downstairs cloakroom was a trompe l'oeil potting shed: 'I painted three of the walls as glasshouse walls, with views to the garden beyond, and a brick wall on the fourth wall with shelves covered in garden equipment, such as gloves and watering cans.'

tronc /trɒŋk/ *noun* E20 **French** (= collecting box). In a hotel or restaurant, a common fund into which tips and service charges are paid for distribution to the staff.

> *attributive* **1981** *Times* The money was massaged by managements and distributed on their behalf to staff . . . or paid into an independent tronc fund.

troppo /ˈtrɒpəʊ/ *adverb* E20 **Italian**. *Music* (In directions:) too much.

■ Especially in adverb phrase *ma non troppo* 'but not too much'.

trotteur /ˈtrɒtəː/ *noun* E20 **French** (from as next). *History* An ankle-length skirt, usually flared at the back for ease of walking.

trottoir /ˈtrɒtwɑː/; *foreign* /trɔtwar/ (*plural same*) *noun* L18 **French** (from *trotter* to trot). Especially in France and French-speaking countries: a pavement.

troubadour /ˈtruːbədɔː/ *noun* E18 **French** (from Provençal *trobador* (= Old French *troveor*), from *trobar* (= Old French *trover*) to find, compose in verse, invent, ultimate origin unknown; cf. TROUVÈRE. **1** E18 *History* Any of a class of French medieval lyric poets composing and singing in Provençal especially on the themes of chivalry and courtly love, living in southern France, eastern Spain, and northern Italy between the eleventh and thirteenth centuries. **2** E19 A person who composes or sings verses.

■ The northern French equivalent of the *troubadour* was the TROUVÈRE.

trousseau /'tru:səʊ/ *noun* plural **trousseaus, trousseaux** /'tru:səʊz/ M19 **French** (from Old French *troussel* diminutive of *trousse* truss). The clothes etc. collected by a bride in preparation for her marriage.

■ Originally (ME) in the sense of 'a bundle or package', later 'a bunch', but long rare or obsolete with this meaning. Old French *troussel* in this sense was also represented in English as *trussell* (LME only).

trouvaille /truvɑj/ *noun* plural pronounced same M19 **French** (from *trouver* to find). A lucky find; a windfall.

1996 *Spectator* It is not only the curious *trouvailles* that make this travel book a special pleasure.

trouvère /tru:'vɛ:/, *foreign* /truvɛr/ (*plural same*) *noun* (also **trouveur** /tru:'və:/, *foreign* /truvœr/ (*plural same*)) L18 **French** (Old French (*trovere* (modern *trouvère*, *trouveur*) from *troveor*, from *trover* (modern *trouver* to find) to compose in verse, invent, find, ultimate origin unknown; cf. TROUBADOUR). *History* Any of a class of French medieval epic poets composing especially *chansons de geste* and fabliaux, living in northern France between the eleventh and fourteenth centuries.

truite au bleu /trɥit o blø/ *noun phrase* M20 **French** (literally, 'trout in the blue'). A dish consisting of trout cooked with vinegar, which turns the fish blue.

■ Also earlier (E20) as *truite bleue* /trɥit blø/, literally, 'blue trout'.

trullo /'trullo/ *noun* plural **trulli** /'trulli/ E20 **Italian**. In Apulia in southern Italy: a small round house built of stone, with a conical roof.

trumeau /tru:'məʊ/ *noun* plural **trumeaux** /tru:'məʊz/ L19 **French** (literally, 'calf of the leg'). **1** L19 A pier-glass. Also *trumeau mirror*. **2** L19 *Architecture* A section of wall or a pillar between two openings, *especially* a pillar supporting the middle of the tympanum of a church doorway.

tsaddik /'tsadɪk/ *noun* (also **tzaddik**) plural **tsaddikim** /'tsadɪkɪm/, **tsaddiks** L19 **Hebrew** (*ṣaddīq* just, righteous). In Judaism, a man of exemplary righteousness; a Hasidic spiritual leader or sage.

tsar /zɑ:/, /tsɑ:/ *noun* (also **czar**; also (especially in titles) with capital initial) M16 **Russian** (*tsar'* Old Church Slavonic *cěsarĭ* ultimately representing Latin *Caesar*, probably through Germanic; the spelling with *cz-* is not Slavonic). **1** *History* (The title of) the former emperor of Russia; (the title of) certain other eastern European rulers. **2** M19 *transferred* A person with great authority or power; a despot.

tsarevich /'zɑ:rɪvɪtʃ/, /tsɑ:'rjeɪvɪtʃ/ *noun* (also **czarevich**; also (especially in titles) with capital initial) E18 **Russian** (from as TSAR + patronymic *-evich*). *History* The eldest son of the former emperor of Russia; the (male) heir of a tsar.

tsarevna /zɑ:'rɛvnə/, /tsɑ:'rɛvnə/ *noun* (also **czarevna**; also (especially in titles) with capital initial) L19 **Russian**. *History* A daughter of a tsar.

tsarina /zɑ:'ri:nə/, /tsɑ:'ri:nə/ *noun* (also **czarina**; also (especially in titles) with capital initial) E18 **Italian and Spanish** (*tzarina* (*c*)*zarina*, French *tsarine*, *czarine*, from German *Zarin*, *Czarin* feminine of *Zar*, *Czar*). The wife of a tsar; *History* (the title of) the former empress of Russia.

tsaritsa /zɑ:'rɪtsə/, /tsɑ:'rɪtsə/ *noun* (also **czaritsa**; also (especially in titles) with capital initial) L17 **Russian**. *History* (The title of) the former empress of Russia.

tsatske /'tsɒtskə/ *noun* (also **tchotchke** /'tʃɒtʃkə/) M20 **Yiddish** (from Slavonic: cf. Russian *tsatska*). A trinket; *transferred* a pretty girl or woman. *United States colloquial*.

1977 *New Yorker* . . . stocked with a careful selection of New York's best tchotchkes. These include thirteen-inch-long matchbooks.

tsimmes variant of TZIMMES.

tsipouro /'tsɪpʊrəʊ/ *noun* M20 **Modern Greek**. A rough Greek liquor resembling RAKI, sometimes flavoured with mastic gum.

tsitsith /'tsɪtsɪt/ *noun* (treated as *singular* or *plural*) (also **tzitzit(h)**) L17 **Hebrew** (*ṣīṣīṯ*). The tassels on the corners of the Jewish tallith or prayer-shawl. Also, (the tassels on each corner of) a small tasselled rectangular garment with a large hole in the middle, worn under the shirt by orthodox male Jews.

tsores /'tsɒrəs/ *noun plural* E20 **Yiddish** (plural of *tsore* trouble, woe, from Hebrew *ṣārāh*). Troubles, worries; (treated as *singular*) trouble, worry. *United States colloquial*.

tsotsi /'tsɒtsi/ *noun* M20 **Bantu** (perhaps from Nguni *-tsotsa* dress in exaggerated clothing). In South Africa: a hoodlum, *es-*

pecially a member of a Black African street gang wearing clothing of exaggerated cut.

tsuba /ˈtsuːba/ *noun* plural same, **tsubas** L19 **Japanese**. A Japanese sword-guard.

tsugi ashi /ˌtsuːɡɪ ˈaʃi/ *noun phrase* M20 **Japanese** (from *tsugi* next, following + *ashi* foot). *Judo* A method of moving in which the same foot always leads rather than both feet alternating. Also in other martial arts.

tsuica /ˈtsuːɪkə/ *noun* (also **tuica** /ˈtuːɪkə/) E20 **Romanian** (*tuică*). A Romanian plum brandy.

tsukemono /tsuːkɪˈmoːno/, /tsuːkɪˈməʊnəʊ/ *noun* L19 **Japanese** (from *tsukeru* pickle + *mono* thing). A Japanese side dish of pickled vegetables, usually served with rice.

tsunami /tsuːˈnɑːmi/ *noun* plural **tsunamis**, same L19 **Japanese** (from *tsu* harbour + *nami* wave). A long high undulation or series of undulations of the surface of the sea caused by an earthquake or similar underwater disturbance, travelling at great speed and in shallow waters often building up enough height and force to flood the land.

1995 *New Scientist* A tsunami—a series of mountainous waves—is generated when a section of the ocean floor lurches upwards during an earthquake and lofts a vast body of water with it.

tsutsumu /tsʊˈtsuːmuː/ *noun* L20 **Japanese** (= wrap). The Japanese art of wrapping items in an attractive and appropriate way.

tuan /tuːˈɑːn/ *noun* L18 **Malay**. In Malaysia and Indonesia: a master, a lord. Also used as a respectful form of address corresponding to *Mr* or *sir*.

tuchis variant of TOKUS.

tufa /ˈtuːfə/, /ˈtjuːfə/ *noun* L18 **Italian** (obsolete local variant of *tufo*, from late Latin *tofus*). *Geology* Originally, a friable porous stone formed of consolidated, often stratified material; tuff, tophus. Now usually *specifically*, a soft porous calcium carbonate rock formed by deposition around mineral springs.

tughra /ˈtʊɡrə/ *noun* (also **toughra**, **tugra**) M19 **Turkish** (*tuğra*). *History* A Turkish ornamental monogram incorporating the name and title of the Sultan.

tuica variant of TSUICA.

tuile /twiːl/, *in sense 2 also foreign* /tɥil/ (*plural same*) *noun* (in sense 1 also **tuille**) LME **French** (or from Old French *tieule* from Latin *tegula* tile). **1** LME *History* In medieval armour, any of two or more steel plates hanging below or forming the lowest part of the tasses, and covering the front of the thighs. **2** M20 A thin curved biscuit, usually made with almonds.

tule /ˈtuːli/ *noun* M19 **Spanish** (from Nahuatl *tollin*, *tullin*). Either of two species of bulrush, *Scirpus lacustris* and *S. acutus*, abundant in flooded marshy areas in south-west North America, especially in California; an area of low-lying ground in the United States dominated by such a plant.

■ The plural, *tules*, has given rise to the Canadian word *toolies* (M20) meaning 'the backwoods'.

tulle /t(j)uːl/ *noun & adjective* E19 **French** (*Tulle*, a town in south-west France where originally made). **A 1** E19 A fine soft silk bobbin-net used for women's dresses, veils, etc. **2** M20 *tulle gras* /ɡrɑː/ (= fatty), a gauze dressing for the skin impregnated with petroleum jelly. **B** *attributive* or as *adjective* M19 Made of tulle.

tumbaga /tʊmˈbɑːɡə/ *noun* (also **tombaga**, **tumbago** /tʊmˈbɑːɡəʊ/, plural **tumbagos**) E17 **Spanish** (from Malay *tembaga* copper, brass). **1** E17–L18 TOMBAC. **2** M20 Chiefly *Archaeology* An alloy of gold and copper commonly used in pre-Columbian South and Central America.

tu-mo /ˈtjuːməʊ/ *noun* L20 **Chinese** (*dū mài* (Wade–Giles *tu mai*)). In Chinese medical theory, the chief passage through which vital energy circulates, located in the spine.

tumulus /ˈtjuːmjʊləs/ *noun* plural **tumuli** /ˈtjuːmjʊlʌɪ/, /ˈtjuːmjʊliː/ LME **Latin** (related to *tumere* to swell). An ancient sepulchral mound, a barrow.

tundra /ˈtʌndrə/ *noun* L16 **Lappish**. A vast, nearly level, treeless Arctic region usually with a marshy surface and underlying permafrost.

tunku /ˈtʊŋkuː/ *noun* (also (especially in titles) **Tunku**) L18 **Malay**. A male title of rank in certain states of Western Malaysia; prince.

tupik /ˈtuːpɪk/ *noun* M19 **Eskimo** ((Inuit) *tupiq*). A hut or tent of skins used by Eskimos as a summer residence. Also called *summer lodge*.

tuque /tu:k/ *noun* L19 **Canadian French** (from French *toque*). In Canada: a close-fitting knitted cap, *especially* a knitted stocking cap sealed at both ends, one end being tucked into the other to form a cap.

tu quoque /tu: 'kwəʊkwi:/, /tju: 'kwɒkweɪ/ *noun phrase* L17 **Latin** (literally, 'thou also' = English slang 'you're another'). An argument which consists of turning an accusation back on the accuser.

turba /'tʊəbə/ *noun* plural **turbae** /'tʊəbi:/ L19 **Latin** (= crowd). *Music* The chorus in passion-plays and other religious oratorios in which crowds participate in the action.

turbeh /'tə:beɪ/, /'tʊəbeɪ/ *noun* L17 **Turkish** (*türbe* from Arabic *turba* tomb). A small building, resembling a mosque, erected over the tomb of a Muslim, especially a person of sanctity or rank.

turlough /'tʊələʊx/ *noun* L17 **Irish** (*turloch*, from *tur* dry + *loch* lake). In Ireland: a low-lying area on limestone which becomes flooded in wet weather through the welling up of groundwater from the rock.

turnverein /'tə:nvərʌɪn/, /'tə:nfərʌɪn/ *noun* M19 **German** (from *turnen* to do gymnastic exercises + *Verein* society, club). In the United States: a gymnastics club, originally for German immigrants.

turron /tʊ'rɒn/ *noun* plural **turrones** /tʊ'rɒneɪs/, **turrons** E20 **Spanish** (*turrón*). A kind of Spanish confectionery resembling nougat, made from almonds and honey; a piece of this.

tusche /'tʊʃə/ *noun* L19 **German** (back-formation from *tuschen* from French *toucher* to touch). A greasy black composition, in liquid form or to be mixed with liquids, used for making lithographic drawings; lithographic drawing ink.

tutoyer /tʊ'twɑ:jeɪ/ *transitive verb* inflected **tutoy-**, past tense also written **tutoyered** /tʊ'twɑ:jeɪd/ L17 **French** (from the singular pronoun *tu*, *toi*, *te*). In French, address with the singular and more familiar pronoun *tu*, *toi*, *te* rather than the plural and more formal *vous*; *generally* treat or address with familiarity.

tutti-frutti /tu:tɪ'fru:ti/ *noun* (also (especially sense 2) **Tutti-frutti** and as two words) M19 **Italian** (= all fruits). **1** M19 A confection of mixed fruits; *specifically* a mixture of chopped preserved fruits, nuts, etc., used to flavour ice-cream; ice-cream so flavoured. **2** M19 (Proprietary name for) a chewing-gum with a mixed fruit flavouring.

tutti quanti /ˌtutti 'kwanti/ *noun phrase* L18 **Italian**. Everyone, everything; all the people or things of this or that kind.

tutu /'tu:tu:/ *noun* E20 **French** (childish alteration of *cucu* diminutive of *cul* buttocks). *Ballet* A skirt made up of layers of stiffened frills that stand out from the dancer's legs (*classic tutu*) or extend to mid-calf (*romantic tutu*).

tuyère /twi:'jɛ:/, /tu:'jɛ:/ *noun* (also **tuyere**, **twyer** /'twʌɪə/) L18 **French** (from *tuyau* pipe). *Metallurgy* A nozzle through which the air is forced into a forge or furnace.

tvorog /'tvɔ:rək/ *noun* E20 **Russian**. A soft Russian cheese similar to cottage or curd cheese.

tycoon /tʌɪ'ku:n/ *noun* M19 **Japanese** (*taikun* great lord or prince, from Chinese *dà* great + *jūn* prince). **1** M19 *History* A title applied by foreigners to the shogun of Japan in power between 1854 and 1868. **2** M19 A business magnate.

tympanum /'tɪmpənəm/ *noun* plural **tympanums**, **tympana** /'tɪmpənə/ E16 **Latin** (from Greek *tumpanon* drum, from nasalized variant of base of *tuptein* to strike). **1** *Medicine* Severe distension of the abdomen by gas in the intestine, tympanites. *rare*. Only in E16. **2** E17 *Anatomy* and *Zoology* The tympanic membrane or eardrum. Also, a membrane in any animal which is thought to form part of a hearing organ. **b** L19 *Ornithology* Either of the two inflatable air-sacs at the sides of the neck in certain birds, such as grouse. *rare*. **3** M17 *Architecture* **a** The die or dado of a pedestal. **b** L17 A vertical recessed area within a pediment; a similar area over a door between the lintel and the arch; a carving on this. **4** L17 A drum, *especially* a hand drum of ancient Greece and Rome. *archaic*. **5** L19 A kind of wheel (originally drum-shaped) with curved radial partitions, used for raising water from a stream.

typhoon /tʌɪ'fu:n/ *noun* L16 **Portuguese** (partly from Portuguese *tufão* from Urdu *ṭūfān* hurricane, tornado, from Arabic, perhaps from Greek *tuphōn*; partly from Chinese dialect *tai fung* big wind, from Chinese *dà* big + *fēng* wind). A violent storm occurring in or around the Indian subcontinent; *especially* a tropical cyclone occurring in the region of the Indian or western Pacific oceans.

tyro, **tyrocinium** variants of TIRO, TIROCINIUM.

tzatziki /tsat'si:ki/ *noun* M20 **Modern Greek** (from Turkish *cacık*). A Greek side dish made with yoghurt, cucumber, garlic, and usually mint.

tzedaka /tse'dɔka/ *noun* (also **tzedakah**) M20 **Hebrew** (*ṣĕḏāqāh* righteousness). The obligation to help fellow Jews; *generally* charity.

tzigane /tsɪ'gɑ:n/ *noun & adjective* M18 **French** (from Hungarian *czigany*, *cigány*). **A** *noun* M18 A Hungarian Gypsy. **B** *adjective* L19 That is a tzigane; consisting of tziganes; characteristic of the tziganes or especially their music.

tzimmes /'tsɪməs/ *noun* (also **tsimmes**, **tzimmis** and other variants) plural same L19 **Yiddish** (*tsimes*, of unknown origin). A Jewish stew of sweetened vegetables or vegetables and fruit, sometimes with meat; *figurative* a fuss, a confusion.

1974 R. L. Simon *Wild Turkey* Why are you making such a *tsimmis*? Hecht is dead.

tzitzit(h) variant of TSITSITH.

U

U-bahn /ˈuːbɑːn/, /ˈjuːbɑːn/ *noun* M20 **German** (from *U* (abbreviation of *Untergrund*) underground + *Bahn* railway). In Germany and Austria: the underground railway in various major cities.

über alles /ˌyːbər ˈaləs/ *adjective & adverb phrase* M20 **German** (from *über* over + *alles* all). Above all else.

■ Generally used with implicit reference to the opening words of the German national anthem *Deutschland über alles*, misunderstood to mean 'Germany supreme'.

Überfremdung /ˌyːbərˈfrɛmdʊŋ/ *noun* M20 **German** (from *überfremden* to give foreign character to (from *über* over + *fremd* foreign)). The admission or presence of too many foreigners.

■ Used particularly by right-wing politicians in Switzerland protesting against immigrant workers.

überhaupt /ˌyːbərˈhaʊpt/ *adverb* L19 **German** (from *über* over + *Haupt* head, (in compounds) main). In general, (taken) as a whole; par excellence.

Übermensch /ˈyːbərmɛnʃ/ *noun* plural **Übermenschen** /ˈyːbərmɛnʃən/ L19 **German** (back-formation from *übermenschlich* superhuman, from *über* over + *menschlich* human, from *Mensch* person). The highest type of human being, superman.

■ The concept was important in the philosophy of Friedrich Nietzsche (1844–1900), from whom George Bernard Shaw borrowed it for his comedy *Man and Superman* (1903). It—and its opposite UNTERMENSCH—subsequently became part of the vocabulary of the Nazi ideology of the master race. In English translations of Nietzsche, Übermensch is often translated as 'Overman', thus sidestepping the cartoon associations of 'Superman'. In jocular use *über* may be attached to an English noun (see quotation).

1996 *Times Magazine* . . . the nadir came with whispers that *Baywatch*'s uber-babe Pamela Anderson was being lined up to star with Eric Idle's Doctor.

uberrima fides /juːˌbɛrɪmə ˈfʌɪdiːz/ *noun phrase* M19 **Latin**. *Law* The utmost good faith.

ubi sunt /ˌʊbɪ ˈsʊnt/ *adjective phrase* E20 **Latin** (= 'where are', the opening words or refrain of certain medieval Latin works). *Literary Criticism* Designating or characterizing a literary theme or passage lamenting the mutability of things.

attributive **1996** *Spectator* The whole thing is in fact a subtle homage to all the classic '*ubi sunt*' poems ever written about deserted places where human life once reverberated . . .

uchiwa /ˈuːtʃiwa/ *noun* L19 **Japanese**. A flat Japanese fan that does not fold.

udon /ˈuːdɒn/ *noun* E20 **Japanese**. In Japanese cookery: a thick strip of pasta made from wheat flour; pasta in this form.

uhlan /ˈuːlɑːn/, /ˈjuːlɑːn/, /ʊˈlɑːn/ *noun* (also **hulan** /ˈh(j)uːlən/) M18 **French** (*uhlan*, German *U(h)lan* from Polish *ułan*, *hułan* from Turkish *oğlan* youth, servant). *History* A type of cavalryman or lancer in certain European armies, especially that of Poland or (later) Germany.

uhuru /ʊˈhuːruː/ *noun* (also **Uhuru**) M20 **Kiswahili** (= freedom). National independence of an African country, *specifically* Kenya.

1984 *Listener* An entire continent has seemed hell-bent on self-destruction, despite uhuru, despite the bright hopes of the many thousands who died seeking it.

Uitlander /ˈeɪtlandə/, /ˈɔɪtlandə/, *foreign* /ˈœytlandər/ *noun* L19 **Afrikaans** (from Dutch *uit* out + *land* land). In South Africa: a foreigner, an alien; *specifically* a British person who went to South Africa before the Boer War of 1899–1902.

ujamaa /ˌʊdʒaˈmɑː/ *noun* M20 **Kiswahili** (= consanguinity, brotherhood, from *jamaa* family, from Arabic *jamāʻa* group (of people), community). A kind of socialism introduced in Tanzania by President Nyerere in the 1960s, in which self-help village cooperatives were established.

ukase /juːˈkeɪz/ *noun* E18 **Russian** (*ukaz* ordinance, edict, from *ukazat'* show, order, decree). **1** E18 A decree or edict, having legal force, issued by the tsarist Russian government. **2** E19 *generally* Any proclamation or decree; an order, an arbitrary command.

2 1995 *Times* . . . when I am made Emperor of the Universe, my first ukase will be to make it a capital offence to complain about anyone's dead relatives . . .

ukeke /uː'keɪkeɪ/ *noun* L19 **Hawaiian** (*'ūkēkē*). A Hawaiian stringed instrument consisting of a strip of wood with two or three strings that are played with the fingers and mouth.

ukelele variant of UKULELE.

ukemi /'uːkeɪmi/ *noun* M20 **Japanese** (from *uke* person held or thrown + *mi* body). *Judo* The art of falling safely.

ukha /ʊ'xa/ *noun* (also **oukha**) E20 **Russian**. A Russian fish soup.

uki /'uːki/ *noun* E20 **Japanese** (= floating). *Judo* Used in the names of various techniques involving a controlled throw in which the opponent's feet and body leave the ground.

ukiyo-e /ˌukijo'jeː/, /ˌuːkɪjəʊ'jeɪ/ *noun* L19 **Japanese** (from *ukiyo* fleeting world (from *uku* float, go by fleetingly + *yo* world) + *e* picture). A Japanese art-form in which everyday subjects are treated simply in woodblock prints or paintings; a work in this art-form.

ukulele /juːkə'leɪli/ *noun* (also **ukelele**) L19 **Hawaiian** (literally, 'jumping flea'). A small four-stringed guitar originating in Hawaii but developed from an earlier Portuguese instrument.

■ Colloquially abbreviated to *uke*.

ulema /'ʊləmə/, /'uːlɪmə/, /uːlə'mɑː/ *noun* (also **ulama** /'ʊləmə/, /uːlə'mɑː/) L17 **Arabic** (Turkish, Persian) (*'ulamā'*, plural of *'ālim*, *'alīm* learned, from *'alima* to have (religious) knowledge). **1** L17 *collectively* or in *plural* The members of a Muslim society or country who are recognized as having specialist knowledge of Islamic sacred law and theology. **2** M19 A person who belongs to a *ulema*.

ulpan /ʊl'pan/ *noun* plural **ulpanim** /ˌʊlpa'niːm/ M20 **Modern Hebrew** (*ulpān*, from Aramaic *allēp* to teach). An intensive course in the Hebrew language, originally for immigrants to the State of Israel; a centre providing such a course; *transferred* any intensive language course.

ult. abbreviation of ULTIMO.

ultima ratio /ˌʌltɪmə 'reɪʃɪəʊ/ *noun phrase* M19 **Latin**. The final sanction.

ultimata plural of ULTIMATUM.

ultima Thule /ˌʌltɪmə 'tjuːli/ *noun phrase* (also **ultima thule**) L18 **Latin** (= farthest Thule). The type of the extreme limit of travel and discovery; *figurative* the highest or uttermost point or degree attained or attainable, the (lowest) limit, the nadir. Cf. THULE.

ultimatum /ʌltɪ'meɪtəm/ *noun* plural **ultimatums**, **ultimata** /ʌltɪ'meɪtə/ M18 **Latin** (use as noun of neuter of late Latin *ultimatus* in the medieval Latin senses 'final, completed'). **1** M18 The final terms presented by one party in a dispute etc. to another, the rejection of which could cause a breakdown in relations, a declaration of war, an end of cooperation, etc. **2** M18 The final point, the extreme limit; an ultimate end or aim. (Followed by *of*.) **3** M19 A primary element beyond which advance or analysis is impossible; something fundamental.

ultimo /'ʌltɪməʊ/ *adjective* L16 **Latin** ((sc. *die* or *mense*) ablative singular masculine of *ultimus* last, final). **1** L16–L17 Designating the last day (of a specified month). **2** E17 Of last month. Frequently written *ult.*, *ulto.*

ultra /'ʌltrə/ *adjective & noun* E19 **Latin** (independent use of *ultra-* lying beyond). **A** *adjective* **1** E19 Of a person or party: holding extreme views in politics or other matters of opinion. **2** E19 Going beyond what is normal or ordinary; excessive, extreme. **B** *noun* **1** E19 A person holding extreme views. **2** L20 A long-distance run of great length. *colloquial*.

■ Originally introduced as an abbreviation for French *ultra-royaliste*, referring to a political party in early nineteenth-century France.

B.1 1996 *Spectator* He hopes to encourage the Thatcherite ultras to continue undermining Mr Major . . .

ultra crepidam /ˌʌltrə 'krɛpɪdam/ *preposition* L19 **Latin**. On matters beyond a person's knowledge.

ultra vires /ˌʌltrə 'vʌɪriːz/, /ˌʊltrɑː 'viːreɪz/ *adverb phrase* L18 **Latin** (= beyond the powers). Chiefly *Law*. Beyond the powers or legal authority of a corporation or person.

■ Opposed to INTRA VIRES.

1996 *Times* The only possible challenge would be to claim Mr Lang's block for the . . . merger was *ultra vires*, that it was not in Mr Lang's power to make such a decision.

ultreya /ul'treja/, /ʊl'treɪə/ *noun* M20 **Spanish** (apparently recalling the medieval cry *(E)ultreya* 'onward!', 'forward!' in the hymn sung by pilgrims to Compostela). *Roman Catholic Church* A regular discussion group held by participants in a CURSILLO.

umbilicus /ʌm'bɪlɪkəs/, /ʌmbɪ'lʌɪkəs/ *noun* plural **umbilici** /ʌm'bɪlɪsʌɪ/, **umbilicuses** L17 **Latin** (from base of UMBO, related to Greek *omphalos* and Indo-European base of navel). **1** L17 *Anatomy* A navel. **b** M19 *Botany* The scar on a seed marking its separation from the placenta; the hilum. Now *rare*. **2** *Mathematics* A focus of an ellipse. Only in E18. **b** M19 An umbilical point. **3** E19 *Biology* A small usually central depression or hole suggestive of a navel.

umbo /'ʌmbəʊ/ *noun* plural **umbones** /ʌm'bəʊniːz/, **umbos** E18 **Latin** (= shield-boss, knob). **1** E18 The boss of a shield. **2** M18 A rounded or conical projection or knob, especially in the centre of a rounded natural structure.

umbra /'ʌmbrə/ *noun* plural **umbras, umbrae** /'ʌmbriː/ L16 **Latin**. **1** L16 A phantom, a ghost. **2** M17 A shadow; *especially* (*Astronomy*) the shadow cast by the moon or earth during an eclipse. **3** An inseparable companion, a hanger-on.

umfaan /'ʊmfɑːn/ *noun* M19 **Zulu** (*umFana* small boy). In South Africa: a young African boy, *especially* one employed in domestic service.

umfundisi /ʊm'fʊndɪsi/, /ˌʊmfʊn'diːzi/ *noun* E19 **Xhosa and Zulu** (*umFundisi*). In South Africa: a teacher, a minister, a missionary. Also used as a respectful form of address.

umiak /'uːmɪak/ *noun* (also **umiaq, oomiak**) M18 **Eskimo** ((Inuit) *umiaq*). A large Eskimo canoe with a wooden frame covered in skins, *especially* one paddled by women.

umlaut /'ʊmlaʊt/ *noun* M19 **German** (from *um-* about + *Laut* sound). **1** M19 *Philology* Vowel change arising historically by partial assimilation to an adjacent sound, usually a vowel or semivowel in a following syllable (often now lost), as in German *Mann, Männer*, or English *man, men*. Also called (*vowel*) *mutation*. **2** M20 A diacritical sign (¨) placed over a vowel, especially in Germanic languages, to indicate such a change.

2 *figurative* **1995** *Spectator* The colour nude photos of her [sc. Mimi Papandreou's] spectacular umlauts have 'graced' the Athenian front pages non-stop . . .

umma /'ʊmə/ *noun* L19 **Arabic** (= people, community, nation). The Muslim community, originally founded by Muhammad at Medina, comprising individuals bound to one another predominantly by religious ties.

umrah /'ʊmrɑː/ *noun* E19 **Arabic** (*'umra*). *Islam* A lesser pilgrimage to Mecca made independently of or at the same time as the HAJJ, and consisting of a number of devotional rituals performed within the city.

Umwelt /'ʊmvɛlt/ *noun* plural **Umwelten** /'ʊmvɛltən/ M20 **German** (= environment). The outer world as it affects and is perceived by the organisms inhabiting it; the environment.

una corda /ˌuːnə 'kɔːdə/ *adverb & adjective phrase* M19 **Italian** (= one string). *Music* (A direction:) using the soft pedal of the piano.

una voce /juːneɪ 'vəʊsiː/, /ˌuːnə 'vəʊkeɪ/ *adverb phrase* M16 **Latin** (*una* ablative singular feminine of *unus* one + *voce* ablative singular of *vox* voice). With one voice; unanimously.

unberufen /ˌʊnbə'ruːfən/ *interjection* M19 **German** (= unauthorized, gratuitous). Touch wood! (to avert ill luck).

unda maris /ˌʌndə 'mɑːrɪs/ *noun phrase* E19 **Latin** (literally, 'wave of the sea'). *Music* A type of organ-stop, usually consisting of two ranks of pipes, one of which is tuned slightly sharp or flat, together producing a slowly undulating tone.

Unding /'ʊndɪŋ/ *noun* M20 **German** (= absurdity). A non-existent thing, a vague abstraction, a concept having no properties.

und so weiter /ˌʊnt zo 'vaɪtər/ *adverb phrase* L19 **German**. And so forth.

unheimlich /ʊn'haɪmlɪç/ *adjective* L19 **German**. Uncanny, weird.

unicum /'juːnɪkəm/ *noun* plural **unica** /'juːnɪkə/ L19 **Latin** (neuter singular of *unicus* unique). A unique example, specimen, or thing.

Untergang /'ʊntərgaŋ/ *noun* M20 **German** (= decline, downfall). An irreversible decline, especially leading to the destruction of culture or civilization.

■ Often used with implicit allusion to Oswald Spengler's *Der Untergang des Abendlandes* (1918), translated as *The Decline of the West*.

Untermensch /'ʊntərˌmɛnʃ/ *noun* plural **Untermenschen** /'ʊntərˌmɛnʃən/ M20

German. Especially in Nazi Germany, a person regarded or classified as racially inferior.

1996 *Country Life* Himmler believed that their [sc. the Austrians'] historical involvement with other races made them more suitable than pure Germans for dealing with the *Untermensch*.

unum necessarium /juːnəm nɛsɪ ˈsɛːrɪəm/ *noun phrase* M20 **Modern Latin** (from (Vulgate) Latin *unum est necessarium* one thing is necessary (Luke 10:42)). The one or only necessary thing, the essential element.

uomo universale /ˌwoːmo univerˈsɑːle/ *noun phrase* plural **uomini universali** /ˌwoːmini univerˈsɑːli/ M20 **Italian** (literally, 'universal man'). A man who excels in the major fields of learning and action. Also called *Renaissance man*.

upsara variant of APSARA.

upsilon /ʌpˈsʌɪlən/, /ˈʊpsɪlɒn/, /juːp ˈsʌɪlən/ *noun* M17 **Greek** (*u psilon* simple or slender u, from *psilos* slender, with reference to the need to distinguish upsilon from the diphthong οι, with which upsilon shared a pronunciation in late Greek). **1** M17 The twentieth letter (Υ, υ) of the Greek alphabet. **2** L20 *Particle Physics* A meson with a mass of about 9.4 GeV. Also *upsilon particle*.

ur- /ʊə/ M19 **German** (combining form). Forming words with the sense 'primitive, original, earliest'.

1983 *Sunday Telegraph* Russell Hoban is an ur-novelist, a maverick voice that is like no other.

uraeus /jʊˈriːəs/ *noun* plural **uraei** /jʊ ˈriːʌɪ/ M19 **Modern Latin** (from Greek *ouraios* (perhaps from *oura* tail), representing Egyptian word for 'cobra'). *Egyptian Antiquities* A representation of the sacred asp or snake, symbolizing supreme power, especially worn on the head-dresses of ancient Egyptian divinities and sovereigns.

urbi et orbi /ˌəːbɪ ɛt ˈɔːbi/ *adverb phrase* M19 **Latin.** (Of a papal proclamation etc.) to the city (of Rome) and to the world; *transferred* for general information or acceptance, to everyone.

1973 M. Bence-Jones *Palaces of Raj* One of the nobles, whose bard would, every two hours of the night, proclaim *urbi et orbi* . . . his titles and honours.

urbs /əːbz/ *noun* M20 **Latin** (= city). The city, especially as a symbol of harsh or busy modern life.

Urfirnis /ˈʊəfəːnɪs/ *noun & adjective* E20 **German** (from UR- + *firnis* varnish, veneer). *Greek Archaeology* (Designating) an early form of Greek pottery characterized by the use of dark lustrous paint.

Urheimat /ˈuːrˌhaɪmat/ *noun* M20 **German** (from UR- + *Heimat* home, homeland). The place of origin of a people or language.

Urim /ˈjʊərɪm/ *noun* M16 **Hebrew** (*'ūrīm* plural of *'ōr*). One of the two objects of a now unknown nature worn on the breastplate of a Jewish high priest. Chiefly in *Urim and Thummim*. Cf. THUMMIM.

figurative **1996** *Oldie* Everybody has to have a say nowadays, and the practitioner who can hit the media headlines becomes a pundit, a Urim and Thummim.

urinoir /yrinwar/ *noun* plural pronounced same M20 **French**. In France: a public urinal.

urlar /ˈʊələ/ *noun* L19 **Gaelic** (*ùrlar* ground, floor). *Music* The ground theme in a pibroch.

urs /ʊəs/ *noun* M19 **Arabic** (*'urs*, literally, 'wedding, wedding feast'). Especially in the Indian subcontinent: a ceremony celebrating the anniversary of the death of a Muslim saint.

Ursprache /ˈuːrˌʃprɑːxə/ *noun* plural **Ursprachen** /ˈuːrˌʃprɑːxən/ E20 **German** (from UR- + *Sprache* speech). A hypothetical early language from which actual languages are derived, a proto-language.

Urtext /ˈuːrtɛkst/ *noun* plural **Urtexte** /ˈuːrtɛkstə/ M20 **German** (from UR- + *Text* text (ultimately from Latin *textus*)). An original or the earliest version of a text.

1983 *London Review of Books* Elaborate versions often point back to the gospel of Mark as a kind of cryptic *Urtext*.

ushabti /uːˈʃabti/ *noun* plural **ushabtiu** /uːˈʃabtɪuː/, **ushabtis** L19 **Egyptian** (*wšbty* answerer, replacing *šwbt(y)* SHAWABTI). *Egyptology* A figurine of a dead person, made of faience, stone, wood, etc., and placed with the body in the tomb to substitute for the dead person in any work required in the afterlife. Also *ushabti-figure*.

usine /juːˈziːn/ *noun* L18 **French** (= factory, (in early use) water-mill). **1** Material used or suitable for a furnace or foundry. Only in L18. **2** M19 A factory; *especially* a West Indian sugar factory.

usque ad nauseam earlier variant of AD NAUSEAM.

uti possidetis /juːtʌɪ pɒsɪˈdiːtɪs/, /juːtʌɪ pɒsɪˈdeɪtɪs/ *noun phrase* L17 **Late Latin** (= as you possess). *Law* A principle whereby property or territory not expressly disposed of in a treaty remains in the hands of the party holding it at the end of hostilities.

1996 M. Anderson *Frontiers* . . . the Organization of African Unity . . . in a . . . 1964 resolution on border disputes accepted the principle of *uti possidetis ita possideatis* (that which you possess, you continue to possess) . . .

utopia /juːˈtəʊpɪə/ *noun* (also **Utopia**) M16 **Modern Latin** (= no-place, from Greek *ou* not + *topos* place). **1** M16 An imaginary place or state of things considered to be perfect; a condition of (ideal) social perfection. **2** M18 An impossibly ideal scheme, especially for social improvement.

■ The origin of the name and of all subsequent *utopias* was the political fable *Utopia* (1516) written in Latin by Sir Thomas More (1477–1535) and translated into English in 1551. The antithesis of a *utopia* is a *dystopia* (modern Latin from Greek *dys-* bad + *topos*), a nightmare society of the kind depicted in, for example, Aldous Huxley's *Brave New World* (1932). The word *dystopia* (M19) was coined originally by J. S. Mill but it has only gained currency since the mid twentieth century, especially in sociological contexts.

1 1996 *Spectator* The narrator, the 'Black Widow', Brady and Chico hope to take the fast lane into that middle-class utopia by robbing a bank.

ut supra /ʊt ˈsuːprə/ *adverb phrase* LME **Latin** (from *ut* as + *supra* above). In a book etc.: as previously, as before, as above. Frequently abbreviated *ut sup.*

uvala /ˈuːvələ/ *noun* E20 **Serbo-Croat** (= hollow, depression). *Physical Geography* A large depression in the ground surface occurring in karstic regions, resulting from the collapse of an underground watercourse.

v. abbreviation of VERSUS.

vaaljapie /'fɑ:ljɑ:pi/ *noun* M20 **Afrikaans** (literally, 'tawny Jake', from Dutch *vaal* pale + *japie* diminutive of male forename *Jaap* from *Jakob* Jacob). In South Africa: rough young wine, cheap or inferior wine.

va banque /va bɑ̃k/ *interjection* M20 **French** (literally, 'go bank'). In baccarat: expressing a player's willingness to bet against the banker's whole stake. Cf. BANCO.

vacherin /vaʃrɛ̃/ *noun* M20 **French**. **1** M20 A soft French or Swiss cheese made from cow's milk. **2** M20 A dessert of a meringue shell filled with whipped cream, fruit, etc.

vade-mecum /ˌvɑ:dɪ'meɪkəm/, /ˌveɪdɪ 'mi:kəm/ *noun* E17 **French** (from modern Latin use as noun of Latin *vade mecum* go with me). **1** E17 A small book or manual carried on one's person for ready reference; a handbook, a guidebook. **2** M17 Anything useful commonly carried about or kept available for use by a person.

vae victis /ˌvʌɪ 'vɪktɪs/ *interjection & noun* E17 **Latin** (= woe to the conquered). (A cry noting or calling for) the humiliation of the vanquished by their conquerors.

■ *Vae* was formerly (M16–M17) used on its own as a denunciation, calling down a curse on someone. *Vae victis* is a quotation from Livy (V. xlviii.9) and is chiefly used as an interjection.

vagantes /və'ganti:z/, /və'ganteɪz/ *noun plural* E20 **Latin** (nominative plural of *vagans* present participle of *vagari* to wander). Itinerant medieval scholar monks.

vagitus /və'dʒʌɪtəs/ *noun* M17 **Latin** (from *vagire* to wail). A cry, a wail, *specifically* that of a newborn child.

vague /vag/ *noun* plural pronounced same M20 **French** (literally, 'wave'). A movement, a trend. Cf. NOUVELLE VAGUE.

vahana /'vɑ:hənə/ *noun* (also **vahan** /'vɑ:hən/) E19 **Sanskrit** (*vāhana*, literally, 'conveyance'). *Indian Mythology* The mount or vehicle of a god.

vahine /va'hine/, /vɑ:'hi:ni/ *noun* M20 **Tahitian** (cf. WAHINE). A Tahitian woman or wife.

vajra /'vʌdʒrə/ *noun* L18 **Sanskrit**. *Hinduism* and *Buddhism* (A representation of) a thunderbolt or mythical weapon, *especially* one wielded by the god Indra.

vale /'vɑ:leɪ/ *interjection & noun* M16 **Latin** (imperative singular of *valere* to be well). **A** *interjection* M16 Farewell. Cf. AVE ATQUE VALE. **B** *noun* L16 A written or spoken farewell.

valet /'valɪt/, /'valeɪ/ *noun & verb* L15 **Old and Modern French** ((also *vaslet*, *varlet* varlet), ultimately related to *vassal* from medieval Latin *vassallus* man-servant, retainer). **A** *noun* **1** L15 *Military* A footman acting as attendant or servant to a horseman. Now *rare* or *obsolete*. **2** M16 A man's personal (usually male) attendant, responsible for his or her master's clothes, appearance, etc. Now also, a hotel employee performing similar duties for guests. **3** M20 A rack on which clothing may be hung to retain its shape. Chiefly *United States*. **B** *verb* **1** *transitive & intransitive verb* M19 Act as a valet (to). **2** *transitive verb* M20 Look after (clothes etc.). **3** *transitive verb* L20 Clean (a motor vehicle).

valeta variant of VELETA.

valet-de-chambre /valɛ də ʃɑ̃br/, /ˌvaleɪ də 'ʃɒmbrə/ *noun* plural **valets-de-chambre** (pronounced same) M17 **French** (literally 'chamber-valet'). A VALET (noun) sense 2.

Valhalla /val'hala/ *noun* L17 **Modern Latin** (from Old Norse *Valhall-*, *Valhǫll*, from *valr* those slain in battle (= Old English *wæl*, Old Saxon, Old High German *wal*) + *hǫll* hall). **1** L17 In Scandinavian mythology, the hall in which the souls of those who have died in battle feast with Odin for eternity. **2** M19 *transferred* and *figurative* A place or sphere assigned to a person or thing worthy of special honour. Also, paradise; a place or state of perfect bliss.

valise /və'li:z/ *noun* E17 **French** (from Italian *valigia* corresponding to medieval Latin *valesia*, of unknown origin). **1** E17 A travelling case or portmanteau, now usually made of leather and of a size suitable for carrying by hand, formerly also for strapping to a horse's saddle. Now chiefly *United States*. **2** M19 *Military* A soldier's cloth or leather kitbag.

vallum /'valəm/ *noun* E17 **Latin** (collectively from *vallus* stake, palisade). **1** E17 A defensive wall or rampart of earth, sods, or stone; *especially* one constructed by the Romans in northern England and central Scotland. **2** E19 *Archaeology* A palisaded bank or rampart, formed of the earth dug up from the ditch or fosse around a Roman military camp.

valse /vɑ:ls/, /vɔ:ls/ *noun* L18 **French** (from German *Walzer* waltz). A waltz; a piece of music for this dance or in its rhythm.

valuta /və'lju:tə/, /və'lu:tə/ *noun* L19 **Italian** (= value). The value of one currency in respect of its exchange rate with another; a currency considered in this way.

Vanitas /'vanɪtɑ:s/ *noun* (also **vanitas**) E20 **Latin** (= vanity). *Art* A still-life painting of a seventeenth-century Dutch genre incorporating symbols of mortality or mutability.

vanitas vanitatum /ˌvanɪtɑ:s vanɪ'tɑ:təm/ *noun phrase* M16 **Late Latin** (= vanity of vanities). Futility.

■ Quotation from the Vulgate version of Ecclesiastes 1:2, often as an exclamation of disillusionment or pessimism.

vaporetto /vapə'rɛtəʊ/ *noun* plural **vaporetti** /vapə'rɛti/, **vaporettos** E20 **Italian** (= small steamboat, diminutive of *vapore* from Latin *vapor* steam). In Venice: a canal boat (originally a steamboat, now a motor-boat) used for public transport.

vaquero /və'kɛ:rəʊ/ *noun* plural **vaqueros** E19 **Spanish** (from *vaca* cow; cf. Portuguese *vaqueiro*). In Spanish-speaking parts of America: a cowboy, a cowherd; a cattle-driver.

■ *Buckaroo*, a now archaic term used (from E19) in the United States for 'a cowboy', was an alteration of *vaquero*.

vardo /'vɑ:dəʊ/ *noun* plural **vardos** (also **varda** /'vɑ:də/) E19 **Romany**. A wagon. Now *specifically* a Gypsy caravan. Originally *slang*.

vargueño /vɑ:'gemjəʊ/ *noun* E20 **Spanish** (*bargueño*, *vargueño* adjective of Bargas, a village near Toledo, the former place of manufacture). A kind of cabinet made in Spain in the sixteenth and seventeenth centuries, with numerous small compartments and drawers behind a fall-front which opens out to form a writing surface.

varia lectio /ˌvɛ:rɪə 'lɛktɪəʊ/ *noun phrase* plural **variae lectiones** /ˌvɛ:rɪʌɪ lɛktɪ'əʊni:z/ M17 **Latin**. A variant reading in a text.

variorum /ˌvɛ:rɪ'ɔ:rəm/ *noun & adjective* E18 **Latin** (literally, 'of various (people)', genitive plural of *varius* various, especially in phrase *editio cum notis variorum* edition with the notes of various (commentators)). **A** *noun* **1 a** E18 An edition, especially of the complete works of a classical author, containing the notes of various commentators or editors. Also *variorum edition*. **b** M20 An edition, usually of an author's complete works, containing variant readings from manuscripts or earlier editions. Also *variorum edition*. **2** L18 Variation; (a) novelty; a source of variety. Also, an unnecessary decoration or flourish. *Scottish*. **B** *attributive* or as *adjective* E18 Of, pertaining to, or designating a variorum; (of matter in a book etc.) obtained or collected from various sources. Also, (of a reading in a text) variant.

varna /'vɑ:nə/, /'vʌrna/ *noun* M19 **Sanskrit** (*varṇa*, literally, 'appearance, aspect, colour'). Each of the four original castes of Hindu society; the system or basis of this division.

varve /vɑ:v/ *noun* E20 **Swedish** (= layer, turn). *Physical Geography* A pair of thin layers of clay and silt of contrasting colour and texture which represent the deposit of a single year (summer and winter) in still water at some time in the past (especially in a lake formed by a retreating ice sheet).

Vaterland /'fɑ:tərlant/ *noun* M19 **German**. Germany as the fatherland.

vates /'veɪti:z/ *noun* E17 **Latin** (= seer, poet, related to Greek *ouateis* (plural) ovate, representing a Gaulish word). A poet, *especially* one divinely inspired; a prophet-poet.

vaudeville /'vɔ:dəvɪl/, /'vəʊdəvɪl/ *noun* M18 **French** (earlier *vau* (plural *vaux*) *de ville*, *vau de vire*, and in full *chanson du Vau de Vire* song of the valley of Vire (in Normandy, north-west France)). **1** M18 A satirical or topical song; *specifically* one sung on the stage. Now *rare*. **2** E19 A light stage play or comedy with interspersed songs.

Also, such plays as a genre; *United States* variety theatre, music hall. Frequently *attributive*.

vedette /vɪˈdɛt/ *noun* L17 **French** (from Italian *vedetta*, alteration (after *vedere* to see) of southern Italian *veletta*, perhaps from Spanish *vela* watch, from *velar* to keep watch, from Latin *vigilare*). **1** L17 *Military* A mounted sentry placed in advance of an army's outposts to observe the movements of the enemy; a scout. **2** L19 In full *vedette boat*. A small vessel used for scouting purposes in naval warfare. Also *generally*, a small motor launch or patrol-boat. **3** M20 A leading star of stage or screen.

veduta /veˈdu:ta/ *noun* plural **vedute** /veˈdu:te/ E20 **Italian** (= a view, from *vedere* to see). In Italian art: a detailed, factually accurate landscape, usually a townscape showing buildings of interest.

veena /ˈvi:nə/ *noun* (also **vina**) L18 **Sanskrit and Hindi** (*vīṇā*). In the Indian subcontinent: a plucked musical instrument with a gourd at one or either end of a fretted finger-board and seven strings.

vega /ˈveɪgə/ *noun* M17 **Spanish and Catalan** (*vega* = Portuguese *veiga*). **1** M17 In Spain and Spanish America: an extensive, usually fertile and grass-covered, plain or valley. **2** L19 In Cuba: a tobacco field.

veilleuse /vɛjøz/ *noun* plural pronounced same E19 **French**. A small and usually highly decorated night-light or night-lamp. Also, a small decorative bedside food-warmer, usually with an enclosed burner under a bowl or teapot, and made of pottery or porcelain so as to give out some light.

veld /vɛlt/ *noun* (also **veldt**) L18 **Afrikaans** (from Dutch = field). Unenclosed country; open grassland.

■ South African; frequently with specifying word, as in *bushveld*, *sandveld*.

veldskoen /ˈfɛltskʊn/, /ˈfɛlskʊn/ *noun* E19 **Afrikaans** (= field-shoe, ultimately by assimilation to VELD of earlier *velschoen*, from *fel* skin, + *schoen* shoe). Formerly, a light shoe made of untanned hide. Now, a strong but usually soft leather or suede boot or shoe for walking etc.

veldt variant of VELD.

veleta /vəˈli:tə/ *noun* (also **valeta**) E20 **Spanish** (= weather-vane). An old-time round dance for couples in triple time, faster than a waltz and with partners side by side.

velours /vəˈlʊə/ *noun* (also **velour**) E18 **French** (= velvet, from Old French *velour*, *velous* from Latin *villosus* hairy, from *villus* hair). **1** E18 A silk or velvet pad for smoothing hats. **2** L18 Any of various plush or pile fabrics similar to velvet and used for hats, garments, upholstery, etc.

■ Cf. PATTE DE VELOURS. The French phrase *velours croché* 'hooked velvet' has given rise to the proprietary name Velcro (M20) for a form of fastening widely used for fabrics, consisting of two strips of nylon with complementary meshed and hooked surfaces which adhere to each other when pressed together.

velouté /vəˈlu:teɪ/ *noun* M19 **French** (= velvety). A rich white sauce made with chicken, veal, or fish stock, and often thickened with cream and egg-yolks. More fully *velouté sauce*.

vendange /vɑ̃dɑ̃ʒ/ *noun* plural pronounced same M18 **Old and Modern French** (cf. VENDEMMIA, VENDIMIA). In France: the grape-harvest; the vintage or grapes harvested; a particular vintage of wine.

vendangeur /vɑ̃dɑ̃ʒœr/ *noun* plural pronounced same L19 **French**. In France: a grape-picker.

1995 *Times* I have travelled the world for half a century gobbling bacteria on biscuits . . . washed down . . . with plonk contaminated by everything from insecticide and cork-mould to *vendangeur's* widdle and Austrian anti-freeze.

vendemmia /venˈdemmja/ *noun* plural **vendemmie** /venˈdemmje/ E19 **Italian** (from Latin *vindemia*; cf. VENDANGE, VENDIMIA). In Italy: the grape-harvest; the vintage or grapes harvested; a particular vintage of wine.

vendetta /vɛnˈdɛtə/ *noun* M19 **Italian** (from Latin *vindicta* vengeance). **1** M19 A blood feud in which the family of a murdered person seeks vengeance on the murderer or the murderer's family, especially as customary in Corsica and Sicily. **2** M19 A similar blood feud, or prosecution of private revenge. Also, a prolonged bitter quarrel with or campaign against a person etc.

vendeuse /vɑ̃døz/ *noun* plural pronounced same E20 **French** (from *vendre* to sell). A saleswoman; *specifically* one employed in a fashion house.

1996 *Times Magazine* Abandoning the stage, she worked as a *vendeuse* for the fashion house Worth.

vendimia /ven'dimja/ *noun* M20 **Spanish** (from Latin *vindemia*; cf. VENDANGE, VENDEMMIA). In Spain: the grape-harvest; the vintage or grapes harvested; a particular vintage of wine. Also, a festival celebrating the vintage.

vendue /vɛn'dju:/ *noun* L17 **Dutch** (*vendu, vendue* from Old and Modern French (now dialect) *vendue* sale, from *vendre* to sell). A public sale; an auction. *United States* and *West Indies*.

veni, vidi, vici /'vemi 'vi:di 'vi:ki/ *interjection* L16 **Latin**. I came, I saw, I conquered.

■ According to the ancient biographer Plutarch, the words in which Julius Caesar reported his victory at Zela over Pharnaces, king of Pontus in Asia Minor, in 47 BC. Used with reference to any swift and overwhelming success.

venire /vɪ'nʌɪri:/ *noun* M17 **Latin** (= to come). **1** M17 *Law* (now *historical*) Elliptically for VENIRE FACIAS sense 1. **2** M20 *United States Law* A panel of people available for jury service.

venire facias /vɪˌnʌɪri: 'feɪʃɪas/ *noun phrase* LME **Latin** (literally, 'to make or cause to come'). *Law* **1** LME A judicial writ directing a sheriff to summon a jury. Now *historical* except *United States*. **2** LME–M18 A writ issuing a summons to appear before a court.

ventre à terre /vɑ̃tr a tɛr/ *adverb phrase* M19 **French** (literally, 'belly to the ground'). **1** M19 Of an animal, especially a horse: represented in a painting etc. with legs stretched out in line with the belly; moving at full speed. **2** M20 Lying on the stomach; prone.

1 1977 E. Crispin *Glimpses of Moon* Man and horse . . . went on to gallop almost *ventre à terre* in the direction of the hedge.

venue /'vɛnju:/ *noun* ME **Old and Modern French** (use as noun of feminine past participle of *venir* to come, from Latin *venire*). **1** ME A sally in order to assault someone, an attack. *rare*. Only in ME. **2** *Law* (now *historical*) The locality within which a cause must be tried. **b** The scene of a real or supposed action or event. **c** An appointed meeting-place, especially for a sporting match or competition; a rendezvous.

■ Also formerly in sense 1 with now obsolete uses in fencing terminology.

vera causa /ˌvɛ:rə 'kaʊzə/ *noun phrase* M19 **Latin** (= real cause). *Philosophy* A true cause which brings about an effect as a minimum independent agency.

vera copula /ˌvɛ:rə 'kɒpjʊlə/ *noun phrase* M19 **Latin** (= true union). *Law* Sexual intercourse with erection and penetration.

veranda /və'randə/ *noun* (also **verandah**; **viranda**, **virando**) E18 **Hindustani** (*varaṇḍā* from Portuguese *varanda* railing, balustrade, balcony, of unknown origin). **1** E18 A usually roofed open portico or gallery extending along a wall of a house or building. **2** M19 A roof or canopy extending over the pavement outside a shop or business establishment. *Australia* and *New Zealand*.

verbatim /və:'beɪtɪm/ *adverb, adjective, & noun* L15 **Medieval Latin** (from Latin *verbum* word; cf. LITERATIM). **A** *adverb* **1** L15 Word for word; in exactly the same words. **2** E16–M17 In so many words; exactly, precisely. **B** *adjective* M18 Corresponding with or following an original word for word. **C** *noun* L19 A full or word-for-word report of a speech etc.

verboten /fɛr'bo:tən/ *adjective* E20 **German**. Forbidden, not allowed.

verbum sapienti /ˌvə:bəm sapˌɪənti 'sat ɛst/ *interjection* E19 **Latin** (*verbum sapienti sat est* a word is sufficient for a wise person). A word to the wise (implying that any further explanation or comment is unnecessary or inadvisable).

■ The expression in its full form is virtually never found; by far the most common variant is *verb. sap.* /və:b 'sap/ (E19), but *verbum sap.* /və:bəm 'sap/ or *verbum sat* /ˌvə:bəm 'sat/ 'a word (is) enough' (M17) are also used.

verd-antique /ˌvə:dan'ti:k/ *noun & adjective* M18 **French** (*verd* (now *vert*) green + *antique* antique). **A 1** M18 An ornamental variety of marble, consisting chiefly of serpentine mixed with calcite and dolomite. **2** M19 A greenish patina or incrustation on brass or copper; verdigris. **3** M19 Greenstone. More fully *oriental verd-antique, verd-antique porphyry*. **B** *attributive* or as *adjective* E19 Made or consisting of verd-antique.

verde antico /ˌverde 'antiko/ *noun phrase* M18 **Italian**. VERD-ANTIQUE sense 1.

Verfremdung /fɛr'frɛmdʊŋ/ *noun* M20 **German**. Chiefly *Theatre* Distancing, alienation, especially of a theatrical audience.

■ Also *Verfremdungseffekt* /fɛr'frɛmduŋsɛ ˌfɛkt/ (= alienation effect). The term was coined by the German dramatist and theatrical producer Bertold Brecht (1898–1956) for his theory of theatrical alienation.

verglas /'vɛːglɑː/ *noun* E19 **French** (from *verre* glass + *glas* (now *glace*) ice). A glassy coating of ice formed on the ground or an exposed surface by rain freezing on impact or the refreezing of thawed ice.

verismo /vɛ'rɪzməʊ/ *noun* E20 **Italian**. Realism or naturalism in the arts, especially with reference to late nineteenth-century Italian opera.

1996 *Times Verismo* is a bogus and self-contradictory term—all theatre is illusion—but there is abundant, near-unbearable human truth in these episodes [of *La Bohème*].

vérité /verite/ *noun* M20 **French** (= truth). Realism or naturalism, especially in cinema, radio, and television; documentary method. Cf. CINÉMA-VÉRITÉ.

verkrampte /fer'kramptə/ *adjective & noun* (also (as predicative adjective) **verkramp** /fer'kramp/) M20 **Afrikaans** (= narrow, cramped). **A** *adjective* M20 Politically or socially conservative or reactionary, especially in racial matters. **B** *noun* M20 Such a conservative or reactionary person.

■ Originally used in South Africa of politicians on the conservative wing of the Nationalist Party, but now more generally of any die-hard reactionary, especially a hardline segregationist Afrikaner. The word often appears in contexts in which it is explicitly or implicitly contrasted with VERLIGTE.

verligte /fer'lɪxtə/ *adjective & noun* (also (as predicative adjective) **verlig** /fer'lɪx/) M20 **Afrikaans** (= enlightened). **A** *adjective* M20 Progressive, enlightened, especially in racial matters. **B** *noun* M20 Such a progressive or enlightened person.

■ In South Africa, the opposite of VERKRAMPTE (see quotation).

1981 *Observer* Like most black African Muslims, Edvis favours a liberal interpretation of the Koran, being *verligte* rather than *verkrampte* in that regard.

vermicelli /ˌvəːmɪ'(t)sɛli/ *noun* M17 **Italian** (plural of *vermicello* diminutive of *verme* worm, from Latin *vermis*). Pasta in the form of long slender threads, often added to soups. Now also (*transferred*), shreds of chocolate used as cake decoration etc.

vernaccia /və'natʃə/ *noun* E19 **Italian**. A strong (usually dry white) wine produced in the San Gimignano area of Italy and in Sardinia; the grape from which this is made.

vernis martin /ˌvɛːniː 'mɑːtan/, *foreign* /vɛrni martɛ̃/ *noun & adjective phrase* L19 **French** (from *vernis* varnish + family name *Martin* of French brothers noted for using the lacquer). **A** *noun phrase* L19 A lacquer or varnish imitating oriental lacquer, used in the eighteenth century. **B** *adjective phrase* L19 Finished in vernis martin.

vernissage /vɛrnisaʒ/ *noun* plural pronounced same E20 **French** (literally, 'varnishing'). Originally, a day before an exhibition of paintings on which exhibitors could retouch and varnish pictures already hung. Now usually, a private view of paintings before public exhibition.

veronique /vɛrə'niːk/, *foreign* /verɔnik/ *postpositive adjective* also **Véronique** E20 **French** (*Véronique* Veronica). *Cookery* Designating a dish, especially of fish or chicken, prepared or garnished with grapes.

verre églomisé /vɛr eglɔmize/ *noun phrase* E20 **French** (*verre* glass + ÉGLOMISÉ). Glass decorated with a layer of engraved gold.

1996 *Country Life* The pair of mirrors with red and gold *verre eglomisé* frames . . . are in the arched alcoves above.

versant /'vəːs(ə)nt/ *noun* M19 **French** (use as noun of present participle of *verser* from Latin *versare* to turn hither and thither). The slope, side, or descent of a mountain or mountain chain; the general slope of an area or region.

vers de société /vɛr də sɔsjete/ *noun phrase* L18 **French** (literally, 'verse of society'). Verse treating topics provided by polite society in a light, often witty style.

vers d'occasion /vɛr dɔkazjɔ̃/ *noun phrase* M19 **French**. Light verse written for a special occasion.

vers libre /vɛr libr/ *noun phrase* plural **vers libres** (pronounced same) E20 **French** (literally, 'free verse'). Unrhymed verse which disregards the traditional rules of prosody; an example of this.

verso /'vəːsəʊ/ *noun* plural **versos** M19 **Latin** (*verso* (sc. *folio*) = (the leaf) being turned, ablative singular neuter of *versus* past participle of *vertere* to turn). **1** M19 The left-hand page of an open book; the back of a leaf in a manuscript or printed book, as opposed to the front or RECTO. **2** L19 The reverse side, especially of a coin or medal.

Versöhnung /fɛr'zø:nʊŋ/ *noun* plural **Versöhnungen** /fɛr'zø:nʊŋən/ M19 **German** (= conciliation, propitiation). A reconciliation of opposites.

1976 G. Talbot *Permission to Speak* It was a jarring note in an evening of festive international *versöhnung*.

Verstandesmensch /fɛr'ʃtandəs,mɛnʃ/ *noun* plural **Verstandesmenschen** /fɛr'ʃtandəs,mɛnʃən/ L19 **German**. A matter-of-fact person; a realist.

Verstehen /fɛr'ʃte:ən/ *noun* M20 **German** (= understanding, comprehension). (The use of empathy in) the sociological or historical understanding of human action and behaviour.

versus /'və:səs/ *preposition* LME **Medieval Latin** (use of Latin *versus* towards, in sense of *adversus* against). Against, in opposition to.

■ Used especially in legal or sporting contexts, where it is generally abbreviated *v.* or *vs*, as in *Rovers v. Wolves*.

vertex /'və:tɛks/ *noun* plural **vertices** /'və:tɪsi:z/, **vertexes** LME **Latin** (= whirl, vortex, crown of the head, highest point, from *vertere* to turn). **1** LME *Anatomy* and *Zoology* The crown or top of the head or skull. **b** E19 *Entomology* The top of the head of an insect. **2** L16 *Geometry* The point opposite to the base of a (plane or solid) figure; the point in a curve or surface at which the axis meets it; an angular point of a triangle, polygon, etc. **b** E18 *Optics* The point where the optical axis intersects the surface of a lens. **c** L19 *Astronomy* The point on the limb of a celestial object where it is intersected by a circle passing through the zenith and the centre of the object. Now also, the point to which a group of stars appears to converge, or from which a shower of meteors appears to radiate. **d** M20 *Mathematics* A junction of two or more lines in a network or graph; a node. **3** M17 The point in the sky directly above a given place; the zenith. **4** M17 The top or highest point of a thing.

vertigo /'və:tɪgəʊ/ *noun* LME **Latin** ((stem *vertigin-*) = whirling about, giddiness, from *vertere* to turn). **1** LME *Medicine* A sensation of whirling motion, tending to result in a loss of balance and sometimes of consciousness; giddiness, dizziness. **2** M17 *figurative* A disordered state of mind or things.

vertu variant of VIRTU.

vesica /'vɛsɪkə/, /'vi:sɪkə/ *noun* M17 **Latin** (= bladder, blister). **1** M17 *Anatomy* A bladder. Usually with Latin specifying word. *rare.* **2** E19 Elliptical for VESICA PISCIS.

vesica piscis /,vɛsɪkə 'pɪskɪs/, /,vi:sɪkə 'pɪskɪs/ *noun phrase* (also **vesica piscium** /,vɛsɪkə 'pɪskɪʌm/) E19 **Latin** (= fish's (or fishes') bladder). A pointed oval figure used as an architectural feature and as an aureole enclosing figures of Christ, the Virgin, etc., in medieval painting and sculpture.

■ The origin of the name is uncertain; one nineteenth-century writer objected that it was not a bladder belonging to a fish but a bladder which, when filled, would be in the shape of a fish. Another attributed the invention of the term to the German artist Albrecht Dürer (1471–1528).

vespasienne /vɛspazjɛn/ *noun* plural pronounced same E20 **French** (abbreviation of *colonne vespasienne* Vespasian column). In France: a public lavatory.

■ The allusion is to the Roman emperor Vespasian, who introduced a tax on public lavatories.

vestigium /vɛ'stɪdʒɪəm/ *noun* plural **vestigia** /vɛ'stɪdʒɪə/ M17 **Latin**. A vestige, a trace. Usually followed by *of*.

veto /'vi:təʊ/ *noun & verb* E17 **Latin** (= I forbid, used by Roman tribunes of the people to oppose measures of the Senate or actions of the magistrates). **A** *noun* E17 plural **vetoes** A prohibition of a proposed or intended act, especially a legislative enactment; the right or power of preventing an act in this way. Frequently in *apply, place,* or *put a veto on* or *to*. **B** *transitive verb* E18 Put a veto on (a measure etc.), refuse consent to, forbid authoritatively; refuse to admit or accept (a person).

ve-tsin /veɪ'tsɪn/ *noun* M20 **Chinese** (*wèijīng*, from *wèi* taste, ingredient + *jīng* refined, essence, extract). Monosodium glutamate, as used in Chinese cookery.

veuve /və:v/, *foreign* /vœv/ *noun* L18 **French**. In France: a widow.

■ Frequently as a title prefixed to a woman's surname and perhaps most familiar as part of a proprietary name of a brand of champagne: *Veuve Clicquot*.

vexata quaestio /vɛk,sɑ:tə 'kwʌɪstɪəʊ/, /vɛk,seɪtə 'kwi:stɪəʊ/ *noun phrase* plural

vexatae quaestiones /vɛkˌsɑːtiː ˌkwʌɪstɪ ˈəʊniːz/ E19 **Latin**. A vexed question.

vexillum /vɛkˈsɪləm/ *noun* plural **vexilla** /vɛkˈsɪlə/ E18 **Latin** (= flag, banner, from *vex-*, *vect-*, *vehere* to carry, convey). **1** E18 *Roman History* A military standard or banner; a body of soldiers grouped under this. **b** L19 *Ecclesiastical* A small piece of linen or silk attached to the upper part of a crozier. **2** E18 *Botany* The standard or large uppermost petal of a papilionaceous flower. **3** M19 *Ornithology* The vane of a feather.

via /ˈvʌɪə/, /ˈviːə/ *preposition* L18 **Latin** (ablative singular of *via* way). **1** L18 By way of; by a route passing through or over. **2** M20 By means of; with the aid of.

via affirmativa /ˌviːə əfəːməˈtʌɪvə/ *noun phrase* M19 **Modern Latin** (= affirmative way). *Theology* The approach to God through positive statements about his nature. Cf. VIA NEGATIVA.

Via Crucis /ˌviːə ˈkruːtʃɪs/ *noun phrase* M19 **Latin** (= way of the cross). The route followed by Christ to Calvary; *Christian Church* the Way of the Cross as a series of devotions or, *especially* in the Roman Catholic Church, a series of 'stations' or shrines set around a church interior for devotion and meditation; *figurative* an extremely painful experience requiring strength or courage to bear.

Via Dolorosa /ˌviːə dɒləˈrəʊzə/ *noun phrase* L19 **Latin** (literally, 'sorrowing way'). **1** L19 The route believed to have been taken by Christ through Jerusalem to Calvary. **2** E20 *figurative* A prolonged ordeal.

2 1996 C. Lis and H. Soly *Disordered Lives* Married life for him was a *via dolorosa*: his wife beat him till the blood flowed, killed their cat and dog, set the household furniture on fire and threw burning embers at passers-by . . .

via media /ˌviːə ˈmiːdɪə/ *noun phrase* M19 **Latin** A middle way; an intermediate course, a compromise.

1996 *Spectator* The Anglican *via media* was almost always Burke's way . . .

via negativa /ˌviːə nɛgəˈtʌɪvə/ *noun phrase* M19 **Modern Latin** (= negative way). *Theology* The approach to God believing no positive statements can be made about his nature; *transferred* a way of denial.

viaticum /vʌɪˈatɪkəm/ *noun* plural **viatica** /vʌɪˈatɪkə/ (formerly also Anglicized as **viatic**) M16 **Latin** (use as noun of neuter of *viaticus* pertaining to a road or journey, from *via* road). **1** M16 *Christian Church* The Eucharist as administered to a person near or in danger of death. **2** L16 A supply or official allowance of money for a journey: travelling expenses. **b** M17 A supply of food for a journey.

vibrato /vɪˈbrɑːtəʊ/ *adverb & noun* M19 **Italian** (past participle of *vibrare* vibrate). *Music* **A** *adverb* M19 With a rapid slight variation in pitch. **B** *noun* L19 plural **vibratos** A rapid slight variation in pitch in the singing or playing of a note. Cf. TREMOLO noun 1.

B 1996 *Times* The real weight lies in the middle of the voice, with the sweetest of vibratos . . .

vice anglais /vis ɑ̃glɛ/ *noun phrase* M20 **French** (literally, 'English vice'). A vice considered characteristic of the English; *especially* the use of corporal punishment for sexual stimulation.

vicereine /ˈvʌɪsreɪn/ *noun* E19 **French** (from *vice-* vice- + *reine* queen). The wife of a viceroy. Also, a female viceroy.

vice versa /ˌvʌɪsə ˈvəːsə/, /ˌvʌɪs/ *adverb phrase* E17 **Latin** (literally, 'the position being reversed', from as *vice* ablative of *vix* change, place, stead + *versa* ablative feminine singular of *versus* past participle of *vertere* to turn). With a reversal of the order of terms or conditions mentioned; contrariwise, conversely.

1996 *Spectator* The medium seems to have chosen him rather than vice versa.

vichyssoise /ˌviːʃiːˈswɑːz/ *noun* M20 **French** (*crême vichyssoise glacée*, literally, 'iced cream soup of Vichy'). A soup made with potatoes, leeks, and cream, and usually served cold.

victor ludorum /ˌvɪktə luːˈdɔːrəm/ *noun phrase* E20 **Latin** (= victor of the games). The overall champion in a sports competition, especially at a school or college; the sports competition itself.

figurative **1996** *Times* Though his former teacher Brunetto Latini is condemned to run forever on the burning marl among the sodomites, Dante treats him as a father figure, and as an intellectual *victor ludorum*.

vicuña /vɪˈkjuːnjə/, /vɪˈkuːnjə/ *noun* (also **vicugna**, **vicuna** /vɪˈkjuːnə/) E17 **Spanish** (from Quechua *wikúña*). **1** E17 A hoofed mammal of the high Andes, *Vicugna vicugna*, which is related to the llama and guanaco and has a fine silky coat used for textile fabrics. **2** M19 A fine fabric made from the wool of the vicuña (also more fully *vicuña cloth*). Also, a garment made of this fabric.

vicus /ˈvʌɪkəs/, /ˈviːkəs/ *noun* plural **vici** /ˈvʌɪkiː/ M19 **Latin** (= village, group of dwellings). *Archaeology* In the Roman Empire, a village, a settlement; *specifically* the smallest unit of ancient Roman municipal administration, consisting of a village, part of a town, etc. Also, a medieval European township.

vide /ˈvʌɪdi/, /ˈvɪdeɪ/ *transitive verb* (*imperative*) M16 **Latin** (imperative singular of *videre* to see). See, refer to, consult.

■ Used as a direction in a text referring the reader to a specified passage, work, etc., for fuller or further information. Also abbreviated to *vid*.

1996 *Spectator* . . . English intellectuals like to define themselves by their philistinism about sport. This is not true of intellectuals elsewhere: *vide* my prized collection of Renaissance goalkeepers, which includes Albert Camus, Vladimir Nabokov, . . .

videlicet /vɪˈdɛlɪsɛt/, /vʌɪˈdɛlɪsɛt/, /vɪ ˈdɛlɪkɛt/ *adverb & noun* LME **Latin** (from *vide-* stem of *videre* to see + *licet* it is permissible; cf. SCILICET). **A** *adverb* LME Usually introducing an amplification or explanation of a previous statement or word; that is to say, namely. **B** *noun* M17 The word 'videlicet' introducing an explanation or amplification, especially in a legal document.

■ Frequently abbreviated to *viz*(.) (M16), the *z* representing the usual medieval Latin symbol of contraction for *-et*.

vidimus /ˈvʌɪdɪməs/ *noun* LME **Latin** (= we have seen, from *videre* to see). **1** LME A copy of a document bearing an attestation of its authenticity or accuracy. **b** M19 An inspection of accounts.

vie de Bohème /vi də bɔɛm/ *noun phrase* L19 **French**. A Bohemian way of life.

vie de château /vi də ʃɑto/ *noun phrase* E20 **French**. The way of life of a large country house; aristocratic social life.

vie d'intérieur /vi dɛ̃terjœr/ *noun phrase* L19 **French**. Private or domestic life.

vie en rose /vi ɑ̃ roz/ *noun phrase* M20 **French**. A life seen through rose-coloured spectacles.

■ A phrase popularized by the French singer Edith Piaf (1915–63), one of whose songs was called 'La Vie en rose'.

1974 M. Cecil *Heroines in Love* So many hopes had tumbled that magazine writers were reluctant to present an unending *vie en rose*.

vie intérieure /vi ɛ̃terjœr/ *noun phrase* E20 **French**. One's inner life, the life of the spirit.

vie intime /vi ɛ̃tim/ *noun phrase* L19 **French**. The intimate private life of a person.

vie romancée /vi rɔmɑ̃se/ *noun phrase plural* **vies romancées** (pronounced same) M20 **French**. A fictionalized biography.

vi et armis /ˌviː ɛt ˈɑːmiːs/ *adverb phrase* E17 **Latin** (= with force and arms). Violently, forcibly, by compulsion; *specifically* in *Law* (now *historical*), with unlawful violence.

vieux jeu /vjø ʒø/ *noun & adjective* plural of noun **vieux jeux** (pronounced same) L19 **French** (literally, 'old game'). (Something or someone) old-fashioned, outmoded, passé.

vieux marcheur /vjø marʃœr/ plural **vieux marcheurs** (pronounced same) E20 **French** (literally, 'old campaigner'). An elderly womanizer.

■ From the title of a play *Le Vieux Marcheur* (1909) by Henri Lavedon.

vieux rose /vjø roz/ *noun & adjective* L19 **French**. (Of) a deep pink colour, old rose.

viga /ˈviːgə/ *noun* M19 **Spanish**. In United States: a rough-hewn roof timber or rafter, especially in a Pueblo building.

vigia /ˈvɪdʒɪə/ *noun* M19 **Portuguese** (= lookout, from *vigiar*, from Latin *vigilia* wakefulness, from *vigil* awake, alert). A warning on a sea chart to denote a reported but as yet unverified danger.

vigilante /vɪdʒɪˈlanti/ *noun* M19 **Spanish** (from Latin *vigilant-* present participial stem of *vigilare* to keep awake). A member of a vigilance committee; any person executing summary justice in the absence or breakdown of legally constituted law enforcement bodies. Now also, a member of a self-appointed group undertaking law enforcement but without legal authority, operating in addition to an existing police force to protect property etc. within a localized area. Originally *United States*.

attributive **1995** *New Scientist* . . . the California-based Sea Shepherd Conservation Society—a kind of marine vigilante squad—threatens to halt the Makah hunt by force.

vigneron /ˈviːnjərɒn/, *foreign* /viɲərɔ̃/ (*plural same*) *noun* LME **French** (from *vigne* vine). A person who cultivates grapevines; a vine-grower.

vignette /viːˈnjɛt/, /vɪˈnjɛt/ *noun & verb* LME **Old and Modern French** (diminutive of *vigne* vine). **A** *noun* **1** LME A usually small decorative design or illustration on a blank space in a book etc., especially at the beginning or end of a chapter or on the title page; *specifically* one not enclosed in a border, or with the edges shading off into the surrounding paper. **2** LME *Architecture* A carved decoration representing the trailing tendrils, branches, or leaves of a vine. **3** M19 A photographic portrait showing only the head or the head and shoulders and with the edges gradually shading into the background. **4** L19 A brief descriptive account, anecdote, or essay; a character sketch; a short evocative episode in a play etc. **B** *transitive verb* **1** M19 Make a vignette of; *specifically* produce (a photograph) in the style of a vignette by softening away or shading off the edges of the subject. **2** M20 *Optics* Cause vignetting of an image.

A.4 1996 *Spectator* The minor characters seem alive; the incidental vignettes are as well told as the climaxes . . .

vignoble /ˈviːnjəʊb(ə)l/ *noun* L15 **Old and Modern French** (from popular Latin, from Latin *vinea* vineyard). A vineyard.

vihara /vɪˈhɑːrə/ *noun* L17 **Sanskrit** (*vihāra*). A Buddhist monastery or nunnery.

villa /ˈvɪlə/ *noun* E17 **Italian and Latin** (partly from Latin *villa* country house, farm, partly from Italian *villa* from Latin). **1** E17 *Roman Antiquities* A large country house with an estate. Now, a country residence; *specifically* a rented or privately owned holiday home, especially abroad. **2** M18 A detached or semi-detached house in a suburban or residential district.

■ In sense 2 often in proper names, as *Villa Ariadne*.

villancico /ˌvi(l)janˈθiko/, /ˌvi(l)janˈsiko/ *noun* plural **villancicos** /ˌvi(l)janˈθikos/, /ˌvi(l)janˈsikos/ E19 **Spanish** (diminutive of *villano* peasant, rustic, from medieval Latin *villanus* villager, from Latin *villa* villa (sense 1)). *Music* A form of Spanish and Portuguese song consisting of short stanzas separated by a refrain, originally a kind of folk-song but later used in sacred music; now *especially* a Christmas carol.

villanella /vɪləˈnɛlə/ *noun* plural **villanelle** /vɪləˈnɛleɪ/, **villanellas** L16 **Italian** (see next). *Music* A form of Italian part-song having a rustic character and a vigorous rhythm.

villanelle /vɪləˈnɛl/ *noun* L16 **French** (from Italian *villanella* feminine of *villanello* rural, rustic, from *villano* peasant, rustic, from medieval Latin *villanus* villager, from Latin *villa* villa (sense 1)). **1** L16–L17 *Music* A VILLANELLA. **2** L19 A usually pastoral or lyric poem consisting normally of five three-line stanzas and a final quatrain, with only two rhymes throughout and some lines repeated.

ville /vɪl/, /vʌɪl/ *noun* M19 **French** (= town). A town, a village.

■ Colloquial, chiefly United States, where *-ville* occurs in the names of many towns (e.g. *Louisville*). Hence used jocularly as a suffix to form the name of a fictitious place that epitomizes the quality concerned (see quotation 1972).

1972 *Publishers' Weekly* There are some who will simply not get the fun of it out there in mass-marketville.

1977 M. Herr *Dispatches* Once we fanned over a little ville that had just been airstruck.

villeggiatura /ˌvilledʤaˈtuːra/ *noun* plural **villeggiature** /ˌvilledʤaˈtuːrə/ M18 **Italian** (from *villeggiare* to live at a villa or in the country, from *villa* villa). Residence at a country villa or in the country, especially in Italy; a holiday spent in this way.

ville lumière /vil lymjɛr/ *noun* E20 **French** (= town or city of light(s)). A brightly lit city or town; an exciting modern city or town; *specifically* (*la Ville Lumière*), Paris.

vim /vɪm/ *noun* M19 **Latin** (probably from *vim* accusative singular of *vis* strength, energy). Vigour, energy, spirit. Originally *United States*.

vimana /vɪˈmɑːnə/ *noun* M19 **Sanskrit**. In the Indian subcontinent: the central tower enclosing the shrine in a temple; *Mythology* a heavenly chariot.

vin /vɛ̃/ *noun* L17 **French**. French wine.

vina variant of VEENA.

vinaigrette /ˌvɪnerˈgrɛt/, /ˌvɪnɪˈgrɛt/ *noun* LME **French** (from *vinaigre* vinegar). **1** A stew, sauce, or other dish made with vinegar. Only in LME. **b** A condiment prepared with vinegar. Only in L17. **2** L17 *History* A small two-wheeled carriage drawn or pushed by people, formerly used in France. **3** E19 A small ornamental bottle or box for holding a sponge saturated with smelling-salts etc. **4** L19 A salad dressing of oil and wine vinegar with seasoning. Also more fully *vinaigrette dressing, vinaigrette sauce.*

vin blanc /vɛ̃ blɑ̃/ *noun phrase* L18 **French**. White wine.

vin compris /vɛ̃ kɔ̃pri/ *noun phrase* L19 **French**. Wine included in the price of a meal or other entertainment.

vin cuit /vɛ̃ kɥi/ *noun phrase* M19 **French** (literally 'cooked, boiled'). **1** M19 Grape juice boiled to a syrup and used to fortify or sweeten other wine. Cf. VINO COTTO. **2** M20 A sweet aperitif wine.

vinculum /'vɪŋkjʊləm/ *noun* plural **vincula** /'viŋkjʊlə/ M17 **Latin** (from *vincire* to bind). **1** M17 A bond, a tie. Chiefly *figurative.* **2** E18 *Mathematics* A horizontal line over two or more terms, denoting that they are to be treated as a unit in the following operation. **3** M19 *Anatomy* A connecting band or bandlike structure; *especially* a narrow tendon.

vindaloo /vɪndə'luː/ *noun* L19 **Portuguese** (probably from Portuguese *vin d'alho* wine and garlic sauce, from *vinho* wine + *alho* garlic). A highly spiced hot Indian curry dish made with meat, fish, or poultry. Also *vindaloo curry.*

vin de paille /vɛ̃ də pɑj/ *noun phrase* M19 **French** (= straw wine). Wine made from grapes that have been dried on straw mats before being pressed.

vin de table /vɛ̃ də tabl/ *noun phrase* M20 **French**. Wine suitable for drinking with a meal, usually one that is not fortified or sparkling.

■ The English phrase *table wine* (L17) is also used, especially of non-French wines; the German equivalent is TAFELWEIN.

vin d'honneur /vɛ̃ dɔnœr/ *noun phrase* E20 **French**. A wine formally offered in honour of a person or persons; the reception at which the wine is offered.

vin doux (naturel) /vɛ̃ du natyrel/ *noun phrase* M20 **French** (literally, 'sweet (natural)'). A sweet fortified wine.

vin du pays /vɛ̃ dy pə(j)i/ *noun phrase* L18 **French** (literally, 'of the country'). A local wine.

vin fou /vɛ̃ fu/ *noun phrase* M19 **French** (literally, 'mad'). A white or rosé sparkling wine from the Jura.

vin gris /vɛ̃ gri/ *noun phrase* M19 **French** (literally, 'grey'). A rosé wine of eastern France.

vingt-et-un /vɛ̃t e œ̃/ *noun* Also written **vingt-un** L18 **French** (= twenty-one). The card-game pontoon.

vinho /'viɲu/, /'viːnəʊ/ *noun* M19 **Portuguese**. Portuguese wine.

vinho branco /ˌviɲu 'braŋku/, /ˌviɲu 'braŋkəʊ/ *noun phrase* M19 **Portuguese**. White wine.

vinho corrente /ˌviɲu kɔ'rrentə/ *noun phrase* L20 **Portuguese** (literally, 'common wine'). Cheap wine equivalent to VIN ORDINAIRE.

vinho da casa /ˌviɲu da 'kaza/ *noun phrase* M20 **Portuguese** (literally, 'wine of the house'). House wine.

vinho de consumo /ˌviɲu də kɔ̃'sumu/ *noun phrase* L20 **Portuguese** (literally, 'wine for consumption'). VINHO CORRENTE.

vinho tinto /ˌviɲu 'tintu/, /ˌviːnəʊ 'tɪntəʊ/ *noun phrase* M19 **Portuguese**. Red wine.

vinho verde /ˌviɲu 'verdə/, /ˌviɲu 'vəːdi/ *noun phrase* M20 **Portuguese** (literally, 'green wine'). Young wine not allowed to mature.

vin jaune /vɛ̃ ʒon/ *noun phrase* M19 **French** (literally, 'yellow'). A yellowish wine from the Jura region of eastern France.

vin mousseux /vɛ̃ musø/ *noun phrase* L18 **French**. A sparkling wine. Also called MOUSSEUX.

vino /'vinɒ/, *especially in sense 3* /ˌvɪːnəʊ/ *noun* L17 **Spanish and Italian** (= wine). **1** L17 Spanish or Italian wine. **2** E20 An alcoholic liquor distilled from nipa-palm sap drunk in the Philippines. **3** E20 Wine, especially of an inferior kind. *colloquial*, often *jocular.*

3 1976 P. Cave *High Flying Birds* I was far too stoned to take much notice of Lloyd's vino-inspired ramblings.

vino blanco /ˌvino 'blaŋko/ *noun phrase* L20 **Spanish**. White wine.

vino corriente /ˌvino ko'rrjente/ *noun phrase* M20 **Spanish** (literally, 'common wine'). Cheap wine equivalent to VIN ORDINAIRE.

vino cotto /ˌvino 'kɔtto/ *noun phrase* M19 **Italian** (literally 'cooked'). Grape juice boiled to a syrup and used to fortify or sweeten other wine, especially marsala. Cf. VIN CUIT.

■ The opposite is *vino crudo* /ˌvino 'kruːdo/ (literally, 'raw wine') or 'wine in its natural state'. The distinction is first mentioned in English by the seventeenth-century English botanist John Ray: 'The boil'd wine, which they call *Vin Cotto*, seemed to us much stronger than the wine unboil'd, which they call *Vin Crudo*' (*Observations* . . . , 1673).

vino de color /ˌvino de ko'lor/ *noun phrase* M19 **Spanish**. A rich sweet wine, used in the blending of sherry and other fortified wines.

vino de pasto /ˌvino de 'pasto/ *noun phrase* L19 **Spanish** (literally, 'pasture wine'). **1** L19 A pale and fairly dry sherry. **2** M20 A table wine for everyday consumption.

vino dolce /ˌvino 'doltʃe/ *noun phrase* E20 **Italian**. Sweet Italian wine.

vino dulce /ˌvino 'dulθe/, /'dulse/ *noun phrase* E20 **Spanish**. Sweet Spanish wine.

vino maestro /ˌvino ma'estro/ *noun phrase* E20 **Spanish** (literally, 'master wine'). A sweet and strong wine used to fortify or sweeten other wines.

vino nero /ˌvino 'ne:ro/ *noun phrase* M20 **Italian** (literally, 'black wine'). Dark red wine.

vin ordinaire /vɛ̃ ɔrdinɛr/ *noun phrase* E19 **French** (literally, 'ordinary wine'). Simple (usually red) table wine for everyday use.

■ Also referred to elliptically as ORDINAIRE (M19).

vino rosso /ˌvino 'rosso/ *noun phrase* M20 **Italian**. Red wine.

vino santo /ˌvino 'santo/ *noun phrase* L17 **Italian** (literally, 'holy wine'). VINSANTO.

vino secco /ˌvino 'sekko/ *noun phrase* E20 **Italian**. Dry wine.

vino tierno /ˌvino 'tjerno/ *noun phrase* E20 **Spanish** (literally, 'tender'). Wine made from partially dried grapes, used especially for fortifying malaga.

vino tinto /ˌvino 'tinto/ *noun phrase* L17 **Spanish**. Red wine.

vin rosé /vɛ̃ roze/, /'rəʊzeɪ/ *noun phrase* M20 **French**. Rosé wine.

vin rouge /vɛ̃ ruʒ/ E20 **French**. Red wine.

vinsanto /vin'santo/, /vɪn'santəʊ/ *noun* M20 **Italian** (from *vino santo* holy wine). A sweet white Italian dessert wine.

viola bastarda /vɪˌəʊlə ba'stɑ:də/ *noun phrase* E18 **Italian** (literally, 'bastard viol'). *Music* A bass viol tuned and played according to a system of tablature. Also called *lyra viol*.

viola da braccio /vɪ'əʊlə da ˌbratʃə/ *noun phrase* M19 **Italian** (literally, 'viol of the arm'). Any member of the violin family, as opposed to a viola da gamba; *specifically* a viol corresponding to the modern viola.

viola da gamba /vɪˌəʊlə də 'gambə/ *noun phrase* (also (earlier) **viol da gamba** /ˌvʌɪəl də 'gambə/) L16 **Italian** (literally, 'leg viol'). **1** L16 A viol held between the player's legs, *especially* one corresponding to the modern cello. **2** M19 An organ-stop resembling this instrument in tone.

viola d'amore /vɪ'əʊlə daˌmɔ:re/ *noun phrase* E18 **Italian** (literally, 'viol of love'). A kind of tenor viol usually having sympathetic strings and no frets.

violetta /vio'lɛtta/ *noun* plural **violette** /vio'lɛtte/ M18 **Italian** (diminutive of *viola* viola). *Music* A small viol.

violette de Parme /vjɔlɛt də parm/ *noun phrase* plural **violettes de Parme** (pronounced same) E20 **French**. Any of various cultivated violets with double, scented, usually light purple flowers, used for perfume or crystallized for food decoration, a Parma violet.

violon /'vʌɪələn/ *noun* M16 **French**. **1** M16–E17 A violin. Also, a violinist. **2** M19 A kind of organ-stop resembling a double bass in tone.

violoncello /ˌvʌɪələn'tʃɛləʊ/, /ˌvi:ələn 'tʃɛləʊ/ *noun* E18 **Italian** (diminutive of *violone*). **1** E18 A cello. **b** M19 A cellist. **2** L19 An organ-stop similar in tone to a cello.

violon d'Ingres /vjɔlɔ̃ dɛ̃gr/ *noun phrase* plural **violons d'Ingres** (pronounced same) M20 **French** (literally, 'Ingres' violin'). An interest or activity other than that for which a person is best known; an occasional pastime.

■ The allusion is to the French painter J.-A.-D. Ingres (1780–1867), who was a keen amateur violinist and said to have been more proud of his violin-playing than of his highly acclaimed pictures.

virage /viraʒ/ *noun* plural pronounced same M20 **French**. A hairpin bend; a sharp turn made in negotiating such a bend.

virago /vɪˈrɑːgəʊ/, /vɪˈreɪgəʊ/ *noun & adjective* LME **Latin** (from *vir* man). **A** *noun* plural **viragos**. **1** LME A woman of masculine strength or spirit; a female warrior, an amazon. *archaic*. **2** LME A domineering woman; a fierce or abusive woman. **B** *adjective* L16 That is a virago; of or pertaining to a virago or viragos.

■ Earlier (OE–L16) meaning 'woman', but only in biblical allusions with reference to the name given by Adam to Eve.

vires plural of VIS.

virga /ˈvəːgə/ *noun* plural **virgae** /ˈvəːgiː/ E20 **Latin** (= rod). **1** E20 *Music* (A symbol designating) a note used in plainsong. **2** M20 *Meteorology*, *singular* and in *plural* Streaks of precipitation that appear to hang from the undersurface of a cloud and usually evaporate before reaching the ground.

virgo intacta /ˌvəːgəʊ ɪnˈtaktə/ *noun phrase* E18 **Latin** (literally, 'untouched virgin'). Chiefly *Law* A girl or woman who has never had sexual intercourse.

virgule /ˈvəːgjuːl/ *noun* M19 **French** (= comma, from Latin *virgula* diminutive of *virga* rod). **1** M19 A slanting or upright line used especially in medieval manuscripts to mark a caesura, or as a punctuation mark equivalent to a comma. Now also a SOLIDUS sense 2. **2** L19 *Watchmaking* A type of escapement in which the teeth of the wheel have the shape of a comma. More fully *virgule escapement*.

virtu /vəːˈtuː/ *noun* (also **vertu, virtù**) E18 **Italian** (*virtù* virtue; the form *vertu* altered as if from French). **1** E18 A love of or interest in works of art; a knowledge of or expertise in the fine arts; the fine arts as a subject of study or interest. **2** M18 *collective* Objects of art; curios. **3** M20 The strength or worth inherent in a person or thing; *especially* inherent moral worth or virtue.

virtuoso /vəːtjʊˈəʊsəʊ/, /vəːtjʊˈəʊzəʊ/ *noun & adjective* E17 **Italian** (= learned, skilful, from late Latin *virtuosus*). **A** *noun* plural **virtuosi** /vəːtjʊˈəʊsiː/, **virtuosos** **1** E17–L18 A person who has a general interest in arts and sciences, or who pursues special investigations in one or more of these; a learned person. **2** M17 A person who has a special knowledge of or interest in the fine arts; a connoisseur, *especially* a person pursuing these interests in a dilettante manner. **3** M18 A person who has special knowledge or skill in the technique of a fine art, especially music. Also, a person with outstanding technical skill in any sphere. **B** *attributive* or as *adjective* M17 Of or pertaining to a virtuoso; displaying the skills of a virtuoso; characterized by virtuosity.

A.3 1996 *Times* The virtuoso in interpersonal skills is the corporate future.

virtute officii /vəːˌtjuːti ɒˈfɪʃɪiː/ *adverb phrase* E19 **Latin**. *Law* By virtue of (one's) office.

vis /vɪs/ *noun* plural **vires** /ˈvʌɪriːz/ E17 **Latin**. **1** E17 Strength, force, energy, vigour. **2** L20 *Law* In *plural* Legal validity; legal authority or power.

■ Chiefly now in various phrases; in the legal sense *vires* occurs earlier in INTRA VIRES and ULTRA VIRES.

visa /ˈviːzə/ *noun* M19 **French** (from Latin = things seen, neuter plural of past participle of *videre* to see). An endorsement on a passport etc. indicating that it has been examined and found correct, especially as permitting the holder to enter or leave a country.

vis a fronte /ˌvɪs ɑː ˈfrɒnteɪ/ *noun phrase* E19 **Latin**. A force operating from in front, as in attraction or suction. Opposite of VIS A TERGO.

visagiste /ˌviːzɑːˈʒiːst/ *noun* (also **visagist** /ˈvɪzədʒɪst/) M20 **French**. A make-up artist.

vis a tergo /ˌvɪs ɑː ˈtəːgəʊ/ *noun phrase* E19 **Latin**. A force operating from behind; a propulsive force. Opposite of VIS A FRONTE.

vis-à-vis /ˌviːzɑːˈviː/ *noun, preposition & adverb* M18 **Old and Modern French** (literally, 'face to face', from Old French *vis* visage + *à* to + *vis*). **A** *noun* plural same. **1** M18 A light horse-drawn carriage for two people sitting face to face. *obsolete* except *historical*. **2** M18 A person or thing facing or situated opposite to another, especially in certain dances. **b** E20 A counterpart, an opposite number. Also (*United States*), a social partner. **3** M19 A face-to-face meeting. **B** *preposition* M18 Regarding, in relation to. Also, opposite to, face to face with. **C** *adverb* E19 Opposite; facing one another.

B 1996 *Times* But the Foreign Office must accept that its own obsessive secrecy . . . has ensured a climate of deep suspicion about anything involving its own role *vis-à-vis* the Jews and their treatment at the hands of the Nazis.

vis comica /ˌvɪs ˈkɒmɪkə/ *noun phrase* M18 **Latin**. Humorous energy; comic force or effect.

visibilia /vɪzɪˈbɪlɪə/ *noun plural* M20 **Latin** (neuter plural of *visibilis* visible). Visible things; visual images.

vis inertiae /ˌvɪs ɪˈnəːʃɪʌɪ/ *noun phrase* E18 **Latin**. *Mechanics* The resistance offered by matter to any force tending to alter its state of rest or motion; *transferred* a tendency to remain inactive or unprogressive.

visitant /ˈvɪzɪt(ə)nt/ *noun & adjective* L16 **French** (present participle of *visiter* to visit, or Latin *visitant-* present participial stem of *visitare*). **A** *noun* **1** L16 A person who visits a place, another person, etc.; a visitor, now *especially* a supernatural one. **2** M18 A thing which affects or comes to a person, especially for a temporary period. **3** L18 A migratory bird or animal that frequents a certain locality only at particular times of year. **B** *adjective* M17 Of the nature of a visitant.

visite de digestion /vizit də diʒɛstjɔ̃/ *noun phrase* E20 **French** (literally, 'visit of digestion'). A formal call paid in return for hospitality received, especially after a dinner party.

vis major /ˌvɪs ˈmeɪdʒə/ *noun phrase* E17 **Latin**. *Law* Overpowering force, especially of nature (used as a reason for damage done to, or loss of, property).

vis medicatrix naturae /ˌvɪs mɛdɪˌkeɪtrɪks ˈnatʃərʌɪ/ *noun phrase* E19 **Latin**. The healing power of nature.

vista /ˈvɪstə/ *noun* M17 **Italian** (= view). **1** M17 A view, a prospect, *especially* one seen through an avenue of trees or other long narrow opening. **2** L17 A long narrow opening, especially one created deliberately in a wood etc., through which a view may be obtained, or in itself affording a pleasant prospect. **b** E18 An open corridor or long passage in or through a large building; an interior portion of a building affording a continuous view. **3** L17 *figurative* A broad prospect or vision presented to the imagination; a mental view, in prospect or retrospect, of an extensive period of time or series of events, experiences, etc.

vis viva /ˌvɪs ˈviːvə/ *noun phrase* L18 **Latin**. *Mechanics* The operative force of a moving or acting body, equal to the mass of the body multiplied by the square of its velocity.

vita /ˈviːtə/ *noun* M20 **Latin** (= life). **1** M20 A biography, a life history, *especially* a short Latin biography of a saint. **2** M20 A CURRICULUM VITAE.

vita nuova /ˌviːtə ˈnwəʊvə/ *noun phrase* M20 **Italian** (= new life). A fresh start or new direction in life, especially after some powerful emotional experience.

■ With allusion to the title of a work by Dante describing his love for Beatrice.

1975 P. Organ *House on Cheyne Walk* Not a very good way to begin *la vita nuova*, with more lies.

vitello tonnato /viˈtɛllo tonˈnɑːto/ *noun phrase* M20 **Italian** (from *vitello* veal + *tonno* tuna). An Italian dish consisting of roast or poached veal served cold in a tuna and anchovy mayonnaise.

viva /ˈviːvə/ *noun 1 & interjection* M17 **Italian** (= live!, 3rd person singular present subjunctive of *vivere* to live, from Latin). (A cry or cheer) wishing long life and prosperity to or expressing approval of an admired person or thing: hurrah! long live! Cf. VIVAT, VIVE (interjection).

viva /ˈvʌɪvə/ *noun 2 & verb* L19 **Latin** (abbreviation of VIVA VOCE). **A** *noun* L19 A VIVA VOCE examination. **B** *transitive verb* L19 past tense *vivaed*, *viva'd* /ˈvʌɪvəd/. Subject to a viva voce examination, examine orally.

A 1996 *Spectator* The candidate in search of a doctorate was not alone in being taken aback by the honesty of Richard at their *viva* when he stated that he had not read all of the thesis.

vivandier /vivɑ̃djə/ *noun* (feminine **vivandière** /vivɑ̃djɛr/) plural pronounced same L16 **French**. *History* In the French and other Continental European armies, a supplier of provisions to troops in the field.

vivarium /vʌɪˈvɛːrɪəm/, /vɪˈvɛːrɪəm/ *noun* plural **vivaria** /vʌɪˈvɛːrɪə/, **vivariums** E17 **Latin** (= warren, fish-pond, use as noun of *vivarius* from *vivus* alive, from *vivere* to live). **1** E17 A place for keeping living animals, especially fish, for food; a fish-pond. *obsolete* except *historical*. **2** L17 A structure used for keeping animals under conditions approximating to the natural conditions, for observation or study.

vivat /ˈvʌɪvat/, /ˈviːvat/ *interjection & noun* L16 **Latin** (= may he or she live, 3rd person singular present subjunctive of *vivere* to live). (A cry or cheer) wishing long life and prosperity to or expressing approval of an admired person or thing: hurrah! long live! Cf. VIVA, VIVE.

viva voce /ˌvʌɪvə ˈvəʊtʃi/ *adverb, adjective, & noun phrase* M16 **Medieval Latin** (literally, 'by or with the living voice'). **A** *adverb phrase* M16 Orally rather than in writing. **B** *adjective phrase* **1** E17 Expressed in speech rather than writing, spoken. **2** E19 Of an examination: conducted orally; *specifically* of a supplementary oral examination following a written one. **C** *noun phrase* M19 A viva voce examination.

▪ In the nominal sense frequently abbreviated to VIVA (noun 2).

vive /viv/ *interjection* L16 **French** (= may he, she, or it live, from *vivre* from Latin *vivere* live). Wishing long life and prosperity to or expressing approval of an admired person or thing; long live! Cf. VIVA (interjection), VIVAT.

vive la bagatelle /viv la bagatɛl/ *interjection* M18 **French** (literally, 'success to frivolity or nonsense'). Expressing a carefree attitude to life.

vive la différence /viv la diferɑ̃s/ *interjection* M20 **French**. Expressing approval of the difference between the sexes.

▪ In jocular use; also transferred (see quotation).

1995 *Times* Three compatriots argued that there was little scope for significant tax cuts . . . But—*vive la différence*—two others argued for *higher* public spending.

viveur /vivœr/ *noun* plural pronounced same M19 **French** (= a living person). A person who lives a fashionable and social life. Cf. BON VIVEUR.

vivier /vivje/ *noun* plural pronounced same. LME **Old and Modern French**. A fish-pond; a tank for storing live fish etc.

viz. abbreviation of VIDELICET.

vlakte /ˈflaktə/ *noun* L18 **Afrikaans** (from Dutch). In South Africa: an extent of flat open country; a plain. Frequently in *plural*.

vlei /fleɪ/, /vlʌɪ/ *noun* L18 **Afrikaans** (from Dutch *vallei* valley). **1** L18 In South Africa: a shallow pool of water; a piece of low-lying ground covered with water during the rainy season. **2** L19 A swamp. *United States local.*

vobla /ˈvɒbla/ *noun* (also **wobla**) M20 **Russian**. Dried and smoked roach eaten in Russia as a delicacy.

voce di gola /ˌvɒtʃe di ˈgoːla/ *noun phrase* L19 **Italian** (literally, 'throat voice'). *Music* A throaty or guttural voice.

voce di petto /ˌvɒtʃe di ˈpɛtto/ *noun phrase* M18 **Italian** (literally, 'chest voice'). *Music* The chest register.

voce di testa /ˌvɒtʃe di ˈtɛsta/ *noun phrase* M18 **Italian** (literally, 'head voice'). *Music* The head register; formerly also, the falsetto voice.

vodka /ˈvɒdkə/ *noun* E19 **Russian** (diminutive of *voda* water). A colourless alcoholic spirit made especially in Russia by distillation of grain etc.; a glass or drink of this.

voetganger /ˈfʊtˌxaŋə/ *noun* E19 **Afrikaans** (from Dutch = pedestrian, from *voet* foot + *ganger* goer). **1** E19 A locust in its immature wingless stage. **2** E20 A pedestrian. Also (*colloquial*), an infantryman. *South African.*

voetsek /ˈfʊtsɛk/ *interjection & verb* (also **voetsak** /ˈfʊtsak/) M19 **Afrikaans** (*voe(r)tsek*, from Dutch *voort zeg ik* be off I say). **A** *interjection* M19 Especially to a dog: go away!, off you go! **B** *verb* **1** *transitive verb* L19 Chase (a dog) away. **2** *intransitive verb* M20 Leave, go away. *South African.*

voeu /vø/, /vəː/ *noun* plural **voeux** (pronounced same) E20 **French** (= vow, wish). A non-mandatory recommendation made by an international conference.

vogue la galère /vɔg la galɛr/ *interjection* M18 **French** (literally, 'let the galley be rowed'). Let's get on with it! Let's give it a go!

voilà /vwala/, /vwɑːˈlɑː/ *transitive & intransitive verb* (*imperative & impersonal*) (also **voila**) M18 **French** (from imperative of *voir* see + *là* there). There is, are, etc.; see there.

▪ Also as an interjection: 'there it is!', 'there you are!'

1996 *New Scientist* Just as there is nothing north of the North Pole, so there was nothing before the Big Bang. Voilà! We are supposed to be convinced by that . . .

voilà tout /tu/, /tuː/ *interjection* E19 **French**. That's all! That's it! There is nothing more to do or say.

voile /vɔɪl/, /vwal/ *noun & adjective* L19 **French** (= veil). **A** *noun* L19 A lightweight open-texture material of cotton, wool, silk, or acetate, used especially for blouses and dresses. **B** *attributive* or as *adjective* L19 Made of voile.

voir dire /ˈvwɑː ˌdɪə/ *noun* (also **voire dire**) L17 **Law French** (from Old French *voir* true, truth + *dire* to say). *Law* A preliminary examination by a judge or counsel of the competence of a witness or (occasionally) a juror; an oath taken by such a witness. Also, an investigation into the truth or admissibility of evidence, held during a trial.

voix céleste /vwa səlɛst/, /ˌvwɑː sɪ'lɛst/ *noun phrase* plural **voix célestes** (pronounced same) L19 **French** (= heavenly voice). An organ-stop having an 8-ft pitch, with 2 pipes to each note, tuned slightly apart, producing an undulating tone traditionally regarded as reminiscent of celestial voices. Also called *vox angelica*.

volage /vɔ'lɑːʒ/ *adjective* LME **Old and Modern French** (from Latin *volaticus* winged, inconstant). Giddy, foolish; fickle, inconstant.

■ Formerly fully naturalized; now in literary use, reintroduced from modern French.

volante /və'lanti/ *noun 1* L18 **Spanish** (from present participle of *volar* to fly, from Latin *volare* to fly). A horse-drawn carriage or wagon, especially of a two-wheeled covered type, used in Cuba and formerly in other Spanish-speaking countries.

volante /və'lanti/ *noun 2* L19 **Italian** (= flying). *Music* The rapid execution of a series of notes in singing or playing; *especially* in violin-playing, a bowing technique in which the bow bounces from the string in a slurred staccato.

vol-au-vent /'vɒlə(ʊ),vɒ̃/ *noun* E19 **French** (literally, 'flight in the wind'). A (usually small and round) flat-bottomed case of puff pastry filled with chopped meat, fish, egg, etc., in sauce.

volens /'vəʊlɛnz/ *adjective* L19 **Latin** (present participle of *velle* to be willing). *Law* Consenting to the risk of injury. Cf. NOLENS VOLENS.

volet /'vɒleɪ/, *foreign* /vɔlɛ/ (*plural same*) *noun* M19 **Old and Modern French** (literally, 'shutter', from *voler* from Latin *volare* to fly). Each of the wings or side-compartments of a triptych. Also called *volant*.

volk /fɒlk/ *noun* (also (German) **Volk**) L19 **Afrikaans** (from Dutch or German = nation, people). **1** L19 The Afrikaner people. Also (frequently *derogatory*), the Coloured employees of a White (especially Afrikaner) master collectively. *South African*. **2** M20 The German people (especially with reference to Nazi ideology).

1 1996 T. Alexander *Unravelling Global Apartheid* . . . was access to global markets amd finance ultimately more important than self-determination and local supremacy for the Afrikaner *volk*?

Völkerwanderung /'føːlkərˌvandərʊŋ/, /'fəːlkəˌvɑːndərʊŋ/ *noun* plural **Völkerwanderungen** /'føːlkərˌvandərʊŋən/ M20 **German** (from *Völker* nations + *Wanderung* migration). A migration of peoples; *specifically* that of Germanic and Slavonic peoples into and across Europe from the second to the eleventh centuries.

völkisch /'føːlkɪʃ/ *adjective* M20 **German**. Populist, nationalist, racialist.

volksgeist /'fɒlksgʌɪst/ *noun* (also **Volksgeist**) M20 **German**. The spirit or genius that marks the thought or feeling of a nation or people.

1995 *Spectator* I first read Herder in a seminar organised by Nazi students at Freiburg in 1938, and it soon became clear to me that Herder's *volksgeist*—the spirit of a nation—could be stretched to cover a dangerous doctrine of racial supremacy.

volkslied /'fɒlksliːd/, /'fɒlksliːt/ *noun* plural **volkslieder** /'fɒlksliːdə/ (also **Volkslied**) M19 **German** (or Afrikaans (from Dutch)). **1** M19 A German folk-song; a song or other piece of music in the style of German folk-songs. **2** L19 A national anthem; *specifically* (*historical*) that of the nineteenth-century Transvaal Republic. Also, a South African folk-song.

volta /'vɒltə/ *noun* L16 **Italian** (= turn; cf. VOLTE). The LAVOLTA.

volte /vɒlt/, /vəʊlt/ *noun* L16 **French** (from Italian *volta* turn, use as noun of feminine past participle of *volgere* to turn, from Latin *volvere* to roll). **1** L16–E17 The LAVOLTA. **2** L17 *Fencing* (now *historical*) A sudden jump or other movement to avoid a thrust. **3** E18 *Horsemanship* A small circle of determined size (proposed with a radius equal to the length of a horse); a movement by a horse sideways around the point of such a circle. **4** E20 (A) complete change. *rare*.

volte-face /vɒlt'fɑːs/, /vɒlt'fas/ *noun* E19 **French** (from Italian *voltafaccia*, from *voltare* to turn (ultimately from frequentative of Latin *volvere* to roll) + *faccia* (ultimately from Latin *facies*) face). The act or an instance of turning so as to face in the opposite direction. Chiefly *figurative*, a complete change of attitude, opinion, or position in an argument.

1995 *Times* This volte-face confirms the suspicion that the earlier limits were set artificially low by the health education industry . . .

volupté /vɔlypte/ *noun* E18 **French**. Voluptuousness.

volute /və'l(j)u:t/ *noun* (also (earlier) in Latin form **voluta**, plural **volutae**) M16 **French** (Latin *voluta* use as noun of feminine of *volutus* past participle of *volvere* to roll, to wrap). **1** M16 *Architecture* A spiral scroll characteristic of Ionic capitals and also used in Corinthian and composite capitals. **2** M18 A spiral part or object; a convolution. **3** M18 (A shell of) any of numerous gastropod molluscs of the family Volutidae.

vomitorium /vɒmɪ'tɔ:rɪəm/ *noun* plural **vomitoria** /vɒmɪ'tɔ:rɪə/ M18 **Late Latin** (use as noun of neuter of Latin *vomitorius* vomitory). *Roman Antiquities* **1** M18 A passage or opening in an amphitheatre or theatre, leading to or from the seats. Usually in *plural*. **2** E20 A room allegedly for vomiting deliberately during feasts, to make way for other food.

voorloper /'fʊəlʊəpə/ *noun* M19 **Afrikaans** (from *voor-* before + *loop* to run). In South Africa: the leader of a span of oxen, usually a young African or Coloured boy.

Voortrekker /'fʊətrɛkə/ *noun* L19 **Afrikaans** (from *voor-* before + *trekken* to trek). *South African History* A Boer pioneer, *especially* one who took part in the Great Trek from Cape Colony *c.*1835.

vorlage /'fɔ:lɑ:gə/ *noun* plural **vorlages**, **vorlagen** /'fɔ:lɑ:gən/ M20 **German**. **1** M20 *Skiing* A position in which the skier leans forward without lifting the heels from the skis. **b** M20 In *plural* Skiing trousers. **2** M20 An original version of a manuscript from which a copy is produced.

vorlaufer /'fɔ:laʊfə/ *noun* M20 **German** (*Vorläufer*, from *vorlaufen* run on ahead). A skier who travels a course before a race to establish that it is within the capacity of the competitors.

Vorspiel /'fo:rʃpi:l/ *noun* plural **Vorspiele** /'fo:rʃpi:lə/ L19 **German** (from *vor* before + *Spiel* play). *Music* A prelude.

Vorstellung /'fo:rʃtɛlʊŋ/ *noun* (also **vorstellung** plural **Vorstellen** /'fo:rʃtɛlən/ E19 **German**. *Philosophy* and *Psychology* An idea, a mental picture.

vortex /'vɔ:tɛks/ *noun* plural **vortexes vortices** /'vɔ:tɪsi:z/ M17 **Latin** ((variant of VERTEX) an eddy of water, wind, or flame, from *vortere*, *vertere* to turn). **1 a** M17 In Cartesian theory: any of the rapidly revolving collections of fine particles supposed to fill all space. Usually in *plural*. **b** M19 *Physics* A rapid motion of particles round an axis; a whirl of atoms, fluid, or vapour. **2** M17 A violent eddy of the air; a cyclone. Also, an eddying mass of fire. **3** E18 A swirling mass of water; a whirlpool. **4** *figurative* **a** M18 A whirl or constant round of frenetic activity, rapid change, etc. **b** L18 A place or state into which people or things are irresistibly drawn. **5** E20 *The Vortex* A group of modernist British artists (*c.*1914–15).

voulu /vuly/ *adjective* L19 **French** (past participle of *vouloir* to wish). Lacking in spontaneity; contrived.

voussoir /'vu:swɑ:/ *noun* ME **Old French** (*vausoir*, *vaussoir*, etc. (modern *voussoir*) from popular Latin *volsorium* ultimately from Latin *vols-* past participial stem of *volvere* to roll, to turn). Each of the wedge-shaped or tapered stones, bricks, etc., forming an arch or vaulting.

vox angelica /ˌvɒks an'ʤɛlɪkə/ *noun phrase* M19 **Latin** (= angelic voice). A VOIX CÉLESTE.

vox humana /ˌvɒks hjʊ'mɑ:nə/ *noun phrase* E18 **Latin** (= human voice). An organ reed-stop, having an 8-ft pitch, producing a tone supposedly resembling the human voice.

vox nihili /ˌvɒks 'nʌɪ(h)ɪlʌɪ/, /ˌvɒks 'nʌɪ(h)ɪli:/ *noun phrase* L19 **Latin** (literally, 'voice of nothing'). A worthless or meaningless word, *especially* one produced by a scribal or printer's error.

vox populi /ˌvɒks 'pɒpjʊlʌɪ/, /ˌvɒks 'pɒpjʊli:/ *noun phrase* M19 **Latin** (= voice of the people). Expressed general opinion; common talk or rumour.

■ In colloquial use abbreviated to *vox pop* (M20), usually (but not always—see quotation) with derogatory connotations of 'uninformed opinion, as expressed in the media by members of the public'. The Latin tag from which the phrase derives, *vox populi, vox Dei* 'the voice of the people is the voice of God' has been cited or alluded to in English from the fifteenth century.

1996 *Times* Vox pop is not, after all, baying for blood; on the contrary, it calls justly for guns to be taken out of our hands.

voyagé /vwajaʒe/ *noun & adjective* plural of noun pronounced same M20 **French** (past participle of *voyager* to travel). *Ballet* (Designating) a movement in which the pose is held during progression.

voyant /vwajɑ̃/ *noun* plural pronounced same M20 **French** (from as next). A visionary; a seer.

voyant /vwajɑ̃/ *adjective* E20 **French** (present participial adjective of *voir* to see). Showy, gaudy, flashy.

voyeur /vwɑːˈjəː/ *noun* E20 **French** (from *voir* to see). A person who obtains sexual satisfaction from covert observation of the sexual organs or actions of others. Also (*transferred*) a powerless or passive spectator.

1996 *Spectator* So there I sit like James Stewart in *Rear Window*, a voyeur in spite of myself . . .

voyou /vwaju/ *noun* plural pronounced same E20 **French**. A street urchin; a lout, a hooligan.

vozhd /vəʊʒd/ *noun* M20 **Russian** (*vozhd'*). A leader, a person in supreme authority; *specifically* (*historical*) Stalin.

vrai réseau /vrɛ rezo/ *noun phrase* plural **vrais réseaux** (pronounced same) M19 **French** (= true net). A fine net ground used in making handmade (especially Brussels) lace. Cf. RÉSEAU sense 1.

vraisemblable /vrɛsɑ̃blabl/ *adjective* M19 **French** (from *vrai* true + *semblable* like). Believable, plausible.

vraisemblance /vrɛsɑ̃blɑ̃s/ *noun* plural pronounced same E19 **French** (from *vrai* true + *semblance* likeness). **1** E19 Verisimilitude. **2** M19 A representation *of* a person or thing.

vrais réseaux plural of VRAI RÉSEAU.

vrouw /vraʊ/ *noun* (also **vrow**) E17 **Dutch** (= German *Frau*). A woman, a wife; *especially* one of Dutch origin. Chiefly *South African*.

vue d'ensemble /vy dɑ̃sɑ̃bl/ *noun phrase* plural **vues d'ensemble** (pronounced same) M19 **French**. A general view of matters; an overview.

vulgarisateur /vylgarizatœr/ *noun* plural pronounced same M20 **French** (from *vulgariser* to popularize, vulgarize). A popularizer, a vulgarizer.

vulgarisation /vylgarizasjɔ̃/ *noun* M20 **French**. Vulgarization. Cf. HAUTE VULGARISATION.

Wabenzi /wɑˈbɛnzi/ *noun plural* (also **Wa-Benzi**) M20 **African languages** (invented to resemble the name of an African people: from human plural prefix *wa-* + Mercedes-*Benz*). In Africa: Black politicians, civil servants, entrepreneurs, etc., whose status is marked by their ownership or use of a Mercedes-Benz or similar luxury car.

wabi /ˈwabi/ *noun* M20 **Japanese** (literally, 'solitude'). In Japanese art, a quality of simple and serene beauty of a slightly austere or melancholy kind expressing a mood of spiritual solitude recognized in Zen Buddhist philosophy. Cf. SABI.

wadi /ˈwɑːdi/, /ˈwɒdi/ *noun* (also **wady**) plural **wadis**, **wadies** E17 **Arabic** (*wādī* valley, river-bed). In certain Arabic-speaking countries, a rocky watercourse which is dry except during the rainy season; the stream running through such a watercourse.

■ French *oued*, a later (M19) introduction, represents the same Arabic word. *Oued* now mainly occurs in English with reference to placenames in Francophone North African territories.

wagon-lit /vagɔ̃ˈliː/ *noun* plural **wagon-lits** /vagɔ̃ˈliːz/, **wagons-lits** /vagɔ̃ˈliː/ L19 **French** (from *wagon* railway coach + *lit* bed). A sleeping-car on a train in Continental Europe.

wagon-restaurant /vagɔ̃ rɛstɔrɑ̃/ *noun* plural **wagons-restaurants** (pronounced same) E20 **French** (from *wagon* railway coach + *restaurant*). A dining-car on a train in Continental Europe.

wahala /wəˈhala/ *noun* L20 **Hausa**. In Nigeria: trouble, inconvenience; fuss, bother.

wahine /wɑːˈhiːni/, *foreign* /waˈhine/ *noun* L18 **Maori** (cf. VAHINE). **1** L18 In New Zealand: a Maori woman or wife. **2** M19 In Polynesia: a VAHINE. **3** M20 A girl surfer. *surfing slang*.

wai see under NAMASKAR.

waka /ˈwaka/ *noun 1* E19 **Maori**. In New Zealand: a Maori canoe.

waka /ˈwakə/ *noun 2* M20 **Japanese**. **1** M20 A form of classic Japanese lyrical poetry developed from ancient traditional ballads. **2** M20 A TANKA.

wakame /ˈwakameɪ/ *noun* L20 **Japanese**. An edible Japanese seaweed.

wakf /wɑːkf/ *noun* (also **waqf**) M19 **Arabic** (*waqf* stoppage, immobilization (sc. of ownership of property), from *waqafa* to stop, come to a standstill). In Islamic countries, endowment or settlement of property under which the proceeds are to be devoted to a religious or charitable purpose; land or property endowed in this way.

waldhorn /ˈvalthɔːn/ *noun* M19 **German**. A French horn. Also, a natural valveless horn.

Waldsterben /ˈvaltˌʃtɛrbən/ *noun* L20 **German** (from *Wald* wood, forest + *Sterben* dying, death). *Ecology* Disease and death in forest trees and vegetation as a result of atmospheric pollution.

■ The term has been current in English since about 1983, originally with reference to dieback through environmental causes affecting Germany's forest trees, but now applied to the same phenomenon elsewhere.

wallah /ˈwɒlə/ *noun* (also **walla**) L18 **Hindi** (*-vālā* suffix expressing relation, from Sanskrit *pālaka* keeper). **1** L18 A person, formerly usually a servant, concerned with or in charge of a usually specified thing, task, etc. Chiefly as second element of combination. **2** M19 An Indian Civil servant appointed by competitive examination. More fully *competition-wallah*. **3** M20 Any functionary doing a routine administrative job; a civil servant, a bureaucrat.

■ The Hindi suffix was commonly apprehended by Europeans as a noun with the sense 'man, fellow'; in Anglo-Indian speech it was used chiefly as the second element in combinations such as *box-wallah* ('an itinerant Indian pedlar'). *Wallah* is now only used colloquially with a derogatory suggestion of 'an office-bound functionary' (see quotation 1974) and generally (harking back to the Anglo-Indian usage) with a defining word (see quotation 1996).

3 1974 *Courier-Mail (Brisbane)* Some wallahs in Canberra are sitting in air-conditioned offices telling us what has been flooded and what hasn't.

3 1996 *Times* As the heritage wallahs lord it in

the media during the summer tourist season, they would do well to reflect upon how shallowly rooted and fragile is their present high status.

Walpurgisnacht /val'pʊrgɪsˌnaxt/ *noun* E19 **German** (genitive of *Walpurga* (name) + *Nacht* night). The eve of May Day, marked (according to German folklore and especially Goethe's *Faust*) by a witches' sabbath or a feast of the powers of darkness; *transferred* an orgiastic celebration or party.

■ St Walpurga (or Walburga) was an eighth-century Anglo-Saxon nun who became abbess of Heidenheim in Germany. May Day marks the occasion of the translation of her bodily remains to Eichstätt, where her shrine became a pilgrimage centre. The connection with the powers of darkness is nothing to do with the saintly abbess but is a fortuitous association with pagan festivities formerly celebrated on that date.

1996 *Spectator* . . . the new freedom she finds is mirrored by the licentiousness of her lover's half-mad identical twin, who turns up at her house to burn her books and caper in a demonic spirit of *Walpurgisnacht*.

wampum /'wɒmpəm/ *noun* M17 **Algonquian** (*wampumpeag* (from *wap* white + *umpe* string + plural suffix *-ag*) abbreviated on the erroneous analysis of the word as *wampum* + *peag*). **1** M17 Chiefly *History*. Beads made from the ends of shells rubbed down, polished, and threaded on strings, worn by North American Indians as decoration or (formerly) used as money or for mnemonic or symbolic purposes. **2** L19 *generally* Money. *slang*.

■ Chiefly North America.

wamus /'wamәs/ *noun* E19 **Dutch** (probably from Dutch *wammes* contraction of *wambuis* from Old French *wambois* gambeson, tunic). In southern and western United States: a warm knitted jacket resembling a cardigan.

Wanderjahr /'vandərjɑ:r/ *noun* plural **Wanderjahre** /'vandərjɑ:rə/ L19 **German** (*wander* wander + *Jahr* year). A year of wandering or travel, especially one undertaken by a young person.

■ Formerly a period of travel by an apprentice to improve his skill and broaden his experience; cf. LEHRJAHR. Also occurs in English form *wanderyear* (L19).

wanderlust /'wɒndəlʌst/ *noun* E20 **German**. An eagerness or fondness for wandering or travelling.

1996 *Times* But what America really seems to suit is her wanderlust, her sparkle.

Wandervogel /'vandərfø:gəl/ *noun* plural **Wandervögel** /'vandərfø:gəl/ E20 **German** (literally, 'bird of passage'). A member of a German youth organization founded at the end of the nineteenth century for the promotion of outdoor activities (especially hiking) and folk culture; *transferred* a rambler, a hiker.

waqf variant of WAKF.

wasabi /wə'sɑ:bi/ *noun* E20 **Japanese**. A cruciferous plant, *Eutrema wasabi*, whose thick green root is used in Japanese cookery, usually ground as an accompaniment to raw fish.

washi /'waʃi/ *noun* L20 **Japanese**. Japanese paper; *specifically* a thin handmade variety used to make lantern shades, kites, etc.

wat /wat/ *noun* M19 **Thai** (from Sanskrit *vāṭa* enclosure). In Thailand or Cambodia (Kampuchea): a Buddhist monastery or temple.

wayang /'wɑ:jaŋ/ *noun* E19 **Javanese** (*wajang*, *wayang*). In Indonesia and Malaysia: a theatrical performance employing puppets or human dancers; *specifically* a Javanese and Balinese shadow puppet play (also *wayang kulit* /'ku:lɪt/ (Javanese = skin, leather)).

wazir /wə'zɪə/ *noun* E18 **Arabic** (*wazīr* helper). *History* A high state official, especially in the Ottoman empire; a vizier.

wedeln /'veɪd(ə)ln/ *noun* (also **wedel** /'veɪd(ə)l/) M20 **German** (see next). *Skiing* A technique using a swaying movement of the hips to make a series of short parallel turns.

wedeln /'veɪd(ə)ln/ *intransitive verb* (also **wedel** /'veɪd(ə)l/) M20 **German** (literally, 'wag (the tail)'). *Skiing* Use the wedeln technique. Also, perform a similar movement on a skateboard.

Wehmut /'ve:mu:t/ *noun* E20 **German**. Sadness, melancholy, wistfulness, nostalgia.

Wehrmacht /'ve:rmaxt/ *noun* M20 **German** (literally, 'defence force'). *History* The German armed forces, especially the army, between 1921 and 1945.

Wehrwirtschaft /'ve:rvɪrtʃaft/ *noun* M20 **German** (from *Wehr* defence + *Wirtschaft* economy). The principle or policy of directing a nation's economic activity towards preparation for or support of a war effort, especially as applied in Germany in the 1930s.

wei ch'i /weɪ 'tʃi:/ *noun* L19 **Chinese** (*wéiqí* (Wade–Giles *wei-ch'i*), from *wei* to surround + *qí* (*ch'i*) chess). A traditional Chinese board game of territorial possession and capture. Cf. GO.

weiner variant of WIENER.

weinkraut /'vʌmkraʊt/ *noun* M20 **German** (from *Wein* wine + *Kraut* cabbage). Pickled cabbage cooked with white wine and apples.

Weinstube /'vamʃtu:bə/, /'vamstu:bə/ *noun* plural **Weinstuben** /'vamʃtu:bən/, **Weinstubes** L19 **German** (from *Wein*, wine + *Stube* room). A small German wine bar or tavern. Cf. BIERSTUBE.

Wein, Weib, und Gesang /'vam 'vaɪp ʊnt gə'zaŋ/ *noun phrase* L19 **German**. Wine, woman, and song.

Weisswurst /'vʌɪsvə:st/, /'vʌɪsvʊəst/ *noun* M20 **German** (from *weiss* white + *Wurst* sausage). (A) whitish German sausage made chiefly of veal.

Weltanschauung /ˌvɛltan'ʃaʊʊŋ/ *noun* plural **Weltanschauungen** /ˌvɛltan 'ʃaʊʊŋən/, **Weltanschauungs** M19 **German** (from *Welt* world + *Anschauung* perception). A particular philosophy or view of life; the world-view of an individual or group.

1996 *Spectator* In my case, of course, this shattering event would have to be something pleasant, since my *Weltanschauung* is one of nihilistic despair—that is to say, I am a realist.

Weltbild /'vɛltbɪlt/ *noun* M20 **German** (from *Welt* world + *Bild* picture). WELTANSCHAUUNG.

Weltliteratur /'vɛltlɪteraˌtu:r/ *noun* (also **Weltlitteratur**) E20 **German** (from *Welt* world + *Literatur* literature). A literature of all nations and peoples; universal literature.

Weltpolitik /'vɛltpoliˌti:k/ *noun* E20 **German** (from *Welt* world + *Politik* politics). International politics; a particular country's policy towards the world at large.

Weltschmerz /'vɛltʃmɛrts/ *noun* L19 **German** (from *Welt* world + *Schmerz* pain). A weary or pessimistic feeling about life; an apathetic or vaguely yearning attitude.

1996 *Times* The music does not have to drip with emotion, but surely a love-song can be allowed to exude Weltschmerz as well as passion.

Weltstadt /'vɛltʃtat/ *noun* plural **Weltstädte** /'vɛltʃtɛ:tə/ L19 **German** (from *Welt* world + *Stadt* town). A city of international importance or cosmopolitan character; a cosmopolis.

wendigo variant of WINDIGO.

wen jen /'wɛn ʒɛn/ *noun phrase plural* M20 **Chinese** (*wénrén* man of letters, from *wén* writing + *rén* (Wade–Giles *jên*) man). Chinese men of letters.

wen-yen /'wɛnjɛn/ *noun* (also **wenyen**, **wenyan**) M20 **Chinese** (*wényán*, from *wén* writing + *yán* speech, words). The traditional literary language or style of China, now superseded by PAI-HUA.

wertfrei /'ve:rtfraɪ/ *adjective* E20 **German** (from *Wert* worth + *frei* free). Free of value judgements; morally neutral.

■ In sociological contexts often in English translation as *value-free*; cf. WERTFREIHEIT.

Wertfreiheit /'ve:rtfraɪhaɪt/ *noun* M20 **German** (from as preceding + *-heit* -hood). The quality of being *wertfrei*.

■ *Wertfreiheit* (also frequently in English 'value-freedom'), was recommended by the German sociologist Max Weber (1864–1920) as an ideal to which sociologists should aspire in that they should not allow their own values to influence their judgements on the people and institutions they study.

Westpolitik /'vɛstpɒlɪˌti:k/ *noun* L20 **German** (from *West* west + *Politik* policy: cf. OSTPOLITIK). *History* In European politics, a policy of establishing or developing diplomatic and trading relations with Western nations, especially formerly on the part of Communist States.

whare /'wɒri/ *noun* E19 **Maori**. In New Zealand: a (Maori) house or hut; *generally* a hut, a shed, *specifically* one on a sheep station, where the hands sleep or eat.

wickiup /'wɪkɪʌp/ *noun* (also **wickyup**) M19 **Algonquian** ((Menominee *wikiop*), perhaps a variant of *wikiwam* wigwam). A rough hut consisting of a frame covered with brushwood, used by nomadic peoples in the west and south-west of the United States; *colloquial* any small hut or shanty.

wiederkom /'vi:dəkɒm/ *noun* (also **wiederkomm**, **Wiederkomm**) L19 **French** (*vidrecome* goblet, ultimately from German *wiederkommen* to return, come again). A tall cylindrical German drinking-vessel made of (usually coloured or painted) glass.

wiener /ˈviːnə/ *noun* (in sense 2 also **weiner** /ˈwiːnə/) L19 **German** (adjective from *Wien* Vienna). **I** *attributive* **1** L19 Used *attributively* to designate things from or associated with Vienna. **II 2** E20 *Elliptically for* WIENERWURST. *North American.*

weiner schnitzel see under SCHNITZEL.

wienerwurst /ˈviːnəˌvəːst/, /ˈwiːnəˌwəːst/ *noun* L19 **German.** Viennese sausage.

wili /ˈvɪli/ *noun* (also **willi**) M20 **German or French** (from Serbo-Croat *vîla* nymph, fairy). *Mythology* In Slavonic and eastern German legends, a spirit of a betrothed girl who has died from grief at being jilted by her lover (used especially with reference to the ballet *Giselle*).

wiliwili /ˈwiːlɪwiːli/ *noun* L19 **Hawaiian.** A coral tree, *Erythrina tahitensis*, of Hawaii and Tahiti, which bears clusters of orange flowers; the wood of this tree, used to make surfboards.

willi variant of WILI.

willy-willy /ˈwɪlɪˌwɪli/ *noun* L19 **Aboriginal.** In North West Australia: a cyclone or dust-storm.

windigo /ˈwɪndɪgəʊ/ *noun* (also **wendigo** /ˈwɛndɪgəʊ/) plural **windigo(e)s** E18 **Ojibwa** (*wintiko*). In the folklore of the northern Algonquian Indians, a cannibalistic giant, the transformation of a person who has eaten human flesh.

Wirtschaft /ˈvɪrtʃaft/ *noun* M19 **German** (in sense 2 abbreviation of *Gastwirtschaft* hotel). **1** M19 (Domestic) economy, housekeeping. **2** E20 A hostelry, inn.

Wirtschaftswunder /ˈvɪrtʃaftsˌvʊndər/ *noun* (also **Wirtschaftwunder**) M20 **German** (*Wirtschaft* economy + *Wunder* miracle). The economic recovery of West Germany after the war of 1939–45. Also *transferred.*

> **1996** *Times* But this ominous comparison makes no impression on the self-confidence of German public and political opinion, still mesmerised by the myth of the *Wirtschaftswunder* of the 1950s.

Wissenschaft /ˈvɪsənʃaft/ *noun* M19 **German.** (The systematic pursuit of) knowledge, science; learning, scholarship.

witblits /ˈvɪtblɪts/ *noun* (also **witblitz**) M20 **Afrikaans** (from *wit* white + *blits* lightning). In South Africa: home-brewed brandy, a strong and colourless raw spirit.

witdoek /ˈvɪtdʊk/ *noun* plural **witdoeke** /ˈvɪtdʊkə/, **witdoeks** L20 **Afrikaans** (from *wit* white + DOEK). In South Africa: a member of a largely Black conservative vigilante movement operating in the townships around Cape Town, identifiable by the wearing of a white cloth or scarf about the head. Usually in *plural.*

witloof /ˈwɪtluːf/ *noun* L19 **Dutch** (literally, 'white leaf'). A variety of chicory grown for blanching, with broad leaves and midribs.

wobla variant of VOBLA.

wok /wɒk/ *noun* M20 **Chinese** (Cantonese). A large bowl-shaped frying-pan used in especially Chinese cookery.

■ The *wok*, introduced into Western kitchens in the 1970s, rapidly became a standard item of kitchen equipment.

> **1988** D. Lodge *Nice Work* 'I thought we could put the electric wok away. We never use it. A microwave would be more useful.'

wongi /ˈwɒŋgi/ *noun* E20 **Aboriginal.** A talk, a chat; a speech. *Australian slang.*

wonton /wɒnˈtɒn/ *noun* (also **won ton**) M20 **Chinese** ((Cantonese) *wān t'ān*). In Chinese cookery, (a dish consisting of) a small round dumpling or roll with a savoury filling (especially of minced pork), usually eaten boiled in soup.

woonerf /ˈvuːnəːf/ *noun* plural **woonerfs, woonerven** /ˈvuːnəːv(ə)n/ L20 **Dutch** (from *woon-* residential (from *wonen* to live) + *erf* ground, premises). A road in a residential area, in which a number of devices are employed to create a safer environment by reducing and slowing the flow of traffic.

Wunderkammer /ˈvʊndərkamər/ *noun* L20 **German** (from *Wunder* wonder + *Kammer* chamber). A chamber or cabinet of wonders; *historical* a place exhibiting the collection of a connoisseur of curiosities.

wunderkind /ˈvʊndəkɪnt/ *noun* (also **Wunderkind**) plural **wunderkinds, wunderkinder** /ˈvʊndəkɪndər/ L19 **German** (from *Wunder* wonder + *Kind* child). **1** L19 A highly talented child; a child prodigy, especially in music. **2** M20 A person who achieves remarkable success at an early age. *colloquial.*

2 1996 *Times* Marion's lyricist, the 20-year-old *wunderkind* Jaime Harding, wails hard and long . . .

wurst /vəːst/, /wəːst/; *foreign* /vʊrst/ *noun* M19 **German**. Sausage, especially of the German or Austrian type; a German or Austrian sausage.

wushu /wuːˈʃuː/ *noun* L20 **Chinese** (*wǔshù*, from *wǔ* military + *shù* technique, art). The Chinese martial arts.

wu ts'ai /wuːˈtsʌɪ/ *noun* E20 **Chinese** (*wǔcǎi* (Wade–Giles *wu ts'ai*), from *wǔ* five + *cǎi* colour). Polychrome; polychrome decoration in enamels applied to porcelain; porcelain with polychrome decoration.

xenodochium /zɛnəˈdɒkiəm/ *noun* plural **xenodochia** /zɛnəˈdɒkiə/ (also *xenodochion*) M16 **Late Latin** (from Late Greek from as *xeno-* stranger + *deskhesthai* to receive). *History* A house of reception for strangers and pilgrims, especially in a monastery.

xoanon /ˈzəʊənɒn/ *noun* plural **xoana** /ˈzəʊənə/ E18 **Greek** (related to *xein* to carve). Chiefly *Greek Antiquities* A primitive simply carved image of a deity, originally of wood, and often said to have fallen from heaven.

xystus /ˈzɪstəs/ *noun* plural **xysti** /ˈzɪstʌɪ/ (also Anglicized as **xyst**) M17 **Latin** (from Greek *xustos* smooth, from *xuein* to scrape). *Classical Antiquities* A long covered portico or court used by ancient Greek athletes for exercises. Also, an open colonnade or terrace walk planted with trees and used by the Romans for recreation and conversation.

yabba /ˈjabə/ *noun* L19 **Twi** (*ayawá* earthen vessel, dish). In Jamaica: a large wooden or earthenware vessel used for cookery or storage.

yacca, **yacker** variants of YAKKA.

yad /jɑːd/ *noun* E20 **Hebrew** (*yād*, literally, 'hand'). *Judaism* A pointer used by a reader of the Torah in a synagogue to follow the text, usually in the form of a rod terminating in a hand with an outstretched index finger.

yager see under JÄGER.

yagna variant of YAJNA.

yahrzeit /ˈjɑːtsʌɪt/ *noun* M19 **Yiddish** (from Middle High German *jarzît* anniversary, from Old High German *jar* (German *Jahr*) year + *zît* (German *Zeit*) time). *Judaism* The anniversary of the death of a person, especially a parent.

yajna /ˈjʌdʒnjə/ *noun* (also **yagna**) E19 **Sanskrit** (*yajña* worship, sacrifice). In Hinduism, a sacrificial rite with a specific objective, often involving the burning of substantial offerings.

yakitori /jakɪˈtɔːri/ *noun* M20 **Japanese** (from *yaki* toasting, grilling + *tori* bird). A Japanese dish consisting of pieces of chicken grilled on a skewer.

yakka /ˈjakə/ *noun* (also **yacca**, **yacker**) L19 **Aboriginal**. Work, toil.

■ Australian slang, especially in the phrase *hard yakka*.

yaksha /ˈjʌkʃə/ *noun* L18 **Sanskrit** (*yakṣa*). *Indian Mythology* (A statue or carving of) any of a class of demigods or nature spirits often serving as tutelary guardians.

yakuza /jəˈkuːzə/ *noun* plural same M20 **Japanese** (from *ya* eight + *ku* nine + *za* three, with reference to the worst kind of hand in a gambling game). A Japanese gangster or racketeer. Usually *plural* meaning such gangsters etc. collectively.

attributive **1995** *Spectator Yakuza* gangsters, with extreme right-wing connections, were instantly recognisable by their dress and demeanour . . .

yang /jaŋ/ *noun & adjective* L17 **Chinese** (*yáng* sun, positive, male genitals). **A** *noun* L17 In Chinese philosophy, the male or active principle of the two opposing forces of the universe. Cf. YIN. **B** *attributive* or as *adjective* L17 That represents yang; masculine.

yang ch'in /jaŋ ˈtʃɪn/ *noun phrase* L19 **Chinese** (*yángqín*, from *yáng* high-sounding, foreign + *qín* (Wade–Giles *ch'in*) musical instrument, zither). A Chinese dulcimer.

1996 *Times* But from the moment Lisa Gerrard appeared on stage, . . . and gracefully glided swan-like over to her *yang-ch'in* (that's Chinese dulcimer to you), I knew this was going to be something special.

yanggona /jaŋˈgəʊnə/ *noun* (also **yaqona**) M19 **Fijian** (*yaqona*). KAVA.

yantra /ˈjantrə/ *noun* L19 **Sanskrit** (= device or mechanism for holding or fastening, from *yam* to hold, support). A geometrical diagram used as an aid to meditation in tantric worship; any object used similarly.

yaourt see under YOGHURT.

yaqona variant of YANGGONA.

yarmulke /ˈjɑːmʊlkə/ *noun* (also **yarmulka**) E20 **Yiddish** (*yarmolke*, from Polish *jarmułka* cap, probably from Turkish *yağmurluk* raincoat, cape, from *yağmur* rain). A skullcap worn by male Jews.

yashmak /ˈjaʃmak/ *noun* M19 **Arabic** (*yašmaḳ* from Turkish *yaşmak* use as noun of *yaşmak* to hide oneself). A veil concealing the face below the eyes, worn by Muslim women in public.

yataghan /ˈjatəgan/ *noun* (also **ataghan** /ˈatəgan/) E19 **Turkish** (*yatağan*). Chiefly *History* In Muslim countries, a sword or long dagger having a handle without a guard and often a double-curved blade.

yenta /ˈjɛntə/ *noun* (also **yente**) E20 **Yiddish** (originally a personal name; see quotation). A gossip, a busybody; a noisy, vulgar person; a scolding woman, a shrew. *North American colloquial*.

1968 *Encounter Yenta*, I am told, was a perfectly acceptable name for a lady, derived from the Italian *gentile*—until some ungracious *yenta* gave it a bad name.

yentz /jɛnts/ *transitive verb* M20 **Yiddish** (from *yentzen* to copulate). Cheat, swindle. *United States slang*.

yerba /ˈjəːbə/ *noun* E19 **Spanish** (= herb). MATÉ sense 2. More fully *yerba maté*.

yeshiva /jəˈʃiːvə/ *noun* plural **yeshivas, yeshivot(h)** /jəˈʃiːvɒt/ M19 **Hebrew** (*yĕšīḇāh*, from *yāšhaḇ* to sit). An Orthodox Jewish college or seminary; a Talmudic academy.

yeso /ˈjɛsəʊ/ *noun* (also **yesso**) M16 **Spanish** (from Latin *gypsum*; cf. GESSO). Gypsum, plaster of Paris; *especially* gypsum-rich dust used to control acidity during the making of sherry.

yeti /ˈjɛti/ *noun* M20 **Tibetan** (*yeh-teh* little manlike animal). A creature said to resemble a large ape, whose tracks have supposedly been found in snow on the Himalayan mountains. Also called *Abominable Snowman*.

yé-yé /jɛˈjɛ/ *adjective & noun* M20 **French** (representing *yeah-yeah* reduplication of *yeah*, common in popular songs of the 1960s). **A** *adjective* M20 Designating or pertaining to a style of popular music, dress, etc., typical of the 1960s, especially in France; associated with or enthusiastic about this or subsequent forms of popular optimistic youth culture. **B** *noun* M20 A person associated with the yé-yé style. Also, rock or pop music.

yichus /ˈjɪkəs/, /ˈjɪxəs/ *noun* E20 **Yiddish** (from Hebrew *yiḥūs* pedigree). Social status, prestige. Chiefly *United States colloquial*.

yin /jɪn/ *noun & adjective* L17 **Chinese** (*yīn* shade, feminine, the moon). **A** *noun* L17 In Chinese philosophy, the female or negative principle of the two opposing forces of the universe. Cf. YANG. **B** *attributive* or as *adjective* M20 That represents yin; feminine.

ying ch'ing /jɪŋ ˈtʃɪŋ/ *adjective & noun phrase* E20 **Chinese** (*yǐngqīng* (Wade–Giles *ying ch'ing*) literally, 'shadowy blue'). (Designating) a type of Chinese porcelain with a bluish-white glaze produced in Jiangxi and other provinces, chiefly during the Song dynasty.

ylang-ylang /iːlaŋˈiːlaŋ/ *noun* (also **ilang-ilang**) L19 **Tagalog** (*ilàng-ílang*). A tree of tropical Asia, *Cananga odorata*, with fragrant greenish-yellow flowers from which a perfume is distilled; the perfume obtained from this tree.

yoga /ˈjəʊgə/ *noun* L18 **Sanskrit** (literally, 'union'). In Hindu philosophy, union of the self with the supreme being; a system of ascetic practice, meditation, etc., designed to achieve this.

■ Frequently specifically HATHA YOGA.

yoghurt /ˈjɒgət/ *noun* (also **yogurt**) E17 **Turkish** (*yoğurt*). A semi-solid, somewhat sour foodstuff, now often fruit-flavoured, made from milk curdled by the addition of certain bacteria; a carton of this substance.

■ The spelling *yaourt* /ˈjaʊət/ (E19) as a representation of the pronunciation of *yoğurt* is now rare or obsolete.

yogi /ˈjəʊgi/ *noun* (in sense 1 also **yogin** /ˈjəʊgɪn/) E17 **Sanskrit** (*yogin*, nominative singular *yogī*, from YOGA). **1** E17 A person practising, or proficient in, yoga. **2** E20 YOGA.

yogini /ˈjəʊgɪniː/ *noun* L18 **Sanskrit** (*yoginī* feminine *yogin* yogi). **1** L18 *Hindu Mythology* A female demon, *especially* one of a group attendant on Durga or Siva. **2** M20 A female yogi.

yokozuna /ˌjəʊkəˈzuːnə/ *noun* M20 **Japanese** (from *yoko* crosswise + *tsuna* rope (originally a kind of belt presented to the champion)). A grand champion sumo wrestler.

yom tov /ˈjɒm tɒv/ *noun phrase* M19 **Yiddish** (from Hebrew *yōm* day + *ṭōḇ* good). A Jewish holiday or holy day.

yoni /ˈjəʊni/ *noun* L18 **Sanskrit**. Chiefly *Hinduism* A figure or representation of the female genitals as a sacred symbol or object.

yordim /jɔːˈdɪm/ *noun plural* L20 **Hebrew** (plural of *yored* person who descends). Emigrants from the State of Israel.

yorgan /jɔːˈgʌn/ *noun* E20 **Turkish**. A Turkish quilt.

yourt variant of YURT.

yuan /jʊˈɑːn/ *noun* (also **Yuan**) plural same E20 **Chinese** (*yuàn* courtyard). In China: any of several government departments.

yüeh ch'in /ˈjʊə tʃɪn/, /kin/ *noun* M19 **Chinese** (*yuèqín* (Wade–Giles *yüeh-ch'in*) literally, 'moon guitar'). A Chinese lute with four strings and a flat circular body.

yuga /ˈjʊgə/ *noun* (also **yug** /jʊg/) L18 **Sanskrit** (*yuga* yoke, an age of the world). In Hindu cosmology, each of four periods, each shorter than and inferior to its predecessor, together totalling 4,320,000 years. Cf. KALPA.

yugen /'ju:g(ə)n/ *noun* E20 **Japanese** (from *jū* faint, distant + *gen* dark, unfathomable). In traditional Japanese court culture and Noh plays, a hidden quality of graceful beauty or mystery; profound aestheticism.

yukata /jʊ'kata/ *noun* E19 **Japanese** (from *yu* hot water, bath + *kata(bira)* light kimono). A light cotton kimono, frequently with stencil designs, worn after a bath, or as a housecoat.

yurt /jʊət/ *noun* (also **yourt**) L18 **Russian** (*yurta* (through French *yourte* or German *Jurte*) from Turkic *jurt*). A circular tent of felt, skins, etc., on a collapsible framework, used by nomads in Mongolia and Siberia. Also, a semi-subterranean hut, usually of timber covered with earth or turf.

Z

zabaglione /zabaˈljəʊni/ *noun* L19 **Italian** (perhaps ultimately from late Latin *sabaia* an Illyrian drink). A dessert consisting of egg-yolks, sugar, and (usually Marsala) wine, whipped to a frothy texture over a gentle heat and served either hot or cold. Cf. SABAYON.

zabuton /zaˈbuːtɒn/ *noun* L19 **Japanese** (from *za* sitting, seat + *buton* variant of FUTON). A flat floor cushion for sitting or kneeling on.

zaftig /ˈzaftɪg/ *adjective* (also **zoftig** /ˈzɒftɪg/) M20 **Yiddish** (from German *saftig* juicy). Of a woman: plump, having a full rounded figure. *North American colloquial.*

zaguan /zaˈgwan/, /saˈgwan/ *noun* M19 **Spanish** (*zaguán* = vestibule, hall, from Arabic *ʼustuwān*, perhaps ultimately from Greek *stoa* porch). In South and Central America and in the south-western United States: a passage running from the front door to the central patio of houses.

zaibatsu /zʌɪˈbatsuː/ *noun* plural same M20 **Japanese** (from *zai* wealth + *batsu* clique). *Commerce* Originally, a Japanese capitalist organization usually based on a single family having controlling interests in a variety of companies. Now, (the members of) a Japanese business cartel or conglomerate.

zaikai /ˈzʌɪkʌɪ/ *noun* M20 **Japanese** (from *zai* wealth + *kai* world). In Japan: (the élite who control) the world of business and high finance.

zaitech /ˈzʌɪtɛk/ *noun* L20 **Japanese** (= financial engineering). Playing the money and stock markets as a business practice to enhance a company's profitability.

zakat /zəˈkɑːt/ *noun* E19 **Persian and Urdu** (*zakā(t)*, Turkish *zekât*, from Arabic *zakā(t)* almsgiving). An obligatory payment made annually under Islamic law on certain kinds of property and used for charitable and religious objects.

zakuska /zaˈkuska/ *noun* (also **zakouska**) plural **zakuskas**, **zakuski** /zaˈkuski/ L19 **Russian** (usually as plural *zakuski*). An hors d'oeuvre.

zamarra /θaˈmarra/, /saˈmarra/ *noun* M19 **Spanish**. In Spain: a kind of sheepskin jacket.

zampogna /zamˈpɒnjə/, *foreign* /tsam ˈpoɲɲa/ *noun* M18 **Italian** (from (late) Latin *symphonia*). *Music* A traditional mouth-blown bagpipe of southern Italy having two chanters and two drones. Also, any of various other woodwind instruments.

zapateado /za,patɪˈɑːdəʊ/, *foreign* /θa,pate ˈado/, /sa,pateˈado/ *noun* plural **zapateados** /za,patɪˈɑːdəʊz/, /sa,patɪˈɑːdos/, /θa,pateˈados/, /sa,pateˈados/ M19 **Spanish** (from *zapato* shoe). **1** M19 A flamenco dance involving complex syncopated stamping of the heels and toes in imitation of castanets. **2** M20 Dancing or footwork of this kind.

zarape variant of SERAPE.

zarda /ˈzɑːdə/ *noun* L19 **Persian and Urdu** (*zardah*, from Persian *zard* yellow). A Persian and Indian sweet dish consisting of rice cooked with saffron and often almonds and raisins or sultanas.

zareba /zəˈriːbə/ *noun* (also **zereba**, **zariba**, **zeriba**) M19 **Arabic** (*zarība* pen or enclosure for cattle). **1** M19 In Sudan and neighbouring countries: (a camp fortified by) a fence, usually made of thorn trees, for defence against enemies or wild animals. **2** L19 *transferred* and *figurative* A defensive force or barrier.

zari /zari/ *noun* M20 **Persian and Urdu** (*zarī*, from Persian *zar* gold). Indian gold and silver brocade; *colloquial* a sari decorated with this.

zariba variant of ZAREBA.

zarzuela /θarˈθwela/, /sarˈswela/ *noun* L19 **Spanish**. **1** L19 A traditional form of operetta in Spain, with spoken dialogue, songs, and dances. **2** M20 A Spanish dish consisting of various kinds of seafood cooked in a rich sauce.

zastruga variant of SASTRUGA.

zawiya /ˈzɑːwɪə/ *noun* (also **zawiyeh**) M19 **Arabic** (*zāwiya* corner, prayer room). In North Africa: a Sufi religious community's mosque, especially when containing the shrine of a holy person.

zazen /zɑː'zɛn/ *noun* E18 **Japanese** (from *za* sitting, a seat + *zen* Zen). Zen meditation.

zearat variant of ZIARAT.

zeitgeber /'tsaɪtgeːbər/, /'zʌɪtgeɪbə/ *noun* plural same, **zeitgebers** M20 **German** (from *Zeit* time + *Geber* giver). *Physiology* A rhythmically occurring event, especially in the environment, which acts as a cue in the regulation of certain biological rhythms in an organism.

Zeitgeist /'tsaɪtgaɪst/, /'zʌɪtgʌɪst/ *noun* M19 **German** (from *Zeit* time + *Geist* spirit). The spirit of the age; the trend of thought or feeling in a period, especially as reflected in its literature, art, etc.

> **1995** *Times* Like the seasoned politician he [sc. M. Mitterand] is, he has once again identified the *zeitgeist* in France, where dying has become the subject of some debate.

zek /zɛk/ *noun* M20 **Russian** (representing pronunciation of *z/k*, abbreviation of *zaklyuchënnyĭ* prisoner). In countries of the former USSR: a person held in a prison or forced labour camp.

zemstvo /'zɛmstvəʊ/, *foreign* /'zemstvo/ *noun* plural **zemstvos**, **zemstva** /'zɛmstvə/ M19 **Russian** (from *zem'* (now *zemlya*) land). *History* Any of the elected district or provincial councils set up in Russia by Alexander II in 1864 as part of his reforms.

Zen /zɛn/ *noun* E18 **Japanese** (from Chinese *chán* quietude, from Sanskrit *dhyāna* meditation). A school of Mahayana Buddhism emphasizing meditation and personal awareness.

■ Also more fully *Zen Buddhism*. Influential in Japanese life from the thirteenth century onwards, *Zen* became significantly fashionable in the West during the 1960s.

zenana /zə'nɑːnə/ *noun* M18 **Persian and Urdu** (*zanānah*, from *zan* woman). **1** M18 In the Indian subcontinent: the part of a house in which high-caste women are or were secluded. **2** E20 A light quilted thin fabric used for women's dresses.

zendo /'zɛndəʊ/ *noun* plural **zendos** M20 **Japanese** (*zendō*, from ZEN + *dō* hall). A place for Zen Buddhist meditation and study.

zeppole /'zɛpɒleɪ/ *noun* plural **zeppoli** /'zɛpɒli/ M20 **Italian**. A kind of doughnut. *United States*.

zereba, **zeriba** variants of ZAREBA.

zeugma /'zjuːgmə/ *noun* LME **Latin** (from Greek, literally, 'yoking', from *zeugnunai* to yoke, related to *zugon* a yoke). A rhetorical figure by which a single word is made to refer to two or more words in a sentence, especially when applying to them in different senses.

ziarat /ziː'ɑːrət/ *noun* (also **zearat**) L18 **Urdu** (from Persian *ziyārat* from Arabic *ziyāra(t)* visit, pilgrimage). A Muslim pilgrimage to a shrine.

zibeline /'zɪbəlɪn/, /'zɪbəliːn/, /'zɪbəlʌɪn/ *noun* L16 **French** (of Slavonic origin). **1** L16 The sable. Now *rare* or *obsolete*. **b** M19 The fur of this animal. **2** L19 A soft smooth woollen material with a long nap pressed flat, used especially for women's coats. Also *zibeline cloth*.

zibib /'zɪbɪb/, /zə'biːb/ *noun* M19 **Arabic** (*zabīb* (Egyptian Arabic *zibīb*) dried grapes, raisins). A strong colourless spirit made in Egypt from raisins.

Zigeuner /tsɪ'gɔɪnə/ *noun* plural same (feminine **Zigeunerin** /tsɪ'gɔɪnərɪn/, plural **Zigeunerinnen** /tsɪ'gɔɪnərɪnən/) M19 **German**. A Gypsy.

zingana /'zɪŋgənə/, /zɪŋ'gɑːnə/, /'tsɪŋgənə/ *noun* E18 **Italian**. **1** E18 (*Zingana*) A Gypsy girl or woman. *rare*. **2** M20 Striped wood furnished by various African trees; zebrano.

Zingaro /'zɪŋgərəʊ/, /'tsɪŋgərəʊ/ *noun* & *adjective* (also **zingaro**) E17 **Italian**. **A** *noun* E17 plural **zingari** /'zɪŋgəri/ (feminine **zingara** /'zɪŋgərə/, plural **zingare** /'zɪŋgəreɪ/). A Gypsy. **B** *attributive* or as *adjective* L18 Of or pertaining to Gypsies.

zita /'ziːtə/ *noun* plural **zite** /'ziːteɪ/, **ziti** /'ziːti/ M19 **Italian**. Pasta in the form of tubes resembling large macaroni.

zocalo /'zɒkələʊ/ *noun* plural **zocalos** L19 **Spanish** (*zócalo*). In Mexico: a public square, a plaza.

zoco /'zɒkəʊ/ *noun* plural **zocos** L19 **Spanish** (from Arabic *sūḳ* souk). In Spain and North Africa: a souk; a market-place.

zoftig variant of ZAFTIG.

zollverein /'tsɔlfəraɪn/ *noun* M19 **German** (from *Zoll* toll + *Verein* union). *History* A union of States with a uniform rate of customs duties from other countries and free trade within the union; *specifically* that between States of the German Empire in the nineteenth century.

zombie /ˈzɒmbi/ *noun & verb* E19 **Bantu** (cf. JUMBY). **A** *noun* **1** E19 Originally, a snake-deity in voodoo cults of or deriving from West Africa and Haiti. Now (especially in the West Indies and southern United States), a soulless corpse said to have been revived by witchcraft. **2** M20 A dull, apathetic, unresponsive, or unthinkingly acquiescent person. *colloquial*. **3** M20 In the war of 1939–45, a man conscripted for home defence. *Canadian military slang* (*derogatory*). **4** M20 A long mixed drink consisting of several kinds of rum, liqueur, and fruit juice. **B** *transitive verb* M20 *zombie out*. Exhaust; disorientate.

zoppa /ˈtsɔppa/ *adjective & adverb* **M18 Italian** (feminine of *zoppo* limping). *Music* In a syncopated rhythm, especially one in which the second quaver of a 2/4 bar is accented.

■ Frequently in the phrase *alla zoppa*.

zori /ˈzɔːri/ *noun* plural **zoris**, same **E19 Japanese** (*zōri*, from *sō* grass, (rice) straw + *ri* footwear, sole). A Japanese sandal, having a simple thong between the toes and a flat sole originally of straw but now often of rubber, felt, etc.

Zouave /zuːˈɑːv/, /zwɑːv/ *noun* M19 **French** (from Kabyle *Zouaoua* name of a tribe). **1** M19 A member of a body of light infantry in the French army, originally formed of Algerian Kabyles, and long retaining the original oriental uniform. **b** M19 *History* More fully *Papal* or *Pontifical Zouave*. A member of a corps of French soldiers formed in Rome for the defence of the pope between 1860 and 1871. **c** M19 *History* A member of any of several volunteer regiments of Union troops in the American Civil War which adopted the name and in part the uniform of the French Zouaves. **2** M19 A garment resembling part of the Zouave uniform; *specifically* **a** *History* (in full *Zouave jacket, bodice*) a woman's short embroidered jacket or bodice, with or without sleeves; **b** in *plural*, peg-top trousers, as worn by men in the late nineteenth century and women in the late twentieth century (also *Zouave trousers, pants*); **c** a wide loose skirt with a looped or tucked up hemline (also *Zouave skirt*).

2.b 1981 *Washington Post* First came the ankle-length Zouaves, looking a bit like baggies gone beserk . . . Then came the shorter Zouaves, like knee-length bloomers.

zouk /zuːk/ *noun* L20 **French** (apparently from Antillean creole *zouk* to party, possibly influenced by United States slang *juke* (or *jook*) to have a good time). An exuberant style of popular music originating in Guadeloupe in the Lesser Antilles.

■ Developed in Paris as a style of Antillean popular music intended to hold its own against Western pop and disco music, *zouk* was popularized in France during the 1980s by the group called Kassav, and began to feature on the British and American music scene at the end of the decade (see quotation).

1987 *Guardian* Tonight, the first ever zouk on British soil kicks off this year's Camden Festival International arts programme . . . Zouk, especially Kassav, is the pulse of Paris streets and the soundtrack for her nightclubs.

zucchetto /tsʊˈkɛtəʊ/ *noun* plural **zucchettos** (also **zucchetta** /tsʊˈkɛtə/) **M19 Italian** (*zucchetta* diminutive of *zucca* gourd, head). The skullcap worn by Roman Catholic ecclesiastics, black for priests, purple for bishops, red for cardinals, and white for the Pope.

zucchini /zʊˈkiːni/ *noun plural* (also **zucchinis**) E20 **Italian** (plural of *zucchino* small marrow, courgette, diminutive of *zucca* gourd). Courgettes.

■ Chiefly in North America and Australia; in Britain *courgettes* is the usual word.

zufolo /ˈtsuːfələʊ/, /ˈzuːfələʊ/ *noun* (also **zuffolo**) plural **zufoli** /ˈtsuːfəli/ **E18 Italian**. *Music* A flageolet, a small flute or whistle.

Zugunruhe /ˈtsuːkˌʊnruːə/ *noun* **M20 German**. *Ornithology* Migratory restlessness; the migratory drive in birds.

zugzwang /ˈzʌgzwaŋ/ *noun* **E20 German** (from *Zug* move + *Zwang* compulsion, obligation). *Chess* A position in which a player must move but cannot do so without disadvantage; the obligation to make a move even when disadvantageous.

■ Frequently in *in zugzwang*.

zuppa di pesce /ˌtsuppa di ˈpeʃe/ *noun phrase* **M20 Italian**. Fish soup.

zuppa inglese /ˌtsuppa iŋˈglese/ *noun phrase* **M20 Italian** (= English soup). A rich Italian dessert resembling trifle.

zurla /ˈzʊələ/ *noun* plural **zurle** /ˈzʊəleɪ/ **M20 Serbo-Croat** (*sûrla*, from (as) next). *Music* A kind of shawm introduced to the

Balkans from the Middle East by Gypsies.

zurna /ˈzʊənə/ *noun* L19 **Turkish** (from Persian *surnā* festival pipe). *Music* A kind of shawm found in Turkey, Arabic-speaking countries, and various neighbouring regions.

zut /zyt/ *interjection* E20 **French.** Expressing irritation, contempt, impatience, etc.

■ Also *zut alors!*, in which *alors* acts as an intensifier.

1996 *Times: Weekend* So just what is it in the end that brings together the woman with the hair lip, the dirty dancer, a quixotic French cameraman—zut alors!—and a group of troglodyte descendants of lost Vikings with a liking for high technology?

zwieback /ˈtsviːbak/ *noun* L19 **German** (= twice-bake). A (sweet) rusk or biscuit made by baking a small loaf, and then toasting slices until they are dry and crisp.

zwischenzug /ˈtsvɪʃənˌtsuːk/ *noun* M20 **German** (from *zwischen* intermediate + *Zug* move). *Chess* A move interposed in a sequence of play in such a way as to alter the outcome.

Appendix

Aboriginal languages

EIGHTEENTH CENTURY

boomerang
cooee
corroboree
gibber
koradji

NINETEENTH CENTURY

alcheringa
billabong
binghi
bunyip
gilgai
goondie
gunyah
mallee
mulga
tjurunga
willy-willy
yakka

TWENTIETH CENTURY

bombora
didgeridoo
wongi

African languages

SEVENTEENTH CENTURY

harmattan
juju

EIGHTEENTH CENTURY

buckra
kierie
marimba

NINETEENTH CENTURY

accra
donga
impi
indaba
induna
inkosi
intombi
inyanga
jumby
lobola
mabele
mbira
nagana
sangoma
tokoloshe
umfaan
umfundisi
yabba
zombie

TWENTIETH CENTURY

alhaji
balafon
dashiki
kalimba
kente
kwashiorkor
kya
lappa
manyatta
mau-mau
patha patha
piri-piri
soukous
tsotsi
Wabenzi
wahala

Afrikaans/Dutch

SEVENTEENTH CENTURY

dagga
jong

EIGHTEENTH CENTURY

doek
hanepoot
kaross
kraal
krans
mebos
naartjie
sjambok
skoff
springbok
stoep
veld
vlakte
vlei

NINETEENTH CENTURY

berg
biltong
bond
dop
hamel
inspan
jukskei
kappie
katel
kêrel
klompie
konfyt
kop
koppie
laager
lammervanger
maas
mealie
meisie
Nagmaal
oblietjie
oom
ou
oubaas
pondok
rand
remskoen
rondavel
rooinek
schlenter
skepsel
sosatie
takhaar
tameletjie
togt
trek
Uitlander
veldskoen
voetganger
voetsek
volk
voorloper
Voortrekker

TWENTIETH CENTURY

apartheid
baasskap
boerewors
braai
braaivleis
dominee
klonkie
koeksister
kragdadig
kwela
lekker
melktert
naat
oudstryder
ouma
oupa
outjie
platteland
swart gevaar
tot siens
vaaljapie
verkrampte
verligte
witblits
witdoek

American Indian languages

SEVENTEENTH CENTURY

moccasin
peag
pocosin
powwow
wampum

EIGHTEENTH CENTURY

coontie
menhaden
pemmican
quipu
shaganappi
tepee
windigo

NINETEENTH CENTURY

cassareep
cheechako
hogan
kachina
kiva
piki
wickiup

TWENTIETH CENTURY

mola

Anglo-Indian

SEVENTEENTH CENTURY

brinjal

EIGHTEENTH CENTURY

chi-chi
serang

NINETEENTH CENTURY

chota
memsahib
topi

Arabic

SIXTEENTH CENTURY

cadi
cafila
faki
hashish
jubba
kebaya
muezzin
mufti
reis
sharif
sheikh

SEVENTEENTH CENTURY

arak
eid
fakir
fatwa
hakim
haram
imam
kebab
khamsin
kiblah
laban
madrasah
mastaba
sakia
salaam
sayyid
sura
ulema
wadi

EIGHTEENTH CENTURY

afreet
bismillah
dhow

fellah
galabiya
ghazi
Hadith
hajj
hanif
id ul-fitr
ihram
khalifa
kohl
naskhi
rebab
simoom
talak
tarboosh
tekbir
wazir

NINETEENTH CENTURY

aba
abaya
agal
alfa
askari
azan
bint
fana
fedai
gandoura
ghibli
gimbri
halal
hammada
hamza
inshallah
izar
jebel
jellaba
jihad
jinnee
kaid
kameez
keffiyeh
khat
khutbah
kief
Kitab
loofah
Mahdi
Majlis
mancala
mashallah
masjid
Maulana
mihrab
mimbar
sabkha
santir
serdab
shadoof
shahada
shahid
sheikha
shott
souk
sudd
tazia
umma
umrah
urs
wakf
yashmak
zareba
zawiya
zibib

TWENTIETH CENTURY

Bedu
burghul
falafel
harka
hijab
hummus
imshi
intifada
ishan
maleesh
mazar
medina
reg
seif
sharifa
shufti
shura
tabbouleh

Aramaic

SEVENTEENTH CENTURY

Kaddish
tefillin

NINETEENTH CENTURY

kiddushin
Kol Nidre

Bantu languages see under African languages

Bengali

NINETEENTH CENTURY

surbahar

TWENTIETH CENTURY

esraj

Breton

NINETEENTH CENTURY

korrigan
menhir

Catalan

NINETEENTH CENTURY

paella
talayot
taula

TWENTIETH CENTURY

sardana

Chinese

SEVENTEENTH CENTURY

ginseng
li
sampan
yang
yin

EIGHTEENTH CENTURY

feng-shui
hong
pe-tsai
souchong
T'ai Chi

NINETEENTH CENTURY

chopsuey
chow mein
k'ai shu
kowtow
kung fu
kylin
Lohan
nien hao
pak-choi
pa-kua
san-hsien
taipan
t'ing
te
ti-tzu
tong
wei ch'i
yang ch'in
yüeh ch'in

TWENTIETH CENTURY

an-hua
cheongsam
dazibao
dim sum
erh hu
fu yung
ganbei
ganbu
gung-ho
hoisin
ko
kuei
kwai-lo
lei
li
ling chih
mah-jong
mee
mei ping
pai-hua
pakapoo
p'an
putonghua
qinghaosu
samfu
san ts'ai
subgum
tou ts'ai
tu-mo
ve-tsin
wen jen
wen-yen
wok
wonton
wushu
wu ts'ai
ying ch'ing
yuan

Corsican

TWENTIETH CENTURY

macchia
tafone

Czech

TWENTIETH CENTURY

háček
kolach

Danish

TWENTIETH CENTURY

landnam
landrace
mor
smørrebrød

Dutch

SIXTEENTH CENTURY

kermis
monsoon

SEVENTEENTH CENTURY

maelstrom
polder
soya
vendue
vrouw

EIGHTEENTH CENTURY

baas
kloof
poort
snoek
stoop

NINETEENTH CENTURY

Boer
matje
poffertje
riem
riempie
rijsttafel
roemer
spruit
stelling
taal
wamus
witloof

TWENTIETH CENTURY

kraak porselein
woonerf

Egyptian (Ancient)

NINETEENTH CENTURY

ankh
shabti
ushabti

TWENTIETH CENTURY

shawabti

Eskimo languages

EIGHTEENTH CENTURY

angekok
kabloona
kayak
parka
umiak

NINETEENTH CENTURY

igloo
nunatak
tupik

TWENTIETH CENTURY
anorak
pingo
qiviut

Fijian

NINETEENTH CENTURY
sulu
yanggona

Finnish

NINETEENTH CENTURY
sauna

TWENTIETH CENTURY
kantele

French

OLD ENGLISH
philosophe

MIDDLE ENGLISH
accidie
amour
avoirdupois
bourdon
chemise
corvée
douce
flèche
fleur-de-lis
godet
haras
hydria
impayable
jupe
langue
largesse
lieu
Madame
ménage
Messiah
noblesse
orfèvrerie
par
parure
patron
peridot
potage
reverie
richesse
sans
sec
sous-
tablier
tache
trebuchet
venue
voussoir

LATE MIDDLE ENGLISH
absinth
adieu
aigre-doux
antipodes
avant-garde
ballade
Bedouin
beguine
bergerette
blancmange
bourg
bruit
cameo
carte
catechumen
ceinture
cenacle
cham
chaperon
chasse
chaussure
chevalier
chevauchée
chevelure
chevron
cicatrice
cohabitation
commissar
confrère
congé
couchant
couleur de rose
coup
crise
dariole
dauphin
difficile
distrait
douceur
droit
envoi
equivoque
fête
finesse
fleuron
gabelle
gourmand
haut-pas
hélas
hydra
introit
jaune
jour
jujube
jupon
lardon
legerdemain
lèse-majesté
lierne
Mademoiselle
meridional
migraine
muscatel
musette
nadir
noir
nonpareil
obit
or
orgeat
oriflamme
oyer
oyez
pain
pavé
péage
pensée
petit
plage
puissance
rebec
regardant
reinette
reprise
rouge
sanglier
tendresse
tisane
toile
triste
tristesse
tuile
vigneron
vignette
vinaigrette
vivier
volage

FIFTEENTH CENTURY
blond
brochette
chanson
cheval
convenance
entremet
faubourg
jumelle
parole
portail
recueil
regime
réplique
sachet
serviette
sou
tambour
tapis
tranche
tourbillion
valet
vignoble

SIXTEENTH CENTURY
abbé
adage
à la
à la mode
aliquot
antes
armoire
auberge
banderole
bastide
baton
bayadère
bibliothèque
bocage
bon
bonjour
bonne
bonze
bourgeois
bourse
bricole
brocard
brunet
burnous
cabochon
cachou
cafard
caloyer
camaieu
canaille
canton
cap-à-pie
capriole
capuche
cartel
cestui
chamois
champignon
chancre
chaton
clientele
commis
concierge
confiture
cordelle
corps
corps de garde
courante
croissant
démenti
demoiselle
diable
divan
doge
dolman
éloge
emir
escritoire
esplanade
esprit
faille
feme covert
feme sole
feuillemorte
framboise
fricassee
fugue
fusee
gabion
gendarme
gendarmerie
gigot
girasol
gnomon
gonfalonier
goût
guidon
haut-goût
hippodrome
jacquerie
kermes
kumis
lien
limaçon
loup-garou
lunette
luxe
maison
maître d'hôtel
malgré
marron
massif
mignon
monad
mot

moustache
muguet
muscat
mystagogue
nacre
naïf
nebulé
paladin
panache
patisserie
pavane
pensionnaire
perdu
petite
phaeton
piquant
pique
pomade
portmanteau
puisne
qui vive
ravelin
reglement
rendezvous
réseau
rondeau
santon
seigneur
sequin
serin
sorbet
sultan
taille
tarot
tercet
terreplein
tilleul
toque
villanelle
violon
visitant
vivandier
vive
volte
volute
zibeline

SEVENTEENTH CENTURY

aide-de-camp
allemande
allumette
amende honorable
ampoule
andouille
andouillette
à outrance
apropos
arabesque
arrêt
assegai
atelier
attentat
aubade
au reste
au revoir
baccalaureate
badinage
bagatelle
ballet
banquette
baragouin
bascule
beau
beau monde
bel esprit
belle
belles-lettres
berceau
bidet
bienséance
bigarreau
bijou
billet-doux
bisque
bizarre
bon vivant
bon voyage
boucan
bouilli
bouillon
bourgade
bourrée
boutade
brouillon
brusque
bureau
burin
burlesque
cabaret
cachet
cadet
caique
caisson
calotte
calumet
capot
caprice
caracole
carousel
carte blanche
cartouche
casque
cassolette
catafalque
cervelat
chaconne
chagrin
chaise
chandelier
chanterelle
charivari
chassis
chef-d'œuvre
chevaux de frise
chicane
ciboule
cirque
clairvoyant
coiffure
colon
commissionaire
compote
comte
console
contretemps
coquet
coquette
corps de logis
cortège
corvette
couchee
coup d'état
coup de grâce
courbette
court bouillon
couscous
creole
cresson
critique
croisette
croupade
culet
curé
cuvette
dégagé
de haut en bas
délicatesse
démarche
dernier
dernier ressort
déshabillé
dey
domino
douane
double entendre
doyen
dragée
éclaircissement
éclat
embarras
embonpoint
enceinte
en déshabillé
en passant
en prince
entre nous
environs
epode
ergot
espalier
estacade
estrade
étourdi
etui
exergue
faïence
fainéant
fainéantise
fanfaronade
farceur
faux pas
feu d'artifice
feu de joie
flageolet
flambeau
forte
fronton
gala
garçon
gare
gavotte
gazette
genie
gens de la robe
gigue
girandole
glacis
globule
goitre
gondolier
grand monarque
grand seigneur
gratin
grillade
gueux
haricot
hauteur
honnête homme
hôtel-Dieu
impromptu
intendant
intime
jalap
jargonelle
je ne sais quoi
jet d'eau
knout
kremlin
lansquenet
legume
levee
liaison
mâche
maladroit
malapropos
mal-entendu
manège
marabout
marc
Mardi gras
marionette
marquise
mascaron
mélange
mêlée
menus plaisirs
minaret
mistral
moire
mon cher
mouche
mousseline
musée
naive
naïveté
neroli
niche
nom de guerre
nonchalance
nouvelle
odalisque
odeum
opuscule
orangerie
ordonnance
ortolan
par excellence
parterre
partie
passade
passementerie
passe-partout
pastille
patois
paysage
penchant

pension
percale
père
peristyle
picot
pignon
piquet
pirogue
pirouette
pis aller
plafond
point
poivrade
politique
porte-cochère
potager
pot-pourri
pour passer le temps
pratique
procès-verbal
ragout
rapport
rasant
ratafia
ratelier
ravissant
rebus
recherché
religieuse
religieux
renversement
reveille
rigadoon
rodomontade
rouleau
routier
sabot
sagamité
sainfoin
salon
sans cérémonie
sans façon
sarabande
saucisson
seigneurie
sobriquet
sottise
sou markee
spirituel
suede
suite
tableau
table d'hôte
tabouret
taille-douce
talus
terre-verte
tête-à-tête
toison d'or
tombac
topinambour
tourniquet
tourte
tracasserie
traineau
treillage
tremblement
trente-et-quarante
tribade
tric-trac
tutoyer
vade-mecum
valet-de-chambre
valise
vedette
vin
voir dire

EIGHTEENTH CENTURY

abatis
accouchement
accoucheur
acharnement
agiotage
agrément
aigrette
aiguille
à la daube
allée
amateur
à merveille
amour propre
ancien régime
aplomb
appliqué
à propos de bottes
assemblé
assemblée
assiette
à tort et à travers
aubergine
au contraire
au courant
au fait
au fond
au pied de la lettre
avalanche
badigeon
baguette
bain-marie
balancé
ballonné
bal masqué
banco
bandeau
barbette
barcarole
bas bleu
batardeau
bateau
batterie
batterie de cuisine
béchamel
bergère
bigarade
bistre
bivouac
blanc
blanquette
bon-bon
bonhomie
bon mot
bonne bouche
bon ton
borné
bosquet
bossage
boudoir
bougie
boulevard
bouleversement
bouquet
bouquetier
bourgeoise
bourgeoisie
boutique
bouts rimés
bravo
brisé
brochure
buffet
cabriole
cabriolet
cache
cadastre
cadeau
café au lait
cannelure
cantaloup
caoutchouc
carafe
carillon
carmagnole
carriole
carte du pays
casserole
cassette
catalogue raisonné
cause célèbre
celadon
centrifuge
chalumeau
chambranle
chanterelle
chapeau-bras
charade
chargé d'affaires
charlotte
chasse
chasseur
château
chatoyant
chenille
chère amie
chez
chiffon
chiffonier
chignon
chou
ci-devant
cipolin
civet
clique
colporteur
comme il faut
compagnon de voyage
compère
compotier
comptoir
connoisseur
conservatoire
contrecoup
cordon bleu
corps diplomatique
coterie
cotillion
coup d'œil
coup de foudre
coup de main
coup de théâtre
coupé
coureur
crèche
crêpe
cretin
critique
cromorne
croquette
croupier
cuisine
cul-de-sac
curette
cyme
dalles
dame de compagnie
daube
débouché
debris
début
dehors
déjeuner
demi-caractère
demilune
demi-saison
denouement
de nouveau
depot
derrière
detour
de trop
dévot
diablerie
Directoire
divertissement
dormeuse
douanier
douche
duchesse
duvet
eau-de-vie
ébauche
echelon
écrevisse
égalité
élégante
élite
embarras de richesse
embouchure
embrasure
émeute
emigré
empressement
en attendant
enceinte
encore
en face
en famille
enfilade
en gros
en l'air
en masse
ennui

ennuyant
ennuyé
enragé
en route
ensemble
en suite
en train
entrechat
entrée
entrepôt
entresol
en ventre sa mère
epaulette
epigramme
épris
esprit de corps
esprit fort
esquisse
etamine
etiquette
étourderie
exigeant
extrados
farce
farouche
faute de mieux
fauteuil
femme de chambre
fête champêtre
fichu
figurant
fille de joie
fourchette
foyer
fracas
fricandeau
frisson
fronde
frondeur
gage d'amour
gaieté de coeur
galère
galette
galipot
gauche
gaucherie
gîte
grande dame
grand monde
grippe
grisette
gros
guillotine
ha-ha
haute noblesse
homme d'affaires
hors d'oeuvre
hors de combat
hôtel de ville
hôtel garni
houri
illuminé
insouciance
intrados
intriguant
jalousie
jeu
jeu d'esprit
jeu de mots
jeu de paume
jeunesse
jongleur
julienne
kaolin
kasbah
lande
langue d'oc
langue d'oïl
lavage
lettre
lettre de cachet
levee
liqueur
locale
loge
longueur
loup
maisonette
majuscule
malaise
mal de mer
mandolin
maniéré
mannequin
manqué
maréchaussée
marinade
marivaudage
matelote
mauvais
mauvais sujet
mentor
meringue
mésalliance
messagerie
métayer
métier
mézair
mezzanine
mignonette
minaudière
mirabelle
molleton
mon ami
monde
moraine
morale
morceau
mordoré
mousquetaire
nacarat
née
negligée
nonchalant
nouvelle
noyau
nuance
oeil-de-boeuf
ombres chinoises
opéra comique
orné
oubliette
outré
palette
panne
papier mâché
papillote
parloir
paroli
parti
partie carrée
pas
pas de deux
pas de trois
passacaille
passé
pâté
patronne
patte
paupiette
paysanne
perruquier
persiflage
petit-maître
petit pain
piaffe
picotee
pièce de résistance
pierrot
pisé
piste
place d'armes
plat
plateau
politesse
polonaise
pompadour
pompon
port-crayon
port de voix
posé
poste restante
postiche
pot-au-feu
pot de chambre
poudre
poupée
pourparler
praline
précieux
précis
preux chevalier
prie-dieu
protégé
purée
quadrille
quatorze
radeau
raisonné
rapporteur
récolte
redingote
régie
restaurateur
reticule
ricochet
rinceau
riposte
rissole
robe de chambre
rôti
rôtisseur
rouge-et-noir
roulade
roulette
rusé
saccade
salep
salle
salle-à-manger
salmi
salpicon
sang-froid
sans pareil
sansculotte
savant
savante
savoir vivre
savonette
secretaire
séjour
sève
siffleur
silhouette
sissonne
socle
soi-disant
soirée
solitaire
Soubise
soubrette
soupçon
soupe
souterrain
souvenir
tafia
tant bien que mal
tant mieux
tant pis
terre-à-terre
terrine
tiers état
tirailleur
ton
tonneau
tontine
toujours gai
toujours perdrix
toupet
tournee
tournure
tout
tout au contraire
tout compris
tout court
tout de suite
tout ensemble
tout le monde
tout seul
traiteur
trajet
triage
tricorne
tricot
tripotage
trottoir
troubadour
trouvère
tuyère
tzigane
uhlan
usine
valse
vaudeville
velours
vendange

verd-antique
vers de société
veuve
vin blanc
vin du pays
vingt-et-un
vin mousseux
vis-à-vis
vive la bagatelle
vogue la galère
voilà
volupté

NINETEENTH CENTURY

à bas
abattoir
abonné
abonnement
abri
à cheval
à contrecœur
à deux
affaire
affiche
à fond
agent provocateur
aide-mémoire
à la brochette
à la carte
à la fourchette
à la lanterne
à la russe
âme damnée
amour courtois
amourette
anis
anonym
aperçu
aperitif
après nous le déluge
après coup
aquarelle
arête
argot
arme blanche
arrière-pensée
arrondissement
artiste
à trois
attaché
au grand sérieux
au gratin
au mieux
aumônière
au naturel
au pair
au sérieux
Av[o]u[é]
baba
baccarat
bagarre
bagasse
bahut
baignoire
bal costumé
ballon
ballon d'essai
barbotine
barège
barré
basse-taille
bassinet
batiste
battement
battue
batture
bavaroise
béarnaise
beau ideal
beau rôle
beau sabreur
beauté du diable
beaux arts
beaux yeux
beignet
berceuse
beret
bertillonage
bête noire
bêtise
beurre noir
bibelot
biberon
bidon
bien entendu
bien-être
bijouterie
blague
blagueur
blancbec
blanc de chine
blanc de perle
blanc fixe
blasé
bleu-du-roi
bois brûlé
boiserie
bombe
bon appétit
bonbonnière
bon enfant
bon gré mal gré
bonheur du jour
bonne femme
bonne fortune
bordereau
bouchée
bouclé
bouffant
bouillabaisse
boulevardier
bouleversé
bouquet garni
bouton
boutonnière
brandade
brasserie
breloque
bretelle
bric-à-brac
brioche
briquette
broché
broderie anglaise
brouhaha
brut
burette
butte
caba
cabane
cabotage
cache-peigne
cache-pot
cadre
café
café chantant
café noir
cafetière
cagnotte
calembour
camaraderie
camisole
canapé
canard
cancan
capable de tout
capitonné
capote
carnet
carte-de-visite
cartonnage
carton-pierre
casse
cassis
causerie
causeuse
celeste
cep
cerise
chacun à son goût
chaise longue
champlevé
changement
chanson de geste
chansonette
chansonnier
chantage
chanteuse
chapelle ardente
charabanc
charcuterie
chargé
charlotte russe
chartreuse
chassé
chassé croisé
Chateaubriand
chatelaine
chaud-froid
chaussée
chechia
chef
chef d'école
chef d'orchestre
chemin de fer
chemisette
cheval de bataille
chevalet
chevet
cheville
chibouk
chic
chiffonnade
chiffonnier
chiné
chinoiserie
chipolata
chocolatier
chose jugée
choucroute
chouette
chronique scandaleuse
chypre
cire perdue
clair-de-lune
clairvoyance
claque
claqueur
clavecin
cliché
cloche
cloisonné
clou
cocasse
coco-de-mer
cocotte
cohue
coiffeur
col
colportage
comble
comédie humaine
comédie larmoyante
comedienne
communard
communiqué
compte rendu
concessionaire
conférencier
confrérie
consigne
consommé
conte
conteur
contredanse
coque
coquillage
coquille
cor anglais
corbeau
corbeille
cordon sanitaire
corniche
corps à corps
corps d'élite
corps de ballet
corsetière
coryphée
costumier
coteau
couac
coudé
coulée
coulisse
couloir
coup de fors
coupe
courge
couvade
couvre-pied
cracovienne
crémaillère
crème

crème brûlée
crème de la crème
crème de noyau
crêpe de Chine
crêpeline
crépinette
crépon
cretonne
crevasse
criard
criblé
crochet
croquis
croustade
croûton
cru
culotte
cupidon
curettage
cuvée
dame d'honneur
danse du ventre
danse macabre
danseur
danseuse
débâcle
débat
débutant
débutante
déclassé
décolletage
décolleté
décor
degras
dégringolade
délassement
de luxe
déménagement
demi-mondaine
demi-monde
demitasse
démodé
dénigrement
de rigueur
dernier cri
dernier mot
détenu
diable au corps
dinanderie
diorama
diseuse
distingué
divorcee
doctrinaire
dolmen
donnée
dos-à-dos
dot
doublé
double entente
doublure
doyenne
drageoir
dramaturge
droit de seigneur
du reste
du tout
duxelles
eau
eau-de-Cologne
eau de Javel
eau-de-Nil
eau sucrée
éboulement
écarté
éclair
écorché
écossaise
ecru
ecuelle
églomisé
élan
email ombrant
embarras de choix
empiecement
emplacement
employé
empressé
en avant
en beau
en bloc
en cabochon
enchaînement
en clair
enclave
encoignure
en échelon
en évidence
enfant gâté
enfantillage
enfant terrible
en fête
engagé
en garçon
engobe
en grande tenue
en grand seigneur
en noir
en pension
en permanence
en place
en plein
en plein air
en prise
en rapport
en règle
en retraite
en revanche
ensilage
entente
entente cordiale
entourage
en tout cas
entrain
entr'acte
entrecôte
entredeux
entrepreneur
épaulement
épée
erg
escargot
esclandre
espacement
espadrille
espagnole
espagnolette
espieglerie
estaminet
estouffade
etagere
étang
étrenne
étude
exalté
exposé
fabliau
façon de parler
façonné
fait accompli
famille de robe
famille jaune
famille noire
famille rose
famille verte
farandole
faux-bourdon
femme de ménage
femme du monde
femme incomprise
femme savante
fer-de-lance
ferronnière
feu
feu follet
feuilleton
fiancé
ficelle
filé
filet
filet de boeuf
fillette
fils
fin de siècle
fine champagne
fines herbes
flacon
flageolet
flambé
flâneur
fleur-de-coin
flic
flicflac
foie gras
folie
folie de grandeur
folie du doute
fondant
fondue
force majeure
foudroyant
fouetté
foulard
foulé
fourreau
franc tireur
frappé
frisé
frotteur
frou-frou
fusain
fusillade
galop
gamin
gamine
gangue
garde champêtre
gare
garigue
gateau
gêné
gêne
genre
gilet
girouette
glacé
glissade
gloire
gloriette
gouache
goujon
gourmet
grand battement
grand coup
grande horizontale
grande passion
grand mal
Grand Prix
grand siècle
graticule
grecque
grenadine
grès
grimoire
griot
grisaille
gros bleu
grosgrain
gros point
guéridon
guichet
guilloche
guimpe
guipure
habitué
hachure
haute bourgeoisie
haute école
haut monde
haut-relief
haut ton
hollandaise
horizontale
hors concours
houp-la
idée fixe
immortelle
impair
impasse
imprévu
inconnu
ingénue
insouciant
intriguante
introuvable
jabot
jacquard
japonaiserie
jardinière
jaspé
j'adoube
jeté
jeu de société
jeune fille
jeune fille bien élevée

jeune premier
jeunesse dorée
joie de vivre
jolie laide
juge d'instruction
juste milieu
kepi
kermesse
La
lacet
laissez-aller
laissez-faire
langouste
langue de chat
larmoyant
lavaliere
layette
lectrice
legionnaire
levée en masse
lever de rideau
lié
lingerie
lisse
littérateur
livraison
lorgnette
louche
luthier
lycée
Lyonnais
macabre
macédoine
madeleine
maillot
maison de santé
maison tolérée
maître
maître d'
maître d'armes
maître de ballet
maîtresse en titre
maîtresse femme
malade imaginaire
maladif
maladresse
mal élevé
mandat
mange-tout
manoir
maquereau
maquillage
maquis
marabou
mariage de convenance
mari complaisant
marmite
marron glacé
martelé
massage
massé
massecuite
masseur
matelassé
matériel
matinée
mauvaise langue
mauvais pas
mauvais quart d'heure
mayonnaise
mazurka
méchant
méfiance
ménage à trois
mère
métairie
métayage
metif
metis
meunière
milieu
millefeuille
mille-fleurs
mirage
mirepoix
mirliton
mise en scène
misère
modiste
moellon
mofette
moiré
mondain
montagnard
montagne russe
mont de piété
mon vieux
moquette
morgue
mot d'ordre
motif
motte
moue
moule
moulin
mousse
mousseux
moyen-âge
museau
musicale
mystique
nappe
naturelle
navarin
nécessaire
Niçois
noblesse oblige
nocturne
noel
noisette
noix
nom de théâtre
nostalgie de la boue
note verbale
nougat
nouille
nous autres
nouveau riche
nouveaux arrivés
noyade
nuit blanche
objet
objet d'art
oeil-de-perdrix
œuvre
ombré
on dit
opéra bouffe
ouvrier
paillette
pair
Palais Royal
paletot
palmette
papeterie
parados
paratonnerre
par éminence
par exemple
parfait
parfumerie
pari-mutuel
parquet
parsemé
parti pris
parvenu
pas d'âne
pas de basque
pas de ciseaux
pas de quatre
passe
pas seul
pastiche
pastourelle
pâte
pâte brisée
pâté de foie gras
pâte dure
pâte-sue-pâte
pâte tendre
patte de velours
pavillon
paysan
peau d'Espagne
peau-de-soie
peignoir
pelure
pendeloque
père de famille
perfide Albion
permis de séjour
persiennes
personnel
pervenche
pétillant
petit bourgeois
petite noblesse
petit four
petit mal
petit point
petits chevaux
petits pois
petits soins
petit verre
pétrissage
pétroleur
physique
picaresque
picayune
pièce d'occasion
pièce de circonstance
pied-à-terre
pierrette
pince-nez
piolet
pipette
piqué
piton
placement
planchette
plastique
plein-air
plein-airiste
plein jeu
plié
plique à jour
plissé
plombière
plumeau
pochade
pochette
poêlée
point d'appui
point d'orgue
point de repère
pointe
polisson
pomme de terre
pompier
pontil
porte-bouquet
portée
porte-monnaie
portière
pose plastique
poseur
potiche
poudré
pouf
poule au pot
poulet
poulette
poult-de-soie
pourboire
pour encourager les autres
pour rire
pousse-café
premier cru
premier danseur
première
première danseuse
pré salé
primeur
printanier
prix fixe
procédé
profiterole
projet
prononcé
pur et simple
pur sang
puy
quadrille
quai
quand même
quantité négligeable
quartier
quel
quenelle
questionnaire

quincaillerie
racloir
raconteur
raconteuse
raffiné
raison d'état
raison d'être
rangé
rappel
rapprochement
rastaquouère
rataplan
ratatouille
ravigote
rayonnant
razzia
réchauffé
récit
réclame
recueillement
reculer pour mieux
sauter
redowa
reflet
régisseur
reine
relâche
relevé
remanié
remarque
remontoir
rémoulade
remplaçant
Renaissance
renseignement
rente
rentier
rentrée
renvers
repoussé
repoussoir
restaurant
résumé
retable
retraite
retroussé
revanche
réveillon
revenant
revers
revolte
revue
rien ne va plus
rillettes
ris de veau
risqué
ritournelle
riverain
rivière
robe de nuit
rocaille
roche moutonnée
rococo
rognon
roi fainéant
roi soleil
roman-à-clef
roman à thése
roman de geste
ronde
rondelle
rond-point
rongeur
rosé
rotisserie
roué
rouget
routinier
roux
ruche
ruse de guerre
sabreur
salle d'armes
salle d'attente
salle des pas perdus
salon des refusés
sang-de-boeuf
sans-gêne
sans peur
sans phrase
sans recours
sans reproche
sans serif
saphir d'eau
sartage
saut
sauté
sauve qui peut
savarin
savate
savoir
savoir faire
scène à faire
secateur
secretariat
secret de
Polichinelle
selon les règles
serein
serré
servante
sévigné
shako
sicilienne
sirop
soigné
soirée dansante
soit
soixante-neuf
sommelier
sommité
soubresaut
soubriquet
soufflé
souffrante
souffre-douleur
soufrière
soupirant
souple
sous-entendu
soutache
soutane
spécialité
succès d'estime
succès de scandale
succès fou
sucrier
suprême
surah
surveillant
svelte
sympathique
tableau vivant
tapotement
tartine
tâtonnement
tel quel
tempête
temps
tenue
terrasse
terre cuite
tête-bêche
tête de boeuf
tête montée
thé dansant
tic
tic douloureux
tierceron
timbale
tirade
tirage
titre
tombola
tonnelle
torchon
torque
torsade
tortillon
tour de force
tourmente
tournasin
tournedos
tragédienne
tranchet
travers
trembleuse
très
tricoteuse
tripot
trompe l'oeil
trousseau
trouvaille
trumeau
tulle
veilleuse
velouté
vendangeur
ventre à terre
verglas
vernis martin
versant
vers d'occasion
vicereine
vie d'intérieur
vie de Bohème
vie intime
vieux jeu
vieux rose
ville
vin compris
vin cuit
vin de paille
vin fou
vin gris
vin jaune
vin ordinaire
virgule
visa
viveur
voilà tout
voile
voix céleste
vol-au-vent
volet
volte-face
voulu
vrai réseau
vraisemblable
vraisemblance
vue d'ensemble
wagon-lit
wiederkom
Zouave

TWENTIETH CENTURY

acte gratuit
actualité
adage
affairé
a gogo
aileron
aioli
à la broche
à la Florentine
à la page
ambiance
amuse-gueule
anomie
à point
appellation
contrôlée
après
après-ski
à rebours
arrivisme
arriviste
art brut
art nouveau
à terre
attentisme
attrait
aubusson
auguste
auteur
autoroute
avant la lettre
ballet blanc
bal musette
barre
barrette
bateau-mouche
beau geste
Beaujolais nouveau
béguin
belle époque
belle laide
belote
beur
beurre manié
bidonville
bien pensant
bistro
blanc de blanc
bled
bloc

blouson
bœuf
bœuf bourguignon
boîte
bombé
bondieuserie
boudin
boule
brassière
bricolage
bricoleur
brise-soleil
bustier
cabotin
cache-sexe
café complet
cagoule
calque
calvados
cambré
camouflage
carte d'identité
cassoulet
c'est la guerre
c'est la vie
chaîné
chaise percée
chambré
charmeuse
chef d'équipe
cherchez la femme
cher maître
chétif
chèvre
chichi
chou moellier
cinéaste
cinematheque
cinéma-vérité
ciné-vérité
cinq-à-sept
ciré
clementine
clochard
cloqué
collage
comédie noire
comme ci, comme ça
commère
communautaire
comtesse
conche
concours d'élégance
contre-jour
coq au vin
coque
couchette
coulis
coupe
courgette
course libre
couture
couverture
craquelure
crème caramel
crème Chantilly
crème de cacao
crème de menthe
crème fraîche
crème renversée
crêpe Suzette
cri de cœur
crime passionnel
crise de conscience
crise de nerfs
croque-monsieur
crotale
croûte
cru classé
crudités
cuir-ciselé
cuivré
danseur noble
debitage
decalage
découpage
déjà entendu
déjà lu
déjà vu
demi-glace
demi-pension
demi-sec
demi-vierge
de nos jours
dépaysé
déraciné
derailleur
désaxé
détente
détraqué
développé
diamanté
digestif
dirigisme
dirigiste
discothèque
dix-huitième
domaine
douçaine
douceur de vivre
dressage
eau de toilette
ébéniste
élan vital
embourgeoisé
embourgeoisement
embusqué
emincé
éminence grise
en brosse
en croûte
en daube
engrenage
en pantoufles
en poste
en primeur
en principe
en regard
entrée en matière
épatant
épater
épater les bourgeois
épicerie
éponge
équipe
escarole
esprit de l'escalier
étalage
etatism
etrier
événement
évolué
explication de texte
extraordinaire
façade d'honneur
façon de Venise
faisandé
faits divers
fantaisiste
farci
fauve
faux
faux amis
faux bonhomme
faux marbre
faux-naïf
femme de trent ans
femme fatale
ferronnerie
fête galante
fiche
filet mignon
film noir
filtre
fin de saison
fine
fléchette
folie à deux
fonctionnaire
force de frappe
fou rire
franc fort
franglais
frisée
froideur
fromage blanc
fromage frais
frottage
fruits de mer
fuselage
gaffe
gaga
galanterie
gaminerie
garconnière
gargouillade
gazon coupé
georgette
gigolo
glissé
grand cru
grand jeté
grande amoureuse
grande sonnerie
Grand Guignol
gratiné
grège
grognard
guêpière
gueule de bois
haute Bohème
haute couture
haute cuisine
haute-luxe
haute vulgarisation
homme moyen sensuel
hotelier
hotel particulier
idée reçue
idiot savant
inédit
intimism
intimist
j'accuse
jeté en tournant
jeton
jus
jusqu'au bout
kir
laissez-passer
lamé
langoustine
lapiés
le tout
lettrisme
levade
lissoir
livre de chevet
livre de circonstance
longeron
madérisé
madrilene
maison clos
maison de couture
maison de passe
mal du siècle
mal vu
manière criblée
maquette
maquillé
maquisard
marcottage
mariage blanc
marocain
marque
marquisette
Marxisant
matelot
matière
maudit
mauvais coucheur
mauvaise foi
médaillon
melusine
merde
messaline
méthode champenoise
metro
metteur en scène
midinette
millegrain
minuterie
mise au point
mise-en-page
mixte
moderne
moeurs
moi
monocoque
monstre sacré
montage

motard
mot de Cambronne
mot juste
mouchette
moulage
mouton enragé
mouvementé
moyen sensuel
musique concrète
mutuel
nacelle
nature morte
navarin printanier
navette
né
négociant
Negritude
ninon
noceur
non
notes inégales
nouveau
nouveau pauvre
nouveau roman
nouvelle cuisine
nouvelle vague
nuancé
nuée ardente
numéro
oeufs en cocotte
œvre de vulgarisation
oursin
ouvert
palais
palais de danse
palmier
panier de crabes
paperasserie
papier collé
papier déchiré
papier poudré
parc fermé
parlementaire
partouse
pas d'action
pas de bourrée
pas de chat
pas de cheval
pas devant
passéisme
pasticheur
pastis
pâté de campagne
pâte de verre
pâté en croûte
pâté maison
patissier
patronat
peloton
pelouse
pelure d'oignon
penchée
pétanque
petit battement
petit beurre
petite amie
petite bourgeoisie
petit marmite
petit poussin
petit suisse
petit tranchet
pièce à thèse
pièce noire
pièce rose
pied d'éléphant
pied noir
pilotis
pinard
piperade
piqûre
pissaladière
pissoir
planche
plastiqueur
plat du jour
plein-airisme
plongeur
plus ça change
poché
pochoir
poète maudit
poilu
point de départ
pointillé
pointillisme
policier
pomme
poncif
popote
port de bras
porteur
portrait parlé
pot-et-fleur
poudreuse
poule
poule de luxe
pour le sport
pourriture noble
pour-soi
poussin
praire
pratiquant
prêt-à-porter
princesse lointaine
problematique
profil perdu
protocolaire
provocateur
prunelle
pudeur
quatre-couleur
quête
quiche
rabat
raccourci
raclette
rafale
raisonneur
rapide
rapportage
rasta
raté
ratine
ravalement
ravinement
razet
razeteur
reblochon
Récamier
réchaud
recherche du temps perdu
règlement de compte
relais
relance
remaniement
remboîtage
remuage
remueur
rendu
repêchage
répétiteur
résistant
retardataire
retiré
retroussage
réussi
reverdie
revirement
rimaye
rite de passage
robe de style
romaine
romancé
roman-fleuve
roman noir
roman policier
rond de cuir
roquette
rouge de fer
rouge flambé
rouille
roulement
sabayon
sabotage
saboteur
salade niçoise
salariat
salaud
salle d'eau
salle de jeux
salle privée
salonnière
salopette
sans blague
saucier
sautoir
semis
sensibilité
sensiblerie
se-tenant
singerie
snobisme
soigneur
soirée musicale
solfège
sondage
sonde
son et lumière
sons bouchés
sorbetière
sottisier
sous vide
souteneur
soutenu
sportif
strapontin
sur place
système D
tabac
tac-au-tac
tailleur
tapénade
tapette
tapis vert
taqueté
tastevin
taupe
taxe de séjour
téléphérique
témoignage
temps perdu
tendu
terrain vague
terre pisée
terroir
tête de cuvée
tête de nègre
thé complet
tiens
tiercé
tiers monde
tole
tomme
torchère
touché
tour d'horizon
tournette
tourtière
tout simple
tragédie lyrique
trahison des clercs
trait d'union
tranche de vie
tranchette
travaux préparatoires
tremie
triptyque
tronc
trotteur
truite au bleu
tutu
urinoir
va banque
vacherin
vague
vendeuse
vérité
vernissage
veronique
verre églomisé
vers libre
vespasienne
vice anglais
vichyssoise
vie de château
vie en rose
vie intérieure
vie romancée
vieux marcheur
ville lumière
vin d'honneur
vin de table

vin doux (naturel)
vin rosé
vin rouge
violette de Parme
violon d'Ingres
virage
visagiste
visite de digestion
vive la différence
voeu
voyagé
voyant
voyeur
voyou
vulgarisateur
vulgarisation
wagon-restaurant
yé-yé
zouk
zut

French (American)

EIGHTEENTH CENTURY
bayou

NINETEENTH CENTURY
jambalaya
tignon
travois

TWENTIETH CENTURY
beguine

French (Canadian)

NINETEENTH CENTURY
babiche
frazil
parfleche
tuque

TWENTIETH CENTURY
joual

French (and German)

NINETEENTH CENTURY
galant

French (and Italian)

SEVENTEENTH CENTURY
bis

NINETEENTH CENTURY
cantatrice

French (or Latin)

SEVENTEENTH CENTURY
concordat

French (or Urdu)

SEVENTEENTH CENTURY
tandoor

Gaelic

LATE MIDDLE ENGLISH
loch
sennachie

SIXTEENTH CENTURY
quaich
strath

SEVENTEENTH CENTURY
deoch an doris
machair

EIGHTEENTH CENTURY
pibroch
sporran
taisch

NINETEENTH CENTURY
piob mhor
slainte
toman
urlar

TWENTIETH CENTURY
glaistig
port-a-beul

Gaelic (and Irish)

LATE MIDDLE ENGLISH
clachan

German

MIDDLE ENGLISH
Hanse

SIXTEENTH CENTURY
junker

SEVENTEENTH CENTURY
automat
Fräulein
Graf
krummhorn
sauerkraut
shaman

EIGHTEENTH CENTURY
gneiss
hausfrau
Heimweh
jäger
landau
meerschaum
noumenon
posaune
pumpernickel
schema
sinter
torte
Totentanz

NINETEENTH CENTURY
Abiturient
ablaut
alpenhorn
alpenstock
althorn
anlaut
Anschauung
an sich
Aufklärung
Auslese
backfisch
barouche
bebung
bergschrund
blutwurst
buhl
bund
conservatorium
Dasein
delicatessen
Ding an sich
docent
dom
doppelgänger
Drang
dummkopf
durchkomponiert
erbswurst
ersatz
euchre
Ewigkeit
Fach
fest
firn
flügelhorn
föhn
Fraktur
frankfurter
Frau
gasthaus
gasthof
Gelehrte
gemshorn
gemütlich
Gemütlichkeit
Gesellschaft
giro
glockenspiel
glühwein
graupel
Grenzbegriff
Grübelsucht
gugelhupf
haff
Heft
horst
Identitäts-philosophie
idioticon
Kaffeeklatsch
Kaiser
kapellmeister
kaput
Karren
Karrenfeld
karst
katzenjammer
kindergarten
kinder, kirche, küche
kirsch
klaberjass
knallgas
Kneipe
knödel
kobold
kohlrabi
Kommers
kraut
kriegspiel
krimmer
krug
kuchen
kulturgeschichte
kulturkampf
kümmel
Kunstforscher
Kunstgeschichte
Kur
Kurhaus
Kurort
kursaal
lager
lammergeyer
ländler
Landsturm
Landwehr
Lebenslust
leberwurst
Lehrjahr
leitmotiv
liebchen
Liebestod
liebling
lied
loess
maar
Märchen
Mettwurst
Minnelied
Minnesinger
mit
Mittelschmerz
mordent
motiviert
Nachlass
Nachschlag
Naturphilosophie
pickelhaube
polka
poltergeist
pralltriller
pretzel
prosit
rackett
rauschpfeife
rinderpest
ritter
Romanze
Sängerfest
sastruga
sauerbraten
Schadenfreude
schappe
schiller
schinken
schlemiel
schloss
schmelz
schnapps
schnitzel
schottische
schrund
Schuhplattler
schwa
schwärmerei
Sehnsucht
singspiel
skat
Spätzle
stadthaus
staffage
stoss
strudel
Sturm und Drang

Tafelmusik
tendenz
tendenzroman
thalweg
tremolant
Trinkhalle
turnverein
tusche
überhaupt
Übermensch
umlaut
unberufen
und so weiter
unheimlich
ur-
Vaterland
Versöhnung
Verstandesmensch
volkslied
Vorspiel
Vorstellung
waldhorn
Walpurgisnacht
Wanderjahr
Weinstube
Wein, Weib, und Gesang
Weltanschauung
Weltschmerz
Weltstadt
wiener
wienerwurst
Wirtschaft
Wissenschaft
wunderkind
wurst
Zeitgeist
Zigeuner
zollverein
zwieback

TWENTIETH CENTURY

Abitur
abseil
angst
Anschluss
apfelstrudel
autobahn
Bauhaus
Beerenauslese
bierhaus
Bierstube
Bildungsroman
blitzkrieg
bratwurst
brei
breitschwanz
buckling
diktat
dirndl
Dobos Torte
doctorand
Drang nach Osten
echt
Einfühlung
Eiswein
Entscheidungsproblem
Erlebnis
Fasching
feldgrau
felsenmeer
Festschrift
Formgeschichte
Frauendienst
führer
führerprinzip
Galgenhumor
Gastarbeiter
Gebrauchsmusik
Gedankenexperiment
Gemeinschaft
Gesamtkunstwerk
gestalt
Gestapo
Gleichschaltung
goldwasser
Götterdämmerung
Hakenkreuz
hausmaler
Heilsgeschichte
Heldentenor
Herrenvolk
heurige
hochgeboren
inselberg
Interimsethik
Judenrat
judenrein
Jugendstil
kamerad
karabiner
keller
kinderspiel
kitsch
klatch
kletterschuh
klippe
klops
konditorei
krummholz
kultur
Kunsthistoriker
Künstlerroman
Kunstprosa
lachsschinken
Land
langlauf
Lebensform
lebensraum
lebensspur
Lebenswelt
lederhosen
Linzertorte
litzendraht
loden
lumpenproletariat
Macht-politik
malerisch
mensur
Methodenstreit
Mischsprache
Mitbestimmung
Mitsein
Mittelstand
Modernismus
Nacht und Nebel
nebelwerfer
Neue Sachlichkeit
nicht wahr
orterde
ortstein
Ostpolitik
panzer
Prägnanz
putz
quark
quatsch
Quellenforschung
randkluft
realpolitik
realpolitiker
Rechtsstaat
Reeperbahn
Reich
ressentiment
riegel
Sachertorte
Sachlichkeit
Schimpfwort
schlag
Schlagobers
schlagsahne
Schlamperei
Schmelzglas
Schmerz
schmierkäse
schnook
Schrecklichkeit
schreierpfeife
schuss
schwarm
Schweinerei
schwerpunkt
Schwung
Seilbahn
Sekt
Sezession
Sezessionsstil
Sicherheitsdienst
Sieg Heil
Sitzfleisch
Sitz im Leben
Spätlese
Spielraum
Sprechgesang
Sprechstimme
spritzer
spritzig
spurlos
Stimmung
stollen
streusel
Stube
sympathisch
Tafelwein
textura
thuringer
Torschlusspanik
treff
Trockenbeerenauslese
U-bahn
über alles
Überfremdung
Umwelt
Unding
Untergang
Untermensch
Urfirnis
Urheimat
Ursprache
Urtext
verboten
Verfremdung
Verstehen
Völkerwanderung
völkisch
volksgeist
vorlage
vorlaufer
Waldsterben
wanderlust
Wandervogel
wedeln
Wehmut
Wehrmacht
Wehrwirtschaft
weinkraut
Weisswurst
Weltbild
Weltliteratur
Weltpolitik
wertfrei
Wertfreiheit
Westpolitik
wili
Wirtschaftswunder
Wunderkammer
zeitgeber
Zugunruhe
zugzwang
zwischenzug

German (Austrian)

NINETEENTH CENTURY

nockerl

TWENTIETH CENTURY

palatschinken

Greek

MIDDLE ENGLISH

cosmos
mu
tau

LATE MIDDLE ENGLISH

eta
iota
kappa
maranatha
pi
pseudo
psi
rho
theta

SIXTEENTH CENTURY

acme
agora
anamnesis
anastrophe
archon
cacodemon
catastasis

ephemeron
gnosis
haltere
Logos
mimesis
nemesis
omega
organon
pathos
peripeteia
telos
tmesis

SEVENTEENTH CENTURY

Aceldama
acropolis
acroterion
agape
agon
agonistes
apokatastasis
atlantes
bema
boustrophedon
eidolon
eureka
euthanasia
exegesis
glaucoma
hapax legomenon
Hebe
hexapla
hoi polloi
horme
ichor
kinesis
lambda
miasma
narcosis
nous
octapla
pentathlon
periegesis
pseudepigrapha
stoa
strophe
threnos
trauma
upsilon

EIGHTEENTH CENTURY

amnesia
anabasis
anagnorisis
analgesia
anamorphosis
anti
bathos
demos
epsilon
eupepsia
hamartia
kudos
laura
martyrion
melos
mythos
naos
onomasticon
peplos
pleroma
protome
xoanon

NINETEENTH CENTURY

agapemone
agraphon
anthemion
aphasia
apo koinou
aryballos
ascesis
ataraxia
benthos
boule
calliope
chi-rho
chiton
chroma
daimon
Diaspora
dromos
dysphoria
epyllion
ethos
eunomia
halma
hetaera
hubris
ion
kelebe
kenosis
koine
kylix
larnax
lebes
lekythos
macron
megaron
melisma
metanoia
micro
nabla
noesis
nostos
odeon
oenochoe
olpe
omphalos
ostracon
Phi Beta Kappa
pithos
pneuma
polis
pou sto
psychopompos
rhyton
sepsis
skene
sphendone
stele
temenos

TWENTIETH CENTURY

cathexis
esoterica
eudaimonia
ganosis
hegemon
kafenion
kairos
kernos
koinonia
kore
kouros
kurtosis
labrys
lekane
lexis
macro
mega
migma
moron
mythopoeia
noema
nomos
orthosis
paideia
philia
polloi
semiosis
skandalon
tephra
topos

Greek (ecclesiastical)

EIGHTEENTH CENTURY

Homoousion

NINETEENTH CENTURY

Homoiousion

Greek (Late)

NINETEENTH CENTURY

gammadion

Greek (Modern)

SEVENTEENTH CENTURY

dolmas

NINETEENTH CENTURY

iconostasis
katavothron
ouzo

TWENTIETH CENTURY

bouzouki
enosis
feta
filo
gyro
katharevousa
keftedes
mastika
mavrodaphne
meltemi
pitta
retsina
saganaki
souvlaki
stifado
tahina
taverna
tsipouro
tzatziki

Haitian (creole)

NINETEENTH CENTURY

mamaloi
papaloi

TWENTIETH CENTURY

loa

Hawaiian

NINETEENTH CENTURY

aa
aloha
hula
kahuna
ki
lanai
lei
luau
pahoehoe
pali
ukeke
ukulele
wiliwili

TWENTIETH CENTURY

kapu
laulau
makai
muu-muu

Hebrew

MIDDLE ENGLISH

aleph

LATE MIDDLE ENGLISH

Methuselah

SIXTEENTH CENTURY

dagesh
sephira
shekel
sheva
Thummim
Urim

SEVENTEENTH CENTURY

bethel
haham
hazzan
Masorah
Megillah
mezuza
mitzvah
mohel
shibboleth
tallith
tohu-bohu
tsitsith

EIGHTEENTH CENTURY

gaon
kiddush
minyan

NINETEENTH CENTURY

bar mitzvah
cherem
chuppah
etrog
genizah
gett
goy
hametz
haroseth
hasid
hebra
heder
ketubah
kosher

lulav
maror
melamed
menorah
Mizpah
nabi
parnas
parochet
pilpul
shalom
shechita
shiva
shochet
shofar
succah
trefa
tsaddik
yeshiva

TWENTIETH CENTURY
bat mitzvah
challah
eruv
halutzim
Kahal
Kashrut
lamdan
lechayim
Magen David
maven
Mitnagged
nahal
olim
rimmon
shomer
simchah
temura
tzedaka
yad
yordim

Hebrew (Modern)

NINETEENTH CENTURY
mazel tov

TWENTIETH CENTURY
kibbutz
kippa
kvutza
moshav
sabra
ulpan

Hindi

SEVENTEENTH CENTURY
pukka

EIGHTEENTH CENTURY
sari
wallah

NINETEENTH CENTURY
apsara
corah
ganja
jheel
mung

TWENTIETH CENTURY
bhaji
darshan
dhania
gherao
goonda
namaskar
namaste

Hindustani

SIXTEENTH CENTURY
achar

SEVENTEENTH CENTURY
dhal
dhoti
ghat
ghee
lakh
pan
puggaree
punkah
ranee

EIGHTEENTH CENTURY
babu
bania
dacoit
dak
veranda

NINETEENTH CENTURY
ankus
bandar-log
basmati
burra
chapatti
chappal
chela
dekko
dhobi
ek dum
haldi
jalebi
jat
kutcha
lassi
lathi
maharani
pachisi
raj
terai
tika

TWENTIETH CENTURY
achkan
choli
dilruba
gharana
hartal
kisan
nimbu-pani
pakora
paratha
puri
raita
roti
thali

Hungarian

NINETEENTH CENTURY
cimbalom
csardas
goulash
paprika

Icelandic

NINETEENTH CENTURY
sandur

Indonesian

TWENTIETH CENTURY
legong
tempeh

Irish

LATE MIDDLE ENGLISH
currach

FIFTEENTH CENTURY
clairschach

SEVENTEENTH CENTURY
crannog
curragh
leprechaun
turlough

EIGHTEENTH CENTURY
caoine
feis
ogham
shebeen

NINETEENTH CENTURY
brogan
ceilidh
immram

Italian

MIDDLE ENGLISH
tramontana

SIXTEENTH CENTURY
alto
amoretto
bagnio
basta
bazaar
biretta
bordello
botargo
bravo
campagna
canto
canto fermo
canzone
cupola
duo
duomo
fresco
gamba
gesso
gondola
illuminato
impresa
inamorato
lavolta
lazaretto
macaroni
Madonna
madrigal
magnifico
majolica
mezzo-relievo
motto
nuncio
pasquinade
per contra
phantasma
piazza
presto
Rialto
saltarello
scagliola
seraglio
signor
signoria
sordino
stanza
stucco
sultana
villanella
viola da gamba
volta

SEVENTEENTH CENTURY
adagio
agio
albergo
allegro
alto-relievo
antipasto
baldachin
basso-relievo
beccafico
campanile
capriccio
chiaroscuro
contadino
Corso
dado
ditto
dogana
felucca
flebile
furioso
generalissimo
ghetto
giro
gusto
inamorata
incognita
incognito
in petto
intaglio
internuncio
largo
lazzaro
lido
lingua franca
manifesto
minestra
monte di pietà
morbidezza
mortadella
orlo
ovolo
padrone
palazzo
palio
passacaglia
pergola
piano
piano piano
Pietà
pietra commessa
portico

prunello
putto
recitativo
regatta
relievo
ritornello
scorzonera
signora
sirocco
sonata
stiletto
tarsia
tempo
vermicelli
vino santo
virtuoso
vista
viva
Zingaro

EIGHTEENTH CENTURY

addio
alfresco
alla breve
alla cappella
allegretto
al segno
andante
appoggiatura
arco
aria
arietta
arioso
arpeggio
a tempo
ballerina
bambino
bassetto
basso
basso continuo
battuta
bravura
breccia
brillante
brio
buffo
cadenza
cantabile
cantata
cantilena
capriccioso
cara sposa
caro sposo
casino
cassino
castrato
cavaliere servente
chitarrone
cicerone
cicisbeo
cinquecento
clavicembalo
coda
cognoscente
coloratura
con amore
concertante
concertino
concerto
concerto grosso
condottiere
conoscente
conservatorio
continuo
contralto
conversazione
cortile
crescendo
da capo
del credere
dilettante
diminuendo
divertimento
divisi
duetto
fagotto
falsetto
falsobordone
fantasia
fantoccini
finale
finocchio
flautino
flauto
forte
forte-piano
fortissimo
furore
giallo antico
imbroglio
impasto
impresario
influenza
intermezzo
larghetto
lazzarone
legato
lentamente
lento
libretto
literato
loggia
maestoso
maestrale
maestro
malaria
maraschino
messa di voce
mezza voce
mezzo
mezzo-soprano
mezzo termine
minuetto
moderato
motivo
moto
mozzetta
obbligato
operetta
oratorio
ottava rima
pasticcio
pastorale
patina
penseroso
pianissimo
piano
pianoforte
più
pococurante
ponticello
portamento
prestissimo
prima
prima donna
primo
pronto
propaganda
rifacimento
ripieno
ripresa
risoluto
riviera
rondo
rosso antico
rubato
scaglia
segue
semplice
senza
sgraffito
siciliana
sinfonia
solfatara
solfeggio
sonatina
soprano
sostenuto
sotto voce
spiccato
staccato
stretto
subito
tarantella
tasto
tempo giusto
tempo rubato
tenore
tenuto
terracotta
terzetto
testo
toccata
toccatina
tondino
torso
tremolo
trio
tufa
tutti quanti
verde antico
villeggiatura
viola bastarda
viola d'amore
violetta
violoncello
virtu
voce di petto
voce di testa
zampogna
zingana
zoppa
zufolo

NINETEENTH CENTURY

a cappella
accelerando
acciaccatura
agitato
albarello
aleatico
alla marcia
allargando
amorino
ancona
andantino
ballabile
basso cantante
basso ostinato
basso profundo
bel canto
ben trovato
bersaglieri
bianco sopra
bianco
brava
calando
Camorra
canzona
capotasto
carabiniere
carissima
cassone
cavatina
cembalo
codetta
commedia dell'arte
commendatore
con brio
confetti
con moto
con sordino
contadina
contessa
contrabasso
contrafagotto
coperta
cotta
credenza
cymbalo
dal segno
decrescendo
disinvoltura
diva
dogaressa
dolce far niente
duettino
espressivo
faenza
far niente
fata morgana
fermata
fianchetto
fiasco
fioritura
fiumara
flautando
flautato
forzando
franco
fresco buono
fresco secco
frottola
fugato
fughetta
fustanella

galleria
giocoso
Giuoco Piano
glissando
gnocchi
graffito
grandioso
granita
grappa
grazioso
grissino
gruppetto
inferno
intarsia
intermedio
intonaco
isolato
karezza
lamentoso
largamente
lasagne
latticinio
leggiero
maestria
Mafia
Mafioso
malebolge
mancando
mandorla
mantelletta
marcato
maremma
martellato
marzacotto
mascara
meno
mesto
mezzani
millefiore
minestrone
molto
Moresca
mosso
moto perpetuo
muta
niello
niente
oboe da caccia
oboe d'amore
ocarina
ombrellino
omertà
opera buffa
opera seria
ossia
ostinato
pallone
panforte
parlando
parmigiana
parroco
partita
pasta
piano
piano nobile
piccolo
pietra dura
pizza
pizzicato
pomposo
precipitato
predella
prima ballerina
prima vista
quattrocento
rallentando
rapido
ravioli
religioso
reticella
reticello
ricotta
rinforzando
Risorgimento
risotto
ritardando
ritenuto
rosalia
rosolio
salami
salto
scampi
scarpetti
scenario
scherzando
scherzo
scordatura
scuola
secco
sempre
sestina
sforzando
sforzato
sfumato
sgraffiato
signorina
sinopia
smorzando
sopra bianco
spaghetti
spianato
stiacciato
stile rappresentativo
stracchino
strepitoso
stretta
stringendo
tagliarini
tagliatelle
tanto
tazza
tedesco
tempera
tempietto
tenebroso
tenore di forza
tenore di grazia
tenore robusto
tenorino
terraglia
terra rosa
terra rossa
terribilità
terza rima
tessitura
tombolo
tondo
tragedietta
tranquillo
trascinando
traverso
trecento
tremolando
tutti-frutti
una corda
valuta
vendemmia
vendetta
vernaccia
vibrato
vino cotto
viola da braccio
voce di gola
volante
zabaglione
zita
zucchetto

TWENTIETH CENTURY

aggiornamento
agnolotti
al dente
autostrada
basso buffo
biennale
bimbo
calamari
calzone
cannelloni
capo
cappuccino
cassata
ciabatta
ciao
classico
contrapposto
Cosa Nostra
crostini
diabolo
dolce vita
doppione
duce
espresso
farfalle
fettucine
focaccia
frittata
fritto misto
fusilli
gelato
gonzo
graffiti
gran turismo
grosso modo
imprimatura
irredenta
ladino
lamento
libero
linguine
lupara
manicotti
marinara
mascarpone
modello
mondo
moscato
mozzarella
mysterioso
noia
novella
numero uno
orzo
osso bucco
ottocento
paliotto
pancetta
panettone
panino
panzanella
papabile
paparazzo
pappardelle
partigiano
passeggiata
pastiglia
pecorino
penne
pensiero
pentimento
pepperoni
pesto
pizzeria
prominenti
pro-nuncio
prosciutto
provolone
pulvino
radicchio
ricordo
rigatoni
romanità
rucola
sacro egoismo
saltimbocca
salumeria
scala mobile
scaloppine
scungille
seicento
settecento
sinfonietta
sopranino
sottoportico
spaghettini
spinto
sprezzatura
spumante
spumoni
stagione
stelline
stile antico
stile concitato
stracciatella
studiolo
taleggio
targa
terra irredenta
terrazzo
tiorba
tiramisu
tombarolo
tortellini
trapunto
trasformismo

tre corde
troppo
trullo
uomo universale
vaporetto
veduta
verismo
vino dolce
vino nero
vino rosso
vino secco
vinsanto
vita nuova
vitello tonnato
zeppole
zucchini
zuppa di pesce
zuppa inglese

Italian (and Latin)

SEVENTEENTH CENTURY
villa

Italian (and Spanish)

SIXTEENTH CENTURY
punto

EIGHTEENTH CENTURY
tsarina

NINETEENTH CENTURY
marina
triduo

TWENTIETH CENTURY
ambiente
punto banco

Italian, Spanish, Portuguese

SIXTEENTH CENTURY
padre

Japanese

SEVENTEENTH CENTURY
inro
kami
kimono
mochi
sake
samisen
shogun
tabi
tatami

EIGHTEENTH CENTURY
adzuki
awabi
daimyo
kana
katakana
katsuo
kirin
koi
koto
miso
samurai
satori
shoyu
tofu
torii
zazen
Zen

NINETEENTH CENTURY
banzai
bugaku
bushido
futon
go
gobang
habutai
haiku
hakama
hara-kiri
hibachi
hiragana
hokku
jinricksha
joruri
judo
ju-jitsu
kabuki
kagura
kakemono
kamikaze
ken
kombu
koro
kudzu
kyogen
makimono
netsuke
Noh
nori
obi
ojime
raku
renga
rikka
ronin
ryu
san
sashimi
satsuma
sayonara
sennin
sensei
seppuku
shakudo
shakuhachi
shiitake
shippo
shogi
soba
soshi
sumo
surimono
sushi
taiko
tanka
temmoku
togidashi
tsuba
tsukemono
tsunami
tycoon
uchiwa
ukiyo-e
yukata
zabuton
zori

TWENTIETH CENTURY
aikido
ama
banzuke
basho
bonsai
Bunraku
butoh
dan
dojo
dotaku
emakimono
fugu
gagaku
gaijin
haniwa
harai-goshi
hibakusha
honcho
ikebana
ippon
janken
jigotai
juku
kaizen
kanban
kanji
karaoke
karate
karoshi
kata
katsura
keiretsu
Kempeitai
kendo
koan
kuzushi
kyu
mama-san
manga
mingei
mompei
mondo
narikin
nembutsu
ninja
ninjutsu
nisei
nogaku
nunchaku
onnagata
origami
orihon
oyama
pachinko
ramen
randori
sabi
sanpaku
sansei
seiza
shabu-shabu
shiatsu
shibui
shosagoto
shosha
shunga
shuriken
sogo shosha
sokaiya
suiboku
sukiya
sukiyaki
sumi
sumotori
suzuribako
takamakie
tamagotchi
tamari
tempura
teppan-yaki
teriyaki
tsugi ashi
tsutsumu
udon
ukemi
uki
wabi
waka
wakame
wasabi
washi
yakitori
yakuza
yokozuna
yugen
zaibatsu
zaikai
zaitech
zendo

Javanese

NINETEENTH CENTURY
batik
gamelan
saron
wayang

TWENTIETH CENTURY
lahar

Kiswahili

NINETEENTH CENTURY
baraza
boma
bwana
safari
shamba

TWENTIETH CENTURY
kanzu
khanga
kiboko
kikoi
ngoma
panga
shauri
shenzi
simba
simi
toto
uhuru
ujamaa

Korean

NINETEENTH CENTURY

kimchi

TWENTIETH CENTURY

chaebol
tae kwon do

Kurdish

TWENTIETH CENTURY

peshmerga

Lappish

SIXTEENTH CENTURY

tundra

Latin

OLD ENGLISH

genesis
paternoster
polenta
rhagades
Te Deum
Thule

MIDDLE ENGLISH

alpha
amphora
ave
Ave Maria
benedicite
beta
credo
cursor
delta
et
et cetera
gloria
jubilate
magnificat
magus
miserere
origanum
pallium
pater
placebo
requiem
solidus

LATE MIDDLE ENGLISH

Agnus Dei
alias
amphisbaena
ampulla
aqua vitae
aura
aurora
bubo
cathedra
cave
chimera
cicada
clepsydra
colossus
consul
contra
corpus
cortex
crepusculum
cum
custos
decemvir
de profundis
ecce
echinus
ergo
fenestella
feria
fiat
finis
foetus
forum
fungus
gamma
genitor
genius
gratis
gutta
gypsum
habeas corpora
habeas corpus
halcyon
herpes
hyperbole
idem
index
in excelsis
in pontificalibus
item
lamia
lanx
lapis
lapis lazuli
lector
limbo
macula
magma
manes
matrix
mausoleum
mea culpa
medusa
memento
mittimus
noli me tangere
obelus
palaestra
palladium
papyrus
pax
per
plectrum
Priapus
pro
proconsul
pro tempore
proviso
quietus
quorum
regimen
salve
sanctum sanctorum
sanctus
sarcophagus
scilicet
scoria
sede vacante
sedile
sepia
sigma
sistrum
speculum
sphinx
stadium
summa
susurrus
synecdoche
synthesis
teste
thorax
tiro
toties quoties
triumvir
tumulus
ut supra
venire facias
vertex
vertigo
videlicet
vidimus
virago
zeugma

FIFTEENTH CENTURY

aqua fortis
aureola
exeunt
memorandum
modicum
mutatis mutandis
patella
paterfamilias
prima facie

SIXTEENTH CENTURY

abacus
ab origine
ab ovo
absit omen
acanthus
acumen
ad hominem
ad idem
ad rem
adsum
albumen
alga
alter ego
ambrosia
anaphora
Anno Domini
annulus
anta
ante meridiem
anthropophagi
antonomasia
a priori
arcanum
armiger
atrium
ballista
basilica
boletus
bona fide
cacoethes
caduceus
caesura
callus
cantor
cantus
caries
caveat
caveat emptor
cerebellum
cestus
cloaca
coccyx
codex
colloquium
colostrum
compendium
coram
coryza
cymatium
daemon
decorum
de jure
delirium
Deo gratias
diaeresis
dictum
dilemma
dixit
domine
ecce signum
Elysium
emporium
encomium
ephemeris
epiphora
epithalamium
epitome
errata
erratum
esse
Et tu, Brute
exit
ex nihilo
ex officio
exordium
ex professo
extempore
facetiae
fasces
fascia
fidus Achates
flora
forma pauperis
garum
genus
gymnasium
helix
helot
hiatus
hippocampus
homo
hyperbaton
iambus
icon
id est
ignoramus
in articulo mortis
indecorum
in esse
in extremis
in fine
infinitum
in infinitum
in nubibus

innuendo
in posse
in rerum natura
interim
interregnum
interrex
interstitium
invita Minerva
ipse dixit
ipso facto
ipso jure
janitor
jure divino
jus gentium
ladanum
lar
lemma
lignum vitae
limes
lunula
lustrum
Lyceum
mater
materia prima
medium
menses
metamorphosis
metope
meum
militia
minimus
miscellanea
modulus
modus
molossus
murex
naumachia
nepenthes
nolens volens
non placet
nonplus
non sequitur
novus homo
nunc dimittis
obiter
occupatio
o tempora, o mores!
panacea
pari passu
paronomasia
passus
peccavi
penates
periphrasis
per se
petitio principii
piscina
placet
pontifex
pontificalia
postscriptum
primus
principium
pro forma
proprium
pro rata
pubes
punctum
quaere
quantum
quid
quid pro quo
quondam
quot homines, tot sententiae
radius
radix
rectum
redivivus
reductio ad impossibile
remora
rhombus
rostrum
sanctum
Saturnalia
scarabaeus
scotia
scrutator
sempervivum
simplex
simulacrum
solus
sortes
sphincter
stigma
stria
striges
summum bonum
summum genus
summum jus
sumpsimus
superficies
supra
Sursum corda
symposium
taenia
talaria
tenet
terminus ad quem
terminus a quo
terrae filius
theatrum mundi
thermae
thesaurus
thyrsus
tiara
torus
transire
triquetra
trochilus
tympanum
ultimo
umbra
una voce
vale
veni, vidi, vici
viaticum
vide
vivat

SEVENTEENTH CENTURY

ab initio
ab urbe condita
addendum
ad hoc
ad infinitum
ad libitum
ad nauseam
ad valorem
ad vivum
adytum
aegis
afflatus
a fortiori
agenda
agnomen
album
alibi
alluvium
Alma Mater
alumnus
amanuensis
a mensa et thoro
analemma
angelus
antenna
apex
apodyterium
a posteriori
aqua regia
arbor vitae
argumentum ad hominem
armilla
auditorium
automaton
brutum fulmen
calyx
canephora
cantoris
caput mortuum
caret
cavea
cella
census
cento
cerebrum
cestus
choragus
chorea
cognomen
collectanea
coma
compos mentis
consensus
continuum
copula
coran judice
coryphaeus
crux
cui bono
culmen
cultus
cumulus
curia
data
decennium
decretum
de facto
Dei gratia
de minimis
de novo
desideratum
dies non juridicus
differentia
digamma
diploma
discus
dithyramb
doli capax
doli incapax
dolus
dominie
donatio mortis causa
duodecimo
duumvir
dyspnoea
Ecce Homo
effluvium
elenchus
embolus
eo ipso
eo nomine
Eros
ex animo
ex cathedra
exempli gratia
exequatur
exit
ex parte
ex pede Herculem
ex post facto
ex relatione
exuviae
facies
facilis descensus Averni
farrago
felo de se
ferae naturae
festina lente
focus
frustum
fulcrum
genius loci
germen
hic jacet
homunculus
honorarium
honoris causa
horresco referens
hortus conclusus
hortus siccus
hypogeum
hysterica passio
ibid
idolum
impedimenta
imperium
impetus
imprimatur
in abstracto
in concreto
index librorum prohibitorum
indicium
in flagrante
in medio
in nomine
in partibus
in perpetuum
in potentia
in propria persona

in puris naturalibus
in re
insignia
insomnia
instanter
in statu quo
inter alia
inter alios
in terrorem
in vacuo
involucrum
jus naturae
juvenilia
lacuna
lamina
lapsus
lapsus linguae
larva
latex
legator
lex talionis
liberum arbitrium
literati
longo intervallo
lues
lumbago
lumen siccum
lusus
mala fide
mala fides
mare clausum
mare liberum
mens sana in corpore sano
minerval
momentum
mons Veneris
more
more majorum
motu proprio
mutato nomine
mystes
narthex
nebula
nemine contradicente
ne plus ultra
nexus
nil desperandum
nimbus
nolle prosequi
non compos mentis
non est factum
non plus ultra
nostrum
numen
nuntius
obiit
odium
oestrus
olim
onus
opprobrium
ovum
pabulum
pancratium
parergon
patera
pelta
penetralia
peplum
perpetuum mobile
philosophia prima
pinax
plenum
post factum
post meridiem
praecognitum
praenomen
praetorium
prolegomenon
pronaos
proscenium
pruritus
psyche
pudendum
pudor
qua
quadra
quadriga
quantum meruit
quantum sufficit
quia timet
quinquennium
quoad
quod erat demonstrandum
quod erat faciendum
quotum
rara avis
Regius
reliquiae
res
res gestae
residuum
resurgam
retiarius
rota
salvo
scintilla
sederunt
septum
serum
silenus
sine die
sine qua non
specie
spectrum
sputum
status
stemma
stimulus
sub judice
sub rosa
sub silentio
sudarium
sui juris
sylva
talio
telamon
tenendum
terra firma
terra incognita
tessera
testimonium
tholos
tirocinium
toga
totidem verbis
toto caelo
triclinium
tu quoque
umbilicus
vae victis
vagitus
vallum
varia lectio
vates
venire
vesica
vestigium
veto
via media
vice versa
vi et armis
vinculum
vis
vis major
vivarium
vortex
xystus

EIGHTEENTH CENTURY

ad captandum vulgus
ad eundem
ad interim
ad litem
ad usum Delphini
adversaria
aegrotat
angina pectoris
apologia
aurora australis
aurora borealis
bibliotheca
bona fides
caldarium
camera lucida
camera obscura
campus
carcinoma
casus foederis
cervix
cilium
cippus
cirrus
cithara
columbarium
comes
conceptus
contra mundum
conversus
crotalum
curiosa felicitas
cursus
datum
decani
dementia
Deo volente
detritus
detur
discobolus
disjecta membra
dominium
dramatis personae
dux
dyspepsia
emeritus
excelsior
exeat
exedra
ex gratia
ex-voto
frigidarium
gradus
habitat
heroon
humus
ibidem
imago
inertia
in flagrante delicto
ingesta
in medias res
in personam
in rem
in situ
in toto
in utero
lapillus
laquear
laudator temporis acti
lavabo
lex loci
literae humaniores
locus
locus poenitentiae
lucus a non lucendo
magna mater
magnum
magnum opus
materfamilias
memorabilia
minutia
morituri te salutamus
multum in parvo
muscae
musica
musica figurata
nemine dissentiente
nil admirari
nota bene
notitia
nucleus
nugae
nugae difficiles
nymphaeum
omnium
optime
opus
opus signinum
ore rotundo
otium
pace
panem et circenses
pars pro toto
pastoralia
pendente lite
periplus

phobia
pileus
podium
pons asinorum
post-mortem
pro bono publico
propugnaculum
propylaeum
prospectus
pullus
quaesitum
quieta non movere
quod vide
re
rectus
reductio ad absurdum
remittitur
restitutio in integrum
rictus
rus in urbe
sacrum
sequela
signum pantheum
simplex munditiis
situs
sola
stela
stet
stylus
succus
sui generis
tacet
taedium vitae
triduum
triforium
ultima Thule
ultimatum
ultra vires
umbo
variorum
vexillum
via
virgo intacta
vis comica
vis inertiae
vis viva
vox humana

NINETEENTH CENTURY

abortus
absurdum
actio in distans
ad lib
aetatis
alumna
animus
ante
ante-bellum
antefix
ante-mortem
anthrax
arbiter elegantiae
arboretum
Arcades ambo
armamentarium
ave atque vale
candelabrum
castrum
casus belli
celebret
circa
circiter
cogito
cognitum
coitus
collegium
compluvium
consortium
conspectus
corrigendum
crux ansata
culpa
cum laude
cunnilingus
curiosa
curriculum
damnosa hereditas
damnum
defluvium
dies irae
dies non
distinguo
dum casta
ego
ejecta
epos
et al.
et seq.
ex
excreta
excursus
exemplum
ex-libris
exotica
extra dictionem
faciendum
facile princeps
famulus
fecit
fides Punica
filioque
flagellum
flagrante delicto
floreat
flore pleno
floruit
fons et origo
functus officio
furor scribendi
generalia
gens
Homo sapiens
horae
idem sonans
imbrex
impluvium
in absentia
in antis
incipit
incognita
in contumaciam
incunabulum
in dictione
indumentum
in extenso
infra
infra dig
ingenium
injuria
in limine
in loco parentis
in memoriam
in nuce
in ovo
in pari materia
in pectore
in se
in statu pupillari
inter partes
inter se
inter vivos
intra vires
intra vitam
in vitro
ipsissima verba
jus cogens
jus primae noctis
lapsus calami
latifundium
lex domicilii
lex fori
litera scripta
loc. cit.
locus classicus
locus standi
loquitur
ludo
magna cum laude
membrum virile
memento mori
mens rea
mirabile dictu
mons pubis
more meo
mores
more suo
musica ficta
naevus
natura naturans
natura naturata
navicula
nisi
nolo contendere
nominatim
nominis umbra
non est
non nobis
notabilia
nova
noxa
nulla bona
nulli secundus
obiit sine prole
obiter dictum
oculus
officina
op. cit.
optimum
opus sectile
oratio obliqua
oratio recta
passim
pax Romana
perceptum
per impossibile
persona designata
philosophia perennis
pinetum
post-bellum
post eventum
post festum
post hoc
post-partum
pre-mortem
primus inter pares
proxime accessit
proximo
pteroma
pulpitum
quadrennium
quadrivium
quasi in rem
raptus
rariora
recte
recto
redux
referendum
requiescat
responsum
rubella
saeva indignatio
sancta simplicitas
secundus
senex
sensibile
sensu stricto
separatum
sequitur
sic
signum
situla
solarium
solatium
status quo
status quo ante
studium generale
sub specie aeternitatis
sub specie temporis
sub voce
summa cum laude
tabula rasa
tacenda
tegula
tepidarium
tertius
tertius gaudens
textus receptus
tinnitus
triennium
trivium
turba
uberrima fides
ultima ratio
ultra
ultra crepidam
unda maris
unicum
urbi et orbi
vera causa
vera copula
verbum sapienti

verso
vesica piscis
vexata quaestio
Via Crucis
Via Dolorosa
vicus
vim
virtute officii
vis a fronte
vis a tergo
vis medicatrix naturae
viva
volens
vox angelica
vox nihili
vox populi

TWENTIETH CENTURY
academia
ad personam
aloe vera
anima
argumentum e silentio
biennium
cancellandum
cancellans
circulus vitiosus
colluvium
compactum
consolatio
contra proferentem
curriculum vitae
cursus honorum
damnatio memoriae
de mortuis
deus absconditus
diabolus in musica
difficilior lectio
dis aliter visum
dissensus
eheu fugaces
ex silentio
ex vivo
felix culpa
figura
filius nullius
furor academicus
furor poeticus
gravida
gravitas
humanitas
id
in corpore
in parvo
intacta
in vivo
lacrimae rerum
Latino sine flexione
lectio difficilior
lente
libido
locum
locus desperatus
media
memento vivere
miles gloriosus
mirabilia
more hispanico
murus gallicus
musica plana
musica reservata
mysterium tremendum
nihil obstat
nomen dubium
nomen nudum
nominatum
numerus clausus
orans
orientalia
patria
persona
personalia
pessimum
pietas
planctus
Pluvius
post coitum
prima materia
proferens
punctum indifferens
punctus
puris naturalibus
rarissime
rectius
refugium
res cogitans
res extensa
res non verba
sensu lato
sententia
sic et non
sigillata
spiritus rector
stricto sensu
sub verbo
terminus ante quem
terminus post quem
terra alba
terra cognita
terra ignota
tertium comparationis
titulus
tremendum
ubi sunt
urbs
vagantes
Vanitas
victor ludorum
virga
visibilia
vita

Latin (ecclesiastical)

OLD ENGLISH
exodus
rabbi

LATE MIDDLE ENGLISH
Abba
Apocrypha

SIXTEENTH CENTURY
anathema
apotheosis
hypostasis

SEVENTEENTH CENTURY
charisma

EIGHTEENTH CENTURY
catechesis

NINETEENTH CENTURY
albedo
coenobium

Latin (Late)

OLD ENGLISH
manna

MIDDLE ENGLISH
incubus

LATE MIDDLE ENGLISH
antithesis
arsis
enchiridion
hydrophobia
hyle
ignotum per ignotius
oedema
syncope
thesis

SIXTEENTH CENTURY
antepenultima
antistrophe
aporia
bolus
cornucopia
dogma
ens
homoeoteleuton
hypothesis
hysteron proteron
in saecula saeculorum
intermedium
latria
litotes
mamzer
metastasis
metathesis
metempsychosis
onomatopoeia
phenomenon
plethora
prosthesis
succuba
trapezium
vanitas vanitatum

SEVENTEENTH CENTURY
ab extra
acedia
anorexia
campana
catheter
colophon
explicit
ex proprio motu
golgotha
gravamen
labarum
melancholia
moloch
phallus
prognosis
psychomachia
sensorium
sigillum
uti possidetis

EIGHTEENTH CENTURY
anacoluthon
herbarium
siglum
tertium quid
vomitorium

NINETEENTH CENTURY
anorexia nervosa
bacillus
exceptis excipiendis
in camera
natatorium
obscurum per obscurius
persona grata
septennium

TWENTIETH CENTURY
persona non grata
realia
romanitas
tabula gratulatoria

Latin (Medieval)

MIDDLE ENGLISH
Kyrie eleison

LATE MIDDLE ENGLISH
cranium
dulia
duodenum
hiera picra
lac
non-obstante
nux vomica
oesophagus
quodlibet
retina
succubus
terra sigillata
versus

FIFTEENTH CENTURY
Magna Carta
primum mobile
seriatim
spermaceti
verbatim

SIXTEENTH CENTURY
affidavit
anima mundi
antependium
cabbala
ciborium
confrater
factotum
hegira
hendiadys
hyperdulia
ignoratio elenchi

morbilli
praxis
regalia
viva voce

SEVENTEENTH CENTURY
ambo
anglice
ephemera
incisor
linctus
literatim
malum in se
paraphernalia
quota
suppositum

EIGHTEENTH CENTURY
cancrizans
dulciana
schola cantorum
scriptorium

NINETEENTH CENTURY
ante rem
cantus firmus
Mater Dolorosa
necessarium
novena
opus Alexandrinum
opus anglicanum
opus araneum
opus consutum
opus Dei

TWENTIETH CENTURY
post rem
significacio

Latin (Modern)

SIXTEENTH CENTURY
cyma
guaiacum
ignis fatuus
larynx
lemur
meiosis
per accidens
per diem
pomatum
scholium
stratum
utopia

SEVENTEENTH CENTURY
ab intra
abscissa
amicus curiae
annus mirabilis
bene esse
catalysis
ceteris paribus
chiasmus
coma
deus ex machina
entasis
euphoria
ex hypothesi
experimentum crucis
florilegium
lachryma Christi
materia medica
meniscus
millennium
modus operandi
necrosis
per annum
per capita
per centum
per mensem
per stirpes
pharmacopoeia
rebus sic stantibus
risus sardonicus
sal volatile
sarcoma
strabismus
substratum
succedaneum
symbiosis
Valhalla

EIGHTEENTH CENTURY
ad referendum
anaesthesia
condominium
currente calamo
fauna
memoria technica
menologium
neurosis
parens patriae
respondentia
stasis
suppressio veri

NINETEENTH CENTURY
advocatus diaboli
amoeba
anacrusis
apparatus criticus
aquarium
asphyxia
axiomata media
bacterium
catharsis
cyanosis
delirium tremens
editio princeps
horribile dictu
horror vacui
inedita
modus vivendi
moratorium
sanatarium
sanatorium
sebum
suggestio falsi
torticollis
uraeus
via affirmativa
via negativa

TWENTIETH CENTURY
annus horribilis
candida
contrafactum
ex ante
ex post
imponderabilia
minifundium
trivia
unum necessarium

Malagasy

EIGHTEENTH CENTURY
raffia

Malay

SIXTEENTH CENTURY
kris

EIGHTEENTH CENTURY
adat
kain
kramat
rambutan
tuan
tunku

NINETEENTH CENTURY
agar-agar
gutta-percha
nasi
parang
sambal
sarong

TWENTIETH CENTURY
ikat
jadam
kathi
merdeka
pahit
satay

Maori

EIGHTEENTH CENTURY
tiki
wahine

NINETEENTH CENTURY
haka
hangi
kai
kapai
korero
kuri
mana
pakeha
pikau
taihoa
waka
whare

TWENTIETH CENTURY
karanga

Maori (and Hawaiian)

NINETEENTH CENTURY
hui

Marathi

TWENTIETH CENTURY
rangoli

Melanesian

TWENTIETH CENTURY
kula

Nepali

NINETEENTH CENTURY
kukri

New Guinea

TWENTIETH CENTURY
kuru

Norwegian

SEVENTEENTH CENTURY
fiord

EIGHTEENTH CENTURY
kraken

NINETEENTH CENTURY
aquavit
fjeld
halling

TWENTIETH CENTURY
gjetost
gravadlax
klister
kril
langeleik
rosemaling
ski-joring
slalom
smørbrød
springar

Old Norse

MIDDLE ENGLISH
kist

EIGHTEENTH CENTURY
Ragnarok
saga
skald

NINETEENTH CENTURY
jotun

Pali

NINETEENTH CENTURY
bhikkhu

TWENTIETH CENTURY
dhamma
nibbana
tathata

Panjabi

TWENTIETH CENTURY
bhangra
gurdwara
jatha
khaddar
kirpan
tikka

Persian

LATE MIDDLE ENGLISH
khan

SIXTEENTH CENTURY
caravanserai
shah

SEVENTEENTH CENTURY
attar
hafiz
hajji
khanum
mullah

EIGHTEENTH CENTURY
baksheesh
durgah

ezan
ghazal
narghile
peri
simurg

NINETEENTH CENTURY
gul
hom
izzat
kanoon
kenaf
qanat

TWENTIETH CENTURY
ayatollah
kulah
takht

Persian (and Urdu)

SIXTEENTH CENTURY
amir
bhang

SEVENTEENTH CENTURY
begum
chadar
charpoy
chokidar
durbar
farrash
havildar
moulvi
sahib
satranji
shikar
syce
tamasha

EIGHTEENTH CENTURY
bundobust
hookah
howdah
khalsa
khidmutgar
masala
mofussil
munshi
nawab
zenana
ziarat

NINETEENTH CENTURY
badmash
bibi
burka
chaprassi
chikan
huma
khaki
kofta
korma
numdah
numnah
purdah
sarod
shalwar
shikari
sitar
tabla
tarkaski
zakat
zarda

TWENTIETH CENTURY
balti
biryani
garam masala
kurta
nan
rogan josh
samosa
shisha
tandoori
zari

Polish

EIGHTEENTH CENTURY
hetman

TWENTIETH CENTURY
kielbasa
oberek

Polynesian

NINETEENTH CENTURY
poi
poipoi

Portuguese

SIXTEENTH CENTURY
amok
banyan
betel
pagoda
typhoon

SEVENTEENTH CENTURY
aldea
copaiba
fidalgo
ipecacuanha
maraca
nabob

EIGHTEENTH CENTURY
auto-da-fé
ayah
commando
cuspidor
elephanta
piranha
senhor

NINETEENTH CENTURY
amah
bucellas
carioca
fazenda
fazendeiro
feijão
garimpeiro
guarana
lingua geral
samba
senhora
senhorita
serra
sertão
vigia
vindaloo
vinho
vinho branco
vinho tinto

TWENTIETH CENTURY
bossa nova
churrasco
fado
favela
favelado
feijoada
lundum
maxixe
pinga
pousada
retornado
saudade
tanga
vinho corrente
vinho da casa
vinho de consumo
vinho verde

Portuguese (Brazilian)

TWENTIETH CENTURY
lambada

Portuguese (and Spanish)

SIXTEENTH CENTURY
copra

SEVENTEENTH CENTURY
peon

TWENTIETH CENTURY
tristeza

Provençal

NINETEENTH CENTURY
alba

TWENTIETH CENTURY
mas
pistou
tian

pseudo-French

EIGHTEENTH CENTURY
bêche-de-mer

NINETEENTH CENTURY
bon viveur
nom de plume

TWENTIETH CENTURY
en travesti

pseudo-German

TWENTIETH CENTURY
sitzkrieg

pseudo-Italian

SIXTEENTH CENTURY
braggadocio

pseudo-Latin

SIXTEENTH CENTURY
mumpsimus
omnium gatherum

NINETEENTH CENTURY
celesta

pseudo-Greek

NINETEENTH CENTURY
agoraphobia

Romanian

TWENTIETH CENTURY
sarmale
tsuica

Romany

NINETEENTH CENTURY
chal
patrin
vardo

Russian

SIXTEENTH CENTURY
boyar
kvass
muzhik
sevruga
tsar

SEVENTEENTH CENTURY
steppe
tsaritsa

EIGHTEENTH CENTURY
balalaika
isba
Raskolnik
tsarevich
ukase
yurt

NINETEENTH CENTURY
artel
ataman
blin
bortsch
chernozem
dacha
droshky
druzhina
duma
feldsher
karakul
kasha
kulak
kurgan
mazut
pirog
polynya
samovar
shchi
starover
taiga
tchin
troika
tsarevna
vodka
zakuska
zemstvo

TWENTIETH CENTURY
agitprop
apparat
apparatchik
babushka
Bolshevik
glasnost
Gulag

intelligentsia
kazachoc
kissel
kolkhoz
kulturny
narod
nekulturny
niet
nilas
nitchevo
nomenklatura
paskha
pelmeny
perestroika
piroshki
podzol
pogrom
Politbureau
Presidium
prisiadka
proletkult
rassolnik
rendzina
residentura
rezident
riza
sambo
samizdat
shashlik
sierozem
skaz
smetana
sobornost
solod
solonchak
solonetz
solyanka
sovkhoz
sputnik
starets
subbotnik
talik
tokamak
tolkach
tovarish
tvorog
ukha
vobla
vozhd
zek

Samoan

NINETEENTH CENTURY
lava-lava

Sanskrit

SIXTEENTH CENTURY
raja

SEVENTEENTH CENTURY
guru
maharaja
puja
sannyasi
vihara
yogi

EIGHTEENTH CENTURY
atman
avatar
brahman
chakra
dharma
gandharva
gopi
kalpa
linga
maharishi
mantra
maya
moksha
mukti
naga
om
om mani padme hum
purusha
raga
rasa
samadhi
soma
suttee
swami
tantra
vajra
veena
yaksha
yoga
yogini
yoni
yuga

NINETEENTH CENTURY
acharya
ahimsa
Arhat
bhakta
bhakti
bhikshu
chaitya
deva
devadasi
dharmsala
garuda
gopura
Jina
jiva
Kama Sutra
karma
kundalini
mahatma
mandala
mudra
nirvana
nritya
padma
padmasana
raja yoga
rakshasa
rasa
sadhu
samsara
samskara
samyama
sangha
sarangi
shanti
shikhara
siddha
stupa
sutra
swastika
tilak
torana
vahana
varna
vimana
yajna
yantra

TWENTIETH CENTURY
ashram
ayurveda
bhajan
brahmacharya
gramdan
hatha yoga
hatha yogi
karana
kumkum
lasya
nada
nritta
panchshila
pata
sabha
satyagraha
shrikhand
sunyata

Sardinian

NINETEENTH CENTURY
nuragh

Serbo-Croat

EIGHTEENTH CENTURY
kolo

NINETEENTH CENTURY
slivovitz

TWENTIETH CENTURY
chetnik
hum
uvala
zurla

Sinhalese

NINETEENTH CENTURY
dagoba
pansala

Somali

TWENTIETH CENTURY
shifta

Spanish

SIXTEENTH CENTURY
alcaide
alcalde
alguacil
armada
bacalao
batata
bonito
cacique
cedilla
copal
cordovan
don
frijoles
hidalgo
infanta
machete
mestizo
Morisco
muchacho
olla podrida
panada
peccadillo
salina
sanbenito
sarsaparilla
sassafras
savannah
señora
seron
sierra
sombrero
tercio
tinaja
tinto
yeso

SEVENTEENTH CENTURY
alcazar
alforja
balsa
bandolero
caldera
chilli
chinchilla
conde
condor
contrayerva
dinero
duenna
embargo
estancia
flota
huaca
jornada
llano
manta
matador
mirador
mondongo
montera
mulatta
olla
paco
picaro
pimento
pimiento
plaza
pundonor
rancheria
santo
señor
siesta
toreador
toro
tortilla
tumbaga
vega
vicuña
vino tinto

EIGHTEENTH CENTURY

adobe
alameda
alpaca
banderilla
banderillero
bolero
carambole
cherimoya
chulo
cordillera
fandango
flotilla
gallinazo
garbanzo
hacienda
hermandad
mantilla
maté
merino
mesa
mescal
noria
oregano
pampas
paramo
picador
posada
presidio
tapia
tasajo
teniente
torero
volante

NINETEENTH CENTURY

adios
aficionado
aguardiente
alfalfa
alpargata
amigo
amontillado
aparejo
arroyo
azotea
azulejo
bajada
barrio
boccaro
bodega
bodegón
bolas
bolson
bonanza
bronco
burro
caballada
caballero
cabana
cabildo
camarilla
camaron
canyon
capataz
carabinero
caramba
cargador
cascara sagrada
caudillo
cavayard
chaparral
chilli con carne
chorizo
claro
compadre
conquistador
coon-can
copita
coquina
coquito
corrida
criollo
cuadrilla
cuartel
cuesta
descamisado
El Niño
embarcadero
encierro
escopette
espada
esparto
estufa
faja
fiesta
fino
flamenco
garrocha
gazpacho
gitana
gitano
gringo
guaracha
guardia civil
guerrilla
guiro
habanera
hacendado
hilo
hombre
honda
horchata
huerta
incommunicado
jaleo
jota
langosta
latigo
laud
lidia
lidiador
lobo
loco
loma
maja
malpais
mañana
manga
manso
manzanilla
mercado
meson
monosabio
Montaña
monte
muchacha
muleta
mustafina
norte
novillada
novillo
oficina
ole
oloroso
pacifico
paisano
palacio
parador
pasear
paseo
patio
pedregal
pelota
perfecto
piñata
piñon
pinto
playa
pollo
potrero
potro
pronunciamento
puchero
pueblo
puro
quebrada
ramada
ranchero
ranchito
rancho
rancio
rasgado
rebozo
regalia
reja
retablo
ria
riata
rodeo
romanza
saladero
salsa
sangre azul
señorita
sereno
silo
simpatico
solera
tapadero
temporale
tendido
tilde
toldo
tonadilla
toril
tule
vaquero
viga
vigilante
villancico
vino de color
vino de pasto
yerba
zaguan
zamarra
zapateado
zarzuela
zocalo
zoco

TWENTIETH CENTURY

abrazo
altiplano
anchoveta
autogiro
autopista
barrera
campesino
canasta
cante hondo
capeador
chicano
cilantro
cogida
cojones
cornada
costa
curandero
cursillo
desaparecido
duende
empanada
estocada
faena
farruca
finca
gamba
gaseosa
hasta la vista
huaco
insurrecto
jai alai
langostino
mano
mano a mano
marinera
masa
matraca
membrillo
meseta
mogote
Morisca
nada
novillero
novio
olé
paso
paso doble
peineta
poblador
pronto
puta
querencia
quesadilla
sangria
santeria
santero
señorito
sillar
sindicato
sol y sombra
son
supremo
tapa

tienta
tonto
tostada
turron
ultreya
vargueño
veleta
vendimia
vino blanco
vino corriente
vino dulce
vino maestro
vino tierno

Spanish (American)

SEVENTEENTH CENTURY
atole
charqui
chicha
chuño
metate
pulque
puna
teocalli
trapiche

EIGHTEENTH CENTURY
calinda

NINETEENTH CENTURY
bombilla
cafeteria
campo
chicharron
chicle
cholo
enchilada
galpon
gaucho
hornito
jarabe
marijuana
panatela
penuche
peyote
pinole
pulperia
remuda
tango
temblor

TWENTIETH CENTURY
bongo
burrito
cha-cha
chino
clave
conga
cueca
exacta
guacamole
mambo
merengue
montuno
palomino
panga
perfecta
quinella
ruana
rumba
sancocho
sopaipilla

Spanish (Mexican)

SEVENTEENTH CENTURY
tamale

EIGHTEENTH CENTURY
Apache
coyote

NINETEENTH CENTURY
alfilaria
amole
cenote
chaparejos
ejido
huarache
jacal
mecate
milpa
octli
pilón
serape
tequila
tilma

TWENTIETH CENTURY
ayahuasca
charro
chipotle
fajita
huevos rancheros
jalapeño
jojoba
machismo
macho
maquiladora
mariachi
menudo
molcajete
mole
mordida
nacho
pachuco
palapa
pochismo
pocho
taco
taqueria
tepache
tomatillo

Spanish (South American)

SEVENTEENTH CENTURY
guano

EIGHTEENTH CENTURY
poncho

NINETEENTH CENTURY
llanero

TWENTIETH CENTURY
basuco
bombachas
pina colada
seviche

Spanish (West Indian)

NINETEENTH CENTURY
dengue
guajiro

TWENTIETH CENTURY
guajira

Spanish (and Italian)

SEVENTEENTH CENTURY
amoroso
vino

NINETEENTH CENTURY
cantina
municipio

Spanish (and Portuguese)

SIXTEENTH CENTURY
auto
corral
infante
mulatto

SEVENTEENTH CENTURY
junta
recado

EIGHTEENTH CENTURY
albino
curare
quinta

NINETEENTH CENTURY
selva

TWENTIETH CENTURY
norteamericano

Swedish

EIGHTEENTH CENTURY
isblink

NINETEENTH CENTURY
polska
smorgasbord

TWENTIETH CENTURY
fartlek
glögg
ombudsman
palsa
pipkrake
rya
tjaele
varve

Swiss French

EIGHTEENTH CENTURY
chalet
ranz-des-vaches

NINETEENTH CENTURY
luge
névé
seiche
serac

Swiss German

TWENTIETH CENTURY
muesli
putsch
roesti

Tagalog

NINETEENTH CENTURY
ylang-ylang

TWENTIETH CENTURY
boondock

Tahitian

TWENTIETH CENTURY
vahine

Tamil

SEVENTEENTH CENTURY
catamaran
pariah

NINETEENTH CENTURY
patchouli
poppadam

TWENTIETH CENTURY
kavadi
sambar

Thai

NINETEENTH CENTURY
wat

Tibetan

SEVENTEENTH CENTURY
lama

NINETEENTH CENTURY
sherpa

TWENTIETH CENTURY
gompa
yeti

Tongan

EIGHTEENTH CENTURY
kava
taboo

Turkic

NINETEENTH CENTURY
barchan
khatun

Turkish

SIXTEENTH CENTURY
aga
bey
caftan
dervish

SEVENTEENTH CENTURY
baklava
bezesteen
effendi
hammam
harem
khoja
pasha
pashalic
pilau
raki
serai
sherbet
tekke
turbeh
yoghurt

NINETEENTH CENTURY
fez
kilim
kismet
konak
macramé
rahat
rayah
tughra
yataghan
zurna

TWENTIETH CENTURY
bulgur
dolmus
doner kebab
imam bayildi
karaburan
lokum
meze
millet
moussaka
mukhtar
sheshbesh
shish kebab
yorgan

Urdu (see Persian (and Urdu))

Vietnamese

TWENTIETH CENTURY
nuoc mam

Welsh

SEVENTEENTH CENTURY
cromlech

EIGHTEENTH CENTURY
Gorsedd

NINETEENTH CENTURY
bach
crwth
cwm

West Indian creole

EIGHTEENTH CENTURY
goombah

TWENTIETH CENTURY
soucouyant

Yiddish

SEVENTEENTH CENTURY
halva

NINETEENTH CENTURY
chutzpah
farfel
frum
gefilte fish
golem
kehilla
kittel
koppel
kreplach
kugel
lokshen
matzo
meshuga
meshumad
mikva
narrischkeit
nebbish
oy
reb
rebbe
rebbitzin
schmuck
schnorrer
shemozzle
shidduch
shiksa
shul
tzimmes
yahrzeit
yom tov

TWENTIETH CENTURY
bagel
blintze
cholent
dreidel
dybbuk
heimisch
kibbutznik
kibitz
kishke
klezmer
klutz
knaidel
knish
kvell
kvetch
landsman
latke
lekach
luftmensch
macher
mazuma
mensch
meshugaas
meshugener
naches
nosh
nudnik
pastrami
platzel
schalet
schlep
schlepper
schlimazel
schlock
schlong
schmaltz
schmooze
schmutz
schnozz
schwartze
shegetz
shlub
shmatte
shmear
shonda
shtetl
shtibl
shtick
shtoom
teiglach
tokus
trombenik
tsatske
tsores
yarmulke
yenta
yentz
yichus
zaftig